American Medical Associa

Physicians dedicated to the health of America

# Current Procedural Terminology

# cpt™ 2000

Celeste G. Kirschner, MHSA
Caryn A. Anderson, ART, CCS
Joyce A. Dalton
Stephanie J. Davis, BA
Desiree Evans
DeHandro Hayden, BS
Jennifer Kopacz, RRA
Grace M. Kotowicz, RN, BS
Marie L. Mindeman, ART
Karen E. O'Hara, BS, CCS-P
Mary R. O'Heron, RRA, CCS-P
Danielle Pavloski, ART
Dan Reyes, BA
Desiree Rozell, MPA
Arletrice A. Watkins
Rejina L. Young
Joan Zacharias

Standard perfect bound ISBN: 1-57947-016-5
Standard spiral ISBN: 1-57947-017-3
ISSN: 0276-8283



1st Edition printed 1966
2nd Edition printed 1970
3rd Edition printed 1973
4th Edition printed 1977
Revised: 1978, 1979, 1980, 1981, 1982, 1984, 1985, 1986, 1987, 1988, 1989, 1990, 1991, 1992, 1993, 1994, 1995, 1996, 1997, 1998, 1999

For information regarding the reprinting or licensing of CPT information, please contact:
CPT Intellectual Property Services
American Medical Association
515 North State Street
Chicago, IL 60610
312 464-5022

Additional books may be purchased from the American Medical Association by calling 800 621-8335.

# Foreword

*Current Procedural Terminology*, Fourth Edition (*CPT*™) is a listing of descriptive terms and identifying codes for reporting medical services and procedures performed by physicians. The purpose of the terminology is to provide a uniform language that will accurately describe medical, surgical, and diagnostic services, and will thereby provide an effective means for reliable nationwide communication among physicians, patients, and third parties. *CPT 2000* is the most recent revision of a work that first appeared in 1966.

CPT descriptive terms and identifying codes currently serve a wide variety of important functions in the field of medical nomenclature. CPT is the most widely accepted nomenclature for the reporting of physician procedures and services under government and private health insurance programs. CPT is also useful for administrative management purposes such as claims processing and for the development of guidelines for medical care review. The uniform language is likewise applicable to medical education and research by providing a useful basis for local, regional, and national utilization comparisons.

The changes that appear in this revision have been prepared by the CPT Editorial Panel with the assistance of physicians representing all specialties of medicine, and with important contributions from many third party payors and governmental agencies.

The American Medical Association trusts that this revision will continue the usefulness of its predecessors in identifying, describing, and coding medical, surgical, and diagnostic services.

E. Ratcliffe Anderson, Jr, MD
Executive Vice President

October 1, 1999

# Dedication

We dedicate *CPT 2000* to the memory of T. Reginald Harris, MD. Vision, leadership and dedication to the profession are Doctor Harris' hallmarks. He selflessly provided these qualities in his service as Chair of the CPT Editorial Panel. Doctor Harris served as the Chair of the Editorial Panel from August 1992 to May 1999. We will miss his warmth, his wisdom and his friendship as we continue our work in CPT.

# AMA CPT Editorial Panel

*Chair*
Tracy R. Gordy, MD*
*Vice-Chair*
Douglas E. Henley, MD*

Karen R. Borman, MD
Simon Philip Cohn, MD
Lee D. Eisenberg, MD
Laurie Feinberg, MD
Robert H. Haralson, MD*
Samuel Hassenbusch, MD**
Carl Anderson Hedberg, MD
Lee Harold Hilborne, MD**
Philipp M. Lippe, MD
Glenn D. Littenberg, MD
Allen J. McBride, MD*
Richard A. Molteni, MD
Gerald E. Silverstein, MD
Robert D. Sowell, DPM
William T. Thorwarth, MD**
James A. Zalla, MD

*Secretary*
Celeste G. Kirschner, MHSA

* Member of the CPT Executive Committee
** New Panel Member August 1999

# AMA CPT Advisory Committee

Donald W. Aaronson, MD
*American Academy of Allergy, Asthma and Immunology*

H. Christopher Alexander, III, MD
*American College of Physicians-American Society of Internal Medicine*

Freda Arlow, MD
*American College of Gastroenterology*

Paul N. Arnold, MD
Stephen S. Lane, MD*
*American Society of Cataract and Refractive Surgery*

Michael Ashcraft, MD
*The Endocrine Society*

Joseph S. Bailes, MD
*American Society of Clinical Oncology*

C. Robert Baisden, MD
*United States and Canadian Academy of Pathology*

Stephen N. Bauer, MD
*College of American Pathologist*

*New Advisor June 1999

J. Sumner Bell, MD
*American Gastroenterological Association*

David I. Berland, MD
*American Academy of Child and Adolescent Psychiatry*

James C. Blankenship, MD
Douglas L. Wood, MD*
*American College of Cardiology*

Neil A. Busis, MD
*American Association of Electrodiagnostic Medicine*

Jeffery B. Carter, MD, DMD
*American Dental Association*

Jean M. Colandrea, MD
*American Society of Cytopathology*

Mark V. Connelly, MD
*American Academy of Facial Plastic and Reconstructive Surgery*

David O. Davis, MD
*Radiology Society of North America*

Robin K. Dore, MD
*American College of Rheumatology*

Gary S. Dorfman, MD
*Society of Cardiovascular and Interventional Radiology*

Philip N. Eskew Jr, MD
*American College of Obstetricians and Gynecologists*

Tom Faciszewski, MD
*North American Spine Society*

Morton H. Field, MD
*American Association of Clinical Endocrinologists*

Blair C. Filler, MD
*American Orthopaedic Association*

David B. Flannery, MD
*American College of Medical Genetics*

William J. Fulkerson, MD
*American Thoracic Society*

Gary F. Gates, MD
*American College of Nuclear Physicians*

Thomas G. Goergen, MD
*American Roentgen Ray Society*

Stanford M. Goldman, MD
*Association of University Radiologists*

Arvind K. Goyal, MD, MPH
*American Association of Public Health Physicians*

Diller B. Groff, MD
*American Pediatric Surgical Association*

Gary N. Gross, MD
*American College of Allergy, Asthma and Immunology*

Richard J. Hamburger, MD
*Renal Physicians Association*

Samuel Hassenbusch, MD
*Congress of Neurological Surgeons*

Curtis Hawkins, MD
*Society for Investigative Dermatology*

Charles E. Hawtrey, MD
*American Urological Association, Inc.*

Charles Haynie, MD
*Society of American Gastrointestinal Endoscopic Surgeons*

George A. Hill, MD
*American Society for Reproductive Medicine*

Thomas Hobbins, MD
*American Sleep Disorders Association*

Peter A. Hollmann, MD
*American Geriatric Society*

Raymond V. Janevicius, MD
*American Society of Plastic and Reconstructive Surgeons*

Blake A. Johnson, MD
*American Society of Neuroradiology*

Christine L. Kasser, MD
*American Society of Addiction Medicine*

Frederick A. Kuhn, MD
*American Academy of Otolaryngology Head and Neck Surgery*

James M. Levett, MD
*American Association for Thoracic Surgery*

Sidney Levitsky, MD
*Society of Thoracic Surgeons*

Thomas B. Logan, MD*
*American Academy of Otolaryngic Allergy*

A. Clinton MacKinney, MD, MS
*American Academy of Family Physicians*

Vivek Mahendru, MD
*American Academy of Pain Medicine*

Robert H. Maisel, MD
*Triological Society*

Kenneth A. McKusick, MD
*Society of Nuclear Medicine*

Joseph P. McNerney, DO
*American Osteopathic Association*

Gregory J. Mulford, MD
*American Academy of Physical Medicine and Rehabilitation*

Daniel J. Nagle, MD
*American Society for Surgery of the Hand*

Fred T. Nobrega, MD
*American College of Preventive Medicine*

Marc Nuwer, MD, PhD
*American Academy of Neurology, American Clinical Neurophysiology Society*

Walter J. O'Donohue Jr, MD
*American College of Chest Physicians*

Walter J. Pedowitz, MD
*American Orthopaedic Foot and Ankle Society*

John T. Preskitt, MD
*American College of Surgeons*

Michael X. Repka, MD
*American Academy of Ophthalmology*

Nigel K. Roberts, MD
*American Academy of Insurance Medicine*

Nicholas L. Rock, MD
*Society of Medical Consultants to the Armed Forces*

Randall K. Roenigk, MD
*American Society for Dermatologic Surgery*

Demostene Romanucci, MD
*American Society of Abdominal Surgeons*

Richard A. Roski, MD
*American Association of Neurological Surgeons*

George A. Sample, MD
*Society of Critical Care Medicine*

Peter L. Sawchuk, MD
*American College of Emergency Physicians*

Chester W. Schmidt, Jr, MD
*American Psychiatric Association*

Charles J. Schulte III, MD
*American Academy of Pediatrics*

Anthony Senagore, MD
*American Society of Colon and Rectal Surgeons*

Alan E. Seyfer, MD
*American Society of Maxillofacial Surgeons*

Jon D. Shanser, MD
*American College of Radiology*

Anton N. Sidawy, MD
*International Society for Cardiovascular Surgery*

Samuel M. Silver, MD, PhD
*American Society of Hematology*

Charles B. Slonim, MD
*Contact Lens Association of Ophthalmologists*

Stanley W. Stead, MD
*American Society of Anesthesiologists*

Dennis L. Stone, MD
*American Medical Directors Association*

Mark S. Synovec, MD
*American Society of Clinical Pathologists*

Susan K. Turney, MD
*American Medical Group Association*

Paul E. Wallner, DO
*American Society for Therapeutic Radiology and Oncology*

Thomas J. Weatherall, Jr, MD
*American College of Radiation Oncology*

Michael L. Weinstein, MD
*American Society for Gastrointestinal Endoscopy*

William N. Werner, MD, MPH
*American College of Medical Quality*

Allan S. Wirtzer, MD
*American Academy of Dermatology*

Richard L. Wixson, MD
*American Academy of Orthopaedic Surgeons*

Robert Wolfson, MD, PhD
*American Institute of Ultrasound in Medicine*

## AMA Health Care Professionals Advisory Committee (HCPAC)

Tracy R. Gordy, MD, Co-Chair
*AMA CPT Editorial Panel*

Robert Sowell, DPM, Co-Chair
*American Podiatric Medical Association*

Linda Botten, OTR, CHT
*American Occupational Therapy Association*

Patrick J. Cafferty, PA-C
*American Academy of Physician Assistants*

Helene Fearon, PT
*American Physical Therapy Association*

Craig S. Little, DC
*American Chiropractic Association*

Douglas C. Morrow, OD
*American Optometric Association*

Antonio Puente, PhD
*American Psychological Association*

Nelda Spyres, ACSW, LCSW
*National Association of Social Workers*

Ann M. Thrailkill, RN
*American Nurses Association*

Marilyn Seif Workinger, PhD
*American Speech-Language Hearing Association*

*New Advisor June 1999

## Acknowledgements

Publication of each annual *CPT* represents many challenges and opportunities. From reconciling the many differences of opinion about the best way to describe a procedure, to last details on the placement of a semicolon, many individuals and organizations devote their energies and expertise to the preparation of this revision.

The editorial staff wishes to express sincere thanks to the many national medical specialty societies, health insurance organizations and agencies, and to the many individual physicians and other health professionals who have made contributions.

Thanks are due to Robert A. Musacchio, PhD, Sr VP, American Medical Association; Mark J. Segal, Vice President, Coding and Medical Information Systems, American Medical Association; Claudia Bonnell, Blue Cross and Blue Shield Association; Nelly Leon-Chisen, American Hospital Association; Thomas Musco, Health Insurance Association of America; and Sue Prophet, RRA, American Health Information Management Association, for their invaluable assistance in enhancing CPT.

And finally, our gratitude to the Publishing and Information Technology Groups of the American Medical Association for their assistance in producing the books, diskettes, magnetic tapes, and CD-ROMs that contain CPT, including Rhonda Taira, Director of Marketing Services, Donald Frye, Senior Print Coordinator, Boon Ai Tan, Production Coordinator, and Todd Feinstein, Application Developer.

# Contents

# Introduction

*Current Procedural Terminology,* Fourth Edition (*CPT*™) is a systematic listing and coding of procedures and services performed by physicians. Each procedure or service is identified with a five-digit code. The use of CPT codes simplifies the reporting of services. With this coding and recording system, the procedure or service rendered by the physician is accurately identified.

Inclusion of a descriptor and its associated specific five-digit identifying code number in *CPT* is generally based upon the procedure being consistent with contemporary medical practice and being performed by many physicians in clinical practice in multiple locations. Inclusion in *CPT* does not represent endorsement by the American Medical Association of any particular diagnostic or therapeutic procedure. Inclusion or exclusion of a procedure does not imply any health insurance coverage or reimbursement policy.

The main body of the material is listed in six sections. Within each section are subsections with anatomic, procedural, condition, or descriptor subheadings. The procedures and services with their identifying codes are presented in numeric order with one exception—the entire **Evaluation and Management** section (99201-99499) has been placed at the beginning of the listed procedures. These items are used by most physicians in reporting a significant portion of their services. The **Medicine** (procedures) section now follows **Pathology and Laboratory**.

## Section Numbers and Their Sequences

**Evaluation and Management** . .99201 to 99499

**Anesthesiology** . . . . . . . . . . . . .00100 to 01999, 99100 to 99140

**Surgery** . . . . . . . . . . . . . . . . . . .10040 to 69990

**Radiology (Including Nuclear Medicine and Diagnostic Ultrasound)** . . .70010 to 79999

**Pathology and Laboratory** . . . .80049 to 89399

**Medicine (except Anesthesiology)** . . . . . .90281 to 99199

The first and last code numbers and the subsection name of the items appear at the top of each page (eg, "11056–11313 Surgery/Integumentary System"). The continuous pagination of *CPT* is found on the lower, outer margin of each page along with the section name.

## Instructions for Use of CPT

Select the name of the procedure or service that most accurately identifies the service performed. In surgery, it may be an operation; in medicine, a diagnostic or therapeutic procedure; in radiology, a radiograph. Other additional procedures performed or pertinent special services are also listed. When necessary, any modifying or extenuating circumstances are added. Any service or procedure should be adequately documented in the medical record.

It is important to recognize that the listing of a service or procedure and its code number in a specific section of this book does not restrict its use to a specific specialty group. Any procedure or service in any section of this book may be used to designate the services rendered by any qualified physician.

### Format of the Terminology

CPT procedure terminology has been developed as stand-alone descriptions of medical procedures. However, some of the procedures in *CPT* are not printed in their entirety but refer back to a common portion of the procedure listed in a preceding entry. This is evident when an entry is followed by one or more indentations. This is done in an effort to conserve space.

***Example***

**25100** Arthrotomy, wrist joint; for biopsy

**25105** for synovectomy

Note that the common part of code 25100 (that part before the semicolon) should be considered part of code 25105. Therefore the full procedure represented by code 25105 should read:

**25105** Arthrotomy, wrist joint; for synovectomy

## Requests to Update CPT

The effectiveness of *Current Procedural Terminology (CPT™)* is dependent upon constant updating to reflect changes in medical practice. This can only be accomplished through the interest and timely suggestions of practicing physicians, medical specialty societies, state medical associations, and other organizations and agencies. Accordingly, the American Medical Association welcomes correspondence, inquiries, and suggestions concerning old and new procedures, as well as other matters such as codes and indices.

For suggestions concerning the introduction of new procedures, or the coding, deleting, or revising of procedures contained in *CPT 2000*, correspondence requesting an application for coding change should be directed to:

CPT Editorial Research & Development
American Medical Association
515 North State Street
Chicago, Illinois 60610

All proposed additions to, or modifications of, *CPT 2000* will be by decision of the CPT Editorial Panel after consultation with appropriate medical specialty societies.

## Guidelines

Specific "Guidelines" are presented at the beginning of each of the six sections. These guidelines define items that are necessary to appropriately interpret and report the procedures and services contained in that section. For example, in the **Medicine** section, specific instructions are provided for handling unlisted services or procedures, special reports, and supplies and materials provided. Guidelines also provide explanations regarding terms that apply only to a particular section. For instance, **Surgery Guidelines** provides an explanation of the use of the star, while in **Radiology**, the unique term, "radiological supervision and interpretation" is defined.

## Starred Procedures

The star "*" is used to identify certain surgical procedures. A description of this reporting mechanism will be found in the **Surgery Guidelines**.

## Modifiers

A modifier provides the means by which the reporting physician can indicate that a service or procedure that has been performed has been altered by some specific circumstance but not changed in its definition or code. The judicious application of modifiers obviates the necessity for separate procedure listings that may describe the modifying circumstance. Modifiers may be used to indicate to the recipient of a report that:

- A service or procedure has both a professional and technical component.
- A service or procedure was performed by more than one physician and/or in more than one location.
- A service or procedure has been increased or reduced.
- Only part of a service was performed.
- An adjunctive service was performed.
- A bilateral procedure was performed.
- A service or procedure was provided more than once.
- Unusual events occurred.

***Example***
A physician providing diagnostic or therapeutic radiology services, ultrasound or nuclear medicine services in a hospital would use either modifier '-26' or 09926 to report the professional component.

73090-26 = Professional component only for an x-ray of the forearm

*or*

73090 AND 09926 = Professional component only for an x-ray of the forearm

***Example***
Two surgeons may be required to manage a specific surgical problem. When two surgeons work together as primary surgeons performing distinct part(s) of a single reportable procedure, each surgeon should report his/her distinct operative work by adding the modifier '-62' to the single definitive procedure code. Each surgeon should report the co-surgery once using the same procedure code. The modifier '-62' or the alternative modifier five-digit code 09962 would be applicable. For instance, a neurological surgeon and an otolaryngologist are working as co-surgeons in performing transsphenoidal excision of a pituitary neoplasm.

61548-62 = Hypophysectomy or excision of pituitary tumor, transnasal or transseptal approach, nonstereotactic + two surgeons modifier

*or*

61548 AND 09962 = Hypophysectomy or excision of pituitary tumor, transnasal or transseptal approach, nonstereotactic + two surgeons modifier

AND the second surgeon would report:

61548-62 = Hypophysectomy or excision of pituitary tumor, transnasal or transseptal approach, nonstereotactic + two surgeons modifier

*or*

61548 AND 09962 = Hypophysectomy or excision of pituitary tumor, transnasal or transseptal approach, nonstereotactic + two surgeons modifier

If additional procedure(s) (including add-on procedure(s)) are performed during the same surgical session, separate code(s) may be reported without the modifier '-62' added. **Note:** If a cosurgeon acts as an assistant in the performance of additional procedure(s) during the same surgical session, those services may be reported using separate procedure code(s) with the modifier '-80' or modifier '-81' added, as appropriate. A complete listing of modifiers is found in Appendix A.

## Unlisted Procedure or Service

It is recognized that there may be services or procedures performed by physicians that are not found in *CPT.* Therefore, a number of specific code numbers have been designated for reporting unlisted procedures. When an unlisted procedure number is used, the service or procedure should be described. Each of these unlisted procedural code numbers (with the appropriate accompanying topical entry) relates to a specific section of the book and is presented in the Guidelines of that section.

## Special Report

A service that is rarely provided, unusual, variable, or new may require a special report in determining medical appropriateness of the service. Pertinent information should include an adequate definition or description of the nature, extent, and need for the procedure; and the time, effort, and equipment necessary to provide the service. Additional items which may be included are:

Complexity of symptoms, final diagnosis, pertinent physical findings, diagnostic and therapeutic procedures, concurrent problems, and follow-up care.

## Code Changes

A summary listing of additions, deletions, and revisions applicable to *CPT 2000* is found in Appendix B. New procedure numbers added to *CPT* are identified throughout the text with the symbol "●" placed before the code number. In instances where a code revision has resulted in a substantially altered procedure descriptor, the symbol "▲" is placed before the code number. The symbols "►◄" are used to indicate new and revised text other than the procedure descriptors. CPT add-on codes are annotated by a "✚" symbol and are listed in **Appendix E**. The "⊘" symbol is used to identify codes that are exempt from the use of modifier '-51', but have not been designated as CPT add-on procedures/services. A list of codes exempt from modifier '-51' usage is included in **Appendix F**.

## Alphabetical Reference Index

A new, expanded alphabetical index is found in the back of the book. It includes listings by procedure and anatomic site. Procedures and services commonly known by their eponyms or other designations are also included.

## CPT in Electronic Formats

*CPT 2000* procedure codes and descriptors are also available on magnetic computer tapes, diskettes, and CD-ROM in various formats. For more information call (800) 621-8335.

**Visit CPT on the AMA Website**
**http://www.ama-assn.org/cpt**

# Evaluation and Management (E/M) Services Guidelines

In addition to the information presented in the **Introduction,** several other items unique to this section are defined or identified here.

## Classification of Evaluation and Management (E/M) Services

The E/M section is divided into broad categories such as office visits, hospital visits, and consultations. Most of the categories are further divided into two or more subcategories of E/M services. For example, there are two subcategories of office visits (new patient and established patient) and there are two subcategories of hospital visits (initial and subsequent). The subcategories of E/M services are further classified into levels of E/M services that are identified by specific codes. This classification is important because the nature of physician work varies by type of service, place of service, and the patient's status.

The basic format of the levels of E/M services is the same for most categories. First, a unique code number is listed. Second, the place and/or type of service is specified, eg, office consultation. Third, the content of the service is defined, eg, comprehensive history and comprehensive examination. (See "Levels of E/M Services," page 2, for details on the content of E/M services.) Fourth, the nature of the presenting problem(s) usually associated with a given level is described. Fifth, the time typically required to provide the service is specified. (A detailed discussion of time is provided on page 4.)

## Definitions of Commonly Used Terms

Certain key words and phrases are used throughout the E/M section. The following definitions are intended to reduce the potential for differing interpretations and to increase the consistency of reporting by physicians in differing specialties.

### New and Established Patient

A new patient is one who has not received any professional services from the physician or another physician of the same specialty who belongs to the same group practice, within the past three years.

An established patient is one who has received professional services from the physician or another physician of the same specialty who belongs to the same group practice, within the past three years.

In the instance where a physician is on call for or covering for another physician, the patient's encounter will be classified as it would have been by the physician who is not available.

No distinction is made between new and established patients in the emergency department. E/M services in the emergency department category may be reported for any new or established patient who presents for treatment in the emergency department.

### Chief Complaint

A concise statement describing the symptom, problem, condition, diagnosis or other factor that is the reason for the encounter, usually stated in the patient's words.

## Concurrent Care

Concurrent care is the provision of similar services, eg, hospital visits, to the same patient by more than one physician on the same day. When concurrent care is provided, no special reporting is required. Modifier '-75' has been deleted.

## Counseling

Counseling is a discussion with a patient and/or family concerning one or more of the following areas:

- diagnostic results, impressions, and/or recommended diagnostic studies;
- prognosis;
- risks and benefits of management (treatment) options;
- instructions for management (treatment) and/or follow-up;
- importance of compliance with chosen management (treatment) options;
- risk factor reduction; and
- patient and family education.

(For psychotherapy, see 90804-90857)

## Family History

A review of medical events in the patient's family that includes significant information about:

- the health status or cause of death of parents, siblings, and children;
- specific diseases related to problems identified in the Chief Complaint or History of the Present Illness, and/or System Review;
- diseases of family members which may be hereditary or place the patient at risk.

## History of Present Illness

A chronological description of the development of the patient's present illness from the first sign and/or symptom to the present. This includes a description of location, quality, severity, timing, context, modifying factors and associated signs and symptoms significantly related to the presenting problem(s).

## Levels of E/M Services

Within each category or subcategory of E/M service, there are three to five levels of E/M services available for reporting purposes. Levels of E/M services are *not* interchangeable among the different categories or subcategories of service. For example, the first level of E/M services in the subcategory of office visit, new patient, does not have the same definition as the first level of E/M services in the subcategory of office visit, established patient.

The levels of E/M services include examinations, evaluations, treatments, conferences with or concerning patients, preventive pediatric and adult health supervision, and similar medical services, such as the determination of the need and/or location for appropriate care. Medical screening includes the history, examination, and medical decision-making required to determine the need and/or location for appropriate care and treatment of the patient (eg, office and other outpatient setting, emergency department, nursing facility, etc.). The levels of E/M services encompass the wide variations in skill, effort, time, responsibility and medical knowledge required for the prevention or diagnosis and treatment of illness or injury and the promotion of optimal health. Each level of E/M services may be used by all physicians.

The descriptors for the levels of E/M services recognize seven components, six of which are used in defining the levels of E/M services. These components are:

- history;
- examination;
- medical decision making;
- counseling;
- coordination of care;
- nature of presenting problem; and
- time.

The first three of these components (history, examination, and medical decision making) are considered the **key** components in selecting a level of E/M services. (See "Determine the Extent of History Obtained," page 6.)

The next three components (counseling, coordination of care, and the nature of the presenting problem) are considered **contributory** factors in the majority of encounters. Although the first two of these contributory factors are important E/M services, it is not required that these services be provided at every patient encounter.

Coordination of care with other providers or agencies without a patient encounter on that day is reported using the case management codes.

The final component, time, is discussed in detail (see page 4).

Any specifically identifiable procedure (ie, identified with a specific CPT code) performed on or subsequent to the date of initial or subsequent "E/M Services" should be reported separately.

The actual performance and/or interpretation of diagnostic tests/studies ordered during a patient encounter are not included in the levels of E/M services. Physician performance of diagnostic tests/studies for which specific CPT codes are available may be reported separately, in addition to the appropriate E/M code. The physician's interpretation of the results of diagnostic tests/studies (ie, professional component) with preparation of a separate distinctly identifiable signed written report may also be reported separately, using the appropriate CPT code with the modifier '-26' appended.

The physician may need to indicate that on the day a procedure or service identified by a CPT code was performed, the patient's condition required a significant separately identifiable E/M service above and beyond other services provided or beyond the usual preservice and postservice care associated with the procedure that was performed. The E/M service may be caused or prompted by the symptoms or condition for which the procedure and/or service was provided. This circumstance may be reported by adding the modifier '-25' to the appropriate level of E/M service. As such, different diagnoses are not required for reporting of the procedure and the E/M services on the same date.

## Nature of Presenting Problem

A presenting problem is a disease, condition, illness, injury, symptom, sign, finding, complaint, or other reason for encounter, with or without a diagnosis being established at the time of the encounter. The E/M codes recognize five types of presenting problems that are defined as follows:

***Minimal:*** A problem that may not require the presence of the physician, but service is provided under the physician's supervision.

***Self-limited or minor:*** A problem that runs a definite and prescribed course, is transient in nature, and is not likely to permanently alter health status OR has a good prognosis with management/compliance.

***Low severity:*** A problem where the risk of morbidity without treatment is low; there is little to no risk of mortality without treatment; full recovery without functional impairment is expected.

***Moderate severity:*** A problem where the risk of morbidity without treatment is moderate; there is moderate risk of mortality without treatment; uncertain prognosis OR increased probability of prolonged functional impairment.

***High severity:*** A problem where the risk of morbidity without treatment is high to extreme; there is a moderate to high risk of mortality without treatment OR high probability of severe, prolonged functional impairment.

## Past History

A review of the patient's past experiences with illnesses, injuries, and treatments that includes significant information about:

- prior major illnesses and injuries;
- prior operations;
- prior hospitalizations;
- current medications;
- allergies (eg, drug, food);
- age appropriate immunization status;
- age appropriate feeding/dietary status.

## Social History

An age appropriate review of past and current activities that includes significant information about:

- marital status and/or living arrangements;
- current employment;
- occupational history;
- use of drugs, alcohol, and tobacco;
- level of education;
- sexual history;
- other relevant social factors.

## System Review (Review of Systems)

An inventory of body systems obtained through a series of questions seeking to identify signs and/or symptoms which the patient may be experiencing or has experienced. For the purposes of CPT the following elements of a system review have been identified:

- Constitutional symptoms (fever, weight loss, etc.)
- Eyes
- Ears, Nose, Mouth, Throat
- Cardiovascular
- Respiratory
- Gastrointestinal
- Genitourinary
- Musculoskeletal
- Integumentary (skin and/or breast)
- Neurological
- Psychiatric
- Endocrine
- Hematologic/Lymphatic
- Allergic/Immunologic

The review of systems helps define the problem, clarify the differential diagnosis, identify needed testing, or serves as baseline data on other systems that might be affected by any possible management options.

## Time

The inclusion of time in the definitions of levels of E/M services has been implicit in prior editions of *CPT*. The inclusion of time as an explicit factor beginning in *CPT 1992* is done to assist physicians in selecting the most appropriate level of E/M services. It should be recognized that the specific times expressed in the visit code descriptors are averages, and therefore represent a range of times which may be higher or lower depending on actual clinical circumstances.

Time is *not* a descriptive component for the emergency department levels of E/M services because emergency department services are typically provided on a variable intensity basis, often involving multiple encounters with several patients over an extended period of time. Therefore, it is often difficult for physicians to provide accurate estimates of the time spent face-to-face with the patient.

Studies to establish levels of E/M services employed surveys of practicing physicians to obtain data on the amount of time and work associated with typical E/M services. Since "work" is not easily quantifiable, the codes must rely on other objective, verifiable measures that correlate with physicians' estimates of their "work". It has been demonstrated that physicians' estimations of **intraservice time** (as explained below), both within and across specialties, is a variable that is predictive of the "work" of E/M services. This same research has shown there is a strong relationship between intra-service time and total time for E/M services. Intra-service time, rather than total time, was chosen for inclusion with the codes because of its relative ease of measurement and because of its direct correlation with measurements of the total amount of time and work associated with typical E/M services.

Intra-service times are defined as **face-to-face** time for office and other outpatient visits and as **unit/floor** time for hospital and other inpatient visits. This distinction is necessary because most of the work of typical office visits takes place during the face-to-face time with the patient, while most of the work of typical hospital visits takes place during the time spent on the patient's floor or unit.

***Face-to-face time (office and other outpatient visits and office consultations):*** For coding purposes, face-to-face time for these services is defined as only that time that the physician spends face-to-face with the patient and/or family. This includes the time in which the physician performs such tasks as obtaining a history, performing an examination, and counseling the patient.

Physicians also spend time doing work before or after the face-to-face time with the patient, performing such tasks as reviewing records and tests, arranging for further services, and communicating further with other professionals and the patient through written reports and telephone contact.

This *non*-face-to-face time for office services—also called pre- and post-encounter time—is not included in the time component described in the E/M codes. However, the pre- and post-face-to-face work associated with an encounter was included in calculating the total work of typical services in physician surveys.

Thus, the face-to-face time associated with the services described by any E/M code is a valid proxy for the total work done before, during, and after the visit.

***Unit/floor time (hospital observation services, inpatient hospital care, initial and follow-up hospital consultations, nursing facility):*** For reporting purposes, intra-service time for these services is defined as unit/floor time, which includes the time that the physician is present on the patient's hospital unit and at the bedside rendering services for that patient. This includes the time in which the physician establishes and/or reviews the patient's chart, examines the patient, writes notes and communicates with other professionals and the patient's family.

In the hospital, pre- and post-time includes time spent off the patient's floor performing such tasks as reviewing pathology and radiology findings in another part of the hospital.

This pre- and post-visit time is not included in the time component described in these codes. However, the pre- and post-work performed during the time spent off the floor or unit was included in calculating the total work of typical services in physician surveys.

Thus, the unit/floor time associated with the services described by any code is a valid proxy for the total work done before, during, and after the visit.

## Unlisted Service

An E/M service may be provided that is not listed in this section of CPT. When reporting such a service, the appropriate "Unlisted" code may be used to indicate the service, identifying it by "Special Report", as discussed in the following paragraph. The "Unlisted Services" and accompanying codes for the E/M section are as follows:

**99429** Unlisted preventive medicine service

**99499** Unlisted evaluation and management service

## Special Report

An unlisted service or one that is unusual, variable, or new may require a special report demonstrating the medical appropriateness of the service. Pertinent information should include an adequate definition or description of the nature, extent, and need for the procedure; and the time, effort, and equipment necessary to provide the service. Additional items which may be included are complexity of symptoms, final diagnosis, pertinent physical findings, diagnostic and therapeutic procedures, concurrent problems, and follow-up care.

## Clinical Examples

Clinical examples of the codes for E/M services are provided to assist physicians in understanding the meaning of the descriptors and selecting the correct code. The clinical examples are listed in Appendix D. Each example was developed by physicians in the specialties shown.

The same problem, when seen by physicians in different specialties, may involve different amounts of work. Therefore, the appropriate level of encounter should be reported using the descriptors rather than the examples.

The examples have been tested for validity and approved by the CPT Editorial Panel. Physicians were given the examples and asked to assign a code or assess the amount of time and work involved. Only those examples that were rated consistently have been included in Appendix D.

## Instructions for Selecting a Level of E/M Service

### Identify the Category and Subcategory of Service

The categories and subcategories of codes available for reporting E/M services are shown in Table 1 on the following page.

### Review the Reporting Instructions for the Selected Category or Subcategory

Most of the categories and many of the subcategories of service have special guidelines or instructions unique to that category or subcategory. Where these are indicated, eg, "Inpatient Hospital Care," special instructions will be presented preceding the levels of E/M services.

Table 1
**Categories and Subcategories of Service**

| Category/Subcategory | Code Numbers |
|---|---|
| Office or Other Outpatient Services | |
| New Patient | 99201-99205 |
| Established Patient | 99211-99215 |
| Hospital Observation Discharge Services | 99217 |
| Hospital Observation Services | 99218-99220 |
| Hospital Observation or Inpatient Care Services (Including Admission and Discharge Services) | 99234-99236 |
| Hospital Inpatient Services | |
| Initial Hospital Care | 99221-99223 |
| Subsequent Hospital Care | 99231-99233 |
| Hospital Discharge Services | 99238-99239 |
| Consultations | |
| Office Consultations | 99241-99245 |
| Initial Inpatient Consultations | 99251-99255 |
| Follow-up Inpatient Consultations | 99261-99263 |
| Confirmatory Consultations | 99271-99275 |
| Emergency Department Services | 99281-99288 |
| Critical Care Services | 99291-99292 |
| Neonatal Intensive Care | 99295-99298 |
| Nursing Facility Services | |
| Comprehensive Nursing Facility Assessments | 99301-99303 |
| Subsequent Nursing Facility Care | 99311-99313 |
| Nursing Facility Discharge Services | 99315-99316 |
| Domiciliary, Rest Home or Custodial Care Services | |
| New Patient | 99321-99323 |
| Established Patient | 99331-99333 |
| Home Services | |
| New Patient | 99341-99345 |
| Established Patient | 99347-99350 |
| Prolonged Services | |
| With Direct Patient Contact | 99354-99357 |
| Without Direct Patient Contact | 99358-99359 |
| Standby Services | 99360 |
| Case Management Services | |
| Team Conferences | 99361-99362 |
| Telephone Calls | 99371-99373 |
| Care Plan Oversight Services | 99374-99380 |
| Preventive Medicine Services | |
| New Patient | 99381-99387 |
| Established Patient | 99391-99397 |
| Individual Counseling | 99401-99404 |
| Group Counseling | 99411-99412 |
| Other | 99420-99429 |
| Newborn Care | 99431-99440 |
| Special E/M Services | 99450-99456 |
| Other E/M Services | 99499 |

## Review the Level of E/M Service Descriptors and Examples in the Selected Category or Subcategory

The descriptors for the levels of E/M services recognize seven components, six of which are used in defining the levels of E/M services. These components are:

- history;
- examination;
- medical decision making;
- counseling;
- coordination of care;
- nature of presenting problem; and
- time.

The first three of these components (ie, history, examination, and medical decision making) should be considered the **key** components in selecting the level of E/M services. An exception to this rule is in the case of visits which consist predominantly of counseling or coordination of care (See numbered paragraph 3, page 8.)

The nature of the presenting problem and time are provided in some levels to assist the physician in determining the appropriate level of E/M service.

## Determine the Extent of History Obtained

The extent of the history is dependent upon clinical judgment and on the nature of the presenting problems(s). The levels of E/M services recognize four types of history that are defined as follows:

***Problem focused:*** chief complaint; brief history of present illness or problem.

***Expanded problem focused:*** chief complaint; brief history of present illness; problem pertinent system review.

***Detailed:*** chief complaint; extended history of present illness; problem pertinent system review extended to include a review of a limited number of additional systems; **pertinent** past, family, and/or social history *directly related to the patient's problems.*

***Comprehensive:*** chief complaint; extended history of present illness; review of systems which is directly related to the problem(s) identified in the history of the present illness plus a review of all additional body systems; **complete** past, family, and social history.

The comprehensive history obtained as part of the preventive medicine evaluation and management service is not problem-oriented and does not involve a chief complaint or present illness. It does, however, include a comprehensive system review and comprehensive or interval past, family, and social history as well as a comprehensive assessment/history of pertinent risk factors.

## Determine the Extent of Examination Performed

The extent of the examination performed is dependent on clinical judgment and on the nature of the presenting problem(s). The levels of E/M services recognize four types of examination that are defined as follows:

***Problem focused:*** a limited examination of the affected body area or organ system.

***Expanded problem focused:*** a limited examination of the affected body area or organ system and other symptomatic or related organ system(s).

***Detailed:*** an extended examination of the affected body area(s) and other symptomatic or related organ system(s).

***Comprehensive:*** a general multi-system examination or a complete examination of a single organ system. **Note:** The comprehensive examination performed as part of the preventive medicine evaluation and management service is multisystem, but its extent is based on age and risk factors identified.

For the purposes of these CPT definitions, the following body areas are recognized:

- Head, including the face
- Neck
- Chest, including breasts and axilla
- Abdomen
- Genitalia, groin, buttocks
- Back
- Each extremity

For the purposes of these CPT definitions, the following organ systems are recognized:

- Eyes
- Ears, Nose, Mouth, and Throat
- Cardiovascular
- Respiratory
- Gastrointestinal
- Genitourinary
- Musculoskeletal
- Skin
- Neurologic
- Psychiatric
- Hematologic/Lymphatic/Immunologic

## Determine the Complexity of Medical Decision Making

Medical decision making refers to the complexity of establishing a diagnosis and/or selecting a management option as measured by:

- the number of possible diagnoses and/or the number of management options that must be considered;
- the amount and/or complexity of medical records, diagnostic tests, and/or other information that must be obtained, reviewed, and analyzed; and
- the risk of significant complications, morbidity, and/or mortality, as well as comorbidities, associated with the patient's presenting problems(s), the diagnostic procedure(s) and/or the possible management options.

Four types of medical decision making are recognized: straightforward; low complexity; moderate complexity; and high complexity. To qualify for a given type of decision making, two of the three elements in Table 2 on the following page must be met or exceeded.

Comorbidities/underlying diseases, in and of themselves, are not considered in selecting a level of E/M services *unless* their presence significantly increases the complexity of the medical decision making.

## Select the Appropriate Level of E/M Services Based on the Following

1. For the following categories/subcategories, **all of the key components,** ie, history, examination, and medical decision making, must meet or exceed the stated requirements to qualify for a particular level of E/M service: office, new patient; hospital observation services; initial hospital care; office consultations; initial inpatient consultations; confirmatory consultations; emergency department services; comprehensive nursing facility assessments; domiciliary care, new patient; and home, new patient.

2. For the following categories/subcategories, **two of the three key components** (ie, history, examination, and medical decision making) must meet or exceed the stated requirements to qualify for a particular level of E/M services: office, established patient; subsequent hospital care; follow-up inpatient consultations; subsequent nursing facility care; domiciliary care, established patient; and home, established patient.

3. When counseling and/or coordination of care dominates (more than 50%) the physician/patient and/or family encounter (face-to-face time in the office or other outpatient setting or floor/unit time in the hospital or nursing facility), then **time** may be considered the key or controlling factor to qualify for a particular level of E/M services. ►This includes time spent with parties who have assumed responsibility for the care of the patient or decision making whether or not they are family members (eg, foster parents, person acting in locum parentis, legal guardian).◄ The extent of counseling and/or coordination of care must be documented in the medical record.

Table 2
**Complexity of Medical Decision Making**

| Number of Diagnoses or Management Options | Amount and/or Complexity of Data to be Reviewed | Risk of Complications and/or Morbidity or Mortality | Type of Decision Making |
|---|---|---|---|
| minimal | minimal or none | minimal | **straightforward** |
| limited | limited | low | **low complexity** |
| multiple | moderate | moderate | **moderate complexity** |
| extensive | extensive | high | **high complexity** |

# Evaluation and Management

## Office or Other Outpatient Services

The following codes are used to report evaluation and management services provided in the physician's office or in an outpatient or other ambulatory facility. A patient is considered an outpatient until inpatient admission to a health care facility occurs.

To report services provided to a patient who is admitted to a hospital or nursing facility in the course of an encounter in the office or other ambulatory facility, see the notes for initial hospital inpatient care (page 12) or comprehensive nursing facility assessments (page 24).

For services provided by physicians in the Emergency Department, see 99281-99285.

For observation care, see 99217-99220.

For observation or inpatient care services (including admission and discharge services), see 99234-99236.

### New Patient

**99201** **Office or other outpatient visit** for the evaluation and management of a new patient, which requires these three key components:

- **a problem focused history;**
- **a problem focused examination; and**
- **straightforward medical decision making.**

Counseling and/or coordination of care with other providers or agencies are provided consistent with the nature of the problem(s) and the patient's and/or family's needs.

Usually, the presenting problems are self limited or minor. Physicians typically spend 10 minutes face-to-face with the patient and/or family.

**99202** **Office or other outpatient visit** for the evaluation and management of a new patient, which requires these three key components:

- **an expanded problem focused history;**
- **an expanded problem focused examination; and**
- **straightforward medical decision making.**

Counseling and/or coordination of care with other providers or agencies are provided consistent with the nature of the problem(s) and the patient's and/or family's needs.

Usually, the presenting problem(s) are of low to moderate severity. Physicians typically spend 20 minutes face-to-face with the patient and/or family.

**99203** **Office or other outpatient visit** for the evaluation and management of a new patient, which requires these three key components:

- **a detailed history;**
- **a detailed examination; and**
- **medical decision making of low complexity.**

Counseling and/or coordination of care with other providers or agencies are provided consistent with the nature of the problem(s) and the patient's and/or family's needs.

Usually, the presenting problem(s) are of moderate severity. Physicians typically spend 30 minutes face-to-face with the patient and/or family.

**99204** **Office or other outpatient visit** for the evaluation and management of a new patient, which requires these three key components:

- **a comprehensive history;**
- **a comprehensive examination; and**
- **medical decision making of moderate complexity.**

Counseling and/or coordination of care with other providers or agencies are provided consistent with the nature of the problem(s) and the patient's and/or family's needs.

Usually, the presenting problem(s) are of moderate to high severity. Physicians typically spend 45 minutes face-to-face with the patient and/or family.

**99205** **Office or other outpatient visit** for the evaluation and management of a new patient, which requires these three key components:

- **a comprehensive history;**
- **a comprehensive examination; and**
- **medical decision making of high complexity.**

Counseling and/or coordination of care with other providers or agencies are provided consistent with the nature of the problem(s) and the patient's and/or family's needs.

Usually, the presenting problem(s) are of moderate to high severity. Physicians typically spend 60 minutes face-to-face with the patient and/or family.

## Established Patient

**99211** **Office or other outpatient visit** for the evaluation and management of an established patient, that may not require the presence of a physician. Usually, the presenting problem(s) are minimal. Typically, 5 minutes are spent performing or supervising these services.

**99212** **Office or other outpatient visit** for the evaluation and management of an established patient, which requires at least two of these three key components:

- **a problem focused history;**
- **a problem focused examination;**
- **straightforward medical decision making.**

Counseling and/or coordination of care with other providers or agencies are provided consistent with the nature of the problem(s) and the patient's and/or family's needs.

Usually, the presenting problem(s) are self limited or minor. Physicians typically spend 10 minutes face-to-face with the patient and/or family.

**99213** **Office or other outpatient visit** for the evaluation and management of an established patient, which requires at least two of these three key components:

- **an expanded problem focused history;**
- **an expanded problem focused examination;**
- **medical decision making of low complexity.**

Counseling and coordination of care with other providers or agencies are provided consistent with the nature of the problem(s) and the patient's and/or family's needs.

Usually, the presenting problem(s) are of low to moderate severity. Physicians typically spend 15 minutes face-to-face with the patient and/or family.

**99214** **Office or other outpatient visit** for the evaluation and management of an established patient, which requires at least two of these three key components:

- **a detailed history;**
- **a detailed examination;**
- **medical decision making of moderate complexity.**

Counseling and/or coordination of care with other providers or agencies are provided consistent with the nature of the problem(s) and the patient's and/or family's needs.

Usually, the presenting problem(s) are of moderate to high severity. Physicians typically spend 25 minutes face-to-face with the patient and/or family.

**99215** **Office or other outpatient visit** for the evaluation and management of an established patient, which requires at least two of these three key components:

- **a comprehensive history;**
- **a comprehensive examination;**
- **medical decision making of high complexity.**

Counseling and/or coordination of care with other providers or agencies are provided consistent with the nature of the problem(s) and the patient's and/or family's needs.

Usually, the presenting problem(s) are of moderate to high severity. Physicians typically spend 40 minutes face-to-face with the patient and/or family.

# Hospital Observation Services

The following codes are used to report evaluation and management services provided to patients designated/admitted as "observation status" in a hospital. It is not necessary that the patient be located in an observation area designated by the hospital.

If such an area does exist in a hospital (as a separate unit in the hospital, in the emergency department, etc.), these codes are to be utilized if the patient is placed in such an area.

For definitions of key components and commonly used terms, please see **Evaluation and Management Services Guidelines.**

Typical times have not yet been established for this category of services.

## Observation Care Discharge Services

Observation care discharge of a patient from "observation status" includes final examination of the patient, discussion of the hospital stay, instructions for continuing care, and preparation of discharge records. For observation or inpatient hospital care including the admission and discharge of the patient on the same date, see codes 99234-99236 as appropriate.

**99217** **Observation care discharge** day management (This code is to be utilized by the physician to report all services provided to a patient on discharge from "observation status" if the discharge is on other than the initial date of "observation status." To report services to a patient designated as "observation status" or "inpatient status" and discharged on the same date, use the codes for Observation or Inpatient Care Services (including Admission and Discharge Services, 99234-99236 as appropriate.))

## Initial Observation Care

### New or Established Patient

The following codes are used to report the encounter(s) by the supervising physician with the patient when designated as "observation status." This refers to the initiation of observation status, supervision of the care plan for observation and performance of periodic reassessments. For observation encounters by other physicians, see Office or Other Outpatient Consultation codes (99241-99245).

To report services provided to a patient who is admitted to the hospital after receiving hospital observation care services on the same date, see the notes for initial hospital inpatient care (page 12). For a patient admitted to the hospital on a date subsequent to the date of observation status, the hospital admission would be reported with the appropriate Initial Hospital Care codes (99221-99223). For a patient admitted and discharged from observation or inpatient status on the same date, the services should be reported with codes 99234-99236 as appropriate. Do not report observation discharge (99217) in conjunction with a hospital admission.

When "observation status" is initiated in the course of an encounter in another site of service (eg, hospital emergency department, physician's office, nursing facility) all evaluation and management services provided by the supervising physician in conjunction with initiating "observation status" are considered part of the initial observation care when performed on the same date. The observation care level of service reported by the supervising physician should include the services related to initiating "observation status" provided in the other sites of service as well as in the observation setting.

Evaluation and management services on the same date provided in sites that are related to initiating "observation status" should NOT be reported separately.

These codes may not be utilized for post-operative recovery if the procedure is considered part of the surgical "package." These codes apply to all evaluation and management services that are provided on the same date of initiating "observation status."

**99218** **Initial observation care,** per day, for the evaluation and management of a patient which requires these three key components:

- **a detailed or comprehensive history;**
- **a detailed or comprehensive examination; and**
- **medical decision making that is straightforward or of low complexity.**

Counseling and/or coordination of care with other providers or agencies are provided consistent with the nature of the problem(s) and the patient's and/or family's needs.

Usually, the problem(s) requiring admission to "observation status" are of low severity.

**99219** **Initial observation care,** per day, for the evaluation and management of a patient, which requires these three key components:

- **a comprehensive history;**
- **a comprehensive examination; and**
- **medical decision making of moderate complexity.**

Counseling and/or coordination of care with other providers or agencies are provided consistent with the nature of the problem(s) and the patient's and/or family's needs.

Usually, the problem(s) requiring admission to "observation status" are of moderate severity.

**99220** **Initial observation care,** per day, for the evaluation and management of a patient, which requires these three key components:

- **a comprehensive history;**
- **a comprehensive examination; and**
- **medical decision making of high complexity.**

Counseling and/or coordination of care with other providers or agencies are provided consistent with the nature of the problem(s) and the patient's and/or family's needs.

Usually, the problem(s) requiring admission to "observation status" are of high severity.

# Hospital Inpatient Services

The following codes are used to report evaluation and management services provided to hospital inpatients. Hospital inpatient services include those services provided to patients in a 'partial hospital' setting. These codes are to be used to report these partial hospitalization services. See also psychiatry notes in the full text of *CPT*.

For definitions of key components and commonly used terms, please see **Evaluation and Management Services Guidelines.** For Hospital Observation Services, see 99218-99220. For a patient admitted and discharged from observation or inpatient status on the same date, the services should be reported with codes 99234-99236 as appropriate.

## Initial Hospital Care

### New or Established Patient

The following codes are used to report the first hospital inpatient encounter with the patient by the admitting physician.

For initial inpatient encounters by physicians other than the admitting physician, see initial inpatient consultation codes (99251-99255) or subsequent hospital care codes (99231-99233) as appropriate.

When the patient is admitted to the hospital as an inpatient in the course of an encounter in another site of service (eg, hospital emergency department, observation status in a hospital, physician's office, nursing facility) all evaluation and management services provided by that physician in conjunction with that admission are considered part of the initial hospital care when performed on the same date as the admission. The inpatient care level of service reported by the admitting physician should include the services related to the admission he/she provided in the other sites of service as well as in the inpatient setting.

Evaluation and management services on the same date provided in sites that are related to the admission "observation status" should NOT be reported separately. For a patient admitted and discharged from observation or inpatient status on the same date, the services should be reported with codes 99234-99236 as appropriate.

**99221** **Initial hospital care,** per day, for the evaluation and management of a patient which requires these three key components:

- **a detailed or comprehensive history;**
- **a detailed or comprehensive examination; and**
- **medical decision making that is straightforward or of low complexity.**

Counseling and/or coordination of care with other providers or agencies are provided consistent with the nature of the problem(s) and the patient's and/or family's needs.

Usually, the problem(s) requiring admission are of low severity. Physicians typically spend 30 minutes at the bedside and on the patient's hospital floor or unit.

**99222** **Initial hospital care,** per day, for the evaluation and management of a patient, which requires these three key components:

- **a comprehensive history;**
- **a comprehensive examination; and**
- **medical decision making of moderate complexity.**

Counseling and/or coordination of care with other providers or agencies are provided consistent with the nature of the problem(s) and the patient's and/or family's needs.

Usually, the problem(s) requiring admission are of moderate severity. Physicians typically spend 50 minutes at the bedside and on the patient's hospital floor or unit.

**99223** **Initial hospital care,** per day, for the evaluation and management of a patient, which requires these three key components:

- **a comprehensive history;**
- **a comprehensive examination; and**
- **medical decision making of high complexity.**

Counseling and/or coordination of care with other providers or agencies are provided consistent with the nature of the problem(s) and the patient's and/or family's needs.

Usually, the problem(s) requiring admission are of high severity. Physicians typically spend 70 minutes at the bedside and on the patient's hospital floor or unit.

## Subsequent Hospital Care

All levels of subsequent hospital care include reviewing the medical record and reviewing the results of diagnostic studies and changes in the patient's status, (ie, changes in history, physical condition and response to management) since the last assessment by the physician.

**99231** **Subsequent hospital care,** per day, for the evaluation and management of a patient, which requires at least two of these three key components:

- **a problem focused interval history;**
- **a problem focused examination;**
- **medical decision making that is straightforward or of low complexity.**

Counseling and/or coordination of care with other providers or agencies are provided consistent with the nature of the problem(s) and the patient's and/or family's needs.

Usually, the patient is stable, recovering or improving. Physicians typically spend 15 minutes at the bedside and on the patient's hospital floor or unit.

**99232** **Subsequent hospital care,** per day, for the evaluation and management of a patient, which requires at least two of these three key components:

- **an expanded problem focused interval history;**
- **an expanded problem focused examination;**
- **medical decision making of moderate complexity.**

Counseling and/or coordination of care with other providers or agencies are provided consistent with the nature of the problem(s) and the patient's and/or family's needs.

Usually, the patient is responding inadequately to therapy or has developed a minor complication. Physicians typically spend 25 minutes at the bedside and on the patient's hospital floor or unit.

**99233** **Subsequent hospital care,** per day, for the evaluation and management of a patient, which requires at least two of these three key components:

- **a detailed interval history;**
- **a detailed examination;**
- **medical decision making of high complexity.**

Counseling and/or coordination of care with other providers or agencies are provided consistent with the nature of the problem(s) and the patient's and/or family's needs.

Usually, the patient is unstable or has developed a significant complication or a significant new problem. Physicians typically spend 35 minutes at the bedside and on the patient's hospital floor or unit.

## Observation or Inpatient Care Services (Including Admission and Discharge Services)

The following codes are used to report observation or inpatient hospital care services provided to patients admitted and discharged on the same date of service. When a patient is admitted to the hospital from observation status on the same date, the physician should report only the initial hospital care code. The initial hospital care code reported by the admitting physician should include the services related to the observation status services he/she provided on the same date of inpatient admission.

When "observation status" is initiated in the course of an encounter in another site of service (eg, hospital emergency department, physician's office, nursing facility) all evaluation and management services provided by the supervising physician in conjunction with initiating "observation status" are considered part of the initial observation care when performed on the same date. The observation care level of service should include the services related to initiating "observation status" provided in the other sites of service as well as in the observation setting when provided by the same physician.

For patients admitted to observation or inpatient care and discharged on a different date, see codes 99218-99220 and 99217, or 99221-99223 and 99238-99239.

**99234** **Observation or inpatient hospital care,** for the evaluation and management of a patient including admission and discharge on the same date which requires these three key components:

- **a detailed or comprehensive history;**
- **a detailed or comprehensive examination; and**
- **medical decision making that is straightforward or of low complexity.**

Counseling and/or coordination of care with other providers or agencies are provided consistent with the nature of the problem(s) and the patient's and/or family's needs.

Usually the presenting problem(s) requiring admission are of low severity.

**99235** **Observation or inpatient hospital care,** for the evaluation and management of a patient including admission and discharge on the same date which requires these three key components:

- **a comprehensive history;**
- **a comprehensive examination; and**
- **medical decision making of moderate complexity.**

Counseling and/or coordination of care with other providers or agencies are provided consistent with the nature of the problem(s) and the patient's and/or family's needs.

Usually the presenting problem(s) requiring admission are of moderate severity.

**99236** **Observation or inpatient hospital care,** for the evaluation and management of a patient including admission and discharge on the same date which requires these three key components:

- **a comprehensive history;**
- **a comprehensive examination; and**
- **medical decision making of high complexity.**

Counseling and/or coordination of care with other providers or agencies are provided consistent with the nature of the problem(s) and the patient's and/or family's needs.

Usually the presenting problem(s) requiring admission are of high severity.

## Hospital Discharge Services

The hospital discharge day management codes are to be used to report the total duration of time spent by a physician for final hospital discharge of a patient. The codes include, as appropriate, final examination of the patient, discussion of the hospital stay, even if the time spent by the physician on that date is not continuous, instructions for continuing care to all relevant caregivers, and preparation of discharge records, prescriptions and referral forms. For a patient admitted and discharged from observation or inpatient status on the same date, the services should be reported with codes 99234-99236 as appropriate.

**99238** **Hospital discharge day management;** 30 minutes or less

**99239** more than 30 minutes

(These codes are to be utilized by the physician to report all services provided to a patient on the date of discharge, if other than the initial date of inpatient status. To report services to a patient who is admitted as an inpatient, and discharged on the same date, see codes 99234-99236 for observation or inpatient hospital care including the admission and discharge of the patient on the same date. To report concurrent care services provided by a physician(s) other than the attending physician, use subsequent hospital care codes (99231-99233) on the day of discharge.)

(For Observation Care Discharge, use 99217)

(For observation or inpatient hospital care including the admission and discharge of the patient on the same date, see 99234-99236)

(For Nursing Facility Care Discharge, see 99315, 99316)

(For discharge services provided to newborns admitted and discharged on the same date, use 99435)

# Consultations

A consultation is a type of service provided by a physician whose opinion or advice regarding evaluation and/or management of a specific problem is requested by another physician or other appropriate source.

A physician consultant may initiate diagnostic and/or therapeutic services ►at the same or subsequent visit.◄

►The written or verbal request for a consult may be made by a physician or other appropriate source and documented in the patient's medical record.◄ The consultant's opinion and any services that were ordered or performed must also be documented in the patient's medical record and communicated ►by written report◄ to the requesting physician or other appropriate source.

A "consultation" initiated by a patient and/or family, and not requested by a physician, is not reported using the initial consultation codes but may be reported using the codes for confirmatory consultation or office visits, as appropriate.

If a confirmatory consultation is required, eg, by a third party payor, the modifier '-32', mandated services, should also be reported.

Any specifically identifiable procedure (ie, identified with a specific CPT code) performed on or subsequent to the date of the initial consultation should be reported separately.

If subsequent to the completion of a consultation, the consultant assumes responsibility for management of a portion or all of the patient's condition(s), the follow-up consultation codes should not be used. In the hospital setting, the ►consulting◄ physician should use the appropriate inpatient hospital consultation code for the initial encounter and then subsequent hospital care codes (not follow-up consultation codes). In the office setting, the appropriate established patient code should be used.

There are four subcategories of consultations: office, initial inpatient, follow-up inpatient, and confirmatory. See each subcategory for specific reporting instructions.

For definitions of key components and commonly used terms, please see **Evaluation and Management Services Guidelines**.

# Office or Other Outpatient Consultations

## New or Established Patient

The following codes are used to report consultations provided in the physician's office or in an outpatient or other ambulatory facility, including hospital observation services, home services, domiciliary, rest home, custodial care, or emergency department (see consultation definition, above). Follow-up visits in the consultant's office or other outpatient facility that are initiated by the physician consultant are reported using office visit codes for established patients (99211-99215). If an additional request for an opinion or advice regarding the same or a new problem is received from the attending physician and documented in the medical record, the office consultation codes may be used again.

**99241** **Office consultation** for a new or established patient, which requires these three key components:

- **a problem focused history;**
- **a problem focused examination; and**
- **straightforward medical decision making.**

Counseling and/or coordination of care with other providers or agencies are provided consistent with the nature of the problem(s) and the patient's and/or family's needs.

Usually, the presenting problem(s) are self limited or minor. Physicians typically spend 15 minutes face-to-face with the patient and/or family.

**99242** **Office consultation** for a new or established patient, which requires these three key components:

- **an expanded problem focused history;**
- **an expanded problem focused examination; and**
- **straightforward medical decision making.**

Counseling and/or coordination of care with other providers or agencies are provided consistent with the nature of the problem(s) and the patient's and/or family's needs.

Usually, the presenting problem(s) are of low severity. Physicians typically spend 30 minutes face-to-face with the patient and/or family.

**99243** **Office consultation** for a new or established patient, which requires these three key components:

- **a detailed history;**
- **a detailed examination; and**
- **medical decision making of low complexity.**

Counseling and/or coordination of care with other providers or agencies are provided consistent with the nature of the problem(s) and the patient's and/or family's needs.

Usually, the presenting problem(s) are of moderate severity. Physicians typically spend 40 minutes face-to-face with the patient and/or family.

**99244** **Office consultation** for a new or established patient, which requires these three key components:

- **a comprehensive history;**
- **a comprehensive examination; and**
- **medical decision making of moderate complexity.**

Counseling and/or coordination of care with other providers or agencies are provided consistent with the nature of the problem(s) and the patient's and/or family's needs.

Usually, the presenting problem(s) are of moderate to high severity. Physicians typically spend 60 minutes face-to-face with the patient and/or family.

**99245** **Office consultation** for a new or established patient, which requires these three key components:

- **a comprehensive history;**
- **a comprehensive examination; and**
- **medical decision making of high complexity.**

Counseling and/or coordination of care with other providers or agencies are provided consistent with the nature of the problem(s) and the patient's and/or family's needs.

Usually, the presenting problem(s) are of moderate to high severity. Physicians typically spend 80 minutes face-to-face with the patient and/or family.

# Initial Inpatient Consultations

## New or Established Patient

The following codes are used to report physician consultations provided to hospital inpatients, residents of nursing facilities, or patients in a partial hospital setting. Only one initial consultation should be reported by a consultant per admission.

**99251** **Initial inpatient consultation** for a new or established patient, which requires these three key components:

- **a problem focused history;**
- **a problem focused examination; and**
- **straightforward medical decision making.**

Counseling and/or coordination of care with other providers or agencies are provided consistent with the nature of the problem(s) and the patient's and/or family's needs.

Usually, the presenting problem(s) are self limited or minor. Physicians typically spend 20 minutes at the bedside and on the patient's hospital floor or unit.

**99252** **Initial inpatient consultation** for a new or established patient, which requires these three key components:

- **an expanded problem focused history;**
- **an expanded problem focused examination; and**
- **straightforward medical decision making.**

Counseling and/or coordination of care with other providers or agencies are provided consistent with the nature of the problem(s) and the patient's and/or family's needs.

Usually, the presenting problem(s) are of low severity. Physicians typically spend 40 minutes at the bedside and on the patient's hospital floor or unit.

**99253** **Initial inpatient consultation** for a new or established patient, which requires these three key components:

- **a detailed history;**
- **a detailed examination; and**
- **medical decision making of low complexity.**

Counseling and/or coordination of care with other providers or agencies are provided consistent with the nature of the problem(s) and the patient's and/or family's needs.

Usually, the presenting problem(s) are of moderate severity. Physicians typically spend 55 minutes at the bedside and on the patient's hospital floor or unit.

**99254** **Initial inpatient consultation** for a new or established patient, which requires three key components:

- **a comprehensive history;**
- **a comprehensive examination; and**
- **medical decision making of moderate complexity.**

Counseling and/or coordination of care with other providers or agencies are provided consistent with the nature of the problem(s) and the patient's and/or family's needs.

Usually, the presenting problem(s) are of moderate to high severity. Physicians typically spend 80 minutes at the bedside and on the patient's hospital floor or unit.

**99255** **Initial inpatient consultation** for a new or established patient, which requires these three key components:

- **a comprehensive history;**
- **a comprehensive examination; and**
- **medical decision making of high complexity.**

Counseling and/or coordination of care with other providers or agencies are provided consistent with the nature of the problem(s) and the patient's and/or family's needs.

Usually, the presenting problem(s) are of moderate to high severity. Physicians typically spend 110 minutes at the bedside and on the patient's hospital floor or unit.

# Follow-Up Inpatient Consultations

## Established Patient

Follow-up consultations are visits to complete the initial consultation OR subsequent consultative visits requested by the attending physician.

A follow-up consultation includes monitoring progress, recommending management modifications or advising on a new plan of care in response to changes in the patient's status.

If the physician consultant has initiated treatment at the initial consultation, and participates thereafter in the patient's management, the codes for subsequent hospital care should be used (99231-99233).

The following codes are used to report follow-up consultations provided to hospital inpatients or nursing facility residents only. For consultative services provided in other settings, the codes for office or other outpatient consultations should be reported (99241-99245).

**99261** **Follow-up inpatient consultation** for an established patient, which requires at least two of these three key components:

- **a problem focused interval history;**
- **a problem focused examination;**
- **medical decision making that is straightforward or of low complexity.**

Counseling and/or coordination of care with other providers or agencies are provided consistent with nature of the problem(s) and the patient's and/or family's needs.

Usually, the patient is stable, recovering or improving. Physicians typically spend 10 minutes at the bedside and on the patient's hospital floor or unit.

**99262** **Follow-up inpatient consultation** for an established patient which requires at least two of these three key components:

- **an expanded problem focused interval history;**
- **an expanded problem focused examination;**
- **medical decision making of moderate complexity.**

Counseling and/or coordination of care with other providers or agencies are provided consistent with the nature of the problem(s) and the patient's and/or family's needs.

Usually, the patient is responding inadequately to therapy or has developed a minor complication. Physicians typically spend 20 minutes at the bedside and on the patient's hospital floor or unit.

**99263** **Follow-up inpatient consultation** for an established patient which requires at least two of these three key components:

- **a detailed interval history;**
- **a detailed examination;**
- **medical decision making of high complexity.**

Counseling and/or coordination of care with other providers or agencies are provided consistent with the nature of the problem(s) and the patient's and/or family's needs.

Usually, the patient is unstable or has developed a significant complication or a significant new problem. Physicians typically spend 30 minutes at the bedside and on the patient's hospital floor or unit.

# Confirmatory Consultations

## New or Established Patient

The following codes are used to report the evaluation and management services provided to patients when the consulting physician is aware of the confirmatory nature of the opinion sought (eg, when a second/third opinion is requested or required on the necessity or appropriateness of a previously recommended medical treatment or surgical procedure).

Confirmatory consultations may be provided in any setting.

A physician consultant providing a confirmatory consultation is expected to provide an opinion and/or advice only. Any services subsequent to the opinion are coded at the appropriate level of office visit, established patient, or subsequent hospital care. If a confirmatory consultation is required, eg, by a third party payor, the modifier '-32', mandated services, should also be reported. (See also Consultation notes, page 15.) Typical times have not yet been established for this subcategory of services.

**99271** **Confirmatory consultation** for a new or established patient, which requires these three key components:

- **a problem focused history;**
- **a problem focused examination; and**
- **straightforward medical decision making.**

Counseling and/or coordination of care with other providers or agencies are provided consistent with the nature of the problem(s) and the patient's and/or family's needs.

Usually, the presenting problem(s) are self limited or minor.

**99272** **Confirmatory consultation** for a new or established patient, which requires these three key components:

- **an expanded problem focused history;**
- **an expanded problem focused examination; and**
- **straightforward medical decision making.**

Counseling and/or coordination of care with other providers or agencies are provided consistent with the nature of the problem(s) and the patient's and/or family's needs.

Usually, the presenting problem(s) are of low severity.

**99273** **Confirmatory consultation** for a new or established patient, which requires these three key components:

- **a detailed history;**
- **a detailed examination; and**
- **medical decision making of low complexity.**

Counseling and/or coordination of care with other providers or agencies are provided consistent with the nature of the problem(s) and the patient's and/or family's needs.

Usually, the presenting problem(s) are of moderate severity.

**99274** **Confirmatory consultation** for a new or established patient, which requires these three key components:

- **a comprehensive history;**
- **a comprehensive examination; and**
- **medical decision making of moderate complexity.**

Counseling and/or coordination of care with other providers or agencies are provided consistent with the nature of the problem(s) and the patient's and/or family's needs.

Usually, the presenting problem(s) are of moderate to high severity.

**99275** **Confirmatory consultation** for a new or established patient, which requires these three key components:

- **a comprehensive history;**
- **a comprehensive examination; and**
- **medical decision making of high complexity.**

Counseling and/or coordination of care with other providers or agencies are provided consistent with the nature of the problem(s) and the patient's and/or family's needs.

Usually, the presenting problem(s) are of moderate to high severity.

# Emergency Department Services

## New or Established Patient

The following codes are used to report evaluation and management services provided in the emergency department. No distinction is made between new and established patients in the emergency department.

An emergency department is defined as an organized hospital-based facility for the provision of unscheduled episodic services to patients who present for immediate medical attention. The facility must be available 24 hours a day.

For critical care services provided in the Emergency Department, see Critical Care notes and 99291, 99292.

For evaluation and management services provided to a patient in an observation area of a hospital, see 99217-99220.

For observation or inpatient care services (including admission and discharge services), see 99234-99236.

**99281** **Emergency department visit** for the evaluation and management of a patient, which requires these three key components:

- **a problem focused history;**
- **a problem focused examination; and**
- **straightforward medical decision making.**

Counseling and/or coordination of care with other providers or agencies are provided consistent with the nature of the problem(s) and the patient's and/or family's needs.

Usually, the presenting problem(s) are self limited or minor.

**99282** **Emergency department visit** for the evaluation and management of a patient, which requires these three key components:

- **an expanded problem focused history;**
- **an expanded problem focused examination; and**
- **medical decision making of low complexity.**

Counseling and/or coordination of care with other providers or agencies are provided consistent with the nature of the problem(s) and the patient's and/or family's needs.

Usually, the presenting problem(s) are of low to moderate severity.

**99283** **Emergency department visit** for the evaluation and management of a patient, which requires these three key components:

- **an expanded problem focused history;**
- **an expanded problem focused examination; and**
- **medical decision making of moderate complexity.**

Counseling and/or coordination of care with other providers or agencies are provided consistent with the nature of the problem(s) and the patient's and/or family's needs.

Usually, the presenting problem(s) are of moderate severity.

**99284** **Emergency department visit** for the evaluation and management of a patient, which requires these three key components:

- **a detailed history;**
- **a detailed examination; and**
- **medical decision making of moderate complexity.**

Counseling and/or coordination of care with other providers or agencies are provided consistent with the nature of the problem(s) and the patient's and/or family's needs.

Usually, the presenting problem(s) are of high severity, and require urgent evaluation by the physician but do not pose an immediate significant threat to life or physiologic function.

▲**99285** **Emergency department visit** for the evaluation and management of a patient, which requires these three key components within the constraints imposed by the urgency of the patient's clinical condition and/or mental status:

- **a comprehensive history;**
- **a comprehensive examination; and**
- **medical decision making of high complexity.**

Counseling and/or coordination of care with other providers or agencies are provided consistent with the nature of the problem(s) and the patient's and/or family's needs.

Usually, the presenting problem(s) are of high severity and pose an immediate significant threat to life or physiologic function.

## Other Emergency Services

In physician directed emergency care, advanced life support, the physician is located in a hospital emergency or critical care department, and is in two-way voice communication with ambulance or rescue personnel outside the hospital. The physician directs the performance of necessary medical procedures, including but not limited to:

telemetry of cardiac rhythm; cardiac and/or pulmonary resuscitation; endotracheal or esophageal obturator airway intubation; administration of intravenous fluids and/or administration of intramuscular, intratracheal or subcutaneous drugs; and/or electrical conversion of arrhythmia.

**99288** **Physician direction of** emergency medical systems (EMS) emergency care, advanced life support

## Critical Care Services

►Critical care is the direct delivery by a physician(s) of medical care for a critically ill or injured patient. A critical illness or injury acutely impairs one or more vital organ systems such that the patient's survival is jeopardized. The care of such patients involves decision making of high complexity to assess, manipulate and support central nervous system failure, circulatory failure, shock-like conditions, renal, hepatic, metabolic or respiratory failure, postoperative complications, overwhelming infection, or other vital system functions to treat single or multiple vital organ system failure or to prevent further deterioration. It may require extensive interpretation of multiple databases and the application of advanced technology to manage the patient. Critical care may be provided on multiple days, even if no changes are made in the treatment rendered to the patient, provided that the patient's condition continues to require the level of physician attention described above.◄

Critical care services ►include◄ but ►are◄ not limited to ►the treatment or prevention or further deterioration◄ of central nervous system failure, circulatory failure, shock-like conditions, renal, hepatic, metabolic, or respiratory failure, postoperative complications, or overwhelming infection. Critical care is usually, but not always, given in a critical care area, such as the coronary care unit, intensive care unit, ►pediatric intensive care unit,◄ respiratory care unit, or the emergency care facility.

►Critical care services provided to infants older than one month of age at the time of admission to an intensive care unit are reported with critical care codes 99291 and 99292. Critical care services provided to neonates (30 days of age or less at the time of admission to an intensive care unit) are reported with the neonatal critical care codes 99295, 99296, 99297 and 99298. The neonatal critical care codes are reported as long as the neonate qualifies for critical care services during the hospital stay. The reporting of neonatal critical care services is not based on time, the type of unit (eg, pediatric or neonatal critical care unit) or the type of provider delivering the care. For additional instructions on reporting these services, see the Neonatal Intensive Care section and codes 99295-99298.◄

Services for a patient who is not critically ill but happens to be in a critical care unit are reported using ►other appropriate E/M codes.◄

The following services are included in reporting critical care when performed during the critical period by the physician(s) providing critical care: the interpretation of cardiac output measurements (93561, 93562), chest x-rays (71010, 71020), blood gases, and information data stored in computers (eg, ECGs, blood pressures, hematologic data (99090)); gastric intubation (91105); temporary transcutaneous pacing (92953); ventilator management (94656, 94657, 94660, 94662); and vascular access procedures (36000, 36410, 36415, 36600). Any services performed which are not listed above should be reported separately.

The critical care codes ►99291 and 99292◄ are used to report the total duration of time spent by a physician providing ►critical care services◄ to a critically ill or critically injured patient, even if the time spent by the physician on that date is not continuous. ►For any given period of time spent providing critical care services, the physician must devote his or her full attention to the patient and, therefore, cannot provide services to any other patient during the same period of time.◄

►Time spent with the individual patient should be recorded in the patient's record. The time that can be reported as critical care is the time spent engaged in work directly related to the individual patient's care whether that time was spent at the immediate bedside or elsewhere on the floor or unit. For example, time spent on the unit or at the nursing station on the floor reviewing test results or imaging studies, discussing the critically ill patient's care with other medical staff or documenting critical care services in the medical record would be reported as critical care, even though it does not occur at the bedside. Also, when the patient is unable or clinically incompetent to participate in discussions, time spent on the floor or unit with family members or surrogate decision makers obtaining a medical history, reviewing the patient's condition or prognosis, or discussing treatment or limitation(s) of treatment may be reported as critical care, provided that the conversation bears directly on the medical decision making.◄

►Time spent in activities that occur outside of the unit or off the floor (eg, telephone calls, whether taken at home, in the office, or elsewhere in the hospital) may not be reported as critical care since the physician is not immediately available to the patient. Time spent in activities that do not directly contribute to the treatment of the patient may not be reported as critical care, even if they are performed in the critical care unit (eg, participation in administrative meetings or telephone calls to discuss other patients).◄

Code 99291 is used to report the first ►30-74 minutes◄ of critical care on a given date. It should be used only once per date even if the time spent by the physician is not continuous on that date. Critical care of less than 30 minutes total duration on a given date should be reported with the appropriate E/M code.

Code 99292 is used to report each additional 30 minutes beyond the first ►74 minutes.◄ It also may be used to report the final 15-30 minutes of critical care on a given date. Critical care of less than 15 minutes beyond the first ►74 minutes◄ or less than 15 minutes beyond the final 30 minutes is not reported separately.

The following examples illustrate the correct reporting of critical care services:

| Total Duration of Critical Care | Codes |
|---|---|
| less than 30 minutes (less than 1/2 hour) | ►appropriate E/M codes◄ |
| 30-74 minutes (1/2 hr. - 1 hr. 14 min.) | 99291 X 1 |
| 75-104 minutes (1 hr. 15 min. - 1 hr. 44 min.) | 99291 X 1 AND 99292 X 1 |
| 105-134 minutes (1 hr. 45 min. - 2 hr. 14 min.) | 99291 X 1 AND 99292 X 2 |
| 135 - 164 minutes (2 hr. 15 min. - 2 hr. 44 min.) | 99291 X 1 AND 99292 X 3 |
| 165 - 194 minutes (2 hr. 45 min. - 3 hr. 14 min.) | 99291 X 1 AND 99292 X 4 |

▲**99291** **Critical care, evaluation and management** of the critically ill or critically injured patient; first 30-74 minutes

+**99292** each additional 30 minutes (List separately in addition to code for primary service)

(Use 99292 in conjunction with 99291)

## Neonatal Intensive Care

The following codes (99295-99298) are used to report services provided by a physician directing the care of a critically ill newborn (or managing the continuing intensive care of the very low birth weight (VLBW) infant). They represent care starting with the date of admission and may be reported only once per day, per patient. Once the neonate is no longer considered to be critically ill and attains a body weight which exceeds 1500 grams, the codes for Subsequent Hospital Care (99231-99233) should be utilized.

These neonatal critical care codes are to be used in addition to codes 99360, 99436 or 99440 as appropriate, when the physician is present for the delivery and newborn resuscitation is required.

►The same definitions for critical care services apply for the adult, child and neonate. The neonatal critical care codes, however, are global

24-hour codes and not reported as hourly services. Services for a patient who is not critically ill but happens to be in a critical care unit are reported using other appropriate E/M codes.◄

►The neonatal critical care codes (99295, 99296, 99297, 99298) are applied to neonates (30 days of age or less) admitted to an intensive care unit. These codes will be applicable as long as the child qualifies for critical care services during this hospital stay. Infants admitted to an intensive care unit older than one month of age would be coded with hourly critical care codes (99291, 99292) if they qualify for critical care services. These neonatal codes are not applied based upon the type of unit (eg, pediatric or neonatal critical care unit) in which the child receives care nor the type of provider delivering the care.◄

Care rendered includes management, monitoring, and treatment of the patient including enteral and parenteral nutritional maintenance, metabolic and hematologic maintenance, pharmacologic control of the circulatory system, parent counseling, case management services, and personal direct supervision of the health care team in the performance of cognitive and procedural activities.

►In addition to those services listed above for adult and pediatric hourly codes, the following procedures are also included in the bundled (global) neonatal codes (99295, 99296, 99297 and 99298):◄ umbilical ►venous (36510) and umbilical arterial (36620) catheters,◄ central ►(36488, 36490)◄ or peripheral vessel catheterization ►(36000),◄ other arterial catheters (36140, 36620),◄ oral or nasogastric tube placement, endotracheal intubation ►(31500),◄ lumbar puncture ►(62270),◄ suprapubic bladder aspiration ►(51000),◄ bladder catheterization ►(53670),◄ initiation and management of mechanical ventilation ►(94656, 94657)◄ or continuous positive airway pressure (CPAP) ►(94660),◄ surfactant administration, intravascular fluid administration, transfusion of blood components ►(36430, 36440),◄ vascular punctures ►(36420, 36600),◄ invasive or non-invasive electronic monitoring of vital signs, bedside pulmonary function testing, and/or monitoring or interpretation of blood gases or oxygen saturation (94760-94762). Any services performed which are not listed above should be reported separately.

For additional instructions, see parenthetical descriptions listed for 99295-99298.

▲99295 **Initial neonatal intensive care,** per day, for the evaluation and management of a critically ill neonate or infant

This code is reserved for the date of admission for neonates who are critically ill. Critically ill neonates require cardiac and/or respiratory support (including ventilator or nasal CPAP when indicated), continuous or frequent vital sign monitoring, laboratory and blood gas interpretations, follow-up physician reevaluations, and constant observation by the health care team under direct physician supervision. Immediate preoperative evaluation and stabilization of neonates with life threatening surgical or cardiac conditions are included under this code.

▲99296 **Subsequent neonatal intensive care,** per day, for the evaluation and management of a critically ill and unstable neonate or infant

A critically ill and unstable neonate will require cardiac and/or respiratory support (including ventilator or nasal CPAP when indicated), continuous or frequent vital sign monitoring, laboratory and blood gas interpretations, follow-up physician re-evaluations throughout a 24-hour period, and constant observation by the health care team under direct physician supervision. In addition, most will require frequent ventilator changes, intravenous fluid alterations, and/or early initiation of parenteral nutrition. Neonates in the immediate post-operative period or those who become critically ill and unstable during the hospital stay will commonly qualify for this level of care.

This code encompasses intensive care provided on dates subsequent to the admission date.

▲**99297** **Subsequent neonatal intensive care,** per day, for the evaluation and management of a critically ill though stable neonate or infant

Critically ill though stable neonates require cardiac and/or respiratory support (including ventilator and nasal CPAP when indicated), continuous or frequent vital sign monitoring, laboratory and blood gas interpretations, follow-up physician re-evaluations throughout a 24 hour period, and constant observation by the health care team under direct physician supervision. Neonates at this level of care would be expected to require less frequent changes in respiratory, cardiovascular and fluid and electrolyte therapy as those included under code 99296.

This code encompasses intensive care provided on dates subsequent to the admission date.

**99298** **Subsequent neonatal intensive care,** per day, for the evaluation and management of the recovering very low birth weight infant (less than 1500 grams)

Very low birth weight neonates who are no longer critically ill continue to require intensive cardiac and respiratory monitoring, continuous and/or frequent vital sign monitoring, heat maintenance, enteral and/or parenteral nutritional adjustments, laboratory and oxygen monitoring and constant observation by the health care team under direct physician supervision. Neonates of this level of care would be expected to require infrequent changes in respiratory, cardiovascular and/or fluid and electrolyte therapy as those induced under 99296 or 99297.

This code encompasses intensive care provided on days subsequent to the admission date.

# Nursing Facility Services

The following codes are used to report evaluation and management services to patients in Nursing Facilities (formerly called Skilled Nursing Facilities (SNFs), Intermediate Care Facilities (ICFs) or Long Term Care Facilities (LTCFs)).

These codes should also be used to report evaluation and management services provided to a patient in a psychiatric residential treatment center (a facility or a distinct part of a facility for psychiatric care, which provides a 24 hour therapeutically planned and professionally staffed group living and learning environment). If procedures such as medical psychotherapy are provided in addition to evaluation and management services, these should be reported in addition to the evaluation and management services provided.

Nursing facilities that provide convalescent, rehabilitative, or long term care are required to conduct comprehensive, accurate, standardized, and reproducible assessments of each resident's functional capacity using a Resident Assessment Instrument (RAI). All RAIs include the Minimum Data Set (MDS), Resident Assessment Protocols (RAPs) and utilization guidelines. The MDS is the primary screening and assessment tool; the RAPs trigger the identification of potential problems and provide guidelines for follow-up assessments.

Physicians have a central role in assuring that all residents receive thorough assessments and that medical plans of care are instituted or revised to enhance or maintain the residents' physical and psychosocial functioning.

Two subcategories of nursing facility services are recognized: Comprehensive Nursing Facility Assessments and Subsequent Nursing Facility Care. Both subcategories apply to new or established patients. Comprehensive Assessments may be performed at one or more sites in the assessment process: the hospital, observation unit, office, nursing facility, domiciliary/non-nursing facility or patient's home.

For definitions of key components and commonly used terms, please see **Evaluation and Management Services Guidelines.**

## Comprehensive Nursing Facility Assessments

### New or Established Patient

When the patient is admitted to the nursing facility in the course of an encounter in another site of service (eg, hospital emergency department, physician's office), all evaluation and management services provided by that physician in conjunction with that admission are considered part of the initial nursing facility care when performed on the same date as the admission or readmission. The nursing facility care level of service reported by the admitting physician should include the services related to the admission he/she provided in the other sites of service as well as in the nursing facility setting.

Hospital discharge or observation discharge services performed on the same date of nursing facility admission or readmission may be reported separately. For a patient discharged from inpatient status on the same date of nursing facility admission or readmission, the hospital discharge services should be reported with codes 99238-99239 as appropriate. For a patient discharged from observation status on the same date of nursing facility admission or readmission, the observation care discharge services should be reported with code 99217. For a patient admitted and discharged from observation or inpatient status on the same date, see codes 99234-99236.

(For nursing facility care discharge, see 99315, 99316)

More than one comprehensive assessment may be necessary during an inpatient confinement.

**99301** **Evaluation and management** of a new or established patient involving an annual nursing facility assessment which requires these three key components:

- **a detailed interval history;**
- **a comprehensive examination; and**
- **medical decision making that is straightforward or of low complexity.**

Counseling and/or coordination of care with other providers or agencies are provided consistent with the nature of the problem(s) and the patient's and/or family's needs.

Usually, the patient is stable, recovering or improving. The review and affirmation of the medical plan of care is required. Physicians typically spend 30 minutes at the bedside and on the patient's facility floor or unit.

**99302** **Evaluation and management** of a new or established patient involving a nursing facility assessment which requires these three key components:

- **a detailed interval history;**
- **a comprehensive examination; and**
- **medical decision making of moderate to high complexity.**

Counseling and/or coordination of care with other providers or agencies are provided consistent with the nature of the problem(s) and the patient's and/or family's needs.

Usually, the patient has developed a significant complication or a significant new problem and has had a major permanent change in status.

The creation of a new medical plan of care is required. Physicians typically spend 40 minutes at the bedside and on the patient's facility floor or unit.

**99303** **Evaluation and management** of a new or established patient involving a nursing facility assessment at the time of initial admission or readmission to the facility, which requires these three key components:

- **a comprehensive history;**
- **a comprehensive examination; and**
- **medical decision making of moderate to high complexity.**

Counseling and/or coordination of care with other providers or agencies are provided consistent with the nature of the problem(s) and the patient's and/or family's needs.

The creation of a medical plan of care is required. Physicians typically spend 50 minutes at the bedside and on the patient's facility floor or unit.

## Subsequent Nursing Facility Care

### New or Established Patient

The following codes are used to report the services provided to residents of nursing facilities who do not require a comprehensive assessment, and/or who have not had a major, permanent change of status.

All levels include reviewing the medical record, noting changes in the resident's status since the last visit, and reviewing and signing orders.

**99311** **Subsequent nursing facility care,** per day, for the evaluation and management of a new or established patient, which requires at least two of these three key components:

- **a problem focused interval history;**
- **a problem focused examination;**
- **medical decision making that is straightforward or of low complexity.**

Counseling and/or coordination of care with other providers or agencies are provided consistent with the nature of the problem(s) and the patient's and/or family's needs.

Usually, the patient is stable, recovering or improving. Physicians typically spend 15 minutes at the bedside and on the patient's facility floor or unit.

**99312** **Subsequent nursing facility care,** per day, for the evaluation and management of a new or established patient, which requires at least two of these three key components:

- **an expanded problem focused interval history;**
- **an expanded problem focused examination;**
- **medical decision making of moderate complexity.**

Counseling and/or coordination of care with other providers or agencies are provided consistent with the nature of the problem(s) and the patient's and/or family's needs.

Usually, the patient is responding inadequately to therapy or has developed a minor complication. Physicians typically spend 25 minutes at the bedside and on the patient's facility floor or unit.

**99313** **Subsequent nursing facility care,** per day, for the evaluation and management of a new or established patient, which requires at least two of these three key components:

- **a detailed interval history;**
- **a detailed examination;**
- **medical decision making of moderate to high complexity.**

Counseling and/or coordination of care with other providers or agencies are provided consistent with the nature of the problem(s) and the patient's and/or family's needs.

Usually, the patient has developed a significant complication or a significant new problem. Physicians typically spend 35 minutes at the bedside and on the patient's facility floor or unit.

## Nursing Facility Discharge Services

The nursing facility discharge day management codes are to be used to report the total duration of time spent by a physician for the final nursing facility discharge of a patient. The codes include, as appropriate, final examination of the patient, discussion of the nursing facility stay, even if the time spent by the physician on that date is not continuous. Instructions are given for continuing care to all relevant caregivers, and preparation of discharge records, prescriptions and referral forms.

**99315** Nursing facility discharge day management; 30 minutes or less

**99316** more than 30 minutes

# Domiciliary, Rest Home (eg, Boarding Home), or Custodial Care Services

The following codes are used to report evaluation and management services in a facility which provides room, board and other personal assistance services, generally on a long-term basis. The facility's services do not include a medical component.

For definitions of key components and commonly used terms, please see **Evaluation and Management Services Guidelines.**

Typical times have not yet been established for this category of services.

### New Patient

**99321** **Domiciliary or rest home visit** for the evaluation and management of a new patient which requires these three key components:

- **a problem focused history;**
- **a problem focused examination; and**
- **medical decision making that is straightforward or of low complexity.**

Counseling and/or coordination of care with other providers or agencies are provided consistent with the nature of the problem(s) and the patient's and/or family's needs.

Usually, the presenting problem(s) are of low severity.

99322 **Domiciliary or rest home visit** for the evaluation and management of a new patient, which requires these three key components:

- **an expanded problem focused history;**
- **an expanded problem focused examination; and**
- **medical decision making of moderate complexity.**

Counseling and/or coordination of care with other providers or agencies are provided consistent with the nature of the problem(s) and the patient's and/or family's needs.

Usually, the presenting problem(s) are of moderate severity.

99323 **Domiciliary or rest home visit** for the evaluation and management of a new patient, which requires these three key components:

- **a detailed history;**
- **a detailed examination; and**
- **medical decision making of high complexity.**

Counseling and/or coordination of care with other providers or agencies are provided consistent with the nature of the problem(s) and the patient's and/or family's needs.

Usually, the presenting problem(s) are of high complexity.

## Established Patient

99331 **Domiciliary or rest home visit** for the evaluation and management of an established patient, which requires at least two of these three key components:

- **a problem focused interval history;**
- **a problem focused examination;**
- **medical decision making that is straightforward or of low complexity.**

Counseling and/or coordination of care with other providers or agencies are provided consistent with the nature of the problem(s) and the patient's and/or family's needs.

Usually, the patient is stable, recovering or improving.

99332 **Domiciliary or rest home visit** for the evaluation and management of an established patient, which requires at least two of these three key components:

- **an expanded problem focused interval history;**
- **an expanded problem focused examination;**
- **medical decision making of moderate complexity.**

Counseling and/or coordination of care with other providers or agencies are provided consistent with the nature of the problem(s) and the patient's and/or family's needs.

Usually, the patient is responding inadequately to therapy or has developed a minor complication.

99333 **Domiciliary or rest home visit** for the evaluation and management of an established patient, which requires at least two of these three key components:

- **a detailed interval history;**
- **a detailed examination;**
- **medical decision making of high complexity.**

Counseling and/or coordination of care with other providers or agencies are provided consistent with the nature of the problem(s) and the patient's and/or family's needs.

Usually, the patient is unstable or has developed a significant complication or a significant new problem.

# Home Services

The following codes are used to report evaluation and management services provided in a private residence.

For definitions of key components and commonly used terms, please see **Evaluation and Management Services Guidelines.**

## New Patient

**99341** **Home visit** for the evaluation and management of a new patient, which requires these three key components:

- **a problem focused history;**
- **a problem focused examination; and**
- **straightforward medical decision making.**

Counseling and/or coordination of care with other providers or agencies are provided consistent with the nature of the problem(s) and the patient's and/or family's needs.

Usually, the presenting problem(s) are of low severity. Physicians typically spend 20 minutes face-to-face with the patient and/or family.

**99342** **Home visit** for the evaluation and management of a new patient, which requires these three key components:

- **an expanded problem focused history;**
- **an expanded problem focused examination; and**
- **medical decision making of low complexity.**

Counseling and/or coordination of care with other providers or agencies are provided consistent with the nature of the problem(s) and the patient's and/or family's needs.

Usually, the presenting problem(s) are of moderate severity. Physicians typically spend 30 minutes face-to-face with the patient and/or family.

**99343** **Home visit** for the evaluation and management of a new patient, which requires these three key components:

- **a detailed history;**
- **a detailed examination; and**
- **medical decision making of moderate complexity.**

Counseling and/or coordination of care with other providers or agencies are provided consistent with the nature of the problem(s) and the patient's and/or family's needs.

Usually, the presenting problem(s) are of moderate to high severity. Physicians typically spend 45 minutes face-to-face with the patient and/or family.

**99344** **Home visit** for the evaluation and management of a new patient, which requires these three components:

- **a comprehensive history;**
- **a comprehensive examination; and**
- **medical decision making of moderate complexity.**

Counseling and/or coordination of care with other providers or agencies are provided consistent with the nature of the problem(s) and the patient's and/or family's needs.

Usually, the presenting problem(s) are of high severity. Physicians typically spend 60 minutes face-to-face with the patient and/or family.

**99345** **Home visit** for the evaluation and management of a new patient, which requires these three key components:

- **a comprehensive history;**
- **a comprehensive examination; and**
- **medical decision making of high complexity.**

Counseling and/or coordination of care with other providers or agencies are provided consistent with the nature of the problem(s) and the patient's and/or family's needs.

Usually, the patient is unstable or has developed a significant new problem requiring immediate physician attention. Physicians typically spend 75 minutes face-to-face with the patient and/or family.

## Established Patient

**99347** **Home visit** for the evaluation and management of an established patient, which requires at least two of these three key components:

- **a problem focused interval history;**
- **a problem focused examination;**
- **straightforward medical decision making.**

Counseling and/or coordination of care with other providers or agencies are provided consistent with the nature of the problem(s) and the patient's and/or family's needs.

Usually, the presenting problem(s) are self-limited or minor. Physicians typically spend 15 minutes face-to-face with the patient and/or family.

**99348** **Home visit** for the evaluation and management of an established patient, which requires at least two of these three key components:

- **an expanded problem focused interval history;**
- **an expanded problem focused examination;**
- **medical decision making of low complexity.**

Counseling and/or coordination of care with other providers or agencies are provided consistent with the nature of the problem(s) and the patient's and/or family's needs.

Usually, the presenting problem(s) are of low to moderate severity. Physicians typically spend 25 minutes face-to-face with the patient and/or family.

**99349** **Home visit** for the evaluation and management of an established patient, which requires at least two of these three key components:

- **a detailed interval history;**
- **a detailed examination;**
- **medical decision making of moderate complexity.**

Counseling and/or coordination of care with other providers or agencies are provided consistent with the nature of the problem(s) and the patient's and/or family's needs.

Usually, the presenting problem(s) are moderate to high severity. Physicians typically spend 40 minutes face-to-face with the patient and/or family.

**99350** **Home visit** for the evaluation and management of an established patient, which requires at least two of these three key components:

- **a comprehensive interval history;**
- **a comprehensive examination;**
- **medical decision making of moderate to high complexity.**

Counseling and/or coordination of care with other providers or agencies are provided consistent with the nature of the problem(s) and the patient's and/or family's needs.

Usually, the presenting problem(s) are of moderate to high severity. The patient may be unstable or may have developed a significant new problem requiring immediate physician attention. Physicians typically spend 60 minutes face-to-face with the patient and/or family.

(99351 has been deleted. To report, use 99347)

(99352 has been deleted. To report, use 99348)

(99353 has been deleted. To report, use 99349)

# Prolonged Services

## Prolonged Physician Service With Direct (Face-To-Face) Patient Contact

Codes 99354-99357 are used when a physician provides prolonged service involving direct (face-to-face) patient contact that is beyond the usual service in either the inpatient or outpatient setting. This service is reported in addition to other physician service, including evaluation and management services at any level. Appropriate codes should be selected for supplies provided or procedures performed in the care of the patient during this period.

Codes 99354-99357 are used to report the total duration of face-to-face time spent by a physician on a given date providing prolonged service, even if the time spent by the physician on that date is not continuous.

Code 99354 or 99356 is used to report the first hour of prolonged service on a given date, depending on the place of service.

Either code also may be used to report a total duration of prolonged service of 30-60 minutes on a given date. Either code should be used only once per date, even if the time spent by the physician is not continuous on that date. Prolonged service of less than 30 minutes total duration on a given date is not separately reported because the work involved is included in the total work of the evaluation and management codes.

Code 99355 or 99357 is used to report each additional 30 minutes beyond the first hour, depending on the place of service. Either code may also be used to report the final 15-30 minutes of prolonged service on a given date. Prolonged service of less than 15 minutes beyond the first hour or less than 15 minutes beyond the final 30 minutes is not reported separately.

The following examples illustrate the correct reporting of prolonged physician service with direct patient contact in the office setting:

| **Total Duration of Prolonged Services** | **Code(s)** |
|---|---|
| less than 30 minutes (less than 1/2 hour) | Not reported separately |
| 30-74 minutes (1/2 hr. - 1 hr. 14 min.) | 99354 X 1 |
| 75-104 minutes (1 hr. 15 min. - 1 hr. 44 min.) | 99354 X 1 AND 99355 X 1 |
| 105-134 minutes (1 hr. 45 min. - 2 hr. 14 min.) | 99354 X 1 AND 99355 X 2 |
| 135-164 minutes (2 hr. 15 min. - 2 hr. 44 min.) | 99354 X 1 AND 99355 X 3 |
| 165-194 minutes (2 hr. 45 min. - 3 hr. 14 min.) | 99354 X 1 AND 99355 X 4 |

**+ 99354** Prolonged physician service in the office or other outpatient setting requiring direct (face-to-face) patient contact beyond the usual service (eg, prolonged care and treatment of an acute asthmatic patient in an outpatient setting); first hour (List separately in addition to code for office or other outpatient Evaluation and Management service)

(Use 99354 in conjunction with codes 99201-99215, 99241-99245, 99301-99350)

**+ 99355** each additional 30 minutes (List separately in addition to code for prolonged physician service)

(Use 99355 in conjunction with codes 99354)

**+ 99356** Prolonged physician service in the inpatient setting, requiring direct (face-to-face) patient contact beyond the usual service (eg, maternal fetal monitoring for high risk delivery or other physiological monitoring, prolonged care of an acutely ill inpatient); first hour (List separately in addition to code for inpatient Evaluation and Management service)

(Use 99356 in conjunction with codes 99221-99233, 99251-99255, 99261-99263)

**+ 99357** each additional 30 minutes (List separately in addition to code for prolonged physician service)

(Use 99357 in conjunction with code 99356)

## Prolonged Physician Service Without Direct (Face-To-Face) Patient Contact

Codes 99358 and 99359 are used when a physician provides prolonged service not involving direct (face-to-face) care that is beyond the usual service in either the inpatient or outpatient setting.

This service is to be reported in addition to other physician service, including evaluation and management services at any level.

Codes 99358 and 99359 are used to report the total duration of non-face-to-face time spent by a physician on a given date providing prolonged service, even if the time spent by the physician on that date is not continuous. Code 99358 is used to report the first hour of prolonged service on a given date regardless of the place of service.

It may also be used to report a total duration of prolonged service of 30-60 minutes on a given date. It should be used only once per date even if the time spent by the physician is not continuous on that date.

Prolonged service of less than 30 minutes total duration on a given date is not separately reported.

Code 99359 is used to report each additional 30 minutes beyond the first hour regardless of the place of service. It may also be used to report the final 15-30 minutes of prolonged service on a given date.

Prolonged service of less than 15 minutes beyond the first hour or less than 15 minutes beyond the final 30 minutes is not reported separately.

**+ 99358** **Prolonged evaluation and management service** before and/or after direct (face-to-face) patient care (eg, review of extensive records and tests, communication with other professionals and/or the patient/family); first hour (List separately in addition to code(s) for other physician service(s) and/or inpatient or outpatient Evaluation and Management service)

**+ 99359** each additional 30 minutes (List separately in addition to code for prolonged physician service)

(Use 99359 in conjunction with code 99358)

(To report telephone calls, see 99371-99373)

## Physician Standby Services

Code 99360 is used to report physician standby service that is requested by another physician and that involves prolonged physician attendance without direct (face-to-face) patient contact. The physician may not be providing care or services to other patients during this period. This code is not used to report time spent proctoring another physician. It is also not used if the period of standby ends with the performance of a procedure subject to a "surgical" package by the physician who was on standby.

Code 99360 is used to report the total duration of time spent by a physician on a given date on standby. Standby service of less than 30 minutes total duration on a given date is not reported separately.

Second and subsequent periods of standby beyond the first 30 minutes may be reported only if a full 30 minutes of standby was provided for each unit of service reported.

**99360** **Physician standby service,** requiring prolonged physician attendance, each 30 minutes (eg, operative standby, standby for frozen section, for cesarean/high risk delivery, for monitoring EEG)

(99360 may be reported in addition to 99431, 99440 as appropriate)

(99360 may not be reported in addition to 99436)

# Case Management Services

Physician case management is a process in which a physician is responsible for direct care of a patient, and for coordinating and controlling access to or initiating and/or supervising other health care services needed by the patient.

## Team Conferences

**99361** **Medical conference** by a physician with interdisciplinary team of health professionals or representatives of community agencies to coordinate activities of patient care (patient not present); approximately 30 minutes

**99362** approximately 60 minutes

## Telephone Calls

**99371** **Telephone call** by a physician to patient or for consultation or medical management or for coordinating medical management with other health care professionals (eg, nurses, therapists, social workers, nutritionists, physicians, pharmacists); simple or brief (eg, to report on tests and/or laboratory results, to clarify or alter previous instructions, to integrate new information from other health professionals into the medical treatment plan, or to adjust therapy)

**99372** intermediate (eg, to provide advice to an established patient on a new problem, to initiate therapy that can be handled by telephone, to discuss test results in detail, to coordinate medical management of a new problem in an established patient, to discuss and evaluate new information and details, or to initiate new plan of care)

**99373** complex or lengthy (eg, lengthy counseling session with anxious or distraught patient, detailed or prolonged discussion with family members regarding seriously ill patient, lengthy communication necessary to coordinate complex services of several different health professionals working on different aspects of the total patient care plan)

## Care Plan Oversight Services

Care Plan Oversight Services are reported separately from codes for office/outpatient, hospital, home, nursing facility or domiciliary services. The complexity and approximate physician time of the care plan oversight services provided within a 30-day period determine code selection. Only one physician may report services for a given period of time, to reflect that physician's sole or predominant supervisory role with a particular patient. These codes should not be reported for supervision of patients in nursing facilities or under the care of home health agencies unless they require recurrent supervision of therapy.

The work involved in providing very low intensity or infrequent supervision services is included in the pre- and post-encounter work for home, office/outpatient and nursing facility or domiciliary visit codes.

**99374** **Physician supervision** of a patient under care of home health agency (patient not present) requiring complex and multidisciplinary care modalities involving regular physician development and/or revision of care plans, review of subsequent reports of patient status, review of laboratory and other studies, communication (including telephone calls) with other health care professionals involved in patient's care, integration of new information into the medical treatment plan and/or adjustment of medical therapy, within a calendar month; 15-29 minutes

**99375** 30 minutes or more

(99376 has been deleted. To report, see 99375, 99378, 99380)

**99377** **Physician supervision** of a hospice patient (patient not present) requiring complex and multidisciplinary care modalities involving regular physician development and/or revision of care plans, review of subsequent reports of patient status, review of related laboratory and other studies, communication (including telephone calls) with other health care professionals involved in patient's care, integration of new information into the medical treatment plan and/or adjustment of medical therapy, within a calendar month; 15-29 minutes

**99378** 30 minutes or more

**99379** **Physician supervision** of a nursing facility patient (patient not present) requiring complex and multidisciplinary care modalities involving regular physician development and/or revision of care plans, review of subsequent reports of patient status, review of related laboratory and other studies, communication (including telephone calls) with other health care professionals involved in patient's care, integration of new information into the medical treatment plan and/or adjustment of medical therapy, within a calendar month; 15-29 minutes

**99380** 30 minutes or more

## Preventive Medicine Services

The following codes are used to report the preventive medicine evaluation and management of infants, children, adolescents and adults.

The extent and focus of the services will largely depend on the age of the patient.

If an abnormality/ies is encountered or a preexisting problem is addressed in the process of performing this preventive medicine evaluation and management service, and if the problem/abnormality is significant enough to require additional work to perform the key components of a problem-oriented E/M service, then the appropriate Office/Outpatient code 99201-99215 should also be reported. Modifier '-25' should be added to the Office/Outpatient code to indicate that a significant, separately identifiable Evaluation and Management service was provided by the same physician on the same day as the preventive medicine service. The appropriate preventive medicine service is additionally reported.

An insignificant or trivial problem/abnormality that is encountered in the process of performing the preventive medicine evaluation and management service and which does not require additional work and the performance of the key components of a problem-oriented E/M service should not be reported.

The "comprehensive" examination of the Preventive Medicine Services codes 99381-99397 is NOT synonymous with the "comprehensive" examination required in Evaluation and Management codes 99201-99350.

Codes 99381-99397 include counseling/anticipatory guidance/risk factor reduction interventions which are provided at the time of the initial or periodic comprehensive preventive medicine examination. (Refer to codes 99401-99412 for reporting those counseling/anticipatory guidance/ risk factor reduction interventions that are provided at an encounter separate from the preventive medicine examination.)

Immunizations and ancillary studies involving laboratory, radiology, other procedures, ►or screening tests identified with a specific CPT code◄ are reported separately. For immunizations, see 90471-90472 and 90476-90749.

## New Patient

**99381** **Initial preventive medicine** evaluation and management of an individual including a comprehensive history, a comprehensive examination, counseling/anticipatory guidance/risk factor reduction interventions, and the ordering of appropriate laboratory/diagnostic procedures, new patient; infant (age under 1 year)

**99382** early childhood (age 1 through 4 years)

**99383** late childhood (age 5 through 11 years)

**99384** adolescent (age 12 through 17 years)

**99385** 18-39 years

**99386** 40-64 years

**99387** 65 years and over

## Established Patient

**99391** **Periodic preventive medicine** reevaluation and management of an individual including a comprehensive history, comprehensive examination, counseling/anticipatory guidance/risk factor reduction interventions, and the ordering of appropriate laboratory/diagnostic procedures, established patient; infant (age under 1 year)

**99392** early childhood (age 1 through 4 years)

**99393** late childhood (age 5 through 11 years)

**99394** adolescent (age 12 through 17 years)

**99395** 18-39 years

**99396** 40-64 years

**99397** 65 years and over

# Counseling and/or Risk Factor Reduction Intervention

## New or Established Patient

These codes are used to report services provided to individuals at a separate encounter for the purpose of promoting health and preventing illness or injury.

Preventive medicine counseling and risk factor reduction interventions provided as a separate encounter will vary with age and should address such issues as family problems, diet and exercise, substance abuse, sexual practices, injury prevention, dental health, and diagnostic and laboratory test results available at the time of the encounter.

These codes are not to be used to report counseling and risk factor reduction interventions provided to patients with symptoms or established illness. For counseling individual patients with symptoms or established illness, use the appropriate office, hospital or consultation or other evaluation and management codes. For counseling groups of patients with symptoms or established illness, use 99078.

## Preventive Medicine, Individual Counseling

**99401** **Preventive medicine counseling** and/or risk factor reduction intervention(s) provided to an individual (separate procedure); approximately 15 minutes

**99402** approximately 30 minutes

**99403** approximately 45 minutes

**99404** approximately 60 minutes

### Preventive Medicine, Group Counseling

**99411** **Preventive medicine counseling** and/or risk factor reduction intervention(s) provided to individuals in a group setting (separate procedure); approximately 30 minutes

**99412** approximately 60 minutes

### Other Preventive Medicine Services

**99420** **Administration and interpretation** of health risk assessment instrument (eg, health hazard appraisal)

**99429** **Unlisted preventive** medicine service

## Newborn Care

The following codes are used to report the services provided to newborns in several different settings.

For newborn hospital discharge services provided on a date subsequent to the admission date of the newborn, use 99238.

For discharge services provided to newborns admitted and discharged on the same date, see 99435.

**99431** **History and examination** of the normal newborn infant, initiation of diagnostic and treatment programs and preparation of hospital records. (This code should also be used for birthing room deliveries.)

**99432** **Normal newborn care** in other than hospital or birthing room setting, including physical examination of baby and conference(s) with parent(s)

**99433** **Subsequent hospital care,** for the evaluation and management of a normal newborn, per day

**99435** **History and examination** of the normal newborn infant, including the preparation of medical records (this code should only be used for newborns assessed and discharged from the hospital or birthing room on the same date)

**99436** **Attendance** at delivery (when requested by delivering physician) and initial stabilization of newborn

(99436 may be reported in addition to 99431)

(99436 may not be reported in addition to 99440)

(99438 has been deleted)

**99440** **Newborn resuscitation:** provision of positive pressure ventilation and/or chest compressions in the presence of acute inadequate ventilation and/or cardiac output

## Special Evaluation and Management Services

The following codes are used to report evaluations performed to establish baseline information prior to life or disability insurance certificates being issued. This service is performed in the office or other setting, and applies to both new and established patients. When using these codes, no active management of the problem(s) is undertaken during the encounter.

If other evaluation and management services and/or procedures are performed on the same date, the appropriate E/M or procedure code(s) should be reported in addition to these codes.

### Basic Life and/or Disability Evaluation Services

**99450** **Basic life** and/or disability examination that includes:

- **measurement of height, weight and blood pressure;**
- **completion of a medical history following a life insurance pro forma;**
- **collection of blood sample and/or urinalysis complying with "chain of custody" protocols; and**
- **completion of necessary documentation/certificates.**

## Work Related or Medical Disability Evaluation Services

**99455** **Work related** or medical disability examination by the treating physician that includes:

- **completion of a medical history commensurate with the patient's condition;**
- **performance of an examination commensurate with the patient's condition;**
- **formulation of a diagnosis, assessment of capabilities and stability, and calculation of impairment;**
- **development of future medical treatment plan; and**
- **completion of necessary documentation/certificates and report.**

**99456** **Work related** or medical disability examination by other than the treating physician that includes:

- **completion of a medical history commensurate with the patient's condition;**
- **performance of an examination commensurate with the patient's condition;**
- **formulation of a diagnosis, assessment of capabilities and stability, and calculation of impairment;**
- **development of future medical treatment plan; and**
- **completion of necessary documentation/certificates and report.**

# Other Evaluation and Management Services

**99499** **Unlisted evaluation and management** service

# Notes

# Anesthesia Guidelines

Services involving administration of anesthesia are reported by the use of the anesthesia five digit procedure code (00100-01999) plus modifier codes (defined under "Anesthesia Modifiers" later in these Guidelines).

The reporting of anesthesia services is appropriate by or under the responsible supervision of a physician. These services may include but are not limited to general, regional, supplementation of local anesthesia, or other supportive services in order to afford the patient the anesthesia care deemed optimal by the anesthesiologist during any procedure. These services include the usual preoperative and postoperative visits, the anesthesia care during the procedure, the administration of fluids and/or blood and the usual monitoring services (eg, ECG, temperature, blood pressure, oximetry, capnography, and mass spectrometry). Unusual forms of monitoring (eg, intra-arterial, central venous, and Swan-Ganz) are not included.

Items used by all physicians in reporting their services are presented in the **Introduction.** Some of the commonalities are repeated here for the convenience of those physicians referring to this section on **Anesthesia.** Other definitions and items unique to anesthesia are also listed.

To report sedation with or without analgesia (conscious sedation) provided by a physician also performing the service for which conscious sedation is being provided, see codes 99141, 99142.

To report regional or general anesthesia provided by a physician also performing the services for which the anesthesia is being provided, see modifier '-47,' Anesthesia by Surgeon, in Appendix A.

## Time Reporting

Time for anesthesia procedures may be reported as is customary in the local area. Anesthesia time begins when the anesthesiologist begins to prepare the patient for the induction of anesthesia in the operating room or in an equivalent area and ends when the anesthesiologist is no longer in personal attendance, that is, when the patient may be safely placed under postoperative supervision.

## Physician's Services

Physician's services rendered in the office, home, or hospital, consultation, and other medical services are listed in the section entitled **Evaluation and Management Services** (99200 series) found in the front of the book, beginning on page 1. "Special Services and Reporting" (99000 series) are presented in the **Medicine** section.

## Materials Supplied by Physician

Supplies and materials provided by the physician (eg, sterile trays, drugs) over and above those usually included with the office visit or other services rendered may be listed separately. List drugs, tray supplies, and materials provided. Identify as 99070.

## Separate or Multiple Procedures

It is appropriate to designate multiple procedures that are rendered on the same date by separate entries. This can be reported by using the multiple procedure modifier ('-51'). See "Anesthesia Modifiers" for modifier definitions.

## Special Report

A service that is rarely provided, unusual, variable, or new may require a special report in determining medical appropriateness of the service. Pertinent information should include an adequate definition or description of the nature, extent, and need for the procedure; and the time, effort, and equipment necessary to provide the service. Additional items which may be included are:

- complexity of symptoms;
- final diagnosis;
- pertinent physical findings;
- diagnostic and therapeutic procedures;
- concurrent problems;
- follow-up care.

## Anesthesia Modifiers

All anesthesia services are reported by use of the anesthesia five digit procedure code (00100-01999) plus the addition of a physical status modifier. The use of other optional modifiers may be appropriate.

### Physical Status Modifiers

Physical Status modifiers are represented by the initial letter 'P' followed by a single digit from 1 to 6 defined below.

P1-A normal healthy patient.

P2-A patient with mild systemic disease.

P3-A patient with severe systemic disease.

P4-A patient with severe systemic disease that is a constant threat to life.

P5-A moribund patient who is not expected to survive without the operation.

P6-A declared brain-dead patient whose organs are being removed for donor purposes.

The above six levels are consistent with the American Society of Anesthesiologists (ASA) ranking of patient physical status. Physical status is included in CPT to distinguish among various levels of complexity of the anesthesia service provided.

Example: 00100-P1

## Qualifying Circumstances

More than one may be selected.

Many anesthesia services are provided under particularly difficult circumstances, depending on factors such as extraordinary condition of patient, notable operative conditions, and/or unusual risk factors. This section includes a list of important qualifying circumstances that significantly impact on the character of the anesthesia service provided. These procedures would not be reported alone but would be reported as additional procedure numbers qualifying an anesthesia procedure or service.

**+ 99100** Anesthesia for patient of extreme age, under one year and over seventy (List separately in addition to code for primary anesthesia procedure)

**+ 99116** Anesthesia complicated by utilization of total body hypothermia (List separately in addition to code for primary anesthesia procedure)

**+ 99135** Anesthesia complicated by utilization of controlled hypotension (List separately in addition to code for primary anesthesia procedure)

**+ 99140** Anesthesia complicated by emergency conditions (specify) (List separately in addition to code for primary anesthesia procedure)

An emergency is defined as existing when delay in treatment of the patient would lead to a significant increase in the threat to life or body part.

# Anesthesia

## Head

▲00100 Anesthesia for procedures on salivary glands, including biopsy

▲00102 Anesthesia for procedures on plastic repair of cleft lip

▲00103 Anesthesia for reconstructive procedures of eyelid (eg, blepharoplasty, ptosis surgery)

00104 Anesthesia for electroconvulsive therapy

00120 Anesthesia for procedures on external, middle, and inner ear including biopsy; not otherwise specified

(00122 has been deleted. To report, use 00120)

00124 otoscopy

00126 tympanotomy

00140 Anesthesia for procedures on eye; not otherwise specified

00142 lens surgery

00144 corneal transplant

00145 vitrectomy

(00146 has been deleted. To report, use 00140)

00147 iridectomy

00148 ophthalmoscopy

00160 Anesthesia for procedures on nose and accessory sinuses; not otherwise specified

00162 radical surgery

00164 biopsy, soft tissue

00170 Anesthesia for intraoral procedures, including biopsy; not otherwise specified

00172 repair of cleft palate

00174 excision of retropharyngeal tumor

00176 radical surgery

00190 Anesthesia for procedures on facial bones; not otherwise specified

00192 radical surgery (including prognathism)

00210 Anesthesia for intracranial procedures; not otherwise specified

00212 subdural taps

▲00214 burr holes, including ventriculography

00215 elevation of depressed skull fracture, extradural (simple or compound)

00216 vascular procedures

00218 procedures in sitting position

00220 spinal fluid shunting procedures

00222 electrocoagulation of intracranial nerve

## Neck

▲00300 Anesthesia for all procedures on the integumentary system, muscles and nerves of head, neck, and posterior trunk, not otherwise specified

00320 Anesthesia for all procedures on esophagus, thyroid, larynx, trachea and lymphatic system of neck; not otherwise specified

00322 needle biopsy of thyroid

(For procedures on cervical spine and cord, see 00600, 00604, 00670)

00350 Anesthesia for procedures on major vessels of neck; not otherwise specified

00352 simple ligation

(For arteriography, use 01916)

## Thorax (Chest Wall and Shoulder Girdle)

▲00400 Anesthesia for procedures on the integumentary system on the extremities, anterior trunk and perineum; not otherwise specified

00402 reconstructive procedures on breast (eg, reduction or augmentation mammoplasty, muscle flaps)

00404 radical or modified radical procedures on breast

00406 radical or modified radical procedures on breast with internal mammary node dissection

00410 electrical conversion of arrhythmias

►(00420 has been deleted. To report, use 00300)◄

00450 Anesthesia for procedures on clavicle and scapula; not otherwise specified

00452 radical surgery

00454 biopsy of clavicle

00470 Anesthesia for partial rib resection; not otherwise specified

00472 thoracoplasty (any type)

00474 radical procedures (eg, pectus excavatum)

(00476 has been deleted. To report, use 00470)

## Intrathoracic

00500 Anesthesia for all procedures on esophagus

▲00520 Anesthesia for closed chest procedures; (including bronchoscopy) not otherwise specified

00522 needle biopsy of pleura

00524 pneumocentesis

(00526 has been deleted. To report, use 00520)

▲00528 mediastinoscopy and diagnostic thoracoscopy

00530 Anesthesia for transvenous pacemaker insertion

00532 Anesthesia for access to central venous circulation

00534 Anesthesia for transvenous insertion or replacement of cardioverter/defibrillator

(For transthoracic approach, use 00560)

00540 Anesthesia for thoracotomy procedures involving lungs, pleura, diaphragm, and mediastinum (including surgical thoracoscopy); not otherwise specified

00542 decortication

00544 pleurectomy

00546 pulmonary resection with thoracoplasty

00548 intrathoracic procedures on the trachea and bronchi

00560 Anesthesia for procedures on heart, pericardium, and great vessels of chest; without pump oxygenator

00562 with pump oxygenator

00580 Anesthesia for heart transplant or heart/lung transplant

## Spine and Spinal Cord

00600 Anesthesia for procedures on cervical spine and cord; not otherwise specified

(For myelography and diskography, see radiological procedures 01906-01914)

00604 posterior cervical laminectomy in sitting position

00620 Anesthesia for procedures on thoracic spine and cord; not otherwise specified

00622 thoracolumbar sympathectomy

**00630** Anesthesia for procedures in lumbar region; not otherwise specified

**00632** lumbar sympathectomy

**00634** chemonucleolysis

(00650 has been deleted. To report, use 00220)

**00670** Anesthesia for extensive spine and spinal cord procedures (eg, Harrington rod technique)

## Upper Abdomen

**00700** Anesthesia for procedures on upper anterior abdominal wall; not otherwise specified

**00702** percutaneous liver biopsy

**00730** Anesthesia for procedures on upper posterior abdominal wall

▲**00740** Anesthesia for upper gastrointestinal endoscopic procedures, endoscope introduced proximal to duodenum

**00750** Anesthesia for hernia repairs in upper abdomen; not otherwise specified

**00752** lumbar and ventral (incisional) hernias and/or wound dehiscence

**00754** omphalocele

**00756** transabdominal repair of diaphragmatic hernia

**00770** Anesthesia for all procedures on major abdominal blood vessels

**00790** Anesthesia for intraperitoneal procedures in upper abdomen including laparoscopy; not otherwise specified

**00792** partial hepatectomy (excluding liver biopsy)

**00794** pancreatectomy, partial or total (eg, Whipple procedure)

**00796** liver transplant (recipient)

(For harvesting of liver, use 01990)

## Lower Abdomen

**00800** Anesthesia for procedures on lower anterior abdominal wall; not otherwise specified

**00802** panniculectomy

(00806 has been deleted. To report, see 00790, 00840)

▲**00810** Anesthesia for lower intestinal endoscopic procedures, endoscope introduced distal to duodenum

**00820** Anesthesia for procedures on lower posterior abdominal wall

**00830** Anesthesia for hernia repairs in lower abdomen; not otherwise specified

**00832** ventral and incisional hernias

**00840** Anesthesia for intraperitoneal procedures in lower abdomen including laparoscopy; not otherwise specified

**00842** amniocentesis

**00844** abdominoperineal resection

**00846** radical hysterectomy

**00848** pelvic exenteration

**00850** cesarean section

**00855** cesarean hysterectomy

▲**00857** Neuraxial analgesia/anesthesia for labor ending in a cesarean delivery (includes any repeat subarachnoid needle placement and drug injection and/or any necessary replacement of an epidural catheter during labor)

**00860** Anesthesia for extraperitoneal procedures in lower abdomen, including urinary tract; not otherwise specified

**00862** renal procedures, including upper 1/3 of ureter, or donor nephrectomy

**00864** total cystectomy

**00865** radical prostatectomy (suprapubic, retropubic)

**00866** adrenalectomy

**00868** renal transplant (recipient)

(For donor nephrectomy, use 00862)

(For harvesting kidney from brain-dead patient, use 01990)

**00870** cystolithotomy

**00872** Anesthesia for lithotripsy, extracorporeal shock wave; with water bath

**00873** without water bath

**00880** Anesthesia for procedures on major lower abdominal vessels; not otherwise specified

**00882** inferior vena cava ligation

**00884** transvenous umbrella insertion

## Perineum

**00900** Anesthesia for procedures on perineal integumentary system (including biopsy of male genital system); not otherwise specified

**00902** anorectal procedure (including endoscopy and/or biopsy)

**00904** radical perineal procedure

**00906** vulvectomy

**00908** perineal prostatectomy

**00910** Anesthesia for transurethral procedures (including urethrocystoscopy); not otherwise specified

**00912** transurethral resection of bladder tumor(s)

**00914** transurethral resection of prostate

**00916** post-transurethral resection bleeding

▲**00918** with fragmentation, manipulation and/or removal of ureteral calculus

**00920** Anesthesia for procedures on male external genitalia; not otherwise specified

**00922** seminal vesicles

**00924** undescended testis, unilateral or bilateral

**00926** radical orchiectomy, inguinal

**00928** radical orchiectomy, abdominal

**00930** orchiopexy, unilateral or bilateral

**00932** complete amputation of penis

**00934** radical amputation of penis with bilateral inguinal lymphadenectomy

**00936** radical amputation of penis with bilateral inguinal and iliac lymphadenectomy

**00938** insertion of penile prosthesis (perineal approach)

**00940** Anesthesia for vaginal procedures (including biopsy of labia, vagina, cervix or endometrium); not otherwise specified

**00942** colpotomy, colpectomy, colporrhaphy

**00944** vaginal hysterectomy

**00946** vaginal delivery

**00948** cervical cerclage

**00950** culdoscopy

▲**00952** hysteroscopy and/or hysterosalpingography

▲**00955** Neuraxial analgesia/anesthesia for labor ending in a vaginal delivery (includes any repeat subarachnoid needle placement and drug injection and/or any necessary replacement of an epidural catheter during labor)

## Pelvis (Except Hip)

►(01000 has been deleted. To report, use 00400)◄

►(01110 has been deleted. To report, use 00300)◄

**01120** Anesthesia for procedures on bony pelvis

(01122 has been deleted. To report, use 01120)

**01130** Anesthesia for body cast application or revision

**01140** Anesthesia for interpelviabdominal (hindquarter) amputation

**01150** Anesthesia for radical procedures for tumor of pelvis, except hindquarter amputation

**01160** Anesthesia for closed procedures involving symphysis pubis or sacroiliac joint

**01170** Anesthesia for open procedures involving symphysis pubis or sacroiliac joint

**01180** Anesthesia for obturator neurectomy; extrapelvic

**01190** intrapelvic

## Upper Leg (Except Knee)

**01200** Anesthesia for all closed procedures involving hip joint

**01202** Anesthesia for arthroscopic procedures of hip joint

**01210** Anesthesia for open procedures involving hip joint; not otherwise specified

**01212** hip disarticulation

**01214** total hip replacement or revision

**01220** Anesthesia for all closed procedures involving upper 2/3 of femur

**01230** Anesthesia for open procedures involving upper 2/3 of femur; not otherwise specified

**01232** amputation

**01234** radical resection

►(01240 has been deleted. To report, use 00400)◄

**01250** Anesthesia for all procedures on nerves, muscles, tendons, fascia, and bursae of upper leg

**01260** Anesthesia for all procedures involving veins of upper leg, including exploration

**01270** Anesthesia for procedures involving arteries of upper leg, including bypass graft; not otherwise specified

**01272** femoral artery ligation

**01274** femoral artery embolectomy

(01276 has been deleted. To report, use 00880)

## Knee and Popliteal Area

►(01300 has been deleted. To report, use 00400)◄

**01320** Anesthesia for all procedures on nerves, muscles, tendons, fascia, and bursae of knee and/or popliteal area

**01340** Anesthesia for all closed procedures on lower 1/3 of femur

**01360** Anesthesia for all open procedures on lower 1/3 of femur

**01380** Anesthesia for all closed procedures on knee joint

**01382** Anesthesia for arthroscopic procedures of knee joint

**01390** Anesthesia for all closed procedures on upper ends of tibia, fibula, and/or patella

**01392** Anesthesia for all open procedures on upper ends of tibia, fibula, and/or patella

**01400** Anesthesia for open procedures on knee joint; not otherwise specified

**01402** total knee replacement

**01404** disarticulation at knee

**01420** Anesthesia for all cast applications, removal, or repair involving knee joint

**01430** Anesthesia for procedures on veins of knee and popliteal area; not otherwise specified

**01432** arteriovenous fistula

**01440** Anesthesia for procedures on arteries of knee and popliteal area; not otherwise specified

**01442** popliteal thromboendarterectomy, with or without patch graft

**01444** popliteal excision and graft or repair for occlusion or aneurysm

## Lower Leg (Below Knee, Includes Ankle and Foot)

►(01460 has been deleted. To report, use 00400)◄

**01462** Anesthesia for all closed procedures on lower leg, ankle, and foot

**01464** Anesthesia for arthroscopic procedures of ankle joint

**01470** Anesthesia for procedures on nerves, muscles, tendons, and fascia of lower leg, ankle, and foot; not otherwise specified

**01472** repair of ruptured Achilles tendon, with or without graft

**01474** gastrocnemius recession (eg, Strayer procedure)

**01480** Anesthesia for open procedures on bones of lower leg, ankle, and foot; not otherwise specified

**01482** radical resection

**01484** osteotomy or osteoplasty of tibia and/or fibula

**01486** total ankle replacement

**01490** Anesthesia for lower leg cast application, removal, or repair

**01500** Anesthesia for procedures on arteries of lower leg, including bypass graft; not otherwise specified

**01502** embolectomy, direct or with catheter

**01520** Anesthesia for procedures on veins of lower leg; not otherwise specified

**01522** venous thrombectomy, direct or with catheter

## Shoulder and Axilla

Includes humeral head and neck, sternoclavicular joint, acromioclavicular joint, and shoulder joint.

►(01600 has been deleted. To report, use 00400)◄

**01610** Anesthesia for all procedures on nerves, muscles, tendons, fascia, and bursae of shoulder and axilla

**01620** Anesthesia for all closed procedures on humeral head and neck, sternoclavicular joint, acromioclavicular joint, and shoulder joint

**01622** Anesthesia for arthroscopic procedures of shoulder joint

**01630** Anesthesia for open procedures on humeral head and neck, sternoclavicular joint, acromioclavicular joint, and shoulder joint; not otherwise specified

**01632** radical resection

**01634** shoulder disarticulation

**01636** interthoracoscapular (forequarter) amputation

**01638** total shoulder replacement

**01650** Anesthesia for procedures on arteries of shoulder and axilla; not otherwise specified

**01652** axillary-brachial aneurysm

**01654** bypass graft

**01656** axillary-femoral bypass graft

**01670** Anesthesia for all procedures on veins of shoulder and axilla

**01680** Anesthesia for shoulder cast application, removal or repair; not otherwise specified

**01682** shoulder spica

## Upper Arm and Elbow

►(01700 has been deleted. To report, use 00400)◄

**01710** Anesthesia for procedures on nerves, muscles, tendons, fascia, and bursae of upper arm and elbow; not otherwise specified

**01712** tenotomy, elbow to shoulder, open

**01714** tenoplasty, elbow to shoulder

**01716** tenodesis, rupture of long tendon of biceps

**01730** Anesthesia for all closed procedures on humerus and elbow

**01732** Anesthesia for arthroscopic procedures of elbow joint

**01740** Anesthesia for open procedures on humerus and elbow; not otherwise specified

**01742** osteotomy of humerus

**01744** repair of nonunion or malunion of humerus

**01756** radical procedures

**01758** excision of cyst or tumor of humerus

**01760** total elbow replacement

**01770** Anesthesia for procedures on arteries of upper arm and elbow; not otherwise specified

**01772** embolectomy

**01780** Anesthesia for procedures on veins of upper arm and elbow; not otherwise specified

**01782** phleborrhaphy

**01784** Anesthesia for repair of arterio-venous (A-V) fistula, congenital or acquired

## Forearm, Wrist, and Hand

►(01800 has been deleted. To report, use 00400)◄

**01810** Anesthesia for all procedures on nerves, muscles, tendons, fascia, and bursae of forearm, wrist, and hand

**01820** Anesthesia for all closed procedures on radius, ulna, wrist, or hand bones

**01830** Anesthesia for open procedures on radius, ulna, wrist, or hand bones; not otherwise specified

**01832** total wrist replacement

**01840** Anesthesia for procedures on arteries of forearm, wrist, and hand; not otherwise specified

**01842** embolectomy

**01844** Anesthesia for vascular shunt, or shunt revision, any type (eg, dialysis)

**01850** Anesthesia for procedures on veins of forearm, wrist, and hand; not otherwise specified

**01852** phleborrhaphy

**01860** Anesthesia for forearm, wrist, or hand cast application, removal, or repair

## Radiological Procedures

►(01900 has been deleted. To report, use 00952)◄

►(01902 has been deleted. To report, use 00214)◄

**01904** Anesthesia for injection procedure for pneumoencephalography

**01906** Anesthesia for injection procedure for myelography; lumbar

**01908** cervical

**01910** posterior fossa

**01912** Anesthesia for injection procedure for diskography; lumbar

**01914** cervical

**01916** Anesthesia for arteriograms, needle; carotid or vertebral

**01918** retrograde, brachial or femoral

**01920** Anesthesia for cardiac catheterization including coronary arteriography and ventriculography (not to include Swan-Ganz catheter)

**01921** Anesthesia for angioplasty

**01922** Anesthesia for non-invasive imaging or radiation therapy

## Other Procedures

**01990** Physiological support for harvesting of organ(s) from brain-dead patient

**01995** Regional IV administration of local anesthetic agent or other medication (upper or lower extremity)

(For intra-arterial or intravenous therapy for pain management, see 90783, 90784)

**01996** Daily management of epidural or subarachnoid drug administration

**01999** Unlisted anesthesia procedure(s)

# Surgery Guidelines

Items used by all physicians in reporting their services are presented in the **Introduction.** Some of the commonalities are repeated here for the convenience of those physicians referring to this section on **Surgery.** Other definitions and items unique to Surgery are also listed.

## Physicians' Services

Physicians' services rendered in the office, home, or hospital, consultations, and other medical services are listed in the section entitled **Evaluation and Management Services** (99200 series) found in the front of the book, beginning on page 9. "Special Services and Reports" (99000 series) is presented in the **Medicine** section.

## Listed Surgical Procedures

Listed surgical procedures include the operation per se, local infiltration, metacarpal/digital block or topical anesthesia when used, and normal, uncomplicated follow-up care. This concept is referred to as a "package" for surgical procedures. To report a postoperative follow-up visit for documentation purposes only, use 99024.

## Follow-Up Care for Diagnostic Procedures

Follow-up care for diagnostic procedures (eg, endoscopy, arthroscopy, injection procedures for radiography) includes only that care related to recovery from the diagnostic procedure itself. Care of the condition for which the diagnostic procedure was performed or of other concomitant conditions is not included and may be listed separately.

## Follow-Up Care for Therapeutic Surgical Procedures

Follow-up care for therapeutic surgical procedures includes only that care which is usually a part of the surgical service. Complications, exacerbations, recurrence, or the presence of other diseases or injuries requiring additional services should be reported with the identification of appropriate procedures.

## Materials Supplied by Physician

Supplies and materials provided by the physician (eg, sterile trays/drugs), over and above those usually included with the office visit or other services rendered may be listed separately. List drugs, trays, supplies, and materials provided. Identify as 99070.

## Reporting More Than One Procedure/Service

When a physician performs more than one procedure/service on the same date, same session or during a post-operative period (subject to the "surgical package" concept), several CPT modifiers may apply. (See Appendix A for definition.)

### -51 Multiple Procedures

When multiple procedures/services (other than evaluation and management) are performed at the same session, report the most significant procedure first, with all other procedures listed with the '-51' modifier appended. For a list of procedures exempt from the use of the '-51' modifier, see Appendices E and F.

### -58 Staged or Related Procedure or Service by the Same Physician During the Postoperative Period

When a procedure(s) is prospectively planned as a staged procedure, or when the secondary and subsequent procedure(s) is more extensive, or to indicate therapy following a diagnostic surgical procedure, use the '-58' modifier with the staged procedure(s).

### -59 Distinct Procedural Service

For procedure(s)/service(s) not ordinarily performed or encountered on the same day by the same physician, but appropriate under certain circumstances (eg, different site or organ system, separate excision or lesion), use the '-59' modifier.

### -76 Repeat Procedure by Same Physician

When a procedure or service is repeated by the same physician subsequent to the original service, use the '-76' modifier.

### -77 Repeat Procedure by Another Physician

When a procedure is repeated by another physician subsequent to the original service, use the '-77' modifier.

### -78 Return to the Operating Room for a Related Procedure During the Postoperative Period

When a procedure, related to the initial procedure, requires a return to the operating room during the postoperative period of that initial procedure, use the '-78' modifier.

### -79 Unrelated Procedure or Service by the Same Physician During the Postoperative Period

When a procedure, unrelated to the initial procedure, is performed by the same physician during the postoperative period of the initial procedure, use the '-79' modifier.

## Add-on Codes

Some of the listed procedures are commonly carried out in addition to the primary procedure performed. These additional or supplemental procedures are designated as "add-on" codes with a "✚" symbol, and are listed in Appendix E of *CPT*. Add-on codes in *CPT* can be readily identified by specific descriptor nomenclature which includes phrases such as "each additional" or "(List separately in addition to primary procedure)".

The "add-on" code concept in *CPT* applies only to add-on procedures/services performed by the same physician. Add-on codes describe additional intra-service work associated with the primary procedure (eg, additional digit(s), lesion(s), neurorrhaphy(s), vertebral segment(s), tendon(s), joint(s)).

Add-on codes are always performed in addition to the primary service/procedure, and must never be reported as a stand-alone code. All add-on codes found in *CPT* are exempt from the multiple procedure concept (see modifier '-51' definition of Surgery Guidelines).

## Separate Procedure

Some of the procedures or services listed in *CPT* that are commonly carried out as an integral component of a total service or procedure have been identified by the inclusion of the term "separate procedure." The codes designated as "separate procedure" should not be reported in addition to the code for the total procedure or service of which it is considered an integral component.

However, when a procedure or service that is designated as a "separate procedure" is carried out independently or considered to be unrelated or distinct from other procedures/services provided at that time, it may be reported by itself, or in addition to other procedures/services by appending the modifier '-59' to the specific "separate procedure" code to indicate that the procedure is not considered to be a component of another procedure, but is a distinct, independent procedure. This may represent a different session or patient encounter, different procedure or surgery, different site or organ system, separate incision/excision, separate lesion, or separate injury (or area of injury in extensive injuries).

## Subsection Information

Several of the subheadings or subsections have special needs or instructions unique to that section. Where these are indicated (eg, "Maternity Care and Delivery"), special **"Notes"** will be presented preceding those procedural terminology listings, referring to that subsection specifically. If there is an "Unlisted Procedure" code number (see below) for the individual subsection, it will also be shown. Those subsections within the **Surgery** section that have **"Notes"** are as follows:

**Removal of Skin Tags** . . . . . . . . . 11200-11201
**Shaving of Lesions** . . . . . . . . . . . 11300-11313
**Excision—Benign Lesions**. . . . . . 11400-11471
**Excision—Malignant Lesions** . . . 11600-11646
**Repair (Closure)** . . . . . . . . . . . . . 12001-13300
**Adjacent Tissue Transfer or Rearrangement** . . . . . . . . . . . . . 14000-14350
**Free Skin Grafts**. . . . . . . . . . . . . 15000-15400
**Flaps (Skin and/or Deep Tissue)** . 15570-15999
**Burns, Local Treatment**. . . . . . . . 16000-16042
**Destruction, Benign Lesions**. . . . 17000-17250
**Destruction, Malignant Lesions** . 17260-17286
**Moh's Micrographic Surgery**. . . . 17304-17310
**Musculoskeletal**. . . . . . . . . . . . . 20000-29909
**Wound Exploration—Trauma**. . . 20100-20103
**Grafts (or Implants)** . . . . . . . . . . 20900-20999
**Spine: Excision** . . . . . . . . . . . . . 22100-22116
**Spine: Osteotomy** . . . . . . . . . . . 22210-22226
**Spine: Fracture/Dislocation**. . . . . 22305-22328
**Arthrodesis** . . . . . . . . . . . . . . . . 22548-22812
**Spinal Instrumentation**. . . . . . . . 22840-22855
**Casting and Strapping**. . . . . . . . . 29000-29750
**Cardiovascular System**. . . . . . . . . 33010-37799
**Pacing Cardioverter-Pacemaker or Defibrillator** . . . . . . . . . . . . . 33200-33249
**Venous—CABG**. . . . . . . . . . . . . . 33510-33516
**Arterial—Venous—CABG**. . . . . . 33517-33530
**Arterial—CABG** . . . . . . . . . . . . . 33533-33545
**Transluminal Angioplasty** . . . . . . 35450-35476
**Transluminal Atherectomy** . . . . . 35480-35495
**Composite Grafts** . . . . . . . . . . . . 35681-35683
**Arteries and Veins** . . . . . . . . . . . . 34001-35907
**Vascular Injection Procedures:**
**Intravenous** . . . . . . . . . . . . . . . . . 36000-36015
**Endoscopy** . . . . . . 31505-31579, 32601-32665, 43200-43272, 44360-44394, 45300-45385, 46600-46615, 47550-47556
**Herniotomy**. . . . . . . . . . . . . . . . . 49495-49611
**Urodynamics**. . . . . . . . . . . . . . . . 51725-51797
**Endoscopy**. . . . . . . . . . . . . . . . . . 52000-52318
**Ureter and Pelvis** . . . . . . . . . . . . . 52320-52339
**Maternity Care and Delivery**. . . . 59000-59899
**Surgery of Skull Base** . . . . . . . . . 61580 61619
**Neurostimulators (Intracranial)** . 61850-61888
**Neurostimulators (Spinal)**. . . . . . 63650-63688
**Neurostimulators (Peripheral Nerve)**. . . . . . . . . . . . 64553-64595
**Secondary Implants(s)**. . . . . . . . . 65125-65175
**Removal Cataract** . . . . . . . . . . . . 66830-66999
**Prophylaxis** . . . . . . . . . . . . . . . . . 67141-67145
**Operating Microscope** . . . . . . . . . . . . . . 69990

## Unlisted Service or Procedure

A service or procedure may be provided that is not listed in this edition of *CPT*. When reporting such a service, the appropriate "Unlisted Procedure" code may be used to indicate the service, identifying it by "Special Report" as discussed in the section below. The "Unlisted Procedures" and accompanying codes for **Surgery** are as follows:

**15999** Unlisted procedure, excision pressure ulcer

**17999** Unlisted procedure, skin, mucous membrane and subcutaneous tissue

**19499** Unlisted procedure, breast

**20999** Unlisted procedure, musculoskeletal system, general

**21089** Unlisted maxillofacial prosthetic procedure

**21299** Unlisted craniofacial and maxillofacial procedure

**21499** Unlisted musculoskeletal procedure, head

21899 Unlisted procedure, neck or thorax
22899 Unlisted procedure, spine
22999 Unlisted procedure, abdomen, musculoskeletal system
23929 Unlisted procedure, shoulder
24999 Unlisted procedure, humerus or elbow
25999 Unlisted procedure, forearm or wrist
26989 Unlisted procedure, hands or fingers
27299 Unlisted procedure, pelvis or hip joint
27599 Unlisted procedure, femur or knee
27899 Unlisted procedure, leg or ankle
28899 Unlisted procedure, foot or toes
29799 Unlisted procedure, casting or strapping
29909 Unlisted procedure, arthroscopy
30999 Unlisted procedure, nose
31299 Unlisted procedure, accessory sinuses
31599 Unlisted procedure, larynx
31899 Unlisted procedure, trachea, bronchi
32999 Unlisted procedure, lungs and pleura
33999 Unlisted procedure, cardiac surgery
36299 Unlisted procedure, vascular injection
37799 Unlisted procedure, vascular surgery
38129 Unlisted laparoscopy procedure, spleen
38589 Unlisted laparoscopy procedure, lymphatic system
38999 Unlisted procedure, hemic or lymphatic system
39499 Unlisted procedure, mediastinum
39599 Unlisted procedure, diaphragm
40799 Unlisted procedure, lips
40899 Unlisted procedure, vestibule of mouth
41599 Unlisted procedure, tongue, floor of mouth
41899 Unlisted procedure, dentoalveolar structures
42299 Unlisted procedure, palate, uvula
42699 Unlisted procedure, salivary glands or ducts
42999 Unlisted procedure, pharynx, adenoids, or tonsils
43289 Unlisted laparoscopy procedure, esophagus
43499 Unlisted procedure, esophagus
43659 Unlisted laparoscopy procedure, stomach
43999 Unlisted procedure, stomach
44209 Unlisted laparoscopy procedure, intestine (except rectum)
44799 Unlisted procedure, intestine
44899 Unlisted procedure, Meckels diverticulum and the mesentery
44979 Unlisted laparoscopy procedure, appendix
45999 Unlisted procedure, rectum
46999 Unlisted procedure, anus
47399 Unlisted procedure, liver
47579 Unlisted laparoscopy procedure, biliary tract
47999 Unlisted procedure, biliary tract
48999 Unlisted procedure, pancreas
49329 Unlisted laparoscopy procedure, abdomen, peritoneum and omentum
49659 Unlisted laparoscopy procedure, hernioplasty, herniorrhaphy, herniotomy
49999 Unlisted procedure, abdomen, peritoneum and omentum
50549 Unlisted laparoscopy procedure, renal
53899 Unlisted procedure, urinary system
54699 Unlisted laparoscopy procedure, testis
55559 Unlisted laparoscopy procedure, spermatic cord
55899 Unlisted procedure, male genital system
58578 Unlisted laparoscopy procedure, uterus
58579 Unlisted hysteroscopy procedure, uterus
58679 Unlisted laparoscopy procedure, oviduct, ovary
58999 Unlisted procedure, female genital system (nonobstetrical)
59898 Unlisted laparoscopy procedure, maternity care and delivery
59899 Unlisted procedure, maternity care and delivery
60659 Unlisted laparoscopy procedure, endocrine system
60699 Unlisted procedure, endocrine system
64999 Unlisted procedure, nervous system
66999 Unlisted procedure, anterior segment of eye
67299 Unlisted procedure, posterior segment
67399 Unlisted procedure, ocular muscle
67599 Unlisted procedure, orbit
67999 Unlisted procedure, eyelids
68399 Unlisted procedure, conjunctiva
68899 Unlisted procedure, lacrimal system
69399 Unlisted procedure, external ear
69799 Unlisted procedure, middle ear
69949 Unlisted procedure, inner ear
69979 Unlisted procedure, temporal bone, middle fossa approach

## Special Report

A service that is rarely provided, unusual, variable, or new may require a special report in determining medical appropriateness of the service. Pertinent information should include an adequate definition or description of the nature, extent, and need for the procedure, and the time, effort, and equipment necessary to provide the service. Additional items which may be included are:

- complexity of symptoms;
- final diagnosis;
- pertinent physical findings (such as size, locations, and number of lesion(s), if appropriate);
- diagnostic and therapeutic procedures (including major and supplementary surgical procedures, if appropriate);
- concurrent problems;
- follow-up care.

## Starred (*) Procedures or Items

Certain relatively small surgical services involve a readily identifiable surgical procedure but include variable preoperative and postoperative services (eg, incision and drainage of an abscess, injection of a tendon sheath, manipulation of a joint under anesthesia, dilation of the urethra). Because of the indefinite pre- and postoperative services the usual "package" concept for surgical services (see above) cannot be applied. Such procedures are identified by a star (*) following the procedure code number.

When a star (*) follows a surgical procedure code number, the following rules apply:

1. *The service as listed includes the surgical procedure only.* Associated pre- and postoperative services are not included in the service as listed.

2. *Preoperative services are considered as one of the following:*

- When the starred (*) procedure is carried out at the time of an initial visit (new patient) and this procedure constitutes the major service at that visit, procedure number 99025 is listed in lieu of the usual initial visit as an additional service.
- When the starred (*) procedure is carried out at the time of an initial or ►established patient◄ visit involving significant identifiable services, the appropriate visit is listed ►with the modifier '-25' appended◄ in addition to the starred (*) procedure and its follow-up care.
- When the starred (*) procedure requires hospitalization, an appropriate hospital visit is listed in addition to the starred (*) procedure and its follow-up care.

3. *All postoperative care is added on a service-by-service basis (eg, office or hospital visit, cast change).*

4. *Complications are added on a service-by-service basis (as with all surgical procedures).*

## Surgical Destruction

Surgical destruction is a part of a surgical procedure and different methods of destruction are not ordinarily listed separately unless the technique substantially alters the standard management of a problem or condition. Exceptions under special circumstances are provided for by separate code numbers.

# Notes

# Surgery

## Integumentary System

### Skin, Subcutaneous and Accessory Structures

#### Incision and Drainage

(For excision, see 11400, et seq)

(10000-10020 have been deleted. To report, see 10060, 10061)

**10040*** Acne surgery (eg, marsupialization, opening or removal of multiple milia, comedones, cysts, pustules)

**10060*** Incision and drainage of abscess (eg, carbuncle, suppurative hidradenitis, cutaneous or subcutaneous abscess, cyst, furuncle, or paronychia); simple or single

**10061** complicated or multiple

**10080*** Incision and drainage of pilonidal cyst; simple

**10081** complicated

(For excision of pilonidal cyst, see 11770-11772)

(10100, 10101 have been deleted. To report, see 10060, 10061)

**10120*** Incision and removal of foreign body, subcutaneous tissues; simple

**10121** complicated

(To report wound exploration due to penetrating trauma without laparotomy or thoracotomy, see 20100-20103, as appropriate)

(To report debridement associated with open fracture(s) and/or dislocation(s), use 11010-11012, as appropriate)

**10140*** Incision and drainage of hematoma, seroma or fluid collection

(10141 has been deleted. To report, use 10140)

**10160*** Puncture aspiration of abscess, hematoma, bulla, or cyst

**10180** Incision and drainage, complex, postoperative wound infection

(For secondary closure of surgical wound, see 12020, 12021, 13160)

#### Excision—Debridement

(For dermabrasions, see 15780-15783)

(For nail debridement, see 11720-11721)

(For burn(s), see 16000-►16035◄)

**11000*** Debridement of extensive eczematous or infected skin; up to 10% of body surface

**+ 11001** each additional 10% of the body surface (List separately in addition to code for primary procedure)

(Use 11001 in conjunction with code 11000)

**11010** Debridement including removal of foreign material associated with open fracture(s) and/or dislocation(s); skin and subcutaneous tissues

**11011** skin, subcutaneous tissue, muscle fascia, and muscle

**11012** skin, subcutaneous tissue, muscle fascia, muscle, and bone

**11040** Debridement; skin, partial thickness

**11041** skin, full thickness

**11042** skin, and subcutaneous tissue

**11043** skin, subcutaneous tissue, and muscle

**11044** skin, subcutaneous tissue, muscle, and bone

## Paring or Cutting

(11050-11052 have been deleted. To report paring, see 11055-11057, or to report destruction, see 17000-17004)

**11055** Paring or cutting of benign hyperkeratotic lesion (eg, corn or callus); single lesion

**11056** two to four lesions

**11057** more than four lesions

(11060-11062 have been deleted. To report, see 11300-11313)

## Biopsy

**11100** Biopsy of skin, subcutaneous tissue and/or mucous membrane (including simple closure), unless otherwise listed (separate procedure); single lesion

**+ 11101** each separate/additional lesion (List separately in addition to code for primary procedure)

(Use 11101 in conjunction with code 11100)

(For biopsy of conjunctiva, use 68100; eyelid, use 67810)

## Removal of Skin Tags

Removal by scissoring or any sharp method, ligature strangulation, electrosurgical destruction or combination of treatment modalities including chemical or electrocauterization of wound, with or without local anesthesia.

**11200*** Removal of skin tags, multiple fibrocutaneous tags, any area; up to and including 15 lesions

**+ 11201** each additional ten lesions (List separately in addition to code for primary procedure)

(Use 11201 in conjunction with code 11200)

## Shaving of Epidermal or Dermal Lesions

Shaving is the sharp removal by transverse incision or horizontal slicing to remove epidermal and dermal lesions without a full-thickness dermal excision. This includes local anesthesia, chemical or electrocauterization of the wound. The wound does not require suture closure.

**11300*** Shaving of epidermal or dermal lesion, single lesion, trunk, arms or legs; lesion diameter 0.5 cm or less

**11301** lesion diameter 0.6 to 1.0 cm

**11302** lesion diameter 1.1 to 2.0 cm

**11303** lesion diameter over 2.0 cm

**11305*** Shaving of epidermal or dermal lesion, single lesion, scalp, neck, hands, feet, genitalia; lesion diameter 0.5 cm or less

**11306** lesion diameter 0.6 to 1.0 cm

**11307** lesion diameter 1.1 to 2.0 cm

**11308** lesion diameter over 2.0 cm

**11310*** Shaving of epidermal or dermal lesion, single lesion, face, ears, eyelids, nose, lips, mucous membrane; lesion diameter 0.5 cm or less

**11311** lesion diameter 0.6 to 1.0 cm

**11312** lesion diameter 1.1 to 2.0 cm

**11313** lesion diameter over 2.0 cm

## Excision—Benign Lesions

Excision (including simple closure) of benign lesions of skin or subcutaneous tissues (eg, cicatricial, fibrous, inflammatory, congenital, cystic lesions), including local anesthesia. See appropriate size and area below.

Excision is defined as full-thickness (through the dermis) removal of the following lesions and includes simple (non-layered) closure. The closure of defects created by incision, excision, or trauma may require intermediate (layered) closure. Layered closure involves dermal closure with separate suture closure of at least one of the deeper layers of subcutaneous and non-muscle fascial tissues. See page 57 and following for repair codes.

(For excision of lesions requiring more than simple closure, ie, requiring intermediate, complex, or reconstructive closure, see 12031-12057, 13100-13160, 14000-14300, 15000-15261, 15570-15770)

(For electrosurgical and other methods, see 17000 et seq)

**11400** Excision, benign lesion, except skin tag (unless listed elsewhere), trunk, arms or legs; lesion diameter 0.5 cm or less

**11401** lesion diameter 0.6 to 1.0 cm

**11402** lesion diameter 1.1 to 2.0 cm

**11403** lesion diameter 2.1 to 3.0 cm

**11404** lesion diameter 3.1 to 4.0 cm

**11406** lesion diameter over 4.0 cm

(For unusual or complicated excision, add modifier '-22')

**11420** Excision, benign lesion, except skin tag (unless listed elsewhere), scalp, neck, hands, feet, genitalia; lesion diameter 0.5 cm or less

**11421** lesion diameter 0.6 to 1.0 cm

**11422** lesion diameter 1.1 to 2.0 cm

**11423** lesion diameter 2.1 to 3.0 cm

**11424** lesion diameter 3.1 to 4.0 cm

**11426** lesion diameter over 4.0 cm

(For unusual or complicated excision, add modifier '-22')

**11440** Excision, other benign lesion (unless listed elsewhere), face, ears, eyelids, nose, lips, mucous membrane; lesion diameter 0.5 cm or less

**11441** lesion diameter 0.6 to 1.0 cm

**11442** lesion diameter 1.1 to 2.0 cm

**11443** lesion diameter 2.1 to 3.0 cm

**11444** lesion diameter 3.1 to 4.0 cm

**11446** lesion diameter over 4.0 cm

(For unusual or complicated excision, add modifier '-22')

(For eyelids involving more than skin, see also 67800 et seq)

**11450** Excision of skin and subcutaneous tissue for hidradenitis, axillary; with simple or intermediate repair

**11451** with complex repair

**11462** Excision of skin and subcutaneous tissue for hidradenitis, inguinal; with simple or intermediate repair

**11463** with complex repair

**11470** Excision of skin and subcutaneous tissue for hidradenitis, perianal, perineal, or umbilical; with simple or intermediate repair

**11471** with complex repair

(When skin graft or flap is used for closure, use appropriate procedure code in addition)

(For bilateral procedure, add modifier '-50')

## Excision—Malignant Lesions

Excision (including simple closure) of malignant lesion of skin or subcutaneous tissues including local anesthesia, each lesion. For removal of malignant lesions of skin by any method other than excision, as defined above, see destruction codes 17000-17999.

Excision is defined as full-thickness (through the dermis) removal of the following lesions and includes simple (non-layered) closure. The closure of defects created by incision, excision, or trauma may require intermediate (layered) closure. Layered closure involves dermal closure with separate suture closure of at least one of the deeper layers of subcutaneous and non-muscle fascial tissues.

(For excision of lesions requiring more than simple closure, ie, requiring intermediate, complex, or reconstructive repair, see 12031-12057, 13100-13160, 14000-14300, 15000-15261, 15570-15770)

**11600** Excision, malignant lesion, trunk, arms, or legs; lesion diameter 0.5 cm or less

**11601** lesion diameter 0.6 to 1.0 cm

**11602** lesion diameter 1.1 to 2.0 cm

**11603** lesion diameter 2.1 to 3.0 cm

**11604** lesion diameter 3.1 to 4.0 cm

**11606** lesion diameter over 4.0 cm

**11620** Excision, malignant lesion, scalp, neck, hands, feet, genitalia; lesion diameter 0.5 cm or less

**11621** lesion diameter 0.6 to 1.0 cm

**11622** lesion diameter 1.1 to 2.0 cm

**11623** lesion diameter 2.1 to 3.0 cm

**11624** lesion diameter 3.1 to 4.0 cm

**11626** lesion diameter over 4.0 cm

**11640** Excision, malignant lesion, face, ears, eyelids, nose, lips; lesion diameter 0.5 cm or less

**11641** lesion diameter 0.6 to 1.0 cm

**11642** lesion diameter 1.1 to 2.0 cm

**11643** lesion diameter 2.1 to 3.0 cm

**11644** lesion diameter 3.1 to 4.0 cm

**11646** lesion diameter over 4.0 cm

(For eyelids involving more than skin, see also 67800 et seq)

## Nails

(For drainage of paronychia or onychia, see 10060, 10061)

(11700, 11701 have been deleted. To report, use 11720, 11721)

(11710, 11711 have been deleted. To report, use 11720, 11721)

**11719** Trimming of nondystrophic nails, any number

**11720** Debridement of nail(s) by any method(s); one to five

**11721** six or more

**11730*** Avulsion of nail plate, partial or complete, simple; single

(11731 has been deleted. To report, use 11732)

**+ 11732** each additional nail plate (List separately in addition to code for primary procedure)

(Use 11732 in conjunction with code 11730)

**11740** Evacuation of subungual hematoma

**11750** Excision of nail and nail matrix, partial or complete, (eg, ingrown or deformed nail) for permanent removal;

**11752** with amputation of tuft of distal phalanx

(For skin graft, if used, use 15050)

**11755** Biopsy of nail unit, any method (eg, plate, bed, matrix, hyponychium, proximal and lateral nail folds) (separate procedure)

**11760** Repair of nail bed

**11762** Reconstruction of nail bed with graft

**11765** Wedge excision of skin of nail fold (eg, for ingrown toenail)

(For incision of pilonidal cyst, see 10080, 10081)

**11770** Excision of pilonidal cyst or sinus; simple

**11771** extensive

**11772** complicated

## Introduction

**11900*** Injection, intralesional; up to and including seven lesions

**11901*** more than seven lesions

►(11900, 11901 are not to be used for preoperative local anesthetic injection)◄

(For veins, see 36470, 36471)

(For intralesional chemotherapy administration, see 96405, 96406)

**11920** Tattooing, intradermal introduction of insoluble opaque pigments to correct color defects of skin, including micropigmentation; 6.0 sq cm or less

**11921** 6.1 to 20.0 sq cm

**+ 11922** each additional 20.0 sq cm (List separately in addition to code for primary procedure)

(Use 11922 in conjunction with code 11921)

**11950** Subcutaneous injection of filling material (eg, collagen); 1 cc or less

**11951** 1.1 to 5.0 cc

**11952** 5.1 to 10.0 cc

**11954** over 10.0 cc

**11960** Insertion of tissue expander(s) for other than breast, including subsequent expansion

(For breast reconstruction with tissue expander(s), use 19357)

**11970** Replacement of tissue expander with permanent prosthesis

**11971** Removal of tissue expander(s) without insertion of prosthesis

**11975** Insertion, implantable contraceptive capsules

**11976** Removal, implantable contraceptive capsules

**11977** Removal with reinsertion, implantable contraceptive capsules

**●11980** Subcutaneous hormone pellet implantation (implantation of estradiol and/or testosterone pellets beneath the skin)

## Repair (Closure)

►Use the codes in this section to designate wound closure utilizing sutures, staples, or tissue adhesives (eg, 2-cyanoacrylate), either singly or in combination with each other, or in combination with adhesive strips. Wound closure utilizing adhesive strips as the sole repair material should be coded using the appropriate E/M code.◄

### Definitions

The repair of wounds may be classified as Simple, Intermediate, or Complex.

***Simple repair*** is used when the wound is superficial; eg, involving primarily epidermis or dermis, or subcutaneous tissues without significant involvement of deeper structures, and requires simple one layer closure. This includes local anesthesia and chemical or electrocauterization of wounds not closed.

***Intermediate repair*** includes the repair of wounds that, in addition to the above, require layered closure of one or more of the deeper layers of subcutaneous tissue and superficial (non-muscle) fascia, in addition to the skin (epidermal and dermal) closure. Single-layer closure of heavily contaminated wounds that have required extensive cleaning or removal of particulate matter also constitutes intermediate repair.

***Complex repair*** includes the repair of wounds requiring more than layered closure, viz., scar revision, debridement, (eg, traumatic lacerations or avulsions), extensive undermining, stents or retention sutures. It may include creation of the defect and necessary preparation for repairs or the debridement and repair of complicated lacerations or avulsions.

Instructions for listing services at time of wound repair:

1. The repaired wound(s) should be measured and recorded in centimeters, whether curved, angular, or stellate.

2. When multiple wounds are repaired, add together the lengths of those in the same classification (see above) ►and from all anatomic sites that are grouped together into the same code descriptor. For example, add together the lengths of intermediate repairs to the trunk and extremities. Do not add lengths of repairs from different groupings of anatomic sites (eg, face and extremities). Also, do not add together lengths of different classifications (eg, intermediate and complex repairs).◄

When more than one classification of wounds is repaired, list the more complicated as the primary procedure and the less complicated as the secondary procedure, using either modifier '-51'.

3. Decontamination and/or debridement: Debridement is considered a separate procedure only when gross contamination requires prolonged cleansing, when appreciable amounts of devitalized or contaminated tissue are removed, or when debridement is carried out separately without immediate primary closure. (For extensive debridement of soft tissue and/or bone, see 11040-11044.)

(For extensive debridement of soft tissue and/or bone, not associated with open fracture(s) and/or dislocation(s) resulting from penetrating and/or blunt trauma, see 11040-11044.)

(For extensive debridement of subcutaneous tissue, muscle fascia, muscle, and/or bone associated with open fracture(s) and/or dislocation(s), see 11010-11012.)

4. Involvement of nerves, blood vessels and tendons: Report under appropriate system (Nervous, Cardiovascular, Musculoskeletal) for repair of these structures. The repair of these associated wounds is included in the primary procedure unless it qualifies as a complex wound, in which case either modifier '-51' applies.

Simple ligation of vessels in an open wound is considered as part of any wound closure.

Simple "exploration" of nerves, blood vessels or tendons exposed in an open wound is also considered part of the essential treatment of the wound and is not a separate procedure unless appreciable dissection is required. If the wound requires enlargement, extension of dissection (to determine penetration), debridement, removal of foreign body(s), ligation or coagulation of minor subcutaneous and/or muscular blood vessel(s) of the subcutaneous tissue, muscle fascia, and/or muscle, not requiring thoracotomy or laparotomy, use codes 20100-20103, as appropriate.

## Repair—Simple

Sum of lengths of repairs ►for each group of anatomic sites.◄

**12001*** Simple repair of superficial wounds of scalp, neck, axillae, external genitalia, trunk and/or extremities (including hands and feet); 2.5 cm or less

**12002*** 2.6 cm to 7.5 cm

**12004*** 7.6 cm to 12.5 cm

**12005** 12.6 cm to 20.0 cm

**12006** 20.1 cm to 30.0 cm

**12007** over 30.0 cm

**12011*** Simple repair of superficial wounds of face, ears, eyelids, nose, lips and/or mucous membranes; 2.5 cm or less

**12013*** 2.6 cm to 5.0 cm

**12014** 5.1 cm to 7.5 cm

**12015** 7.6 cm to 12.5 cm

**12016** 12.6 cm to 20.0 cm

**12017** 20.1 cm to 30.0 cm

**12018** over 30.0 cm

**12020** Treatment of superficial wound dehiscence; simple closure

**12021** with packing

(For extensive or complicated secondary wound closure, use 13160)

## Repair—Intermediate

Sum of lengths of repairs ►for each group of anatomic sites.◄

**12031*** Layer closure of wounds of scalp, axillae, trunk and/or extremities (excluding hands and feet); 2.5 cm or less

**12032*** 2.6 cm to 7.5 cm

**12034** 7.6 cm to 12.5 cm

**12035** 12.6 cm to 20.0 cm

**12036** 20.1 cm to 30.0 cm

**12037** over 30.0 cm

**12041*** Layer closure of wounds of neck, hands, feet and/or external genitalia; 2.5 cm or less

**12042** 2.6 cm to 7.5 cm

**12044** 7.6 cm to 12.5 cm

**12045** 12.6 cm to 20.0 cm

**12046** 20.1 cm to 30.0 cm

**12047** over 30.0 cm

**12051*** Layer closure of wounds of face, ears, eyelids, nose, lips and/or mucous membranes; 2.5 cm or less

**12052** 2.6 cm to 5.0 cm

**12053** 5.1 cm to 7.5 cm

**12054** 7.6 cm to 12.5 cm

**12055** 12.6 cm to 20.0 cm

**12056** 20.1 cm to 30.0 cm

**12057** over 30.0 cm

## Repair—Complex

Reconstructive procedures, complicated wound closure.

Sum of lengths of repairs ►for each group of anatomic sites.◄

(For full thickness repair of lip or eyelid, see respective anatomical subsections)

**13100** Repair, complex, trunk; 1.1 cm to 2.5 cm

(For 1.0 cm or less, see simple or intermediate repairs)

**13101** 2.6 cm to 7.5 cm

**+ ●13102** each additional 5 cm or less (List separately in addition to code for primary procedure)

►(Use 13102 in conjunction with code 13101)◄

**13120** Repair, complex, scalp, arms, and/or legs; 1.1 cm to 2.5 cm

(For 1.0 cm or less, see simple or intermediate repairs)

**13121** 2.6 cm to 7.5 cm

**+ ●13122** each additional 5 cm or less (List separately in addition to code for primary procedure)

►(Use 13122 in conjunction with code 13121)◄

**13131** Repair, complex, forehead, cheeks, chin, mouth, neck, axillae, genitalia, hands and/or feet; 1.1 cm to 2.5 cm

(For 1.0 cm or less, see simple or intermediate repairs)

**13132** 2.6 cm to 7.5 cm

**+ ●13133** each additional 5 cm or less (List separately in addition to code for primary procedure)

►(Use 13133 in conjunction with code 13132)◄

**13150** Repair, complex, eyelids, nose, ears and/or lips; 1.0 cm or less

(See also 40650-40654, 67961-67975)

**13151** 1.1 cm to 2.5 cm

**13152** 2.6 cm to 7.5 cm

**+ ●13153** each additional 5 cm or less (List separately in addition to code for primary procedure)

►(Use 13153 in conjunction with code 13152)◄

**13160** Secondary closure of surgical wound or dehiscence, extensive or complicated

(For packing or simple secondary wound closure, see 12020, 12021)

►(13300 has been deleted. To report, see 13102, 13122, 13133 and 13153)◄

## Adjacent Tissue Transfer or Rearrangement

For full thickness repair of lip or eyelid, see respective anatomical subsections.

Excision (including lesion) and/or repair by adjacent tissue transfer or rearrangement (eg, Z-plasty, W-plasty, V-Y plasty, rotation flap, advancement flap, double pedicle flap). When applied in repairing lacerations, the procedures listed must be developed by the surgeon to accomplish the repair. They do not apply when direct closure or rearrangement of traumatic wounds incidentally result in these configurations.

Skin graft necessary to close secondary defect is considered an additional procedure.

**14000** Adjacent tissue transfer or rearrangement, trunk; defect 10 sq cm or less

**14001** defect 10.1 sq cm to 30.0 sq cm

**14020** Adjacent tissue transfer or rearrangement, scalp, arms and/or legs; defect 10 sq cm or less

**14021** defect 10.1 sq cm to 30.0 sq cm

**14040** Adjacent tissue transfer or rearrangement, forehead, cheeks, chin, mouth, neck, axillae, genitalia, hands and/or feet; defect 10 sq cm or less

**14041** defect 10.1 sq cm to 30.0 sq cm

**14060** Adjacent tissue transfer or rearrangement, eyelids, nose, ears and/or lips; defect 10 sq cm or less

**14061** defect 10.1 sq cm to 30.0 sq cm

(For eyelid, full thickness, see 67961 et seq)

**14300** Adjacent tissue transfer or rearrangement, more than 30 sq cm, unusual or complicated, any area

**14350** Filleted finger or toe flap, including preparation of recipient site

## Free Skin Grafts

Identify by size and location of the defect (recipient area) and the type of graft; includes simple debridement of granulations or recent avulsion.

When a primary procedure such as orbitectomy, radical mastectomy, or deep tumor removal requires skin graft for definitive closure, see appropriate anatomical subsection for primary procedure and this section for skin graft.

For tissue-cultured skin grafts, including bilaminate skin substitutes/neodermis, use 15100-15121. These codes include harvesting of keratinocytes and/or application of skin substitute/neodermis. Procedures are coded by recipient site.

Repair of donor site requiring skin graft or local flaps is to be added as an additional procedure.

Codes 15000, 15001, 15350, 15351, 15400, 15401 describe burn and wound preparation and management procedures. The following definition should be applied to codes 15000, 15001, 15100, 15101, 15120, 15121 when determining the involvement of body size. The measurement of 100 sq cm is applicable to adults and children age 10 and over, percentages apply to infants and children under the age of 10.

(For microvascular flaps, see 15756-15758)

**15000** Surgical preparation or creation of recipient site by excision of open wounds, burn eschar, or scar (including subcutaneous tissues); first 100 sq cm or one percent of body area of infants and children

(For appropriate skin grafts, see 15050-15261; list the free graft separately by its procedure number when the graft, immediate or delayed, is applied)

**+ 15001** each additional 100 sq cm or each additional one percent of body area of infants and children (List separately in addition to code for primary procedure)

(Use code 15001 in conjunction with code 15000)

(For excision of benign lesions, see 11400-11471)

(For excision of malignant lesions, see 11600-11646)

(For excision with alloplastic dressing, use 15000 only)

(For excision with immediate skin grafting use 15050-15261 in addition to 15000)

(For excision with immediate allograft placement use 15350 in addition to 15000)

(For excision with immediate xenograft placement use 15400 in addition to 15000)

**15050** Pinch graft, single or multiple, to cover small ulcer, tip of digit, or other minimal open area (except on face), up to defect size 2 cm diameter

**15100** Split graft, trunk, arms, legs; first 100 sq cm or less, or one percent of body area of infants and children (except 15050)

**+ 15101** each additional 100 sq cm, or each additional one percent of body area of infants and children, or part thereof (List separately in addition to code for primary procedure)

(Use 15101 in conjunction with code 15100)

**15120** Split graft, face, scalp, eyelids, mouth, neck, ears, orbits, genitalia, hands, feet and/or multiple digits; first 100 sq cm or less, or one percent of body area of infants and children (except 15050)

**+ 15121** each additional 100 sq cm, or each additional one percent of body area of infants and children, or part thereof (List separately in addition to code for primary procedure)

(Use 15121 in conjunction with code 15120)

(For eyelids, see also 67961 et seq)

**15200** Full thickness graft, free, including direct closure of donor site, trunk; 20 sq cm or less

**+ 15201** each additional 20 sq cm (List separately in addition to code for primary procedure)

(Use 15201 in conjunction with code 15200)

**15220** Full thickness graft, free, including direct closure of donor site, scalp, arms, and/or legs; 20 sq cm or less

**+ 15221** each additional 20 sq cm (List separately in addition to code for primary procedure)

(Use 15221 in conjunction with code 15220)

**15240** Full thickness graft, free, including direct closure of donor site, forehead, cheeks, chin, mouth, neck, axillae, genitalia, hands, and/or feet; 20 sq cm or less

(For finger tip graft, use 15050)

(For repair of syndactyly, fingers, see 26560-26562)

**+ 15241** each additional 20 sq cm (List separately in addition to code for primary procedure)

(Use 15241 in conjunction with code 15240)

**15260** Full thickness graft, free, including direct closure of donor site, nose, ears, eyelids, and/or lips; 20 sq cm or less

**+ 15261** each additional 20 sq cm (List separately in addition to code for primary procedure)

(Use 15261 in conjunction with code 15260)

(For eyelids, see also 67961 et seq)

(Repair of donor site requiring skin graft or local flaps, to be added as additional separate procedure)

**15350** Application of allograft, skin; 100 sq cm or less

(For staged tissue graft implantation, use modifier '-58')

**+ 15351** each additional 100 sq cm (List separately in addition to code for primary procedure)

(Use 15351 in conjunction with code 15350)

**15400** Application of xenograft, skin; 100 sq cm or less

(15410-15416 have been deleted. To report, see 15756-15758)

**+ 15401** each additional 100 sq cm (List separately in addition to code for primary procedure)

(Use 15401 in conjunction with code 15400)

## Flaps (Skin and/or Deep Tissues)

Regions listed refer to recipient area (not donor site) when flap is being attached in transfer or to final site.

Regions listed refer to donor site when tube is formed for later or when "delay" of flap is prior to transfer.

Procedures 15570-15738 do not include extensive immobilization (eg, large plaster casts and other immobilizing devices are considered additional separate procedures).

Repair of donor site requiring skin graft or local flaps is considered an additional separate procedure.

(For microvascular flaps, see 15756-15758)

(15500-15515 have been deleted. To report, use 15000)

(15540-15555 have been deleted. To report, see 15570-15576)

**15570** Formation of direct or tubed pedicle, with or without transfer; trunk

**15572** scalp, arms, or legs

**15574** forehead, cheeks, chin, mouth, neck, axillae, genitalia, hands or feet

**15576** eyelids, nose, ears, lips, or intraoral

►(15580 has been deleted. To report, use 15574)◄

**15600** Delay of flap or sectioning of flap (division and inset); at trunk

**15610** at scalp, arms, or legs

**15620** at forehead, cheeks, chin, neck, axillae, genitalia, hands, or feet

►(15625 has been deleted. To report, use 15620)◄

**15630** at eyelids, nose, ears, or lips

**15650** Transfer, intermediate, of any pedicle flap (eg, abdomen to wrist, Walking tube), any location

(15700-15730 have been deleted. To report, see 15570-15576)

(For eyelids, nose, ears, or lips, see also anatomical area)

(For revision, defatting or rearranging of transferred pedicle flap or skin graft, see 13100-14300)

(Procedures 15732-15738 are described by donor site of the muscle, myocutaneous, or fasciocutaneous flap)

**15732** Muscle, myocutaneous, or fasciocutaneous flap; head and neck (eg, temporalis, masseter, sternocleidomastoid, levator scapulae)

**15734** trunk

**15736** upper extremity

**15738** lower extremity

## Other Flaps and Grafts

Repair of donor site requiring skin graft or local flaps should be reported as an additional procedure.

**15740** Flap; island pedicle

(15745 has been deleted. To report, see 15732-15738)

**15750** neurovascular pedicle

(15755 has been deleted. To report, see 15756-15758)

**15756** Free muscle flap with or without skin with microvascular anastomosis

(Do not report code 69990 in addition to code 15756)

**15757** Free skin flap with microvascular anastomosis

(Do not report code 69990 in addition to code 15757)

**15758** Free fascial flap with microvascular anastomosis

(Do not report code 69990 in addition to code 15758)

**15760** Graft; composite (eg, full thickness of external ear or nasal ala), including primary closure, donor area

**15770** derma-fat-fascia

**15775** Punch graft for hair transplant; 1 to 15 punch grafts

**15776** more than 15 punch grafts

(For strip transplant, use 15220)

## Other Procedures

**15780** Dermabrasion; total face (eg, for acne scarring, fine wrinkling, rhytids, general keratosis)

**15781** segmental, face

**15782** regional, other than face

**15783** superficial, any site, (eg, tattoo removal)

(15785 has been deleted. To report, see 15781, 15782)

**15786*** Abrasion; single lesion (eg, keratosis, scar)

**+ 15787** each additional four lesions or less (List separately in addition to code for primary procedure)

(Use 15787 in conjunction with 15786)

**15788** Chemical peel, facial; epidermal

**15789** dermal

(15790, 15791 have been deleted. To report, see 15788-15793)

**15792** Chemical peel, nonfacial; epidermal

**15793** dermal

(15800 has been deleted)

**15810** Salabrasion; 20 sq cm or less

**15811** over 20 sq cm

**15819** Cervicoplasty

**15820** Blepharoplasty, lower eyelid;

**15821** with extensive herniated fat pad

**15822** Blepharoplasty, upper eyelid;

**15823** with excessive skin weighting down lid

(For bilateral blepharoplasty, add modifier '-50')

(See also 67916, 67917, 67923, 67924)

**15824** Rhytidectomy; forehead

(For repair of brow ptosis, use 67900)

**15825** neck with platysmal tightening (platysmal flap, P-flap)

**15826** glabellar frown lines

(15827 has been deleted. To report, use 15838)

**15828** cheek, chin, and neck

**15829** superficial musculoaponeurotic system (SMAS) flap

(For bilateral rhytidectomy, add modifier '-50')

**15831** Excision, excessive skin and subcutaneous tissue (including lipectomy); abdomen (abdominoplasty)

**15832** thigh

**15833** leg

**15834** hip

**15835** buttock

**15836** arm

**15837** forearm or hand

**15838** submental fat pad

**15839** other area

(For bilateral procedure, add modifier '-50')

**15840** Graft for facial nerve paralysis; free fascia graft (including obtaining fascia)

(For bilateral procedure, add modifier '-50')

**15841** free muscle graft (including obtaining graft)

**15842** free muscle graft by microsurgical technique

**15845** regional muscle transfer

(For intravenous fluorescein examination of blood flow in graft or flap, use 15860)

(For nerve transfers, decompression, or repair, see 64830-64876, 64905, 64907, 69720, 69725, 69740, 69745, 69955)

**15850** Removal of sutures under anesthesia (other than local), same surgeon

**15851** Removal of sutures under anesthesia (other than local), other surgeon

**15852** Dressing change (for other than burns) under anesthesia (other than local)

**15860** Intravenous injection of agent (eg, fluorescein) to test blood flow in flap or graft

(15875 has been deleted. To report, see 15876-15879)

**15876** Suction assisted lipectomy; head and neck

**15877** trunk

**15878** upper extremity

**15879** lower extremity

## Pressure Ulcers (Decubitus Ulcers)

**15920** Excision, coccygeal pressure ulcer, with coccygectomy; with primary suture

**15922** with flap closure

(15930 has been deleted. To report, use 15934)

**15931** Excision, sacral pressure ulcer, with primary suture;

(15932 has been deleted)

**15933** with ostectomy

**15934** Excision, sacral pressure ulcer, with skin flap closure;

**15935** with ostectomy

**15936** Excision, sacral pressure ulcer, in preparation for muscle or myocutaneous flap or skin graft closure;

**15937** with ostectomy

(For repair of defect using muscle or myocutaneous flap, use code(s) 15734 and/or 15738 in addition to 15936, 15937. For repair of defect using split skin graft, use codes 15100 and/or 15101 in addition to 15936, 15937)

**15940** Excision, ischial pressure ulcer, with primary suture;

**15941** with ostectomy (ischiectomy)

(15942, 15943 have been deleted. To report, see 15944-15946)

**15944** Excision, ischial pressure ulcer, with skin flap closure;

**15945** with ostectomy

**15946** Excision, ischial pressure ulcer, with ostectomy, in preparation for muscle or myocutaneous flap or skin graft closure

(For repair of defect using muscle or myocutaneous flap, use code(s) 15734 and/or 15738 in addition to 15946. For repair of defect using split skin graft, use codes 15100 and/or 15101 in addition to 15946)

**15950** Excision, trochanteric pressure ulcer, with primary suture;

**15951** with ostectomy

**15952** Excision, trochanteric pressure ulcer, with skin flap closure;

**15953** with ostectomy

(15954 and 15955 have been deleted. To report, use appropriate debridement, closure or flap codes)

**15956** Excision, trochanteric pressure ulcer, in preparation for muscle or myocutaneous flap or skin graft closure;

**15958** with ostectomy

(For repair of defect using muscle or myocutaneous flap, use code(s) 15734 and/or 15738 in addition to 15956, 15958. For repair of defect using split skin graft, use codes 15100 and/or 15101 in addition to 15956, 15958)

(15960-15983 have been deleted. To report, use appropriate debridement, closure or flap codes)

**15999** Unlisted procedure, excision pressure ulcer

(For free skin graft to close ulcer or donor site, see 15000 et seq)

## Burns, Local Treatment

Procedures 16000-16035 refer to local treatment of burned surface only.

List percentage of body surface involved and depth of burn.

For necessary related medical services (eg, hospital visits, detention) in management of burned patients, see appropriate services in **Evaluation and Management** and **Medicine** sections.

(For skin graft, see 15100-15650)

**16000** Initial treatment, first degree burn, when no more than local treatment is required

**16010** Dressings and/or debridement, initial or subsequent; under anesthesia, small

**16015** under anesthesia, medium or large, or with major debridement

**16020*** without anesthesia, office or hospital, small

**16025*** without anesthesia, medium (eg, whole face or whole extremity)

**16030** without anesthesia, large (eg, more than one extremity)

**16035** Escharotomy

(16040-16042 have been deleted. To report, use 15000)

(For debridement, curettement of burn wound, see 16010-16030)

# Destruction

Destruction means the ablation of benign, premalignant or malignant tissues by any method, with or without curettement, including local anesthesia, and not usually requiring closure.

Any method includes electrosurgery, cryosurgery, laser and chemical treatment. Lesions include condylomata, papillomata, molluscum contagiosum, herpetic lesions, warts (ie, common, plantar, flat), milia, or other benign, premalignant (eg, actinic keratoses), or malignant lesions.

(For destruction of lesion(s) in specific anatomic sites, see 40820, 46900-46917, 46924, 54050-54057, 54065, 56501, 56515, 57061, 57065, 67850, 68135)

(For paring or cutting of benign hyperkeratotic lesions (eg, corns or calluses), see 11055-11057)

(For sharp removal or electrosurgical destruction of skin tags and fibrocutaneous tags, see 11200, 11201)

(For cryotherapy of acne, use 17340)

(For initiation or follow-up care of topical chemotherapy (eg, 5-FU or similar agents), see appropriate office visits)

(For shaving of epidermal or dermal lesions, see 11300-11313)

## Destruction, Benign or Premalignant Lesions

**17000*** Destruction by any method, including laser, with or without surgical curettement, all benign or premalignant lesions (eg, actinic keratoses) other than skin tags or cutaneous vascular proliferative lesions, including local anesthesia; first lesion

(17001, 17002 have been deleted. To report, see 17003, 17004)

**+ 17003** second through 14 lesions, each (List separately in addition to code for first lesion)

(Use 17003 in conjunction with code 17000)

**⊘ 17004** Destruction by any method, including laser, with or without surgical curettement, all benign or premalignant lesions (eg, actinic keratoses) other than skin tags or cutaneous vascular proliferative lesions, including local anesthesia, 15 or more lesions

(Do not report 17004 in conjunction with codes 17000-17003)

(17010 has been deleted. To report, see specific anatomic site code)

(17100-17105 have been deleted. To report, see 17000, 17003, 17004)

**17106** Destruction of cutaneous vascular proliferative lesions (eg, laser technique); less than 10 sq cm

**17107** 10.0 - 50.0 sq cm

**17108** over 50.0 sq cm

**17110*** Destruction by any method of flat warts, molluscum contagiosum, or milia; up to 14 lesions

**17111** 15 or more lesions

(For destruction of common or plantar warts, see 17000, 17003, 17004)

(17200, 17201 have been deleted. To report, see 11200, 11201)

**17250*** Chemical cauterization of granulation tissue (proud flesh, sinus or fistula)

(17250 is not to be used with removal or excision codes for the same lesion)

## Destruction, Malignant Lesions, Any Method

**17260*** Destruction, malignant lesion, any method, trunk, arms or legs; lesion diameter 0.5 cm or less

**17261** lesion diameter 0.6 to 1.0 cm

**17262** lesion diameter 1.1 to 2.0 cm

**17263** lesion diameter 2.1 to 3.0 cm

**17264** lesion diameter 3.1 to 4.0 cm

**17266** lesion diameter over 4.0 cm

**17270*** Destruction, malignant lesion, any method, scalp, neck, hands, feet, genitalia; lesion diameter 0.5 cm or less

**17271** lesion diameter 0.6 to 1.0 cm

**17272** lesion diameter 1.1 to 2.0 cm

**17273** lesion diameter 2.1 to 3.0 cm

**17274** lesion diameter 3.1 to 4.0 cm

**17276** lesion diameter over 4.0 cm

**17280*** Destruction, malignant lesion, any method, face, ears, eyelids, nose, lips, mucous membrane; lesion diameter 0.5 cm or less

**17281** lesion diameter 0.6 to 1.0 cm

**17282** lesion diameter 1.1 to 2.0 cm

**17283** lesion diameter 2.1 to 3.0 cm

**17284** lesion diameter 3.1 to 4.0 cm

**17286** lesion diameter over 4.0 cm

## Mohs' Micrographic Surgery

Mohs' micrographic surgery, for the removal of complex or ill-defined skin cancer, requires a single physician to act in two integrated, but separate and distinct capacities: surgeon and pathologist. If either of these responsibilities are delegated to another physician who reports his services separately, these codes are not appropriate. If repair is performed, use separate repair, flap, or graft codes.

(17300-17302 have been deleted. To report, use 17304-17310)

(17303 has been deleted)

⦸ **17304** Chemosurgery (Mohs micrographic technique), including removal of all gross tumor, surgical excision of tissue specimens, mapping, color coding of specimens, microscopic examination of specimens by the surgeon, and complete histopathologic preparation; first stage, fresh tissue technique, up to 5 specimens

⦸ **17305** second stage, fixed or fresh tissue, up to 5 specimens

⦸ **17306** third stage, fixed or fresh tissue, up to 5 specimens

⦸ **17307** additional stage(s), up to 5 specimens, each stage

⦸ **17310** more than 5 specimens, fixed or fresh tissue, any stage

## Other Procedures

**17340*** Cryotherapy ($CO_2$ slush, liquid $N_2$) for acne

**17360*** Chemical exfoliation for acne (eg, acne paste, acid)

**17380*** Electrolysis epilation, each 1/2 hour

(For actinotherapy, use 96900)

**17999** Unlisted procedure, skin, mucous membrane and subcutaneous tissue

# Breast

## Incision

**19000*** Puncture aspiration of cyst of breast;

**+ 19001** each additional cyst (List separately in addition to code for primary procedure)

(Use 19001 in conjunction with code 19000)

**19020** Mastotomy with exploration or drainage of abscess, deep

**19030** Injection procedure only for mammary ductogram or galactogram

(For radiological supervision and interpretation, see 76086, 76088)

## Excision

(All codes for bilateral procedures have been deleted. To report, add modifier '-50')

**19100*** Biopsy of breast; needle core (separate procedure)

(For fine needle aspiration, use 88170)

(For stereotactic breast biopsy, see 19100, 19101, 88170)

(For radiologic guidance performed in conjunction with breast biopsy, see 76095, 76942)

**19101** incisional

**19110** Nipple exploration, with or without excision of a solitary lactiferous duct or a papilloma lactiferous duct

**19112** Excision of lactiferous duct fistula

**19120** Excision of cyst, fibroadenoma, or other benign or malignant tumor aberrant breast tissue, duct lesion, nipple or areolar lesion (except 19140), male or female, one or more lesions

**19125** Excision of breast lesion identified by preoperative placement of radiological marker; single lesion

**+ 19126** each additional lesion separately identified by a radiological marker (List separately in addition to code for primary procedure)

(Use 19126 in conjunction with code 19125)

**19140** Mastectomy for gynecomastia

**19160** Mastectomy, partial;

**19162** with axillary lymphadenectomy

**19180** Mastectomy, simple, complete

(For immediate or delayed insertion of implant, use 19340 or 19342)

(For gynecomastia, see 19140)

**19182** Mastectomy, subcutaneous

(19184-19187 have been deleted. To report, use 19182 with 19340 or 19342)

**19200** Mastectomy, radical, including pectoral muscles, axillary lymph nodes

(19211-19216 have been deleted. To report, use 19200 with 19340 or 19342)

**19220** Mastectomy, radical, including pectoral muscles, axillary and internal mammary lymph nodes (Urban type operation)

(19224-19229 have been deleted. To report, use 19220 with 19340 or 19342)

**19240** Mastectomy, modified radical, including axillary lymph nodes, with or without pectoralis minor muscle, but excluding pectoralis major muscle

(19250-19255 have been deleted. To report, use 19240 with 19340 or 19342)

**19260** Excision of chest wall tumor including ribs

**19271** Excision of chest wall tumor involving ribs, with plastic reconstruction; without mediastinal lymphadenectomy

**19272** with mediastinal lymphadenectomy

## Introduction

**19290** Preoperative placement of needle localization wire, breast;

**+ 19291** each additional lesion (List separately in addition to code for primary procedure)

(Use 19291 in conjunction with code 19290)

(For radiological supervision and interpretation, use 76096)

## Repair and/or Reconstruction

(19300-19304 have been deleted. To report, see 19316, 19318)

(19310, 19311 have been deleted. To report, use 19325)

(All codes for bilateral procedures have been deleted. To report, add modifier '-50')

**19316** Mastopexy

**19318** Reduction mammaplasty

**19324** Mammaplasty, augmentation; without prosthetic implant

**19325** with prosthetic implant

(For flap or graft, use also appropriate number)

**19328** Removal of intact mammary implant

**19330** Removal of mammary implant material

**19340** Immediate insertion of breast prosthesis following mastopexy, mastectomy or in reconstruction

**19342** Delayed insertion of breast prosthesis following mastopexy, mastectomy or in reconstruction

(For supply of implant, use 99070)

(For preparation of custom breast implant, use 19396)

**19350** Nipple/areola reconstruction

**19355** Correction of inverted nipples

**19357** Breast reconstruction, immediate or delayed, with tissue expander, including subsequent expansion

(19360 has been deleted)

**19361** Breast reconstruction with latissimus dorsi flap, with or without prosthetic implant

(19362 has been deleted. To report, see 19367-19369)

**19364** Breast reconstruction with free flap

(Do not report code 69990 in addition to code 19364)

(19364 includes harvesting of the flap, microvascular transfer, closure of the donor site, and inset shaping the flap into a breast)

**19366** Breast reconstruction with other technique

(For operating microscope, use 69990)

(For insertion of prosthesis, use also 19340 or 19342)

**19367** Breast reconstruction with transverse rectus abdominis myocutaneous flap (TRAM), single pedicle, including closure of donor site;

**19368** with microvascular anastomosis (supercharging)

(Do not report code 69990 in addition to code 19368)

**19369** Breast reconstruction with transverse rectus abdominis myocutaneous flap (TRAM), double pedicle, including closure of donor site

**19370** Open periprosthetic capsulotomy, breast

**19371** Periprosthetic capsulectomy, breast

**19380** Revision of reconstructed breast

**19396** Preparation of moulage for custom breast implant

## Other Procedures

**19499** Unlisted procedure, breast

# Musculoskeletal System

Cast and strapping procedures appear at the end of this section.

The services listed below include the application and removal of the first cast or traction device only. Subsequent replacement of cast and/or traction device may require an additional listing.

**Definitions**

The terms "closed treatment," "open treatment," and "percutaneous skeletal fixation" have been carefully chosen to accurately reflect current orthopaedic procedural treatments.

***Closed treatment*** specifically means that the fracture site is not surgically opened (exposed to the external environment and directly visualized). This terminology is used to describe procedures that treat fractures by three methods: 1) without manipulation 2) with manipulation 3) with or without traction.

***Open treatment*** is used when the fracture is surgically opened (exposed to the external environment). In this instance, the fracture (bone ends) is visualized and internal fixation may be used.

***Percutaneous skeletal fixation*** describes fracture treatment which is neither open nor closed. In this procedure, the fracture fragments are not visualized, but fixation (eg, pins) is placed across the fracture site, usually under x-ray imaging.

The type of fracture (eg, open, compound, closed) does not have any coding correlation with the type of treatment (eg, closed, open, or percutaneous) provided.

The codes for treatment of fractures and joint injuries (dislocations) are categorized by the type of manipulation (reduction) and stabilization (fixation or immobilization). These codes can apply to either open (compound) or closed fractures or joint injuries.

Skeletal traction is the application of a force (distracting or traction force) to a limb segment through a wire, pin, screw, or clamp that is attached (eg, penetrates) to bone.

Skin traction is the application of a force (longitudinal) to a limb using felt or strapping applied directly to skin only.

External fixation is the usage of skeletal pins plus an attaching mechanism/device used for temporary or definitive treatment of acute or chronic bony deformity.

Codes for obtaining autogenous bone grafts, cartilage, tendon, fascia lata grafts or other tissues through separate incisions are to be used only when the graft is not already listed as part of the basic procedure.

Re-reduction of a fracture and/or dislocation performed by the primary physician may be identified by either the addition of the modifier '-76' to the usual procedure number to indicate "Repeat Procedure by Same Physician." (See Guidelines.)

Codes for external fixation are to be used only when external fixation is not already listed as part of the basic procedure.

All codes for suction irrigation have been deleted. To report, list only the primary surgical procedure performed (eg, sequestrectomy, deep incision).

***Manipulation*** is used throughout the musculoskeletal fracture and dislocation subsections to specifically mean the attempted reduction or restoration of a fracture or joint dislocation to its normal anatomic alignment by the application of manually applied forces.

## General

### Incision

**20000*** Incision of soft tissue abscess (eg, secondary to osteomyelitis); superficial

**20005** deep or complicated

(20010 has been deleted)

### Wound Exploration—Trauma (eg, Penetrating Gunshot, Stab Wound)

20100-20103 relate to wound(s) resulting from penetrating trauma. These codes describe surgical exploration and enlargement of the wound, extension of dissection (to determine penetration), debridement, removal of foreign body(s), ligation or coagulation of minor subcutaneous and/or muscular blood vessel(s), of the subcutaneous tissue, muscle fascia, and/or muscle, not requiring thoracotomy or laparotomy. If a repair is done to major structure(s) or major blood vessel(s) requiring thoracotomy or laparotomy, then those specific code(s) would supersede the use of codes 20100-20103. To report Simple, Intermediate, or Complex repair of wound(s) that do not require enlargement of the wound, extension of dissection, etc., as stated above, use specific Repair code(s) in the Integumentary System section.

**20100** Exploration of penetrating wound (separate procedure); neck

**20101** chest

**20102** abdomen/flank/back

**20103** extremity

## Excision

**20150** Excision of epiphyseal bar, with or without autogenous soft tissue graft obtained through same fascial incision

(For aspiration of bone marrow, use 85095)

**20200** Biopsy, muscle; superficial

**20205** deep

**20206*** Biopsy, muscle, percutaneous needle

(For radiological supervision and interpretation, see 76360, 76942)

(For fine needle aspiration, preparation, and interpretation of smears, see 88170-88173)

(For excision of muscle tumor, deep, see specific anatomic section)

**20220** Biopsy, bone, trocar, or needle; superficial (eg, ilium, sternum, spinous process, ribs)

**20225** deep (vertebral body, femur)

(For bone marrow biopsy, use 85102)

**20240** Biopsy, bone, excisional; superficial (eg, ilium, sternum, spinous process, ribs, trochanter of femur)

**20245** deep (eg, humerus, ischium, femur)

**20250** Biopsy, vertebral body, open; thoracic

**20251** lumbar or cervical

(For sequestrectomy, osteomyelitis or drainage of bone abscess, see anatomical area)

## Introduction or Removal

(For injection procedure for arthrography, see anatomical area)

**20500*** Injection of sinus tract; therapeutic (separate procedure)

**20501*** diagnostic (sinogram)

(For radiological supervision and interpretation, use 76080)

**20520*** Removal of foreign body in muscle or tendon sheath; simple

**20525** deep or complicated

**20550*** Injection, tendon sheath, ligament, trigger points or ganglion cyst

**20600*** Arthrocentesis, aspiration and/or injection; small joint, bursa or ganglion cyst (eg, fingers, toes)

**20605*** intermediate joint, bursa or ganglion cyst (eg, temporomandibular, acromioclavicular, wrist, elbow or ankle, olecranon bursa)

**20610*** major joint or bursa (eg, shoulder, hip, knee joint, subacromial bursa)

**20615** Aspiration and injection for treatment of bone cyst

**20650*** Insertion of wire or pin with application of skeletal traction, including removal (separate procedure)

⊘ **20660** Application of cranial tongs, caliper, or stereotactic frame, including removal (separate procedure)

**20661** Application of halo, including removal; cranial

**20662** pelvic

**20663** femoral

**20664** Application of halo, including removal, cranial, 6 or more pins placed, for thin skull osteology (eg, pediatric patients, hydrocephalus, osteogenesis imperfecta), requiring general anesthesia

**20665*** Removal of tongs or halo applied by another physician

**20670*** Removal of implant; superficial, (eg, buried wire, pin or rod) (separate procedure)

**20680** deep (eg, buried wire, pin, screw, metal band, nail, rod or plate)

⊘ **20690** Application of a uniplane (pins or wires in one plane), unilateral, external fixation system

(20691 has been deleted. To report, use 20690)

⊘ **20692** Application of a multiplane (pins or wires in more than one plane), unilateral, external fixation system (eg, Ilizarov, Monticelli type)

**20693** Adjustment or revision of external fixation system requiring anesthesia (eg, new pin(s) or wire(s) and/or new ring(s) or bar(s))

**20694** Removal, under anesthesia, of external fixation system

## Replantation

**20802** Replantation, arm (includes surgical neck of humerus through elbow joint), complete amputation

(20804 has been deleted. To report, see specific code(s) for repair of bone(s), ligament(s), tendon(s), nerve(s), or blood vessel(s) with modifier '-52')

**20805** Replantation, forearm (includes radius and ulna to radial carpal joint), complete amputation

(20806 has been deleted. To report, see specific code(s) for repair of bone(s), ligament(s), tendon(s), nerve(s), or blood vessel(s) with modifier '-52')

**20808** Replantation, hand (includes hand through metacarpophalangeal joints), complete amputation

(20812 has been deleted. To report, see specific code(s) for repair of bone(s), ligament(s), tendon(s), nerve(s), or blood vessel(s) with modifier '-52')

**20816** Replantation, digit, excluding thumb (includes metacarpophalangeal joint to insertion of flexor sublimis tendon), complete amputation

(20820 has been deleted. To report, see specific code(s) for repair of bone(s), ligament(s), tendon(s), nerve(s), or blood vessel(s) with modifier '-52')

**20822** Replantation, digit, excluding thumb (includes distal tip to sublimis tendon insertion), complete amputation

(20823 has been deleted. To report, see specific code(s) for repair of bone(s), ligament(s), tendon(s), nerve(s), or blood vessel(s) with modifier '-52')

**20824** Replantation, thumb (includes carpometacarpal joint to MP joint), complete amputation

(20826 has been deleted. To report, see specific code(s) for repair of bone(s), ligament(s), tendon(s), nerve(s), or blood vessel(s) with modifier '-52')

**20827** Replantation, thumb (includes distal tip to MP joint), complete amputation

(20828 has been deleted. To report, see specific code(s) for repair of bone(s), ligament(s), tendon(s), nerve(s), or blood vessel(s) with modifier '-52')

(20832 has been deleted. To report, see specific code(s) for repair of bone(s), ligament(s), tendon(s), nerve(s), or blood vessel(s) with modifier '-52')

(20834 has been deleted. To report, see specific code(s) for repair of bone(s), ligament(s), tendon(s), nerve(s), or blood vessel(s) with modifier '-52')

**20838** Replantation, foot, complete amputation

(20840 has been deleted. To report, see specific code(s) for repair of bone(s), ligament(s), tendon(s), nerve(s), or blood vessel(s) with modifier '-52')

## Grafts (or Implants)

Codes for obtaining autogenous bone, cartilage, tendon, fascia lata grafts, or other tissues through separate incisions are to be used only when graft is not already listed as part of basic procedure.

(For spinal surgery bone graft(s) see codes 20930-20938)

⊘**20900** Bone graft, any donor area; minor or small (eg, dowel or button)

⊘**20902** major or large

⊘**20910** Cartilage graft; costochondral

⊘**20912** nasal septum

(For ear cartilage, use 21235)

⊘**20920** Fascia lata graft; by stripper

⊘**20922** by incision and area exposure, complex or sheet

⊘**20924** Tendon graft, from a distance (eg, palmaris, toe extensor, plantaris)

⊘**20926** Tissue grafts, other (eg, paratenon, fat, dermis)

(Codes 20930-20938 are reported in addition to codes for the definitive procedure(s) without modifier '-51')

⊘**20930** Allograft for spine surgery only; morselized

⊘**20931** structural

⊘**20936** Autograft for spine surgery only (includes harvesting the graft); local (eg, ribs, spinous process, or laminar fragments) obtained from same incision

⊘**20937** morselized (through separate skin or fascial incision)

⊘**20938** structural, bicortical or tricortical (through separate skin or fascial incision)

(For needle aspiration of bone marrow for the purpose of bone grafting, use 85095)

## Other Procedures

**20950** Monitoring of interstitial fluid pressure (includes insertion of device, eg, wick catheter technique, needle manometer technique) in detection of muscle compartment syndrome

**20955** Bone graft with microvascular anastomosis; fibula

**20956** iliac crest

**20957** metatarsal

(20960 has been deleted. To report, use 20962)

**20962** other than fibula, iliac crest, or metatarsal

(Do not report code 69990 in addition to codes 20955-20962)

**20969** Free osteocutaneous flap with microvascular anastomosis; other than iliac crest, metatarsal, or great toe

**20970** iliac crest

(20971 has been deleted. To report, use 20969)

**20972** metatarsal

**20973** great toe with web space

(Do not report code 69990 in addition to codes 20969-20973)

(For great toe, wrap-around procedure, use 26551)

⊘**20974** Electrical stimulation to aid bone healing; noninvasive (nonoperative)

⊘**20975** invasive (operative)

(20976 has been deleted)

●**20979** Low intensity ultrasound stimulation to aid bone healing, noninvasive (nonoperative)

**20999** Unlisted procedure, musculoskeletal system, general

# Head

Skull, facial bones and temporomandibular joint.

## Incision

(For drainage of superficial abscess and hematoma, use 20000)

(For removal of embedded foreign body from dentoalveolar structure, see 41805, 41806)

**21010** Arthrotomy, temporomandibular joint

(21011 has been deleted. To report, use 21010 with modifier '-50')

## Excision

(For biopsy, see 20220, 20240)

**21015** Radical resection of tumor (eg, malignant neoplasm), soft tissue of face or scalp

(21020 has been deleted. To report, use 61501)

**21025** Excision of bone (eg, for osteomyelitis or bone abscess); mandible

**21026** facial bone(s)

**21029** Removal by contouring of benign tumor of facial bone (eg, fibrous dysplasia)

**21030** Excision of benign tumor or cyst of facial bone other than mandible

**21031** Excision of torus mandibularis

**21032** Excision of maxillary torus palatinus

**21034** Excision of malignant tumor of facial bone other than mandible

**21040** Excision of benign cyst or tumor of mandible; simple

**21041** complex

**21044** Excision of malignant tumor of mandible;

**21045** radical resection

(For bone graft, use 21215)

**21050** Condylectomy, temporomandibular joint (separate procedure)

(21051 has been deleted. To report, use 21050 with modifier '-50')

**21060** Meniscectomy, partial or complete, temporomandibular joint (separate procedure)

(21061 has been deleted. To report, use 21060 with modifier '-50')

**21070** Coronoidectomy (separate procedure)

(21071 has been deleted. To report, use 21070 with modifier '-50')

## Introduction or Removal

(For application or removal of caliper or tongs, see 20660, 20665.) Codes 21076-21089 describe professional services for the rehabilitation of patients with oral, facial or other anatomical deficiencies by means of prostheses such as an artificial eye, ear, or nose or intraoral obturator to close a cleft. Codes 21076-21089 should only be used when the physician actually designs and prepares the prosthesis (ie, not prepared by an outside laboratory).

**21076** Impression and custom preparation; surgical obturator prosthesis

**21077** orbital prosthesis

**21079** interim obturator prosthesis

**21080** definitive obturator prosthesis

**21081** mandibular resection prosthesis

**21082** palatal augmentation prosthesis

**21083** palatal lift prosthesis

**21084** speech aid prosthesis

**21085** oral surgical splint

**21086** auricular prosthesis

**21087** nasal prosthesis

**21088** facial prosthesis

**21089** Unlisted maxillofacial prosthetic procedure

**21100*** Application of halo type appliance for maxillofacial fixation, includes removal (separate procedure)

**21110** Application of interdental fixation device for conditions other than fracture or dislocation, includes removal

(For removal of interdental fixation by another physician, see 20670-20680)

**21116** Injection procedure for temporomandibular joint arthrography

(For radiological supervision and interpretation, use 70332)

## Repair, Revision, and/or Reconstruction

(For cranioplasty, see 21179, 21180 and 62116, 62120, 62140-62147)

**21120** Genioplasty; augmentation (autograft, allograft, prosthetic material)

**21121** sliding osteotomy, single piece

**21122** sliding osteotomies, two or more osteotomies (eg, wedge excision or bone wedge reversal for asymmetrical chin)

**21123** sliding, augmentation with interpositional bone grafts (includes obtaining autografts)

**21125** Augmentation, mandibular body or angle; prosthetic material

**21127** with bone graft, onlay or interpositional (includes obtaining autograft)

**21137** Reduction forehead; contouring only

**21138** contouring and application of prosthetic material or bone graft (includes obtaining autograft)

**21139** contouring and setback of anterior frontal sinus wall

**21141** Reconstruction midface, LeFort I; single piece, segment movement in any direction (eg, for Long Face Syndrome), without bone graft

**21142** two pieces, segment movement in any direction, without bone graft

**21143** three or more pieces, segment movement in any direction, without bone graft

(21144 has been deleted. To report, use 21141)

**21145** single piece, segment movement in any direction, requiring bone grafts (includes obtaining autografts)

**21146** two pieces, segment movement in any direction, requiring bone grafts (includes obtaining autografts) (eg, ungrafted unilateral alveolar cleft)

**21147** three or more pieces, segment movement in any direction, requiring bone grafts (includes obtaining autografts) (eg, ungrafted bilateral alveolar cleft or multiple osteotomies)

**21150** Reconstruction midface, LeFort II; anterior intrusion (eg, Treacher-Collins Syndrome)

**21151** any direction, requiring bone grafts (includes obtaining autografts)

**21154** Reconstruction midface, LeFort III (extracranial), any type, requiring bone grafts (includes obtaining autografts); without LeFort I

**21155** with LeFort I

**21159** Reconstruction midface, LeFort III (extra and intracranial) with forehead advancement (eg, mono bloc), requiring bone grafts (includes obtaining autografts); without LeFort I

**21160** with LeFort I

**21172** Reconstruction superior-lateral orbital rim and lower forehead, advancement or alteration, with or without grafts (includes obtaining autografts)

(For frontal or parietal craniotomy performed for craniosynostosis, use 61556)

**21175** Reconstruction, bifrontal, superior-lateral orbital rims and lower forehead, advancement or alteration (eg, plagiocephaly, trigonocephaly, brachycephaly), with or without grafts (includes obtaining autografts)

(For bifrontal craniotomy performed for craniosynostosis, use 61557)

**21179** Reconstruction, entire or majority of forehead and/or supraorbital rims; with grafts (allograft or prosthetic material)

**21180** with autograft (includes obtaining grafts)

(For extensive craniectomy for multiple suture craniosynostosis, use only 61558 or 61559)

**21181** Reconstruction by contouring of benign tumor of cranial bones (eg, fibrous dysplasia), extracranial

**21182** Reconstruction of orbital walls, rims, forehead, nasoethmoid complex following intra- and extracranial excision of benign tumor of cranial bone (eg, fibrous dysplasia), with multiple autografts (includes obtaining grafts); total area of bone grafting less than 40 $cm^2$

**21183** total area of bone grafting greater than 40 $cm^2$ but less than 80 $cm^2$

**21184** total area of bone grafting greater than 80 $cm^2$

(For excision of benign tumor of cranial bones, see 61563, 61564)

**21188** Reconstruction midface, osteotomies (other than LeFort type) and bone grafts (includes obtaining autografts)

**21193** Reconstruction of mandibular rami, horizontal, vertical, C, or L osteotomy; without bone graft

**21194** with bone graft (includes obtaining graft)

**21195** Reconstruction of mandibular rami and/or body, sagittal split; without internal rigid fixation

**21196** with internal rigid fixation

**21198** Osteotomy, mandible, segmental

(21200, 21202, 21203 have been deleted. To report, see 21193-21198)

(21204 has been deleted. To report, see 21141-21160)

**21206** Osteotomy, maxilla, segmental (eg, Wassmund or Schuchard)

(21207 has been deleted. To report, use 21209)

**21208** Osteoplasty, facial bones; augmentation (autograft, allograft, or prosthetic implant)

**21209** reduction

**21210** Graft, bone; nasal, maxillary or malar areas (includes obtaining graft)

(For cleft palate repair, see 42200-42225)

**21215** mandible (includes obtaining graft)

**21230** Graft; rib cartilage, autogenous, to face, chin, nose or ear (includes obtaining graft)

**21235** ear cartilage, autogenous, to nose or ear (includes obtaining graft)

(21239 has been deleted. To report, use 21208)

**21240** Arthroplasty, temporomandibular joint, with or without autograft (includes obtaining graft)

(21241 has been deleted. To report, use 21240)

**21242** Arthroplasty, temporomandibular joint, with allograft

**21243** Arthroplasty, temporomandibular joint, with prosthetic joint replacement

**21244** Reconstruction of mandible, extraoral, with transosteal bone plate (eg, mandibular staple bone plate)

**21245** Reconstruction of mandible or maxilla, subperiosteal implant; partial

**21246** complete

**21247** Reconstruction of mandibular condyle with bone and cartilage autografts (includes obtaining grafts) (eg, for hemifacial microsomia)

**21248** Reconstruction of mandible or maxilla, endosteal implant (eg, blade, cylinder); partial

**21249** complete

(21250, 21254 have been deleted. To report, see 21141-21160)

**21255** Reconstruction of zygomatic arch and glenoid fossa with bone and cartilage (includes obtaining autografts)

**21256** Reconstruction of orbit with osteotomies (extracranial) and with bone grafts (includes obtaining autografts) (eg, micro-ophthalmia)

**21260** Periorbital osteotomies for orbital hypertelorism, with bone grafts; extracranial approach

**21261** combined intra- and extracranial approach

**21263** with forehead advancement

**21267** Orbital repositioning, periorbital osteotomies, unilateral, with bone grafts; extracranial approach

**21268** combined intra- and extracranial approach

**21270** Malar augmentation, prosthetic material

(For malar augmentation with bone graft, use 21210)

**21275** Secondary revision of orbitocraniofacial reconstruction

**21280** Medial canthopexy (separate procedure)

(For medial canthoplasty, use 67950)

**21282** Lateral canthopexy

**21295** Reduction of masseter muscle and bone (eg, for treatment of benign masseteric hypertrophy); extraoral approach

**21296** intraoral approach

## Other Procedures

**21299** Unlisted craniofacial and maxillofacial procedure

## Fracture and/or Dislocation

**21300** Closed treatment of skull fracture without operation

(For operative repair, see 62000-62010)

**21310** Closed treatment of nasal bone fracture without manipulation

**21315*** Closed treatment of nasal bone fracture; without stabilization

**21320** with stabilization

**21325** Open treatment of nasal fracture; uncomplicated

**21330** complicated, with internal and/or external skeletal fixation

**21335** with concomitant open treatment of fractured septum

**21336** Open treatment of nasal septal fracture, with or without stabilization

**21337** Closed treatment of nasal septal fracture, with or without stabilization

**21338** Open treatment of nasoethmoid fracture; without external fixation

**21339** with external fixation

**21340** Percutaneous treatment of nasoethmoid complex fracture, with splint, wire or headcap fixation, including repair of canthal ligaments and/or the nasolacrimal apparatus

**21343** Open treatment of depressed frontal sinus fracture

**21344** Open treatment of complicated (eg, comminuted or involving posterior wall) frontal sinus fracture, via coronal or multiple approaches

**21345** Closed treatment of nasomaxillary complex fracture (LeFort II type), with interdental wire fixation or fixation of denture or splint

**21346** Open treatment of nasomaxillary complex fracture (LeFort II type); with wiring and/or local fixation

**21347** requiring multiple open approaches

**21348** with bone grafting (includes obtaining graft)

(21350 has been deleted. If necessary to report, use appropriate Evaluation and Management code)

**21355*** Percutaneous treatment of fracture of malar area, including zygomatic arch and malar tripod, with manipulation

**21356** Open treatment of depressed zygomatic arch fracture (eg, Gillies approach)

**21360** Open treatment of depressed malar fracture, including zygomatic arch and malar tripod

**21365** Open treatment of complicated (eg, comminuted or involving cranial nerve foramina) fracture(s) of malar area, including zygomatic arch and malar tripod; with internal fixation and multiple surgical approaches

**21366** with bone grafting (includes obtaining graft)

(21380 has been deleted. If necessary to report, use appropriate Evaluation and Management code)

**21385** Open treatment of orbital floor blowout fracture; transantral approach (Caldwell-Luc type operation)

**21386** periorbital approach

**21387** combined approach

**21390** periorbital approach, with alloplastic or other implant

**21395** periorbital approach with bone graft (includes obtaining graft)

**21400** Closed treatment of fracture of orbit, except blowout; without manipulation

**21401** with manipulation

**21406** Open treatment of fracture of orbit, except blowout; without implant

**21407** with implant

**21408** with bone grafting (includes obtaining graft)

(21420 has been deleted. If necessary to report, use appropriate Evaluation and Management code)

**21421** Closed treatment of palatal or maxillary fracture (LeFort I type), with interdental wire fixation or fixation of denture or splint

**21422** Open treatment of palatal or maxillary fracture (LeFort I type);

**21423** complicated (comminuted or involving cranial nerve foramina), multiple approaches

**21431** Closed treatment of craniofacial separation (LeFort III type) using interdental wire fixation of denture or splint

**21432** Open treatment of craniofacial separation (LeFort III type); with wiring and/or internal fixation

**21433** complicated (eg, comminuted or involving cranial nerve foramina), multiple surgical approaches

**21435** complicated, utilizing internal and/or external fixation techniques (eg, head cap, halo device, and/or intermaxillary fixation)

(For removal of internal or external fixation device, use 20670)

**21436** complicated, multiple surgical approaches, internal fixation, with bone grafting (includes obtaining graft)

**21440** Closed treatment of mandibular or maxillary alveolar ridge fracture (separate procedure)

**21445** Open treatment of mandibular or maxillary alveolar ridge fracture (separate procedure)

**21450** Closed treatment of mandibular fracture; without manipulation

**21451** with manipulation

**21452** Percutaneous treatment of mandibular fracture, with external fixation

**21453** Closed treatment of mandibular fracture with interdental fixation

**21454** Open treatment of mandibular fracture with external fixation

(21455 has been deleted. To report, use 21453)

**21461** Open treatment of mandibular fracture; without interdental fixation

**21462** with interdental fixation

**21465** Open treatment of mandibular condylar fracture

**21470** Open treatment of complicated mandibular fracture by multiple surgical approaches including internal fixation, interdental fixation, and/or wiring of dentures or splints

**21480** Closed treatment of temporomandibular dislocation; initial or subsequent

**21485** complicated (eg, recurrent requiring intermaxillary fixation or splinting), initial or subsequent

**21490** Open treatment of temporomandibular dislocation

(For interdental wire fixation, use 21497)

**21493** Closed treatment of hyoid fracture; without manipulation

**21494** with manipulation

**21495** Open treatment of hyoid fracture

(For treatment of fracture of larynx, see 31584-31586)

**21497** Interdental wiring, for condition other than fracture

### Other Procedures

**21499** Unlisted musculoskeletal procedure, head

(For unlisted craniofacial or maxillofacial procedure, use 21299)

## Neck (Soft Tissues) and Thorax

(For cervical spine and back, see 21920 et seq)

(For injection of fracture site or trigger point, use 20550)

### Incision

(For incision and drainage of abscess or hematoma, superficial, see 10060, 10140)

**21501** Incision and drainage, deep abscess or hematoma, soft tissues of neck or thorax;

**21502** with partial rib ostectomy

**21510** Incision, deep, with opening of bone cortex (eg, for osteomyelitis or bone abscess), thorax

(21511 has been deleted)

### Excision

(For bone biopsy, see 20220-20251)

**21550** Biopsy, soft tissue of neck or thorax

(For needle biopsy of soft tissue, use 20206)

**21555** Excision tumor, soft tissue of neck or thorax; subcutaneous

**21556** deep, subfascial, intramuscular

**21557** Radical resection of tumor (eg, malignant neoplasm), soft tissue of neck or thorax

**21600** Excision of rib, partial

(For radical resection of chest wall and rib cage for tumor, use 19260)

(For radical debridement of chest wall and rib cage for injury, see 11040-11044)

**21610** Costotransversectomy (separate procedure)

**21615** Excision first and/or cervical rib;

**21616** with sympathectomy

**21620** Ostectomy of sternum, partial

**21627** Sternal debridement

(For debridement and closure, use 21750)

**21630** Radical resection of sternum;

**21632** with mediastinal lymphadenectomy

(21633 has been deleted. To report, use 21630)

### Repair, Revision, and/or Reconstruction

(For superficial wound, see **Integumentary System** section under Repair—Simple)

**21700** Division of scalenus anticus; without resection of cervical rib

**21705** with resection of cervical rib

**21720** Division of sternocleidomastoid for torticollis, open operation; without cast application

(For transection of spinal accessory and cervical nerves, see 63191, 64722)

**21725** with cast application

**21740** Reconstructive repair of pectus excavatum or carinatum

(21741 has been deleted. To report, use 21899)

**21750** Closure of sternotomy separation with or without debridement (separate procedure)

### Fracture and/or Dislocation

**21800** Closed treatment of rib fracture, uncomplicated, each

**21805** Open treatment of rib fracture without fixation, each

**21810** Treatment of rib fracture requiring external fixation (flail chest)

**21820** Closed treatment of sternum fracture

**21825** Open treatment of sternum fracture with or without skeletal fixation

(For sternoclavicular dislocation, see 23520-23532)

### Other Procedures

**21899** Unlisted procedure, neck or thorax

## Back and Flank

### Excision

**21920** Biopsy, soft tissue of back or flank; superficial

**21925** deep

(For needle biopsy of soft tissue, use 20206)

**21930** Excision, tumor, soft tissue of back or flank

**21935** Radical resection of tumor (eg, malignant neoplasm), soft tissue of back or flank

## Spine (Vertebral Column)

Cervical, thoracic, and lumbar spine.

Within the SPINE section, bone grafting procedures are reported separately and in addition to arthrodesis. For bone grafts in other Musculoskeletal sections, see specific code(s) descriptor(s) and/or accompanying guidelines.

To report bone grafts performed after arthrodesis, see codes 20930-20938. Bone graft codes are reported without modifier '-51' (multiple procedure).

*Example:*

Posterior arthrodesis of L5-S1 for degenerative disc disease utilizing morselized autogenous iliac bone graft harvested through a separate fascial incision.

Report as 22612 and 20937.

Within the SPINE section, instrumentation is reported separately and in addition to arthrodesis. To report instrumentation procedures performed with definitive vertebral procedure(s), see codes 22840-22855. Instrumentation procedure codes 22840-22848 and 22851 are reported in addition to the definitive procedure(s) without modifier '-51'.

*Example:*

Posterior arthrodesis of L4-S1, utilizing morselized autogenous iliac bone graft harvested through separate fascial incision, and pedicle screw fixation.

Report as 22612, 22614, 22842, and 20937.

Vertebral procedures are sometimes followed by arthrodesis and in addition may include bone grafts and instrumentation.

When arthrodesis is performed in addition to another procedure, the arthrodesis should be reported in addition to the original procedure with a modifier '-51' (multiple procedures). Examples are after osteotomy, fracture care, vertebral corpectomy and laminectomy. Since bone grafts and instrumentation are never performed without arthrodesis, modifier '-51' (multiple procedures) is not used.

Arthrodesis, however, may be performed in the absence of other procedures and therefore when it is combined with another definitive procedure, modifier '-51' (multiple procedure) is appropriate.

*Example:*

Treatment of a burst fracture of L2 by corpectomy followed by arthrodesis of L1-L3, utilizing anterior instrumentation L1-L3 and structural allograft.

Report as 63090, 22558-51, ►22585,◄ 22845, and 20931.

(For injection procedure for myelography, use 62284)

(For injection procedure for diskography, see 62290, 62291)

(For injection procedure, chemonucleolysis, single or multiple levels, use 62292)

(For injection procedure for facet joints, see ►64470-64476, 64622-64627◄)

(For needle or trocar biopsy, see 20220-20225)

## Excision

(For bone biopsy, see 20220-20251)

(22010 has been deleted. To report, use 21920)

(22011 has been deleted. To report, use 21925)

(22012 has been deleted. To report, use 20206)

(22030-22033 have been deleted. To report, use 21930)

**22100** Partial excision of posterior vertebral component (eg, spinous process, lamina or facet) for intrinsic bony lesion, single vertebral segment; cervical

**22101** thoracic

**22102** lumbar

**+ 22103** each additional segment (List separately in addition to code for primary procedure)

(Use 22103 in conjunction with codes 22100, 22101, 22102)

(22105 has been deleted. To report, use 22100)

(22106 has been deleted. To report, use 22101)

(22107 has been deleted. To report, use 22102)

**22110** Partial excision of vertebral body, for intrinsic bony lesion, without decompression of spinal cord or nerve root(s), single vertebral segment; cervical

(22111 has been deleted)

**22112** thoracic

(22113 has been deleted)

**22114** lumbar

(22115 has been deleted)

**+ 22116** each additional vertebral segment (List separately in addition to code for primary procedure)

(Use 22116 in conjunction with codes 22110, 22112, 22114)

(22120-22130 have been deleted. For complete or near complete resection of vertebral body, see vertebral corpectomy, 63081-63091)

(22140 has been deleted. To report, use 63081 and 22554 and 20931 or 20938)

(22141 has been deleted. To report, use 63085 or 63087 and 22556 and 20931 or 20938)

(22142 has been deleted. To report, use 63087 or 63090 and 22558 and 20931 or 20938)

(22145 has been deleted. To report, use 63082 or 63086 or 63088 or 63091, and 22585)

(22148 has been deleted. To report, see 20931 or 20938)

(22150 has been deleted. To report, use 63081 and 22554 and 20931 or 20938 and 22851)

(22151 has been deleted. To report, use 63085 or 63087 and 22556 and 20931 or 20938 and 22851)

(22152 has been deleted. To report, use 63087 or 63090 and 22558, and 20931 or 20938 and 22851)

(22200-22207 have been deleted. For osteotomy of spine, see 22210-22226)

## Osteotomy

To report arthrodesis, see codes 22590-22632. (Report in addition to code(s) for the definitive procedure with modifier '-51'.)

To report instrumentation procedures, see codes 22840-22855. (Report in addition to code(s) for the definitive procedure(s) without modifier '-51'.)

To report bone graft procedures, see codes 20930-20938. (Report in addition to code(s) for the definitive procedure(s) without modifier '-51'.)

**22210** Osteotomy of spine, posterior or posterolateral approach, one vertebral segment; cervical

**22212** thoracic

**22214** lumbar

+ **22216** each additional vertebral segment (List separately in addition to primary procedure)

(Use 22216 in conjunction with codes 22210, 22212, 22214)

**22220** Osteotomy of spine, including diskectomy, anterior approach, single vertebral segment; cervical

**22222** thoracic

**22224** lumbar

+ **22226** each additional vertebral segment (List separately in addition to code for primary procedure)

(Use 22226 in conjunction with codes 22220, 22222, 22224)

(22230 has been deleted. To report, use 22216 or 22226)

(22250, 22251 have been deleted. For vertebral corpectomy, see 63081-63091)

## Fracture and/or Dislocation

To report arthrodesis, see codes 22590-22632. (Report in addition to code(s) for the definitive procedure with modifier '-51'.)

To report instrumentation procedures, see codes 22840-22855. (Report in addition to code(s) for the definitive procedure(s) without modifier '-51'.)

To report bone graft procedures, see codes 20930-20938. (Report in addition to code(s) for the definitive procedure(s) without modifier '-51'.)

**22305** Closed treatment of vertebral process fracture(s)

**22310** Closed treatment of vertebral body fracture(s), without manipulation, requiring and including casting or bracing

**22315** Closed treatment of vertebral fracture(s) and/or dislocation(s) requiring casting or bracing, with and including casting and/or bracing, with or without anesthesia, by manipulation or traction

(For spinal subluxation, use ►97140◄)

● **22318** Open treatment and/or reduction of odontoid fracture(s) and or dislocation(s) (including os odontoideum), anterior approach, including placement of internal fixation; without grafting

● **22319** with grafting

**22325** Open treatment and/or reduction of vertebral fracture(s) and/or dislocation(s), posterior approach, one fractured vertebrae or dislocated segment; lumbar

**22326** cervical

**22327** thoracic

+ **22328** each additional fractured vertebrae or dislocated segment (List separately in addition to code for primary procedure)

(Use 22328 in conjunction with codes 22325, 22326, 22327)

(For treatment of vertebral fracture by the anterior approach, see corpectomy 63081-63091, and appropriate arthrodesis, bone graft and instrument codes)

(22330-22379 have been deleted. For decompression of spine following fracture, see 63001-63091; for arthrodesis of spine following fracture, see 22548-22632)

## Manipulation

(22500 has been deleted. To report, use 97260)

**22505** Manipulation of spine requiring anesthesia, any region

## Arthrodesis

Arthrodesis may be performed in the absence of other procedures and therefore when it is combined with another definitive procedure (eg, osteotomy, fracture care, vertebral corpectomy or laminectomy), modifier '-51' is appropriate. However, arthrodesis codes 22585, 22614, and 22632 are considered add-on procedure codes and should not be used with modifier '-51'.

To report instrumentation procedures, see codes 22840-22855. (Report in addition to code(s) for the definitive procedure(s) without modifier '-51'.)

To report bone graft procedures, see codes 20930-20938. (Report in addition to code(s) for the definitive procedure(s) without modifier '-51'.)

## Anterior or Anterolateral Approach Technique

Procedure codes 22554-22558 are for SINGLE interspace; for additional interspaces, use 22585. ►A vertebral interspace is the non-bony compartment between two adjacent vertebral bodies, which contains the intervertebral disk, and includes the nucleus pulposus, annulus fibrosus, and two cartilagenous endplates.◄

**22548** Arthrodesis, anterior transoral or extraoral technique, clivus-C1-C2 (atlas-axis), with or without excision of odontoid process

(22550, 22552, 22555, 22560, 22561, 22565 have been deleted. For intervertebral disk excision by laminotomy or laminectomy, see 63020-63042. For arthrodesis, see 22548-22632)

**22554** Arthrodesis, anterior interbody technique, including minimal diskectomy to prepare interspace (other than for decompression); cervical below C2

**22556** thoracic

**22558** lumbar

**+ 22585** each additional interspace (List separately in addition to code for primary procedure)

(Use 22585 in conjunction with codes 22554, 22556, 22558)

## Posterior, Posterolateral or Lateral Transverse Process Technique

To report instrumentation procedures, see codes 22840-22855. (Report in addition to code(s) for the definitive procedure(s) without modifier '-51'.)

To report bone graft procedures, see codes 20930-20938. (Report in addition to code(s) for the definitive procedure(s) without modifier '-51'.) ►A vertebral segment describes the basic constituent part into which the spine may be divided. It represents a single complete vertebral bone with its associated articular processes and laminae. A vertebral interspace is the non-bony compartment between two adjacent vertebral bodies which contains the intervertebral disk, and includes the nucleus pulposus, annulus fibrosus, and two cartilagenous endplates.◄

**22590** Arthrodesis, posterior technique, craniocervical (occiput-C2)

**22595** Arthrodesis, posterior technique, atlas-axis (C1-C2)

**22600** Arthrodesis, posterior or posterolateral technique, single level; cervical below C2 segment

(22605 has been deleted. To report, use 22600)

**22610** thoracic (with or without lateral transverse technique)

**22612** lumbar (with or without lateral transverse technique)

**+ 22614** each additional vertebral segment (List separately in addition to code for primary procedure)

(Use 22614 in conjunction with codes 22600, 22610, 22612)

(22615 has been deleted. To report, use 22554 and 20930-20938)

(22617 has been deleted. To report, use 22548 and 20930-20938)

(22620 has been deleted. To report, use 22590 and 20930-20938)

(22625 has been deleted. To report, use 22612 and 22840-22855, and 20930-20938)

**▲22630** Arthrodesis, posterior interbody technique, including laminectomy and/or diskectomy to prepare interspace (other than for decompression), single interspace; lumbar

**+ 22632** each additional interspace (List separately in addition to code for primary procedure)

(Use 22632 in conjunction with code 22630)

(22640-22645 have been deleted. To report, see 22610, 22612, and 20930-20938)

(22650 has been deleted. To report, use 22614)

(22655 has been deleted. To report, see 22630, 22632 and 20930-20938)

(22670 has been deleted. To report, see 22610 or 22612 and 22840-22855, and 20930-20938)

(22680 has been deleted. To report, see 22556-22585 and 20930-20938)

(22700 has been deleted. To report, see 22558 and 20930-20938)

(22720 has been deleted. To report, see 22612 and 20930-20938)

(22730 has been deleted. To report, see 22585, 22614)

(22735 has been deleted. To report, see 22585, 22614)

## Spine Deformity (eg, Scoliosis, Kyphosis)

To report instrumentation procedures, see codes 22840-22855. (Report in addition to code(s) for the definitive procedure(s) without modifier '-51'.)

To report bone graft procedures, see codes 20930-20938. (Report in addition to code(s) for the definitive procedure(s) without modifier '-51'.)

►A vertebral segment describes the basic constituent part into which the spine may be divided. It represents a single complete vertebral bone with its associated articular processes and laminae.◄

**22800** Arthrodesis, posterior, for spinal deformity, with or without cast; up to 6 vertebral segments

(22801 has been deleted. To report, use 22800)

**22802** 7 to 12 vertebral segments

(22803 has been deleted. To report, use 22802)

**22804** 13 or more vertebral segments

**22808** Arthrodesis, anterior, for spinal deformity, with or without cast; 2 to 3 vertebral segments

**22810** 4 to 7 vertebral segments

**22812** 8 or more vertebral segments

**22818** Kyphectomy, circumferential exposure of spine and resection of vertebral segment(s) (including body and posterior elements); single or 2 segments

**22819** 3 or more segments

(To report arthrodesis, see 22800-22804 and add modifier '-51')

## Exploration

(22820 has been deleted. To report, see 20930-20938)

**22830** Exploration of spinal fusion

## Spinal Instrumentation

Segmental instrumentation is defined as fixation at each end of the construct and at least one additional interposed bony attachment.

Non-segmental instrumentation is defined as fixation at each end of the construct and may span several vertebral segments without attachment to the intervening segments.

Insertion of spinalinstrumentation is reported separately and in addition to arthrodesis. Instrumentation procedure codes 22840-22848, 22851 are reported in addition to the definitive procedure(s) without modifier '-51'.

To report bone graft procedures, see codes 20930-20938. (Report in addition to code(s) for definitive procedure(s) without modifier '-51'.)

►A vertebral segment describes the basic constituent part into which the spine may be divided. It represents a single complete vertebral bone with its associated articular processes and laminae. A vertebral interspace is the non-bony compartment between two adjacent vertebral bodies, which contains the intervertebral disk, and includes the nucleus pulposus, annulus fibrosus, and two cartilagenous endplates.◄

(List codes 22840-22848, 22851 separately, in addition to code for fracture, dislocation, or arthrodesis of the spine, 22325, 22326, 22327, 22548-22812)

⊘▲**22840** Posterior non-segmental instrumentation (eg, Harrington rod technique), pedicle fixation across one interspace, atlantoaxial transarticular screw fixation, sublaminar wiring at C1, facet screw fixation

⊘**22841** Internal spinal fixation by wiring of spinous processes

⊘**22842** Posterior segmental instrumentation (eg, pedicle fixation, dual rods with multiple hooks and sublaminar wires); 3 to 6 vertebral segments

⊘**22843** 7 to 12 vertebral segments

⊘**22844** 13 or more vertebral segments

⊘**22845** Anterior instrumentation; 2 to 3 vertebral segments

⊘**22846** 4 to 7 vertebral segments

⊘**22847** 8 or more vertebral segments

⊘**22848** Pelvic fixation (attachment of caudal end of instrumentation to pelvic bony structures) other than sacrum

**22849** Reinsertion of spinal fixation device

**22850** Removal of posterior nonsegmental instrumentation (eg, Harrington rod)

⊘▲**22851** Application of intervertebral biomechanical device(s) (eg, synthetic cage(s), threaded bone dowel(s), methylmethacrylate) to vertebral defect or interspace

**22852** Removal of posterior segmental instrumentation

**22855** Removal of anterior instrumentation

## Other Procedures

**22899** Unlisted procedure, spine

# Abdomen

## Excision

**22900** Excision, abdominal wall tumor, subfascial (eg, desmoid)

(22910 has been deleted. To report, use 22999)

## Other Procedures

**22999** Unlisted procedure, abdomen, musculoskeletal system

# Shoulder

Clavicle, scapula, humerus head and neck, sterno-clavicular joint, acromioclavicular joint and shoulder joint.

## Incision

**23000** Removal of subdeltoid (or intratendinous) calcareous deposits, any method

**23020** Capsular contracture release (eg, Sever type procedure)

(For incision and drainage procedures, superficial, see 10040-10160)

**23030** Incision and drainage, shoulder area; deep abscess or hematoma

**23031** infected bursa

**23035** Incision, bone cortex (eg, osteomyelitis or bone abscess), shoulder area

(23036 has been deleted)

**23040** Arthrotomy, glenohumeral joint, including exploration, drainage, or removal of foreign body

(23042 has been deleted)

**23044** Arthrotomy, acromioclavicular, sternoclavicular joint, including exploration, drainage, or removal of foreign body

## Excision

**23065** Biopsy, soft tissue of shoulder area; superficial

**23066** deep

(For needle biopsy of soft tissue, use 20206)

**23075** Excision, soft tissue tumor, shoulder area; subcutaneous

**23076** deep, subfascial, or intramuscular

**23077** Radical resection of tumor (eg, malignant neoplasm), soft tissue of shoulder area

**23100** Arthrotomy, glenohumeral joint, including biopsy

**23101** Arthrotomy, acromioclavicular joint or sternoclavicular joint, including biopsy and/or excision of torn cartilage

**23105** Arthrotomy; glenohumeral joint, with synovectomy, with or without biopsy

**23106** sternoclavicular joint, with synovectomy, with or without biopsy

**23107** Arthrotomy, glenohumeral joint, with joint exploration, with or without removal of loose or foreign body

(23110 has been deleted. To report, use 23929)

**23120** Claviculectomy; partial

**23125** total

**23130** Acromioplasty or acromionectomy, partial, with or without coracoacromial ligament release

**23140** Excision or curettage of bone cyst or benign tumor of clavicle or scapula;

**23145** with autograft (includes obtaining graft)

**23146** with allograft

**23150** Excision or curettage of bone cyst or benign tumor of proximal humerus;

**23155** with autograft (includes obtaining graft)

**23156** with allograft

**23170** Sequestrectomy (eg, for osteomyelitis or bone abscess), clavicle

(23171 has been deleted)

**23172** Sequestrectomy (eg, for osteomyelitis or bone abscess), scapula

(23173 has been deleted)

**23174** Sequestrectomy (eg, for osteomyelitis or bone abscess), humeral head to surgical neck

(23175 has been deleted)

**23180** Partial excision (craterization, saucerization, or diaphysectomy) bone (eg, osteomyelitis), clavicle

(23181 has been deleted)

**23182** Partial excision (craterization, saucerization, or diaphysectomy) bone (eg, osteomyelitis), scapula

(23183 has been deleted)

**23184** Partial excision (craterization, saucerization, or diaphysectomy) bone (eg, osteomyelitis), proximal humerus

(23185 has been deleted)

**23190** Ostectomy of scapula, partial (eg, superior medial angle)

**23195** Resection, humeral head

(For replacement with implant, use 23470)

**23200** Radical resection for tumor; clavicle

**23210** scapula

**23220** Radical resection of bone tumor, proximal humerus;

**23221** with autograft (includes obtaining graft)

**23222** with prosthetic replacement

## Introduction or Removal

(For arthrocentesis or needling of bursa, use 20610)

(For K-wire or pin insertion or removal, see 20650, 20670, 20680)

**23330** Removal of foreign body, shoulder; subcutaneous

**23331** deep (eg, Neer hemiarthroplasty removal)

**23332** complicated (eg, total shoulder)

**23350** Injection procedure for shoulder arthrography

(For radiological supervision and interpretation, use 73040)

(23355-23358 have been deleted. To report, see 29815-29825)

## Repair, Revision, and/or Reconstruction

**23395** Muscle transfer, any type, shoulder or upper arm; single

**23397** multiple

**23400** Scapulopexy (eg, Sprengels deformity or for paralysis)

**23405** Tenotomy, shoulder area; single tendon

**23406** multiple tendons through same incision

**23410** Repair of ruptured musculotendinous cuff (eg, rotator cuff); acute

**23412** chronic

**23415** Coracoacromial ligament release, with or without acromioplasty

**23420** Reconstruction of complete shoulder (rotator) cuff avulsion, chronic (includes acromioplasty)

**23430** Tenodesis of long tendon of biceps

**23440** Resection or transplantation of long tendon of biceps

**23450** Capsulorrhaphy, anterior; Putti-Platt procedure or Magnuson type operation

**23455** with labral repair (eg, Bankart procedure)

**23460** Capsulorrhaphy, anterior, any type; with bone block

**23462** with coracoid process transfer

**23465** Capsulorrhaphy, glenohumeral joint, posterior, with or without bone block

(For sternoclavicular and acromioclavicular reconstruction, see 23530, 23550)

**23466** Capsulorrhaphy, glenohumeral joint, any type multi-directional instability

**23470** Arthroplasty, glenohumeral joint; hemiarthroplasty

**23472** total shoulder (glenoid and proximal humeral replacement (eg, total shoulder))

(For removal of total shoulder implants, see 23331, 23332)

(For osteotomy, proximal humerus, use 24400)

**23480** Osteotomy, clavicle, with or without internal fixation;

**23485** with bone graft for nonunion or malunion (includes obtaining graft and/or necessary fixation)

**23490** Prophylactic treatment (nailing, pinning, plating or wiring) with or without methylmethacrylate; clavicle

**23491** proximal humerus

## Fracture and/or Dislocation

**23500** Closed treatment of clavicular fracture; without manipulation

**23505** with manipulation

(23510 has been deleted. To report, see 23500, 23505, 23515)

**23515** Open treatment of clavicular fracture, with or without internal or external fixation

**23520** Closed treatment of sternoclavicular dislocation; without manipulation

**23525** with manipulation

**23530** Open treatment of sternoclavicular dislocation, acute or chronic;

**23532** with fascial graft (includes obtaining graft)

**23540** Closed treatment of acromioclavicular dislocation; without manipulation

**23545** with manipulation

**23550** Open treatment of acromioclavicular dislocation, acute or chronic;

**23552** with fascial graft (includes obtaining graft)

**23570** Closed treatment of scapular fracture; without manipulation

**23575** with manipulation, with or without skeletal traction (with or without shoulder joint involvement)

(23580 has been deleted. To report, see 23570, 23575, 23585)

**23585** Open treatment of scapular fracture (body, glenoid or acromion) with or without internal fixation

**23600** Closed treatment of proximal humeral (surgical or anatomical neck) fracture; without manipulation

**23605** with manipulation, with or without skeletal traction

(23610 has been deleted. To report, see 23600, 23605, 23615)

**23615** Open treatment of proximal humeral (surgical or anatomical neck) fracture, with or without internal or external fixation, with or without repair of tuberosity(-ies);

**23616** with proximal humeral prosthetic replacement

**23620** Closed treatment of greater humeral tuberosity fracture; without manipulation

**23625** with manipulation

**23630** Open treatment of greater humeral tuberosity fracture, with or without internal or external fixation

**23650** Closed treatment of shoulder dislocation, with manipulation; without anesthesia

**23655** requiring anesthesia

(23658 has been deleted. To report, see 23650, 23655, 23660, 23665, 23670)

**23660** Open treatment of acute shoulder dislocation

(Repairs for recurrent dislocations, see 23450-23466)

**23665** Closed treatment of shoulder dislocation, with fracture of greater humeral tuberosity, with manipulation

**23670** Open treatment of shoulder dislocation, with fracture of greater humeral tuberosity, with or without internal or external fixation

**23675** Closed treatment of shoulder dislocation, with surgical or anatomical neck fracture, with manipulation

**23680** Open treatment of shoulder dislocation, with surgical or anatomical neck fracture, with or without internal or external fixation

## Manipulation

**23700*** Manipulation under anesthesia, shoulder joint, including application of fixation apparatus (dislocation excluded)

## Arthrodesis

**23800** Arthrodesis, glenohumeral joint;

**23802** with autogenous graft (includes obtaining graft)

## Amputation

**23900** Interthoracoscapular amputation (forequarter)

**23920** Disarticulation of shoulder;

**23921** secondary closure or scar revision

## Other Procedures

**23929** Unlisted procedure, shoulder

# Humerus (Upper Arm) and Elbow

Elbow area includes head and neck of radius and olecranon process.

## Incision

(For incision and drainage procedures, superficial, see 10040-10160)

**23930** Incision and drainage, upper arm or elbow area; deep abscess or hematoma

**23931** bursa

**23935** Incision, deep, with opening of bone cortex (eg, for osteomyelitis or bone abscess), humerus or elbow

(23936 has been deleted)

**24000** Arthrotomy, elbow, including exploration, drainage, or removal of foreign body

(24001 has been deleted)

**24006** Arthrotomy of the elbow, with capsular excision for capsular release (separate procedure)

## Excision

**24065** Biopsy, soft tissue of upper arm or elbow area; superficial

**24066** deep (subfascial or intramuscular)

(For needle biopsy of soft tissue, use 20206)

**24075** Excision, tumor, upper arm or elbow area; subcutaneous

**24076** deep, subfascial or intramuscular

**24077** Radical resection of tumor (eg, malignant neoplasm), soft tissue of upper arm or elbow area

**24100** Arthrotomy, elbow; with synovial biopsy only

**24101** with joint exploration, with or without biopsy, with or without removal of loose or foreign body

**24102** with synovectomy

**24105** Excision, olecranon bursa

**24110** Excision or curettage of bone cyst or benign tumor, humerus;

**24115** with autograft (includes obtaining graft)

**24116** with allograft

**24120** Excision or curettage of bone cyst or benign tumor of head or neck of radius or olecranon process;

**24125** with autograft (includes obtaining graft)

**24126** with allograft

**24130** Excision, radial head

(For replacement with implant, use 24366)

**24134** Sequestrectomy (eg, for osteomyelitis or bone abscess), shaft or distal humerus

(24135 has been deleted)

**24136** Sequestrectomy (eg, for osteomyelitis or bone abscess), radial head or neck

(24137 has been deleted)

**24138** Sequestrectomy (eg, for osteomyelitis or bone abscess), olecranon process

(24139 has been deleted)

**24140** Partial excision (craterization, saucerization, or diaphysectomy) bone (eg, osteomyelitis), humerus

(24144 has been deleted)

**24145** Partial excision (craterization, saucerization, or diaphysectomy) bone (eg, osteomyelitis), radial head or neck

(24146 has been deleted)

**24147** Partial excision (craterization, saucerization, or diaphysectomy) bone (eg, osteomyelitis), olecranon process

(24148 has been deleted)

**24149** Radical resection of capsule, soft tissue, and heterotopic bone, elbow, with contracture release (separate procedure)

(For capsular and soft tissue release only, use 24006)

**24150** Radical resection for tumor, shaft or distal humerus;

**24151** with autograft (includes obtaining graft)

**24152** Radical resection for tumor, radial head or neck;

**24153** with autograft (includes obtaining graft)

**24155** Resection of elbow joint (arthrectomy)

## Introduction or Removal

(For K-wire or pin insertion or removal, see 20650, 20670, 20680)

(For arthrocentesis or needling of bursa or joint, use 20605)

**24160** Implant removal; elbow joint

**24164** radial head

**24200** Removal of foreign body, upper arm or elbow area; subcutaneous

**24201** deep (subfascial or intramuscular)

**24220** Injection procedure for elbow arthrography

(For radiological supervision and interpretation, use 73085)

(For injection of tennis elbow, use 20550)

## Repair, Revision, and/or Reconstruction

**24301** Muscle or tendon transfer, any type, upper arm or elbow, single (excluding 24320-24331)

**24305** Tendon lengthening, upper arm or elbow, each tendon

**24310** Tenotomy, open, elbow to shoulder, each tendon

**24320** Tenoplasty, with muscle transfer, with or without free graft, elbow to shoulder, single (Seddon-Brookes type procedure)

**24330** Flexor-plasty, elbow (eg, Steindler type advancement);

**24331** with extensor advancement

**24340** Tenodesis of biceps tendon at elbow (separate procedure)

**24341** Repair, tendon or muscle, upper arm or elbow, each tendon or muscle, primary or secondary (excludes rotator cuff)

**24342** Reinsertion of ruptured biceps or triceps tendon, distal, with or without tendon graft

**24350** Fasciotomy, lateral or medial (eg, tennis elbow or epicondylitis);

**24351** with extensor origin detachment

**24352** with annular ligament resection

**24354** with stripping

**24356** with partial ostectomy

**24360** Arthroplasty, elbow; with membrane (eg, fascial)

**24361** with distal humeral prosthetic replacement

**24362** with implant and fascia lata ligament reconstruction

**24363** with distal humerus and proximal ulnar prosthetic replacement (eg, total elbow)

**24365** Arthroplasty, radial head;

**24366** with implant

**24400** Osteotomy, humerus, with or without internal fixation

**24410** Multiple osteotomies with realignment on intramedullary rod, humeral shaft (Sofield type procedure)

**24420** Osteoplasty, humerus (eg, shortening or lengthening) (excluding 64876)

**24430** Repair of nonunion or malunion, humerus; without graft (eg, compression technique)

**24435** with iliac or other autograft (includes obtaining graft)

(For proximal radius and/or ulna, see 25400-25420)

**24470** Hemiepiphyseal arrest (eg, cubitus varus or valgus, distal humerus)

**24495** Decompression fasciotomy, forearm, with brachial artery exploration

**24498** Prophylactic treatment (nailing, pinning, plating or wiring), with or without methylmethacrylate, humeral shaft

## Fracture and/or Dislocation

**24500** Closed treatment of humeral shaft fracture; without manipulation

**24505** with manipulation, with or without skeletal traction

(24506 has been deleted. To report, use 24516)

(24510 has been deleted. To report, see 24500, 24505, 24515, 24516)

**24515** Open treatment of humeral shaft fracture with plate/screws, with or without cerclage

**24516** Open treatment of humeral shaft fracture, with insertion of intramedullary implant, with or without cerclage and/or locking screws

**24530** Closed treatment of supracondylar or transcondylar humeral fracture, with or without intercondylar extension; without manipulation

(24531 has been deleted. To report, use 24535)

**24535** with manipulation, with or without skin or skeletal traction

(24536 has been deleted. To report, use 24535)

**24538** Percutaneous skeletal fixation of supracondylar or transcondylar humeral fracture, with or without intercondylar extension

(24540 and 24542 have been deleted. To report, see 24530, 24535, 24538, 24545, 24546)

**24545** Open treatment of humeral supracondylar or transcondylar fracture, with or without internal or external fixation; without intercondylar extension

**24546** with intercondylar extension

**24560** Closed treatment of humeral epicondylar fracture, medial or lateral; without manipulation

**24565** with manipulation

**24566** Percutaneous skeletal fixation of humeral epicondylar fracture, medial or lateral, with manipulation

(24570 has been deleted. To report, see 24560, 24565, 24575)

**24575** Open treatment of humeral epicondylar fracture, medial or lateral, with or without internal or external fixation

**24576** Closed treatment of humeral condylar fracture, medial or lateral; without manipulation

**24577** with manipulation

(24578 has been deleted. To report, see 24576, 24577, 24579)

**24579** Open treatment of humeral condylar fracture, medial or lateral, with or without internal or external fixation

(24580 has been deleted. To report, see 24530, 24560, 24576, 24650, 24670)

(24581 has been deleted. To report, see 24535, 24565, 24577, 24675)

**24582** Percutaneous skeletal fixation of humeral condylar fracture, medial or lateral, with manipulation

(24583 has been deleted. To report, see 24535, 24538, 24545, 24560, 24565, 24577)

(24585 has been deleted. To report, see 24538, 24545, 24575, 24579, 24665, 24666, 24685)

**24586** Open treatment of periarticular fracture and/or dislocation of the elbow (fracture distal humerus and proximal ulna and/ or proximal radius);

**24587** with implant arthroplasty

(See also 24361)

(24588 has been deleted. To report, see 24586, 24587)

**24600** Treatment of closed elbow dislocation; without anesthesia

**24605** requiring anesthesia

(24610 has been deleted. To report, see 24586, 24600, 24605, 24615)

**24615** Open treatment of acute or chronic elbow dislocation

**24620** Closed treatment of Monteggia type of fracture dislocation at elbow (fracture proximal end of ulna with dislocation of radial head), with manipulation

(24625 has been deleted. To report, see 24620, 24635)

**24635** Open treatment of Monteggia type of fracture dislocation at elbow (fracture proximal end of ulna with dislocation of radial head), with or without internal or external fixation

**24640*** Closed treatment of radial head subluxation in child, nursemaid elbow, with manipulation

**24650** Closed treatment of radial head or neck fracture; without manipulation

**24655** with manipulation

(24660 has been deleted. To report, see 24650, 24655, 24665, 24666)

**24665** Open treatment of radial head or neck fracture, with or without internal fixation or radial head excision;

**24666** with radial head prosthetic replacement

**24670** Closed treatment of ulnar fracture, proximal end (olecranon process); without manipulation

**24675** with manipulation

(24680 has been deleted. To report, see 24670, 24675, 24685)

**24685** Open treatment of ulnar fracture proximal end (olecranon process), with or without internal or external fixation

(24700 has been deleted. To report, use 24999)

## Arthrodesis

**24800** Arthrodesis, elbow joint; local

**24802** with autogenous graft (includes obtaining graft)

## Amputation

**24900** Amputation, arm through humerus; with primary closure

**24920** open, circular (guillotine)

**24925** secondary closure or scar revision

**24930** re-amputation

**24931** with implant

**24935** Stump elongation, upper extremity

**24940** Cineplasty, upper extremity, complete procedure

## Other Procedures

**24999** Unlisted procedure, humerus or elbow

# Forearm and Wrist

Radius, ulna, carpal bones and joints.

## Incision

**25000** Incision, extensor tendon sheath, wrist (eg, deQuervains disease)

(For decompression median nerve or for carpal tunnel syndrome, use 64721)

(25005 has been deleted. To report, use 25000)

**25020** Decompression fasciotomy, forearm and/or wrist; flexor or extensor compartment

**25023** with debridement of nonviable muscle and/or nerve

(For decompression fasciotomy with brachial artery exploration, use 24495)

(For incision and drainage procedures, superficial, see 10040-10160)

(For debridement, see also 11000-11044)

**25028** Incision and drainage, forearm and/or wrist; deep abscess or hematoma

**25031** bursa

**25035** Incision, deep, bone cortex, forearm and/or wrist (eg, osteomyelitis or bone abscess)

(25036 has been deleted)

**25040** Arthrotomy, radiocarpal or midcarpal joint, with exploration, drainage, or removal of foreign body

(25041 has been deleted)

## Excision

**25065** Biopsy, soft tissue of forearm and/or wrist; superficial

**25066** deep (subfascial or intramuscular)

(For needle biopsy of soft tissue, use 20206)

**25075** Excision, tumor, forearm and/or wrist area; subcutaneous

**25076** deep, subfascial or intramuscular

**25077** Radical resection of tumor (eg, malignant neoplasm), soft tissue of forearm and/or wrist area

**25085** Capsulotomy, wrist (eg, contracture)

**25100** Arthrotomy, wrist joint; with biopsy

**25101** with joint exploration, with or without biopsy, with or without removal of loose or foreign body

**25105** with synovectomy

**25107** Arthrotomy, distal radioulnar joint including repair of triangular cartilage, complex

**25110** Excision, lesion of tendon sheath, forearm and/or wrist

**25111** Excision of ganglion, wrist (dorsal or volar); primary

**25112** recurrent

(For hand or finger, use 26160)

**25115** Radical excision of bursa, synovia of wrist, or forearm tendon sheaths (eg, tenosynovitis, fungus, Tbc, or other granulomas, rheumatoid arthritis); flexors

**25116** extensors, with or without transposition of dorsal retinaculum

(For finger synovectomies, use 26145)

**25118** Synovectomy, extensor tendon sheath, wrist, single compartment;

**25119** with resection of distal ulna

**25120** Excision or curettage of bonc cyst or benign tumor of radius or ulna (excluding head or neck of radius and olecranon process);

(For head or neck of radius or olecranon process, see 24120-24126)

**25125** with autograft (includes obtaining graft)

**25126** with allograft

**25130** Excision or curettage of bone cyst or benign tumor of carpal bones;

**25135** with autograft (includes obtaining graft)

**25136** with allograft

**25145** Sequestrectomy (eg, for osteomyelitis or bone abscess), forearm and/or wrist

(25146 has been deleted)

**25150** Partial excision (craterization, saucerization, or diaphysectomy) of bone (eg, for osteomyelitis); ulna

**25151** radius

(25153 has been deleted)

(For head or neck of radius or olecranon process, see 24145, 24147)

**25170** Radical resection for tumor, radius or ulna

**25210** Carpectomy; one bone

(For carpectomy with implant, see 25441-25445)

**25215** all bones of proximal row

**25230** Radial styloidectomy (separate procedure)

**25240** Excision distal ulna partial or complete (eg, Darrach type or matched resection)

(For implant replacement, distal ulna, use 25442)

(For obtaining fascia for interposition, see 20920, 20922)

## Introduction or Removal

(For K-wire, pin or rod insertion or removal, see 20650, 20670, 20680)

**25246** Injection procedure for wrist arthrography

(For radiological supervision and interpretation, use 73115)

(For foreign body removal, superficial use 20520)

**25248** Exploration with removal of deep foreign body, forearm or wrist

**25250** Removal of wrist prosthesis; (separate procedure)

**25251** complicated, including total wrist

## Repair, Revision, and/or Reconstruction

**25260** Repair, tendon or muscle, flexor, forearm and/or wrist; primary, single, each tendon or muscle

**25263** secondary, single, each tendon or muscle

**25265** secondary, with free graft (includes obtaining graft), each tendon or muscle

**25270** Repair, tendon or muscle, extensor, forearm and/or wrist; primary, single, each tendon or muscle

**25272** secondary, single, each tendon or muscle

**25274** Repair, tendon or muscle, extensor, secondary, with tendon graft (includes obtaining graft), forearm and/or wrist, each tendon or muscle

**25280** Lengthening or shortening of flexor or extensor tendon, forearm and/or wrist, single, each tendon

**25290** Tenotomy, open, flexor or extensor tendon, forearm and/or wrist, single, each tendon

**25295** Tenolysis, flexor or extensor tendon, forearm and/or wrist, single, each tendon

**25300** Tenodesis at wrist; flexors of fingers

**25301** extensors of fingers

**25310** Tendon transplantation or transfer, flexor or extensor, forearm and/or wrist, single; each tendon

**25312** with tendon graft(s) (includes obtaining graft), each tendon

**25315** Flexor origin slide (eg, for cerebral palsy, Volkmann contracture), forearm and/or wrist;

**25316** with tendon(s) transfer

(25317, 25318 have been deleted. To report, see 25315, 25316)

**25320** Capsulorrhaphy or reconstruction, wrist, any method (eg, capsulodesis, ligament repair, tendon transfer or graft) (includes synovectomy, capsulotomy and open reduction) for carpal instability

(25330, 25331 have been deleted. To report, see 25332 and 25441-25446)

**25332** Arthroplasty, wrist, with or without interposition, with or without external or internal fixation

(For obtaining fascia for interposition, see 20920, 20922)

(For prosthetic replacement arthroplasty, see 25441- 25446)

**25335** Centralization of wrist on ulna (eg, radial club hand)

**25337** Reconstruction for stabilization of unstable distal ulna or distal radioulnar joint, secondary by soft tissue stabilization (eg, tendon transfer, tendon graft or weave, or tenodesis) with or without open reduction of distal radioulnar joint

(For harvesting of fascia lata graft, see 20920, 20922)

**25350** Osteotomy, radius; distal third

**25355** middle or proximal third

**25360** Osteotomy; ulna

**25365** radius AND ulna

**25370** Multiple osteotomies, with realignment on intramedullary rod (Sofield type procedure); radius OR ulna

**25375** radius AND ulna

**25390** Osteoplasty, radius OR ulna; shortening

**25391** lengthening with autograft

**25392** Osteoplasty, radius AND ulna; shortening (excluding 64876)

**25393** lengthening with autograft

**25400** Repair of nonunion or malunion, radius OR ulna; without graft (eg, compression technique)

**25405** with iliac or other autograft (includes obtaining graft)

**25415** Repair of nonunion or malunion, radius AND ulna; without graft (eg, compression technique)

**25420** with iliac or other autograft (includes obtaining graft)

**25425** Repair of defect with autograft; radius OR ulna

**25426** radius AND ulna

**25440** Repair of nonunion, scaphoid (navicular) bone, with or without radial styloidectomy (includes obtaining graft and necessary fixation)

**25441** Arthroplasty with prosthetic replacement; distal radius

**25442** distal ulna

**25443** scaphoid (navicular)

**25444** lunate

**25445** trapezium

**25446** distal radius and partial or entire carpus (total wrist)

**25447** Arthroplasty, interposition, intercarpal or carpometacarpal joints

(For wrist arthroplasty, use 25332)

**25449** Revision of arthroplasty, including removal of implant, wrist joint

**25450** Epiphyseal arrest by epiphysiodesis or stapling; distal radius OR ulna

**25455** distal radius AND ulna

**25490** Prophylactic treatment (nailing, pinning, plating or wiring) with or without methylmethacrylate; radius

**25491** ulna

**25492** radius AND ulna

## Fracture and/or Dislocation

**25500** Closed treatment of radial shaft fracture; without manipulation

**25505** with manipulation

(25510 has been deleted. To report, see 25500, 25505, 25515)

**25515** Open treatment of radial shaft fracture, with or without internal or external fixation

**25520** Closed treatment of radial shaft fracture, with dislocation of distal radio-ulnar joint (Galeazzi fracture/dislocation)

**25525** Open treatment of radial shaft fracture, with internal and/ or external fixation and closed treatment of dislocation of distal radio-ulnar joint (Galeazzi fracture/dislocation), with or without percutaneous skeletal fixation

**25526** Open treatment of radial shaft fracture, with internal and/or external fixation and open treatment, with or without internal or external fixation of distal radio-ulnar joint (Galeazzi fracture/dislocation), includes repair of triangular cartilage

**25530** Closed treatment of ulnar shaft fracture; without manipulation

**25535** with manipulation

(25540 has been deleted. To report, see 25530, 25535, 25545)

**25545** Open treatment of ulnar shaft fracture, with or without internal or external fixation

**25560** Closed treatment of radial and ulnar shaft fractures; without manipulation

**25565** with manipulation

(25570 has been deleted. To report, see 25560, 25565, 25574, 25575)

**25574** Open treatment of radial AND ulnar shaft fractures, with internal or external fixation; of radius OR ulna

**25575** of radius AND ulna

**25600** Closed treatment of distal radial fracture (eg, Colles or Smith type) or epiphyseal separation, with or without fracture of ulnar styloid; without manipulation

**25605** with manipulation

(25610 has been deleted. To report, use 25605)

**25611** Percutaneous skeletal fixation of distal radial fracture (eg, Colles or Smith type) or epiphyseal separation, with or without fracture of ulnar styloid, requiring manipulation, with or without external fixation

(25615 has been deleted. To report, see 25600, 25605, 25611, 25620)

**25620** Open treatment of distal radial fracture (eg, Colles or Smith type) or epiphyseal separation, with or without fracture of ulnar styloid, with or without internal or external fixation

**25622** Closed treatment of carpal scaphoid (navicular) fracture; without manipulation

**25624** with manipulation

(25626 has been deleted. To report, see 25622, 25624, 25628)

**25628** Open treatment of carpal scaphoid (navicular) fracture, with or without internal or external fixation

**25630** Closed treatment of carpal bone fracture (excluding carpal scaphoid (navicular)); without manipulation, each bone

**25635** with manipulation, each bone

(25640 has been deleted. To report, see 25630, 25635, 25645)

**25645** Open treatment of carpal bone fracture (excluding carpal scaphoid (navicular)), each bone

**25650** Closed treatment of ulnar styloid fracture

**25660** Closed treatment of radiocarpal or intercarpal dislocation, one or more bones, with manipulation

(25665 has been deleted. To report, see 25650, 25660, 25670)

**25670** Open treatment of radiocarpal or intercarpal dislocation, one or more bones

**25675** Closed treatment of distal radioulnar dislocation with manipulation

**25676** Open treatment of distal radioulnar dislocation, acute or chronic

**25680** Closed treatment of trans-scaphoperilunar type of fracture dislocation, with manipulation

**25685** Open treatment of trans-scaphoperilunar type of fracture dislocation

**25690** Closed treatment of lunate dislocation, with manipulation

**25695** Open treatment of lunate dislocation

(25700 has been deleted. To report, use 25999)

## Arthrodesis

**25800** Arthrodesis, wrist; complete, without bone graft (includes radiocarpal and/or intercarpal and/or carpometacarpal joints)

**25805** with sliding graft

**25810** with iliac or other autograft (includes obtaining graft)

(25815 has been deleted. To report, see 25820, 25825)

**25820** Arthrodesis, wrist; limited, without bone graft (eg, intercarpal or radiocarpal)

**25825** with autograft (includes obtaining graft)

**25830** Arthrodesis, distal radioulnar joint with segmental resection of ulna, with or without bone graft (eg, Sauve-Kapandji procedure)

## Amputation

**25900** Amputation, forearm, through radius and ulna;

**25905** open, circular (guillotine)

**25907** secondary closure or scar revision

**25909** re-amputation

**25915** Krukenberg procedure

**25920** Disarticulation through wrist;

**25922** secondary closure or scar revision

**25924** re-amputation

**25927** Transmetacarpal amputation;

**25929** secondary closure or scar revision

**25931** re-amputation

## Other Procedures

**25999** Unlisted procedure, forearm or wrist

# Hand and Fingers

## Incision

**26010*** Drainage of finger abscess; simple

**26011*** complicated (eg, felon)

**26020** Drainage of tendon sheath, digit and/or palm, each

**26025** Drainage of palmar bursa; single, bursa

**26030** multiple bursa

(26032 has been deleted)

**26034** Incision, bone cortex, hand or finger (eg, osteomyelitis or bone abscess)

**26035** Decompression fingers and/or hand, injection injury (eg, grease gun)

**26037** Decompressive fasciotomy, hand (excludes 26035)

(For injection injury, use 26035)

**26040** Fasciotomy, palmar (eg, Dupuytren's contracture); percutaneous

**26045** open, partial

(For fasciectomy, see 26121-26125)

**26055** Tendon sheath incision (eg, for trigger finger)

**26060** Tenotomy, percutaneous, single, each digit

**26070** Arthrotomy, with exploration, drainage, or removal of loose or foreign body; carpometacarpal joint

**26075** metacarpophalangeal joint, each

**26080** interphalangeal joint, each

## Excision

**26100** Arthrotomy with biopsy; carpometacarpal joint, each

**26105** metacarpophalangeal joint, each

**26110** interphalangeal joint, each

**26115** Excision, tumor or vascular malformation, hand or finger; subcutaneous

**26116** deep, subfascial, intramuscular

**26117** Radical resection of tumor (eg, malignant neoplasm), soft tissue of hand or finger

(26120 has been deleted. To report, see 26121-26125)

**26121** Fasciectomy, palm only, with or without Z-plasty, other local tissue rearrangement, or skin grafting (includes obtaining graft)

(26122 has been deleted. To report, use 26121-26125)

**26123** Fasciectomy, partial palmar with release of single digit including proximal interphalangeal joint, with or without Z-plasty, other local tissue rearrangement, or skin grafting (includes obtaining graft);

(26124 has been deleted. To report, use 26121-26125)

**+ 26125** each additional digit (List separately in addition to code for primary procedure)

(Use 26125 in conjunction with code 26123)

(26126, 26128 have been deleted. To report, use 26121-26125)

(For fasciotomy, see 26040, 26045)

**26130** Synovectomy, carpometacarpal joint

**26135** Synovectomy, metacarpophalangeal joint including intrinsic release and extensor hood reconstruction, each digit

**26140** Synovectomy, proximal interphalangeal joint, including extensor reconstruction, each interphalangeal joint

**26145** Synovectomy, tendon sheath, radical (tenosynovectomy), flexor tendon, palm and/or finger, each tendon

(For tendon sheath synovectomies at wrist, see 25115, 25116)

**26160** Excision of lesion of tendon sheath or capsule (eg, cyst, mucous cyst, or ganglion), hand or finger

(For wrist ganglion, see 25111, 25112)

(For trigger digit, use 26055)

**26170** Excision of tendon, palm, flexor, single (separate procedure), each

**26180** Excision of tendon, finger, flexor (separate procedure), each tendon

**26185** Sesamoidectomy, thumb or finger (separate procedure)

**26200** Excision or curettage of bone cyst or benign tumor of metacarpal;

**26205** with autograft (includes obtaining graft)

(26206 has been deleted. To report, use 26989)

**26210** Excision or curettage of bone cyst or benign tumor of proximal, middle, or distal phalanx of finger;

**26215** with autograft (includes obtaining graft)

(26216 has been deleted. To report, use 26989)

**26230** Partial excision (craterization, saucerization, or diaphysectomy) bone (eg, osteomyelitis); metacarpal

**26235** proximal or middle phalanx of finger

**26236** distal phalanx of finger

**26250** Radical resection, metacarpal; (eg, tumor)

**26255** with autograft (includes obtaining graft)

**26260** Radical resection, proximal or middle phalanx of finger (eg, tumor);

**26261** with autograft (includes obtaining graft)

**26262** Radical resection, distal phalanx of finger (eg, tumor)

## Introduction or Removal

**26320** Removal of implant from finger or hand

(For removal of foreign body in hand or finger, see 20520, 20525)

## Repair, Revision, and/or Reconstruction

**26350** Repair or advancement, flexor tendon, not in digital flexor tendon sheath (eg, no man's land); primary or secondary without free graft, each tendon

**26352** secondary with free graft (includes obtaining graft), each tendon

**26356** Repair or advancement, flexor tendon, in digital flexor tendon sheath (eg, no man's land); primary, each tendon

**26357** secondary, each tendon

**26358** secondary with free graft (includes obtaining graft), each tendon

**26370** Repair or advancement of profundus tendon, with intact superficialis tendon; primary, each tendon

**26372** secondary with free graft (includes obtaining graft), each tendon

**26373** secondary without free graft, each tendon

**26390** Excision flexor tendon, implantation of prosthetic rod for delayed tendon graft, hand or finger, each tendon

**26392** Removal of prosthetic rod and insertion of flexor tendon graft, hand or finger (includes obtaining graft), each tendon

**26410** Repair, extensor tendon, hand, primary or secondary; without free graft, each tendon

**26412** with free graft (includes obtaining graft), each tendon

**26415** Excision of extensor tendon, implantation of prosthetic rod for delayed tendon graft, hand or finger

▲**26416** Removal of prosthetic rod and insertion of extensor tendon graft (includes obtaining graft), hand or finger, each tendon

**26418** Repair, extensor tendon, finger, primary or secondary; without free graft, each tendon

**26420** with free graft (includes obtaining graft) each tendon

**26426** Repair of extensor tendon, central slip, secondary (eg, boutonniere deformity); using local tissue(s), including lateral band(s), each tendon

**26428** with free graft (includes obtaining graft), each tendon

**26432** Closed treatment of distal extensor tendon insertion, with or without percutaneous pinning (eg, mallet finger)

**26433** Repair of extensor tendon, distal insertion, primary or secondary; without graft (eg, mallet finger)

**26434** with free graft (includes obtaining graft)

(For tenovaginotomy for trigger finger, see 26055)

**26437** Realignment of extensor tendon, hand, each tendon

**26440** Tenolysis, flexor tendon; palm OR finger; each tendon

**26442** palm AND finger, each tendon

**26445** Tenolysis, extensor tendon, hand or finger; each tendon

**26449** Tenolysis, complex, extensor tendon, finger, including forearm, each tendon

**26450** Tenotomy, flexor, palm, open, each tendon

**26455** Tenotomy, flexor, finger, open, each tendon

**26460** Tenotomy, extensor, hand or finger, open, each tendon

**26471** Tenodesis; of proximal interphalangeal joint, each joint

**26474** of distal joint, each joint

**26476** Lengthening of tendon, extensor, hand or finger, each tendon

**26477** Shortening of tendon, extensor, hand or finger, each tendon

**26478** Lengthening of tendon, flexor, hand or finger, each tendon

**26479** Shortening of tendon, flexor, hand or finger, each tendon

**26480** Transfer or transplant of tendon, carpometacarpal area or dorsum of hand; without free graft, each tendon

**26483** with free tendon graft (includes obtaining graft), each tendon

**26485** Transfer or transplant of tendon, palmar; without free tendon graft, each tendon

**26489** with free tendon graft (includes obtaining graft), each tendon

**26490** Opponensplasty; superficialis tendon transfer type, each tendon

**26492** tendon transfer with graft (includes obtaining graft), each tendon

**26494** hypothenar muscle transfer

**26496** other methods

(For thumb fusion in opposition, use 26820)

**26497** Transfer of tendon to restore intrinsic function; ring and small finger

**26498** all four fingers

**26499** Correction claw finger, other methods

**26500** Reconstruction of tendon pulley, each tendon; with local tissues (separate procedure)

**26502** with tendon or fascial graft (includes obtaining graft) (separate procedure)

**26504** with tendon prosthesis (separate procedure)

**26508** Release of thenar muscle(s) (eg, thumb contracture)

**26510** Cross intrinsic transfer

**26516** Capsulodesis, metacarpophalangeal joint; single digit

**26517** two digits

**26518** three or four digits

**26520** Capsulectomy or capsulotomy; metacarpophalangeal joint, each joint

**26525** interphalangeal joint, each joint

(26527 has been deleted. To report, use 25447)

**26530** Arthroplasty, metacarpophalangeal joint; each joint

**26531** with prosthetic implant, each joint

**26535** Arthroplasty, interphalangeal joint; each joint

**26536** with prosthetic implant, each joint

**26540** Repair of collateral ligament, metacarpophalangeal or interphalangeal joint

**26541** Reconstruction, collateral ligament, metacarpophalangeal joint, single; with tendon or fascial graft (includes obtaining graft)

**26542** with local tissue (eg, adductor advancement)

**26545** Reconstruction, collateral ligament, interphalangeal joint, single, including graft, each joint

**26546** Repair non-union, metacarpal or phalanx, (includes obtaining bone graft with or without external or internal fixation)

**26548** Repair and reconstruction, finger, volar plate, interphalangeal joint

**26550** Pollicization of a digit

**26551** Transfer, toe-to-hand with microvascular anastomosis; great toe wrap-around with bone graft

(For great toe with web space, use 20973)

(26552 has been deleted. To report, see 20973 or 26551, 26553, 26554)

**26553** other than great toe, single

**26554** other than great toe, double

(Do not report code 69990 in addition to codes 26551-26554)

**26555** Transfer, finger to another position without microvascular anastomosis

**26556** Transfer, free toe joint, with microvascular anastomosis

(Do not report code 69990 in addition to code 26556)

(26557-26559 have been deleted. To report, see 20973 or 26551, 26553, 26554)

**26560** Repair of syndactyly (web finger) each web space; with skin flaps

**26561** with skin flaps and grafts

**26562** complex (eg, involving bone, nails)

**26565** Osteotomy; metacarpal, each

**26567** phalanx of finger, each

**26568** Osteoplasty, lengthening, metacarpal or phalanx

(26570, 26574 have been deleted. To report, use 26989)

**26580** Repair cleft hand

**26585** Repair bifid digit

**26587** Reconstruction of supernumerary digit, soft tissue and bone

(For excision of supernumerary digit, soft tissue only, use 11200)

**26590** Repair macrodactylia

**26591** Repair, intrinsic muscles of hand, each muscle

**26593** Release, intrinsic muscles of hand, each muscle

**26596** Excision of constricting ring of finger, with multiple Z-plasties

**26597** Release of scar contracture, flexor or extensor, with skin grafts, rearrangement flaps, or Z-plasties, hand and/or finger

## Fracture and/or Dislocation

**26600** Closed treatment of metacarpal fracture, single; without manipulation, each bone

**26605** with manipulation, each bone

**26607** Closed treatment of metacarpal fracture, with manipulation, with internal or external fixation, each bone

**26608** Percutaneous skeletal fixation of metacarpal fracture, each bone

(26610 has been deleted. To report, see 26605, 26607, 26608)

**26615** Open treatment of metacarpal fracture, single, with or without internal or external fixation, each bone

**26641** Closed treatment of carpometacarpal dislocation, thumb, with manipulation

**26645** Closed treatment of carpometacarpal fracture dislocation, thumb (Bennett fracture), with manipulation

**26650** Percutaneous skeletal fixation of carpometacarpal fracture dislocation, thumb (Bennett fracture), with manipulation, with or without external fixation

(26655 has been deleted. To report, see 26645, 26650, 26665)

(26660 has been deleted. To report, see 26650, 26665)

**26665** Open treatment of carpometacarpal fracture dislocation, thumb (Bennett fracture), with or without internal or external fixation

**26670** Closed treatment of carpometacarpal dislocation, other than thumb (Bennett fracture), single, with manipulation; without anesthesia

**26675** requiring anesthesia

**26676** Percutaneous skeletal fixation of carpometacarpal dislocation, other than thumb (Bennett fracture), single, with manipulation

(26680 has been deleted. To report, see 26670, 26675, 26676, 26685)

**26685** Open treatment of carpometacarpal dislocation, other than thumb (Bennett fracture); single, with or without internal or external fixation

**26686** complex, multiple or delayed reduction

**26700** Closed treatment of metacarpophalangeal dislocation, single, with manipulation; without anesthesia

**26705** requiring anesthesia

**26706** Percutaneous skeletal fixation of metacarpophalangeal dislocation, single, with manipulation

(26710 has been deleted. To report, see 26700, 26705, 26706, 26715)

**26715** Open treatment of metacarpophalangeal dislocation, single, with or without internal or external fixation

**26720** Closed treatment of phalangeal shaft fracture, proximal or middle phalanx, finger or thumb; without manipulation, each

**26725** with manipulation, with or without skin or skeletal traction, each

**26727** Percutaneous skeletal fixation of unstable phalangeal shaft fracture, proximal or middle phalanx, finger or thumb, with manipulation, each

(26730 has been deleted. To report, see 26720, 26725, 26727, 26735)

**26735** Open treatment of phalangeal shaft fracture, proximal or middle phalanx, finger or thumb, with or without internal or external fixation, each

**26740** Closed treatment of articular fracture, involving metacarpophalangeal or interphalangeal joint; without manipulation, each

**26742** with manipulation, each

(26743 has been deleted. To report, use 26989)

(26744 has been deleted. To report, see 26740, 26742, 26746)

**26746** Open treatment of articular fracture, involving metacarpophalangeal or interphalangeal joint, with or without internal or external fixation, each

**26750** Closed treatment of distal phalangeal fracture, finger or thumb; without manipulation, each

**26755** with manipulation, each

**26756** Percutaneous skeletal fixation of distal phalangeal fracture, finger or thumb, each

(26760 has been deleted. To report, see 26750, 26755, 26756, 26765)

**26765** Open treatment of distal phalangeal fracture, finger or thumb, with or without internal or external fixation, each

**26770** Closed treatment of interphalangeal joint dislocation, single, with manipulation; without anesthesia

**26775** requiring anesthesia

**26776** Percutaneous skeletal fixation of interphalangeal joint dislocation, single, with manipulation

(26780 has been deleted. To report, see 26770, 26775, 26776, 26785)

**26785** Open treatment of interphalangeal joint dislocation, with or without internal or external fixation, single

## Arthrodesis

**26820** Fusion in opposition, thumb, with autogenous graft (includes obtaining graft)

**26841** Arthrodesis, carpometacarpal joint, thumb, with or without internal fixation;

**26842** with autograft (includes obtaining graft)

26843 Arthrodesis, carpometacarpal joint, digits, other than thumb;

26844 with autograft (includes obtaining graft)

26850 Arthrodesis, metacarpophalangeal joint, with or without internal fixation;

26852 with autograft (includes obtaining graft)

26860 Arthrodesis, interphalangeal joint, with or without internal fixation;

+ 26861 each additional interphalangeal joint (List separately in addition to code for primary procedure)

(Use 26861 in conjunction with code 26860)

26862 with autograft (includes obtaining graft)

+ 26863 with autograft (includes obtaining graft), each additional joint (List separately in addition to code for primary procedure)

(Use 26863 in conjunction with code 26862)

## Amputation

(For hand through metacarpal bones, use 25927)

26910 Amputation, metacarpal, with finger or thumb (ray amputation), single, with or without interosseous transfer

(For repositioning, see 26550, 26555)

26951 Amputation, finger or thumb, primary or secondary, any joint or phalanx, single, including neurectomies; with direct closure

26952 with local advancement flaps (V-Y, hood)

(For repair of soft tissue defect requiring split or full thickness graft or other pedicle flaps, see 15050-15758)

## Other Procedures

26989 Unlisted procedure, hands or fingers

# Pelvis and Hip Joint

Including head and neck of femur.

## Incision

(For incision and drainage procedures, superficial, see 10040-10160)

26990 Incision and drainage, pelvis or hip joint area; deep abscess or hematoma

26991 infected bursa

26992 Incision, bone cortex, pelvis and/or hip joint (eg, osteomyelitis or bone abscess)

(26995 has been deleted)

27000 Tenotomy, adductor of hip, percutaneous (separate procedure)

27001 Tenotomy, adductor of hip, open

(27002 has been deleted. To report, use 27001 with modifier '-50')

27003 Tenotomy, adductor, subcutaneous, open, with obturator neurectomy

(27004 has been deleted. To report, use 27003 with modifier '-50')

27005 Tenotomy, hip flexor(s), open (separate procedure)

27006 Tenotomy, abductors and/or extensor(s) of hip, open (separate procedure)

(27010, 27015 have been deleted. To report, use 27025)

27025 Fasciotomy, hip or thigh, any type

(27026 has been deleted. To report, use 27025 with modifier '-50')

27030 Arthrotomy, hip, with drainage (eg, infection)

(27031 has been deleted)

27033 Arthrotomy, hip, including exploration or removal of loose or foreign body

**27035** Denervation, hip joint, intrapelvic or extrapelvic intra-articular branches of sciatic, femoral, or obturator nerves

(For obturator neurectomy, see 64763, 64766)

**27036** Capsulectomy or capsulotomy, hip, with or without excision of heterotopic bone, with release of hip flexor muscles (ie, gluteus medius, gluteus minimus, tensor fascia latae, rectus femoris, sartorius, iliopsoas)

## Excision

**27040** Biopsy, soft tissue of pelvis and hip area; superficial

**27041** deep, subfascial or intramuscular

(For needle biopsy of soft tissue, use 20206)

**27047** Excision, tumor, pelvis and hip area; subcutaneous tissue

**27048** deep, subfascial, intramuscular

**27049** Radical resection of tumor, soft tissue of pelvis and hip area (eg, malignant neoplasm)

**27050** Arthrotomy, with biopsy; sacroiliac joint

**27052** hip joint

**27054** Arthrotomy with synovectomy, hip joint

**27060** Excision; ischial bursa

**27062** trochanteric bursa or calcification

(For arthrocentesis or needling of bursa, use 20610)

**27065** Excision of bone cyst or benign tumor; superficial (wing of ilium, symphysis pubis, or greater trochanter of femur) with or without autograft

**27066** deep, with or without autograft

**27067** with autograft requiring separate incision

**27070** Partial excision (craterization, saucerization) (eg, osteomyelitis or bone abscess); superficial (eg, wing of ilium, symphysis pubis, or greater trochanter of femur)

**27071** deep (subfascial or intramuscular)

**27075** Radical resection of tumor or infection; wing of ilium, one pubic or ischial ramus or symphysis pubis

**27076** ilium, including acetabulum, both pubic rami, or ischium and acetabulum

**27077** innominate bone, total

**27078** ischial tuberosity and greater trochanter of femur

**27079** ischial tuberosity and greater trochanter of femur, with skin flaps

**27080** Coccygectomy, primary

(For pressure (decubitus) ulcer, see 15920, 15922 and 15931-15958)

## Introduction or Removal

**27086*** Removal of foreign body, pelvis or hip; subcutaneous tissue

**27087** deep (subfascial or intramuscular)

(27088 has been deleted. To report, use 27087)

**27090** Removal of hip prosthesis; (separate procedure)

**27091** complicated, including total hip prosthesis, methylmethacrylate with or without insertion of spacer

**27093** Injection procedure for hip arthrography; without anesthesia

(For radiological supervision and interpretation, use 73525)

**27095** with anesthesia

(For radiological supervision and interpretation, use 73525)

●**27096** Injection procedure for sacroiliac joint, arthrography and/or anesthetic/steroid

►(For radiological supervision and interpretation, use 73542. If formal arthrography is not performed, recorded, and a formal radiologic report is not issued, use 76005 for fluoroscopic guidance for sacroiliac joint injections)◄

## Repair, Revision, and/or Reconstruction

**27097** Release or recession, hamstring, proximal

**27098** Transfer, adductor to ischium

**27100** Transfer external oblique muscle to greater trochanter including fascial or tendon extension (graft)

**27105** Transfer paraspinal muscle to hip (includes fascial or tendon extension graft)

**27110** Transfer iliopsoas; to greater trochanter

**27111** to femoral neck

(27115 has been deleted. To report, use 27299)

**27120** Acetabuloplasty; (eg, Whitman, Colonna, Haygroves, or cup type)

**27122** resection, femoral head (eg, Girdlestone procedure)

**27125** Hemiarthroplasty, hip, partial (eg, femoral stem prosthesis, bipolar arthroplasty)

(For prosthetic replacement following fracture of the hip, use 27236)

(27126, 27127 have been deleted. To report, use 27120)

**27130** Arthroplasty, acetabular and proximal femoral prosthetic replacement (total hip replacement), with or without autograft or allograft

(27131 has been deleted. To report, use 27132)

**27132** Conversion of previous hip surgery to total hip replacement, with or without autograft or allograft

**27134** Revision of total hip arthroplasty; both components, with or without autograft or allograft

(27135 has been deleted. To report, see 27134, 27137, 27138)

**27137** acetabular component only, with or without autograft or allograft

**27138** femoral component only, with or without allograft

**27140** Osteotomy and transfer of greater trochanter (separate procedure)

**27146** Osteotomy, iliac, acetabular or innominate bone;

**27147** with open reduction of hip

**27151** with femoral osteotomy

**27156** with femoral osteotomy and with open reduction of hip

(27157 has been deleted)

**27158** Osteotomy, pelvis, bilateral (eg, congenital malformation)

**27161** Osteotomy, femoral neck (separate procedure)

**27165** Osteotomy, intertrochanteric or subtrochanteric including internal or external fixation and/or cast

**27170** Bone graft, femoral head, neck, intertrochanteric or subtrochanteric area (includes obtaining bone graft)

**27175** Treatment of slipped femoral epiphysis; by traction, without reduction

**27176** by single or multiple pinning, in situ

**27177** Open treatment of slipped femoral epiphysis; single or multiple pinning or bone graft (includes obtaining graft)

**27178** closed manipulation with single or multiple pinning

**27179** osteoplasty of femoral neck (Heyman type procedure)

**27181** osteotomy and internal fixation

**27185** Epiphyseal arrest by epiphysiodesis or stapling, greater trochanter

**27187** Prophylactic treatment (nailing, pinning, plating or wiring) with or without methylmethacrylate, femoral neck and proximal femur

## Fracture and/or Dislocation

(27190, 27191 have been deleted. To report, see 27193, 27194)

(27192 has been deleted. To report, see 27215, 27216)

**27193** Closed treatment of pelvic ring fracture, dislocation, diastasis or subluxation; without manipulation

**27194** with manipulation, requiring more than local anesthesia

(27195 has been deleted. To report, use 27193)

(27196 has been deleted. To report, use 27194)

**27200** Closed treatment of coccygeal fracture

(27201 has been deleted. To report, see 27200, 27202)

**27202** Open treatment of coccygeal fracture

(27210, 27211, 27212 have been deleted. To report, see 27193, 27194, 27215, 27216, 27217, 27218)

(27214 has been deleted. To report, see 27215, 27216, 27217, 27218)

**27215** Open treatment of iliac spine(s), tuberosity avulsion, or iliac wing fracture(s) (eg, pelvic fracture(s) which do not disrupt the pelvic ring), with internal fixation

**27216** Percutaneous skeletal fixation of posterior pelvic ring fracture and/or dislocation (includes ilium, sacroiliac joint and/or sacrum)

**27217** Open treatment of anterior ring fracture and/or dislocation with internal fixation (includes pubic symphysis and/or rami)

**27218** Open treatment of posterior ring fracture and/or dislocation with internal fixation (includes ilium, sacroiliac joint and/ or sacrum)

**27220** Closed treatment of acetabulum (hip socket) fracture(s); without manipulation

**27222** with manipulation, with or without skeletal traction

(27224 has been deleted. To report, see 27226, 27227)

(27225 has been deleted. To report, see 27227, 27228)

**27226** Open treatment of posterior or anterior acetabular wall fracture, with internal fixation

**27227** Open treatment of acetabular fracture(s) involving anterior or posterior (one) column, or a fracture running transversely across the acetabulum, with internal fixation

**27228** Open treatment of acetabular fracture(s) involving anterior and posterior (two) columns, includes T-fracture and both column fracture with complete articular detachment, or single column or transverse fracture with associated acetabular wall fracture, with internal fixation

**27230** Closed treatment of femoral fracture, proximal end, neck; without manipulation

**27232** with manipulation, with or without skeletal traction

(27234 has been deleted. To report, see 27230, 27232, 27235, 27236)

**27235** Percutaneous skeletal fixation of femoral fracture, proximal end, neck, undisplaced, mildly displaced, or impacted fracture

**27236** Open treatment of femoral fracture, proximal end, neck, internal fixation or prosthetic replacement (direct fracture exposure)

**27238** Closed treatment of intertrochanteric, pertrochanteric, or subtrochanteric femoral fracture; without manipulation

**27240** with manipulation, with or without skin or skeletal traction

(27242 has been deleted. To report, see 27238, 27240, 27244, 27245)

**27244** Open treatment of intertrochanteric, pertrochanteric, or subtrochanteric femoral fracture; with plate/screw type implant, with or without cerclage

**27245** with intramedullary implant, with or without interlocking screws and/or cerclage

**27246** Closed treatment of greater trochanteric fracture, without manipulation

**27248** Open treatment of greater trochanteric fracture, with or without internal or external fixation

**27250** Closed treatment of hip dislocation, traumatic; without anesthesia

**27252** requiring anesthesia

**27253** Open treatment of hip dislocation, traumatic, without internal fixation

**27254** Open treatment of hip dislocation, traumatic, with acetabular wall and femoral head fracture, with or without internal or external fixation

(27255 has been deleted. To report, see 27226, 27227, 27253, 27254)

**27256*** Treatment of spontaneous hip dislocation (developmental, including congenital or pathological), by abduction, splint or traction; without anesthesia, without manipulation

**27257*** with manipulation, requiring anesthesia

**27258** Open treatment of spontaneous hip dislocation (developmental, including congenital or pathological), replacement of femoral head in acetabulum (including tenotomy, etc);

**27259** with femoral shaft shortening

**27265** Closed treatment of post hip arthroplasty dislocation; without anesthesia

**27266** requiring regional or general anesthesia

### Manipulation

**27275*** Manipulation, hip joint, requiring general anesthesia

### Arthrodesis

**27280** Arthrodesis, sacroiliac joint (including obtaining graft)

(27281 has been deleted. To report, use 27280 with modifier '-50')

**27282** Arthrodesis, symphysis pubis (including obtaining graft)

**27284** Arthrodesis, hip joint (including obtaining graft);

**27286** with subtrochanteric osteotomy

### Amputation

**27290** Interpelviabdominal amputation (hindquarter amputation)

**27295** Disarticulation of hip

### Other Procedures

**27299** Unlisted procedure, pelvis or hip joint

## Femur (Thigh Region) and Knee Joint

Including tibial plateaus.

### Incision

(For incision and drainage of abscess or hematoma, superficial, see 10040-10160)

**27301** Incision and drainage, deep abscess, bursa, or hematoma, thigh or knee region

**27303** Incision, deep, with opening of bone cortex, femur or knee (eg, osteomyelitis or bone abscess)

(27304 has been deleted)

**27305** Fasciotomy, iliotibial (tenotomy), open

(For combined Ober-Yount fasciotomy, use 27025)

**27306** Tenotomy, percutaneous, adductor or hamstring; single tendon (separate procedure)

**27307** multiple tendons

**27310** Arthrotomy, knee, with exploration, drainage, or removal of foreign body (eg, infection)

(27311 has been deleted)

**27315** Neurectomy, hamstring muscle

**27320** Neurectomy, popliteal (gastrocnemius)

## Excision

**27323** Biopsy, soft tissue of thigh or knee area; superficial

**27324** deep (subfascial or intramuscular)

(For needle biopsy of soft tissue, use 20206)

**27327** Excision, tumor, thigh or knee area; subcutaneous

**27328** deep, subfascial, or intramuscular

**27329** Radical resection of tumor (eg, malignant neoplasm), soft tissue of thigh or knee area

**27330** Arthrotomy, knee; with synovial biopsy only

**27331** including joint exploration, biopsy, or removal of loose or foreign bodies

**27332** Arthrotomy, with excision of semilunar cartilage (meniscectomy) knee; medial OR lateral

**27333** medial AND lateral

**27334** Arthrotomy, with synovectomy, knee; anterior OR posterior

**27335** anterior AND posterior including popliteal area

**27340** Excision, prepatellar bursa

**27345** Excision of synovial cyst of popliteal space (eg, Baker's cyst)

**27347** Excision of lesion of meniscus or capsule (eg, cyst, ganglion), knee

**27350** Patellectomy or hemipatellectomy

**27355** Excision or curettage of bone cyst or benign tumor of femur;

**27356** with allograft

**27357** with autograft (includes obtaining graft)

**+ 27358** with internal fixation (List in addition to code for primary procedure)

(Use 27358 in conjunction with codes 27355, 27356, or 27357)

**27360** Partial excision (craterization, saucerization, or diaphysectomy) bone, femur, proximal tibia and/or fibula (eg, osteomyelitis or bone abscess)

(27361 has been deleted)

**27365** Radical resection of tumor, bone, femur or knee

(For radical resection of tumor, soft tissue, use 27329)

## Introduction or Removal

**27370** Injection procedure for knee arthrography

(For radiological supervision and interpretation, use 73580)

**27372** Removal of foreign body, deep, thigh region or knee area

(For removal of knee prosthesis including "total knee," use 27488)

(27373-27379 have been deleted. To report, see 29870-29887)

## Repair, Revision, and/or Reconstruction

**27380** Suture of infrapatellar tendon; primary

**27381** secondary reconstruction, including fascial or tendon graft

**27385** Suture of quadriceps or hamstring muscle rupture; primary

**27386** secondary reconstruction, including fascial or tendon graft

**27390** Tenotomy, open, hamstring, knee to hip; single tendon

**27391** multiple tendons, one leg

**27392** multiple tendons, bilateral

**27393** Lengthening of hamstring tendon; single tendon

**27394** multiple tendons, one leg

**27395** multiple tendons, bilateral

**27396** Transplant, hamstring tendon to patella; single tendon

**27397** multiple tendons

**27400** Transfer, tendon or muscle, hamstrings to femur (eg, Egger's type procedure)

**27403** Arthrotomy with meniscus repair, knee

(For arthroscopic repair, use 29882)

**27405** Repair, primary, torn ligament and/or capsule, knee; collateral

**27407** cruciate

(27408 has been deleted. To report, use 27427)

**27409** collateral and cruciate ligaments

(27410-27416 have been deleted. To report, see 27427-27429)

**27418** Anterior tibial tubercleplasty (eg, Maquet type procedure)

**27420** Reconstruction of dislocating patella; (eg, Hauser type procedure)

**27422** with extensor realignment and/or muscle advancement or release (eg, Campbell, Goldwaite type procedure)

**27424** with patellectomy

**27425** Lateral retinacular release (any method)

**27427** Ligamentous reconstruction (augmentation), knee; extra-articular

**27428** intra-articular (open)

**27429** intra-articular (open) and extra-articular

►(For primary repair of ligament(s) performed in addition to reconstruction, report 27405, 27407 or 27409 in addition to code 27427, 27428 or 27429)◄

**27430** Quadricepsplasty (eg, Bennett or Thompson type)

**27435** Capsulotomy, posterior capsular release, knee

(27436 has been deleted. To report, use 29887)

**27437** Arthroplasty, patella; without prosthesis

**27438** with prosthesis

**27440** Arthroplasty, knee, tibial plateau;

**27441** with debridement and partial synovectomy

**27442** Arthroplasty, femoral condyles or tibial plateau(s), knee;

**27443** with debridement and partial synovectomy

(27444 has been deleted. To report, see 27445-27447)

**27445** Arthroplasty, knee, hinge prosthesis (eg, Walldius type)

**27446** Arthroplasty, knee, condyle and plateau; medial OR lateral compartment

**27447** medial AND lateral compartments with or without patella resurfacing (total knee replacement)

(For revision of total knee arthroplasty, use 27487)

(For removal of total knee prosthesis, use 27488)

**27448** Osteotomy, femur, shaft or supracondylar; without fixation

(27449 has been deleted. To report, use 27448 with modifier '-50')

**27450** with fixation

(27452 has been deleted. To report, use 27450 with modifier '-50')

**27454** Osteotomy, multiple, with realignment on intramedullary rod, femoral shaft (eg, Sofield type procedure)

**27455** Osteotomy, proximal tibia, including fibular excision or osteotomy (includes correction of genu varus (bowleg) or genu valgus (knock-knee)); before epiphyseal closure

**27457** after epiphyseal closure

(27460 has been deleted. To report, use 27455 with modifier '-50')

(27462 has been deleted. To report, use 27457 with modifier '-50')

**27465** Osteoplasty, femur; shortening (excluding 64876)

**27466** lengthening

**27468** combined, lengthening and shortening with femoral segment transfer

**27470** Repair, nonunion or malunion, femur, distal to head and neck; without graft (eg, compression technique)

**27472** with iliac or other autogenous bone graft (includes obtaining graft)

**27475** Arrest, epiphyseal, any method (eg, epiphydiodesis); distal femur

**27477** tibia and fibula, proximal

**27479** combined distal femur, proximal tibia and fibula

**27485** Arrest, hemiepiphyseal, distal femur or proximal tibia or fibula (eg, genu varus or valgus)

**27486** Revision of total knee arthroplasty, with or without allograft; one component

**27487** femoral and entire tibial component

**27488** Removal of prosthesis, including total knee prosthesis, methylmethacrylate with or without insertion of spacer, knee

(27490 has been deleted. To report, use 29882)

**27495** Prophylactic treatment (nailing, pinning, plating or wiring) with or without methylmethacrylate, femur

**27496** Decompression fasciotomy, thigh and/or knee, one compartment (flexor or extensor or adductor);

**27497** with debridement of nonviable muscle and/or nerve

**27498** Decompression fasciotomy, thigh and/or knee, multiple compartments;

**27499** with debridement of nonviable muscle and/or nerve

## Fracture and/or Dislocation

(For arthroscopic treatment of intercondylar spine(s) and tuberosity fracture(s) of the knee, see 29850, 29851)

(For arthroscopic treatment of tibial fracture, see 29855, 29856)

**27500** Closed treatment of femoral shaft fracture, without manipulation

**27501** Closed treatment of supracondylar or transcondylar femoral fracture with or without intercondylar extension, without manipulation

**27502** Closed treatment of femoral shaft fracture, with manipulation, with or without skin or skeletal traction

**27503** Closed treatment of supracondylar or transcondylar femoral fracture with or without intercondylar extension, with manipulation, with or without skin or skeletal traction

(27504 has been deleted. To report, see 27500, 27501, 27502, 27503, 27506, 27507, 27509, 27511, 27513)

**27506** Open treatment of femoral shaft fracture, with or without external fixation, with insertion of intramedullary implant, with or without cerclage and/or locking screws

**27507** Open treatment of femoral shaft fracture with plate/screws, with or without cerclage

**27508** Closed treatment of femoral fracture, distal end, medial or lateral condyle, without manipulation

**27509** Percutaneous skeletal fixation of femoral fracture, distal end, medial or lateral condyle, or supracondylar or transcondylar, with or without intercondylar extension, or distal femoral epiphyseal separation

**27510** Closed treatment of femoral fracture, distal end, medial or lateral condyle, with manipulation

**27511** Open treatment of femoral supracondylar or transcondylar fracture without intercondylar extension, with or without internal or external fixation

(27512 has been deleted. To report, see 27508, 27510, 27514)

**27513** Open treatment of femoral supracondylar or transcondylar fracture with intercondylar extension, with or without internal or external fixation

**27514** Open treatment of femoral fracture, distal end, medial or lateral condyle, with or without internal or external fixation

**27516** Closed treatment of distal femoral epiphyseal separation; without manipulation

**27517** with manipulation, with or without skin or skeletal traction

(27518 has been deleted. To report, see 27516, 27517, 27519)

**27519** Open treatment of distal femoral epiphyseal separation, with or without internal or external fixation

**27520** Closed treatment of patellar fracture, without manipulation

(27522 has been deleted. To report, see 27520, 27524)

**27524** Open treatment of patellar fracture, with internal fixation and/or partial or complete patellectomy and soft tissue repair

**27530** Closed treatment of tibial fracture, proximal (plateau); without manipulation

**27532** with or without manipulation, with skeletal traction

(27534 has been deleted. To report, see 27530, 27532, 27535, 27536)

(For arthroscopic treatment, see 29855, 29856)

**27535** Open treatment of tibial fracture, proximal (plateau); unicondylar, with or without internal or external fixation

**27536** bicondylar, with or without internal fixation

(For arthroscopic treatment, see 29855, 29856)

(27537 has been deleted. To report, see 27535, 27536)

**27538** Closed treatment of intercondylar spine(s) and/or tuberosity fracture(s) of knee, with or without manipulation

(For arthroscopic treatment, see 29850, 29851)

**27540** Open treatment of intercondylar spine(s) and/or tuberosity fracture(s) of the knee, with or without internal or external fixation

**27550** Closed treatment of knee dislocation; without anesthesia

**27552** requiring anesthesia

(27554 has been deleted. To report, see 27550, 27552, 27556, 27557, 27558)

**27556** Open treatment of knee dislocation, with or without internal or external fixation; without primary ligamentous repair or augmentation/reconstruction

**27557** with primary ligamentous repair

**27558** with primary ligamentous repair, with augmentation/reconstruction

**27560** Closed treatment of patellar dislocation; without anesthesia

(For recurrent dislocation, see 27420-27424)

**27562** requiring anesthesia

(27564 has been deleted. To report, see 27560, 27562, 27566)

**27566** Open treatment of patellar dislocation, with or without partial or total patellectomy

## Manipulation

**27570*** Manipulation of knee joint under general anesthesia (includes application of traction or other fixation devices)

## Arthrodesis

**27580** Arthrodesis, knee, any technique

## Amputation

**27590** Amputation, thigh, through femur, any level;

**27591** immediate fitting technique including first cast

**27592** open, circular (guillotine)

**27594** secondary closure or scar revision

**27596** re-amputation

**27598** Disarticulation at knee

## Other Procedures

**27599** Unlisted procedure, femur or knee

# Leg (Tibia and Fibula) and Ankle Joint

## Incision

**27600** Decompression fasciotomy, leg; anterior and/or lateral compartments only

**27601** posterior compartment(s) only

**27602** anterior and/or lateral, and posterior compartment(s)

(For incision and drainage procedures, superficial, see 10040-10160)

(For decompression fasciotomy with debridement, see 27892-27894)

**27603** Incision and drainage, leg or ankle; deep abscess or hematoma

**27604** infected bursa

**27605*** Tenotomy, percutaneous, Achilles tendon (separate procedure); local anesthesia

**27606** general anesthesia

**27607** Incision (eg, osteomyelitis or bone abscess), leg or ankle

(27608 has been deleted)

**27610** Arthrotomy, ankle, including exploration, drainage, or removal of foreign body

(27611 has been deleted)

**27612** Arthrotomy, posterior capsular release, ankle, with or without Achilles tendon lengthening

(See also 27685)

## Excision

**27613** Biopsy, soft tissue of leg or ankle area; superficial

**27614** deep (subfascial or intramuscular)

(For needle biopsy of soft tissue, use 20206)

**27615** Radical resection of tumor (eg, malignant neoplasm), soft tissue of leg or ankle area

**27618** Excision, tumor, leg or ankle area; subcutaneous tissue

**27619** deep (subfascial or intramuscular)

**27620** Arthrotomy, ankle, with joint exploration, with or without biopsy, with or without removal of loose or foreign body

**27625** Arthrotomy, with synovectomy, ankle;

**27626** including tenosynovectomy

**27630** Excision of lesion of tendon sheath or capsule (eg, cyst or ganglion), leg and/or ankle

**27635** Excision or curettage of bone cyst or benign tumor, tibia or fibula;

**27637** with autograft (includes obtaining graft)

**27638** with allograft

**27640** Partial excision (craterization, saucerization, or diaphysectomy) bone (eg, osteomyelitis or exostosis); tibia

**27641** fibula

**27645** Radical resection of tumor, bone; tibia

**27646** fibula

**27647** talus or calcaneus

## Introduction or Removal

**27648** Injection procedure for ankle arthrography

(For radiological supervision and interpretation, use 73615)

(For ankle arthroscopy, see 29894-29898)

## Repair, Revision, and/or Reconstruction

**27650** Repair, primary, open or percutaneous, ruptured Achilles tendon;

**27652** with graft (includes obtaining graft)

**27654** Repair, secondary, Achilles tendon, with or without graft

**27656** Repair, fascial defect of leg

**27658** Repair, flexor tendon, leg; primary, without graft, each tendon

**27659** secondary, with or without graft, each tendon

**27664** Repair, extensor tendon, leg; primary, without graft, each tendon

**27665** secondary, with or without graft, each tendon

**27675** Repair, dislocating peroneal tendons; without fibular osteotomy

**27676** with fibular osteotomy

**27680** Tenolysis, flexor or extensor tendon, leg and/or ankle; single, each tendon

**27681** multiple tendons (through separate incision(s))

**27685** Lengthening or shortening of tendon, leg or ankle; single tendon (separate procedure)

**27686** multiple tendons (through same incision), each

**27687** Gastrocnemius recession (eg, Strayer procedure)

(Toe extensors are considered as a group to be a single tendon when transplanted into midfoot)

**27690** Transfer or transplant of single tendon (with muscle redirection or rerouting); superficial (eg, anterior tibial extensors into midfoot)

**27691** deep (eg, anterior tibial or posterior tibial through interosseous space, flexor digitorum longus, flexor hallucis longus, or peroneal tendon to midfoot or hindfoot)

**+ 27692** each additional tendon (List separately in addition to code for primary procedure)

(Use 27692 in conjunction with codes 27690, 27691)

**27695** Repair, primary, disrupted ligament, ankle; collateral

**27696** both collateral ligaments

**27698** Repair, secondary disrupted ligament, ankle, collateral (eg, Watson-Jones procedure)

**27700** Arthroplasty, ankle;

**27702** with implant (total ankle)

**27703** revision, total ankle

**27704** Removal of ankle implant

**27705** Osteotomy; tibia

**27707** fibula

**27709** tibia and fibula

**27712** multiple, with realignment on intramedullary rod (eg, Sofield type procedure)

(For osteotomy to correct genu varus (bowleg) or genu valgus (knock-knee), see 27455-27457)

**27715** Osteoplasty, tibia and fibula, lengthening or shortening

**27720** Repair of nonunion or malunion, tibia; without graft, (eg, compression technique)

**27722** with sliding graft

**27724** with iliac or other autograft (includes obtaining graft)

**27725** by synostosis, with fibula, any method

**27727** Repair of congenital pseudarthrosis, tibia

**27730** Arrest, epiphyseal (epiphysiodesis), any method; distal tibia

**27732** distal fibula

**27734** distal tibia and fibula

**27740** Arrest, epiphyseal (epiphysiodesis), any method, combined, proximal and distal tibia and fibula;

**27742** and distal femur

(For epiphyseal arrest of proximal tibia and fibula, use 27477)

**27745** Prophylactic treatment (nailing, pinning, plating or wiring) with or without methylmethacrylate, tibia

## Fracture and/or Dislocation

**27750** Closed treatment of tibial shaft fracture (with or without fibular fracture); without manipulation

**27752** with manipulation, with or without skeletal traction

(27754 has been deleted. To report, see 27750, 27752, 27756, 27758)

**27756** Percutaneous skeletal fixation of tibial shaft fracture (with or without fibular fracture) (eg, pins or screws)

**27758** Open treatment of tibial shaft fracture, (with or without fibular fracture) with plate/screws, with or without cerclage

**27759** Open treatment of tibial shaft fracture (with or without fibular fracture) by intramedullary implant, with or without interlocking screws and/or cerclage

**27760** Closed treatment of medial malleolus fracture; without manipulation

**27762** with manipulation, with or without skin or skeletal traction

(27764 has been deleted. To report, see 27762, 27766)

**27766** Open treatment of medial malleolus fracture, with or without internal or external fixation

**27780** Closed treatment of proximal fibula or shaft fracture; without manipulation

**27781** with manipulation

(27782 has been deleted. To report, see 27780, 27781, 27784)

**27784** Open treatment of proximal fibula or shaft fracture, with or without internal or external fixation

**27786** Closed treatment of distal fibular fracture (lateral malleolus); without manipulation

**27788** with manipulation

(27790 has been deleted. To report, see 27786, 27788, 27792)

**27792** Open treatment of distal fibular fracture (lateral malleolus), with or without internal or external fixation

(27800 has been deleted. To report, use 27750)

(27802 has been deleted. To report, use 27752)

(27804 has been deleted. To report, see 27750, 27752, 27756, 27758, 27759)

(27806 has been deleted. To report, see 27756, 27758, 27759)

**27808** Closed treatment of bimalleolar ankle fracture, (including Potts); without manipulation

**27810** with manipulation

(27812 has been deleted. To report, see 27808, 27810, 27814)

**27814** Open treatment of bimalleolar ankle fracture, with or without internal or external fixation

**27816** Closed treatment of trimalleolar ankle fracture; without manipulation

**27818** with manipulation

(27820 has been deleted. To report, see 27816, 27818, 27822, 27823)

**27822** Open treatment of trimalleolar ankle fracture, with or without internal or external fixation, medial and/or lateral malleolus; without fixation of posterior lip

**27823** with fixation of posterior lip

**27824** Closed treatment of fracture of weight bearing articular portion of distal tibia (eg, pilon or tibial plafond), with or without anesthesia; without manipulation

**27825** with skeletal traction and/or requiring manipulation

**27826** Open treatment of fracture of weight bearing articular surface/portion of distal tibia (eg, pilon or tibial plafond), with internal or external fixation; of fibula only

**27827** of tibia only

**27828** of both tibia and fibula

**27829** Open treatment of distal tibiofibular joint (syndesmosis) disruption, with or without internal or external fixation

**27830** Closed treatment of proximal tibiofibular joint dislocation; without anesthesia

**27831** requiring anesthesia

**27832** Open treatment of proximal tibiofibular joint dislocation, with or without internal or external fixation, or with excision of proximal fibula

**27840** Closed treatment of ankle dislocation; without anesthesia

**27842** requiring anesthesia, with or without percutaneous skeletal fixation

(27844 has been deleted. To report, see 27840, 27842, 27846, 27848)

**27846** Open treatment of ankle dislocation, with or without percutaneous skeletal fixation; without repair or internal fixation

**27848** with repair or internal or external fixation

(27850-27853 have been deleted. To report, see 29894-29898)

## Manipulation

**27860*** Manipulation of ankle under general anesthesia (includes application of traction or other fixation apparatus)

## Arthrodesis

**27870** Arthrodesis, ankle, any method

**27871** Arthrodesis, tibiofibular joint, proximal or distal

## Amputation

**27880** Amputation, leg, through tibia and fibula;

**27881** with immediate fitting technique including application of first cast

**27882** open, circular (guillotine)

**27884** secondary closure or scar revision

**27886** re-amputation

**27888** Amputation, ankle, through malleoli of tibia and fibula (eg, Syme, Pirogoff type procedures), with plastic closure and resection of nerves

**27889** Ankle disarticulation

## Other Procedures

**27892** Decompression fasciotomy, leg; anterior and/or lateral compartments only, with debridement of nonviable muscle and/or nerve

(For decompression fasciotomy of the leg without debridement, use 27600)

**27893** posterior compartment(s) only, with debridement of nonviable muscle and/or nerve

(For decompression fasciotomy of the leg without debridement, use 27601)

**27894** anterior and/or lateral, and posterior compartment(s), with debridement of nonviable muscle and/or nerve

(For decompression fasciotomy of the leg without debridement, use 27602)

**27899** Unlisted procedure, leg or ankle

# Foot and Toes

## Incision

(For incision and drainage procedures, superficial, see 10040-10160)

**28001*** Incision and drainage, bursa, foot

**28002*** Incision and drainage below fascia, with or without tendon sheath involvement, foot; single bursal space

**28003** multiple areas

(28004 has been deleted)

**28005** Incision, bone cortex (eg, osteomyelitis or bone abscess), foot

(28006 has been deleted)

**28008** Fasciotomy, foot and/or toe

(See also 28060, 28062, 28250)

**28010** Tenotomy, percutaneous, toe; single tendon

**28011** multiple tendons

(For open tenotomy, see 28230-28234)

**28020** Arthrotomy, including exploration, drainage, or removal of loose or foreign body; intertarsal or tarsometatarsal joint

**28022** metatarsophalangeal joint

**28024** interphalangeal joint

**28030** Neurectomy, intrinsic musculature of foot

**28035** Release, tarsal tunnel (posterior tibial nerve decompression)

(For other nerve entrapments, see 64704, 64722)

## Excision

**28043** Excision, tumor, foot; subcutaneous tissue

**28045** deep, subfascial, intramuscular

**28046** Radical resection of tumor (eg, malignant neoplasm), soft tissue of foot

**28050** Arthrotomy with biopsy; intertarsal or tarsometatarsal joint

**28052** metatarsophalangeal joint

**28054** interphalangeal joint

**28060** Fasciectomy, plantar fascia; partial (separate procedure)

**28062** radical (separate procedure)

(For plantar fasciotomy, see 28008, 28250)

**28070** Synovectomy; intertarsal or tarsometatarsal joint, each

**28072** metatarsophalangeal joint, each

**28080** Excision, interdigital (Morton) neuroma, single, each

**28086** Synovectomy, tendon sheath, foot; flexor

**28088** extensor

**28090** Excision of lesion, tendon, tendon sheath, or capsule (including synovectomy) (eg, cyst or ganglion); foot

**28092** toe(s), each

**28100** Excision or curettage of bone cyst or benign tumor, talus or calcaneus;

**28102** with iliac or other autograft (includes obtaining graft)

**28103** with allograft

**28104** Excision or curettage of bone cyst or benign tumor, tarsal or metatarsal bones, except talus or calcaneus;

**28106** with iliac or other autograft (includes obtaining graft)

**28107** with allograft

**28108** Excision or curettage of bone cyst or benign tumor, phalanges of foot

(For ostectomy, partial (eg, hallux valgus, Silver type procedure), use 28290)

(28109 has been deleted. To report, use 28899)

**28110** Ostectomy, partial excision, fifth metatarsal head (bunionette) (separate procedure)

**28111** Ostectomy, complete excision; first metatarsal head

**28112** other metatarsal head (second, third or fourth)

**28113** fifth metatarsal head

**28114** all metatarsal heads, with partial proximal phalangectomy, excluding first metatarsal (eg, Clayton type procedure)

**28116** Ostectomy, excision of tarsal coalition

**28118** Ostectomy, calcaneus;

**28119** for spur, with or without plantar fascial release

**28120** Partial excision (craterization, saucerization, sequestrectomy, or diaphysectomy) bone (eg, osteomyelitis or bossing); talus or calcaneus

(28121 has been deleted)

**28122** tarsal or metatarsal bone, except talus or calcaneus

(For partial excision of talus or calcaneus, use 28120)

(For cheilectomy for hallux rigidus, use 28289)

(28123 has been deleted)

**28124** phalanx of toe

**28126** Resection, partial or complete, phalangeal base, each toe

**28130** Talectomy (astragalectomy)

(28135 has been deleted. To report, use 28118)

**28140** Metatarsectomy

**28150** Phalangectomy, toe, each toe

**28153** Resection, condyle(s), distal end of phalanx, each toe

**28160** Hemiphalangectomy or interphalangeal joint excision, toe, proximal end of phalanx, each

**28171** Radical resection of tumor, bone; tarsal (except talus or calcaneus)

**28173** metatarsal

**28175** phalanx of toe

(For talus or calcaneus, use 27647)

## Introduction or Removal

**28190*** Removal of foreign body, foot; subcutaneous

**28192** deep

**28193** complicated

## Repair, Revision, and/or Reconstruction

**28200** Repair, tendon, flexor, foot; primary or secondary, without free graft, each tendon

**28202** secondary with free graft, each tendon (includes obtaining graft)

**28208** Repair, tendon, extensor, foot; primary or secondary, each tendon

**28210** secondary with free graft, each tendon (includes obtaining graft)

**28220** Tenolysis, flexor, foot; single tendon

**28222** multiple tendons

**28225** Tenolysis, extensor, foot; single tendon

**28226** multiple tendons

**28230** Tenotomy, open, tendon flexor; foot, single or multiple tendon(s) (separate procedure)

**28232** toe, single tendon (separate procedure)

**28234** Tenotomy, open, extensor, foot or toe, each tendon

(28236 has been deleted. To report, see 27690, 27691)

**28238** Reconstruction (advancement), posterior tibial tendon with excision of accessory navicular bone (eg, Kidner type procedure)

(For subcutaneous tenotomy, see 28010, 28011)

(For transfer or transplant of tendon with muscle redirection or rerouting, see 27690-27692)

(For extensor hallucis longus transfer with great toe IP fusion (Jones procedure), use 28760)

**28240** Tenotomy, lengthening, or release, abductor hallucis muscle

**28250** Division of plantar fascia and muscle (eg, Steindler stripping) (separate procedure)

**28260** Capsulotomy, midfoot; medial release only (separate procedure)

**28261** with tendon lengthening

**28262** extensive, including posterior talotibial capsulotomy and tendon(s) lengthening (eg, resistant clubfoot deformity)

**28264** Capsulotomy, midtarsal (eg, Heyman type procedure)

**28270** Capsulotomy; metatarsophalangeal joint, with or without tenorrhaphy, each joint (separate procedure)

**28272** interphalangeal joint, each joint (separate procedure)

**28280** Syndactylization, toes (eg, webbing or Kelikian type procedure)

**28285** Correction, hammertoe (eg, interphalangeal fusion, partial or total phalangectomy)

**28286** Correction, cock-up fifth toe, with plastic skin closure (eg, Ruiz-Mora type procedure)

**28288** Ostectomy, partial, exostectomy or condylectomy, metatarsal head, each metatarsal head

**28289** Hallux rigidus correction with cheilectomy, debridement and capsular release of the first metatarsophalangeal joint

**28290** Correction, hallux valgus (bunion), with or without sesamoidectomy; simple exostectomy (eg, Silver type procedure)

**28292** Keller, McBride, or Mayo type procedure

**28293** resection of joint with implant

**28294** with tendon transplants (eg, Joplin type procedure)

**28296** with metatarsal osteotomy (eg, Mitchell, Chevron, or concentric type procedures)

**28297** Lapidus type procedure

**28298** by phalanx osteotomy

**28299** by other methods (eg, double osteotomy)

**28300** Osteotomy; calcaneus (eg, Dwyer or Chambers type procedure), with or without internal fixation

**28302** talus

**28304** Osteotomy, tarsal bones, other than calcaneus or talus;

**28305** with autograft (includes obtaining graft) (eg, Fowler type)

**28306** Osteotomy, with or without lengthening, shortening or angular correction, metatarsal; first metatarsal

**28307** first metatarsal with autograft (other than first toe)

**28308** other than first metatarsal, each

**28309** multiple (eg, Swanson type cavus foot procedure)

**28310** Osteotomy, shortening, angular or rotational correction; proximal phalanx, first toe (separate procedure)

**28312** other phalanges, any toe

**28313** Reconstruction, angular deformity of toe, soft tissue procedures only (eg, overlapping second toe, fifth toe, curly toes)

**28315** Sesamoidectomy, first toe (separate procedure)

**28320** Repair, nonunion or malunion; tarsal bones

**28322** metatarsal, with or without bone graft (includes obtaining graft)

**28340** Reconstruction, toe, macrodactyly; soft tissue resection

**28341** requiring bone resection

**28344** Reconstruction, toe(s); polydactyly

**28345** syndactyly, with or without skin graft(s), each web

**28360** Reconstruction, cleft foot

## Fracture and/or Dislocation

**28400** Closed treatment of calcaneal fracture; without manipulation

**28405** with manipulation

**28406** Percutaneous skeletal fixation of calcaneal fracture, with manipulation

(28410 has been deleted. To report, see 28400, 28405, 28406, 28415, 28420)

**28415** Open treatment of calcaneal fracture, with or without internal or external fixation;

**28420** with primary iliac or other autogenous bone graft (includes obtaining graft)

**28430** Closed treatment of talus fracture; without manipulation

**28435** with manipulation

**28436** Percutaneous skeletal fixation of talus fracture, with manipulation

(28440 has been deleted. To report, see 28430, 28435, 28436, 28445)

**28445** Open treatment of talus fracture, with or without internal or external fixation

**28450** Treatment of tarsal bone fracture (except talus and calcaneus); without manipulation, each

**28455** with manipulation, each

**28456** Percutaneous skeletal fixation of tarsal bone fracture (except talus and calcaneus), with manipulation, each

(28460 has been deleted. To report, see 28450, 28455, 28456, 28465)

**28465** Open treatment of tarsal bone fracture (except talus and calcaneus), with or without internal or external fixation, each

**28470** Closed treatment of metatarsal fracture; without manipulation, each

**28475** with manipulation, each

**28476** Percutaneous skeletal fixation of metatarsal fracture, with manipulation, each

(28480 has been deleted. To report, see 28470, 28475, 28476, 28485)

**28485** Open treatment of metatarsal fracture, with or without internal or external fixation, each

**28490** Closed treatment of fracture great toe, phalanx or phalanges; without manipulation

**28495** with manipulation

**28496** Percutaneous skeletal fixation of fracture great toe, phalanx or phalanges, with manipulation

(28500 has been deleted. To report, see 28490, 28495, 28496, 28505)

**28505** Open treatment of fracture great toe, phalanx or phalanges, with or without internal or external fixation

**28510** Closed treatment of fracture, phalanx or phalanges, other than great toe; without manipulation, each

**28515** with manipulation, each

(28520 has been deleted. To report, see 28510, 28515, 28525)

**28525** Open treatment of fracture, phalanx or phalanges, other than great toe, with or without internal or external fixation, each

**28530** Closed treatment of sesamoid fracture

**28531** Open treatment of sesamoid fracture, with or without internal fixation

**28540** Closed treatment of tarsal bone dislocation, other than talotarsal; without anesthesia

**28545** requiring anesthesia

**28546** Percutaneous skeletal fixation of tarsal bone dislocation, other than talotarsal, with manipulation

(28550 has been deleted. To report, see 28540, 28545, 28546, 28555)

**28555** Open treatment of tarsal bone dislocation, with or without internal or external fixation

**28570** Closed treatment of talotarsal joint dislocation; without anesthesia

**28575** requiring anesthesia

**28576** Percutaneous skeletal fixation of talotarsal joint dislocation, with manipulation

(28580 has been deleted. To report, see 28570, 28575, 28576, 28585)

**28585** Open treatment of talotarsal joint dislocation, with or without internal or external fixation

**28600** Closed treatment of tarsometatarsal joint dislocation; without anesthesia

**28605** requiring anesthesia

**28606** Percutaneous skeletal fixation of tarsometatarsal joint dislocation, with manipulation

(28610 has been deleted. To report, see 28600, 28605, 28606, 28615)

**28615** Open treatment of tarsometatarsal joint dislocation, with or without internal or external fixation

**28630*** Closed treatment of metatarsophalangeal joint dislocation; without anesthesia

**28635*** requiring anesthesia

**28636** Percutaneous skeletal fixation of metatarsophalangeal joint dislocation, with manipulation

(28640 has been deleted. To report, see 28630, 28635, 28636, 28645)

**28645** Open treatment of metatarsophalangeal joint dislocation, with or without internal or external fixation

**28660*** Closed treatment of interphalangeal joint dislocation; without anesthesia

**28665*** requiring anesthesia

**28666** Percutaneous skeletal fixation of interphalangeal joint dislocation, with manipulation

(28670 has been deleted. To report, see 28660, 28665, 28666, 28675)

**28675** Open treatment of interphalangeal joint dislocation, with or without internal or external fixation

## Arthrodesis

**28705** Arthrodesis; pantalar

**28715** triple

**28725** subtalar

**28730** Arthrodesis, midtarsal or tarsometatarsal, multiple or transverse;

**28735** with osteotomy (eg, flatfoot correction)

**28737** Arthrodesis, with tendon lengthening and advancement, midtarsal navicular-cuneiform (eg, Miller type procedure)

**28740** Arthrodesis, midtarsal or tarsometatarsal, single joint

**28750** Arthrodesis, great toe; metatarsophalangeal joint

**28755** interphalangeal joint

**28760** Arthrodesis, with extensor hallucis longus transfer to first metatarsal neck, great toe, interphalangeal joint (eg, Jones type procedure)

(For hammertoe operation or interphalangeal fusion, use 28285)

## Amputation

**28800** Amputation, foot; midtarsal (eg, Chopart type procedure)

**28805** transmetatarsal

**28810** Amputation, metatarsal, with toe, single

**28820** Amputation, toe; metatarsophalangeal joint

**28825** interphalangeal joint

(For amputation of tuft of distal phalanx, use 11752)

## Other Procedures

**28899** Unlisted procedure, foot or toes

# Application of Casts and Strapping

The listed procedures apply when the cast application or strapping is a replacement procedure used during or after the period of follow-up care, or when the cast application or strapping is an initial service performed without a restorative treatment or procedure(s) to stabilize or protect a fracture, injury, or dislocation and/or to afford comfort to a patient. Restorative treatment or procedure(s) rendered by another physician following the application of the initial cast/splint/strap may be reported with a treatment of fracture and/or dislocation code.

A physician who applies the initial cast, strap or splint and also assumes all of the subsequent fracture, dislocation, or injury care cannot use the application of casts and strapping codes as an initial service, since the first cast/splint or strap application is included in the treatment of fracture and/or dislocation codes. (See notes under Musculoskeletal System, page 69). A temporary cast/splint/strap is not considered to be part of the preoperative care, and the use of the modifier '-56' is not applicable. Additional evaluation and management services are reportable only if significant identifiable further services are provided at the time of the cast application or strapping.

If cast application or strapping is provided as an initial service (eg, casting of a sprained ankle or knee) in which no other procedure or treatment (eg, surgical repair, reduction of a fracture or joint dislocation) is performed or is expected to be performed by a physician rendering the initial care only, use the casting, strapping and/or supply code (99070) in addition to an evaluation and management code as appropriate.

Listed procedures include removal of cast or strapping.

(For orthotics fitting and training, use 97504)

## Body and Upper Extremity

### Casts

**29000** Application of halo type body cast (see 20661-20663 for insertion)

**29010** Application of Risser jacket, localizer, body; only

**29015** including head

**29020** Application of turnbuckle jacket, body; only

**29025** including head

**29035** Application of body cast, shoulder to hips;

**29040** including head, Minerva type

**29044** including one thigh

**29046** including both thighs

**29049** Application; plaster figure-of-eight

**29055** shoulder spica

**29058** plaster Velpeau

**29065** shoulder to hand (long arm)

**29075** elbow to finger (short arm)

**29085** hand and lower forearm (gauntlet)

### Splints

**29105** Application of long arm splint (shoulder to hand)

29125 Application of short arm splint (forearm to hand); static

29126 dynamic

29130 Application of finger splint; static

29131 dynamic

### Strapping—Any Age

29200 Strapping; thorax

29220 low back

29240 shoulder (eg, Velpeau)

29260 elbow or wrist

29280 hand or finger

## Lower Extremity

### Casts

29305 Application of hip spica cast; one leg

29325 one and one-half spica or both legs

(For hip spica (body) cast, including thighs only, use 29046)

29345 Application of long leg cast (thigh to toes);

29355 walker or ambulatory type

29358 Application of long leg cast brace

29365 Application of cylinder cast (thigh to ankle)

29405 Application of short leg cast (below knee to toes);

29425 walking or ambulatory type

29435 Application of patellar tendon bearing (PTB) cast

29440 Adding walker to previously applied cast

29445 Application of rigid total contact leg cast

29450 Application of clubfoot cast with molding or manipulation, long or short leg

(29455 has been deleted. To report, use 29450 with modifier '-50')

### Splints

29505 Application of long leg splint (thigh to ankle or toes)

29515 Application of short leg splint (calf to foot)

### Strapping—Any Age

29520 Strapping; hip

29530 knee

29540 ankle

29550 toes

29580 Unna boot

29590 Denis-Browne splint strapping

## Removal or Repair

Codes for cast removals should be employed only for casts applied by another physician.

29700 Removal or bivalving; gauntlet, boot or body cast

29705 full arm or full leg cast

29710 shoulder or hip spica, Minerva, or Risser jacket, etc.

29715 turnbuckle jacket

29720 Repair of spica, body cast or jacket

29730 Windowing of cast

29740 Wedging of cast (except clubfoot casts)

29750 Wedging of clubfoot cast

(29751 has been deleted. To report, use 29750 with modifier '-50')

## Other Procedures

29799 Unlisted procedure, casting or strapping

## Endoscopy/Arthroscopy

Surgical arthroscopy always includes a diagnostic arthroscopy.

When arthroscopy is performed in conjunction with arthrotomy, add modifier '-51'.

**29800** Arthroscopy, temporomandibular joint, diagnostic, with or without synovial biopsy (separate procedure)

**29804** Arthroscopy, temporomandibular joint, surgical

**29815** Arthroscopy, shoulder, diagnostic, with or without synovial biopsy (separate procedure)

**29819** Arthroscopy, shoulder, surgical; with removal of loose body or foreign body

**29820** synovectomy, partial

**29821** synovectomy, complete

**29822** debridement, limited

**29823** debridement, extensive

**29825** with lysis and resection of adhesions, with or without manipulation

**29826** decompression of subacromial space with partial acromioplasty, with or without coracoacromial release

**29830** Arthroscopy, elbow, diagnostic, with or without synovial biopsy (separate procedure)

**29834** Arthroscopy, elbow, surgical; with removal of loose body or foreign body

**29835** synovectomy, partial

**29836** synovectomy, complete

**29837** debridement, limited

**29838** debridement, extensive

**29840** Arthroscopy, wrist, diagnostic, with or without synovial biopsy (separate procedure)

**29843** Arthroscopy, wrist, surgical; for infection, lavage and drainage

**29844** synovectomy, partial

**29845** synovectomy, complete

**29846** excision and/or repair of triangular fibrocartilage and/or joint debridement

**29847** internal fixation for fracture or instability

**29848** Endoscopy, wrist, surgical, with release of transverse carpal ligament

(For open procedure, use 64721)

**29850** Arthroscopically aided treatment of intercondylar spine(s) and/or tuberosity fracture(s) of the knee, with or without manipulation; without internal or external fixation (includes arthroscopy)

**29851** with internal or external fixation (includes arthroscopy)

(For bone graft, use 20900, 20902)

**29855** Arthroscopically aided treatment of tibial fracture, proximal (plateau); unicondylar, with or without internal or external fixation (includes arthroscopy)

**29856** bicondylar, with or without internal or external fixation (includes arthroscopy)

(For bone graft, use 20900, 20902)

**29860** Arthroscopy, hip, diagnostic with or without synovial biopsy (separate procedure)

**29861** Arthroscopy, hip, surgical; with removal of loose body or foreign body

**29862** with debridement/shaving of articular cartilage (chondroplasty), abrasion arthroplasty, and/or resection of labrum

**29863** with synovectomy

**29870** Arthroscopy, knee, diagnostic, with or without synovial biopsy (separate procedure)

**29871** Arthroscopy, knee, surgical; for infection, lavage and drainage

(29872 has been deleted)

**29874** for removal of loose body or foreign body (eg, osteochondritis dissecans fragmentation, chondral fragmentation)

**29875** synovectomy, limited (eg, plica or shelf resection) (separate procedure)

**29876** synovectomy, major, two or more compartments (eg, medial or lateral)

**29877** debridement/shaving of articular cartilage (chondroplasty)

▲**29879** abrasion arthroplasty (includes chondroplasty where necessary) or multiple drilling or microfracture

**29880** with meniscectomy (medial AND lateral, including any meniscal shaving)

**29881** with meniscectomy (medial OR lateral, including any meniscal shaving)

**29882** with meniscus repair (medial OR lateral)

**29883** with meniscus repair (medial AND lateral)

**29884** with lysis of adhesions, with or without manipulation (separate procedure)

**29885** drilling for osteochondritis dissecans with bone grafting, with or without internal fixation (including debridement of base of lesion)

**29886** drilling for intact osteochondritis dissecans lesion

**29887** drilling for intact osteochondritis dissecans lesion with internal fixation

**29888** Arthroscopically aided anterior cruciate ligament repair/augmentation or reconstruction

**29889** Arthroscopically aided posterior cruciate ligament repair/augmentation or reconstruction

(Procedures 29888 and 29889 should not be used with reconstruction procedures 27427-27429)

(29890 has been deleted)

**29891** Arthroscopy, ankle, surgical; excision of osteochondral defect of talus and/or tibia, including drilling of the defect

**29892** Arthroscopically aided repair of large osteochondritis dissecans lesion, talar dome fracture, or tibial plafond fracture, with or without internal fixation (includes arthroscopy)

**29893** Endoscopic plantar fasciotomy

**29894** Arthroscopy, ankle (tibiotalar and fibulotalar joints), surgical; with removal of loose body or foreign body

**29895** synovectomy, partial

(29896 has been deleted)

**29897** debridement, limited

**29898** debridement, extensive

**29909** Unlisted procedure, arthroscopy

# Notes

# Respiratory System

## Nose

### Incision

**30000*** Drainage abscess or hematoma, nasal, internal approach

(For external approach, see 10060, 10140)

**30020*** Drainage abscess or hematoma, nasal septum

(For lateral rhinotomy, see specific application (eg, 30118, 30320))

### Excision

**30100** Biopsy, intranasal

(For biopsy skin of nose, see 11100, 11101)

**30110** Excision, nasal polyp(s), simple

(30110 would normally be completed in an office setting)

(30111 has been deleted. To report, use 30110 with modifier '-50')

**30115** Excision, nasal polyp(s), extensive

(30115 would normally require the facilities available in a hospital setting)

(30116 has been deleted. To report, use 30115 with modifier '-50')

**30117** Excision or destruction, any method (including laser), intranasal lesion; internal approach

**30118** external approach (lateral rhinotomy)

**30120** Excision or surgical planing of skin of nose for rhinophyma

**30124** Excision dermoid cyst, nose; simple, skin, subcutaneous

**30125** complex, under bone or cartilage

**30130** Excision turbinate, partial or complete, any method

**30140** Submucous resection turbinate, partial or complete, any method

(For submucous resection of nasal septum, use 30520)

(For reduction of turbinates, use 30140 with modifier '-52')

**30150** Rhinectomy; partial

**30160** total

(For closure and/or reconstruction, primary or delayed, see **Integumentary System,** 13150-13153, 14060-14300, 15120, 15121, 15260, 15261, 15760, 20900-20912)

### Introduction

**30200*** Injection into turbinate(s), therapeutic

**30210*** Displacement therapy (Proetz type)

**30220** Insertion, nasal septal prosthesis (button)

### Removal of Foreign Body

**30300*** Removal foreign body, intranasal; office type procedure

**30310** requiring general anesthesia

**30320** by lateral rhinotomy

### Repair

(For obtaining tissues for graft, see 20900-20926, 21210)

**30400** Rhinoplasty, primary; lateral and alar cartilages and/or elevation of nasal tip

(For columellar reconstruction, see 13150 et seq)

**30410** complete, external parts including bony pyramid, lateral and alar cartilages, and/or elevation of nasal tip

**30420** including major septal repair

**30430** Rhinoplasty, secondary; minor revision (small amount of nasal tip work)

**30435** intermediate revision (bony work with osteotomies)

**30450** major revision (nasal tip work and osteotomies)

**30460** Rhinoplasty for nasal deformity secondary to congenital cleft lip and/or palate, including columellar lengthening; tip only

**30462** tip, septum, osteotomies

(30500 has been deleted. To report, use 30520)

**30520** Septoplasty or submucous resection, with or without cartilage scoring, contouring or replacement with graft

(For submucous resection of turbinates, use 30140)

**30540** Repair choanal atresia; intranasal

**30545** transpalatine

**30560*** Lysis intranasal synechia

**30580** Repair fistula; oromaxillary (combine with 31030 if antrotomy is included)

**30600** oronasal

**30620** Septal or other intranasal dermatoplasty (does not include obtaining graft)

**30630** Repair nasal septal perforations

## Destruction

(30800 has been deleted. To report, see 30801 and 30802)

**30801*** Cauterization and/or ablation, mucosa of turbinates, unilateral or bilateral, any method, (separate procedure); superficial

**30802** intramural

(30805, 30820 have been deleted. To report, see 30801 and 30802)

## Other Procedures

(30900 has been deleted. To report, see 30901, 30903)

**30901*** Control nasal hemorrhage, anterior, simple (limited cautery and/or packing) any method

(30902 has been deleted. To report, use 30901 with modifier '-50')

**30903*** Control nasal hemorrhage, anterior, complex (extensive cautery and/or packing) any method

(30904 has been deleted. To report, use 30903 with modifier '-50')

**30905*** Control nasal hemorrhage, posterior, with posterior nasal packs and/or cauterization, any method; initial

**30906*** subsequent

**30915** Ligation arteries; ethmoidal

**30920** internal maxillary artery, transantral

(For ligation external carotid artery, use 37600)

**30930** Fracture nasal turbinate(s), therapeutic

**30999** Unlisted procedure, nose

# Accessory Sinuses

## Incision

**31000*** Lavage by cannulation; maxillary sinus (antrum puncture or natural ostium)

(31001 has been deleted. To report, use 31000 with modifier '-50')

**31002*** sphenoid sinus

**31020** Sinusotomy, maxillary (antrotomy); intranasal

(31021 has been deleted. To report, use 31020 with modifier '-50')

**31030** radical (Caldwell-Luc) without removal of antrochoanal polyps

(31031 has been deleted. To report, use 31030 with modifier '-50')

**31032** radical (Caldwell-Luc) with removal of antrochoanal polyps

(31033 has been deleted. To report, use 31032 with modifier '-50')

**31040** Pterygomaxillary fossa surgery, any approach

(For transantral ligation of internal maxillary artery, use 30920)

**31050** Sinusotomy, sphenoid, with or without biopsy;

**31051** with mucosal stripping or removal of polyp(s)

**31070** Sinusotomy frontal; external, simple (trephine operation)

(31071 has been deleted. To report, use 31276)

**31075** transorbital, unilateral (for mucocele or osteoma, Lynch type)

**31080** obliterative without osteoplastic flap, brow incision (includes ablation)

**31081** obliterative, without osteoplastic flap, coronal incision (includes ablation)

**31084** obliterative, with osteoplastic flap, brow incision

**31085** obliterative, with osteoplastic flap, coronal incision

**31086** nonobliterative, with osteoplastic flap, brow incision

**31087** nonobliterative, with osteoplastic flap, coronal incision

**31090** Sinusotomy, unilateral, three or more paranasal sinuses (frontal, maxillary, ethmoid, sphenoid)

## Excision

**31200** Ethmoidectomy; intranasal, anterior

**31201** intranasal, total

**31205** extranasal, total

**31225** Maxillectomy; without orbital exenteration

**31230** with orbital exenteration (en bloc)

(For orbital exenteration only, see 65110 et seq)

(For skin grafts, see 15120 et seq)

## Endoscopy

A surgical sinus endoscopy includes a sinusotomy (when appropriate) and diagnostic endoscopy.

Codes 31231-31294 are used to report unilateral procedures unless otherwise specified.

The codes 31231-31235 for diagnostic evaluation refer to employing a nasal/sinus endoscope to inspect the interior of the nasal cavity and the middle and superior meatus, the turbinates, and the spheno-ethmoid recess. Any time a diagnostic evaluation is performed all these areas would be inspected and a separate code is not reported for each area.

**31231** Nasal endoscopy, diagnostic, unilateral or bilateral (separate procedure)

**31233** Nasal/sinus endoscopy, diagnostic with maxillary sinusoscopy (via inferior meatus or canine fossa puncture)

**31235** Nasal/sinus endoscopy, diagnostic with sphenoid sinusoscopy (via puncture of sphenoidal face or cannulation of ostium)

**31237** Nasal/sinus endoscopy, surgical; with biopsy, polypectomy or debridement (separate procedure)

**31238** with control of epistaxis

**31239** with dacryocystorhinostomy

**31240** with concha bullosa resection

(31245 has been deleted. To report, use 31254)

(31246 has been deleted. To report, use 31254 and 31256)

(31247 has been deleted. To report, use 31254 and 31267)

(31248 has been deleted. To report, use 31254 and 31276)

(31249 has been deleted. To report, use 31254, 31256, and 31276)

(31250 has been deleted. To report, see 31231-31235)

(31251 has been deleted. To report, use 31254, 31267, and 31276)

(31252 has been deleted. To report, use 31237)

**31254** Nasal/sinus endoscopy, surgical; with ethmoidectomy, partial (anterior)

**31255** with ethmoidectomy, total (anterior and posterior)

**31256** Nasal/sinus endoscopy, surgical, with maxillary antrostomy;

(31258 has been deleted. To report, use 31237)

(31260 has been deleted. To report, use 31233)

(31261 has been deleted. To report, use 31255)

(31262 has been deleted. To report, use 31255 and 31256)

(31263 has been deleted. To report, use 31267)

(31264 has been deleted. To report, use 31255 and 31267)

(31265 has been deleted. To report, use 31267)

(31266 has been deleted. To report, use 31255 and 31276)

**31267** with removal of tissue from maxillary sinus

(31268 has been deleted. To report, use 31267)

(31269 has been deleted. To report, use 31255, 31256, and 31276)

(31270 has been deleted. To report, use 31235)

(31271 has been deleted. To report, use 31255, 31267, and 31276)

(31275 has been deleted. To report, use 31287)

**31276** Nasal/sinus endoscopy, surgical with frontal sinus exploration, with or without removal of tissue from frontal sinus

(31277 has been deleted. To report, use 31288)

(31280 has been deleted. To report, use 31255, and 31287 or 31288)

(31281 has been deleted. To report, use 31255, 31256, and 31287 or 31288)

(31282 has been deleted. To report, use 31255, 31267, and 31287 or 31288)

(31283 has been deleted. To report, use 31255, 31287 or 31288, and 31276)

(31284 has been deleted. To report, use 31255, 31256, 31287 or 31288, and 31276)

(31285 has been deleted. To report, see 31231-31235)

(31286 has been deleted. To report, use 31255, 31267, 31287 or 31288, and 31276)

**31287** Nasal/sinus endoscopy, surgical, with sphenoidotomy;

**31288** with removal of tissue from the sphenoid sinus

**31290** Nasal/sinus endoscopy, surgical, with repair of cerebrospinal fluid leak; ethmoid region

**31291** sphenoid region

**31292** Nasal/sinus endoscopy, surgical; with medial or inferior orbital wall decompression

**31293** with medial orbital wall and inferior orbital wall decompression

**31294** with optic nerve decompression

## Other Procedures

(For hypophysectomy, transantral or transeptal approach, use 61548)

(For transcranial hypophysectomy, use 61546)

**31299** Unlisted procedure, accessory sinuses

# Larynx

## Excision

**31300** Laryngotomy (thyrotomy, laryngofissure); with removal of tumor or laryngocele, cordectomy

**31320** diagnostic

**31360** Laryngectomy; total, without radical neck dissection

**31365** total, with radical neck dissection

**31367** subtotal supraglottic, without radical neck dissection

**31368** subtotal supraglottic, with radical neck dissection

**31370** Partial laryngectomy (hemilaryngectomy); horizontal

**31375** laterovertical

**31380** anterovertical

**31382** antero-latero-vertical

**31390** Pharyngolaryngectomy, with radical neck dissection; without reconstruction

**31395** with reconstruction

**31400** Arytenoidectomy or arytenoidopexy, external approach

(For endoscopic arytenoidectomy, use 31560)

**31420** Epiglottidectomy

## Introduction

⊘ **31500** Intubation, endotracheal, emergency procedure

(For injection procedure for bronchography, see 31656, 31708, 31710)

**31502** Tracheotomy tube change prior to establishment of fistula tract

## Endoscopy

For endoscopic procedures, code appropriate endoscopy of each anatomic site examined.

**31505** Laryngoscopy, indirect; diagnostic (separate procedure)

**31510** with biopsy

**31511** with removal of foreign body

**31512** with removal of lesion

**31513** with vocal cord injection

**31515** Laryngoscopy direct, with or without tracheoscopy; for aspiration

**31520** diagnostic, newborn

**31525** diagnostic, except newborn

**31526** diagnostic, with operating microscope

(Do not report code 69990 in addition to code 31526)

**31527** with insertion of obturator

**31528** with dilatation, initial

**31529** with dilatation, subsequent

**31530** Laryngoscopy, direct, operative, with foreign body removal;

**31531** with operating microscope

(Do not report code 69990 in addition to code 31531)

**31535** Laryngoscopy, direct, operative, with biopsy;

**31536** with operating microscope

(Do not report code 69990 in addition to code 31536)

**31540** Laryngoscopy, direct, operative, with excision of tumor and/or stripping of vocal cords or epiglottis;

**31541** with operating microscope

(Do not report code 69990 in addition to code 31541)

**31560** Laryngoscopy, direct, operative, with arytenoidectomy;

**31561** with operating microscope

(Do not report code 69990 in addition to code 31561)

**31570** Laryngoscopy, direct, with injection into vocal cord(s), therapeutic;

**31571** with operating microscope

(Do not report code 69990 in addition to code 31571)

**31575** Laryngoscopy, flexible fiberoptic; diagnostic

**31576** with biopsy

**31577** with removal of foreign body

**31578** with removal of lesion

**31579** Laryngoscopy, flexible or rigid fiberoptic, with stroboscopy

### Repair

**31580** Laryngoplasty; for laryngeal web, two stage, with keel insertion and removal

**31582** for laryngeal stenosis, with graft or core mold, including tracheotomy

**31584** with open reduction of fracture

**31585** Treatment of closed laryngeal fracture; without manipulation

**31586** with closed manipulative reduction

**31587** Laryngoplasty, cricoid split

**31588** Laryngoplasty, not otherwise specified (eg, for burns, reconstruction after partial laryngectomy)

**31590** Laryngeal reinnervation by neuromuscular pedicle

### Destruction

**31595** Section recurrent laryngeal nerve, therapeutic (separate procedure), unilateral

### Other Procedures

**31599** Unlisted procedure, larynx

## Trachea and Bronchi

### Incision

**31600** Tracheostomy, planned (separate procedure);

**31601** under two years

**31603** Tracheostomy, emergency procedure; transtracheal

**31605** cricothyroid membrane

**31610** Tracheostomy, fenestration procedure with skin flaps

(For endotracheal intubation, use 31500)

(For tracheal aspiration under direct vision, use 31515)

**31611** Construction of tracheoesophageal fistula and subsequent insertion of an alaryngeal speech prosthesis (eg, voice button, Blom-Singer prosthesis)

**31612** Tracheal puncture, percutaneous with transtracheal aspiration and/or injection

**31613** Tracheostoma revision; simple, without flap rotation

**31614** complex, with flap rotation

### Endoscopy

For endoscopy procedures, code appropriate endoscopy of each anatomic site examined. ►Surgical bronchoscopy always includes diagnostic bronchoscopy when performed by the same physician.◄ Codes 31622-31646 include fluoroscopic guidance, when performed.

(For tracheoscopy, see laryngoscopy codes 31515-31578)

**31615** Tracheobronchoscopy through established tracheostomy incision

(31620, 31621 have been deleted. To report, use 31622)

**▲31622** Bronchoscopy, (rigid or flexible); diagnostic, with or without cell washing (separate procedure)

**31623** with brushing or protected brushings

**31624** with bronchial alveolar lavage

**31625** with biopsy

(31626 has been deleted. To report, use 31625)

(31627 has been deleted. To report, use 31622)

**31628** with transbronchial lung biopsy, with or without fluoroscopic guidance

**31629** with transbronchial needle aspiration biopsy

**31630** with tracheal or bronchial dilation or closed reduction of fracture

**31631** with tracheal dilation and placement of tracheal stent

**31635** with removal of foreign body

**31640** with excision of tumor

**31641** with destruction of tumor or relief of stenosis by any method other than excision (eg, laser)

►(For bronchoscopic photodynamic therapy, report 31641 in addition to 96570, 96571 as appropriate)◄

**31643** with placement of catheter(s) for intracavitary radioelement application

(For intracavitary radioelement application, see 77761-77763, 77781-77784)

**31645** with therapeutic aspiration of tracheobronchial tree, initial (eg, drainage of lung abscess)

**31646** with therapeutic aspiration of tracheobronchial tree, subsequent

(For catheter aspiration of tracheobronchial tree at bedside, use 31725)

(31650, 31651 have been deleted. To report, see 31645, 31646)

**31656** with injection of contrast material for segmental bronchography (fiberscope only)

(For radiological supervision and interpretation, see 71040, 71060)

(31659 has been deleted)

## Introduction

(For endotracheal intubation, use 31500)

(For tracheal aspiration under direct vision, see 31515)

**31700** Catheterization, transglottic (separate procedure)

**31708** Instillation of contrast material for laryngography or bronchography, without catheterization

(For radiological supervision and interpretation, see 70373, 71040, 71060)

**31710** Catheterization for bronchography, with or without instillation of contrast material

(For bronchoscopic catheterization for bronchography, fiberscope only, use 31656)

(For radiological supervision and interpretation, see 71040, 71060)

**31715** Transtracheal injection for bronchography

(For radiological supervision and interpretation, see 71040, 71060)

(For prolonged services, see 99354-99360)

**31717** Catheterization with bronchial brush biopsy

(31719 has been deleted. To report, use 31730)

**31720** Catheter aspiration (separate procedure); nasotracheal

**31725** tracheobronchial with fiberscope, bedside

**31730** Transtracheal (percutaneous) introduction of needle wire dilator/stent or indwelling tube for oxygen therapy

## Repair

**31750** Tracheoplasty; cervical

**31755** tracheopharyngeal fistulization, each stage

**31760** intrathoracic

**31766** Carinal reconstruction

**31770** Bronchoplasty; graft repair

**31775** excision stenosis and anastomosis

(For lobectomy and bronchoplasty, use 32501)

**31780** Excision tracheal stenosis and anastomosis; cervical

**31781** cervicothoracic

**31785** Excision of tracheal tumor or carcinoma; cervical

**31786** thoracic

**31800** Suture of tracheal wound or injury; cervical

**31805** intrathoracic

**31820** Surgical closure tracheostomy or fistula; without plastic repair

**31825** with plastic repair

(For repair tracheoesophageal fistula, see 43305, 43312)

**31830** Revision of tracheostomy scar

## Other Procedures

**31899** Unlisted procedure, trachea, bronchi

# Lungs and Pleura

## Incision

⊘ **32000*** Thoracentesis, puncture of pleural cavity for aspiration, initial or subsequent

(For radiological supervision and interpretation, see 76003, 76360, 76934)

►(32001 has been deleted. To report, use 32997)◄

⊘ **32002** Thoracentesis with insertion of tube with or without water seal (eg, for pneumothorax) (separate procedure)

**32005** Chemical pleurodesis (eg, for recurrent or persistent pneumothorax)

⊘ **32020** Tube thoracostomy with or without water seal (eg, for abscess, hemothorax, empyema) (separate procedure)

**32035** Thoracostomy; with rib resection for empyema

**32036** with open flap drainage for empyema

**32095** Thoracotomy, limited, for biopsy of lung or pleura

(To report wound exploration due to penetrating trauma without thoractomy, use 20102)

**32100** Thoracotomy, major; with exploration and biopsy

**32110** with control of traumatic hemorrhage and/or repair of lung tear

**32120** for postoperative complications

**32124** with open intrapleural pneumonolysis

**32140** with cyst(s) removal, with or without a pleural procedure

**32141** with excision-plication of bullae, with or without any pleural procedure

(For lung volume reduction, use 32491)

**32150** with removal of intrapleural foreign body or fibrin deposit

**32151** with removal of intrapulmonary foreign body

**32160** with cardiac massage

(For segmental or other resections of lung, see 32480-32525)

**32200** Pneumonostomy; with open drainage of abscess or cyst

**32201** with percutaneous drainage of abscess or cyst

(For radiological supervision and interpretation, use 75989)

**32215** Pleural scarification for repeat pneumothorax

**32220** Decortication, pulmonary (separate procedure); total

**32225** partial

## Excision

**32310** Pleurectomy, parietal (separate procedure)

(32315 has been deleted. To report, use 32310)

**32320** Decortication and parietal pleurectomy

**32400*** Biopsy, pleura; percutaneous needle

(For radiological supervision and interpretation, see 71036, 76360, 76942)

(For fine needle aspiration, preparation, and interpretation of smears, see 88170-88173)

**32402** open

**32405** Biopsy, lung or mediastinum, percutaneous needle

(For radiological supervision and interpretation, see 71036, 76360, 76942)

(For fine needle aspiration, preparation, and interpretation of smears, see 88170-88173)

**32420*** Pneumonocentesis, puncture of lung for aspiration

**32440** Removal of lung, total pneumonectomy;

**32442** with resection of segment of trachea followed by broncho-tracheal anastomosis (sleeve pneumonectomy)

**32445** extrapleural

(32450 has been deleted. To report, use 32445 and 32540)

**32480** Removal of lung, other than total pneumonectomy; single lobe (lobectomy)

**32482** two lobes (bilobectomy)

**32484** single segment (segmentectomy)

(32485 has been deleted. To report, use 32501)

**32486** with circumferential resection of segment of bronchus followed by broncho-bronchial anastomosis (sleeve lobectomy)

**32488** all remaining lung following previous removal of a portion of lung (completion pneumonectomy)

(32490 has been deleted. To report, use 32320 and the appropriate removal of lung code)

**32491** excision-plication of emphysematous lung(s) (bullous or non-bullous) for lung volume reduction, sternal split or transthoracic approach, with or without any pleural procedure

**32500** wedge resection, single or multiple

**+ 32501** Resection and repair of portion of bronchus (bronchoplasty) when performed at time of lobectomy or segmentectomy (List separately in addition to code for primary procedure)

(Use 32501 in conjunction with codes 32480, 32482, 32484)

(32501 is to be used when a portion of the bronchus to preserved lung is removed and requires plastic closure to preserve function of that preserved lung. It is not to be used for closure for the proximal end of a resected bronchus.)

**32520** Resection of lung; with resection of chest wall

**32522** with reconstruction of chest wall, without prosthesis

**32525** with major reconstruction of chest wall, with prosthesis

**32540** Extrapleural enucleation of empyema (empyemectomy)

(32545 has been deleted. To report, use 32540 and the appropriate removal of lung code)

## Endoscopy

Surgical thoracoscopy always includes diagnostic thoracoscopy.

For endoscopic procedures, code appropriate endoscopy of each anatomic site examined.

**32601** Thoracoscopy, diagnostic (separate procedure); lungs and pleural space, without biopsy

**32602** lungs and pleural space, with biopsy

**32603** pericardial sac, without biopsy

**32604** pericardial sac, with biopsy

**32605** mediastinal space, without biopsy

**32606** mediastinal space, with biopsy

(Surgical thoracoscopy always includes diagnostic thoracoscopy)

**32650** Thoracoscopy, surgical; with pleurodesis, any method

**32651** with partial pulmonary decortication

**32652** with total pulmonary decortication, including intrapleural pneumonolysis

**32653** with removal of intrapleural foreign body or fibrin deposit

**32654** with control of traumatic hemorrhage

**32655** with excision-plication of bullae, including any pleural procedure

**32656** with parietal pleurectomy

**32657** with wedge resection of lung, single or multiple

**32658** with removal of clot or foreign body from pericardial sac

**32659** with creation of pericardial window or partial resection of pericardial sac for drainage

**32660** with total pericardiectomy

**32661** with excision of pericardial cyst, tumor, or mass

**32662** with excision of mediastinal cyst, tumor, or mass

**32663** with lobectomy, total or segmental

**32664** with thoracic sympathectomy

**32665** with esophagomyotomy (Heller type)

(32700 and 32705 have been deleted. To report, see 32601-32606)

## Repair

**32800** Repair lung hernia through chest wall

**32810** Closure of chest wall following open flap drainage for empyema (Clagett type procedure)

**32815** Open closure of major bronchial fistula

**32820** Major reconstruction, chest wall (posttraumatic)

## Lung Transplantation

**32850** Donor pneumonectomy(ies) with preparation and maintenance of allograft (cadaver)

**32851** Lung transplant, single; without cardiopulmonary bypass

**32852** with cardiopulmonary bypass

**32853** Lung transplant, double (bilateral sequential or en bloc); without cardiopulmonary bypass

**32854** with cardiopulmonary bypass

## Surgical Collapse Therapy; Thoracoplasty

(See also 32520-32525)

**32900** Resection of ribs, extrapleural, all stages

**32905** Thoracoplasty, Schede type or extrapleural (all stages);

**32906** with closure of bronchopleural fistula

(For open closure of major bronchial fistula, use 32815)

(For resection of first rib for thoracic outlet compression, see 21615, 21616)

**32940** Pneumonolysis, extraperiosteal, including filling or packing procedures

**32960*** Pneumothorax, therapeutic, intrapleural injection of air

●**32997** Total lung lavage (unilateral)

►(For bronchoscopic bronchial alveolar lavage, use 31624)◄

## Other Procedures

**32999** Unlisted procedure, lungs and pleura

# Notes

# Cardiovascular System

Selective vascular catheterizations should be coded to include introduction and all lesser order selective catheterizations used in the approach (eg, the description for a selective right middle cerebral artery catheterization includes the introduction and placement catheterization of the right common and internal carotid arteries).

Additional second and/or third order arterial catheterizations within the same family of arteries supplied by a single first order artery should be expressed by 36218 or 36248. Additional first order or higher catheterizations in vascular families supplied by a first order vessel different from a previously selected and coded family should be separately coded using the conventions described above.

(For monitoring, operation of pump and other nonsurgical services, see 99190-99192, 99291, 99292, 99354-99360)

(For other medical or laboratory related services, see appropriate section)

(For radiological supervision and interpretation, see 75600-75978)

## Heart and Pericardium

### Pericardium

**33010*** Pericardiocentesis; initial

(For radiological supervision and interpretation, use 76930)

**33011*** subsequent

(For radiological supervision and interpretation, use 76930)

**33015** Tube pericardiostomy

**33020** Pericardiotomy for removal of clot or foreign body (primary procedure)

**33025** Creation of pericardial window or partial resection for drainage

**33030** Pericardiectomy, subtotal or complete; without cardiopulmonary bypass

**33031** with cardiopulmonary bypass

(33035 has been deleted. To report, use 33031)

**33050** Excision of pericardial cyst or tumor

(33100 has been deleted. To report, see 33030, 33031)

### Cardiac Tumor

**33120** Excision of intracardiac tumor, resection with cardiopulmonary bypass

**33130** Resection of external cardiac tumor

### ▸Transmyocardial Revascularization◂

●**33140** Transmyocardial laser revascularization, by thoracotomy (separate procedure)

### Pacemaker or ▸Pacing Cardioverter-◂ Defibrillator

A pacemaker system includes a pulse generator containing electronics and a battery, and one or more electrodes (leads). Pulse generators ▸are◂ placed in a subcutaneous "pocket" created in either a subclavicular site ▸or underneath the abdominal muscles just below the ribcage.◂ Electrodes may be inserted through a vein (transvenous) or ▸they may be placed◂ on the surface of the heart (epicardial). ▸The epicardial location of electrodes requires a thoracotomy for electrode insertion.◂

A single chamber ▸pacemaker◂ system includes a pulse generator and one electrode inserted in either the atrium or ventricle. A dual chamber ▸pacemaker◂ system includes a pulse generator and one electrode inserted in the atrium and one electrode inserted in the ventricle.

▸Like a pacemaker system,◂ a ▸pacing cardioverter-◂defibrillator system includes a pulse generator and electrodes, ▸although pacing cardioverter-defibrillators may require multiple leads, even when only a single chamber is being paced. A pacing cardioverter-defibrillator system may be inserted in a single chamber (pacing in the ventricle) or in dual chambers (pacing in atrium and ventricle). These devices use a combination of antitachycardia pacing, low energy cardioversion or defibrillating shocks to treat ventricular tachycardia or ventricular fibrillation.◀

▶Pacing cardioverter-defibrillator◀ pulse generators may be ▶implanted◀ in a subcutaneous ▶infraclavicular pocket◀ or ▶in an abdominal◀ pocket. ▶Removal of a pacing cardioverter-defibrillator pulse generator requires opening of the existing subcutaneous pocket and disconnection of the pulse generator from its electrode(s). A thoracotomy (or laparotomy in the case of abdominally placed pulse generators) is not required to remove the pulse generator.◀

The electrodes ▶(leads) of a pacing cardioverter-defibrillator system are positioned in the heart via the venous system (transvenously), in most circumstances. Electrode positioning on the epicardial surface of the heart requires a thoracotomy (codes 33245-33246). Removal of electrode(s) may first be attempted by transvenous extraction (code 33244). However, if transvenous extraction is unsuccessful, a thoracotomy may be required to remove the electrodes (code 33243).◀

When the "battery" ▶of a pacemaker or pacing cardioverter-defibrillator◀ is changed, it is actually the pulse generator that is changed. Replacement of a pulse generator ▶should be reported with◀ a code for removal of the pulse generator and another code for insertion of a pulse generator.

These procedures include repositioning or replacement in the first 14 days after the insertion (or replacement) of the device.

Modifiers '-76' and '-77' are not reported with pacemaker or ▶pacing cardioverter-◀defibrillator codes after 14 days as these are considered new, not repeat, services.

(For electronic, telephonic analysis of internal pacemaker system, see 93731-93736)

(For radiological supervision and interpretation with insertion of pacemaker, use 71090)

**33200** Insertion of permanent pacemaker with epicardial electrode(s); by thoracotomy

**33201** by xiphoid approach

(33205 has been deleted. To report, see 33206-33208)

**33206** Insertion or replacement of permanent pacemaker with transvenous electrode(s); atrial

**33207** ventricular

**33208** atrial and ventricular

▶(Codes 33206-33208 include subcutaneous insertion of the pulse generator and transvenous placement of electrode(s))◀

**33210** Insertion or replacement of temporary transvenous single chamber cardiac electrode or pacemaker catheter (separate procedure)

**33211** Insertion or replacement of temporary transvenous dual chamber pacing electrodes (separate procedure)

**33212** Insertion or replacement of pacemaker pulse generator only; single chamber, atrial or ventricular

**33213** dual chamber

**33214** Upgrade of implanted pacemaker system, conversion of single chamber system to dual chamber system (includes removal of previously placed pulse generator, testing of existing lead, insertion of new lead, insertion of new pulse generator)

**▲33216** Insertion or repositioning of a transvenous electrode (15 days or more after initial insertion); single chamber (one electrode) permanent pacemaker or single chamber pacing cardioverter-defibrillator

**▲33217** dual chamber (two electrodes) permanent pacemaker or dual chamber pacing cardioverter-defibrillator

▶(Do not report 33216-33217 in conjunction with code 33214)◀

**▲33218** Repair of single transvenous electrode for a single chamber, permanent pacemaker or single chamber pacing cardioverter-defibrillator

(33219 has been deleted. To report, see 33212 or 33213 and 33218 or 33220)

**▲33220** Repair of two transvenous electrodes for a dual chamber permanent pacemaker or dual chamber pacing cardioverter-defibrillator

**33222** Revision or relocation of skin pocket for pacemaker

**▲33223** Revision of skin pocket for single or dual chamber pacing cardioverter-defibrillator

(33232 has been deleted. To report, see 33233, 33234, 33236)

**33233** Removal of permanent pacemaker pulse generator

**33234** Removal of transvenous pacemaker electrode(s); single lead system, atrial or ventricular

**33235** dual lead system

**33236** Removal of permanent epicardial pacemaker and electrodes by thoracotomy; single lead system, atrial or ventricular

**33237** dual lead system

**33238** Removal of permanent transvenous electrode(s) by thoracotomy

**▲33240** Insertion of single or dual chamber pacing cardioverter-defibrillator pulse generator

**▲33241** Subcutaneous removal of single or dual chamber pacing cardioverter-defibrillator pulse generator

►(For removal of electrode(s) by thoracotomy, use 33243 in conjunction with code 33241)◄

►(For removal of electrode(s) by transvenous extraction, use 33244 in conjunction with code 33241)◄

►(For removal and reinsertion of a pacing cardioverter-defibrillator system (pulse generator and electrodes), report 33241 and 33243 or 33244 and 33249)◄

►(33242 has been deleted. To report, see 33218, 33220)◄

**▲33243** Removal of single or dual chamber pacing cardioverter-defibrillator electrode(s); by thoracotomy

**▲33244** by transvenous extraction

►(For subcutaneous removal of the pulse generator, use 33241 in conjunction with code 33243 or 33244)◄

**▲33245** Insertion of epicardial single or dual chamber pacing cardioverter-defibrillator electrodes by thoracotomy;

**▲33246** with insertion of pulse generator

►(33247 has been deleted. To report, use 33216)◄

(33248 has been deleted. To report, see 33242, 33243, 33244)

**▲33249** Insertion or repositioning of electrode lead(s) for single or dual chamber pacing cardioverter-defibrillator and insertion of pulse generator

►(For removal and reinsertion of a pacing cardioverter-defibrillator system (pulse generator and electrodes), report 33241 and 33243 or 33244 and 33249)◄

## ►Electrophysiologic Operative Procedures◄

**33250** Operative ablation of supraventricular arrhythmogenic focus or pathway (eg, Wolff-Parkinson-White, A-V node re-entry), tract(s) and/or focus (foci); without cardiopulmonary bypass

**33251** with cardiopulmonary bypass

**33253** Operative incisions and reconstruction of atria for treatment of atrial fibrillation or atrial flutter (eg, maze procedure)

(33260 has been deleted. To report, use 33261)

**33261** Operative ablation of ventricular arrhythmogenic focus with cardiopulmonary bypass

## ►Patient-Activated Event Recorder◄

**●33282** Implantation of patient-activated cardiac event recorder

►(Initial implantation includes programming. For subsequent electronic analysis and/or reprogramming, use 93727)◄

**●33284** Removal of an implantable, patient-activated cardiac event recorder

## Wounds of the Heart and Great Vessels

**33300** Repair of cardiac wound; without bypass

**33305** with cardiopulmonary bypass

**33310** Cardiotomy, exploratory (includes removal of foreign body); without bypass

**33315** with cardiopulmonary bypass

**33320** Suture repair of aorta or great vessels; without shunt or cardiopulmonary bypass

**33321** with shunt bypass

**33322** with cardiopulmonary bypass

**33330** Insertion of graft, aorta or great vessels; without shunt, or cardiopulmonary bypass

**33332** with shunt bypass

**33335** with cardiopulmonary bypass

(33350 has been deleted)

## Cardiac Valves

### Aortic Valve

**33400** Valvuloplasty, aortic valve; open, with cardiopulmonary bypass

**33401** open, with inflow occlusion

**33403** using transventricular dilation, with cardiopulmonary bypass

**33404** Construction of apical-aortic conduit

▲**33405** Replacement, aortic valve, with cardiopulmonary bypass; with prosthetic valve other than homograft or stentless valve

**33406** with homograft valve (freehand)

(33407 has been deleted. To report, use 33403)

(33408 has been deleted. To report, use 33401)

●**33410** with stentless tissue valve

**33411** Replacement, aortic valve; with aortic annulus enlargement, noncoronary cusp

**33412** with transventricular aortic annulus enlargement (Konno procedure)

**33413** by translocation of autologous pulmonary valve with homograft replacement of pulmonary valve (Ross procedure)

**33414** Repair of left ventricular outflow tract obstruction by patch enlargement of the outflow tract

**33415** Resection or incision of subvalvular tissue for discrete subvalvular aortic stenosis

**33416** Ventriculomyotomy (-myectomy) for idiopathic hypertrophic subaortic stenosis (eg, asymmetric septal hypertrophy)

**33417** Aortoplasty (gusset) for supravalvular stenosis

### Mitral Valve

**33420** Valvotomy, mitral valve; closed heart

**33422** open heart, with cardiopulmonary bypass

**33425** Valvuloplasty, mitral valve, with cardiopulmonary bypass;

**33426** with prosthetic ring

**33427** radical reconstruction, with or without ring

**33430** Replacement, mitral valve, with cardiopulmonary bypass

### Tricuspid Valve

(33450 has been deleted. To report, see 33463, 33464)

(33452 has been deleted. To report, see 33463, 33464)

**33460** Valvectomy, tricuspid valve, with cardiopulmonary bypass

**33463** Valvuloplasty, tricuspid valve; without ring insertion

**33464** with ring insertion

**33465** Replacement, tricuspid valve, with cardiopulmonary bypass

**33468** Tricuspid valve repositioning and plication for Ebstein anomaly

### Pulmonary Valve

**33470** Valvotomy, pulmonary valve, closed heart; transventricular

**33471** via pulmonary artery

(To report percutaneous valvuloplasty of pulmonary valve, use 92990)

**33472** Valvotomy, pulmonary valve, open heart; with inflow occlusion

**33474** with cardiopulmonary bypass

**33475** Replacement, pulmonary valve

**33476** Right ventricular resection for infundibular stenosis, with or without commissurotomy

**33478** Outflow tract augmentation (gusset), with or without commissurotomy or infundibular resection

(33480-33492 have been deleted. To report, see 33400-33478 and add modifier -51 to the secondary valve procedure code when multiple valve procedures are performed.)

## Other Valvular Procedures

**33496** Repair of non-structural prosthetic valve dysfunction with cardiopulmonary bypass (separate procedure)

(For reoperation, use 33530 in addition to 33496)

## Coronary Artery Anomalies

Basic procedures include endarterectomy or angioplasty.

**33500** Repair of coronary arteriovenous or arteriocardiac chamber fistula; with cardiopulmonary bypass

**33501** without cardiopulmonary bypass

**33502** Repair of anomalous coronary artery; by ligation

**33503** by graft, without cardiopulmonary bypass

**33504** by graft, with cardiopulmonary bypass

**33505** with construction of intrapulmonary artery tunnel (Takeuchi procedure)

**33506** by translocation from pulmonary artery to aorta

## Venous Grafting Only for Coronary Artery Bypass

The following codes are used to report coronary artery bypass procedures using venous grafts only. These codes should NOT be used to report the performance of coronary artery bypass procedures using arterial grafts and venous grafts during the same procedure. See 33517-33523 and 33533-33536 for reporting combined arterial-venous grafts.

Procurement of the saphenous vein graft is included in the description of the work for 33510-33516 and should not be reported as a separate service or co-surgery. When graft procurement is performed by surgical assistant, add modifier '-80' to 33510-33516.

**33510** Coronary artery bypass, vein only; single coronary venous graft

**33511** two coronary venous grafts

**33512** three coronary venous grafts

**33513** four coronary venous grafts

**33514** five coronary venous grafts

**33516** six or more coronary venous grafts

## Combined Arterial-Venous Grafting for Coronary Bypass

The following codes are used to report coronary artery bypass procedures using venous grafts and arterial grafts during the same procedure. These codes may NOT be used alone.

To report combined arterial-venous grafts it is necessary to report two codes: 1) the appropriate combined arterial-venous graft code (33517-33523); and 2) the appropriate arterial graft code (33533-33536).

Procurement of the saphenous vein graft is included in the description of the work for 33517-33523 and should not be reported as a separate service or co-surgery. ►Procurement of the artery for grafting is included in the description of the work for 33533-33536 and should not be reported as a separate service or co-surgery.◄ When ►arterial and/or venous graft◄ procurement is performed by surgical assistant, add modifier '-80' to 33517-33523, ►33533-33536, as appropriate.◄

⊘ **33517** Coronary artery bypass, using venous graft(s) and arterial graft(s); single vein graft (List separately in addition to code for arterial graft)

⊘ **33518** two venous grafts (List separately in addition to code for arterial graft)

⊘ **33519** three venous grafts (List separately in addition to code for arterial graft)

(33520 has been deleted)

⊘ **33521** four venous grafts (List separately in addition to code for arterial graft)

⊘ **33522** five venous grafts (List separately in addition to code for arterial graft)

⊘ **33523** six or more venous grafts (List separately in addition to code for arterial graft)

(33525, 33528 have been deleted)

✚ **33530** Reoperation, coronary artery bypass procedure or valve procedure, more than one month after original operation (List separately in addition to code for primary procedure)

(Use 33530 in conjunction with codes 33400-33496; 33510-33536, 33863)

(33532 has been deleted. To report, use 33999)

## Arterial Grafting for Coronary Artery Bypass

The following codes are used to report coronary artery bypass procedures using either arterial grafts only or a combination of arterial-venous grafts. The codes include the use of the internal mammary artery, gastroepiploic artery, epigastric artery, radial artery, and arterial conduits procured from other sites.

To report combined arterial-venous grafts it is necessary to report two codes: 1) the appropriate arterial graft code (33533-33536); and 2) the appropriate combined arterial-venous graft code (33517-33523).

►Procurement of the artery for grafting is included in the description of the work for 33533-33536 and should not be reported as a separate service or co-surgery. Procurement of the saphenous vein graft is included in the description of the work for 33517-33523 and should not be reported as a separate service or co-surgery. When arterial and/or venous graft procurement is performed by surgical assistant, add modifier '-80' to 33517-33523, 33533-33536, as appropriate.◄

**33533** Coronary artery bypass, using arterial graft(s); single arterial graft

**33534** two coronary arterial grafts

**33535** three coronary arterial grafts

**33536** four or more coronary arterial grafts

**33542** Myocardial resection (eg, ventricular aneurysmectomy)

**33545** Repair of postinfarction ventricular septal defect, with or without myocardial resection

(33560 has been deleted)

## Coronary Endarterectomy

(33570 has been deleted. To report, see 33510-33536 and 33572)

✚ **33572** Coronary endarterectomy, open, any method, of left anterior descending, circumflex, or right coronary artery performed in conjunction with coronary artery bypass graft procedure, each vessel (List separately in addition to primary procedure)

(Use 33572 in conjunction with 33510-33516, 33533-33536)

(33575 has been deleted. To report, see 33510-33536 and 33572)

## Single Ventricle and Other Complex Cardiac Anomalies

**33600** Closure of atrioventricular valve (mitral or tricuspid) by suture or patch

**33602** Closure of semilunar valve (aortic or pulmonary) by suture or patch

**33606** Anastomosis of pulmonary artery to aorta (Damus-Kaye-Stansel procedure)

**33608** Repair of complex cardiac anomaly other than pulmonary atresia with ventricular septal defect by construction or replacement of conduit from right or left ventricle to pulmonary artery

(For repair of pulmonary atresia with ventricular septal defect, see 33918, 33919, 33920)

**33610** Repair of complex cardiac anomalies (eg, single ventricle with subaortic obstruction) by surgical enlargement of interventricular septal defect

**33611** Repair of double outlet right ventricle with intraventricular tunnel repair;

**33612** with repair of right ventricular outflow tract obstruction

**33615** Repair of complex cardiac anomalies (eg, tricuspid atresia) by closure of atrial septal defect and anastomosis of atria or vena cava to pulmonary artery (simple Fontan procedure)

**33617** Repair of complex cardiac anomalies (eg, single ventricle) by modified Fontan procedure

**33619** Repair of single ventricle with aortic outflow obstruction and aortic arch hypoplasia (hypoplastic left heart syndrome) (eg, Norwood procedure)

## Septal Defect

(33640 has been deleted. To report, use 33641)

**33641** Repair atrial septal defect, secundum, with cardiopulmonary bypass, with or without patch

(33643 has been deleted. To report, use 33641)

**33645** Direct or patch closure, sinus venosus, with or without anomalous pulmonary venous drainage

**33647** Repair of atrial septal defect and ventricular septal defect, with direct or patch closure

(33649 has been deleted. To report, use 33615)

**33660** Repair of incomplete or partial atrioventricular canal (ostium primum atrial septal defect), with or without atrioventricular valve repair

**33665** Repair of intermediate or transitional atrioventricular canal, with or without atrioventricular valve repair

**33670** Repair of complete atrioventricular canal, with or without prosthetic valve

**33681** Closure of ventricular septal defect, with or without patch;

(33682 has been deleted. To report, use 33681)

**33684** with pulmonary valvotomy or infundibular resection (acyanotic)

**33688** with removal of pulmonary artery band, with or without gusset

**33690** Banding of pulmonary artery

**33692** Complete repair tetralogy of Fallot without pulmonary atresia;

**33694** with transannular patch

(33696 has been deleted. To report, use 33924)

**33697** Complete repair tetralogy of Fallot with pulmonary atresia including construction of conduit from right ventricle to pulmonary artery and closure of ventricular septal defect

(33698 has been deleted. To report, use 33924)

## Sinus of Valsalva

**33702** Repair sinus of Valsalva fistula, with cardiopulmonary bypass;

**33710** with repair of ventricular septal defect

**33720** Repair sinus of Valsalva aneurysm, with cardiopulmonary bypass

**33722** Closure of aortico-left ventricular tunnel

## Total Anomalous Pulmonary Venous Drainage

**33730** Complete repair of anomalous venous return (supracardiac, intracardiac, or infracardiac types)

(For partial anomalous return, see atrial septal defect)

**33732** Repair of cor triatriatum or supravalvular mitral ring by resection of left atrial membrane

## Shunting Procedures

**33735** Atrial septectomy or septostomy; closed heart (Blalock-Hanlon type operation)

**33736** open heart with cardiopulmonary bypass

**33737** open heart, with inflow occlusion

(33738 has been deleted. To report, use 92992)

(33739 has been deleted. To report, use 92993)

**33750** Shunt; subclavian to pulmonary artery (Blalock-Taussig type operation)

**33755** ascending aorta to pulmonary artery (Waterston type operation)

**33762** descending aorta to pulmonary artery (Potts-Smith type operation)

**33764** central, with prosthetic graft

**33766** superior vena cava to pulmonary artery for flow to one lung (classical Glenn procedure)

**33767** superior vena cava to pulmonary artery for flow to both lungs (bidirectional Glenn procedure)

## Transposition of the Great Vessels

**33770** Repair of transposition of the great arteries with ventricular septal defect and subpulmonary stenosis; without surgical enlargement of ventricular septal defect

**33771** with surgical enlargement of ventricular septal defect

**33774** Repair of transposition of the great arteries, atrial baffle procedure (eg, Mustard or Senning type) with cardiopulmonary bypass;

**33775** with removal of pulmonary band

**33776** with closure of ventricular septal defect

**33777** with repair of subpulmonic obstruction

**33778** Repair of transposition of the great arteries, aortic pulmonary artery reconstruction (eg, Jatene type);

**33779** with removal of pulmonary band

**33780** with closure of ventricular septal defect

**33781** with repair of subpulmonic obstruction

(33782, 33783, 33784, 33785 have been deleted. To report, see 33774-33781)

## Truncus Arteriosus

**33786** Total repair, truncus arteriosus (Rastelli type operation)

**33788** Reimplantation of an anomalous pulmonary artery

(For pulmonary artery band, use 33690)

## Aortic Anomalies

**33800** Aortic suspension (aortopexy) for tracheal decompression (eg, for tracheomalacia) (separate procedure)

**33802** Division of aberrant vessel (vascular ring);

**33803** with reanastomosis

(33810, 33812 have been deleted)

**33813** Obliteration of aortopulmonary septal defect; without cardiopulmonary bypass

**33814** with cardiopulmonary bypass

**33820** Repair of patent ductus arteriosus; by ligation

**33822** by division, under 18 years

**33824** by division, 18 years and older

(33830 has been deleted. To report, see 33820-33824)

**33840** Excision of coarctation of aorta, with or without associated patent ductus arteriosus; with direct anastomosis

**33845** with graft

(33850 has been deleted. To report, use 33999)

**33851** repair using either left subclavian artery or prosthetic material as gusset for enlargement

**33852** Repair of hypoplastic or interrupted aortic arch using autogenous or prosthetic material; without cardiopulmonary bypass

**33853** with cardiopulmonary bypass

(33855 has been deleted. To report, use 33619)

## Thoracic Aortic Aneurysm

**33860** Ascending aorta graft, with cardiopulmonary bypass, with or without valve suspension;

**33861** with coronary reconstruction

**33863** with aortic root replacement using composite prosthesis and coronary reconstruction

(33865 has been deleted. To report, see 33860 or 33861 and 33405 or 33406)

**33870** Transverse arch graft, with cardiopulmonary bypass

**33875** Descending thoracic aorta graft, with or without bypass

**33877** Repair of thoracoabdominal aortic aneurysm with graft, with or without cardiopulmonary bypass

## Pulmonary Artery

**33910** Pulmonary artery embolectomy; with cardiopulmonary bypass

**33915** without cardiopulmonary bypass

**33916** Pulmonary endarterectomy, with or without embolectomy, with cardiopulmonary bypass

**33917** Repair of pulmonary artery stenosis by reconstruction with patch or graft

**33918** Repair of pulmonary atresia with ventricular septal defect, by unifocalization of pulmonary arteries; without cardiopulmonary bypass

**33919** with cardiopulmonary bypass

**33920** Repair of pulmonary atresia with ventricular septal defect, by construction or replacement of conduit from right or left ventricle to pulmonary artery

(For repair of other complex cardiac anomalies by construction or replacement of right or left ventricle to pulmonary artery conduit, see 33608)

**33922** Transection of pulmonary artery with cardiopulmonary bypass

**+ 33924** Ligation and takedown of a systemic-to-pulmonary artery shunt, performed in conjunction with a congenital heart procedure (List separately in addition to code for primary procedure)

(Use 33924 in conjunction with 33470-33475, 33600-33619, 33684-33688, 33692-33697, 33735-33767, 33770-33781, 33786, 33918-33922)

## Heart/Lung Transplantation

**33930** Donor cardiectomy-pneumonectomy, with preparation and maintenance of allograft

**33935** Heart-lung transplant with recipient cardiectomy-pneumonectomy

**33940** Donor cardiectomy, with preparation and maintenance of allograft

**33945** Heart transplant, with or without recipient cardiectomy

(33950 has been deleted. To report, see 33940, 33945)

## Cardiac Assist

**33960** Prolonged extracorporeal circulation for cardiopulmonary insufficiency; initial 24 hours

**+ 33961** each additional 24 hours (List separately in addition to code for primary procedure)

(Use 33961 in conjunction with code 33960)

(For insertion of cannula for prolonged extracorporeal circulation, use 36822)

**● 33968** Removal of intra-aortic balloon assist device, percutaneous

►(For percutaneous insertion, use 93536)◄

**33970** Insertion of intra-aortic balloon assist device through the femoral artery, open approach

**33971** Removal of intra-aortic balloon assist device including repair of femoral artery, with or without graft

(33972 has been deleted. To report, use appropriate E/M code)

**33973** Insertion of intra-aortic balloon assist device through the ascending aorta

**33974** Removal of intra-aortic balloon assist device from the ascending aorta, including repair of the ascending aorta, with or without graft

**33975** Implantation of ventricular assist device; single ventricle support

**33976** biventricular support

**33977** Removal of ventricular assist device; single ventricle support

**33978** biventricular support

## Other Procedures

**33999** Unlisted procedure, cardiac surgery

# Arteries and Veins

Primary vascular procedure listings include establishing both inflow and outflow by whatever procedures necessary. Also included is that portion of the operative arteriogram performed by the surgeon, as indicated. Sympathectomy, when done, is included in the listed aortic procedures. For unlisted vascular procedure, use 37799.

## Embolectomy/Thrombectomy

### Arterial, With or Without Catheter

**34001** Embolectomy or thrombectomy, with or without catheter; carotid, subclavian or innominate artery, by neck incision

**34051** innominate, subclavian artery, by thoracic incision

**34101** axillary, brachial, innominate, subclavian artery, by arm incision

**34111** radial or ulnar artery, by arm incision

**34151** renal, celiac, mesentery, aortoiliac artery, by abdominal incision

**34201** femoropopliteal, aortoiliac artery, by leg incision

**34203** popliteal-tibio-peroneal artery, by leg incision

### Venous, Direct or With Catheter

**34401** Thrombectomy, direct or with catheter; vena cava, iliac vein, by abdominal incision

**34421** vena cava, iliac, femoropopliteal vein, by leg incision

**34451** vena cava, iliac, femoropopliteal vein, by abdominal and leg incision

**34471** subclavian vein, by neck incision

**34490** axillary and subclavian vein, by arm incision

## Venous Reconstruction

**34501** Valvuloplasty, femoral vein

**34502** Reconstruction of vena cava, any method

**34510** Venous valve transposition, any vein donor

**34520** Cross-over vein graft to venous system

**34530** Saphenopopliteal vein anastomosis

## Direct Repair of Aneurysm or Excision (Partial or Total) and Graft Insertion for Aneurysm, False Aneurysm, Ruptured Aneurysm, and Associated Occlusive Disease

Procedures 35001-35162 include preparation of artery for anastomosis including endarterectomy.

(For direct repairs associated with occlusive disease only, see 35201-35286)

(For intracranial aneurysm, see 61700 et seq)

(For thoracic aortic aneurysm, see 33860-33875)

**35001** Direct repair of aneurysm, false aneurysm, or excision (partial or total) and graft insertion, with or without patch graft; for aneurysm and associated occlusive disease, carotid, subclavian artery, by neck incision

**35002** for ruptured aneurysm, carotid, subclavian artery, by neck incision

**35005** for aneurysm, false aneurysm, and associated occlusive disease, vertebral artery

**35011** for aneurysm and associated occlusive disease, axillary-brachial artery, by arm incision

**35013** for ruptured aneurysm, axillary-brachial artery, by arm incision

**35021** for aneurysm, false aneurysm, and associated occlusive disease, innominate, subclavian artery, by thoracic incision

**35022** for ruptured aneurysm, innominate, subclavian artery, by thoracic incision

**35045** for aneurysm, false aneurysm, and associated occlusive disease, radial or ulnar artery

**35081** for aneurysm, false aneurysm, and associated occlusive disease, abdominal aorta

**35082** for ruptured aneurysm, abdominal aorta

**35091** for aneurysm, false aneurysm, and associated occlusive disease, abdominal aorta involving visceral vessels (mesenteric, celiac, renal)

**35092** for ruptured aneurysm, abdominal aorta involving visceral vessels (mesenteric, celiac, renal)

**35102** for aneurysm, false aneurysm, and associated occlusive disease, abdominal aorta involving iliac vessels (common, hypogastric, external)

**35103** for ruptured aneurysm, abdominal aorta involving iliac vessels (common, hypogastric, external)

**35111** for aneurysm, false aneurysm, and associated occlusive disease, splenic artery

**35112** for ruptured aneurysm, splenic artery

**35121** for aneurysm, false aneurysm, and associated occlusive disease, hepatic, celiac, renal, or mesenteric artery

**35122** for ruptured aneurysm, hepatic, celiac, renal, or mesenteric artery

**35131** for aneurysm, false aneurysm, and associated occlusive disease, iliac artery (common, hypogastric, external)

**35132** for ruptured aneurysm, iliac artery (common, hypogastric, external)

**35141** for aneurysm, false aneurysm, and associated occlusive disease, common femoral artery (profunda femoris, superficial femoral)

**35142** for ruptured aneurysm, common femoral artery (profunda femoris, superficial femoral)

**35151** for aneurysm, false aneurysm, and associated occlusive disease, popliteal artery

**35152** for ruptured aneurysm, popliteal artery

**35161** for aneurysm, false aneurysm, and associated occlusive disease, other arteries

**35162** for ruptured aneurysm, other arteries

## Repair Arteriovenous Fistula

**35180** Repair, congenital arteriovenous fistula; head and neck

**35182** thorax and abdomen

**35184** extremities

**35188** Repair, acquired or traumatic arteriovenous fistula; head and neck

**35189** thorax and abdomen

**35190** extremities

## Repair Blood Vessel Other Than for Fistula, With or Without Patch Angioplasty

(For AV fistula repair, see 35180-35190)

**35201** Repair blood vessel, direct; neck

**35206** upper extremity

**35207** hand, finger

**35211** intrathoracic, with bypass

**35216** intrathoracic, without bypass

**35221** intra-abdominal

**35226** lower extremity

**35231** Repair blood vessel with vein graft; neck

**35236** upper extremity

**35241** intrathoracic, with bypass

**35246** intrathoracic, without bypass

**35251** intra-abdominal

**35256** lower extremity

**35261** Repair blood vessel with graft other than vein; neck

**35266** upper extremity

**35271** intrathoracic, with bypass

**35276** intrathoracic, without bypass

**35281** intra-abdominal

**35286** lower extremity

## Thromboendarterectomy

(For coronary artery, see 33510-33536 and 33572)

**35301** Thromboendarterectomy, with or without patch graft; carotid, vertebral, subclavian, by neck incision

**35311** subclavian, innominate, by thoracic incision

**35321** axillary-brachial

**35331** abdominal aorta

**35341** mesenteric, celiac, or renal

**35351** iliac

**35355** iliofemoral

**35361** combined aortoiliac

**35363** combined aortoiliofemoral

**35371** common femoral

**35372** deep (profunda) femoral

**35381** femoral and/or popliteal, and/or tibioperoneal

✚ **35390** Reoperation, carotid, thromboendarterectomy, more than one month after original operation (List separately in addition to code for primary procedure)

(Use 35390 in conjunction with code 35301)

## Angioscopy

✚ **35400** Angioscopy (non-coronary vessels or grafts) during therapeutic intervention (List separately in addition to code for primary procedure)

## Transluminal Angioplasty

If done as part of another operation, use modifier '-51' or use modifier '-52'.

(For radiological supervision and interpretation, see 75962-75968 and 75978)

### Open

**35450** Transluminal balloon angioplasty, open; renal or other visceral artery

**35452** aortic

**35454** iliac

**35456** femoral-popliteal

**35458** brachiocephalic trunk or branches, each vessel

**35459** tibioperoneal trunk and branches

**35460** venous

### Percutaneous

**35470** Transluminal balloon angioplasty, percutaneous; tibioperoneal trunk or branches, each vessel

**35471** renal or visceral artery

**35472** aortic

**35473** iliac

**35474** femoral-popliteal

**35475** brachiocephalic trunk or branches, each vessel

**35476** venous

(For radiological supervision and interpretation, use 75978)

## Transluminal Atherectomy

If done as part of another operation, use modifier '-51' or use modifier '-52'.

(For radiological supervision and interpretation, see 75992-75996)

### Open

**35480** Transluminal peripheral atherectomy, open; renal or other visceral artery

**35481** aortic

**35482** iliac

**35483** femoral-popliteal

**35484** brachiocephalic trunk or branches, each vessel

**35485** tibioperoneal trunk and branches

### Percutaneous

**35490** Transluminal peripheral atherectomy, percutaneous; renal or other visceral artery

**35491** aortic

**35492** iliac

**35493** femoral-popliteal

**35494** brachiocephalic trunk or branches, each vessel

**35495** tibioperoneal trunk and branches

## Bypass Graft

### Vein

**▲35500** Harvest of upper extremity vein, one segment, for lower extremity or coronary artery bypass procedure (List separately in addition to code for primary procedure)

(For harvest of more than one vein segment, see 35682, 35683)

**35501** Bypass graft, with vein; carotid

**35506** carotid-subclavian

**35507** subclavian-carotid

**35508** carotid-vertebral

**35509** carotid-carotid

**35511** subclavian-subclavian

**35515** subclavian-vertebral

**35516** subclavian-axillary

**35518** axillary-axillary

**35521** axillary-femoral

(For bypass graft performed with synthetic graft, use 35621)

**35526** aortosubclavian or carotid

(For bypass graft performed with synthetic graft, use 35626)

**35531** aortoceliac or aortomesenteric

**35533** axillary-femoral-femoral

(For bypass graft performed with synthetic graft, use 35654)

**35536** splenorenal

**35541** aortoiliac or bi-iliac

(For bypass graft performed with synthetic graft, use 35641)

**35546** aortofemoral or bifemoral

(For bypass graft performed with synthetic graft, use 35646)

**35548** aortoiliofemoral, unilateral

(For bypass graft performed with synthetic graft, use 37799)

**35549** aortoiliofemoral, bilateral

(For bypass graft performed with synthetic graft, use 37799)

**35551** aortofemoral-popliteal

**35556** femoral-popliteal

**35558** femoral-femoral

**35560** aortorenal

**35563** ilioiliac

**35565** iliofemoral

**35566** femoral-anterior tibial, posterior tibial, peroneal artery or other distal vessels

**35571** popliteal-tibial, -peroneal artery or other distal vessels

## In-Situ Vein

**35582** In-situ vein bypass; aortofemoral-popliteal (only femoral-popliteal portion in-situ)

**35583** femoral-popliteal

**35585** femoral-anterior tibial, posterior tibial, or peroneal artery

**35587** popliteal-tibial, peroneal

## Other Than Vein

**35601** Bypass graft, with other than vein; carotid

**35606** carotid-subclavian

**35612** subclavian-subclavian

**35616** subclavian-axillary

**35621** axillary-femoral

**35623** axillary-popliteal or -tibial

**35626** aortosubclavian or carotid

**35631** aortoceliac, aortomesenteric, aortorenal

**35636** splenorenal (splenic to renal arterial anastomosis)

(35637 has been deleted. To report, use 35691)

(35638 has been deleted. To report, use 35693)

**35641** aortoiliac or bi-iliac

**35642** carotid-vertebral

**35645** subclavian-vertebral

**35646** aortofemoral or bifemoral

**35650** axillary-axillary

**35651** aortofemoral-popliteal

**35654** axillary-femoral-femoral

**35656** femoral-popliteal

**35661** femoral-femoral

**35663** ilioiliac

**35665** iliofemoral

**35666** femoral-anterior tibial, posterior tibial, or peroneal artery

**35671** popliteal-tibial or -peroneal artery

## Composite Grafts

Codes 35682-35683 are used to report harvest and anastomosis of multiple vein segments from distant sites for use as arterial bypass graft conduits. These codes are intended for use when the two or more vein segments are harvested from a limb other than that undergoing bypass. Add-on codes 35682 and 35683 are reported in addition to bypass graft codes 35501-35587.

**+ 35681** Bypass graft; composite, prosthetic and vein (List separately in addition to code for primary procedure)

(Do not report 35681 in addition to 35682, 35683)

**+ 35682** autogenous composite, two segments of veins from two locations (List separately in addition to code for primary procedure)

(Do not report 35682 in addition to 35681, 35683)

**+ 35683** autogenous composite, three or more segments of vein from two or more locations (List separately in addition to code for primary procedure)

(Do not report 35683 in addition to 35681, 35682)

## Arterial Transposition

**35691** Transposition and/or reimplantation; vertebral to carotid artery

**35693** vertebral to subclavian artery

**35694** subclavian to carotid artery

**35695** carotid to subclavian artery

## Exploration►/Revision◄

**+ 35700** Reoperation, femoral-popliteal or femoral (popliteal)-anterior tibial, posterior tibial, peroneal artery or other distal vessels, more than one month after original operation (List separately in addition to code for primary procedure)

(Use 35700 in conjunction with codes 35556, 35566, 35571, 35583, 35585, 35587, 35656, 35666, 35671)

**35701** Exploration (not followed by surgical repair), with or without lysis of artery; carotid artery

**35721** femoral artery

**35741** popliteal artery

**35761** other vessels

**35800** Exploration for postoperative hemorrhage, thrombosis or infection; neck

**35820** chest

**35840** abdomen

**35860** extremity

**35870** Repair of graft-enteric fistula

**35875** Thrombectomy of arterial or venous graft (other than hemodialysis graft or fistula);

**35876** with revision of arterial or venous graft

(For thrombectomy of hemodialysis graft or fistula, see 36831, 36833)

(35880 has been deleted. To report, use 35875)

(35900 has been deleted. To report, see 35901-35907 and appropriate revascularization code)

►Codes 35879 and 35881 describe open revision of graft-threatening stenoses of lower extremity arterial bypass graft(s) (previously constructed with autogenous vein conduit) using vein patch angioplasty or segmental vein interposition techniques. For thrombectomy with revision of any non-coronary arterial or venous graft, including those of the lower extremity, (other than hemodialysis graft or fistula), use 35876. For direct repair (other than for fistula) of a lower extremity blood vessel (with or without patch angioplasty), use 35226. For repair (other than for fistula) of a lower extremity blood vessel using a vein graft, use 35256.◄

●35879 Revision, lower extremity arterial bypass, without thrombectomy, open; with vein patch angioplasty

●35881 with segmental vein interposition

35901 Excision of infected graft; neck

35903 extremity

35905 thorax

35907 abdomen

(35910 has been deleted. To report, see 35901-35907 and appropriate revascularization code)

## Vascular Injection Procedures

Listed services for injection procedures include necessary local anesthesia, introduction of needles or catheter, injection of contrast media with or without automatic power injection, and/or necessary pre- and postinjection care specifically related to the injection procedure.

Catheters, drugs, and contrast media are not included in the listed service for the injection procedures.

Selective vascular catheterization should be coded to include introduction and all lesser order selective catheterization used in the approach (eg, the description for a selective right middle cerebral artery catheterization includes the introduction and placement catheterization of the right common and internal carotid arteries).

Additional second and/or third order arterial catheterization within the same family of arteries or veins supplied by a single first order vessel should be expressed by 36012, 36218 or 36248.

Additional first order or higher catheterization in vascular families supplied by a first order vessel different from a previously selected and coded family should be separately coded using the conventions described above.

(For radiological supervision and interpretation, see **Radiology**)

(For injection procedures in conjunction with cardiac catheterization, see 93541-93545)

(For chemotherapy of malignant disease, see 96400-96549)

## Intravenous

An intracatheter is a sheathed combination of needle and short catheter.

36000* Introduction of needle or intracatheter, vein

(36001 has been deleted. To report, use 36000 with modifier '-50')

36005 Injection procedure for contrast venography (including introduction of needle or intracatheter)

36010 Introduction of catheter, superior or inferior vena cava

36011 Selective catheter placement, venous system; first order branch (eg, renal vein, jugular vein)

36012 second order, or more selective, branch (eg, left adrenal vein, petrosal sinus)

36013 Introduction of catheter, right heart or main pulmonary artery

36014 Selective catheter placement, left or right pulmonary artery

36015 Selective catheter placement, segmental or subsegmental pulmonary artery

(For insertion of flow directed catheter (eg, Swan-Ganz), use 93503)

(For venous catheterization for selective organ blood sampling, use 36500)

## Intra-Arterial—Intra-Aortic

(For radiological supervision and interpretation, see **Radiology**)

36100 Introduction of needle or intracatheter, carotid or vertebral artery

(36101 has been deleted. To report, use 36100 with modifier '-50')

**36120** Introduction of needle or intracatheter; retrograde brachial artery

**36140** extremity artery

**36145** arteriovenous shunt created for dialysis (cannula, fistula, or graft)

(For insertion of arteriovenous cannula, see 36810-36821)

**36160** Introduction of needle or intracatheter, aortic, translumbar

**36200** Introduction of catheter, aorta

(36210 has been deleted. To report, see 36215-36218)

**36215** Selective catheter placement, arterial system; each first order thoracic or brachiocephalic branch, within a vascular family

(For catheter placement for coronary angiography, use 93508)

**36216** initial second order thoracic or brachiocephalic branch, within a vascular family

**36217** initial third order or more selective thoracic or brachiocephalic branch, within a vascular family

**+ 36218** additional second order, third order, and beyond, thoracic or brachiocephalic branch, within a vascular family (List in addition to code for initial second or third order vessel as appropriate)

(Use 36218 in conjunction with codes 36216, 36217)

(For angiography, see 75600-75790)

(For angioplasty, see 35470-35475)

(For transcatheter therapies, see 37200-37208, 61624, 61626)

(36220 has been deleted. To report, see 36215-36218)

(36230 has been deleted. When coronary artery, arterial conduit (eg, internal mammary, inferior epigastric or free radial artery) or venous bypass graft angiography is performed in conjunction with cardiac catheterization, see the appropriate cardiac catheterization code(s) (93501-93556) in the **Medicine** section of *CPT.* When coronary artery, arterial coronary conduit or venous bypass graft angiography is performed without concomitant left heart cardiac catheterization, use 93508. When internal mammary artery angiography only is performed without a concomitant left heart cardiac catheterization, use 36216 or 36217 as appropriate.)

(36240 has been deleted. To report, use 36248)

**36245** Selective catheter placement, arterial system; each first order abdominal, pelvic, or lower extremity artery branch, within a vascular family

**36246** initial second order abdominal, pelvic, or lower extremity artery branch, within a vascular family

**36247** initial third order or more selective abdominal, pelvic, or lower extremity artery branch, within a vascular family

**+ 36248** additional second order, third order, and beyond, abdominal, pelvic, or lower extremity artery branch, within a vascular family (List in addition to code for initial second or third order vessel as appropriate)

(Use 36248 in conjunction with codes 36246, 36247)

(36250 has been deleted. To report, use 36248)

**36260** Insertion of implantable intra-arterial infusion pump (eg, for chemotherapy of liver)

**36261** Revision of implanted intra-arterial infusion pump

**36262** Removal of implanted intra-arterial infusion pump

**36299** Unlisted procedure, vascular injection

## Venous

Venipuncture, needle or catheter for diagnostic study or intravenous therapy, percutaneous.

**36400** Venipuncture, under age 3 years; femoral, jugular or sagittal sinus

**36405*** scalp vein

**36406** other vein

**36410*** Venipuncture, child over age 3 years or adult, necessitating physician's skill (separate procedure), for diagnostic or therapeutic purposes. Not to be used for routine venipuncture.

**36415*** Routine venipuncture or finger/heel/ear stick for collection of specimen(s)

**36420** Venipuncture, cutdown; under age 1 year

**36425** age 1 or over

**36430** Transfusion, blood or blood components

(36431 has been deleted)

**36440*** Push transfusion, blood, 2 years or under

**36450** Exchange transfusion, blood; newborn

**36455** other than newborn

**36460** Transfusion, intrauterine, fetal

(For radiological supervision and interpretation, use 76941)

**36468** Single or multiple injections of sclerosing solutions, spider veins (telangiectasia); limb or trunk

**36469** face

**36470*** Injection of sclerosing solution; single vein

**36471*** multiple veins, same leg

(36480 has been deleted. To report, use 36488 or 36489)

**36481** Percutaneous portal vein catheterization by any method

(36485 has been deleted. To report, use 36490 or 36491)

⊘ **36488*** Placement of central venous catheter (subclavian, jugular, or other vein) (eg, for central venous pressure, hyperalimentation, hemodialysis, or chemotherapy); percutaneous, age 2 years or under

⊘ **36489*** percutaneous, over age 2

⊘ **36490*** cutdown, age 2 years or under

⊘ **36491*** cutdown, over age 2

(For examination of patient and instruction to patient, review of prescription of fluids for long-term or permanent hyperalimentation, use **Evaluation and Management** codes for office or hospital inpatient category or follow-up inpatient consultation codes as appropriate)

**36493** Repositioning of previously placed central venous catheter under fluoroscopic guidance

(36495-36497 have been deleted. To report, see 36530-36535)

**36500** Venous catheterization for selective organ blood sampling

(For catheterization in superior or inferior vena cava, use 36010)

(For radiological supervision and interpretation, use 75893)

**36510*** Catheterization of umbilical vein for diagnosis or therapy, newborn

**36520** Therapeutic apheresis; plasma and/or cell exchange

● **36521** with extracorporeal affinity column adsorption and plasma reinfusion

**36522** Photopheresis, extracorporeal

**36530** Insertion of implantable intravenous infusion pump

**36531** Revision of implantable intravenous infusion pump

**36532** Removal of implantable intravenous infusion pump

**▲36533** Insertion of implantable venous access device, with or without subcutaneous reservoir

►(For removal, use 36535)◄

►(For refilling and maintenance of an implantable venous access device reservoir, use 96530)◄

**▲36534** Revision of implantable venous access device, and/or subcutaneous reservoir

►(For removal, use 36535)◄

**▲36535** Removal of implantable venous access device, and/or subcutaneous reservoir

►(Use 36535 in conjunction with codes 36533, 36534, as appropriate)◄

►(Do not use 36535 in conjunction with codes 36488-36491)◄

**●36550** Declotting by thrombolytic agent of implanted vascular access device or catheter

## Arterial

**36600*** Arterial puncture, withdrawal of blood for diagnosis

**⊘36620** Arterial catheterization or cannulation for sampling, monitoring or transfusion (separate procedure); percutaneous

**36625** cutdown

**36640** Arterial catheterization for prolonged infusion therapy (chemotherapy), cutdown

(See also 96420-96425)

(For arterial catheterization for occlusion therapy, see 75894)

**⊘36660*** Catheterization, umbilical artery, newborn, for diagnosis or therapy

## Intraosseous

**36680** Placement of needle for intraosseous infusion

## Intervascular Cannulization or Shunt

**36800** Insertion of cannula for hemodialysis, other purpose (separate procedure); vein to vein

**36810** arteriovenous, external (Scribner type)

**36815** arteriovenous, external revision, or closure

(36820 has been deleted. To report, use 36821)

**●36819** Arteriovenous anastomosis, open; by basilic vein transposition

**▲36821** direct, any site (eg, Cimino type) (separate procedure)

**36822** Insertion of cannula(s) for prolonged extracorporeal circulation for cardiopulmonary insufficiency (ECMO) (separate procedure)

(For maintenance of prolonged extracorporeal circulation, use 33960)

**36823** Insertion of arterial and venous cannula(s) for isolated extracorporeal circulation and regional chemotherapy perfusion to an extremity, with or without hyperthermia, with removal of cannula(s) and repair of arteriotomy and venotomy sites

**36825** Creation of arteriovenous fistula by other than direct arteriovenous anastomosis (separate procedure); autogenous graft

(For direct arteriovenous anastomosis, use 36821)

**36830** nonautogenous graft

(For direct arteriovenous anastomosis, use 36821)

**36831** Thrombectomy, arteriovenous fistula without revision, autogenous or nonautogenous dialysis graft (separate procedure)

**36832** Revision, arteriovenous fistula; without thrombectomy, autogenous or nonautogenous dialysis graft (separate procedure)

**36833** with thrombectomy, autogenous or nonautogenous dialysis graft (separate procedure)

**36834** Plastic repair of arteriovenous aneurysm (separate procedure)

**36835** Insertion of Thomas shunt (separate procedure)

(36840 has been deleted)

(36845 has been deleted)

**36860** External cannula declotting (separate procedure); without balloon catheter

**36861** with balloon catheter

## Portal Decompression Procedures

**37140** Venous anastomosis; portocaval

(For peritoneal-venous shunt, use 49425)

**37145** renoportal

**37160** caval-mesenteric

**37180** splenorenal, proximal

**37181** splenorenal, distal (selective decompression of esophagogastric varices, any technique)

(37190 has been ►deleted. To report, use 36834◄)

## Transcatheter Procedures

(For radiological supervision and interpretation, see **Radiology**)

**37195** Thrombolysis, cerebral, by intravenous infusion

**37200** Transcatheter biopsy

(For radiological supervision and interpretation, use 75970)

**37201** Transcatheter therapy, infusion for thrombolysis other than coronary

**37202** Transcatheter therapy, infusion other than for thrombolysis, any type (eg, spasmolytic, vasoconstrictive)

(For thrombolysis of coronary vessels, see 92975, 92977)

**37203** Transcatheter retrieval, percutaneous, of intravascular foreign body (eg, fractured venous or arterial catheter)

(For radiological supervision and interpretation, use 75961)

**37204** Transcatheter occlusion or embolization (eg, for tumor destruction, to achieve hemostasis, to occlude a vascular malformation), percutaneous, any method, non-central nervous system, non-head or neck

(See also 61624, 61626)

(For radiological supervision and interpretation, use 75894)

**37205** Transcatheter placement of an intravascular stent(s), (non-coronary vessel), percutaneous; initial vessel

**+ 37206** each additional vessel (List separately in addition to code for primary procedure)

(Use 37206 in conjunction with code 37205)

**37207** Transcatheter placement of an intravascular stent(s), (non-coronary vessel), open; initial vessel

**+ 37208** each additional vessel (List separately in addition to code for primary procedure)

(Use 37208 in conjunction with code 37207)

(For radiological supervision and interpretation, use 75960)

(For catheterizations, see 36215-36248)

(For transcatheter placement of intracoronary stent(s), see 92980, 92981)

**37209** Exchange of a previously placed arterial catheter during thrombolytic therapy

(For radiological supervision and interpretation, use 75900)

## Intravascular Ultrasound Services

Intravascular ultrasound services include all transducer manipulations and repositioning within the specific vessel being examined, both before and after therapeutic intervention (eg, stent placement).

Vascular access for intravascular ultrasound performed during a therapeutic intervention is not reported separately.

+▲**37250** Intravascular ultrasound (non-coronary vessel) during diagnostic evaluation and/or therapeutic intervention; initial vessel (List separately in addition to code for primary procedure)

+**37251** each additional vessel (List separately in addition to code for primary procedure)

(Use 37251 in conjunction with code 37250)

(For catheterizations, see 36215-36248)

(For transcatheter therapies, see 37200-37208, 61624, 61626)

(For radiological supervision and interpretation see 75945, 75946)

## Ligation and Other Procedures

(37400-37560 have been deleted. To report, see 35201-35286)

**37565** Ligation, internal jugular vein

**37600** Ligation; external carotid artery

**37605** internal or common carotid artery

**37606** internal or common carotid artery, with gradual occlusion, as with Selverstone or Crutchfield clamp

(For ligation treatment of intracranial aneurysm, use 61703)

**37607** Ligation or banding of angioaccess arteriovenous fistula

**37609** Ligation or biopsy, temporal artery

**37615** Ligation, major artery (eg, post-traumatic, rupture); neck

**37616** chest

**37617** abdomen

**37618** extremity

**37620** Interruption, partial or complete, of inferior vena cava by suture, ligation, plication, clip, extravascular, intravascular (umbrella device)

(For radiological supervision and interpretation, use 75940)

**37650** Ligation of femoral vein

(37651 has been deleted. To report, use 37650 with modifier '-50')

**37660** Ligation of common iliac vein

**37700** Ligation and division of long saphenous vein at saphenofemoral junction, or distal interruptions

(37701 has been deleted. To report, use 37700 with modifier '-50')

**37720** Ligation and division and complete stripping of long or short saphenous veins

(37721 has been deleted. To report, use 37720 with modifier '-50')

**37730** Ligation and division and complete stripping of long and short saphenous veins

(37731 has been deleted. To report, use 37730 with modifier '-50')

**37735** Ligation and division and complete stripping of long or short saphenous veins with radical excision of ulcer and skin graft and/or interruption of communicating veins of lower leg, with excision of deep fascia

(37737 has been deleted. To report, use 37735 with modifier '-50')

**37760** Ligation of perforators, subfascial, radical (Linton type), with or without skin graft

**37780** Ligation and division of short saphenous vein at saphenopopliteal junction (separate procedure)

(37781 has been deleted. To report, use 37780 with modifier '-50')

**37785** Ligation, division, and/or excision of recurrent or secondary varicose veins (clusters), one leg

(37787 has been deleted. To report, use 37785 with modifier '-50')

**37788** Penile revascularization, artery, with or without vein graft

**37790** Penile venous occlusive procedure

**37799** Unlisted procedure, vascular surgery

# Hemic and Lymphatic Systems

## Spleen

### Excision

(38090 has been deleted. To report, use 38999)

**38100** Splenectomy; total (separate procedure)

**38101** partial (separate procedure)

**+ 38102** total, en bloc for extensive disease, in conjunction with other procedure (List in addition to code for primary procedure)

### Repair

**38115** Repair of ruptured spleen (splenorrhaphy) with or without partial splenectomy

### ►Laparoscopy◄

►Surgical laparoscopy always includes diagnostic laparoscopy. To report a diagnostic laparoscopy (peritoneoscopy) (separate procedure), use 49320.◄

**●38120** Laparoscopy, surgical, splenectomy

**●38129** Unlisted laparoscopy procedure, spleen

### Introduction

**38200** Injection procedure for splenoportography

(For radiological supervision and interpretation, use 75810)

## Bone Marrow or Stem Cell Transplantation Services

**38230** Bone marrow harvesting for transplantation

**38231** Blood-derived peripheral stem cell harvesting for transplantation, per collection

**38240** Bone marrow or blood-derived peripheral stem cell transplantation; allogenic

**38241** autologous

(For bone marrow aspiration, use 85095)

(For modification, treatment, and processing of bone marrow ►or blood-derived stem cell◄ specimens for transplantation, use 86915)

(For cryopreservation, freezing and storage of blood-derived stem cells for transplantation, use 88240)

(For thawing and expansion of blood-derived stem cells for transplantation, use 88241)

(For compatibility studies, see 86812-86822)

## Lymph Nodes and Lymphatic Channels

### Incision

**38300*** Drainage of lymph node abscess or lymphadenitis; simple

**38305** extensive

**38308** Lymphangiotomy or other operations on lymphatic channels

**38380** Suture and/or ligation of thoracic duct; cervical approach

**38381** thoracic approach

**38382** abdominal approach

## Excision

(For injection for sentinel node identification, use 38792)

**38500** Biopsy or excision of lymph node(s); superficial (separate procedure)

**38505** by needle, superficial (eg, cervical, inguinal, axillary)

(For fine needle aspiration, use 88170)

**38510** deep cervical node(s)

**38520** deep cervical node(s) with excision scalene fat pad

**38525** deep axillary node(s)

**38530** internal mammary node(s) (separate procedure)

(For percutaneous needle biopsy, retroperitoneal lymph node or mass, use 49180; for fine needle aspiration, use 88171)

(38540 has been deleted. To report, see 38510, 38520)

**38542** Dissection, deep jugular node(s)

(For radical cervical neck dissection, use 38720)

**38550** Excision of cystic hygroma, axillary or cervical; without deep neurovascular dissection

**38555** with deep neurovascular dissection

## Limited Lymphadenectomy for Staging

**38562** Limited lymphadenectomy for staging (separate procedure); pelvic and para-aortic

(When combined with prostatectomy, use 55812 or 55842)

(When combined with insertion of radioactive substance into prostate, use 55862)

**38564** retroperitoneal (aortic and/or splenic)

## ►Laparoscopy◄

►Surgical laparoscopy always includes diagnostic laparoscopy. To report a diagnostic laparoscopy (peritoneoscopy) (separate procedure), use 49320.◄

●**38570** Laparoscopy, surgical; with retroperitoneal lymph node sampling (biopsy), single or multiple

●**38571** with bilateral total pelvic lymphadenectomy

●**38572** with bilateral total pelvic lymphadenectomy and peri-aortic lymph node sampling (biopsy), single or multiple

►(For drainage of lymphocele to peritoneal cavity, use 49323)◄

●**38589** Unlisted laparoscopy procedure, lymphatic system

## Radical Lymphadenectomy (Radical Resection of Lymph Nodes)

(For limited pelvic and retroperitoneal lymphadenectomies, see 38562, 38564)

**38700** Suprahyoid lymphadenectomy

(38701 has been deleted. To report, use 38700 with modifier '-50')

**38720** Cervical lymphadenectomy (complete)

(38721 has been deleted. To report, use 38720 with modifier '-50')

**38724** Cervical lymphadenectomy (modified radical neck dissection)

**38740** Axillary lymphadenectomy; superficial

**38745** complete

+ **38746** Thoracic lymphadenectomy, regional, including mediastinal and peritracheal nodes (List separately in addition to code for primary procedure)

+ **38747** Abdominal lymphadenectomy, regional, including celiac, gastric, portal, peripancreatic, with or without para-aortic and vena caval nodes (List separately in addition to code for primary procedure)

**38760** Inguinofemoral lymphadenectomy, superficial, including Cloquets node (separate procedure)

(38761 has been deleted. To report, use 38760 with modifier '-50')

**38765** Inguinofemoral lymphadenectomy, superficial, in continuity with pelvic lymphadenectomy, including external iliac, hypogastric, and obturator nodes (separate procedure)

(38766 has been deleted. To report, use 38765 with modifier '-50')

**38770** Pelvic lymphadenectomy, including external iliac, hypogastric, and obturator nodes (separate procedure)

(38771 has been deleted. To report, use 38770 with modifier '-50')

**38780** Retroperitoneal transabdominal lymphadenectomy, extensive, including pelvic, aortic, and renal nodes (separate procedure)

(For excision and repair of lymphedematous skin and subcutaneous tissue, see 15000, 15570-15650)

### Introduction

**38790** Injection procedure; lymphangiography

(For radiological supervision and interpretation, see 75801-75807)

(38791 has been deleted. To report, use 38790 with modifier '-50')

⊘ **38792** for identification of sentinel node

(For excision of sentinel node, see 38500-38542)

(For nuclear medicine lymphatics and lymph gland imaging, use 78195)

**38794** Cannulation, thoracic duct

### Other Procedures

**38999** Unlisted procedure, hemic or lymphatic system

# Mediastinum and Diaphragm

## Mediastinum

### Incision

**39000** Mediastinotomy with exploration, drainage, removal of foreign body, or biopsy; cervical approach

**39010** transthoracic approach, including either transthoracic or median sternotomy

(39020 has been deleted. To report, use 39010)

(39050-39070 have been deleted. To report, see 39000-39010)

### Excision

**39200** Excision of mediastinal cyst

**39220** Excision of mediastinal tumor

(For substernal thyroidectomy, use 60270)

(For thymectomy, use 60520)

### Endoscopy

**39400** Mediastinoscopy, with or without biopsy

### Other Procedures

**39499** Unlisted procedure, mediastinum

## Diaphragm

### Repair

(39500 has been deleted. To report, see 43324, 43325)

**39501** Repair, laceration of diaphragm, any approach

**39502** Repair, paraesophageal hiatus hernia, transabdominal, with or without fundoplasty, vagotomy, and/or pyloroplasty, except neonatal

**39503** Repair, neonatal diaphragmatic hernia, with or without chest tube insertion and with or without creation of ventral hernia

(39510 has been deleted. To report, see 43324, 43325)

**39520** Repair, diaphragmatic hernia (esophageal hiatal); transthoracic

**39530** combined, thoracoabdominal

**39531** combined, thoracoabdominal, with dilation of stricture (with or without gastroplasty)

**39540** Repair, diaphragmatic hernia (other than neonatal), traumatic; acute

**39541** chronic

**39545** Imbrication of diaphragm for eventration, transthoracic or transabdominal, paralytic or nonparalytic

(39547 has been deleted. To report, use 39545)

●**39560** Resection, diaphragm; with simple repair (eg, primary suture)

●**39561** with complex repair (eg, prosthetic material, local muscle flap)

## Other Procedures

**39599** Unlisted procedure, diaphragm

# Notes

# Digestive System

## Lips

(For procedures on skin of lips, see 10040 et seq)

### Excision

**40490** Biopsy of lip

**40500** Vermilionectomy (lip shave), with mucosal advancement

**40510** Excision of lip; transverse wedge excision with primary closure

**40520** V-excision with primary direct linear closure

(For excision of mucous lesions, see 40810-40816)

**40525** full thickness, reconstruction with local flap (eg, Estlander or fan)

**40527** full thickness, reconstruction with cross lip flap (Abbe-Estlander)

**40530** Resection of lip, more than one-fourth, without reconstruction

(For reconstruction, see 13131 et seq)

### Repair (Cheiloplasty)

**40650** Repair lip, full thickness; vermilion only

**40652** up to half vertical height

**40654** over one-half vertical height, or complex

**40700** Plastic repair of cleft lip/nasal deformity; primary, partial or complete, unilateral

**40701** primary bilateral, one stage procedure

**40702** primary bilateral, one of two stages

**40720** secondary, by recreation of defect and reclosure

(To report rhinoplasty only for nasal deformity secondary to congenital cleft lip, see 30460, 30462)

(40740 has been deleted. To report, use 40720 with modifier '-50')

(40760 has been deleted. To report, use 40527)

**40761** with cross lip pedicle flap (Abbe-Estlander type), including sectioning and inserting of pedicle

(For repair cleft palate, see 42200 et seq)

(For other reconstructive procedures, see 14060, 14061, 15120-15261, 15574, 15576, 15630)

### Other Procedures

**40799** Unlisted procedure, lips

## Vestibule of Mouth

The vestibule is the part of the oral cavity outside the dentoalveolar structures; it includes the mucosal and submucosal tissue of lips and cheeks.

### Incision

**40800*** Drainage of abscess, cyst, hematoma, vestibule of mouth; simple

**40801** complicated

**40804*** Removal of embedded foreign body, vestibule of mouth; simple

**40805** complicated

**40806** Incision of labial frenum (frenotomy)

### Excision, Destruction

**40808** Biopsy, vestibule of mouth

**40810** Excision of lesion of mucosa and submucosa, vestibule of mouth; without repair

**40812** with simple repair

**40814** with complex repair

**40816** complex, with excision of underlying muscle

**40818** Excision of mucosa of vestibule of mouth as donor graft

**40819** Excision of frenum, labial or buccal (frenumectomy, frenulectomy, frenectomy)

**40820** Destruction of lesion or scar of vestibule of mouth by physical methods (eg, laser, thermal, cryo, chemical)

## Repair

**40830** Closure of laceration, vestibule of mouth; 2.5 cm or less

**40831** over 2.5 cm or complex

**40840** Vestibuloplasty; anterior

**40842** posterior, unilateral

**40843** posterior, bilateral

**40844** entire arch

**40845** complex (including ridge extension, muscle repositioning)

(For skin grafts, see 15000 et seq)

## Other Procedures

**40899** Unlisted procedure, vestibule of mouth

# Tongue and Floor of Mouth

## Incision

**41000*** Intraoral incision and drainage of abscess, cyst, or hematoma of tongue or floor of mouth; lingual

**41005*** sublingual, superficial

**41006** sublingual, deep, supramylohyoid

**41007** submental space

**41008** submandibular space

**41009** masticator space

**41010** Incision of lingual frenum (frenotomy)

**41015** Extraoral incision and drainage of abscess, cyst, or hematoma of floor of mouth; sublingual

**41016** submental

**41017** submandibular

**41018** masticator space

(For frenoplasty, use 41520)

## Excision

**41100** Biopsy of tongue; anterior two-thirds

**41105** posterior one-third

**41108** Biopsy of floor of mouth

**41110** Excision of lesion of tongue without closure

**41112** Excision of lesion of tongue with closure; anterior two-thirds

**41113** posterior one-third

**41114** with local tongue flap

(List 41114 in addition to code 41112 or 41113)

**41115** Excision of lingual frenum (frenectomy)

**41116** Excision, lesion of floor of mouth

**41120** Glossectomy; less than one-half tongue

**41130** hemiglossectomy

**41135** partial, with unilateral radical neck dissection

**41140** complete or total, with or without tracheostomy, without radical neck dissection

**41145** complete or total, with or without tracheostomy, with unilateral radical neck dissection

**41150** composite procedure with resection floor of mouth and mandibular resection, without radical neck dissection

**41153** composite procedure with resection floor of mouth, with suprahyoid neck dissection

**41155** composite procedure with resection floor of mouth, mandibular resection, and radical neck dissection (Commando type)

### Repair

**41250*** Repair of laceration 2.5 cm or less; floor of mouth and/or anterior two-thirds of tongue

**41251*** posterior one-third of tongue

**41252*** Repair of laceration of tongue, floor of mouth, over 2.6 cm or complex

### Other Procedures

**41500** Fixation of tongue, mechanical, other than suture (eg, K-wire)

**41510** Suture of tongue to lip for micrognathia (Douglas type procedure)

**41520** Frenoplasty (surgical revision of frenum, eg, with Z-plasty)

(For frenotomy, see 40806, 41010)

**41599** Unlisted procedure, tongue, floor of mouth

## Dentoalveolar Structures

### Incision

**41800*** Drainage of abscess, cyst, hematoma from dentoalveolar structures

**41805** Removal of embedded foreign body from dentoalveolar structures; soft tissues

**41806** bone

### Excision, Destruction

**41820** Gingivectomy, excision gingiva, each quadrant

**41821** Operculectomy, excision pericoronal tissues

**41822** Excision of fibrous tuberosities, dentoalveolar structures

**41823** Excision of osseous tuberosities, dentoalveolar structures

**41825** Excision of lesion or tumor (except listed above), dentoalveolar structures; without repair

**41826** with simple repair

**41827** with complex repair

(For nonexcisional destruction, use 41850)

**41828** Excision of hyperplastic alveolar mucosa, each quadrant (specify)

**41830** Alveolectomy, including curettage of osteitis or sequestrectomy

**41850** Destruction of lesion (except excision), dentoalveolar structures

### Other Procedures

**41870** Periodontal mucosal grafting

**41872** Gingivoplasty, each quadrant (specify)

**41874** Alveoloplasty, each quadrant (specify)

(For closure of lacerations, see 40830, 40831)

(For segmental osteotomy, use 21206)

(For reduction of fractures, see 21421-21490)

**41899** Unlisted procedure, dentoalveolar structures

## Palate and Uvula

### Incision

**42000*** Drainage of abscess of palate, uvula

### Excision, Destruction

**42100** Biopsy of palate, uvula

**42104** Excision, lesion of palate, uvula; without closure

**42106** with simple primary closure

**42107** with local flap closure

(For skin graft, see 14040-14300)

(For mucosal graft, use 40818)

**42120** Resection of palate or extensive resection of lesion

(For reconstruction of palate with extraoral tissue, see 14040-14300, 15050, 15120, 15240, 15576)

**42140** Uvulectomy, excision of uvula

**42145** Palatopharyngoplasty (eg, uvulopalatopharyngoplasty, uvulopharyngoplasty)

(42150 has been deleted. To report, see 21031, 21032)

**42160** Destruction of lesion, palate or uvula (thermal, cryo or chemical)

## Repair

**42180** Repair, laceration of palate; up to 2 cm

**42182** over 2 cm or complex

**42200** Palatoplasty for cleft palate, soft and/or hard palate only

**42205** Palatoplasty for cleft palate, with closure of alveolar ridge; soft tissue only

**42210** with bone graft to alveolar ridge (includes obtaining graft)

**42215** Palatoplasty for cleft palate; major revision

**42220** secondary lengthening procedure

**42225** attachment pharyngeal flap

**42226** Lengthening of palate, and pharyngeal flap

**42227** Lengthening of palate, with island flap

**42235** Repair of anterior palate, including vomer flap

(42250 has been deleted. To report, use 30600)

**42260** Repair of nasolabial fistula

(For repair of cleft lip, see 40700 et seq)

**42280** Maxillary impression for palatal prosthesis

**42281** Insertion of pin-retained palatal prosthesis

## Other Procedures

**42299** Unlisted procedure, palate, uvula

# Salivary Gland and Ducts

## Incision

**42300*** Drainage of abscess; parotid, simple

**42305** parotid, complicated

**42310*** Drainage of abscess; submaxillary or sublingual, intraoral

**42320*** submaxillary, external

**42325** Fistulization of sublingual salivary cyst (ranula);

**42326** with prosthesis

**42330** Sialolithotomy; submandibular (submaxillary), sublingual or parotid, uncomplicated, intraoral

**42335** submandibular (submaxillary), complicated, intraoral

**42340** parotid, extraoral or complicated intraoral

## Excision

**42400*** Biopsy of salivary gland; needle

**42405** incisional

**42408** Excision of sublingual salivary cyst (ranula)

**42409** Marsupialization of sublingual salivary cyst (ranula)

(For fistulization of sublingual salivary cyst, use 42325)

**42410** Excision of parotid tumor or parotid gland; lateral lobe, without nerve dissection

**42415** lateral lobe, with dissection and preservation of facial nerve

**42420** total, with dissection and preservation of facial nerve

**42425** total, en bloc removal with sacrifice of facial nerve

**42426** total, with unilateral radical neck dissection

(For suture or grafting of facial nerve, see 64864, 64865, 69740, 69745)

**42440** Excision of submandibular (submaxillary) gland

**42450** Excision of sublingual gland

## Repair

**42500** Plastic repair of salivary duct, sialodochoplasty; primary or simple

**42505** secondary or complicated

**42507** Parotid duct diversion, bilateral (Wilke type procedure);

**42508** with excision of one submandibular gland

**42509** with excision of both submandibular glands

**42510** with ligation of both submandibular (Wharton's) ducts

## Other Procedures

**42550** Injection procedure for sialography

(For radiological supervision and interpretation, use 70390)

**42600** Closure salivary fistula

**42650*** Dilation salivary duct

**42660*** Dilation and catheterization of salivary duct, with or without injection

**42665** Ligation salivary duct, intraoral

**42699** Unlisted procedure, salivary glands or ducts

# Pharynx, Adenoids, and Tonsils

## Incision

**42700*** Incision and drainage abscess; peritonsillar

**42720** retropharyngeal or parapharyngeal, intraoral approach

**42725** retropharyngeal or parapharyngeal, external approach

## Excision, Destruction

**42800** Biopsy; oropharynx

**42802** hypopharynx

**42804** nasopharynx, visible lesion, simple

**42806** nasopharynx, survey for unknown primary lesion

(For laryngoscopic biopsy, see 31510, 31535, 31536)

**42808** Excision or destruction of lesion of pharynx, any method

**42809** Removal of foreign body from pharynx

**42810** Excision branchial cleft cyst or vestige, confined to skin and subcutaneous tissues

**42815** Excision branchial cleft cyst, vestige, or fistula, extending beneath subcutaneous tissues and/or into pharynx

**42820** Tonsillectomy and adenoidectomy; under age 12

**42821** age 12 or over

**42825** Tonsillectomy, primary or secondary; under age 12

**42826** age 12 or over

**42830** Adenoidectomy, primary; under age 12

**42831** age 12 or over

**42835** Adenoidectomy, secondary; under age 12

**42836** age 12 or over

**42842** Radical resection of tonsil, tonsillar pillars, and/or retromolar trigone; without closure

**42844** closure with local flap (eg, tongue, buccal)

**42845** closure with other flap

(For closure with other flap(s), use appropriate number for flap(s))

(When combined with radical neck dissection, use also 38720)

**42860** Excision of tonsil tags

**42870** Excision or destruction lingual tonsil, any method (separate procedure)

(42880 has been deleted. For resection of the nasopharynx (eg, juvenile angiofibroma) by bicoronal and/or transzygomatic approach, see 61586 and 61600)

**42890** Limited pharyngectomy

**42892** Resection of lateral pharyngeal wall or pyriform sinus, direct closure by advancement of lateral and posterior pharyngeal walls

(When combined with radical neck dissection, use also 38720)

**42894** Resection of pharyngeal wall requiring closure with myocutaneous flap

(When combined with radical neck dissection, use also 38720)

(42895 has been deleted. To report, use 38720 with 42890)

## Repair

**42900** Suture pharynx for wound or injury

**42950** Pharyngoplasty (plastic or reconstructive operation on pharynx)

(For pharyngeal flap, use 42225)

**42953** Pharyngoesophageal repair

(For closure with myocutaneous or other flap, use appropriate number in addition)

## Other Procedures

**42955** Pharyngostomy (fistulization of pharynx, external for feeding)

**42960** Control oropharyngeal hemorrhage, primary or secondary (eg, post-tonsillectomy); simple

**42961** complicated, requiring hospitalization

**42962** with secondary surgical intervention

**42970** Control of nasopharyngeal hemorrhage, primary or secondary (eg, postadenoidectomy); simple, with posterior nasal packs, with or without anterior packs and/or cauterization

**42971** complicated, requiring hospitalization

**42972** with secondary surgical intervention

**42999** Unlisted procedure, pharynx, adenoids, or tonsils

# Esophagus

## Incision

(For esophageal intubation with laparotomy, use 43510)

(43000 has been deleted)

**43020** Esophagotomy, cervical approach, with removal of foreign body

**43030** Cricopharyngeal myotomy

(43040 has been deleted)

**43045** Esophagotomy, thoracic approach, with removal of foreign body

## Excision

(For gastrointestinal reconstruction for previous esophagectomy, see 43360, 43361)

**43100** Excision of lesion, esophagus, with primary repair; cervical approach

**43101** thoracic or abdominal approach

(43105 has been deleted. To report, see 43107, 43116, 43124, and 31360)

(43106 has been deleted. To report, see 43107, 43116, 43124, and 31365)

**43107** Total or near total esophagectomy, without thoracotomy; with pharyngogastrostomy or cervical esophagogastrostomy, with or without pyloroplasty (transhiatal)

**43108** with colon interposition or small bowel reconstruction, including bowel mobilization, preparation and anastomosis(es)

(43110 has been deleted. To report, see 43107-43113)

(43111 has been deleted. To report, see 43107-43113)

**43112** Total or near total esophagectomy, with thoracotomy; with pharyngogastrostomy or cervical esophagogastrostomy, with or without pyloroplasty

**43113** with colon interposition or small bowel reconstruction, including bowel mobilization, preparation, and anastomosis(es)

(43115 has been deleted. To report, see 43116-43118)

**43116** Partial esophagectomy, cervical, with free intestinal graft, including microvascular anastomosis, obtaining the graft and intestinal reconstruction

(Do not report code 69990 in addition to code 43116)

(Report 43116 with the modifier '-52' appended if intestinal or free jejunal graft with microvascular anastomosis is performed by another physician)

(For free jejunal graft with microvascular anastomosis performed by another physician, use 43496)

**43117** Partial esophagectomy, distal two-thirds, with thoracotomy and separate abdominal incision, with or without proximal gastrectomy; with thoracic esophagogastrostomy, with or without pyloroplasty (Ivor Lewis)

**43118** with colon interposition or small bowel reconstruction, including bowel mobilization, preparation, and anastomosis(es)

(43119 has been deleted. To report, see 43107, 43124)

(43120 has been deleted. To report, use 43122)

**43121** Partial esophagectomy, distal two-thirds, with thoracotomy only, with or without proximal gastrectomy, with thoracic esophagogastrostomy, with or without pyloroplasty

**43122** Partial esophagectomy, thoracoabdominal or abdominal approach, with or without proximal gastrectomy; with esophagogastrostomy, with or without pyloroplasty

**43123** with colon interposition or small bowel reconstruction, including bowel mobilization, preparation, and anastomosis(es)

**43124** Total or partial esophagectomy, without reconstruction (any approach), with cervical esophagostomy

**43130** Diverticulectomy of hypopharynx or esophagus, with or without myotomy; cervical approach

**43135** thoracic approach

(43136 has been deleted. To report, use 43499)

## Endoscopy

For endoscopic procedures, code appropriate endoscopy of each anatomic site examined.

Surgical endoscopy always includes diagnostic endoscopy.

**43200** Esophagoscopy, rigid or flexible; diagnostic, with or without collection of specimen(s) by brushing or washing (separate procedure)

**43202** with biopsy, single or multiple

**43204** with injection sclerosis of esophageal varices

**43205** with band ligation of esophageal varices

**43215** with removal of foreign body

(For radiological supervision and interpretation, use 74235)

**43216** with removal of tumor(s), polyp(s), or other lesion(s) by hot biopsy forceps or bipolar cautery

**43217** with removal of tumor(s), polyp(s), or other lesion(s) by snare technique

(43218 has been deleted. To report, use 43499)

**43219** with insertion of plastic tube or stent

**43220** with balloon dilation (less than 30 mm diameter)

(For endoscopic dilation with balloon 30 mm diameter or larger, use 43458)

(For dilation without visualization, see 43450-43453)

(43221 has been deleted. To report, use 43200 or 43235)

(43222 has been deleted. To report, use 43200, 43202, 43235, or 43239)

(43223 has been deleted. To report, use 43215 or 43247)

(43224 has been deleted. To report, use 43217 or 43251)

(43225 has been deleted. To report, use 43499)

**43226** with insertion of guide wire followed by dilation over guide wire

(For radiological supervision and interpretation, use 74360)

**43227** with control of bleeding, any method

**43228** with ablation of tumor(s), polyp(s), or other lesion(s), not amenable to removal by hot biopsy forceps, bipolar cautery or snare technique

►(For esophagoscopic photodynamic therapy, report 43228 in addition to 96570, 96571 as appropriate)◄

**43234** Upper gastrointestinal endoscopy, simple primary examination (eg, with small diameter flexible endoscope) (separate procedure)

**43235** Upper gastrointestinal endoscopy including esophagus, stomach, and either the duodenum and/or jejunum as appropriate; diagnostic, with or without collection of specimen(s) by brushing or washing (separate procedure)

**43239** with biopsy, single or multiple

**43241** with transendoscopic tube or catheter placement

**43243** with injection sclerosis of esophageal and/or gastric varices

**43244** with band ligation of esophageal and/or gastric varices

**43245** with dilation of gastric outlet for obstruction, any method

**43246** with directed placement of percutaneous gastrostomy tube

(For radiological supervision and interpretation, use 74350)

**43247** with removal of foreign body

(For radiological supervision and interpretation, use 74235)

**43248** with insertion of guide wire followed by dilation of esophagus over guide wire

**43249** with balloon dilation of esophagus (less than 30 mm diameter)

**43250** with removal of tumor(s), polyp(s), or other lesion(s) by hot biopsy forceps or bipolar cautery

**43251** with removal of tumor(s), polyp(s), or other lesion(s) by snare technique

**43255** with control of bleeding, any method

**43258** with ablation of tumor(s), polyp(s), or other lesion(s) not amenable to removal by hot biopsy forceps, bipolar cautery or snare technique

(For injection sclerosis of esophageal varices, use 43204 or 43243)

**43259** with endoscopic ultrasound examination

(For radiological supervision and interpretation, use 76975)

(Surgical endoscopy always includes diagnostic endoscopy)

**43260** Endoscopic retrograde cholangiopancreatography (ERCP); diagnostic, with or without collection of specimen(s) by brushing or washing (separate procedure)

(For radiological supervision and interpretation, see 74328, 74329, 74330)

**43261** with biopsy, single or multiple

**43262** with sphincterotomy/papillotomy

(For radiological supervision and interpretation, see 74328, 74329, 74330)

**43263** with pressure measurement of sphincter of Oddi (pancreatic duct or common bile duct)

(For radiological supervision and interpretation, see 74328, 74329, 74330)

**43264** with endoscopic retrograde removal of stone(s) from biliary and/or pancreatic ducts

(When done with sphincterotomy, also use 43262)

(For radiological supervision and interpretation, see 74328, 74329, 74330)

**43265** with endoscopic retrograde destruction, lithotripsy of stone(s), any method

(When done with sphincterotomy, also use 43262)

(For radiological supervision and interpretation, see 74328, 74329, 74330)

**43267** with endoscopic retrograde insertion of nasobiliary or nasopancreatic drainage tube

(When done with sphincterotomy, also use 43262)

(For radiological supervision and interpretation, see 74328, 74329, 74330)

**43268** with endoscopic retrograde insertion of tube or stent into bile or pancreatic duct

(When done with sphincterotomy, also use 43262)

(For radiological supervision and interpretation, see 74328, 74329, 74330)

**43269** with endoscopic retrograde removal of foreign body and/or change of tube or stent

(When done with sphincterotomy, also use 43262)

(For radiological supervision and interpretation, see 74328, 74329, 74330)

**43271** with endoscopic retrograde balloon dilation of ampulla, biliary and/or pancreatic duct(s)

(When done with sphincterotomy, also use 43262)

(For radiological supervision and interpretation, see 74328, 74329, 74330)

**43272** with ablation of tumor(s), polyp(s), or other lesion(s) not amenable to removal by hot biopsy forceps, bipolar cautery or snare technique

(For radiological supervision and interpretation, see 74328, 74329, 74330)

## ►Laparoscopy◄

►Surgical laparoscopy always includes diagnostic laparoscopy. To report a diagnostic laparoscopy (peritoneoscopy) (separate procedure), use 49320.◄

●**43280** Laparoscopy, surgical, esophagogastric fundoplasty (eg, Nissen, Toupet procedures)

►(For open approach, use 43324)◄

●**43289** Unlisted laparoscopy procedure, esophagus

## Repair

**43300** Esophagoplasty, (plastic repair or reconstruction), cervical approach; without repair of tracheoesophageal fistula

**43305** with repair of tracheoesophageal fistula

**43310** Esophagoplasty, (plastic repair or reconstruction), thoracic approach; without repair of tracheoesophageal fistula

**43312** with repair of tracheoesophageal fistula

**43320** Esophagogastrostomy (cardioplasty), with or without vagotomy and pyloroplasty, transabdominal or transthoracic approach

(43321 has been deleted. To report, use 43320)

**43324** Esophagogastric fundoplasty (eg, Nissen, Belsey IV, Hill procedures)

►(For laparoscopic procedure, use 43280)◄

**43325** Esophagogastric fundoplasty; with fundic patch (Thal-Nissen procedure)

(For cricopharyngeal myotomy, use 43030)

**43326** with gastroplasty (eg, Collis)

**43330** Esophagomyotomy (Heller type); abdominal approach

**43331** thoracic approach

►(For thoracoscopic esophagomyotomy, use 32665)◄

**43340** Esophagojejunostomy (without total gastrectomy); abdominal approach

**43341** thoracic approach

**43350** Esophagostomy, fistulization of esophagus, external; abdominal approach

**43351** thoracic approach

**43352** cervical approach

**43360** Gastrointestinal reconstruction for previous esophagectomy, for obstructing esophageal lesion or fistula, or for previous esophageal exclusion; with stomach, with or without pyloroplasty

**43361** with colon interposition or small bowel reconstruction, including bowel mobilization, preparation, and anastomosis(es)

**43400** Ligation, direct, esophageal varices

**43401** Transection of esophagus with repair, for esophageal varices

**43405** Ligation or stapling at gastroesophageal junction for pre-existing esophageal perforation

**43410** Suture of esophageal wound or injury; cervical approach

**43415** transthoracic or transabdominal approach

**43420** Closure of esophagostomy or fistula; cervical approach

**43425** transthoracic or transabdominal approach

(For repair of esophageal hiatal hernia, see 39520 et seq)

## Manipulation

(For associated esophagogram, use 74220)

**43450*** Dilation of esophagus, by unguided sound or bougie, single or multiple passes

(43451 has been deleted. To report, use 43450)

**43453** Dilation of esophagus, over guide wire

(For dilation with direct visualization, use 43220)

(43455 has been deleted. To report, see 43220, 43458, 74360)

**43456** Dilation of esophagus, by balloon or dilator, retrograde

**43458** Dilation of esophagus with balloon (30 mm diameter or larger) for achalasia

(For dilation with balloon less than 30 mm diameter, use 43220)

(For radiological supervision and interpretation, use 74360)

**43460** Esophagogastric tamponade, with balloon (Sengstaaken type)

(For removal of esophageal foreign body by balloon catheter, see 43215, 43247, 74235)

## Other Procedures

**43496** Free jejunum transfer with microvascular anastomosis

(Do not report code 69990 in addition to code 43496)

**43499** Unlisted procedure, esophagus

# Stomach

## Incision

**43500** Gastrotomy; with exploration or foreign body removal

**43501** with suture repair of bleeding ulcer

**43502** with suture repair of pre-existing esophagogastric laceration (eg, Mallory-Weiss)

**43510** with esophageal dilation and insertion of permanent intraluminal tube (eg, Celestin or Mousseaux-Barbin)

**43520** Pyloromyotomy, cutting of pyloric muscle (Fredet-Ramstedt type operation)

## Excision

**43600** Biopsy of stomach; by capsule, tube, peroral (one or more specimens)

**43605** by laparotomy

**43610** Excision, local; ulcer or benign tumor of stomach

**43611** malignant tumor of stomach

**43620** Gastrectomy, total; with esophagoenterostomy

**43621** with Roux-en-Y reconstruction

**43622** with formation of intestinal pouch, any type

(43625 has been deleted. To report, use 43622)

(43630 has been deleted. To report, see 43631-43634)

**43631** Gastrectomy, partial, distal; with gastroduodenostomy

**43632** with gastrojejunostomy

**43633** with Roux-en-Y reconstruction

**43634** with formation of intestinal pouch

**+ 43635** Vagotomy when performed with partial distal gastrectomy (List separately in addition to code(s) for primary procedure)

(Use 43635 in conjunction with codes 43631, 43632, 43633, 43634)

**43638** Gastrectomy, partial, proximal, thoracic or abdominal approach including esophagogastrostomy, with vagotomy;

**43639** with pyloroplasty or pyloromyotomy

(For regional thoracic lymphadenectomy, use 38746)

(For regional abdominal lymphadenectomy, use 38747)

**43640** Vagotomy including pyloroplasty, with or without gastrostomy; truncal or selective

(For pyloroplasty, use 43800)

(For vagotomy, see 64752-64760)

**43641** parietal cell (highly selective)

(For upper gastrointestinal endoscopy, see 43234-43259)

(43700 has been deleted. To report, use 43235)

(43702 has been deleted. To report, use 43239)

(43709 has been deleted. To report, use 43247)

(43711 has been deleted. To report, use 43251)

(43712 has been deleted. To report, use 43255)

(43714 has been deleted. To report, use 43258)

## ▸Laparoscopy◂

▸Surgical laparoscopy always includes diagnostic laparoscopy. To report a diagnostic laparoscopy (peritoneoscopy) (separate procedure), use 49320.◂

●**43651** Laparoscopy, surgical; transection of vagus nerves, truncal

●**43652** transection of vagus nerves, selective or highly selective

●**43653** gastrostomy, without construction of gastric tube (eg, Stamm procedure) (separate procedure)

●**43659** Unlisted laparoscopy procedure, stomach

## Introduction

**43750** Percutaneous placement of gastrostomy tube

(For radiological supervision and interpretation, use 74350)

**43760*** Change of gastrostomy tube

(For endoscopic placement of gastrostomy tube, use 43246)

(For radiological supervision and interpretation, use 75984)

▲**43761** Repositioning of the gastric feeding tube, any method, through the duodenum for enteric nutrition

(43765 has been deleted. To report, use 43760)

## Other Procedures

**43800** Pyloroplasty

(For pyloroplasty and vagotomy, use 43640)

**43810** Gastroduodenostomy

**43820** Gastrojejunostomy; without vagotomy

**43825** with vagotomy, any type

▲**43830** Gastrostomy, open; without construction of gastric tube (eg, Stamm procedure) (separate procedure)

**43831** neonatal, for feeding

(For change of gastrostomy tube, use 43760)

▲**43832** with construction of gastric tube (eg, Janeway procedure)

(43834 has been deleted. To report, use 43246)

**43840** Gastrorrhaphy, suture of perforated duodenal or gastric ulcer, wound, or injury

**43842** Gastric restrictive procedure, without gastric bypass, for morbid obesity; vertical-banded gastroplasty

**43843** other than vertical-banded gastroplasty

(43844 has been deleted. To report, use 43847)

(43845 has been deleted. To report, see 43842, 43843)

**43846** Gastric restrictive procedure, with gastric bypass for morbid obesity; with short limb (less than 100 cm) Roux-en-Y gastro enterostomy

**43847** with small bowel reconstruction to limit absorption

**43848** Revision of gastric restrictive procedure for morbid obesity (separate procedure)

**43850** Revision of gastroduodenal anastomosis (gastroduodenostomy) with reconstruction; without vagotomy

**43855** with vagotomy

**43860** Revision of gastrojejunal anastomosis (gastrojejunostomy) with reconstruction, with or without partial gastrectomy or bowel resection; without vagotomy

**43865** with vagotomy

**43870** Closure of gastrostomy, surgical

**43880** Closure of gastrocolic fistula

(43885 has been deleted)

**43999** Unlisted procedure, stomach

# Intestines (Except Rectum)

## Incision

(44000 has been deleted)

**44005** Enterolysis (freeing of intestinal adhesion) (separate procedure)

(For laparoscopic approach, use ►44200◄)

**44010** Duodenotomy, for exploration, biopsy(s), or foreign body removal

**+ 44015** Tube or needle catheter jejunostomy for enteral alimentation, intraoperative, any method (List separately in addition to primary procedure)

**44020** Enterotomy, small bowel, other than duodenum; for exploration, biopsy(s), or foreign body removal

**44021** for decompression (eg, Baker tube)

**44025** Colotomy, for exploration, biopsy(s), or foreign body removal

(44040 has been deleted. To report, see 44602-44605)

**44050** Reduction of volvulus, intussusception, internal hernia, by laparotomy

**44055** Correction of malrotation by lysis of duodenal bands and/or reduction of midgut volvulus (eg, Ladd procedure)

(44060 has been deleted. To report, use 44799)

## Excision

**44100** Biopsy of intestine by capsule, tube, peroral (one or more specimens)

**44110** Excision of one or more lesions of small or large bowel not requiring anastomosis, exteriorization, or fistulization; single enterotomy

**44111** multiple enterotomies

(44115 has been deleted. To report, use 44799)

**44120** Enterectomy, resection of small intestine; single resection and anastomosis

**+ 44121** each additional resection and anastomosis (List separately in addition to code for primary procedure)

(Use 44121 in conjunction with code 44120)

**44125** with enterostomy

**44130** Enteroenterostomy, anastomosis of intestine, with or without cutaneous enterostomy (separate procedure)

(44131 has been deleted)

**+ 44139** Mobilization (take-down) of splenic flexure performed in conjunction with partial colectomy (List separately in addition to primary procedure)

(Use 44139 in conjunction with codes 44140-44147)

**44140** Colectomy, partial; with anastomosis

**44141** with skin level cecostomy or colostomy

**44143** with end colostomy and closure of distal segment (Hartmann type procedure)

**44144** with resection, with colostomy or ileostomy and creation of mucofistula

**44145** with coloproctostomy (low pelvic anastomosis)

**44146** with coloproctostomy (low pelvic anastomosis), with colostomy

**44147** abdominal and transanal approach

**44150** Colectomy, total, abdominal, without proctectomy; with ileostomy or ileoproctostomy

**44151** with continent ileostomy

**44152** with rectal mucosectomy, ileoanal anastomosis, with or without loop ileostomy

**44153** with rectal mucosectomy, ileoanal anastomosis, creation of ileal reservoir (S or J), with or without loop ileostomy

**44155** Colectomy, total, abdominal, with proctectomy; with ileostomy

**44156** with continent ileostomy

**44160** Colectomy with removal of terminal ileum and ileocolostomy

## ▸Laparoscopy◂

▸Surgical laparoscopy always includes diagnostic laparoscopy. To report a diagnostic laparoscopy (peritoneoscopy) (separate procedure), use 49320.◂

●**44200** Laparoscopy, surgical; enterolysis (freeing of intestinal adhesion) (separate procedure)

▸(For laparoscopy with salpingolysis, ovariolysis, use 58660)◂

●**44201** jejunostomy (eg, for decompression or feeding)

●**44202** intestinal resection, with anastomosis (intra or extracorporeal)

●**44209** Unlisted laparoscopy procedure, intestine (except rectum)

## Enterostomy—External Fistulization of Intestines

**44300** Enterostomy or cecostomy, tube (eg, for decompression or feeding) (separate procedure)

(44305 has been deleted)

(44308 has been deleted. To report, use 44799)

**44310** Ileostomy or jejunostomy, non-tube (separate procedure)

**44312** Revision of ileostomy; simple (release of superficial scar) (separate procedure)

**44314** complicated (reconstruction in-depth) (separate procedure)

**44316** Continent ileostomy (Kock procedure) (separate procedure)

(For fiberoptic evaluation, use 44385)

**44320** Colostomy or skin level cecostomy; (separate procedure)

**44322** with multiple biopsies (eg, for Hirschsprung disease) (separate procedure)

**44340** Revision of colostomy; simple (release of superficial scar) (separate procedure)

**44345** complicated (reconstruction in-depth) (separate procedure)

**44346** with repair of paracolostomy hernia (separate procedure)

## Endoscopy, Small Bowel and Stomal

Surgical endoscopy always includes diagnostic endoscopy.

(For upper gastrointestinal endoscopy, see 43234-43258)

**44360** Small intestinal endoscopy, enteroscopy beyond second portion of duodenum, not including ileum; diagnostic, with or without collection of specimen(s) by brushing or washing (separate procedure)

**44361** with biopsy, single or multiple

**44363** with removal of foreign body

**44364** with removal of tumor(s), polyp(s), or other lesion(s) by snare technique

**44365** with removal of tumor(s), polyp(s), or other lesion(s) by hot biopsy forceps or bipolar cautery

**44366** with control of bleeding, any method

**44369** with ablation of tumor(s), polyp(s), or other lesion(s) not amenable to removal by hot biopsy forceps, bipolar cautery or snare technique

**44372** with placement of percutaneous jejunostomy tube

**44373** with conversion of percutaneous gastrostomy tube to percutaneous jejunostomy tube

(44375 has been deleted. To report, use 43235)

(Surgical endoscopy always includes diagnostic endoscopy)

**44376** Small intestinal endoscopy, enteroscopy beyond second portion of duodenum, including ileum; diagnostic, with or without collection of specimen(s) by brushing or washing (separate procedure)

**44377** with biopsy, single or multiple

**44378** with control of bleeding, any method

(Surgical endoscopy always includes diagnostic endoscopy)

**44380** Ileoscopy, through stoma; diagnostic, with or without collection of specimen(s) by brushing or washing (separate procedure)

**44382** with biopsy, single or multiple

**44385** Endoscopic evaluation of small intestinal (abdominal or pelvic) pouch; diagnostic, with or without collection of specimen(s) by brushing or washing (separate procedure)

**44386** with biopsy, single or multiple

(Surgical endoscopy always includes diagnostic endoscopy)

**44388** Colonoscopy through stoma; diagnostic, with or without collection of specimen(s) by brushing or washing (separate procedure)

**44389** with biopsy, single or multiple

**44390** with removal of foreign body

**44391** with control of bleeding, any method

**44392** with removal of tumor(s), polyp(s), or other lesion(s) by hot biopsy forceps or bipolar cautery

**44393** with ablation of tumor(s), polyp(s), or other lesion(s) not amenable to removal by hot biopsy forceps, bipolar cautery or snare technique

**44394** with removal of tumor(s), polyp(s), or other lesion(s) by snare technique

(For colonoscopy per rectum, see 45330-45385)

(44400, 44405 have been deleted. To report, use 44799)

## Introduction

⊘ **44500** Introduction of long gastrointestinal tube (eg, Miller-Abbott) (separate procedure)

(For radiological supervision and interpretation, use 74340)

## Repair

(44600 has been deleted. To report, see 44602, 44604)

**44602** Suture of small intestine (enterorrhaphy) for perforated ulcer, diverticulum, wound, injury or rupture; single perforation

**44603** multiple perforations

**44604** Suture of large intestine (colorrhaphy) for perforated ulcer, diverticulum, wound, injury or rupture (single or multiple perforations); without colostomy

**44605** with colostomy

(44610 has been deleted. To report, see 44603, 44604)

**44615** Intestinal stricturoplasty (enterotomy and enterorrhaphy) with or without dilation, for intestinal obstruction

**44620** Closure of enterostomy, large or small intestine;

**44625** with resection and anastomosis other than colorectal

**44626** with resection and colorectal anastomosis (eg, closure of Hartmann type procedure)

**44640** Closure of intestinal cutaneous fistula

**44650** Closure of enteroenteric or enterocolic fistula

**44660** Closure of enterovesical fistula; without intestinal or bladder resection

**44661** with bowel and/or bladder resection

(For closure of renocolic fistula, see 50525, 50526)

(For closure of gastrocolic fistula, use 43880)

(For closure of rectovesical fistula, see 45800, 45805)

**44680** Intestinal plication (separate procedure)

### Other Procedures

**44700** Exclusion of small bowel from pelvis by mesh or other prosthesis, or native tissue (eg, bladder or omentum)

(For therapeutic radiation clinical treatment, see **Radiation Oncology** section)

**44799** Unlisted procedure, intestine

## Meckel's Diverticulum and the Mesentery

### Excision

**44800** Excision of Meckel's diverticulum (diverticulectomy) or omphalomesenteric duct

**44820** Excision of lesion of mesentery (separate procedure)

(With bowel resection, see 44120 or 44140 et seq)

### Suture

**44850** Suture of mesentery (separate procedure)

(For reduction and repair of internal hernia, use 44050)

### Other Procedures

**44899** Unlisted procedure, Meckel's diverticulum and the mesentery

## Appendix

### Incision

**44900** Incision and drainage of appendiceal abscess; open

**44901** percutaneous

(For radiological supervision and interpretation, use 75989)

### Excision

**44950** Appendectomy;

(Incidental appendectomy during intra-abdominal surgery does not usually warrant a separate identification. If necessary to report, add modifier '-52')

✚ **44955** when done for indicated purpose at time of other major procedure (not as separate procedure) (List separately in addition to code for primary procedure)

**44960** for ruptured appendix with abscess or generalized peritonitis

### ►Laparoscopy◄

►Surgical laparoscopy always includes diagnostic laparoscopy. To report a diagnostic laparoscopy (peritoneoscopy) (separate procedure), use 49320.◄

● **44970** Laparoscopy, surgical, appendectomy

● **44979** Unlisted laparoscopy procedure, appendix

## Rectum

### Incision

**45000** Transrectal drainage of pelvic abscess

**45005** Incision and drainage of submucosal abscess, rectum

**45020** Incision and drainage of deep supralevator, pelvirectal, or retrorectal abscess

(See also 46050, 46060)

### Excision

**45100** Biopsy of anorectal wall, anal approach (eg, congenital megacolon)

(45105 has been deleted. To report, use 45100)

(For endoscopic biopsy, use 45305)

**45108** Anorectal myomectomy

**45110** Proctectomy; complete, combined abdominoperineal, with colostomy

**45111** partial resection of rectum, transabdominal approach

**45112** Proctectomy, combined abdominoperineal, pull-through procedure (eg, colo-anal anastomosis)

(For colo-anal anastomosis with colonic reservoir or pouch, use 45119)

**45113** Proctectomy, partial, with rectal mucosectomy, ileoanal anastomosis, creation of ileal reservoir (S or J), with or without loop ileostomy

**45114** Proctectomy, partial, with anastomosis; abdominal and transsacral approach

**45116** transsacral approach only (Kraske type)

**45119** Proctectomy, combined abdominoperineal pull-through procedure (eg, colo-anal anastomosis), with creation of colonic reservoir (eg, J-pouch), with or without proximal diverting ostomy

**45120** Proctectomy, complete (for congenital megacolon), abdominal and perineal approach; with pull-through procedure and anastomosis (eg, Swenson, Duhamel, or Soave type operation)

**45121** with subtotal or total colectomy, with multiple biopsies

**45123** Proctectomy, partial, without anastomosis, perineal approach

**45126** Pelvic exenteration for colorectal malignancy, with proctectomy (with or without colostomy), with removal of bladder and ureteral transplantations, and/or hysterectomy, or cervicectomy, with or without removal of tube(s), with or without removal of ovary(s), or any combination thereof

**45130** Excision of rectal procidentia, with anastomosis; perineal approach

**45135** abdominal and perineal approach

**45150** Division of stricture of rectum

**45160** Excision of rectal tumor by proctotomy, transsacral or transcoccygeal approach

**45170** Excision of rectal tumor, transanal approach

(45180, 45181 have been deleted. To report, see 45170, 45190)

## Destruction

**45190** Destruction of rectal tumor, any method (eg, electrodesiccation) transanal approach

## Endoscopy

### Definitions

***Proctosigmoidoscopy*** is the examination of the rectum and sigmoid colon.

***Sigmoidoscopy*** is the examination of the entire rectum, sigmoid colon and may include examination of a portion of the descending colon.

***Colonoscopy*** is the examination of the entire colon, from the rectum to the cecum, and may include the examination of the terminal ileum.

For an incomplete colonoscopy, with full preparation for a colonoscopy, use a colonoscopy code with the modifier '-52' and provide documentation.

Surgical endoscopy always includes diagnostic endoscopy.

**45300** Proctosigmoidoscopy, rigid; diagnostic, with or without collection of specimen(s) by brushing or washing (separate procedure)

(45302 has been deleted. To report, use 45300)

**45303** with dilation, any method

(For radiological supervision and interpretation, use 74360)

**45305** with biopsy, single or multiple

**45307** with removal of foreign body

**45308** with removal of single tumor, polyp, or other lesion by hot biopsy forceps or bipolar cautery

**45309** with removal of single tumor, polyp, or other lesion by snare technique

(45310 has been deleted. To report, see 45308, 45309)

**45315** with removal of multiple tumors, polyps, or other lesions by hot biopsy forceps, bipolar cautery or snare technique

**45317** with control of bleeding, any method

(45319 has been deleted. To report, use 45999)

**45320** with ablation of tumor(s), polyp(s), or other lesion(s) not amenable to removal by hot biopsy forceps, bipolar cautery or snare technique (eg, laser)

**45321** with decompression of volvulus

(45325 colonoscopy has been renumbered 45355 without change in terminology)

(Surgical endoscopy always includes diagnostic endoscopy)

**45330** Sigmoidoscopy, flexible; diagnostic, with or without collection of specimen(s) by brushing or washing (separate procedure)

**45331** with biopsy, single or multiple

**45332** with removal of foreign body

**45333** with removal of tumor(s), polyp(s), or other lesion(s) by hot biopsy forceps or bipolar cautery

**45334** with control of bleeding, any method

(45336 has been deleted. To report, use 45339)

**45337** with decompression of volvulus, any method

**45338** with removal of tumor(s), polyp(s), or other lesion(s) by snare technique

**45339** with ablation of tumor(s), polyp(s), or other lesion(s) not amenable to removal by hot biopsy forceps, bipolar cautery or snare technique

**45355** Colonoscopy, rigid or flexible, transabdominal via colotomy, single or multiple

(45360-45372 have been deleted. To report, see 45330-45337)

(Surgical endoscopy always includes diagnostic endoscopy)

**45378** Colonoscopy, flexible, proximal to splenic flexure; diagnostic, with or without collection of specimen(s) by brushing or washing, with or without colon decompression (separate procedure)

**45379** with removal of foreign body

**45380** with biopsy, single or multiple

**45382** with control of bleeding, any method

**45383** with ablation of tumor(s), polyp(s), or other lesion(s) not amenable to removal by hot biopsy forceps, bipolar cautery or snare technique

**45384** with removal of tumor(s), polyp(s), or other lesion(s) by hot biopsy forceps or bipolar cautery

**45385** with removal of tumor(s), polyp(s), or other lesion(s) by snare technique

(45386 has been deleted. To report, use 44799)

(For small bowel and stomal endoscopy, see 44360-44393)

## Repair

**45500** Proctoplasty; for stenosis

**45505** for prolapse of mucous membrane

**45520** Perirectal injection of sclerosing solution for prolapse

(45521 has been deleted)

**45540** Proctopexy for prolapse; abdominal approach

**45541** perineal approach

**45550** Proctopexy combined with sigmoid resection, abdominal approach

**45560** Repair of rectocele (separate procedure)

(For repair of rectocele with posterior colporrhaphy, use 57250)

**45562** Exploration, repair, and presacral drainage for rectal injury;

**45563** with colostomy

**45800** Closure of rectovesical fistula;

**45805** with colostomy

**45820** Closure of rectourethral fistula;

**45825** with colostomy

(For rectovaginal fistula closure, see 57300-57308)

## Manipulation

**45900*** Reduction of procidentia (separate procedure) under anesthesia

**45905*** Dilation of anal sphincter (separate procedure) under anesthesia other than local

**45910** Dilation of rectal stricture (separate procedure) under anesthesia other than local

**45915*** Removal of fecal impaction or foreign body (separate procedure) under anesthesia

## Other Procedures

**45999** Unlisted procedure, rectum

# Anus

## Incision

(46000 has been deleted. To report, use 46270)

**46030*** Removal of anal seton, other marker

(46032 has been deleted. To report, use 46999)

**46040** Incision and drainage of ischiorectal and/or perirectal abscess (separate procedure)

**46045** Incision and drainage of intramural, intramuscular, or submucosal abscess, transanal, under anesthesia

**46050*** Incision and drainage, perianal abscess, superficial

(See also 45020, 46060)

**46060** Incision and drainage of ischiorectal or intramural abscess, with fistulectomy or fistulotomy, submuscular, with or without placement of seton

(See also 45020)

**46070** Incision, anal septum (infant)

(For anoplasty, see 46700-46705)

**46080*** Sphincterotomy, anal, division of sphincter (separate procedure)

**46083** Incision of thrombosed hemorrhoid, external

## Excision

**46200** Fissurectomy, with or without sphincterotomy

**46210** Cryptectomy; single

**46211** multiple (separate procedure)

**46220** Papillectomy or excision of single tag, anus (separate procedure)

**46221** Hemorrhoidectomy, by simple ligature (eg, rubber band)

**46230** Excision of external hemorrhoid tags and/or multiple papillae

**46250** Hemorrhoidectomy, external, complete

**46255** Hemorrhoidectomy, internal and external, simple;

**46257** with fissurectomy

**46258** with fistulectomy, with or without fissurectomy

**46260** Hemorrhoidectomy, internal and external, complex or extensive;

**46261** with fissurectomy

**46262** with fistulectomy, with or without fissurectomy

**46270** Surgical treatment of anal fistula (fistulectomy/fistulotomy); subcutaneous

**46275** submuscular

**46280** complex or multiple, with or without placement of seton

(46281 has been renumbered to 46288 without change in terminology)

**46285** second stage

**46288** Closure of anal fistula with rectal advancement flap

**46320*** Enucleation or excision of external thrombotic hemorrhoid

## Introduction

**46500*** Injection of sclerosing solution, hemorrhoids

(46510, 46530 have been deleted. To report, use 46999)

## Endoscopy

Surgical endoscopy always includes diagnostic endoscopy.

**46600** Anoscopy; diagnostic, with or without collection of specimen(s) by brushing or washing (separate procedure)

(46602 has been deleted. To report, use 46600)

**46604** with dilation, any method

**46606** with biopsy, single or multiple

**46608** with removal of foreign body

**46610** with removal of single tumor, polyp, or other lesion by hot biopsy forceps or bipolar cautery

**46611** with removal of single tumor, polyp, or other lesion by snare technique

**46612** with removal of multiple tumors, polyps, or other lesions by hot biopsy forceps, bipolar cautery or snare technique

**46614** with control of bleeding, any method

**46615** with ablation of tumor(s), polyp(s), or other lesion(s) not amenable to removal by hot biopsy forceps, bipolar cautery or snare technique

## Repair

**46700** Anoplasty, plastic operation for stricture; adult

**46705** infant

(For simple incision of anal septum, use 46070)

**46715** Repair of low imperforate anus; with anoperineal fistula (cut-back procedure)

**46716** with transposition of anoperineal or anovestibular fistula

**46730** Repair of high imperforate anus without fistula; perineal or sacroperineal approach

**46735** combined transabdominal and sacroperineal approaches

**46740** Repair of high imperforate anus with rectourethral or rectovaginal fistula; perineal or sacroperineal approach

**46742** combined transabdominal and sacroperineal approaches

**46744** Repair of cloacal anomaly by anorectovaginoplasty and urethroplasty, sacroperineal approach

**46746** Repair of cloacal anomaly by anorectovaginoplasty and urethroplasty, combined abdominal and sacroperineal approach;

**46748** with vaginal lengthening by intestinal graft or pedicle flaps

**46750** Sphincteroplasty, anal, for incontinence or prolapse; adult

**46751** child

**46753** Graft (Thiersch operation) for rectal incontinence and/or prolapse

**46754** Removal of Thiersch wire or suture, anal canal

**46760** Sphincteroplasty, anal, for incontinence, adult; muscle transplant

**46761** levator muscle imbrication (Park posterior anal repair)

**46762** implantation artificial sphincter

## Destruction

**46900*** Destruction of lesion(s), anus (eg, condyloma, papilloma, molluscum contagiosum, herpetic vesicle), simple; chemical

**46910*** electrodesiccation

**46916** cryosurgery

**46917** laser surgery

(46920 has been deleted. To report, use 46922)

**46922** surgical excision

**46924** Destruction of lesion(s), anus (eg, condyloma, papilloma, molluscum contagiosum, herpetic vesicle), extensive, any method

(46930 has been deleted. To report, use 46924)

(46932 has been deleted. To report, use 46916)

(46933 has been deleted. To report, use 46924)

**46934** Destruction of hemorrhoids, any method; internal

**46935** external

**46936** internal and external

**46937** Cryosurgery of rectal tumor; benign

**46938** malignant

**46940** Curettage or cauterization of anal fissure, including dilation of anal sphincter (separate procedure); initial

**46942** subsequent

## Suture

**46945** Ligation of internal hemorrhoids; single procedure

**46946** multiple procedures

## Other Procedures

**46999** Unlisted procedure, anus

# Liver

## Incision

**47000*** Biopsy of liver, needle; percutaneous

(For radiological supervision and interpretation, see 76003, 76360, 76942)

**+ 47001** when done for indicated purpose at time of other major procedure (List separately in addition to code for primary procedure)

(For radiological supervision and interpretation, see 76003, 76360, 76942)

(For fine needle aspiration, preparation, and interpretation of smears, see 88170-88173)

**47010** Hepatotomy; for open drainage of abscess or cyst, one or two stages

**47011** for percutaneous drainage of abscess or cyst, one or two stages

(For radiological supervision and interpretation, use 75989)

**47015** Laparotomy, with aspiration and/or injection of hepatic parasitic (eg, amoebic or echinococcal) cyst(s) or abscess(es)

## Excision

**47100** Biopsy of liver, wedge

**47120** Hepatectomy, resection of liver; partial lobectomy

**47122** trisegmentectomy

**47125** total left lobectomy

**47130** total right lobectomy

**47133** Donor hepatectomy, with preparation and maintenance of allograft; from cadaver donor

**47134** partial, from living donor

**47135** Liver allotransplantation; orthotopic, partial or whole, from cadaver or living donor, any age

**47136** heterotopic, partial or whole, from cadaver or living donor, any age

## Repair

**47300** Marsupialization of cyst or abscess of liver

**47350** Management of liver hemorrhage; simple suture of liver wound or injury

(47355 has been deleted)

**47360** complex suture of liver wound or injury, with or without hepatic artery ligation

**47361** exploration of hepatic wound, extensive debridement, coagulation and/or suture, with or without packing of liver

**47362** re-exploration of hepatic wound for removal of packing

## Other Procedures

**47399** Unlisted procedure, liver

# Biliary Tract

## Incision

**47400** Hepaticotomy or hepaticostomy with exploration, drainage, or removal of calculus

**47420** Choledochotomy or choledochostomy with exploration, drainage, or removal of calculus, with or without cholecystotomy; without transduodenal sphincterotomy or sphincteroplasty

**47425** with transduodenal sphincterotomy or sphincteroplasty

(47440 has been deleted)

**47460** Transduodenal sphincterotomy or sphincteroplasty, with or without transduodenal extraction of calculus (separate procedure)

**47480** Cholecystotomy or cholecystostomy with exploration, drainage, or removal of calculus (separate procedure)

**47490** Percutaneous cholecystostomy

(For radiological supervision and interpretation, use 75989)

## Introduction

**47500** Injection procedure for percutaneous transhepatic cholangiography

(For radiological supervision and interpretation, use 74320)

**47505** Injection procedure for cholangiography through an existing catheter (eg, percutaneous transhepatic or T-tube)

**47510** Introduction of percutaneous transhepatic catheter for biliary drainage

(For radiological supervision and interpretation, use 75980)

**47511** Introduction of percutaneous transhepatic stent for internal and external biliary drainage

(For radiological supervision and interpretation, use 75982)

**47525** Change of percutaneous biliary drainage catheter

(For radiological supervision and interpretation, use 75984)

**47530** Revision and/or reinsertion of transhepatic tube

(For radiological supervision and interpretation, use 75984)

## Endoscopy

Surgical endoscopy always includes diagnostic endoscopy.

**+ 47550** Biliary endoscopy, intraoperative (choledochoscopy) (List separately in addition to code for primary procedure)

**47552** Biliary endoscopy, percutaneous via T-tube or other tract; diagnostic, with or without collection of specimen(s) by brushing and/or washing (separate procedure)

**47553** with biopsy, single or multiple

**47554** with removal of stone(s)

**47555** with dilation of biliary duct stricture(s) without stent

(For ERCP, see 43260-43272, 74363)

**47556** with dilation of biliary duct stricture(s) with stent

(For radiological supervision and interpretation, use 75982)

## ►Laparoscopy◄

►Surgical laparoscopy always includes diagnostic laparoscopy. To report a diagnostic laparoscopy (peritoneoscopy) (separate procedure), use 49320.◄

●**47560** Laparoscopy, surgical; with guided transhepatic cholangiography, without biopsy

●**47561** with guided transhepatic cholangiography with biopsy

●**47562** cholecystectomy

●**47563** cholecystectomy with cholangiography

●**47564** cholecystectomy with exploration of common duct

●**47570** cholecystoenterostomy

●**47579** Unlisted laparoscopy procedure, biliary tract

## Excision

**47600** Cholecystectomy;

**47605** with cholangiography

(For laparoscopic ►approach,◄ see ►47562-47564◄)

**47610** Cholecystectomy with exploration of common duct;

(47611 has been deleted. To report, use 47610 and 47550)

**47612** with choledochoenterostomy

**47620** with transduodenal sphincterotomy or sphincteroplasty, with or without cholangiography

**47630** Biliary duct stone extraction, percutaneous via T-tube tract, basket, or snare (eg, Burhenne technique)

(For radiological supervision and interpretation, use 74327)

**47700** Exploration for congenital atresia of bile ducts, without repair, with or without liver biopsy, with or without cholangiography

**47701** Portoenterostomy (eg, Kasai procedure)

(47710 has been deleted. To report, see 47711, 47712)

**47711** Excision of bile duct tumor, with or without primary repair of bile duct; extrahepatic

**47712** intrahepatic

(For anastomosis, see 47760-47800)

**47715** Excision of choledochal cyst

**47716** Anastomosis, choledochal cyst, without excision

## Repair

**47720** Cholecystoenterostomy; direct

►(For laparoscopic approach, use 47570)◄

**47721** with gastroenterostomy

**47740** Roux-en-Y

**47741** Roux-en-Y with gastroenterostomy

**47760** Anastomosis, of extrahepatic biliary ducts and gastrointestinal tract

**47765** Anastomosis, of intrahepatic ducts and gastrointestinal tract

**47780** Anastomosis, Roux-en-Y, of extrahepatic biliary ducts and gastrointestinal tract

**47785** Anastomosis, Roux-en-Y, of intrahepatic biliary ducts and gastrointestinal tract

**47800** Reconstruction, plastic, of extrahepatic biliary ducts with end-to-end anastomosis

**47801** Placement of choledochal stent

**47802** U-tube hepaticoenterostomy

(47810 has been deleted. To report, use 47999)

(47850, 47855 have been deleted. To report, use 47999)

**47900** Suture of extrahepatic biliary duct for pre-existing injury (separate procedure)

### Other Procedures

**47999** Unlisted procedure, biliary tract

## Pancreas

(For peroral pancreatic endoscopic procedures, see 43260-43272)

### Incision

**48000** Placement of drains, peripancreatic, for acute pancreatitis;

**48001** with cholecystostomy, gastrostomy, and jejunostomy

**48005** Resection or debridement of pancreas and peripancreatic tissue for acute necrotizing pancreatitis

**48020** Removal of pancreatic calculus

### Excision

**48100** Biopsy of pancreas, open, any method (eg, fine needle aspiration, needle core biopsy, wedge biopsy)

**48102*** Biopsy of pancreas, percutaneous needle

(For radiological supervision and interpretation, see 76003, 76360, 76942)

(For fine needle aspiration, preparation, and interpretation of smears, see 88170-88173)

**48120** Excision of lesion of pancreas (eg, cyst, adenoma)

**48140** Pancreatectomy, distal subtotal, with or without splenectomy; without pancreaticojejunostomy

**48145** with pancreaticojejunostomy

**48146** Pancreatectomy, distal, near-total with preservation of duodenum (Child-type procedure)

**48148** Excision of ampulla of Vater

**48150** Pancreatectomy, proximal subtotal with total duodenectomy, partial gastrectomy, choledochoenterostomy and gastrojejunostomy (Whipple-type procedure); with pancreatojejunostomy

(48151 has been deleted. To report, use 48146)

**48152** without pancreatojejunostomy

**48153** Pancreatectomy, proximal subtotal with near-total duodenectomy, choledochoenterostomy and duodenojejunostomy (pylorus-sparing, Whipple-type procedure); with pancreatojejunostomy

**48154** without pancreatojejunostomy

**48155** Pancreatectomy, total

**48160** Pancreatectomy, total or subtotal, with autologous transplantation of pancreas or pancreatic islets

**48180** Pancreaticojejunostomy, side-to-side anastomosis (Puestow-type operation)

### Introduction

**+ 48400** Injection procedure for intraoperative pancreatography (List separately in addition to code for primary procedure)

(For radiological supervision and interpretation, see 74300-74305)

### Repair

**48500** Marsupialization of cyst of pancreas

**48510** External drainage, pseudocyst of pancreas; open

**48511** percutaneous

(For radiological supervision and interpretation, use 75989)

**48520** Internal anastomosis of pancreatic cyst to gastrointestinal tract; direct

**48540** Roux-en-Y

**48545** Pancreatorrhaphy for trauma

**48547** Duodenal exclusion with gastrojejunostomy for pancreatic trauma

## Pancreas Transplantation

**48550** Donor pancreatectomy, with preparation and maintenance of allograft from cadaver donor, with or without duodenal segment for transplantation

**48554** Transplantation of pancreatic allograft

**48556** Removal of transplanted pancreatic allograft

## Other Procedures

**48999** Unlisted procedure, pancreas

# Abdomen, Peritoneum, and Omentum

## Incision

**49000** Exploratory laparotomy, exploratory celiotomy with or without biopsy(s) (separate procedure)

(To report wound exploration due to penetrating trauma without laparotomy, use 20102)

**49002** Reopening of recent laparotomy

(To report re-exploration of hepatic wound for removal of packing, use 47362)

**49010** Exploration, retroperitoneal area with or without biopsy(s) (separate procedure)

(To report wound exploration due to penetrating trauma without laparotomy, use 20102)

**49020** Drainage of peritoneal abscess or localized peritonitis, exclusive of appendiceal abscess; open

(For appendiceal abscess, use 44900)

**49021** percutaneous

**49040** Drainage of subdiaphragmatic or subphrenic abscess; open

**49041** percutaneous

(For radiological supervision and interpretation, use 75989)

**49060** Drainage of retroperitoneal abscess; open

**49061** percutaneous

►(For laparoscopic drainage, use 49323)◄

(For radiological supervision and interpretation, use 75989)

**49062** Drainage of extraperitoneal lymphocele to peritoneal cavity, open

**49080*** Peritoneocentesis, abdominal paracentesis, or peritoneal lavage (diagnostic or therapeutic); initial

**49081*** subsequent

**49085** Removal of peritoneal foreign body from peritoneal cavity

(For lysis of intestinal adhesions, use 44005)

## Excision, Destruction

**49180*** Biopsy, abdominal or retroperitoneal mass, percutaneous needle

(For radiological supervision and interpretation, see 76003, 76360, 76365, 76942)

(For fine needle aspiration, preparation, and interpretation of smears, see 88170-88173)

**49200** Excision or destruction by any method of intra-abdominal or retroperitoneal tumors or cysts or endometriomas;

**49201** extensive

**49215** Excision of presacral or sacrococcygeal tumor

**49220** Staging celiotomy (laparotomy) for Hodgkins disease or lymphoma (includes splenectomy, needle or open biopsies of both liver lobes, possibly also removal of abdominal nodes, abdominal node and/or bone marrow biopsies, ovarian repositioning)

**49250** Umbilectomy, omphalectomy, excision of umbilicus (separate procedure)

**49255** Omentectomy, epiploectomy, resection of omentum (separate procedure)

(49300 has been deleted. To report, use ►49320◄)

(49301 has been deleted. To report, use ►49321◄)

(49302 has been deleted. To report, use ►47560◄)

(49303 has been deleted. To report, use ►47561◄)

(49310 has been deleted. To report, use ►47562◄)

(49311 has been deleted. To report, use ►47563◄)

(49315 has been deleted. To report, use ►44970◄)

## ►Laparoscopy◄

►Surgical laparoscopy always includes diagnostic laparoscopy. To report a diagnostic laparoscopy (peritoneoscopy), (separate procedure), use 49320.◄

►For laparoscopic fulguration or excision of lesions of the ovary, pelvic viscera, or peritoneal surface use 58662.◄

●**49320** Laparoscopy, surgical, abdomen, peritoneum, and omentum; diagnostic, with or without collection of specimen(s) by brushing or washing (separate procedure)

●**49321** with biopsy (single or multiple)

●**49322** with aspiration of cavity or cyst (eg, ovarian cyst) (single or multiple)

●**49323** with drainage of lymphocele to peritoneal cavity

►(For percutaneous or open drainage, see 49060, 49061)◄

●**49329** Unlisted laparoscopy procedure, abdomen, peritoneum and omentum

## Introduction, Revision, and/or Removal

**49400*** Injection of air or contrast into peritoneal cavity (separate procedure)

(For radiological supervision and interpretation, use 74190)

(49401 has been deleted. To report, use 49400)

**49420*** Insertion of intraperitoneal cannula or catheter for drainage or dialysis; temporary

**49421** permanent

**49422** Removal of permanent intraperitoneal cannula or catheter

(For removal of a temporary catheter/cannula, use appropriate E/M code)

**49423** Exchange of previously placed abscess or cyst drainage catheter under radiological guidance (separate procedure)

(For radiological supervision and interpretation, use 75984)

**49424** Contrast injection for assessment of abscess or cyst via previously placed catheter (separate procedure)

(For radiological supervision and interpretation, use 76080)

**49425** Insertion of peritoneal-venous shunt

**49426** Revision of peritoneal-venous shunt

(For shunt patency test, use 78291)

**49427** Injection procedure (eg, contrast media) for evaluation of previously placed peritoneal-venous shunt

(For radiological supervision and interpretation, use 75809)

**49428** Ligation of peritoneal-venous shunt

**49429** Removal of peritoneal-venous shunt

(49430, 49440 have been deleted. To report, use 49999)

## Repair

### Hernioplasty, Herniorrhaphy, Herniotomy

The hernia repair codes in this section are categorized primarily by the type of hernia (inguinal, femoral, incisional, etc.).

Some types of hernias are further categorized as "initial" or "recurrent" based on whether or not the hernia has required previous repair(s).

Additional variables accounted for by some of the codes include patient age and clinical presentation (reducible vs. incarcerated or strangulated).

With the exception of the incisional hernia repairs (see 49560-49566) the use of mesh or other prostheses is not separately reported.

The excision/repair of strangulated organs or structures such as testicle(s), intestine, ovaries are reported by using the appropriate code for the excision/repair (eg, 44120, 54520, and 58940) in addition to the appropriate code for the repair of the strangulated hernia.

(For reduction and repair of intra-abdominal hernia, use 44050)

(For debridement of abdominal wall, see 11042, 11043)

(All codes for bilateral procedures in hernia repair have been deleted. To report, add modifier '-50')

**49495** Repair initial inguinal hernia, under age 6 months, with or without hydrocelectomy; reducible

**49496** incarcerated or strangulated

**49500** Repair initial inguinal hernia, age 6 months to under 5 years, with or without hydrocelectomy; reducible

**49501** incarcerated or strangulated

**49505** Repair initial inguinal hernia, age 5 years or over; reducible

**49507** incarcerated or strangulated

(49510 has been deleted. To report, see 49505 or 49507 and 54520)

(49515 has been deleted. To report, see 49505 or 49507 and 54840 or 55040)

**49520** Repair recurrent inguinal hernia, any age; reducible

**49521** incarcerated or strangulated

**49525** Repair inguinal hernia, sliding, any age

(49530 has been deleted. To report, see 49496, 49501, 49507, 49521)

(49535 has been deleted. To report, see 49496, 49501, 49507, 49521)

**49540** Repair lumbar hernia

**49550** Repair initial femoral hernia, any age; reducible

(49552 has been deleted. To report, see 49550 or 49553)

**49553** incarcerated or strangulated

**49555** Repair recurrent femoral hernia; reducible

**49557** incarcerated or strangulated

**49560** Repair initial incisional or ventral hernia; reducible

**49561** incarcerated or strangulated

**49565** Repair recurrent incisional or ventral hernia; reducible

**49566** incarcerated or strangulated

**+ 49568** Implantation of mesh or other prosthesis for incisional or ventral hernia repair (List separately in addition to code for the incisional or ventral hernia repair)

**49570** Repair epigastric hernia (eg, preperitoneal fat); reducible (separate procedure)

**49572** incarcerated or strangulated

(49575 has been deleted. To report, use 49572)

**49580** Repair umbilical hernia, under age 5 years; reducible

(49581 has been deleted. To report, see 49585 or 49587)

**49582** incarcerated or strangulated

**49585** Repair umbilical hernia, age 5 years or over; reducible

**49587** incarcerated or strangulated

**49590** Repair spigelian hernia

**49600** Repair of small omphalocele, with primary closure

**49605** Repair of large omphalocele or gastroschisis; with or without prosthesis

**49606** with removal of prosthesis, final reduction and closure, in operating room

**49610** Repair of omphalocele (Gross type operation); first stage

**49611** second stage

(For diaphragmatic or hiatal hernia repair, see 39502-39541)

(49630-49640 have been deleted. For surgical repair of omentum, use 49999)

## ►Laparoscopy◄

►Surgical laparoscopy always includes diagnostic laparoscopy. To report a diagnostic laparoscopy (peritoneoscopy) (separate procedure), use 49320.◄

●**49650** Laparoscopy, surgical; repair initial inguinal hernia

●**49651** repair recurrent inguinal hernia

●**49659** Unlisted laparoscopy procedure, hernioplasty, herniorrhaphy, herniotomy

## Suture

**49900** Suture, secondary, of abdominal wall for evisceration or dehiscence

(For suture of ruptured diaphragm, see 39540, 39541)

(For debridement of abdominal wall, see 11042, 11043)

## Other Procedures

✚ **49905** Omental flap (eg, for reconstruction of sternal and chest wall defects) (List separately in addition to code for primary procedure)

(49910 has been deleted. To report, use 49999)

**49906** Free omental flap with microvascular anastomosis

(Do not report code 69990 in addition to code 49906)

**49999** Unlisted procedure, abdomen, peritoneum and omentum

# Urinary System

(For provision of chemotherapeutic agents, use 96545 in addition to code for primary procedure)

## Kidney

### Incision

(For retroperitoneal exploration, abscess, tumor, or cyst, see 49010, 49060, 49200, 49201)

**50010** Renal exploration, not necessitating other specific procedures

**50020** Drainage of perirenal or renal abscess; open

**50021** percutaneous

(For radiological supervision and interpretation, use 75989)

**50040** Nephrostomy, nephrotomy with drainage

**50045** Nephrotomy, with exploration

(For renal endoscopy performed in conjunction with this procedure, see 50570-50580)

**50060** Nephrolithotomy; removal of calculus

**50065** secondary surgical operation for calculus

**50070** complicated by congenital kidney abnormality

**50075** removal of large staghorn calculus filling renal pelvis and calyces (including anatrophic pyelolithotomy)

**50080** Percutaneous nephrostolithotomy or pyelostolithotomy, with or without dilation, endoscopy, lithotripsy, stenting, or basket extraction; up to 2 cm

**50081** over 2 cm

(For establishment of nephrostomy without nephrostolithotomy, see 50040, 50395, 52334)

(For fluoroscopic guidance, see 76000, 76001)

**50100** Transection or repositioning of aberrant renal vessels (separate procedure)

**50120** Pyelotomy; with exploration

(For renal endoscopy performed in conjunction with this procedure, see 50570-50580)

**50125** with drainage, pyelostomy

**50130** with removal of calculus (pyelolithotomy, pelviolithotomy, including coagulum pyelolithotomy)

**50135** complicated (eg, secondary operation, congenital kidney abnormality)

(For supply of anticarcinogenic agents, use 99070 in addition to code for primary procedure)

### Excision

(For excision of retroperitoneal tumor or cyst, see 49200, 49201)

**50200*** Renal biopsy; percutaneous, by trocar or needle

(For radiological supervision and interpretation, see 76003, 76360, 76942)

(For fine needle aspiration, preparation, and interpretation of smears, see 88170-88173)

**50205** by surgical exposure of kidney

**50220** Nephrectomy, including partial ureterectomy, any approach including rib resection;

**50225** complicated because of previous surgery on same kidney

**50230** radical, with regional lymphadenectomy and/or vena caval thrombectomy

(When vena caval resection with reconstruction is necessary, use 37799)

**50234** Nephrectomy with total ureterectomy and bladder cuff; through same incision

**50236** through separate incision

**50240** Nephrectomy, partial

**50280** Excision or unroofing of cyst(s) of kidney

►(For laparoscopic ablation of renal cysts, use 50541)◄

**50290** Excision of perinephric cyst

## Renal Transplantation

(For dialysis, see 90935-90999)

►(For laparoscopic donor nephrectomy, use 50547)◄

►(For laparoscopic drainage of lymphocele to peritoneal cavity, use 49323)◄

**50300** Donor nephrectomy, with preparation and maintenance of allograft, from cadaver donor, unilateral or bilateral

▲**50320** Donor nephrectomy, open from living donor (excluding preparation and maintenance of allograft)

**50340** Recipient nephrectomy (separate procedure)

(50341 has been deleted. To report, use 50340 with modifier '-50')

**50360** Renal allotransplantation, implantation of graft; excluding donor and recipient nephrectomy

**50365** with recipient nephrectomy

(50366 has been deleted. To report, use 50365 with modifier '-50')

**50370** Removal of transplanted renal allograft

**50380** Renal autotransplantation, reimplantation of kidney

(For extra-corporeal "bench" surgery, use autotransplantation as the primary procedure and add the secondary procedure (eg, partial nephrectomy, nephrolithotomy), and use the modifier '-51')

## Introduction

**50390*** Aspiration and/or injection of renal cyst or pelvis by needle, percutaneous

(For radiological supervision and interpretation, see 74425, 74470, 76003, 76365, 76938)

(For fine needle aspiration, preparation, and interpretation of smears, see 88170-88173)

**50392** Introduction of intracatheter or catheter into renal pelvis for drainage and/or injection, percutaneous

(For radiological supervision and interpretation, see 74475, 76365, 76938)

**50393** Introduction of ureteral catheter or stent into ureter through renal pelvis for drainage and/or injection, percutaneous

(For radiological supervision and interpretation, see 74480, 76003, 76365, 76938)

**50394** Injection procedure for pyelography (as nephrostogram, pyelostogram, antegrade pyeloureterograms) through nephrostomy or pyelostomy tube, or indwelling ureteral catheter

(For radiological supervision and interpretation, use 74425)

**50395** Introduction of guide into renal pelvis and/or ureter with dilation to establish nephrostomy tract, percutaneous

(For radiological supervision and interpretation, see 74475, 74480, 74485)

(For nephrostolithotomy, see 50080, 50081)

(For retrograde percutaneous nephrostomy, use 52334)

(For endoscopic surgery, see 50551-50561)

**50396** Manometric studies through nephrostomy or pyelostomy tube, or indwelling ureteral catheter

(For radiological supervision and interpretation, see 74425, 74475, 74480)

**50398*** Change of nephrostomy or pyelostomy tube

(For fluoroscopic guidance, use 76000)

(For radiological supervision and interpretation, use 75984)

## Repair

**50400** Pyeloplasty (Foley Y-pyeloplasty), plastic operation on renal pelvis, with or without plastic operation on ureter, nephropexy, nephrostomy, pyelostomy, or ureteral splinting; simple

**50405** complicated (congenital kidney abnormality, secondary pyeloplasty, solitary kidney, calycoplasty)

►(For laparoscopic approach, use 50544)◄

(50420 has been deleted)

**50500** Nephrorrhaphy, suture of kidney wound or injury

**50520** Closure of nephrocutaneous or pyelocutaneous fistula

**50525** Closure of nephrovisceral fistula (eg, renocolic), including visceral repair; abdominal approach

**50526** thoracic approach

**50540** Symphysiotomy for horseshoe kidney with or without pyeloplasty and/or other plastic procedure, unilateral or bilateral (one operation)

## ►Laparoscopy◄

►Surgical laparoscopy always includes diagnostic laparoscopy. To report a diagnostic laparoscopy (peritoneoscopy) (separate procedure), use 49320.◄

●**50541** Laparoscopy, surgical; ablation of renal cysts

●**50544** pyeloplasty

●**50546** nephrectomy

●**50547** donor nephrectomy from living donor (excluding preparation and maintenance of allograft)

●**50548** Laparoscopically assisted nephroureterectomy

●**50549** Unlisted laparoscopy procedure, renal

►(For laparoscopic drainage of lymphocele to peritoneal cavity, use 49323)◄

## Endoscopy

(For supplies and materials, use 99070)

(References to office and hospital have been deleted)

**50551** Renal endoscopy through established nephrostomy or pyelostomy, with or without irrigation, instillation, or ureteropyelography, exclusive of radiologic service;

**50553** with ureteral catheterization, with or without dilation of ureter

**50555** with biopsy

**50557** with fulguration and/or incision, with or without biopsy

**50559** with insertion of radioactive substance with or without biopsy and/or fulguration

**50561** with removal of foreign body or calculus

(When procedures 50570-50580 provide a significant identifiable service, they may be added to 50045 and 50120)

**50570** Renal endoscopy through nephrotomy or pyelotomy, with or without irrigation, instillation, or ureteropyelography, exclusive of radiologic service;

(For nephrotomy, use 50045)

(For pyelotomy, use 50120)

**50572** with ureteral catheterization, with or without dilation of ureter

**50574** with biopsy

**50575** with endopyelotomy (includes cystoscopy, ureteroscopy, dilation of ureter and ureteral pelvic junction, incision of ureteral pelvic junction and insertion of endopyelotomy stent)

**50576** with fulguration and/or incision, with or without biopsy

**50578** with insertion of radioactive substance, with or without biopsy and/or fulguration

**50580** with removal of foreign body or calculus

## Other Procedures

**50590** Lithotripsy, extracorporeal shock wave

# Ureter

## Incision

**50600** Ureterotomy with exploration or drainage (separate procedure)

(For ureteral endoscopy performed in conjunction with this procedure, see 50970-50980)

**50605** Ureterotomy for insertion of indwelling stent, all types

**50610** Ureterolithotomy; upper one-third of ureter

**50620** middle one-third of ureter

**50630** lower one-third of ureter

►(For laparoscopic approach, use 50945)◄

(For transvesical ureterolithotomy, use 51060)

(For cystotomy with stone basket extraction of ureteral calculus, use 51065)

(For endoscopic extraction or manipulation of ureteral calculus, see 50080, 50081, 50561, 50961, 50980, 52320-52330, 52336, 52337)

## Excision

(For ureterocele, see 51535, 52300)

**50650** Ureterectomy, with bladder cuff (separate procedure)

**50660** Ureterectomy, total, ectopic ureter, combination abdominal, vaginal and/or perineal approach

## Introduction

**50684** Injection procedure for ureterography or ureteropyelography through ureterostomy or indwelling ureteral catheter

(For radiological supervision and interpretation, use 74425)

**50686** Manometric studies through ureterostomy or indwelling ureteral catheter

**50688*** Change of ureterostomy tube

(For radiological supervision and interpretation, use 74425)

**50690** Injection procedure for visualization of ileal conduit and/or ureteropyelography, exclusive of radiologic service

(For radiological supervision and interpretation, use 74425)

## Repair

**50700** Ureteroplasty, plastic operation on ureter (eg, stricture)

**50715** Ureterolysis, with or without repositioning of ureter for retroperitoneal fibrosis

(50716 has been deleted. To report, use 50715 with modifier '-50')

**50722** Ureterolysis for ovarian vein syndrome

**50725** Ureterolysis for retrocaval ureter, with reanastomosis of upper urinary tract or vena cava

**50727** Revision of urinary-cutaneous anastomosis (any type urostomy);

**50728** with repair of fascial defect and hernia

**50740** Ureteropyelostomy, anastomosis of ureter and renal pelvis

**50750** Ureterocalycostomy, anastomosis of ureter to renal calyx

**50760** Ureteroureterostomy

**50770** Transureteroureterostomy, anastomosis of ureter to contralateral ureter

(Codes 50780-50785 include minor procedures to prevent vesicoureteral reflux)

**50780** Ureteroneocystostomy; anastomosis of single ureter to bladder

(50781 has been deleted. To report, use 50780 with modifier '-50')

(When combined with cystourethroplasty or vesical neck revision, use 51820)

**50782** anastomosis of duplicated ureter to bladder

**50783** with extensive ureteral tailoring

**50785** with vesico-psoas hitch or bladder flap

(50786 has been deleted. To report, use 50785 with modifier '-50')

**50800** Ureteroenterostomy, direct anastomosis of ureter to intestine

(50801 has been deleted. To report, use 50800 with modifier '-50')

**50810** Ureterosigmoidostomy, with creation of sigmoid bladder and establishment of abdominal or perineal colostomy, including bowel anastomosis

**50815** Ureterocolon conduit, including bowel anastomosis

(50816 has been deleted. To report, use 50815 with modifier '-50')

**50820** Ureteroileal conduit (ileal bladder), including bowel anastomosis (Bricker operation)

(50821 has been deleted. To report, use 50820 with modifier '-50')

(For combination of 50800-50820 with cystectomy, see 51580-51595)

**50825** Continent diversion, including bowel anastomosis using any segment of small and/or large bowel (Kock pouch or Camey enterocystoplasty)

**50830** Urinary undiversion (eg, taking down of ureteroileal conduit, ureterosigmoidostomy or ureteroenterostomy with ureteroureterostomy or ureteroneocystostomy)

**50840** Replacement of all or part of ureter by bowel segment, including bowel anastomosis

(50841 has been deleted. To report, use 50840 with modifier '-50')

**50845** Cutaneous appendico-vesicostomy

**50860** Ureterostomy, transplantation of ureter to skin

(50861 has been deleted. To report, use 50860 with modifier '-50')

**50900** Ureterorrhaphy, suture of ureter (separate procedure)

**50920** Closure of ureterocutaneous fistula

**50930** Closure of ureterovisceral fistula (including visceral repair)

**50940** Deligation of ureter

(For ureteroplasty, ureterolysis, see 50700-50860)

## ▸Laparoscopy◂

▸Surgical laparoscopy always includes diagnostic laparoscopy. To report a diagnostic laparoscopy (peritoneoscopy) (separate procedure), use 49320.◂

●**50945** Laparoscopy, surgical, ureterolithotomy

## Endoscopy

(References to office and hospital have been deleted)

**50951** Ureteral endoscopy through established ureterostomy, with or without irrigation, instillation, or ureteropyelography, exclusive of radiologic service;

**50953** with ureteral catheterization, with or without dilation of ureter

**50955** with biopsy

**50957** with fulguration and/or incision, with or without biopsy

**50959** with insertion of radioactive substance, with or without biopsy and/or fulguration (not including provision of material)

**50961** with removal of foreign body or calculus

(When procedures 50970-50980 provide a significant identifiable service, they may be added to 50600)

**50970** Ureteral endoscopy through ureterotomy, with or without irrigation, instillation, or ureteropyelography, exclusive of radiologic service;

(For ureterotomy, use 50600)

**50972** with ureteral catheterization, with or without dilation of ureter

**50974** with biopsy

**50976** with fulguration and/or incision, with or without biopsy

**50978** with insertion of radioactive substance, with or without biopsy and/or fulguration (not including provision of material)

**50980** with removal of foreign body or calculus

# Bladder

## Incision

**51000*** Aspiration of bladder by needle

**51005*** Aspiration of bladder; by trocar or intracatheter

**51010** with insertion of suprapubic catheter

**51020** Cystotomy or cystostomy; with fulguration and/or insertion of radioactive material

**51030** with cryosurgical destruction of intravesical lesion

**51040** Cystostomy, cystotomy with drainage

**51045** Cystotomy, with insertion of ureteral catheter or stent (separate procedure)

**51050** Cystolithotomy, cystotomy with removal of calculus, without vesical neck resection

**51060** Transvesical ureterolithotomy

**51065** Cystotomy, with stone basket extraction and/or ultrasonic or electrohydraulic fragmentation of ureteral calculus

**51080** Drainage of perivesical or prevesical space abscess

## Excision

**51500** Excision of urachal cyst or sinus, with or without umbilical hernia repair

**51520** Cystotomy; for simple excision of vesical neck (separate procedure)

**51525** for excision of bladder diverticulum, single or multiple (separate procedure)

**51530** for excision of bladder tumor

(For transurethral resection, see 52234-52240, 52305)

**51535** Cystotomy for excision, incision, or repair of ureterocele

(For transurethral excision, use 52300)

(51536 has been deleted. To report, use 51535 with modifier -50)

**51550** Cystectomy, partial; simple

**51555** complicated (eg, postradiation, previous surgery, difficult location)

**51565** Cystectomy, partial, with reimplantation of ureter(s) into bladder (ureteroneocystostomy)

**51570** Cystectomy, complete; (separate procedure)

**51575** with bilateral pelvic lymphadenectomy, including external iliac, hypogastric, and obturator nodes

**51580** Cystectomy, complete, with ureterosigmoidostomy or ureterocutaneous transplantations;

**51585** with bilateral pelvic lymphadenectomy, including external iliac, hypogastric, and obturator nodes

**51590** Cystectomy, complete, with ureteroileal conduit or sigmoid bladder, including bowel anastomosis;

**51595** with bilateral pelvic lymphadenectomy, including external iliac, hypogastric, and obturator nodes

**51596** Cystectomy, complete, with continent diversion, any technique, using any segment of small and/or large bowel to construct neobladder

**51597** Pelvic exenteration, complete, for vesical, prostatic or urethral malignancy, with removal of bladder and ureteral transplantations, with or without hysterectomy and/or abdominoperineal resection of rectum and colon and colostomy, or any combination thereof

(For pelvic exenteration for gynecologic malignancy, use 58240)

## Introduction

(For bladder catheterization, see 53670, 53675)

**51600*** Injection procedure for cystography or voiding urethrocystography

(For radiological supervision and interpretation, see 74430, 74455)

**51605** Injection procedure and placement of chain for contrast and/or chain urethrocystography

(For radiological supervision and interpretation, use 74430)

**51610** Injection procedure for retrograde urethrocystography

(For radiological supervision and interpretation, use 74450)

**51700*** Bladder irrigation, simple, lavage and/or instillation

**51705*** Change of cystostomy tube; simple

**51710*** complicated

**51715** Endoscopic injection of implant material into the submucosal tissues of the urethra and/or bladder neck

**51720** Bladder instillation of anticarcinogenic agent (including detention time)

## Urodynamics

The following section (51725-51797) lists procedures that may be used separately or in many and varied combinations.

When multiple procedures are performed in the same investigative session, modifier '-51' should be employed.

All procedures in this section imply that these services are performed by, or are under the direct supervision of, a physician and that all instruments, equipment, fluids, gases, probes, catheters, technician's fees, medications, gloves, trays, tubing and other sterile supplies be provided by the physician. When the physician only interprets the results and/or operates the equipment, a professional component, modifier '-26', should be used to identify physicians' services.

**51725** Simple cystometrogram (CMG) (eg, spinal manometer)

**51726** Complex cystometrogram (eg, calibrated electronic equipment)

(51727-51733 have been deleted. To report, use 51726)

**51736** Simple uroflowmetry (UFR) (eg, stop-watch flow rate, mechanical uroflowmeter)

(51737, 51738 have been deleted. To report, use 51736)

(51739 has been deleted)

**51741** Complex uroflowmetry (eg, calibrated electronic equipment)

(51742-51749 have been deleted. To report, use 51741)

(51751-51769 have been deleted. To report, use 53899)

**51772** Urethral pressure profile studies (UPP) (urethral closure pressure profile), any technique

(51773-51783 have been deleted. To report, use 51772)

**51784** Electromyography studies (EMG) of anal or urethral sphincter, other than needle, any technique

**51785** Needle electromyography studies (EMG) of anal or urethral sphincter, any technique

(51786-51791 have been deleted. To report, use 51785)

**51792** Stimulus evoked response (eg, measurement of bulbocavernosus reflex latency time)

**51795** Voiding pressure studies (VP); bladder voiding pressure, any technique

(51796 has been deleted. To report, use 51795)

**51797** intra-abdominal voiding pressure (AP) (rectal, gastric, intraperitoneal)

## Repair

**51800** Cystoplasty or cystourethroplasty, plastic operation on bladder and/or vesical neck (anterior Y-plasty, vesical fundus resection), any procedure, with or without wedge resection of posterior vesical neck

**51820** Cystourethroplasty with unilateral or bilateral ureteroneocystostomy

**51840** Anterior vesicourethropexy, or urethropexy (eg, Marshall-Marchetti-Krantz, Burch); simple

**51841** complicated (eg, secondary repair)

(For urethropexy (Pereyra type), use 57289)

**51845** Abdomino-vaginal vesical neck suspension, with or without endoscopic control (eg, Stamey, Raz, modified Pereyra)

**51860** Cystorrhaphy, suture of bladder wound, injury or rupture; simple

**51865** complicated

**51880** Closure of cystostomy (separate procedure)

**51900** Closure of vesicovaginal fistula, abdominal approach

(For vaginal approach, see 57320-57330)

**51920** Closure of vesicouterine fistula;

**51925** with hysterectomy

(For closure of vesicoenteric fistula, see 44660, 44661)

(For closure of rectovesical fistula, see 45800-45805)

**51940** Closure of bladder exstrophy

(See also 54390)

**51960** Enterocystoplasty, including bowel anastomosis

**51980** Cutaneous vesicostomy

## ►Laparoscopy◄

►Surgical laparoscopy always includes diagnostic laparoscopy. To report a diagnostic laparoscopy (peritoneoscopy) (separate procedure), use 49320.◄

●**51990** Laparoscopy, surgical; urethral suspension for stress incontinence

●**51992** sling operation for stress incontinence (eg, fascia or synthetic)

## Endoscopy—Cystoscopy, Urethroscopy, Cystourethroscopy

Endoscopic descriptions are listed so that the main procedure can be identified without having to list all the minor related functions performed at the same time. For example: meatotomy, urethral calibration and/or dilation, urethroscopy, and cystoscopy prior to a transurethral resection of prostate; ureteral catheterization following extraction of ureteral calculus; internal urethrotomy and bladder neck fulguration when performing a cystourethroscopy for the female urethral syndrome. When the secondary procedure requires significant additional time and effort, it may be identified by the addition of modifier '-22'.

For example: urethrotomy performed for a documented pre-existing stricture or bladder neck contracture.

(References to office and hospital have been deleted)

**52000** Cystourethroscopy (separate procedure)

**52005** Cystourethroscopy, with ureteral catheterization, with or without irrigation, instillation, or ureteropyelography, exclusive of radiologic service;

**52007** with brush biopsy of ureter and/or renal pelvis

**52010** Cystourethroscopy, with ejaculatory duct catheterization, with or without irrigation, instillation, or duct radiography, exclusive of radiologic service

(For radiological supervision and interpretation, use 74440)

(52190 has been deleted)

## Transurethral Surgery

### Urethra and Bladder

(References to office and hospital have been deleted)

**52204** Cystourethroscopy, with biopsy

**52214** Cystourethroscopy, with fulguration (including cryosurgery or laser surgery) of trigone, bladder neck, prostatic fossa, urethra, or periurethral glands

**52224** Cystourethroscopy, with fulguration (including cryosurgery or laser surgery) or treatment of MINOR (less than 0.5 cm) lesion(s) with or without biopsy

**52234** Cystourethroscopy, with fulguration (including cryosurgery or laser surgery) and/or resection of; SMALL bladder tumor(s) (0.5 to 2.0 cm)

**52235** MEDIUM bladder tumor(s) (2.0 to 5.0 cm)

**52240** LARGE bladder tumor(s)

**52250** Cystourethroscopy with insertion of radioactive substance, with or without biopsy or fulguration

**52260** Cystourethroscopy, with dilation of bladder for interstitial cystitis; general or conduction (spinal) anesthesia

**52265** local anesthesia

**52270** Cystourethroscopy, with internal urethrotomy; female

**52275** male

**52276** Cystourethroscopy with direct vision internal urethrotomy

**52277** Cystourethroscopy, with resection of external sphincter (sphincterotomy)

**52281** Cystourethroscopy, with calibration and/or dilation of urethral stricture or stenosis, with or without meatotomy, with or without injection procedure for cystography, male or female

**52282** Cystourethroscopy, with insertion of urethral stent

**52283** Cystourethroscopy, with steroid injection into stricture

**52285** Cystourethroscopy for treatment of the female urethral syndrome with any or all of the following: urethral meatotomy, urethral dilation, internal urethrotomy, lysis of urethrovaginal septal fibrosis, lateral incisions of the bladder neck, and fulguration of polyp(s) of urethra, bladder neck, and/or trigone

**52290** Cystourethroscopy; with ureteral meatotomy, unilateral or bilateral

**52300** with resection or fulguration of orthotopic ureterocele(s), unilateral or bilateral

**52301** with resection or fulguration of ectopic ureterocele(s), unilateral or bilateral

**52305** with incision or resection of orifice of bladder diverticulum, single or multiple

**52310** Cystourethroscopy, with removal of foreign body, calculus, or ureteral stent from urethra or bladder (separate procedure); simple

**52315** complicated

**52317** Litholapaxy: crushing or fragmentation of calculus by any means in bladder and removal of fragments; simple or small (less than 2.5 cm)

**52318** complicated or large (over 2.5 cm)

## Ureter and Pelvis

The insertion and removal of a temporary stent during diagnostic or therapeutic cystourethroscopic intervention(s) is included in 52320-52339 and should not be reported separately.

To report insertion of a self-retaining, indwelling stent performed during cystourethroscopic diagnostic or therapeutic intervention(s), use code 52332, in addition to primary procedure(s) performed, and append the modifier '-51'. Code 52332 is used to report a unilateral procedure unless otherwise specified.

For bilateral insertion of self-retaining, indwelling ureteral stents, use code 52332, and append the modifier '-50'.

To report cystourethroscopic removal of a self-retaining, indwelling ureteral stent, see codes 52310, 52315, and append the modifier '-58'.

**52320** Cystourethroscopy (including ureteral catheterization); with removal of ureteral calculus

**52325** with fragmentation of ureteral calculus (eg, ultrasonic or electro-hydraulic technique)

**52327** with subureteric injection of implant material

**52330** with manipulation, without removal of ureteral calculus

**52332** Cystourethroscopy, with insertion of indwelling ureteral stent (eg, Gibbons or double-J type)

**52334** Cystourethroscopy with insertion of ureteral guide wire through kidney to establish a percutaneous nephrostomy, retrograde

(For percutaneous nephrostolithotomy, see 50080, 50081; for establishment of nephrostomy tract only, use 50395)

**52335** Cystourethroscopy, with ureteroscopy and/or pyeloscopy (includes dilation of the ureter and/or pyeloureteral junction by any method);

(For radiological supervision and interpretation, use 74485)

**52336** with removal or manipulation of calculus (ureteral catheterization is included)

**52337** with lithotripsy (ureteral catheterization is included)

**52338** with biopsy and/or fulguration of lesion

**52339** with resection of tumor

## Vesical Neck and Prostate

**52340** Cystourethroscopy with incision, fulguration, or resection of congenital posterior urethral valves, or congenital obstructive hypertrophic mucosal folds

**52450** Transurethral incision of prostate

**52500** Transurethral resection of bladder neck (separate procedure)

**52510** Transurethral balloon dilation of the prostatic urethra, any method

**52601** Transurethral electrosurgical resection of prostate, including control of postoperative bleeding, complete (vasectomy, meatotomy, cystourethroscopy, urethral calibration and/or dilation, and internal urethrotomy are included)

(For other approaches, see 55801-55845)

(52605 has been deleted. To report, use 52606)

**52606** Transurethral fulguration for postoperative bleeding occurring after the usual follow-up time

**52612** Transurethral resection of prostate; first stage of two-stage resection (partial resection)

**52614** second stage of two-stage resection (resection completed)

**52620** Transurethral resection; of residual obstructive tissue after 90 days postoperative

**52630** of regrowth of obstructive tissue longer than one year postoperative

**52640** of postoperative bladder neck contracture

**52647** Non-contact laser coagulation of prostate, including control of postoperative bleeding, complete (vasectomy, meatotomy, cystourethroscopy, urethral calibration and/or dilation, and internal urethrotomy are included)

**52648** Contact laser vaporization with or without transurethral resection of prostate, including control of postoperative bleeding, complete (vasectomy, meatotomy, cystourethroscopy, urethral calibration and/or dilation, and internal urethrotomy are included)

(52650 has been deleted)

**52700** Transurethral drainage of prostatic abscess

(52800, 52805 have been deleted. To report, see 52317, 52318)

# Urethra

(For endoscopy, see cystoscopy, urethroscopy, cystourethroscopy, 52000-52700)

(For injection procedure for urethrocystography, see 51600-51610)

## Incision

**53000** Urethrotomy or urethrostomy, external (separate procedure); pendulous urethra

**53010** perineal urethra, external

**53020** Meatotomy, cutting of meatus (separate procedure); except infant

(53021 has been deleted. To report, use 53020)

**53025** infant

**53040** Drainage of deep periurethral abscess

(For subcutaneous abscess, see 10060, 10061)

**53060** Drainage of Skene's gland abscess or cyst

**53080** Drainage of perineal urinary extravasation; uncomplicated (separate procedure)

**53085** complicated

## Excision

**53200** Biopsy of urethra

**53210** Urethrectomy, total, including cystostomy; female

**53215** male

**53220** Excision or fulguration of carcinoma of urethra

**53230** Excision of urethral diverticulum (separate procedure); female

**53235** male

**53240** Marsupialization of urethral diverticulum, male or female

**53250** Excision of bulbourethral gland (Cowper's gland)

**53260** Excision or fulguration; urethral polyp(s), distal urethra

(For endoscopic approach, see 52214, 52224)

**53265** urethral caruncle

**53270** Skene's glands

**53275** urethral prolapse

## Repair

(For hypospadias, see 54300-54352)

**53400** Urethroplasty; first stage, for fistula, diverticulum, or stricture (eg, Johannsen type)

**53405** second stage (formation of urethra), including urinary diversion

**53410** Urethroplasty, one-stage reconstruction of male anterior urethra

**53415** Urethroplasty, transpubic or perineal, one stage, for reconstruction or repair of prostatic or membranous urethra

**53420** Urethroplasty, two-stage reconstruction or repair of prostatic or membranous urethra; first stage

**53425** second stage

**53430** Urethroplasty, reconstruction of female urethra

**53440** Operation for correction of male urinary incontinence, with or without introduction of prosthesis

**53442** Removal of perineal prosthesis introduced for continence

**53443** Urethroplasty with tubularization of posterior urethra and/ or lower bladder for incontinence (eg, Tenago, Leadbetter procedure)

**53445** Operation for correction of urinary incontinence with placement of inflatable urethral or bladder neck sphincter, including placement of pump and/or reservoir

**53447** Removal, repair, or replacement of inflatable sphincter including pump and/or reservoir and/or cuff

**53449** Surgical correction of hydraulic abnormality of inflatable sphincter device

**53450** Urethromeatoplasty, with mucosal advancement

(For meatotomy, see 53020, 53025)

**53460** Urethromeatoplasty, with partial excision of distal urethral segment (Richardson type procedure)

**53502** Urethrorrhaphy, suture of urethral wound or injury, female

**53505** Urethrorrhaphy, suture of urethral wound or injury; penile

**53510** perineal

**53515** prostatomembranous

**53520** Closure of urethrostomy or urethrocutaneous fistula, male (separate procedure)

(For closure of urethrovaginal fistula, use 57310)

(For closure of urethrorectal fistula, see 45820, 45825)

## Manipulation

(For radiological supervision and interpretation, use 74485)

**53600*** Dilation of urethral stricture by passage of sound or urethral dilator, male; initial

**53601*** subsequent

**53605** Dilation of urethral stricture or vesical neck by passage of sound or urethral dilator, male, general or conduction (spinal) anesthesia

**53620*** Dilation of urethral stricture by passage of filiform and follower, male; initial

**53621*** subsequent

(53640 has been deleted. To report, use 53620)

**53660*** Dilation of female urethra including suppository and/or instillation; initial

**53661*** subsequent

**53665** Dilation of female urethra, general or conduction (spinal) anesthesia

**53670*** Catheterization, urethra; simple

**53675*** complicated (may include difficult removal of balloon catheter)

## Other Procedures

(53800 has been deleted. To report, use 81020)

**53850** Transurethral destruction of prostate tissue; by microwave thermotherapy

**53852** by radiofrequency thermotherapy

**53899** Unlisted procedure, urinary system

# Male Genital System

## Penis

### Incision

**54000** Slitting of prepuce, dorsal or lateral (separate procedure); newborn

**54001** except newborn

**54015** Incision and drainage of penis, deep

(For skin and subcutaneous abscess, see 10060-10160)

### Destruction

**54050*** Destruction of lesion(s), penis (eg, condyloma, papilloma, molluscum contagiosum, herpetic vesicle), simple; chemical

**54055*** electrodesiccation

**54056** cryosurgery

**54057** laser surgery

**54060** surgical excision

**54065** Destruction of lesion(s), penis (eg, condyloma, papilloma, molluscum contagiosum, herpetic vesicle), extensive, any method

(For destruction or excision of other lesions, see **Integumentary System**)

### Excision

▲**54100** Biopsy of penis; (separate procedure)

**54105** deep structures

**54110** Excision of penile plaque (Peyronie disease);

**54111** with graft to 5 cm in length

**54112** with graft greater than 5 cm in length

**54115** Removal foreign body from deep penile tissue (eg, plastic implant)

**54120** Amputation of penis; partial

**54125** complete

**54130** Amputation of penis, radical; with bilateral inguinofemoral lymphadenectomy

**54135** in continuity with bilateral pelvic lymphadenectomy, including external iliac, hypogastric and obturator nodes

(For lymphadenectomy (separate procedure), see 38760-38770)

**54150** Circumcision, using clamp or other device; newborn

**54152** except newborn

(54154 has been deleted. To report, use 54152)

**54160** Circumcision, surgical excision other than clamp, device or dorsal slit; newborn

**54161** except newborn

### Introduction

**54200*** Injection procedure for Peyronie disease;

**54205** with surgical exposure of plaque

**54220** Irrigation of corpora cavernosa for priapism

**54230** Injection procedure for corpora cavernosography

(For radiological supervision and interpretation, use 74445)

**54231** Dynamic cavernosometry, including intracavernosal injection of vasoactive drugs (eg, papaverine, phentolamine)

**54235** Injection of corpora cavernosa with pharmacologic agent(s) (eg, papaverine, phentolamine)

**54240** Penile plethysmography

**54250** Nocturnal penile tumescence and/or rigidity test

## Repair

(For other urethroplasties, see 53400-53430)

(For penile revascularization, use 37788)

**54300** Plastic operation of penis for straightening of chordee (eg, hypospadias), with or without mobilization of urethra

**54304** Plastic operation on penis for correction of chordee or for first stage hypospadias repair with or without transplantation of prepuce and/or skin flaps

(54305 has been deleted. To report, see 54304 et seq)

**54308** Urethroplasty for second stage hypospadias repair (including urinary diversion); less than 3 cm

**54312** greater than 3 cm

**54316** Urethroplasty for second stage hypospadias repair (including urinary diversion) with free skin graft obtained from site other than genitalia

**54318** Urethroplasty for third stage hypospadias repair to release penis from scrotum (eg, third stage Cecil repair)

(54320 has been deleted. To report, see 54308 et seq)

**54322** One stage distal hypospadias repair (with or without chordee or circumcision); with simple meatal advancement (eg, Magpi, V-flap)

**54324** with urethroplasty by local skin flaps (eg, flip-flap, prepucial flap)

(54325 has been deleted. To report, see 54308 et seq)

**54326** with urethroplasty by local skin flaps and mobilization of urethra

**54328** with extensive dissection to correct chordee and urethroplasty with local skin flaps, skin graft patch, and/or island flap

(54330 has been deleted. To report, use 54308)

**54332** One stage proximal penile or penoscrotal hypospadias repair requiring extensive dissection to correct chordee and urethroplasty by use of skin graft tube and/or island flap

**54336** One stage perineal hypospadias repair requiring extensive dissection to correct chordee and urethroplasty by use of skin graft tube and/or island flap

**54340** Repair of hypospadias complications (ie, fistula, stricture, diverticula); by closure, incision, or excision, simple

**54344** requiring mobilization of skin flaps and urethroplasty with flap or patch graft

**54348** requiring extensive dissection and urethroplasty with flap, patch or tubed graft (includes urinary diversion)

**54352** Repair of hypospadias cripple requiring extensive dissection and excision of previously constructed structures including re-release of chordee and reconstruction of urethra and penis by use of local skin as grafts and island flaps and skin brought in as flaps or grafts

**54360** Plastic operation on penis to correct angulation

**54380** Plastic operation on penis for epispadias distal to external sphincter;

**54385** with incontinence

**54390** with exstrophy of bladder

**54400** Insertion of penile prosthesis; non-inflatable (semi-rigid)

**54401** inflatable (self-contained)

**54402** Removal or replacement of non-inflatable (semi-rigid) or inflatable (self-contained) penile prosthesis

**54405** Insertion of inflatable (multi-component) penile prosthesis, including placement of pump, cylinders, and/or reservoir

**54407** Removal, repair, or replacement of inflatable (multi-component) penile prosthesis, including pump and/or reservoir and/or cylinders

**54409** Surgical correction of hydraulic abnormality of inflatable (multi-component) prosthesis including pump and/or reservoir and/or cylinders

**54420** Corpora cavernosa-saphenous vein shunt (priapism operation), unilateral or bilateral

**54430** Corpora cavernosa-corpus spongiosum shunt (priapism operation), unilateral or bilateral

**54435** Corpora cavernosa-glans penis fistulization (eg, biopsy needle, Winter procedure, rongeur, or punch) for priapism

**54440** Plastic operation of penis for injury

## Manipulation

**54450** Foreskin manipulation including lysis of preputial adhesions and stretching

# Testis

## Excision

**54500** Biopsy of testis, needle (separate procedure)

(For fine needle aspiration, preparation, and interpretation of smears, see 88170-88173)

**54505** Biopsy of testis, incisional (separate procedure)

(When combined with vasogram, seminal vesiculogram, or epididymogram, use 55300)

(54506 has been deleted. To report, use 54505 with modifier '-50')

**54510** Excision of local lesion of testis

**54520** Orchiectomy, simple (including subcapsular), with or without testicular prosthesis, scrotal or inguinal approach

(54521 has been deleted. To report, use 54520 with modifier '-50')

**54530** Orchiectomy, radical, for tumor; inguinal approach

**54535** with abdominal exploration

(For orchiectomy with repair of hernia, see 49505 or 49507 and 54520)

(For radical retroperitoneal lymphadenectomy, use 38780)

**54550** Exploration for undescended testis (inguinal or scrotal area)

(54555 has been deleted. To report, use 54550 with modifier '-50')

**54560** Exploration for undescended testis with abdominal exploration

(54565 has been deleted. To report, use 54560 with modifier '-50')

## Repair

**54600** Reduction of torsion of testis, surgical, with or without fixation of contralateral testis

**54620** Fixation of contralateral testis (separate procedure)

**54640** Orchiopexy, inguinal approach, with or without hernia repair

(54641 has been deleted. To report, use 54640 with modifier '-50')

(54645 has been deleted)

**54650** Orchiopexy, abdominal approach, for intra-abdominal testis (eg, Fowler-Stephens)

►(For laparoscopic approach, use 54692)◄

**54660** Insertion of testicular prosthesis (separate procedure)

(54661 has been deleted. To report, use 54660 with modifier '-50')

**54670** Suture or repair of testicular injury

**54680** Transplantation of testis(es) to thigh (because of scrotal destruction)

## ►Laparoscopy◄

►Surgical laparoscopy always includes diagnostic laparoscopy. To report a diagnostic laparoscopy (peritoneoscopy) (separate procedure), use 49320.◄

●54690 Laparoscopy, surgical; orchiectomy

●54692 orchiopexy for intra-abdominal testis

●54699 Unlisted laparoscopy procedure, testis

# Epididymis

## Incision

**54700** Incision and drainage of epididymis, testis and/or scrotal space (eg, abscess or hematoma)

## Excision

**54800** Biopsy of epididymis, needle

(For fine needle aspiration, preparation, and interpretation of smears, see 88170-88173)

**54820** Exploration of epididymis, with or without biopsy

**54830** Excision of local lesion of epididymis

**54840** Excision of spermatocele, with or without epididymectomy

**54860** Epididymectomy; unilateral

**54861** bilateral

## Repair

**54900** Epididymovasostomy, anastomosis of epididymis to vas deferens; unilateral

**54901** bilateral

(For operating microscope, use 69990)

# Tunica Vaginalis

## Incision

**55000*** Puncture aspiration of hydrocele, tunica vaginalis, with or without injection of medication

## Excision

**55040** Excision of hydrocele; unilateral

**55041** bilateral

(With hernia repair, see 49495-49501)

## Repair

**55060** Repair of tunica vaginalis hydrocele (Bottle type)

# Scrotum

## Incision

**55100*** Drainage of scrotal wall abscess

(See also 54700)

**55110** Scrotal exploration

**55120** Removal of foreign body in scrotum

## Excision

(For excision of local lesion of skin of scrotum, see **Integumentary System**)

**55150** Resection of scrotum

## Repair

(55170 has been deleted. To report, see 55175, 55180)

**55175** Scrotoplasty; simple

**55180** complicated

# Vas Deferens

## Incision

**55200** Vasotomy, cannulization with or without incision of vas, unilateral or bilateral (separate procedure)

## Excision

**55250** Vasectomy, unilateral or bilateral (separate procedure), including postoperative semen examination(s)

## Introduction

**55300** Vasotomy for vasograms, seminal vesiculograms, or epididymograms, unilateral or bilateral

(For radiological supervision and interpretation, use 74440)

(When combined with biopsy of testis, see 54505 and use modifier '-51')

## Repair

**55400** Vasovasostomy, vasovasorrhaphy

(For operating microscope, use 69990)

(55401 has been deleted. To report, use 55400 with modifier '-50')

## Suture

**55450** Ligation (percutaneous) of vas deferens, unilateral or bilateral (separate procedure)

# Spermatic Cord

## Excision

**55500** Excision of hydrocele of spermatic cord, unilateral (separate procedure)

**55520** Excision of lesion of spermatic cord (separate procedure)

**55530** Excision of varicocele or ligation of spermatic veins for varicocele; (separate procedure)

**55535** abdominal approach

**55540** with hernia repair

## ►Laparoscopy◄

►Surgical laparoscopy always includes diagnostic laparoscopy. To report a diagnostic laparoscopy (peritoneoscopy) (separate procedure), use 49320.◄

●**55550** Laparoscopy, surgical, with ligation of spermatic veins for varicocele

●**55559** Unlisted laparoscopy procedure, spermatic cord

# Seminal Vesicles

## Incision

**55600** Vesiculotomy;

(55601 has been deleted. To report, use 55600 with modifier '-50')

**55605** complicated

## Excision

**55650** Vesiculectomy, any approach

(55651 has been deleted. To report, use 55650 with modifier '-50')

**55680** Excision of Mullerian duct cyst

(For injection procedure, see 52010, 55300)

# Prostate

## Incision

**55700** Biopsy, prostate; needle or punch, single or multiple, any approach

(For fine needle aspiration, preparation, and interpretation of smears, see 88170-88173)

**55705** incisional, any approach

**55720** Prostatotomy, external drainage of prostatic abscess, any approach; simple

**55725** complicated

(For transurethral drainage, use 52700)

(55740 has been deleted. To report, use 55899)

## Excision

(For transurethral removal of prostate, see 52601-52640)

(For transurethral destruction of prostate, see 53850-53852)

(For limited pelvic lymphadenectomy for staging (separate procedure), use 38562)

(For independent node dissection, see 38770-38780)

**55801** Prostatectomy, perineal, subtotal (including control of postoperative bleeding, vasectomy, meatotomy, urethral calibration and/or dilation, and internal urethrotomy)

**55810** Prostatectomy, perineal radical;

**55812** with lymph node biopsy(s) (limited pelvic lymphadenectomy)

**55815** with bilateral pelvic lymphadenectomy, including external iliac, hypogastric and obturator nodes

(If 55815 is carried out on separate days, use 38770 with modifier '-50' and 55810)

**55821** Prostatectomy (including control of postoperative bleeding, vasectomy, meatotomy, urethral calibration and/or dilation, and internal urethrotomy); suprapubic, subtotal, one or two stages

**55831** retropubic, subtotal

**55840** Prostatectomy, retropubic radical, with or without nerve sparing;

**55842** with lymph node biopsy(s) (limited pelvic lymphadenectomy)

**55845** with bilateral pelvic lymphadenectomy, including external iliac, hypogastric, and obturator nodes

(If 55845 is carried out on separate days, use 38770 with modifier '-50' and 55840)

**55859** Transperineal placement of needles or catheters into prostate for interstitial radioelement application, with or without cystoscopy

(For interstitial radioelement application, see 77776-77778)

(For ultrasonic guidance for interstitial radioelement application, use 76965)

**55860** Exposure of prostate, any approach, for insertion of radioactive substance;

(For application of interstital radioelement, see 77776-77778)

**55862** with lymph node biopsy(s) (limited pelvic lymphadenectomy)

**55865** with bilateral pelvic lymphadenectomy, including external iliac, hypogastric and obturator nodes

## Other Procedures

(For artificial insemination, see 58321, 58322)

**55870** Electroejaculation

**55899** Unlisted procedure, male genital system

# Intersex Surgery

**55970** Intersex surgery; male to female

**55980** female to male

►(56300 has been deleted. To report, use 49320)◄

►(56301 has been deleted. To report, use 58670)◄

►(56302 has been deleted. To report, use 58671)◄

►(56303 has been deleted. To report, use 58662)◄

►(56304 has been deleted. To report, use 58660)◄

►(56305 has been deleted. To report, use 49321)◄

►(56306 has been deleted. To report, use 49322)◄

►(56307 has been deleted. To report, use 58661)◄

►(56308 has been deleted. To report, use 58550)◄

►(56309 has been deleted. To report, use 58551)◄

►(56310 has been deleted. To report, use 44200)◄

►(56311 has been deleted. To report, use 38570)◄

►(56312 has been deleted. To report, use 38571)◄

►(56313 has been deleted. To report, use 38572)◄

►(56314 has been deleted. To report, use 49323)◄

►(56315 has been deleted. To report, use 44970)◄

►(56316 has been deleted. To report, use 49650)◄

►(56317 has been deleted. To report, use 49651)◄

►(56318 has been deleted. To report, use 54690)◄

►(56320 has been deleted. To report, use 55550)◄

►(56321 has been deleted. To report, use 60650)◄

►(56322 has been deleted. To report, use 43651)◄

►(56323 has been deleted. To report, use 43652)◄

►(56324 has been deleted. To report, use 47570)◄

►(56340 has been deleted. To report, use 47562)◄

►(56341 has been deleted. To report, use 47563)◄

►(56342 has been deleted. To report, use 47564)◄

►(56343 has been deleted. To report, use 58673)◄

►(56344 has been deleted. To report, use 58672)◄

►(56345 has been deleted. To report, use 38120)◄

►(56346 has been deleted. To report, use 43653)◄

►(56347 has been deleted. To report, use 44201)◄

►(56348 has been deleted. To report, use 44202)◄

►(56349 has been deleted. To report, use 43280)◄

►(56350 has been deleted. To report, use 58555)◄

►(56351 has been deleted. To report, use 58558)◄

►(56352 has been deleted. To report, use 58559)◄

►(56353 has been deleted. To report, use 58560)◄

►(56354 has been deleted. To report, use 58561)◄

►(56355 has been deleted. To report, use 58562)◄

►(56356 has been deleted. To report, use 58563)◄

►(56360 has been deleted. To report, use 49320)◄

►(56361 has been deleted. To report, use 49321)◄

►(56362 has been deleted. To report, use 47560)◄

►(56363 has been deleted. To report, use 47561)◄

►(56399 has been deleted. To report, see site-specific unlisted laparoscopy/hysteroscopy procedure codes)◄

# Female Genital System

(For pelvic laparotomy, use 49000)

(For excision or destruction of endometriomas, open method, see 49200, 49201)

(For paracentesis, see 49080, 49081)

(For secondary closure of abdominal wall evisceration or disruption, use 49900)

(For fulguration or excision of lesions, laparoscopic approach, use ►58662◄)

(For chemotherapy, see 96400-96549)

(56000 has been deleted. To report, use 56405)

(56100 has been deleted. To report, use 56605)

(56200 has been deleted. To report, use 56810)

## Vulva, Perineum and Introitus

**Definitions**

The following definitions apply to the vulvectomy codes (56620-56640).

A ***simple*** procedure is the removal of skin and superficial subcutaneous tissues.

A ***radical*** procedure is the removal of skin and deep subcutaneous tissue.

A ***partial*** procedure is the removal of less than 80% of the vulvar area.

A ***complete*** procedure is the removal of greater than 80% of the vulvar area.

### Incision

(For incision and drainage of sebaceous cyst, furuncle, or abscess, see 10040, 10060, 10061)

(56400 has been deleted. To report, use 56405)

**56405*** Incision and drainage of vulva or perineal abscess

**56420*** Incision and drainage of Bartholin's gland abscess

(For incision and drainage of Skene's gland abscess or cyst, use 53060)

**56440** Marsupialization of Bartholin's gland cyst

**56441** Lysis of labial adhesions

### Destruction

(56500 has been deleted. To report, use 56501)

**56501** Destruction of lesion(s), vulva; simple, any method

(56505-56507, 56510 have been deleted. To report, use 56501)

**56515** extensive, any method

(56520, 56521 have been deleted. To report, use 56501 or 56515)

(For destruction of Skene's gland cyst or abscess, use 53270)

(For cautery destruction of urethral caruncle, use 53265)

### Excision

(56600 has been deleted. To report, use 56605)

**56605*** Biopsy of vulva or perineum (separate procedure); one lesion

**+ 56606*** each separate additional lesion (List separately in addition to code for primary procedure)

(Use 56606 in conjunction with code 56605)

(For excision of local lesion, see 11420-11426, 11620-11626)

**56620** Vulvectomy simple; partial

**56625** complete

(For skin graft, see 15000 et seq)

**56630** Vulvectomy, radical, partial;

(For skin graft, if used, see 15000, 15120, 15121, 15240, 15241)

**56631** with unilateral inguinofemoral lymphadenectomy

**56632** with bilateral inguinofemoral lymphadenectomy

**56633** Vulvectomy, radical, complete;

**56634** with unilateral inguinofemoral lymphadenectomy

(56635 has been deleted. To report, see 56634, 56637)

(56636 has been deleted. To report, see 56634, 56637)

**56637** with bilateral inguinofemoral lymphadenectomy

**56640** Vulvectomy, radical, complete, with inguinofemoral, iliac, and pelvic lymphadenectomy

(56641 has been deleted. To report, use 56640 with modifier '-50')

(For lymphadenectomy, see 38760-38780)

(56680, 56685 have been deleted)

**56700** Partial hymenectomy or revision of hymenal ring

(56710 has been deleted. To report, use 56700)

**56720*** Hymenotomy, simple incision

**56740** Excision of Bartholin's gland or cyst

(For excision of Skene's gland, use 53270)

(For excision of urethral caruncle, use 53265)

(For excision or fulguration of urethral carcinoma, use 53220)

(For excision or marsupialization of urethral diverticulum, see 53230, 53240)

## Repair

(For repair of urethra for mucosal prolapse, use 53275)

**56800** Plastic repair of introitus

**56805** Clitoroplasty for intersex state

**56810** Perineoplasty, repair of perineum, nonobstetrical (separate procedure)

(See also 56800)

(For repair of wounds to genitalia, see 12001-12007, 12041-12047, 13131-13133)

(For repair of recent injury of vagina and perineum, nonobstetrical, use 57210)

(For anal sphincteroplasty, see 46750, 46751)

(For episiorrhaphy, episioperineorrhaphy for recent injury of vulva and/or perineum, nonobstetrical, use 57210)

# Vagina

## Incision

**57000** Colpotomy; with exploration

**57010** with drainage of pelvic abscess

**57020*** Colpocentesis (separate procedure)

## Destruction

(57050, 57057, 57060 have been deleted. To report, use 57061 or 57065)

**57061** Destruction of vaginal lesion(s); simple, any method

(57063 has been deleted. To report, use 57061 or 57065)

**57065** extensive, any method

## Excision

**57100*** Biopsy of vaginal mucosa; simple (separate procedure)

**57105** extensive, requiring suture (including cysts)

**57106** Vaginectomy, partial removal of vaginal wall;

**57107** with removal of paravaginal tissue (radical vaginectomy)

(57108 has been deleted. To report, use 57106)

**57109** with removal of paravaginal tissue (radical vaginectomy) with bilateral total pelvic lymphadenectomy and para-aortic lymph node sampling (biopsy)

**57110** Vaginectomy, complete removal of vaginal wall;

**57111** with removal of paravaginal tissue (radical vaginectomy)

**57112** with removal of paravaginal tissue (radical vaginectomy) with bilateral total pelvic lymphadenectomy and para-aortic lymph node sampling (biopsy)

**57120** Colpocleisis (Le Fort type)

**57130** Excision of vaginal septum

**57135** Excision of vaginal cyst or tumor

## Introduction

**57150*** Irrigation of vagina and/or application of medicament for treatment of bacterial, parasitic, or fungoid disease

**57160*** Fitting and insertion of pessary or other intravaginal support device

**57170** Diaphragm or cervical cap fitting with instructions

**57180** Introduction of any hemostatic agent or pack for spontaneous or traumatic nonobstetrical vaginal hemorrhage (separate procedure)

## Repair

(For urethral suspension, Marshall-Marchetti-Krantz type, abdominal approach, see 51840, 51841)

►(For laparoscopic suspension, use 51990)◄

**57200** Colporrhaphy, suture of injury of vagina (nonobstetrical)

**57210** Colpoperineorrhaphy, suture of injury of vagina and/or perineum (nonobstetrical)

**57220** Plastic operation on urethral sphincter, vaginal approach (eg, Kelly urethral plication)

**57230** Plastic repair of urethrocele

**57240** Anterior colporrhaphy, repair of cystocele with or without repair of urethrocele

**57250** Posterior colporrhaphy, repair of rectocele with or without perineorrhaphy

(For repair of rectocele (separate procedure) without posterior colporrhaphy, use 45560)

**57260** Combined anteroposterior colporrhaphy;

**57265** with enterocele repair

**57268** Repair of enterocele, vaginal approach (separate procedure)

**57270** Repair of enterocele, abdominal approach (separate procedure)

**57280** Colpopexy, abdominal approach

**57282** Sacrospinous ligament fixation for prolapse of vagina

**57284** Paravaginal defect repair (including repair of cystocele, stress urinary incontinence, and/or incomplete vaginal prolapse)

**57288** Sling operation for stress incontinence (eg, fascia or synthetic)

►(For laparoscopic approach, use 51992)◄

**57289** Pereyra procedure, including anterior colporrhaphy

(57290 has been deleted. To report, use 57291 or 57292)

**57291** Construction of artificial vagina; without graft

**57292** with graft

**57300** Closure of rectovaginal fistula; vaginal or transanal approach

**57305** abdominal approach

**57307** abdominal approach, with concomitant colostomy

**57308** transperineal approach, with perineal body reconstruction, with or without levator plication

**57310** Closure of urethrovaginal fistula;

**57311** with bulbocavernosus transplant

**57320** Closure of vesicovaginal fistula; vaginal approach

(For concomitant cystostomy, see 51005-51040)

**57330** transvesical and vaginal approach

(For abdominal approach, use 51900)

**57335** Vaginoplasty for intersex state

## Manipulation

**57400*** Dilation of vagina under anesthesia

**57410*** Pelvic examination under anesthesia

**57415** Removal of impacted vaginal foreign body (separate procedure) under anesthesia

(For removal without anesthesia of an impacted vaginal foreign body, use the appropriate E/M code)

## Endoscopy

(57450, 57451 have been deleted)

**57452*** Colposcopy (vaginoscopy); (separate procedure)

**57454*** with biopsy(s) of the cervix and/or endocervical curettage

**57460** with loop electrode excision procedure of the cervix

# Cervix Uteri

## Excision

(For radical surgical procedures, see 58200-58240)

**57500*** Biopsy, single or multiple, or local excision of lesion, with or without fulguration (separate procedure)

**57505** Endocervical curettage (not done as part of a dilation and curettage)

**57510** Cauterization of cervix; electro or thermal

**57511*** cryocautery, initial or repeat

**57513** laser ablation

**57520** Conization of cervix, with or without fulguration, with or without dilation and curettage, with or without repair; cold knife or laser

(See also 58120)

**57522** loop electrode excision

**57530** Trachelectomy (cervicectomy), amputation of cervix (separate procedure)

**57531** Radical trachelectomy, with bilateral total pelvic lymphadenectomy and para-aortic lymph node sampling biopsy, with or without removal of tube(s), with or without removal of ovary(s)

(For radical abdominal hysterectomy, use 58210)

**57540** Excision of cervical stump, abdominal approach;

**57545** with pelvic floor repair

**57550** Excision of cervical stump, vaginal approach;

**57555** with anterior and/or posterior repair

**57556** with repair of enterocele

(For insertion of intrauterine device, use 58300)

(57600-57620 have been deleted. For insertion of any hemostatic agent or pack for control of spontaneous non-obstetrical hemorrhage, use 57180)

## Repair

**57700** Cerclage of uterine cervix, nonobstetrical

**57720** Trachelorrhaphy, plastic repair of uterine cervix, vaginal approach

## Manipulation

**57800*** Dilation of cervical canal, instrumental (separate procedure)

**57820** Dilation and curettage of cervical stump

# Corpus Uteri

## Excision

**58100*** Endometrial sampling (biopsy) with or without endocervical sampling (biopsy), without cervical dilation, any method (separate procedure)

(For endocervical curettage only, use 57505)

(58101, 58102, 58103 have been deleted)

**58120** Dilation and curettage, diagnostic and/or therapeutic (nonobstetrical)

(For postpartum hemorrhage, use 59160)

**58140** Myomectomy, excision of fibroid tumor of uterus, single or multiple (separate procedure); abdominal approach

**58145** vaginal approach

**58150** Total abdominal hysterectomy (corpus and cervix), with or without removal of tube(s), with or without removal of ovary(s);

**58152** with colpo-urethrocystopexy (eg, Marshall-Marchetti-Krantz, Burch)

(For urethrocystopexy without hysterectomy, see 51840, 51841)

**58180** Supracervical abdominal hysterectomy (subtotal hysterectomy), with or without removal of tube(s), with or without removal of ovary(s)

**58200** Total abdominal hysterectomy, including partial vaginectomy, with para-aortic and pelvic lymph node sampling, with or without removal of tube(s), with or without removal of ovary(s)

(58205 has been deleted. For hysterectomy with pelvic lymphadenectomy, use 58210)

**58210** Radical abdominal hysterectomy, with bilateral total pelvic lymphadenectomy and para-aortic lymph node sampling (biopsy), with or without removal of tube(s), with or without removal of ovary(s)

(For radical hysterectomy with ovarian transposition, use also 58825)

**58240** Pelvic exenteration for gynecologic malignancy, with total abdominal hysterectomy or cervicectomy, with or without removal of tube(s), with or without removal of ovary(s), with removal of bladder and ureteral transplantations, and/or abdominoperineal resection of rectum and colon and colostomy, or any combination thereof

(For pelvic exenteration for lower urinary tract or male genital malignancy, use 51597)

**58260** Vaginal hysterectomy;

**58262** with removal of tube(s), and/or ovary(s)

**58263** with removal of tube(s), and/or ovary(s), with repair of enterocele

(58265 has been deleted. To report, see 57240, 57250, 57260, 57265)

**58267** with colpo-urethrocystopexy (Marshall-Marchetti-Krantz type, Pereyra type, with or without endoscopic control)

**58270** with repair of enterocele

(For repair of enterocele with removal of tubes and/or ovaries, use 58263)

**58275** Vaginal hysterectomy, with total or partial colpectomy;

**58280** with repair of enterocele

**58285** Vaginal hysterectomy, radical (Schauta type operation)

## Introduction

(For insertion/removal of implantable contraceptive capsules, see 11975, 11976, 11977)

**58300*** Insertion of intrauterine device (IUD)

**58301** Removal of intrauterine device (IUD)

(58310 has been deleted. To report, see 58321, 58322)

(58311 has been deleted. To report, use 58323)

(58320 has been deleted)

**58321** Artificial insemination; intra-cervical

**58322** intra-uterine

**58323** Sperm washing for artificial insemination

**58340*** Catheterization and introduction of saline or contrast material for hysterosonography or hysterosalpingography

(For radiological supervision and interpretation of hysterosonography, use 76831)

(For radiological supervision and interpretation of hysterosalpingography, use 74740)

**58345** Transcervical introduction of fallopian tube catheter for diagnosis and/or re-establishing patency (any method), with or without hysterosalpingography

(For radiological supervision and interpretation, use 74742)

**58350*** Chromotubation of oviduct, including materials

(For materials supplied by physician, use 99070)

## Repair

**58400** Uterine suspension, with or without shortening of round ligaments, with or without shortening of sacrouterine ligaments; (separate procedure)

**58410** with presacral sympathectomy

(58430 has been deleted. To report, use 58999)

(58500 has been deleted. To report, use 58752)

**58520** Hysterorrhaphy, repair of ruptured uterus (nonobstetrical)

**58540** Hysteroplasty, repair of uterine anomaly (Strassman type)

(For closure of vesicouterine fistula, use 51920)

## ►Laparoscopy/Hysteroscopy◄

►Surgical laparoscopy always includes diagnostic laparoscopy. To report a diagnostic laparoscopy (peritoneoscopy) (separate procedure), use 49320. To report a diagnostic hysteroscopy (separate procedure), use 58555.◄

●**58550** Laparoscopy, surgical; with vaginal hysterectomy with or without removal of tube(s), with or without removal of ovary(s) (laparoscopic assisted vaginal hysterectomy)

●**58551** with removal of leiomyomata (single or multiple)

●**58555** Hysteroscopy, diagnostic (separate procedure)

●**58558** Hysteroscopy, surgical; with sampling (biopsy) of endometrium and/or polypectomy, with or without D & C

●**58559** with lysis of intrauterine adhesions (any method)

●**58560** with division or resection of intrauterine septum (any method)

●**58561** with removal of leiomyomata

●**58562** with removal of impacted foreign body

●**58563** with endometrial ablation (any method)

●**58578** Unlisted laparoscopy procedure, uterus

●**58579** Unlisted hysteroscopy procedure, uterus

# Oviduct►/Ovary◄

## Incision

**58600** Ligation or transection of fallopian tube(s), abdominal or vaginal approach, unilateral or bilateral

**58605** Ligation or transection of fallopian tube(s), abdominal or vaginal approach, postpartum, unilateral or bilateral, during same hospitalization (separate procedure)

(For laparoscopic procedures, use ►58670, 58671◄)

(58610 has been deleted. To report, see 58600-58611)

+ **58611** Ligation or transection of fallopian tube(s) when done at the time of cesarean section or intra-abdominal surgery (not a separate procedure) (List separately in addition to code for primary procedure)

**58615** Occlusion of fallopian tube(s) by device (eg, band, clip, Falope ring) vaginal or suprapubic approach

(For laparoscopic approach, use ►58671◄)

(58618 has been deleted. To report, use 58740)

## ►Laparoscopy◄

►Surgical laparoscopy always includes diagnostic laparoscopy. To report a diagnostic laparoscopy (peritoneoscopy) (separate procedure), use 49320.◄

►(For laparoscopic biopsy of the ovary or fallopian tube, use 49321)◄

● **58660** Laparoscopy, surgical; with lysis of adhesions (salpingolysis, ovariolysis) (separate procedure)

● **58661** with removal of adnexal structures (partial or total oophorectomy and/or salpingectomy)

● **58662** with fulguration or excision of lesions of the ovary, pelvic viscera, or peritoneal surface by any method

● **58670** with fulguration of oviducts (with or without transection)

● **58671** with occlusion of oviducts by device (eg, band, clip, or Falope ring)

● **58672** with fimbrioplasty

● **58673** with salpingostomy (salpingoneostomy)

►(Codes 58672 and 58673 are used to report unilateral procedures. For bilateral procedure, use modifier '-50')◄

● **58679** Unlisted laparoscopy procedure, oviduct, ovary

## Excision

**58700** Salpingectomy, complete or partial, unilateral or bilateral (separate procedure)

**58720** Salpingo-oophorectomy, complete or partial, unilateral or bilateral (separate procedure)

## Repair

**58740** Lysis of adhesions (salpingolysis, ovariolysis)

(For laparoscopic approach, ►use 58660◄)

(For excision or destruction of endometriomas, open method, see 49200, 49201)

(For fulguration or excision of lesions, laparoscopic approach, ►use 58662◄)

**58750** Tubotubal anastomosis

**58752** Tubouterine implantation

**58760** Fimbrioplasty

►(For laparoscopic approach, use 58672)◄

**58770** Salpingostomy (salpingoneostomy)

►(For laparoscopic approach, use 58673)◄

# Ovary

## Incision

**58800** Drainage of ovarian cyst(s), unilateral or bilateral, (separate procedure); vaginal approach

**58805** abdominal approach

**58820** Drainage of ovarian abscess; vaginal approach, open

**58822** abdominal approach

**58823** Drainage of pelvic abscess, transvaginal or transrectal approach, percutaneous (eg, ovarian, pericolic)

(For radiological supervision and interpretation, use 75989)

**58825** Transposition, ovary(s)

## Excision

**58900** Biopsy of ovary, unilateral or bilateral (separate procedure)

►(For laparoscopic biopsy of the ovary or fallopian tube, use 49321)◄

**58920** Wedge resection or bisection of ovary, unilateral or bilateral

**58925** Ovarian cystectomy, unilateral or bilateral

**58940** Oophorectomy, partial or total, unilateral or bilateral;

(58942 has been deleted. To report, use 58952)

**58943** for ovarian malignancy, with para-aortic and pelvic lymph node biopsies, peritoneal washings, peritoneal biopsies, diaphragmatic assessments, with or without salpingectomy(s), with or without omentectomy

(58945 has been deleted. To report, use 58950)

**58950** Resection of ovarian malignancy with bilateral salpingo-oophorectomy and omentectomy;

**58951** with total abdominal hysterectomy, pelvic and limited para-aortic lymphadenectomy

**58952** with radical dissection for debulking

**58960** Laparotomy, for staging or restaging of ovarian malignancy (second look), with or without omentectomy, peritoneal washing, biopsy of abdominal and pelvic peritoneum, diaphragmatic assessment with pelvic and limited para-aortic lymphadenectomy

# In Vitro Fertilization

**58970** Follicle puncture for oocyte retrieval, any method

(For radiological supervision and interpretation, use 76948)

(58972 has been deleted. To report, use 89250)

**58974** Embryo transfer, intrauterine

**58976** Gamete, zygote, or embryo intrafallopian transfer, any method

(58980 has been deleted. To report, use ►49320◄)

(58982 has been deleted. To report, use ►58670◄)

(58983 has been deleted. To report, use ►58671◄)

(58984 has been deleted. To report, use ►58662◄)

(58985 has been deleted. To report, use ►58660◄)

(58986 has been deleted. To report, use ►49321◄)

(58987 has been deleted. To report, use ►49322◄)

(58988 has been deleted. To report, use ►58661◄)

(58990 has been deleted. To report, use ►58555◄)

(58992 has been deleted. To report, see ►58559, 58560◄)

(58994 has been deleted. To report, use ►58561◄)

(58995 has been deleted. To report, see ►58559, 58561, 58563◄)

(58996 has been deleted. To report, use ►58563◄)

## Other Procedures

**58999** Unlisted procedure, female genital system (nonobstetrical)

# Maternity Care and Delivery

The services normally provided in uncomplicated maternity cases include antepartum care, delivery, and postpartum care.

Antepartum care includes the initial and subsequent history, physical examinations, recording of weight, blood pressures, fetal heart tones, routine chemical urinalysis, and monthly visits up to 28 weeks gestation, biweekly visits to 36 weeks gestation, and weekly visits until delivery. Any other visits or services within this time period should be coded separately.

Delivery services include admission to the hospital, the admission history and physical examination, management of uncomplicated labor, vaginal delivery (with or without episiotomy, with or without forceps), or cesarean delivery. Medical problems complicating labor and delivery management may require additional resources and should be identified by utilizing the codes in the **Medicine** and **Evaluation and Management Services** section in addition to codes for maternity care.

Postpartum care includes hospital and office visits following vaginal or cesarean section delivery.

For medical complications of pregnancy (eg, cardiac problems, neurological problems, diabetes, hypertension, toxemia, hyperemesis, pre-term labor, premature rupture of membranes), see services in the **Medicine** and **Evaluation and Management Services** section.

For surgical complications of pregnancy (eg, appendectomy, hernia, ovarian cyst, Bartholin cyst), see services in the **Surgery** section.

If a physician provides all or part of the antepartum and/or postpartum patient care but does not perform delivery due to termination of pregnancy by abortion or referral to another physician for delivery, see the antepartum and postpartum care codes 59425-59426 and 59430.

(For circumcision of newborn, see 54150, 54160)

## Antepartum Services

**59000*** Amniocentesis, any method

(For radiological supervision and interpretation, use 76946)

(59010, 59011 have been deleted)

**59012** Cordocentesis (intrauterine), any method

(For radiological supervision and interpretation, use 76941)

**59015** Chorionic villus sampling, any method

(For radiological supervision and interpretation, use 76945)

**59020*** Fetal contraction stress test

**59025** Fetal non-stress test

**59030*** Fetal scalp blood sampling

(59031 has been deleted. To report, use 59030 and see modifiers '-76' and '-77')

**59050** Fetal monitoring during labor by consulting physician (ie, non-attending physician) with written report; supervision and interpretation

**59051** interpretation only

## Excision

**59100** Hysterotomy, abdominal (eg, for hydatidiform mole, abortion)

(When tubal ligation is performed at the same time as hysterotomy, use 58611 in addition to 59100)

(59101, 59105, 59106 have been deleted. To report, see 59100, 58611)

**59120** Surgical treatment of ectopic pregnancy; tubal or ovarian, requiring salpingectomy and/or oophorectomy, abdominal or vaginal approach

**59121** tubal or ovarian, without salpingectomy and/or oophorectomy

(59125, 59126 have been deleted. To report, see 59120, 59121)

**59130** abdominal pregnancy

**59135** interstitial, uterine pregnancy requiring total hysterectomy

**59136** interstitial, uterine pregnancy with partial resection of uterus

**59140** cervical, with evacuation

**59150** Laparoscopic treatment of ectopic pregnancy; without salpingectomy and/or oophorectomy

**59151** with salpingectomy and/or oophorectomy

**59160** Curettage, postpartum

## Introduction

(For intrauterine fetal transfusion, use 36460)

(For introduction of hypertonic solution and/or prostaglandins to initiate labor, see 59850-59857)

**59200** Insertion of cervical dilator (eg, laminaria, prostaglandin) (separate procedure)

## Repair

(For tracheloplasty, use 57700)

**59300** Episiotomy or vaginal repair, by other than attending physician

(59305 has been deleted)

**59320** Cerclage of cervix, during pregnancy; vaginal

**59325** abdominal

**59350** Hysterorrhaphy of ruptured uterus

(59351 has been deleted)

## Vaginal Delivery, Antepartum and Postpartum Care

**59400** Routine obstetric care including antepartum care, vaginal delivery (with or without episiotomy, and/or forceps) and postpartum care

**59409** Vaginal delivery only (with or without episiotomy and/or forceps);

**59410** including postpartum care

**59412** External cephalic version, with or without tocolysis (List in addition to code(s) for delivery)

**59414** Delivery of placenta (separate procedure)

(59420 has been deleted. To report, see 59425, 59426 or appropriate E/M code(s))

(For 1-3 antepartum care visits, see appropriate E/M code(s))

**59425** Antepartum care only; 4-6 visits

**59426** 7 or more visits

**59430** Postpartum care only (separate procedure)

## Cesarean Delivery

(For standby attendance for infant, use 99360)

(59500, 59501 have been deleted. To report, see 59510, 59515, 59525)

**59510** Routine obstetric care including antepartum care, cesarean delivery, and postpartum care

**59514** Cesarean delivery only;

**59515** including postpartum care

(59520, 59521 have been deleted. To report, see 59510, 59515, 59525)

**+ 59525** Subtotal or total hysterectomy after cesarean delivery (List separately in addition to code for primary procedure)

(Use 59525 in conjunction with codes 59510, 59514, 59515, 59618, 59620, 59622)

(59540, 59541, 59560, 59561, 59580, 59581 have been deleted. To report, see 59510, 59515, 59525)

## Delivery After Previous Cesarean Delivery

Patients who have had a previous cesarean delivery and now present with the expectation of a vaginal delivery are coded using codes 59610-59622. If the patient has a successful vaginal delivery after a previous cesarean delivery (VBAC), use codes 59610-59614. If the attempt is unsuccessful and another cesarean delivery is carried out, use codes 59618-59622. To report elective cesarean deliveries use code 59510, 59514 or 59515.

**59610** Routine obstetric care including antepartum care, vaginal delivery (with or without episiotomy, and/or forceps) and postpartum care, after previous cesarean delivery

**59612** Vaginal delivery only, after previous cesarean delivery (with or without episiotomy and/or forceps);

**59614** including postpartum care

**59618** Routine obstetric care including antepartum care, cesarean delivery, and postpartum care, following attempted vaginal delivery after previous cesarean delivery

**59620** Cesarean delivery only, following attempted vaginal delivery after previous cesarean delivery;

**59622** including postpartum care

## Abortion

(For medical treatment of spontaneous complete abortion, any trimester, use E/M codes 99201-99233)

(59800, 59810 have been deleted. To report, see 99201-99233)

(59801, 59811 have been deleted. To report, use 59812)

**59812** Treatment of incomplete abortion, any trimester, completed surgically

**59820** Treatment of missed abortion, completed surgically; first trimester

**59821** second trimester

**59830** Treatment of septic abortion, completed surgically

**59840** Induced abortion, by dilation and curettage

**59841** Induced abortion, by dilation and evacuation

**59850** Induced abortion, by one or more intra-amniotic injections (amniocentesis-injections), including hospital admission and visits, delivery of fetus and secundines;

**59851** with dilation and curettage and/or evacuation

**59852** with hysterotomy (failed intra-amniotic injection)

(For insertion of cervical dilator, use 59200)

**59855** Induced abortion, by one or more vaginal suppositories (eg, prostaglandin) with or without cervical dilation (eg, laminaria), including hospital admission and visits, delivery of fetus and secundines;

**59856** with dilation and curettage and/or evacuation

**59857** with hysterotomy (failed medical evacuation)

## Other Procedures

**59866** Multifetal pregnancy reduction(s) (MPR)

**59870** Uterine evacuation and curettage for hydatidiform mole

**59871** Removal of cerclage suture under anesthesia (other than local)

● **59898** Unlisted laparoscopy procedure, maternity care and delivery

**59899** Unlisted procedure, maternity care and delivery

# Notes

# Endocrine System

(For pituitary and pineal surgery, see **Nervous System**)

## Thyroid Gland

### Incision

**60000*** Incision and drainage of thyroglossal cyst, infected

### Excision

**60001** Aspiration and/or injection, thyroid cyst

(For fine needle aspiration, see 88170, 88171)

**60100*** Biopsy thyroid, percutaneous core needle

(For radiological supervision and interpretation, see 76360, 76942)

(For fine needle aspiration, preparation, and interpretation of smears, see 88170-88173)

**60200** Excision of cyst or adenoma of thyroid, or transection of isthmus

**60210** Partial thyroid lobectomy, unilateral; with or without isthmusectomy

(For fine needle aspiration, see 88170, 88171)

**60212** with contralateral subtotal lobectomy, including isthmusectomy

(For fine needle aspiration, see 88170, 88171)

**60220** Total thyroid lobectomy, unilateral; with or without isthmusectomy

**60225** with contralateral subtotal lobectomy, including isthmusectomy

**60240** Thyroidectomy, total or complete

(60242 has been deleted. To report, see 60210-60225)

(60245 has been deleted. To report, see 60210-60225)

(60246 has been deleted. To report, use 60271)

**60252** Thyroidectomy, total or subtotal for malignancy; with limited neck dissection

**60254** with radical neck dissection

**60260** Thyroidectomy, removal of all remaining thyroid tissue following previous removal of a portion of thyroid

(60261 has been deleted. To report, use 60260 with modifier '-50')

**60270** Thyroidectomy, including substernal thyroid gland; sternal split or transthoracic approach

**60271** cervical approach

**60280** Excision of thyroglossal duct cyst or sinus;

**60281** recurrent

(For thyroid ultrasonography, use 76536)

## Parathyroid, Thymus, Adrenal Glands, and Carotid Body

### Excision

(For pituitary and pineal surgery, see **Nervous System**)

**60500** Parathyroidectomy or exploration of parathyroid(s);

**60502** re-exploration

**60505** with mediastinal exploration, sternal split or transthoracic approach

(60510 has been deleted)

**+ 60512** Parathyroid autotransplantation (List separately in addition to code for primary procedure)

(Use 60512 in conjunction with codes 60500, 60502, 60505, 60212, 60225, 60240, 60252, 60254, 60260, 60270, 60271)

**60520** Thymectomy, partial or total; transcervical approach (separate procedure)

**60521** sternal split or transthoracic approach, without radical mediastinal dissection (separate procedure)

**60522** sternal split or transthoracic approach, with radical mediastinal dissection (separate procedure)

**60540** Adrenalectomy, partial or complete, or exploration of adrenal gland with or without biopsy, transabdominal, lumbar or dorsal (separate procedure);

**60545** with excision of adjacent retroperitoneal tumor

(For excision of remote or disseminated pheochromocytoma, see 49200, 49201)

(For laparoscopic approach, use 56321)

(60550, 60555 have been deleted. To report, use 60540 with modifier '-50')

**60600** Excision of carotid body tumor; without excision of carotid artery

**60605** with excision of carotid artery

## ►Laparoscopy◄

►Surgical laparoscopy always includes diagnostic laparoscopy. To report a diagnostic laparoscopy (peritoneoscopy) (separate procedure), use 49320.◄

● **60650** Laparoscopy, surgical, with adrenalectomy, partial or complete, or exploration of adrenal gland with or without biopsy, transabdominal, lumbar or dorsal

● **60659** Unlisted laparoscopy procedure, endocrine system

## Other Procedures

**60699** Unlisted procedure, endocrine system

# Nervous System

## Skull, Meninges, and Brain

(For injection procedure for cerebral angiography, see 36100-36218)

(For injection procedure for ventriculography, see 61026, 61120, 61130)

(For injection procedure for pneumoencephalography, use 61055)

### Injection, Drainage, or Aspiration

**61000*** Subdural tap through fontanelle, or suture, infant, unilateral or bilateral; initial

**61001*** subsequent taps

**61020*** Ventricular puncture through previous burr hole, fontanelle, suture, or implanted ventricular catheter/reservoir; without injection

(61025 has been deleted. To report, use 61026)

**61026*** with injection of drug or other substance for diagnosis or treatment

(61030, 61045 have been deleted. To report, use 61026)

**61050*** Cisternal or lateral cervical (C1-C2) puncture; without injection (separate procedure)

(61051, 61052, 61053 have been deleted. To report, use 61055)

**61055*** with injection of drug or other substance for diagnosis or treatment (eg, C1-C2)

(For radiological supervision and interpretation, see **Radiology**)

**61070*** Puncture of shunt tubing or reservoir for aspiration or injection procedure

(For radiological supervision and interpretation, use 75809)

### Twist Drill, Burr Hole(s), or Trephine

**61105*** Twist drill hole for subdural or ventricular puncture;

(61106 has been deleted)

⊘**61107*** for implanting ventricular catheter or pressure recording device

**61108** for evacuation and/or drainage of subdural hematoma

**61120** Burr hole(s) for ventricular puncture (including injection of gas, contrast media, dye, or radioactive material)

(61130 has been deleted)

**61140** Burr hole(s) or trephine; with biopsy of brain or intracranial lesion

**61150** with drainage of brain abscess or cyst

**61151** with subsequent tapping (aspiration) of intracranial abscess or cyst

**61154** Burr hole(s) with evacuation and/or drainage of hematoma, extradural or subdural

(61155 has been deleted. To report, use 61154 with modifier '-50')

**61156** Burr hole(s); with aspiration of hematoma or cyst, intracerebral

⊘**61210*** for implanting ventricular catheter, reservoir, EEG electrode(s) or pressure recording device (separate procedure)

**61215** Insertion of subcutaneous reservoir, pump or continuous infusion system for connection to ventricular catheter

(For chemotherapy, use 96450)

**61250** Burr hole(s) or trephine, supratentorial, exploratory, not followed by other surgery

(61251 has been deleted. To report, use 61250 with modifier '-50')

**61253** Burr hole(s) or trephine, infratentorial, unilateral or bilateral

(If burr hole(s) or trephine are followed by craniotomy at same operative session, use 61304-61321; do not use 61250 or 61253)

## Craniectomy or Craniotomy

**61304** Craniectomy or craniotomy, exploratory; supratentorial

**61305** infratentorial (posterior fossa)

(61310, 61311 have been deleted. To report, see 61312-61315)

**61312** Craniectomy or craniotomy for evacuation of hematoma, supratentorial; extradural or subdural

**61313** intracerebral

**61314** Craniectomy or craniotomy for evacuation of hematoma, infratentorial; extradural or subdural

**61315** intracerebellar

**61320** Craniectomy or craniotomy, drainage of intracranial abscess; supratentorial

**61321** infratentorial

**61330** Decompression of orbit only, transcranial approach

(61331 has been deleted. To report, use 61330 with modifier '-50')

**61332** Exploration of orbit (transcranial approach); with biopsy

**61333** with removal of lesion

**61334** with removal of foreign body

**61340** Other cranial decompression (eg, subtemporal), supratentorial

(61341 has been deleted. To report, use 61340 with modifier '-50')

**61343** Craniectomy, suboccipital with cervical laminectomy for decompression of medulla and spinal cord, with or without dural graft (eg, Arnold-Chiari malformation)

**61345** Other cranial decompression, posterior fossa

(For orbital decompression by lateral wall approach, Kroenlein type, use 67445)

**61440** Craniotomy for section of tentorium cerebelli (separate procedure)

**61450** Craniectomy, subtemporal, for section, compression, or decompression of sensory root of gasserian ganglion

**61458** Craniectomy, suboccipital; for exploration or decompression of cranial nerves

**61460** for section of one or more cranial nerves

**61470** for medullary tractotomy

**61480** for mesencephalic tractotomy or pedunculotomy

**61490** Craniotomy for lobotomy, including cingulotomy

(61491 has been deleted. To report, use 61490 with modifier '-50')

**61500** Craniectomy; with excision of tumor or other bone lesion of skull

**61501** for osteomyelitis

**61510** Craniectomy, trephination, bone flap craniotomy; for excision of brain tumor, supratentorial, except meningioma

**61512** for excision of meningioma, supratentorial

**61514** for excision of brain abscess, supratentorial

**61516** for excision or fenestration of cyst, supratentorial

(For excision of pituitary tumor or craniopharyngioma, see 61545, 61546, 61548)

**61518** Craniectomy for excision of brain tumor, infratentorial or posterior fossa; except meningioma, cerebellopontine angle tumor, or midline tumor at base of skull

**61519** meningioma

**61520** cerebellopontine angle tumor

**61521** midline tumor at base of skull

**61522** Craniectomy, infratentorial or posterior fossa; for excision of brain abscess

**61524** for excision or fenestration of cyst

**61526** Craniectomy, bone flap craniotomy, transtemporal (mastoid) for excision of cerebellopontine angle tumor;

**61530** combined with middle/posterior fossa craniotomy/craniectomy

**61531** Subdural implantation of strip electrodes through one or more burr or trephine hole(s) for long term seizure monitoring

(For stereotactic implantation of electrodes, use 61760)

(61532 has been deleted. To report, see 61680-61692)

**61533** Craniotomy with elevation of bone flap; for subdural implantation of an electrode array, for long term seizure monitoring

(For continuous EEG monitoring, see 95950-95954)

**61534** for excision of epileptogenic focus without electrocorticography during surgery

**61535** for removal of epidural or subdural electrode array, without excision of cerebral tissue (separate procedure)

**61536** for excision of cerebral epileptogenic focus, with electrocorticography during surgery (includes removal of electrode array)

**61538** for lobectomy with electrocorticography during surgery, temporal lobe

**61539** for lobectomy with electrocorticography during surgery, other than temporal lobe, partial or total

**61541** for transection of corpus callosum

**61542** for total hemispherectomy

**61543** for partial or subtotal hemispherectomy

**61544** for excision or coagulation of choroid plexus

**61545** for excision of craniopharyngioma

**61546** Craniotomy for hypophysectomy or excision of pituitary tumor, intracranial approach

**61548** Hypophysectomy or excision of pituitary tumor, transnasal or transseptal approach, nonstereotactic

(Do not report code 69990 in addition to code 61548)

**61550** Craniectomy for craniosynostosis; single cranial suture

**61552** multiple cranial sutures

(61553 has been deleted. To report, see 61552, 61558, 61559)

(61555 has been deleted. To report, see 21172-21180, 61552, 61558, 61559)

(For cranial reconstruction for orbital hypertelorism, see 21260-21263)

**61556** Craniotomy for craniosynostosis; frontal or parietal bone flap

**61557** bifrontal bone flap

**61558** Extensive craniectomy for multiple cranial suture craniosynostosis (eg, cloverleaf skull); not requiring bone grafts

**61559** recontouring with multiple osteotomies and bone autografts (eg, barrel-stave procedure) (includes obtaining grafts)

(61561 has been deleted. To report, see 21172-21180)

**61563** Excision, intra and extracranial, benign tumor of cranial bone (eg, fibrous dysplasia); without optic nerve decompression

**61564** with optic nerve decompression

(For reconstruction, see 21181-21183)

**61570** Craniectomy or craniotomy; with excision of foreign body from brain

**61571** with treatment of penetrating wound of brain

(For sequestrectomy for osteomyelitis, use 61501)

**61575** Transoral approach to skull base, brain stem or upper spinal cord for biopsy, decompression or excision of lesion;

**61576** requiring splitting of tongue and/or mandible (including tracheostomy)

(For arthrodesis, use 22548)

## Surgery of Skull Base

The surgical management of lesions involving the skull base (base of anterior, middle, and posterior cranial fossae) often requires the skills of several surgeons of different surgical specialties working together or in tandem during the operative session. These operations are usually not staged because of the need for definitive closure of dura, subcutaneous tissues, and skin to avoid serious infections such as osteomyelitis and/or meningitis.

The procedures are categorized according to: 1) ***approach procedure*** necessary to obtain adequate exposure to the lesion (pathologic entity), 2) ***definitive procedure(s)*** necessary to biopsy, excise or otherwise treat the lesion, and 3) ***repair/reconstruction*** of the defect present following the definitive procedure(s).

The ***approach procedure*** is described according to anatomical area involved, ie, anterior cranial fossa, middle cranial fossa, posterior cranial fossa, and brain stem or upper spinal cord.

The ***definitive procedure(s)*** describes the repair, biopsy, resection, or excision of various lesions of the skull base and, when appropriate, primary closure of the dura, mucous membranes, and skin.

The ***repair/reconstruction procedure(s)*** is reported separately if extensive dural grafting, cranioplasty, local or regional myocutaneous pedicle flaps, or extensive skin grafts are required.

For primary closure, see the appropriate codes, ie, 15732, 15755.

When one surgeon performs the approach procedure, another surgeon performs the definitive procedure, and another surgeon performs the repair/reconstruction procedure, each surgeon reports only the code for the specific procedure performed.

If one surgeon performs more than one procedure (ie, approach procedure and definitive procedure), then both codes are reported, adding modifier '-51' to the secondary, additional procedure(s).

## Approach Procedures

### Anterior Cranial Fossa

**61580** Craniofacial approach to anterior cranial fossa; extradural, including lateral rhinotomy, ethmoidectomy, sphenoidectomy, without maxillectomy or orbital exenteration

**61581** extradural, including lateral rhinotomy, orbital exenteration, ethmoidectomy, sphenoidectomy and/or maxillectomy

**61582** extradural, including unilateral or bifrontal craniotomy, elevation of frontal lobe(s), osteotomy of base of anterior cranial fossa

**61583** intradural, including unilateral or bifrontal craniotomy, elevation or resection of frontal lobe, osteotomy of base of anterior cranial fossa

**61584** Orbitocranial approach to anterior cranial fossa, extradural, including supraorbital ridge osteotomy and elevation of frontal and/or temporal lobe(s); without orbital exenteration

**61585** with orbital exenteration

**61586** Bicoronal, transzygomatic and/or LeFort I osteotomy approach to anterior cranial fossa with or without internal fixation, without bone graft

### Middle Cranial Fossa

**61590** Infratemporal pre-auricular approach to middle cranial fossa (parapharyngeal space, infratemporal and midline skull base, nasopharynx), with or without disarticulation of the mandible, including parotidectomy, craniotomy, decompression and/or mobilization of the facial nerve and/or petrous carotid artery

**61591** Infratemporal post-auricular approach to middle cranial fossa (internal auditory meatus, petrous apex, tentorium, cavernous sinus, parasellar area, infratemporal fossa) including mastoidectomy, resection of sigmoid sinus, with or without decompression and/or mobilization of contents of auditory canal or petrous carotid artery

**61592** Orbitocranial zygomatic approach to middle cranial fossa (cavernous sinus and carotid artery, clivus, basilar artery or petrous apex) including osteotomy of zygoma, craniotomy, extra- or intradural elevation of temporal lobe

### Posterior Cranial Fossa

**61595** Transtemporal approach to posterior cranial fossa, jugular foramen or midline skull base, including mastoidectomy, decompression of sigmoid sinus and/or facial nerve, with or without mobilization

**61596** Transcochlear approach to posterior cranial fossa, jugular foramen or midline skull base, including labyrinthectomy, decompression, with or without mobilization of facial nerve and/or petrous carotid artery

**61597** Transcondylar (far lateral) approach to posterior cranial fossa, jugular foramen or midline skull base, including occipital condylectomy, mastoidectomy, resection of C1-C3 vertebral body(s), decompression of vertebral artery, with or without mobilization

**61598** Transpetrosal approach to posterior cranial fossa, clivus or foramen magnum, including ligation of superior petrosal sinus and/or sigmoid sinus

## Definitive Procedures

### Base of Anterior Cranial Fossa

**61600** Resection or excision of neoplastic, vascular or infectious lesion of base of anterior cranial fossa; extradural

**61601** intradural, including dural repair, with or without graft

### Base of Middle Cranial Fossa

**61605** Resection or excision of neoplastic, vascular or infectious lesion of infratemporal fossa, parapharyngeal space, petrous apex; extradural

**61606** intradural, including dural repair, with or without graft

**61607** Resection or excision of neoplastic, vascular or infectious lesion of parasellar area, cavernous sinus, clivus or midline skull base; extradural

**61608** intradural, including dural repair, with or without graft

Codes 61609-61612 are reported in addition to code(s) for primary procedure(s) 61605-61608. Report only one transection or ligation of carotid artery code per operative session.

**+ 61609** Transection or ligation, carotid artery in cavernous sinus; without repair (List separately in addition to code for primary procedure)

**+ 61610** with repair by anastomosis or graft (List separately in addition to code for primary procedure)

**+ 61611** Transection or ligation, carotid artery in petrous canal; without repair (List separately in addition to code for primary procedure)

**+ 61612** with repair by anastomosis or graft (List separately in addition to code for primary procedure)

**61613** Obliteration of carotid aneurysm, arteriovenous malformation, or carotid-cavernous fistula by dissection within cavernous sinus

### Base of Posterior Cranial Fossa

**61615** Resection or excision of neoplastic, vascular or infectious lesion of base of posterior cranial fossa, jugular foramen, foramen magnum, or C1-C3 vertebral bodies; extradural

**61616** intradural, including dural repair, with or without graft

## Repair and/or Reconstruction of Surgical Defects of Skull Base

**61618** Secondary repair of dura for CSF leak, anterior, middle or posterior cranial fossa following surgery of the skull base; by free tissue graft (eg, pericranium, fascia, tensor fascia lata, adipose tissue, homologous or synthetic grafts)

**61619** by local or regionalized vascularized pedicle flap or myocutaneous flap (including galea, temporalis, frontalis or occipitalis muscle)

## Endovascular Therapy

**61624** Transcatheter occlusion or embolization (eg, for tumor destruction, to achieve hemostasis, to occlude a vascular malformation), percutaneous, any method; central nervous system (intracranial, spinal cord)

(See also 37204)

(For radiological supervision and interpretation, use 75894)

**61626** non-central nervous system, head or neck (extracranial, brachiocephalic branch)

(See also 37204)

(For radiological supervision and interpretation, use 75894)

## Surgery for Aneurysm, Arteriovenous Malformation or Vascular Disease

Includes craniotomy when appropriate for procedure.

**61680** Surgery of intracranial arteriovenous malformation; supratentorial, simple

**61682** supratentorial, complex

**61684** infratentorial, simple

**61686** infratentorial, complex

**61690** dural, simple

**61692** dural, complex

**61700** Surgery of intracranial aneurysm, intracranial approach; carotid circulation

**61702** vertebral-basilar circulation

**61703** Surgery of intracranial aneurysm, cervical approach by application of occluding clamp to cervical carotid artery (Selverstone-Crutchfield type)

(For cervical approach for direct ligation of carotid artery, see 37600-37606)

**61705** Surgery of aneurysm, vascular malformation or carotid-cavernous fistula; by intracranial and cervical occlusion of carotid artery

**61708** by intracranial electrothrombosis

(For ligation or gradual occlusion of internal/common carotid artery, see 37605, 37606)

**61710** by intra-arterial embolization, injection procedure, or balloon catheter

**61711** Anastomosis, arterial, extracranial-intracranial (eg, middle cerebral/cortical) arteries

(For carotid or vertebral thromboendarterectomy, use 35301)

(61712 has been deleted. Use 69990 when the surgical microscope is employed for the microsurgical procedure. Do not use 69990 for visualization with magnifying loupes or corrected vision.)

## Stereotaxis

**61720** Creation of lesion by stereotactic method, including burr hole(s) and localizing and recording techniques, single or multiple stages; globus pallidus or thalamus

**61735** subcortical structure(s) other than globus pallidus or thalamus

**61750** Stereotactic biopsy, aspiration, or excision, including burr hole(s), for intracranial lesion;

**▲61751** with computerized axial tomography and/or magnetic resonance guidance

►(For radiological supervision and interpretation of computerized tomography, see 70450, 70460, or 70470 as appropriate)◄

►(For radiological supervision and interpretation of magnetic resonance imaging, see 70551, 70552, or 70553 as appropriate)◄

**61760** Stereotactic implantation of depth electrodes into the cerebrum for long term seizure monitoring

**61770** Stereotactic localization, any method, including burr hole(s), with insertion of catheter(s) for brachytherapy

(61780 has been deleted. To report, use 61760)

**61790** Creation of lesion by stereotactic method, percutaneous, by neurolytic agent (eg, alcohol, thermal, electrical, radiofrequency); gasserian ganglion

**61791** trigeminal medullary tract

**61793** Stereotactic radiosurgery (particle beam, gamma ray or linear accelerator), one or more sessions

**+▲61795** Stereotactic computer assisted volumetric (navigational) procedure, intracranial, extracranial, or spinal (List separately in addition to code for primary procedure)

## Neurostimulators (Intracranial)

Codes 61850-61888 apply to both simple and complex neurostimulators. For initial or subsequent electronic analysis and programming of neurostimulator pulse generators, see codes 95970-95975.

**61850** Twist drill or burr hole(s) for implantation of neurostimulator electrodes, cortical

►(61855 has been deleted. To report, use 61862)◄

**61860** Craniectomy or craniotomy for implantation of neurostimulator electrodes, cerebral, cortical

**●61862** Twist drill, burr hole, craniotomy, or craniectomy for stereotactic implantation of one neurostimulator array in subcortical site (eg, thalamus, globus pallidus, subthalamic nucleus, periventricular, periaqueductal gray)

►(61865 has been deleted. To report, use 61862)◄

**61870** Craniectomy for implantation of neurostimulator electrodes, cerebellar; cortical

**61875** subcortical

**61880** Revision or removal of intracranial neurostimulator electrodes

**▲61885** Incision and subcutaneous placement of cranial neurostimulator pulse generator or receiver, direct or inductive coupling; with connection to a single electrode array

**●61886** with connection to two or more electrode arrays

►(For open placement of cranial nerve (eg, vagal, trigeminal) neurostimulator electrode(s), use 64573)◄

►(For percutaneous placement of cranial nerve (eg, vagal, trigeminal) neurostimulator electrode(s), use 64553)◄

►(For revision or removal of cranial nerve (eg, vagal, trigeminal) neurostimulator electrode(s), use 64585)◄

**61888** Revision or removal of cranial neurostimulator pulse generator or receiver

## Repair

**62000** Elevation of depressed skull fracture; simple, extradural

**62005** compound or comminuted, extradural

**62010** with repair of dura and/or debridement of brain

**62100** Craniotomy for repair of dural/CSF leak, including surgery for rhinorrhea/otorrhea

(For repair of spinal dural/CSF leak, see 63707, 63709)

**62115** Reduction of craniomegalic skull (eg, treated hydrocephalus); not requiring bone grafts or cranioplasty

**62116** with simple cranioplasty

**62117** requiring craniotomy and reconstruction with or without bone graft (includes obtaining grafts)

**62120** Repair of encephalocele, skull vault, including cranioplasty

**62121** Craniotomy for repair of encephalocele, skull base

**62140** Cranioplasty for skull defect; up to 5 cm diameter

**62141** larger than 5 cm diameter

**62142** Removal of bone flap or prosthetic plate of skull

**62143** Replacement of bone flap or prosthetic plate of skull

**62145** Cranioplasty for skull defect with reparative brain surgery

**62146** Cranioplasty with autograft (includes obtaining bone grafts); up to 5 cm diameter

**62147** larger than 5 cm diameter

## CSF Shunt

**62180** Ventriculocisternostomy (Torkildsen type operation)

**62190** Creation of shunt; subarachnoid/subdural-atrial, -jugular, -auricular

**62192** subarachnoid/subdural-peritoneal, -pleural, other terminus

**62194** Replacement or irrigation, subarachnoid/subdural catheter

**62200** Ventriculocisternostomy, third ventricle;

**62201** stereotactic method

**62220** Creation of shunt; ventriculo-atrial, -jugular, -auricular

**62223** ventriculo-peritoneal, -pleural, other terminus

**62225** Replacement or irrigation, ventricular catheter

**62230** Replacement or revision of CSF shunt, obstructed valve, or distal catheter in shunt system

**62256** Removal of complete CSF shunt system; without replacement

**62258** with replacement by similar or other shunt at same operation

(For percutaneous irrigation or aspiration of shunt reservoir, use 61070)

# Spine and Spinal Cord

(For application of caliper or tongs, use 20660)

(For treatment of fracture or dislocation of spine, see 22305-22327)

## Injection, Drainage, or Aspiration

►Injection of contrast during fluoroscopic guidance and localization is an inclusive component of codes 62270-62273, 62280-62282, 62310-62319. Fluoroscopic guidance and localization is reported by code 76005, unless a formal contrast study (myelography, epidurography, or arthrography) is performed, in which case the use of fluoroscopy is included in the supervision and interpretation codes.

For radiologic supervision and interpretation of epidurography, use 72275. Code 72275 is only to be used when an epidurogram is performed, recorded, and a formal radiologic report is issued.

For codes 62318 and 62319, use code 01996 for subsequent daily management of epidural or subarachnoid catheter drug administration.◄

●**62263** Percutaneous lysis of epidural adhesions using solution injection (eg, hypertonic saline, enzyme) or mechanical means (eg, spring-wound catheter) including radiologic localization (includes contrast when administered)

**62268*** Percutaneous aspiration, spinal cord cyst or syrinx

(For radiological supervision and interpretation, see 76003, 76365, 76938)

**62269*** Biopsy of spinal cord, percutaneous needle

(For radiological supervision and interpretation, see 76003, 76360, 76942)

**62270*** Spinal puncture, lumbar, diagnostic

**62272*** Spinal puncture, therapeutic, for drainage of spinal fluid (by needle or catheter)

**▲62273*** Injection, epidural, of blood or clot patch

►(62274 has been deleted. To report, see 62310, 62311)◄

►(62275 has been deleted. To report, use 62310)◄

►(62276 has been deleted. To report, see 62318, 62319)◄

►(62277 has been deleted. To report, see 62318, 62319)◄

►62278 has been deleted. To report, use 62311)◄

►(62279 has been deleted. To report, use 62319)◄

**▲62280*** Injection/infusion of neurolytic substance (eg, alcohol, phenol, iced saline solutions), with or without other therapeutic substance; subarachnoid

**62281*** epidural, cervical or thoracic

**▲62282*** epidural, lumbar, sacral (caudal)

**⊘62284*** Injection procedure for myelography and/or computerized axial tomography, spinal (other than C1-C2 and posterior fossa)

(For injection procedure at C1-C2, use 61055)

(For radiological supervision and interpretation, see **Radiology**)

(62286 has been deleted. To report, use 64999)

**▲62287** Aspiration or decompression procedure, percutaneous, of nucleus pulposus of intervertebral disk, any method, single or multiple levels, lumbar (eg, manual or automated percutaneous diskectomy, percutaneous laser diskectomy)

►(For fluoroscopic guidance, use 76003)◄

►(62288 has been deleted. To report, see 62310, 62311)◄

►(62289 has been deleted. To report, use 62311)◄

**62290*** Injection procedure for diskography, each level; lumbar

**▲62291*** cervical or thoracic

(For radiological supervision and interpretation, see 72285, 72295)

**62292** Injection procedure for chemonucleolysis, including diskography, intervertebral disk, single or multiple levels, lumbar

(62293 has been deleted)

**62294** Injection procedure, arterial, for occlusion of arteriovenous malformation, spinal

(62295-62297 have been deleted. To report, see 63001-63017)

►(62298 has been deleted. To report, use 62310)◄

**●62310** Injection, single (not via indwelling catheter), not including neurolytic substances, with or without contrast (for either localization or epidurography), of diagnostic or therapeutic substance(s) (including anesthetic, antispasmodic, opioid, steroid, other solution), epidural or subarachnoid; cervical or thoracic

**●62311** lumbar, sacral (caudal)

**●62318** Injection, including catheter placement, continuous infusion or intermittent bolus, not including neurolytic substances, with or without contrast (for either localization or epidurography), of diagnostic or therapeutic substance(s) (including anesthetic, antispasmodic, opioid, steroid, other solution), epidural or subarachnoid; cervical or thoracic

**●62319** lumbar, sacral (caudal)

►(For transforaminal epidural injection, see 64479-64484)◄

## Catheter Implantation

(For percutaneous placement of intrathecal or epidural catheter, see codes ►62270-62273, 62280-62284, 62310-62319◄)

(62301-62303 have been deleted. To report, see 63001-63017)

**▲62350** Implantation, revision or repositioning of tunneled intrathecal or epidural catheter, for long-term pain management via an external pump or implantable reservoir/infusion pump; without laminectomy

**62351** with laminectomy

►(For refilling and maintenance of an implantable reservoir or infusion pump, use 96530)◄

**62355** Removal of previously implanted intrathecal or epidural catheter

## Reservoir/Pump Implantation

**62360** Implantation or replacement of device for intrathecal or epidural drug infusion; subcutaneous reservoir

**62361** non-programmable pump

**62362** programmable pump, including preparation of pump, with or without programming

**62365** Removal of subcutaneous reservoir or pump, previously implanted for intrathecal or epidural infusion

**62367** Electronic analysis of programmable, implanted pump for intrathecal or epidural drug infusion (includes evaluation of reservoir status, alarm status, drug prescription status); without reprogramming

**62368** with reprogramming

(To report implantable pump or reservoir refill, use 96530)

## Posterior Extradural Laminotomy or Laminectomy for Exploration/ Decompression of Neural Elements or Excision of Herniated Intervertebral Disks

(When 63001-63048 are followed by arthrodesis, see 22590-22614)

**63001** Laminectomy with exploration and/or decompression of spinal cord and/or cauda equina, without facetectomy, foraminotomy or diskectomy, (eg, spinal stenosis), one or two vertebral segments; cervical

**63003** thoracic

**63005** lumbar, except for spondylolisthesis

(63010 has been deleted. To report, use 63012)

**63011** sacral

**63012** Laminectomy with removal of abnormal facets and/or pars inter-articularis with decompression of cauda equina and nerve roots for spondylolisthesis, lumbar (Gill type procedure)

**63015** Laminectomy with exploration and/or decompression of spinal cord and/or cauda equina, without facetectomy, foraminotomy or diskectomy, (eg, spinal stenosis), more than 2 vertebral segments; cervical

**63016** thoracic

**63017** lumbar

**63020** Laminotomy (hemilaminectomy), with decompression of nerve root(s), including partial facetectomy, foraminotomy and/or excision of herniated intervertebral disk; one interspace, cervical

(63021 has been deleted. To report, use 63020 with modifier '-50')

**▲63030** one interspace, lumbar (including open or endoscopically-assisted approach)

(63031 has been deleted. To report, use 63030 with modifier '-50')

**+ 63035** each additional interspace, cervical or lumbar (List separately in addition to code for primary procedure)

(Use 63035 in conjunction with codes 63020-63030)

**63040** Laminotomy (hemilaminectomy), with decompression of nerve root(s), including partial facetectomy, foraminotomy and/or excision of herniated intervertebral disk, reexploration; cervical

(63041 has been deleted)

**63042** lumbar

**63045** Laminectomy, facetectomy and foraminotomy (unilateral or bilateral with decompression of spinal cord, cauda equina and/or nerve root(s), (eg, spinal or lateral recess stenosis)), single vertebral segment; cervical

**63046** thoracic

**63047** lumbar

**+ 63048** each additional segment, cervical, thoracic, or lumbar (List separately in addition to code for primary procedure)

(Use 63048 in conjunction with codes 63045-63047)

## Transpedicular or Costovertebral Approach for Posterolateral Extradural Exploration/Decompression

**63055** Transpedicular approach with decompression of spinal cord, equina and/or nerve root(s) (eg, herniated intervertebral disk), single segment; thoracic

**▲63056** lumbar (including transfacet, or lateral extraforaminal approach) (eg, far lateral herniated intervertebral disk)

**+ 63057** each additional segment, thoracic or lumbar (List separately in addition to code for primary procedure)

(Use 63057 in conjunction with codes 63055, 63056)

(63060 has been deleted)

**63064** Costovertebral approach with decompression of spinal cord or nerve root(s), (eg, herniated intervertebral disk), thoracic; single segment

(63065 has been deleted)

**+ 63066** each additional segment (List separately in addition to code for primary procedure)

(Use 63066 in conjunction with code 63064)

(For excision of thoracic intraspinal lesions by laminectomy, see 63266, 63271, 63276, 63281, 63286)

## Anterior or Anterolateral Approach for Extradural Exploration/Decompression

**63075** Diskectomy, anterior, with decompression of spinal cord and/or nerve root(s), including osteophytectomy; cervical, single interspace

**+ 63076** cervical, each additional interspace (List separately in addition to code for primary procedure)

(Use 63076 in conjunction with code 63075)

**63077** thoracic, single interspace

**+ 63078** thoracic, each additional interspace (List separately in addition to code for primary procedure)

(Use 63078 in conjunction with code 63077)

(Do not report code 69990 in addition to codes 63075-63078)

**63081** Vertebral corpectomy (vertebral body resection), partial or complete, anterior approach with decompression of spinal cord and/or nerve root(s); cervical, single segment

**+ 63082** cervical, each additional segment (List separately in addition to code for primary procedure)

(Use 63082 in conjunction with code 63081)

(For transoral approach, see 61575, 61576)

**63085** Vertebral corpectomy (vertebral body resection), partial or complete, transthoracic approach with decompression of spinal cord and/or nerve root(s); thoracic, single segment

**+ 63086** thoracic, each additional segment (List separately in addition to code for primary procedure)

(Use 63086 in conjunction with code 63085)

**63087** Vertebral corpectomy (vertebral body resection), partial or complete, combined thoracolumbar approach with decompression of spinal cord, cauda equina or nerve root(s), lower thoracic or lumbar; single segment

**+ 63088** each additional segment (List separately in addition to code for primary procedure)

(Use 63088 in conjunction with code 63087)

**63090** Vertebral corpectomy (vertebral body resection), partial or complete, transperitoneal or retroperitoneal approach with decompression of spinal cord, cauda equina or nerve root(s), lower thoracic, lumbar, or sacral; single segment

**+ 63091** each additional segment (List separately in addition to code for primary procedure)

(Use 63091 in conjunction with code 63090)

(Procedures 63081-63091 include diskectomy above and/or below vertebral segment)

(If followed by arthrodesis, see 22548-22812)

(For reconstruction of spine, use appropriate vertebral corpectomy codes 63081-63091, bone graft codes 20930-20938, arthrodesis codes 22548-22812, and spinal instrumentation codes 22840-22855)

## Incision

**63170** Laminectomy with myelotomy (eg, Bischof or DREZ type), cervical, thoracic, or thoracolumbar

**63172** Laminectomy with drainage of intramedullary cyst/syrinx; to subarachnoid space

**63173** to peritoneal space

**63180** Laminectomy and section of dentate ligaments, with or without dural graft, cervical; one or two segments

**63182** more than two segments

**63185** Laminectomy with rhizotomy; one or two segments

**63190** more than two segments

**63191** Laminectomy with section of spinal accessory nerve

(63192 has been deleted. To report, use 63191 with modifier '-50')

(For resection of sternocleidomastoid muscle, use 21720)

**63194** Laminectomy with cordotomy, with section of one spinothalamic tract, one stage; cervical

**63195** thoracic

**63196** Laminectomy with cordotomy, with section of both spinothalamic tracts, one stage; cervical

**63197** thoracic

**63198** Laminectomy with cordotomy with section of both spinothalamic tracts, two stages within 14 days; cervical

**63199** thoracic

**63200** Laminectomy, with release of tethered spinal cord, lumbar

## Excision by Laminectomy of Lesion Other Than Herniated Disk

(63210-63242 have been deleted. To report, see 63265-63290)

**63250** Laminectomy for excision or occlusion of arteriovenous malformation of spinal cord; cervical

**63251** thoracic

**63252** thoracolumbar

**63265** Laminectomy for excision or evacuation of intraspinal lesion other than neoplasm, extradural; cervical

**63266** thoracic

**63267** lumbar

**63268** sacral

**63270** Laminectomy for excision of intraspinal lesion other than neoplasm, intradural; cervical

**63271** thoracic

**63272** lumbar

**63273** sacral

**63275** Laminectomy for biopsy/excision of intraspinal neoplasm; extradural, cervical

**63276** extradural, thoracic

**63277** extradural, lumbar

**63278** extradural, sacral

**63280** intradural, extramedullary, cervical

**63281** intradural, extramedullary, thoracic

**63282** intradural, extramedullary, lumbar

**63283** intradural, sacral

**63285** intradural, intramedullary, cervical

**63286** intradural, intramedullary, thoracic

**63287** intradural, intramedullary, thoracolumbar

**63290** combined extradural-intradural lesion, any level

(For drainage of intramedullary cyst/syrinx, use 63172, 63173)

## Excision, Anterior or Anterolateral Approach, Intraspinal Lesion

(For arthrodesis, see 22548-22585)

(For reconstruction of spine, see 20930-20938)

**63300** Vertebral corpectomy (vertebral body resection), partial or complete, for excision of intraspinal lesion, single segment; extradural, cervical

**63301** extradural, thoracic by transthoracic approach

**63302** extradural, thoracic by thoracolumbar approach

**63303** extradural, lumbar or sacral by transperitoneal or retroperitoneal approach

**63304** intradural, cervical

**63305** intradural, thoracic by transthoracic approach

**63306** intradural, thoracic by thoracolumbar approach

**63307** intradural, lumbar or sacral by transperitoneal or retroperitoneal approach

**+ 63308** each additional segment (List separately in addition to codes for single segment)

(Use 63308 in conjunction with codes 63300-63307)

## Stereotaxis

**63600** Creation of lesion of spinal cord by stereotactic method, percutaneous, any modality (including stimulation and/or recording)

**63610** Stereotactic stimulation of spinal cord, percutaneous, separate procedure not followed by other surgery

**63615** Stereotactic biopsy, aspiration, or excision of lesion, spinal cord

## Neurostimulators (Spinal)

Codes 63650-63688 apply to both simple and complex neurostimulators. For initial or subsequent electronic analysis and programming of neurostimulator pulse generators, see codes 95970-95975.

Codes 63650, 63655, and 63660 describe the operative placement, revision, or removal of the spinal neurostimulator system components to provide spinal electrical stimulation. A neurostimulator system includes an implanted neurostimulator, external controller, extension, and collection of contacts. Multiple contacts or electrodes (4 or more) provide the actual electrical stimulation in the epidural space.

For percutaneously placed neurostimulator systems (63650, 63660), the contacts are on a catheter-like lead. An array defines the collection of contacts that are on one catheter.

For systems placed via an open surgical exposure (63655, 63660), the contacts are on a plate or paddle-shaped surface.

**63650** Percutaneous implantation of neurostimulator electrode array, epidural

(63652 has been deleted)

**63655** Laminectomy for implantation of neurostimulator electrodes, plate/paddle, epidural

(63656 has been deleted)

(63657 and 63658 have been deleted)

**63660** Revision or removal of spinal neurostimulator electrode percutaneous array(s) or plate/paddle(s)

**63685** Incision and subcutaneous placement of spinal neurostimulator pulse generator or receiver, direct or inductive coupling

**63688** Revision or removal of implanted spinal neurostimulator pulse generator or receiver

(63690, 63691 have been deleted. To report, see 95970-►95975◄)

## Repair

**63700** Repair of meningocele; less than 5 cm diameter

**63702** larger than 5 cm diameter

**63704** Repair of myelomeningocele; less than 5 cm diameter

**63706** larger than 5 cm diameter

(For complex skin closure, see **Integumentary System**)

**63707** Repair of dural/CSF leak, not requiring laminectomy

(63708 has been deleted. To report, see 63707, 63709)

**63709** Repair of dural/CSF leak or pseudomeningocele, with laminectomy

**63710** Dural graft, spinal

(For laminectomy and section of dentate ligaments, with or without dural graft, cervical, see 63180, 63182)

## Shunt, Spinal CSF

**63740** Creation of shunt, lumbar, subarachnoid-peritoneal, -pleural, or other; including laminectomy

**63741** percutaneous, not requiring laminectomy

**63744** Replacement, irrigation or revision of lumbosubarachnoid shunt

**63746** Removal of entire lumbosubarachnoid shunt system without replacement

(63750 has been deleted. To report, see 62351 and 62360, 62361 or 62362)

(63780 has been deleted. To report, see 62350 and 62360, 62361 or 62362)

# Extracranial Nerves, Peripheral Nerves, and Autonomic Nervous System

(For intracranial surgery on cranial nerves, see 61450, 61460, 61790)

## Introduction/Injection of Anesthetic Agent (Nerve Block), Diagnostic or Therapeutic

### Somatic Nerves

**64400*** Injection, anesthetic agent; trigeminal nerve, any division or branch

**64402*** facial nerve

**64405*** greater occipital nerve

**64408*** vagus nerve

**64410*** phrenic nerve

**64412*** spinal accessory nerve

**64413*** cervical plexus

**64415*** brachial plexus

**64417*** axillary nerve

**64418*** suprascapular nerve

**64420*** intercostal nerve, single

**64421*** intercostal nerves, multiple, regional block

**64425*** ilioinguinal, iliohypogastric nerves

**64430*** pudendal nerve

**64435*** paracervical (uterine) nerve

►(64440 has been deleted. To report, see 64479, 64483)◄

►(64441 has been deleted. To report, see 64480, 64484)◄

►(64442 has been deleted. To report, use 64475)◄

►(64443 has been deleted. To report, use 64476)◄

**64445*** sciatic nerve

**64450*** other peripheral nerve or branch

(For phenol destruction, see ►62310-62319◄)

(For subarachnoid or subdural injection, see ►62310-62319◄)

(For epidural or caudal injection, see ►62310-62319◄)

►(Codes 64470-64484 are unilateral procedures. For bilateral procedures, use modifier '-50')◄

►(For fluoroscopic guidance and localization for needle placement and injection in conjunction with codes 64470-64484, use code 76005)◄

●**64470** Injection, anesthetic agent and/or steroid, paravertebral facet joint or facet joint nerve; cervical or thoracic, single level

+●**64472** cervical or thoracic, each additional level (List separately in addition to code for primary procedure)

►(Use code 64472 in conjunction with code 64470)◄

●**64475** lumbar or sacral, single level

+●**64476** lumbar or sacral, each additional level (List separately in addition to code for primary procedure)

►(Use code 64476 in conjunction with code 64475)◄

●**64479** Injection, anesthetic agent and/or steroid, transforaminal epidural; cervical or thoracic, single level

+●**64480** cervical or thoracic, each additional level (List separately in addition to code for primary procedure)

►(Use code 64480 in conjunction with code 64479)◄

●**64483** lumbar or sacral, single level

+●**64484** lumbar or sacral, each additional level (List separately in addition to code for primary procedure)

►(Use code 64484 in conjunction with code 64483)◄

### Sympathetic Nerves

**64505*** Injection, anesthetic agent; sphenopalatine ganglion

**64508*** carotid sinus (separate procedure)

**64510*** stellate ganglion (cervical sympathetic)

**64520*** lumbar or thoracic (paravertebral sympathetic)

**64530*** celiac plexus, with or without radiologic monitoring

## Neurostimulators (Peripheral Nerve)

Codes 64553-64595 apply to both simple and complex neurostimulators. For initial or subsequent electronic analysis and programming of neurostimulator pulse generators, see codes 95970-95975.

**64550** Application of surface (transcutaneous) neurostimulator

**64553** Percutaneous implantation of neurostimulator electrodes; cranial nerve

►(For open placement of cranial nerve (eg, vagal, trigeminal) neurostimulator pulse generator or receiver, see 61885, 61886, as appropriate)◄

**64555** peripheral nerve

**64560** autonomic nerve

**64565** neuromuscular

**64573** Incision for implantation of neurostimulator electrodes; cranial nerve

►(For open placement of cranial nerve (eg, vagal, trigeminal) neurostimulator pulse generator or receiver, see 61885, 61886, as appropriate)◄

►(For revision or removal of cranial nerve (eg, vagal, trigeminal) neurostimulator pulse generator or receiver, use 61888)◄

**64575** peripheral nerve

**64577** autonomic nerve

**64580** neuromuscular

**64585** Revision or removal of peripheral neurostimulator electrodes

**64590** Incision and subcutaneous placement of peripheral neurostimulator pulse generator or receiver, direct or inductive coupling

**64595** Revision or removal of peripheral neurostimulator pulse generator or receiver

## Destruction by Neurolytic Agent (eg, Chemical, Thermal, Electrical, Radiofrequency)

### Somatic Nerves

**64600** Destruction by neurolytic agent, trigeminal nerve; supraorbital, infraorbital, mental, or inferior alveolar branch

**64605** second and third division branches at foramen ovale

**64610** second and third division branches at foramen ovale under radiologic monitoring

**64612** Destruction by neurolytic agent (chemodenervation of muscle endplate); muscles innervated by facial nerve (eg, for blepharospasm, hemifacial spasm)

**64613** cervical spinal muscles (eg, for spasmodic torticollis)

(For chemodenervation for strabismus involving the extraocular muscles, use 67345)

**64620** Destruction by neurolytic agent, intercostal nerve

►(Codes 64622-64627 are unilateral procedures. For bilateral procedures, use modifier '-50')◄

►(For fluoroscopic guidance and localization for needle placement and neurolysis in conjunction with codes 64622-64627, use 76005)◄

**▲64622** Destruction by neurolytic agent, paravertebral facet joint nerve; lumbar or sacral, single level

**+▲64623** lumbar or sacral, each additional level (List separately in addition to code for primary procedure)

►(Use 64623 in conjunction with code 64622)◄

**●64626** cervical or thoracic, single level

**+●64627** cervical or thoracic, each additional level (List separately in addition to code for primary procedure)

►(Use 64627 in conjunction with code 64626)◄

**64630** pudendal nerve

**64640** other peripheral nerve or branch

### Sympathetic Nerves

**64680** Destruction by neurolytic agent, celiac plexus, with or without radiologic monitoring

## Neuroplasty (Exploration, Neurolysis or Nerve Decompression)

Neuroplasty is the decompression or freeing of intact nerve from scar tissue, including external neurolysis and/or transposition.

(For internal neurolysis requiring use of operating microscope, use 64727)

(For facial nerve decompression, use 69720)

**64702** Neuroplasty; digital, one or both, same digit

**64704** nerve of hand or foot

**64708** Neuroplasty, major peripheral nerve, arm or leg; other than specified

**64712** sciatic nerve

**64713** brachial plexus

**64714** lumbar plexus

**64716** Neuroplasty and/or transposition; cranial nerve (specify)

**64718** ulnar nerve at elbow

**64719** ulnar nerve at wrist

**64721** median nerve at carpal tunnel

(For arthroscopic procedure, use 29848)

**64722** Decompression; unspecified nerve(s) (specify)

**64726** plantar digital nerve

**+ 64727** Internal neurolysis, requiring use of operating microscope (List separately in addition to code for neuroplasty) (Neuroplasty includes external neurolysis)

(Do not report code 69990 in addition to code 64727)

## Transection or Avulsion

(For stereotactic lesion of gasserian ganglion, use 61790)

**64732** Transection or avulsion of; supraorbital nerve

**64734** infraorbital nerve

**64736** mental nerve

**64738** inferior alveolar nerve by osteotomy

**64740** lingual nerve

**64742** facial nerve, differential or complete

**64744** greater occipital nerve

**64746** phrenic nerve

(For section of recurrent laryngeal nerve, use 31595)

**64752** vagus nerve (vagotomy), transthoracic

**64755** vagi limited to proximal stomach (selective proximal vagotomy, proximal gastric vagotomy, parietal cell vagotomy, supra- or highly selective vagotomy)

►(For laparoscopic approach, use 43652)◄

**64760** vagus nerve (vagotomy), abdominal

►(For laparoscopic approach, use 43651)◄

**64761** pudendal nerve

(64762 has been deleted. To report, use 64761 with modifier '-50')

**64763** Transection or avulsion of obturator nerve, extrapelvic, with or without adductor tenotomy

(64764 has been deleted. To report, use 64763 with modifier '-50')

**64766** Transection or avulsion of obturator nerve, intrapelvic, with or without adductor tenotomy

(64768 has been deleted. To report, use 64766 with modifier '-50')

**64771** Transection or avulsion of other cranial nerve, extradural

**64772** Transection or avulsion of other spinal nerve, extradural

(For excision of tender scar, skin and subcutaneous tissue, with or without tiny neuroma, see 11400-11446, 13100-►13153◄)

## Excision

### Somatic Nerves

(For Morton neurectomy, use 28080)

**64774** Excision of neuroma; cutaneous nerve, surgically identifiable

**64776** digital nerve, one or both, same digit

**+ 64778** digital nerve, each additional digit (List separately in addition to code for primary procedure)

(Use 64778 in conjunction with code 64776)

**64782** hand or foot, except digital nerve

**+ 64783** hand or foot, each additional nerve, except same digit (List separately in addition to code for primary procedure)

(Use 64783 in conjunction with code 64782)

**64784** major peripheral nerve, except sciatic

**64786** sciatic nerve

**+ 64787** Implantation of nerve end into bone or muscle (List separately in addition to neuroma excision)

(Use 64787 in conjunction with codes 64774-64786)

**64788** Excision of neurofibroma or neurolemmoma; cutaneous nerve

**64790** major peripheral nerve

**64792** extensive (including malignant type)

**64795** Biopsy of nerve

### Sympathetic Nerves

**64802** Sympathectomy, cervical

(64803 has been deleted. To report, use 64802 with modifier '-50')

**64804** Sympathectomy, cervicothoracic

(64806 has been deleted. To report, use 64804 with modifier '-50')

**64809** Sympathectomy, thoracolumbar

(64811 has been deleted. To report, use 64809 with modifier '-50')

(64814 has been deleted. To report, use 64999)

**64818** Sympathectomy, lumbar

(64819 has been deleted. To report, use 64818 with modifier '-50')

**64820** Sympathectomy, digital arteries, with magnification, each digit

(64824 has been deleted. To report, use 64999)

## Neurorrhaphy

(64830 has been deleted. Use 69990 when the surgical microscope is employed for the microsurgical procedure. Do not use 69990 for visualization with magnifying loupes or corrected vision)

**64831** Suture of digital nerve, hand or foot; one nerve

**+ 64832** each additional digital nerve (List separately in addition to code for primary procedure)

(Use 64832 in conjunction with code 64831)

**64834** Suture of one nerve, hand or foot; common sensory nerve

**64835** median motor thenar

**64836** ulnar motor

**+ 64837** Suture of each additional nerve, hand or foot (List separately in addition to code for primary procedure)

(Use 64837 in conjunction with codes 64834-64836)

**64840** Suture of posterior tibial nerve

**64856** Suture of major peripheral nerve, arm or leg, except sciatic; including transposition

**64857** without transposition

**64858** Suture of sciatic nerve

**+ 64859** Suture of each additional major peripheral nerve (List separately in addition to code for primary procedure)

(Use 64859 in conjunction with codes 64856, 64857)

**64861** Suture of; brachial plexus

**64862** lumbar plexus

**64864** Suture of facial nerve; extracranial

**64865** infratemporal, with or without grafting

**64866** Anastomosis; facial-spinal accessory

**64868** facial-hypoglossal

**64870** facial-phrenic

**+ 64872** Suture of nerve; requiring secondary or delayed suture (List separately in addition to code for primary neurorrhaphy)

(Use 64872 in conjunction with codes 64831-64865)

**+ 64874** requiring extensive mobilization, or transposition of nerve (List separately in addition to code for nerve suture)

(Use 64874 in conjunction with codes 64831-64865)

**+ 64876** requiring shortening of bone of extremity (List separately in addition to code for nerve suture)

(Use 64876 in conjunction with codes 64831-64865)

## Neurorrhaphy With Nerve Graft

**64885** Nerve graft (includes obtaining graft), head or neck; up to 4 cm in length

**64886** more than 4 cm length

**64890** Nerve graft (includes obtaining graft), single strand, hand or foot; up to 4 cm length

**64891** more than 4 cm length

**64892** Nerve graft (includes obtaining graft), single strand, arm or leg; up to 4 cm length

**64893** more than 4 cm length

**64895** Nerve graft (includes obtaining graft), multiple strands (cable), hand or foot; up to 4 cm length

**64896** more than 4 cm length

**64897** Nerve graft (includes obtaining graft), multiple strands (cable), arm or leg; up to 4 cm length

**64898** more than 4 cm length

**+ 64901** Nerve graft, each additional nerve; single strand (List separately in addition to code for primary procedure)

(Use 64901 in conjunction with codes 64885-64893)

**+ 64902** multiple strands (cable) (List separately in addition to code for primary procedure)

(Use 64902 in conjunction with codes 64885, 64886, 64895-64898)

**64905** Nerve pedicle transfer; first stage

**64907** second stage

## Other Procedures

**64999** Unlisted procedure, nervous system

# Notes

# Eye and Ocular Adnexa

(For diagnostic and treatment ophthalmological services, see **Medicine, Ophthalmology,** and 92002 et seq)

(Do not report code 69990 in addition to codes 65091-68850)

## Eyeball

### Removal of Eye

**65091** Evisceration of ocular contents; without implant

**65093** with implant

**65101** Enucleation of eye; without implant

**65103** with implant, muscles not attached to implant

**65105** with implant, muscles attached to implant

(For conjunctivoplasty after enucleation, see 68320 et seq)

**65110** Exenteration of orbit (does not include skin graft), removal of orbital contents; only

**65112** with therapeutic removal of bone

**65114** with muscle or myocutaneous flap

(For skin graft to orbit (split skin), see 15120, 15121; free, full thickness, see 15260, 15261)

(For eyelid repair involving more than skin, see 67930 et seq)

### Secondary Implant(s) Procedures

An ocular implant is an implant inside muscular cone; an orbital implant is an implant outside muscular cone.

**65125** Modification of ocular implant with placement or replacement of pegs (eg, drilling receptacle for prosthesis appendage) (separate procedure)

**65130** Insertion of ocular implant secondary; after evisceration, in scleral shell

**65135** after enucleation, muscles not attached to implant

**65140** after enucleation, muscles attached to implant

**65150** Reinsertion of ocular implant; with or without conjunctival graft

**65155** with use of foreign material for reinforcement and/or attachment of muscles to implant

**65175** Removal of ocular implant

(For orbital implant (implant outside muscle cone) insertion, use 67550; removal, use 67560)

### Removal of Foreign Body

(For removal of implanted material: ocular implant, use 65175; anterior segment implant, use 65920; posterior segment implant, use 67120; orbital implant, use 67560)

(For diagnostic x-ray for foreign body, use 70030)

(For diagnostic echography for foreign body, use 76529)

(For removal of foreign body from orbit: frontal approach, use 67413; lateral approach, use 67430; transcranial approach, use 61334)

(For removal of foreign body from eyelid, embedded, use 67938)

(For removal of foreign body from lacrimal system, use 68530)

**65205*** Removal of foreign body, external eye; conjunctival superficial

**65210*** conjunctival embedded (includes concretions), subconjunctival, or scleral nonperforating

**65220*** corneal, without slit lamp

**65222*** corneal, with slit lamp

(For repair of corneal laceration with foreign body, use 65275)

(65230 has been deleted. To report, use 65235)

**65235** Removal of foreign body, intraocular; from anterior chamber or lens

(65240, 65245 have been deleted. To report, use 65235)

(For removal of implanted material from anterior segment, use 65920)

**65260** from posterior segment, magnetic extraction, anterior or posterior route

**65265** from posterior segment, nonmagnetic extraction

(For removal of implanted material from posterior segment, use 67120)

## Repair of Laceration

(For fracture of orbit, see 21385 et seq)

(For repair of wound of eyelid, skin, linear, simple, see 12011-12018; intermediate, layered closure, see 12051-12057; linear, complex, see 13150-13300; other, see 67930, 67935)

(For repair of wound of lacrimal system, use 68700)

(For repair of operative wound, use 66250)

**65270*** Repair of laceration; conjunctiva, with or without nonperforating laceration sclera, direct closure

**65272** conjunctiva, by mobilization and rearrangement, without hospitalization

**65273** conjunctiva, by mobilization and rearrangement, with hospitalization

**65275** cornea, nonperforating, with or without removal foreign body

**65280** cornea and/or sclera, perforating, not involving uveal tissue

**65285** cornea and/or sclera, perforating, with reposition or resection of uveal tissue

**65286** application of tissue glue, wounds of cornea and/or sclera

(Repair of laceration includes use of conjunctival flap and restoration of anterior chamber, by air or saline injection when indicated)

(For repair of iris or ciliary body, use 66680)

**65290** Repair of wound, extraocular muscle, tendon and/or Tenon's capsule

# Anterior Segment

## Cornea

### Excision

(65300 has been deleted)

**65400** Excision of lesion, cornea (keratectomy, lamellar, partial), except pterygium

**65410*** Biopsy of cornea

**65420** Excision or transposition of pterygium; without graft

**65426** with graft

### Removal or Destruction

**65430*** Scraping of cornea, diagnostic, for smear and/or culture

**65435*** Removal of corneal epithelium; with or without chemocauterization (abrasion, curettage)

**65436** with application of chelating agent (eg, EDTA)

(65445 has been deleted. To report, use 65450)

**65450** Destruction of lesion of cornea by cryotherapy, photocoagulation or thermocauterization

(65455 has been deleted. To report, use 65450)

**65600** Multiple punctures of anterior cornea (eg, for corneal erosion, tattoo)

### Keratoplasty

Corneal transplant includes use of fresh or preserved grafts, and preparation of donor material.

(Keratoplasty excludes refractive keratoplasty procedures, 65760, 65765, and 65767)

**65710** Keratoplasty (corneal transplant); lamellar

(65720, 65725 have been deleted. To report, use 65710)

**65730** penetrating (except in aphakia)

(65740, 65745 have been deleted. To report, use 65730)

**65750** penetrating (in aphakia)

**65755** penetrating (in pseudophakia)

### Other Procedures

**65760** Keratomileusis

**65765** Keratophakia

**65767** Epikeratoplasty

**65770** Keratoprosthesis

**65771** Radial keratotomy

**65772** Corneal relaxing incision for correction of surgically induced astigmatism

**65775** Corneal wedge resection for correction of surgically induced astigmatism

(For fitting of contact lens for treatment of disease, use 92070)

(For unlisted procedures on cornea, use 66999)

## Anterior Chamber

### Incision

**65800*** Paracentesis of anterior chamber of eye (separate procedure); with diagnostic aspiration of aqueous

**65805*** with therapeutic release of aqueous

**65810** with removal of vitreous and/or discission of anterior hyaloid membrane, with or without air injection

**65815** with removal of blood, with or without irrigation and/or air injection

(For injection, see 66020-66030)

(For removal of blood clot, use 65930)

**65820** Goniotomy

(65825, 65830 have been deleted)

**65850** Trabeculotomy ab externo

**65855** Trabeculoplasty by laser surgery, one or more sessions (defined treatment series)

(If re-treatment is necessary after several months because of disease progression, a new treatment or treatment series should be reported with a modifier, if necessary, to indicate lesser or greater complexity)

(For trabeculectomy, use 66170)

**65860** Severing adhesions of anterior segment, laser technique (separate procedure)

### Other Procedures

**65865** Severing adhesions of anterior segment of eye, incisional technique (with or without injection of air or liquid) (separate procedure); goniosynechiae

(For trabeculoplasty by laser surgery, use 65855)

**65870** anterior synechiae, except goniosynechiae

**65875** posterior synechiae

**65880** corneovitreal adhesions

(For laser surgery, use 66821)

**65900** Removal of epithelial downgrowth, anterior chamber eye

**65920** Removal of implanted material, anterior segment eye

**65930** Removal of blood clot, anterior segment eye

**66020** Injection, anterior chamber (separate procedure); air or liquid

**66030*** medication

(For unlisted procedures on anterior segment, use 66999)

## Anterior Sclera

### Excision

(For removal of intraocular foreign body, use 65235)

(For operations on posterior sclera, use 67250, 67255)

**66130** Excision of lesion, sclera

**66150** Fistulization of sclera for glaucoma; trephination with iridectomy

**66155** thermocauterization with iridectomy

**66160** sclerectomy with punch or scissors, with iridectomy

**66165** iridencleisis or iridotasis

**66170** trabeculectomy ab externo in absence of previous surgery

(For trabeculotomy ab externo, use 65850)

(For repair of operative wound, use 66250)

**66172** trabeculectomy ab externo with scarring from previous ocular surgery or trauma (includes injection of antifibrotic agents)

**66180** Aqueous shunt to extraocular reservoir (eg, Molteno, Schocket, Denver-Krupin)

**66185** Revision of aqueous shunt to extraocular reservoir

(For removal of implanted shunt, use 67120)

### Repair or Revision

(For scleral procedures in retinal surgery, see 67101 et seq)

**66220** Repair of scleral staphyloma; without graft

**66225** with graft

(For scleral reinforcement, see 67250, 67255)

**66250** Revision or repair of operative wound of anterior segment, any type, early or late, major or minor procedure

(For unlisted procedures on anterior sclera, use 66999)

## Iris, Ciliary Body

### Incision

**66500** Iridotomy by stab incision (separate procedure); except transfixion

**66505** with transfixion as for iris bombe

(For iridotomy by photocoagulation, use 66761)

### Excision

**66600** Iridectomy, with corneoscleral or corneal section; for removal of lesion

**66605** with cyclectomy

**66625** peripheral for glaucoma (separate procedure)

**66630** sector for glaucoma (separate procedure)

**66635** optical (separate procedure)

(For coreoplasty by photocoagulation, use 66762)

### Repair

**66680** Repair of iris, ciliary body (as for iridodialysis)

(For reposition or resection of uveal tissue with perforating wound of cornea or sclera, use 65285)

**66682** Suture of iris, ciliary body (separate procedure) with retrieval of suture through small incision (eg, McCannel suture)

### Destruction

**66700** Ciliary body destruction; diathermy

(66701, 66702 have been deleted. To report, see 66700, 66710, 66720, 66740)

**66710** cyclophotocoagulation

**66720** cryotherapy

(66721 has been deleted. To report, see 66700, 66710, 66720, 66740)

**66740** cyclodialysis

(66741 has been deleted. To report, see 66700, 66710, 66720, 66740)

**66761** Iridotomy/iridectomy by laser surgery (eg, for glaucoma) (one or more sessions)

**66762** Iridoplasty by photocoagulation (one or more sessions) (eg, for improvement of vision, for widening of anterior chamber angle)

**66770** Destruction of cyst or lesion iris or ciliary body (nonexcisional procedure)

(For excision lesion iris, ciliary body, see 66600, 66605; for removal of epithelial downgrowth, use 65900)

(For unlisted procedures on iris, ciliary body, use 66999)

## Lens

### Incision

(66800, 66801 have been deleted. To report, use 66999)

(66802 has been deleted)

**66820** Discission of secondary membranous cataract (opacified posterior lens capsule and/or anterior hyaloid); stab incision technique (Ziegler or Wheeler knife)

**66821** laser surgery (eg, YAG laser) (one or more stages)

**66825** Repositioning of intraocular lens prosthesis, requiring an incision (separate procedure)

### Removal Cataract

Lateral canthotomy, iridectomy, iridotomy, anterior capsulotomy, posterior capsulotomy, the use of viscoelastic agents, enzymatic zonulysis, use of other pharmacologic agents, and subconjunctival or sub-tenon injections are included as part of the code for the extraction of lens.

**66830** Removal of secondary membranous cataract (opacified posterior lens capsule and/or anterior hyaloid) with corneo-scleral section, with or without iridectomy (iridocapsulotomy, iridocapsulectomy)

**66840** Removal of lens material; aspiration technique, one or more stages

**66850** phacofragmentation technique (mechanical or ultrasonic) (eg, phacoemulsification), with aspiration

**66852** pars plana approach, with or without vitrectomy

(66915 has been deleted)

**66920** intracapsular

**66930** intracapsular, for dislocated lens

**66940** extracapsular (other than 66840, 66850, 66852)

(66945 has been deleted. To report, see 66920-66940)

(For removal of intralenticular foreign body without lens extraction, use 65235)

(For repair of operative wound, use 66250)

(66980 has been deleted. To report, see 66983, 66984)

**66983** Intracapsular cataract extraction with insertion of intraocular lens prosthesis (one stage procedure)

**66984** Extracapsular cataract removal with insertion of intraocular lens prosthesis (one stage procedure), manual or mechanical technique (eg, irrigation and aspiration or phacoemulsification)

**66985** Insertion of intraocular lens prosthesis (secondary implant), not associated with concurrent cataract removal

(To code implant at time of concurrent cataract surgery, use 66983 or 66984)

(For intraocular lens prosthesis supplied by physician, use 99070)

(For ultrasonic determination of intraocular lens power, use 76519)

(For removal of implanted material from anterior segment, use 65920)

(For secondary fixation (separate procedure), use 66682)

**66986** Exchange of intraocular lens

### Other Procedures

**66999** Unlisted procedure, anterior segment of eye

## Posterior Segment

### Vitreous

**67005** Removal of vitreous, anterior approach (open sky technique or limbal incision); partial removal

**67010** subtotal removal with mechanical vitrectomy

(For removal of vitreous by paracentesis of anterior chamber, use 65810)

(For removal of corneovitreal adhesions, use 65880)

**67015** Aspiration or release of vitreous, subretinal or choroidal fluid, pars plana approach (posterior sclerotomy)

**67025** Injection of vitreous substitute, pars plana or limbal approach, (fluid-gas exchange), with or without aspiration (separate procedure)

**67027** Implantation of intravitreal drug delivery system (eg, ganciclovir implant), includes concomitant removal of vitreous

(For removal, use 67121)

**67028** Intravitreal injection of a pharmacologic agent (separate procedure)

**67030** Discission of vitreous strands (without removal), pars plana approach

**67031** Severing of vitreous strands, vitreous face adhesions, sheets, membranes or opacities, laser surgery (one or more stages)

(67035 has been deleted. To report, use 67036)

**67036** Vitrectomy, mechanical, pars plana approach;

**67038** with epiretinal membrane stripping

**67039** with focal endolaser photocoagulation

**67040** with endolaser panretinal photocoagulation

(For associated lensectomy, use 66850)

(For use of vitrectomy in retinal detachment surgery, use 67108)

(For associated removal of foreign body, see 65260, 65265)

(For unlisted procedures on vitreous, use 67299)

### Retina or Choroid

#### Repair

(If diathermy, cryotherapy and/or photocoagulation are combined, report under principal modality used)

**67101** Repair of retinal detachment, one or more sessions; cryotherapy or diathermy, with or without drainage of subretinal fluid

(67102, 67103 have been deleted. To report, use 67101)

(67104 has been deleted. To report, use 67105)

**67105** photocoagulation, with or without drainage of subretinal fluid

(67106 has been deleted. To report, use 67105)

**67107** Repair of retinal detachment; scleral buckling (such as lamellar scleral dissection, imbrication or encircling procedure), with or without implant, with or without cryotherapy, photocoagulation, and drainage of subretinal fluid

**67108** with vitrectomy, any method, with or without air or gas tamponade, focal endolaser photocoagulation, cryotherapy, drainage of subretinal fluid, scleral buckling, and/or removal of lens by same technique

(67109 has been deleted. To report, use 67299)

**67110** by injection of air or other gas (eg, pneumatic retinopexy)

**67112** by scleral buckling or vitrectomy, on patient having previous ipsilateral retinal detachment repair(s) using scleral buckling or vitrectomy techniques

(For aspiration or drainage of subretinal or subchoroidal fluid, use 67015)

**67115** Release of encircling material (posterior segment)

**67120** Removal of implanted material, posterior segment; extraocular

**67121** intraocular

(For removal from anterior segment, use 65920)

(For removal of foreign body, see 65260, 65265)

### Prophylaxis

Repetitive services. The services listed below are often performed in multiple sessions or groups of sessions. The methods of reporting vary.

The following descriptors are intended to include all sessions in a defined treatment period.

**67141** Prophylaxis of retinal detachment (eg, retinal break, lattice degeneration) without drainage, one or more sessions; cryotherapy, diathermy

(67142, 67143 have been deleted. To report, use 67141)

(67144 has been deleted. To report, use 67145)

**67145** photocoagulation (laser or xenon arc)

(67146 has been deleted. To report, use 67145)

### Destruction

**67208** Destruction of localized lesion of retina (eg, macular edema, tumors), one or more sessions; cryotherapy, diathermy

**67210** photocoagulation

(67212, 67213 have been deleted. To report, use 67208)

(67214, 67216 have been deleted. To report, use 67210)

**67218** radiation by implantation of source (includes removal of source)

**▲67220** Destruction of localized lesion of choroid (eg, choroidal neovascularization), one or more session, photocoagulation (eg, laser, ocular photodynamic therapy)

(67222, 67223 have been deleted. To report, use 67227)

(67224, 67226 have been deleted. To report, use 67228)

**67227** Destruction of extensive or progressive retinopathy (eg, diabetic retinopathy), one or more sessions; cryotherapy, diathermy

**67228** photocoagulation (laser or xenon arc)

(For unlisted procedures on retina, use 67299)

## Sclera

### Repair

(For excision lesion sclera, use 66130)

**67250** Scleral reinforcement (separate procedure); without graft

**67255** with graft

(For repair scleral staphyloma, see 66220, 66225)

## Other Procedures

**67299** Unlisted procedure, posterior segment

# Ocular Adnexa

## Extraocular Muscles

**67311** Strabismus surgery, recession or resection procedure; one horizontal muscle

**67312** two horizontal muscles

(67313 has been deleted)

**67314** one vertical muscle (excluding superior oblique)

**67316** two or more vertical muscles (excluding superior oblique)

(For adjustable sutures, use 67335 in addition to codes 67311-67334 for primary procedure reflecting number of muscles operated on)

**67318** Strabismus surgery, any procedure, superior oblique muscle

**+ 67320** Transposition procedure (eg, for paretic extraocular muscle), any extraocular muscle (specify) (List separately in addition to code for primary procedure)

(Use 67320 in conjunction with codes 67311-67318)

**+ 67331** Strabismus surgery on patient with previous eye surgery or injury that did not involve the extraocular muscles (List separately in addition to code for primary procedure)

(Use 67331 in conjunction with codes 67311-67318)

**+ 67332** Strabismus surgery on patient with scarring of extraocular muscles (eg, prior ocular injury, strabismus or retinal detachment surgery) or restrictive myopathy (eg, dysthyroid ophthalmopathy) (List separately in addition to code for primary procedure)

(Use 67332 in conjunction with codes 67311-67318)

**+ 67334** Strabismus surgery by posterior fixation suture technique, with or without muscle recession (List separately in addition to code for primary procedure)

(Use 67334 in conjunction with codes 67311-67318)

**+ 67335** Placement of adjustable suture(s) during strabismus surgery, including postoperative adjustment(s) of suture(s) (List separately in addition to code for specific strabismus surgery)

(Use 67335 only for code(s) for conventional muscle surgery, 67311-67334, to identify number of muscles involved)

**+ 67340** Strabismus surgery involving exploration and/or repair of detached extraocular muscle(s) (List separately in addition to code for primary procedure)

(Use 67340 in conjunction with codes 67311-67334)

**67343** Release of extensive scar tissue without detaching extraocular muscle (separate procedure)

(Use 67343 in conjunction with codes 67311-67340, when such procedures are performed other than on the affected muscle)

**67345** Chemodenervation of extraocular muscle

(For chemodenervation for blepharospasm and other neurological disorders, see 64612 and 64613)

### Other Procedures

**67350** Biopsy of extraocular muscle

(For repair of wound, extraocular muscle, tendon or Tenon's capsule, use 65290)

**67399** Unlisted procedure, ocular muscle

## Orbit

### Exploration, Excision, Decompression

**67400** Orbitotomy without bone flap (frontal or transconjunctival approach); for exploration, with or without biopsy

**67405** with drainage only

**67412** with removal of lesion

**67413** with removal of foreign body

**67414** with removal of bone for decompression

**67415** Fine needle aspiration of orbital contents

(For exenteration, enucleation, and repair, see 65101 et seq; for optic nerve decompression, use 67570)

**67420** Orbitotomy with bone flap or window, lateral approach (eg, Kroenlein); with removal of lesion

**67430** with removal of foreign body

**67440** with drainage

**67445** with removal of bone for decompression

(For optic nerve sheath decompression, use 67570)

**67450** for exploration, with or without biopsy

(For orbitotomy, transcranial approach, see 61330-61334)

(For orbital implant, see 67550, 67560)

(For removal of eyeball or for repair after removal, see 65091-65175)

### Other Procedures

**67500*** Retrobulbar injection; medication (separate procedure, does not include supply of medication)

**67505** alcohol

(67510 has been deleted. To report, use 67599)

**67515*** Injection of therapeutic agent into Tenon's capsule

(For subconjunctival injection, use 68200)

**67550** Orbital implant (implant outside muscle cone); insertion

**67560** removal or revision

(For ocular implant (implant inside muscle cone), see 65093-65105, 65130-65175)

(For treatment of fractures of malar area, orbit, see 21355 et seq)

**67570** Optic nerve decompression (eg, incision or fenestration of optic nerve sheath)

**67599** Unlisted procedure, orbit

## Eyelids

### Incision

**67700*** Blepharotomy, drainage of abscess, eyelid

**67710*** Severing of tarsorrhaphy

**67715*** Canthotomy (separate procedure)

(For canthoplasty, use 67950)

(For division of symblepharon, use 68340)

### Excision

Codes for removal of lesion include more than skin (ie, involving lid margin, tarsus, and/or palpebral conjunctiva).

(For removal of lesion, involving mainly skin of eyelid, see 11310-11313; 11440-11446, 11640-11646; 17000-17004)

(For repair of wounds, blepharoplasty, grafts, reconstructive surgery, see 67930-67975)

**67800** Excision of chalazion; single

**67801** multiple, same lid

**67805** multiple, different lids

**67808** under general anesthesia and/or requiring hospitalization, single or multiple

**67810*** Biopsy of eyelid

**67820*** Correction of trichiasis; epilation, by forceps only

**67825*** epilation by other than forceps (eg, by electrosurgery, cryotherapy, laser surgery)

**67830** incision of lid margin

**67835** incision of lid margin, with free mucous membrane graft

**67840*** Excision of lesion of eyelid (except chalazion) without closure or with simple direct closure

(For excision and repair of eyelid by reconstructive surgery, see 67961, 67966)

**67850*** Destruction of lesion of lid margin (up to 1 cm)

(For Mohs' micrographic surgery, see 17304-17310)

(For initiation or follow-up care of topical chemotherapy (eg, 5-FU or similar agents), see appropriate office visits)

### Tarsorrhaphy

**67875** Temporary closure of eyelids by suture (eg, Frost suture)

**67880** Construction of intermarginal adhesions, median tarsorrhaphy, or canthorrhaphy;

**67882** with transposition of tarsal plate

(For severing of tarsorrhaphy, use 67710)

(For canthoplasty, reconstruction canthus, use 67950)

(For canthotomy, use 67715)

## Repair (Brow Ptosis, Blepharoptosis, Lid Retraction, Ectropion, Entropion)

**67900** Repair of brow ptosis (supraciliary, mid-forehead or coronal approach)

(For forehead rhytidectomy, use 15824)

**67901** Repair of blepharoptosis; frontalis muscle technique with suture or other material

**67902** frontalis muscle technique with fascial sling (includes obtaining fascia)

**67903** (tarso)levator resection or advancement, internal approach

**67904** (tarso)levator resection or advancement, external approach

**67906** superior rectus technique with fascial sling (includes obtaining fascia)

(67907 has been deleted. To report, use 67999)

**67908** conjunctivo-tarso-Muller's muscle-levator resection (eg, Fasanella-Servat type)

**67909** Reduction of overcorrection of ptosis

**67911** Correction of lid retraction

(For obtaining autogenous graft materials, see 20920, 20922 or 20926)

(For correction of trichiasis by mucous membrane graft, use 67835)

**67914** Repair of ectropion; suture

**67915** thermocauterization

**67916** blepharoplasty, excision tarsal wedge

**67917** blepharoplasty, extensive (eg, Kuhnt-Szymanowski or tarsal strip operations)

(For correction of everted punctum, use 68705)

**67921** Repair of entropion; suture

**67922** thermocauterization

**67923** blepharoplasty, excision tarsal wedge

**67924** blepharoplasty, extensive (eg, Wheeler operation)

(For repair of cicatricial ectropion or entropion requiring scar excision or skin graft, see also 67961 et seq)

## Reconstruction

Codes for blepharoplasty involve more than skin (ie, involving lid margin, tarsus, and/or palpebral conjunctiva).

**67930** Suture of recent wound, eyelid, involving lid margin, tarsus, and/or palpebral conjunctiva direct closure; partial thickness

**67935** full thickness

**67938** Removal of embedded foreign body, eyelid

(For repair of skin of eyelid, see 12011-12018; 12051-12057; 13150-13153)

(For tarsorrhaphy, canthorrhaphy, see 67880, 67882)

(For repair of blepharoptosis and lid retraction, see 67901-67911)

(For blepharoplasty for entropion, ectropion, see 67916, 67917, 67923, 67924)

(For correction of blepharochalasis (blepharorhytidectomy), see 15820-15823)

(For repair of skin of eyelid, adjacent tissue transfer, see 14060, 14061; preparation for graft, use 15000; free graft, see 15120, 15121, 15260, 15261)

(For excision of lesion of eyelid, use 67800 et seq)

(For repair of lacrimal canaliculi, use 68700)

**67950** Canthoplasty (reconstruction of canthus)

**67961** Excision and repair of eyelid, involving lid margin, tarsus, conjunctiva, canthus, or full thickness, may include preparation for skin graft or pedicle flap with adjacent tissue transfer or rearrangement; up to one-fourth of lid margin

**67966** over one-fourth of lid margin

(For canthoplasty, use 67950)

(For free skin grafts, see 15120, 15121, 15260, 15261)

(For tubed pedicle flap preparation, see 15576; for delay, see 15630; for attachment, see 15650)

**67971** Reconstruction of eyelid, full thickness by transfer of tarsoconjunctival flap from opposing eyelid; up to two-thirds of eyelid, one stage or first stage

**67973** total eyelid, lower, one stage or first stage

**67974** total eyelid, upper, one stage or first stage

**67975** second stage

### Other Procedures

**67999** Unlisted procedure, eyelids

## Conjunctiva

(For removal of foreign body, see 65205 et seq)

### Incision and Drainage

**68020** Incision of conjunctiva, drainage of cyst

**68040** Expression of conjunctival follicles (eg, for trachoma)

### Excision and/or Destruction

**68100** Biopsy of conjunctiva

**68110** Excision of lesion, conjunctiva; up to 1 cm

**68115** over 1 cm

**68130** with adjacent sclera

**68135*** Destruction of lesion, conjunctiva

### Injection

(For injection into Tenon's capsule or retrobulbar injection, see 67500-67515)

**68200*** Subconjunctival injection

### Conjunctivoplasty

(For wound repair, see 65270-65273)

**68320** Conjunctivoplasty; with conjunctival graft or extensive rearrangement

**68325** with buccal mucous membrane graft (includes obtaining graft)

**68326** Conjunctivoplasty, reconstruction cul-de-sac; with conjunctival graft or extensive rearrangement

**68328** with buccal mucous membrane graft (includes obtaining graft)

**68330** Repair of symblepharon; conjunctivoplasty, without graft

**68335** with free graft conjunctiva or buccal mucous membrane (includes obtaining graft)

**68340** division of symblepharon, with or without insertion of conformer or contact lens

### Other Procedures

**68360** Conjunctival flap; bridge or partial (separate procedure)

**68362** total (such as Gunderson thin flap or purse string flap)

(For conjunctival flap for perforating injury, see 65280, 65285)

(For repair of operative wound, use 66250)

(For removal of conjunctival foreign body, see 65205, 65210)

**68399** Unlisted procedure, conjunctiva

## Lacrimal System

### Incision

**68400** Incision, drainage of lacrimal gland

**68420** Incision, drainage of lacrimal sac (dacryocystotomy or dacryocystostomy)

**68440*** Snip incision of lacrimal punctum

### Excision

**68500** Excision of lacrimal gland (dacryoadenectomy), except for tumor; total

**68505** partial

**68510** Biopsy of lacrimal gland

**68520** Excision of lacrimal sac (dacryocystectomy)

**68525** Biopsy of lacrimal sac

**68530** Removal of foreign body or dacryolith, lacrimal passages

**68540** Excision of lacrimal gland tumor; frontal approach

**68550** involving osteotomy

### Repair

**68700** Plastic repair of canaliculi

**68705** Correction of everted punctum, cautery

**68720** Dacryocystorhinostomy (fistulization of lacrimal sac to nasal cavity)

**68745** Conjunctivorhinostomy (fistulization of conjunctiva to nasal cavity); without tube

**68750** with insertion of tube or stent

**68760** Closure of the lacrimal punctum; by thermocauterization, ligation, or laser surgery

**68761** by plug, each

**68770** Closure of lacrimal fistula (separate procedure)

### Probing and/or Related Procedures

(68800 has been deleted. To report, use 68801)

**68801*** Dilation of lacrimal punctum, with or without irrigation

(To report a bilateral procedure, use 68801 with modifier '-50')

**68810*** Probing of nasolacrimal duct, with or without irrigation;

**68811** requiring general anesthesia

**68815** with insertion of tube or stent

(See also 92018)

(To report a bilateral procedure, use 68810, 68811, or 68815 with modifier '-50')

(68820, 68825, 68830 have been deleted. To report, see 68810, 68811, or 68815)

**68840*** Probing of lacrimal canaliculi, with or without irrigation

**68850*** Injection of contrast medium for dacryocystography

(For radiological supervision and interpretation, use 70170)

### Other Procedures

**68899** Unlisted procedure, lacrimal system

# Auditory System

(For diagnostic services (eg, audiometry, vestibular tests), see 92502 et seq)

## External Ear

### Incision

**69000*** Drainage external ear, abscess or hematoma; simple

**69005** complicated

**69020*** Drainage external auditory canal, abscess

**69090** Ear piercing

### Excision

**69100** Biopsy external ear

**69105** Biopsy external auditory canal

**69110** Excision external ear; partial, simple repair

**69120** complete amputation

(For reconstruction of ear, see 15120 et seq)

**69140** Excision exostosis(es), external auditory canal

**69145** Excision soft tissue lesion, external auditory canal

**69150** Radical excision external auditory canal lesion; without neck dissection

**69155** with neck dissection

(For resection of temporal bone, use 69535)

(For skin grafting, see 15000-15261)

### Removal of Foreign Body

**69200** Removal foreign body from external auditory canal; without general anesthesia

**69205** with general anesthesia

**69210** Removal impacted cerumen (separate procedure), one or both ears

**69220** Debridement, mastoidectomy cavity, simple (eg, routine cleaning)

(69221 has been deleted. To report, use 69220 with modifier '-50')

**69222** Debridement, mastoidectomy cavity, complex (eg, with anesthesia or more than routine cleaning)

(69223 has been deleted. To report, use 69222 with modifier '-50')

### Repair

(For suture of wound or injury of external ear, see 12011-14300)

**69300** Otoplasty, protruding ear, with or without size reduction

(69301 has been deleted. To report, use 69300 with modifior ' 50')

**69310** Reconstruction of external auditory canal (meatoplasty) (eg, for stenosis due to trauma, infection) (separate procedure)

**69320** Reconstruction external auditory canal for congenital atresia, single stage

(For combination with middle ear reconstruction, see 69631, 69641)

(For other reconstructive procedures with grafts (eg, skin, cartilage, bone), see 13150-15760, 21230-21235)

### Other Procedures

(For otoscopy under general anesthesia, use 92502)

**69399** Unlisted procedure, external ear

## Middle Ear

### Introduction

**69400** Eustachian tube inflation, transnasal; with catheterization

**69401** without catheterization

**69405** Eustachian tube catheterization, transtympanic

**69410** Focal application of phase control substance, middle ear (baffle technique)

## Incision

**69420*** Myringotomy including aspiration and/or eustachian tube inflation

**69421*** Myringotomy including aspiration and/or eustachian tube inflation requiring general anesthesia

**69424** Ventilating tube removal when originally inserted by another physician

(69425 has been deleted. To report, use 69424 with modifier '-50')

(Tympanostomy 69431-69435 has been revised as 69433, 69436)

**69433*** Tympanostomy (requiring insertion of ventilating tube), local or topical anesthesia

(69434 has been deleted. To report, use 69433 with modifier '-50')

**69436** Tympanostomy (requiring insertion of ventilating tube), general anesthesia

(69437 has been deleted. To report, use 69436 with modifier '-50')

**69440** Middle ear exploration through postauricular or ear canal incision

(For atticotomy, see 69601 et seq)

**69450** Tympanolysis, transcanal

## Excision

**69501** Transmastoid antrotomy (simple mastoidectomy)

**69502** Mastoidectomy; complete

**69505** modified radical

**69511** radical

(For skin graft, see 15000 et seq)

(For mastoidectomy cavity debridement, see 69220, 69222)

**69530** Petrous apicectomy including radical mastoidectomy

**69535** Resection temporal bone, external approach

(For middle fossa approach, see 69950-69970)

**69540** Excision aural polyp

**69550** Excision aural glomus tumor; transcanal

**69552** transmastoid

**69554** extended (extratemporal)

## Repair

**69601** Revision mastoidectomy; resulting in complete mastoidectomy

**69602** resulting in modified radical mastoidectomy

**69603** resulting in radical mastoidectomy

**69604** resulting in tympanoplasty

(For planned secondary tympanoplasty after mastoidectomy, see 69631, 69632)

**69605** with apicectomy

(For skin graft, see 15120, 15121, 15260, 15261)

**69610** Tympanic membrane repair, with or without site preparation or perforation for closure, with or without patch

(69611 has been deleted. To report, use 69610)

**69620** Myringoplasty (surgery confined to drumhead and donor area)

**69631** Tympanoplasty without mastoidectomy (including canalplasty, atticotomy and/or middle ear surgery), initial or revision; without ossicular chain reconstruction

**69632** with ossicular chain reconstruction (eg, postfenestration)

**69633** with ossicular chain reconstruction and synthetic prosthesis (eg, partial ossicular replacement prosthesis (PORP), total ossicular replacement prosthesis (TORP))

**69635** Tympanoplasty with antrotomy or mastoidotomy (including canalplasty, atticotomy, middle ear surgery, and/or tympanic membrane repair); without ossicular chain reconstruction

**69636** with ossicular chain reconstruction

**69637** with ossicular chain reconstruction and synthetic prosthesis (eg, partial ossicular replacement prosthesis (PORP), total ossicular replacement prosthesis (TORP))

**69641** Tympanoplasty with mastoidectomy (including canalplasty, middle ear surgery, tympanic membrane repair); without ossicular chain reconstruction

**69642** with ossicular chain reconstruction

**69643** with intact or reconstructed wall, without ossicular chain reconstruction

**69644** with intact or reconstructed canal wall, with ossicular chain reconstruction

**69645** radical or complete, without ossicular chain reconstruction

**69646** radical or complete, with ossicular chain reconstruction

**69650** Stapes mobilization

**69660** Stapedectomy or stapedotomy with reestablishment of ossicular continuity, with or without use of foreign material;

**69661** with footplate drill out

**69662** Revision of stapedectomy or stapedotomy

**69666** Repair oval window fistula

**69667** Repair round window fistula

**69670** Mastoid obliteration (separate procedure)

(69675 Tympanic neurectomy has been revised as 69676)

**69676** Tympanic neurectomy

(69677 has been deleted. To report, use 69676 with modifier '-50')

## Other Procedures

**69700** Closure postauricular fistula, mastoid (separate procedure)

**69710** Implantation or replacement of electromagnetic bone conduction hearing device in temporal bone

(Replacement procedure includes removal of old device)

**69711** Removal or repair of electromagnetic bone conduction hearing device in temporal bone

**69720** Decompression facial nerve, intratemporal; lateral to geniculate ganglion

**69725** including medial to geniculate ganglion

**69740** Suture facial nerve, intratemporal, with or without graft or decompression; lateral to geniculate ganglion

**69745** including medial to geniculate ganglion

(For extracranial suture of facial nerve, use 64864)

**69799** Unlisted procedure, middle ear

# Inner Ear

## Incision and/or Destruction

**69801** Labyrinthotomy, with or without cryosurgery including other nonexcisional destructive procedures or perfusion of vestibuloactive drugs (single or multiple perfusions); transcanal

(69801 includes all required infusions performed on initial and subsequent days of treatment)

**69802** with mastoidectomy

**69805** Endolymphatic sac operation; without shunt

**69806** with shunt

**69820** Fenestration semicircular canal

**69840** Revision fenestration operation

### Excision

**69905** Labyrinthectomy; transcanal

**69910** with mastoidectomy

**69915** Vestibular nerve section, translabyrinthine approach

(For transcranial approach, use 69950)

### Introduction

**69930** Cochlear device implantation, with or without mastoidectomy

### Other Procedures

**69949** Unlisted procedure, inner ear

## Temporal Bone, Middle Fossa Approach

(For external approach, use 69535)

**69950** Vestibular nerve section, transcranial approach

**69955** Total facial nerve decompression and/or repair (may include graft)

**69960** Decompression internal auditory canal

(69965 has been deleted. To report, use 69979)

**69970** Removal of tumor, temporal bone

### Other Procedures

**69979** Unlisted procedure, temporal bone, middle fossa approach

# Operating Microscope

The surgical microscope is employed when the surgical services are performed using the techniques of microsurgery. Code 69990 should be reported (without the modifier '-51' appended) in addition to the code for the primary procedure performed. Do not use 69990 for visualization with magnifying loupes or corrected vision. Do not report code 69990 in addition to procedures where use of the operating microscope is an inclusive component (15756-15758, 19364, 19368, 20955-20962, 20969-20973, 26551-26554, 26556, 31526, 31531, 31536, 31541, 31561, 31571, 43116, 43496, 49906, 61548, 63075-63078, 64727, 65091-68850).

**+ 69990** Use of operating microscope (List separately in addition to code for primary procedure)

# Radiology Guidelines (Including Nuclear Medicine and Diagnostic Ultrasound)

Items used by all physicians in reporting their services are presented in the **Introduction.** Some of the commonalities are repeated here for the convenience of those physicians referring to this section on **Radiology (Including Nuclear Medicine and Diagnostic Ultrasound).** Other definitions and items unique to Radiology are also listed.

## Subject Listings

Subject listings apply when radiological services are performed by or under the responsible supervision of a physician.

## Multiple Procedures

It is appropriate to designate multiple procedures that are rendered on the same date by separate entries. This can be reported by using the multiple procedure modifier '-51'. See Appendix A for modifier definitions.

## Separate Procedures

Some of the procedures or services listed in *CPT* that are commonly carried out as an integral component of a total service or procedure have been identified by the inclusion of the term "separate procedure." The codes designated as "separate procedure" should not be reported in addition to the code for the total procedure or service of which it is considered an integral component.

However, when a procedure or service that is designated as a "separate procedure" is carried out independently or considered to be unrelated or distinct from other procedures/services provided at that time, it may be reported by itself, or in addition to other procedures/services by appending the modifier '-59' to the specific "separate procedure" code to indicate that the procedure is not considered to be a component of another procedure, but is a distinct, independent procedure. This may represent a different session or patient encounter, different procedure or surgery, different site or organ system, separate incision/excision, separate lesion, or separate injury (or area of injury in extensive injuries).

## Subsection Information

Several of the subheadings or subsections have special needs or instructions unique to that section. Where these are indicated (eg, "Radiation Oncology") special **"Notes"** will be presented preceding those procedural terminology listings, referring to that subsection specifically. If there is an "Unlisted Procedure" code number (see section below) for the individual subsection, it will be shown. Those subsections with **"Notes"** are as follows:

**Diagnostic Radiology (Diagnostic Imaging)** . . . . . . . . . . . . . . . . . .70010-76499
**Aorta and Arteries** . . . . . . . . . . . .75600-75790
**Diagnostic Ultrasound** . . . . . . . .76506-76999
**Radiation Oncology** . . . . . . . . . .77261-77799
**Clinical Treatment Planning** . . . .77261-77299
**►Radiation◄ Treatment Management** . . . . . . . . . . . . . . . .77427-77499
**►Proton Beam Treatment Delivery** . . . . . . . . . . . . . . . . . . .77520-77523◄

## Unlisted Service or Procedure

A service or procedure may be provided that is not listed in this edition of *CPT*. When reporting such a service, the appropriate "Unlisted Procedure" code may be used to indicate the service, identifying it by "Special Report" as discussed below. The "Unlisted Procedures" and accompanying codes for **Radiology (Including Nuclear Medicine and Diagnostic Ultrasound)** are as follows:

**76499** Unlisted diagnostic radiologic procedure

**76999** Unlisted ultrasound procedure

**77299** Unlisted procedure, therapeutic radiology clinical treatment planning

**77399** Unlisted procedure, medical radiation physics, dosimetry and treatment devices, and special services

**77499** Unlisted procedure, therapeutic radiology treatment management

**77799** Unlisted procedure, clinical brachytherapy

**78099** Unlisted endocrine procedure, diagnostic nuclear medicine

**78199** Unlisted hematopoietic, reticuloendothelial and lymphatic procedure, diagnostic nuclear medicine

**78299** Unlisted gastrointestinal procedure, diagnostic nuclear medicine

**78399** Unlisted musculoskeletal procedure, diagnostic nuclear medicine

**78499** Unlisted cardiovascular procedure, diagnostic nuclear medicine

**78599** Unlisted respiratory procedure, diagnostic nuclear medicine

**78699** Unlisted nervous system procedure, diagnostic nuclear medicine

**78799** Unlisted genitourinary procedure, diagnostic nuclear medicine

**78999** Unlisted miscellaneous procedure, diagnostic nuclear medicine

**79999** Unlisted radiopharmaceutical therapeutic procedure

## Special Report

A service that is rarely provided, unusual, variable, or new may require a special report in determining medical appropriateness of the service. Pertinent information should include an adequate definition or description of the nature, extent, and need for the procedure; and the time, effort, and equipment necessary to provide the service. Additional items which may be included are:

- complexity of symptoms;
- final diagnosis;
- pertinent physical findings;
- diagnostic and therapeutic procedures;
- concurrent problems;
- follow-up care.

## Supervision and Interpretation

When a procedure is performed by two physicians, the radiologic portion of the procedure is designated as "radiological supervision and interpretation." When a physician performs both the procedure and provides imaging supervision and interpretation, a combination of procedure codes outside the 70000 series and imaging supervision and interpretation codes are to be used.

(The Radiological Supervision and Interpretation codes are not applicable to the Radiation Oncology subsection.)

## Administration of Contrast Material(s)

Some of the listed procedures are commonly carried out without the use of contrast material for imaging enhancement. For those codes that may or may not be performed using contrast material for imaging enhancement, the phrase "with contrast" represents contrast material administered intravascularly.

►For spine examinations using computerized tomography, magnetic resonance imaging, magnetic resonance angiography, "with contrast" includes intrathecal or intravascular injection. For intrathecal injection, use also 61055 or 62284.◄

►Injection of contrast material is part of the "with contrast" CT, MRI, MRA procedure.◄

Oral and ►/or◄ rectal contrast ►administration alone does not qualify as a study "with contrast."◄

## Written Report(s)

A written report, signed by the interpreting physician, should be considered an integral part of a radiologic procedure or interpretation.

# Notes

# Radiology

## Diagnostic Radiology (Diagnostic Imaging)

### Head and Neck

(70002, 70003 have been deleted. To report, use 76499)

**70010** Myelography, posterior fossa, radiological supervision and interpretation

(70011 (complete procedure) has been deleted, see 61055, 62284, 70010)

**70015** Cisternography, positive contrast, radiological supervision and interpretation

(70016 (complete procedure) has been deleted, see 61055, 62284, 70015)

(70020, 70021 have been deleted. To report, use 76499)

(70022 has been deleted. To report CT guidance for stereotactic localization, use 76355)

**70030** Radiologic examination, eye, for detection of foreign body

(70040, 70050 have been deleted)

**70100** Radiologic examination, mandible; partial, less than four views

**70110** complete, minimum of four views

**70120** Radiologic examination, mastoids; less than three views per side

**70130** complete, minimum of three views per side

**70134** Radiologic examination, internal auditory meati, complete

**70140** Radiologic examination, facial bones; less than three views

**70150** complete, minimum of three views

**70160** Radiologic examination, nasal bones, complete, minimum of three views

**70170** Dacryocystography, nasolacrimal duct, radiological supervision and interpretation

(70171 (complete procedure) has been deleted, see 68850, 70170)

**70190** Radiologic examination; optic foramina

**70200** orbits, complete, minimum of four views

**70210** Radiologic examination, sinuses, paranasal, less than three views

**70220** Radiologic examination, sinuses, paranasal, complete, minimum of three views

(70230, 70231 have been deleted. To report, use 76499)

**70240** Radiologic examination, sella turcica

**70250** Radiologic examination, skull; less than four views, with or without stereo

**70260** complete, minimum of four views, with or without stereo

**70300** Radiologic examination, teeth; single view

**70310** partial examination, less than full mouth

**70320** complete, full mouth

**70328** Radiologic examination, temporomandibular joint, open and closed mouth; unilateral

**70330** bilateral

**70332** Temporomandibular joint arthrography, radiological supervision and interpretation

(70333 (complete procedure) has been deleted, see 21116, 70332)

**70336** Magnetic resonance (eg, proton) imaging, temporomandibular joint

**70350** Cephalogram, orthodontic

**70355** Orthopantogram

**70360** Radiologic examination; neck, soft tissue

**70370** pharynx or larynx, including fluoroscopy and/or magnification technique

**70371** Complex dynamic pharyngeal and speech evaluation by cine or video recording

**70373** Laryngography, contrast, radiological supervision and interpretation

(70374 (complete procedure) has been deleted, see 31708, 70373)

**70380** Radiologic examination, salivary gland for calculus

**70390** Sialography, radiological supervision and interpretation

(70391 (complete procedure) has been deleted, see 42550, 70390)

(70400, 70401 have been deleted. To report, use 76499)

**70450** Computerized axial tomography, head or brain; without contrast material

**70460** with contrast material(s)

**70470** without contrast material, followed by contrast material(s) and further sections

(For coronal, sagittal, and/or oblique sections, use 76375)

**70480** Computerized axial tomography, orbit, sella, or posterior fossa or outer, middle, or inner ear; without contrast material

**70481** with contrast material(s)

**70482** without contrast material, followed by contrast material(s) and further sections

(For coronal, sagittal, and/or oblique sections, use 76375)

**70486** Computerized axial tomography, maxillofacial area; without contrast material

**70487** with contrast material(s)

**70488** without contrast material, followed by contrast material(s) and further sections

(For coronal, sagittal, and/or oblique sections, use 76375)

**70490** Computerized axial tomography, soft tissue neck; without contrast material

**70491** with contrast material(s)

**70492** without contrast material followed by contrast material(s) and further sections

(For coronal, sagittal, and/or oblique sections, use 76375)

(For cervical spine, see 72125, 72126)

**70540** Magnetic resonance (eg, proton) imaging, orbit, face, and neck

**70541** Magnetic resonance angiography, head and/or neck, with or without contrast material(s)

(70550 has been deleted. To report, use 70551)

**70551** Magnetic resonance (eg, proton) imaging, brain (including brain stem); without contrast material

**70552** with contrast material(s)

**70553** without contrast material, followed by contrast material(s) and further sequences

(For magnetic spectroscopy, use 76390)

# Chest

(71000 has been deleted)

**71010** Radiologic examination, chest; single view, frontal

**71015** stereo, frontal

**71020** Radiologic examination, chest, two views, frontal and lateral;

**71021** with apical lordotic procedure

**71022** with oblique projections

**71023** with fluoroscopy

**71030** Radiologic examination, chest, complete, minimum of four views;

**71034** with fluoroscopy

(For separate chest fluoroscopy, use 76000)

**71035** Radiologic examination, chest, special views (eg, lateral decubitus, Bucky studies)

**71036** Needle biopsy of intrathoracic lesion, including follow-up films, fluoroscopic localization only, radiological supervision and interpretation

(71037 (complete procedure) has been deleted, see 32400, 32405, 71036)

(71038 has been deleted. To report, use 31628)

**71040** Bronchography, unilateral, radiological supervision and interpretation

(71041 (complete procedure) has been deleted, see 31656, 31708, 31710, 31715, 71040)

**71060** Bronchography, bilateral, radiological supervision and interpretation

(71061 (complete procedure) has been deleted, see 31656, 31708, 31710, 31715, 71060)

**71090** Insertion pacemaker, fluoroscopy and radiography, radiological supervision and interpretation

**71100** Radiologic examination, ribs, unilateral; two views

**71101** including posteroanterior chest, minimum of three views

**71110** Radiologic examination, ribs, bilateral; three views

**71111** including posteroanterior chest, minimum of four views

**71120** Radiologic examination; sternum, minimum of two views

**71130** sternoclavicular joint or joints, minimum of three views

**71250** Computerized axial tomography, thorax; without contrast material

**71260** with contrast material(s)

**71270** without contrast material, followed by contrast material(s) and further sections

(For coronal, sagittal, and/or oblique sections, use 76375)

**71550** Magnetic resonance (eg, proton) imaging, chest (eg, for evaluation of hilar and mediastinal lymphadenopathy)

(For breast MRI, see 76093 and 76094)

**71555** Magnetic resonance angiography, chest (excluding myocardium), with or without contrast material(s)

## Spine and Pelvis

**72010** Radiologic examination, spine, entire, survey study, anteroposterior and lateral

**72020** Radiologic examination, spine, single view, specify level

**72040** Radiologic examination, spine, cervical; anteroposterior and lateral

**72050** minimum of four views

**72052** complete, including oblique and flexion and/or extension studies

**72069** Radiologic examination, spine, thoracolumbar, standing (scoliosis)

**72070** Radiologic examination, spine; thoracic, anteroposterior and lateral

**72072** thoracic, anteroposterior and lateral, including swimmer's view of the cervicothoracic junction

**72074** thoracic, complete, including obliques, minimum of four views

**72080** thoracolumbar, anteroposterior and lateral

**72090** scoliosis study, including supine and erect studies

**72100** Radiologic examination, spine, lumbosacral; anteroposterior and lateral

**72110** complete, with oblique views

**72114** complete, including bending views

**72120** Radiologic examination, spine, lumbosacral, bending views only, minimum of four views

(Contrast material in CT of spine is either by intrathecal or intravenous injection. For intrathecal injection, use also 61055 or 62284. IV injection of contrast material is part of the CT procedure)

**72125** Computerized axial tomography, cervical spine; without contrast material

**72126** with contrast material

**72127** without contrast material, followed by contrast material(s) and further sections

(For intrathecal injection procedure, see 61055, 62284)

**72128** Computerized axial tomography, thoracic spine; without contrast material

**72129** with contrast material

(For intrathecal injection procedure, see 61055, 62284)

**72130** without contrast material, followed by contrast material(s) and further sections

(For intrathecal injection procedure, see 61055, 62284)

**72131** Computerized axial tomography, lumbar spine; without contrast material

**72132** with contrast material

**72133** without contrast material, followed by contrast material(s) and further sections

(For intrathecal injection procedure, see 61055, 62284)

(For coronal, sagittal, and/or oblique sections, use 76375)

(72140 has been deleted. To report, see 72141-72149)

**72141** Magnetic resonance (eg, proton) imaging, spinal canal and contents, cervical; without contrast material

**72142** with contrast material(s)

(For cervical spinal canal imaging without contrast material followed by contrast material, use 72156)

(72143 has been deleted. To report, see 72146, 72147)

(72144 has been deleted. To report, see 72148, 72149)

(72145 has been deleted. To report, see 72125-72133)

**72146** Magnetic resonance (eg, proton) imaging, spinal canal and contents, thoracic; without contrast material

**72147** with contrast material(s)

(For thoracic spinal canal imaging without contrast material followed by contrast material, use 72157)

**72148** Magnetic resonance (eg, proton) imaging, spinal canal and contents, lumbar; without contrast material

**72149** with contrast material(s)

(For lumbar spinal canal imaging without contrast material followed by contrast material, use 72158)

**72156** Magnetic resonance (eg, proton) imaging, spinal canal and contents, without contrast material, followed by contrast material(s) and further sequences; cervical

**72157** thoracic

**72158** lumbar

**72159** Magnetic resonance angiography, spinal canal and contents, with or without contrast material(s)

**72170** Radiologic examination, pelvis; anteroposterior only

(72180 has been deleted. To report, use 72170)

**72190** complete, minimum of three views

(For pelvimetry, use 74710)

**72192** Computerized axial tomography, pelvis; without contrast material

**72193** with contrast material(s)

**72194** without contrast material, followed by contrast material(s) and further sections

(For coronal, sagittal, and/or oblique sections, use 76375)

**72196** Magnetic resonance (eg, proton) imaging, pelvis

**72198** Magnetic resonance angiography, pelvis, with or without contrast material(s)

**72200** Radiologic examination, sacroiliac joints; less than three views

**72202** three or more views

**72220** Radiologic examination, sacrum and coccyx, minimum of two views

**72240** Myelography, cervical, radiological supervision and interpretation

(72241 (complete procedure) has been deleted, see 61055, 62284, 72240)

**72255** Myelography, thoracic, radiological supervision and interpretation

(72256 (complete procedure) has been deleted, see 61055, 62284, 72255)

**72265** Myelography, lumbosacral, radiological supervision and interpretation

(72266 (complete procedure) has been deleted, see 61055, 62284, 72265)

**72270** Myelography, entire spinal canal, radiological supervision and interpretation

(72271 (complete procedure) has been deleted, see 61055, 62284, 72270)

●**72275** Epidurography, radiological supervision and interpretation

►(For injection procedure, see 62280-62282, 62310-62319, 64479-64484)◄

▲**72285** Diskography, cervical or thoracic, radiological supervision and interpretation

(72286 (complete procedure) has been deleted, see 62291, 72285)

**72295** Diskography, lumbar, radiological supervision and interpretation

(72296 (complete procedure) has been deleted, see 62290, 72295)

# Upper Extremities

(For stress views, any joint, use 76006)

**73000** Radiologic examination; clavicle, complete

**73010** scapula, complete

**73020** Radiologic examination, shoulder; one view

**73030** complete, minimum of two views

**73040** Radiologic examination, shoulder, arthrography, radiological supervision and interpretation

(73041 (complete procedure) has been deleted, see 23350, 73040)

**73050** Radiologic examination; acromioclavicular joints, bilateral, with or without weighted distraction

**73060** humerus, minimum of two views

**73070** Radiologic examination, elbow; anteroposterior and lateral views

**73080** complete, minimum of three views

**73085** Radiologic examination, elbow, arthrography, radiological supervision and interpretation

(73086 (complete procedure) has been deleted, see 24220, 73085)

**73090** Radiologic examination; forearm, anteroposterior and lateral views

**73092** upper extremity, infant, minimum of two views

**73100** Radiologic examination, wrist; anteroposterior and lateral views

**73110** complete, minimum of three views

**73115** Radiologic examination, wrist, arthrography, radiological supervision and interpretation

(73116 (complete procedure) has been deleted, see 25246, 73115)

**73120** Radiologic examination, hand; two views

**73130** minimum of three views

**73140** Radiologic examination, finger(s), minimum of two views

**73200** Computerized axial tomography, upper extremity; without contrast material

**73201** with contrast material(s)

**73202** without contrast material, followed by contrast material(s) and further sections

(For coronal, sagittal, and/or oblique sections, use 76375)

**73220** Magnetic resonance (eg, proton) imaging, upper extremity, other than joint

**73221** Magnetic resonance (eg, proton) imaging, any joint of upper extremity

**73225** Magnetic resonance angiography, upper extremity, with or without contrast material(s)

## Lower Extremities

(For stress views, any joint, use 76006)

**73500** Radiologic examination, hip, unilateral; one view

**73510** complete, minimum of two views

**73520** Radiologic examination, hips, bilateral, minimum of two views of each hip, including anteroposterior view of pelvis

**73525** Radiologic examination, hip, arthrography, radiological supervision and interpretation

(73526 (complete procedure) has been deleted, see 27093, 27095, 73525)

**73530** Radiologic examination, hip, during operative procedure

(73531 has been deleted. To report, use 73530)

**73540** Radiologic examination, pelvis and hips, infant or child, minimum of two views

●**73542** Radiological examination, sacroiliac joint arthrography, radiological supervision and interpretation

►(For procedure, use 27096. If formal arthrography is not performed, recorded, and a formal radiologic report is not issued, use 76005 for fluoroscopic guidance for sacroiliac joint injections)◄

**73550** Radiologic examination, femur, anteroposterior and lateral views

**73560** Radiologic examination, knee; one or two views

**73562** three views

**73564** complete, four or more views

**73565** both knees, standing, anteroposterior

(73570 has been deleted. To report, see 73562, 73564)

**73580** Radiologic examination, knee, arthrography, radiological supervision and interpretation

(73581 (complete procedure) has been deleted, see 27370, 73580)

**73590** Radiologic examination; tibia and fibula, anteroposterior and lateral views

**73592** lower extremity, infant, minimum of two views

**73600** Radiologic examination, ankle; anteroposterior and lateral views

**73610** complete, minimum of three views

**73615** Radiologic examination, ankle, arthrography, radiological supervision and interpretation

(73616 (complete procedure) has been deleted, see 27648, 73615)

**73620** Radiologic examination, foot; anteroposterior and lateral views

**73630** complete, minimum of three views

**73650** Radiologic examination; calcaneus, minimum of two views

**73660** toe(s), minimum of two views

**73700** Computerized axial tomography, lower extremity; without contrast material

**73701** with contrast material(s)

**73702** without contrast material, followed by contrast material(s) and further sections

(For coronal, sagittal, and/or oblique sections, use 76375)

**73720** Magnetic resonance (eg, proton) imaging, lower extremity, other than joint

**73721** Magnetic resonance (eg, proton) imaging, any joint of lower extremity

**73725** Magnetic resonance angiography, lower extremity, with or without contrast material(s)

# Abdomen

**74000** Radiologic examination, abdomen; single anteroposterior view

**74010** anteroposterior and additional oblique and cone views

**74020** complete, including decubitus and/or erect views

**74022** complete acute abdomen series, including supine, erect, and/ or decubitus views, upright PA chest

**74150** Computerized axial tomography, abdomen; without contrast material

**74160** with contrast material(s)

**74170** without contrast material, followed by contrast material(s) and further sections

(For coronal, sagittal, and/or oblique sections, use 76375)

**74181** Magnetic resonance (eg, proton) imaging, abdomen

**74185** Magnetic resonance angiography, abdomen, with or without contrast material(s)

**74190** Peritoneogram (eg, after injection of air or contrast), radiological supervision and interpretation

(For procedure, use 49400)

(For computerized axial tomography, see 72192 or 74150)

# Gastrointestinal Tract

(For percutaneous placement of gastrostomy tube, use 43750)

**74210** Radiologic examination; pharynx and/or cervical esophagus

**74220** esophagus

**74230** Swallowing function, pharynx and/or esophagus, with cineradiography and/or video

**74235** Removal of foreign body(s), esophageal, with use of balloon catheter, radiological supervision and interpretation

(For procedure, see 43215, 43247)

**74240** Radiologic examination, gastrointestinal tract, upper; with or without delayed films, without KUB

**74241** with or without delayed films, with KUB

**74245** with small bowel, includes multiple serial films

**74246** Radiological examination, gastrointestinal tract, upper, air contrast, with specific high density barium, effervescent agent, with or without glucagon; with or without delayed films, without KUB

**74247** with or without delayed films, with KUB

**74249** with small bowel follow-through

**74250** Radiologic examination, small bowel, includes multiple serial films;

**74251** via enteroclysis tube

**74260** Duodenography, hypotonic

**74270** Radiologic examination, colon; barium enema, with or without KUB

(74275 has been deleted. To report, use 76499)

**74280** air contrast with specific high density barium, with or without glucagon

**74283** Therapeutic enema, contrast or air, for reduction of intussusception or other intraluminal obstruction (eg, meconium ileus)

(74285 has been deleted. To report, see 74270, 74280)

**74290** Cholecystography, oral contrast;

**74291** additional or repeat examination or multiple day examination

**74300** Cholangiography and/or pancreatography; intraoperative, radiological supervision and interpretation

**+ 74301** additional set intraoperative, radiological supervision and interpretation (List separately in addition to code for primary procedure)

(Use 74301 in conjunction with code 74300)

**74305** postoperative, radiological supervision and interpretation

(For procedure, see 47505, 48400, ►47560-47561, 47563◄)

(For biliary duct stone extraction, percutaneous, see 47630, 74327)

(74310, 74315 have been deleted. To report, use 76499)

**74320** Cholangiography, percutaneous, transhepatic, radiological supervision and interpretation

(74321 (complete procedure) has been deleted, see 47500, 74320)

(74325, 74326 have been deleted. To report, use 76499)

**74327** Postoperative biliary duct stone removal, percutaneous via T-tube tract, basket, or snare (eg, Burhenne technique), radiological supervision and interpretation

(For procedure, use 47630)

**74328** Endoscopic catheterization of the biliary ductal system, radiological supervision and interpretation

(For procedure, see 43260-43272 as appropriate)

**74329** Endoscopic catheterization of the pancreatic ductal system, radiological supervision and interpretation

(For procedure, see 43260-43272 as appropriate)

**74330** Combined endoscopic catheterization of the biliary and pancreatic ductal systems, radiological supervision and interpretation

(For procedure, see 43260-43272 as appropriate)

(74331 has been deleted. To report, use 43262)

**74340** Introduction of long gastrointestinal tube (eg, Miller-Abbott), including multiple fluoroscopies and films, radiological supervision and interpretation

(For tube placement, use 44500)

**74350** Percutaneous placement of gastrostomy tube, radiological supervision and interpretation

**74355** Percutaneous placement of enteroclysis tube, radiological supervision and interpretation

(74356 (complete procedure) has been deleted, see 44015, 74355)

**74360** Intraluminal dilation of strictures and/or obstructions (eg, esophagus), radiological supervision and interpretation

(74361 (complete procedure) has been deleted, see 43220, 43458, 74360)

**74363** Percutaneous transhepatic dilatation of biliary duct stricture with or without placement of stent, radiological supervision and interpretation

(For procedure, see 47510, 47511, 47555, 47556)

## Urinary Tract

**74400** Urography (pyelography), intravenous, with or without KUB, with or without tomography

(74405 has been deleted. To report, see 74400, 74410 or 74415)

**74410** Urography, infusion, drip technique and/or bolus technique;

**74415** with nephrotomography

**74420** Urography, retrograde, with or without KUB

**74425** Urography, antegrade, (pyelostogram, nephrostogram, loopogram), radiological supervision and interpretation

(74426 (complete procedure) has been deleted, see 50394, 50684, 50690, 74425)

**74430** Cystography, minimum of three views, radiological supervision and interpretation

(74431 (complete procedure) has been deleted, see 51600, 51605, 74430)

**74440** Vasography, vesiculography, or epididymography, radiological supervision and interpretation

(74441 (complete procedure) has been deleted, see 52010, 55300, 74440)

**74445** Corpora cavernosography, radiological supervision and interpretation

(74446 (complete procedure) has been deleted, see 54230, 74445)

**74450** Urethrocystography, retrograde, radiological supervision and interpretation

(74451 (complete procedure) has been deleted, see 51610, 74450)

**74455** Urethrocystography, voiding, radiological supervision and interpretation

(74456 (complete procedure) has been deleted, see 51600, 74455)

(74460, 74461 have been deleted. To report, use 76499)

**74470** Radiologic examination, renal cyst study, translumbar, contrast visualization, radiological supervision and interpretation

(74471 (complete procedure) has been deleted, see 50390, 74470)

**74475** Introduction of intracatheter or catheter into renal pelvis for drainage and/or injection, percutaneous, radiological supervision and interpretation

(74476 (complete procedure) has been deleted, see 50392-50398, 74475)

**74480** Introduction of ureteral catheter or stent into ureter through renal pelvis for drainage and/or injection, percutaneous, radiological supervision and interpretation

(74481 (complete procedure) has been deleted, see 50392-50398, 74480)

(For transurethral surgery (ureter and pelvis), see 52320-52338)

**74485** Dilation of nephrostomy, ureters, or urethra, radiological supervision and interpretation

(74486 (complete procedure) has been deleted, see 50395, 53600-53621, 74485)

(For dilation of ureter without radiologic guidance, use 52335)

(For change of nephrostomy or pyelostomy tube, use 50398)

## Gynecological and Obstetrical

(For abdomen and pelvis, see 72170-72190, 74000-74170)

**74710** Pelvimetry, with or without placental localization

(74720, 74725 have been deleted. To report, use 74000)

(74730, 74731 have been deleted. To report, use 76499)

**74740** Hysterosalpingography, radiological supervision and interpretation

(For introduction of saline or contrast for hysterosalpingography, see 58340)

(74741 (complete procedure) has been deleted, see 58340, 74740)

**74742** Transcervical catheterization of fallopian tube, radiological supervision and interpretation

(For procedure, use 58345)

(74760, 74761, 74770, 74771 have been deleted. To report, use 76499)

**74775** Perineogram (eg, vaginogram, for sex determination or extent of anomalies)

## Heart

(For separate injection procedures for vascular radiology, see **Surgery** section, 36000-36299)

(For cardiac catheterization procedures, see 93501-93556)

(75500 has been deleted. To report, use 93555)

(75501 (complete procedure) has been deleted, see 93501-93536, 93542, 93543, 93555)

(75505 has been deleted. To report, use 93555)

(75506 (complete procedure) has been deleted, see 36400-36425 for intravenous procedure, 36100-36248 for intra-arterial procedure and 93501-93536, 93542, 93543, 93555)

(75507 has been deleted. To report, use 93555)

(75509 (complete procedure) has been deleted. To report, see 36400-36425 for intravenous procedure, 36100-36248 for intra-arterial procedure and 93501-93536, 93542, 93543)

(75510, 75511 have been deleted. To report, use 76499)

(75519 has been deleted. To report, use 93555)

(75520 (complete procedure) has been deleted, see 36400-36425 for intravenous procedure, 36100-36248 for intra-arterial procedure, and 93501, 93542)

(75523 has been deleted. To report, use 93555)

(75524 has been deleted, see 36400-36425 for intravenous procedure, 36100-36248 for intra-arterial procedure, and 93510-93514, 93524, 93543)

(75527 has been deleted. To report, use 93555)

(75528 has been deleted, see 36400-36425 for intravenous procedure, 36100-36248 for intra-arterial procedure, and 93526-93529, 93543, and 93555)

**75552** Cardiac magnetic resonance imaging for morphology; without contrast material

**75553** with contrast material

**75554** Cardiac magnetic resonance imaging for function, with or without morphology; complete study

**75555** limited study

**75556** Cardiac magnetic resonance imaging for velocity flow mapping

## Aorta and Arteries

Selective vascular catheterizations should be coded to include introduction and all lesser order selective catheterizations used in the approach (eg, the description for a selective right middle cerebral artery catheterization includes the introduction and placement catheterization of the right common and internal carotid arteries).

Additional second and/or third order arterial catheterizations within the same family of arteries supplied by a single first order artery should be expressed by 36218 or 36248. Additional first order or higher catheterizations in vascular families supplied by a first order vessel different from a previously selected and coded family should be separately coded using the conventions described above.

(For intravenous procedure, see 36000-36013, 36400-36425 and 36100-36248 for intra-arterial procedure)

(For radiological supervision and interpretation, see 75600-75978)

**75600** Aortography, thoracic, without serialography, radiological supervision and interpretation

(75601 (complete procedure) has been deleted, see 36000-36013, 36400-36425 for intravenous procedure, and 36100-36200 for intra-arterial procedure and 75600)

(For injection procedure, use 93544)

**75605** Aortography, thoracic, by serialography, radiological supervision and interpretation

(75606 (complete procedure) has been deleted, see 36000-36013, 36400-36425 for intravenous procedure, and 36100-36200 for intra-arterial procedure and 75605)

(For injection procedure, use 93544)

(75620, 75621, 75622, 75623 have been deleted. To report, use 76499)

**75625** Aortography, abdominal, by serialography, radiological supervision and interpretation

(75626, 75627 and 75628 have been deleted, see 36000-36013, 36400-36425 for intravenous procedure, and 36100-36200 for intra-arterial procedure and 75625)

(For injection procedure, use 93544)

**75630** Aortography, abdominal plus bilateral iliofemoral lower extremity, catheter, by serialography, radiological supervision and interpretation

(75631 (complete procedure) has been deleted, see 36000-36013, 36400-36425 for intravenous procedure, and 36100-36200 and 36245-36248 for intra-arterial procedure and 75630)

**75650** Angiography, cervicocerebral, catheter, including vessel origin, radiological supervision and interpretation

(75651-75657 (complete procedure) have been deleted, see 36000-36013, 36400-36425 for intravenous procedure, and 36100-36218 for intra-arterial procedure and 75650, 75660-75685 as appropriate)

**75658** Angiography, brachial, retrograde, radiological supervision and interpretation

(75659 (complete procedure) has been deleted, see 36000-36013, 36400-36425 for intravenous procedure, and 36100-36218 for intra-arterial procedure and 75658)

**75660** Angiography, external carotid, unilateral, selective, radiological supervision and interpretation

(75661 (complete procedure) has been deleted, see 36000-36013, 36400-36425 for intravenous procedure, and 36100-36218 and 75660)

**75662** Angiography, external carotid, bilateral, selective, radiological supervision and interpretation

(75663 (complete procedure) has been deleted, see 36000-36013, 36400-36425 for intravenous procedure, and 36100-36218 for intra-arterial procedure and 75662)

**75665** Angiography, carotid, cerebral, unilateral, radiological supervision and interpretation

(75667, 75669 (complete procedure) have been deleted, see 36000-36013, 36400-36425 for intravenous procedure, and 36100-36218 for intra-arterial procedure and 75665)

**75671** Angiography, carotid, cerebral, bilateral, radiological supervision and interpretation

(75672, 75673 (complete procedure) have been deleted, see 36000-36013, 36400-36425 for intravenous procedure, and 36100-36218 for intra-arterial procedure and 75671)

**75676** Angiography, carotid, cervical, unilateral, radiological supervision and interpretation

(75677, 75678 (complete procedure) have been deleted, see 36000-36013, 36400-36425 for intravenous procedure, and 36100-36218 for intra-arterial procedure and 75676)

**75680** Angiography, carotid, cervical, bilateral, radiological supervision and interpretation

(75681, 75682 (complete procedure) have been deleted, see 36000-36013, 36400-36425 for intravenous procedure, and 36100-36218 for intra-arterial procedure and 75680)

**75685** Angiography, vertebral, cervical, and/or intracranial, radiological supervision and interpretation

(75686 has been deleted)

(75687 (complete procedure) has been deleted, see 36000-36013, 36400-36425 for intravenous procedure, and 36100-36218 for intra-arterial procedure and 75685)

(75690 (complete procedure) has been deleted, see 36000-36013, 36400-36425 for intravenous procedure, and 36100-36218 for intra-arterial procedure and 75685)

(75691 has been deleted)

(75692 (complete procedure) has been deleted, see 36000-36013, 36400-36425 for intravenous procedure, and 36100-36218 for intra-arterial procedure and 75685)

(75695 (complete procedure) has been deleted, see 36000-36013, 36400-36425 for intravenous procedure, and 36100-36218 for intra-arterial procedure and 75685)

(75696 has been deleted)

(75697 (complete procedure) has been deleted, see 36000-36013, 36400-36425 for intravenous procedure, and 36100-36218 for intra-arterial procedure and 75685)

**75705** Angiography, spinal, selective, radiological supervision and interpretation

(75706 (complete procedure) has been deleted, see 36000-36013, 36400-36425 for intravenous procedure, and 36100-36248 for intra-arterial procedure and 75705)

**75710** Angiography, extremity, unilateral, radiological supervision and interpretation

(75711, 75712 (complete procedure) have been deleted, see 36000-36013, 36400-36425 for intravenous procedure, and 36100-36248 for intra-arterial procedure and 75710)

**75716** Angiography, extremity, bilateral, radiological supervision and interpretation

(75717, 75718 (complete procedure) have been deleted, see 36000-36013, 36400-36425 for intravenous procedure, and 36100-36248 for intra-arterial procedure and 75716)

**75722** Angiography, renal, unilateral, selective (including flush aortogram), radiological supervision and interpretation

(75723 (complete procedure) has been deleted, see 36000-36013, 36400-36425 for intravenous procedure, and 36100-36200 and 36245-36248 for intra-arterial procedure and 75722)

**75724** Angiography, renal, bilateral, selective (including flush aortogram), radiological supervision and interpretation

(75725 (complete procedure) has been deleted, see 36000-36013, 36400-36425 for intravenous procedure, and 36100-36200 and 36245-36248 for intra-arterial procedure and 75724)

**75726** Angiography, visceral, selective or supraselective, (with or without flush aortogram), radiological supervision and interpretation

(For selective angiography, each additional visceral vessel studied after basic examination, use 75774)

(75727, 75728 (complete procedure) have been deleted, see 36000-36013, 36400-36425 for intravenous procedure, and 36100-36248 for intra-arterial procedure and 75726)

**75731** Angiography, adrenal, unilateral, selective, radiological supervision and interpretation

(75732 (complete procedure) has been deleted, see 36000-36013, 36400-36425 for intravenous procedure, and 36100-36200 and 36245-36248 for intra-arterial procedure and 75731)

**75733** Angiography, adrenal, bilateral, selective, radiological supervision and interpretation

(75734 (complete procedure) has been deleted, see 36000-36013, 36400-36425 for intravenous procedure, and 36100-36200 and 36245-36248 for intra-arterial procedure and 75733)

**75736** Angiography, pelvic, selective or supraselective, radiological supervision and interpretation

(75737, 75738 (complete procedure) have been deleted, see 36000-36013, 36400-36425 for intravenous procedure, and 36100-36200 and 36245-36248 for intra-arterial procedure and 75736)

**75741** Angiography, pulmonary, unilateral, selective, radiological supervision and interpretation

(75742 (complete procedure) has been deleted, see 36000-36015, 36400-36425 for intravenous procedure and 75741)

(For injection procedure, use 93541)

**75743** Angiography, pulmonary, bilateral, selective, radiological supervision and interpretation

(75744 (complete procedure) has been deleted, see 36000-36015, 36400-36425 for intravenous procedure and 75743)

(For injection procedure, use 93541)

**75746** Angiography, pulmonary, by nonselective catheter or venous injection, radiological supervision and interpretation

(75747, 75748 (complete procedure) have been deleted, see 36000-36013, 36400-36425 for intravenous procedure, and 36100-36200 for intra-arterial procedure and 75746)

(For injection procedure, use 93541)

(75750 has been deleted. To report, use 93556)

(75751 (complete procedure) has been deleted, see 36000-36013, 36400-36425 for intravenous procedure, and 36100-36200 for intra-arterial procedure and 93556)

(For introduction of catheter, injection procedure, see 93501-93536, 93539, 93540, 93545, 93556)

(75752 has been deleted. To report, use 93556)

(75753 (complete procedure) has been deleted, see 36100-36218 for intra-arterial procedure and 93556)

(For introduction of catheter, injection procedure, see 93501-93536, 93545, 93556)

(75754 has been deleted. To report, use 93556)

(75755 (complete procedure) has been deleted, see 36100-36218 for intra-arterial procedure and 93556)

(For introduction of catheter, injection procedure, see 93501-93536, 93539, 93540, 93545, 93556)

**75756** Angiography, internal mammary, radiological supervision and interpretation

(75757 (complete procedure) has been deleted, see 36000-36013, 36400-36425 for intravenous procedure, and 36100-36218 for intra-arterial procedure and 93556)

(75762 has been deleted. To report, use 93556)

(75764 (complete procedure) has been deleted, see 36000-36013, 36400-36425 for intravenous procedure, and 36100-36218 for intra-arterial procedure and 93556)

(For introduction of catheter, injection procedure, see 93501-93536, 93545, 93556)

(75766 has been deleted. To report, use 93556)

(75767 has been deleted. To report, see 36000-36013, 36400-36425 for intravenous procedure, and 36100-36218 for intra-arterial procedure and 93556)

(For introduction of catheter, injection procedure, see 93501-93536, 93545, 93556)

(75772, 75773 have been deleted. To report, use 75774)

**+ 75774** Angiography, selective, each additional vessel studied after basic examination, radiological supervision and interpretation (List separately in addition to code for primary procedure)

(Use 75774 in addition to code for specific initial vessel studied)

(For angiography, see codes 75600-75790)

(For catheterizations, see codes 36215-36248)

(75775 (complete procedure) has been deleted, see 36000-36015, 36400-36425 for intravenous procedure, and 36100-36248 for intra-arterial procedure and 75774)

(For introduction of catheter, injection procedure, see 93501-93536, 93545, 93555, 93556)

**75790** Angiography, arteriovenous shunt (eg, dialysis patient), radiological supervision and interpretation

(For introduction of catheter, use 36140, 36145, 36215-36217, 36245-36247)

# Veins and Lymphatics

(For injection procedure for venous system, see 36000-36015, 36400-36510)

(For injection procedure for lymphatic system, use 38790)

**75801** Lymphangiography, extremity only, unilateral, radiological supervision and interpretation

(75802 (complete procedure) has been deleted, see 38790, 75801)

**75803** Lymphangiography, extremity only, bilateral, radiological supervision and interpretation

(75804 (complete procedure) has been deleted, see 38790, 75803)

**75805** Lymphangiography, pelvic/abdominal, unilateral, radiological supervision and interpretation

(75806 (complete procedure) has been deleted, see 38790, 75805)

**75807** Lymphangiography, pelvic/abdominal, bilateral, radiological supervision and interpretation

(75808 (complete procedure) has been deleted, see 38790, 75807)

**75809** Shuntogram for investigation of previously placed indwelling nonvascular shunt (eg, LeVeen shunt, ventriculoperitoneal shunt), radiological supervision and interpretation

(For procedure, see 49427 or 61070)

**75810** Splenoportography, radiological supervision and interpretation

(75811 (complete procedure) has been deleted, see 38200, 75810)

**75820** Venography, extremity, unilateral, radiological supervision and interpretation

(75821 (complete procedure) has been deleted, see 36000, 36406, 36410, 36420, 36425, 75820)

**75822** Venography, extremity, bilateral, radiological supervision and interpretation

(75823 (complete procedure) has been deleted, see 36000, 36406, 36410, 36420, 36425, 75822)

**75825** Venography, caval, inferior, with serialography, radiological supervision and interpretation

(75826 (complete procedure) has been deleted, see 36010, 75825)

**75827** Venography, caval, superior, with serialography, radiological supervision and interpretation

(75828 (complete procedure) has been deleted, see 36010, 75827)

**75831** Venography, renal, unilateral, selective, radiological supervision and interpretation

(75832 (complete procedure) has been deleted, see 36000-36012, 75831)

**75833** Venography, renal, bilateral, selective, radiological supervision and interpretation

(75834 (complete procedure) has been deleted, see 36000-36012, 75833)

**75840** Venography, adrenal, unilateral, selective, radiological supervision and interpretation

(75841 (complete procedure) has been deleted, see 36000-36012, 75840)

**75842** Venography, adrenal, bilateral, selective, radiological supervision and interpretation

(75843 (complete procedure) has been deleted, see 36000-36012, 75842)

(75845, 75846, 75847, 75850, 75851 have been deleted)

**75860** Venography, sinus or jugular, catheter, radiological supervision and interpretation

(75861 (complete procedure) has been deleted, see 36000-36012 for intravenous procedure and 36100-36218 for intra-arterial procedure, 75860)

**75870** Venography, superior sagittal sinus, radiological supervision and interpretation

(75871 (complete procedure) has been deleted, see 36000-36012 for intravenous procedure and 36100-36218 for intra-arterial procedure, 75870)

**75872** Venography, epidural, radiological supervision and interpretation

(75873 (complete procedure) has been deleted, see 36000-36012 for intravenous procedure and 36100-36218 for intra-arterial procedure, 75872)

**75880** Venography, orbital, radiological supervision and interpretation

(75881 (complete procedure) has been deleted, see 36000-36012 for intravenous procedure and 36100-36218 for intra-arterial procedure, 75880)

**75885** Percutaneous transhepatic portography with hemodynamic evaluation, radiological supervision and interpretation

(75886 (complete procedure) has been deleted, see 36011, 36012, 36481, 75885)

**75887** Percutaneous transhepatic portography without hemodynamic evaluation, radiological supervision and interpretation

(75888 (complete procedure) has been deleted, see 36011, 36012, 36481, 75887)

**75889** Hepatic venography, wedged or free, with hemodynamic evaluation, radiological supervision and interpretation

(75890 (complete procedure) has been deleted, see 36000-36012, 75889)

**75891** Hepatic venography, wedged or free, without hemodynamic evaluation, radiological supervision and interpretation

(75892 (complete procedure) has been deleted, see 36000-36012, 75891)

**75893** Venous sampling through catheter, with or without angiography (eg, for parathyroid hormone, renin), radiological supervision and interpretation

(For procedure, use 36500)

## Transcatheter Procedures

**75894** Transcatheter therapy, embolization, any method, radiological supervision and interpretation

(75895 (complete procedure) has been deleted, see 37204, 61624, 61626, 75894)

**75896** Transcatheter therapy, infusion, any method (eg, thrombolysis other than coronary), radiological supervision and interpretation

(75897 (complete procedure) has been deleted, see 37201, 37202, 75896)

(For infusion for coronary disease, see 92975, 92977)

**75898** Angiogram through existing catheter for follow-up study for transcatheter therapy, embolization or infusion

**75900** Exchange of a previously placed arterial catheter during thrombolytic therapy with contrast monitoring, radiological supervision and interpretation

(For procedure, use 37209)

**75940** Percutaneous placement of IVC filter, radiological supervision and interpretation

(75941 (complete procedure) has been deleted, see 37620, 75940)

**75945** Intravascular ultrasound (non-coronary vessel), radiological supervision and interpretation; initial vessel

**+ 75946** each additional non-coronary vessel (List separately in addition to code for primary procedure)

(Use 75946 in conjunction with code 75945)

(For catheterizations, see codes 36215-36248)

(For transcatheter therapies, see codes 37200-37208, 61624, 61626)

(For procedure, see 37250, 37251)

(75950, 75951, 75955, 75956 (complete procedure) have been deleted, see 37204, 61624, 61626, 75894)

**75960** Transcatheter introduction of intravascular stent(s), (non-coronary vessel), percutaneous and/or open, radiological supervision and interpretation, each vessel

(For procedure, see 37205-37208)

**75961** Transcatheter retrieval, percutaneous, of intravascular foreign body (eg, fractured venous or arterial catheter), radiological supervision and interpretation

(For procedure, use 37203)

**75962** Transluminal balloon angioplasty, peripheral artery, radiological supervision and interpretation

(75963 (complete procedure) has been deleted, see 35450-35460 or 35470-35476 and 75962)

**+ 75964** Transluminal balloon angioplasty, each additional peripheral artery, radiological supervision and interpretation (List separately in addition to code for primary procedure)

(Use 75964 in conjunction with code 75962)

(75965 (complete procedure) has been deleted, see 35450-35460 or 35470-35476 and 75964)

**75966** Transluminal balloon angioplasty, renal or other visceral artery, radiological supervision and interpretation

(75967 (complete procedure) has been deleted, see 35450-35460 or 35470-35476 and 75966)

**+ 75968** Transluminal balloon angioplasty, each additional visceral artery, radiological supervision and interpretation (List separately in addition to code for primary procedure)

(Use 75968 in conjunction with code 75966)

(75969 (complete procedure) has been deleted, see 35450-35460 or 35470-35476 and 75968)

(For percutaneous transluminal coronary angioplasty, see 92982-92984)

**75970** Transcatheter biopsy, radiological supervision and interpretation

(For injection procedure only for transcatheter therapy or biopsy, see 36100-36299)

(75971 (complete procedure) has been deleted, see 37200, 75970)

(For transcatheter renal and ureteral biopsy, use 52007)

(For percutaneous needle biopsy of pancreas, use 48102; of retroperitoneal lymph node or mass, use 49180)

(75972-75977 have been deleted. To report, see 75962-75968)

**75978** Transluminal balloon angioplasty, venous (eg, subclavian stenosis), radiological supervision and interpretation

(75979 (complete procedure) has been deleted, see 35460, 35476, 75978)

**75980** Percutaneous transhepatic biliary drainage with contrast monitoring, radiological supervision and interpretation

(75981 (complete procedure) has been deleted, see 47510, 47511, 75980)

**75982** Percutaneous placement of drainage catheter for combined internal and external biliary drainage or of a drainage stent for internal biliary drainage in patients with an inoperable mechanical biliary obstruction, radiological supervision and interpretation

(75983 (complete procedure) has been deleted, see 47511, 75982)

**75984** Change of percutaneous tube or drainage catheter with contrast monitoring (eg, gastrointestinal system, genitourinary system, abscess), radiological supervision and interpretation

(75985 (complete procedure) has been deleted, see 43760, 47525, 47530, 50398, 50688, 75984)

(For change of nephrostomy or pyelostomy tube only, use 50398)

(For introduction procedure only for percutaneous biliary drainage, see 47510, 47511)

(For percutaneous cholecystostomy, use 47490)

(For change of percutaneous biliary drainage catheter only, use 47525)

(For percutaneous nephrostolithotomy or pyelostolithotomy, see 50080, 50081)

**75989** Radiological guidance for percutaneous drainage of abscess, or specimen collection (ie, fluoroscopy, ultrasound, or computed tomography), with placement of indwelling catheter, radiological supervision and interpretation

(75990 (complete procedure) has been deleted, see appropriate organ or site and 75989)

## Transluminal Atherectomy

**75992** Transluminal atherectomy, peripheral artery, radiological supervision and interpretation

(For procedure, see 35481-35485, 35491-35495)

**+ 75993** Transluminal atherectomy, each additional peripheral artery, radiological supervision and interpretation (List separately in addition to code for primary procedure)

(Use 75993 in conjunction with code 75992)

(For procedure, see 35481-35485, 35491-35495)

**75994** Transluminal atherectomy, renal, radiological supervision and interpretation

(For procedure, see 35480, 35490)

**75995** Transluminal atherectomy, visceral, radiological supervision and interpretation

(For procedure, see 35480, 35490)

**+ 75996** Transluminal atherectomy, each additional visceral artery, radiological supervision and interpretation (List separately in addition to code for primary procedure)

(Use 75996 in conjunction with code 75995)

(For procedure, see 35480, 35490)

## Other Procedures

(For arthrography of shoulder, use 73040; elbow, use 73085; wrist, use 73115; hip, use 73525; knee, use 73580; ankle, use 73615)

**76000** Fluoroscopy (separate procedure), up to one hour physician time, other than 71023 or 71034 (eg, cardiac fluoroscopy)

**76001** Fluoroscopy, physician time more than one hour, assisting a non-radiologic physician (eg, nephrostolithotomy, ERCP, bronchoscopy, transbronchial biopsy)

**76003** Fluoroscopic localization for needle biopsy or fine needle aspiration

(See appropriate surgical code for location, eg, 20220, 20225, 32400, 32405, 47000, 47001, 48102, 50200, 50390, 60100)

**● 76005** Fluoroscopic guidance and localization of needle or catheter tip for spine or paraspinous diagnostic or therapeutic injection procedures (epidural, transforaminal epidural, subarachnoid, paravertebral facet joint, paravertebral facet joint nerve or sacroiliac joint), including neurolytic agent destruction

►(Injection of contrast during fluoroscopic guidance and localization is an inclusive component of codes 62270-62273, 62280-62282, 62310-62319)◄

►(Fluoroscopic guidance for subarachnoid puncture for diagnostic radiographic myelography is included in supervision and interpretation codes 72240, 72255, 72265, 72270)◄

►(For epidural or subarachnoid needle or catheter placement and injection, see codes 62270-62273, 62280-62282, 62310-62319)◄

►(For sacroiliac joint arthrography, see 27096, 73542. If formal arthrography is not performed, recorded, and a formal radiographic report is not issued, use 76005 for fluoroscopic guidance for sacroiliac joint injections)◄

►(For paravertebral facet joint injection, see 64470-64476. For transforaminal epidural needle placement and injection, see 64479-64484)◄

►(For destruction by neurolytic agent, see 64600-64680)◄

**76006** Radiologic examination, stress view(s), any joint, stress applied by a physician (includes comparison views)

**76010** Radiologic examination from nose to rectum for foreign body, single film, child

**76020** Bone age studies

**76040** Bone length studies (orthoroentgenogram, scanogram)

(76060 has been deleted. See 76061, 76062)

**76061** Radiologic examination, osseous survey; limited (eg, for metastases)

**76062** complete (axial and appendicular skeleton)

**76065** Radiologic examination, osseous survey, infant

**76066** Joint survey, single view, one or more joints (specify)

**76070** Computerized tomography bone mineral density study, one or more sites

**76075** Dual energy x-ray absorptiometry (DEXA), bone density study, one or more sites; axial skeleton (eg, hips, pelvis, spine)

**76076** appendicular skeleton (peripheral) (eg, radius, wrist, heel)

**76078** Radiographic absorptiometry (photodensitometry), one or more sites

**76080** Radiologic examination, abscess, fistula or sinus tract study, radiological supervision and interpretation

(76081 (complete procedure) has been deleted, see 20501, 49424, 76080)

**76086** Mammary ductogram or galactogram, single duct, radiological supervision and interpretation

(76087 (complete procedure) has been deleted, see 19030, 76086)

**76088** Mammary ductogram or galactogram, multiple ducts, radiological supervision and interpretation

(76089 (complete procedure) has been deleted, see 19030, 76088)

**76090** Mammography; unilateral

**76091** bilateral

**76092** Screening mammography, bilateral (two view film study of each breast)

**76093** Magnetic resonance imaging, breast, without and/or with contrast material(s); unilateral

**76094** bilateral

**76095** Stereotactic localization for breast biopsy, each lesion, radiological supervision and interpretation

(For procedure, see 19100, 19101, 88170)

**76096** Preoperative placement of needle localization wire, breast, radiological supervision and interpretation

(For placement, see 19290, 19291)

(76097 has been deleted. To report, see 19291, 76096)

**76098** Radiological examination, surgical specimen

**76100** Radiologic examination, single plane body section (eg, tomography), other than with urography

**76101** Radiologic examination, complex motion (ie, hypercycloidal) body section (eg, mastoid polytomography), other than with urography; unilateral

**76102** bilateral

(For nephrotomography, use 74415)

**76120** Cineradiography, except where specifically included

**+ 76125** Cineradiography to complement routine examination (List separately in addition to code for primary procedure)

(76127 has been deleted. The use of photographic media is not reported separately but is considered to be a component of the basic procedure)

(76130-76137 have been deleted. To report, use code for specific radiologic examination)

**76140** Consultation on x-ray examination made elsewhere, written report

**76150** Xeroradiography

(76150 is to be used for non-mammographic studies only)

(76300 has been deleted. To report, use 76499)

**76350** Subtraction in conjunction with contrast studies

**76355** Computerized tomography guidance for stereotactic localization

**76360** Computerized tomography guidance for needle biopsy, radiological supervision and interpretation

(76361 (complete procedure) has been deleted, see appropriate organ or site and 76360)

**76365** Computerized tomography guidance for cyst aspiration, radiological supervision and interpretation

(76366 (complete procedure) has been deleted, see appropriate organ or site and 76365)

**76370** Computerized tomography guidance for placement of radiation therapy fields

**76375** Coronal, sagittal, multiplanar, oblique, 3-dimensional and/or holographic reconstruction of computerized tomography, magnetic resonance imaging, or other tomographic modality

(Use 76375 in addition to code for imaging procedure)

**76380** Computerized tomography, limited or localized follow-up study

**76390** Magnetic resonance spectroscopy

(For magnetic resonance imaging, use appropriate MRI body site code)

**76400** Magnetic resonance (eg, proton) imaging, bone marrow blood supply

**76499** Unlisted diagnostic radiologic procedure

# Diagnostic Ultrasound

### Definitions

***A-mode*** implies a one-dimensional ultrasonic measurement procedure.

***M-mode*** implies a one-dimensional ultrasonic measurement procedure with movement of the trace to record amplitude and velocity of moving echo-producing structures.

***B-scan*** implies a two-dimensional ultrasonic scanning procedure with a two-dimensional display.

***Real-time scan*** implies a two-dimensional ultrasonic scanning procedure with display of both two-dimensional structure and motion with time.

## Head and Neck

(76500, 76505 have been deleted. To report, use 76999)

**76506** Echoencephalography, B-scan and/or real time with image documentation (gray scale) (for determination of ventricular size, delineation of cerebral contents and detection of fluid masses or other intracranial abnormalities), including A-mode encephalography as secondary component where indicated

**76511** Ophthalmic ultrasound, echography, diagnostic; A-scan only, with amplitude quantification

**76512** contact B-scan (with or without simultaneous A-scan)

**▲76513** anterior segment ultrasound, immersion (water bath) B-scan or high resolution biomicroscopy

(76515 has been deleted. To report, use 76999)

**76516** Ophthalmic biometry by ultrasound echography, A-scan;

(76517 has been deleted. To report, use 76999)

**76519** with intraocular lens power calculation

**76529** Ophthalmic ultrasonic foreign body localization

(76530 has been deleted. To report, use 76999)

(76535 has been deleted. To report, use 76536)

**76536** Echography, soft tissues of head and neck (eg, thyroid, parathyroid, parotid), B-scan and/or real time with image documentation

(76550 has been deleted. To report, see 93880-93888)

## Chest

(76601 has been deleted. To report, use 76999)

**76604** Echography, chest, B-scan (includes mediastinum) and/or real time with image documentation

(76620, 76625 have been deleted)

(76627, 76628 have been deleted. To report, see 93307, 93308)

(76629 has been deleted)

(76632 has been deleted. To report, see 93320, 93321)

(76640 has been deleted. To report, use 76999)

**76645** Echography, breast(s) (unilateral or bilateral), B-scan and/ or real time with image documentation

## Abdomen and Retroperitoneum

**76700** Echography, abdominal, B-scan and/or real time with image documentation; complete

**76705** limited (eg, single organ, quadrant, follow-up)

**76770** Echography, retroperitoneal (eg, renal, aorta, nodes), B-scan and/or real time with image documentation; complete

**76775** limited

**76778** Echography of transplanted kidney, B-scan and/or real time with image documentation, with or without duplex Doppler studies

## Spinal Canal

**76800** Echography, spinal canal and contents

## Pelvis

**76805** Echography, pregnant uterus, B-scan and/or real time with image documentation; complete (complete fetal and maternal evaluation)

**76810** complete (complete fetal and maternal evaluation), multiple gestation, after the first trimester

**76815** limited (fetal size, heart beat, placental location, fetal position, or emergency in the delivery room)

**76816** follow-up or repeat

**76818** Fetal biophysical profile

**76825** Echocardiography, fetal, cardiovascular system, real time with image documentation (2D), with or without M-mode recording;

**76826** follow-up or repeat study

**76827** Doppler echocardiography, fetal, cardiovascular system, pulsed wave and/or continuous wave with spectral display; complete

**76828** follow-up or repeat study

(To report the use of color mapping, use 93325)

**76830** Echography, transvaginal

(76855 has been deleted. To report, see 93975-93979)

**76831** Hysterosonography, with or without color flow Doppler

(For introduction of saline or contrast for hysterosonography, use 58340)

**76856** Echography, pelvic (nonobstetric), B-scan and/or real time with image documentation; complete

**76857** limited or follow-up (eg, for follicles)

## Genitalia

**76870** Echography, scrotum and contents

**76872** Echography, transrectal;

● **76873** prostate volume study for brachytherapy treatment planning (separate procedure)

## Extremities

**76880** Echography, extremity, non-vascular, B-scan and/or real time with image documentation

**76885** Echography of infant hips, real time with imaging documentation; dynamic (eg, requiring manipulation)

**76886** limited, static (eg, not requiring manipulation)

## Vascular Studies

(76900-76920 have been deleted. To report, see 93922-93971; for cerebrovascular studies, see 93875-93888)

(76925 has been deleted. To report, see 93922-93931 or 93965-93971)

(76926 has been deleted. To report, see 93875-93888 or 93975-93979)

## Ultrasonic Guidance Procedures

**76930** Ultrasonic guidance for pericardiocentesis, radiological supervision and interpretation

(76931 (complete procedure) has been deleted, see 33010, 33011, 76930)

**76932** Ultrasonic guidance for endomyocardial biopsy, radiological supervision and interpretation

(76933 (complete procedure) has been deleted, see 93505, 76932)

**76934** Ultrasonic guidance for thoracentesis or abdominal paracentesis, radiological supervision and interpretation

(76935 (complete procedure) has been deleted, see 32000, 76934)

**76936** Ultrasound guided compression repair of arterial pseudo-aneurysm or arteriovenous fistulae (includes diagnostic ultrasound evaluation, compression of lesion and imaging)

**76938** Ultrasonic guidance for cyst (any location) or renal pelvis aspiration, radiological supervision and interpretation

(76939 (complete procedure) has been deleted, see appropriate organ or site and 76938)

**76941** Ultrasonic guidance for intrauterine fetal transfusion or cordocentesis, radiological supervision and interpretation

(For procedure, see 36460, 59012)

**76942** Ultrasonic guidance for needle biopsy, radiological supervision and interpretation

(76943 (complete procedure) has been deleted, see appropriate organ or site and 76942)

(76944 has been deleted. To report, use 75989)

**76945** Ultrasonic guidance for chorionic villus sampling, radiological supervision and interpretation

(For procedure, use 59015)

**76946** Ultrasonic guidance for amniocentesis, radiological supervision and interpretation

(76947 (complete procedure) has been deleted, see 59000, 76946)

**76948** Ultrasonic guidance for aspiration of ova, radiological supervision and interpretation

(76949 (complete procedure) has been deleted, see 58970, 76948)

**76950** Echography for placement of radiation therapy fields, B-scan

**76960** Ultrasonic guidance for placement of radiation therapy fields, except for B-scan echography

**76965** Ultrasonic guidance for interstitial radioelement application

## Other Procedures

**76970** Ultrasound study follow-up (specify)

**76975** Gastrointestinal endoscopic ultrasound, radiological supervision and interpretation

(For procedure, use 43259)

**76977** Ultrasound bone density measurement and interpretation, peripheral site(s), any method

(76980 has been deleted. To report, use code for specific ultrasound examination)

(76985 has been deleted. To report, use 76986)

**76986** Echography, intraoperative

(76990 has been deleted. To report, use 76999)

(76991 has been deleted. To report, see 76830, 76872)

**76999** Unlisted ultrasound procedure

# Radiation Oncology

Listings for Radiation Oncology provide for teletherapy and brachytherapy to include initial consultation, clinical treatment planning, simulation, medical radiation physics, dosimetry, treatment devices, special services, and clinical treatment management procedures. They include normal follow-up care during course of treatment and for three months following its completion.

When a service or procedure is provided that is not listed in this edition of *CPT* it should be identified by a Special Report (see page 300) and one of the unlisted procedure codes listed below:

77299 Unlisted procedure, therapeutic radiology clinical treatment planning
77399 Unlisted procedure, medical radiation physics, dosimetry and treatment devices, and special services
77499 Unlisted procedure, therapeutic radiology treatment management
77799 Unlisted procedure, clinical brachytherapy

For treatment by injectable or ingestible isotopes, see subsection **Nuclear Medicine**.

## Consultation: Clinical Management

Preliminary consultation, evaluation of patient prior to decision to treat, or full medical care (in addition to treatment management) when provided by the therapeutic radiologist may be identified by the appropriate procedure codes from **Evaluation and Management, Medicine,** or **Surgery** sections.

## Clinical Treatment Planning (External and Internal Sources)

The clinical treatment planning process is a complex service including interpretation of special testing, tumor localization, treatment volume determination, treatment time/dosage determination, choice of treatment modality, determination of number and size of treatment ports, selection of appropriate treatment devices, and other procedures.

**Definitions**

***Simple*** planning requires a single treatment area of interest encompassed in a single port or simple parallel opposed ports with simple or no blocking.

***Intermediate*** planning requires three or more converging ports, two separate treatment areas, multiple blocks, or special time dose constraints.

***Complex*** planning requires highly complex blocking, custom shielding blocks, tangential ports, special wedges or compensators, three or more separate treatment areas, rotational or special beam considerations, combination of therapeutic modalities.

(77260, 77265, 77270, 77275 have been deleted. To report, see 77261-77263)

**77261** Therapeutic radiology treatment planning; simple

**77262** intermediate

**77263** complex

**Definitions**

***Simple*** simulation of a single treatment area with either a single port or parallel opposed ports. Simple or no blocking.

***Intermediate*** simulation of three or more converging ports, two separate treatment areas, multiple blocks.

***Complex*** simulation of tangential portals, three or more treatment areas, rotation or arc therapy, complex blocking, custom shielding blocks, brachytherapy source verification, hyperthermia probe verification, any use of contrast materials.

***Three-dimensional*** computer-generated three dimensional reconstruction of tumor volume and surrounding critical normal tissue structures from direct CT scans and/or MRI data in preparation for non-coplanar or coplanar therapy. The simulation utilizes documented three-dimensional beam's eye view volume-dose displays of multiple or moving beams. Documentation with three-dimensional volume reconstruction and dose distribution is required.

Simulation may be carried out on a dedicated simulator, a radiation therapy treatment unit, or diagnostic x-ray machine.

**77280** Therapeutic radiology simulation-aided field setting; simple

**77285** intermediate

**77290** complex

**77295** three-dimensional

**77299** Unlisted procedure, therapeutic radiology clinical treatment planning

## Medical Radiation Physics, Dosimetry, Treatment Devices, and Special Services

**77300** Basic radiation dosimetry calculation, central axis depth dose, TDF, NSD, gap calculation, off axis factor, tissue inhomogeneity factors, as required during course of treatment, only when prescribed by the treating physician

**77305** Teletherapy, isodose plan (whether hand or computer calculated); simple (one or two parallel opposed unmodified ports directed to a single area of interest)

**77310** intermediate (three or more treatment ports directed to a single area of interest)

**77315** complex (mantle or inverted Y, tangential ports, the use of wedges, compensators, complex blocking, rotational beam, or special beam considerations)

(Only one teletherapy isodose plan may be reported for a given course of therapy to a specific treatment area)

(77320 has been deleted. To report, see 77300-77399)

**77321** Special teletherapy port plan, particles, hemibody, total body

(77325 has been deleted. To report, see 77300-77399)

**77326** Brachytherapy isodose calculation; simple (calculation made from single plane, one to four sources/ ribbon application, remote afterloading brachytherapy, 1 to 8 sources)

(For definition of source/ribbon, see page 330)

**77327** intermediate (multiplane dosage calculations, application involving 5 to 10 sources/ribbons, remote afterloading brachytherapy, 9 to 12 sources)

**77328** complex (multiplane isodose plan, volume implant calculations, over 10 sources/ribbons used, special spatial reconstruction, remote afterloading brachytherapy, over 12 sources)

(77330 has been deleted. To report, see 77300-77399)

**77331** Special dosimetry (eg, TLD, microdosimetry) (specify), only when prescribed by the treating physician

**77332** Treatment devices, design and construction; simple (simple block, simple bolus)

**77333** intermediate (multiple blocks, stents, bite blocks, special bolus)

**77334** complex (irregular blocks, special shields, compensators, wedges, molds or casts)

(77335 has been deleted. To report, see 77300-77399)

**77336** Continuing medical physics consultation, including assessment of treatment parameters, quality assurance of dose delivery, and review of patient treatment documentation in support of the radiation oncologist, reported per week of therapy

(77340 has been deleted. To report, see 77300-77399)

(77345-77360 have been deleted. To report, see 77300-77399)

**77370** Special medical radiation physics consultation

►(77380 has been deleted. To report, use 77520)◄

►(77381 has been deleted. To report, use 77523)◄

**77399** Unlisted procedure, medical radiation physics, dosimetry and treatment devices, and special services

## Radiation Treatment Delivery

(Radiation treatment delivery (77401-77416) recognizes the technical component and the various energy levels.)

(77400 has been deleted)

**77401** Radiation treatment delivery, superficial and/or ortho voltage

**77402** Radiation treatment delivery, single treatment area, single port or parallel opposed ports, simple blocks or no blocks; up to 5 MeV

**77403** 6-10 MeV

**77404** 11-19 MeV

(77405 has been deleted)

**77406** 20 MeV or greater

**77407** Radiation treatment delivery, two separate treatment areas, three or more ports on a single treatment area, use of multiple blocks; up to 5 MeV

**77408** 6-10 MeV

**77409** 11-19 MeV

(77410 has been deleted)

**77411** 20 MeV or greater

**77412** Radiation treatment delivery, three or more separate treatment areas, custom blocking, tangential ports, wedges, rotational beam, compensators, special particle beam (eg, electron or neutrons); up to 5 MeV

**77413** 6-10 MeV

**77414** 11-19 MeV

(77415 has been deleted. To report, use 77417)

**77416** 20 MeV or greater

**77417** Therapeutic radiology port film(s)

## ►Radiation◄ Treatment Management

►Radiation treatment management is reported in units of five fractions or treatment sessions, regardless of the actual time period in which the services are furnished. The services need not be furnished on consecutive days. Multiple fractions representing two or more treatment sessions furnished on the same day may be counted separately as long as there has been a distinct break in therapy sessions, and the fractions are of the character usually furnished on different days. Code 77427 is also reported if there are three or four fractions beyond a multiple of five at the end of a course of treatment; one or two fractions beyond a multiple of five at the end of a course of treatment are not reported separately. The professional services furnished during treatment management typically consists of:

- Review of port films;
- Review of dosimetry, dose delivery, and treatment parameters;
- Review of patient treatment set-up;
- Examination of patient for medical evaluation and management (eg, assessment of the patient's response to treatment, coordination of care and treatment, review of imaging and/or lab test results).◄

►(77419, 77420, 77425, and 77430 have been deleted. To report radiation treatment management, use 77427)◄

●**77427** Radiation treatment management, five treatments

**77431** Radiation therapy management with complete course of therapy consisting of one or two fractions only

(77431 is not to be used to fill in the last week of a long course of therapy)

**77432** Stereotactic radiation treatment management of cerebral lesion(s) (complete course of treatment consisting of one session)

(77435-77460 have been deleted. To report, see 77401-77499)

(77465 has been deleted)

**77470** Special treatment procedure (eg, total body irradiation, hemibody irradiation, per oral, vaginal cone irradiation)

(77470 assumes that the procedure is performed one or more times during the course of therapy, in addition to daily or weekly patient management)

▲**77499** Unlisted procedure, therapeutic radiology treatment management

## ▸Proton Beam Treatment Delivery◂

●**77520** Proton beam delivery to a single treatment area, single port, custom block, with or without compensation, with treatment set-up and verification images

●**77523** Proton beam delivery to one or two treatment areas, two or more ports, two or more custom blocks, and two or more compensators, with treatment set-up and verification images

## Hyperthermia

Hyperthermia treatments as listed in this section include external (superficial and deep), interstitial, and intracavitary.

Radiation therapy when given concurrently is listed separately.

Hyperthermia is used only as an adjunct to radiation therapy or chemotherapy. It may be induced by a variety of sources (eg, microwave, ultrasound, low energy radio-frequency conduction, or by probes).

The listed treatments include management during the course of therapy and follow-up care for three months after completion.

Preliminary consultation is not included (see **Medicine** 99241-99263).

Physics planning and interstitial insertion of temperature sensors, and use of external or interstitial heat generating sources are included.

The following descriptors are included in the treatment schedule:

**77600** Hyperthermia, externally generated; superficial (ie, heating to a depth of 4 cm or less)

**77605** deep (ie, heating to depths greater than 4 cm)

**77610** Hyperthermia generated by interstitial probe(s); 5 or fewer interstitial applicators

**77615** more than 5 interstitial applicators

## Clinical Intracavitary Hyperthermia

**77620** Hyperthermia generated by intracavitary probe(s)

## Clinical Brachytherapy

Clinical brachytherapy requires the use of either natural or man-made radioelements applied into or around a treatment field of interest. The supervision of radioelements and dose interpretation are performed solely by the therapeutic radiologist.

When a procedure requires the service of a surgeon(s) in addition, either modifier '-66' or modifier '-62' may be used (see Appendix A for modifier definitions).

Services 77750-77799 include admission to the hospital and daily visits.

**Definitions**

(Sources refer to intracavitary placement or permanent interstitial placement; ribbons refer to temporary interstitial placement)

***A simple*** application has one to four sources/ribbons.

***An intermediate*** application has five to ten sources/ribbons.

***A complex*** application has greater than ten sources/ribbons.

(77700-77749 have been deleted. To report, see 77761-77799)

**77750** Infusion or instillation of radioelement solution

(77755, 77760 have been deleted. To report, see 77761-77799)

**77761** Intracavitary radioelement application; simple

**77762** intermediate

**77763** complex

(77765, 77770, 77775 have been deleted. To report, see 77761-77799)

**77776** Interstitial radioelement application; simple

**77777** intermediate

**77778** complex

(77780 has been deleted. To report, see 77761-77799)

**77781** Remote afterloading high intensity brachytherapy; 1-4 source positions or catheters

**77782** 5-8 source positions or catheters

**77783** 9-12 source positions or catheters

**77784** over 12 source positions or catheters

(77785 has been deleted. To report, see 77761-77799)

**77789** Surface application of radioelement

**77790** Supervision, handling, loading of radioelement

**77799** Unlisted procedure, clinical brachytherapy

(77800 has been deleted. To report, use 77331)

(77805-77810 have been deleted. To report, see 77305-77321 or 77326-77328)

(77850 has been deleted. To report, see 77300, 77336, 77370)

(77860 has been deleted. To report, use 77336)

(77999 has been deleted. To report, use 77399)

# Nuclear Medicine

Listed procedures may be performed independently or in the course of overall medical care. If the physician providing these services is also responsible for diagnostic work-up and/or follow-up care of patient, see appropriate sections also.

Radioimmunoassay tests are found in the **Clinical Pathology** section (codes 82000-84999). These codes can be appropriately used by any specialist performing such tests in a laboratory licensed and/or certified for radioimmunoassays. The reporting of these tests is not confined to clinical pathology laboratories alone.

The services listed do not include the provision of radium or other radioelements. Those materials supplied by the physician should be listed separately and identified by the code 78990 for diagnostic radiopharmaceutical and 79900 for therapeutic radiopharmaceutical.

## Diagnostic

### Endocrine System

**78000** Thyroid uptake; single determination

**78001** multiple determinations

**78003** stimulation, suppression or discharge (not including initial uptake studies)

**78006** Thyroid imaging, with uptake; single determination

**78007** multiple determinations

**78010** Thyroid imaging; only

**78011** with vascular flow

**78015** Thyroid carcinoma metastases imaging; limited area (eg, neck and chest only)

**78016** with additional studies (eg, urinary recovery)

(78017 has been deleted. To report, use 78018)

**78018** whole body

(For triiodothyronine (true TT-3), use 84480)

(For calcitonin, use 82308)

(For triiodothyronine, free (FT-3), (unbound T-3 only), use 84481)

(For TT-4 thyroxine, use 84436)

(For T-4 thyroxine, neonatal, use 84437)

(For FT-4 thyroxine, free, (unbound T-4 only), use 84439)

**+ 78020** Thyroid carcinoma metastases uptake (List separately in addition to code for primary procedure)

(Use 78020 in conjunction with 78018 only)

**78070** Parathyroid imaging

(For parathormone (parathyroid hormone), use 83970)

**78075** Adrenal imaging, cortex and/or medulla

(For cortisol, plasma, use 82533)

(For cortisol, urine, use 82533)

(For aldosterone, double isotope technique, use 82088)

(For aldosterone, blood, use 82088)

(For aldosterone, urine, use 82088)

(For 17-ketosteroids, use 83586)

(For 17-OH ketosteroids, use 83586)

(For 17-hydroxycorticosteroids, use 83491)

(For insulin, use 83525)

(For insulin antibodies, use 86337)

(For proinsulin, use 84206)

(For glucagon, use 82943)

(For adrenocorticotropic hormone (ACTH), use 82024)

(For human growth hormone (HGH), (somatotropin), use 83003)

(For human growth antibody, use 86277)

(For thyroglobulin antibody, use 86800)

(For thyroid microsomal antibody, use 86376)

(For thyroid stimulating hormone (TSH), use 84443)

(For thyrotropin releasing factor, see 80438, 80439)

(For plus long-acting thyroid stimulator (LATS), use 84445)

(For follicle stimulating hormone (FSH component of pituitary gonadotropin), use 83001)

(For luteinizing hormone (LH component of pituitary gonadotropin), (ICSH), use 83002)

(For luteinizing releasing factor (LRH), use 83727)

(For prolactin level (mammotropin), use 84146)

(For vasopressin level (antidiuretic hormone), use 84588)

(For estradiol, use 82670)

(For progesterone, use 84144)

(For testosterone, blood, use 84403)

(For testosterone, urine, use 84403)

(For etiocholanolone, use 82696)

**78099** Unlisted endocrine procedure, diagnostic nuclear medicine

(For chemical analysis, see **Chemistry** section)

## Hematopoietic, Reticuloendothelial and Lymphatic System

**78102** Bone marrow imaging; limited area

**78103** multiple areas

**78104** whole body

**78110** Plasma volume, radiopharmaceutical volume-dilution technique (separate procedure); single sampling

**78111** multiple samplings

**78120** Red cell volume determination (separate procedure); single sampling

**78121** multiple samplings

**78122** Whole blood volume determination, including separate measurement of plasma volume and red cell volume (radiopharmaceutical volume-dilution technique)

**78130** Red cell survival study;

**78135** differential organ/tissue kinetics, (eg, splenic and/or hepatic sequestration)

**78140** Labeled red cell sequestration, differential organ/tissue, (eg, splenic and/or hepatic)

**78160** Plasma radioiron disappearance (turnover) rate

**78162** Radioiron oral absorption

**78170** Radioiron red cell utilization

**78172** Chelatable iron for estimation of total body iron

(78180 has been deleted. To report, use 78199)

(For hemosiderin, use 83071)

(For intrinsic factor antibodies, use 86340)

(For cyanocobalamin (vitamin B-12), use 82607)

(For folic acid (folate) serum, use 82746)

(For hepatitis B antigen, see 87340, 87350)

(For hepatitis A antibody (HAAb), see 86708, 86709)

(For hepatitis B core antibody (HBcAb), see 86704, 86705)

(For hepatitis B surface antigen (HBsAb), use 87340)

(For hepatitis B surface antibody (HBsAb), use 86706)

(For hepatitis Be antigen (HBeAg), use 87350)

(For hepatitis Be antibody (HBeAb), use 86707)

**78185** Spleen imaging only, with or without vascular flow

(If combined with liver study, use procedures 78215 and 78216)

(78186 has been deleted)

**78190** Kinetics, study of platelet survival, with or without differential organ/tissue localization

**78191** Platelet survival study

(78192 has been deleted. To report, use 78805)

(78193 has been deleted. To report, use 78806)

**78195** Lymphatics and lymph glands imaging

(For sentinel node ►identification without scintigraphy imaging,◄ use 38792)

(For sentinal node excision, see 38500-38542)

**78199** Unlisted hematopoietic, reticuloendothelial and lymphatic procedure, diagnostic nuclear medicine

(For chemical analysis, see **Chemistry** section)

## Gastrointestinal System

**78201** Liver imaging; static only

**78202** with vascular flow

(For spleen imaging only, use 78185)

**78205** Liver imaging (SPECT);

**78206** with vascular flow

**78215** Liver and spleen imaging; static only

**78216** with vascular flow

**78220** Liver function study with hepatobiliary agents, with serial images

(78221 has been deleted. To report, use 78299)

**78223** Hepatobiliary ductal system imaging, including gallbladder, with or without pharmacologic intervention, with or without quantitative measurement of gallbladder function

(78225 has been deleted)

**78230** Salivary gland imaging;

**78231** with serial images

**78232** Salivary gland function study

(78240 has been deleted. To report pancreas imaging, use 78299)

**78258** Esophageal motility

**78261** Gastric mucosa imaging

**78262** Gastroesophageal reflux study

**78264** Gastric emptying study

●**78267** Urea breath test, C-14; acquisition for analysis

●**78268** analysis

**78270** Vitamin B-12 absorption study (eg, Schilling test); without intrinsic factor

**78271** with intrinsic factor

**78272** Vitamin B-12 absorption studies combined, with and without intrinsic factor

(78276 has been deleted)

**78278** Acute gastrointestinal blood loss imaging

(78280 has been deleted)

**78282** Gastrointestinal protein loss

(78285, 78286 have been deleted. To report, use 78299)

(For gastrin, use 82941)

(For intrinsic factor level, use 83528)

(For carcinoembryonic antigen level (CEA), use 82378)

**78290** Bowel imaging (eg, ectopic gastric mucosa, Meckels localization, volvulus)

**78291** Peritoneal-venous shunt patency test (eg, for LeVeen, Denver shunt)

**78299** Unlisted gastrointestinal procedure, diagnostic nuclear medicine

(For chemical analysis, see **Chemistry** section)

## Musculoskeletal System

Bone and joint imaging can be used in the diagnosis of a variety of infectious inflammatory diseases (eg, osteomyelitis), as well as for localization of primary and/or metastatic neoplasms.

**78300** Bone and/or joint imaging; limited area

**78305** multiple areas

**78306** whole body

(78310 has been deleted. To report, use 78445)

**78315** three phase study

**78320** tomographic (SPECT)

**78350** Bone density (bone mineral content) study, one or more sites; single photon absorptiometry

**78351** dual photon absorptiometry, one or more sites

(78380, 78381 have been deleted. To report, see 78300, 78305)

(For radiographic bone density (photodensitometry), use 76078)

**78399** Unlisted musculoskeletal procedure, diagnostic nuclear medicine

## Cardiovascular System

Myocardial perfusion and cardiac blood pool imaging studies may be performed at rest and/or during stress. When performed during exercise and/or pharmacologic stress, the appropriate stress testing code from the 93015-93018 series should be reported in addition to code(s) 78460-78465, 78472, 78473, ►78478, 78480,◄ 78481, 78483, ►78491, and 78492◄.

(78401-78412 have been deleted. To report, see 78472-78483)

**78414** Determination of central c-v hemodynamics (non-imaging) (eg, ejection fraction with probe technique) with or without pharmacologic intervention or exercise, single or multiple determinations

(78415 has been deleted. To report, use 78472)

(78418-78424 have been deleted. To report, see 78460-78469)

(78425 has been deleted. To report, use 78472)

**78428** Cardiac shunt detection

(78435 has been deleted. To report, use 78481)

**78445** Non-cardiac vascular flow imaging (ie, angiography, venography)

**78455** Venous thrombosis study (eg, radioactive fibrinogen)

● **78456** Acute venous thrombosis imaging, peptide

▲ **78457** Venous thrombosis imaging, venogram; unilateral

**78458** bilateral

**78459** Myocardial imaging, positron emission tomography (PET), metabolic evaluation

(For myocardial perfusion study, see 78491-78492)

**78460** Myocardial perfusion imaging; (planar) single study, at rest or stress (exercise and/or pharmacologic), with or without quantification

**78461** multiple studies, (planar) at rest and/or stress (exercise and/or pharmacologic), and redistribution and/or rest injection, with or without quantification

(78462, 78463 have been deleted. To report, see 78460, 78461)

**78464** tomographic (SPECT), single study at rest or stress (exercise and/or pharmacologic), with or without quantification

**78465** tomographic (SPECT), multiple studies, at rest and/or stress (exercise and/or pharmacologic) and redistribution and/or rest injection, with or without quantification

**78466** Myocardial imaging, infarct avid, planar; qualitative or quantitative

(78467 has been deleted. To report, use 78466)

**78468** with ejection fraction by first pass technique

**78469** tomographic SPECT with or without quantification

(78470 has been deleted. To report, see 78472, 78473, or 78481)

(78471 has been deleted. To report, use 78472)

**78472** Cardiac blood pool imaging, gated equilibrium; planar, single study at rest or stress (exercise and/or pharmacologic), wall motion study plus ejection fraction, with or without additional quantitative processing

(For ►assessment of cardiac function◄ by first pass technique, use 78496)

**78473** multiple studies, wall motion study plus ejection fraction, at rest and stress (exercise and/or pharmacologic), with or without additional quantification

(78474 has been deleted. To report, use 78472)

(78475-78477 have been deleted. To report, use 78473)

✚ **78478** Myocardial perfusion study with wall motion, qualitative or quantitative study (List separately in addition to code for primary procedure)

(Use 78478 in conjunction with codes 78460, 78461, 78464, ►78465◄)

(78479 has been deleted)

✚ **78480** Myocardial perfusion study with ejection fraction (List separately in addition to code for primary procedure)

(Use 78480 in conjunction with codes 78460, 78461, 78464, 78465)

**78481** Cardiac blood pool imaging, (planar), first pass technique; single study, at rest or with stress (exercise and/or pharmacologic), wall motion study plus ejection fraction, with or without quantification

**78483** multiple studies, at rest and with stress (exercise and/ or pharmacologic), wall motion study plus ejection fraction, with or without quantification

(78484 has been deleted. To report, use 78481)

(78485, 78486 have been deleted. To report, use 78483)

(78487 and 78489 have been deleted. To report, use 78483)

(78490 has been deleted. To report, use 78499)

(For digoxin, use 80162)

(For cerebral blood flow study, use 78615)

**78491** Myocardial imaging, positron emission tomography (PET), perfusion; single study at rest or stress

**78492** multiple studies at rest and/or stress

**78494** Cardiac blood pool imaging, gated equilibrium, SPECT, at rest, wall motion study plus ejection fraction, with or without quantitative processing

**+ 78496** Cardiac blood pool imaging, gated equilibrium, single study, at rest, with right ventricular ejection fraction by first pass technique (List separately in addition to code for primary procedure)

(Use 78496 in conjunction with code 78472)

**78499** Unlisted cardiovascular procedure, diagnostic nuclear medicine

(For chemical analysis, see **Chemistry** section)

## Respiratory System

**78580** Pulmonary perfusion imaging, particulate

(78581 and 78582 have been deleted)

**78584** Pulmonary perfusion imaging, particulate, with ventilation; single breath

**78585** rebreathing and washout, with or without single breath

**78586** Pulmonary ventilation imaging, aerosol; single projection

**78587** multiple projections (eg, anterior, posterior, lateral views)

**78588** Pulmonary perfusion imaging, particulate, with ventilation imaging, aerosol, one or multiple projections

**78591** Pulmonary ventilation imaging, gaseous, single breath, single projection

**78593** Pulmonary ventilation imaging, gaseous, with rebreathing and washout with or without single breath; single projection

**78594** multiple projections (eg, anterior, posterior, lateral views)

**78596** Pulmonary quantitative differential function (ventilation/perfusion) study

**78599** Unlisted respiratory procedure, diagnostic nuclear medicine

## Nervous System

**78600** Brain imaging, limited procedure; static

**78601** with vascular flow

**78605** Brain imaging, complete study; static

**78606** with vascular flow

**78607** tomographic (SPECT)

**78608** Brain imaging, positron emission tomography (PET); metabolic evaluation

**78609** perfusion evaluation

**78610** Brain imaging, vascular flow only

**78615** Cerebral blood flow

**78630** Cerebrospinal fluid flow, imaging (not including introduction of material); cisternography

(For injection procedure, see 61000-61070, 62270-62294)

**78635** ventriculography

(For injection procedure, see 61000-61070, 62270-62294)

(78640 has been deleted. To report, use 78699)

**78645** shunt evaluation

(For injection procedure, see 61000-61070, 62270-62294)

**78647** tomographic (SPECT)

**78650** CSF leakage detection and localization

(For injection procedure, see 61000-61070, 62270-62294)

(For myelin basic protein, CSF, use 83873)

(78652 has been deleted. To report, use 78647)

(78655 has been deleted. To report, use 78800)

**78660** Radiopharmaceutical dacryocystography

**78699** Unlisted nervous system procedure, diagnostic nuclear medicine

## Genitourinary System

**78700** Kidney imaging; static only

**78701** with vascular flow

**78704** with function study (ie, imaging renogram)

**78707** Kidney imaging with vascular flow and function; single study without pharmacological intervention

**78708** single study, with pharmacological intervention (eg, angiotensin converting enzyme inhibitor and/or diuretic)

**78709** multiple studies, with and without pharmacological intervention (eg, angiotensin converting enzyme inhibitor and/or diuretic)

(For introduction of radioactive substance in association with renal endoscopy, see 50559, 50578)

**78710** Kidney imaging, tomographic (SPECT)

**78715** Kidney vascular flow only

(78720 has been deleted. To report, use 78704)

**78725** Kidney function study, non-imaging radioisotopic study

(78726 has been deleted. To report, use 78799)

(78727 has been deleted. To report, see 78700-78707)

(For renin (angiotensin I), use 84244)

(For angiotensin II, use 82163)

(For beta-2 microglobulin, use 82232)

**78730** Urinary bladder residual study

(For introduction of radioactive substance in association with cystotomy or cystostomy, use 51020; in association with cystourethroscopy, use 52250)

**78740** Ureteral reflux study (radiopharmaceutical voiding cystogram)

(For estradiol, use 82670)

(For estriol, use 82677)

(For progesterone, use 84144)

(For prostatic acid phosphatase, use 84066)

**78760** Testicular imaging;

**78761** with vascular flow

(For testosterone, blood or urine, use 84403)

(For introduction of radioactive substance in association with ureteral endoscopy, see 50959, 50978)

(78770, 78775 have been deleted. To report, use 78799)

(For lactogen, human placental (HPL) chorionic somatomammotropin, use 83632)

(For chorionic gonadotropin, beta subunit, see 84702, 84703)

(For pregnanediol, use 84135)

(For pregnanetriol, use 84138)

**78799** Unlisted genitourinary procedure, diagnostic nuclear medicine

(For chemical analysis, see **Chemistry** section)

## Other Procedures

(For specific organ, see appropriate heading)

(For radiophosphorus tumor identification, ocular, see 78800)

**78800** Radiopharmaceutical localization of tumor; limited area

(For specific organ, see appropriate heading)

**78801** multiple areas

**78802** whole body

**78803** tomographic (SPECT)

**78805** Radiopharmaceutical localization of abscess; limited area

**78806** whole body

(For imaging bone infectious ►or◄ inflammatory disease ►with a bone imaging radiopharmaceutical,◄ see 78300, 78305, ►78306◄)

(For RAST, see 82785, 83518, 86003, 86005)

(For gamma-E immunoglobulin, use 82785)

(For gamma-G immunoglobulin, use 82784)

(For alpha-1 antitrypsin, see 82103, 82104)

(For alpha-1 fetoprotein, see 82105, 82106)

(For amikacin, use 80150)

(For aminophylline, use 80198)

(For amitriptyline, use 80152)

(For amphetamine, chemical quantitative, use 82145)

(For chlordiazepoxide, see code for specific method)

(For chlorpromazine, see phenothiazine, urine 84022)

(For clonazepam, use 80154)

(For cocaine, quantitative, use 82520)

(For diazepam, use 80154)

(For dihydromorphinone, quantitative, use 82649)

(For diphenylhydantoin, use 80185)

(For flucytosine, see code for specific method)

(For gentamicin, use 80170)

(For lactic dehydrogenase, use 83615)

(For lysergic acid diethylamide (LSD), see 80100-80103, 80299)

(For morphine (heroin), see 80100-80103, 83925)

(For phencyclidine (PCP), see 80100-80103, 83992)

(For phenobarbital, see barbiturates 80100-80103, 82205)

(For phenytoin (diphenylthydantoin), use 80185)

(For tobramycin, use 80200)

**78807** tomographic (SPECT)

**78810** Tumor imaging, positron emission tomography (PET), metabolic evaluation

**78890** Generation of automated data: interactive process involving nuclear physician and/or allied health professional personnel; simple manipulations and interpretation, not to exceed 30 minutes

**78891** complex manipulations and interpretation, exceeding 30 minutes

(Use 78890 or 78891 in addition to primary procedure)

(78895 has been deleted)

**78990** Provision of diagnostic radiopharmaceutical(s)

**78999** Unlisted miscellaneous procedure, diagnostic nuclear medicine

## Therapeutic

**79000** Radiopharmaceutical therapy, hyperthyroidism; initial, including evaluation of patient

**79001** subsequent, each therapy

(For follow-up visit, see 99211-99215)

**79020** Radiopharmaceutical therapy, thyroid suppression (euthyroid cardiac disease), including evaluation of patient

**79030** Radiopharmaceutical ablation of gland for thyroid carcinoma

**79035** Radiopharmaceutical therapy for metastases of thyroid carcinoma

**79100** Radiopharmaceutical therapy, polycythemia vera, chronic leukemia, each treatment

**79200** Intracavitary radioactive colloid therapy

**79300** Interstitial radioactive colloid therapy

**79400** Radiopharmaceutical therapy, nonthyroid, nonhematologic

**79420** Intravascular radiopharmaceutical therapy, particulate

**79440** Intra-articular radiopharmaceutical therapy

**79900** Provision of therapeutic radiopharmaceutical(s)

**79999** Unlisted radiopharmaceutical therapeutic procedure

# Notes

# Notes

# Pathology and Laboratory Guidelines

Items used by all physicians in reporting their services are presented in the **Introduction.** Some of the commonalities are repeated here for the convenience of those physicians referring to this section on **Pathology and Laboratory.** Other definitions and items unique to Pathology and Laboratory are also listed.

## Services in Pathology and Laboratory

Services in Pathology and Laboratory are provided by a physician or by technologists under responsible supervision of a physician.

## Separate or Multiple Procedures

It is appropriate to designate multiple procedures that are rendered on the same date by separate entries.

## Subsection Information

Several of the subheadings or subsections have special needs or instructions unique to that section. Where these are indicated, (eg, "Panel Tests"), special **"Notes"** will be presented preceding those procedural terminology listings referring to that subsection specifically. If there is an "Unlisted Procedure" code number (see section below) for the individual subsection, it will be shown. Those subsections with **"Notes"** are as follows:

**Organ or Disease Panels** .......80048-80090
**Drug Testing** ...............80100-80103
**Therapeutic Drug Assays** ......80150-80299
**Evocative/Suppression Testing** . . .80400-80440
**Consultations**
**(Clinical Pathology)** ........80500-80502
**Urinalysis** .................81000-81099
**Chemistry** .................82000-84999
**Molecular**
**Diagnostics** . . .83890-83912, 87470-87799
**Infectious Agent Antibodies** . . . .86602-86804
**Microbiology Infectious Agent**
**Detection** ...............87260-87799
**Anatomic Pathology** .........88000-88099
**Cytopathology** ..............88141-88167
**Surgical Pathology** ..........88300-88399

## Unlisted Service or Procedure

A service or procedure may be provided that is not listed in this edition of *CPT.* When reporting such a service, the appropriate "Unlisted Procedure" code may be used to indicate the service, identifying it by "Special Report" as discussed below. The "Unlisted Procedures" and accompanying codes for **Pathology and Laboratory** are as follows:

**80299** Quantitation of drug, not elsewhere specified
**81099** Unlisted urinalysis procedure
**84999** Unlisted chemistry procedure
**85999** Unlisted hematology and coagulation procedure
**86586** Unlisted antigen, each
**86849** Unlisted immunology procedure
**86999** Unlisted transfusion medicine procedure
**87999** Unlisted microbiology procedure

**88099** Unlisted necropsy (autopsy) procedure
**88199** Unlisted cytopathology procedure
**88299** Unlisted cytogenetic study
**88399** Unlisted surgical pathology procedure
**89399** Unlisted miscellaneous pathology test

## Special Report

A service that is rarely provided, unusual, variable, or new may require a special report in determining medical appropriateness of the service. Pertinent information should include an adequate definition or description of the nature, extent, and need for the procedure; and the time, effort, and equipment necessary to provide the service. Additional items which may be included are:

- complexity of symptoms;
- final diagnosis;
- pertinent physical findings;
- diagnostic and therapeutic procedures;
- concurrent problems;
- follow-up care.

# Pathology and Laboratory

(80002-80019 have been deleted. To report, see codes under Organ or Disease Oriented Panels)

(80031-80034 have been deleted. To report, see Therapeutic Drug Assays)

(80040 has been deleted. To report, see 80150-80299)

(80042 has been deleted. For serum cidal level, see 87197)

## Organ or Disease Oriented Panels

These panels were developed for coding purposes only and should not be interpreted as clinical parameters. The tests listed with each panel identify the defined components of that panel.

These panel components are not intended to limit the performance of other tests. If one performs tests in addition to those specifically indicated for a particular panel, those tests should be reported separately in addition to the panel code.

●**80048** Basic metabolic panel

This panel must include the following:

Calcium (82310)

Carbon dioxide (82374)

Chloride (82435)

Creatinine (82565)

Glucose (82947)

Potassium (84132)

Sodium (84295)

Urea Nitrogen (BUN) (84520)

►(Do not use 80048 in addition to 80053)◄

►(80049 has been deleted. To report, use 80048)◄

**80050** General health panel

This panel must include the following:

Comprehensive metabolic panel (80054)

Hemogram, automated, and manual differential WBC count (CBC) (85022) OR

Hemogram and platelet count, automated, and automated complete differential WBC count (CBC) (85025)

Thyroid stimulating hormone (TSH) (84443)

**80051** Electrolyte panel

This panel must include the following:

Carbon dioxide (82374)

Chloride (82435)

Potassium (84132)

Sodium (84295)

(80052 has been deleted. To report, see codes for specific tests)

(80053 has been deleted. To report, see 80050 and codes for individual tests)

●**80053** Comprehensive metabolic panel

This panel must include the following:

Albumin (82040)

Bilirubin, total (82247)

Calcium (82310)

Carbon dioxide (bicarbonate) (82374)

Chloride (82435)

Creatinine (82565)

Glucose (82947)

Phosphatase, alkaline (84075)

Potassium (84132)

Protein, total (84155)

Sodium (84295)

Transferase, alanine amino (ALT) (SGPT) (84460)

Transferase, aspartate amino (AST) (SGOT) (84450)

Urea Nitrogen (BUN) (84520)

►(Do not use 80053 in addition to 80048, 80076)◄

►(80054 has been deleted. To report, use 80053)◄

**80055** Obstetric panel

This panel must include the following:

Hemogram, automated, and manual differential WBC count (CBC) (85022) OR

Hemogram and platelet count, automated, and automated complete differential WBC count (CBC) (85025)

Hepatitis B surface antigen (HBsAg) (87340)

Antibody, rubella (86762)

Syphilis test, qualitative (eg, VDRL, RPR, ART) (86592)

Antibody screen, RBC, each serum technique (86850)

Blood typing, ABO (86900) AND

Blood typing, Rh (D) (86901)

(80056 has been deleted. To report, see codes for specific tests)

(80057 has been deleted. To report, see codes for specific tests)

►(80058 has been deleted. To report, use 80076)◄

►(80059 has been deleted. To report, use 80074)◄

(80060 has been deleted. To report, see codes for specific tests)

**80061** Lipid panel

This panel must include the following:

Cholesterol, serum, total (82465)

Lipoprotein, direct measurement, high density cholesterol (HDL cholesterol) (83718)

Triglycerides (84478)

(80062 has been deleted. To report, see 80061 and/or codes for specific tests)

(80063 has been deleted. To report, see codes for specific tests)

(80064 has been deleted. To report, see codes for specific tests)

(80065 has been deleted. To report, see codes for specific tests)

(80066 has been deleted. To report, see codes for specific tests)

(80067 has been deleted. To report, see codes for specific tests)

(80068 has been deleted. To report, see codes for specific tests)

●**80069** Renal function panel

This panel must include the following:

Albumin (82040)

Calcium (82310)

Carbon dioxide (bicarbonate) (82374)

Chloride (82435)

Creatinine (82565)

Glucose (82947)

Phosphorus inorganic (phosphate) (84100)

Potassium (84132)

Sodium (84295)

Urea nitrogen (BUN) (84520)

(80070 has been deleted. To report, use 80091)

(80071 has been deleted. To report, see codes for specific tests)

**80072** Arthritis panel

This panel must include the following:

Uric acid, blood, chemical (84550)

Sedimentation rate, erythrocyte, non-automated (85651)

Fluorescent noninfectious agent, screen, each antibody (86255)

Rheumatoid factor, qualitative (86430)

(80073 has been deleted. To report, see codes for specific tests)

●**80074** Acute hepatitis panel

This panel must include the following:

Hepatitis A antibody (HAAb), IgM antibody (86709)

Hepatitis B core antibody (HbcAb), IgM antibody (86705)

Hepatitis B surface antigen (HbsAg) (87340)

Hepatitis C antibody (86803)

(80075 has been deleted. To report, see codes for specific tests)

●**80076** Hepatic function panel

This panel must include the following:

Albumin (82040)

Bilirubin, total (82247)

Bilirubin, direct (82248)

Phosphatase, alkaline (84075)

Protein, total (84155)

Transferase, alanine amino (ALT) (SGPT) (84460)

Transferase, aspartate amino (AST) (SGOT) (84450)

►(Do not use 80076 in addition to 80053)◄

(80080 has been deleted. To report PSA, use 84153)

(80082 has been deleted. To report, see codes for specific tests)

(80084 has been deleted. To report, see codes for specific tests)

(80085 has been deleted. To report, see codes for specific tests)

(80086 has been deleted. To report, see codes for specific tests)

(80088 has been deleted. To report, see codes for specific tests)

(80089 has been deleted. To report, see codes for specific tests)

**80090** TORCH antibody panel

This panel must include the following tests:

Antibody, cytomegalovirus (CMV) (86644)

Antibody, herpes simplex, non-specific type test (86694)

Antibody, rubella (86762)

Antibody, toxoplasma (86777)

►(80091 has been deleted. To report, see codes for specific tests)◄

►(80092 has been deleted. To report, see codes for specific test)◄

(80099 has been deleted. To report, see codes for specific tests)

## Drug Testing

The following list contains examples of drugs or classes of drugs that are commonly assayed by qualitative screen, followed by confirmation with a second method.

Alcohols

Amphetamines

Barbiturates

Benzodiazepines

Cocaine and Metabolites

Methadones

Methaqualones

Opiates

Phencyclidines

Phenothiazines

Propoxyphenes

Tetrahydrocannabinoids

Tricyclic Antidepressants

Confirmed drugs may also be quantitated. Qualitative screening tests are coded by procedure, not method or analyte. For example, if chromatography is being used, code each combination of stationary and mobile phases separately using 80100 if the analysis is designed to detect multiple drug classes or 80101 if the procedure is capable of detecting a single class of drugs.

Use 80102 for each procedure necessary for confirmation, eg, if confirmation of three drugs by chromatography requires three stationary or mobile phases, use 80102 three (3) times. However, if multiple drugs can be confirmed using a single analysis, use 80102 only once.

For quantitation of drugs screened, use appropriate code in **Chemistry** section (82000-84999) or **Therapeutic Drug Assay** section (80150-80299).

The following codes (80100-80103) should be used for testing of other drugs which may not be listed above.

**80100** Drug, screen; multiple drug classes, each procedure

**80101** single drug class, each drug class

**80102** Drug, confirmation, each procedure

**80103** Tissue preparation for drug analysis

## Therapeutic Drug Assays

The material for examination may be from any source. Examination is quantitative. For nonquantitative testing, see Drug Testing (80100-80103).

**80150** Amikacin

**80152** Amitriptyline

**80154** Benzodiazepines

**80156** Carbamazepine

**80158** Cyclosporine

**80160** Desipramine

**80162** Digoxin

**80164** Dipropylacetic acid (valproic acid)

**80166** Doxepin

**80168** Ethosuximide

**80170** Gentamicin

**80172** Gold

**80174** Imipramine

**80176** Lidocaine

**80178** Lithium

**80182** Nortriptyline

**80184** Phenobarbital

**80185** Phenytoin; total

**80186** free

**80188** Primidone

**80190** Procainamide;

**80192** with metabolites (eg, n-acetyl procainamide)

**80194** Quinidine

**80196** Salicylate

**80197** Tacrolimus

**80198** Theophylline

**80200** Tobramycin

**80201** Topiramate

**80202** Vancomycin

**80299** Quantitation of drug, not elsewhere specified

## Evocative/Suppression Testing

The following test panels involve the administration of evocative or suppressive agents, and the baseline and subsequent measurement of their effects on chemical constituents. These codes are to be used for the reporting of the laboratory component of the overall testing protocol. For the physician's administration of the evocative or suppressive agents, see 90780-90784; for the supplies and drugs, see 99070. To report physician attendance and monitoring during the testing, use the appropriate evaluation and management code, including the prolonged physician care codes if required. Prolonged physician care codes are not separately reported when evocative/suppression testing involves prolonged infusions reported with 90780 and 90781. In the code descriptors where reference is made to a particular analyte (eg, Cortisol (82533 x 2)) the "x 2" refers to the number of times the test for that particular analyte is performed.

**80400** ACTH stimulation panel; for adrenal insufficiency

This panel must include the following:

Cortisol (82533 x 2)

**80402** for 21 hydroxylase deficiency

This panel must include the following:

Cortisol (82533 x 2)

17 hydroxyprogesterone (83498 x 2)

**80406** for 3 beta-hydroxydehydrogenase deficiency

This panel must include the following:

Cortisol (82533 x 2)

17 hydroxypregnenolone (84143 x 2)

**80408** Aldosterone suppression evaluation panel (eg, saline infusion)

This panel must include the following:

Aldosterone (82088 x 2)

Renin (84244 x 2)

**80410** Calcitonin stimulation panel (eg, calcium, pentagastrin)

This panel must include the following:

Calcitonin (82308 x 3)

**80412** Corticotropic releasing hormone (CRH) stimulation panel

This panel must include the following:

Cortisol (82533 x 6)

Adrenocorticotropic hormone (ACTH) (82024 x 6)

**80414** Chorionic gonadotropin stimulation panel; testosterone response

This panel must include the following:

Testosterone (84403 x 2 on three pooled blood samples)

**80415** estradiol response

This panel must include the following:

Estradiol (82670 x 2 on three pooled blood samples)

**80416** Renal vein renin stimulation panel (eg, captopril)

This panel must include the following:

Renin (84244 x 6)

**80417** Peripheral vein renin stimulation panel (eg, captopril)

This panel must include the following:

Renin (84244 x 2)

**80418** Combined rapid anterior pituitary evaluation panel

This panel must include the following:

Adrenocorticotropic hormone (ACTH) (82024 x 4)

Luteinizing hormone (LH) (83002 x 4)

Follicle stimulating hormone (FSH) (83001 x 4)

Prolactin (84146 x 4)

Human growth hormone (HGH) (83003 x 4)

Cortisol (82533 x 4)

Thyroid stimulating hormone (TSH) (84443 x 4)

**80420** Dexamethasone suppression panel, 48 hour

This panel must include the following:

Free cortisol, urine (82530 x 2)

Cortisol (82533 x 2)

Volume measurement for timed collection (81050 x 2)

(For single dose dexamethasone, use 82533)

**80422** Glucagon tolerance panel; for insulinoma

This panel must include the following:

Glucose (82947 x 3)

Insulin (83525 x 3)

**80424** for pheochromocytoma

This panel must include the following:

Catecholamines, fractionated (82384 x 2)

**80426** Gonadotropin releasing hormone stimulation panel

This panel must include the following:

Follicle stimulating hormone (FSH) (83001 x 4)

Luteinizing hormone (LH) (83002 x 4)

**80428** Growth hormone stimulation panel (eg, arginine infusion, l-dopa administration)

This panel must include the following:

Human growth hormone (HGH) (83003 x 4)

**80430** Growth hormone suppression panel (glucose administration)

This panel must include the following:

Glucose (82947 x 3)

Human growth hormone (HGH) (83003 x 4)

**80432** Insulin-induced C-peptide suppression panel

This panel must include the following:

Insulin (83525)

C-peptide (84681 x 5)

Glucose (82947 x 5)

**80434** Insulin tolerance panel; for ACTH insufficiency

This panel must include the following:

Cortisol (82533 x 5)

Glucose (82947 x 5)

**80435** for growth hormone deficiency

This panel must include the following:

Glucose (82947 x 5)

Human growth hormone (HGH) (83003 x 5)

**80436** Metyrapone panel

This panel must include the following:

Cortisol (82533 x 2)

11 deoxycortisol (82634 x 2)

**80438** Thyrotropin releasing hormone (TRH) stimulation panel; one hour

This panel must include the following:

Thyroid stimulating hormone (TSH) (84443 x 3)

**80439** two hour

This panel must include the following:

Thyroid stimulating hormone (TSH) (84443 x 4)

**80440** for hyperprolactinemia

This panel must include the following:

Prolactin (84146 x 3)

## Consultations (Clinical Pathology)

A clinical pathology consultation is a service, including a written report, rendered by the pathologist in response to a request from an attending physician in relation to a test result(s) requiring additional medical interpretive judgment.

Reporting of a test result(s) without medical interpretive judgment is not considered a clinical pathology consultation.

**80500** Clinical pathology consultation; limited, without review of patients history and medical records

**80502** comprehensive, for a complex diagnostic problem, with review of patients history and medical records

(These codes may also be used for pharmacokinetic consultations)

(For consultations involving the examination and evaluation of the patient, see 99241-99275)

## Urinalysis

For specific analyses, see appropriate section.

**81000** Urinalysis, by dip stick or tablet reagent for bilirubin, glucose, hemoglobin, ketones, leukocytes, nitrite, pH, protein, specific gravity, urobilinogen, any number of these constituents; non-automated, with microscopy

**81001** automated, with microscopy

**81002** non-automated, without microscopy

**81003** automated, without microscopy

(81004 has been deleted. To report, use 81000)

**81005** Urinalysis; qualitative or semiquantitative, except immunoassays

(For non-immunoassay reagent strip urinalysis, see 81000, 81002)

(For immunoassay, qualitative or semiquantitative, use 83518)

(81006 has been deleted. To report, use 81099)

(For microalbumin, see 82043, 82044)

**81007** bacteriuria screen, by non-culture technique, commercial kit (specify type)

(81010, 81011, and 81012 have been deleted)

**81015** microscopic only

**81020** two or three glass test

**81025** Urine pregnancy test, by visual color comparison methods

(81030 has been deleted)

**81050** Volume measurement for timed collection, each

**81099** Unlisted urinalysis procedure

## Chemistry

The material for examination may be from any source. When an analyte is measured in multiple specimens from different sources, or in specimens that are obtained at different times, the analyte is reported separately for each source and for each specimen. The examination is quantitative unless specified. To report an organ or disease oriented panel, see codes 80048-80090.

When a code describes a method where measurement of multiple analytes may require one or several procedures, each procedure is coded separately (eg, 82491-82492, 82541-82544). For example, if two (2) analytes are measured using column chromatography using a single stationary or mobile phase, use 82492. If the same two analytes are measured using different stationary or mobile phase conditions, 82491 would be used twice. If a total of four (4) analytes are measured where two (2) analytes are measured with a single stationary and mobile phase, and the other two (2) analytes are measured using a different stationary and mobile phase, use 82492 twice. If a total of three (3) analytes are measured where two (2) analytes are measured using a single stationary or mobile phase condition, and the third analyte is measured separately using a different stationary or mobile phase procedure, use 82492 once for the (2) analytes measured under the same condition, and use 82491 once for the third analyte measured separately.

Clinical information derived from the results of laboratory data that is mathematically calculated (eg, free thyroxine index (T7)) is considered part of the test procedure and therefore is not a separately reportable service.

**82000** Acetaldehyde, blood

**82003** Acetaminophen

(82005 has been deleted)

**82009** Acetone or other ketone bodies, serum; qualitative

**82010** quantitative

(82011 has been deleted. To report, use 80196)

(82012 has been deleted)

**82013** Acetylcholinesterase

(Acid, gastric, see gastric acid, 82926, 82928)

(Acid phosphatase, see 84060-84066)

(82015 has been deleted)

**82016** Acylcarnitines; qualitative, each specimen

**82017** quantitative, each specimen

►(For carnitine, use 82379)◄

**82024** Adrenocorticotropic hormone (ACTH)

**82030** Adenosine, 5-monophosphate, cyclic (cyclic AMP)

(82035 has been deleted)

**82040** Albumin; serum

**82042** urine, quantitative

**82043** urine, microalbumin, quantitative

**82044** urine, microalbumin, semiquantitative (eg, reagent strip assay)

(For prealbumin, use 84134)

**82055** Alcohol (ethanol); any specimen except breath

(For other volatiles, alcohol, use 84600)

(82060, 82065, 82070 have been deleted. To report, use 82055)

(82072 has been deleted)

**82075** breath

(82076, 82078 have been deleted. For ethanol, use 82055; for volatiles, use 84600)

**82085** Aldolase

(82086 has been deleted. To report, use 82085)

(82087 has been deleted. To report, use 82088)

**82088** Aldosterone

(82089 has been deleted. To report, use 82088)

(82091 has been deleted. To report, use 80408)

(82095 has been deleted. To report, see 80100, 80101, and 80103)

(82096 has been deleted. To report, use code for specific drug and 80103)

(82100 has been deleted. To report, use 80100 and 80101)

(Alkaline phosphatase, see 84075, 84080)

**82101** Alkaloids, urine, quantitative

(Alphaketoglutarate, see 82009, 82010)

(Alpha tocopherol (Vitamin E), use 84446)

**82103** Alpha-1-antitrypsin; total

**82104** phenotype

**82105** Alpha-fetoprotein; serum

**82106** amniotic fluid

**82108** Aluminum

(82112 has been deleted. To report, use 80150)

(82126 has been deleted)

●**82120** Amines, vaginal fluid, qualitative

►(For combined pH and amines test for vaginitis, use 82120 and 83986)◄

**82127** Amino acids; single, qualitative, each specimen

**82128** multiple, qualitative, each specimen

(82130 has been deleted. To report, see 82131, 82136, 82139)

**82131** single, quantitative, each specimen

(82134 has been deleted)

**82135** Aminolevulinic acid, delta (ALA)

**82136** Amino acids, 2 to 5 amino acids, quantitative, each specimen

(82137 has been deleted. To report, use 80198)

(82138 has been deleted. To report, use 80152)

**82139** Amino acids, 6 or more amino acids, quantitative, each specimen

**82140** Ammonia

(82141 has been deleted. To report, use 82140)

(82142 has been deleted)

**82143** Amniotic fluid scan (spectrophotometric)

(For L/S ratio, use 83661)

(Amobarbital, see 80100-80103 for qualitative analysis, 82205 for quantitative analysis)

**82145** Amphetamine or methamphetamine

(For qualitative analysis, see 80100-80103)

**82150** Amylase

**82154** Androstanediol glucuronide

(82155 has been deleted)

(82156 has been deleted. To report, use 82150)

**82157** Androstenedione

(82159 has been deleted. To report, use 82160)

**82160** Androsterone

**82163** Angiotensin II

**82164** Angiotensin I - converting enzyme (ACE)

(82165 has been deleted)

(Antidiuretic hormone (ADH), use 84588)

(82168 has been deleted. For antihistamines, see code for specific method)

(82170 has been deleted. To report, see 83015, 83018)

(Antimony, use 83015)

(Antitrypsin, alpha-1-, see 82103, 82104)

**82172** Apolipoprotein, each

(82173 has been deleted. To report, use 80428)

**82175** Arsenic

(For heavy metal screening, see 83015)

**82180** Ascorbic acid (Vitamin C), blood

(Aspirin, see acetylsalicylic acid, 80196)

(Atherogenic index, blood, ultracentrifugation, quantitative, use 83717)

**82190** Atomic absorption spectroscopy, each analyte

**82205** Barbiturates, not elsewhere specified

(For qualitative analysis, see 80100-80103)

(82210 has been deleted. To report, see 80100-80103, 82205)

(82225, 82230 have been deleted. To report, see 83015, 83018)

(82231 has been deleted. To report, use 82232)

**82232** Beta-2 microglobulin

(82235, 82236 have been deleted)

(Bicarbonate, use 82374)

**82239** Bile acids; total

**82240** cholylglycine

(For bile pigments, urine, see 81000-81005)

(82245 has been deleted. To report, see 81000, 81002, 81005)

**82247** Bilirubin; total

**82248** direct

(82250 has been deleted. To report, see 82247, 82248 as appropriate)

**82251** total AND direct

**82252** feces, qualitative

(82260 has been deleted. To report, ►see 81000-81003, 82247, 82248, 82251◄)

**82261** Biotinidase, each specimen

(82265 has been deleted. To report spectrophotometric scan, use 82143)

(82268 has been deleted. To report, see 83015, 83018)

**82270** Blood, occult; feces, 1-3 simultaneous determinations

**82273** other sources, qualitative

(Blood urea nitrogen (BUN), see 84520, 84525)

(82280, 82285 have been deleted. To report, see code for specific method)

**82286** Bradykinin

(82290, 82291 have been deleted. To report, use 84311)

**82300** Cadmium

(82305 has been deleted. To report, see 82486, 82491)

**82306** Calcifediol (25-OH Vitamin D-3)

**82307** Calciferol (Vitamin D)

(For 1,25-Dihydroxyvitamin D, use 82652)

**82308** Calcitonin

**82310** Calcium; total

(82315, 82320, 82325 have been deleted. To report, use 82310)

**82330** ionized

**82331** after calcium infusion test

(82335 has been deleted)

**82340** urine quantitative, timed specimen

(82345 has been deleted)

**82355** Calculus (stone); qualitative analysis

**82360** quantitative analysis, chemical

**82365** infrared spectroscopy

**82370** x-ray diffraction

(82372 has been deleted. To report, use 80156)

(Carbamates, see individual listings)

**82374** Carbon dioxide (bicarbonate)

(See also 82803)

**82375** Carbon monoxide, (carboxyhemoglobin); quantitative

**82376** qualitative

**82378** Carcinoembryonic antigen (CEA)

**82379** Carnitine (total and free), quantitative, each specimen

(For acylcarnitine, see 82016, 82017)

**82380** Carotene

**82382** Catecholamines; total urine

**82383** blood

**82384** fractionated

(For urine metabolites, see 83835, 84585)

**82387** Cathepsin-D

**82390** Ceruloplasmin

**82397** Chemiluminescent assay

(82400 has been deleted. To report, see code for specific method)

(82405 has been deleted)

**82415** Chloramphenicol

(82418, 82420, 82425 have been deleted. To report, see code for specific method)

**82435** Chloride; blood

**82436** urine

(82437 has been deleted)

**82438** other source

(For sweat collection by iontophoresis, use 89360)

**82441** Chlorinated hydrocarbons, screen

(82443 has been deleted. To report, see code for specific method)

(Chlorpromazine, use 84022)

(Cholecalciferol (Vitamin D), use 82307)

**82465** Cholesterol, serum, total

(For high density lipoprotein (HDL), use 83718)

(82470 has been deleted)

**82480** Cholinesterase; serum

**82482** RBC

(82484 has been deleted. To report, use 82480 and 82482)

**82485** Chondroitin B sulfate, quantitative

(Chorionic gonadotropin, see gonadotropin, 84702, 84703)

**82486** Chromatography, qualitative; column (eg, gas liquid or HPLC), analyte not elsewhere specified

**82487** paper, 1-dimensional, analyte not elsewhere specified

**82488** paper, 2-dimensional, analyte not elsewhere specified

**82489** thin layer, analyte not elsewhere specified

(82490 has been deleted)

**82491** Chromatography, quantitative, column (eg, gas liquid or HPLC); single analyte not elsewhere specified, single stationary and mobile phase

**82492** multiple analytes, single stationary and mobile phase

**82495** Chromium

(82505 has been deleted)

**82507** Citrate

(82512 has been deleted. To report, use 80154)

**82520** Cocaine or metabolite

(Cocaine, qualitative analysis, see 80100-80103)

(Codeine, qualitative analysis, see 80100-80103)

(Codeine, quantitative analysis, see 82101)

(Complement, see 86160-86162)

**82523** Collagen cross links, any method

**82525** Copper

(82526 has been deleted. To report, use 82525)

(Coproporphyrin, see 84119, 84120)

(Corticosteroids, use 83491)

**82528** Corticosterone

(82529 has been deleted. To report, use 82533)

**82530** Cortisol; free

(82531, 82532 have been deleted)

**82533** total

(82534 has been deleted. To report, use 82533)

(82536 has been deleted. To report, see 80400-80406)

(82537 has been deleted. To report, see 80400-80406)

(82538 has been deleted. To report, use 80436)

(82539 has been deleted. To report, use 80420)

(C-peptide, use 84681)

**82540** Creatine

**82541** Column chromatography/mass spectometry (eg, GC/MS, or HPLC/MS), analyte not elsewhere specified; qualitative, single stationary and mobile phase

**82542** quantitative, single stationary and mobile phase

**82543** stable isotope dilution, single analyte, quantitative, single stationary and mobile phase

**82544** stable isotope dilution, multiple analytes, quantitative, single stationary and mobile phase

(82545 has been deleted. To report, use 82540)

(82546 has been deleted. To report, see 82540, 82565)

**82550** Creatine kinase (CK), (CPK); total

**82552** isoenzymes

**82553** MB fraction only

**82554** isoforms

(82555 has been deleted)

**82565** Creatinine; blood

**82570** other source

**82575** clearance

**82585** Cryofibrinogen

**82595** Cryoglobulin

(Crystals, pyrophosphate vs. urate, use 89060)

**82600** Cyanide

(82601 has been deleted. To report, see 80103, 82600)

(82606 has been deleted)

**82607** Cyanocobalamin (Vitamin B-12);

**82608** unsaturated binding capacity

(Cyclic AMP, use 82030)

(Cyclic GMP, use 83008)

(Cyclosporine, use 80158)

(82610, 82614 have been deleted)

**82615** Cystine and homocystine, urine, qualitative

(82620 has been deleted. For cystine and homocystine, quantitative, use 82130)

(82624 has been deleted)

**82626** Dehydroepiandrosterone (DHEA)

**82627** Dehydroepiandrosterone-sulfate (DHEA-S)

(82628 has been deleted. To report, see 80100-80103 for qualitative analysis; see 80160 for quantitative analysis)

(Delta-aminolevulinic acid (ALA), use 82135)

**82633** Desoxycorticosterone, 11-

**82634** Deoxycortisol, 11-

(Dexamethasone suppression test, use 80420)

(82635 has been deleted)

(Diastase, urine, use 82150)

(82636 has been deleted. To report, see 80100-80103, 80154)

**82638** Dibucaine number

(82639 has been deleted. To report, use code for specific method)

(Dichloroethane, use 84600)

(Dichloromethane, use 84600)

(Diethylether, use 84600)

(82640, 82641 have been deleted)

(82643 has been deleted. To report, use 80162)

**82646** Dihydrocodeinone

(For qualitative analysis, see 80100-80103)

**82649** Dihydromorphinone

(For qualitative analysis, see 80100-80103)

**82651** Dihydrotestosterone (DHT)

**82652** Dihydroxyvitamin D, 1,25-

**82654** Dimethadione

(For qualitative analysis, see 80100-80103)

(Diphenylhydantoin, use 80185)

(Dipropylacetic acid, use 80164)

(Dopamine, see 82382-82384)

(82656 has been deleted. To report, use 80166)

(Duodenal contents, see individual enzymes; for intubation and collection, use 89100)

**82657** Enzyme activity in blood cells, cultured cells, or tissue, not elsewhere specified; nonradioactive substrate, each specimen

**82658** radioactive substrate, each specimen

(82660 has been deleted. To report, see 80100, 80101)

(82662 has been deleted. To report, see 80100-80103)

**82664** Electrophoretic technique, not elsewhere specified

(Endocrine receptor assays, see 84233-84235)

**82666** Epiandrosterone

(Epinephrine, see 82382-82384)

**82668** Erythropoietin

**82670** Estradiol

**82671** Estrogens; fractionated

**82672** total

(82673, 82674, 82676 have been deleted. To report, use 82677)

(Estrogen receptor assay, use 84233)

**82677** Estriol

(82678 has been deleted. To report, use 82679)

**82679** Estrone

(Ethanol, see 82055 and 82075)

**82690** Ethchlorvynol

(82691 has been deleted. To report, use 82690)

(82692 has been deleted. To report, use 80168)

(Ethyl alcohol, see 82055 and 82075)

**82693** Ethylene glycol

(82694 has been deleted. To report, use 82696)

**82696** Etiocholanolone

(For fractionation of ketosteroids, use 83593)

**82705** Fat or lipids, feces; qualitative

**82710** quantitative

**82715** Fat differential, feces, quantitative

(82720 has been deleted)

**82725** Fatty acids, nonesterified

**82726** Very long chain fatty acids

(82727 has been deleted. To report ferric chloride test, urine, use 81005)

**82728** Ferritin

(Fetal hemoglobin, see hemoglobin 83030, 83033, and 85460)

(Fetoprotein, alpha-1, see 82105, 82106)

(82730 has been deleted. To report fibrinogen, see 85384, 85385)

**82731** Fetal fibronectin, cervicovaginal secretions, semi-quantitative

**82735** Fluoride

(82740 has been deleted. To report, use 82735)

(82741 has been deleted. To report, see code for specific method)

**82742** Flurazepam

(For qualitative analysis, see 80100-80103)

(Foam stability test, use 83662)

(82745 has been deleted)

**82746** Folic acid; serum

**82747** RBC

(Follicle stimulating hormone (FSH), use 83001)

(82750 has been deleted. To report, see code for specific method)

(82755, 82756 have been deleted)

**82757** Fructose, semen

(Fructosamine, use 82985)

(Fructose, TLC screen, use 84375)

**82759** Galactokinase, RBC

**82760** Galactose

(82763 has been deleted. To report, use 82760 and codes for administration)

(82765 has been deleted. To report, use 82760)

**82775** Galactose-1-phosphate uridyl transferase; quantitative

**82776** screen

(82780 has been deleted. To report gallium, see code for specific method)

**82784** Gammaglobulin; IgA, IgD, IgG, IgM, each

**82785** IgE

(For allergen specific IgE, see 86003, 86005)

(82786 has been deleted)

**82787** immunoglobulin subclasses, (IgG1, 2, 3, and 4)

(Gamma-glutamyltransferase (GGT), use 82977)

(82790, 82791 have been deleted)

(82792 has been deleted. To report, see 82805, 82810)

(82793, 82795 have been deleted)

**82800** Gases, blood, pH only

(82801, 82802 have been deleted. To report, use 82803)

**82803** Gases, blood, any combination of pH, $pCO_2$, $pO_2$, $CO_2$, $HCO_3$ (including calculated $O_2$ saturation);

(Use 82803 for two or more of the above listed analytes)

(82804 has been deleted. To report, use 82803)

**82805** with $O_2$ saturation, by direct measurement, except pulse oximetry

**82810** Gases, blood, $O_2$ saturation only, by direct measurement, except pulse oximetry

(For pulse oximetry, use 94760)

(82812 has been deleted. To report, use 82803)

(82817 has been deleted. To report, use 82803)

**82820** Hemoglobin-oxygen affinity ($pO_2$ for 50% hemoglobin saturation with oxygen)

**82926** Gastric acid, free and total, each specimen

(82927 has been deleted. To report, use 82926)

**82928** Gastric acid, free or total; each specimen

(82929, 82931, and 82932 have been deleted. To report, use 82928)

**82938** Gastrin after secretin stimulation

**82941** Gastrin

(Gentamicin, use 80170)

(GGT, use 82977)

(GLC, gas liquid chromatography, use 82486)

(82942 has been deleted)

**82943** Glucagon

(82944 has been deleted)

**82946** Glucagon tolerance test

**82947** Glucose; quantitative

**82948** blood, reagent strip

(82949 has been deleted)

**82950** post glucose dose (includes glucose)

**82951** tolerance test (GTT), three specimens (includes glucose)

**82952** tolerance test, each additional beyond three specimens

**82953** tolbutamide tolerance test

(For insulin tolerance test, see 80434, 80435)

(For leucine tolerance test, use 80428)

(For semiquantitative urine glucose, see 81000, 81002, 81005, 81099)

(82954 has been deleted. To report, use 82947)

**82955** Glucose-6-phosphate dehydrogenase (G6PD); quantitative

**82960** screen

(82961 has been deleted)

(For glucose tolerance test with medication, use 90784 in addition)

**82962** Glucose, blood by glucose monitoring device(s) cleared by the FDA specifically for home use

**82963** Glucosidase, beta

**82965** Glutamate dehydrogenase

**82975** Glutamine (glutamic acid amide)

**82977** Glutamyltransferase, gamma (GGT)

**82978** Glutathione

**82979** Glutathione reductase, RBC

**82980** Glutethimide

(Glycohemoglobin, use 83036)

**82985** Glycated protein

(82995 has been deleted. To report, use 80172)

(82996-82998 have been deleted. To report, see 84702, 84703)

(Gonadotropin, chorionic, see 84702, 84703)

(83000 has been deleted)

**83001** Gonadotropin; follicle stimulating hormone (FSH)

**83002** luteinizing hormone (LH)

(For luteinizing releasing factor (LRH), use 83727)

**83003** Growth hormone, human (HGH) (somatotropin)

(83004 has been deleted. To report, use 80430)

(For antibody to human growth hormone, use 86277)

(83005 has been deleted)

**83008** Guanosine monophosphate (GMP), cyclic

**83010** Haptoglobin; quantitative

(83011 has been deleted. To report, use 83010)

**83012** phenotypes

**▲83013** Helicobacter pylori, breath test analysis (mass spectrometry);

**83014** drug administration and sample collection

**83015** Heavy metal (arsenic, barium, beryllium, bismuth, antimony, mercury); screen

**83018** quantitative, each

(83019 has been deleted. To report, see 83013, 83014)

**83020** Hemoglobin fractionation and quantitation; electrophoresis (eg, A2, S, C, and/or F)

**83021** chromotography (eg, A2, S, C, and/or F)

**83026** Hemoglobin; by copper sulfate method, non-automated

**83030** F (fetal), chemical

**83033** F (fetal), qualitative (APT) test, fecal

**83036** glycated

(83040 has been deleted. To report, use 83050)

**83045** methemoglobin, qualitative

**83050** methemoglobin, quantitative

**83051** plasma

(83052, 83053 have been deleted. To report, use 85660)

**83055** sulfhemoglobin, qualitative

**83060** sulfhemoglobin, quantitative

**83065** thermolabile

**83068** unstable, screen

**83069** urine

**83070** Hemosiderin; qualitative

**83071** quantitative

(Heroin, see 80100-80103)

(HIAA, use 83497)

(High performance liquid chromatography (HPLC), use 82486)

**83080** b-Hexosaminidase, each assay

(83086, 83087 have been deleted. To report, use 82128)

**83088** Histamine

(Hollander test, use 91052)

(Homocystine, see 82128, 82130)

(83093, 83095 have been deleted. For homogentisic acid, qualitative urine screen, see 81005. For quantitative assay, see code for specific method)

**83150** Homovanillic acid (HVA)

(Hormones, see individual alphabetic listings in **Chemistry** section)

(Hydrogen breath test, use 91065)

(83485, 83486 have been deleted)

**83491** Hydroxycorticosteroids, 17- (17-OHCS)

(For cortisol, see 82530, 82533. For deoxycortisol, use 82634)

(83492 has been deleted. To report, use 83491)

(83493 has been deleted)

(83494-83496 have been deleted. To report, use 83491)

**83497** Hydroxyindolacetic acid, 5-(HIAA)

(For urine qualitative test, use 81005)

(5-Hydroxytryptamine, use 84260)

**83498** Hydroxyprogesterone, 17-d

**83499** Hydroxyprogesterone, 20-

**83500** Hydroxyproline; free

**83505** total

(83510 has been deleted. To report, use 83500 and 83505)

**83516** Immunoassay for analyte other than infectious agent antibody or infectious agent antigen, qualitative or semiquantitative; multiple step method

**83518** single step method (eg, reagent strip)

**83519** Immunoassay, analyte, quantitative; by radiopharmaceutical technique (eg, RIA)

**83520** not otherwise specified

(83523 has been deleted. To report, use 80174)

(For immunoassays for antibodies to infectious agent antigens, see analyte and method specific codes in the **Immunology** section)

(For immunoassay of tumor antigen not elsewhere specified, use 86316)

(Immunoglobulins, see 82784, 82785)

(83524 has been deleted)

**83525** Insulin; total

(For proinsulin, use 84206)

(83526 has been deleted. To report, see 80434, 80435)

**83527** free

**83528** Intrinsic factor

(For intrinsic factor antibodies, use 86340)

(83530 has been deleted)

(83533, 83534 have been deleted. To report, use 84999)

**83540** Iron

(83545, 83546 have been deleted. To report, use 83540)

**83550** Iron binding capacity

(83555, 83565 have been deleted. To report, use 83550)

**83570** Isocitric dehydrogenase (IDH)

(Isonicotinic acid hydrazide, INH, see code for specific method)

(Isopropyl alcohol, use 84600)

(83571 has been deleted. To report, use 83570)

(83576 has been deleted. To report, see code for specific method)

(83578 has been deleted)

**83582** Ketogenic steroids, fractionation

(83583, 83584 have been deleted)

(Ketone bodies, for serum, see 82009, 82010; for urine, see 81000-81003)

**83586** Ketosteroids, 17- (17-KS); total

(83587 has been deleted. To report, use 83593)

(83588, 83589 have been deleted. To report, use 83586)

(83590 has been deleted)

**83593** fractionation

(83596 has been deleted)

(83597 has been deleted)

(83599 has been deleted. To report, use 83586)

(83600 has been deleted. To report, see code for specific method)

**83605** Lactate (lactic acid)

(83610 has been deleted. To report, use 83615)

**83615** Lactate dehydrogenase (LD), (LDH);

(83620 has been deleted. To report, use 83615)

(83624 has been deleted)

**83625** isoenzymes, separation and quantitation

(83626 has been deleted)

(83628 has been deleted. To report, use 83625)

(83629, 83631 have been deleted. To report, use 83615)

**83632** Lactogen, human placental (HPL) human chorionic somatomammotropin

**83633** Lactose, urine; qualitative

**83634** quantitative

(For tolerance, see 82951, 82952)

(For breath hydrogen test for lactase deficiency, use 91065)

(83645 has been deleted. To report, see quantitative code or screening for toxicity)

(83650 has been deleted)

**83655** Lead

(83660 has been deleted. To report, use 83655)

**83661** Lecithin-sphingomyelin ratio (L/S ratio); quantitative

**83662** foam stability test

**83670** Leucine aminopeptidase (LAP)

(83675, 83680 have been deleted. To report, use 83670)

(83681 has been deleted. To report, use 80428)

(83685 has been deleted. To report, use 80176)

**83690** Lipase

(83700, 83705 have been deleted. For cholesterol, see 82465, 83718-83721. For triglycerides, use 84478)

**83715** Lipoprotein, blood; electrophoretic separation and quantitation

**83716** high resolution fractionation and quantitation of lipoprotein cholesterols (eg, electrophoresis, nuclear magnetic resonance, ultracentrifugation)

(83717 has been deleted. To report, use 83716)

**83718** Lipoprotein, direct measurement; high density cholesterol (HDL cholesterol)

**83719** direct measurement, VLDL cholesterol

(83720 has been deleted)

**83721** direct measurement, LDL cholesterol

(For fractionation by nuclear magnetic resonance or high resolution electrophoresis, use 83716)

(Luteinizing hormone (LH), use 83002)

(83725 has been deleted. To report, use 80178)

**83727** Luteinizing releasing factor (LRH)

(83728 has been deleted. To report, see 80100-80103, 80299)

(83730 has been deleted)

(For qualitative analysis, see 80100-80103)

(Macroglobulins, alpha-2, use 86329)

**83735** Magnesium

(83740, 83750, 83755, 83760, 83765 have been deleted. To report, use 83735)

**83775** Malate dehydrogenase

(Maltose tolerance, see 82951, 82952)

(Mammotropin, use 84146)

**83785** Manganese

(83790 has been deleted)

(Marijuana, see 80100-80103)

(83795 has been deleted)

(83799 has been deleted. To report, use 83925)

**83788** Mass spectrometry and tandem mass spectrometry (MS, MS/MS), analyte not elsewhere specified; qualitative, each specimen

**83789** quantitative, each specimen

**83805** Meprobamate

(For qualitative analysis, see 80100-80103)

**83825** Mercury, quantitative

(83830 has been deleted. To report, use 83825)

(Mercury screen, use 83015)

**83835** Metanephrines

(For catecholamines, see 82382-82384)

**83840** Methadone

(For methadone qualitative analysis, see 80100-80103)

(Methamphetamine, see 80100-80103, 82145)

(Methanol, use 84600)

(83842 has been deleted. To report, see code for specific method)

(83845 has been deleted. To report, see 80101-80103)

**83857** Methemalbumin

(Methemoglobin, see hemoglobin 83045, 83050)

**83858** Methsuximide

(Methyl alcohol, use 84600)

(Microalbumin, see 82043 for quantitative, see 82044 for semiquantitative)

(Microglobulin, beta-2, use 82232)

(83859 has been deleted)

(83860-83862 have been deleted. To report, see 80100-80103 for qualitative analysis, 83925 for quantitative analysis)

**83864** Mucopolysaccharides, acid; quantitative

(83865 has been deleted. To report, use 83864)

**83866** screen

(83870 has been deleted. To report, use 84999)

**83872** Mucin, synovial fluid (Ropes test)

**83873** Myelin basic protein, CSF

(For oligoclonal bands, use 83916)

**83874** Myoglobin

(83875 has been deleted)

(83880 has been deleted. To report, use 83925)

**83883** Nephelometry, each analyte not elsewhere specified

**83885** Nickel

**83887** Nicotine

Codes 83890-83912 are intended for use with molecular diagnostic techniques for analysis of nucleic acids.

Codes 83890-83912 are coded by procedure rather than analyte.

Code separately for each procedure used in an analysis. For example, a procedure requiring isolation of DNA, restriction endonuclease digestion, electrophoresis, and nucleic acid probe amplification would be coded 83890, 83892, 83894, and 83898.

(For microbial identification, see 87797, 87798)

**83890** Molecular diagnostics; molecular isolation or extraction

**83891** isolation or extraction of highly purified nucleic acid

**83892** enzymatic digestion

**83893** dot/slot blot production

**83894** separation by gel electrophoresis (eg, agarose, polyacrylamide)

(83895 has been deleted)

**83896** nucleic acid probe, each

**83897** nucleic acid transfer (eg, Southern, Northern)

**83898** amplification of patient nucleic acid (eg, PCR, LCR, RT-PCR), single primer pair, each primer pair

(83900 has been deleted)

**83901** amplification of patient nucleic acid, multiplex, each multiplex reaction

**83902** reverse transcription

**83903** mutation scanning, by physical properties (eg, single strand conformational polymorphisms (SSCP), heteroduplex, denaturing gradient gel electrophoresis (DGGE), RNA'ase A), single segment, each

**83904** mutation identification by sequencing, single segment, each segment

**83905** mutation identification by allele specific transcription, single segment, each segment

**83906** mutation identification by allele specific translation, single segment, each segment

(83910 has been deleted)

**83912** interpretation and report

(83913 has been deleted. To report, use 83898)

**83915** Nucleotidase 5-

**83916** Oligoclonal immunoglobulin (oligoclonal bands)

(83917 has been deleted)

**83918** Organic acids; quantitative, each specimen

**83919** qualitative, each specimen

(83920 has been deleted. To report, use code for specific method)

**83925** Opiates, (eg, morphine, meperidine)

**83930** Osmolality; blood

**83935** urine

**83937** Osteocalcin (bone g1a protein)

(83938 has been deleted)

**83945** Oxalate

(83946 has been deleted. To report, use 80154)

(83947 has been deleted. To report, see 82009, 82010)

(83948 has been deleted. To report, see 80100-80103, 83925)

(83949 has been deleted)

(83965 has been deleted. To report, see code for specific method)

**83970** Parathormone (parathyroid hormone)

(83971, 83972 have been deleted. To report, see code for specific method)

(83973 has been deleted. To report, use 84375)

(83974 has been deleted)

(83975, 83985 have been deleted. To report, see code for specific method)

(Pesticide, quantitative, see code for specific method. For screen for chlorinated hydrocarbons, use 82441)

**83986** pH, body fluid, except blood

(For blood pH, see 82800, 82803)

**83992** Phencyclidine (PCP)

(For qualitative analysis, see 80100-80103)

(Phenobarbital, use 80184)

(83995 has been deleted. To report, see code for specific method)

(84005 has been deleted)

(84021 has been deleted. To report, see 80100, 80101, 84022)

**84022** Phenothiazine

(For qualitative analysis, see 80100, 80101)

**84030** Phenylalanine (PKU), blood

(Phenylalanine-tyrosine ratio, see 84030, 84510)

(84031 has been deleted)

(84033 has been deleted. To report, see code for specific method)

**84035** Phenylketones, qualitative

(84037 has been deleted. To report, use 84035)

(84038 has been deleted. To report, see code for specific method)

(84039, 84040 have been deleted)

(84045 has been deleted. To report, see 80185, 80186)

**84060** Phosphatase, acid; total

**84061** forensic examination

(84065 has been deleted. To report, use 84066)

**84066** prostatic

**84075** Phosphatase, alkaline;

**84078** heat stable (total not included)

**84080** isoenzymes

**84081** Phosphatidylglycerol

(84082 has been deleted)

(Phosphates inorganic, use 84100)

(Phosphates, organic, see code for specific method. For cholinesterase, see 82480, 82482)

(84083 has been deleted)

**84085** Phosphogluconate, 6-, dehydrogenase, RBC

**84087** Phosphohexose isomerase

(84090 has been deleted)

**84100** Phosphorus inorganic (phosphate);

**84105** urine

(Pituitary gonadotropins, see 83001-83002)

(PKU, see 84030, 84035)

**84106** Porphobilinogen, urine; qualitative

**84110** quantitative

(84118 has been deleted. To report, use 84120)

**84119** Porphyrins, urine; qualitative

**84120** quantitation and fractionation

(84121 has been deleted. To report, use 84120)

**84126** Porphyrins, feces; quantitative

**84127** qualitative

(84128 has been deleted)

(Porphyrin precursors, see 82135, 84106, 84110)

(For protoporphyrin, RBC, see 84202, 84203)

**84132** Potassium; serum

**84133** urine

**84134** Prealbumin

(For microalbumin, see 82043, 82044)

**84135** Pregnanediol

(84136 has been deleted. To report, use 84135)

**84138** Pregnanetriol

(84139 has been deleted. To report, use 84138)

**84140** Pregnenolone

(84141 has been deleted. To report, use 80188)

(84142 has been deleted. To report, see 80190, 80192)

**84143** 17-hydroxypregnenolone

**84144** Progesterone

(Progesterone receptor assay, use 84234)

(For proinsulin, use 84206)

**84146** Prolactin

(84147 has been deleted. To report, see 80100-80103)

(84149 has been deleted)

**84150** Prostaglandin, each

**84153** Prostate specific antigen (PSA); total

**84154** free

**84155** Protein; total, except refractometry

**84160** refractometric

**84165** electrophoretic fractionation and quantitation

(84170 has been deleted)

(84175 has been deleted. To report, use 84165)

(84176 has been deleted)

(84180 has been deleted. To report, use 81050 and 84155)

**84181** Western Blot, with interpretation and report, blood or other body fluid

**84182** Western Blot, with interpretation and report, blood or other body fluid, immunological probe for band identification, each

(For Western Blot tissue analysis, use 88371)

(84185 has been deleted)

(84190 has been deleted. To report, use 84165)

(84195 has been deleted)

(84200 has been deleted. To report, use 84165)

(84201 has been deleted. To report, see 80438, 80439)

**84202** Protoporphyrin, RBC; quantitative

**84203** screen

(84205 has been deleted. To report, use code for specific method)

**84206** Proinsulin

(Pseudocholinesterase, use 82480)

**84207** Pyridoxal phosphate (Vitamin B-6)

(84208 has been deleted. To report, use 89060)

**84210** Pyruvate

**84220** Pyruvate kinase

**84228** Quinine

(84230 has been deleted. To report, use 80194)

(84231 has been deleted. To report radioimmunoassay not elsewhere specified, use 83519)

(84232 has been deleted)

**84233** Receptor assay; estrogen

**84234** progesterone

**84235** endocrine, other than estrogen or progesterone (specify hormone)

(84236 has been deleted. To report, use 84233 and 84234)

**84238** non-endocrine (eg, acetylcholine) (specify receptor)

**84244** Renin

(84246 has been deleted)

(84250, 84251 have been deleted. To report, use 84479)

**84252** Riboflavin (Vitamin B-2)

(Salicylates, use 80196)

(Secretin test, see 99070, 89100 and appropriate analyses)

**84255** Selenium

**84260** Serotonin

(For urine metabolites (HIAA), use 83497)

**84270** Sex hormone binding globulin (SHBG)

**84275** Sialic acid

(Sickle hemoglobin, use 85660)

**84285** Silica

**84295** Sodium; serum

**84300** urine

(Somatomammotropin, use 83632)

(Somatotropin, use 83003)

**84305** Somatomedin

**84307** Somatostatin

(84310 has been deleted)

**84311** Spectrophotometry, analyte not elsewhere specified

**84315** Specific gravity (except urine)

(For specific gravity, urine, see 81000-81003)

(84317 has been deleted)

(84318 has been deleted)

(Stone analysis, see 82355-82370)

(84324 has been deleted. To report, see code for specific method)

**84375** Sugars, chromatographic, TLC or paper chromatography

(Sulfhemoglobin, see hemoglobin, 83055, 83060)

(84382 has been deleted)

**84376** Sugars (mon-, di, and oligosaccharides); single qualitative, each specimen

**84377** multiple qualitative, each specimen

**84378** single quantitative, each specimen

**84379** multiple quantitative, each specimen

**84392** Sulfate, urine

(84395 has been deleted)

(84397 has been deleted)

(T-3, see 84479-84481)

(T-4, see 84436-84439)

(84401 has been deleted)

**84402** Testosterone; free

**84403** total

(84404 has been deleted)

(84405 has been deleted. To report, use 84403)

(84406 has been deleted. For testosterone binding protein, use sex hormone binding globulin, 84270)

(84407 has been deleted. To report, see code for specific method)

(84408 has been deleted. To report, see 80100-80103, 80299)

(84409, 84410 have been deleted. To report, see code for specific method)

(84420 has been deleted. To report, use 80198)

**84425** Thiamine (Vitamin B-1)

**84430** Thiocyanate

**84432** Thyroglobulin

(Thyroglobulin, antibody, use 86800)

(84434 has been deleted. To report, use 84022)

(Thyrotropin releasing hormone (TRH) test, see 80438, 80439)

(84435 has been deleted. To report, use 84436)

**84436** Thyroxine; total

**84437** requiring elution (eg, neonatal)

**84439** free

(84441 has been deleted. To report, see 84436-84439)

**84442** Thyroxine binding globulin (TBG)

**84443** Thyroid stimulating hormone (TSH)

(84444 has been deleted. To report, see 80438, 80439)

**84445** Thyroid stimulating immunoglobulins (TSI)

(Tobramycin, use 80200)

**84446** Tocopherol alpha (Vitamin E)

(Tolbutamide tolerance, use 82953)

(84447, 84448 have been deleted. To report, see 80100-80103)

**84449** Transcortin (cortisol binding globulin)

**84450** Transferase; aspartate amino (AST) (SGOT)

(84455 has been deleted. To report, use 84450)

**84460** alanine amino (ALT) (SGPT)

(84465 has been deleted. To report, use 84460)

**84466** Transferrin

(Iron binding capacity, use 83550)

(84472 has been deleted. To report, see code for specific method)

(84474 has been deleted. To report, see code for specific method)

(84476 has been deleted. To report, use 84022)

**84478** Triglycerides

**84479** Thyroid hormone (T3 or T4) uptake or thyroid hormone binding ratio (THBR)

**84480** Triiodothyronine T3; total (TT-3)

**84481** free

**84482** reverse

(84483 has been deleted. To report, see 80100-80103, 80299)

**84484** Troponin, quantitative

(For Troponin, qualitative assay, use 84512)

**84485** Trypsin; duodenal fluid

**84488** feces, qualitative

**84490** feces, quantitative, 24-hour collection

**84510** Tyrosine

(Urate crystal identification, use 89060)

**84512** Troponin, qualitative

(For Troponin, quantitative assay, use 84484)

**84520** Urea nitrogen; quantitative

**84525** semiquantitative (eg, reagent strip test)

**84540** Urea nitrogen, urine

**84545** Urea nitrogen, clearance

**84550** Uric acid; blood

(84555 has been deleted. To report, use 84550)

**84560** other source

(84565, 84570, 84575 have been deleted)

**84577** Urobilinogen, feces, quantitative

**84578** Urobilinogen, urine; qualitative

**84580** quantitative, timed specimen

**84583** semiquantitative

(84584 has been deleted)

(Uroporphyrins, use 84120)

(Valproic acid (dipropylacetic acid), use 80164)

**84585** Vanillylmandelic acid (VMA), urine

**84586** Vasoactive intestinal peptide (VIP)

**84588** Vasopressin (antidiuretic hormone, ADH)

(84589 has been deleted. To report, use 85810)

**84590** Vitamin A

(84595 has been deleted. To report, use 82380 and 84590)

(Vitamin B-1, use 84425)

(Vitamin B-2, use 84252)

(Vitamin B-6, use 84207)

(Vitamin B-12, use 82607)

(Vitamin B-12, absorption (Schilling), see 78270, 78271)

(Vitamin C, use 82180)

(Vitamin D, see 82306, 82307, 82652)

(Vitamin E, use 84446)

**84597** Vitamin K

(VMA, use 84585)

**84600** Volatiles (eg, acetic anhydride, carbon tetrachloride, dichloroethane, dichloromethane, diethylether, isopropyl alcohol, methanol)

(For acetaldehyde, use 82000)

(84605 has been deleted)

(84610 has been deleted)

(Volume, blood, RISA or Cr-51, see 78110, 78111)

(84613 has been deleted)

(84615 has been deleted. To report, see code for specific method)

**84620** Xylose absorption test, blood and/or urine

(For administration, use 99070)

**84630** Zinc

(84635 has been deleted. To report, use 84630)

(84645 has been deleted)

(84680 has been deleted. To report, use 82677)

**84681** C-peptide

(84695 has been deleted. To report, use 80170)

(84701 has been deleted. To report, see 84702-84703)

**84702** Gonadotropin, chorionic (hCG); quantitative

**84703** qualitative

(For urine pregnancy test by visual color comparison, use 81025)

(84800 has been deleted. To report, use 84443)

(84810 has been deleted. To report, use 80200)

**84830** Ovulation tests, by visual color comparison methods for human luteinizing hormone

**84999** Unlisted chemistry procedure

## Hematology and Coagulation

(For blood banking procedures, see **Transfusion Medicine**)

(Agglutinins, see **Immunology**)

(Antiplasmin, use 85410)

(Antithrombin III, see 85300, 85301)

(85000 has been deleted. To report, use 85002)

**85002** Bleeding time

(85003 has been deleted. To report, use 85999)

(85005 has been deleted)

**85007** Blood count; manual differential WBC count (includes RBC morphology and platelet estimation)

**85008** manual blood smear examination without differential parameters

(See also 85585)

(For other fluids (eg, CSF), see 89050, 89051)

**85009** differential WBC count, buffy coat

(85012 has been deleted)

(Eosinophils, nasal smear, use 89190)

**85013** spun microhematocrit

**85014** other than spun hematocrit

**85018** hemoglobin

(For other hemoglobin determination, see 83020-83069)

**85021** hemogram, automated (RBC, WBC, Hgb, Hct and indices only)

**85022** hemogram, automated, and manual differential WBC count (CBC)

**85023** hemogram and platelet count, automated, and manual differential WBC count (CBC)

**85024** hemogram and platelet count, automated, and automated partial differential WBC count (CBC)

**85025** hemogram and platelet count, automated, and automated complete differential WBC count (CBC)

**85027** hemogram and platelet count, automated

(85028 has been deleted. To report, see 85023-85025)

(85029, 85030 have been deleted. To report, see 85021-85027)

**85031** Blood count; hemogram, manual, complete CBC (RBC, WBC, Hgb, Hct, differential and indices)

**85041** red blood cell (RBC) only

(See also 85021-85031, 89050)

**85044** reticulocyte count, manual

**85045** reticulocyte count, flow cytometry

**85046** reticulocytes, hemoglobin concentration

**85048** white blood cell (WBC)

(See also 85021-85031)

**85060** Blood smear, peripheral, interpretation by physician with written report

**85095** Bone marrow; aspiration only

(85096 has been deleted. For interpretation of smear, use 85097; for cell block interpretation, use 88305)

**85097** smear interpretation only, with or without differential cell count

(85100 has been deleted. To report, use 85095 and 85097)

(85101 has been deleted. For aspiration, use 85095)

(For special stains, see 85540, 88312, 88313)

**85102** Bone marrow biopsy, needle or trocar

(For bone biopsy, see 20220, 20225, 20240, 20245, 20250, 20251)

(85103, 85105 have been deleted. For bone marrow biopsy interpretation, use 88305)

(85109 has been deleted)

(85120 has been deleted. To report, see 38230-38240)

**85130** Chromogenic substrate assay

(85150, 85160, 85165 have been deleted)

(Circulating anti-coagulant screen (mixing studies), see 85611, 85732)

**85170** Clot retraction

(85171, 85172 have been deleted)

**85175** Clot lysis time, whole blood dilution

(Clotting factor I (fibrinogen), see 85384, 85385)

**85210** Clotting; factor II, prothrombin, specific

(See also 85610-85613)

**85220** factor V (AcG or proaccelerin), labile factor

**85230** factor VII (proconvertin, stable factor)

**85240** factor VIII (AHG), one stage

(85242 has been deleted)

**85244** factor VIII related antigen

**85245** factor VIII, VW factor, ristocetin cofactor

**85246** factor VIII, VW factor antigen

**85247** factor VIII, Von Willebrands factor, multimetric analysis

**85250** factor IX (PTC or Christmas)

**85260** factor X (Stuart-Prower)

**85270** factor XI (PTA)

**85280** factor XII (Hageman)

**85290** factor XIII (fibrin stabilizing)

**85291** factor XIII (fibrin stabilizing), screen solubility

**85292** prekallikrein assay (Fletcher factor assay)

**85293** high molecular weight kininogen assay (Fitzgerald factor assay)

**85300** Clotting inhibitors or anticoagulants; antithrombin III, activity

**85301** antithrombin III, antigen assay

**85302** protein C, antigen

**85303** protein C, activity

**85305** protein S, total

**85306** protein S, free

(85310, 85311 have been deleted)

(85320 has been deleted)

(85330 has been deleted. To report, use 85335)

**85335** Factor inhibitor test

**85337** Thrombomodulin

(For mixing studies for inhibitors, use 85732)

(85340, 85341 have been deleted)

**85345** Coagulation time; Lee and White

**85347** activated

**85348** other methods

(Differential count, see 85007 et seq)

(Duke bleeding time, use 85002)

(Eosinophils, nasal smear, use 89190)

**85360** Euglobulin lysis

(Fetal hemoglobin, see 83030, 83033, 85460)

**85362** Fibrin(ogen) degradation (split) products (FDP)(FSP); agglutination slide, semiquantitative

(85363, 85364 have been deleted)

(85365 has been deleted. To report, use 86320)

(Immunoelectrophoresis, use 86320)

**85366** paracoagulation

(85367 has been deleted)

(85368 has been deleted. To report, use 85366)

(85369 has been deleted)

**85370** quantitative

(85371 has been deleted. To report, see 85384, 85385)

(85372 has been deleted)

(85376, 85377 have been deleted. To report, see 85384, 85385)

**85378** Fibrin degradation products, D-dimer; semiquantitative

**85379** quantitative

**85384** Fibrinogen; activity

**85385** antigen

**85390** Fibrinolysins or coagulopathy screen, interpretation and report

(85392 has been deleted)

(85395 has been deleted)

(85398 has been deleted)

**85400** Fibrinolytic factors and inhibitors; plasmin

**85410** alpha-2 antiplasmin

**85415** plasminogen activator

**85420** plasminogen, except antigenic assay

**85421** plasminogen, antigenic assay

(85426 has been deleted. For von Willebrand factor assay, see 85245-85247)

(Fragility, red blood cell, see 85547, 85555-85557)

**85441** Heinz bodies; direct

**85445** induced, acetyl phenylhydrazine

(Hematocrit (PCV), see 85014, 85021-85031)

(Hemoglobin, see 83020-83068, 85018-85031)

**85460** Hemoglobin or RBCs, fetal, for fetomaternal hemorrhage; differential lysis (Kleihauer-Betke)

(See also 83030, 83033)

(Hemogram, see 85021-85031)

(Hemolysins, see 86940, 86941)

**85461** rosette

**85475** Hemolysin, acid

(See also 86940, 86941)

**85520** Heparin assay

**85525** Heparin neutralization

**85530** Heparin-protamine tolerance test

**85535** Iron stain (RBC or bone marrow smears)

(85538 has been deleted. For leder stain, esterase, blood or bone marrow, use 88319)

**85540** Leukocyte alkaline phosphatase with count

(85544 has been deleted)

**85547** Mechanical fragility, RBC

(85548 has been deleted. To report, use 85008)

**85549** Muramidase

(Nitroblue tetrazolium dye test, use 86384)

**85555** Osmotic fragility, RBC; unincubated

(85556 has been deleted)

**85557** incubated

(Packed cell volume, use 85013)

(Partial thromboplastin time, see 85730, 85732)

(Parasites, blood (eg, malaria smears), use 87207)

(Plasmin, use 85400)

(Plasminogen, use 85420)

(Plasminogen activator, use 85415)

(85560 has been deleted. For peroxidase stain, WBC, use 88319)

(85575 has been deleted)

**85576** Platelet; aggregation (in vitro), each agent

(85577 has been deleted)

(85580 has been deleted. To report, use 85590)

**85585** estimation on smear, only

(See also 85008)

**85590** manual count

**85595** automated count

**85597** Platelet neutralization

**85610** Prothrombin time;

**85611** substitution, plasma fractions, each

**85612** Russell viper venom time (includes venom); undiluted

**85613** diluted

(85614 has been deleted)

(85615 has been deleted)

(85618 has been deleted)

(Red blood cell count, see 85021, 85031, 85041)

(85630 has been deleted. To report, see 85021- 85027)

(85632 has been deleted)

**85635** Reptilase test

(Reticulocyte count, see 85044, 85045)

(85650 has been deleted)

**85651** Sedimentation rate, erythrocyte; non-automated

**85652** automated

**85660** Sickling of RBC, reduction

(Hemoglobin electrophoresis, use 83020)

(Smears (eg, for parasites, malaria), use 87207)

(85665 has been deleted. For plasminogen activator, use 85415)

(85667 has been deleted)

**85670** Thrombin time; plasma

**85675** titer

(85700 has been deleted)

**85705** Thromboplastin inhibition; tissue

(85710, 85711 have been deleted)

(85720 has been deleted)

(For individual clotting factors, see 85245-85247)

**85730** Thromboplastin time, partial (PTT); plasma or whole blood

**85732** substitution, plasma fractions, each

**85810** Viscosity

(85820 has been deleted. To report, use 85810)

(Von Willebrand factor assay, see 85245-85247)

(WBC count, see 85021-85031, 85048, 89050)

**85999** Unlisted hematology and coagulation procedure

# Immunology

(Acetylcholine receptor antibody, see 86255, 86256)

(Actinomyces, antibodies to, use 86602)

(Adrenal cortex antibodies, see 86255, 86256)

**86000** Agglutinins, febrile (eg, Brucella, Francisella, Murine typhus, Q fever, Rocky Mountain spotted fever, scrub typhus), each antigen

(For antibodies to infectious agents, see 86602-86804)

(86002 has been deleted)

(Agglutinins and autohemolysins, see 86940, 86941)

**86003** Allergen specific IgE; quantitative or semiquantitative, each allergen

(For total quantitative IgE, use 82785)

(86004 has been deleted. To report, see 86940, 86941)

**86005** qualitative, multiallergen screen (dipstick, paddle or disk)

(For total qualitative IgE, use 83518)

(Alpha-1 antitrypsin, see 82103, 82104)

(Alpha-1 feto-protein, see 82105, 82106)

(Anti-AChR (acetylcholine receptor) antibody titer, see 86255, 86256)

(86006 has been deleted. To report, see 83519, 86318, 86403)

(86007, 86008, 86009 have been deleted)

(86011 has been deleted. To report, use 86021)

(86012 has been deleted. To report, use 86978)

(86013 has been deleted)

(86014 has been deleted. To report, use 86022)

(86016 has been deleted. To report, use 86850)

(86017 has been deleted. To report, see 86850 and 86901)

(86018 has been deleted)

(86019 has been deleted. To report, use 86860)

(Anticardiolipin antibody, use 86147)

(Anti-DNA, use 86225)

(Anti-deoxyribonuclease titer, use 86215)

**86021** Antibody identification; leukocyte antibodies

**86022** platelet antibodies

**86023** platelet associated immunoglobulin assay

(86024 has been deleted. For RBC antibodies, use 86870)

(86026, 86028 have been deleted)

(86031 has been deleted. To report, use 86880)

(86032 has been deleted. To report, use 86885)

(86033 has been deleted. To report, use 86886)

(86034 has been deleted. To report, see 86880-86886 and 86971)

(86035 has been deleted. To report, use 86970)

**86038** Antinuclear antibodies (ANA);

**86039** titer

(86045 has been deleted)

(Antistreptococcal antibody, ie, anti-DNAse, use 86215)

(Antistreptokinase titer, use 86590)

**86060** Antistreptolysin 0; titer

(For antibodies to infectious agents, see 86602-86804)

**86063** screen

(For antibodies to infectious agents, see 86602-86804)

(86064 has been deleted. For antitrypsin, alpha-1 use 82103, for phenotyping use 82104)

(86066 has been deleted. To report, use 82104)

(86067 has been deleted. To report, use 82103)

(86068 has been deleted. For blood compatibility test, see 86920-86922)

(Blastomyces, antibodies to, use 86612)

(86069 has been deleted)

(86070 has been deleted. To report, use 86920)

(86072 has been deleted)

(86073 has been deleted. To report, see 86156, 86157, 86904)

(86074 has been deleted)

(86075, 86076 have been deleted)

**86077** Blood bank physician services; difficult cross match and/or evaluation of irregular antibody(s), interpretation and written report

**86078** investigation of transfusion reaction including suspicion of transmissible disease, interpretation and written report

**86079** authorization for deviation from standard blood banking procedures (eg, use of outdated blood, transfusion of Rh incompatible units), with written report

(86080 has been deleted. For blood typing, see 86900-86910)

(86082 has been deleted. To report, see 86900, 86901)

(86083 has been deleted. To report, use 86850 and 86900 or 86901)

(86084 has been deleted. To report, use 86903)

(86085 has been deleted. To report, use 86904)

(86090 has been deleted)

(86095 has been deleted. To report, use 86905)

(86096 has been deleted)

(86100 has been deleted. To report, use 86901)

(86105 has been deleted. To report, use 86906)

(86115 has been deleted)

(86120 has been deleted. To report, use 86905)

(86128 has been deleted. To report, use 86890)

(86129 has been deleted)

(86130 has been deleted. To report, use 86891)

(86131, 86134, 86138 and 86139 have been deleted)

(Brucella, antibodies to, use 86622)

(Candida, antibodies to, use 86628. For skin testing, use 86485)

**86140** C-reactive protein

(Candidiasis, use 86628)

**86147** Cardiolipin (phospholipid) antibody

(86149 has been deleted. To report, use 82378)

(86151 has been deleted. To report, use 82378)

**86148** Anti-phosphatidylserine (phospholipid) antibody

**86155** Chemotaxis assay, specify method

(Clostridium difficile toxin, use 87230)

(Coccidioides, antibodies to, see 86635. For skin testing, use 86490)

**86156** Cold agglutinin; screen

**86157** titer

(86158 has been deleted)

(86159 has been deleted. To report, see 86160 and 86161)

**86160** Complement; antigen, each component

**86161** functional activity, each component

**86162** total hemolytic (CH50)

(86163, 86164 have been deleted. To report, see 86160 and 86161)

**86171** Complement fixation tests, each antigen

(Coombs test, see 86880-86886)

**86185** Counterimmunoelectrophoresis, each antigen

(86201, 86202 have been deleted)

(Cryptococcus, antibodies to, use 86641)

(86209 has been deleted. To report, use 86999)

**86215** Deoxyribonuclease, antibody

**86225** Deoxyribonucleic acid (DNA) antibody; native or double stranded

(Echinococcus, antibodies to, see code for specific method)

(For HIV antibody tests, see 86701-86703)

**86226** single stranded

(Anti D.S., DNA, IFA, eg, using C.Lucilae, see 86255 and 86256)

(86227, 86228 have been deleted. To report, use 86317)

(86229 has been deleted)

**86235** Extractable nuclear antigen, antibody to, any method (eg, nRNP, SS-A, SS-B, Sm, RNP, Sc170, J01), each antibody

(86240, 86241 have been deleted)

**86243** Fc receptor

(86244 has been deleted. To report fetoprotein, alpha-1, see 82105, 82106)

(86245 has been deleted)

(Filaria, antibodies to, see code for specific method)

**86255** Fluorescent noninfectious agent antibody; screen, each antibody

**86256** titer, each antibody

(Fluorescent technique for antigen identification in tissue, use 88346; for indirect fluorescence, use 88347)

(86265 has been deleted. To report, use 86930)

(86266 has been deleted. To report, use 86931)

(FTA, see 86781)

(86267 has been deleted. To report, use 86932)

(Gel (agar) diffusion tests, use 86331)

(86272, 86273 have been deleted)

(86274 has been deleted. To report, use 90742)

**86277** Growth hormone, human (HGH), antibody

**86280** Hemagglutination inhibition test (HAI)

(For rubella, use 86762)

(86281 has been deleted. To report, use 85475)

(86282 has been deleted. To report, use 86940)

(86283 has been deleted. To report, use 86941)

(86285, 86286 have been deleted)

(86287 has been deleted. To report, use 87340)

(86289 has been deleted. To report, use 86704)

(For antibodies to infectious agents, see 86602-86804)

(86290 has been deleted. To report, use 86705)

(86291 has been deleted. To report, use 86706)

(86293 has been deleted. To report, use 87350)

(86295 has been deleted. To report, use 86707)

(86296 has been deleted. To report, use 86708)

(86297 has been deleted. To report, use 86708)

(86299 has been deleted. To report, use 86709)

(86302 has been deleted. To report, use 86803)

(86303 has been deleted. To report, use 86804)

(86306 has been deleted. To report, use 87380)

(For hepatitis delta agent, antibody, use 86692)

**86308** Heterophile antibodies; screening

(For antibodies to infectious agents, see 86602-86804)

**86309** titer

(For antibodies to infectious agents, see 86602-86804)

**86310** titers after absorption with beef cells and guinea pig kidney

(Histoplasma, antibodies to, use 86698. For skin testing, use 86510)

(For antibodies to infectious agents, see 86602-86804)

(86311 has been deleted. To report, see 87390, 87391)

(86312 has been deleted. To report, see 86701-86703)

(86313 has been deleted. To report, use 87449)

(86314 has been deleted. To report, use 86689)

(86315 has been deleted. To report, use 87450)

(Human growth hormone antibody, use 86277)

**86316** Immunoassay for tumor antigen (eg, cancer antigen 125), each

**86317** Immunoassay for infectious agent antibody, quantitative, not otherwise specified

(For immunoassay techniques for antigens, see 83516, 83518, 83519, 83520, 87301-87450, 87810-87899)

(For particle agglutination procedures, use 86403)

**86318** Immunoassay for infectious agent antibody, qualitative or semiquantitative, single step method (eg, reagent strip)

(86319 has been deleted. To report immunoassays for drugs, see 80100-80103)

**86320** Immunoelectrophoresis; serum

**86325** other fluids (eg, urine, CSF) with concentration

**86327** crossed (2-dimensional assay)

**86329** Immunodiffusion; not elsewhere specified

**86331** gel diffusion, qualitative (Ouchterlony), each antigen or antibody

**86332** Immune complex assay

(86333 has been deleted. To report, use 86332)

**86334** Immunofixation electrophoresis

(86335 has been deleted)

**86337** Insulin antibodies

(86338 has been deleted. To report, use 86337)

**86340** Intrinsic factor antibodies

(Leptospira, antibodies to, use 86720)

(Leukoagglutinins, use 86021)

**86341** Islet cell antibody

(86342 has been deleted. To report, use 86945)

**86343** Leukocyte histamine release test (LHR)

**86344** Leukocyte phagocytosis

(86345, 86346, 86347 have been deleted)

(86349 has been deleted. To report, use 86950)

(86351 has been deleted)

**86353** Lymphocyte transformation, mitogen (phytomitogen) or antigen induced blastogenesis

(Lymphocytes immunophenotyping, use 88180 for cytometry; see 88342, 88346 for microscopic techniques)

(86357 has been deleted. To report, see 88180, 88342, 88346)

(86358 has been deleted. To report, see 88180, 88342, 88346)

(Malaria antibodies, use 86750)

**86359** T cells; total count

**86360** absolute CD4 and CD8 count, including ratio

**86361** absolute CD4 count

(86365 has been deleted)

**86376** Microsomal antibodies (eg, thyroid or liver-kidney), each

(86377 has been deleted. To report, use 86376)

**86378** Migration inhibitory factor test (MIF)

(Mitochondrial antibody, liver, see 86255, 86256)

(Mononucleosis, see 86308-86310)

**86382** Neutralization test, viral

**86384** Nitroblue tetrazolium dye test (NTD)

(Ouchterlony diffusion, use 86331)

(86385, 86386 have been deleted. To report, see 86910, 86911)

(86388, 86389, 86391 have been deleted)

(Platelet antibodies, see 86022, 86023)

(86392, 86393, 86398 have been deleted)

(86402 has been deleted)

**86403** Particle agglutination; screen, each antibody

(86404 has been deleted. To report, use 86965)

(86405 has been deleted)

**86406** titer, each antibody

(Pregnancy test, see 84702, 84703)

(86410 has been deleted. To report, use 86970)

(86411 has been deleted. To report, use 86971)

(86412 has been deleted. To report, use 86972)

(86415, 86416 have been deleted)

(86417 has been deleted. To report, use 86975)

(86418 has been deleted. To report, use 86976)

(86419 has been deleted. To report, use 86977)

(86420 has been deleted. To report, use 86978)

(86421-86423 have been deleted. To report, see 82785, 83518, 86003, 86005)

(86424, 86425, 86427 have been deleted)

(Rapid plasma reagin test (RPR), see 86592, 86593)

**86430** Rheumatoid factor; qualitative

**86431** quantitative

(Serologic test for syphilis, see 86592, 86593)

(86450 has been deleted)

(86455 has been deleted. To report, use 86586)

(86460, 86470, 86480 have been deleted)

**86485** Skin test; candida

(For antibody, candida, use 86628)

**86490** coccidioidomycosis

(86495, 86500 have been deleted)

**86510** histoplasmosis

(For histoplasma, antibody, use 86698)

(86520, 86530 have been deleted)

(86540 has been deleted. For mumps antibody, use 86735)

(86550, 86565, 86570 have been deleted)

**86580** tuberculosis, intradermal

**86585** tuberculosis, tine test

(For skin tests for allergy, see 95010-95199)

(Smooth muscle antibody, see 86255, 86256)

(Sporothrix, antibodies to, see code for specific method)

**86586** unlisted antigen, each

(86587 has been deleted. To report, use 86985)

►(86588 has been deleted. To report, see 86403, 87081, 87430, or 87880)◄

**86590** Streptokinase, antibody

(For antibodies to infectious agents, see 86602-86804)

(Streptolysin O antibody, see antistreptolysin O, 86060, 86063)

**86592** Syphilis test; qualitative (eg, VDRL, RPR, ART)

(For antibodies to infectious agents, see 86602-86804)

**86593** quantitative

(For antibodies to infectious agents, see 86602-86804)

(Tetanus antibody, use 86774)

(Thyroglobulin antibody, use 86800)

(Thyroglobulin, use 84432)

(Thyroid microsomal antibody, use 86376)

(86594 has been deleted. To report, see 86376 and 86800)

(86595 has been deleted)

(86597 has been deleted. To report see 86812-86822)

(86600 has been deleted)

(For toxoplasma antibody, see 86777-86778)

The following codes (86602-86804) are qualitative or semiquantitative immunoassays performed by multiple step methods for the detection of antibodies to infectious agents. For immunoassays by single step method (eg, reagent strips), use code 86318. Procedures for the identification of antibodies should be coded as precisely as possible. For example, an antibody to a virus could be coded with increasing specificity for virus, family, genus, species, or type. In some cases, further precision may be added to codes by specifying the class of immunoglobulin being detected. When multiple tests are done to detect antibodies to organisms classified more precisely than the specificity allowed by available codes, it is appropriate to code each as a separate service. For example, a test for antibody to an enterovirus is coded as 86658. Coxsackie viruses are enteroviruses, but there are no codes for the individual species of enterovirus. If assays are performed for antibodies to coxsackie A and B species, each assay should be separately coded. Similarly, if multiple assays are performed for antibodies of different immunoglobulin classes, each assay should be coded separately.

For the detection of antibodies other than those to infectious agents, see specific antibody (eg, 86021, 86022, 86023, 86376, 86800, 86850-86870) or specific method (eg, 83516, 86255, 86256).

(For infectious agent/antigen detection, see 87260-87899)

**86602** Antibody; actinomyces

**86603** adenovirus

**86606** Aspergillus

**86609** bacterium, not elsewhere specified

**86612** Blastomyces

**86615** Bordetella

**86617** Borrelia burgdorferi (Lyme disease) confirmatory test (eg, Western blot or immunoblot)

**86618** Borrelia burgdorferi (Lyme disease)

**86619** Borrelia (relapsing fever)

**86622** Brucella

**86625** Campylobacter

**86628** Candida

(For skin test, candida, use 86485)

(86630 has been deleted)

**86631** Chlamydia

**86632** Chlamydia, IgM

(For chlamydia antigen, see 87270, 87320. For fluorescent antibody technique, see 86255, 86256)

**86635** Coccidioides

**86638** Coxiella Brunetii (Q fever)

**86641** Cryptococcus

**86644** cytomegalovirus (CMV)

(For TORCH panel, use 80090)

**86645** cytomegalovirus (CMV), IgM

**86648** Diphtheria

(86650 has been deleted. To report, use 86781)

**86651** encephalitis, California (La Crosse)

**86652** encephalitis, Eastern equine

**86653** encephalitis, St. Louis

**86654** encephalitis, Western equine

**86658** enterovirus (eg, coxsackie, echo, polio)

(86662 has been deleted. To report, use 86781)

(Trichinella, antibodies to, use 86784)

(Trypanosoma, antibodies to, see code for specific method)

(Tuberculosis, use 86580 for skin testing)

(Viral antibodies, see code for specific method)

**86663** Epstein-Barr (EB) virus, early antigen (EA)

**86664** Epstein-Barr (EB) virus, nuclear antigen (EBNA)

**86665** Epstein-Barr (EB) virus, viral capsid (VCA)

**86668** Francisella Tularensis

**86671** fungus, not elsewhere specified

**86674** Giardia Lamblia

**86677** Helicobacter Pylori

(86681 has been deleted. To report, see 86255, 86256)

**86682** helminth, not elsewhere specified

**86684** Hemophilus influenza

(86685 has been deleted. To report, see 86255, 86256)

**86687** HTLV-I

**86688** HTLV-II

**86689** HTLV or HIV antibody, confirmatory test (eg, Western Blot)

**86692** hepatitis, delta agent

(For hepatitis delta agent, antigen, use 87380)

**86694** herpes simplex, non-specific type test

(For TORCH panel, use 80090)

**86695** herpes simplex, type I

**86698** histoplasma

**86701** HIV-1

**86702** HIV-2

**86703** HIV-1 and HIV-2, single assay

(For HIV-1 antigen, use 87390)

(For HIV-2 antigen, use 87391)

(For confirmatory test for HIV antibody (eg, Western Blot), use 86689)

**86704** Hepatitis B core antibody (HBcAb); IgG and IgM

**86705** IgM antibody

**86706** Hepatitis B surface antibody (HBsAb)

**86707** Hepatitis Be antibody (HBeAb)

**86708** Hepatitis A antibody (HAAb); IgG and IgM

**86709** IgM antibody

**86710** Antibody; influenza virus

**86713** Legionella

**86717** Leishmania

**86720** Leptospira

**86723** Listeria monocytogenes

**86727** lymphocytic choriomeningitis

**86729** Lymphogranuloma Venereum

**86732** mucormycosis

**86735** mumps

**86738** Mycoplasma

**86741** Neisseria meningitidis

**86744** Nocardia

**86747** parvovirus

**86750** Plasmodium (malaria)

**86753** protozoa, not elsewhere specified

**86756** respiratory syncytial virus

86759 rotavirus

86762 rubella

86765 rubeola

86768 Salmonella

86771 Shigella

86774 tetanus

86777 Toxoplasma

86778 Toxoplasma, IgM

86781 Treponema Pallidum, confirmatory test (eg, FTA-abs)

86784 trichinella

86787 varicella-zoster

86790 virus, not elsewhere specified

86793 Yersinia

86800 Thyroglobulin antibody

(For thyroglobulin, use 84432)

86803 Hepatitis C antibody;

86804 confirmatory test (eg, immunoblot)

## Tissue Typing

(For pretransplant cross-match, see appropriate code or codes)

86805 Lymphocytotoxicity assay, visual crossmatch; with titration

86806 without titration

86807 Serum screening for cytotoxic percent reactive antibody (PRA); standard method

86808 quick method

(86810 has been deleted)

86812 HLA typing; A, B, or C (eg, A10, B7, B27), single antigen

86813 A, B, or C, multiple antigens

86816 DR/DQ, single antigen

86817 DR/DQ, multiple antigens

86821 lymphocyte culture, mixed (MLC)

86822 lymphocyte culture, primed (PLC)

86849 Unlisted immunology procedure

## Transfusion Medicine

(For apheresis, use 36520)

(For therapeutic phlebotomy, use 99195)

86850 Antibody screen, RBC, each serum technique

86860 Antibody elution (RBC), each elution

86870 Antibody identification, RBC antibodies, each panel for each serum technique

86880 Antihuman globulin test (Coombs test); direct, each antiserum

86885 indirect, qualitative, each antiserum

86886 indirect, titer, each antiserum

86890 Autologous blood or component, collection processing and storage; predeposited

86891 intra- or postoperative salvage

(For physician services to autologous donors, see 99201-99204)

86900 Blood typing; ABO

86901 Rh (D)

86903 antigen screening for compatible blood unit using reagent serum, per unit screened

86904 antigen screening for compatible unit using patient serum, per unit screened

86905 RBC antigens, other than ABO or Rh (D), each

86906 Rh phenotyping, complete

86910 Blood typing, for paternity testing, per individual; ABO, Rh and MN

86911 each additional antigen system

**▲86915** Bone marrow or peripheral stem cell harvest, modification or treatment to eliminate cell type(s) (eg, T-cells, metastatic carcinoma)

**86920** Compatibility test each unit; immediate spin technique

**86921** incubation technique

**86922** antiglobulin technique

**86927** Fresh frozen plasma, thawing, each unit

**86930** Frozen blood, preparation for freezing, each unit;

**86931** with thawing

**86932** with freezing and thawing

**86940** Hemolysins and agglutinins; auto, screen, each

**86941** incubated

**86945** Irradiation of blood product, each unit

**86950** Leukocyte transfusion

(For leukapheresis, use 36520)

**86965** Pooling of platelets or other blood products

**86970** Pretreatment of RBCs for use in RBC antibody detection, identification, and/or compatibility testing; incubation with chemical agents or drugs, each

**86971** incubation with enzymes, each

**86972** by density gradient separation

**86975** Pretreatment of serum for use in RBC antibody identification; incubation with drugs, each

**86976** by dilution

**86977** incubation with inhibitors, each

**86978** by differential red cell absorption using patient RBCs or RBCs of known phenotype, each absorption

**86985** Splitting of blood or blood products, each unit

**86999** Unlisted transfusion medicine procedure

# Microbiology

Includes bacteriology, mycology, parasitology, and virology.

**87001** Animal inoculation, small animal; with observation

**87003** with observation and dissection

**87015** Concentration (any type), for parasites, ova, or tubercle bacillus (TB, AFB)

**87040** Culture, bacterial, definitive; blood (includes anaerobic screen)

**87045** stool

**87060** throat or nose

**87070** any other source

(For urine, see 87086-87088)

**87072** Culture or direct bacterial identification method, each organism, by commercial kit, any source except urine

(For urine, use 87087)

**87075** Culture, bacterial, any source; anaerobic (isolation)

**87076** definitive identification, each anaerobic organism, including gas chromatography

(For anaerobe without GC, use 87072)

**87081** Culture, bacterial, screening only, for single organisms

**87082** Culture, presumptive, pathogenic organisms, screening only, by commercial kit (specify type); for single organisms

**87083** multiple organisms

**87084** with colony estimation from density chart

**87085** with colony count

(For urine colony count, use 87086)

**87086** Culture, bacterial, urine; quantitative, colony count

**87087** commercial kit

**87088** identification, in addition to quantitative or commercial kit

**87101** Culture, fungi, isolation (with or without presumptive identification); skin

**87102** other source (except blood)

**87103** blood

**87106** Culture, fungi, definitive identification of each fungus (use in addition to codes 87101, 87102, or 87103 when appropriate)

**87109** Culture, mycoplasma, any source

**87110** Culture, chlamydia

**87116** Culture, tubercle or other acid-fast bacilli (eg, TB, AFB, mycobacteria); any source, isolation only

**87117** concentration plus isolation

**87118** Culture, mycobacteria, definitive identification of each organism

**87140** Culture, typing; fluorescent method, each antiserum

**87143** gas liquid chromatography (GLC) method

**87145** phage method

**87147** serologic method, agglutination grouping, per antiserum

**87151** serologic method, speciation

**87155** precipitin method, grouping, per antiserum

**87158** other methods

**+ 87163** Culture, any source, additional identification methods required (use in addition to primary culture code)

**87164** Dark field examination, any source (eg, penile, vaginal, oral, skin); includes specimen collection

**87166** without collection

(87173 has been deleted)

**87174** Endotoxin, bacterial (pyrogens); chemical

**87175** biological assay (eg, Limulus lysate)

**87176** homogenization, tissue, for culture

**87177** Ova and parasites, direct smears, concentration and identification

(Individual smears and procedures, see 87015, 87208-87211)

(Trichrome, iron hemotoxylin and other special stains, use 88312)

(For nucleic acid probes in cytologic material, use 88365)

(For molecular diagnostics, see 83890-83898, 87470-87799)

(87178 has been deleted. To report, use 87797)

(87179 has been deleted. To report, use 87798)

**87181** Sensitivity studies, antibiotic; agar diffusion method, per antibiotic

**87184** disk method, per plate (12 or fewer disks)

**87186** microtiter, minimum inhibitory concentration (MIC), any number of antibiotics

**87187** minimum bactericidal concentration (MBC) (use in addition to 87186 or 87188)

**87188** macrotube dilution method, each antibiotic

**87190** tubercle bacillus (TB, AFB), each drug

**87192** fungi, each drug

**87197** Serum bactericidal titer (Schlicter test)

**87205** Smear, primary source, with interpretation; routine stain for bacteria, fungi, or cell types

**87206** fluorescent and/or acid fast stain for bacteria, fungi, or cell types

**87207** special stain for inclusion bodies or intracellular parasites (eg, malaria, kala azar, herpes)

**87208** direct or concentrated, dry, for ova and parasites

(For concentration, use 87015; complete examination, use 87177)

(For complex special stains, see 88312, 88313)

(For fat, meat, fibers, nasal eosinophils, and starch, see miscellaneous section)

**87210** wet mount with simple stain, for bacteria, fungi, ova, and/or parasites

**87211** wet and dry mount, for ova and parasites

**87220** Tissue examination for fungi (eg, KOH slide)

**87230** Toxin or antitoxin assay, tissue culture (eg, Clostridium difficile toxin)

**87250** Virus identification; inoculation of embryonated eggs, or small animal, includes observation and dissection

**87252** tissue culture inoculation and observation

**87253** tissue culture, additional studies (eg, hemabsorption, neutralization) each isolate

(Electron microscopy, use 88348)

(Inclusion bodies in tissue sections, see 88304-88309; in smears, see 87207-87210; in fluids, use 88106)

(87300 has been deleted. To report, use 87999)

Infectious agents by antigen detection, direct fluorescence microscopy, or nucleic acid probe techniques should be reported as precisely as possible. The most specific code possible should be reported. If there is no specific agent code, the general methodology code (eg, 87299, 87449, 87450, 87797, 87798, 87799, 87899) should be used. For identification of antibodies to many of the listed infectious agents, see 86602-86804.

**87260** Infectious agent antigen detection by direct fluorescent antibody technique; adenovirus

**87265** Bordetella pertussis/parapertussis

**87270** Chlamydia trachomatis

**87272** cryptosporidium/giardia

**87274** Herpes simplex virus

**87276** influenza A virus

**87278** Legionella pneumophila

**87280** respiratory syncytial virus

**87285** Treponema pallidum

**87290** Varicella zoster virus

**87299** Infectious agent antigen detection by direct fluorescent antibody technique, not otherwise specified

**87301** Infectious agent antigen detection by enzyme immunoassay technique, qualitative or semiquantitative, multiple step method; adenovirus enteric types 40/41

**87320** Chlamydia trachomatis

**87324** Clostridium difficile toxin A

**87328** cryptosporidium/giardia

**87332** cytomegalovirus

**87335** Escherichia coli 0157

(For giardia antigen, use 87328)

●**87338** Helicobacter pylori, stool

**87340** hepatitis B surface antigen (HBsAg)

**87350** hepatitis Be antigen (HBeAg)

**87380** hepatitis, delta agent

**87385** Histoplasma capsulatum

**87390** HIV-1

**87391** HIV-2

**87420** respiratory syncytial virus

**87425** rotavirus

**87430** Streptococcus, group A

**87449** Infectious agent antigen detection by enzyme immunoassay technique qualitative or semiquantitative; multiple step method, not otherwise specified

**87450** single step method, not otherwise specified

**87470** Infectious agent detection by nucleic acid (DNA or RNA); Bartonella henselae and Bartonella quintana, direct probe technique

**87471** Bartonella henselae and Bartonella quintana, amplified probe technique

**87472** Bartonella henselae and Bartonella quintana, quantification

**87475** Borrelia burgdorferi, direct probe technique

**87476** Borrelia burgdorferi, amplified probe technique

**87477** Borrelia burgdorferi, quantification

**87480** Candida species, direct probe technique

**87481** Candida species, amplified probe technique

**87482** Candida species, quantification

**87485** Chlamydia pneumoniae, direct probe technique

**87486** Chlamydia pneumoniae, amplified probe technique

**87487** Chlamydia pneumoniae, quantification

**87490** Chlamydia trachomatis, direct probe technique

**87491** Chlamydia trachomatis, amplified probe technique

**87492** Chlamydia trachomatis, quantification

**87495** cytomegalovirus, direct probe technique

**87496** cytomegalovirus, amplified probe technique

**87497** cytomegalovirus, quantification

**87510** Gardnerella vaginalis, direct probe technique

**87511** Gardnerella vaginalis, amplified probe technique

**87512** Gardnerella vaginalis, quantification

**87515** hepatitis B virus, direct probe technique

**87516** hepatitis B virus, amplified probe technique

**87517** hepatitis B virus, quantification

**87520** hepatitis C, direct probe technique

**87521** hepatitis C, amplified probe technique

**87522** hepatitis C, quantification

**87525** hepatitis G, direct probe technique

**87526** hepatitis G, amplified probe technique

**87527** hepatitis G, quantification

**87528** Herpes simplex virus, direct probe technique

**87529** Herpes simplex virus, amplified probe technique

**87530** Herpes simplex virus, quantification

**87531** Herpes virus-6, direct probe technique

**87532** Herpes virus-6, amplified probe technique

**87533** Herpes virus-6, quantification

**87534** HIV-1, direct probe technique

**87535** HIV-1, amplified probe technique

**87536** HIV-1, quantification

**87537** HIV-2, direct probe technique

**87538** HIV-2, amplified probe technique

**87539** HIV-2, quantification

**87540** Legionella pneumophila, direct probe technique

**87541** Legionella pneumophila, amplified probe technique

**87542** Legionella pneumophila, quantification

**87550** Mycobacteria species, direct probe technique

**87551** Mycobacteria species, amplified probe technique

**87552** Mycobacteria species, quantification

**87555** Mycobacteria tuberculosis, direct probe technique

**87556** Mycobacteria tuberculosis, amplified probe technique

**87557** Mycobacteria tuberculosis, quantification

**87560** Mycobacteria avium-intracellulare, direct probe technique

**87561** Mycobacteria avium-intracellulare, amplified probe technique

**87562** Mycobacteria avium-intracellulare, quantification

**87580** Mycoplasma pneumoniae, direct probe technique

**87581** Mycoplasma pneumoniae, amplified probe technique

**87582** Mycoplasma pneumoniae, quantification

**87590** Neisseria gonorrhoeae, direct probe technique

**87591** Neisseria gonorrhoeae, amplified probe technique

**87592** Neisseria gonorrhoeae, quantification

**87620** papillomavirus, human, direct probe technique

**87621** papillomavirus, human, amplified probe technique

**87622** papillomavirus, human, quantification

**87650** Streptococcus, group A, direct probe technique

**87651** Streptococcus, group A, amplified probe technique

**87652** Streptococcus, group A, quantification

**87797** Infectious agent detection by nucleic acid (DNA or RNA); not otherwise specified, direct probe technique

**87798** not otherwise specified, amplified probe technique

**87799** not otherwise specified, quantification

**87810** Infectious agent detection by immunoassay with direct optical observation; Chlamydia trachomatis

**87850** Neisseria gonorrhoeae

**87880** Streptococcus, group A

**87899** not otherwise specified

**87999** Unlisted microbiology procedure

# Anatomic Pathology

## Postmortem Examination

Procedures 88000 through 88099 represent physician services only. Use modifier '-90' or 09990 for outside laboratory services.

**88000** Necropsy (autopsy), gross examination only; without CNS

**88005** with brain

**88007** with brain and spinal cord

**88012** infant with brain

**88014** stillborn or newborn with brain

**88016** macerated stillborn

**88020** Necropsy (autopsy), gross and microscopic; without CNS

**88025** with brain

**88027** with brain and spinal cord

**88028** infant with brain

**88029** stillborn or newborn with brain

**88036** Necropsy (autopsy), limited, gross and/or microscopic; regional

**88037** single organ

**88040** Necropsy (autopsy); forensic examination

**88045** coroner's call

**88099** Unlisted necropsy (autopsy) procedure

# Cytopathology

**88104** Cytopathology, fluids, washings or brushings, except cervical or vaginal; smears with interpretation

**88106** filter method only with interpretation

**88107** smears and filter preparation with interpretation

**88108** Cytopathology, concentration technique, smears and interpretation (eg, Saccomanno technique)

(88109 has been deleted. For interpretation of smear, use 88104; for cell block interpretation, use 88305)

(For cervical or vaginal smears, see 88150-88155)

(For gastric intubation with lavage, see 89130-89141, 91055)

(For x-ray localization, use 74340)

**88125** Cytopathology, forensic (eg, sperm)

**88130** Sex chromatin identification; Barr bodies

**88140** peripheral blood smear, polymorphonuclear drumsticks

(For Guard stain, use 88313)

Codes 88141-88155, 88164-88167 are used to report cervical or vaginal screening by various methods and to report physician interpretation services. Use codes 88150-88154 to report Pap smears that are examined using non-Bethesda reporting. Use codes 88164-88167 to report Pap smears that are examined using the Bethesda System of reporting. Use codes 88142-88145 to report specimens collected in fluid medium with automated thin layer preparation that are examined using any system of reporting (Bethesda or non-Bethesda). Within each of these three code families choose the one code that describes the screening method(s) used. Codes 88141 and 88155 should be reported in addition to the screening code chosen when the additional services are provided.

**+ 88141** Cytopathology, cervical or vaginal (any reporting system); requiring interpretation by physician (List separately in addition to code for technical service)

(Use 88141 in conjunction with codes 88142-88154, 88164-88167)

**88142** Cytopathology, cervical or vaginal (any reporting system), collected in preservative fluid, automated thin layer preparation; manual screening under physician supervision

**88143** with manual screening and rescreening under physician supervision

**88144** with manual screening and computer-assisted rescreening under physician supervision

**88145** with manual screening and computer-assisted rescreening using cell selection and review under physician supervision

**88147** Cytopathology smears, cervical or vaginal; screening by automated system under physician supervision

**▲88148** screening by automated system with manual rescreening under physician supervision

**88150** Cytopathology, slides, cervical or vaginal; manual screening under physician supervision

(88151 has been deleted. To report, use 88141)

**88152** with manual screening and computer-assisted rescreening under physician supervision

**88153** with manual screening and rescreening under physician supervision

**88154** with manual screening and computer-assisted rescreening using cell selection and review under physician supervision

**+ 88155** Cytopathology, slides, cervical or vaginal, definitive hormonal evaluation (eg, maturation index, karyopyknotic index, estrogenic index) (List separately in addition to code(s) for other technical and interpretation services)

(Use 88155 in conjunction with 88142-88154, 88164-88167)

(88156 has been deleted. To report, use 88164)

(88157 has been deleted. To report, use 88141)

(88158 has been deleted. To report, use 88166)

**88160** Cytopathology, smears, any other source; screening and interpretation

**88161** preparation, screening and interpretation

**88162** extended study involving over 5 slides and/or multiple stains

(For obtaining specimen, see percutaneous needle biopsy under individual organ in **Surgery**)

(For aerosol collection of sputum, use 89350)

(For special stains, see 88312-88314)

**88164** Cytopathology, slides, cervical or vaginal (the Bethesda System); manual screening under physician supervision

**88165** with manual screening and rescreening under physician supervision

**88166** with manual screening and computer-assisted rescreening under physician supervision

**88167** with manual screening and computer-assisted rescreening using cell selection and review under physician supervision

**88170** Fine needle aspiration with or without preparation of smears; superficial tissue (eg, thyroid, breast, prostate)

(For percutaneous needle biopsy, see 60100 for thyroid, 19100 for breast, 55700 for prostate)

**88171** deep tissue under radiologic guidance

(For radiological supervision and interpretation, see 76003, 76360, 76942)

(For percutaneous needle biopsy, see 32405 for lung, 47000, 47001 for liver, 48102 for pancreas, 49180 for abdominal or retroperitoneal mass)

**88172** Evaluation of fine needle aspirate with or without preparation of smears; immediate cytohistologic study to determine adequacy of specimen(s)

**88173** interpretation and report

**88180** Flow cytometry; each cell surface marker

**88182** cell cycle or DNA analysis

(For tumor morphometry and DNA and ploidy analysis by imaging techniques, use 88358)

**88199** Unlisted cytopathology procedure

(For electron microscopy, see 88348, 88349)

## Cytogenetic Studies

(For acetylcholinesterase, use 82013)

(For alpha-fetoprotein, serum or amniotic fluid, see 82105, 82106)

**88230** Tissue culture for non-neoplastic disorders; lymphocyte

**88233** skin or other solid tissue biopsy

**88235** amniotic fluid or chorionic villus cells

**88237** Tissue culture for neoplastic disorders; bone marrow, blood cells

**88239** solid tumor

**88240** Cryopreservation, freezing and storage of cells, each cell line

**88241** Thawing and expansion of frozen cells, each aliquot

**88245** Chromosome analysis for breakage syndromes; baseline Sister Chromatid Exchange (SCE), 20-25 cells

**88248** baseline breakage, score 50-100 cells, count 20 cells, 2 karyotypes (eg, for ataxia telangiectasia, Fanconi anemia, fragile X)

**88249** score 100 cells, clastogen stress (eg, diepoxybutane, mitomycin C, ionizing radiation, UV radiation)

(88250 has been deleted. To report, use 88248)

(88260 has been deleted. To report, use 88261)

**88261** Chromosome analysis; count 5 cells, 1 karyotype, with banding

**88262** count 15-20 cells, 2 karyotypes, with banding

**88263** count 45 cells for mosaicism, 2 karyotypes, with banding

**88264** analyze 20-25 cells

(88265 has been deleted. To report, use 88262)

**88267** Chromosome analysis, amniotic fluid or chorionic villus, count 15 cells, 1 karyotype, with banding

(88268 has been deleted. To report, use 88261)

**88269** Chromosome analysis, in situ for amniotic fluid cells, count cells from 6-12 colonies, 1 karyotype, with banding

(88270 has been deleted. To report, use 88261)

**88271** Molecular cytogenetics; DNA probe, each (eg, FISH)

**88272** chromosomal in situ hybridization, analyze 3-5 cells (eg, for derivatives and markers)

**88273** chromosomal in situ hybridization, analyze 10-30 cells (eg, for microdeletions)

**88274** interphase in situ hybridization, analyze 25-99 cells

**88275** interphase in situ hybridization, analyze 100-300 cells

**88280** Chromosome analysis; additional karyotypes, each study

**88283** additional specialized banding technique (eg, NOR, C-banding)

**88285** additional cells counted, each study

**88289** additional high resolution study

**88291** Cytogenetics and molecular cytogenetics, interpretation and report

**88299** Unlisted cytogenetic study

## Surgical Pathology

Services 88300 through 88309 include accession, examination, and reporting. They do not include the services designated in codes 88311 through 88365 and 88399, which are coded in addition when provided.

The unit of service for codes 88300 through 88309 is the specimen.

A specimen is defined as tissue or tissues that is (are) submitted for individual and separate attention, requiring individual examination and pathologic diagnosis. Two or more such specimens from the same patient (eg, separately identified endoscopic biopsies, skin lesions, etc.) are each appropriately assigned an individual code reflective of its proper level of service.

Service code 88300 is used for any specimen that in the opinion of the examining pathologist can be accurately diagnosed without microscopic examination. Service code 88302 is used when gross and microscopic examination is performed on a specimen to confirm identification and the absence of disease. Service codes 88304 through 88309 describe all other specimens requiring gross and microscopic examination, and represent additional ascending levels of physician work. Levels 88302 through 88309 are specifically defined by the assigned specimens.

Any unlisted specimen should be assigned to the code which most closely reflects the physician work involved when compared to other specimens assigned to that code.

**88300** **Level I -** Surgical pathology, gross examination only

**88302** **Level II -** Surgical pathology, gross and microscopic examination

Appendix, Incidental

Fallopian Tube, Sterilization

Fingers/Toes, Amputation, Traumatic

Foreskin, Newborn

Hernia Sac, Any Location

Hydrocele Sac

Nerve

Skin, Plastic Repair

Sympathetic Ganglion

Testis, Castration

Vaginal Mucosa, Incidental

Vas Deferens, Sterilization

**88304** **Level III -** Surgical pathology, gross and microscopic examination

Abortion, Induced

Abscess

Aneurysm - Arterial/Ventricular

Anus, Tag

Appendix, Other than Incidental

Artery, Atheromatous Plaque

Bartholin's Gland Cyst

Bone Fragment(s), Other than Pathologic Fracture

Bursa/Synovial Cyst

Carpal Tunnel Tissue

Cartilage, Shavings

Cholesteatoma

Colon, Colostomy Stoma

Conjunctiva - Biopsy/Pterygium

Cornea

Diverticulum - Esophagus/Small Bowel

Dupuytren's Contracture Tissue

Femoral Head, Other than Fracture

Fissure/Fistula

Foreskin, Other than Newborn

Gallbladder

Ganglion Cyst

Hematoma

Hemorrhoids

Hydatid of Morgagni

Intervertebral Disc

Joint, Loose Body

Meniscus

Mucocele, Salivary

Neuroma - Morton's/Traumatic

Pilonidal Cyst/Sinus

Polyps, Inflammatory - Nasal/Sinusoidal

Skin - Cyst/Tag/Debridement

Soft Tissue, Debridement

Soft Tissue, Lipoma

Spermatocele

Tendon/Tendon Sheath

Testicular Appendage

Thrombus or Embolus

Tonsil and/or Adenoids

Varicocele

Vas Deferens, Other than Sterilization

Vein, Varicosity

**88305** **Level IV -** Surgical pathology, gross and microscopic examination

Abortion - Spontaneous/Missed

Artery, Biopsy

Bone Marrow, Biopsy

Bone Exostosis

Brain/Meninges, Other than for Tumor Resection

Breast, Biopsy, Not Requiring Microscopic Evaluation of Surgical Margins

Breast, Reduction Mammoplasty

Bronchus, Biopsy

Cell Block, Any Source

Cervix, Biopsy

Colon, Biopsy

Duodenum, Biopsy

Endocervix, Curettings/Biopsy

Endometrium, Curettings/Biopsy

Esophagus, Biopsy

Extremity, Amputation, Traumatic

Fallopian Tube, Biopsy

Fallopian Tube, Ectopic Pregnancy

Femoral Head, Fracture

Fingers/Toes, Amputation, Non-traumatic

Gingiva/Oral Mucosa, Biopsy

Heart Valve

Joint, Resection

Kidney, Biopsy

Larynx, Biopsy

Leiomyoma(s), Uterine Myomectomy - without Uterus

Lip, Biopsy/Wedge Resection

Lung, Transbronchial Biopsy

Lymph Node, Biopsy

Muscle, Biopsy

Nasal Mucosa, Biopsy

Nasopharynx/Oropharynx, Biopsy

Nerve, Biopsy

Odontogenic/Dental Cyst

Omentum, Biopsy

Ovary with or without Tube, Non-neoplastic

Ovary, Biopsy/Wedge Resection

Parathyroid Gland

Peritoneum, Biopsy

Pituitary Tumor

Placenta, Other than Third Trimester

Pleura/Pericardium - Biopsy/Tissue

Polyp, Cervical/Endometrial

Polyp, Colorectal

Polyp, Stomach/Small Bowel

Prostate, Needle Biopsy

Prostate, TUR

Salivary Gland, Biopsy

Sinus, Paranasal Biopsy

Skin, Other than Cyst/Tag/Debridement/ Plastic Repair

Small Intestine, Biopsy

Soft Tissue, Other than Tumor/Mass/Lipoma/ Debridement

Spleen

Stomach, Biopsy

Synovium

Testis, Other than Tumor/Biopsy/Castration

Thyroglossal Duct/Brachial Cleft Cyst

Tongue, Biopsy

Tonsil, Biopsy

Trachea, Biopsy

Ureter, Biopsy

Urethra, Biopsy

Urinary Bladder, Biopsy

Uterus, with or without Tubes and Ovaries, for Prolapse

Vagina, Biopsy

Vulva/Labia, Biopsy

**88307** **Level V -** Surgical pathology, gross and microscopic examination

Adrenal, Resection

Bone - Biopsy/Curettings

Bone Fragment(s), Pathologic Fracture

Brain, Biopsy

Brain/Meninges, Tumor Resection

Breast, Excision of Lesion, Requiring Microscopic Evaluation of Surgical Margins

Breast, Mastectomy - Partial/Simple

Cervix, Conization

Colon, Segmental Resection, Other than for Tumor

Extremity, Amputation, Non-traumatic

Eye, Enucleation

Kidney, Partial/Total Nephrectomy

Larynx, Partial/Total Resection

Liver, Biopsy - Needle/Wedge

Liver, Partial Resection

Lung, Wedge Biopsy

Lymph Nodes, Regional Resection

Mediastinum, Mass

Myocardium, Biopsy

Odontogenic Tumor

Ovary with or without Tube, Neoplastic

Pancreas, Biopsy

Placenta, Third Trimester

Prostate, Except Radical Resection

Salivary Gland

Small Intestine, Resection, Other than for Tumor

Soft Tissue Mass (except Lipoma) - Biopsy/Simple Excision

Stomach - Subtotal/Total Resection, Other than for Tumor

Testis, Biopsy

Thymus, Tumor

Thyroid, Total/Lobe

Ureter, Resection

Urinary Bladder, TUR

Uterus, with or without Tubes and Ovaries, Other than Neoplastic/Prolapse

**88309** **Level VI -** Surgical pathology, gross and microscopic examination

Bone Resection

Breast, Mastectomy - with Regional Lymph Nodes

Colon, Segmental Resection for Tumor

Colon, Total Resection

Esophagus, Partial/Total Resection

Extremity, Disarticulation

Fetus, with Dissection

Larynx, Partial/Total Resection - with Regional Lymph Nodes

Lung - Total/Lobe/Segment Resection

Pancreas, Total/Subtotal Resection

Prostate, Radical Resection

Small Intestine, Resection for Tumor

Soft Tissue Tumor, Extensive Resection

Stomach - Subtotal/Total Resection for Tumor

Testis, Tumor

Tongue/Tonsil - Resection for Tumor

Urinary Bladder, Partial/Total Resection

Uterus, with or without Tubes and Ovaries, Neoplastic

Vulva, Total/Subtotal Resection

(For fine needle aspiration, preparation, and interpretation of smears, see 88170-88173)

**+ 88311** Decalcification procedure (List separately in addition to code for surgical pathology examination)

**+ 88312** Special stains (List separately in addition to code for surgical pathology examination); Group I for microorganisms (eg, Gridley, acid fast, methenamine silver), each

**+ 88313** Group II, all other, (eg, iron, trichrome), except immunocytochemistry and immunoperoxidase stains, each

(For immunocytochemistry and immunoperoxidase tissue studies, use 88342)

**+ 88314** histochemical staining with frozen section(s)

(88316 has been deleted. To report, use 99070)

(88317 has been deleted)

**88318** Determinative histochemistry to identify chemical components (eg, copper, zinc)

**88319** Determinative histochemistry or cytochemistry to identify enzyme constituents, each

**88321** Consultation and report on referred slides prepared elsewhere

**88323** Consultation and report on referred material requiring preparation of slides

**88325** Consultation, comprehensive, with review of records and specimens, with report on referred material

**88329** Pathology consultation during surgery;

**88331** with frozen section(s), single specimen

**88332** each additional tissue block with frozen section(s)

**88342** Immunocytochemistry (including tissue immunoperoxidase), each antibody

(88345 has been deleted. To report, use 88346)

**88346** Immunofluorescent study, each antibody; direct method

**88347** indirect method

**88348** Electron microscopy; diagnostic

**88349** scanning

**88355** Morphometric analysis; skeletal muscle

**88356** nerve

**88358** tumor

(When semi-thin plastic-embedded sections are performed in conjunction with morphometric analysis, only the morphometric analysis should be coded; if performed as an independent procedure, see codes 88300-88309 for surgical pathology.)

(88360 has been deleted. To report, use 88399)

**88362** Nerve teasing preparations

(For physician interpretation of peripheral blood smear, use 85060)

**88365** Tissue in situ hybridization, interpretation and report

(88370 has been deleted. To report, use 88342)

**88371** Protein analysis of tissue by Western Blot, with interpretation and report;

**88372** immunological probe for band identification, each

**88399** Unlisted surgical pathology procedure

## Other Procedures

(Basal metabolic rate has been deleted. If necessary to report, use 89399)

(89005-89007 have been deleted)

**89050** Cell count, miscellaneous body fluids (eg, CSF, joint fluid), except blood;

**89051** with differential count

**89060** Crystal identification by light microscopy with or without polarizing lens analysis, any body fluid (except urine)

(89070, 89080 have been deleted)

**89100** Duodenal intubation and aspiration; single specimen (eg, simple bile study or afferent loop culture) plus appropriate test procedure

**89105** collection of multiple fractional specimens with pancreatic or gallbladder stimulation, single or double lumen tube

(For radiological localization, use 74340)

(For chemical analyses, see **Chemistry,** this section)

(Electrocardiogram, see 93000-93268)

(Esophagus acid perfusion test (Bernstein), see 91030)

**89125** Fat stain, feces, urine, or sputum

**89130** Gastric intubation and aspiration, diagnostic, each specimen, for chemical analyses or cytopathology;

**89132** after stimulation

**89135** Gastric intubation, aspiration, and fractional collections (eg, gastric secretory study); one hour

**89136** two hours

**89140** two hours including gastric stimulation (eg, histalog, pentagastrin)

**89141** three hours, including gastric stimulation

(For gastric lavage, therapeutic, use 91105)

(For radiologic localization of gastric tube, use 74340)

(For chemical analyses, see 82926, 82928)

(Joint fluid chemistry, see **Chemistry,** this section)

**89160** Meat fibers, feces

(89180 has been deleted. To report, use 89190)

**89190** Nasal smear for eosinophils

(89205 has been deleted. To report, use 82273)

(Occult blood, feces, use 82270)

(Paternity tests, use 86910)

(89210 has been deleted)

**89250** Culture and fertilization of oocyte(s);

**89251** with co-culture of embryos

**89252** Assisted oocyte fertilization, microtechnique (any method)

**89253** Assisted embryo hatching, microtechniques (any method)

**89254** Oocyte identification from follicular fluid

**89255** Preparation of embryo for transfer (any method)

**89256** Preparation of cryopreserved embryos for transfer (includes thaw)

**89257** Sperm identification from aspiration (other than seminal fluid)

(For semen analysis, see 89300-89320)

(For sperm identification from testis tissue, use 89264)

**89258** Cryopreservation; embryo

**89259** sperm

**89260** Sperm isolation; simple prep (eg, sperm wash and swim-up) for insemination or diagnosis with semen analysis

**89261** complex prep (eg, Percoll gradient, albumin gradient) for insemination or diagnosis with semen analysis

(For semen analysis without sperm wash or swim-up, use 89320)

**89264** Sperm identification from testis tissue, fresh or cryopreserved

(For biopsy of testis, see 54500, 54505)

(For sperm identification from aspiration, use 89257)

(For semen analysis, see 89300-89320)

**89300** Semen analysis; presence and/or motility of sperm including Huhner test (post coital)

**89310** motility and count

**89320** complete (volume, count, motility, and differential)

(Skin tests, see 86485-86585 and 95010-95199)

(89323 has been deleted. To report, use 89325)

**89325** Sperm antibodies

(For medicolegal identification of sperm, use 88125)

**89329** Sperm evaluation; hamster penetration test

**89330** cervical mucus penetration test, with or without spinnbarkeit test

(89345 has been deleted)

**89350** Sputum, obtaining specimen, aerosol induced technique (separate procedure)

**89355** Starch granules, feces

**89360** Sweat collection by iontophoresis

(For chloride and sodium analysis, use 84295)

**89365** Water load test

**89399** Unlisted miscellaneous pathology test

# Notes

# Notes

# Medicine Guidelines

In addition to the definitions and commonly used terms presented in the **Introduction,** several other items unique to this section on **Medicine** are defined or identified here.

## Multiple Procedures

It is appropriate to designate multiple procedures that are rendered on the same date by separate entries. For example: If individual medical psychotherapy (90841) is rendered in addition to subsequent hospital care (eg, 99231), the psychotherapy would be reported separately from the hospital visit. In this instance, both 99231 and 90841 would be reported.

## Add-on Codes

Some of the listed procedures are commonly carried out in addition to the primary procedure performed. All add-on codes found in CPT are exempt from the multiple procedure concept. They are exempt from the use of the Modifier '-51', as these procedures are not reported as stand-alone codes. These additional or supplemental procedures are designated as "add-on" codes. Add-on codes in CPT can be readily identified by specific descriptor nomenclature which includes phrases such as "each additional" or "(List separately in addition to primary procedure)."

## Separate Procedures

Some of the procedures or services listed in CPT that are commonly carried out as an integral component of a total service or procedure have been identified by the inclusion of the term "separate procedure." The codes designated as "separate procedure" should not be reported in addition to the code for the total procedure or service of which it is considered an integral component.

However, when a procedure or service that is designated as a "separate procedure" is carried out independently or considered to be unrelated or distinct from other procedures/services provided at that time, it may be reported by itself, or in addition to other procedures/services by appending the modifier '-59' to the specific "separate procedure" code to indicate that the procedure is not considered to be a component of another procedure, but is a distinct, independent procedure. This may represent a different session or patient encounter, different procedure or surgery, different site or organ system, separate incision/excision, separate lesion, or separate injury (or area of injury in extensive injuries).

## Subsection Information

Several of the subheadings or subsections have special instructions unique to that section. These special instructions will be presented preceding those procedural terminology listings, referring to that subsection specifically. If there is an "Unlisted Procedure" code number (see section below) for the individual subsection, it will also be shown. Those subsections within the **Medicine** section that have special instructions are as follows:

**Immune Globulins** . . . . . . . . . . .90281-90399
**Immunization Administration for Vaccines/Toxoids** . . . . . . . . . .90471-90472
**Vaccines, Toxoids** . . . . . . . . . . . .90476-90749
**Therapeutic, ►Prophylactic◄ or Diagnostic Infusions** . . . . . . . . . . . . . . . . . . .90780-90781
**Psychiatry** . . . . . . . . . . . . . . . . .90801-90899
**Dialysis** . . . . . . . . . . . . . . . . . . .90918-90999
**Ophthalmology** . . . . . . . . . . . . . .92002-92499
**Otorhinolaryngology** . . . . . . . . .92502-92599
**Echocardiography** . . . . . . . . . . . .93303-93350
**Cardiac Catheterization** . . . . . . .93501-93556
**Non-Invasive Vascular Diagnostic Studies** . . . . . . . . .93875-93990
**Pulmonary** . . . . . . . . . . . . . . . . .94010-94799
**Allergy and Clinical Immunology** . . . . . . .95004-95199

**Neurology and Neuromuscular** . .95805-95999
**Neurostimulators,**
**Analysis-Programming** . . . . . .95970-95975
**Central Nervous System**
**Assessments/Tests** . . . . . . . . . .96100-96117
**Chemotherapy Administration** . .96400-96549
**Dermatological Procedures** . . . . .96900-96999
**Physical Medicine and Rehabilitation**
**Modalities** . . . . . . . . . . . . . . .97001-97028
**Constant Attendance** . . . . . . .97032-97039
**Therapeutic Procedures** . . . . .97110-97546
**Osteopathic Manipulative**
**Treatment** . . . . . . . . . . . . . . . .98925-98929
**Chiropractic Manipulative**
**Treatment** . . . . . . . . . . . . . . . .98940-98943
**Special Services, ►Procedures◄ and**
**Reports** . . . . . . . . . . . . . . . . . . . .99000-99199

## Unlisted Service or Procedure

A service or procedure may be provided that is not listed in this edition of *CPT*. When reporting such a service, the appropriate "Unlisted Procedure" code may be used to indicate the service, identifying it by "Special Report" as discussed on this page. The "Unlisted Procedures" and accompanying codes for **Medicine** are as follows:

**90399** Unlisted immune globulin
**90749** Unlisted vaccine/toxoid
**90799** Unlisted therapeutic, prophylactic or diagnostic injection
**90899** Unlisted psychiatric service or procedure
**90999** Unlisted dialysis procedure, inpatient or outpatient
**91299** Unlisted diagnostic gastroenterology procedure
**92499** Unlisted ophthalmological service or procedure
**92599** Unlisted otorhinolaryngological service or procedure
**93799** Unlisted cardiovascular service or procedure
**94799** Unlisted pulmonary service or procedure
**95199** Unlisted allergy/clinical immunologic service or procedure
**95999** Unlisted neurological or neuromuscular diagnostic procedure
**96549** Unlisted chemotherapy procedure
**96999** Unlisted special dermatological service or procedure
**97039** Unlisted modality (specify type and time if constant attendance)
**97139** Unlisted therapeutic procedure (specify)
**97799** Unlisted physical medicine/rehabilitation service or procedure
**99199** Unlisted special service, procedure or report

## Special Report

A service that is rarely provided, unusual, variable, or new may require a special report in determining medical appropriateness of the service. Pertinent information should include an adequate definition or description of the nature, extent, and need for the procedure; and the time, effort, and equipment necessary to provide the service. Additional items which may be included are:

- complexity of symptoms;
- final diagnosis;
- pertinent physical findings;
- diagnostic and therapeutic procedures;
- concurrent problems;
- follow-up care.

## Materials Supplied by Physician

Supplies and materials provided by the physician (eg, sterile trays/drugs), over and above those usually included with the office visit or other services rendered may be listed separately. List drugs, trays, supplies, and materials provided. Identify as 99070.

# Medicine

(90000-90080 have been deleted. To report, see 99201-99215)

(90100-90170 have been deleted. To report, see 99341-99350)

(90200-90220 have been deleted. To report, see 99221-99223)

(90225 has been deleted. To report, use 99431)

(90240-90280 have been deleted. To report, see 99231-99233)

(90282 has been deleted. To report, use 99433)

(90292 has been deleted. To report, use 99238)

(90300-90370 have been deleted. To report, see 99301-99313)

(90400-90470 have been deleted. To report, see 99321-99333)

(90500-90580 have been deleted. To report, see 99281-99288)

(90590 has been deleted. To report, use 99288)

(90600-90630 have been deleted. To report, see 99241-99255)

(90640-90643 have been deleted. To report, see 99241-99245 or 99261-99263)

(90650-90654 have been deleted. To report, see 99271-99275)

(90699 has been deleted. To report, use 99499)

## Immune Globulins

Codes 90281-90399 identify the immune globulin product only and must be reported in addition to the administration codes 90780-90784 as appropriate. Immune globulin products listed here include broad-spectrum and anti-infective immune globulins, antitoxins, and ►various◄ isoantibodies.

⊘ **90281** Immune globulin (Ig), human, for intramuscular use

⊘ **90283** Immune globulin (IgIV), human, for intravenous use

⊘ **90287** Botulinum antitoxin, equine, any route

⊘ **90288** Botulism immune globulin, human, for intravenous use

⊘ **90291** Cytomegalovirus immune globulin (CMV-IgIV), human, for intravenous use

⊘ **90296** Diphtheria antitoxin, equine, any route

⊘ **90371** Hepatitis B immune globulin (HBIg), human, for intramuscular use

⊘ **90375** Rabies immune globulin (RIg), human, for intramuscular and/or subcutaneous use

⊘ **90376** Rabies immune globulin, heat-treated (RIg-HT), human, for intramuscular and/or subcutaneous use

⊘ ● **90378** Respiratory syncytial virus immune globulin (RSV-IgIM), for intramuscular use

⊘ **90379** Respiratory syncytial virus immune globulin (RSV-IgIV), human, for intravenous use

⊘ **90384** Rho(D) immune globulin (RhIg), human, full-dose, for intramuscular use

⊘ **90385** Rho(D) immune globulin (RhIg), human, mini-dose, for intramuscular use

⊘ **90386** Rho(D) immune globulin (RhIgIV), human, for intravenous use

⊘ **90389** Tetanus immune globulin (TIg), human, for intramuscular use

⊘ **90393** Vaccinia immune globulin, human, for intramuscular use

⊘ **90396** Varicella-zoster immune globulin, human, for intramuscular use

⊘ **90399** Unlisted immune globulin

## Immunization Administration for Vaccines/Toxoids

Codes 90471-90472 must be reported in addition to the vaccine and toxoid code(s) 90476-90749.

If a significant separately identifiable Evaluation and Management service ►(eg, office or other outpatient services, preventive medicine services)◄ is performed, the appropriate E/M service code should be reported in addition to the vaccine and toxoid administration codes.

(For allergy testing, see 95004 et seq)

(For skin testing of bacterial, viral, fungal extracts, see 86485-86586)

(For therapeutic or diagnostic injections, see 90782-90799)

▲**90471** Immunization administration (includes percutaneous, intradermal, subcutaneous, intramuscular and jet injections and/or intranasal or oral administration); one vaccine (single or combination vaccine/toxoid)

+▲**90472** each additional vaccine (single or combination vaccine/toxoid) (List separately in addition to code for primary procedure)

►(Use 90472 in conjunction with code 90471)◄

(For administration of immune globulins, use 90780-90784, and see 90281-90399)

(For intravesical administration of BCG vaccine, use 51720, and see 90586)

## Vaccines, Toxoids

Codes 90476-90748 identify the vaccine product **only.** ►To report the administration of a vaccine/toxoid, the vaccine/toxoid product codes 90476-90749 must be used in addition to an immunization administration code(s) 90471, 90472. Do not append the modifier '-51' to the vaccine/toxoid product codes 90476-90749.

If a significantly separately identifiable Evaluation and Management service (eg, office or other outpatient services, preventive medicine services) is performed, the appropriate E/M service code should be reported in addition to the vaccine and toxoid administration codes.◄

To meet the reporting requirements of immunization registries, vaccine distribution programs, and reporting systems (eg, Vaccine Adverse Event Reporting System) the exact vaccine product administered needs to be reported. Multiple codes for a particular vaccine are provided in CPT when the schedule (number of doses or timing) differs for two or more products of the same vaccine type (eg, hepatitis A, Hib) or the vaccine product is available in more than one chemical formulation, dosage, or route of administration.

Separate codes are available for combination vaccines (eg, DTP-Hib, DtaP-Hib, HepB-Hib). It is inappropriate to code each component of a combination vaccine separately. If a specific vaccine code is not available, the unlisted procedure code should be reported, until a new code becomes available.

(For immune globulins, see codes 90281-90399, and 90780-90784 for administration of immune globulins)

⊘ **90476** Adenovirus vaccine, type 4, live, for oral use

⊘ **90477** Adenovirus vaccine, type 7, live, for oral use

⊘ **90581** Anthrax vaccine, for subcutaneous use

⊘ **90585** Bacillus Calmette-Guerin vaccine (BCG) for tuberculosis, live, for percutaneous use

⊘ **90586** Bacillus Calmette-Guerin vaccine (BCG) for bladder cancer, live, for intravesical use

►(90592 has been deleted)◄

⊘ **90632** Hepatitis A vaccine, adult dosage, for intramuscular use

⊘ **90633** Hepatitis A vaccine, pediatric/adolescent dosage-2 dose schedule, for intramuscular use

⊘ **90634** Hepatitis A vaccine, pediatric/adolescent dosage-3 dose schedule, for intramuscular use

⊘ **90636** Hepatitis A and hepatitis B vaccine (HepA-HepB), adult dosage, for intramuscular use

⊘ **90645** Hemophilus influenza b vaccine (Hib), HbOC conjugate (4 dose schedule), for intramuscular use

⊘ **90646** Hemophilus influenza b vaccine (Hib), PRP-D conjugate, for booster use only, intramuscular use

⊘ **90647** Hemophilus influenza b vaccine (Hib), PRP-OMP conjugate (3 dose schedule), for intramuscular use

⊘ **90648** Hemophilus influenza b vaccine (Hib),PRP-T conjugate (4 dose schedule), for intramuscular use

⊘ **90657** Influenza virus vaccine, split virus, 6-35 months dosage, for intramuscular or jet injection use

⊘ **90658** Influenza virus vaccine, split virus, 3 years and above dosage, for intramuscular or jet injection use

⊘ **90659** Influenza virus vaccine, whole virus, for intramuscular or jet injection use

⊘ **90660** Influenza virus vaccine, live, for intranasal use

⊘ **90665** Lyme disease vaccine, adult dosage, for intramuscular use

⊘ **90669** Pneumococcal conjugate vaccine, polyvalent, for intramuscular use

⊘ **90675** Rabies vaccine, for intramuscular use

⊘ **90676** Rabies vaccine, for intradermal use

⊘ **90680** Rotavirus vaccine, tetravalent, live, for oral use

⊘ **90690** Typhoid vaccine, live, oral

⊘ **90691** Typhoid vaccine, Vi capsular polysaccharide (ViCPs), for intramuscular use

⊘ **90692** Typhoid vaccine, heat- and phenol-inactivated (H-P), for subcutaneous or intradermal use

⊘ **90693** Typhoid vaccine, acetone-killed, dried (AKD), for subcutaneous or jet injection use (U.S. military)

⊘ **90700** Diphtheria, tetanus toxoids, and acellular pertussis vaccine (DTaP), for intramuscular use

⊘ **90701** Diphtheria, tetanus toxoids, and whole cell pertussis vaccine (DTP), for intramuscular use

⊘ **90702** Diphtheria and tetanus toxoids (DT) adsorbed for pediatric use, for intramuscular use

⊘ **90703** Tetanus toxoid adsorbed, for intramuscular or jet injection use

⊘ **90704** Mumps virus vaccine, live, for subcutaneous or jet injection use

⊘ **90705** Measles virus vaccine, live, for subcutaneous or jet injection use

⊘ **90706** Rubella virus vaccine, live, for subcutaneous or jet injection use

⊘ **90707** Measles, mumps and rubella virus vaccine (MMR), live, for subcutaneous or jet injection use

⊘ **90708** Measles and rubella virus vaccine, live, for subcutaneous or jet injection use

⊘ **90709** Rubella and mumps virus vaccine, live, for subcutaneous use

⊘ **90710** Measles, mumps, rubella, and varicella vaccine (MMRV), live, for subcutaneous use

(90711 has been deleted)

⊘ **90712** Poliovirus vaccine, (any type(s)) (OPV), live, for oral use

⊘ **90713** Poliovirus vaccine, inactivated, (IPV), for subcutaneous use

(90714 has been deleted. To report, see 90690-90693)

⊘ **90716** Varicella virus vaccine, live, for subcutaneous use

⊘ **90717** Yellow fever vaccine, live, for subcutaneous use

⊘ **90718** Tetanus and diphtheria toxoids (Td) adsorbed for adult use, for intramuscular or jet injection

⊘ **90719** Diphtheria toxoid, for intramuscular use

⊘ **90720** Diphtheria, tetanus toxoids, and whole cell pertussis vaccine and Hemophilus influenza B vaccine (DTP-Hib), for intramuscular use

⊘ **90721** Diphtheria, tetanus toxoids, and acellular pertussis vaccine and Hemophilus influenza B vaccine (DtaP-Hib), for intramuscular use

(90724 has been deleted. To report, see 90657-90660)

⊘ **90725** Cholera vaccine for injectable use

(For oral cholera, use 90592)

(90726 has been deleted. To report, see 90675, 90676)

⊘ **90727** Plague vaccine, for intramuscular or jet injection use

(90728 has been deleted. To report, see 90585, 90586)

(90730 has been deleted. To report, see 90632-90634)

(90731 has been deleted. To report, see 90744-90747)

⊘ **90732** Pneumococcal polysaccharide vaccine, 23-valent, adult dosage, for subcutaneous or intramuscular use

⊘ **90733** Meningocococcal polysaccharide vaccine (any group(s)), for subcutaneous or jet injection use

⊘ **90735** Japanese encephalitis virus vaccine, for subcutaneous use

(90737 has been deleted. To report, see 90645-90648)

(90741 has been deleted. To report, see 90281-90283)

(90742 has been deleted. To report, see 90287-90399)

⊘ ▲ **90744** Hepatitis B vaccine, pediatric/adolescent dosage, for intramuscular use

►(90745 has been deleted)◄

⊘ **90746** Hepatitis B vaccine, adult dosage, for intramuscular use

⊘ **90747** Hepatitis B vaccine, dialysis or immunosuppressed patient dosage, for intramuscular use

⊘ **90748** Hepatitis B and Hemophilus influenza b vaccine (HepB-Hib), for intramuscular use

⊘ **90749** Unlisted vaccine/toxoid

(90750-90754 have been deleted. To report, see 99381-99387)

(90755 has been deleted)

(90757 has been deleted. To report, use 99432)

(90760-90764 have been deleted. To report, see 99391-99397)

(90774 has been deleted. To report, use 96110)

(90778 has been deleted. To report, use 94772)

## Therapeutic or Diagnostic Infusions (Excludes Chemotherapy)

These procedures encompass prolonged intravenous injections.

These codes require the presence of the physician during the infusion. These codes are not to be used for intradermal, subcutaneous or intramuscular or routine IV drug injections. For these services, see 90782-90788.

These codes may not be used in addition to prolonged services codes.

**90780** IV infusion for therapy/diagnosis, administered by physician or under direct supervision of physician; up to one hour

**+ 90781** each additional hour, up to eight (8) hours (List separately in addition to code for primary procedure)

(Use 90781 in conjunction with code 90780)

## Therapeutic, ▸Prophylactic◂ or Diagnostic Injections

**▲90782** Therapeutic, prophylactic or diagnostic injection (specify material injected); subcutaneous or intramuscular

▸(For administration of vaccines/toxoids, see 90471-90472)◂

**90783** intra-arterial

**90784** intravenous

(90782-90784 do not include injections for allergen immunotherapy. For allergen immunotherapy injections, see 95115-95117)

**90788** Intramuscular injection of antibiotic (specify)

(90790-90796 have been deleted. To report, see 96408-96414, 96420-96425, 96440, 96450, 96530, 96545, 96549)

(90798 has been deleted. To report, see 90780, 90781, 90784)

**▲90799** Unlisted therapeutic, prophylactic or diagnostic injection

(For allergy immunizations, see 95004 et seq)

## Psychiatry

Hospital care by the attending physician in treating a psychiatric inpatient or partial hospitalization may be initial or subsequent in nature (see 99221-99233) and may include exchanges with nursing and ancillary personnel. Hospital care services involve a variety of responsibilities unique to the medical management of inpatients, such as physician hospital orders, interpretation of laboratory or other medical diagnostic studies and observations.

Some patients receive hospital evaluation and management services only and others receive evaluation and management services and other procedures. If other procedures such as electroconvulsive therapy or psychotherapy are rendered in addition to hospital evaluation and management services, these should be listed separately (ie, hospital care service plus electroconvulsive therapy or when psychotherapy is done, an appropriate code defining psychotherapy with medical evaluation and management services). The modifier '-22' may be used to indicate a more extensive service. The modifier '-52' may be used to signify a service that is reduced or less extensive than the usual procedure.

Other evaluation and management services, such as office medical service or other patient encounters, may be described as listed in the section on **Evaluation and Management,** if appropriate.

The Evaluation and Management services should not be reported separately, when reporting codes 90805, 90807, 90809, 90811, 90813, 90815, 90817, 90819, 90822, 90824, 90827, 90829.

Consultation for psychiatric evaluation of a patient includes examination of a patient and exchange of information with the primary physician and other informants such as nurses or family members, and preparation of a report. These consultation services (99241-99263) are limited to initial or follow-up evaluation and do not involve psychiatric treatment.

### Psychiatric Diagnostic or Evaluative Interview Procedures

Psychiatric diagnostic interview examination includes a history, mental status, and a disposition, and may include communication with family or other sources, ordering and medical interpretation of laboratory or other medical diagnostic studies. In certain circumstances other informants will be seen in lieu of the patient.

Interactive psychiatric diagnostic interview examination is typically furnished to children. It involves the use of physical aids and non-verbal communication to overcome barriers to therapeutic interaction between the clinician and a patient who has not yet developed, or has lost, either the expressive language communication skills to explain his/her symptoms and response to treatment, or the receptive communication skills to understand the clinician if he/she were to use ordinary adult language for communication.

**90801** Psychiatric diagnostic interview examination

**90802** Interactive psychiatric diagnostic interview examination using play equipment, physical devices, language interpreter, or other mechanisms of communication

## Psychiatric Therapeutic Procedures

Psychotherapy is the treatment for mental illness and behavioral disturbances in which the clinician establishes a professional contract with the patient and, through definitive therapeutic communication, attempts to alleviate the emotional disturbances, reverse or change maladaptive patterns of behavior, and encourage personality growth and development. The codes for reporting psychotherapy are divided into two broad categories: Interactive Psychotherapy; and Insight Oriented, Behavior Modifying and/or Supportive Psychotherapy.

Interactive psychotherapy is typically furnished to children. It involves the use of physical aids and non-verbal communication to overcome barriers to therapeutic interaction between the clinician and a patient who has not yet developed, or has lost, either the expressive language communication skills to explain his/her symptoms and response to treatment, or the receptive communication skills to understand the clinician if he/she were to use ordinary adult language for communication.

Insight oriented, behavior modifying and/or supportive psychotherapy refers to the development of insight or affective understanding, the use of behavior modification techniques, the use of supportive interactions, the use of cognitive discussion of reality, or any combination of the above to provide therapeutic change.

Some patients receive psychotherapy only and others receive psychotherapy and medical evaluation and management services. These evaluation and management services involve a variety of responsibilities unique to the medical management of psychiatric patients, such as medical diagnostic evaluation (eg, evaluation of comorbid medical conditions, drug interactions, and physical examinations), drug management when indicated, physician orders, interpretation of laboratory or other medical diagnostic studies and observations.

In reporting psychotherapy, the appropriate code is chosen on the basis of the type of psychotherapy (interactive using non-verbal techniques versus insight oriented, behavior modifying and/or supportive using verbal techniques), the place of service (office versus inpatient), the face-to-face time spent with the patient during psychotherapy, and whether evaluation and management services are furnished on the same date of service as psychotherapy.

To report medical evaluation and management services furnished on a day when psychotherapy is not provided, select the appropriate code from the **Evaluation and Management Services Guidelines.**

### Office or Other Outpatient Facility

#### Insight Oriented, Behavior Modifying and/or Supportive Psychotherapy

**90804** Individual psychotherapy, insight oriented, behavior modifying and/or supportive, in an office or outpatient facility, approximately 20 to 30 minutes face-to-face with the patient;

**90805** with medical evaluation and management services

**90806** Individual psychotherapy, insight oriented, behavior modifying and/or supportive, in an office or outpatient facility, approximately 45 to 50 minutes face-to-face with the patient;

**90807** with medical evaluation and management services

**90808** Individual psychotherapy, insight oriented, behavior modifying and/or supportive, in an office or outpatient facility, approximately 75 to 80 minutes face-to-face with the patient;

**90809** with medical evaluation and management services

### Interactive Psychotherapy

**90810** Individual psychotherapy, interactive, using play equipment, physical devices, language interpreter, or other mechanisms of non-verbal communication, in an office or outpatient facility, approximately 20 to 30 minutes face-to-face with the patient;

**90811** with medical evaluation and management services

**90812** Individual psychotherapy, interactive, using play equipment, physical devices, language interpreter, or other mechanisms of non-verbal communication, in an office or outpatient facility, approximately 45 to 50 minutes face-to-face with the patient;

**90813** with medical evaluation and management services

**90814** Individual psychotherapy, interactive, using play equipment, physical devices, language interpreter, or other mechanisms of non-verbal communication, in an office or outpatient facility, approximately 75 to 80 minutes face-to-face with the patient;

**90815** with medical evaluation and management services

## Inpatient Hospital, Partial Hospital or Residential Care Facility

### Insight Oriented, Behavior Modifying and/or Supportive Psychotherapy

**90816** Individual psychotherapy, insight oriented, behavior modifying and/or supportive, in an inpatient hospital, partial hospital or residential care setting, approximately 20 to 30 minutes face-to-face with the patient;

**90817** with medical evaluation and management services

**90818** Individual psychotherapy, insight oriented, behavior modifying and/or supportive, in an inpatient hospital, partial hospital or residential care setting, approximately 45 to 50 minutes face-to-face with the patient;

**90819** with medical evaluation and management services

(90820 has been deleted. To report, use 90802)

**90821** Individual psychotherapy, insight oriented, behavior modifying and/or supportive, in an inpatient hospital, partial hospital or residential care setting, approximately 75 to 80 minutes face-to-face with the patient;

**90822** with medical evaluation and management services

### Interactive Psychotherapy

**90823** Individual psychotherapy, interactive, using play equipment, physical devices, language interpreter, or other mechanisms of non-verbal communication, in an inpatient hospital, partial hospital or residential care setting, approximately 20 to 30 minutes face-to-face with the patient;

**90824** with medical evaluation and management services

(90825 has been deleted. To report, use 90885)

**90826** Individual psychotherapy, interactive, using play equipment, physical devices, language interpreter, or other mechanisms of non-verbal communication, in an inpatient hospital, partial hospital or residential care setting, approximately 45 to 50 minutes face-to-face with the patient;

**90827** with medical evaluation and management services

**90828** Individual psychotherapy, interactive, using play equipment, physical devices, language interpreter, or other mechanisms of non-verbal communication, in an inpatient hospital, partial hospital or residential care setting, approximately 75 to 80 minutes face-to-face with the patient;

**90829** with medical evaluation and management services

(90830 has been deleted. To report, use 96100)

(90831 has been deleted. To report, see 99371-99373)

(90835 has been deleted. To report, use 90865)

(90841 has been deleted)

(90842 has been deleted. To report, see 90808, 90809, 90821, 90822)

(90843 has been deleted. To report, see 90804, 90805, 90816, 90817)

(90844 has been deleted. To report, see 90806, 90807, 90818, 90819)

## Other Psychotherapy

**90845** Psychoanalysis

**90846** Family psychotherapy (without the patient present)

**90847** Family psychotherapy (conjoint psychotherapy) (with patient present)

(90848 has been deleted. To report, use 90847)

**90849** Multiple-family group psychotherapy

**90853** Group psychotherapy (other than of a multiple-family group)

(90855 has been deleted. To report, see 90810-90815, and 90823-90829)

**90857** Interactive group psychotherapy

## Other Psychiatric Services or Procedures

**90862** Pharmacologic management, including prescription, use, and review of medication with no more than minimal medical psychotherapy

**90865** Narcosynthesis for psychiatric diagnostic and therapeutic purposes (eg, sodium amobarbital (Amytal) interview)

**90870** Electroconvulsive therapy (includes necessary monitoring); single seizure

**90871** multiple seizures, per day

(90872 has been deleted. To report, use 90899)

**90875** Individual psychophysiological therapy incorporating biofeedback training by any modality (face-to-face with the patient), with psychotherapy (eg, insight oriented, behavior modifying or supportive psychotherapy); approximately 20-30 minutes

**90876** approximately 45-50 minutes

**90880** Hypnotherapy

**90882** Environmental intervention for medical management purposes on a psychiatric patients behalf with agencies, employers, or institutions

**90885** Psychiatric evaluation of hospital records, other psychiatric reports, psychometric and/or projective tests, and other accumulated data for medical diagnostic purposes

**90887** Interpretation or explanation of results of psychiatric, other medical examinations and procedures, or other accumulated data to family or other responsible persons, or advising them how to assist patient

**90889** Preparation of report of patients psychiatric status, history, treatment, or progress (other than for legal or consultative purposes) for other physicians, agencies, or insurance carriers

**90899** Unlisted psychiatric service or procedure

# Biofeedback

(For psychophysiological therapy incorporating biofeedback training, see 90875, 90876)

(90900 has been deleted. To report, use 90901)

**90901** Biofeedback training by any modality

(90902, 90904, 90906, 90908, 90910 have been deleted. To report, use 90901)

**90911** Biofeedback training, perineal muscles, anorectal or urethral sphincter, including EMG and/or manometry

(90915 has been deleted. To report, use 90901)

# Dialysis

Evaluation and management services unrelated to the dialysis procedure that cannot be rendered during the dialysis session may be reported in addition to the dialysis procedure. All evaluation and management services related to the patient's end stage renal disease that are rendered on a day when dialysis is performed and all other patient care services that are rendered during the dialysis procedure are included in the dialysis procedure, 90935-90947.

## End Stage Renal Disease Services

**90918** End stage renal disease (ESRD) related services per full month; for patients under two years of age to include monitoring for the adequacy of nutrition, assessment of growth and development, and counseling of parents

**90919** for patients between two and eleven years of age to include monitoring for the adequacy of nutrition, assessment of growth and development, and counseling of parents

**90920** for patients between twelve and nineteen years of age to include monitoring for the adequacy of nutrition, assessment of growth and development, and counseling of parents

**90921** for patients twenty years of age and over

**90922** End stage renal disease (ESRD) related services (less than full month), per day; for patients under two years of age

**90923** for patients between two and eleven years of age

**90924** for patients between twelve and nineteen years of age

**90925** for patients twenty years of age and over

## Hemodialysis

(For cannula declotting, see ►36831, 36833◄ 36860, 36861)

►(For declotting of implanted vascular access device or catheter by thrombolytic agent, use 36550)◄

(For prolonged physician attendance, see 99354-99360)

**90935** Hemodialysis procedure with single physician evaluation

**90937** Hemodialysis procedure requiring repeated evaluation(s) with or without substantial revision of dialysis prescription

(90941-90944 have been deleted. To report, see 90935-90937)

## Miscellaneous Dialysis Procedures

(For insertion of intraperitoneal cannula or catheter, see 49420, 49421)

(For prolonged physician attendance, see 99354-99360)

**90945** Dialysis procedure other than hemodialysis (eg, peritoneal, hemofiltration), with single physician evaluation

**90947** Dialysis procedure other than hemodialysis (eg, peritoneal, hemofiltration) requiring repeated evaluations, with or without substantial revision of dialysis prescription

(90951-90958 have been deleted. To report, see 90935, 90937)

(90966-90985 have been deleted. To report, see 90945, 90947)

(90988, 90991 and 90994 have been deleted. To report, see 90918-90921)

**90989** Dialysis training, patient, including helper where applicable, any mode, completed course

(90990, 90992 have been deleted. To report, see 90989 and 90993)

**90993** Dialysis training, patient, including helper where applicable, any mode, course not completed, per training session

(90995 has been deleted. To report, see 90918-90921)

**90997** Hemoperfusion (eg, with activated charcoal or resin)

(90998 has been deleted. To report, use 90922)

**90999** Unlisted dialysis procedure, inpatient or outpatient

## Gastroenterology

(For duodenal intubation and aspiration, see 89100-89105)

(For gastrointestinal radiologic procedures, see 74210-74363)

(For esophagoscopy procedures, see 43200-43228; upper GI endoscopy 43234-43259; endoscopy, small bowel and stomal 44360-44393; proctosigmoidoscopy 45300-45321; sigmoidoscopy 45330-45339; colonoscopy 45355-45385; anoscopy 46600-46615)

**91000** Esophageal intubation and collection of washings for cytology, including preparation of specimens (separate procedure)

**91010** Esophageal motility (manometric study of the esophagus and/or gastroesophageal junction) study;

**91011** with mecholyl or similar stimulant

**91012** with acid perfusion studies

**91020** Gastric motility (manometric) studies

**91030** Esophagus, acid perfusion (Bernstein) test for esophagitis

**91032** Esophagus, acid reflux test, with intraluminal pH electrode for detection of gastroesophageal reflux;

**91033** prolonged recording

**91052** Gastric analysis test with injection of stimulant of gastric secretion (eg, histamine, insulin, pentagastrin, calcium and secretin)

(For gastric biopsy by capsule, peroral, via tube, one or more specimens, use 43600)

(For gastric laboratory procedures, see also 89130-89141)

**91055** Gastric intubation, washings, and preparing slides for cytology (separate procedure)

(For gastric lavage, therapeutic, use 91105)

**91060** Gastric saline load test

(For biopsy by capsule, small intestine, per oral, via tube (one or more specimens), use 44100)

**91065** Breath hydrogen test (eg, for detection of lactase deficiency)

(91090 has been deleted)

**91100** Intestinal bleeding tube, passage, positioning and monitoring

**91105** Gastric intubation, and aspiration or lavage for treatment (eg, for ingested poisons)

(For cholangiography, see 47500, 74320)

(For abdominal paracentesis, see 49080, 49081; with instillation of medication, see 96440, 96445)

(For peritoneoscopy, use ►49320◄; with biopsy, use ►49321◄)

(For peritoneoscopy and guided transhepatic cholangiography, use ►47560◄; with biopsy, use ►47561◄)

(For splenoportography, see 38200, 75810)

**91122** Anorectal manometry

**91299** Unlisted diagnostic gastroenterology procedure

# Ophthalmology

(For surgical procedures, see **Surgery,** Eye and Ocular Adnexa, 65091 et seq)

**Definitions**

***Intermediate ophthalmological services*** describes an evaluation of a new or existing condition complicated with a new diagnostic or management problem not necessarily relating to the primary diagnosis, including history, general medical observation, external ocular and adnexal examination and other diagnostic procedures as indicated; may include the use of mydriasis for ophthalmoscopy.

*For example:*

a. Review of history, external examination, ophthalmoscopy, biomicroscopy for an acute complicated condition (eg, iritis) not requiring comprehensive ophthalmological services.

b. Review of interval history, external examination, ophthalmoscopy, biomicroscopy and tonometry in established patient with known cataract not requiring comprehensive ophthalmological services.

***Comprehensive ophthalmological services*** describes a general evaluation of the complete visual system. The comprehensive services constitute a single service entity but need not be performed at one session. The service includes history, general medical observation, external and ophthalmoscopic examinations, gross visual fields and basic sensorimotor examination. It often includes, as indicated: biomicroscopy, examination with cycloplegia or mydriasis and tonometry. It always includes initiation of diagnostic and treatment programs.

Intermediate and comprehensive ophthalmological services constitute integrated services in which medical decision making cannot be separated from the examining techniques used. Itemization of service components, such as slit lamp examination, keratometry, routine ophthalmoscopy, retinoscopy, tonometry, or motor evaluation is not applicable.

*For example:*

The comprehensive services required for diagnosis and treatment of a patient with symptoms indicating possible disease of the visual system, such as glaucoma, cataract or retinal disease, or to rule out disease of the visual system, new or established patient.

*Initiation of diagnostic and treatment program* includes the prescription of medication, and arranging for special ophthalmological diagnostic or treatment services, consultations, laboratory procedures and radiological services.

***Special ophthalmological services*** describes services in which a special evaluation of part of the visual system is made, which goes beyond the services included under general ophthalmological services, or in which special treatment is given. Special ophthalmological services may be reported in addition to the general ophthalmological services or evaluation and management services.

*For example:*

Fluorescein angioscopy, quantitative visual field examination, refraction or extended color vision examination (such as Nagel's anomaloscope) should be separately reported.

Prescription of lenses, when required is included in 92015 Determination of refractive state. It includes specification of lens type (monofocal, bifocal, other), lens power, axis, prism, absorptive factor, impact resistance, and other factors.

Interpretation and report by the physician is an integral part of special ophthalmological services where indicated. Technical procedures (which may or may not be performed by the physician personally) are often part of the service, but should not be mistaken to constitute the service itself.

## General Ophthalmological Services

### New Patient

A new patient is one who has not received any professional services from the physician or another physician of the same specialty who belongs to the same group practice within the past three years.

**92002** Ophthalmological services: medical examination and evaluation with initiation of diagnostic and treatment program; intermediate, new patient

**92004** comprehensive, new patient, one or more visits

## Established Patient

An established patient is one who has received professional services from the physician or another physician of the same specialty who belongs to the same group practice within the past three years.

**92012** Ophthalmological services: medical examination and evaluation, with initiation or continuation of diagnostic and treatment program; intermediate, established patient

**92014** comprehensive, established patient, one or more visits

(For surgical procedures, see **Surgery,** Eye and Ocular Adnexa, 65091 et seq)

# Special Ophthalmological Services

**92015** Determination of refractive state

**92018** Ophthalmological examination and evaluation, under general anesthesia, with or without manipulation of globe for passive range of motion or other manipulation to facilitate diagnostic examination; complete

**92019** limited

**92020** Gonioscopy (separate procedure)

(For gonioscopy under general anesthesia, use 92018)

**92060** Sensorimotor examination with multiple measurements of ocular deviation (eg, restrictive or paretic muscle with diplopia) with interpretation and report (separate procedure)

**92065** Orthoptic and/or pleoptic training, with continuing medical direction and evaluation

**92070** Fitting of contact lens for treatment of disease, including supply of lens

**92081** Visual field examination, unilateral or bilateral, with interpretation and report; limited examination (eg, tangent screen, Autoplot, arc perimeter, or single stimulus level automated test, such as Octopus 3 or 7 equivalent)

**92082** intermediate examination (eg, at least 2 isopters on Goldmann perimeter, or semiquantitative, automated suprathreshold screening program, Humphrey suprathreshold automatic diagnostic test, Octopus program 33)

**92083** extended examination (eg, Goldmann visual fields with at least 3 isopters plotted and static determination within the central 30°, or quantitative, automated threshold perimetry, Octopus program G-1, 32 or 42, Humphrey visual field analyzer full threshold programs 30-2, 24-2, or 30/60-2)

(Gross visual field testing (eg, confrontation testing) is a part of general ophthalmological services and is not reported separately)

**92100** Serial tonometry (separate procedure) with multiple measurements of intraocular pressure over an extended time period with interpretation and report, same day (eg, diurnal curve or medical treatment of acute elevation of intraocular pressure)

**92120** Tonography with interpretation and report, recording indentation tonometer method or perilimbal suction method

**92130** Tonography with water provocation

**92135** Scanning computerized ophthalmic diagnostic imaging (eg, scanning laser) with interpretation and report, unilateral

**92140** Provocative tests for glaucoma, with interpretation and report, without tonography

## Ophthalmoscopy

Routine ophthalmoscopy is part of general and special ophthalmologic services whenever indicated. It is a non-itemized service and is not reported separately.

**92225** Ophthalmoscopy, extended, with retinal drawing (eg, for retinal detachment, melanoma), with interpretation and report; initial

**92226** subsequent

**92230** Fluorescein angioscopy with interpretation and report

**92235** Fluorescein angiography (includes multiframe imaging) with interpretation and report

**92240** Indocyanine-green angiography (includes multiframe imaging) with interpretation and report

**92250** Fundus photography with interpretation and report

**92260** Ophthalmodynamometry

(For ophthalmoscopy under general anesthesia, use 92018)

## Other Specialized Services

**92265** Needle oculoelectromyography, one or more extraocular muscles, one or both eyes, with interpretation and report

**92270** Electro-oculography with interpretation and report

**92275** Electroretinography with interpretation and report

(92280 has been deleted. To report visual evoked potential testing of the central nervous system, use 95930)

(For electronystagmography for vestibular function studies, see 92541 et seq)

(For ophthalmic echography (diagnostic ultrasound), see 76511-76529)

**92283** Color vision examination, extended, eg, anomaloscope or equivalent

(Color vision testing with pseudoisochromatic plates (such as HRR or Ishihara) is not reported separately. It is included in the appropriate general or ophthalmological service.)

**92284** Dark adaptation examination with interpretation and report

**92285** External ocular photography with interpretation and report for documentation of medical progress (eg, close-up photography, slit lamp photography, goniophotography, stereo-photography)

**92286** Special anterior segment photography with interpretation and report; with specular endothelial microscopy and cell count

**92287** with fluorescein angiography

## Contact Lens Services

The prescription of contact lens includes specification of optical and physical characteristics (such as power, size, curvature, flexibility, gas-permeability). It is NOT a part of the general ophthalmological services.

The fitting of contact lens includes instruction and training of the wearer and incidental revision of the lens during the training period.

Follow-up of successfully fitted extended wear lenses is reported as part of a general ophthalmological service (92012 et seq).

The supply of contact lenses may be reported as part of the service of fitting. It may also be reported separately by using 92391 or 92396 and modifier '-26' for the service of fitting without supply.

(For therapeutic or surgical use of contact lens, see 68340, 92070)

**92310** Prescription of optical and physical characteristics of and fitting of contact lens, with medical supervision of adaptation; corneal lens, both eyes, except for aphakia

(For prescription and fitting of one eye, add modifier '-52')

**92311** corneal lens for aphakia, one eye

**92312** corneal lens for aphakia, both eyes

**92313** corneoscleral lens

**92314** Prescription of optical and physical characteristics of contact lens, with medical supervision of adaptation and direction of fitting by independent technician; corneal lens, both eyes except for aphakia

(For prescription and fitting of one eye, add modifier '-52')

**92315** corneal lens for aphakia, one eye

**92316** corneal lens for aphakia, both eyes

**92317** corneoscleral lens

**92325** Modification of contact lens (separate procedure), with medical supervision of adaptation

**92326** Replacement of contact lens

## Ocular Prosthetics, Artificial Eye

**92330** Prescription, fitting, and supply of ocular prosthesis (artificial eye), with medical supervision of adaptation

(If supply is not included, use modifier '-26'; to report supply separately, use 92393)

**92335** Prescription of ocular prosthesis (artificial eye) and direction of fitting and supply by independent technician, with medical supervision of adaptation

## Spectacle Services (Including Prosthesis for Aphakia)

Prescription of lenses, when required, is included in 92015 Determination of refractive state. It includes specification of lens type (monofocal, bifocal, other), lens power, axis, prism, absorptive factor, impact resistance, and other factors.

Fitting of spectacles is a separate service; when provided by the physician, it is reported as indicated by 92340-92371.

Fitting includes measurement of anatomical facial characteristics, the writing of laboratory specifications, and the final adjustment of the spectacles to the visual axes and anatomical topography. Presence of physician is not required.

Supply of materials is a separate service component; it is not part of the service of fitting spectacles.

**92340** Fitting of spectacles, except for aphakia; monofocal

**92341** bifocal

**92342** multifocal, other than bifocal

**92352** Fitting of spectacle prosthesis for aphakia; monofocal

**92353** multifocal

**92354** Fitting of spectacle mounted low vision aid; single element system

**92355** telescopic or other compound lens system

**92358** Prosthesis service for aphakia, temporary (disposable or loan, including materials)

**92370** Repair and refitting spectacles; except for aphakia

**92371** spectacle prosthesis for aphakia

## Supply of Materials

**92390** Supply of spectacles, except prosthesis for aphakia and low vision aids

**92391** Supply of contact lenses, except prosthesis for aphakia

(For supply of contact lenses reported as part of the service of fitting, see 92310-92313)

(For replacement of contact lens, use 92326)

**92392** Supply of low vision aids (A low vision aid is any lens or device used to aid or improve visual function in a person whose vision cannot be normalized by conventional spectacle correction. Includes reading additions up to 4D.)

**92393** Supply of ocular prosthesis (artificial eye)

(For supply reported as part of the service of fitting, use 92330)

**92395** Supply of permanent prosthesis for aphakia; spectacles

(For temporary spectacle correction, use 92358)

**92396** contact lenses

(For supply reported as part of the service of fitting, see 92311, 92312)

(Use 99070 for the supply of other materials, drugs, trays, etc.)

## Other Procedures

**92499** Unlisted ophthalmological service or procedure

# Special Otorhinolaryngologic Services

Diagnostic or treatment procedures usually included in a comprehensive otorhinolaryngologic evaluation or office visit, are reported as an integrated medical service, using appropriate descriptors from the 99201 series. Itemization of component procedures (eg, otoscopy, rhinoscopy, tuning fork test) does not apply.

Special otorhinolaryngologic services are those diagnostic and treatment services not usually included in a comprehensive otorhinolaryngologic evaluation or office visit. These services are reported separately, using descriptors from the 92500 series.

All services include medical diagnostic evaluation. Technical procedures (which may or may not be performed by the physician personally) are often part of the service, but should not be mistaken to constitute the service itself.

(For laryngoscopy with stroboscopy, use 31579)

**92502** Otolaryngologic examination under general anesthesia

**92504** Binocular microscopy (separate diagnostic procedure)

**92506** Evaluation of speech, language, voice, communication, auditory processing, and/or aural rehabilitation status

**92507** Treatment of speech, language, voice, communication, and/ or auditory processing disorder (includes aural rehabilitation); individual

**92508** group, two or more individuals

**92510** Aural rehabilitation following cochlear implant (includes evaluation of aural rehabilitation status and hearing, therapeutic services) with or without speech processor programming

**92511** Nasopharyngoscopy with endoscope (separate procedure)

**92512** Nasal function studies (eg, rhinomanometry)

**92516** Facial nerve function studies (eg, electroneuronography)

**92520** Laryngeal function studies

**92525** Evaluation of swallowing and oral function for feeding

**92526** Treatment of swallowing dysfunction and/or oral function for feeding

## Vestibular Function Tests, With Observation and Evaluation by Physician, Without Electrical Recording

**92531** Spontaneous nystagmus, including gaze

**92532** Positional nystagmus

**92533** Caloric vestibular test, each irrigation (binaural, bithermal stimulation constitutes four tests)

**92534** Optokinetic nystagmus

## Vestibular Function Tests, With Recording (eg, ENG, PENG), and Medical Diagnostic Evaluation

**92541** Spontaneous nystagmus test, including gaze and fixation nystagmus, with recording

**92542** Positional nystagmus test, minimum of 4 positions, with recording

**92543** Caloric vestibular test, each irrigation (binaural, bithermal stimulation constitutes four tests), with recording

**92544** Optokinetic nystagmus test, bidirectional, foveal or peripheral stimulation, with recording

**92545** Oscillating tracking test, with recording

**92546** Sinusoidal vertical axis rotational testing

**+ 92547** Use of vertical electrodes (List separately in addition to code for primary procedure)

(Use 92547 in conjunction with codes 92541-92546)

(For unlisted vestibular tests, use 92599)

**92548** Computerized dynamic posturography

## Audiologic Function Tests With Medical Diagnostic Evaluation

The audiometric tests listed below imply the use of calibrated electronic equipment. Other hearing tests (such as whispered voice, tuning fork) are considered part of the general otorhinolaryngologic services and are not reported separately. All descriptors refer to testing both ears. Use the modifier '-52' if a test is applied to one ear instead of to two ears. All descriptors (except 92559) apply to testing of individuals; for testing of groups, use 92559 and specify test(s) used.

(For evaluation of speech, language and/or hearing problems through observation and assessment of performance, use 92506)

**92551** Screening test, pure tone, air only

**92552** Pure tone audiometry (threshold); air only

**92553** air and bone

**92555** Speech audiometry threshold;

**92556** with speech recognition

**92557** Comprehensive audiometry threshold evaluation and speech recognition (92553 and 92556 combined)

(For hearing aid evaluation and selection, see 92590-92595)

**92559** Audiometric testing of groups

**92560** Bekesy audiometry; screening

**92561** diagnostic

**92562** Loudness balance test, alternate binaural or monaural

**92563** Tone decay test

**92564** Short increment sensitivity index (SISI)

**92565** Stenger test, pure tone

(92566 has been deleted. To report, use 92567)

**92567** Tympanometry (impedance testing)

**92568** Acoustic reflex testing

**92569** Acoustic reflex decay test

**92571** Filtered speech test

**92572** Staggered spondaic word test

**92573** Lombard test

(92574 has been deleted)

**92575** Sensorineural acuity level test

**92576** Synthetic sentence identification test

**92577** Stenger test, speech

(92578 has been deleted)

**92579** Visual reinforcement audiometry (VRA)

(92580 has been deleted)

(92581 has been deleted. To report, use 92585)

**92582** Conditioning play audiometry

**92583** Select picture audiometry

**92584** Electrocochleography

**92585** Auditory evoked potentials for evoked response audiometry and/or testing of the central nervous system

**92587** Evoked otoacoustic emissions; limited (single stimulus level, either transient or distortion products)

**92588** comprehensive or diagnostic evaluation (comparison of transient and/or distortion product otoacoustic emissions at multiple levels and frequencies)

**92589** Central auditory function test(s) (specify)

**92590** Hearing aid examination and selection; monaural

**92591** binaural

**92592** Hearing aid check; monaural

**92593** binaural

**92594** Electroacoustic evaluation for hearing aid; monaural

**92595** binaural

**92596** Ear protector attenuation measurements

**92597** Evaluation for use and/or fitting of voice prosthetic or augmentative/alternative communication device to supplement oral speech

**92598** Modification of voice prosthetic or augmentative/alternative communication device to supplement oral speech

## Other Procedures

**92599** Unlisted otorhinolaryngological service or procedure

# Cardiovascular

## Therapeutic Services

**92950** Cardiopulmonary resuscitation (eg, in cardiac arrest)

(See also critical care services, 99291, 99292)

**92953** Temporary transcutaneous pacing

(For physician direction of ambulance or rescue personnel outside the hospital, use 99288)

**92960** Cardioversion, elective, electrical conversion of arrhythmia; external

●**92961** internal (separate procedure)

►(Do not report 92961 in addition to codes 93618-93624, 93631, 93640-93642, 93650-93652, 93741-93744)◄

**92970** Cardioassist-method of circulatory assist; internal

**92971** external

(For balloon atrial-septostomy, use 92992)

(For placement of catheters for use in circulatory assist devices such as intra-aortic balloon pump, use 33970)

**92975** Thrombolysis, coronary; by intracoronary infusion, including selective coronary angiography

**92977** by intravenous infusion

(For thrombolysis of vessels other than coronary, see 37201, 75896)

(For cerebral thrombolysis, use 37195)

+▲**92978** Intravascular ultrasound (coronary vessel or graft) during diagnostic evaluation and/or therapeutic intervention including imaging supervision, interpretation and report; initial vessel (List separately in addition to code for primary procedure)

+ **92979** each additional vessel (List separately in addition to code for primary procedure)

(Use 92979 in conjunction with code 92978)

(Intravascular ultrasound services include all transducer manipulations and repositioning within the specific vessel being examined, both before and after therapeutic intervention (eg, stent placement))

**92980** Transcatheter placement of an intracoronary stent(s), percutaneous, with or without other therapeutic intervention, any method; single vessel

+ **92981** each additional vessel (List separately in addition to code for primary procedure)

(Use 92981 in conjunction with code 92980)

(To report additional vessels treated by angioplasty or atherectomy only during the same session, see 92984, 92996)

**92982** Percutaneous transluminal coronary balloon angioplasty; single vessel

**+ 92984** each additional vessel (List separately in addition to code for primary procedure)

(Use 92984 in conjunction with code(s) 92980, 92982, 92995)

(For stent placement following completion of angioplasty or atherectomy, see 92980, 92981)

**92986** Percutaneous balloon valvuloplasty; aortic valve

**92987** mitral valve

**92990** pulmonary valve

**92992** Atrial septectomy or septostomy; transvenous method, balloon (eg, Rashkind type) (includes cardiac catheterization)

**92993** blade method (Park septostomy) (includes cardiac catheterization)

**92995** Percutaneous transluminal coronary atherectomy, by mechanical or other method, with or without balloon angioplasty; single vessel

**+ 92996** each additional vessel (List separately in addition to code for primary procedure)

(Use 92996 in conjunction with code(s) 92980, 92982, 92995)

(For stent placement following completion of angioplasty or atherectomy, see 92980, 92981)

(To report additional vessels treated by angioplasty only during the same session, use 92984)

**92997** Percutaneous transluminal pulmonary artery balloon angioplasty; single vessel

**+ 92998** each additional vessel (List separately in addition to code for primary procedure)

(Use 92998 in conjunction with code 92997)

# Cardiography

(For echocardiography, see 93303-93350)

**93000** Electrocardiogram, routine ECG with at least 12 leads; with interpretation and report

**93005** tracing only, without interpretation and report

**93010** interpretation and report only

(For ECG monitoring, see 99354-99360)

**93012** Telephonic transmission of post-symptom electrocardiogram rhythm strip(s), per 30 day period of time; tracing only

**93014** physician review with interpretation and report only

**93015** Cardiovascular stress test using maximal or submaximal treadmill or bicycle exercise, continuous electrocardiographic monitoring, and/or pharmacological stress; with physician supervision, with interpretation and report

**93016** physician supervision only, without interpretation and report

**93017** tracing only, without interpretation and report

**93018** interpretation and report only

**93024** Ergonovine provocation test

**93040** Rhythm ECG, one to three leads; with interpretation and report

**93041** tracing only without interpretation and report

**93042** interpretation and report only

(93045 has been deleted. To report, use 93615)

(93201, 93202, 93204, 93205, 93208, 93209 and 93210 have been deleted. To report, use 93799)

(93220, 93221, 93222 have been deleted. To report, use 93799)

**93224** Electrocardiographic monitoring for 24 hours by continuous original ECG waveform recording and storage, with visual superimposition scanning; includes recording, scanning analysis with report, physician review and interpretation

**93225** recording (includes hook-up, recording, and disconnection)

**93226** scanning analysis with report

**93227** physician review and interpretation

**93230** Electrocardiographic monitoring for 24 hours by continuous original ECG waveform recording and storage without superimposition scanning utilizing a device capable of producing a full miniaturized printout; includes recording, microprocessor-based analysis with report, physician review and interpretation

**93231** recording (includes hook-up, recording, and disconnection)

**93232** microprocessor-based analysis with report

**93233** physician review and interpretation

**93235** Electrocardiographic monitoring for 24 hours by continuous computerized monitoring and non-continuous recording, and real-time data analysis utilizing a device capable of producing intermittent full-sized waveform tracings, possibly patient activated; includes monitoring and real-time data analysis with report, physician review and interpretation

**93236** monitoring and real-time data analysis with report

**93237** physician review and interpretation

(93255 has been deleted)

(93258, 93259, 93262, 93263, 93266 have been deleted. To report, see 93224-93237)

**93268** Patient demand single or multiple event recording with presymptom memory loop, per 30 day period of time; includes transmission, physician review and interpretation

(93269 has been deleted. To report, use 93268)

**93270** recording (includes hook-up, recording, and disconnection)

**93271** monitoring, receipt of transmissions, and analysis

**93272** physician review and interpretation only

(For postsymptom recording, see 93012, 93014)

►(For implanted patient activated cardiac event recording, see 33282, 93727)◄

(93273-93277 have been deleted. To report, see 93224-93237)

**93278** Signal-averaged electrocardiography (SAECG), with or without ECG

(For interpretation and report only, use 93278 with modifier '-26')

(For unlisted cardiographic procedure, use 93799)

(93280 has been deleted. To report, use 76000)

## Echocardiography

Echocardiography includes obtaining ultrasonic signals from the heart and great arteries, with two-dimensional image and/or Doppler ultrasonic signal documentation, and interpretation and report. When interpretation is performed separately use modifier '-26'.

(For fetal echocardiography, see 76825-76828)

(93300 has been deleted)

**93303** Transthoracic echocardiography for congenital cardiac anomalies; complete

**93304** follow-up or limited study

(93305 has been deleted)

**93307** Echocardiography, transthoracic, real-time with image documentation (2D) with or without M-mode recording; complete

**93308** follow-up or limited study

(93309 has been deleted. To report, see 93307, 93308)

**93312** Echocardiography, transesophageal, real time with image documentation (2D) (with or without M-mode recording); including probe placement, image acquisition, interpretation and report

**93313** placement of transesophageal probe only

**93314** image acquisition, interpretation and report only

**93315** Transesophageal echocardiography for congenital cardiac anomalies; including probe placement, image acquisition, interpretation and report

**93316** placement of transesophageal probe only

**93317** image acquisition, interpretation and report only

**+ 93320** Doppler echocardiography, pulsed wave and/or continuous wave with spectral display (List separately in addition to codes for echocardiographic imaging); complete

(Use 93320 in conjunction with codes 93303, 93304, 93307, 93308, 93312, 93314, 93315, 93317, 93350)

**+ 93321** follow-up or limited study (List separately in addition to codes for echocardiographic imaging)

(Use 93321 in conjunction with codes 93303, 93304, 93307, 93308, 93312, 93314, 93315, 93317, 93950)

**+ 93325** Doppler echocardiography color flow velocity mapping (List separately in addition to codes for echocardiography)

(Use 93325 in conjunction with codes 76825, 76826, 76827, 76828, 93303, 93304, 93307, 93308, 93312, 93314, 93315, 93317, 93320, 93321, 93350)

**93350** Echocardiography, transthoracic, real-time with image documentation (2D), with or without M-mode recording, during rest and cardiovascular stress test using treadmill, bicycle exercise and/or pharmacologically induced stress, with interpretation and report

(The appropriate stress testing code from the 93015-93018 series should be reported in addition to 93350 to capture the exercise stress portion of the study)

# Cardiac Catheterization

Cardiac catheterization is a diagnostic medical procedure which includes introduction, positioning and repositioning of catheter(s), when necessary, recording of intracardiac and intravascular pressure, obtaining blood samples for measurement of blood gases or dilution curves and cardiac output measurements (Fick or other method, with or without rest and exercise and/or studies) with or without electrode catheter placement, final evaluation and report of procedure. When selective injection procedures are performed without a preceding cardiac catheterization, these services should be reported using codes in the Vascular Injection Procedures section, 36011-36015 and 36215-36218.

When coronary artery, arterial coronary conduit or venous bypass graft angiography is performed without concomitant left heart cardiac catheterization, use 93508. Injection procedures 93539, 93540, 93544, and 93545 represent separate identifiable services and may be coded in conjunction with one another in addition to code 93508, as appropriate. To report imaging supervision, interpretation and report in conjunction with code 93508, use code 93556.

Modifier '-51' should not be appended to codes 93501-93533, 93539-93556.

**⊘ 93501** Right heart catheterization

(For bundle of His recording, use 93600)

**⊘ 93503** Insertion and placement of flow directed catheter (eg, Swan-Ganz) for monitoring purposes

(For subsequent monitoring, see 99354-99360)

**⊘ 93505** Endomyocardial biopsy

**⊘ 93508** Catheter placement in coronary artery(s), arterial coronary conduit(s), and/or venous coronary bypass graft(s) for coronary angiography without concomitant left heart catheterization

(93508 is to be used only when left heart catheterization 93510, 93511, 93524, 93526 is not performed)

(93508 is to be used only once per procedure)

⊘ **93510** Left heart catheterization, retrograde, from the brachial artery, axillary artery or femoral artery; percutaneous

⊘ **93511** by cutdown

⊘ **93514** Left heart catheterization by left ventricular puncture

(93515 has been deleted. To report, use 93524)

⊘ **93524** Combined transseptal and retrograde left heart catheterization

⊘ **93526** Combined right heart catheterization and retrograde left heart catheterization

⊘ **93527** Combined right heart catheterization and transseptal left heart catheterization through intact septum (with or without retrograde left heart catheterization)

⊘ **93528** Combined right heart catheterization with left ventricular puncture (with or without retrograde left heart catheterization)

⊘ **93529** Combined right heart catheterization and left heart catheterization through existing septal opening (with or without retrograde left heart catheterization)

⊘ **93530** Right heart catheterization, for congenital cardiac anomalies

⊘ **93531** Combined right heart catheterization and retrograde left heart catheterization, for congenital cardiac anomalies

⊘ **93532** Combined right heart catheterization and transseptal left heart catheterization through intact septum with or without retrograde left heart catheterization, for congenital cardiac anomalies

⊘ **93533** Combined right heart catheterization and transseptal left heart catheterization through existing septal opening, with or without retrograde left heart catheterization, for congenital cardiac anomalies

(93535 has been deleted. To report, see 33971, 93536)

**93536** Percutaneous insertion of intra-aortic balloon catheter

(When injection procedures are performed in conjunction with cardiac catheterization, these services do not include introduction of catheters but do include repositioning of catheters when necessary and use of automatic power injectors. Injection procedures 93539-93545 represent separate identifiable services and may be coded in conjunction with one another when appropriate. The technical details of angiography, supervision of filming and processing, interpretation and report are not included. To report imaging supervision, interpretation and report, use 93555 and/or 93556. Modifier '-51' should not be appended to 93539-93556.)

⊘ **93539** Injection procedure during cardiac catheterization; for selective opacification of arterial conduits (eg, internal mammary), whether native or used for bypass

⊘ **93540** for selective opacification of aortocoronary venous bypass grafts, one or more coronary arteries

⊘ **93541** for pulmonary angiography

⊘ **93542** for selective right ventricular or right atrial angiography

⊘ **93543** for selective left ventricular or left atrial angiography

⊘ **93544** for aortography

⊘ **93545** for selective coronary angiography (injection of radiopaque material may be by hand)

(93546 has been deleted. To report, use 93510 and 93543)

(To report imaging supervision and interpretation, use 93555)

(93547 has been deleted. To report, use 93510, 93543, and 93545)

(To report imaging supervision and interpretation, use 93555 and 93556)

(93548 has been deleted. To report, use 93510, 93543, 93544, 93545)

(To report imaging supervision and interpretation, use 93555 and 93556)

(93549 has been deleted. To report, use 93526, 93527 or 93528; 93543, 93545)

(To report imaging supervision and interpretation, use 93555 and 93556)

(93550 has been deleted. To report, use 93526 or 93527 or 93528; 93540, 93543; and 93545)

(To report imaging supervision and interpretation, use 93555 and 93556)

(93551 has been deleted. To report, use 93539 or 93540)

(93552 has been deleted. To report, use 93510; 93539 or 93540; 93543 and 93545)

(To report imaging supervision and interpretation, use 93555 and 93556)

(93553 has been deleted. To report, use 93510; 93539 or 93540; 93543, 93544, 93545)

(To report imaging supervision and interpretation, use 93555 and 93556)

⦸ **93555** Imaging supervision, interpretation and report for injection procedure(s) during cardiac catheterization; ventricular and/or atrial angiography

⦸ **93556** pulmonary angiography, aortography, and/or selective coronary angiography including venous bypass grafts and arterial conduits (whether native or used in bypass)

(Codes 93561 and 93562 are not to be used with cardiac catheterization codes)

**93561** Indicator dilution studies such as dye or thermal dilution, including arterial and/or venous catheterization; with cardiac output measurement (separate procedure)

**93562** subsequent measurement of cardiac output

(For radioisotope method of cardiac output, see 78472, 78473, or 78481)

(93570 has been deleted. To report, use 92982)

✚ **93571** Intravascular doppler velocity and/or pressure derived coronary flow reserve measurement (coronary vessel or graft) during coronary angiography including pharmacologically induced stress; initial vessel (List separately in addition to code for primary procedure)

✚ **93572** each additional vessel (List separately in addition to code for primary procedure)

(Intravascular distal coronary blood flow velocity measurements include all Doppler transducer manipulations and repositioning within the specific vessel being examined, during coronary angiography or therapeutic intervention (eg, angioplasty))

(For unlisted cardiac catheterization procedure, use 93799)

## Intracardiac Electrophysiological Procedures

►Modifier '-51' should not be appended to 93600-93660.◄

⦸ **93600** Bundle of His recording

⦸ **93602** Intra-atrial recording

⦸ **93603** Right ventricular recording

(93604, 93606 have been deleted. To report, see 93603, 93607, and 93609 as appropriate)

(93605 has been deleted. To report, use 93609)

⦸ **93607** Left ventricular recording

(93608 has been deleted. To report, use 93609)

⦸ **93609** Intraventricular and/or intra-atrial mapping of tachycardia site(s) with catheter manipulation to record from multiple sites to identify origin of tachycardia

⦸ **93610** Intra-atrial pacing

⦸ **93612** Intraventricular pacing

(93614 has been deleted)

⦸ **93615** Esophageal recording of atrial electrogram with or without ventricular electrogram(s);

⊘**93616** with pacing

⊘**93618** Induction of arrhythmia by electrical pacing

(For intracardiac phonocardiogram, use 93799)

⊘**93619** Comprehensive electrophysiologic evaluation with right atrial pacing and recording, right ventricular pacing and recording, His bundle recording, including insertion and repositioning of multiple electrode catheters; without induction or attempted induction of arrhythmia (This code is to be used when 93600 is combined with 93602, 93603, 93610, 93612)

⊘**93620** with induction or attempted induction of arrhythmia (This code is to be used when 93618 is combined with 93619)

⊘**93621** with left atrial recordings from coronary sinus or left atrium, with or without pacing, with induction or attempted induction of arrhythmia

⊘**93622** with left ventricular recordings, with or without pacing, with induction or attempted induction of arrhythmia

**+ 93623** Programmed stimulation and pacing after intravenous drug infusion (List separately in addition to code for primary procedure)

(Use 93623 in conjunction with codes 93620, 93621, 93622)

⊘**93624** Electrophysiologic follow-up study with pacing and recording to test effectiveness of therapy, including induction or attempted induction of arrhythmia

(93630 has been deleted. To report, use 93631 and 33261)

⊘**93631** Intra-operative epicardial and endocardial pacing and mapping to localize the site of tachycardia or zone of slow conduction for surgical correction

⊘▲**93640** Electrophysiologic evaluation of single or dual chamber pacing cardioverter-defibrillator leads including defibrillation threshold evaluation (induction of arrhythmia, evaluation of sensing and pacing for arrhythmia termination) at time of initial implantation or replacement;

⊘▲**93641** with testing of single or dual chamber pacing cardioverter-defibrillator pulse generator

►(For subsequent or periodic electronic analysis and/or reprogramming of single or dual chamber pacing cardioverter-defibrillators, see 93642, 93741-93744)◄

⊘▲**93642** Electrophysiologic evaluation of single or dual chamber pacing cardioverter-defibrillator (includes defibrillation threshold evaluation, induction of arrhythmia, evaluation of sensing and pacing for arrhythmia termination, and programming or reprogramming of sensing or therapeutic parameters)

⊘**93650** Intracardiac catheter ablation of atrioventricular node function, atrioventricular conduction for creation of complete heart block, with or without temporary pacemaker placement

⊘**93651** Intracardiac catheter ablation of arrhythmogenic focus; for treatment of supraventricular tachycardia by ablation of fast or slow atrioventricular pathways, accessory atrioventricular connections or other atrial foci, singly or in combination

⊘**93652** for treatment of ventricular tachycardia

⊘**93660** Evaluation of cardiovascular function with tilt table evaluation, with continuous ECG monitoring and intermittent blood pressure monitoring, with or without pharmacological intervention

(For testing of autonomic nervous system function, see 95921-95923)

## Other Vascular Studies

(For arterial cannulization and recording of direct arterial pressure, use 36620)

(For radiographic injection procedures, see 36000-36299)

(For vascular cannulization for hemodialysis, see 36800-36821)

(For chemotherapy for malignant disease, see 96408-96549)

(For penile plethysmography, use 54240)

(93700 has been deleted)

(93710 has been deleted)

**93720** Plethysmography, total body; with interpretation and report

**93721** tracing only, without interpretation and report

**93722** interpretation and report only

(For regional plethysmography, see 93875-93931)

**93724** Electronic analysis of antitachycardia pacemaker system (includes electrocardiographic recording, programming of device, induction and termination of tachycardia via implanted pacemaker, and interpretation of recordings)

(93725-93730 have been deleted. To report, see 93875-93971)

● **93727** Electronic analysis of implantable loop recorder (ILR) system (includes retrieval of recorded and stored ECG data, physician review and interpretation of retrieved ECG data and reprogramming)

**93731** Electronic analysis of dual-chamber pacemaker system (includes evaluation of programmable parameters at rest and during activity where applicable, using electrocardiographic recording and interpretation of recordings at rest and during exercise, analysis of event markers and device response); without reprogramming

**93732** with reprogramming

**93733** Electronic analysis of dual chamber internal pacemaker system (may include rate, pulse amplitude and duration, configuration of wave form, and/or testing of sensory function of pacemaker), telephonic analysis

**93734** Electronic analysis of single chamber pacemaker system (includes evaluation of programmable parameters at rest and during activity where applicable, using electrocardiographic recording and interpretation of recordings at rest and during exercise, analysis of event markers and device response); without reprogramming

**93735** with reprogramming

**93736** Electronic analysis of single chamber internal pacemaker system (may include rate, pulse amplitude and duration, configuration of wave form, and/or testing of sensory function of pacemaker), telephonic analysis

▲ **93737** Electronic analysis of single or dual chamber pacing cardioverter-defibrillator only (interrogation, evaluation of pulse generator status); without reprogramming

**93738** with reprogramming

**93740** Temperature gradient studies

(93750 has been deleted. To report, see 93875-93971)

● **93741** Electronic analysis of pacing cardioverter-defibrillator (includes interrogation, evaluation of pulse generator status, evaluation of programmable parameters at rest and during activity where applicable, using electrocardiographic recording and interpretation of recordings at rest and during exercise, analysis of event markers and device response); single chamber, without reprogramming

● **93742** single chamber, with reprogramming

● **93743** dual chamber, without reprogramming

● **93744** dual chamber, with reprogramming

**93760** Thermogram; cephalic

**93762** peripheral

**93770** Determination of venous pressure

(For central venous cannulization and pressure measurements, see 36488-36491, 36500)

(93780, 93781 have been deleted)

**93784** Ambulatory blood pressure monitoring, utilizing a system such as magnetic tape and/or computer disk, for 24 hours or longer; including recording, scanning analysis, interpretation and report

**93786** recording only

**93788** scanning analysis with report

**93790** physician review with interpretation and report

(93791-93796 have been deleted. To report, see 93731-93736)

## Other Procedures

**93797** Physician services for outpatient cardiac rehabilitation; without continuous ECG monitoring (per session)

**93798** with continuous ECG monitoring (per session)

**93799** Unlisted cardiovascular service or procedure

# Non-Invasive Vascular Diagnostic Studies

Vascular studies include patient care required to perform the studies, supervision of the studies and interpretation of study results with copies for patient records of hard copy output with analysis of all data, including bidirectional vascular flow or imaging when provided.

The use of a simple hand-held or other Doppler device that does not produce hard copy output, or that produces a record that does not permit analysis of bidirectional vascular flow, is considered to be part of the physical examination of the vascular system and is not separately reported.

***Duplex scan*** describes an ultrasonic scanning procedure with display of both two-dimensional structure and motion with time and Doppler ultrasonic signal documentation with spectral analysis and/or color flow velocity mapping or imaging.

## Cerebrovascular Arterial Studies

(93850, 93860 have been deleted. To report, see 93875-93882)

(93870 has been deleted. To report, see 93880 and 93882)

**93875** Non-invasive physiologic studies of extracranial arteries, complete bilateral study (eg, periorbital flow direction with arterial compression, ocular pneumoplethysmography, Doppler ultrasound spectral analysis)

**93880** Duplex scan of extracranial arteries; complete bilateral study

**93882** unilateral or limited study

**93886** Transcranial Doppler study of the intracranial arteries; complete study

**93888** limited study

## Extremity Arterial Studies (Including Digits)

(93890, 93910 have been deleted. To report, see 93922-93931)

(93920, 93921 have been deleted. To report, see 93922-93924)

**93922** Non-invasive physiologic studies of upper or lower extremity arteries, single level, bilateral (eg, ankle/brachial indices, Doppler waveform analysis, volume plethysmography, transcutaneous oxygen tension measurement)

**93923** Non-invasive physiologic studies of upper or lower extremity arteries, multiple levels or with provocative functional maneuvers, complete bilateral study (eg, segmental blood pressure measurements, segmental Doppler waveform analysis, segmental volume plethysmography, segmental transcutaneous oxygen tension measurements, measurements with postural provocative tests, measurements with reactive hyperemia)

**93924** Non-invasive physiologic studies of lower extremity arteries, at rest and following treadmill stress testing, complete bilateral study

**93925** Duplex scan of lower extremity arteries or arterial bypass grafts; complete bilateral study

**93926** unilateral or limited study

**93930** Duplex scan of upper extremity arteries or arterial bypass grafts; complete bilateral study

**93931** unilateral or limited study

## Extremity Venous Studies (Including Digits)

(93950, 93960 have been deleted. To report, see 93965-93971)

**93965** Non-invasive physiologic studies of extremity veins, complete bilateral study (eg, Doppler waveform analysis with responses to compression and other maneuvers, phleborheography, impedance plethysmography)

**93970** Duplex scan of extremity veins including responses to compression and other maneuvers; complete bilateral study

**93971** unilateral or limited study

## Visceral and Penile Vascular Studies

**93975** Duplex scan of arterial inflow and venous outflow of abdominal, pelvic, scrotal contents and/or retroperitoneal organs; complete study

**93976** limited study

**93978** Duplex scan of aorta, inferior vena cava, iliac vasculature, or bypass grafts; complete study

**93979** unilateral or limited study

**93980** Duplex scan of arterial inflow and venous outflow of penile vessels; complete study

**93981** follow-up or limited study

## Extremity Arterial-Venous Studies

**93990** Duplex scan of hemodialysis access (including arterial inflow, body of access and venous outflow)

# Pulmonary

Items 94010-94799 include laboratory procedure(s) and interpretation of test results. If a separate identifiable Evaluation and Management service is performed, the appropriate E/M service code should be reported in addition to 94010-94799.

**94010** Spirometry, including graphic record, total and timed vital capacity, expiratory flow rate measurement(s), with or without maximal voluntary ventilation

**94014** Patient-initiated spirometric recording per 30-day period of time; includes reinforced education, transmission of spirometric tracing, data capture, analysis of transmitted data, periodic recalibration and physician review and interpretation

**94015** recording (includes hook-up, reinforced education, data transmission, data capture, trend analysis, and periodic recalibration)

**94016** physician review and interpretation only

**94060** Bronchospasm evaluation: spirometry as in 94010, before and after bronchodilator (aerosol or parenteral)

(For prolonged exercise test for bronchospasm with pre- and post-spirometry, use 94620)

**94070** Prolonged postexposure evaluation of bronchospasm with multiple spirometric determinations after antigen, cold air, methacholine or other chemical agent, with subsequent spirometrics

**94150** Vital capacity, total (separate procedure)

(94160 has been deleted. For vital capacity measurement only, use 94150. For spirometry with timed expiratory volumes, use 94010)

**94200** Maximum breathing capacity, maximal voluntary ventilation

**94240** Functional residual capacity or residual volume: helium method, nitrogen open circuit method, or other method

**94250** Expired gas collection, quantitative, single procedure (separate procedure)

**94260** Thoracic gas volume

(For plethysmography, see 93720-93722)

**94350** Determination of maldistribution of inspired gas: multiple breath nitrogen washout curve including alveolar nitrogen or helium equilibration time

**94360** Determination of resistance to airflow, oscillatory or plethysmographic methods

**94370** Determination of airway closing volume, single breath tests

**94375** Respiratory flow volume loop

**94400** Breathing response to $CO_2$ ($CO_2$ response curve)

**94450** Breathing response to hypoxia (hypoxia response curve)

**94620** Pulmonary stress testing; simple (eg, prolonged exercise test for bronchospasm with pre- and post-spirometry)

**94621** complex (including measurements of $CO_2$ production, $O_2$ uptake, and electrocardiographic recordings)

**94640** Nonpressurized inhalation treatment for acute airway obstruction

**94642** Aerosol inhalation of pentamidine for pneumocystis carinii pneumonia treatment or prophylaxis

**94650** Intermittent positive pressure breathing (IPPB) treatment, air or oxygen, with or without nebulized medication; initial demonstration and/or evaluation

**94651** subsequent

**94652** newborn infants

**94656** Ventilation assist and management, initiation of pressure or volume preset ventilators for assisted or controlled breathing; first day

**94657** subsequent days

**94660** Continuous positive airway pressure ventilation (CPAP), initiation and management

**94662** Continuous negative pressure ventilation (CNP), initiation and management

**94664** Aerosol or vapor inhalations for sputum mobilization, bronchodilation, or sputum induction for diagnostic purposes; initial demonstration and/or evaluation

**94665** subsequent

**94667** Manipulation chest wall, such as cupping, percussing, and vibration to facilitate lung function; initial demonstration and/or evaluation

**94668** subsequent

**94680** Oxygen uptake, expired gas analysis; rest and exercise, direct, simple

**94681** including $CO_2$ output, percentage oxygen extracted

**94690** rest, indirect (separate procedure)

(94700, 94705, 94710 have been deleted. For analysis of arterial blood gas results, see appropriate Evaluation and Management code. For test procedure, see 82800-82817)

(For single arterial puncture, use 36600)

(94715 has been deleted. To report, use 82820)

**94720** Carbon monoxide diffusing capacity, any method

**94725** Membrane diffusion capacity

**94750** Pulmonary compliance study, any method

**94760** Noninvasive ear or pulse oximetry for oxygen saturation; single determination

(For blood gases, see 82803-82810)

**94761** multiple determinations (eg, during exercise)

**94762** by continuous overnight monitoring (separate procedure)

**94770** Carbon dioxide, expired gas determination by infrared analyzer

(For bronchoscopy, see 31622-31659)

(For placement of flow directed catheter, use 93503)

(For venipuncture, use 36410)

(For central venous catheter placement, see 36488-36491)

(For arterial puncture, use 36600)

(For arterial catheterization, use 36620)

(For thoracentesis, use 32000)

(For phlebotomy, therapeutic, use 99195)

(For lung biopsy, needle, use 32405)

(For intubation, orotracheal or nasotracheal, use 31500)

**94772** Circadian respiratory pattern recording (pediatric pneumogram), 12 to 24 hour continuous recording, infant

(Separate procedure codes for electromyograms, EEG, ECG, and recordings of respiration are excluded when 94772 is reported)

**94799** Unlisted pulmonary service or procedure

# Allergy and Clinical Immunology

### Definitions

***Allergy sensitivity tests*** describe the performance and evaluation of selective cutaneous and mucous membrane tests in correlation with the history, physical examination, and other observations of the patient. The number of tests performed should be judicious and dependent upon the history, physical findings, and clinical judgment. All patients should not necessarily receive the same tests nor the same number of sensitivity tests.

***Immunotherapy (desensitization, hyposensitization)*** is the parenteral administration of allergenic extracts as antigens at periodic intervals, usually on an increasing dosage scale to a dosage which is maintained as maintenance therapy. Indications for immunotherapy are determined by appropriate diagnostic procedures coordinated with clinical judgment and knowledge of the natural history of allergic diseases.

***Other therapy:*** for medical conferences on the use of mechanical and electronic devices (precipitators, air conditioners, air filters, humidifiers, dehumidifiers), climatotherapy, physical therapy, occupational and recreational therapy, see **Evaluation and Management** section.

## Allergy Testing

(95000-95003 have been deleted. To report, use 95004)

**95004** Percutaneous tests (scratch, puncture, prick) with allergenic extracts, immediate type reaction, specify number of tests

(95005-95007 have been deleted. To report, use 95010)

**95010** Percutaneous tests (scratch, puncture, prick) sequential and incremental, with drugs, biologicals or venoms, immediate type reaction, specify number of tests

(95011 has been deleted. To report, use 95010)

(95014 has been deleted. To report, use 95015)

**95015** Intracutaneous (intradermal) tests, sequential and incremental, with drugs, biologicals, or venoms, immediate type reaction, specify number of tests

(95016-95018 have been deleted. To report, use 95015)

(95020-95023 have been deleted. To report, use 95024)

**95024** Intracutaneous (intradermal) tests with allergenic extracts, immediate type reaction, specify number of tests

**95027** Skin end point titration

**95028** Intracutaneous (intradermal) tests with allergenic extracts, delayed type reaction, including reading, specify number of tests

(95030-95034 have been deleted. To report, use 95028)

(95040-95043 have been deleted. To report, use 95044)

**95044** Patch or application test(s) (specify number of tests)

(95050, 95051 have been deleted. To report, use 95052)

**95052** Photo patch test(s) (specify number of tests)

**95056** Photo tests

**95060** Ophthalmic mucous membrane tests

**95065** Direct nasal mucous membrane test

**95070** Inhalation bronchial challenge testing (not including necessary pulmonary function tests); with histamine, methacholine, or similar compounds

**95071** with antigens or gases, specify

(For pulmonary function tests, see 94060, 94070)

**95075** Ingestion challenge test (sequential and incremental ingestion of test items, eg, food, drug or other substance such as metabisulfite)

(95077 has been deleted)

**95078** Provocative testing (eg, Rinkel test)

(95080-95082 have been deleted)

(For allergy laboratory tests, see 86000-86999)

(For intravenous therapy for severe or intractable allergic disease, see 90780, 90781, 90784)

(95105 has been deleted. To report, see appropriate E/M code(s))

## Allergen Immunotherapy

Codes 95115-95199 include the professional services necessary for allergen immunotherapy. Office visit codes may be used in addition to allergen immunotherapy if other identifiable services are provided at that time.

**95115** Professional services for allergen immunotherapy not including provision of allergenic extracts; single injection

**95117** two or more injections

**95120** Professional services for allergen immunotherapy in prescribing physicians office or institution, including provision of allergenic extract; single injection

**95125** two or more injections

**95130** single stinging insect venom

**95131** two stinging insect venoms

**95132** three stinging insect venoms

**95133** four stinging insect venoms

**95134** five stinging insect venoms

(95135 has been deleted. To report, use 95144)

(95140 has been deleted. To report, use 95144)

**95144** Professional services for the supervision and provision of antigens for allergen immunotherapy, single or multiple antigens, single dose vials (specify number of vials)

**95145** Professional services for the supervision and provision of antigens for allergen immunotherapy (specify number of doses); single stinging insect venom

**95146** two single stinging insect venoms

**95147** three single stinging insect venoms

**95148** four single stinging insect venoms

**95149** five single stinging insect venoms

(95150, 95155 have been deleted. To report, use 95165)

(95160 has been deleted. To report, see 95145-95149)

**95165** Professional services for the supervision and provision of antigens for allergen immunotherapy; single or multiple antigens (specify number of doses)

**95170** whole body extract of biting insect or other arthropod (specify number of doses)

**95180** Rapid desensitization procedure, each hour (eg, insulin, penicillin, horse serum)

**95199** Unlisted allergy/clinical immunologic service or procedure

(For skin testing of bacterial, viral, fungal extracts, see 95028, 86485-86586)

(For special reports on allergy patients, use 99080)

(For testing procedures such as radioallergosorbent testing (RAST), rat mast cell technique (RMCT), mast cell degranulation test (MCDT), lymphocytic transformation test (LTT), leukocyte histamine release (LHR), migration inhibitory factor test (MIF), transfer factor test (TFT), nitroblue tetrazolium dye test (NTD), see Immunology section in **Pathology** or use 95199)

# Neurology and Neuromuscular Procedures

Neurologic services are typically consultative, and any of the levels of consultation (99241-99263) may be appropriate.

In addition, services and skills outlined under **Evaluation and Management** levels of service appropriate to neurologic illnesses should be coded similarly.

The EEG, evoked potential and sleep services (95805-95829, 95920-95925 and 95950-95962) include tracing, interpretation and report. For interpretation only, use modifier '-26'.

Modifier '-51,' multiple procedures, is not appropriate when reporting nerve conduction studies (95900-95904) performed on multiple nerves.

## Sleep Testing

Sleep studies and polysomnography refer to the continuous and simultaneous monitoring and recording of various physiological and pathophysiological parameters of sleep for 6 or more hours with physician review, interpretation and report. The studies are performed to diagnose a variety of sleep disorders and to evaluate a patient's response to therapies such as nasal continuous positive airway pressure (NCPAP). Polysomnography is distinguished from sleep studies by the inclusion of sleep staging which is defined to include a 1-4 lead electroencephalogram (EEG), an electro-oculogram (EOG), and a submental electromyogram (EMG). Additional parameters of sleep include: 1) ECG; 2) airflow; 3) ventilation and respiratory effort; 4) gas exchange by oximetry, transcutaneous monitoring, or end tidal gas analysis; 5) extremity muscle activity, motor activity-movement; 6) extended EEG monitoring; 7) penile tumescence; 8) gastroesophageal reflux; 9) continuous blood pressure monitoring; 10) snoring; 11) body positions; etc.

For a study to be reported as polysomnography, sleep must be recorded and staged.

(Report with a '-52' modifier if less than 6 hours of recording or in other cases of reduced services as appropriate)

(For unattended sleep study, use 95806)

**95805** Multiple sleep latency or maintenance of wakefulness testing, recording, analysis and interpretation of physiological measurements of sleep during multiple trials to assess sleepiness

**95806** Sleep study, simultaneous recording of ventilation, respiratory effort, ECG or heart rate, and oxygen saturation, unattended by a technologist

**95807** Sleep study, simultaneous recording of ventilation, respiratory effort, ECG or heart rate, and oxygen saturation, attended by a technologist

**95808** Polysomnography; sleep staging with 1-3 additional parameters of sleep, attended by a technologist

**95810** sleep staging with 4 or more additional parameters of sleep, attended by a technologist

**95811** sleep staging with 4 or more additional parameters of sleep, with initiation of continuous positive airway pressure therapy or bilevel ventilation, attended by a technologist

**95812** Electroencephalogram (EEG) extended monitoring; up to one hour

**95813** greater than one hour

**▲95816** Electroencephalogram (EEG) including recording awake and drowsy (including hyperventilation and/or photic stimulation when appropriate)

(For extended EEG monitoring, see 95812, 95813)

(95817 has been deleted. To report, use 95816)

**▲95819** Electroencephalogram (EEG) including recording awake and asleep (including hyperventilation and/or photic stimulation when appropriate)

(For extended EEG monitoring, see 95812, 95813)

(For digital analysis of EEG, use 95957)

(95821 has been deleted. To report, use 95819)

**95822** Electroencephalogram (EEG); sleep only

(For extended EEG monitoring, see 95812, 95813)

(95823 has been deleted. To report, use 95954)

**95824** cerebral death evaluation only

(95826 has been deleted. To report, use 95829, 95951 or 95956)

**95827** all night sleep only

(For ambulatory 24-hour EEG monitoring, use 95950)

(For EEG during nonintracranial surgery, use 95955)

(For Wada activation test, use 95958)

(95828 has been deleted. To report, see 95807-95810)

(For recording of circadian respiratory patterns of infants, use 94772)

**95829** Electrocorticogram at surgery (separate procedure)

**95830** Insertion by physician of sphenoidal electrodes for electroencephalographic (EEG) recording

**▲95831** Muscle testing, manual (separate procedure) with report; extremity (excluding hand) or trunk

**95832** hand, with or without comparison with normal side

**95833** total evaluation of body, excluding hands

**95834** total evaluation of body, including hands

(95842 has been deleted. To report, use 95999)

**95851** Range of motion measurements and report (separate procedure); each extremity (excluding hand) or each trunk section (spine)

**95852** hand, with or without comparison with normal side

**95857** Tensilon test for myasthenia gravis;

**95858** with electromyographic recording

**95860** Needle electromyography, one extremity with or without related paraspinal areas

**95861** Needle electromyography, two extremities with or without related paraspinal areas

**95863** Needle electromyography, three extremities with or without related paraspinal areas

**95864** Needle electromyography, four extremities with or without related paraspinal areas

**95867** Needle electromyography, cranial nerve supplied muscles, unilateral

**95868** Needle electromyography, cranial nerve supplied muscles, bilateral

**95869** Needle electromyography; thoracic paraspinal muscles

**▲95870** limited study of muscles in one extremity or non-limb (axial) muscles (unilateral or bilateral), other than thoracic paraspinal, cranial nerve supplied muscles, or sphincters

►(To report a complete study of the extremities, see 95860-95864)◄

►(For needle electromyography of cranial supplied muscles, see 95867, 95868)◄

(For anal or urethral sphincter, detrusor, urethra, perineum musculature, see 51785-51792)

(For eye muscles, use 92265)

**95872** Needle electromyography using single fiber electrode, with quantitative measurement of jitter, blocking and/or fiber density, any/all sites of each muscle studied

**95875** Ischemic limb exercise with needle electromyography, with lactic acid determination

(95880 has been deleted. To report, use 96105)

(95881 has been deleted. To report, use 96111)

(95882 has been deleted. To report, use 96115)

(95883 has been deleted. To report, use 96117)

⊘▲ **95900** Nerve conduction, amplitude and latency/velocity study, each nerve; motor, without F-wave study

⊘ **95903** motor, with F-wave study

⊘▲ **95904** sensory or mixed

►(Report 95900, 95903, and/or 95904 only once when multiple sites on the same nerve are stimulated or recorded)◄

✚ **95920** Intraoperative neurophysiology testing, per hour (List separately in addition to code for primary procedure)

(Use code 95920 in conjunction with the study performed, 92585, ►95860, 95861, 95867, 95868, 95900, 95904,◄ 95925, 95926, 95927, 95930, 95933, 95934, 95936, 95937)

**95921** Testing of autonomic nervous system function; cardiovagal innervation (parasympathetic function), including two or more of the following: heart rate response to deep breathing with recorded R-R interval, Valsalva ratio, and 30:15 ratio

**95922** vasomotor adrenergic innervation (sympathetic adrenergic function), including beat-to-beat blood pressure and R-R interval changes during Valsalva maneuver and at least five minutes of passive tilt

**95923** sudomotor, including one or more of the following: quantitative sudomotor axon reflex test (QSART), silastic sweat imprint, thermoregulatory sweat test, and changes in sympathetic skin potential

**95925** Short-latency somatosensory evoked potential study, stimulation of any/all peripheral nerves or skin sites, recording from the central nervous system; in upper limbs

**95926** in lower limbs

**95927** in the trunk or head

(To report a unilateral study, use modifier '-52')

(For visual evoked potentials, use 95930)

(For brainstem evoked response recording, use 92585)

(For auditory evoked potentials, use 92585)

**95930** Visual evoked potential (VEP) testing central nervous system, checkerboard or flash

**95933** Orbicularis oculi (blink) reflex, by electrodiagnostic testing

**95934** H-reflex, amplitude and latency study; record gastrocnemius/soleus muscle

(95935 has been deleted. To report, see 95903, 95934, 95936)

**95936** record muscle other than gastrocnemius/soleus muscle

(To report a bilateral study, use modifier '-50')

**95937** Neuromuscular junction testing (repetitive stimulation, paired stimuli), each nerve, any one method

**95950** Monitoring for identification and lateralization of cerebral seizure focus, electroencephalographic (eg, 8 channel EEG) recording and interpretation, each 24 hours

**95951** Monitoring for localization of cerebral seizure focus by cable or radio, 16 or more channel telemetry, combined electroencephalographic (EEG) and video recording and interpretation (eg, for presurgical localization), each 24 hours

(95952 has been deleted. To report, use 95950)

**95953** Monitoring for localization of cerebral seizure focus by computerized portable 16 or more channel EEG, electroencephalographic (EEG) recording and interpretation, each 24 hours

**95954** Pharmacological or physical activation requiring physician attendance during EEG recording of activation phase (eg, thiopental activation test)

(For digital analysis of EEG, use 95957)

**95955** Electroencephalogram (EEG) during nonintracranial surgery (eg, carotid surgery)

**95956** Monitoring for localization of cerebral seizure focus by cable or radio, 16 or more channel telemetry, electroencephalographic (EEG) recording and interpretation, each 24 hours

**95957** Digital analysis of electroencephalogram (EEG) (eg, for epileptic spike analysis)

**95958** Wada activation test for hemispheric function, including electroencephalographic (EEG) monitoring

**▲95961** Functional cortical and subcortical mapping by stimulation and/or recording of electrodes on brain surface, or of depth electrodes, to provoke seizures or identify vital brain structures; initial hour of physician attendance

**+ 95962** each additional hour of physician attendance (List separately in addition to code for primary procedure)

(Use 95962 in conjunction with code 95961)

# Neurostimulators, Analysis-Programming

A simple neurostimulator pulse generator/transmitter (95970, 95971) is one capable of affecting 3 or fewer of the following: pulse amplitude, pulse duration, pulse frequency, 8 or more electrode contacts, cycling, stimulation train duration, train spacing, number of programs, number of channels, phase angle, alternating electrode polarities, configuration of wave form, more than 1 clinical feature (eg, rigidity, dyskinesia, tremor). A complex neurostimulator pulse generator/transmitter (95970, 95972, 95973, 95974, 95975) is one capable of affecting more than 3 of the above.

►Code 95970 describes subsequent electronic analysis of a previously-implanted simple or complex brain, spinal cord, or peripheral neurostimulator pulse generator system, without reprogramming. Code 95971 describes intraoperative or subsequent electronic analysis of an implanted simple brain, spinal cord, or peripheral (ie, peripheral nerve, autonomic nerve, neuromuscular) neurostimulator pulse generator system, with programming. Codes 95972 and 95973 describe intraoperative (at initial insertion/revision) or subsequent electronic analysis of an implanted simple or complex brain, spinal cord or peripheral (except cranial nerve) neurostimulator pulse generator system, with programming. Codes 95974 and 95975 describe intraoperative (at initial insertion/revision) or subsequent electronic analysis of an implanted complex cranial nerve neurostimulator pulse generator system, with programming.◄

(For insertion of neurostimulator pulse generator, see 61885, 63685, 63688, 64590)

(For revision or removal of neurostimulator pulse generator or receiver, see 61888, 63688, 64595)

(For implantation of neurostimulator electrodes, see 61850-61875, 63650-63655, 64553-64580. For revision or removal of neurostimulator electrodes, see 61880, 63660, 64585)

**▲95970** Electronic analysis of implanted neurostimulator pulse generator system (eg, rate, pulse amplitude and duration, configuration of wave form, battery status, electrode selectability, output modulation, cycling, impedance and patient compliance measurements); simple or complex brain, spinal cord, or peripheral (ie, cranial nerve, peripheral nerve, autonomic nerve, neuromuscular) neurostimulator pulse generator/transmitter, without reprogramming

**▲95971** simple brain, spinal cord, or peripheral (ie, peripheral nerve, autonomic nerve, neuromuscular) neurostimulator pulse generator/transmitter, with intraoperative or subsequent programming

**▲95972** complex brain, spinal cord, or peripheral (except cranial nerve) neurostimulator pulse generator/transmitter, with intraoperative or subsequent programming, first hour

**+▲95973** complex brain, spinal cord, or peripheral (except cranial nerve) neurostimulator pulse generator/transmitter, with intraoperative or subsequent programming, each additional 30 minutes after first hour (List separately in addition to code for primary procedure)

(Use 95973 in conjunction with code 95972)

**95974** complex cranial nerve neurostimulator pulse generator/transmitter, with intraoperative or subsequent programming, with or without nerve interface testing, first hour

**+ 95975** complex cranial nerve neurostimulator pulse generator/transmitter, with intraoperative or subsequent programming, each additional 30 minutes after first hour (List separately in addition to code for primary procedure)

(Use 95975 in conjunction with code 95974)

## ►Other Procedures◄

**95999** Unlisted neurological or neuromuscular diagnostic procedure

## Central Nervous System Assessments/Tests (eg, Neuro-Cognitive, Mental Status, Speech Testing)

The following codes are used to report the services provided during testing of the cognitive function of the central nervous system. The testing of cognitive processes, visual motor responses, and abstractive abilities is accomplished by the combination of several types of testing procedures. It is expected that the administration of these tests will generate material that will be formulated into a report.

(For development of cognitive skills, use 97770)

**96100** Psychological testing (includes psychodiagnostic assessment of personality, psychopathology, emotionality, intellectual abilities, eg, WAIS-R, Rorschach, MMPI) with interpretation and report, per hour

**96105** Assessment of aphasia (includes assessment of expressive and receptive speech and language function, language comprehension, speech production ability, reading, spelling, writing, eg, by Boston Diagnostic Aphasia Examination) with interpretation and report, per hour

**96110** Developmental testing; limited (eg, Developmental Screening Test II, Early Language Milestone Screen), with interpretation and report

**96111** extended (includes assessment of motor, language, social, adaptive and/or cognitive functioning by standardized developmental instruments, eg, Bayley Scales of Infant Development) with interpretation and report, per hour

**96115** Neurobehavioral status exam (clinical assessment of thinking, reasoning and judgment, eg, acquired knowledge, attention, memory, visual spatial abilities, language functions, planning) with interpretation and report, per hour

**96117** Neuropsychological testing battery (eg, Halstead-Reitan, Luria, WAIS-R) with interpretation and report, per hour

# Chemotherapy Administration

Procedures 96400-96549 are independent of the patient's visit.

If signficant separately identifiable Evaluation and Management service is performed, the appropriate E/M service code should be reported in addition to 96400-96549.

Either may occur independently on any date of service, or they may occur sequentially on the same day.

Preparation of chemotherapy agent(s) is included in the service for administration of the agent.

Regional (isolation) chemotherapy perfusion should be reported using the codes for arterial infusion. Placement of the intra-arterial catheter should be reported using the appropriate code from the **Cardiovascular Surgery** section.

Report separate codes for each parenteral method of administration employed when chemotherapy is administered by different techniques. Medications (eg, antibiotics, steroidal agents, antiemetics, narcotics, analgesics, biological agents) administered independently or sequentially as supportive management of chemotherapy administration, should be separately reported using 90780-90788, as appropriate.

**96400** Chemotherapy administration, subcutaneous or intramuscular, with or without local anesthesia

**96405** Chemotherapy administration, intralesional; up to and including 7 lesions

**96406** more than 7 lesions

**96408** Chemotherapy administration, intravenous; push technique

**96410** infusion technique, up to one hour

**+ 96412** infusion technique, one to 8 hours, each additional hour (List separately in addition to code for primary procedure)

(Use 96412 in conjunction with code 96410)

**96414** infusion technique, initiation of prolonged infusion (more than 8 hours), requiring the use of a portable or implantable pump

(For pump or reservoir refilling, see 96520, 96530)

**96420** Chemotherapy administration, intra-arterial; push technique

**96422** infusion technique, up to one hour

**+ 96423** infusion technique, one to 8 hours, each additional hour (List separately in addition to code for primary procedure)

(Use 96423 in conjunction with code 96422)

(For regional chemotherapy perfusion to an extremity, use 36823)

**96425** infusion technique, initiation of prolonged infusion (more than 8 hours), requiring the use of a portable or implantable pump

(For ►implanted◄ pump or reservoir refilling, see 96520, 96530)

**96440** Chemotherapy administration into pleural cavity, requiring and including thoracentesis

**96445** Chemotherapy administration into peritoneal cavity, requiring and including peritoneocentesis

**96450** Chemotherapy administration, into CNS (eg, intrathecal), requiring and including lumbar puncture

(For intravesical (bladder) chemotherapy administration, use 51720)

(For insertion of subarachnoid catheter and reservoir for infusion of drug, see 62350, 62351, 62360, 62361, 62362; for insertion of intraventricular catheter and reservoir, see 61210, 61215)

(96500-96512 have been deleted. To report, see 96408-96414)

**96520** Refilling and maintenance of portable pump

(96524, 96526 have been deleted. To report, see 96420-96425)

**96530** Refilling and maintenance of implantable pump or reservoir

(Access of pump port is included in filling of implantable pump)

(96535 has been deleted. To report, see 96440, 96445)

(96540 has been deleted. To report, use 96542)

**96542** Chemotherapy injection, subarachnoid or intraventricular via subcutaneous reservoir, single or multiple agents

**96545** Provision of chemotherapy agent

(For radioactive isotope therapy, see 79000-79999)

**96549** Unlisted chemotherapy procedure

## ▸Photodynamic Therapy◂

►(96570, 96571 are to be used in addition to bronchoscopy, endoscopy codes)◄

**+ ●96570** Photodynamic therapy by endoscopic application of light to ablate abnormal tissue via activation of photosensitive drug(s); first 30 minutes (List separately in addition to code for endoscopy or bronchoscopy procedures of lung and esophagus)

**+ ●96571** each additional 15 minutes (List separately in addition to code for endoscopy or bronchoscopy procedures of lung and esophagus)

►(Use 96570, 96571 in conjunction with codes 31641, 43228 as appropriate)◄

## Special Dermatological Procedures

Dermatologic services are typically consultative, and any of the five levels of consultation (99241-99263) may be appropriate.

In addition, services and skills outlined under **Evaluation and Management** levels of service appropriate to dermatologic illnesses should be coded similarly.

(For intralesional injections, see 11900, 11901)

(For Tzanck smear, use 87207)

**96900** Actinotherapy (ultraviolet light)

**96902** Microscopic examination of hairs plucked or clipped by the examiner (excluding hair collected by the patient) to determine telogen and anagen counts, or structural hair shaft abnormality

**96910** Photochemotherapy; tar and ultraviolet B (Goeckerman treatment) or petrolatum and ultraviolet B

**96912** psoralens and ultraviolet A (PUVA)

**96913** Photochemotherapy (Goeckerman and/or PUVA) for severe photoresponsive dermatoses requiring at least four to eight hours of care under direct supervision of the physician (includes application of medication and dressings)

**96999** Unlisted special dermatological service or procedure

## Physical Medicine and Rehabilitation

(97000 has been deleted. To report, see 97010-97039)

(For muscle testing, range of joint motion, electromyography, see 95831 et seq)

(For biofeedback training by EMG, use 90901)

(For transcutaneous nerve stimulation (TNS), use 64550)

**97001** Physical therapy evaluation

**97002** Physical therapy re-evaluation

**97003** Occupational therapy evaluation

**97004** Occupational therapy re-evaluation

# Modalities

Any physical agent applied to produce therapeutic changes to biologic tissue; includes but not limited to thermal, acoustic, light, mechanical, or electric energy.

## Supervised

The application of a modality that does not require direct (one on one) patient contact by the provider.

**97010** Application of a modality to one or more areas; hot or cold packs

**97012** traction, mechanical

**97014** electrical stimulation (unattended)

(For acupuncture with electrical stimulation, use 97781)

**97016** vasopneumatic devices

**97018** paraffin bath

**97020** microwave

**97022** whirlpool

**97024** diathermy

**97026** infrared

**97028** ultraviolet

## Constant Attendance

The application of a modality that requires direct (one on one) patient contact by the provider.

**97032** Application of a modality to one or more areas; electrical stimulation (manual), each 15 minutes

**97033** iontophoresis, each 15 minutes

**97034** contrast baths, each 15 minutes

**97035** ultrasound, each 15 minutes

**97036** Hubbard tank, each 15 minutes

**97039** Unlisted modality (specify type and time if constant attendance)

# Therapeutic Procedures

A manner of effecting change through the application of clinical skills and/or services that attempt to improve function.

Physician or therapist required to have direct (one on one) patient contact.

(97100 has been deleted. To report, see 97110-97139)

(97101 has been deleted. To report, see 97110-97139)

**97110** Therapeutic procedure, one or more areas, each 15 minutes; therapeutic exercises to develop strength and endurance, range of motion and flexibility

**97112** neuromuscular reeducation of movement, balance, coordination, kinesthetic sense, posture, and proprioception

**97113** aquatic therapy with therapeutic exercises

(97114 has been deleted. To report, use 97530)

**97116** gait training (includes stair climbing)

(97118 has been deleted. To report, use 97032)

(97120 has been deleted. To report, use 97033)

(97122 has been deleted. To report, use 97140)

**97124** massage, including effleurage, petrissage and/or tapotement (stroking, compression, percussion)

(For myofascial release, use 97250)

(97126 has been deleted. To report, use 97034)

(97128 has been deleted. To report, use 97035)

**97139** unlisted therapeutic procedure (specify)

**97140** Manual therapy techniques (eg, mobilization/manipulation, manual lymphatic drainage, manual traction), one or more regions, each 15 minutes

(97145 has been deleted. To report, see 97110-97139)

**97150** Therapeutic procedure(s), group (2 or more individuals)

►(Report 97150 for each member of group)◄

►(Group therapy procedures involve constant attendance of the physician or therapist, but by definition do not require one-on-one patient contact by the physician or therapist)◄

(97200, 97201 have been deleted. To report, see 97010-97039, 97110-97139)

(97220, 97221 have been deleted. To report, use 97036)

(97240, 97241 have been deleted. To report, see 97036, 97113)

(97250 has been deleted. To report, use 97140)

(97260, 97261 have been deleted. To report, use 97140)

(97265 has been deleted. To report, use 97140)

(For manipulation under general anesthesia, see appropriate anatomic section in **Musculoskeletal System**)

(For osteopathic manipulative treatment (OMT), see 98925-98929)

(97500, 97501 have been deleted. To report, use 97504)

**97504** Orthotics fitting and training, upper and/or lower extremities, each 15 minutes

(Code 97504 should not be reported with 97116)

(For casting and strapping of fracture, injury or dislocation, see 29000, 29590)

**97520** Prosthetic training, upper and/or lower extremities, each 15 minutes

(97521 has been deleted. To report, use 97520)

**97530** Therapeutic activities, direct (one on one) patient contact by the provider (use of dynamic activities to improve functional performance), each 15 minutes

(97531 has been deleted. To report, use 97530)

**97535** Self care/home management training (eg, activities of daily living (ADL) and compensatory training, meal preparation, safety procedures, and instructions in use of adaptive equipment) direct one on one contact by provider, each 15 minutes

**97537** Community/work reintegration training (eg, shopping, transportation, money management, avocational activities and/or work environment/modification analysis, work task analysis), direct one on one contact by provider, each 15 minutes

(97540 has been deleted. To report, see 97535, 97537)

(97541 has been deleted. To report, see 97535, 97537)

(For wheelchair management/propulsion training, use 97542)

**97542** Wheelchair management/propulsion training, each 15 minutes

**97545** Work hardening/conditioning; initial 2 hours

**+ 97546** each additional hour (List separately in addition to code for primary procedure)

(Use 97546 in conjunction with code 97545)

## Tests and Measurements

(For muscle testing, manual or electrical, joint range of motion, electromyography or nerve velocity determination, see 95831-95904)

(97700, 97701 have been deleted. To report, use 97703)

**97703** Checkout for orthotic/prosthetic use, established patient, each 15 minutes

(97720, 97721 have been deleted. To report, use 97750)

(97740, 97741 have been deleted. To report, use 97530)

**97750** Physical performance test or measurement (eg, musculoskeletal, functional capacity), with written report, each 15 minutes

(97752 has been deleted. To report, use 97750)

## Other Procedures

**97770** Development of cognitive skills to improve attention, memory, problem solving, includes compensatory training and/or sensory integrative activities, direct (one on one) patient contact by the provider, each 15 minutes

**97780** Acupuncture, one or more needles; without electrical stimulation

**97781** with electrical stimulation

**97799** Unlisted physical medicine/rehabilitation service or procedure

(98900-98902 have been deleted. To report, use appropriate category and level of **Evaluation and Management** codes)

(98910-98912 have been deleted. To report, see 99361-99362)

(98920-98922 have been deleted. To report, see 99371-99373)

## Osteopathic Manipulative Treatment

Osteopathic manipulative treatment is a form of manual treatment applied by a physician to eliminate or alleviate somatic dysfunction and related disorders. This treatment may be accomplished by a variety of techniques.

Evaluation and Management services may be reported separately if, using the modifier '-25,' the patient's condition requires a significant separately identifiable E/M service, above and beyond the usual preservice and postservice work associated with the procedure. The E/M service may be caused or prompted by the same symptoms or condition for which the OMT service was provided. As such, different diagnoses are not required for the reporting of the OMT and E/M service on the same date.

Body regions referred to are: head region; cervical region; thoracic region; lumbar region; sacral region; pelvic region; lower extremities; upper extremities; rib cage region; abdomen and viscera region.

**98925** Osteopathic manipulative treatment (OMT); one to two body regions involved

**98926** three to four body regions involved

**98927** five to six body regions involved

**98928** seven to eight body regions involved

**98929** nine to ten body regions involved

## Chiropractic Manipulative Treatment

Chiropractic manipulative treatment (CMT) is a form of manual treatment to influence joint and neurophysiological function. This treatment may be accomplished using a variety of techniques.

The chiropractic manipulative treatment codes include a pre-manipulation patient assessment. Additional Evaluation and Management services may be reported separately using the modifier '-25', if the patient's condition requires a significant separately identifiable E/M service, above and beyond the usual preservice and postservice work associated with the procedure. ►The E/M service may be caused or prompted by the same symptoms or condition for which the CMT service was provided. As such, different diagnoses are not required for the reporting of the CMT and E/M service on the same date.◄

For purposes of CMT, the five spinal regions referred to are: cervical region (includes atlanto-occipital joint); thoracic region (includes costovertebral and costotransverse joints); lumbar region; sacral region; and pelvic (sacro-iliac joint) region. The five extraspinal regions referred to are: head (including temporomandibular joint, excluding atlanto-occipital) region; lower extremities; upper extremities; rib cage (excluding costotransverse and costovertebral joints) and abdomen.

**98940** Chiropractic manipulative treatment (CMT); spinal, one to two regions

**98941** spinal, three to four regions

**98942** spinal, five regions

**98943** extraspinal, one or more regions

# Special Services, ▸Procedures◂ and Reports

The procedures with code numbers 99000 through 99090 provide the reporting physician with the means of identifying the completion of special reports and services that are an adjunct to the basic services rendered. The specific number assigned indicates the special circumstances under which a basic procedure is performed.

## Miscellaneous Services

**99000** Handling and/or conveyance of specimen for transfer from the physician's office to a laboratory

**99001** Handling and/or conveyance of specimen for transfer from the patient in other than a physician's office to a laboratory (distance may be indicated)

**99002** Handling, conveyance, and/or any other service in connection with the implementation of an order involving devices (eg, designing, fitting, packaging, handling, delivery or mailing) when devices such as orthotics, protectives, prosthetics are fabricated by an outside laboratory or shop but which items have been designed, and are to be fitted and adjusted by the attending physician

(For routine collection of venous blood, use 36415)

(99012, 99013, 99014, 99015 have been deleted. To report, see 99371-99373)

**99024** Postoperative follow-up visit, included in global service

(As a component of a surgical "package," see **Surgery** guidelines)

**99025** Initial (new patient) visit when starred (*) surgical procedure constitutes major service at that visit

**99050** Services requested after office hours in addition to basic service

**99052** Services requested between 10:00 PM and 8:00 AM in addition to basic service

**99054** Services requested on Sundays and holidays in addition to basic service

**99056** Services provided at request of patient in a location other than physician's office which are normally provided in the office

**99058** Office services provided on an emergency basis

(99062, 99064, 99065 have been deleted. To report, see 99281-99285)

**99070** Supplies and materials (except spectacles), provided by the physician over and above those usually included with the office visit or other services rendered (list drugs, trays, supplies, or materials provided)

(For spectacles, see 92390-92395)

**99071** Educational supplies, such as books, tapes, and pamphlets, provided by the physician for the patient's education at cost to physician

**99075** Medical testimony

**99078** Physician educational services rendered to patients in a group setting (eg, prenatal, obesity, or diabetic instructions)

**99080** Special reports such as insurance forms, more than the information conveyed in the usual medical communications or standard reporting form

**99082** Unusual travel (eg, transportation and escort of patient)

**99090** Analysis of information data stored in computers (eg, ECGs, blood pressures, hematologic data)

## Qualifying Circumstances for Anesthesia

(For explanation of these services, see **Anesthesia** guidelines)

**+ 99100** Anesthesia for patient of extreme age, under one year and over seventy (List separately in addition to code for primary anesthesia procedure)

**+ 99116** Anesthesia complicated by utilization of total body hypothermia (List separately in addition to code for primary anesthesia procedure)

**+ 99135** Anesthesia complicated by utilization of controlled hypotension (List separately in addition to code for primary anesthesia procedure)

**+ 99140** Anesthesia complicated by emergency conditions (specify) (List separately in addition to code for primary anesthesia procedure)

(An emergency is defined as existing when delay in treatment of the patient would lead to a significant increase in the threat to life or body part.)

## Sedation With or Without Analgesia (Conscious Sedation)

Sedation with or without analgesia (conscious sedation) is used to achieve a medically controlled state of depressed consciousness while maintaining the patient's airway, protective reflexes and ability to respond to stimulation or verbal commands. Conscious sedation includes performance and documentation of pre- and post-sedation evaluations of the patient, administration of the sedation and/or analgesic agent(s), and monitoring of cardiorespiratory function (ie, pulse oximetry, cardiorespiratory monitor, and blood pressure). The use of these codes requires the presence of an independent trained observer to assist the physician in monitoring the patient's level of consciousness and physiological status.

(If the sedation with or without analgesia (conscious sedation) is administered in support of a procedure provided by another physician, see **Anesthesia** section)

**⊘ 99141** Sedation with or without analgesia (conscious sedation); intravenous, intramuscular or inhalation

(94760-94762 may not be reported in addition to 99141)

**⊘ 99142** oral, rectal and/or intranasal

(94760-94762 may not be reported in addition to 99142)

(99150, 99151 have been deleted. To report, see 99354-99360)

## Other Services ▸and Procedures◂

**● 99170** Anogenital examination with colposcopic magnification in childhood for suspected trauma

▸(For conscious sedation, use 99141, 99142)◂

**● 99173** Screening test of visual acuity, quantitative, bilateral

▸(The screening test used must employ graduated visual acuity stimuli that allow a quantitative estimate of visual acuity (eg, Snellen chart). Other identifiable services unrelated to this screening test provided at the same time may be reported separately (eg, preventive medicine services). When acuity is measured as part of a general ophthalmological service or of an E/M service of the eye, it is a diagnostic examination and not a screening test.)◂

**99175** Ipecac or similar administration for individual emesis and continued observation until stomach adequately emptied of poison

(For diagnostic intubation, see 82926-82928, 89130-89141)

(For gastric lavage for diagnostic purposes, see 91055)

(99178 has been deleted. To report, use 96110)

(99180 has been deleted. To report, use 99183)

(99182 has been deleted. To report, use 99183)

**99183** Physician attendance and supervision of hyperbaric oxygen therapy, per session

(Evaluation and Management services and/or procedures (eg, wound debridement) provided in a hyperbaric oxygen treatment facility in conjunction with a hyperbaric oxygen therapy session should be reported separately)

**99185** Hypothermia; regional

**99186** total body

**99190** Assembly and operation of pump with oxygenator or heat exchanger (with or without ECG and/or pressure monitoring); each hour

**99191** 3/4 hour

**99192** 1/2 hour

**99195** Phlebotomy, therapeutic (separate procedure)

▲**99199** Unlisted special service, procedure or report

# Notes

# Notes

# Appendix A

## Modifiers

This list includes all of the modifiers applicable to *CPT 2000* codes.

**-21 Prolonged Evaluation and Management Services:** When the face-to-face or floor/unit service(s) provided is prolonged or otherwise greater than that usually required for the highest level of evaluation and management service within a given category, it may be identified by adding modifier '-21' to the evaluation and management code number or by use of the separate five digit modifier code 09921. A report may also be appropriate.

**-22 Unusual Procedural Services:** When the service(s) provided is greater than that usually required for the listed procedure, it may be identified by adding modifier '-22' to the usual procedure number or by use of the separate five digit modifier code 09922. A report may also be appropriate.

**-23 Unusual Anesthesia:** Occasionally, a procedure, which usually requires either no anesthesia or local anesthesia, because of unusual circumstances must be done under general anesthesia. This circumstance may be reported by adding the modifier '-23' to the procedure code of the basic service or by use of the separate five digit modifier code 09923.

**-24 Unrelated Evaluation and Management Service by the Same Physician During a Postoperative Period:** The physician may need to indicate that an evaluation and management service was performed during a postoperative period for a reason(s) unrelated to the original procedure. This circumstance may be reported by adding the modifier '-24' to the appropriate level of E/M service, or the separate five digit modifier 09924 may be used.

**-25 Significant, Separately Identifiable Evaluation and Management Service by the Same Physician on the Same Day of the Procedure or Other Service:** The physician may need to indicate that on the day a procedure or service identified by a CPT code was performed, the patient's condition required a significant, separately identifiable E/M service above and beyond the other service provided or beyond the usual preoperative and postoperative care associated with the procedure that was performed. The E/M service may be prompted by the symptom or condition for which the procedure and/or service was provided. As such, different diagnoses are not required for reporting of the E/M services on the same date. This circumstance may be reported by adding the modifier '-25' to the appropriate level of E/M service, or the separate five digit modifier 09925 may be used. **Note:** This modifier is not used to report an E/M service that resulted in a decision to perform surgery. See modifier '-57.'

**-26 Professional Component:** Certain procedures are a combination of a physician component and a technical component. When the physician component is reported separately, the service may be identified by adding the modifier '-26' to the usual procedure number or the service may be reported by use of the five digit modifier code 09926.

**-32 Mandated Services:** Services related to *mandated* consultation and/or related services (eg, PRO, third party payer, ►governmental, legislative or regulatory requirement◄) may be identified by adding the modifier '-32' to the basic procedure or the service may be reported by use of the five digit modifier 09932.

**-47 Anesthesia by Surgeon:** Regional or general anesthesia provided by the surgeon may be reported by adding the modifier '-47' to the basic service or by use of the separate five digit modifier code 09947. (This does not include local anesthesia.) **Note:** Modifier '-47' or 09947 would not be used as a modifier for the anesthesia procedures 00100-01999.

**-50 Bilateral Procedure:** Unless otherwise identified in the listings, bilateral procedures that are performed at the same operative session should be identified by adding the modifier '-50' to the appropriate five digit code or by use of the separate five digit modifier code 09950.

**-51 Multiple Procedures:** When multiple procedures, other than Evaluation and Management Services, are performed at the same session by the same provider, the primary procedure or service may be reported as listed. The additional procedure(s) or service(s) may be identified by appending the modifier '-51' to the additional procedure or service code(s) or by the use of the separate five digit modifier 09951. **Note:** This modifier should not be appended to designated "add-on" codes (see Appendix E).

**-52 Reduced Services:** Under certain circumstances a service or procedure is partially reduced or eliminated at the physician's discretion. Under these circumstances the service provided can be identified by its usual procedure number and the addition of the modifier '-52', signifying that the service is reduced. This provides a means of reporting reduced services without disturbing the identification of the basic service. Modifier code 09952 may be used as an alternative to modifier '-52.' **Note:** For hospital outpatient reporting of a previously scheduled procedure/service that is partially reduced or cancelled as a result of extenuating circumstances or those that threaten the well-being of the patient prior to or after administration of anesthesia, see modifiers '-73' and '-74' (see modifiers approved for ASC hospital outpatient use).

**-53 Discontinued Procedure:** Under certain circumstances, the physician may elect to terminate a surgical or diagnostic procedure. Due to extenuating circumstances or those that threaten the well being of the patient, it may be necessary to indicate that a surgical or diagnostic procedure was started but discontinued. This circumstance may be reported by adding the modifier '-53' to the code reported by the physician for the discontinued procedure or by use of the separate five digit modifier code 09953. **Note:** This modifier is not used to report the elective cancellation of a procedure prior to the patient's anesthesia induction and/or surgical preparation in the operating suite. For outpatient hospital/ambulatory surgery center (ASC) reporting of a previously scheduled procedure/service that is partially reduced or cancelled as a result of extenuating circumstances or those that threaten the well being of the patient prior to or after administration of anesthesia, see modifiers '-73' and '-74' (see modifiers approved for ASC hospital outpatient use).

**-54 Surgical Care Only:** When one physician performs a surgical procedure and another provides preoperative and/or postoperative management, surgical services may be identified by adding the modifier '-54' to the usual procedure number or by use of the separate five digit modifier code 09954.

**-55 Postoperative Management Only:** When one physician performs the postoperative management and another physician has performed the surgical procedure, the postoperative component may be identified by adding the modifier '-55' to the usual procedure number or by use of the separate five digit modifier code 09955.

**-56 Preoperative Management Only:** When one physician performs the preoperative care and evaluation and another physician performs the surgical procedure, the preoperative component may be identified by adding the modifier '-56' to the usual procedure number or by use of the separate five digit modifier code 09956.

**-57 Decision for Surgery:** An evaluation and management service that resulted in the initial decision to perform the surgery may be identified by adding the modifier '-57' to the appropriate level of E/M service, or the separate five digit modifier 09957 may be used.

**-58 Staged or Related Procedure or Service by the Same Physician During the Postoperative Period:** The physician may need to indicate that the performance of a procedure or service during the postoperative period was:

a) planned prospectively at the time of the original procedure (staged); b) more extensive than the original procedure; or c) for therapy following a diagnostic surgical procedure. This circumstance may be reported by adding the modifier '-58' to the staged or related procedure, or the separate five digit modifier 09958 may be used. **Note:** This modifier is not used to report the treatment of a problem that requires a return to the operating room. See modifier '-78.'

**-59 Distinct Procedural Service:** Under certain circumstances, the physician may need to indicate that a procedure or service was distinct or independent from other services performed on the same day. Modifier '-59' is used to identify procedures/services that are not normally reported together, but are appropriate under the circumstances. This may represent a different session or patient encounter, different procedure or surgery, different site or organ system, separate incision/excision, separate lesion, or separate injury (or area of injury in extensive injuries) not ordinarily encountered or performed on the same day by the same physician. However, when another already established modifier is appropriate it should be used rather than modifier '-59.' Only if no more descriptive modifier is available, and the use of modifier '-59' best explains the circumstances, should modifier '-59' be used. Modifier code 09959 may be used as an alternative to modifier '-59.'

**-62 Two Surgeons:** When two surgeons work together as primary surgeons performing distinct part(s) of a single reportable procedure, each surgeon should report his/her distinct operative work by adding the modifier '-62' to the single definitive procedure code. Each surgeon should report the co-surgery once using the same procedure code. If additional procedure(s) (including add-on procedure(s)) are performed during the same surgical session, separate code(s) may be reported without the modifier '-62' added. Modifier code 09962 may be used as an alternative to modifier '-62'. **Note:** If a co-surgeon acts as an assistant in the performance of additional procedure(s) during the same surgical session, those services may be reported using separate procedure code(s) with the modifier '-80' or modifier '-81' added, as appropriate.

**-66 Surgical Team:** Under some circumstances, highly complex procedures (requiring the concomitant services of several physicians, often of different specialties, plus other highly skilled, specially trained personnel, various types of complex equipment) are carried out under the "surgical team" concept. Such circumstances may be identified by each participating physician with the addition of the modifier '-66' to the basic procedure number used for reporting services. Modifier code 09966 may be used as an alternative to modifier '-66.'

**-76 Repeat Procedure by Same Physician:** The physician may need to indicate that a procedure or service was repeated subsequent to the original procedure or service. This circumstance may be reported by adding the modifier '-76' to the repeated procedure/service or the separate five digit modifier code 09976 may be used.

**-77 Repeat Procedure by Another Physician:** The physician may need to indicate that a basic procedure or service performed by another physician had to be repeated. This situation may be reported by adding modifier '-77' to the repeated procedure/service or the separate five digit modifier code 09977 may be used.

**-78 Return to the Operating Room for a Related Procedure During the Postoperative Period:** The physician may need to indicate that another procedure was performed during the postoperative period of the initial procedure. When this subsequent procedure is related to the first, and requires the use of the operating room, it may be reported by adding the modifier '-78' to the related procedure, or by using the separate five digit modifier 09978. (For repeat procedures on the same day, see '-76'.)

**-79 Unrelated Procedure or Service by the Same Physician During the Postoperative Period:** The physician may need to indicate that the performance of a procedure or service during the postoperative period was unrelated to the original procedure. This circumstance may be reported by using the modifier '-79' or by using the separate five digit modifier 09979. (For repeat procedures on the same day, see '-76'.)

**-80 Assistant Surgeon:** Surgical assistant services may be identified by adding the modifier '-80' to the usual procedure number(s) or by use of the separate five digit modifier code 09980.

**-81 Minimum Assistant Surgeon:** Minimum surgical assistant services are identified by adding the modifier '-81' to the usual procedure number or by use of the separate five digit modifier code 09981.

**-82 Assistant Surgeon (when qualified resident surgeon not available):** The unavailability of a qualified resident surgeon is a prerequisite for use of modifier '-82' appended to the usual procedure code number(s) or by use of the separate five digit modifier code 09982.

**-90 Reference (Outside) Laboratory:** When laboratory procedures are performed by a party other than the treating or reporting physician, the procedure may be identified by adding the modifier '-90' to the usual procedure number or by use of the separate five digit modifier code 09990.

►**-91 Repeat Clinical Diagnostic Laboratory Test:** In the course of treatment of the patient, it may be necessary to repeat the same laboratory test on the same day to obtain subsequent (multiple) test results. Under these circumstances, the laboratory test performed can be identified by its usual procedure number and the addition of the modifier '-91'. **Note:** This modifier may not be used when tests are rerun to confirm initial results; due to testing problems with specimens or equipment; or for any other reason when a normal, one-time, reportable result is all that is required. This modifier may not be used when other code(s) describe a series of test results (eg, glucose tolerance tests, evocative/suppression testing). This modifier may only be used for laboratory test(s) performed more than once on the same day on the same patient.◄

**-99 Multiple Modifiers:** Under certain circumstances two or more modifiers may be necessary to completely delineate a service. In such situations modifier '-99' should be added to the basic procedure, and other applicable modifiers may be listed as part of the description of the service. Modifier code 09999 may be used as an alternative to modifier '-99.'

# Modifiers Approved for Ambulatory Surgery Center (ASC) Hospital Outpatient Use

## CPT Level I Modifiers

**-50 Bilateral Procedure:** Unless otherwise identified in the listings, bilateral procedures that are performed at the same operative session should be identified by adding the modifier '-50' to the appropriate five digit code or by use of the separate five digit modifier code 09950.

**-52 Reduced Services:** Under certain circumstances a service or procedure is partially reduced or eliminated at the physician's discretion. Under these circumstances the service provided can be identified by its usual procedure number and the addition of the modifier '-52', signifying that the service is reduced. This provides a means of reporting reduced services without disturbing the identification of the basic service. Modifier code 09952 may be used as an alternative to modifier '-52.' **Note:** For hospital outpatient reporting of a previously scheduled procedure/service that is partially reduced or cancelled as a result of extenuating circumstances or those that threaten the well-being of the patient prior to or after administration of anesthesia, see modifiers '-73' and '-74' (see modifiers approved for ASC hospital outpatient use).

**-59 Distinct Procedural Service:** Under certain circumstances, the physician may need to indicate that a procedure or service was distinct or independent from other services performed on the same day. Modifier '-59' is used to identify procedures/services that are not normally reported together, but are appropriate under the circumstances. This may represent a different session or patient encounter, different procedure or surgery, different site or organ system, separate incision/excision, separate lesion, or separate injury (or area of injury in extensive injuries) not ordinarily encountered or performed on the same day by the same physician. However, when another already established modifier is appropriate it should be used rather than modifier '-59.' Only if no more descriptive modifier is available, and the use of modifier '-59' best explains the circumstances, should modifier '-59' be used. Modifier code 09959 may be used as an alternative to modifier '-59.'

**-73 Discontinued Out-Patient Hospital/ Ambulatory Surgery Center (ASC) Procedure Prior to the Administration of Anesthesia:** Due to extenuating circumstances or those that threaten the well being of the patient, the physician may cancel a surgical or diagnostic procedure subsequent to the patient's surgical preparation (including sedation when provided, and being taken to the room where the procedure is to be performed), but prior to the administration of anesthesia (local, regional block(s) or general). Under these circumstances, the intended service that is prepared for but cancelled can be reported by its usual procedure number and the addition of the modifier '-73' or by use of the separate five digit modifier code 09973. **Note:** The elective cancellation of a service prior to the administration of anesthesia and/or surgical preparation of the patient should not be reported. For physician reporting of a discontinued procedure, see modifier '-53.'

**-74 Discontinued Out-Patient Hospital/ Ambulatory Surgery Center (ASC) Procedure After Administration of Anesthesia:** Due to extenuating circumstances or those that threaten the well being of the patient, the physician may terminate a surgical or diagnostic procedure after the administration of anesthesia (local, regional block(s), general) or after the procedure was started (incision made, intubation started, scope inserted, etc). Under these circumstances, the procedure started but terminated can be reported by its usual procedure number and the addition of the modifier '-74' or by use of the separate five digit modifier code 09974. **Note:** The elective cancellation of a service prior to the administration of anesthesia and/or surgical preparation of the patient should not be reported. For physician reporting of a discontinued procedure, see modifier '-53.'

**-76 Repeat Procedure by Same Physician:** The physician may need to indicate that a procedure or service was repeated subsequent to the original procedure or service. This circumstance may be reported by adding the modifier '-76' to the repeated procedure/ service or the separate five digit modifier code 09976 may be used.

**-77 Repeat Procedure by Another Physician:** The physician may need to indicate that a basic procedure or service performed by another physician had to be repeated. This situation may be reported by adding modifier '-77' to the repeated procedure/service or the separate five digit modifier code 09977 may be used.

**►-91 Repeat Clinical Diagnostic Laboratory Test:** In the course of treatment of the patient, it may be necessary to repeat the same laboratory test on the same day to obtain subsequent (multiple) test results. Under these circumstances, the laboratory test performed can be identified by its usual procedure number and the addition of the modifier '-91'. **Note:** This modifier may not be used when tests are rerun to confirm initial results; due to testing problems with specimens or equipment; or for any other reason when a normal, one-time, reportable result is all that is required. This modifier may not be used when other code(s) describe a series of test results (eg, glucose tolerance tests, evocative/suppression testing). This modifier may only be used for laboratory test(s) performed more than once on the same day on the same patient.◄

## Level II (HCPCS/National) Modifiers

**-LT Left side (used to identify procedures performed on the left side of the body)**

**-RT Right side (used to identify procedures performed on the right side of the body)**

**-E1 Upper left, eyelid**

**-E2 Lower left, eyelid**

**-E3 Upper right, eyelid**

**-E4 Lower right, eyelid**

**-FA Left hand, thumb**

**-F1 Left hand, second digit**

**-F2 Left hand, third digit**

**-F3** Left hand, fourth digit

**-F4** Left hand, fifth digit

**-F5** Right hand, thumb

**-F6** Right hand, second digit

**-F7** Right hand, third digit

**-F8** Right hand, fourth digit

**-F9** Right hand, fifth digit

**-LC** Left circumflex coronary artery (Hospitals use with codes 92980-92984, 92995, 92996)

**-LD** Left anterior descending coronary artery (Hospitals use with codes 92980-92984, 92995, 92996)

**-RC** Right coronary artery (Hospitals use with codes 92980-92984, 92995, 92996)

**-QM** Ambulance service provided under arrangement by a provider of services

**-QN** Ambulance service furnished directly by a provider of services

**-QR** Repeat laboratory test performed on the same day

**-TA** Left foot, great toe

**-T1** Left foot, second digit

**-T2** Left foot, third digit

**-T3** Left foot, fourth digit

**-T4** Left foot, fifth digit

**-T5** Right foot, great toe

**-T6** Right foot, second digit

**-T7** Right foot, third digit

**-T8** Right foot, fourth digit

**-T9** Right foot, fifth digit

# Appendix B

## Summary of Additions, Deletions, and Revisions

This listing is a summary of additions, deletions, and revisions applicable to *CPT 2000* codes.

The notes, introductory paragraphs, and cross-references that have been revised or added to *CPT 2000* are not included in Appendix B, but are identified in the main text of *CPT* with "▶ ◀" symbols.

The descriptors of the codes listed as "grammatical change" have not been substantially altered, but involve placement of the semicolon, ▶or other punctuation, or a similar minor change.◀ These codes will not be identified in *CPT* with a ▲ symbol.

**'-32'** Modifier revised

**'-91'** Modifier added

**00100** Terminology revised

**00102** Terminology revised

**00103** Terminology revised

**00214** Terminology revised

**00300** Terminology revised

**00400** Terminology revised

**00420** Code deleted. To report, use 00300

**00520** Terminology revised

**00528** Terminology revised

**00740** Terminology revised

**00810** Terminology revised

**00857** Terminology revised

**00918** Terminology revised

**00952** Terminology revised

**00955** Terminology revised

**01000** Code deleted. To report, use 00400

**01110** Code deleted. To report, use 00300

**01240** Code deleted. To report, use 00400

**01300** Code deleted. To report, use 00400

**01460** Code deleted. To report, use 00400

**01600** Code deleted. To report, use 00400

**01700** Code deleted. To report, use 00400

**01800** Code deleted. To report, see 00400

**01900** Code deleted. To report, use 00952

**01902** Code deleted. To report, use 00214

**11980** Hormone pellet implantation code added

**13102** Complex repair add-on code added

**13122** Complex repair add-on code added

**13133** Complex repair add-on code added

**13153** Complex repair add-on code added

**13300** Code deleted. To report, see 13102, 13122, 13133 and 13153

**15580** Code deleted. To report, use 15574

**15625** Code deleted. To report, use 15620

**20979** Ultrasound bone stimulation code added

**22318** Odontoid fracture treatment code added

**22319** Odontoid fracture treatment code added

**22630** Terminology revised

**22840** Terminology revised

**22851** Terminology revised

**26416** Terminology revised

**26476** Grammatical change

**27096** Injection for sacroiliac joint arthrography code added

**27334** Grammatical change

**29879** Terminology revised

**31505** Grammatical change

**31622** Terminology revised

**32001** Code deleted. To report, use 32997

**32997** Total lung lavage code added

**33140** Transmyocardial revascularization code added

**33216** Terminology revised

**33217** Terminology revised

**33218** Terminology revised

**33220** Terminology revised

**33223** Terminology revised

**33240** Terminology revised

**33241** Terminology revised

**33242** Code deleted. To report, see 33218, 33220

**33243** Terminology revised

**33244** Terminology revised

**33245** Terminology revised

**33246** Terminology revised

**33247** Code deleted. To report, use 33216

**33249** Terminology revised

**33282** Implant of patient-activated event recorder code added

**33284** Removal of patient-activated event recorder code added

**33405** Terminology revised

**33410** Aortic valve replacement code added

**33968** Removal of intra-aortic assist device code added

**35500** Terminology revised

**35879** Revision of lower extremity arterial bypass graft code added

**35881** Revision of lower extremity arterial bypass graft code added

**36520** Terminology revised

**36521** Extracorporeal column adsorption code added

**36533** Terminology revised

**36534** Terminology revised

**36535** Terminology revised

**36550** Vascular access device declotting code added

**36819** AV anastomosis by basilic vein code added

**36821** Terminology revised

**36832** Grammatical change

**37250** Terminology revised

**38120** Laparoscopy splenectomy code added

**38129** Laparoscopy unlisted spleen procedure code added

**38570** Laparoscopy retroperitoneal lymph node biopsy code added

**38571** Laparoscopy pelvic lymphadenectomy code added

**38572** Laparoscopy pelvic lymphadenectomy with biopsy code added

**38589** Laparoscopy unlisted lymphatic procedure code added

**39560** Resection of diaphragm code added

**39561** Resection of diaphragm code added

**43280** Laparoscopy esophagogastric fundoplasty code added

**43289** Laparoscopy unlisted esophagus procedure code added

**43651** Laparoscopy transection of vagus nerves, truncal code added

**43652** Laparoscopy transection of vagus nerves, selective code added

**43653** Laparoscopy gastrostomy code added

**43659** Laparoscopy unlisted stomach procedure code added

**43761** Terminology revised

**43830** Terminology revised

**43832** Terminology revised

**44200** Laparoscopy enterolysis code added

**44201** Laparoscopy jejunostomy code added

**44202** Laparoscopy jejunostomy, intestinal resection code added

**44209** Laparoscopy unlisted intestine procedure code added

**44970** Laparoscopy appendectomy code added

**44979** Laparoscopy unlisted appendix procedure code added

**47560** Laparoscopy cholangiography code added

**47561** Laparoscopy cholangiography with biopsy code added

**47562** Laparoscopy cholecystectomy code added

**47563** Laparoscopy cholecystectomy with cholangiography code added

**47564** Laparoscopy cholecystectomy with exploration code added

**47570** Laparoscopy cholecystoenterostomy code added

**47579** Laparoscopy unlisted biliary tract procedure code added

**49320** Laparoscopy/peritoneoscopy diagnostic procedure code added

**49321** Laparoscopy/peritoneoscopy with biopsy code added

**49322** Laparoscopy/peritoneoscopy with aspiration code added

**49323** Laparoscopy/peritoneoscopy with drainage code added

**49329** Laparoscopy/peritoneoscopy unlisted abdomen code added

**49650** Laparoscopy inquinal hernia repair code added

**49651** Laparoscopy inquinal hernia repair code added

**49659** Laparoscopy unlisted hernia procedure code added

**50300** Grammatical change

**50320** Terminology revised

**50541** Laparoscopy ablation of renal cysts code added

**50544** Laparoscopy pyeloplasty code added

**50546** Laparoscopy nephrectomy code added

**50547** Laparoscopy donor nephrectomy code added

**50548** Laparopscopy, nephroureteroectomy code added

**50549** Laparoscopy unlisted renal procedure code added

**50945** Laparoscopy ureterolithotomy code added

**51990** Laparoscopy urethral suspension code added

**51992** Laparoscopy sling operation code added

**54100** Terminology revised

**54690** Laparoscopy orchiectomy code added

**54692** Laparoscopy orchiopexy code added

**54699** Laparoscopy unlisted testis procedure code added

**55550** Laparoscopy ligation of spermatic veins code added

**55559** Laparoscopy unlisted spermatic cord procedure code added

**56300** Code deleted. To report, use 49320

**56301** Code deleted. To report, use 58670

**56302** Code deleted. To report, use 58671

**56303** Code deleted. To report, use 58662

**56304** Code deleted. To report, use 58660

**56305** Code deleted. To report, use 49321

**56306** Code deleted. To report, use 49322

**56307** Code deleted. To report, use 58661

**56308** Code deleted. To report, use 58550

**56309** Code deleted. To report, use 58551

**56310** Code deleted. To report, use 44200

**56311** Code deleted. To report, use 38570

**56312** Code deleted. To report, use 38571

**56313** Code deleted. To report, use 38572

**56314** Code deleted. To report, use 49323

**56315** Code deleted. To report, use 44970

**56316** Code deleted. To report, use 49650

**56317** Code deleted. To report, use 49651

**56318** Code deleted. To report, use 54690

**56320** Code deleted. To report, use 55550

**56321** Code deleted. To report, use 60650

**56322** Code deleted. To report, use 43651

**56323** Code deleted. To report, use 43652

**56324** Code deleted. To report, use 47570

**56340** Code deleted. To report, use 47562

**56341** Code deleted. To report, use 47563

**56342** Code deleted. To report, use 47564

**56343** Code deleted. To report, use 58673

**56344** Code deleted. To report, use 58672

**56345** Code deleted. To report, use 38120

**56346** Code deleted. To report, use 43653

**56347** Code deleted. To report, use 44201

**56348** Code deleted. To report, use 44202

**56349** Code deleted. To report, use 43280

**56350** Code deleted. To report, use 58555

**56351** Code deleted. To report, use 58558

**56352** Code deleted. To report, use 58559

**56353** Code deleted. To report, use 58560

**56354** Code deleted. To report, use 58561

**56355** Code deleted. To report, use 58562

**56356** Code deleted. To report, use 58563

**56362** Code deleted. To report, use 47560

**56363** Code deleted. To report, use 47561

**56399** Code deleted. To report, see site-specific unlisted laparoscopy/hysteroscopy codes

**56606** Grammatical change

**58550** Laparoscopy hysterectomy code added

**58551** Laparoscopy leimyomata removal code added

**58555** Hysteroscopy diagnostic code added

**58558** Hysteroscopy biopsy code added

**58559** Hysteroscopy lysis of adhesions code added

**58560** Hysteroscopy resect intrauterine septum code added

**58561** Hysteroscopy leimyomata removal code added

**58562** Hysteroscopy foreign body removal code added

**58563** Hysteroscopy endometrial ablation code added

**58578** Laparoscopy unlisted uterus procedure code added

**58579** Hysteroscopy unlisted uterus procedure code added

**58660** Laparoscopy lysis of adhesions code added

**58661** Laparoscopy oophorectomy/salpingectomy code added

**58662** Laparoscopy fulguration/excision of lesions code added

**58670** Laparoscopy fulguration of oviducts code added

**58671** Laparoscopy occlusion of oviducts code added

**58672** Laparoscopy fimbrioplasty code added

**58673** Laparoscopy salpingostomy code added

**58679** Laparoscopy unlisted oviduct/ovary procedure code added

**59898** Laparoscopy unlisted OB care/delivery procedure code added

**60650** Laparoscopy adrenalectomy code added

**60659** Laparoscopy unlisted endocrine procedure code added

**61751** Terminology revised

**61795** Terminology revised

**61850** Grammatical change

**61855** Code deleted. To report, use 61862

**61860** Grammatical change

**61862** Stereotactic implant of neurostimulator array code added

**61865** Code deleted. To report, use 61862

**61885** Terminology revised

**61886** Placement of cranial neurostimulator device code added

**62263** Lysis of epidural adhesions code added

**62273** Terminology revised

**62274** Code deleted. To report, see 62310, 62311

**62275** Code deleted. To report, use 62310

**62276** Code deleted. To report, see 62318, 62319

**62277** Code deleted. To report, see 62318, 62319

**62278** Code deleted. To report, use 62311

**62279** Code deleted. To report, use 62319

**62280** Terminology revised

**62282** Terminology revised

**62287** Terminology revised

**62288** Code deleted. To report, see 62310, 62311

**62289** Code deleted. To report, use 62311

**62291** Terminology revised

**62298** Code deleted. To report, use 62310

**62310** Epidural or subarachnoid injection code added

**62311** Epidural or subarachnoid injection code added

**62318** Epidural or subarachnoid injection with indwelling catheter code added

**62319** Epidural or subarachnoid injection with indwelling catheter code added

**62350** Terminology revised

**63030** Terminology revised

**63056** Terminology revised

**64440** Code deleted. To report, see 64479, 64483

**64441** Code deleted. To report, see 64480, 64484

**64442** Code deleted. To report, use 64475

**64443** Code deleted. To report, use 64476

**64470** Paravertebral cervical or thoracic facet joint/nerve injection code added

**64472** Paravertebral cervical or thoracic facet joint/nerve injection add-on code added

**64475** Paravertebral lumbar or sacral facet joint/nerve injection code added

**64476** Paravertebral lumbar or sacral facet joint nerve/injection add-on code added

**64479** Transforaminal cervical or thoracic epidural injection code added

**64480** Transforaminal cervical or thoracic epidural injection add-on code added

**64483** Transforaminal lumbar or sacral epidural injection code added

**64484** Transforaminal lumbar or sacral epidural injection add-on code added

**64612** Grammatical change

**64620** Grammatical change

**64622** Terminology revised

**64623** Terminology revised

**64626** Paravertebral facet joint nerve destruction code added

**64627** Paravertebral facet joint nerve destruction add-on code added

**67220** Terminology revised

**72275** Epidurography code added

**72285** Terminology revised

**73542** Sacroiliac joint arthrography radiologic examination code added

**76005** Fluoroscopic guidance for spine injection code added

**76513** Terminology revised

**76872** Grammatical change

**76873** Prostate volume study code added

**77380** Code deleted. To report, use 77520

| | |
|---|---|
| **77381** | Code deleted. To report, use 77523 |
| **77419** | Code deleted. To report, use 77427 |
| **77420** | Code deleted. To report, use 77427 |
| **77425** | Code deleted. To report, use 77427 |
| **77427** | Radiation treatment management code added |
| **77430** | Code deleted. To report, use 77427 |
| **77499** | Terminology revised |
| **77520** | Proton beam delivery code added |
| **77523** | Proton beam delivery code added |
| **78267** | Urea breath test, C-14 code added |
| **78268** | Urea breath test, C-14 code added |
| **78456** | Venous thrombosis imaging code added |
| **78457** | Terminology revised |
| **80048** | Basic metabolic panel code added |
| **80049** | Code deleted. To report, use 80048 |
| **80053** | Comprehensive metabolic panel code added |
| **80054** | Code deleted. To report, use 80053 |
| **80058** | Code deleted. To report, use 80076 |
| **80059** | Code deleted. To report, use 80074 |
| **80069** | Renal function panel code added |
| **80072** | Grammatical change |
| **80074** | Acute hepatitis panel code added |
| **80076** | Hepatic function panel code added |
| **80091** | Code deleted. To report, see specific codes for specific tests |
| **80092** | Code deleted. To report, see specific codes for specific test |
| **82017** | Grammatical change |
| **82120** | Amines, vaginal fluid code added |
| **83013** | Terminology revised |
| **86586** | Grammatical change |
| **86588** | Code deleted. To report, see 86403, 87081, 87430 or 87880 |
| **86915** | Terminology revised |
| **87338** | H. pylori enzyme immunoassay code added |
| **88148** | Terminology revised |
| **90378** | RSV immune globulin, IM code added |
| **90471** | Terminology revised |
| **90472** | Terminology revised |
| **90592** | Code deleted |
| **90721** | Grammatical change |
| **90744** | Terminology revised |
| **90745** | Code deleted |
| **90782** | Terminology revised |
| **90799** | Terminology revised |
| **92960** | Grammatical change |
| **92961** | Internal cardioversion code added |
| **92978** | Terminology revised |
| **93640** | Terminology revised |
| **93641** | Terminology revised |
| **93642** | Terminology revised |
| **93727** | Implantable loop recorder analysis code added |
| **93737** | Terminology revised |
| **93741** | Cardiac pacing device analysis code added |
| **93742** | Cardiac pacing device analysis code added |
| **93743** | Cardiac pacing device analysis code added |
| **93744** | Cardiac pacing device analysis code added |
| **94014** | Grammatical change |
| **95816** | Terminology revised |
| **95819** | Terminology revised |
| **95831** | Terminology revised |
| **95870** | Terminology revised |
| **95900** | Terminology revised |
| **95904** | Terminology revised |
| **95961** | Terminology revised |
| **95970** | Terminology revised |
| **95971** | Terminology revised |
| **95972** | Terminology revised |
| **95973** | Terminology revised |
| **96570** | Photodynamic therapy code added |
| **96571** | Photodynamic therapy code added |
| **99170** | Anogenital examination in child code added |
| **99173** | Vision screening code added |
| **99199** | Terminology revised |
| **99242** | Grammatical change |
| **99285** | Terminology revised |
| **99291** | Terminology revised |
| **99295** | Terminology revised |
| **99296** | Terminology revised |
| **99297** | Terminology revised |

# Appendix C

## Update to Short Descriptors

This listing includes changes necessary to update the short descriptors on the *CPT 2000* data file.

The descriptors have been changed to reflect additions, revisions, or deletions to the *CPT 2000* codes, or to enhance or correct the data file.

The descriptors which have been enhanced, but do not necessarily reflect a change to the *CPT 2000* codes, are indicated with an asterisk.

**00100** Revise: ANESTH, SALIVARY GLAND
***00104** Revise: ANESTH, ELECTROSHOCK
***00120** Revise: ANESTH, EAR SURGERY
***00124** Revise: ANESTH, EAR EXAM
***00142** Revise: ANESTH, LENS SURGERY
***00148** Revise: ANESTH, EYE EXAM
***00160** Revise: ANESTH, NOSE/SINUS SURGERY
***00162** Revise: ANESTH, NOSE/SINUS SURGERY
**00300** Revise: ANESTH, HEAD/NECK/PTRUNK
**00400** Revise: ANESTH, SKIN, EXT/PER/ATRUNK
**00420** Delete
***00580** Revise: ANESTH HEART/LUNG TRANSPLANT
**00740** Revise: ANESTH, UPPER GI VISUALIZE
**00810** Revise: ANESTH, LOW INTESTINE SCOPE
***00862** Revise: ANESTH, KIDNEY/URETER SURG
***00872** Revise: ANESTH KIDNEY STONE DESTRUCT
***00873** Revise: ANESTH KIDNEY STONE DESTRUCT
**00952** Revise: ANESTH, HYSTEROSCOPE/GRAPH
**01000** Delete
**01110** Delete
**01240** Delete
**01300** Delete
**01460** Delete
***01502** Revise: ANESTH, LWR LEG EMBOLECTOMY
**01600** Delete
**01700** Delete
***01712** Revise: ANESTH, UPPR ARM TENDON SURG
***01714** Revise: ANESTH, UPPR ARM TENDON SURG
***01730** Revise: ANESTH, UPPR ARM PROCEDURE
***01770** Revise: ANESTH, UPPR ARM ARTERY SURG
***01772** Revise: ANESTH, UPPR ARM EMBOLECTOMY
***01782** Revise: ANESTH, UPPR ARM VEIN REPAIR
**01800** Delete
***01840** Revise: ANESTH, LWR ARM ARTERY SURG
***01842** Revise: ANESTH, LWR ARM EMBOLECTOMY
***01852** Revise: ANESTH, LWR ARM VEIN REPAIR
**01900** Delete
**01902** Delete
***01912** Revise: ANESTH, LUMBAR DISKOGRAPHY
***01914** Revise: ANESTH, CERVICAL DISKOGRAPHY
***11001** Revise: DEBRIDE INFECTED SKIN ADD-ON
***11040** Revise: DEBRIDE SKIN, PARTIAL
***11041** Revise: DEBRIDE SKIN, FULL
***11056** Revise: TRIM SKIN LESIONS, 2 TO 4
***11057** Revise: TRIM SKIN LESIONS, OVER 4
***11732** Revise: REMOVE NAIL PLATE, ADD-ON
***11760** Revise: REPAIR OF NAIL BED
**11980** Add: IMPLANT HORMONE PELLET(S)
**13102** Add: REPAIR WOUND/LESION ADD-ON
**13122** Add: REPAIR WOUND/LESION ADD-ON
**13133** Add: REPAIR WOUND/LESION ADD-ON
**13153** Add: REPAIR WOUND/LESION ADD-ON
**13300** Delete
**15580** Delete
**15625** Delete
***15940** Revise: REMOVE HIP PRESSURE SORE
***15941** Revise: REMOVE HIP PRESSURE SORE
***15944** Revise: REMOVE HIP PRESSURE SORE
***15945** Revise: REMOVE HIP PRESSURE SORE
***15946** Revise: REMOVE HIP PRESSURE SORE
***17003** Revise: DESTROY LESIONS, 2-14
***17004** Revise: DESTROY LESIONS, 15 OR MORE
***19126** Revise: EXCISION, ADDL BREAST LESION
***20550** Revise: INJECT TENDON/LIGAMENT/CYST

*20600 Revise: DRAIN/INJECT, JOINT/BURSA
*20605 Revise: DRAIN/INJECT, JOINT/BURSA
*20610 Revise: DRAIN/INJECT, JOINT/BURSA
*20805 Revise: REPLANT, FOREARM, COMPLETE
*20808 Revise: REPLANTATION HAND, COMPLETE
*20838 Revise: REPLANTATION FOOT, COMPLETE
*20950 Revise: FLUID PRESSURE, MUSCLE
*20972 Revise: BONE/SKIN GRAFT, METATARSAL
*20973 Revise: BONE/SKIN GRAFT, GREAT TOE
20979 Add: US BONE STIMULATION
*21125 Revise: AUGMENTATION, LOWER JAW BONE
*21127 Revise: AUGMENTATION, LOWER JAW BONE
*21270 Revise: AUGMENTATION, CHEEK BONE
*21275 Revise: REVISION, ORBITOFACIAL BONES
*21325 Revise: TREATMENT OF NOSE FRACTURE
*21330 Revise: TREATMENT OF NOSE FRACTURE
*21335 Revise: TREATMENT OF NOSE FRACTURE
*21336 Revise: TREAT NASAL SEPTAL FRACTURE
*21337 Revise: TREAT NASAL SEPTAL FRACTURE
*21338 Revise: TREAT NASOETHMOID FRACTURE
*21339 Revise: TREAT NASOETHMOID FRACTURE
21340 Revise: TREATMENT OF NOSE FRACTURE
*21343 Revise: TREATMENT OF SINUS FRACTURE
*21344 Revise: TREATMENT OF SINUS FRACTURE
*21345 Revise: TREAT NOSE/JAW FRACTURE
*21346 Revise: TREAT NOSE/JAW FRACTURE
*21347 Revise: TREAT NOSE/JAW FRACTURE
*21348 Revise: TREAT NOSE/JAW FRACTURE
*21355 Revise: TREAT CHEEK BONE FRACTURE
*21356 Revise: TREAT CHEEK BONE FRACTURE
*21360 Revise: TREAT CHEEK BONE FRACTURE
*21365 Revise: TREAT CHEEK BONE FRACTURE
*21366 Revise: TREAT CHEEK BONE FRACTURE
*21385 Revise: TREAT EYE SOCKET FRACTURE
*21386 Revise: TREAT EYE SOCKET FRACTURE
*21387 Revise: TREAT EYE SOCKET FRACTURE
*21390 Revise: TREAT EYE SOCKET FRACTURE
*21395 Revise: TREAT EYE SOCKET FRACTURE
*21401 Revise: TREAT EYE SOCKET FRACTURE
*21406 Revise: TREAT EYE SOCKET FRACTURE
*21407 Revise: TREAT EYE SOCKET FRACTURE
*21408 Revise: TREAT EYE SOCKET FRACTURE
*21422 Revise: TREAT MOUTH ROOF FRACTURE
*21423 Revise: TREAT MOUTH ROOF FRACTURE
*21432 Revise: TREAT CRANIOFACIAL FRACTURE
*21433 Revise: TREAT CRANIOFACIAL FRACTURE
*21435 Revise: TREAT CRANIOFACIAL FRACTURE
*21436 Revise: TREAT CRANIOFACIAL FRACTURE
*21440 Revise: TREAT DENTAL RIDGE FRACTURE
*21445 Revise: TREAT DENTAL RIDGE FRACTURE
*21461 Revise: TREAT LOWER JAW FRACTURE
*21462 Revise: TREAT LOWER JAW FRACTURE
*21465 Revise: TREAT LOWER JAW FRACTURE
*21470 Revise: TREAT LOWER JAW FRACTURE
*21494 Revise: TREAT HYOID BONE FRACTURE
*21495 Revise: TREAT HYOID BONE FRACTURE
*21555 Revise: REMOVE LESION, NECK/CHEST
*21556 Revise: REMOVE LESION, NECK/CHEST
*21557 Revise: REMOVE TUMOR, NECK/CHEST
*21825 Revise: TREAT STERNUM FRACTURE
*21935 Revise: REMOVE TUMOR, BACK
22318 Add: TREAT ODONTOID FX W/O GRAFT
22319 Add: TREAT ODONTOID FX W/GRAFT
*22325 Revise: TREAT SPINE FRACTURE
*22326 Revise: TREAT NECK SPINE FRACTURE
*22327 Revise: TREAT THORAX SPINE FRACTURE
*22328 Revise: TREAT EACH ADD SPINE FX
*22819 Revise: KYPHECTOMY, 3 OR MORE
*22848 Revise: INSERT PELV FIXATION DEVICE
*23107 Revise: EXPLORE TREAT SHOULDER JOINT
*23125 Revise: REMOVAL OF COLLAR BONE
*23130 Revise: REMOVE SHOULDER BONE, PART
*23170 Revise: REMOVE COLLAR BONE LESION
*23210 Revise: REMOVAL OF SHOULDER BLADE
*23440 Revise: REMOVE/TRANSPLANT TENDON
*23480 Revise: REVISION OF COLLAR BONE
*23515 Revise: TREAT CLAVICLE FRACTURE
*23530 Revise: TREAT CLAVICLE DISLOCATION
*23532 Revise: TREAT CLAVICLE DISLOCATION
*23550 Revise: TREAT CLAVICLE DISLOCATION

*23552 Revise: TREAT CLAVICLE DISLOCATION
*23570 Revise: TREAT SHOULDER BLADE FX
*23575 Revise: TREAT SHOULDER BLADE FX
*23585 Revise: TREAT SCAPULA FRACTURE
*23615 Revise: TREAT HUMERUS FRACTURE
*23616 Revise: TREAT HUMERUS FRACTURE
*23630 Revise: TREAT HUMERUS FRACTURE
*23660 Revise: TREAT SHOULDER DISLOCATION
*23670 Revise: TREAT DISLOCATION/FRACTURE
*23680 Revise: TREAT DISLOCATION/FRACTURE
*24341 Revise: REPAIR ARM TENDON/MUSCLE
*24515 Revise: TREAT HUMERUS FRACTURE
*24516 Revise: TREAT HUMERUS FRACTURE
*24545 Revise: TREAT HUMERUS FRACTURE
*24546 Revise: TREAT HUMERUS FRACTURE
*24575 Revise: TREAT HUMERUS FRACTURE
*24579 Revise: TREAT HUMERUS FRACTURE
*24586 Revise: TREAT ELBOW FRACTURE
*24587 Revise: TREAT ELBOW FRACTURE
*24615 Revise: TREAT ELBOW DISLOCATION
*24635 Revise: TREAT ELBOW FRACTURE
*24665 Revise: TREAT RADIUS FRACTURE
*24666 Revise: TREAT RADIUS FRACTURE
*24670 Revise: TREAT ULNAR FRACTURE
*24675 Revise: TREAT ULNAR FRACTURE
*24685 Revise: TREAT ULNAR FRACTURE
*25390 Revise: SHORTEN RADIUS OR ULNA
*25391 Revise: LENGTHEN RADIUS OR ULNA
*25515 Revise: TREAT FRACTURE OF RADIUS
*25520 Revise: TREAT FRACTURE OF RADIUS
*25525 Revise: TREAT FRACTURE OF RADIUS
*25526 Revise: TREAT FRACTURE OF RADIUS
*25545 Revise: TREAT FRACTURE OF ULNA
*25575 Revise: TREAT FRACTURE RADIUS/ULNA
*25611 Revise: TREAT FRACTURE RADIUS/ULNA
*25620 Revise: TREAT FRACTURE RADIUS/ULNA
*25628 Revise: TREAT WRIST BONE FRACTURE
*25645 Revise: TREAT WRIST BONE FRACTURE
*25650 Revise: TREAT WRIST BONE FRACTURE
*25670 Revise: TREAT WRIST DISLOCATION
*25676 Revise: TREAT WRIST DISLOCATION
*25685 Revise: TREAT WRIST FRACTURE
*25695 Revise: TREAT WRIST DISLOCATION
*25825 Revise: FUSE HAND BONES WITH GRAFT
*25830 Revise: FUSION, RADIOULNAR JNT/ULNA
*26546 Revise: REPAIR NONUNION HAND
*26553 Revise: SINGLE TRANSFER, TOE-HAND
*26554 Revise: DOUBLE TRANSFER, TOE-HAND
*26615 Revise: TREAT METACARPAL FRACTURE
*26650 Revise: TREAT THUMB FRACTURE
*26665 Revise: TREAT THUMB FRACTURE
*26685 Revise: TREAT HAND DISLOCATION
*26686 Revise: TREAT HAND DISLOCATION
*26715 Revise: TREAT KNUCKLE DISLOCATION
*26735 Revise: TREAT FINGER FRACTURE, EACH
*26746 Revise: TREAT FINGER FRACTURE, EACH
*26765 Revise: TREAT FINGER FRACTURE, EACH
*26785 Revise: TREAT FINGER DISLOCATION
*26861 Revise: FUSION OF FINGER JNT, ADD-ON
27096 Add: INJECT SACROILIAC JOINT
*27140 Revise: TRANSPLANT FEMUR RIDGE
*27177 Revise: TREAT SLIPPED EPIPHYSIS
*27178 Revise: TREAT SLIPPED EPIPHYSIS
*27181 Revise: TREAT SLIPPED EPIPHYSIS
*27202 Revise: TREAT TAIL BONE FRACTURE
*27215 Revise: TREAT PELVIC FRACTURE(S)
*27230 Revise: TREAT THIGH FRACTURE
*27232 Revise: TREAT THIGH FRACTURE
*27235 Revise: TREAT THIGH FRACTURE
*27236 Revise: TREAT THIGH FRACTURE
*27238 Revise: TREAT THIGH FRACTURE
*27240 Revise: TREAT THIGH FRACTURE
*27244 Revise: TREAT THIGH FRACTURE
*27245 Revise: TREAT THIGH FRACTURE
*27246 Revise: TREAT THIGH FRACTURE
*27248 Revise: TREAT THIGH FRACTURE
*27253 Revise: TREAT HIP DISLOCATION
*27254 Revise: TREAT HIP DISLOCATION
*27256 Revise: TREAT HIP DISLOCATION
*27257 Revise: TREAT HIP DISLOCATION

*27258 Revise: TREAT HIP DISLOCATION
*27259 Revise: TREAT HIP DISLOCATION
*27265 Revise: TREAT HIP DISLOCATION
*27266 Revise: TREAT HIP DISLOCATION
*27323 Revise: BIOPSY, THIGH SOFT TISSUES
*27324 Revise: BIOPSY, THIGH SOFT TISSUES
*27330 Revise: BIOPSY, KNEE JOINT LINING
*27360 Revise: PARTIAL REMOVAL, LEG BONE(S)
*27486 Revise: REVISE/REPLACE KNEE JOINT
*27487 Revise: REVISE/REPLACE KNEE JOINT
*27506 Revise: TREATMENT OF THIGH FRACTURE
*27514 Revise: TREATMENT OF THIGH FRACTURE
*27516 Revise: TREAT THIGH FX GROWTH PLATE
*27517 Revise: TREAT THIGH FX GROWTH PLATE
*27519 Revise: TREAT THIGH FX GROWTH PLATE
*27524 Revise: TREAT KNEECAP FRACTURE
*27530 Revise: TREAT KNEE FRACTURE
*27532 Revise: TREAT KNEE FRACTURE
*27535 Revise: TREAT KNEE FRACTURE
*27536 Revise: TREAT KNEE FRACTURE
*27540 Revise: TREAT KNEE FRACTURE
*27556 Revise: TREAT KNEE DISLOCATION
*27557 Revise: TREAT KNEE DISLOCATION
*27558 Revise: TREAT KNEE DISLOCATION
*27566 Revise: TREAT KNEECAP DISLOCATION
*27620 Revise: EXPLORE/TREAT ANKLE JOINT
*27756 Revise: TREATMENT OF TIBIA FRACTURE
*27758 Revise: TREATMENT OF TIBIA FRACTURE
*27759 Revise: TREATMENT OF TIBIA FRACTURE
*27766 Revise: TREATMENT OF ANKLE FRACTURE
*27784 Revise: TREATMENT OF FIBULA FRACTURE
*27792 Revise: TREATMENT OF ANKLE FRACTURE
*27814 Revise: TREATMENT OF ANKLE FRACTURE
*27822 Revise: TREATMENT OF ANKLE FRACTURE
*27823 Revise: TREATMENT OF ANKLE FRACTURE
*27832 Revise: TREAT LOWER LEG DISLOCATION
*27846 Revise: TREAT ANKLE DISLOCATION
*27848 Revise: TREAT ANKLE DISLOCATION
*28020 Revise: EXPLORATION OF FOOT JOINT
*28022 Revise: EXPLORATION OF FOOT JOINT
*28024 Revise: EXPLORATION OF TOE JOINT
*28060 Revise: PARTIAL REMOVAL, FOOT FASCIA
*28415 Revise: TREAT HEEL FRACTURE
*28420 Revise: TREAT/GRAFT HEEL FRACTURE
*28445 Revise: TREAT ANKLE FRACTURE
*28456 Revise: TREAT MIDFOOT FRACTURE
*28465 Revise: TREAT MIDFOOT FRACTURE, EACH
*28476 Revise: TREAT METATARSAL FRACTURE
*28485 Revise: TREAT METATARSAL FRACTURE
*28496 Revise: TREAT BIG TOE FRACTURE
*28505 Revise: TREAT BIG TOE FRACTURE
*28525 Revise: TREAT TOE FRACTURE
*29505 Revise: APPLICATION, LONG LEG SPLINT
*29870 Revise: KNEE ARTHROSCOPY, DX
*30801 Revise: CAUTERIZATION, INNER NOSE
*30802 Revise: CAUTERIZATION, INNER NOSE
*30915 Revise: LIGATION, NASAL SINUS ARTERY
*30920 Revise: LIGATION, UPPER JAW ARTERY
*30930 Revise: THERAPY, FRACTURE OF NOSE
*31000 Revise: IRRIGATION, MAXILLARY SINUS
*31002 Revise: IRRIGATION, SPHENOID SINUS
*31020 Revise: EXPLORATION, MAXILLARY SINUS
*31030 Revise: EXPLORATION, MAXILLARY SINUS
*31050 Revise: EXPLORATION, SPHENOID SINUS
*31276 Revise: SINUS ENDOSCOPY, SURGICAL
*31320 Revise: DIAGNOSTIC INCISION, LARYNX
*31584 Revise: TREAT LARYNX FRACTURE
*31585 Revise: TREAT LARYNX FRACTURE
*31586 Revise: TREAT LARYNX FRACTURE
*31643 Revise: DIAG BRONCHOSCOPE/CATHETER
*31646 Revise: BRONCHOSCOPY, RECLEAR AIRWAY
*31656 Revise: BRONCHOSCOPY, INJ FOR XRAY
*31730 Revise: INTRO, WINDPIPE WIRE/TUBE
32001 Delete
*32124 Revise: EXPLORE CHEST FREE ADHESIONS
*32200 Revise: DRAIN, OPEN, LUNG LESION
*32201 Revise: DRAIN, PERCUT, LUNG LESION
*32501 Revise: REPAIR BRONCHUS ADD-ON
*32852 Revise: LUNG TRANSPLANT WITH BYPASS
*32854 Revise: LUNG TRANSPLANT WITH BYPASS

**32997** Add: TOTAL LUNG LAVAGE
**33140** Add: HEART REVASCULARIZE (TMR)
**33216** Revise: REVISE ELTRD PACING-DEFIB
**33217** Revise: REVISE ELTRD PACING-DEFIB
**33218** Revise: REVISE ELTRD PACING-DEFIB
**33220** Revise: REVISE ELTRD PACING-DEFIB
***33222** Revise: REVISE POCKET, PACEMAKER
**33223** Revise: REVISE POCKET, PACING-DEFIB
**33240** Revise: INSERT PULSE GENERATOR
**33241** Revise: REMOVE PULSE GENERATOR
**33242** Delete
**33243** Revise: REMOVE ELTRD/THORACOTOMY
**33244** Revise: REMOVE ELTRD, TRANSVEN
**33245** Revise: INSERT EPIC ELTRD PACE-DEFIB
**33246** Revise: INSERT EPIC ELTRD/GENERATOR
**33247** Delete
**33249** Revise: ELTRD/INSERT PACE-DEFIB
**33282** Add: IMPLANT PAT-ACTIVE HT RECORD
**33284** Add: REMOVE PAT-ACTIVE HT RECORD
***33406** Revise: REPLACEMENT OF AORTIC VALVE
**33410** Add: REPLACEMENT OF AORTIC VALVE
***33413** Revise: REPLACEMENT OF AORTIC VALVE
***33414** Revise: REPAIR OF AORTIC VALVE
***33516** Revise: CABG, VEIN, SIX OR MORE
***33523** Revise: CABG, ART-VEIN, SIX OR MORE
***33536** Revise: CABG, ARTERIAL, FOUR OR MORE
***33615** Revise: REPAIR, SIMPLE FONTAN
***33617** Revise: REPAIR, MODIFIED FONTAN
***33860** Revise: ASCENDING AORTIC GRAFT
***33861** Revise: ASCENDING AORTIC GRAFT
***33863** Revise: ASCENDING AORTIC GRAFT
***33875** Revise: THORACIC AORTIC GRAFT
**33968** Add: REMOVE AORTIC ASSIST DEVICE
***34502** Revise: RECONSTRUCT VENA CAVA
**35879** Add: REVISE GRAFT W/VEIN
**35881** Add: REVISE GRAFT W/VEIN
***36468** Revise: INJECTION(S), SPIDER VEINS
***36469** Revise: INJECTION(S), SPIDER VEINS
**36521** Add: APHERESIS W/ ADSORP/REINFUSE
**36533** Revise: INSERTION OF ACCESS DEVICE
**36534** Revise: REVISION OF ACCESS DEVICE
**36535** Revise: REMOVAL OF ACCESS DEVICE
**36550** Add: DECLOT VASCULAR DEVICE
**36819** Add: AV FUSION BY BASILIC VEIN
**36821** Revise: AV FUSION DIRECT ANY SITE
***36823** Revise: INSERTION OF CANNULA(S)
**37250** Revise: IV US FIRST VESSEL ADD-ON
***37251** Revise: IV US EACH ADD VESSEL ADD-ON
***37607** Revise: LIGATION OF A-V FISTULA
**38120** Add: LAPAROSCOPY, SPLENECTOMY
**38129** Add: LAPAROSCOPE PROC, SPLEEN
***38300** Revise: DRAINAGE, LYMPH NODE LESION
***38305** Revise: DRAINAGE, LYMPH NODE LESION
***38500** Revise: BIOPSY/REMOVAL, LYMPH NODES
***38505** Revise: NEEDLE BIOPSY, LYMPH NODES
***38510** Revise: BIOPSY/REMOVAL, LYMPH NODES
***38520** Revise: BIOPSY/REMOVAL, LYMPH NODES
***38525** Revise: BIOPSY/REMOVAL, LYMPH NODES
***38530** Revise: BIOPSY/REMOVAL, LYMPH NODES
***38550** Revise: REMOVAL, NECK/ARMPIT LESION
***38555** Revise: REMOVAL, NECK/ARMPIT LESION
**38570** Add: LAPAROSCOPY, LYMPH NODE BIOP
**38571** Add: LAPAROSCOPY, LYMPHADENECTOMY
**38572** Add: LAPAROSCOPY, LYMPHADENECTOMY
**38589** Add: LAPAROSCOPE PROC, LYMPHATIC
***38745** Revise: REMOVE ARMPIT LYMPH NODES
***38790** Revise: INJECT FOR LYMPHATIC X-RAY
**39560** Add: RESECT DIAPHRAGM, SIMPLE
**39561** Add: RESECT DIAPHRAGM, COMPLEX
***40804** Revise: REMOVAL, FOREIGN BODY, MOUTH
***40805** Revise: REMOVAL, FOREIGN BODY, MOUTH
***41145** Revise: TONGUE REMOVAL, NECK SURGERY
***42145** Revise: REPAIR PALATE, PHARYNX/UVULA
***42440** Revise: EXCISE SUBMAXILLARY GLAND
***42450** Revise: EXCISE SUBLINGUAL GLAND
***43220** Revise: ESOPH ENDOSCOPY, DILATION
***43226** Revise: ESOPH ENDOSCOPY, DILATION
***43227** Revise: ESOPH ENDOSCOPY, REPAIR
***43228** Revise: ESOPH ENDOSCOPY, ABLATION
***43235** Revise: UPPR GI ENDOSCOPY, DIAGNOSIS

*43243 Revise: UPPER GI ENDOSCOPY & INJECT
*43248 Revise: UPPR GI ENDOSCOPY/GUIDE WIRE
*43249 Revise: ESOPH ENDOSCOPY, DILATION
*43260 Revise: ENDO CHOLANGIOPANCREATOGRAPH
*43261 Revise: ENDO CHOLANGIOPANCREATOGRAPH
*43262 Revise: ENDO CHOLANGIOPANCREATOGRAPH
*43263 Revise: ENDO CHOLANGIOPANCREATOGRAPH
*43264 Revise: ENDO CHOLANGIOPANCREATOGRAPH
*43265 Revise: ENDO CHOLANGIOPANCREATOGRAPH
*43267 Revise: ENDO CHOLANGIOPANCREATOGRAPH
*43268 Revise: ENDO CHOLANGIOPANCREATOGRAPH
*43269 Revise: ENDO CHOLANGIOPANCREATOGRAPH
*43271 Revise: ENDO CHOLANGIOPANCREATOGRAPH
*43272 Revise: ENDO CHOLANGIOPANCREATOGRAPH
43280 Add: LAPAROSCOPY, FUNDOPLASTY
43289 Add: LAPAROSCOPE PROC, ESOPH
*43458 Revise: DILATE ESOPHAGUS
*43632 Revise: REMOVAL OF STOMACH, PARTIAL
*43633 Revise: REMOVAL OF STOMACH, PARTIAL
*43634 Revise: REMOVAL OF STOMACH, PARTIAL
*43635 Revise: REMOVAL OF STOMACH, PARTIAL
*43638 Revise: REMOVAL OF STOMACH, PARTIAL
*43639 Revise: REMOVAL OF STOMACH, PARTIAL
43651 Add: LAPAROSCOPY, VAGUS NERVE
43652 Add: LAPAROSCOPY, VAGUS NERVE
43653 Add: LAPAROSCOPY, GASTROSTOMY
43659 Add: LAPAROSCOPE PROC, STOM
*44015 Revise: INSERT NEEDLE CATH BOWEL
*44155 Revise: REMOVAL OF COLON/ILEOSTOMY
44200 Add: LAPAROSCOPY, ENTEROLYSIS
44201 Add: LAPAROSCOPY, JEJUNOSTOMY
44202 Add: LAPARO, RESECT INTESTINE
44209 Add: LAPAROSCOPE PROC, INTESTINE
*44361 Revise: SMALL BOWEL ENDOSCOPY/BIOPSY
*44377 Revise: SMALL BOWEL ENDOSCOPY/BIOPSY
*44386 Revise: ENDOSCOPY, BOWEL POUCH/BIOP
*44900 Revise: DRAIN APP ABSCESS, OPEN
*44901 Revise: DRAIN APP ABSCESS, PERCUT
44970 Add: LAPAROSCOPY, APPENDECTOMY
44979 Add: LAPAROSCOPE PROC, APP
*45119 Revise: REMOVE RECTUM W/RESERVOIR
*45305 Revise: PROCTOSIGMOIDOSCOPY & BIOPSY
*45330 Revise: DIAGNOSTIC SIGMOIDOSCOPY
*45337 Revise: SIGMOIDOSCOPY & DECOMPRESS
*45382 Revise: COLONOSCOPY/CONTROL BLEEDING
*45383 Revise: LESION REMOVAL COLONOSCOPY
*45385 Revise: LESION REMOVAL COLONOSCOPY
*45550 Revise: REPAIR RECTUM/REMOVE SIGMOID
*45800 Revise: REPAIR RECT/BLADDER FISTULA
*45805 Revise: REPAIR FISTULA W/COLOSTOMY
*45825 Revise: REPAIR FISTULA W/COLOSTOMY
*46608 Revise: ANOSCOPY/ REMOVE FOR BODY
*46610 Revise: ANOSCOPY/REMOVE LESION
*46612 Revise: ANOSCOPY/ REMOVE LESIONS
*46614 Revise: ANOSCOPY/CONTROL BLEEDING
*46742 Revise: REPAIR OF IMPERFORATED ANUS
*46744 Revise: REPAIR OF CLOACAL ANOMALY
*46746 Revise: REPAIR OF CLOACAL ANOMALY
*46748 Revise: REPAIR OF CLOACAL ANOMALY
*46917 Revise: LASER SURGERY, ANAL LESIONS
*47530 Revise: REVISE/REINSERT BILE TUBE
*47552 Revise: BILIARY ENDOSCOPY THRU SKIN
*47553 Revise: BILIARY ENDOSCOPY THRU SKIN
*47554 Revise: BILIARY ENDOSCOPY THRU SKIN
*47555 Revise: BILIARY ENDOSCOPY THRU SKIN
*47556 Revise: BILIARY ENDOSCOPY THRU SKIN
47560 Add: LAPAROSCOPY W/CHOLANGIO
47561 Add: LAPARO W/CHOLANGIO/BIOPSY
47562 Add: LAPAROSCOPIC CHOLECYSTECTOMY
47563 Add: LAPARO CHOLECYSTECTOMY/GRAPH
47564 Add: LAPARO CHOLECYSTECTOMY/EXPLR
47570 Add: LAPARO CHOLECYSTOENTEROSTOMY
47579 Add: LAPAROSCOPE PROC, BILIARY
*48160 Revise: PANCREAS REMOVAL/TRANSPLANT
*48554 Revise: TRANSPL ALLOGRAFT PANCREAS
*49040 Revise: DRAIN, OPEN, ABDOM ABSCESS
*49041 Revise: DRAIN, PERCUT, ABDOM ABSCESS
*49060 Revise: DRAIN, OPEN, RETROP ABSCESS
*49061 Revise: DRAIN, PERCUT, RETROPER ABSC
49320 Add: DIAG LAPARO SEPARATE PROC

49321 Add: LAPAROSCOPY, BIOPSY
49322 Add: LAPAROSCOPY, ASPIRATION
49323 Add: LAPARO DRAIN LYMPHOCELE
49329 Add: LAPARO PROC, ABDM/PER/OMENT
*49423 Revise: EXCHANGE DRAINAGE CATHETER
*49424 Revise: ASSESS CYST, CONTRAST INJECT
*49507 Revise: REPAIR INGUINAL HERNIA
*49572 Revise: REPAIR EPIGASTRIC HERNIA
49650 Add: LAPARO HERNIA REPAIR INITIAL
49651 Add: LAPARO HERNIA REPAIR RECUR
49659 Add: LAPARO PROC, HERNIA REPAIR
*50020 Revise: RENAL ABSCESS, OPEN DRAIN
*50021 Revise: RENAL ABSCESS, PERCUT DRAIN
50541 Add: LAPARO ABLATE RENAL CYST
50544 Add: LAPAROSCOPY, PYELOPLASTY
50546 Add: LAPAROSCOPIC NEPHRECTOMY
50547 Add: LAPARO REMOVAL DONOR KIDNEY
50548 Add: LAPARO-ASST REMOVE K/URETER
50549 Add: LAPAROSCOPE PROC, RENAL
*50559 Revise: RENAL ENDOSCOPY/RADIOTRACER
*50578 Revise: RENAL ENDOSCOPY/RADIOTRACER
50945 Add: LAPAROSCOPY URETEROLITHOTOMY
*51045 Revise: INCISE BLADDER/DRAIN URETER
*51580 Revise: REMOVE BLADDER/REVISE TRACT
*51590 Revise: REMOVE BLADDER/REVISE TRACT
*51595 Revise: REMOVE BLADDER/REVISE TRACT
*51596 Revise: REMOVE BLADDER/CREATE POUCH
51990 Add: LAPARO URETHRAL SUSPENSION
51992 Add: LAPARO SLING OPERATION
*52250 Revise: CYSTOSCOPY AND RADIOTRACER
*52260 Revise: CYSTOSCOPY AND TREATMENT
*52265 Revise: CYSTOSCOPY AND TREATMENT
*53400 Revise: REVISE URETHRA, STAGE 1
*53405 Revise: REVISE URETHRA, STAGE 2
*54328 Revise: REVISE PENIS/URETHRA
*54332 Revise: REVISE PENIS/URETHRA
*54336 Revise: REVISE PENIS/URETHRA
*54352 Revise: RECONSTRUCT URETHRA/PENIS
54690 Add: LAPAROSCOPY, ORCHIECTOMY
54692 Add: LAPAROSCOPY, ORCHIOPEXY
54699 Add: LAPAROSCOPE PROC, TESTIS
*55300 Revise: PREPARE, SPERM DUCT X-RAY
55550 Add: LAPARO LIGATE SPERMATIC VEIN
55559 Add: LAPARO PROC, SPERMATIC CORD
56300 Delete
56301 Delete
56302 Delete
56303 Delete
56304 Delete
56305 Delete
56306 Delete
56307 Delete
56308 Delete
56309 Delete
56310 Delete
56311 Delete
56312 Delete
56313 Delete
56314 Delete
56315 Delete
56316 Delete
56317 Delete
56318 Delete
56320 Delete
56321 Delete
56322 Delete
56323 Delete
56324 Delete
56340 Delete
56341 Delete
56342 Delete
56343 Delete
56344 Delete
56345 Delete
56346 Delete
56347 Delete
56348 Delete
56349 Delete
56350 Delete
56351 Delete

56352 Delete
56353 Delete
56354 Delete
56355 Delete
56356 Delete
56362 Delete
56363 Delete
56399 Delete
*57107 Revise: REMOVE VAGINA TISSUE, PART
*57111 Revise: REMOVE VAGINA TISSUE, COMPL
*57112 Revise: VAGINECTOMY W/NODES, COMPL
*57160 Revise: INSERT PESSARY/OTHER DEVICE
*57415 Revise: REMOVE VAGINAL FOREIGN BODY
*57545 Revise: REMOVE CERVIX/REPAIR PELVIS
*57555 Revise: REMOVE CERVIX/REPAIR VAGINA
*57820 Revise: D & C OF RESIDUAL CERVIX
*58120 Revise: DILATION AND CURETTAGE
*58275 Revise: HYSTERECTOMY/REVISE VAGINA
*58280 Revise: HYSTERECTOMY/REVISE VAGINA
58550 Add: LAPARO-ASST VAG HYSTERECTOMY
58551 Add: LAPAROSCOPY, REMOVE MYOMA
58555 Add: HYSTEROSCOPY, DX, SEP PROC
58558 Add: HYSTEROSCOPY, BIOPSY
58559 Add: HYSTEROSCOPY, LYSIS
58560 Add: HYSTEROSCOPY, RESECT SEPTUM
58561 Add: HYSTEROSCOPY, REMOVE MYOMA
58562 Add: HYSTEROSCOPY, REMOVE FB
58563 Add: HYSTEROSCOPY, ABLATION
58578 Add: LAPARO PROC, UTERUS
58579 Add: HYSTEROSCOPE PROCEDURE
58660 Add: LAPAROSCOPY, LYSIS
58661 Add: LAPAROSCOPY, REMOVE ADNEXA
58662 Add: LAPAROSCOPY, EXCISE LESIONS
58670 Add: LAPAROSCOPY, TUBAL CAUTERY
58671 Add: LAPAROSCOPY, TUBAL BLOCK
58672 Add: LAPAROSCOPY, FIMBRIOPLASTY
58673 Add: LAPAROSCOPIC SALPINGOSTOMY
58679 Add: LAPARO PROC, OVIDUCT-OVARY
*58820 Revise: DRAIN OVARY ABSCESS, OPEN
*58822 Revise: DRAIN OVARY ABSCESS, PERCUT
*58823 Revise: DRAIN PELVIC ABSCESS, PERCUT
*59160 Revise: D & C AFTER DELIVERY
*59866 Revise: ABORTION (MPR)
59898 Add: LAPARO PROC, OB CARE/DELIVER
*60210 Revise: PARTIAL THYROID EXCISION
*60512 Revise: AUTOTRANSPLANT PARATHYROID
*60521 Revise: REMOVAL OF THYMUS GLAND
60650 Add: LAPAROSCOPY ADRENALECTOMY
60659 Add: LAPARO PROC, ENDOCRINE
*61154 Revise: PIERCE SKULL & REMOVE CLOT
*61210 Revise: PIERCE SKULL, IMPLANT DEVICE
*61333 Revise: EXPLORE ORBIT/REMOVE LESION
*61334 Revise: EXPLORE ORBIT/REMOVE OBJECT
*61343 Revise: INCISE SKULL (PRESS RELIEF)
*61570 Revise: REMOVE FOREIGN BODY, BRAIN
*61609 Revise: TRANSECT ARTERY, SINUS
*61610 Revise: TRANSECT ARTERY, SINUS
*61611 Revise: TRANSECT ARTERY, SINUS
*61612 Revise: TRANSECT ARTERY, SINUS
*61750 Revise: INCISE SKULL/BRAIN BIOPSY
61751 Revise: BRAIN BIOPSY W/ CT/MR GUIDE
61855 Delete
61862 Add: IMPLANT NEUROSTIMUL, SUBCORT
61865 Delete
61885 Revise: IMPLANT NEUROSTIM ONE ARRAY
61886 Add: IMPLANT NEUROSTIM ARRAYS
*62000 Revise: TREAT SKULL FRACTURE
*62005 Revise: TREAT SKULL FRACTURE
62263 Add: LYSIS EPIDURAL ADHESIONS
*62269 Revise: NEEDLE BIOPSY, SPINAL CORD
62273 Revise: TREAT EPIDURAL SPINE LESION
62274 Delete
62275 Delete
62276 Delete
62277 Delete
62278 Delete
62279 Delete
62288 Delete
62289 Delete
62298 Delete

**62310** Add: INJECT SPINE C/T
**62311** Add: INJECT SPINE L/S (CD)
**62318** Add: INJECT SPINE W/CATH, C/T
**62319** Add: INJECT SPINE W/CATH L/S (CD)
**62350** Revise: IMPLANT SPINAL CANAL CATH
***62351** Revise: IMPLANT SPINAL CANAL CATH
**64440** Delete
**64441** Delete
**64442** Delete
**64443** Delete
**64470** Add: INJ PARAVERTEBRAL C/T
**64472** Add: INJ PARAVERTEBRAL C/T ADD-ON
**64475** Add: INJ PARAVERTEBRAL L/S
**64476** Add: INJ PARAVERTEBRAL L/S ADD-ON
**64479** Add: INJ FORAMEN EPIDURAL C/T
**64480** Add: INJ FORAMEN EPIDURAL ADD-ON
**64483** Add: INJ FORAMEN EPIDURAL L/S
**64484** Add: INJ FORAMEN EPIDURAL ADD-ON
**64622** Revise: DESTR PARAVERTEBRL NERVE L/S
**64623** Revise: DESTR PARAVERTEBRAL N ADD-ON
**64626** Add: DESTR PARAVERTEBRL NERVE C/T
**64627** Add: DESTR PARAVERTEBRAL N ADD-ON
***64876** Revise: REPAIR NERVE/SHORTEN BONE
***65112** Revise: REMOVE EYE/REVISE SOCKET
***65114** Revise: REMOVE EYE/REVISE SOCKET
***66682** Revise: REPAIR IRIS & CILIARY BODY
***66983** Revise: REMOVE CATARACT/INSERT LENS
***66984** Revise: REMOVE CATARACT/INSERT LENS
***67101** Revise: REPAIR DETACHED RETINA
***67105** Revise: REPAIR DETACHED RETINA
***67112** Revise: REREPAIR DETACHED RETINA
***67115** Revise: RELEASE ENCIRCLING MATERIAL
***67220** Revise: TREATMENT OF CHOROID LESION
***67414** Revise: EXPLR/DECOMPRESS EYE SOCKET
***67415** Revise: ASPIRATION, ORBITAL CONTENTS
***67445** Revise: EXPLR/DECOMPRESS EYE SOCKET
***68505** Revise: PARTIAL REMOVAL, TEAR GLAND
***69110** Revise: REMOVE EXTERNAL EAR, PARTIAL
***69410** Revise: INSET MIDDLE EAR (BAFFLE)
***70240** Revise: X-RAY EXAM, PITUITARY SADDLE
***70336** Revise: MAGNETIC IMAGE, JAW JOINT
***70486** Revise: CAT SCAN OF FACE/JAW
***70488** Revise: CONTRAST CAT SCANS, FACE/JAW
***70540** Revise: MAGNETIC IMAGE, FACE/NECK
***70553** Revise: MAGNETIC IMAGE, BRAIN (MRI)
***71015** Revise: CHEST X-RAY
***71034** Revise: CHEST X-RAY AND FLUOROSCOPY
***71101** Revise: X-RAY EXAM OF RIBS/CHEST
***71111** Revise: X-RAY EXAM OF RIBS/ CHEST
***71550** Revise: MAGNETIC IMAGE, CHEST (MRI)
***71555** Revise: MAGNETIC IMAGE, CHEST (MRA)
***72070** Revise: X-RAY EXAM OF THORACIC SPINE
***72133** Revise: CONTRST CAT SCANS, LOW SPINE
***72159** Revise: MAGNETIC IMAGE, SPINE (MRA)
***72198** Revise: MAGNETIC IMAGE, PELVIS (MRA)
***72255** Revise: CONTRAST X-RAY, THORAX SPINE
***72265** Revise: CONTRAST X-RAY, LOWER SPINE
**72275** Add: EPIDUROGRAPHY
**72285** Revise: X-RAY C/T SPINE DISK
***73000** Revise: X-RAY EXAM OF COLLAR BONE
***73220** Revise: MAGNETIC IMAGE, ARM/HAND
***73225** Revise: MAGNETIC IMAGE, UPPER (MRA)
**73542** Add: X-RAY EXAM, SACROILIAC JOINT
***73564** Revise: X-RAY EXAM, KNEE, 4 OR MORE
***73565** Revise: X-RAY EXAM OF KNEES
***73720** Revise: MAGNETIC IMAGE, LEG/FOOT
***73725** Revise: MAGNETIC IMAGE/LOWER (MRA)
***74181** Revise: MAGNETIC IMAGE/ABDOMEN (MRI)
***74210** Revise: CONTRST X-RAY EXAM OF THROAT
***74220** Revise: CONTRAST X-RAY, ESOPHAGUS
***74230** Revise: CINEMA X-RAY, THROAT/ESOPH
***74240** Revise: X-RAY EXAM, UPPER GI TRACT
***74241** Revise: X-RAY EXAM, UPPER GI TRACT
***74245** Revise: X-RAY EXAM, UPPER GI TRACT
***74246** Revise: CONTRST X-RAY UPPR GI TRACT
***74247** Revise: CONTRST X-RAY UPPR GI TRACT
***74249** Revise: CONTRST X-RAY UPPR GI TRACT
***74300** Revise: X-RAY BILE DUCTS/PANCREAS
***74305** Revise: X-RAY BILE DUCTS/PANCREAS
***74327** Revise: X-RAY BILE STONE REMOVAL

*74328 Revise: XRAY BILE DUCT ENDOSCOPY
*74330 Revise: X-RAY BILE/PANC ENDOSCOPY
*74400 Revise: CONTRST X-RAY, URINARY TRACT
*74410 Revise: CONTRST X-RAY, URINARY TRACT
*74415 Revise: CONTRST X-RAY, URINARY TRACT
*74420 Revise: CONTRST X-RAY, URINARY TRACT
*74425 Revise: CONTRST X-RAY, URINARY TRACT
*74430 Revise: CONTRAST X-RAY, BLADDER
*74440 Revise: X-RAY, MALE GENITAL TRACT
*74450 Revise: X-RAY, URETHRA/BLADDER
*74455 Revise: X-RAY, URETHRA/BLADDER
*74475 Revise: X-RAY CONTROL, CATH INSERT
*74480 Revise: X-RAY CONTROL, CATH INSERT
*74740 Revise: X-RAY, FEMALE GENITAL TRACT
*74742 Revise: X-RAY, FALLOPIAN TUBE
*75658 Revise: ARTERY X-RAYS, ARM
*75733 Revise: ARTERY X-RAYS, ADRENALS
*75894 Revise: X-RAYS, TRANSCATH THERAPY
*75896 Revise: X-RAYS, TRANSCATH THERAPY
76005 Add: FLUOROGUIDE FOR SPINE INJECT
*76645 Revise: ECHO EXAM OF BREAST(S)
*76816 Revise: ECHO EXAM FOLLOW-UP/REPEAT
76873 Add: ECHOGRAP TRANS R, PROS STUDY
77380 Delete
77381 Delete
77419 Delete
77420 Delete
77425 Delete
77427 Add: RADIATION TX MANAGEMENT, X5
77430 Delete
77520 Add: PROTON BEAM DELIVERY
77523 Add: PROTON BEAM DELIVERY
*78006 Revise: THYROID IMAGING WITH UPTAKE
*78007 Revise: THYROID IMAGE, MULT UPTAKES
*78018 Revise: THYROID MET IMAGING, BODY
*78206 Revise: LIVER IMAGE (3D) W/FLOW
*78216 Revise: LIVER & SPLEEN IMAGE/FLOW
78267 Add: BREATH TST ATTAIN/ANAL C-14
78268 Add: BREATH TEST ANALYSIS, C-14
78456 Add: ACUTE VENOUS THROMBUS IMAGE
*78460 Revise: HEART MUSCLE BLOOD, SINGLE
*78461 Revise: HEART MUSCLE BLOOD, MULTIPLE
*78464 Revise: HEART IMAGE (3D), SINGLE
*78465 Revise: HEART IMAGE (3D), MULTIPLE
*78468 Revise: HEART INFARCT IMAGE (EF)
*78472 Revise: GATED HEART, PLANAR, SINGLE
*78481 Revise: HEART FIRST PASS, SINGLE
*78483 Revise: HEART FIRST PASS, MULTIPLE
*78491 Revise: HEART IMAGE (PET), SINGLE
*78492 Revise: HEART IMAGE (PET), MULTIPLE
*78601 Revise: BRAIN IMAGING, LTD W/ FLOW
*78606 Revise: BRAIN IMAGING, COMPL W/FLOW
*78707 Revise: KIDNEY FLOW/FUNCTION IMAGE
*78708 Revise: KIDNEY FLOW/FUNCTION IMAGE
*78709 Revise: KIDNEY FLOW/FUNCTION IMAGE
*78761 Revise: TESTICULAR IMAGING/FLOW
*79000 Revise: INIT HYPERTHYROID THERAPY
*79200 Revise: INTRACAVITARY NUCLEAR TRMT
*79420 Revise: INTRAVASCULAR NUCLEAR THER
80048 Add: BASIC METABOLIC PANEL
80049 Delete
80053 Add: COMPREHEN METABOLIC PANEL
80054 Delete
80058 Delete
80059 Delete
80069 Add: RENAL FUNCTION PANEL
80074 Add: ACUTE HEPATITIS PANEL
80076 Add: HEPATIC FUNCTION PANEL
80091 Delete
80092 Delete
*80156 Revise: ASSAY OF CARBAMAZEPINE
*80162 Revise: ASSAY OF DIGOXIN
*80170 Revise: ASSAY OF GENTAMICIN
*80172 Revise: ASSAY OF GOLD
*80176 Revise: ASSAY OF LIDOCAINE
*80178 Revise: ASSAY OF LITHIUM
*80182 Revise: ASSAY OF NORTRIPTYLINE
*80184 Revise: ASSAY OF PHENOBARBITAL
*80185 Revise: ASSAY OF PHENYTOIN, TOTAL
*80186 Revise: ASSAY OF PHENYTOIN, FREE

*80188 Revise: ASSAY OF PRIMIDONE
*80190 Revise: ASSAY OF PROCAINAMIDE
*80192 Revise: ASSAY OF PROCAINAMIDE
*80194 Revise: ASSAY OF QUINIDINE
*80196 Revise: ASSAY OF SALICYLATE
*80197 Revise: ASSAY OF TACROLIMUS
*80198 Revise: ASSAY OF THEOPHYLLINE
*80200 Revise: ASSAY OF TOBRAMYCIN
*80201 Revise: ASSAY OF TOPIRAMATE
*80202 Revise: ASSAY OF VANCOMYCIN
*81000 Revise: URINALYSIS, NONAUTO W/SCOPE
*81001 Revise: URINALYSIS, AUTO W/SCOPE
*82000 Revise: ASSAY OF BLOOD ACETALDEHYDE
*82003 Revise: ASSAY OF ACETAMINOPHEN
*82024 Revise: ASSAY OF ACTH
*82030 Revise: ASSAY OF ADP & AMP
*82040 Revise: ASSAY OF SERUM ALBUMIN
*82042 Revise: ASSAY OF URINE ALBUMIN
*82055 Revise: ASSAY OF ETHANOL
*82075 Revise: ASSAY OF BREATH ETHANOL
*82088 Revise: ASSAY OF ALDOSTERONE
*82106 Revise: ALPHA-FETOPROTEIN, AMNIOTIC
*82108 Revise: ASSAY OF ALUMINUM
82120 Add: AMINES, VAGINAL FLUID QUAL
*82136 Revise: AMINO ACIDS, QUANT, 2-5
*82139 Revise: AMINO ACIDS, QUAN, 6 OR MORE
*82160 Revise: ASSAY OF ANDROSTERONE
*82172 Revise: ASSAY OF APOLIPOPROTEIN
*82232 Revise: ASSAY OF BETA-2 PROTEIN
*82247 Revise: BILIRUBIN, TOTAL
*82248 Revise: BILIRUBIN, DIRECT
*82251 Revise: ASSAY OF BILIRUBIN
*82261 Revise: ASSAY OF BIOTINIDASE
*82270 Revise: TEST FOR BLOOD, FECES
*82300 Revise: ASSAY OF CADMIUM
*82310 Revise: ASSAY OF CALCIUM
*82330 Revise: ASSAY OF CALCIUM
*82340 Revise: ASSAY OF CALCIUM IN URINE
*82370 Revise: X-RAY ASSAY, CALCULUS
*82374 Revise: ASSAY, BLOOD CARBON DIOXIDE
*82375 Revise: ASSAY, BLOOD CARBON MONOXIDE
*82379 Revise: ASSAY OF CARNITINE
*82380 Revise: ASSAY OF CAROTENE
*82382 Revise: ASSAY, URINE CATECHOLAMINES
*82383 Revise: ASSAY, BLOOD CATECHOLAMINES
*82384 Revise: ASSAY, THREE CATECHOLAMINES
*82387 Revise: ASSAY OF CATHEPSIN-D
*82390 Revise: ASSAY OF CERULOPLASMIN
*82415 Revise: ASSAY OF CHLORAMPHENICOL
*82435 Revise: ASSAY OF BLOOD CHLORIDE
*82436 Revise: ASSAY OF URINE CHLORIDE
*82438 Revise: ASSAY, OTHER FLUID CHLORIDES
*82465 Revise: ASSAY OF SERUM CHOLESTEROL
*82480 Revise: ASSAY, SERUM CHOLINESTERASE
*82482 Revise: ASSAY, RBC CHOLINESTERASE
*82485 Revise: ASSAY, CHONDROITIN SULFATE
*82491 Revise: CHROMOTOGRAPHY, QUANT, SING
*82495 Revise: ASSAY OF CHROMIUM
*82507 Revise: ASSAY OF CITRATE
*82520 Revise: ASSAY OF COCAINE
*82525 Revise: ASSAY OF COPPER
*82528 Revise: ASSAY OF CORTICOSTERONE
*82540 Revise: ASSAY OF CREATINE
*82541 Revise: COLUMN CHROMOTOGRAPHY, QUAL
*82542 Revise: COLUMN CHROMOTOGRAPHY, QUANT
*82550 Revise: ASSAY OF CK (CPK)
*82552 Revise: ASSAY OF CPK IN BLOOD
*82565 Revise: ASSAY OF CREATININE
*82570 Revise: ASSAY OF URINE CREATININE
*82585 Revise: ASSAY OF CRYOFIBRINOGEN
*82595 Revise: ASSAY OF CRYOGLOBULIN
*82600 Revise: ASSAY OF CYANIDE
*82638 Revise: ASSAY OF DIBUCAINE NUMBER
*82651 Revise: ASSAY OF DIHYDROTESTOSTERONE
*82652 Revise: ASSAY OF DIHYDROXYVITAMIN D
*82658 Revise: ENZYME CELL ACTIVITY, RA
*82666 Revise: ASSAY OF EPIANDROSTERONE
*82668 Revise: ASSAY OF ERYTHROPOIETIN
*82670 Revise: ASSAY OF ESTRADIOL
*82671 Revise: ASSAY OF ESTROGENS

***82672** Revise: ASSAY OF ESTROGEN
***82677** Revise: ASSAY OF ESTRIOL
***82679** Revise: ASSAY OF ESTRONE
***82690** Revise: ASSAY OF ETHCHLORVYNOL
***82693** Revise: ASSAY OF ETHYLENE GLYCOL
***82696** Revise: ASSAY OF ETIOCHOLANOLONE
***82705** Revise: FATS/LIPIDS, FECES, QUAL
***82710** Revise: FATS/LIPIDS, FECES, QUANT
***82715** Revise: ASSAY OF FECAL FAT
***82725** Revise: ASSAY OF BLOOD FATTY ACIDS
***82728** Revise: ASSAY OF FERRITIN
***82731** Revise: ASSAY OF FETAL FIBRONECTIN
***82735** Revise: ASSAY OF FLUORIDE
***82747** Revise: ASSAY OF FOLIC ACID, RBC
***82757** Revise: ASSAY OF SEMEN FRUCTOSE
***82759** Revise: ASSAY OF RBC GALACTOKINASE
***82760** Revise: ASSAY OF GALACTOSE
***82784** Revise: ASSAY OF GAMMAGLOBULIN IGM
***82785** Revise: ASSAY OF GAMMAGLOBULIN IGE
***82787** Revise: IGG 1, 2, 3 and 4
***82926** Revise: ASSAY OF GASTRIC ACID
***82928** Revise: ASSAY OF GASTRIC ACID
***82947** Revise: ASSAY OF GLUCOSE, QUANT
***82955** Revise: ASSAY OF G6PD ENZYME
***82963** Revise: ASSAY OF GLUCOSIDASE
***82965** Revise: ASSAY OF GDH ENZYME
***82975** Revise: ASSAY OF GLUTAMINE
***82978** Revise: ASSAY OF GLUTATHIONE
***82979** Revise: ASSAY, RBC GLUTATHIONE
***83003** Revise: ASSAY, GROWTH HORMONE (HGH)
***83008** Revise: ASSAY OF GUANOSINE
***83010** Revise: ASSAY OF HAPTOGLOBIN, QUANT
***83012** Revise: ASSAY OF HAPTOGLOBINS
**83013** Revise: H PYLORI BREATH TST ANALYSIS
***83051** Revise: ASSAY OF PLASMA HEMOGLOBIN
***83065** Revise: ASSAY OF HEMOGLOBIN HEAT
***83069** Revise: ASSAY OF URINE HEMOGLOBIN
***83070** Revise: ASSAY OF HEMOSIDERIN, QUAL
***83071** Revise: ASSAY OF HEMOSIDERIN, QUANT
***83080** Revise: ASSAY OF B HEXOSAMINIDASE
***83088** Revise: ASSAY OF HISTAMINE
***83150** Revise: ASSAY OF FOR HVA
***83497** Revise: ASSAY OF 5-HIAA
***83500** Revise: ASSAY, FREE HYDROXYPROLINE
***83505** Revise: ASSAY, TOTAL HYDROXYPROLINE
***83516** Revise: IMMUNOASSAY, NONANTIBODY
***83519** Revise: IMMUNOASSAY, NONANTIBODY
***83528** Revise: ASSAY OF INTRINSIC FACTOR
***83540** Revise: ASSAY OF IRON
***83570** Revise: ASSAY OF IDH ENZYME
***83582** Revise: ASSAY OF KETOGENIC STEROIDS
***83586** Revise: ASSAY 17- KETOSTEROIDS
***83593** Revise: FRACTIONATION, KETOSTEROIDS
***83605** Revise: ASSAY OF LACTIC ACID
***83625** Revise: ASSAY OF LDH ENZYMES
***83634** Revise: ASSAY OF URINE FOR LACTOSE
***83655** Revise: ASSAY OF LEAD
***83661** Revise: ASSAY OF L/S RATIO
***83670** Revise: ASSAY OF LAP ENZYME
***83690** Revise: ASSAY OF LIPASE
***83715** Revise: ASSAY OF BLOOD LIPOPROTEINS
***83716** Revise: ASSAY OF BLOOD LIPOPROTEINS
***83718** Revise: ASSAY OF LIPOPROTEIN
***83719** Revise: ASSAY OF BLOOD LIPOPROTEIN
***83721** Revise: ASSAY OF BLOOD LIPOPROTEIN
***83727** Revise: ASSAY OF LRH HORMONE
***83735** Revise: ASSAY OF MAGNESIUM
***83825** Revise: ASSAY OF MERCURY
***83835** Revise: ASSAY OF METANEPHRINES
***83840** Revise: ASSAY OF METHADONE
***83857** Revise: ASSAY OF METHEMALBUMIN
***83858** Revise: ASSAY OF METHSUXIMIDE
***83873** Revise: ASSAY OF CSF PROTEIN
***83874** Revise: ASSAY OF MYOGLOBIN
***83883** Revise: ASSAY, NEPHELOMETRY NOT SPEC
***83885** Revise: ASSAY OF NICKEL
***83887** Revise: ASSAY OF NICOTINE
***83898** Revise: MOLECULE NUCLEIC AMPLI
***83901** Revise: MOLECULE NUCLEIC AMPLI
***83915** Revise: ASSAY OF NUCLEOTIDASE

*83918 Revise: ASSAY, ORGANIC ACIDS QUANT
*83919 Revise: ASSAY, ORGANIC ACIDS QUAL
*83925 Revise: ASSAY OF OPIATES
*83930 Revise: ASSAY OF BLOOD OSMOLALITY
*83935 Revise: ASSAY OF URINE OSMOLALITY
*83937 Revise: ASSAY OF OSTEOCALCIN
*83945 Revise: ASSAY OF OXALATE
*83986 Revise: ASSAY OF BODY FLUID ACIDITY
*84030 Revise: ASSAY OF BLOOD PKU
*84035 Revise: ASSAY OF PHENYLKETONES
*84085 Revise: ASSAY OF RBC PG6D ENZYME
*84087 Revise: ASSAY PHOSPHOHEXOSE ENZYMES
*84100 Revise: ASSAY OF PHOSPHORUS
*84105 Revise: ASSAY OF URINE PHOSPHORUS
*84110 Revise: ASSAY OF PORPHOBILINOGEN
*84120 Revise: ASSAY OF URINE PORPHYRINS
*84126 Revise: ASSAY OF FECES PORPHYRINS
*84127 Revise: ASSAY OF FECES PORPHYRINS
*84132 Revise: ASSAY OF SERUM POTASSIUM
*84133 Revise: ASSAY OF URINE POTASSIUM
*84134 Revise: ASSAY OF PREALBUMIN
*84135 Revise: ASSAY OF PREGNANEDIOL
*84138 Revise: ASSAY OF PREGNANETRIOL
*84140 Revise: ASSAY OF PREGNENOLONE
*84143 Revise: ASSAY OF 17-HYDROXYPREGNENO
*84144 Revise: ASSAY OF PROGESTERONE
*84146 Revise: ASSAY OF PROLACTIN
*84153 Revise: ASSAY OF PSA, TOTAL
*84154 Revise: ASSAY OF PSA, FREE
*84155 Revise: ASSAY OF PROTEIN
*84160 Revise: ASSAY OF SERUM PROTEIN
*84165 Revise: ASSAY OF SERUM PROTEINS
*84207 Revise: ASSAY OF VITAMIN B-6
*84210 Revise: ASSAY OF PYRUVATE
*84220 Revise: ASSAY OF PYRUVATE KINASE
*84228 Revise: ASSAY OF QUININE
*84233 Revise: ASSAY OF ESTROGEN
*84234 Revise: ASSAY OF PROGESTERONE
*84235 Revise: ASSAY OF ENDOCRINE HORMONE
*84238 Revise: ASSAY, NONENDOCRINE RECEPTOR
*84252 Revise: ASSAY OF VITAMIN B-2
*84255 Revise: ASSAY OF SELENIUM
*84260 Revise: ASSAY OF SEROTONIN
*84270 Revise: ASSAY OF SEX HORMONE GLOBUL
*84275 Revise: ASSAY OF SIALIC ACID
*84285 Revise: ASSAY OF SILICA
*84295 Revise: ASSAY OF SERUM SODIUM
*84300 Revise: ASSAY OF URINE SODIUM
*84305 Revise: ASSAY OF SOMATOMEDIN
*84307 Revise: ASSAY OF SOMATOSTATIN
*84376 Revise: SUGARS, SINGLE, QUAL
*84377 Revise: SUGARS, MULTIPLE, QUAL
*84392 Revise: ASSAY OF URINE SULFATE
*84402 Revise: ASSAY OF TESTOSTERONE
*84403 Revise: ASSAY OF TOTAL TESTOSTERONE
*84425 Revise: ASSAY OF VITAMIN B-1
*84430 Revise: ASSAY OF THIOCYANATE
*84432 Revise: ASSAY OF THYROGLOBULIN
*84436 Revise: ASSAY OF TOTAL THYROXINE
*84437 Revise: ASSAY OF NEONATAL THYROXINE
*84439 Revise: ASSAY OF FREE THYROXINE
*84442 Revise: ASSAY OF THYROID ACTIVITY
*84445 Revise: ASSAY OF TSI
*84446 Revise: ASSAY OF VITAMIN E
*84449 Revise: ASSAY OF TRANSCORTIN
*84466 Revise: ASSAY OF TRANSFERRIN
*84478 Revise: ASSAY OF TRIGLYCERIDES
*84479 Revise: ASSAY OF THYROID (T3 OR T4)
*84480 Revise: ASSAY, TRIIODOTHYRONINE (T3)
*84484 Revise: ASSAY OF TROPONIN, QUANT
*84490 Revise: ASSAY OF FECES FOR TRYPSIN
*84510 Revise: ASSAY OF TYROSINE
*84512 Revise: ASSAY OF TROPONIN, QUAL
*84520 Revise: ASSAY OF UREA NITROGEN
*84540 Revise: ASSAY OF URINE/UREA-N
*84550 Revise: ASSAY OF BLOOD/URIC ACID
*84560 Revise: ASSAY OF URINE/URIC ACID
*84577 Revise: ASSAY OF FECES/UROBILINOGEN
*84580 Revise: ASSAY OF URINE UROBILINOGEN
*84583 Revise: ASSAY OF URINE UROBILINOGEN

***84585** Revise: ASSAY OF URINE VMA
***84586** Revise: ASSAY OF VIP
***84588** Revise: ASSAY OF VASOPRESSIN
***84590** Revise: ASSAY OF VITAMIN A
***84597** Revise: ASSAY OF VITAMIN K
***84600** Revise: ASSAY OF VOLATILES
***84630** Revise: ASSAY OF ZINC
***84681** Revise: ASSAY OF C-PEPTIDE
***85031** Revise: MANUAL HEMOGRAM, CBC
***85046** Revise: RETICYTE/HGB CONCENTRATE
***85441** Revise: HEINZ BODIES, DIRECT
***85445** Revise: HEINZ BODIES, INDUCED
***85590** Revise: PLATELET COUNT, MANUAL
***85651** Revise: RBC SED RATE, NONAUTOMATED
***85652** Revise: RBC SED RATE, AUTOMATED
***86000** Revise: AGGLUTININS, FEBRILE
***86060** Revise: ANTISTREPTOLYSIN O, TITER
***86063** Revise: ANTISTREPTOLYSIN O, SCREEN
***86156** Revise: COLD AGGLUTININ, SCREEN
***86255** Revise: FLUORESCENT ANTIBODY, SCREEN
***86256** Revise: FLUORESCENT ANTIBODY, TITER
***86359** Revise: T CELLS, TOTAL COUNT
***86360** Revise: T CELL, ABSOLUTE COUNT/RATIO
***86361** Revise: T CELL, ABSOLUTE COUNT
**86588** Delete
***86603** Revise: ADENOVIRUS ANTIBODY
***86609** Revise: BACTERIUM ANTIBODY
***86612** Revise: BLASTOMYCES ANTIBODY
***86622** Revise: BRUCELLA ANTIBODY
***86625** Revise: CAMPYLOBACTER ANTIBODY
***86628** Revise: CANDIDA ANTIBODY
***86631** Revise: CHLAMYDIA ANTIBODY
***86632** Revise: CHLAMYDIA IGM ANTIBODY
***86635** Revise: COCCIDIOIDES ANTIBODY
***86653** Revise: ENCEPHALITIS ANTIBODY
***86654** Revise: ENCEPHALITIS ANTIBODY
***86658** Revise: ENTEROVIRUS ANTIBODY
***86665** Revise: EPSTEIN-BARR ANTIBODY
***86671** Revise: FUNGUS ANTIBODY
***86674** Revise: GIARDIA LAMBLIA ANTIBODY
***86682** Revise: HELMINTH ANTIBODY
***86687** Revise: HTLV-I ANTIBODY
***86688** Revise: HTLV-II ANTIBODY
***86704** Revise: HEP B CORE ANTIBODY, IGG/IGM
***86705** Revise: HEP B CORE ANTIBODY, IGM
***86706** Revise: HEP B SURFACE ANTIBODY
***86707** Revise: HEP BE ANTIBODY
***86708** Revise: HEP A ANTIBODY, IGG/IGM
***86709** Revise: HEP A ANTIBODY, IGM
***86710** Revise: INFLUENZA VIRUS ANTIBODY
***86713** Revise: LEGIONELLA ANTIBODY
***86717** Revise: LEISHMANIA ANTIBODY
***86720** Revise: LEPTOSPIRA ANTIBODY
***86723** Revise: LISTERIA MONOCYTOGENES AB
***86727** Revise: LYMPH CHORIOMENINGITIS AB
***86729** Revise: LYMPHO VENEREUM ANTIBODY
***86732** Revise: MUCORMYCOSIS ANTIBODY
***86735** Revise: MUMPS ANTIBODY
***86738** Revise: MYCOPLASMA ANTIBODY
***86744** Revise: NOCARDIA ANTIBODY
***86747** Revise: PARVOVIRUS ANTIBODY
***86750** Revise: MALARIA ANTIBODY
***86753** Revise: PROTOZOA ANTIBODY NOS
***86756** Revise: RESPIRATORY VIRUS ANTIBODY
***86759** Revise: ROTAVIRUS ANTIBODY
***86762** Revise: RUBELLA ANTIBODY
***86765** Revise: RUBEOLA ANTIBODY
***86768** Revise: SALMONELLA ANTIBODY
***86771** Revise: SHIGELLA ANTIBODY
***86774** Revise: TETANUS ANTIBODY
***86777** Revise: TOXOPLASMA ANTIBODY
***86778** Revise: TOXOPLASMA ANTIBODY, IGM
***86781** Revise: TREPONEMA PALLIDUM, CONFIRM
***86784** Revise: TRICHINELLA ANTIBODY
***86787** Revise: VARICELLA-ZOSTER ANTIBODY
***86790** Revise: VIRUS ANTIBODY NOS
***86793** Revise: YERSINIA ANTIBODY
**86915** Revise: BONE MARROW/STEM CELL PREP
***86932** Revise: FROZEN BLOOD FREEZE/THAW
***86940** Revise: HEMOLYSINS/AGGLUTININS, AUTO

*87060 Revise: NOSE/THROAT CULTURE, BACT
*87086 Revise: URINE CULTURE/COLONY COUNT
87338 Add: HPYLORI, STOOL, EIA
*87350 Revise: HEPATITIS BE AG, EIA
*88141 Revise: CYTOPATH, C/V, INTERPRET
*88142 Revise: CYTOPATH, C/V, THIN LAYER
*88143 Revise: CYTOPATH C/V THIN LAYER REDO
*88144 Revise: CYTOPATH, C/V THIN LYR REDO
*88145 Revise: CYTOPATH, C/V THIN LYR SEL
*88147 Revise: CYTOPATH, C/V, AUTOMATED
*88150 Revise: CYTOPATH, C/V, MANUAL
*88152 Revise: CYTOPATH, C/V, AUTO REDO
*88153 Revise: CYTOPATH, C/V, REDO
*88154 Revise: CYTOPATH, C/V, SELECT
*88155 Revise: CYTOPATH, C/V, INDEX ADD-ON
*88164 Revise: CYTOPATH TBS, C/V, MANUAL
*88165 Revise: CYTOPATH TBS, C/V, REDO
*88166 Revise: CYTOPATH TBS, C/V, AUTO REDO
*88167 Revise: CYTOPATH TBS, C/V, SELECT
*88267 Revise: CHROMOSOME ANALYS, PLACENTA
*88269 Revise: CHROMOSOME ANALYS, AMNIOTIC
*88285 Revise: CHROMOSOME COUNT, ADDITIONAL
*88289 Revise: CHROMOSOME STUDY, ADDITIONAL
*88300 Revise: SURGICAL PATH, GROSS
*89264 Revise: IDENTIFY SPERM TISSUE
*90371 Revise: HEP B IG, IM
90378 Add: RSV IG, IM
90471 Revise: IMMUNIZATION ADMIN
90472 Revise: IMMUNIZATION ADMIN, EACH ADD
90592 Delete
*90632 Revise: HEP A VACCINE, ADULT IM
*90633 Revise: HEP A VACC, PED/ADOL, 2 DOSE
*90634 Revise: HEP A VACC, PED/ADOL, 3 DOSE
*90636 Revise: HEP A/HEP B VACC, ADULT IM
*90708 Revise: MEASLES-RUBELLA VACCINE, SC
*90709 Revise: RUBELLA & MUMPS VACCINE, SC
90744 Revise: HEP B VACCINE, PED/ADOL, IM
90745 Delete
*90746 Revise: HEP B VACCINE, ADULT, IM
*90747 Revise: HEP B VACCINE, ILL PAT, IM
*90748 Revise: HEP B/HIB VACCINE, IM
90782 Revise: INJECTION, SC/IM
*90783 Revise: INJECTION, IA
*90784 Revise: INJECTION, IV
90799 Revise: THER/PROPHYLACTIC/DX INJECT
*90804 Revise: PSYTX, OFFICE, 20-30 MIN
*90805 Revise: PSYTX, OFF, 20-30 MIN W/E&M
*90806 Revise: PSYTX, OFF, 45-50 MIN
*90807 Revise: PSYTX, OFF, 45-50 MIN W/E&M
*90808 Revise: PSYTX, OFFICE, 75-80 MIN
*90809 Revise: PSYTX, OFF, 75-80, W/E&M
*90810 Revise: INTAC PSYTX, OFF, 20-30 MIN
*90811 Revise: INTAC PSYTX, 20-30, W/E&M
*90812 Revise: INTAC PSYTX, OFF, 45-50 MIN
*90813 Revise: INTAC PSYTX, 45-50 MIN W/E&M
*90814 Revise: INTAC PSYTX, OFF, 75-80 MIN
*90815 Revise: INTAC PSYTX, 75-80 W/E&M
*90816 Revise: PSYTX, HOSP, 20-30 MIN
*90817 Revise: PSYTX, HOSP, 20-30 MIN W/E&M
*90818 Revise: PSYTX, HOSP, 45-50 MIN
*90819 Revise: PSYTX, HOSP, 45-50 MIN W/E&M
*90821 Revise: PSYTX, HOSP, 75-80 MIN
*90822 Revise: PSYTX, HOSP, 75-80 MIN W/E&M
*90823 Revise: INTAC PSYTX, HOSP, 20-30 MIN
*90824 Revise: INTAC PSYTX, HSP 20-30 W/E&M
*90826 Revise: INTAC PSYTX, HOSP, 45-50 MIN
*90827 Revise: INTAC PSYTX, HSP 45-50 W/E&M
*90828 Revise: INTAC PSYTX, HOSP, 75-80 MIN
*90829 Revise: INTAC PSYTX, HSP 75-80 W/E&M
*90901 Revise: BIOFEEDBACK TRAIN, ANY METH
*90937 Revise: HEMODIALYSIS, REPEATED EVAL
*90947 Revise: DIALYSIS, REPEATED EVAL
*90989 Revise: DIALYSIS TRAINING, COMPLETE
*90993 Revise: DIALYSIS TRAINING, INCOMPL
*92012 Revise: EYE EXAM ESTABLISHED PAT
*92506 Revise: SPEECH/HEARING EVALUATION
*92594 Revise: ELECTRO HEARNG AID TEST, ONE
*92595 Revise: ELECTRO HEARNG AID TST, BOTH
*92950 Revise: HEART/LUNG RESUSCITATION CPR
*92960 Revise: CARDIOVERSION ELECTRIC, EXT

**92961** Add: CARDIOVERSION, ELECTRIC, INT
**92978** Revise: INTRAVASC US, HEART ADD-ON
* **92979** Revise: INTRAVASC US, HEART ADD-ON
* **92997** Revise: PUL ART BALLOON REPR, PERCUT
* **92998** Revise: PUL ART BALLOON REPR, PERCUT
* **93545** Revise: INJECT FOR CORONARY X-RAYS
**93727** Add: ANALYZE ILR SYSTEM
* **93733** Revise: TELEPHONE ANALY, PACEMAKER
* **93736** Revise: TELEPHONE ANALY, PACEMAKER
**93741** Add: ANALYZE HT PACE DEVICE SNGL
**93742** Add: ANALYZE HT PACE DEVICE SNGL
**93743** Add: ANALYZE HT PACE DEVICE DUAL
**93744** Add: ANALYZE HT PACE DEVICE DUAL
* **94657** Revise: CONTINUED VENTILATOR MGMT
* **94662** Revise: NEG PRESS VENTILATION, CNP
* **94680** Revise: EXHALED AIR ANALYSIS, O2
* **94681** Revise: EXHALED AIR ANALYSIS, O2/CO2
**95870** Revise: MUSCLE TEST, NON-PARASPINAL
**95904** Revise: SENSE/MIXED N CONDUCTION TST
* **95921** Revise: AUTONOMIC NERV FUNCTION TEST
* **95922** Revise: AUTONOMIC NERV FUNCTION TEST
* **95923** Revise: AUTONOMIC NERV FUNCTION TEST
* **95934** Revise: H-REFLEX TEST
* **95936** Revise: H-REFLEX TEST
* **95956** Revise: EEG MONITORING, CABLE/RADIO
* **95962** Revise: ELECTRODE STIM, BRAIN ADD-ON
**95970** Revise: ANALYZE NEUROSTIM, NO PROG
**95971** Revise: ANALYZE NEUROSTIM, SIMPLE
**95972** Revise: ANALYZE NEUROSTIM, COMPLEX
**95973** Revise: ANALYZE NEUROSTIM, COMPLEX
* **95974** Revise: CRANIAL NEUROSTIM, COMPLEX
* **95975** Revise: CRANIAL NEUROSTIM, COMPLEX
* **96400** Revise: CHEMOTHERAPY, SC/IM
* **96412** Revise: CHEMO, INFUSE METHOD ADD-ON
* **96414** Revise: CHEMO, INFUSE METHOD ADD-ON
* **96423** Revise: CHEMO, INFUSE METHOD ADD-ON
**96570** Add: PHOTODYNAMIC TX, 30 MIN
**96571** Add: PHOTODYNAMIC TX, ADDL 15 MIN
* **97542** Revise: WHEELCHAIR MNGMENT TRAINING
* **97780** Revise: ACUPUNCTURE W/O STIMUL
* **97781** Revise: ACUPUNCTURE W/STIMUL
* **99024** Revise: POSTOP FOLLOW-UP VISIT
* **99054** Revise: MEDICAL SERVCS, UNUSUAL HRS
**99170** Add: ANOGENITAL EXAM, CHILD
**99173** Add: VISUAL SCREENING TEST
**99199** Revise: SPECIAL SERVICE/PROC/REPORT
* **99311** Revise: NURSING FAC CARE, SUBSEQ
* **99312** Revise: NURSING FAC CARE, SUBSEQ
* **99313** Revise: NURSING FAC CARE, SUBSEQ
* **99331** Revise: REST HOME VISIT, EST PAT
* **99332** Revise: REST HOME VISIT, EST PAT
* **99333** Revise: REST HOME VISIT, EST PAT
* **99347** Revise: HOME VISIT, EST PATIENT
* **99348** Revise: HOME VISIT, EST PATIENT
* **99349** Revise: HOME VISIT, EST PATIENT
* **99350** Revise: HOME VISIT, EST PATIENT
* **99381** Revise: PREV VISIT, NEW, INFANT
* **99382** Revise: PREV VISIT, NEW, AGE 1-4
* **99383** Revise: PREV VISIT, NEW, AGE 5-11
* **99384** Revise: PREV VISIT, NEW, AGE 12-17
* **99385** Revise: PREV VISIT, NEW, AGE 18-39
* **99386** Revise: PREV VISIT, NEW, AGE 40-64
* **99387** Revise: PREV VISIT, NEW, 65 & OVER
* **99391** Revise: PREV VISIT, EST, INFANT
* **99392** Revise: PREV VISIT, EST, AGE 1-4
* **99393** Revise: PREV VISIT, EST, AGE 5-11
* **99394** Revise: PREV VISIT, EST, AGE 12-17
* **99395** Revise: PREV VISIT, EST, AGE 18-39
* **99396** Revise: PREV VISIT, EST, AGE 40-64
* **99397** Revise: PREV VISIT, EST, 65 & OVER
* **99432** Revise: NEWBORN CARE, NOT IN HOSP
* **99433** Revise: NORMAL NEWBORN CARE/HOSPITAL
* **99435** Revise: NEWBORN DISCHARGE DAY HOSP
* **99499** Revise: UNLISTED E&M SERVICE

# Appendix D

## Clinical Examples

As described in *CPT 2000,* clinical examples of the CPT codes for Evaluation and Management (E/M) services are intended to be an important element of the coding system. The clinical examples, when used with the E/M descriptors contained in the full text of *CPT,* provide a comprehensive and powerful new tool for physicians to report the services provided to their patients.

The American Medical Association is pleased to provide you with these clinical examples ment to *CPT 2000.* The clinical examples that are provided in this supplement are limited to Office or Other Outpatient Services, Hospital Inpatient Services, Consultations, Critical Care, Prolonged Services and Care Plan Oversight.

It is important to note that these clinical examples do not encompass the entire scope of medical practice. Inclusion or exclusion of any particular specialty group does not infer any judgment of importance or lack thereof, nor does it limit the applicability of the example to any particular specialty.

Of utmost importance is the fact that these clinical examples are just that: examples. A particular patient encounter, depending on the specific circumstances, must be judged by the services provided by the physician for that particular patient. Simply because the patient's complaints, symptoms, or diagnoses match those of a particular clinical example, does not automatically assign that patient encounter to that particular level of service. It is important that the three key components (history, examination, and medical decision making) be met and documented in the medical record to report a particular level of service.

## Office or Other Outpatient Services

### New Patient

**99201** Initial office visit for a 50-year-old male from out-of-town who needs a prescription refill for a nonsteroidal anti-inflammatory drug. (Anesthesiology)

Initial office visit for a 40-year-old female, new patient, requesting information about local pain clinics. (Anesthesiology/Pain Medicine)

Initial office visit for a 10-year-old girl for determination of visual acuity as part of a summer camp physical (does not include determination of refractive error). (Ophthalmology)

Initial office visit for an out-of-town patient requiring topical refill. (Dermatology)

Initial office visit for a 65-year-old male for reassurance about an isolated seborrheic keratosis on upper back. (Plastic Surgery)

Initial office visit for an out-of-state visitor who needs refill of topical steroid to treat lichen planus. (Dermatology)

Initial office visit for an 86-year-old male, out-of-town visitor, who needs prescription refilled for an anal skin preparation that he forgot. (General Surgery/Colon & Rectal Surgery)

Initial office visit for a transient patient with alveolar osteitis for repacking. (Oral & Maxillofacial Surgery)

Initial office visit for a patient with a pedunculated lesion of the neck which is unsightly. (Dermatology)

Initial office visit for a 10-year-old male, for limited subungual hematoma not requiring drainage. (Internal Medicine)

Initial office visit with an out-of-town visitor who needs a prescription refilled because she forgot her hay fever medication. (Allergy & Immunology/Internal Medicine)

Initial office visit with a 9-month-old female with diaper rash. (Pediatrics)

Initial office visit with a 10-year-old male with severe rash and itching for the past 24 hours, positive history for contact with poison oak 48 hours prior to the visit. (Family Medicine)

Initial office visit with a 5-year-old female to remove sutures from simple wound placed by another physician. (Plastic Surgery)

Initial office visit for a 22-year-old male with a small area of sunburn requiring first aid. (Dermatology/Family Medicine/Internal Medicine)

Initial office visit for the evaluation and management of a contusion of a finger. (Orthopaedic Surgery)

**99202** Initial office visit for a 13-year-old patient with comedopapular acne of the face unresponsive to over-the-counter medications. (Family Medicine)

Initial office visit for a patient with a clinically benign lesion or nodule of the lower leg which has been present for many years. (Dermatology)

Initial office visit for a patient with a circumscribed patch of dermatitis of the leg. (Dermatology)

Initial office visit for a patient with papulosquamous eruption of elbows. (Dermatology)

Initial office visit for a 9-year-old patient with erythematous, grouped, vesicular eruption of the lip of three days' duration. (Pediatrics)

Initial office visit for an 18-year-old male referred by an orthodontist for advice regarding removal of four wisdom teeth. (Oral & Maxillofacial Surgery)

Initial office visit for a 14-year-old male, who was referred by his orthodontist, for advice on the exposure of impacted maxillary cuspids. (Oral & Maxillofacial Surgery)

Initial office visit for a patient presenting with itching patches on the wrists and ankles. (Dermatology)

Initial office visit for a 30-year-old male for evaluation and discussion of treatment of rhinophyma. (Plastic Surgery)

Initial office visit for a 16-year-old male with severe cystic acne, new patient. (Dermatology)

Initial office evaluation for gradual hearing loss, 58-year-old male, history and physical examination, with interpretation of complete audiogram, air bone, etc. (Otolaryngology)

Initial evaluation and management of recurrent urinary infection in female. (Internal Medicine)

Initial office visit with a 10-year-old girl with history of chronic otitis media and a draining ear. (Pediatrics)

Initial office visit for a 10-year-old female with acute maxillary sinusitis. (Family Medicine)

Initial office visit for a patient with recurring episodes of herpes simplex who has developed a clustering of vesicles on the upper lip. (Internal Medicine)

Initial office visit for a 25-year-old patient with single season allergic rhinitis. (Allergy & Immunology)

Initial office visit to plan transient dialysis for a 56-year-old stable dialysis patient who has accompanying records. (Nephrology)

**99203** Initial office visit for a 76-year-old male with a stasis ulcer of three months' duration. (Dermatology)

Initial office visit for a 30-year-old female with pain in the lateral aspect of the forearm. (Physical Medicine & Rehabilitation)

Initial office visit for a 15-year-old patient with a four-year history of moderate comedopapular acne of the face, chest, and back with early scarring. Discussion of use of systemic medication. (Dermatology)

Initial office visit for a patient with papulosquamous eruption of the elbow with pitting of nails and itchy scalp. (Dermatology)

Initial office visit for a 57-year-old female who complains of painful parotid swelling for one week's duration. (Oral & Maxillofacial Surgery)

Initial office visit for a patient with an ulcerated non-healing lesion or nodule on the tip of the nose. (Dermatology)

Initial office visit for a patient with dermatitis of the antecubital and popliteal fossae. (Dermatology)

Initial office visit for a 22-year-old female with irregular menses. (Family Medicine)

Initial office visit for a 50-year-old female with dyspepsia and nausea. (Family Medicine)

Initial office visit for a 53-year-old laborer with degenerative joint disease of the knee with no prior treatment. (Orthopaedic Surgery)

Initial office visit for a 60-year-old male with Dupuytren's contracture of one hand with multiple digit involvement. (Orthopaedic Surgery)

Initial office visit for a 33-year-old male with painless gross hematuria without cystoscopy. (Internal Medicine)

Initial office visit for a 55-year-old female with chronic blepharitis. There is a history of use of many medications. (Ophthalmology)

Initial office visit for an 18-year-old female with a two-day history of acute conjunctivitis. Extensive history of possible exposures, prior normal ocular history, and medication use is obtained. (Ophthalmology)

Initial office visit for a 14-year-old male with unilateral anterior knee pain. (Physical Medicine & Rehabilitation)

Initial office visit of an adult who presents with symptoms of an upper-respiratory infection that has progressed to unilateral purulent nasal discharge and discomfort in the right maxillary teeth. (Otolaryngology, Head & Neck Surgery)

Initial office visit of a 40-year-old female with symptoms of atopic allergies including eye and sinus congestion, often associated with infections. She would like to be tested for allergies. (Otolaryngology, Head & Neck Surgery)

Initial office visit of a 65-year-old with nasal stuffiness. (Otolaryngology, Head & Neck Surgery)

Initial office visit for initial evaluation of a 48-year-old man with recurrent low back pain radiating to the leg. (General Surgery)

Initial office visit for evaluation, diagnosis and management of painless gross hematuria in new patient, without cystoscopy. (Internal Medicine)

Initial office visit with couple for counseling concerning voluntary vasectomy for sterility. Spent 30 minutes discussing procedure, risks and benefits, and answering questions. (Urology)

Initial office visit of a 49-year-old male with nasal obstruction. Detailed exam with topical anesthesia. (Plastic Surgery)

Initial office visit for evaluation of a 13-year-old female with progressive scoliosis. (Physical Medicine & Rehabilitation)

Initial office visit for a 21-year-old female desiring counseling and evaluation of initiation of contraception. (Family Practice/Internal Medicine/Obstetrics & Gynecology)

Initial office visit for a 49-year-old male presenting with painless blood per rectum associated with bowel movement. (Colon & Rectal Surgery)

Initial office visit for a 19-year-old football player with three-day-old acute knee injury; now with swelling and pain. (Orthopaedic Surgery)

**99204** Initial office visit for a 13-year-old female with progressive scoliosis. (Orthopaedic Surgery)

Initial office visit for a 34-year-old female with primary infertility for evaluation and counseling. (Obstetrics & Gynecology)

Initial office visit for a 6-year-old male with multiple upper respiratory infections. (Allergy & Immunology)

Initial office visit for a patient with generalized dermatitis of 80 percent of the body surface area. (Dermatology)

Initial office visit for an adolescent who was referred by school counselor because of repeated skipping school. (Psychiatry)

Initial office visit for a 50-year-old machinist with a generalized eruption. (Dermatology)

Initial office visit for a 45-year-old female who has been abstinent from alcohol and benzodiazepines for three months but complains of headaches, insomnia, and anxiety. (Psychiatry)

Initial office visit for a 60-year-old male with recent change in bowel habits, weight loss, and abdominal pain. (Abdominal Surgery/General Surgery)

Initial office visit for a 50-year-old male with an aortic aneurysm who is considering surgery. (General Surgery)

Initial office visit for a 17-year-old female with depression. (Internal Medicine)

Initial office visit of a 40-year-old with chronic draining ear, imbalance, and probable cholesteatoma. (Otolaryngology, Head & Neck Surgery)

Initial office visit for initial evaluation of a 63-year-old male with chest pain on exertion. (Cardiology/Internal Medicine)

Initial office visit for evaluation of a 70-year-old patient with recent onset of episodic confusion. (Internal Medicine)

Initial office visit for a 7-year-old female with juvenile diabetes mellitus, new to area, past history of hospitalization times three. (Pediatrics)

Initial office visit of a 50-year-old female with progressive solid food dysphagia. (Gastroenterology)

Initial office visit for a 34-year-old patient with primary infertility, including counseling. (Obstetrics & Gynecology)

Initial office visit for evaluation of a 70-year-old female with polyarthralgia. (Rheumatology)

Initial office visit for a patient with papulosquamous eruption involving 60 percent of the cutaneous surface with joint pain. Combinations of topical and systemic treatments discussed. (Dermatology)

**99205** Initial office visit for a patient with disseminated lupus erythematosus with kidney disease, edema, purpura, and scarring lesions on the extremities plus cardiac symptoms. (Dermatology/General Surgery/Internal Medicine)

Initial office visit for a 25-year-old female with systemic lupus erythematosus, fever, seizures, and profound thrombocytopenia. (Rheumatology/Allergy & Immunology)

Initial office visit for an adult with multiple cutaneous blisters, denuded secondarily infected ulcerations, oral lesions, weight loss, and increasing weakness refractory to high dose corticosteroid. Initiation of new immunosuppressive therapy. (Dermatology)

Initial office visit for a 28-year-old male with systemic vasculitis and compromised circulation to the limbs. (Rheumatology)

Initial office visit for a 41-year-old female new to the area requesting rheumatologic care, on disability due to scleroderma and recent hospitalization for malignant hypertension. (Rheumatology)

Initial office visit for a 52-year-old female with acute four extremity weakness and shortness of breath one week post-flu vaccination. (Physical Medicine & Rehabilitation)

Initial office visit for a 60-year-old male with previous back surgery; now presents with back and pelvic pain, two-month history of bilateral progressive calf and thigh tightness and weakness when walking, causing several falls. (Orthopaedic Surgery)

Initial office visit for an adolescent referred from ER after making suicide gesture. (Psychiatry)

Initial office visit for a 49-year-old female with a history of headaches and dependence on opioids. She reports weight loss, progressive headache, and depression. (Psychiatry)

Initial office visit for a 50-year-old female with symptoms of rash, swellings, recurrent arthritic complaints, and diarrhea and lymphadenopathy. Patient has had a 25 lb. weight loss and was recently camping in the Amazon. (Allergy & Immunology)

Initial office visit for a 34-year-old uremic Type I diabetic patient referred for ESRD modality assessment and planning. (Nephrology)

Initial office visit for a 75-year-old female with neck and bilateral shoulder pain, brisk deep tendon reflexes, and stress incontinence. (Physical Medicine & Rehabilitation)

Initial office visit for an 8-year-old male with cerebral palsy and spastic quadriparesis. (Physical Medicine & Rehabilitation)

Initial office visit for a 73-year-old male with known prostate malignancy, who presents with severe back pain and a recent onset of lower extremity weakness. (Physical Medicine & Rehabilitation)

Initial office visit for a 38-year-old male with paranoid delusions and a history of alcohol abuse. (Psychiatry)

Initial office visit for a 12-week-old with bilateral hip dislocations and bilateral club feet. (Orthopaedic Surgery)

Initial office visit for a 29-year-old female with acute orbital congestion, eyelid retraction, and bilateral visual loss from optic neuropathy. (Ophthalmology)

Initial office visit for a 70-year-old diabetic patient with progressive visual field loss, advanced optic disc cupping and neovascularization of retina. (Ophthalmology)

Initial office visit for a newly diagnosed Type I diabetic patient. (Endocrinology)

Initial office evaluation of a 65-year-old female with exertional chest pain, intermittent claudication, syncope and a murmur of aortic stenosis. (Cardiology)

Initial office visit for a 73-year-old male with an unexplained 20 lb. weight loss. (Hematology/Oncology)

Initial office evaluation, patient with systemic lupus erythematosus, fever, seizures and profound thrombocytopenia. (Allergy & Immunology/Internal Medicine/Rheumatology)

Initial office evaluation and management of patient with systemic vasculitis and compromised circulation to the limbs. (Rheumatology)

Initial office visit for a 24-year-old homosexual male who has a fever, a cough, and shortness of breath. (Infectious Disease)

Initial outpatient evaluation of a 69-year-old male with severe chronic obstructive pulmonary disease, congestive heart failure, and hypertension. (Family Medicine)

Initial office visit for a 17-year-old female, who is having school problems and has told a friend she is considering suicide. The patient and her family are consulted in regard to treatment options. (Psychiatry)

Initial office visit for a female with severe hirsutism, amenorrhea, weight loss and a desire to have children. (Endocrinology/Obstetrics & Gynecology)

Initial office visit for a 42-year-old male on hypertensive medication, newly arrived to the area, with diastolic blood pressure of 110, history of recurrent calculi, episodic headaches, intermittent chest pain and orthopnea. (Internal Medicine)

## Established Patient

**99211** Office visit for an 82-year-old female, established patient, for a monthly B12 injection with documented Vitamin B12 deficiency. (Geriatrics/Internal Medicine/Family Medicine)

Office visit for a 50-year-old male, established patient, for removal of uncomplicated facial sutures. (Plastic Surgery)

Office visit for an established patient who lost prescription for lichen planus. Returned for new copy. (Dermatology)

Office visit for an established patient undergoing orthodontics who complains of a wire which is irritating his/her cheek and asks you to check it. (Oral & Maxillofacial Surgery)

Office visit for a 50-year-old female, established patient, seen for her gold injection by the nurse. (Rheumatology)

Office visit for a 73-year-old female, established patient, with pernicious anemia for weekly B12 injection. (Gastroenterology)

Office visit for an established patient for dressing change on a skin biopsy. (Dermatology)

Office visit for a 19-year-old, established patient, for removal of sutures from a two cm. laceration of forehead, which you placed four days ago in ER. (Plastic Surgery)

Office visit of a 20-year-old female, established patient, who receives an allergy vaccine injection and is observed for a reaction by the nurse. (Otolaryngology, Head & Neck Surgery)

Office visit for a 45-year-old male, established patient, with chronic renal failure for the administration of erythropoietin. (Nephrology)

Office visit for an established patient, a Peace Corps enlistee, who requests documentation that third molars have been removed. (Oral & Maxillofacial Surgery)

Office visit for a 69-year-old female, established patient, for partial removal of antibiotic gauze from an infected wound site. (Plastic Surgery)

Office visit for a 9-year-old, established patient, successfully treated for impetigo, requiring release to return to school. (Dermatology/Pediatrics)

Office visit for an established patient requesting a return-to-work certificate for resolving contact dermatitis. (Dermatology)

Office visit for an established patient who is performing glucose monitoring and wants to check accuracy of machine with lab blood glucose by technician who checks accuracy and function of patient machine. (Endocrinology)

Follow-up office visit for a 65-year-old female with a chronic indwelling percutaneous nephrostomy catheter seen for routine pericatheter skin care and dressing change. (Interventional Radiology)

Outpatient visit with 19-year-old male, established patient, for supervised drug screen. (Addiction Medicine)

Office visit with 12-year-old male, established patient, for cursory check of hematoma one day after venipuncture. (Internal Medicine)

Office visit with 31-year-old female, established patient, for return to work certificate. (Anesthesiology)

Office visit for a 42-year-old, established patient, to read tuberculin test results. (Allergy & Immunology)

Office visit for 14-year-old, established patient, to re-dress an abrasion. (Orthopaedic Surgery)

Office visit for a 45-year-old female, established patient, for a blood pressure check. (Obstetrics & Gynecology)

Office visit for a 23-year-old, established patient, for instruction in use of peak flow meter. (Allergy & Immunology)

Office visit for prescription refill for a 35-year-old female, established patient, with schizophrenia who is stable but has run out of neuroleptic and is scheduled to be seen in a week. (Psychiatry)

**99212** Office visit for an 11-year-old, established patient, seen in follow-up for mild comedonal acne of the cheeks on topical desquamating agents. (Dermatology/Family Medicine/Pediatrics)

Office visit for a 10-year-old female, established patient, who has been swimming in a lake, now presents with a one-day history of left ear pain with purulent drainage. (Family Medicine)

Office visit of a child, established patient, with chronic secretory otitis media. (Otolaryngology, Head & Neck Surgery)

Office visit for an established patient seen in follow-up of clearing patch of localized contact dermatitis. (Family Medicine/Dermatology)

Office visit for an established patient returning for evaluation of response to treatment of lichen planus on wrists and ankles. (Dermatology)

Office visit for an established patient with tinea pedis being treated with topical therapy. (Dermatology)

Office visit for an established patient with localized erythematous plaque of psoriasis with topical hydration. (Dermatology)

Office visit for a 50-year-old male, established patient, recently seen for acute neck pain, diagnosis of spondylosis, responding to physical therapy and intermittent cervical traction. Returns for evaluation for return to work. (Neurology)

Office visit for an established patient with recurring episodes of herpes simplex who has developed a clustering of vesicles on the upper lip. (Oral & Maxillofacial Surgery)

Evaluation for a 50-year-old male, established patient, who has experienced a recurrence of knee pain after he discontinued NSAID. (Anesthesiology/Pain Medicine)

Office visit for an established patient with an irritated skin tag for reassurance. (Dermatology)

Office visit for a 40-year-old, established patient, who has experienced a systemic allergic reaction following administration of immunotherapy. The dose must be readjusted. (Allergy & Immunology)

Office visit for a 33-year-old, established patient, for contusion and abrasion of lower extremity. (Orthopaedic Surgery)

Office visit for a 22-year-old male, established patient, one month after I & D of "wrestler's ear." (Plastic Surgery)

Office visit for a 21-year-old, established patient, who is seen in follow-up after antibiotic therapy for acute bacterial tonsillitis. (Otolaryngology, Head & Neck Surgery)

Office visit for a 4-year-old, established patient, with tympanostomy tubes, check-up. (Otolaryngology, Head & Neck Surgery)

Office visit for an established patient who has had needle aspiration of a peritonsillar abscess. (Otolaryngology, Head & Neck Surgery)

Follow-up office examination for evaluation and treatment of acute draining ear in a 5-year-old with tympanotomy tubes. (Otolaryngology, Head & Neck Surgery)

Office visit, established patient, 6-year-old with sore throat and headache. (Family Medicine/Pediatrics)

Office evaluation for possible purulent bacterial conjunctivitis with one- to two-day history of redness and discharge, 16-year-old female, established patient. (Pediatrics/Internal Medicine/Family Medicine)

Office visit with a 65-year-old female, established patient, returns for three-week follow-up for resolving severe ankle sprain. (Orthopaedic Surgery)

Office visit, sore throat, fever and fatigue in a 19-year-old college student, established patient. (Internal Medicine)

Office visit with a 33-year-old female, established patient, recently started on treatment for hemorrhoidal complaints, for re-evaluation. (Colon & Rectal Surgery)

Office visit with a 36-year-old male, established patient, for follow-up on effectiveness of medicine management of oral candidiasis. (Oral & Maxillofacial Surgery)

Office visit for a 27-year-old female, established patient, with complaints of vaginal itching. (Obstetrics & Gynecology)

Office visit for a 65-year-old male, established patient, with eruptions on both arms from poison oak exposure. (Allergy & Immunology/Internal Medicine)

**99213** Office visit for an established patient with new lesions of lichen planus in spite of topical therapies. (Dermatology)

Office visit for the quarterly follow-up of a 45-year-old male with stable chronic asthma requiring regular drug therapy. (Allergy & Immunology)

Office visit for a 13-year-old, established patient, with comedopapular acne of the face which has shown poor response to topical medication. Discussion of use of systemic medication. (Dermatology)

Office visit for a 62-year-old female, established patient, for follow-up for stable cirrhosis of the liver. (Internal Medicine/Family Medicine)

Office visit for a 3-year-old, established patient, with atopic dermatitis and food hypersensitivity for quarterly follow-up evaluation. The patient is on topical lotions and steroid creams as well as oral antihistamines. (Allergy & Immunology)

Office visit for an 80-year-old female, established patient, to evaluate medical management of osteoarthritis of the temporomandibular joint. (Rheumatology)

Office visit for a 70-year-old female, established patient, one year post excision of basal cell carcinoma of nose with nasolabial flap. Now presents with new suspicious recurrent lesion and suspicious lesion of the back. (Plastic Surgery)

Office visit for a 68-year-old female, established patient, with polymyalgia rheumatic, maintained on chronic low-dose corticosteroid, with no new complaints. (Rheumatology)

Office visit for a 3-year-old female, established patient, for earache and dyshidrosis of feet. (Pediatrics/Family Medicine)

Office visit for an established patient for 18 months post-operative follow-up of TMJ repair. (Oral & Maxillofacial Surgery)

Office visit for a 45-year-old male, established patient, being re-evaluated for recurrent acute prostatitis. (Urology)

Office visit for a 43-year-old male, established patient, with known reflex sympathetic dystrophy. (Anesthesiology)

Office visit for an established patient with an evenly pigmented superficial nodule of leg which is symptomatic. (Dermatology)

Office visit for an established patient with psoriasis involvement of the elbows, pitting of the nails, and itchy scalp. (Dermatology)

Office visit for a 27-year-old male, established patient, with deep follicular and perifollicular inflammation unable to tolerate systemic antibiotics due to GI upset, requires change of systemic medication. (Dermatology)

Office visit for a 16-year-old male, established patient, who is on medication for exercise-induced bronchospasm. (Allergy & Immunology)

Office visit for a 60-year-old, established patient, with chronic essential hypertension on multiple drug regimen, for blood pressure check. (Family Medicine)

Office visit for a 20-year-old male, established patient, for removal of sutures in hand. (Family Medicine)

Office visit for a 58-year-old female, established patient, with unilateral painful bunion. (Orthopaedic Surgery)

Office visit for a 45-year-old female, established patient, with known osteoarthritis and painful swollen knees. (Rheumatology)

Office visit for a 25-year-old female, established patient, complaining of bleeding and heavy menses. (Obstetrics & Gynecology)

Office visit for a 55-year-old male, established patient, with hypertension managed by a beta blocker/thiazide regime; now experiencing mild fatigue. (Nephrology)

Office visit for a 65-year-old female, established patient, with primary glaucoma for interval determination of intraocular pressure and possible adjustment of medication. (Ophthalmology)

Office visit for a 56-year-old man, established patient, with stable exertional angina who complains of new onset of calf pain while walking. (Cardiology)

Office visit for a 63-year-old female, established patient, with rheumatoid arthritis on auranofin and ibuprofin, seen for routine follow-up visit. (Rheumatology)

Office visit for an established patient with Graves' disease, three months post I-131 therapy, who presents with lassitude and malaise. (Endocrinology)

Office visit for the quarterly follow-up of a 63-year-old male, established patient, with chronic myofascial pain syndrome, effectively managed by doxepin, who presents with new onset urinary hesitancy. (Pain Medicine)

Office visit for the biannual follow-up of an established patient with migraine variant having infrequent, intermittent, moderate to severe headaches with nausea and vomiting, which are sometimes effectively managed by ergotamine tartrate and an antiemetic, but occasionally requiring visits to an emergency department. (Pain Medicine)

Office visit for an established patient after discharge from a pain rehabilitation program to review and adjust medication dosage. (Pain Medicine)

Office visit with 55-year-old male, established patient, for management of hypertension, mild fatigue, on beta blocker/thiazide regimen. (Family Medicine/Internal Medicine)

Outpatient visit with 37-year-old male, established patient, who is three years post total colectomy for chronic ulcerative colitis, presents for increased irritation at his stoma. (General Surgery)

Office visit for a 70-year-old diabetic hypertensive established patient with recent change in insulin requirement. (Internal Medicine/Nephrology)

Office visit with 80-year-old female, established patient, for follow-up osteoporosis, status-post compression fractures. (Rheumatology)

Office visit for an established patient with stable cirrhosis of the liver. (Gastroenterology)

Routine, follow-up office evaluation at a three-month interval for a 77-year-old female, established patient, with nodular small cleaved-cell lymphoma. (Hematology/Oncology)

Quarterly follow-up office visit for a 45-year-old male, established patient, with stable chronic asthma, on steroid and bronchodilator therapy. (Pulmonary Medicine)

Office visit for a 50-year-old female, established patient, with insulin-dependent diabetes mellitus and stable coronary artery disease, for monitoring. (Family Medicine/Internal Medicine)

**99214** Office visit for an established patient now presenting with generalized dermatitis of 80 percent of the body surface area. (Dermatology)

Office visit for a 32-year-old female, established patient, with new onset RLQ pain. (Family Medicine)

Office visit for reassessment and reassurance/ counseling of a 40-year-old female, established patient, who is experiencing increased symptoms while on a pain management treatment program. (Pain Medicine)

Office visit for a 30-year-old, established patient, under management for intractable low back pain, who now presents with new onset right posterior thigh pain. (Pain Medicine)

Office visit for an established patient with frequent intermittent, moderate to severe headaches requiring beta blocker or tricyclic antidepressant prophylaxis, as well as four symptomatic treatments, but who is still experiencing headaches at a frequency of several times a month that are unresponsive to treatment. (Pain Medicine)

Office visit for an established patient with psoriasis with extensive involvement of scalp, trunk, palms, and soles with joint pain. Combinations of topical and systemic treatments discussed and instituted. (Dermatology)

Office visit for a 55-year-old male, established patient, with increasing night pain, limp, and progressive varus of both knees. (Orthopaedic Surgery)

Follow-up visit for a 15-year-old withdrawn patient with four-year history of papulocystic acne of the face, chest, and back with early scarring and poor response to past treatment. Discussion of use of systemic medication. (Dermatology)

Office visit for a 28-year-old male, established patient, with regional enteritis, diarrhea, and low-grade fever. (Internal Medicine)

Office visit for a 25-year-old female, established patient, following recent arthrogram and MR imaging for TMJ pain. (Oral & Maxillofacial Surgery)

Office visit for a 32-year-old female, established patient, with large obstructing stone in left mid-ureter, to discuss management options including urethroscopy with extraction or ESWL. (Urology)

Evaluation for a 28-year-old male, established patient, with new onset of low back pain. (Anesthesiology/Pain Medicine)

Office visit for a 28-year-old female, established patient, with right lower quadrant abdominal pain, fever, and anorexia. (Internal Medicine/Family Medicine)

Office visit for a 45-year-old male, established patient, four months follow-up of L4-5 diskectomy, with persistent incapacitating low back and leg pain. (Orthopaedic Surgery)

Outpatient visit for a 77-year-old male, established patient, with hypertension, presenting with a three month history of episodic substernal chest pain on exertion. (Cardiology)

Office visit for a 25-year-old female, established patient, for evaluation of progressive saddle nose deformity of unknown etiology. (Plastic Surgery)

Office visit for a 65-year-old male, established patient, with BPH and severe bladder outlet obstruction, to discuss management options such as TURP. (Urology)

Office visit for an adult diabetic established patient with a past history of recurrent sinusitis who presents with a one-week history of double vision. (Otolaryngology, Head & Neck Surgery)

Office visit for an established patient with lichen planus and 60 percent of the cutaneous surface involved, not responsive to systemic steroids, as well as developing symptoms of progressive heartburn and paranoid ideation. (Dermatology)

Office visit for a 52-year-old male, established patient, with a 12-year history of bipolar disorder responding to lithium carbonate and brief psychotherapy. Psychotherapy and prescription provided. (Psychiatry)

Office visit for a 63-year-old female, established patient, with a history of familial polyposis, status post-colectomy with sphincter sparing procedure, who now presents with rectal bleeding and increase in stooling frequency. (General Surgery)

Office visit for a 68-year-old male, established patient, with the sudden onset of multiple flashes and floaters in the right eye due to a posterior vitreous detachment. (Ophthalmology)

Office visit for a 55-year-old female, established patient, on cyclosporin for treatment of resistant, small vessel vasculitis. (Rheumatology)

Follow-up office visit for a 55-year-old male, two months after iliac angioplasty with new onset of contralateral extremity claudication. (Interventional Radiology)

Office visit for a 68-year-old male, established patient, with stable angina, two months post myocardial infarction, who is not tolerating one of his medications. (Cardiology)

Weekly office visit for 5FU therapy for an ambulatory established patient with metastatic colon cancer and increasing shortness of breath. (Hematology/Oncology)

Follow-up office visit for a 60-year-old male, established patient, whose post-traumatic seizures have disappeared on medication and who now raises the question of stopping the medication (Neurology)

Office evaluation on new onset RLQ pain in a 32-year-oldwoman, established patient. (Urology/General Surgery/Internal Medicine/Family Medicine)

Office evaluation of 28-year-old, established patient, with regional enteritis, diarrhea and low-grade fever. (Family Medicine/Internal Medicine)

Office visit with 50-year-old female, established patient, diabetic, blood sugar controlled by diet. She now complains of frequency of urination and weight loss, blood sugar of 320 and negative ketones on dipstick. (Internal Medicine)

Follow-up office visit for a 45-year-old, established patient, with rheumatoid arthritis on gold, methotrexate, or immunosuppressive therapy. (Rheumatology)

Office visit for a 60-year-old male, established patient, two years post-removal of intracranial meningioma, now with new headaches and visual disturbance. (Neurosurgery)

Office visit for a 68-year-old female, established patient, for routine review and follow-up of non-insulin dependent diabetes, obesity, hypertension and congestive heart failure. Complains of vision difficulties and admits dietary noncompliance. Patient is counseled concerning diet and current medications adjusted. (Family Medicine)

**99215** Office visit for an established patient who developed persistent cough, rectal bleeding, weakness, and diarrhea plus pustular infection on skin. Patient on immunosuppressive therapy. (Dermatology)

Office visit for an established patient with disseminated lupus erythematosus, extensive edema of extremities kidney disease, and weakness requiring monitored course on azathioprene, corticosteroid and complicated by acute depression. (Dermatology/Internal Medicine/Rheumatology)

Office visit for an established patient with progressive dermatomyositis and recent onset of fever, nasal speech, and regurgitation of fluids through the nose. (Dermatology)

Office visit for a 28-year-old female, established patient, who is abstinent from previous cocaine dependence, but reports progressive panic attacks and chest pains. (Psychiatry)

Office visit for an established adolescent patient with history of bipolar disorder treated with lithium; seen on urgent basis at family's request because of severe depressive symptoms. (Psychiatry)

Office visit for an established patient having acute migraine with new onset neurological symptoms and whose headaches are unresponsive to previous attempts at management with a combination of preventive and abortive medication. (Pain Medicine)

Office visit for an established patient with exfoliative lichen planus with daily fever spikes, disorientation, and shortness of breath. (Dermatology)

Office visit for a 25-year-old, established patient, two years post-burn with bilateral ectropion, hypertrophic facial burn scars, near absence of left breast, and burn syndactyly of both hands. Discussion of treatment options following examination. (Plastic Surgery)

Office visit for a 6-year-old, established patient, to review newly diagnosed immune deficiency with recommendations for therapy including IV immunoglobulin and chronic antibiotics. (Allergy & Immunology)

Office visit for a 36-year-old, established patient, three months status post-transplant, with new onset of peripheral edema, increased blood pressure, and progressive fatigue. (Nephrology)

Office visit for an established patient with Kaposi's sarcoma who presents with fever and widespread vesicles. (Dermatology)

Office visit for a 27-year-old female, established patient, with bipolar disorder who was stable on lithium carbonate and monthly supportive psychotherapy but now has developed symptoms of hypomania. (Psychiatry)

Office visit for a 25-year-old male, established patient with a history of schizophrenia who has been seen bi-monthly but is complaining of auditory hallucinations. (Psychiatry)

Office visit for a 62-year-old male, established patient, three years post-op abdominal perineal resection, now with a rising CEA, weight loss, and pelvic pain. (Abdominal Surgery)

Office visit for a 42-year-old male, established patient, nine months post-op emergency vena cava shunt for variceal bleeding, now presents with complaints of one episode of "dark" bowel movement, weight gain, tightness in abdomen, whites of eyes seem "yellow" and occasional drowsiness after eating hamburgers. (Abdominal Surgery)

Office visit for a 68-year-old male, established patient, with biopsy-proven rectal carcinoma, for evaluation and discussion of treatment options. (General Surgery)

Office visit for a 60-year-old, established patient, with diabetic nephropathy with increasing edema and dyspnea. (Endocrinology)

Office visit with 30-year-old male, established patient for three-month history of fatigue, weight loss, intermittent fever, and presenting with diffuse adenopathy and splenomegaly. (Family Medicine)

Office visit for restaging of an established patient with new lymphadenopathy one year post-therapy for lymphoma. (Hematology/Oncology)

Office visit for evaluation of recent onset syncopal attacks in a 70-year-old woman, established patient. (Internal Medicine)

Follow-up visit, 40-year-old mother of three, established patient, with acute rheumatoid arthritis, anatomical Stage 3, ARA function Class 3 rheumatoid arthritis, and deteriorating function. (Rheumatology)

Office evaluation and discussion of treatment options for a 68-year-old male, established patient, with a biopsy-proven rectal carcinoma. (General Surgery)

Follow-up office visit for a 65-year-old male, established patient, with a fever of recent onset while on outpatient antibiotic therapy for endocarditis. (Infectious Disease)

Office visit for a 75-year-old, established patient, with ALS (amyotrophic lateral sclerosis), who is no longer able to swallow. (Neurology)

Office visit for a 70-year-old female, established patient, with diabetes mellitus and hypertension, presenting with a two-month history of increasing confusion, agitation and short-term memory loss. (Family Medicine/Internal Medicine)

# Hospital Inpatient Services

## Initial Hospital Care

### New or Established Patient

**99221** Initial hospital visit following admission for a 42-year-old male for observation following an uncomplicated mandible fracture. (Plastic Surgery/Oral & Maxillofacial Surgery)

Initial hospital visit for a 40-year-old patient with a thrombosed synthetic AV conduit. (Nephrology)

Initial hospital visit for a healthy 24-year-old male with an acute onset of low back pain following a lifting injury. (Internal Medicine/Anesthesiology/Pain Medicine)

Initial hospital visit for a 69-year-old female with controlled hypertension, scheduled for surgery. (Internal Medicine/Cardiology)

Initial hospital visit for a 24-year-old healthy female with benign tumor of palate. (Oral & Maxillofacial Surgery)

Initial hospital visit for a 14-year-old female with infectious mononucleosis and dehydration. (Internal Medicine)

Initial hospital visit for a 62-year-old female with stable rheumatoid arthritis, admitted for total joint replacement. (Rheumatology)

Initial hospital visit for a 12-year-old patient with a laceration of the upper eyelid, involving the lid margin and superior canaliculus, admitted prior to surgery for IV antibiotic therapy. (Plastic Surgery)

Initial hospital visit for a 69-year-old female with controlled hypertension, scheduled for surgery. (Cardiology)

Hospital admission, examination, and initiation of treatment program for a 67-year-old male with uncomplicated pneumonia who requires IV antibiotic therapy. (Internal Medicine)

Hospital admission for an 18-month-old with 10 percent dehydration. (Pediatrics)

Hospital admission for a 12-year-old with a laceration of the upper eyelid involving the lid margin and superior canaliculus, admitted prior to surgery for IV antibiotic therapy. (Ophthalmology)

Hospital admission for a 32-year-old female with severe flank pain, hematuria and presumed diagnosis of ureteral calculus as determined by Emergency Department physician. (Urology)

Initial hospital visit for a patient with several large venous stasis ulcers not responding to outpatient therapy. (Dermatology)

Initial hospital visit for 21-year-old pregnant patient (nine weeks gestation) with hyperemesis gravidarum. (Obstetrics & Gynecology)

Initial hospital visit for a 73-year-old female with acute pyelonephritis who is otherwise generally healthy. (Geriatrics)

Initial hospital visit for 62-year-old patient with cellulitis of the foot requiring bedrest and intravenous antibiotics. (Orthopaedic Surgery)

**99222** Initial hospital visit for a 50-year-old patient with lower quadrant abdominal pain and increased temperature, but without septic picture. (General Surgery/Abdominal Surgery/Colon & Rectal Surgery)

Initial hospital visit for airway management, due to a benign laryngeal mass. (Otolaryngology, Head & Neck Surgery)

Initial hospital visit for a 66-year-old female with an L-2 vertebral compression fracture with acute onset of paralytic ileus; seen in the office two days previously. (Orthopaedic Surgery)

Initial hospital visit and evaluation of a 15-year-old male admitted with peritonsillar abscess or cellulitis requiring intravenous antibiotic therapy. (Otolaryngology, Head & Neck Surgery)

Initial hospital visit for a 42-year-old male with vertebral compression fracture following a motor vehicle accident. (Orthopaedic Surgery)

Initial hospital visit for a patient with generalized atopic dermatitis and secondary infection. (Dermatology)

Initial hospital visit for a 3-year-old patient with high temperature, limp, and painful hip motion of 18 hours' duration. (Pediatrics/Orthopaedic Surgery)

Initial hospital visit for a young adult, presenting with an acute asthma attack unresponsive to outpatient therapy. (Allergy & Immunology)

Initial hospital visit for an 18-year-old male who has suppurative sialoadenitis and dehydration. (Oral & Maxillofacial Surgery)

Initial hospital visit for a 65-year-old female for acute onset of thrombotic cerebrovascular accident with contralateral paralysis and aphasia. (Neurology)

Initial hospital visit for a 50-year-old male chronic paraplegic patient with pain and spasm below the lesion. (Anesthesiology)

Partial hospital admission for an adolescent patient from chaotic blended family, transferred from inpatient setting, for continued treatment to control symptomatic expressions of hostility and depression. (Psychiatry)

Initial hospital visit for a 15-year-old male with acute status asthmaticus, unresponsive to outpatient therapy. (Internal Medicine)

Initial hospital visit for a 61-year-old male with history of previous myocardial infarction, who now complains of chest pain. (Internal Medicine)

Initial hospital visit of a 15-year-old on medications for a sore throat over the last two weeks. The sore throat has worsened and now has dysphagia. The exam shows large necrotic tonsils with an adequate airway and small palpable nodes. The initial mono test was negative. (Otolaryngology, Head & Neck Surgery)

Initial hospital evaluation of a 23-year-old allergy patient admitted with eyelid edema and pain on fifth day of oral antibiotic therapy. (Otolaryngology, Head & Neck Surgery)

Hospital admission, young adult patient, failed previous therapy and now presents in acute asthmatic attack. (Family Medicine/Allergy & Immunology)

Hospital admission of a 62-year-old smoker, established patient, with bronchitis in acute respiratory distress. (Internal Medicine/Pulmonary Medicine)

Hospital admission, examination, and initiation of a treatment program for a 65-year-old female with new onset of right-sided paralysis and aphasia. (Neurology)

Hospital admission for a 50-year-old with left lower quadrant abdominal pain and increased temperature, but without septic picture. (General Surgery)

Hospital admission, examination, and initiation of treatment program for a 66-year-old chronic hemodialysis patient with fever and a new pulmonary infiltrate. (Nephrology)

Hospital admission for an 8-year-old febrile patient with chronic sinusitis and severe headache, unresponsive to oral antibiotics. (Allergy & Immunology)

Hospital admission for a 40-year-old male with submaxillary cellulitis and trismus from infected lower molar. (Oral & Maxillofacial Surgery)

**99223** Initial hospital visit for a 45-year-old female, who has a history of rheumatic fever as a child and now has anemia, fever, and congestive heart failure. (Cardiology)

Initial hospital visit for a 50-year-old male with acute chest pain and diagnostic electrocardiographic changes of an acute anterior myocardial infarction. (Cardiology/Family Medicine/Internal Medicine)

Initial hospital visit of a 75-year-old with progressive stridor and dysphagia with history of cancer of the larynx treated by radiation therapy in the past. Exam shows a large recurrent tumor of the glottis with a mass in the neck. (Otolaryngology, Head & Neck Surgery)

Initial hospital visit for a 70-year-old male admitted with chest pain, complete heart block, and congestive heart failure. (Cardiology)

Initial hospital visit for an 82-year-old male who presents with syncope, chest pain, and ventricular arrhythmias. (Cardiology)

Initial hospital visit for a 75-year-old male with history of ASCVD, who is severely dehydrated, disoriented, and experiencing auditory hallucinations. (Psychiatry)

Initial hospital visit for a 70-year-old male with alcohol and sedative-hypnotic dependence, admitted by family for severe withdrawal, hypertension, and diabetes mellitus. (Psychiatry)

Initial hospital visit for a persistently suicidal latency-aged child whose parents have requested admission to provide safety during evaluation, but are anxious about separation from her. (Psychiatry)

Initial psychiatric visit for an adolescent patient without previous psychiatric history, who was transferred from the medical ICU after a significant overdose. (Psychiatry)

Initial hospital visit for a 35-year-old female with severe systemic lupus erythematosus on corticosteroid and cyclophosphamide, with new onset of fever, chills, rash, and chest pain. (Rheumatology)

Initial hospital visit for a 52-year-old male with known rheumatic heart disease who presents with anasarca, hypertension, and history of alcohol abuse. (Cardiology)

Initial hospital visit for a 55-year-old female with a history of congenital heart disease; now presents with cyanosis. (Cardiology)

Initial hospital visit for a psychotic, hostile, violently combative adolescent, involuntarily committed, for seclusion and restraint in order to provide for safety on unit. (Psychiatry)

Initial hospital visit for a now subdued and sullen teenage male with six-month history of declining school performance, increasing self-endangerment, and resistance of parental expectations, including running away past weekend after physical fight with father. (Psychiatry)

Initial partial hospital admission for a 17-year-old female with history of borderline mental retardation who has developed auditory hallucinations. Parents are known to abuse alcohol, and Child Protective Services is investigating allegations of sexual abuse of a younger sibling. (Psychiatry)

Initial hospital visit of a 67-year old male admitted with a large neck mass, dysphagia, and history of myocardial infarction three months before. (Otolaryngology, Head & Neck Surgery)

Initial hospital visit for a patient with suspected cerebrospinal fluid rhinorrhea which developed two weeks after head injury. (Otolaryngology, Head & Neck Surgery)

Initial hospital visit for a 25-year-old female with history of poly-substance abuse and psychiatric disorder. The patient appears to be psychotic with markedly elevated vital signs. (Psychiatry)

Initial hospital visit for a 70-year-old male with cutaneous T-cell lymphoma who has developed fever and lymphadenopathy. (Internal Medicine)

Initial hospital visit for a 62-year-old female with known coronary artery disease, for evaluation of increasing edema, dyspnea on exertion, confusion, and sudden onset of fever with productive cough. (Internal Medicine)

Initial hospital visit for a 3-year-old female with 36-hour history of sore throat and high fever; now with sudden onset of lethargy, irritability, photophobia, and nuchal rigidity. (Pediatrics)

Initial hospital visit for a 26-year-old female for evaluation of severe facial fractures (LeFort's II/III). (Plastic Surgery)

Initial hospital visit for a 55-year-old female for bilateral mandibular fractures resulting in flail mandible and airway obstruction. (Plastic Surgery)

Initial hospital visit for a 71-year-old patient with a red painful eye four days following uncomplicated cataract surgery due to endophthalmitis. (Ophthalmology)

Initial hospital visit for a 45-year-old patient involved in a motor vehicle accident who suffered a perforating corneoscleral laceration with loss of vision. (Ophthalmology)

Initial hospital visit for a 58-year-old male who has Ludwig's angina and progressive airway compromise. (Oral & Maxillofacial Surgery)

Initial hospital visit for a patient with generalized systemic sclerosis, receiving immunosuppressive therapy because of recent onset of cough, fever, and inability to swallow. (Dermatology)

Initial hospital visit for an 82-year-old male who presents with syncope, chest pain, and ventricular arrhythmias. (Cardiology)

Initial hospital visit for a 62-year-old male with history of previous myocardial infarction, comes in with recurrent, sustained ventricular tachycardia. (Cardiology)

Initial hospital visit for a chronic dialysis patient with infected PTFE fistula, septicemia, and shock. (Nephrology)

Initial hospital visit for a 1-year-old male, victim of child abuse, with central nervous system depression, skull fracture, and retinal hemorrhage. (Family Medicine/Neurology)

Initial hospital visit for a 25-year-old female with recent C4-5 quadriplegia, admitted for rehabilitation. (Physical Medicine & Rehabilitation)

Initial hospital visit for an 18-year-old male, post-traumatic brain injury with multiple impairment. (Physical Medicine & Rehabilitation)

Initial partial hospital admission for 16-year-old male, sullen and subdued, with six-month history of declining school performance, increasing self-endangerment, and resistance to parental expectations. (Psychiatry)

Initial hospital visit for a 16-year-old primigravida at 32 weeks gestation with severe hypertension (200/110), thrombocytopenia, and headache. (Obstetrics & Gynecology)

Initial hospital visit for a 49-year-old male with cirrhosis of liver with hematemesis, hepatic encephalopathy, and fever. (Gastroenterology)

Initial hospital visit for a 55-year-old female in chronic pain who has attempted suicide. (Psychiatry)

Initial hospital visit for a 70-year-old male, with multiple organ system disease, admitted with history of being aneuric and septic for 24 hours prior to admission. (Urology)

Initial hospital visit for a 3-year-old female with 36-hour history of sore throat and high fever, now with sudden onset of lethargy, irritability, photophobia, and nuchal rigidity. (Internal Medicine)

Initial hospital visit for a 78-year-old male, transfers from nursing home with dysuria and pyuria, increasing confusion, and high fever. (Internal Medicine)

Initial hospital visit for a 1-day-old male with cyanosis, respiratory distress, and tachypnea. (Cardiology)

Initial hospital visit for a 3-year-old female with recurrent tachycardia and syncope. (Cardiology)

Initial hospital visit for a thyrotoxic patient who presents with fever, atrial fibrillation, and delirium. (Endocrinology)

Initial hospital visit for a 50-year-old Type I diabetic who presents with diabetic ketoacidosis with fever and obtundation. (Endocrinology)

Initial hospital visit for a 40-year-old female with anatomical stage 3, ARA functional class 3 rheumatoid arthritis on methotrexate, corticosteroid, and nonsteroidal anti-inflammatory drugs. Patient presents with severe arthritis flare, new oral ulcers, abdominal pain, and leukopenia. (Rheumatology)

Initial hospital exam of a pediatric patient with high fever and proptosis. (Otolaryngology, Head & Neck Surgery)

Initial hospital visit for a 25-year-old patient admitted for the first time to the rehab unit, with recent C-4-5 quadriplegia. (Physical Medicine & Rehabilitation)

Hospital admission, examination, and initiation of treatment program for a previously unknown 58-year-old male who presents with acute chest pain (Cardiology)

Hospital admission, examination, and initiation of induction chemotherapy for a 42-year-old patient with newly diagnosed acute myelogenous leukemia. (Hematology/Oncology)

Hospital admission following a motor vehicle accident of a 24-year-old male with fracture dislocation of C5-6; neurologically intact. (Neurosurgery)

Hospital admission for a 78-year-old female with left lower lobe pneumonia and a history of coronary artery disease, congestive heart failure, osteoarthritis and gout. (Family Medicine)

Hospital admission, examination, and initiation of treatment program for a 65-year-old immunosuppressed male with confusion, fever, and a headache. (Infectious Disease)

Hospital admission for a 9-year-old with vomiting, dehydration, fever, tachypnea and an admitting diagnosis of diabetic ketoacidosis. (Pediatrics)

Initial hospital visit for a 65-year-old male who presents with acute myocardial infarction, oliguria, hypotension, and altered state of consciousness. (Cardiology)

Initial hospital visit for a hostile/resistant adolescent patient who is severely depressed and involved in poly-substance abuse. Patient is experiencing significant conflict in his chaotic family situation and was suspended from school following an attack on a teacher with a baseball bat. (Psychiatry)

Initial hospital visit for 89-year-old female with fulminant hepatic failure and encephalopathy. (Gastroenterology)

Initial hospital visit for a 42-year-old female with rapidly progressing scleroderma, malignant hypertension, digital infarcts, and oligurea. (Rheumatology)

# Subsequent Hospital Care

**99231** Subsequent hospital visit for a 65-year-old female, post-open reduction and internal fixation of a fracture. (Physical Medicine & Rehabilitation)

Subsequent hospital visit for a 33-year-old patient with pelvic pain who is responding to pain medication and observation. (Obstetrics & Gynecology)

Subsequent hospital visit for a 21-year-old female with hyperemesis who has responded well to intravenous fluids. (Obstetrics & Gynecology)

Subsequent hospital visit to re-evaluate post-op pain and titrate patient-controlled analgesia for a 27-year-old female. (Anesthesiology)

Follow-up hospital visit for a 35-year-old female, status post-epidural analgesia. (Anesthesiology/Pain Medicine)

Subsequent hospital visit for a 56-year-old male, post-gastrectomy, for maintenance of analgesia using an intravenous dilaudid infusion. (Anesthesiology)

Subsequent hospital visit for a 4-year-old on day three receiving medication for uncomplicated pneumonia. (Allergy & Immunology)

Subsequent hospital visit for a 30-year-old female with urticaria which has stabilized with medication. (Allergy & Immunology)

Subsequent hospital visit for a 76-year-old male with venous stasis ulcers. (Dermatology)

Subsequent hospital visit for a 24-year-old female with otitis externa, seen two days before in consultation, now to have otic wick removal. (Otolaryngology, Head & Neck Surgery)

Subsequent hospital visit for a 27-year-old with acute labyrinthitis. (Otolaryngology, Head & Neck Surgery)

Subsequent hospital visit for a 10-year-old male admitted for lobar pneumonia with vomiting and dehydration; is becoming afebrile and tolerating oral fluids. (Family Medicine/Pediatrics)

Subsequent hospital visit for a 62-year-old patient with resolving cellulitis of the foot. (Orthopaedic Surgery)

Subsequent hospital visit for a 25-year-old male admitted for supra-ventricular tachycardia and converted on medical therapy. (Cardiology)

Subsequent hospital visit for a 27-year-old male two days after open reduction and internal fixation for malar complex fracture. (Plastic Surgery)

Subsequent hospital visit for a 76-year-old male with venous stasis ulcers. (Geriatrics)

Subsequent hospital visit for a 67-year-old female admitted three days ago with bleeding gastric ulcer; now stable. (Gastroenterology)

Subsequent hospital visit for stable 33-year-old male, status post-lower gastrointestinal bleeding. (General Surgery/Gastroenterology)

Subsequent hospital visit for a 29-year-old auto mechanic with effort thrombosis of left upper extremity. (General Surgery)

Subsequent hospital visit for a 14-year-old female in middle phase of inpatient treatment, who is now behaviorally stable and making satisfactory progress in treatment. (Psychiatry)

Subsequent hospital visit for an 18-year-old male with uncomplicated asthma who is clinically stable. (Allergy & Immunology)

Subsequent hospital visit for a 55-year-old male with rheumatoid arthritis, two days following an uncomplicated total joint replacement. (Rheumatology)

Subsequent hospital visit for a 60-year-old dialysis patient with an access infection, now afebrile on antibiotic. (Nephrology)

Subsequent hospital visit for a 36-year-old female with stable post-rhinoplasty epistaxis. (Plastic Surgery)

Subsequent hospital visit for a 66-year-old female with L-2 vertebral compression fracture with resolving ileus. (Orthopaedic Surgery)

Subsequent hospital visit for a 3-year-old patient in traction for congenital (developmental) dislocation of the hip. (Orthopaedic Surgery)

Subsequent hospital visit for a patient with peritonsillar abscess. (Otolaryngology, Head & Neck Surgery)

Subsequent hospital visit for an 18-year-old female responding to intravenous antibiotic therapy for ear or sinus infection. (Otolaryngology, Head & Neck Surgery)

Subsequent hospital visit for a 70-year-old male admitted with congestive heart failure who has responded to therapy. (Cardiology)

Follow-up hospital visit for a 32-year-old female with left ureteral calculus; being followed in anticipation of spontaneous passage. (Urology)

Subsequent hospital visit for a 4-year-old female, admitted for acute gastroenteritis and dehydration, requiring IV hydration; now stable. (Family Medicine)

Subsequent hospital visit for a 50-year-old Type II diabetic who is clinically stable and without complications requiring regulation of a single dose of insulin daily. (Endocrinology)

Subsequent hospital visit to reassesses the status of a 65-year-old patient post-open reduction and internal fixation of hip fracture, on the rehab unit. (Physical Medicine & Rehabilitation)

Subsequent hospital visit for a 78-year-old male with cholangiocarcinoma managed by biliary drainage. (Interventional Radiology)

Subsequent hospital visit for a 50-year-old male with uncomplicated myocardial infarction who is clinically stable and without chest pain. (Family Medicine/Cardiology/Internal Medicine)

Subsequent hospital visit for a stable 72-year-old lung cancer patient undergoing a five-day course of infusion chemotherapy. (Hematology/Oncology)

Subsequent hospital visit, two days post admission for a 65-year-old male with a CVA (cerebral vascular accident) and left hemiparesis, who is clinically stable. (Neurology/Physical Medicine and Rehabilitation)

Subsequent hospital visit for now stable, 33-year-old male, status post lower gastrointestinal bleeding. (General Surgery)

Subsequent visit on third day of hospitalization for a 60-year-old female recovering from an uncomplicated pneumonia. (Infectious Disease/Internal Medicine/Pulmonary Medicine)

Subsequent hospital visit for a 3-year-old patient in traction for a congenital dislocation of the hip. (Orthopaedic Surgery)

Subsequent hospital visit for a 4-year-old female, admitted for acute gastroenteritis and dehydration, requiring IV hydration; now stable. (Family Medicine/Internal Medicine)

Subsequent hospital visit for 50-year-old female with resolving uncomplicated acute pancreatitis. (Gastroenterology)

**99232** Subsequent hospital visit for a patient with venous stasis ulcers who developed fever and red streaks adjacent to the ulcer. (Dermatology/Internal Medicine/Family Medicine)

Subsequent hospital visit for a 66-year-old male for dressing changes and observation. Patient has had a myocutaneous flap to close a pharyngeal fistula and now has a low-grade fever. (Plastic Surgery)

Subsequent hospital visit for a 54-year-old female admitted for myocardial infarction, but who is now having frequent premature ventricular contractions. (Internal Medicine)

Subsequent hospital visit for an 80-year-old patient with a pelvic rim fracture, inability to walk, and severe pain; now 36 hours post-injury, experiencing urinary retention. (Orthopaedic Surgery)

Subsequent hospital visit for a 17-year-old female with fever, pharyngitis, and airway obstruction, who after 48 hours develops a maculopapular rash. (Pediatrics/Family Medicine)

Follow-up hospital visit for a 32-year-old patient admitted the previous day for corneal ulcer. (Dermatology)

Follow-up visit for a 67-year-old male with CHF who has responded to antibiotics and diuretics, and has now developed a monoarthropathy. (Internal Medicine)

Follow-up hospital visit for a 58-year-old male receiving continuous opioids who is experiencing severe nausea and vomiting. (Pain Medicine)

Subsequent hospital visit for a patient after an auto accident who is slow to respond to ambulation training. (Physical Medicine & Rehabilitation)

Subsequent hospital visit for a 14-year-old with unstable bronchial asthma complicated by pneumonia. (Allergy & Immunology)

Subsequent hospital visit for a 50-year-old diabetic, hypertensive male with back pain not responding to conservative inpatient management with continued radiation of pain to the lower left extremity. (Orthopaedic Surgery)

Subsequent hospital visit for a 37-year-old female on day five of antibiotics for bacterial endocarditis, who still has low-grade fever.

Subsequent hospital visit for a 54-year-old patient, post MI (myocardial infarction), who is out of the CCU (coronary care unit) but is now having frequent premature ventricular contractions on telemetry. (Cardiology/Internal Medicine)

Subsequent hospital visit for a patient with neutropenia, a fever responding to antibiotics, and continued slow gastrointestinal bleeding on platelet support. (Hematology/Oncology)

Subsequent hospital visit for a 50-year-old male admitted two days ago for sub-acute renal allograft rejection. (Nephrology)

Subsequent hospital visit for a 35-year-old drug addict, not responding to initial antibiotic therapy for pyelonephritis. (Urology)

Subsequent hospital visit of an 81-year-old male with abdominal distention, nausea, and vomiting. (General Surgery)

Subsequent hospital care for a 62-year-old female with congestive heart failure, who remains dyspneic and febrile. (Internal Medicine)

Subsequent hospital visit for a 73-year-old female with recently diagnosed lung cancer, who complains of unsteady gait. (Pulmonary Medicine)

Subsequent hospital visit for a 20-month-old male with bacterial meningitis treated one week with antibiotic therapy; has now developed a temperature of 101.0. (Pediatrics)

Subsequent hospital visit for 13-year-old male admitted with left lower quadrant abdominal pain and fever, not responding to therapy. (General Surgery)

Subsequent hospital visit for a 65-year-old male with hemiplegia and painful paretic shoulder. (Physical Medicine & Rehabilitation)

**99233** Subsequent hospital visit for a 38-year-old male, quadriplegic with acute autonomic hyperreflexia, who is not responsive to initial care. (Physical Medicine & Rehabilitation)

Follow-up hospital visit for a teenage female who continues to experience severely disruptive, violent and life-threatening symptoms in a complicated multi-system illness. Family/social circumstances also a contributing factor. (Psychiatry)

Subsequent hospital visit for a 42-year-old female with progressive systemic sclerosis (scleroderma), renal failure on dialysis, congestive heart failure, cardiac arrhythmias, and digital ulcers. (Allergy & Immunology)

Subsequent hospital visit for a 50-year-old diabetic, hypertensive male with nonresponding back pain and radiating pain to the lower left extremity, who develops chest pain, cough, and bloody sputum. (Orthopaedic Surgery)

Subsequent hospital visit for a 64-year-old female, status post-abdominal aortic aneurysm resection, with non-responsive coagulopathy, who has now developed lower GI bleeding. (Abdominal Surgery/Colon & Rectal Surgery/General Surgery)

Follow-up hospital care of a patient with pansinusitis infection complicated by a brain abscess and asthma; no response to current treatment. (Otolaryngology, Head & Neck Surgery)

Subsequent hospital visit for a patient with a laryngeal neoplasm who develops airway compromise, suspected metastasis. (Otolaryngology, Head & Neck Surgery)

Subsequent hospital visit for a 49-year-old male with significant rectal bleeding, etiology undetermined, not responding to treatment. (Abdominal Surgery/General Surgery/Colon & Rectal Surgery)

Subsequent hospital visit for a 50-year-old male, post-aortocoronary bypass surgery; now develops hypotension and oliguria. (Cardiology)

Subsequent hospital visit for an adolescent patient who is violent, unsafe, and noncompliant, with multiple expectations for participation in treatment plan and behavior on the treatment unit. (Psychiatry)

Subsequent hospital visit for an 18-year-old male being treated for presumed PCP psychosis. Patient is still moderately symptomatic with auditory hallucinations and is insisting on signing out against medical advice. (Psychiatry)

Subsequent hospital visit for an 8-year-old female with caustic ingestion, who now has fever, dyspnea, and dropping hemoglobin. (Gastroenterology)

Follow-up hospital visit for a chronic renal failure patient on dialysis who develops chest pain and shortness of breath and a new onset pericardial friction rub. (Nephrology)

Subsequent hospital visit for a 44-year-old patient with electrical burns to the left arm with ascending infection. (Orthopaedic Surgery)

Subsequent hospital visit for a patient with systemic sclerosis who has aspirated and is short of breath. (Dermatology)

Subsequent hospital visit for a 65-year-old female, status post-op resection of abdominal aortic aneurysm, with suspected ischemic bowel. (General Surgery)

Subsequent hospital visit for a 50-year-old male, post-aortocoronary bypass surgery, now develops hypotension and oliguria. (Cardiology)

Subsequent hospital visit for a 65-year-old male, following an acute myocardial infarction, who complains of shortness of breath and new chest pain. (Cardiology)

Subsequent hospital visit for a 65-year-old female with rheumatoid arthritis (stage 3, class 3) admitted for urosepsis. On the third hospital day, chest pain, dyspnea and fever develop. (Rheumatology)

Follow-up hospital care of a pediatric case with stridor, laryngomalcia, established tracheostomy, complicated by multiple medical problems in PICU. (Otolaryngology, Head & Neck Surgery)

Subsequent hospital visit for a 60-year-old female, four days post uncomplicated inferior myocardial infarction who has developed severe chest pain, dyspnea, diaphoresis and nausea. (Family Medicine)

Subsequent hospital visit for a patient with AML (acute myelogenous leukemia), fever, elevated white count and uric acid undergoing induction chemotherapy. (Hematology/Oncology)

Subsequent hospital visit for a 38-year-old quadriplegic male with acute autonomic hyperreflexia, who is not responsive to initial care. (Physical Medicine & Rehabilitation)

Subsequent hospital visit for a 65-year-old female post-op resection of abdominal aortic aneurysm, with suspected ischemic bowel. (General Surgery)

Subsequent hospital visit for a 60-year-old female with persistent leukocytosis and a fever seven day's after a sigmoid colon resection for carcinoma. (Infectious Disease)

Subsequent hospital visit for a chronic renal failure patient on dialysis, who develops chest pain, shortness of breath and new onset of pericardial friction rub. (Nephrology)

Subsequent hospital visit for a 65-year-old male with acute myocardial infarction who now demonstrates complete heart block and congestive heart failure. (Cardiology)

Subsequent hospital visit for a 25-year-old female with hypertension and systemic lupus erythmatosus, admitted for fever and respiratory distress. On the third hospital day, the patient presented with purpuric skin lesions and acute renal failure. (Allergy & Immunology)

Subsequent hospital visit for a 55-year-old male with severe chronic obstructive pulmonary disease and bronchospasm; initially admitted for acute respiratory distress requiring ventilatory support in the ICU. The patient was stabilized, extubated and transferred to the floor, but has now developed acute fever, dyspnea, left lower lobe rhonchi and laboratory evidence of carbon dioxide retention and hypoxemia. (Family Medicine/Internal Medicine)

Subsequent hospital visit for 46-year-old female, known liver cirrhosis patient, with recent upper gastrointestinal hemorrhage from varices; now with worsening ascites and encephalopathy. (Gastroenterology)

Subsequent hospital visit for 62-year-old female admitted with acute subarachnoid hemorrhage, negative cerebral arteriogram, increased lethargy and hemiparesis with fever. (Neurosurgery)

# Consultations

## Office or Other Outpatient Consultations

### New or Established Patient

**99241** Initial office consultation for a 40-year-old female in pain from blister on lip following a cold. (Oral & Maxillofacial Surgery)

Initial office consultation for a 62-year-old construction worker with olecranon bursitis. (Orthopaedic Surgery)

Office consultation with 25-year-old postpartum female with severe symptomatic hemorrhoids. (Colon & Rectal Surgery)

Office consultation with 58-year-old male, referred for follow-up of creatinine level and evaluation of obstructive uropathy, relieved two months ago. (Nephrology)

Office consultation for 30-year-old female tennis player with sprain or contusion of the forearm. (Orthopaedic Surgery)

Office consultation for a 45-year-old male, requested by his internist, with asymptomatic torus palatinus requiring no further treatment. (Oral & Maxillofacial Surgery)

**99242** Initial office consultation for a 20-year-old male with acute upper respiratory tract symptoms. (Allergy & Immunology)

Initial office consultation for a 29-year-old soccer player with painful proximal thigh/groin injury. (Orthopaedic Surgery)

Initial office consultation for a 66-year-old female with wrist and hand pain, numbness of finger tips, suspected median nerve compression by carpal tunnel syndrome. (Plastic Surgery)

Initial office consultation for a patient with a solitary lesion of discoid lupus erythematosus on left cheek to rule out malignancy of self-induced lesion. (Dermatology)

Office consultation for management of systolic hypertension in a 70-year-old male scheduled for elective prostate resection. (Geriatrics)

Office consultation with 27-year-old female, with old amputation, for evaluation of existing above-knee prosthesis. (Physical Medicine & Rehabilitation)

Office consultation with 66-year-old female with wrist and hand pain, and finger numbness, secondary to suspected carpal tunnel syndrome. (Orthopaedic Surgery)

Office consultation for 61-year-old female, recently on antibiotic therapy, now with diarrhea and leukocytosis. (Abdominal Surgery)

Office consultation for a patient with papulosquamous eruption of elbow with pitting of nails and itchy scalp. (Dermatology)

Office consultation for a 30-year-old female with single season allergic rhinitis. (Allergy & Immunology)

**99243** Initial office consultation for a 60-year-old male with avascular necrosis of the left femoral head with increasing pain. (Orthopaedic Surgery)

Office consultation for a 31-year-old woman complaining of palpitations and chest pains. Her internist had described a mild systolic click. (Cardiology)

Office consultation for a 65-year-old female with persistent bronchitis. (Infectious Disease)

Office consultation for a 65-year-old man with chronic low-back pain radiating to the leg. (Neurosurgery)

Office consultation for 23-year-old female with Crohn's disease not responding to therapy. (Abdominal Surgery/Colon & Rectal Surgery)

Office consultation for 25-year-old patient with symptomatic knee pain and swelling, with torn anterior cruciate ligament and/or torn meniscus. (Orthopaedic Surgery)

Office consultation for a 67-year-old patient with osteoporosis and mandibular atrophy with regard to reconstructive alternatives. (Oral & Maxillofacial Surgery)

Office consultation for 39-year-old patient referred at a perimenopausal age for irregular menses and menopausal symptoms. (Obstetrics & Gynecology)

**99244** Initial office consultation for a 28-year-old male, HIV+, with a recent change in visual acuity. (Ophthalmology)

Initial office consultation for a 15-year-old male with failing grades, suspected drug abuse. (Pediatrics)

Initial office consultation for a 36-year-old factory worker, status four months post-occupational low back injury and requires management of intractable low back pain. (Pain Medicine)

Initial office consultation for a 45-year-old female with a history of chronic arthralgia of TMJ and associated myalgia and sudden progressive symptomatology over last two to three months. (Oral & Maxillofacial Surgery)

Initial office consultation for evaluation of a 70-year-old male with appetite loss and diminished energy. (Psychiatry)

Initial office consultation for an elementary school-aged patient, referred by pediatrician, with multiple systematic complaints and recent onset of behavioral discontrol. (Psychiatry)

Initial office consultation for a 23-year-old female with developmental facial skeletal anomaly and subsequent abnormal relationship of jaw(s) to cranial base. (Oral & Maxillofacial Surgery)

Initial office consultation for a 45-year-old myopic patient with a one-week history of floaters and a partial retinal detachment. (Ophthalmology)

Initial office consultation for a 65-year-old female with moderate dementia, mild unsteadiness, back pain fatigue on ambulation, intermittent urinary incontinence. (Neurosurgery)

Initial office consultation for a 33-year-old female referred by endocrinologist with amenorrhea and galactorrhea, for evaluation of pituitary tumor. (Neurosurgery)

Initial office consultation for a 34-year-old male with new onset nephrotic syndrome. (Nephrology)

Initial office consultation for a 39-year-old female with intractable chest wall pain secondary to metastatic breast cancer. (Anesthesiology/Pain Medicine)

Initial office consultation for a patient with multiple giant tumors of jaws. (Oral & Maxillofacial Surgery)

Initial office consultation for a patient with a failed total hip replacement with loosening and pain upon walking. (Orthopaedic Surgery)

Initial office consultation for a 60-year-old female with three-year history of intermittent tic-like unilateral facial pain; now constant pain for six weeks without relief by adequate carbamazepine dosage. (Neurosurgery)

Initial office consultation for a 45-year-old male heavy construction worker with prior lumbar disk surgery two years earlier; now gradually recurring low back and unilateral leg pain for three months, unable to work for two weeks. (Neurosurgery)

Initial office consultation of a patient who presents with a 30-year history of smoking and right neck mass. (Otolaryngology, Head & Neck Surgery)

Office consultation with 38-year-old female, with inflammatory bowel disease, who now presents with right lower quadrant pain and suspected intra-abdominal abscess. (General Surgery/Colon & Rectal Surgery)

Office consultation with 72-year-old male with esophageal carcinoma, symptoms of dysphagia and reflux. (Thoracic Surgery)

Office consultation for discussion of treatment options for a 40-year-old female with a two-centimeter adenocarcinoma of the breast. (Radiation Oncology)

Office consultation for young patient referred by pediatrician because of patient's short attention span, easy distractibility and hyperactivity. (Psychiatry)

Office consultation for 66-year-old female, history of colon resection for adenocarcinoma six years earlier, now with severe mid-back pain; x-rays showing osteoporosis and multiple vertebral compression fractures. (Neurosurgery)

Office consultation for a patient with chronic pelvic inflammatory disease who now has left lower quadrant pain with a palpable pelvic mass. (Obstetrics & Gynecology)

Office consultation for a patient with long-standing psoriasis with acute onset of erythroderma, pustular lesions, chills and fever. Combinations of topical and systemic treatments discussed and instituted. (Dermatology)

**99245** Initial office consultation for a 35-year-old multiple-trauma male patient with complex pelvic fractures, for evaluation and formulation of management plan. (Orthopaedic Surgery)

Initial emergency room consultation for 10-year-old male in status epilepticus, recent closed head injury, information about medication not available. (Neurosurgery)

Initial emergency room consultation for a 23-year-old patient with severe abdominal pain, guarding, febrile, and unstable vital signs. (Obstetrics & Gynecology)

Office consultation for a 67-year-old female longstanding uncontrolled diabetic who presents with retinopathy, nephropathy, and a foot ulcer. (Endocrinology)

Office consultation for a 37-year-old male for initial evaluation and management of Cushing's disease. (Endocrinology)

Office consultation for a 60-year-old male who presents with thyrotoxicosis, exophthalmos, frequent premature ventricular contractions and CHF. (Endocrinology)

Initial office consultation for a 36-year-old patient, one year status post occupational herniated cervical disk treated by laminectomy, requiring management of multiple sites of intractable pain, depression, and narcotic dependence. (Pain Medicine)

Office consultation for a 58-year-old man with a history of MI and CHF who complains of the recent onset of rest angina and shortness of breath. The patient has a systolic blood pressure of 90mmHG and is in Class IV heart failure. (Cardiology)

Emergency room consultation for a 1-year-old with a three-day history of fever with increasing respiratory distress who is thought to have cardiac tamponade by the ER physician. (Cardiology)

Office consultation in the emergency room for a 25-year-old male with severe, acute, closed head injury. (Neurosurgery)

Office consultation for a 23-year-old female with Stage II A Hodgkins disease with positive supraclavicular and mediastinal nodes. (Radiation Oncology)

Office consultation for a 27-year-old juvenile diabetic patient with severe diabetic retinopathy, gastric atony, nephrotic syndrome and progressive renal failure, now with a serum creatinine of 2.7, and a blood pressure of 170/114. (Nephrology)

Office consultation for independent medical evaluation of a patient with a history of complicated low back and neck problems with previous multiple failed back surgeries. (Orthopaedic Surgery)

Office consultation for an adolescent referred by pediatrician for recent onset of violent and self-injurious behavior. (Psychiatry)

Office consultation for a 6-year-old male for evaluation of severe muscle and joint pain and a diffuse rash. Well until four-six weeks earlier, when he developed arthralgia, myalgias, and a fever of 102 for one week. (Rheumatology)

# Initial Inpatient Consultations

## New or Established Patient

**99251** Initial hospital consultation for a 27-year-old female with fractured incisor post-intubation. (Oral & Maxillofacial Surgery)

Initial hospital consultation for an orthopaedic patient on IV antibiotics who has developed an apparent candida infection of the oral cavity. (Oral & Maxillofacial Surgery)

Initial inpatient consultation for a 30-year-old female complaining of vaginal itching, post orthopaedic surgery. (Obstetrics & Gynecology)

Initial inpatient consultation for a 36-year-old male on orthopaedic service with complaint of localized dental pain. (Oral & Maxillofacial Surgery)

**99252** Initial hospital consultation for a 45-year-old male, previously abstinent alcoholic, who relapsed and was admitted for management of gastritis. The patient readily accepts the need for further treatment. (Addiction Medicine)

Initial hospital consultation for a 35-year-old dialysis patient with episodic oral ulcerations. (Oral & Maxillofacial Surgery)

Initial inpatient preoperative consultation for a 43-year-old woman with cholecystitis and well-controlled hypertension. (Cardiology)

Initial inpatient consultation for recommendation of antibiotic prophylaxis for a patient with a synthetic heart valve who will undergo urologic surgery. (Internal Medicine)

Initial inpatient consultation for possible drug eruption in 50-year-old male. (Dermatology)

Preoperative inpatient consultation for evaluation of hypertension in a 60-year-old male who will undergo a cholecystectomy. Patient had a normal annual check-up in your office four months ago. (Internal Medicine)

Initial inpatient consultation for 66-year-old patient with wrist and hand pain and finger numbness, secondary to carpal tunnel syndrome. (Orthopaedic Surgery/Plastic Surgery)

Initial inpatient consultation for a 66-year-old male smoker referred for pain management immediately status post-biliary tract surgery done via sub-costal incision. (Anesthesiology/Pain Medicine)

**99253** Initial hospital consultation for a 50-year-old female with incapacitating knee pain due to generalized rheumatoid arthritis. (Orthopaedic Surgery)

Initial hospital consultation for a 60-year-old male with avascular necrosis of the left femoral heel with increasing pain. (Orthopaedic Surgery)

Initial hospital consultation for a 45-year-old female with compound mandibular fracture and concurrent head, abdominal and/or orthopaedic injuries. (Oral & Maxillofacial Surgery)

Initial hospital consultation for a 22-year-old female, paraplegic, to evaluate wrist and hand pain. (Orthopaedic Surgery)

Initial hospital consultation for a 40-year-old male with 10-day history of incapacitating unilateral sciatica, unable to walk now, not improved by bed rest. (Neurosurgery)

Initial hospital consultation, requested by pediatrician, for treatment recommendations for a patient admitted with persistent inability to walk following soft tissue injury to ankle. (Physiatry)

Initial hospital consultation for a 27-year-old previously healthy male who vomited during IV sedation and may have aspirated gastric contents. (Anesthesiology)

Initial hospital consultation for a 33-year-old female, post-abdominal surgery, who now has a fever. (Internal Medicine)

Initial inpatient consultation for a 57-year-old male, post lower endoscopy, for evaluation of abdominal pain and fever. (General Surgery)

Initial inpatient consultation for rehabilitation of a 73-year-old female one week after surgical management of a hip fracture. (Physical Medicine & Rehabilitation)

Initial inpatient consultation for diagnosis/management of fever following abdominal surgery. (Internal Medicine)

Initial inpatient consultation for a 35-year-old female with a fever and pulmonary infiltrate following cesarean section. (Pulmonary Medicine)

Initial inpatient consultation for a 42-year-old non-diabetic patient, post-op cholecystectomy, now with an acute urinary tract infection. (Nephrology)

Initial inpatient consultation for 53-year-old female with moderate uncomplicated pancreatitis. (Gastroenterology)

Initial inpatient consultation for 45-year-old patient with chronic neck pain with radicular pain of the left arm. (Orthopaedic Surgery)

Initial inpatient consultation for 8-year-old patient with new onset of seizures who has a normal examination and previous history. (Neurology)

**99254** Initial hospital consultation for a 15-year-old patient with painless swelling of proximal humerus with lytic lesion by x-ray. (Orthopaedic Surgery)

Initial hospital consultation for evaluation of a 29-year-old female with a diffusely positive medical review of systems and history of multiple surgeries. (Psychiatry)

Initial hospital consultation for a 70-year-old diabetic female with gangrene of the foot. (Orthopaedic Surgery)

Initial inpatient consultation for a 47-year-old female with progressive pulmonary infiltrate, hypoxemia, and diminished urine output. (Anesthesiology)

Initial hospital consultation for a 13-month-old with spasmodic cough, respiratory distress, and fever. (Allergy & Immunology)

Initial hospital consultation for a patient with failed total hip replacement with loosening and pain upon walking. (Orthopaedic Surgery)

Initial hospital consultation for a 62-year-old female with metastatic breast cancer to the femoral neck and thoracic vertebra. (Orthopaedic Surgery)

Initial hospital consultation for a 39-year-old female with nephrolithiasis requiring extensive opioid analgesics, whose vital signs are now elevated. She initially denied any drug use, but today gives history of multiple substance abuse, including opioids and prior treatment for a personality disorder. (Psychiatry)

Initial hospital consultation for a 70-year-old female without previous psychiatric history, who is now experiencing nocturnal confusion and visual hallucinations following hip replacement surgery. (Psychiatry)

Initial inpatient consultation for evaluation of a 63-year-old in the ICU with diabetes and chronic renal failure who develops acute respiratory distress syndrome 36 hours after a mitral valve replacement. (Anesthesiology)

Initial inpatient consultation for a 66-year-old female with enlarged supraclavicular lymph nodes, found on biopsy to be malignant. (Hematology/Oncology)

Initial inpatient consultation for a 43-year-old female for evaluation of sudden painful visual loss, optic neuritis and episodic paresthesia. (Ophthalmology)

Initial inpatient consultation for evaluation of a 71-year-old male with hyponatremia (serum sodium 114)who was admitted to the hospital with pneumonia. (Nephrology)

Initial inpatient consultation for a 72-year-old male with emergency admission for possible bowel obstruction. (Internal Medicine/General Surgery)

Initial inpatient consultation for a 35-year-old female with fever, swollen joints, and rash of one-week duration. (Rheumatology)

**99255** Initial inpatient consultation for a 76-year-old female with massive, life-threatening gastrointestinal hemorrhage and chest pain. (Gastroenterology)

Initial inpatient consultation for a 75-year-old female, admitted to intensive care with acute respiratory distress syndrome, who is hypersensitive, has a moderate metabolic acidosis, and a rising serum creatinine. (Nephrology)

Initial hospital consultation for patient with a history of complicated low back pain and neck problems with previous multiple failed back surgeries. (Orthopaedic Surgery/Neurosurgery)

Initial hospital consultation for a 66-year-old female, two days post-abdominal aneurysm repair, with oliguria and hypertension of one-day duration. (Nephrology/Internal Medicine)

Initial hospital consultation for a patient with shotgun wound to face with massive facial trauma and airway obstruction. (Oral & Maxillofacial Surgery)

Initial hospital consultation for patient with severe pancreatitis complicated by respiratory insufficiency, acute renal failure, and abscess formation. (General Surgery/Colon & Rectal Surgery)

Initial hospital consultation for a 35-year-old multiple-trauma male patient with complex pelvic fractures to evaluate and formulate management plan. (Orthopaedic Surgery)

Initial inpatient consultation for adolescent patient with fractured femur and pelvis who pulled out IVs and disconnected traction in attempt to elope from hospital. (Psychiatry)

Initial hospital consultation for a 16-year-old primigravida at 32 weeks gestation requested by a family practitioner for evaluation of severe hypertension, thrombocytopenia, and headache. (Obstetrics & Gynecology)

Initial hospital consultation for a 58-year-old insulin-dependent diabetic with multiple antibiotic allergies, now with multiple fascial plane abscesses and airway obstruction. (Oral & Maxillofacial Surgery)

Initial inpatient consultation for a 55-year-old male with known cirrhosis and ascites, now with jaundice, encephalopathy, and massive hematemesis. (Gastroenterology)

Initial hospital consultation for a 25-year-old male, seen in emergency room with severe, closed head injury. (Neurosurgery)

Initial hospital consultation for a 2-day-old male with single ventricle physiology and subaortic obstruction. Family counseling following evaluation for multiple, staged surgical procedures. (Thoracic Surgery)

Initial hospital consultation for a 45-year-old male admitted with subarachnoid hemorrhage and intracranial aneurysm on angiogram. (Neurosurgery)

Initial inpatient consultation for myxedematous patient who is hypoventilating and obtunded. (Endocrinology)

Initial hospital consultation for a 45-year-old patient with widely metastatic lung carcinoma, intractable back pain, and a history that includes substance dependence, NSAID allergy, and two prior laminectomies with fusion for low back pain. (Pain Medicine)

Initial hospital consultation for evaluation of treatment options in a 50-year-old patient with cirrhosis, known peptic ulcer disease, hypotension, encephalopathy, and massive acute upper gastrointestinal bleeding which cannot be localized by endoscopy. (Interventional Radiology)

Initial inpatient consultation in the ICU for a 70-year-old male who experienced a cardiac arrest during surgery and was resuscitated. (Cardiology)

Initial inpatient consultation for a patient with severe pancreatitis complicated by respiratory insufficiency, acute renal failure and abscess formation. (Gastroenterology)

Initial inpatient consultation for a 70-year-old cirrhotic male admitted with ascites, jaundice, encephalopathy, and massive hematemesis. (Gastroenterology)

Initial inpatient consultation in the ICU for a 51-year-old patient who is on a ventilator and has a fever two weeks after a renal transplantation. (Infectious Disease)

Initial inpatient consultation for evaluation and formulation of plan for management of multiple trauma patient with complex pelvic fracture, 35-year-old male. (General Surgery/Orthopaedic Surgery)

Initial inpatient consultation for a 50-year-old male with a history of previous myocardial infarction, now with acute pulmonary edema and hypotension. (Cardiology)

Initial inpatient consultation for 45-year-old male with recent, acute subarachnoid hemorrhage, hesitant speech, mildly confused, drowsy. High risk group for HIV+ status. (Neurosurgery)

Initial inpatient consultation for 36-year-old female referred by her internist to evaluate a patient being followed for abdominal pain and fever. The patient has developed diffuse abdominal pain, guarding, rigidity and increased fever. (Obstetrics & Gynecology)

# Follow-up Inpatient Consultations

## Established Patient

**99261** Follow-up consultation for a 78-year-old female nursing home resident for evaluation of medical management of pruritus ani. (Colon & Rectal Surgery/ Geriatrics/General Surgery)

Follow-up hospital consultation on first post-op day for a 64-year-old male who has undergone uneventful CABG. (Anesthesiology)

Follow-up inpatient consultation for a 67-year-old female admitted several days ago for bleeding ulcer; now stable. (Gastroenterology)

Follow-up hospital consultation for a 35-year-old female with history of mitral valve prolapse. (Cardiology)

Follow-up inpatient consultation to complete initial consultation for dental pain after review of radiographs. (Oral & Maxillofacial Surgery)

Follow-up inpatient consultation for evaluation of response to therapy for moniliasis. (Oral & Maxillofacial Surgery)

Follow-up inpatient consultation for a 22-year-old female with recurrent aphthous ulcers. (Oral & Maxillofacial Surgery)

Follow-up hospital consultation for a 37-year-old female to complete review of previously unavailable studies. (Therapeutic Radiology & Oncology)

Follow-up consultation for a highly functional 75-year-old female with urinary incontinence to review preliminary results of diagnostic evaluation. (Geriatrics)

Follow-up inpatient consultation for a 1-week-old premature female with patent ductus arteriosus. The murmur has disappeared. (Cardiology)

Follow-up hospital consultation to review the results of an audiogram. (Otolaryngology, Head & Neck Surgery)

Follow-up inpatient consultation with 35-year-old female with pulmonary embolism post-op cesarean section, now stable, for assessment of response to anticoagulation and recommended adjustment of heparin dose. (Pulmonary Medicine)

Follow-up inpatient consultation for a 74-year-old male whose postoperative facial paralysis after a cholecystectomy is now resolving. (Neurology)

Follow-up inpatient consultation with 67-year-old female, established patient, for review of diagnostic studies ordered at time of first contact. (Internal Medicine)

Follow-up inpatient consultation for 78-year-old female nursing home resident for evaluation of medical management of pruritis ani. (General Surgery/Colon & Rectal Surgery)

Follow-up inpatient consultation for a 36-year-old female two days after spontaneous passage of 3mm stone. (Urology)

Follow-up inpatient consultation for a 94-year-old male nursing home resident for re-evaluation of hemorrhoids following conservative therapy. (Colon & Rectal Surgery/General Surgery/Geriatrics)

Follow-up inpatient consultation for a 50-year-old male, asymptomatic with borderline ECG abnormality, needs preoperative opinion after a thallium exercise perfusion scan. (Cardiology)

**99262** Follow-up inpatient consultation for a 6-year-old female, established patient, with endocarditis and changing heart murmur. (Cardiology)

Follow-up inpatient consultation on a 2-year-old male, one day postoperative ventricular septal defect closure with signs of tachycardia. (Cardiology)

Follow-up inpatient consultation for a 63-year-old man, established patient, with moderately severe pulmonary insufficiency, 10 days postoperative coronary artery bypass for unstable angina. Patient has developed severe dyspnea, fever, and a new exudative right pleural effusion. (Cardiology)

Follow-up inpatient consultation for a 67-year-old woman with lung cancer and syndrome of inappropriate secretion of antidiuretic hormone (SIADH) who has had a seizure following intravenous saline. (Endocrinology)

Follow-up inpatient consultation for a 22-year-old female, established patient, with steroid-dependent systemic lupus erythematosus, arthritis, and glomerulonephritis. Patient is re-evaluated for loss of consciousness and chest pain. (Rheumatology)

Follow-up inpatient consultation for a 75-year-old diabetic with fever, chills, a gangrenous heel ulcer, rhonchi, and dyspnea who appears lethargic and tachypneic. (Endocrinology)

Follow-up inpatient consultation for a 30-year-old, established patient, with intractable neck and low back pain, who is excessively sedated after institution of methadone therapy. (Pain Medicine)

Follow-up inpatient consultation for a 65-year-old man with a history of hypertension and MI who is five days post uncomplicated GI procedure with an unremarkable postoperative recovery. He has just been resuscitated from a cardiopulmonary arrest. (Cardiology)

Follow-up inpatient consultation with 72-year-old female, established patient with bullous pemphigoid on combined oral therapy steroids and immunosuppressive to evaluate progress of cutaneous care orders and adjustment of oral/parenteral therapy dosages. (Dermatology)

Follow-up inpatient consultation for a 71-year-old male who has developed a maculopapular skin rash while on antibiotics recommended for an uncomplicated pneumonia. (Infectious Disease)

Follow-up inpatient consultation with 68-year-old, incapacitated male with spinal stenosis and failure to respond to bedrest, analgesics, and PT. (Neurosurgery)

Follow-up inpatient consultation with 51-year-old male for evaluation and determination of the etiology of postoperative hyponatremia following TURP. (Family Medicine)

Follow-up inpatient consultation for re-evaluation of a stroke patient, and development of plan for initial rehabilitation services. (Neurology)

Follow-up inpatient consultation with 45-year-old male, established patient for discussion of CT scan which demonstrates a cavernous hemangioma. (Ophthalmology)

Follow-up inpatient consultation for an asymptomatic 35-year-old Type I diabetic patient with hyperkalemic, hyperchloremia acidosis, to review lab results. (Nephrology)

Follow-up inpatient consultation for an elderly male with a perioperative myocardial infarction requiring adjustment of vasoactive medications. (Anesthesiology)

**99263** Follow-up hospital consultation of an AIDS patient admitted with a sore throat who now has enlarging neck mass. (Otolaryngology, Head & Neck Surgery)

Follow-up hospital consultation of a pansinusitis patient with sudden onset of proptosis. (Otolaryngology, Head & Neck Surgery)

Follow-up inpatient consultation for a 53-year-old man with known angina who develops crescendo angina post cholecystectomy. (Cardiology)

Follow-up inpatient consultation with 72-year-old male established patient admitted for management of alcohol withdrawal, now confused and febrile. (Addiction Medicine)

Follow-up inpatient consultation for an HIV+ patient with an increasing fever following 10 days of antibiotic therapy for pneumocystis carinii pneumonia. (Infectious Disease)

Follow-up inpatient consultation with 58-year-old diabetic female, with bacterial endocarditis, continuedfever after two weeks of intravenous antibiotic therapy, and new onset ventricular ectopia. (Cardiology)

Follow-up inpatient consultation for a 90-year-old female with urinary incontinence who has a complicated medical history requiring reassessment of multiple medical problems, recommendations for placement, further recommendation for management of incontinence and reevaluation of cognitive status because of competency issues. (Geriatrics/Psychiatry)

Follow-up inpatient consultation for 42-year-old male with persistent gastrointestinal bleeding, etiology undetermined, not responding to conservative therapy of transfusions. (General Surgery/Colon & Rectal Surgery)

Follow-up inpatient consultation for a 62-year-old female with steroid-dependent asthma, diabetes mellitus, thyrotoxicosis, abdominal pain and possible vasculitis. (Rheumatology)

Follow-up inpatient consultation for a 62-year-old male, status post-op acute small bowel obstruction; now with acute renal failure. (Family Medicine)

# Emergency Department Services

## New or Established Patient

**99281** Emergency department visit for a patient for removal of sutures from a well-healed, uncomplicated laceration. (Emergency Medicine)

Emergency department visit for a patient for tetanus toxoid immunization. (Emergency Medicine)

Emergency department visit for a patient with several uncomplicated insect bites. (Emergency Medicine)

**99282** Emergency department visit for a 20-year-old student who presents with a painful sunburn with blister formation on the back. (Emergency Medicine)

Emergency department visit for a child presenting with impetigo localized to the face. (Emergency Medicine)

Emergency department visit for a patient with a minor traumatic injury of an extremity with localized pain, swelling, and bruising. (Emergency Medicine)

Emergency department visit for an otherwise healthy patient whose chief complaint is a red, swollen cystic lesion on his/her back. (Emergency Medicine)

Emergency department visit for a patient presenting with a rash on both legs after exposure to poison ivy. (Emergency Medicine)

Emergency department visit for a young adult patient with infected sclera and purulent discharge from both eyes without pain, visual disturbance or history of foreign body in either eye. (Emergency Medicine)

**99283** Emergency department visit for a sexually active female complaining of vaginal discharge who is afebrile and denies experiencing abdominal or back pain. (Emergency Medicine)

Emergency department visit for a well-appearing 8-year-old who has a fever, diarrhea and abdominal cramps, is tolerating oral fluids and is not vomiting. (Emergency Medicine)

Emergency department visit for a patient with an inversion ankle injury, who is unable to bear weight on the injured foot and ankle. (Emergency Medicine)

Emergency department visit for a patient who has a complaint of acute pain associated with a suspected foreign body in the painful eye. (Emergency Medicine)

Emergency department visit for a healthy, young adult patient who sustained a blunt head injury with local swelling and bruising without subsequent confusion, loss of consciousness or memory deficit. (Emergency Medicine)

**99284** Emergency department visit for a 4-year-old who fell off a bike sustaining a head injury with brief loss of consciousness. (Emergency Medicine)

Emergency department visit for an elderly female who has fallen and is now complaining of pain in her right hip and is unable to walk. (Emergency Medicine)

Emergency department visit for a patient with flank pain and hematuria. (Emergency Medicine)

Emergency department visit for a female presenting with lower abdominal pain and a vaginal discharge. (Emergency Medicine)

**99285** Emergency department visit for a patient with a complicated overdose requiring aggressive management to prevent side effects from the ingested materials. (Emergency Medicine)

Emergency department visit for a patient with a new onset of rapid heart rate requiring IV drugs. (Emergency Medicine)

Emergency department visit for a patient exhibiting active, upper gastrointestinal bleeding. (Emergency Medicine)

Emergency department visit for a previously healthy young adult patient who is injured in an automobile accident and is brought to the emergency department immobilized and has symptoms compatible with intra-abdominal injuries or multiple extremity injuries. (Emergency Medicine)

Emergency department visit for a patient with an acute onset of chest pain compatible with symptoms of cardiac ischemia and/or pulmonary embolus. (Emergency Medicine)

Emergency department visit for a patient who presents with a sudden onset of "the worst headache of her life," and complains of a stiff neck, nausea, and inability to concentrate. (Emergency Medicine)

Emergency department visit for a patient with a new onset of a cerebral vascular accident. (Emergency Medicine)

Emergency department visit for acute febrile illness in an adult, associated with shortness of breath and an altered level of alertness. (Emergency Medicine)

# Critical Care Services

**99291** First hour of critical care of a 65-year-old man with septic shock following relief of ureteral obstruction caused by a stone.

First hour of critical care of a 15-year-old with acute respiratory failure from asthma.

First hour of critical care of a 45-year-old who sustained a liver laceration, cerebral hematoma, flailed chest, and pulmonary contusion after being struck by an automobile.

First hour of critical care of a 65-year-old woman who, following a hysterectomy, suffered a cardiac arrest associated with a pulmonary embolus.

First hour of critical care of a 6-month-old with hypovolemic shock secondary to diarrhea and dehydration.

First hour of critical care of a 3-year-old with respiratory failure secondary to pneumocystis carinii pneumonia.

# Comprehensive Nursing Facility Assessments

## New or Established Patient

**99301** Annual nursing facility history and physical and MDS/RAI evaluation for a two-year nursing facility resident who is an 84-year-old female with multiple chronic health problems, including: stable controlled hypertension, chronic constipation, osteoarthritis, and moderated stable dementia.

Nursing facility visit for an assessment of a resident with non-insulin dependent diabetes, stable angina, and chronic obstructive pulmonary disease (COPD) one year after previous MDS/RAI.

**99302** Nursing facility visit one year after previous MDS/RAI to assess an 80-year-old woman with Parkinson's disease, chronic hypertension, and degenerative arthritis. Visit reveals Stage II decubitus.

Nursing facility assessment of a 28-year-old diabetic, male resident with a new Stage IV pressure ulcer on his left lateral malleolus that is unresponsive to treatment, thus triggering the need for a new MDS/RAI and new medical plan of care.

Nursing facility assessment of an 88-year-old male resident with a permanent change in status following a new cerebral vascular accident (CVA) that has triggered the need for a new MDS/RAI and medical plan of care.

Nursing facility visit and assessment to take over the primary care of a 75-year-old diabetic, previously stable, who was on oral hypoglycemic agents, but who now requires initiation of insulin therapy, a new MDS/RAI, and medical plan of care.

Nursing facility visit and assessment for an 81-year-old female resident with dementia who under structured guidance and intensive nutritional support has regained significant levels of function in three activities of daily living and is now able to feed and dress herself and ambulate with appliance and who now thus requires a new MDS/RAI and medical plan of care.

**99303** Initial nursing facility assessment (MDS/RAI and medical plan of care) of a 72-year-old insulin dependent diabetic amputee with hearing and visual impairments and possible dementia seen in the office the day before and judged to require nursing facility care.

Sub-acute nursing facility assessment of a previously independently living 90-year-old male who suffered a recent cerebral vascular accident (CVA) and is transferred to the hospital sub-acute rehabilitation unit for further rehabilitation supportive services.

Initial nursing facility visit to evaluate a 72-year-old woman found confused and wandering, admitted by Adult Protective Services without a qualifying hospital stay or inpatient diagnostic work. The patient lives alone and has no relatives or significant others in the community.

Nursing facility assessment and creation of medical plan of care upon readmission to the nursing facility of an 82-year-old male who was previously discharged. The patient has just been discharged from the hospital where he had been treated for an acute gastric ulcer bleed associated with transient delirium. The patient returns to the nursing facility debilitated, protein depleted, and with a Stage III coccygeal decubitus.

# Subsequent Nursing Facility Care

## New or Established Patient

**99311** Scheduled follow-up visit for a known 70-year-old stable paraplegic with no status change noted during visit.

Scheduled monthly nursing home visit with a patient who has mild senile dementia, Alzheimers' type, with no change in status, stable hypertension, and who is ambulating with a walker one year past stroke.

Follow-up in skilled nursing facility with a 70-year-old patient following a 10-day treatment of a cellulitis of the foot.

**99312** Scheduled follow-up visit to a resident with controlled dementia, hypertension, and diabetes. During visit, patient seems to exhibit flu symptoms.

Scheduled nursing facility visit with an afebrile demented resident who also has a mild cough, requiring no change in the medical plan of care.

Subsequent visit in a skilled nursing facility with a patient who is six months post stroke and now has a fever and mild cough.

Scheduled nursing facility visit for an 84-year-old male with chronic renal insufficiency, on digitalis and diuretics, requiring adjustment of medications and revision of medical plan of care.

Nursing facility visit of a resident with multiple chronic health problems who is six months post stroke and now has a fever and mild cough, to evaluate for possible pneumonia. Requires the development of a new medical plan of care, but not a revised MDS/RAI.

**99313** Follow-up nursing facility visit to evaluate the reason for frequent falls by a 90-year-old ataxic resident, and to determine possible need for change in medications and medical care plan.

Re-admission of a 75-year-old man with stroke who was hospitalized with pneumonia for his illness and who returns to the nursing facility with no permanent change in status from his condition prior to hospitalization; no new MDS/RAI is required.

Nursing facility visit with a diabetic resident who has developed Stage II decubitus ulcers with cellulitis, requiring a revision in the medical plan of care.

Nursing facility visit to develop a new plan of care for an amputee with atherosclerosis obliterans who has refused to eat for three days and has developed decreased urinary output.

Nursing facility visit for a 78-year-old resident with chronic atrial fibrillation and a history of heart failure to evaluate an acute confusional state and to revise the medical plan of care.

Unscheduled nursing facility visit for evaluation of a patient with fever and obtundation who is determined not to require hospital admission or new MDS, but who does require workup and revision of medical plan of care.

# Prolonged Services

## Prolonged Physician Service With Direct (Face-to-Face) Patient Contact

### Office or Other Outpatient

**99354/ 99355** A 20-year-old female with history of asthma presents with acute bronchospasm and moderate respiratory distress. Initial evaluation shows respiratory rate 30, labored breathing and wheezing heard in all lung fields. Office treatment is initiated which includes intermittent bronchial dilation and subcutaneous epinephrine. Requires intermittent physician face-to-face time with patient over a period of two-three hours. (Family Medicine/Internal Medicine)

### Inpatient

**99356** A 34-year-old primigravida presents to hospital in early labor. Admission history and physical reveals severe preeclampsia. Physician supervises management of preeclampsia, IV magnesium initiation and maintenance, labor augmentation with pitocin, and close maternal-fetal monitoring. Physician face-to-face involvement includes 40 minutes of continuous bedside care until the patient is stable, then is intermittent over several hours until the delivery. (Family Medicine/Internal Medicine/Obstetrics & Gynecology)

## Prolonged Physician Service Without Direct Patient (Face-to-Face) Contact

**99358/ 99359** A 65-year-old new patient with multiple problems is seen and evaluated. After the visit, the physician requires extensive time to talk with the patient's daughter, to review complex, detailed medical records transferred from previous physicians and to complete a comprehensive treatment plan. This plan also requires the physician to personally initiate and coordinate the care plan with a local home health agency and a dietician. (Family Medicine/Internal Medicine)

# Physician Standby Services

**99360** A 24-year-old patient is admitted to OB unit attempting VBAC. Fetal monitoring shows increasing fetal distress. Patient's blood pressure is rising and labor progressing slowly. A primary care physician is requested by the OB/GYN to standby in the unit for possible cesarean delivery and neonatal resuscitation. (Family Medicine/Internal Medicine)

# Care Plan Oversight Services

**99375** First month of care plan oversight for terminal care of a 58-year-old woman with advanced intraabdominal ovarian cancer. Care plan includes home oxygen, diuretics IV for edema and ascites control and pain control management involving IV morphine infusion when progressive ileus occurred. Physician phone contacts with nurse, family, and MSW. Discussion with MSW concerning plans to withdraw supportive measures per patient wishes. Documentation includes review and modification of care plan and certifications from nursing, MSW, pharmacy, and DME. (Family Medicine/Internal Medicine)

# Appendix E

## Summary of CPT Add-on Codes

This listing is a summary of CPT add-on codes for *CPT 2000*. The codes listed below are identified in *CPT 2000* with a ✚ symbol.

11001
11101
11201
11732
11922
13102
13122
13133
13153
15001
15101
15121
15201
15221
15241
15261
15351
15401
15787
17003
19001
19126
19291
22103
22116
22216
22226
22328
22585
22614
22632
26125
26861
26863
27358
27692
32501
33530
33572
33924
33961
35390
35400
35500
35681
35682
35683
35700
36218
36248
37206
37208
37250
37251
38102
38746
38747
43635
44015
44121
44139
44955
47001
47550
48400
49568
49905
56606
58611
59525
60512
61609
61610
61611
61612
61795
63035
63048
63057
63066
63076
63078
63082
63086
63088
63091
63308
64472
64476
64480
64484
64623
64627
64727
64778
64783
64787
64832
64837
64859
64872
64874
64876
64901
64902
67320
67331
67332
67334
67335
67340
69990
75774
74301
75946
75964
75968
75993
75996
76125
78020
78478
78480
78496
87163
88141
88155
88311
88312
88313
88314
90472
90781
92547
92978
92979
92981
92984
92996
92998
93320
93321
93325
93571
93572
93623
95920
95962
95973
95975
96412
96423
96570
96571
97546
99100
99116
99135
99140
99292
99354
99355
99356
99357
99358
99359

# Appendix F

## Summary of CPT Codes Exempt from Modifier '-51'

This listing is a summary of CPT codes that are exempt from the use of modifier '-51' but have NOT been designated as CPT add-on procedures/services. The codes listed below are identified in *CPT 2000* with a ⊘ symbol.

**17004**
**17304**
**17305**
**17306**
**17307**
**17310**
**20660**
**20690**
**20692**
**20900**
**20902**
**20910**
**20912**
**20920**
**20922**
**20924**
**20926**
**20930**
**20931**
**20936**
**20937**
**20938**
**20974**
**20975**
**22840**
**22841**
**22842**
**22843**
**22844**
**22845**
**22846**
**22847**
**22848**
**22851**
**31500**
**32000**
**32002**
**32020**
**33517**
**33518**
**33519**
**33521**
**33522**
**33523**
**36488**
**36489**
**36490**
**36491**
**36620**
**36660**
**37250**
**38792**
**44500**
**61107**
**61210**
**62284**
**90281**
**90283**
**90287**
**90288**
**90291**
**90296**
**90371**
**90375**
**90376**
**90378**
**90379**
**90384**
**90385**
**90386**
**90389**
**90393**
**90396**
**90399**
**90476**
**90477**
**90581**
**90585**
**90586**
**90632**
**90633**
**90634**
**90636**
**90645**
**90646**
**90647**
**90648**
**90657**
**90658**
**90659**
**90660**
**90665**
**90669**
**90675**
**90676**
**90680**
**90690**
**90691**
**90692**
**90693**
**90700**
**90701**
**90702**
**90703**
**90704**
**90705**
**90706**
**90707**
**90708**
**90709**
**90710**
**90712**
**90713**
**90716**
**90717**
**90718**
**90719**
**90720**
**90721**
**90725**
**90727**
**90732**
**90733**
**90735**
**90744**
**90746**
**90747**
**90748**
**90749**
**93501**
**93503**
**93505**
**93508**
**93510**

93511
93514
93524
93526
93527
93528
93529
93530
93531
93532
93533
93539
93540
93541
93542
93543
93544
93545
93555
93556
93600
93602
93603
93607
93609
93610
93612
93615
93616
93618
93619
93620
93621
93622
93624
93631
93640
93641
93642
93650
93651
93652
93660
95900
95903
95904
99141
99142

# Index

## Instructions for the Use of the CPT Index

### Main Terms

The index is organized by main terms. Each main term can stand alone, or be followed by up to three modifying terms. There are four primary classes of main entries:

1. Procedure or service.
   For example: Endoscopy; Anastomosis; Splint
2. Organ or other anatomic site.
   For example: Tibia; Colon; Salivary Gland
3. Condition.
   For example: Abscess; Entropion; Tetralogy of Fallot
4. Synonyms, Eponyms and Abbreviations.
   For example: EEG; Bricker Operation; Clagett Procedure

### Modifying Terms

A main term may be followed by a series of up to three indented terms that modify the main term. When modifying terms appear, one should review the list, as these subterms do have an effect on the selection of the appropriate code for the procedure.

### Code Ranges

Whenever more than one code applies to a given index entry, a code range is listed. If two sequential codes or several non-sequential codes apply, they will be separated by a comma. For example:

Debridement
  Mastoid Cavity . . . . . . . . .69220, 69222

If more than two sequential codes apply, they will be separated by a hyphen. For example:

Antibody
  Antitrypsin, Alpha-1 . . . . . .86064-86067

### Conventions

As a space saving convention, certain words infer some meaning. This convention is primarily used when a procedure or service is listed as a subterm. For example:

Knee
  Incision (of)

In this example, the word in parentheses (of) does not appear in the index, but it is inferred. As another example:

Pancreas
  Anesthesia (for procedures on)

In this example, as there is no such entity as pancreas anesthesia, the words in parentheses are inferred. That is, anesthesia for procedures on the pancreas.

**The alphabetic index is NOT a substitute for the main text of CPT. Even if only one code appears, the user must refer to the main text to ensure that the code selection is accurate.**

# A

Elbow
Incision and Drainage . . . .23930-23931, 23935
Epididymis
Incision and Drainage . . . . . . . . . .54700
Excision
Olecranon Process . . . . . . . . . . . . .24138
Radius . . . . . . . . . . . . . . . . . . . . .24136
Ulna . . . . . . . . . . . . . . . . . . . . . . .24138
Eyelid
Incision and Drainage . . . . . . . . . .67700
Facial Bones
Excision . . . . . . . . . . . . . . . . . . . .21026
Finger . . . . . . . . . . . . . . . . . . . .26010-26011
Incision and Drainage . . . . . . . . . .26034
Foot
Incision . . . . . . . . . . . . . . . . . . . .28005
Gums
Incision and Drainage . . . . . . . . . .41800
Hand
Incision and Drainage . . . . . . . . . .26034
Hematoma
Incision and Drainage . . . . . . . . . .27603
Hip
Incision and Drainage . . . .26990-26992
Humeral Head . . . . . . . . . . . . . . . . . .23174
Humerus
Excision . . . . . . . . . . . . . . . . . . . .24134
Incision and Drainage . . . . . . . . . .23935
Kidney
Incision and Drainage . . . . . . . . . .50020
Open . . . . . . . . . . . . . . . . . . . . .50020
Percutaneous . . . . . . . . . . . . . . .50021
Leg, Lower
Incision and Drainage . . . . . . . . . .27603
Liver . . . . . . . . . . . . . . . . . . . . . . . . . .47010
Drainage
Open . . . . . . . . . . . . . . . . . . . . . .47010
Injection . . . . . . . . . . . . . . . . . . . .47015
Repair . . . . . . . . . . . . . . . . . . . . .47300
Localization
Nuclear Medicine . . . . . . .78805-78807
Lung
Percutaneous Drainage . . .32200-32201
Lymphocele Drainage . . . . . . . . . . . .49062
Lymph Node
Incision and Drainage . . . .38300-38305
Mandible
Excision . . . . . . . . . . . . . . . . . . . .21025
Mouth
Incision and Drainage . . . .40800-40801, 41005-41009, 41015-41018
Nasal Septum
Incision and Drainage . . . . . . . . . .30020
Neck
Incision and Drainage . . . .21501-21502
Ovarian
Incision and Drainage . . . .58820-58822
Abdominal Approach . . . . . . . . .58822
Vaginal Approach . . . . . . . . . . . .58820
Ovary
Drainage
Percutaneous . . . . . . . . . . . . . . .58823
Palate
Incision and Drainage . . . . . . . . . .42000
Paraurethral Gland
Incision and Drainage . . . . . . . . . .53060
Parotid Gland Drainage . . . . . .42300, 42305
Pelvic
Drainage
Percutaneous . . . . . . . . . . . . . . .58823
Pelvis
Incision and Drainage . . . .26990-26992, 45000
Pericolic
Drainage
Percutaneous . . . . . . . . . . . . . . .58823
Perineum
Incision and Drainage . . . . . . . . . .56405
Perirenal or Renal
Drainage . . . . . . . . . . . . . . .50020-50021
Percutaneous . . . . . . . . . . . . . . .50021
Peritoneum
Incision and Drainage
Open . . . . . . . . . . . . . . . . . . . . . .49020
Percutaneous . . . . . . . . . . . . . . .49021
Prostate
Incision and Drainage . . . .55720-55725
Transurethral Drainage . . . . . . . . .52700
Radius
Incision, Deep . . . . . . . . . . . . . . . .25035
Rectum
Incision and Drainage . . .45005, 45020, 46040, 46060
Retroperitoneal . . . . . . . . . . . .49060-49061
Drainage
Open . . . . . . . . . . . . . . . . . . . . . .49060
Percutaneous . . . . . . . . . . . . . . .49061
Salivary Gland
Drainage . . . . . . . . . . . . . . .42300-42320
Scapula
Sequestrectomy . . . . . . . . . . . . . .23172
Scrotum
Incision and Drainage . . . .54700, 55100
Shoulder
Drainage . . . . . . . . . . . . . . . . . . . .23030
Skene's Gland
Incision and Drainage . . . . . . . . . .53060
Skin
Incision and Drainage . . . .10060-10061
Puncture Aspiration . . . . . . . . . . . .10160
Soft Tissue
Incision . . . . . . . . . . . . . . . . .20000-20005
Subdiaphragmatic . . . . . . . . . .49040-49041
Sublingual Gland
Drainage . . . . . . . . . . . . . .42310, 42320
Submaxillary Gland
Drainage . . . . . . . . . . . . . .42310, 42320
Subphrenic . . . . . . . . . . . . . . . .49040-49041
Testis
Incision and Drainage . . . . . . . . . .54700
Thoracostomy . . . . . . . . . . . . . . . . . .32020
Thorax
Incision and Drainage . . . .21501-21502
Throat
Incision and Drainage . . . .42700-42725
Tongue
Incision and Drainage . . . .41000-41006
Tonsil
Incision and Drainage . . . . . . . . . .42700
Ulna
Incision, Deep . . . . . . . . . . . . . . . .25035
Urethra
Incision and Drainage . . . . . . . . . .53040
Uvula
Incision and Drainage . . . . . . . . . .42000
Vagina
Incision and Drainage . . . . . . . . . .57010
Vulva
Incision and Drainage . . . . . . . . . .56405
Wrist
Excision . . . . . . . . . . . . . . . . . . . .25145
Incision and Drainage . . . .25028, 25035
X-Ray . . . . . . . . . . . . . . . . . . . . . . . . .76080

**Abscess, Nasal**
*See* Nose, Abscess

**Abscess, Parotid Gland**
*See* Parotid Gland, Abscess

**Absorptiometry**
Dual Energy
Bone . . . . . . . . . . . . . . . . . . . . . .76075
Appendicular . . . . . . . . . . . . . . .76076
Axial Skeleton . . . . . . . . . . . . . .76075
Dual Photon
Bone . . . . . . . . . . . . . . . . . . . . . .78351
Radiographic
Photodensity . . . . . . . . . . . . . . . .76078
Single Photon
Bone . . . . . . . . . . . . . . . . . . . . . .78350

**Absorption Spectrophotometry, Atomic**
*See* Atomic Absorption Spectroscopy

**Accessory, Toes**
*See* Polydactyly, Toes

**Accessory Nerve, Spinal**
*See* Nerves, Spinal Accessory

**ACE**
*See* Angiotensin Converting Enzyme

**Acetabuloplasty** . . . . . . . .27120-27122

**Acetabulum**
Fracture
Closed Treatment . . . . . . .27220, 27222
Open Treatment . . . . . . . . .27226-27228

**Adenosine Monophosphate (AMP)**
Blood . . . . . . . . . . . . . . . . . . . . . . . . .82030

**Adenovirus**
Antibody . . . . . . . . . . . . . . . . . . . . . . .86603
Antigen Detection
Direct Fluorescence . . . . . . . . . . . .87260
Enzyme Immunoassay . . . . . . . . . .87301

**Adenovirus Vaccine**

**Adenylic Acid**
*See* Adenosine Monophosphate (AMP)

**ADH**
*See* Antidiuretic Hormone

**Adhesions**
Epidural . . . . . . . . . . . . . . . . . . . . . . . .62263
Eye
Incision
Anterior Segment . . . . . . . . . . .65860, 65865, 65870
Corneovitreal . . . . . . . . . . . . . . . . .65880
Posterior Segment . . . . . . . . . . . . .65875
Intermarginal
Construction . . . . . . . . . . . . . . . . .67880
Transposition of Tarsal Plate . . .67882
Intestinal
Enterolysis . . . . . . . . . . . . . . . . . . .44005
Laparoscopic . . . . . . . . . . . . . . .44200
Intrauterine
Lysis . . . . . . . . . . . . . . . . . . . . . . . .58559
Labial
Lysis . . . . . . . . . . . . . . . . . . . . . . . .56441
Lungs
Lysis . . . . . . . . . . . . . . . . . . . . . . . .32124
Pelvic
Lysis . . . . . . . . . . .58660, 58662, 58740
Preputial
Lysis . . . . . . . . . . . . . . . . . . . . . . . .54450

**Adipectomy**
*See* Lipectomy

**ADL**
*See* Activities of Daily Living

**Administration**
Immunization
One Vaccine/Toxoid . . . . . . . . . . . .90471
Each Additional Vaccine/Toxoid . .90472

**ADP**
*See* Adenosine Diphosphate

**ADP Phosphocreatine Phosphotransferase**
*See* CPK

**Adrenalectomy** . . . . . . . . . . . . . . .60540
Anesthesia . . . . . . . . . . . . . . . . . . . .00866

**Adrenalin**
*See* Catecholamines
Blood . . . . . . . . . . . . . . . . . . . . . . . . .82383
Urine . . . . . . . . . . . . . . . . . . . . . . . . .82384

**Adrenaline-Noradrenaline**
Testing . . . . . . . . . . . . . . . . . . .82382-82384

**Adrenal Cortex Hormone**
*See* Corticosteroids

**Adrenal Gland**
Biopsy . . . . . . . . . . . . . . . . . . . .60540-60545
Excision
Laparoscopy . . . . . . . . . . . . . . . . .60650
Retroperitoneal Tumor . . . . . . . . .60545
Exploration . . . . . . . . . . . . . . . .60540-60545
Nuclear Medicine
Imaging . . . . . . . . . . . . . . . . . . . . .78075

**Adrenal Medulla**
*See* Medulla

**Adrenocorticotropic Hormone (ACTH)** . . . . . . . . . . . . . . . . .80400-80406, 80412, 80418, 82024
Blood or Urine . . . . . . . . . . . . . . . . . . .82024
Stimulation Panel . . . . . . . . . . .80400-80406

**Adrenogenital Syndrome** . . . . . . . . . . . . . .56805, 57335

**Adult T Cell Leukemia Lymphoma Virus I**
*See* HTLV I

**Advanced Life Support**
*See* Emergency Department Services
Physician Direction . . . . . . . . . . . . . . .99288

**Advancement**
Tendon
Foot . . . . . . . . . . . . . . . . . . . . . . . .28238

**Advancement Flap**
*See* Skin, Adjacent Tissue Transfer

**Aerosol Inhalation**
*See* Pulmonology, Therapeutic
Pentamidine . . . . . . . . . . . . . . . . . . . .94642

**AFB**
*See* Acid Fast Bacilli (AFB)

**Afferent Nerve**
*See* Sensory Nerve

**AFP**
*See* Alpha-Fetoprotein

**After Hours Medical Services** . . . . . . . . . . . . . . . .99050-99054

**Agents, Anticoagulant**
*See* Clotting Inhibitors

**Agglutinin**
Cold . . . . . . . . . . . . . . . . . . . . .86156-86157
Febrile . . . . . . . . . . . . . . . . . . . . . . . . .86000

**Aggregation**
Platelet . . . . . . . . . . . . . . . . . . . . . . . .85576

**AHG**
*See* Clotting Factor

**AICD (Pacing Cardioverter-Defibrillator)**
*See* Defibrillator, Heart; Pacemaker, Heart

**Aid, Hearing**
*See* Hearing Aid

**AIDS Antibodies**
*See* Antibody, HIV

**AIDS Virus**
*See* HIV-1

**Akin Operation**
*See* Bunion Repair

**ALA**
*See* Aminolevulinic Acid (ALA)

**Alanine 2 Oxoglutarate Aminotransferase**
*See* Transaminase, Glutamic Pyruvic

**Alanine Amino (ALT)** . . . . . . . . . .84460

**Alanine Transaminase**
*See* Transaminase, Glutamic Pyruvic

**Albarran Test**
*See* Water Load Test

**Albumin**
Serum . . . . . . . . . . . . . . . . . . . . . . . . .82040
Urine . . . . . . . . . . . . . . . . . . . . . . . . . .82042

**Alcohol**
Breath . . . . . . . . . . . . . . . . . . . . . . . . .82075
Ethyl
Blood . . . . . . . . . . . . . . . . . . . . . . .82055
Urine . . . . . . . . . . . . . . . . . . . . . . .82055
Ethylene Glycol . . . . . . . . . . . . . . . . . .82693

**Alcohol, Isopropyl**
*See* Isopropyl Alcohol

**Alcohol, Methyl**
*See* Methanol

**Alcohol Dehydrogenase**
*See* Antidiuretic Hormone

**Aldolase**
Blood . . . . . . . . . . . . . . . . . . . . . . . . . .82085

**Aldosterone**
Blood . . . . . . . . . . . . . . . . . . . . . . . . . .82088
Suppression Evaluation . . . . . . . . . . .80408
Urine . . . . . . . . . . . . . . . . . . . . . . . . . .82088

**Alimentary Canal**
*See* Gastrointestinal Tract

**Alkaline Phosphatase** . . .84075-84080
Leukocyte . . . . . . . . . . . . . . . . . . . . . .85540
WBC . . . . . . . . . . . . . . . . . . . . . . . . . .85540

**Alkaloids**
*See* Specific Drug
Urine . . . . . . . . . . . . . . . . . . . . . . . . . .82101

**Allergen Immunotherapy**
Allergen
Prescription/Supply/Injection . . . 95120-95125
with Extract Supply . . . 95144
Injection . . . 95115, 95117
Antigens . . . 95144
IgE . . . 86003-86005
Insect Venom
Prescription/Supply . . . 95145-95149
Prescription/Supply/Injection . . . 95130-95134
Prescription/Supply . . . 95165
Insect, Whole Body . . . 95170
Rapid Desensitization . . . 95180

**Allergy Services/Procedures**
*See* Office and/or Other Outpatient Services; Allergen and Immunotherapy
Education and Counseling . . . 99201-99215
Unlisted Services and Procedures . . . 95199

**Allergy Tests**
Challenge Test
Bronchial . . . 95070-95071
Ingestion . . . 95075
Eye Allergy . . . 95060
Food Allergy . . . 95075
Intradermal
Allergen Extract . . . 95024, 95028
Biologicals . . . 95015
Drugs . . . 95015
Venoms . . . 95015
Nasal Mucous Membrane Test . . . 95065
Nose Allergy . . . 95065
Patch
Application Tests . . . 95044
Photo Patch . . . 95052
Photosensitivity . . . 95056
Provocative Testing . . . 95078
Skin Tests
Allergen Extract . . . 95004
Biologicals . . . 95010
Drugs . . . 95010
End Point Titration . . . 95027
Venoms . . . 95010

**Allogeneic Transplantation**
*See* Homograft

**Allograft**
Bone
Structural . . . 20931
Skin . . . 15350, 15351
Spine Surgery
Morselized . . . 20930
Structural . . . 20931
Lung Transplant . . . 32850

**Alloplastic Dressing**
Burns . . . 15000, 15001

**Allotransplantation**
Renal . . . 50360-50365
Removal . . . 50370

**Almen Test**
*See* Blood, Feces

**Alpha-1 Antitrypsin** . . . 82103-82104

**Alpha-2 Antiplasmin** . . . 85410

**Alpha-Fetoprotein**
Amniotic Fluid . . . 82106
Serum . . . 82105

**Alphatocopherol** . . . 84446

**ALT**
*See* Transaminase, Glutamic Pyruvic

**Altemeier Procedure**
*See* Anus; Rectum, Prolapse, Excision

**Aluminum**
Blood . . . 82108

**Alveola**
Fracture
Closed Treatment . . . 21421
Open Treatment . . . 21422-21423

**Alveolar Cleft**
Ungrafted Bilateral . . . 21147
Ungrafted Unilateral . . . 21146

**Alveolar Nerve**
Avulsion . . . 64738
Incision . . . 64738
Transection . . . 64738

**Alveolar Ridge**
Fracture
Closed Treatment . . . 21440
Open Treatment . . . 21445

**Alveolectomy** . . . 41830

**Alveoloplasty** . . . 41874

**Alveolus**
Excision . . . 41830

**Amide, Procaine**
*See* Procainamide

**Amikacin**
Assay . . . 80150

**Aminolevulinic Acid (ALA)**
Blood or Urine . . . 82135

**Aminotransferase**
*See* Transaminase

**Aminotransferase, Alanine**
*See* Transaminase, Glutamic Pyruvic

**Aminotransferase, Aspartate**
*See* Transaminase, Glutamic Oxaloacetic

**Amine**
Vaginal Fluid . . . 82120

**Amino Acids** . . . 82127-82131, 82135, 82136, 82139

**Amitriptyline**
Assay . . . 80152

**Ammonia**
Blood . . . 82140
Urine . . . 82140

**Amniocenteses**
*See* Amniocentesis

**Amniocentesis** . . . 59000
*See* Chromosome Analysis
Induced Abortion . . . 59850
with Dilation and Curettage . . . 59851
with Dilation and Evacuation . . . 59851
with Hysterectomy . . . 59852

**Amnion**
Amniocentesis . . . 59000

**Amniotic Fluid**
Alpha-Fetoprotein . . . 82106
Scan . . . 82143
Testing . . . 83661

**Amniotic Membrane**
*See* Amnion

**Amobarbital** . . . 82205

**AMP**
*See* Adenosine Monophosphate (AMP)

**AMP, Cyclic**
*See* Cyclic AMP

**Amphetamine**
Blood or Urine . . . 82145

**Amputation**
*See* Radical Resection; Replantation
Ankle . . . 27888
Arm, Lower . . . 25900, 25905, 25915
Revision . . . 25907, 25909
Arm, Upper . . . 24900-24920
and Shoulder . . . 23900-23921
Revision . . . 24925-24930
with Implant . . . 24931-24935
Cervix
Total . . . 57530
Ear
Partial . . . 69110
Total . . . 69120
Finger . . . 26910, 26951-26952
Foot . . . 28800-28805
Hand at Metacarpal . . . 25927
at Wrist . . . 25920
Revision . . . 25922
Revision . . . 25924, 25929, 25931
Interpelviabdominal . . . 27290
Interthoracoscapular . . . 23900
Leg, Lower . . . 27598, 27880-27882
Revision . . . 27884-27886
Leg, Upper . . . 27590-27592
at Hip . . . 27290-27295
Revision . . . 27594, 27596
Metacarpal . . . 26910
Metatarsal . . . 28810

Bursa
- Incision and Drainage .......... 27604

Disarticulation .......... 27889
Dislocation
- Closed Treatment .......... 27840-27842
- Open Treatment .......... 27846-27848

Exploration .......... 27610, 27620
Fracture
- Lateral .......... 27786-27788, 27792, 27808-27810, 27814
- Medial .......... 27760-27762, 27766, 27808-27810, 27814
- Trimalleolar .......... 27816-27818, 27822-27823

Fusion .......... 27870
Hematoma
- Incision and Drainage .......... 27603

Incision .......... 27607
Injection
- Radial .......... 27648

Lesion
- Excision .......... 27630

Magnetic Resonance Imaging (MRI) .......... 73721
Manipulation .......... 27860
Removal
- Forcign Body .......... 27610, 27620
- Implant .......... 27704
- Loose Body .......... 27620

Repair
- Achilles Tendon .......... 27650-27654
- Ligament .......... 27695-27698
- Tendon .......... 27612, 27680-27681, 27685-27687

Strapping .......... 29540
Synovium
- Excision .......... 27625-27626

Tenotomy .......... 27605-27606
Tumor
- Excision .......... 27615, 27618-27619

Unlisted Services and Procedures .......... 27899
X-Ray .......... 73600-73610
- with Contrast .......... 73615

**Ankylosis (Surgical)**
*See* Arthrodesis

**Anogenital Region**
*See* Perineum

**Anoplasty**
Stricture .......... 46700, 46705

**Anorectal Myectomy**
*See* Myomectomy, Anorectal

**Anorectal Procedure**
Biofeedback .......... 90911

**Anorectovaginoplasty** .......... 46744, 46746

**Anoscopy**
Ablation
- Polyp .......... 46615
- Tumor .......... 46615

Biopsy .......... 46606
Dilation .......... 46604
Exploration .......... 46600
Hemorrhage .......... 46614
Removal
- Foreign Body .......... 46608
- Polyp .......... 46610-46612
- Tumor .......... 46610-46612

**Antebrachium**
*See* Forearm

**Antecedent, Plasma Thromboplastin**
*See* Plasma Thromboplastin, Antecedent

**Antepartum Care**
Cesarean Delivery .......... 59510
- Previous .......... 59610, 59618

Vaginal Delivery .......... 59425-59426

**Anterior Ramus of Thoracic Nerve**
*See* Intercostal Nerve

**Anthrax Vaccine**
*See* Vaccines

**Anthrogon**
*See* Follicle Stimulating Hormone (FSH)

**Anti-Human Globulin Consumption Test**
*See* Coombs Test

**Anti-Phospholipid Antibody**
*See* Antibody, Phospholipid

**Antiactivator, Plasmin**
*See* Alpha-2 Antiplasmin

**Antibiotic Administration**
Injection .......... 90788

**Antibiotic Sensitivity** .......... 87181, 87184, 87188, 87192
Minimum Bactericidal Concentration .......... 87187
Minimum Inhibitory Concentration .......... 87186

**Antibodies, Thyroid-Stimulating**
*See* Immunoglobulin, Thyroid Stimulating

**Antibodies, Viral**
*See* Viral Antibodies

**Antibody**
*See* Antibody Identification; Microsomal Antibody
Actinomyces .......... 86602
Adenovirus .......... 86603
Antinuclear .......... 86038-86039
Antiphosphatidylserine (Phospholipid) .......... 86148
Antistreptolysin O .......... 86060-86063
Aspergillus .......... 86606
Bacterium .......... 86609
Blastomyces .......... 86612
Blood Crossmatch .......... 86920-86922
Bordetella .......... 86615
Borrelia .......... 86618, 86619
Brucella .......... 86622
Campylobacter .......... 86625
Candida .......... 86628
Cardiolipin .......... 86147
Chlamydia .......... 86631-86632
Coccidioides .......... 86635
Coxiella Burnetii .......... 86638
Cryptococcus .......... 86641
Cytomegalovirus .......... 86644-86645
Cytotoxic Screen .......... 86807-86808
Deoxyribonuclease .......... 86215
Deoxyribonucleic Acid (DNA) .......... 86225-86226
Diphtheria .......... 86648
Encephalitis .......... 86651-86654
Enterovirus .......... 86658
Epstein-Barr Virus .......... 86663-86665
Fluorescent .......... 86255-86256
Francisella Tularensis .......... 86668
Fungus .......... 86671
Giardia Lamblia .......... 86674
Growth Hormone .......... 86277
Helicobacter Pylori .......... 86677
Helminth .......... 86682
Hemophilus Influenza .......... 86684
Hepatitis
- Delta Agent .......... 86692

Hepatitis A .......... 86708-86709
Hepatitis B
- Core .......... 86704
- IgM .......... 86705
- Surface .......... 86706

Hepatitis Be .......... 86707
Hepatitis C .......... 86803-86804
Herpes Simplex .......... 86694-86695
Heterophile .......... 86308-86310
Histoplasma .......... 86698
HIV .......... 86689, 86701-86703
HIV-1 .......... 86701, 86703
HIV-2 .......... 86702, 86703
HTLV-I .......... 86687, 86689
HTLV-II .......... 86688
Influenza Virus .......... 86710
Insulin .......... 86337
Intrinsic Factor .......... 86340
Islet Cell .......... 86341
Legionella .......... 86713
Leishmania .......... 86717
Leptospira .......... 86720
Listeria Monocytogenes .......... 86723
Lyme Disease .......... 86617
Lymphocytic Choriomeningitis .......... 86727
Lymphogranuloma Venereum .......... 86729
Microsomal .......... 86376
Mucormycosis .......... 86732
Mumps .......... 86735
Mycoplasma .......... 86738
Neisseria Meningitidis .......... 86741
Nocardia .......... 86744
Nuclear Antigen .......... 86235
Other Virus .......... 86790

Hemorrhage
  Endoscopic Control ........... 46614
Hemorrhoids
  Clot Excision ................ 46320
  Destruction ............ 46934-46936
  Excision ............. 46250-46262
  Injection .................... 46500
  Ligation ......... 46221, 46945-46946
  Suture ............... 46945-46946
Imperforated
  Repair ............... 46715-46742
Incision
  Septum ..................... 46070
Lesion
  Destruction ........... 46900, 46910, 46916-46917, 46924
  Excision ............... 45108, 46922
Manometry ..................... 91122
Reconstruction ................. 46742
  Congenital Absence ...... 46730-46740
  Sphincter . . . 46750-46751, 46760-46762
  with Graft ................... 46753
  with Implant ................. 46762
Removal
  Foreign Body ................. 46608
  Seton ....................... 46030
  Suture ...................... 46754
  Wire ........................ 46754
Repair
  Anovaginal Fistula ....... 46715-46716
  Cloacal Anomaly .............. 46748
  Stricture ............... 46700, 46705
Sphincter
  Electromyography ....... 51784-51785
  Needle ...................... 51785
Unlisted Services and Procedures . . . 46999

**Aorta**
Abdominal
  Aneurysm .............. 35081-35103
  Thromboendarterectomy ........ 35331
Anastomosis
  to Pulmonary Artery .......... 33606
Angiogram
  Radiologic Injection ........... 93544
    *See* Cardiac Catheterization, Injection
Angioplasty ................... 35452
Aortography ......... 75600-75625, 75630
Balloon ...................... 33970
Catheterization
  Catheter ..................... 36200
  Intracatheter/Needle ......... 36160
Circulation Assist .............. 33970
Conduit to Heart ............... 33404
Excision
  Coarctation ............ 33840-33851
Insertion
  Graft ................. 33330-33335
  Intracatheter/Needle ......... 36160
Removal
  Balloon Assist Device .... 33968, 33971
Repair ........ 33320-33322, 33802-33803
  Coarctation ............ 33840-33851
  Hypoplastic or Interrupted Aortic Arch
    with Cardiopulmonary Bypass . . 33853
    without Cardiopulmonary
    Bypass .................... 33852
  Graft ................. 33860-33877
  Sinus of Valsalva ........ 33702-33720
Suspension .................... 33800
Suture ................... 33320-33322
Valve
  Incision ..................... 33415
  Repair ................ 33400-33403
    Left Ventricle .............. 33414
    Supravalvular Stenosis ....... 33417
  Replacement ........... 33405-33413
X-Ray with Contrast ......... 75600-75630

**Aorta-Pulmonary ART Transposition**
*See* Transposition, Great Arteries

**Aortic Sinus**
*See* Sinus of Valsalva

**Aortic Stenosis**
Repair ........................ 33415
  Supravalvular ................ 33417

**Aortic Valve**
*See* Heart, Aortic Valve

**Aortic Valve Replacement**
*See* Replacement, Aortic Valve

**Aortocoronary Bypass for Heart Revascularization**
*See* Artery, Coronary, Bypass

**Aortography** ...... 75600-75605, 75630, 93544
*See* Angiography
Serial ........................ 75625
with Iliofemoral Artery ........... 75630

**Aortoiliac**
Embolectomy ............. 34151-34201
Thrombectomy ............ 34151-34201

**Aortopexy** ................... 33800

**Aortoplasty**
Supravalvular Stenosis ........... 33417

**AP**
*See* Voiding Pressure Studies

**Apert-Gallais Syndrome**
*See* Adrenogenital Syndrome

**Aphasia Testing** ............. 96105
*See* Neurology, Diagnostic

**Apheresis**
Therapeutic .............. 36520-36521

**Apical-Aortic Conduit** ........ 33404

**Apicectomy**
with Mastoidectomy ............. 69605
  Petrous ..................... 69530

**Apoaminotransferase, Aspartate**
*See* Transaminase, Glutamic Oxaloacetic

**Apolipoprotein**
Blood or Urine ................. 82172

**Appendectomy** .......... 44950-44960
Laparoscopic ................... 44970

**Appendiceal Abscess**
*See* Abscess, Appendix

**Appendico-Vesicostomy**
Cutaneous ..................... 50845

**Appendix**
Abscess
  Incision and Drainage
    Open ...................... 44900
    Percutaneous ............... 44901
Excision ........... 44950, 44955, 44960

**Application**
Allergy Tests ................... 95044
Bone Fixation Device
  Multiplane ................... 20692
  Uniplane .................... 20690
Caliper ....................... 20660
Cranial Tongs .................. 20660
Fixation Device
  Shoulder .................... 23700
Halo
  Cranial ..................... 20661
    Thin Skull Osteology ......... 20664
  Femoral ..................... 20663
  Maxillofacial Fixation ......... 21100
  Pelvic ...................... 20662
Interdental Fixation Device ........ 21110
Neurostimulation ............... 64550
Radioelement ............. 77761-77778
  Surface ..................... 77789
  with Ultrasound .............. 76965
Stereotactic Frame .............. 20660

**Application of External Fixation Device**
*See* Fixation Device, Application, External

**APPT**
*See* Thromboplastin, Partial, Time

**APTT**
*See* Thromboplastin, Partial, Time

**Aquatic Therapy**
*See* Physical Medicine/Therapy/
Occupational Therapy ............ 97113

**Aqueous Shunt**
to Extraocular Reservoir .......... 66180
  Revision .................... 66185

Adrenal
  Angiography . . . . . . . . . . . .75731-75733
Anastomosis
  Cranial . . . . . . . . . . . . . . . . . . . . . .61711
Angioplasty . . . . . . . . . . . . . . .75962-75968
Aorta
  Angioplasty . . . . . . . . . . . . . . . . . .35452
  Atherectomy . . . . . . . . . . .35481, 35491
Aortoiliac
  Embolectomy . . . . . . . . . . .34151-34201
  Thrombectomy . . . . . . . . . .34151-34201
Aortoiliofemoral . . . . . . . . . . . . . . . . .35363
Arm
  Angiography . . . . . . . . . . . .75710-75716
Atherectomy
  Open . . . . . . . . . . . . . . . . . .35480-35485
  Percutaneous . . . . . . . . . . .35490-35495
Axillary
  Aneurysm . . . . . . . . . . . . . .35011-35013
  Angioplasty . . . . . . . . . . . . . . . . . .35458
  Bypass Graft . . . . .35516-35521, 35533, 35616-35623, 35650, 35654
  Embolectomy . . . . . . . . . . . . . . . . .34101
  Thrombectomy . . . . . . . . . . . . . . . .34101
  Thromboendarterectomy . . . . . . . .35321
Basilar
  Aneurysm . . . . . . . . . . . . . . . . . . .61702
Biopsy
  Transcatheter . . . . . . . . . . . . . . . .75970
Brachial
  Aneurysm . . . . . . . . . . . . . .35011-35013
  Angiography . . . . . . . . . . . . . . . . .75658
  Catheterization . . . . . . . . . . . . . . .36120
  Embolectomy . . . . . . . . . . . . . . . . .34101
  Exploration . . . . . . . . . . . . . . . . . .24495
  Thrombectomy . . . . . . . . . . . . . . . .34101
  Thromboendarterectomy . . . . . . . .35321
Brachiocephalic
  Angioplasty . . . . . . . . . . . . . . . . . .35458
  Atherectomy . . . . . . . . . . .35484, 35494
  Catheterization . . . . . . . . . .36215-36218
Bypass Graft
  with Composite Graft . . . . .35681-35683
Cannulization
  for Extra Corporeal Circulation . . .36823
  to Vein . . . . . . . . . . . . . . . .36810-36815
Carotid
  Aneurysm . .35001-35002, 61700-61705
    Vascular Malformation or Carotid-Cavernous Fistula . . . . . . . . . . . .61710
  Angiography . . . . . . . . . . . .75660-75680
  Bypass Graft . . . . .35501-35509, 35526, 35601-35606, 35626, 35642
  Catheterization . . . . . . . . . . . . . . .36100
  Decompression . . . . . . . . .61590-61591, 61595-61596
  Embolectomy . . . . . . . . . . . . . . . . .34001
  Exploration . . . . . . . . . . . . . . . . . .35701
  Ligation . . . .37600-37606, 61611-61612
  Thrombectomy . . . . . . . . . . . . . . . .34001
  Thromboendarterectomy . .35301, 35390
  Transection . . . . . . . . . . . . .61611-61612
Celiac
  Aneurysm . . . . . . . . . . . . . .35121-35122
  Bypass Graft . . . . . . . . . . .35531, 35631
  Embolectomy . . . . . . . . . . . . . . . . .34151
  Thrombectomy . . . . . . . . . . . . . . . .34151
  Thromboendarterectomy . . . . . . . .35341
Chest
  Ligation . . . . . . . . . . . . . . . . . . . . .37616
Coronary
  Angiography . . . . . . . . . . . . . . . . .93556
  Atherectomy . . . . . . . . . . . .92995-92996
  Bypass . . . . . . . . . . . . . . . .33517-33519
    Arterial . . . . . . . . . . . . . .33533-33536
  Bypass Venous Graft . . . . .33510-33516
  Graft . . . . . . . . . . . . . . . . . .33503-33505
  Ligation . . . . . . . . . . . . . . . . . . . . .33502
  Repair . . . . . . . . . . . . . . . . .33500-33506
Digital
  Sympathectomy . . . . . . . . . . . . . . .64820
Ethmoidal
  Ligation . . . . . . . . . . . . . . . . . . . . .30915
Extracranial
  Vascular Studies
    Non-Invasive, Physiologic . . . . .93875
Extra Corporeal Circulation
  for Regional Chemotherapy of Extremity . . . . . . . . . . . . . . . . . .36823
Extremities
  Vascular Studies . . . . . . . .93922-93923
Extremity
  Bypass graft revision . . . . .35879, 35881
  Catheterization . . . . . . . . . . . . . . .36140
  Ligation . . . . . . . . . . . . . . . . . . . . .37618
Femoral
  Aneurysm . . . . . . . . . . . . . .35141-35142
  Angioplasty . . . . . . . . . . . . . . . . . .35456
  Atherectomy . . . . . . . . . . .35483, 35493
  Bypass Graft . . . . .35521, 35533, 35546, 35551-35558, 35558, 35566, 35621, 35646, 35651-35661, 35666, 35700
  Bypass In-Situ . . . . . . . . . .35582-35585
  Embolectomy . . . . . . . . . . . . . . . . .34201
  Exploration . . . . . . . . . . . . . . . . . .35721
  Thrombectomy . . . . . . . . . . . . . . . .34201
  Thromboendarterectomy . .35371-35381
Great Vessel
  Repair . . . . . . . . . . . . . . . . .33770-33781
Head
  Angiography . . . . . . . . . . . . . . . . .75650
Hepatic
  Aneurysm . . . . . . . . . . . . . .35121-35122
Iliac
  Aneurysm . . . . . . . . . . . . . .35131-35132
  Angioplasty . . . . . . . . . . . . . . . . . .35454
  Atherectomy . . . . . . . . . . .35482, 35492
  Bypass Graft . . . . .35541, 35563, 35641, 35663
  Embolectomy . . . . . . . . . . .34151-34201
  Thrombectomy . . . . . . . . . .34151-34201
  Thromboendarterectomy . . . . . . .35351, 35361, 35363
Iliofemoral
  Bypass Graft . . . . .35548-35549, 35565, 35665
  Thromboendarterectomy . .35355, 35363
  X-Ray with Contrast . . . . . . . . . . .75630
Innominate
  Aneurysm . . . . . . . . . . . . . .35021-35022
  Embolectomy . . . . . . . . . . .34001-34101
  Thrombectomy . . . . . . . . . .34001-34101
  Thromboendarterectomy . . . . . . . .35311
Leg
  Angiography . . . . . . . . . . . .75710-75716
  Catheterization . . . . . . . . . .36245-36248
Mammary
  Angiography . . . . . . . . . . . . . . . . .75756
Maxillary
  Ligation . . . . . . . . . . . . . . . . . . . . .30920
Mesenteric
  Aneurysm . . . . . . . . . . . . . .35121-35122
  Bypass Graft . . . . . . . . . . .35531, 35631
  Embolectomy . . . . . . . . . . . . . . . . .34151
  Thrombectomy . . . . . . . . . . . . . . . .34151
  Thromboendarterectomy . . . . . . . .35341
Neck
  Angiography . . . . . . . . . . . . . . . . .75650
  Ligation . . . . . . . . . . . . . . . . . . . . .37615
Nose
  Incision . . . . . . . . . . . . . . . .30915-30920
Other Angiography . . . . . . . . . . . . . . .75774
Other Artery
  Aneurysm . . . . . . . . . . . . . .35161-35162
  Exploration . . . . . . . . . . . . . . . . . .35761
  Occlusive Disease . . . . . . . . . . . . .35161
Pelvic
  Angiography . . . . . . . . . . . . . . . . .75736
  Catheterization . . . . . . . . . .36245-36248
Peroneal
  Bypass Graft . . . . .35566, 35571, 35666, 35671
  Bypass In-Situ . . . . . . . . . .35585, 35587
  Embolectomy . . . . . . . . . . . . . . . . .34203
  Thrombectomy . . . . . . . . . . . . . . . .34203
  Thromboendarterectomy . . . . . . . .35381
Popliteal
  Aneurysm . . . . . . . . . . . . . .35151-35152
  Angioplasty . . . . . . . . . . . . . . . . . .35456
  Atherectomy . . . . . . . . . . .35483, 35493
  Bypass Graft . . . . .35551-35556, 35571, 35623, 35651, 35656, 35671, 35700
  Bypass In-Situ . . . .35582-35583, 35587
  Embolectomy . . . . . . . . . . . . . . . . .34203
  Exploration . . . . . . . . . . . . . . . . . .35741
  Thrombectomy . . . . . . . . . . . . . . . .34203
  Thromboendarterectomy . . . . . . . .35381
Pulmonary
  Anastomosis . . . . . . . . . . . . . . . . .33606
  Angiography . . . . . . . . . . . .75741-75746
  Repair . . . . . . . . . . . . . . . . . . . . . .33690

## Artery Catheterization, Pulmonary



## Arthrectomy



## Arthrocentesis



## Arthrodeses



## Arthrodesis



## Arthrography

External
  Abscess
    Incision and Drainage ........69020
  Biopsy ......................69105
  Lesion
    Excision .............69140, 69145, 69150-69155
  Reconstruction
    for Congenital Atresia ........69320
    for Stenosis ................69310
  Removal
    Cerumen ...................69210
    Ear Wax ...................69210
    Foreign Body ..........69200, 69205
Internal
  Decompression ...............69960

**Auditory Canal Atresia, External**
*See* Atresia, Congenital, Auditory Canal, External

**Auditory Evoked Otoacoustic Emission** ...............92587, 92588

**Auditory Evoked Potentials** ...92585
*See* Audiologic Function Tests

**Auditory Labyrinth**
*See* Ear, Inner

**Auditory Meatus**
X-Ray ..........................70134

**Auditory Tube**
*See* Eustachian Tube

**Augmentation**
Chin .....................21120, 21123
Malar ..........................21270
Mandibular Body
  with Bone Graft ...............21127
  with Prosthesis ...............21125
Osteoplasty
  Facial Bones ..................21208

**Augmentation Mammoplasty**
*See* Breast, Augmentation

**Augmented Histamine Test** ...91052
*See* Gastric Analysis Test

**Aural Rehabilitation** ..........92510

**Auricle (Heart)**
*See* Atria

**Auricular Fibrillation**
*See* Fibrillation, Atrial

**Auricular Prosthesis** ..........21086

**Australia Antigen**
*See* Hepatitis Antigen, B Surface

**Autograft**
Bone
  for Spine Surgery
    Local ......................20936
    Morselized ..................20937
    Structural ..................20938

**Autologous Blood Transfusion**
*See* Autotransfusion

**Autologous Transplantation**
*See* Autograft

**Automated Data**
Nuclear Medicine ..........78890-78891

**Autonomic Nervous System Function**
*See* Neurology, Diagnostic; Neurophysiologic Testing

**Autoprothrombin C**
*See* Thrombokinase

**Autoprothrombin I**
*See* Proconvertin

**Autoprothrombin II**
*See* Christmas Factor

**Autoprothrombin III**
*See* Stuart-Prower Factor

**Autopsy**
Coroner's Exam .................88045
Forensic Exam ..................88040
Gross and Micro Exam .......88020-88029
Gross Exam ..............88000-88016
Organ ..........................88037
Regional .......................88036
Unlisted Services and Procedures ...88099

**Autotransfusion**
Blood ...................86890, 86891

**Autotransplant**
*See* Autograft

**Autotransplantation**
Renal ..........................50380

**Avulsion**
Nails ....................11730-11732
Nerve ...................64732-64772

**AV Fistula**
*See* Arteriovenous Fistula

**AV Shunt**
*See* Arteriovenous Shunt

**Axillary Arteries**
*See* Artery, Axillary

**Axillary Nerve**
Injection
  Anesthetic ...................64417

**Axis, Dens**
*See* Odontoid Process

**A Vitamin**
*See* Vitamin, A

# B

**B-DNA**
*See* Deoxyribonucleic Acid

**b-Hexosaminidase** ............83080

**B1 Vitamin**
*See* Thiamine

**B6 Vitamin**
*See* Vitamin, B-6

**Babcock Operation**
*See* Ligation, Vein, Saphenous

**Bacillus Calmette Guerin Vaccine**
*See* BCG Vaccine

**Back/Flank**
Biopsy ...................21920-21925
Repair
  Hernia .......................49540
Strapping ......................29220
Tumor
  Excision .....................21930
  Radical Resection .............21935
Wound Exploration
  Penetrating ..................20102

**Backbone**
*See* Spine

**Bacterial Endotoxins** ....87174-87176

**Bacteria Culture**
Anaerobic ...............87075-87076
Blood ..........................87040
by Kit .........................87072
Feces ..........................87045
Other Source ...................87070
Screening ......................87081
Throat/Nose ....................87060
Urine ...................87086-87088

**Bactericidal Titer, Serum** .....87197

**Bacterium**
Antibody .......................86609

**BAER**
*See* Evoked Potential, Auditory Brainstem

**Baker's Cyst** .................27345

**Baker Tube**
Intestine Decompression ..........44021

**Balanoplasty**
*See* Penis, Repair

**Baldy-Webster Operation**
*See* Uterus, Repair, Suspension

**Balkan Grippe**
*See* Q Fever

**Balloon Angioplasties, Coronary**
*See* Percutaneous Transluminal Angioplasty

**Balloon Angioplasty**
*See* Angioplasty

**Balloon Assisted Device**
Aorta .............. 33968-33974, 93727

**Band, Pulmonary Artery**
*See* Banding, Artery, Pulmonary

**Banding**
Artery
  Fistula ...................... 37607
  Pulmonary ................... 33690

**Bank, Blood**
*See* Blood Banking

**Bankart Procedure**
*See* Capsulorrhaphy, Anterior

**Barany Caloric Test**
*See* Caloric Vestibular Test

**Barbiturates**
Blood or Urine ................... 82205

**Bardenheurer Operation**
*See* Ligation, Artery, Chest

**Barium** ....................... 83015

**Barium Enema** .......... 74270-74280

**Barker Operation**
*See* Talus, Excision

**Barr Bodies** .................. 88130

**Barr Procedure**
*See* Tendon, Transfer, Leg, Lower

**Bartholin's Gland**
Abscess
  Incision and Drainage .......... 56420
Cyst
  Repair ...................... 56440
Excision ........................ 56740
Marsupialization ................ 56440

**Bartonella Detection** .... 87470-87472

**Basic Life Services** ........... 99450

**Basic Proteins, Myelin**
*See* Myelin Basic Protein

**Basilar Arteries**
*See* Artery, Basilar

**Batch-Spittler-McFaddin Operation**
*See* Disarticulation, Knee

**BCG Vaccine**
*See* Vaccines

**Bed Sores**
*See* Debridement; Pressure Ulcer (Decubitus); Skin Graft and Flap

**Bekesy Audiometry**
*See* Audiometry, Bekesy

**Belsey IV Procedure**
*See* Fundoplasty

**Bender-Gestalt Test** ........... 96100

**Benedict Test for Urea**
*See* Urinalysis, Qualitative

**Benign Cystic Mucinous Tumour**
*See* Ganglion

**Benign Neoplasm of Cranial Nerves**
*See* Cranial Nerve

**Bennett Fracture**
*See* Phalanx; Thumb, Fracture

**Bennett Procedure**
*See* Repair, Leg, Upper, Muscle; Revision

**Benzidine Test**
*See* Blood, Feces

**Benzodiazepine**
Assay ......................... 80154

**Benzoyl Cholinesterase**
*See* Cholinesterase

**Bernstein Test**
*See* Acid Perfusion Test, Esophagus

**Beryllium** .................... 83015

**Beta-2-Microglobulin**
Blood ......................... 82232
Urine ......................... 82232

**Beta-hydroxydehydrogenase** .80406

**Beta Glucosidase** ............. 82963

**Beta Hypophamine**
*See* Antidiuretic Hormone

**Beta Lipoproteins**
*See* Lipoprotein, LDL

**Beta Test** .................... 96100
*See* Psychiatric Diagnosis

**Bethesda System** ....... 88164-88167

**Be Antigens, Hepatitis**
*See* Hepatitis Antigen, Be

**Bicarbonate** .................. 82374

**Biceps Tendon**
Insertion ...................... 24342

**Bichloride, Methylene**
*See* Dichloromethane

**Bicuspid Valve**
*See* Mitral Valve

**Bifid Digit**
Repair ........................ 26585

**Bifrontal Craniotomy** .......... 61557

**Bile Acids** .................... 82239
Blood ......................... 82240

**Bile Duct**
*See* Gallbladder
Anastomosis
  Cyst ........................ 47716
  with Intestines ... 47760, 47780, 47785
Biopsy
  Endoscopy ................... 47553
Catheterization ................. 75982
Change Catheter Tube ............ 75984
Cyst
  Excision .................... 47715
  Repair ...................... 47716
Destruction
  Calculi (Stone) ............... 43265
Dilation
  Endoscopy ...... 43271, 47555-47556
Drainage
  Transhepatic ................. 75980
Endoscopy
  Biopsy ...................... 47553
  Destruction
    Calculi (Stone) ............. 43265
    Tumor ..................... 43272
  Dilation .......... 43271, 47555-47556
  Exploration .................. 47552
  Intraoperative ................ 47550
  Removal
    Calculi (Stone) ........ 43264, 47554
    Foreign Body ................ 43269
    Stent ...................... 43269
  Specimen Collection ........... 43260
  Sphincterotomy ............... 43262
  Sphincter Pressure ............ 43263
  Tube Placement ......... 43267-43268
Exploration
  Atresia ...................... 47700
  Endoscopy ................... 47552
Incision
  Sphincter .............. 43262, 47460
Incision and Drainage ....... 47420, 47425
Insertion
  Catheter ......... 47510, 47525, 75982
    Revision ................... 47530
  Stent ................. 47511, 47801
Nuclear Medicine
  Imaging ..................... 78223
Reconstruction
  Anastomosis ................. 47800
Removal
  Calculi (Stone) ... 43264, 47420, 47425,
    Percutaneous ............... 47630
  Foreign Body ................. 43269
  Stent ....................... 43269
Repair ......................... 47701
  Cyst ........................ 47716
  Gastrointestinal Tract .......... 47785
  with Intestines ......... 47760, 47780
Tube Placement
  Nasobiliary .................. 43267
  Stent ....................... 43268

Tumor
  Destruction .................. 43271
  Excision ............... 47711-47712
Unlisted Services and Procedures ... 47999
X-Ray
  Guide Dilation ................ 74360
  with Contrast ........... 74300-74320
    Guide Catheter ........ 74328, 74330
    Guide Stone Removal ......... 74327

**Bile Duct, Common, Cystic Dilatation**
*See* Cyst, Choledochal

**Bilirubin**
Blood .................... 82247-82251
Feces ........................ 82252
Total
  Direct ................. 82247-82248

**Billroth I or II**
*See* Gastrectomy, Partial

**Bilobectomy** .................. 32482

**Bimone**
*See* Testosterone

**Binding Globulin, Testosterone-Estradiol**
*See* Globulin, Sex Hormone Binding

**Binet-Simon Test** ............ 96100

**Binet Test** .................... 96100

**Binocular Microscopy** ........ 92504

**Biofeedback**
Anorectal ..................... 90911
Psychiatric Treatment ....... 90875-90876

**Biofeedback Training**
*See* Training, Biofeedback

**Biological Skin Grafts**
*See* Allograft, Skin

**Biometry**
Eye ..................... 76516-76519

**Biopsies, Needle**
*See* Needle Biopsy

**Biopsy**
*See* Brush Biopsy; Needle Biopsy
Abdomen ...................... 49000
Adrenal Gland ............ 60540-60545
Anal
  Endoscopy .................. 46606
Ankle ............. 27613-27614, 27620
Arm, Lower ............... 25065-25066
Arm, Upper ............... 24065-24066
Artery
  Temporal ................... 37609
Auditory Canal, External .......... 69105
Back/Flank ............... 21920-21925
Bile Duct
  Endoscopy .................. 47553
Bladder
  Cystourethroscope ............ 52204
  Cystourethroscopy ....... 52224, 52250
Blood Vessel
  Transcatheter ............... 75970
Bone .................... 20220-20245
Bone Marrow .................. 85102
Brain ......................... 61140
  Stereotactic ........... 61750-61751
Brainstem ................ 61575-61576
Breast ................... 19100-19101
  Stereotactic Localization ........ 76095
Bronchi
  Catheterization .............. 31717
  Endoscopic ............. 31625-31629
Brush
  Bronchi ..................... 31717
  Renal Pelvis ................. 52007
  Ureter ...................... 52007
  with Cystourethroscopy .. 52204, 52338
Carpometacarpal Joint
  Synovium ................... 26100
Cervix ................... 57500, 57520
Chorionic Villus ................ 59015
Colon .................... 44025, 44100
  Endoscopy ............. 44389, 45380
  Multiple
    with Colostomy, Cecostomy .... 44322
Colon-Sigmoid
  Endoscopy ............. 45305, 45331
Conjunctiva .................... 68100
Cornea ........................ 65410
Duodenum ..................... 44010
Ear
  External .................... 69100
Elbow ............. 24065-24066, 24101
  Synovium ................... 24100
Endometrium ............. 58100, 58558
Epididymis .............. 54800-54820
Esophagus
  Endoscopy .................. 43202
Eyelid ........................ 67810
Eye Muscle .................... 67350
Forearm
  Soft Tissue ............ 25065-25066
Gallbladder
  Endoscopy .................. 43261
Gastrointestinal, Upper
  Endoscopy .................. 43239
Hand Joint
  Synovium ................... 26100
Heart ......................... 93505
Hip ..................... 27040-27041
  Joint ....................... 27052
Hypopharynx ................... 42802
Ileum
  Endoscopy .................. 44382
Interphalangeal Joint
  Finger ...................... 26110
  Toe ......................... 28054
Intertarsal Joint
  Toe ......................... 28050
Intestines, Small .......... 44020, 44100
  Endoscopy ............. 44361, 44377
Kidney .................. 50200-50205
  Endoscopic ............ 50555, 50557, 50559, 50574-50578
Knee .................... 27323-27324
  Synovium ................... 27330
Knee Joint
  Synovium ................... 27330
Lacrimal Gland ................ 68510
Lacrimal Sac .................. 68525
Larynx
  Endoscopy ............. 31510, 31576
Leg
  Lower ................. 27613-27614
  Upper ................. 27323-27324
Lip ........................... 40490
Liver ............... 47000, 47001, 47100
  Percutaneous ................ 00702
Lung
  Needle ..................... 32405
  Thoracotomy ........... 32095-32100
Lymph Nodes ............. 38510-38530
  Injection Procedure
    for Identification of
    Sentinel Node .............. 38792
  Laparoscopic ........... 38570-38572
  Needle ..................... 38505
  Superficial .................. 38500
Mediastinum ................... 39400
  Needle ..................... 32405
Metacarpophalangeal Joint ........ 26105
Metatarsophalangeal Joint ........ 28052
Mouth ................... 40808, 41108
Muscle .................. 20200-20206
Nail .......................... 11755
Nasopharynx ............. 42804, 42806
Neck .......................... 21550
Nerve ......................... 64795
Nose
  Endoscopic .................. 31237
  Intranasal .................. 30100
Orbit ......................... 61332
  Exploration ........... 67400, 67450
  Fine Needle Aspiration ......... 67415
Oropharynx .................... 42800
Ovary ......................... 58900
  Laparoscopic ................ 49321
Palate ........................ 42100
Pancreas ...................... 48100
Pelvis .................. 27040-27041
  Endoscopic .................. 49321
Penis ......................... 54100
  Deep Structures .............. 54105

**Blast Cells**
*See* Stem Cell

**Blast Transformation**
*See* Blastogenesis

**Bleeding**
*See* Hemorrhage

**Bleeding, Anal**
*See* Anus, Hemorrhage

**Bleeding, Uterine**
*See* Hemorrhage, Uterus

**Bleeding Disorder**
*See* Coagulopathy

**Bleeding Time** ................85002

**Bleeding Tube**
Passage and Placement ...........91100

**Bleeding Vaginal**
*See* Hemorrhage, Vagina

**Blepharoplasty** .........15820-15823
*See* Canthoplasty
Anesthesia .....................00103
Ectropion
  Excision Tarsal Wedge .........67916
  Extensive ....................67917
Entropion ................67923-67924
  Excision Tarsal Wedge .........67923
  Extensive ....................67924

**Blepharoptosis**
Repair ....................67901-67909
  Frontalis Muscle Technique .....67901
    with Fascial Sling ...........67902
  Superior Rectus Technique with
  Fascial Sling ................67906
  Tarso Levator Resection/Advancement
    External Approach ...........67904
    Internal Approach ...........67903

**Blepharorrhaphy**
*See* Tarsorrhaphy

**Blepharospasm**
Chemodenervation ...............64612

**Blepharotomy** ................67700

**Blister**
*See* Bulla

**Blom-Singer Prosthesis** ......31611

**Blood**
Bleeding Time ..................85002
Collection, for Autotransfusion
  Intraoperative ...............86891
  Preoperative .................86890
Feces ..........................82270
Gastric Contents ...............82273
Harvesting of Stem Cells ..........38231
Hemoglobin Concentration .........85046
Nuclear Medicine
  Flow Imaging ................78445
  Plasma Iron ..................78160
  Red Cell .....................78140
  Red Cell Survival ........78130-78135
Osmolality .....................83930
Other Source ...................82273
Plasma
  Exchange ..............36520-36521
Platelet
  Aggregation ..................85576
  Automated Count .............85595
  Count ........................85585
  Manual Count ................85590
Stem Cell
  Transplantation .........38240-38241
    Cryopreservation ...........88240
    Modification ................86915
    Thawing ....................88241
Transfusion .....................36430
  Exchange ....................36455
    Newborn ...................36450
  Fetal ........................36460
  Push
    Infant .....................36440
Unlisted Services and Procedures ...85999
Urine ..........................83491
Viscosity ......................85810

**Blood, Occult**
*See* Occult Blood

**Blood Banking**
Frozen Blood Preparation .....86930-86932
Frozen Plasma Preparation .........86927
Physician Services ..........86077-86079

**Blood Cell**
CD4 and CD8
  Including Ratio ...............86360
Enzyme Activity .................82657
Exchange ................36520-36521
Sedimentation Rate
  Automated ...................85652
  Manual ......................85651
Stem ...........................38231

**Blood Cell, Red**
*See* Red Blood Cell (RBC)

**Blood Cell, White**
*See* Leukocyte

**Blood Cell Count** .............85014
Differential WBC Count .....85007, 85009
Hemoglobin .....................85018
Hemogram
  Added Indices ..........85021-85027
  Automated .............85021-85027
  Manual .....................85031
Manual Blood Smear ............85008
Microhematocrit .................85013
Other ..........................85014
Red Blood Cells .................85041
Reticulocyte ...............85044-85045
T-Cells ...................86359-86361
White Blood Cells ...............85048

**Blood Cell Count, Red**
*See* Red Blood Cell (RBC), Count

**Blood Cell Count, White**
*See* White Blood Cell, Count

**Blood Clot**
Clotting Factor .............85250-85293
Clotting Factor Test .........85210-85244
Clotting Inhibitors ....85300-85302, 85305
Clot Lysis Time .................85175
Clot Retraction .................85170
Coagulation Time ...........85345-85348

**Blood Coagulation Defect**
*See* Coagulopathy

**Blood Coagulation Factor**
*See* Clotting Factor

**Blood Coagulation Factor I**
*See* Fibrinogen

**Blood Coagulation Factor II**
*See* Prothrombin

**Blood Coagulation Factor III**
*See* Thromboplastin

**Blood Coagulation Factor IV**
*See* Calcium

**Blood Coagulation Factor IX**
*See* Christmas Factor

**Blood Coagulation Factor VII**
*See* Proconvertin

**Blood Coagulation Factor VIII**
*See* Clotting Factor

**Blood Coagulation Factor X**
*See* Stuart-Prower Factor

**Blood Coagulation Factor X, Activated**
*See* Thrombokinase

**Blood Coagulation Factor XI**
*See* Plasma Thromboplastin, Antecedent

**Blood Coagulation Factor XIII**
*See* Fibrin Stabilizing Factor

**Blood Coagulation Test**
*See* Coagulation

**Blood Component Removal**
*See* Apheresis

**Blood Count, Complete**
*See* Complete Blood Count (CBC)

**Blood Flow Check, Graft** ......15860

**Blood Gases**
CO2 ............................82803
HCO3 ...........................82803
O2 Saturation .............82805-82810
pCO2 ...........................82803
pH ......................82800-82803
pO2 ............................82803

**Blood Letting**
*See* Phlebotomy

**Blood Lipoprotein**
*See* Lipoprotein

Multiplane . . . . 20692
Pin/Wire . . . . 20650
Skeletal
Humeral Epicondyle
Percutaneous . . . . 24566
Stereotactic Frame . . . . 20660
Uniplane . . . . 20690
Insertion
Needle . . . . 36680
Nuclear Medicine
Density Study . . . . 78350-78351
Imaging . . . . 78300-78315, 78320
SPECT . . . . 78320
Unlisted Services and Procedures . . . . 78399
Protein . . . . 83937
Removal
Fixation Device . . . . 20670-20680
X-Ray
Age Study . . . . 76020
Dual Energy Absorptiometry . . . . 76075-76076
Length Study . . . . 76040
Osseous Survey . . . . 76061-76065

**Bone, Carpal**
*See* Carpal Bone

**Bone, Cheek**
*See* Cheekbone

**Bone, Facial**
*See* Facial Bone

**Bone, Foot Navicular**
*See* Navicular

**Bone, Hyoid**
*See* Hyoid Bone

**Bone, Metatarsal**
*See* Metatarsal

**Bone, Nasal**
*See* Nasal Bone

**Bone, Scan**
*See* Bone, Nuclear Medicine; Nuclear Medicine Imaging

**Bone, Semilunar**
*See* Lunate

**Bone, Sesamoid**
*See* Sesamoid Bone

**Bone, Tarsal**
*See* Ankle Bone

**Bone, Temporal**
*See* Temporal Bone

**Bone 4-Carboxyglutamic Protein**
*See* Osteocalcin

**Bone Conduction Hearing Device, Electromagnetic**
Implantation/Replacement . . . . 69710
Removal/Repair . . . . 69711

**Bone Density Study**
Appendicular Skeleton . . . . 76076
Axial Skeleton . . . . 76075
Ultrasound . . . . 76977

**Bone Graft**
Augmentation
Mandibular Body . . . . 21127
Femur . . . . 27170
Fracture
Orbit . . . . 21408
Harvesting . . . . 20900-20902
Malar Area . . . . 21210
Mandible . . . . 21215
Mandibular Ramus . . . . 21194
Maxilla . . . . 21210
Microvascular Anastomosis
Fibula . . . . 20955
Other . . . . 20962
Nasal Area . . . . 21210
Nasomaxillary Complex Fracture . . . . 21348
Open Treatment
Craniofacial Separation . . . . 21436
Osteocutaneous Flap . . . . 20969-20973
Reconstruction
Mandibular Rami . . . . 21194
Midface . . . . 21145-21160
Spine Surgery
Allograft
Morselized . . . . 20930
Structural . . . . 20931
Autograft
Local . . . . 20936
Morselized . . . . 20937
Structural . . . . 20938

**Bone Healing**
Electrical Stimulation
Invasive . . . . 20975
Noninvasive . . . . 20974
Ultrasound Stimulation . . . . 20979

**Bone Infection**
*See* Osteomyelitis

**Bone Marrow**
Aspiration . . . . 85095
Harvesting . . . . 38230
Magnetic Resonance Imaging (MRI) . . . . 76400
Needle Biopsy . . . . 85102
Nuclear Medicine
Imaging . . . . 78102-78104
Smear . . . . 85097
T-Cell
Depletion . . . . 86915
Transplantation . . . . 38240-38241
Trocar Biopsy . . . . 85102

**Bone Plate**
Mandible . . . . 21244

**Bone Scan**
*See* Bone, Nuclear Medicine; Nuclear Medicine

**Bone Spur**
*See* Exostosis

**Bone Wedge Reversal**
Osteotomy . . . . 21122

**Bordetella**
Antibody . . . . 86615
Antigen Detection
Direct Fluorescence . . . . 87265

**Borrelia**
Antibody . . . . 86618, 86619

**Borrelia burgdorferi ab**
*See* Antibody, Lyme Disease

**Borreliosis, Lyme**
*See* Lyme Disease

**Borthen Operation**
*See* Iridotasis

**Bost Fusion**
*See* Arthrodesis, Wrist

**Bosworth Operation**
*See* Acromioclavicular Joint, Dislocation; Arthrodesis, Vertebrae; Fasciotomy, Elbow

**Bottle Type Procedure** . . . . 55060

**Botulinum Toxin**
*See* Chemodenervation

**Boutonniere Deformity** . . 26426, 26428

**Bowel**
*See* Intestine

**Bowleg Repair** . . . . 27455-27457

**Boyce Operation**
*See* Nephrotomy

**Boyd Hip Disarticulation**
*See* Amputation, Leg, Upper; Radical Resection; Replantation

**Brace**
*See* Cast
for Leg Cast . . . . 29358

**Brachial Arteries**
*See* Artery, Brachial

**Brachial Plexus**
Decompression . . . . 64713
Injection
Anesthetic . . . . 64415
Neuroplasty . . . . 64713
Release . . . . 64713
Repair/Suture . . . . 64861

**Brachiocephalic Artery**
*See* Artery, Brachiocephalic

**Brachycephaly** . . . . 21175

**Brachytherapy** . . . . 77761-77778, 77789
Dose Plan . . . . 77326-77328
Remote Afterloading
1-4 Positions . . . . 77781
5-8 Positions . . . . 77782
9-12 Positions . . . . 77783
Over 12 Positions . . . . 77784
Over 4 Positions . . . . 77781-77784

# C

**Cadmium**
Urine . . . . . . . . . . 82300

**Calcaneal Spur**
*See* Heel Spur

**Calcaneus**
Craterization . . . . . . . . . . 28120
Cyst
  Excision . . . . . . . . . . 28100-28103
Diaphysectomy . . . . . . . . . . 28120
Excision . . . . . . . . . . 28118-28120
Fracture
  Open Treatment . . . . . . . . . . 28415-28420
  Percutaneous Fixation . . . . . . . . . . 28406
  without Manipulation . . . . . . . . . . 28400
  with Manipulation . . . . . . . . . . 28405-28406
Repair
  Osteotomy . . . . . . . . . . 28300
Saucerization . . . . . . . . . . 28120
Tumor
  Excision . . . . . . . . . . 27647, 28100-28103
X-Ray . . . . . . . . . . 73650

**Calcareous Deposits**
Subdeltoid
  Removal . . . . . . . . . . 23000

**Calcifediol**
Blood or Urine . . . . . . . . . . 82306

**Calcifediol Assay**
*See* Calciferol

**Calciferol**
Blood or Urine . . . . . . . . . . 82307

**Calcification**
*See* Calcium, Deposits

**Calciol**
*See* Vitamin, D-3

**Calcitonin**
Blood or Urine . . . . . . . . . . 82308
Stimulation Panel . . . . . . . . . . 80410

**Calcium**
Blood
  Infusion Test . . . . . . . . . . 82331
Deposits
  *See* Removal, Calculi (Stone); Removal, Foreign Bodies
Ionized . . . . . . . . . . 82330
Total . . . . . . . . . . 82310
Urine . . . . . . . . . . 82340

**Calcium-Binding Protein, Vitamin K-Dependent**
*See* Osteocalcin

**Calcium-Pentagastrin Stimulation** . . . . . . . . . . 80410

**Calculus**
Analysis . . . . . . . . . . 82355-82370
Removal
  Bladder . . . . . . . . . . 51050, 52310-52315, 52317-52318
  Kidney . . . . . . . . . . 50060-50081, 50130, 50561, 50580
  Ureter . . . . . . . . . . 50610-50630, 50961, 50980, 51060-51065, 52320-52325, 52336
  Urethra . . . . . . . . . . 52310-52315

**Calculus of Kidney**
*See* Calculus, Removal, Kidney

**Caldwell-Luc Procedure**
*See* Sinus, Maxillary; Sinusotomy; Sternum, Fracture
Orbital Floor Blowout Fracture . . . . . . . . . . 21385
Sinusotomy . . . . . . . . . . 31030-31032

**Caliper**
Application/Removal . . . . . . . . . . 20660

**Callander Knee Disarticulation**
*See* Disarticulation, Knee

**Callosum, Corpus**
*See* Corpus Callosum

**Calmette Guerin Bacillus Vaccine**
*See* BCG Vaccine

**Caloric Vestibular Test** . . . . . . . . . . 92533

**Calycoplasty** . . . . . . . . . . 50405

**Camey Enterocystoplasty** . . . . . . . . . . 50825

**CAMP**
*See* Cyclic AMP

**Campbell Procedure** . . . . . . . . . . 27422

**Campylobacter**
Antibody . . . . . . . . . . 86625

**Campylobacter Pylori**
*See* Helicobacter Pylori

**Canal, Ear**
*See* Auditory Canal

**Canal, Semicircular**
*See* Semicircular Canal

**Canaloplasty** . . . . . . . . . . 69631, 69635

**Candida**
Antibody . . . . . . . . . . 86628
Skin Test . . . . . . . . . . 86485

**Cannulation** . . . . . . . . . . 36821
Arterial . . . . . . . . . . 36620, 36625
Sinus
  Maxillary . . . . . . . . . . 31000
  Sphenoid . . . . . . . . . . 31002
Thoracic Duct . . . . . . . . . . 38794

**Cannulation, Renoportal**
*See* Anastomosis, Renoportal

**Cannulization**
*See* Catheterization
Arteriovenous . . . . . . . . . . 36145, 36810, 36815
Declotting . . . . . . . . . . 36550, 36860-36861
ECMO . . . . . . . . . . 36822
External
  Declotting . . . . . . . . . . 36860-36861
Vas Deferens . . . . . . . . . . 55200
Vein to Vein . . . . . . . . . . 36800

**Canthocystostomy**
*See* Conjunctivorhinostomy

**Canthopexy**
Lateral . . . . . . . . . . 21282
Medial . . . . . . . . . . 21280

**Canthoplasty** . . . . . . . . . . 67950

**Canthorrhaphy** . . . . . . . . . . 67880, 67882

**Canthotomy** . . . . . . . . . . 67715

**Canthus**
Reconstruction . . . . . . . . . . 67950

**Cap, Cervical**
*See* Cervical Cap

**Capsule**
*See* Capsulodesis
Elbow
  Arthrotomy . . . . . . . . . . 24006
  Excision . . . . . . . . . . 24006
Foot . . . . . . . . . . 28264
Interphalangeal Joint
  Excision . . . . . . . . . . 26525
  Incision . . . . . . . . . . 26525
Knee . . . . . . . . . . 27435
Metacarpophalangeal Joint
  Excision . . . . . . . . . . 26520
  Incision . . . . . . . . . . 26520
Metatarsophalangeal Joint
  Release . . . . . . . . . . 28289
Shoulder
  Incision . . . . . . . . . . 23020
Wrist
  Excision . . . . . . . . . . 25320

**Capsulectomy**
Breast
  Periprosthetic . . . . . . . . . . 19371

**Capsulodesis**
Metacarpophalangeal Joint . . 26516-26518

**Capsulorrhaphy**
Anterior . . . . . . . . . . 23450-23462
Multi-Directional Instability . . . . . . . . . . 23466
Posterior . . . . . . . . . . 23465
Wrist . . . . . . . . . . 25320

**Capsulotomy**
Breast
  Periprosthetic . . . . . . . . . . 19370
Foot . . . . . . . . . . 28260-28262
Hip
  with Release, Flexor Muscles . . . . 27036
Interphalangeal Joint . . . . . . . . . . 28272
Knee . . . . . . . . . . 27435
Metacarpophalangeal Joint . . . . . . . . . . 26520
Metatarsophalangeal Joint . . . . . . . . . . 28270
Toe . . . . . . . . . . 28270, 28272
Wrist . . . . . . . . . . 25085

**Captopril** . . . . . . . . . . 80416, 80417

**Carbamazepine**
Assay . . . . . . . . . . 80156

**Carbazepin**
*See* Carbamazepine

**Carbinol**
*See* Methanol

**Carbon Dioxide**
Blood or Urine ..................82374

**Carbon Monoxide**
Blood ..................82375-82376

**Carbon Tetrachloride** .........84600

**Carboxycathepsin**
*See* Angiotensin Converting Enzyme (ACE)

**Carboxyhemoglobin** .....82375-82376

**Carbuncle**
Incision and Drainage .......10060-10061

**Carcinoembryonal Antigen**
*See* Antigen, Carcinoembryonic

**Carcinoembryonic Antigen** ...82378

**Cardiac**
*See* Coronary

**Cardiac Arrhythmia, Tachycardia**
*See* Tachycardia

**Cardiac Atria**
*See* Atria

**Cardiac Catheterization**
Balloon Catheter, Insertion ........93536
Combined Left and Right
Heart ..................93526-93529
Combined Right and Retrograde Left
Congenital Cardiac Anomalies ...93531
Combined Right and Transseptal Left
Congenital Cardiac Anomalies ..93532-93533
for Biopsy ....................93505
for Dilution Studies .........93561-93562
Imaging ..................93555-93556
Injection ..................93539-93545
*See* Catheterization, Cardiac
Left Heart ..................93510-93524
Pacemaker ....................33210
Right
Congenital Cardiac Anomalies ...93530
Right Heart ..................93501-93503

**Cardiac Electroversion**
*See* Cardioversion

**Cardiac Event Recorder**
Implantation ....................33282
Removal ....................33284

**Cardiac Magnetic Resonance Imaging (CMRI)**
Complete Study ..................75554
Limited Study ..................75555
Morphology ....................75553
Velocity Flow Mapping ...........75556

**Cardiac Massage**
Thoracotomy ....................32160

**Cardiac Muscle**
*See* Myocardium

**Cardiac Neoplasm**
*See* Heart, Tumor

**Cardiac Output**
Indicator Dilution ...........93561-93562

**Cardiac Pacemaker**
*See* Heart, Pacemaker

**Cardiac Rehabilitation** ..93797-93798

**Cardiac Septal Defect**
*See* Septal Defect

**Cardiac Transplantation**
*See* Heart, Transplantation

**Cardiectomy**
Donor ....................33930, 33940

**Cardioassist** ............92970-92971

**Cardiolipin Antibody** ..........86147

**Cardiology**
*See* Electrocardiography
Diagnostic
Atrial Electrogram
Esophageal Recording ..93615-93616
Cardio-Defibrillator
Evaluation and Testing ..93640-93642, 93741-93744
Echocardiography
Doppler ..93303-93317, 93320-93321
Transthoracic .........93303-93304, 93303-93317, 93350
Electrocardiogram
Evaluation ......93000, 93010, 93014
Monitoring ...........93224-93237
Patient-Demand .......93268-93272
Rhythm ..............93040-93042
Tracing ....................93005
Transmission ...............93012
Ergonovine Provocation Test .....93024
Implantable Loop Recorder
System ......................93727
Intracardiac Pacing and
Mapping ....................93631
Follow-up Study ............93624
Stimulation and Pacing .......93623
Intracardiac Pacing and Recording
Arrhythmia Induction ..93618-93620
Bundle of His ...............93600
Comprehensive ........93619-93622
Intra-Atrial ...........93602, 93610
Left Ventricle ...............93607
Right Ventricle .............93603
Tachycardia Sites ...........93609
Ventricular ................93612
Intravascular Ultrasound ..92978-92979
Pacemaker Testing ...........93642
Antitachycardia System .......93724
Dual Chamber .........93731-93733
Leads ......................93641
Single Chamber ........93734-93736
Perfusion Imaging .......78460-78461
*See* Nuclear Medicine
Stress Tests
Cardiovascular ........93015-93018
Drug Induced ...............93024
Multiple Gated Acquisition
(MUGA) ....................78473
Tilt Table Evaluation ...........93660
Therapeutic
Cardioassist ............92970-92971
Cardioversion ...........92960-92961
Intravascular Ultrasound ..92978-92979
Pacing
Transcutaneous, Temporary ....92953
Thrombolysis ...........92975-92977
Thrombolysis, Coronary .........92977
Valvuloplasty
Percutaneous .........92986-92990

**Cardiomyotomy**
*See* Esophagomyotomy

**Cardioplasty** ..................43320

**Cardiopulmonary Bypass**
*See* Heart; Lung, Transplantation

**Cardiopulmonary Resuscitation** ................92950

**Cardiotomy** .............33310, 33315

**Cardiovascular Stress Test**
*See* Exercise Stress Tests

**Cardioversion** ...........92960-92961

**Care, Custodial**
*See* Nursing Facility Services

**Care, Intensive**
*See* Intensive Care

**Care, Neonatal Intensive**
*See* Intensive Care, Neonatal

**Care, Self**
*See* Self Care

**Care Plan Oversight Services**
*See* Physician Services

**Carneous Mole**
*See* Abortion

**Carnitine** ....................82379

**Carotene** ....................82380

**Caroticum, Glomus**
*See* Carotid Body

**Carotid Artery**
Aneurysm Repair
Vascular Malformation or Carotid-Cavernous Fistula ............61710
Excision ........................60605
Ligation .................37600-37606

**Celiac Trunk Artery**
*See* Artery, Celiac

**Celioscopy**
*See* Endoscopy, Peritoneum

**Celiotomy** .................... 49000
Abdomen
for Staging .................... 49220

**Cell, Blood**
*See* Blood Cell

**Cell, Islet**
*See* Islet Cell

**Cell, Mother**
*See* Stem Cell

**Cell-Stimulating Hormone, Interstitial**
*See* Luteinizing Hormone (LH)

**Cellobiase**
*See* Beta Glucosidase

**Cellular Inclusion**
*See* Inclusion Bodies

**Cell Count**
Body Fluid .................. 89050-89051

**Central Shunt** .................. 33764

**Central Venous Catheter Placement**
Cutdown
Child/Adult .................. 36491
Infant .................. 36490
Percutaneous
Child/Adult .................. 36489
Infant .................. 36488
Repositioning .................. 36493

**Cephalic Version**
of Fetus
External .................. 59412

**Cephalocele**
*See* Encephalocele

**Cephalogram, Orthodontic**
*See* Orthodontic Cephalogram

**Cerclage**
Cervix .................. 57700
Abdominal .................. 59325
Removal Under Anesthesia ...... 59871
Vaginal .................. 59320

**Cerebellopontine Angle Tumor**
*See* Brain, Tumor, Excision; Brainstem; Mesencephalon; Skull Base Surgery

**Cerebral Cortex Decortication**
*See* Decortication

**Cerebral Death**
*See* Brain Death

**Cerebral Hernia**
*See* Encephalocele

**Cerebral Thermography**
*See* Thermogram, Cephalic

**Cerebral Ventriculographies**
*See* Ventriculography

**Cerebrose**
*See* Galactose

**Cerebrospinal Fluid** ........... 86325
Nuclear Imaging ............ 78630-78650

**Cerebrospinal Fluid Leak** ..... 63744
Brain
Repair ........... 61618-61619, 62100
Nasal/Sinus Endoscopy
Repair .................. 31290-31291
Spinal Cord
Repair ................ 63707, 63709

**Cerebrospinal Fluid Shunt** .... 63740, 63746
Creation ...... 62180-62192, 62200-62223
Irrigation .................. 62194
Removal .................. 62256, 62258
Replacement ........ 62194, 62225, 62230

**Ceruloplasmin** ................ 82390

**Cerumen**
Removal .................. 69210

**Cervical Cap** .................. 57170

**Cervical Lymphadenectomy** ...... 38720-38724

**Cervical Mucus Penetration Test** .................. 89330

**Cervical Plexus**
Injection
Anesthetic .................. 64413

**Cervical Pregnancy** ........... 59140

**Cervical Puncture** ...... 61050, 61055

**Cervical Smears** ........ 88141-88155, 88164-88167
*See* Cytopathology

**Cervical Spine**
*See* Vertebra, Cervical

**Cervical Sympathectomy**
*See* Sympathectomy, Cervical

**Cervicectomy** ................ 57530

**Cervicoplasty** ................ 15819

**Cervicothoracic Ganglia**
*See* Stellate Ganglion

**Cervix**
*See* Cytopathology
Amputation
Total .................. 57530
Biopsy .................. 57500, 57520
Cauterization .................. 57522
Cryocautery .................. 57511
Electro or Thermal ............ 57510
Laser Ablation ................ 57513
Cerclage .................. 57700
Abdominal .................. 59325
Removal Under Anesthesia ...... 59871
Vaginal .................. 59320
Conization ................ 57520-57522
Curettage
Endocervical ........... 57454, 57505
Dilation
Canal .................. 57800
Stump .................. 57820
Dilation and Curettage ............ 57820
Ectopic Pregnancy ................ 59140
Excision
Electrode .................. 57460
Radical .................. 57531
Stump
Abdominal Approach ... 57540-57545
Vaginal Approach ...... 57550-57556
Total .................. 57530
Insertion
Dilation .................. 59200
Laminaria .................. 59200
Prostaglandin .................. 59200
Repair
Cerclage .................. 57700
Abdominal .................. 59325
Vaginal .................. 59320
Suture .................. 57720
Unlisted Services and Procedures ... 58999

**Cesarean Delivery**
Antepartum Care ........... 59610, 59618
Delivery after Previous
after Attempted Vaginal Delivery . 59618
Delivery Only .................. 59620
Postpartum Care ............ 59622
Routine Care .......... 59610, 59618
Delivery Only .................. 59514
Postpartum Care .................. 59515
Routine Care .................. 59510
Tubal Ligation at Time of ........... 58611
with Hysterectomy ............... 59525

**CGMP**
*See* Cyclic GMP

**Chalazion**
Excision .................. 67805
Multiple
Different Lids ............... 67805
Same Lid .................. 67801
Single .................. 67800
Under Anesthesia ............ 67808

**Challenge Tests**
Bronchial Ingestion ......... 95070-95075

**Chambers Procedure** ......... 28300

**Change**
Catheter
Bile Duct ....................75984
Fetal Position
by Manipulation ..............59412
Tube or Stent
Endoscopic
Bile or Pancreatic Duct ........43269

**Change, Gastrostomy Tube**
*See* Gastrostomy Tube, Change of

**Change of, Dressing**
*See* Dressings, Change

**Cheek**
Bone
Fracture
Closed Treatment with
Manipulation ...............21355
Open Treatment .......21360-21366
Reconstruction ...............21270
Fascia Graft .....................15840
Muscle Graft ..............15841-15845
Muscle Transfer .................15845

**Cheilectomy**
Metatarsophalangeal Joint
Release .........................28289

**Cheiloplasty**
*See* Lip, Repair

**Cheiloschisis**
*See* Cleft Lip

**Cheilotomy**
*See* Incision, Lip

**Chemical Cauterization**
Granulation Tissue ..............17250

**Chemical Exfoliation** .........17360

**Chemical Peel** ..........15788-15793

**Chemiluminescent Assay** .....82397

**Chemistry Tests**
Clinical
Automated
Unlisted Services and
Procedures ...................84999

**Chemocauterization**
Corneal Epithelium ...............65435
with Chelating Agent ..........65436

**Chemodenervation**
Cervical Spinal Muscle ...........64613
Extraocular Muscle ...............67345
Facial Muscle ...................64612

**Chemonucleolysis** ...........62292

**Chemosurgery**
Moh's Technique ...........17304-17310

**Chemotaxis Assay** ...........86155

**Chemotherapy**
Arterial Catheterization ............36640
Bladder Instillation ...............51720
CNS ............................96450
Extracorporeal Circulation
Extremity ....................36823
Intra-Arterial ..............96420-96425
Intralesional ...............96405-96406
Intramuscular ...................96400
Intravenous ...............96408-96414
Peritoneal Cavity ................96445
Pleural Cavity ...................96440
Pump Services
Implantable ..................96530
Portable .....................96520
Reservoir Filling .................96542
Subcutaneous ...................96400
Supply of Agent .................96545
Unlisted Services and Procedures ...96549

**Chest**
*See* Mediastinum; Thorax
Artery
Ligation .....................37616
CAT Scan .................71250-71270
Exploration
Blood Vessel .................35820
Magnetic Resonance Imaging
(MRI) ..........................71550
Repair
Blood Vessel ...........35211-35216
with Other Graft .......35271-35276
with Vein Graft ........35241-35246
Ultrasound .....................76604
Wound Exploration
Penetrating ..................20101
X-Ray ....................71010-71035
Complete (four Views)
with Fluoroscopy ...........71034
Insertion Pacemaker ...........71090
Needle Biopsy ................71036
Partial (Two Views)
with Fluoroscopy ...........71023
Stereo ......................71015
with Fluoroscopy ..............71090

**Chest, Funnel**
*See* Pectus Excavatum

**Chest Cavity**
Bypass Graft ....................35905
Endoscopy
Exploration .............32601-32606
Surgical ...............32650-32665

**Chest Wall**
*See* Pulmonology, Therapeutic
Manipulation ..............94667-94668
Reconstruction .................49905
Trauma ......................32820
Repair .........................32905
Closure ......................32810
Fistula ......................32906

Tumor
Excision ...............19260-19272
Unlisted Services and Procedures ...32999

**Chest Wall Fistula**
*See* Fistula, Chest Wall

**Chevron Procedure** ...........28296

**Chiari Osteotomy of the Pelvis**
*See* Osteotomy, Pelvis

**Chicken Pox Vaccine**

**Child Procedure**
*See* Excision, Pancreas, Partial

**Chin**
Repair
Augmentation ................21120
Osteotomy .............21121-21123

**Chinidin**
*See* Quinidine

**Chiropractic Manipulation**
*See* Manipulation, Chiropractic

**Chiropractic Treatment**
Spinal
Extraspinal .............98940-98943

**Chlamydia**
Antibody ..................86631-86632
Antigen Detection
Direct Fluorescence ............87270
Enzyme Immunoassay ..........87320
Culture ........................87110

**Chloramphenicol** .............82415

**Chloride**
Blood ..........................82435
Other Source ...................82438
Spinal Fluid ....................82438
Urine ..........................82436

**Chloride, Methylene**
*See* Dichloromethane

**Chlorinated Hydrocarbons** ....82441

**Chlorohydrocarbon**
*See* Chlorinated Hydrocarbons

**Chlorpromazine** ...............84022

**Choanal Atresia**
Repair ....................30540-30545

**Cholangiography**
Injection ..................47500, 47505
Intraoperative .............74300, 74301
Percutaneous ...................74320
with Laparoscopy ........47560-47561
Postoperative ..................74305
Repair
with Bile Duct Exploration ......47700
with Cholecystectomy .........47563,
47605, 47620

**Cholangiopancreatography** . . .43260
*See* Bile Duct; Pancreatic Duct
with Biopsy . . . . . . . . . . . . . . . . . .43261
with Surgery . . . . .43262-43265, 43267, 43269

**Cholangiostomy**
*See* Hepaticostomy

**Cholangiotomy**
*See* Hepaticostomy

**Cholecalciferol**
*See* Vitamin, D-3

**Cholecystectomy** . . . . . . .47562-47564, 47600-47620
Any Method . . . . . . . . . . . . . . .47562-47564
with Cholangiography . . . . . . . . .47563, 47605, 47620
with Exploration Common Duct . . . . . . . . . . . . . . . . . .47610, 47564

**Cholecystoenterostomy** . . . . . .47570, 47720-47741

**Cholecystography** . . . . . . .74290-74291

**Cholecystotomy** . . . . . . 47480, 48001
Percutaneous . . . . . . . . . . . . . . . . . . . .47490

**Choledochoplasty**
*See* Bile Duct, Repair

**Choledochoscopy** . . . . . . . . . . . .47550

**Choledochostomy** . . . . . . .47420-47425

**Choledochotomy** . . . . . . . .47420-47425

**Choledochus, Cyst**
*See* Cyst, Choledochal

**Cholera Vaccine**
Injectable . . . . . . . . . . . . . . . . . . . . . .90725

**Cholesterol**
Measurement . . . . . . . . . . . . . . . . . . .83721
Serum . . . . . . . . . . . . . . . . . . . . . . . . .82465
Testing . . . . . . . . . . . . . . . . . . .83718-83719

**Cholinesterase**
Blood . . . . . . . . . . . . . . . . . . . .82480-82482

**Choline Esterase I**
*See* Acetylcholinesterase

**Choline Esterase II**
*See* Cholinesterase

**Cholylglycine**
Blood . . . . . . . . . . . . . . . . . . . . . . . . . .82240

**Chondroitin Sulfate** . . . . . . . . . . .82485

**Chondromalacia Patella**
Repair . . . . . . . . . . . . . . . . . . . . . . . . .27418

**Chondropathia Patellae**
*See* Chondromalacia Patella

**Chondrosteoma**
*See* Exostosis

**Chopart Procedure** . . . . . .28800-28805
*See* Amputation, Foot; Radical Resection; Replantation

**Chordotomies**
*See* Cordotomy

**Chorioangioma**
*See* Lesion, Skin

**Choriogonadotropin**
*See* Chorionic Gonadotropin

**Choriomeningitides, Lymphocytic**
*See* Lymphocytic Choriomeningitis

**Chorionic Gonadotropin** . . . . .80414, 84702-84703
Stimulation . . . . . . . . . . . . . . . .80414-80415

**Chorionic Growth Hormone**
*See* Lactogen, Human Placental

**Chorionic Tumor**
*See* Hydatidiform Mole

**Chorionic Villi**
*See* Biopsy, Chorionic Villus

**Chorionic Villus**
Biopsy . . . . . . . . . . . . . . . . . . . . . . . . .59015

**Choroid**
Destruction
Lesion . . . . . . . . . . . . . . . . . . . . . .67220

**Choroid Plexus**
Excision . . . . . . . . . . . . . . . . . . . . . . . .61544

**Christmas Factor** . . . . . . . . . . . . .85250

**Chromaffinoma, Medullary**
*See* Pheochromocytoma

**Chromatin, Sex**
*See* Barr Bodies

**Chromatography**
Column/Mass Spectrometry . .82541-82544
Gas Liquid or HPLC . . . .82486, 82491-82492
Paper . . . . . . . . . . . . . . . . . . . .82487-82488
Thin-Layer . . . . . . . . . . . . . . . . . . . . . .82489

**Chromium** . . . . . . . . . . . . . . . . . . . .82495

**Chromogenic Substrate Assay** . . . . . . . . . . . . . . . . . . . . . . .85130

**Chromosome Analysis**
*See* Amniocentesis
Added Study . . . . . . . . . . . . . .88280-88289
Amniotic Fluid . . . . . . . . . . . . .88267, 88269
Culture . . . . . . . . . . . . . . . . . . . . . .88235
Biopsy Culture
Tissue . . . . . . . . . . . . . . . . . . . . . .88233
Bone Marrow Culture . . . . . . . . . . . .88237
Chorionic Villus . . . . . . . . . . . . . . . . .88267
15-20 Cells . . . . . . . . . . . . . . . . . .88262
20-25 Cells . . . . . . . . . . . . . . . . . .88264
45 Cells . . . . . . . . . . . . . . . . . . . . .88263
5 Cells . . . . . . . . . . . . . . . . . . . . . .88261
Culture . . . . . . . . . . . . . . . . . . . . . .88235
for Breakage Syndromes . . . . .88245-88249
Fragile-X . . . . . . . . . . . . . . . . . . . . . . .88248
Lymphocyte Culture . . . . . . . . . . . . . .88230
Skin Culture
Tissue . . . . . . . . . . . . . . . . . . . . . .88233
Tissue Culture . . . . . . . . . . . . . . . . . . .88239
Unlisted Services and Procedures . . .88299

**Chromotubation** . . . . . . . . . . . . . .58350
Oviduct . . . . . . . . . . . . . . . . . . . . . . . .58350

**Chronic Erection**
*See* Priapism

**Chronic Interstitial Cystitides**
*See* Cystitis, Interstitial

**Ciliary Body**
Cyst
Destruction
Cryotherapy . . . . . . . . . . . . . . . .66720
Cyclodialysis . . . . . . . . . . . . . . . .66740
Cyclophotocoagulation . . . . . . . .66710
Diathermy . . . . . . . . . . . . . . . . . .66700
Nonexcisional . . . . . . . . . . . . . . .66770
Lesion
Destruction . . . . . . . . . . . . . . . . . .66770
Repair . . . . . . . . . . . . . . . . . . . . . . . . .66680

**Cimino Type Procedure** . . . . . . .36821

**Cinefluorographies**
*See* Cineradiography

**Cineplasty**
Arm, Lower or Upper . . . . . . . . . . . . . .24940

**Cineradiography**
Esophagus . . . . . . . . . . . . . . . . . . . . .74230
Pharynx . . . . . . . . . . . . . . . . . .70371, 74230
Speech Evaluation . . . . . . . . . . . . . . . .70371
Swallowing Evaluation . . . . . . . . . . . .74230
Unlisted Services and Procedures . . . . . . . . . . . . . . . .76120-76125

**Circulation, Extracorporeal**
*See* Extracorporeal Circulation

**Circulation Assist**
Aortic . . . . . . . . . . . . . . . . . . . . . . . . . .33970
Balloon . . . . . . . . . . . . . . . . . . . . . . . .33970
External . . . . . . . . . . . . . . . . . .33960-33961

**Circulatory Assist**
*See* Circulation Assist

**Circumcision**
Surgical Excision . . . . . . . . . . . . . . . .54161
Newborn . . . . . . . . . . . . . . . . . . . . .54160
with Clamp or Other Device . . . . . . . .54152
Newborn . . . . . . . . . . . . . . . . . . . . .54150

**Cisternal Puncture** . . . . . .61050, 61055

**Cisternography** . . . . . . . . . . . . . . .70015
Nuclear . . . . . . . . . . . . . . . . . . . . . . . .78630

**Citrate**
Blood or Urine . . . . . . . . . . . . . . . . . .82507

**Coagulation Factor X**
*See* Stuart-Prower Factor

**Coagulation Factor Xa**
*See* Thrombokinase

**Coagulation Factor XI**
*See* Plasma Thromboplastin, Antecedent

**Coagulation Factor XII**
*See* Hageman Factor

**Coagulation Factor XIII**
*See* Fibrin Stabilizing Factor

**Coagulation Time** .......85345-85348

**Coagulin**
*See* Thromboplastin

**Coagulopathy** .................85390
Assay ...........................85130

**Cocaine**
Blood or Urine ...................82520
Screen ..........................82486

**Coccidioides**
Antibody .......................86635

**Coccidioidin Test**
*See* Streptokinase, Antibody

**Coccidioidomycosis**
Skin Test .......................86490

**Coccygeal Spine Fracture**
*See* Coccyx, Fracture

**Coccygectomy** ....15920-15922, 27080

**Coccyx**
Excision ........................27080
Fracture
  Closed Treatment .............27200
  Open Treatment ...............27202
Tumor
  Excision .....................49215
X-Ray ..........................72220

**Cochlear Device**
Insertion .......................69930

**Codeine**
Alkaloid Screening ...............82101

**Codeine Screen** ..............82486

**Cofactor Protein s**
*See* Protein S

**Coffey Operation**
*See* Uterus, Repair, Suspension

**Cognitive Function Tests** ......96115
*See* Neurology, Diagnostic

**Cognitive Skills Development** ................97770
*See* Physical Medicine/Therapy/ Occupational Therapy

**Cold Agglutinin** .........86156-86157

**Cold Pack Treatment** ..........97010

**Cold Preservation**
*See* Cryopreservation

**Cold Therapies**
*See* Cryotherapy

**Colectomy**
Partial .........................44140
  with Anastomosis .............44140
  with Coloproctostomy ....44145-44146
  with Colostomy ...44141, 44143-44144
  with Ileostomy ................44144
  with Transcanal Approach ......44147
Total
  with Anastomosis .............44152
  with Complete Proctectomy .....45121
  with Ileal Reservoir ............44153
  with Ileostomy ..........44150-44151
  with Ileum Removal ...........44160
  with Proctectomy ........44155-44156

**Collagen Cross Links** .........82523

**Collagen Injection** ......11950-11954

**Collar Bone**
*See* Clavicle

**Collateral Ligament**
Ankle
  Repair .................27695-27698
Interphalangeal Joint .............26545
Knee Joint
  Repair .......................27409
Knee Repair .....................27405
Metacarpophalangeal Joint ..26540-26542
Repair
  Ankle .................27695-27698

**Collection and Processing**
Autologous Blood
  Harvesting of Stem Cells .......38231
  Intraoperative ................86891
  Preoperative .................86890
Specimen
  Venous Blood ................36415
Washings
  Esophagus ...................91000
  Stomach .....................91055

**Colles' Fracture Reversed**
*See* Smith Fracture

**Colles Fracture** .........25600, 25605, 25611, 25620

**Collins Syndrome, Treacher**
*See* Treacher-Collins Syndrome

**Collis Procedure**
*See* Gastroplasty with Esophagogastric Fundoplasty

**Colon**
*See* Colon-Sigmoid
Biopsy .............44025, 44100, 44322
  Endoscopic ............44389, 45380
Colostomy
  Revision .........44340, 44345-44346
Colotomy .......................44322
  Colostomy ...................44320
Destruction
  Lesion ................44393, 45383
  Tumor .................44393, 45383
Endoscopy
  Biopsy ................44389, 45380
  Destruction
    Lesion .....................44393
    Tumor ...............44393, 45383
  Exploration ............44388, 45378
  Hemorrhage ............44391, 45382
  Removal
    Foreign Body ..........44390, 45379
    Polyp .........44392, 45384-45385
    Tumor ...............45384-45385
  Specimen Collection ...........45380
  via Colotomy .................45355
  via Stoma ..............44388-44394
Excision
  Partial .....44140-44141, 44143-44147
  Total ..................44150-44160
Exploration .....................44025
  Endoscopy .............44388, 45378
Hemorrhage
  Endoscopic Control ......44391, 45382
Hernia ..........................44050
Incision
  Creation
    Stoma ...............44320, 44322
  Exploration ..................44025
  Revision
    Stoma .........44340, 44345-44346
Lesion
  Destruction ..................45383
  Excision ...............44110-44111
Lysis
  Adhesions ....................44005
Obstruction ...............44025, 44050
Reconstruction
  Bladder from .................50810
Removal
  Foreign Body .....44025, 44390, 45379
  Polyp ........................44392
Repair
  Diverticula ...................44605
  Fistula ...........44650, 44660-44661
  Hernia .......................44050
  Malrotation ..................44055
  Obstruction ..................44050
  Ulcer ........................44605
  Volvulus .....................44050
  Wound .......................44605
Stoma Closure .............44620, 44625
Suture
  Diverticula ...................44605
  Fistula ...........44650, 44660-44661
  Plication .....................44680

**Computed Axial Tomography (CAT)**
*See* CAT Scan; Specific Anatomic Site

**Computed Tomographic Scintigraphy**
*See* Emission Computerized Tomography

**Computerized Emission Tomography**
*See* Emission Computerized Tomography

**Computer Data Analysis** ......99090

**Concentration, Hydrogen-Ion**
*See* pH

**Concentration, Minimum Inhibitory**
*See* Minimum Inhibitory Concentration

**Concentration of Specimen** ...87015

**Concentric Procedure** ........28296

**Conchae Nasale**
*See* Nasal Turbinate

**Concha Bullosa Resection**
with Nasal/Sinus Endoscopy .......31240

**Conduction, Nerve**
*See* Nerve Conduction

**Conduit, Ileal**
*See* Ileal Conduit

**Condyle**
Humerus
  Fracture
    Closed Treatment ......24576-24577
    Open Treatment .............24579
    Percutaneous ...............24582
Metatarsal
  Excision .....................28288
Phalanges
  Toe
    Excision ...................28126

**Condyle, Mandibular**
*See* Mandibular Condyle

**Condylectomy**
Temporomandibular Joint ..........21050
with Skull Base Surgery ......61596-61597

**Condyloma**
Destruction ................54050-54065

**Conference**
Medical
  with Interdisciplinary
  Team ..................99361-99373

**Confirmation**
Drug ...........................80102

**Confirmatory Consultations**
*See* Consultations
New or Established Patient ...99271-99275

**Congenital Arteriovenous Malformation**
*See* Arteriovenous Malformation

**Congenital Elevation of Scapula**
*See* Sprengel's Deformity

**Congenital Heart Septum Defect**
*See* Septal Defect

**Congenital Kidney Abnormality**
Nephrolithotomy ................50070
Pyeloplasty .....................50405
Pyelotomy ......................50135

**Congenital Laryngocele**
*See* Laryngocele

**Congenital Vascular Anomaly**
*See* Vascular Malformation

**Conisation**
*See* Cervix, Conization

**Conization**
Cervix ....................57520-57522

**Conjoint Psychotherapy** ......90847
*See* Psychiatric Treatment, Family

**Conjunctiva**
Biopsy .........................68100
Cyst
  Incision and Drainage ..........68020
Fistulize for Drainage
  without Tube ................68745
  with Tube ....................68750
Insertion Stent ..................68750
Lesion
  Destruction ..................68135
  Excision ...............68110-68130
    Over 1cm ..................68115
    with Adjacent Sclera .........68130
Reconstruction ............68320-68335
  Symblepharon
    with Graft .................68335
  with Flap
    Bridge or Partial .............68360
    Total ......................68362
Repair
  Symblepharon
    Division ...................68340
    without Graft ...............68330
    with Graft .................68335
  Wound
    Direct Closure ...............65270
    Mobilization and
    Rearrangement .......65272-65273
Unlisted Services and Procedures ...68399

**Conjunctivo-Tarso-Muller Resection** ....................67908

**Conjunctivocystorhinostomy**
*See* Conjunctivorhinostomy

**Conjunctivodacryocystostomy**
*See* Conjunctivorhinostomy

**Conjunctivoplasty** .......68320-68330
Reconstruction Cul de Sac
  with Extensive Rearrangement ...68326
  with Graft ...................68326
    Buccal Mucous Membrane ....68328
with Extensive Rearrangement ......68320
with Graft .......................68320
  Buccal Mucous Membrane ......68325

**Conjunctivorhinostomy**
without Tube ....................68745
with Tube .......................68750

**Conscious Sedation**
*See* Sedation

**Construction**
Finger
  Toe to Hand Transfer .....26551-26556
Neobladder ......................51596
Vagina
  without Graft .................57291
  with Graft ....................57292

**Consultation**
*See* Second Opinion; Third Opinion
Clinical Pathology ..........80500-80502
Confirmatory ..............99271-99275
  New or Established
  Patient ................99271-99275
Follow-up Inpatient
  Established Patient ......99261-99263
Initial Inpatient ............99251-99255
  New or Established
  Patient ................99251-99255
Office and/or Other
Outpatient ................99241-99245
  New or Established
  Patient ................99241-99245
Psychiatric, with Family ...........90887
Radiation Therapy
  Radiation Physics .......77336, 77370
Surgical Pathology ..........88321-88325
  Intraoperation ..........88329-88332
X-Ray .........................76140

**Consumption Test, Antiglobulin**
*See* Coombs Test

**Contact Lens Services**
Fittings and Prescription ..........92070, 92310-92313
Modification ....................92325
Prescription ...............92314-92317
Replacement ....................92326
Supply ...................92391, 92396

**Correction of Ureteropelvic Junction**
*See* Pyeloplasty

**Cortex Decortication, Cerebral**
*See* Decortication

**Cortical Mapping**
Transection
by Electric Stimulation ....95961-95962

**Corticoids**
*See* Corticosteroids

**Corticoliberin**
*See* Corticotropic Releasing Hormone (CRH)

**Corticosteroids**
Blood ....83491
Urine ....83491

**Corticosteroid Binding Globulin**
*See* Transcortin

**Corticosterone**
Blood or Urine ....82528

**Corticotropic Releasing Hormone (CRH)** ....80412

**Cortisol** ....80400-80406, 80418-80420, 80436, 82530
Stimulation ....80412
Total ....82533

**Cortisol Binding Globulin** ....84449

**Costectomy**
*See* Resection, Ribs

**Costen Syndrome**
*See* Temporomandibular Joint (TMJ)

**Costotransversectomy** ....21610

**Cothromboplastin**
*See* Proconvertin

**Cotte Operation** ....58400-58410
*See* Repair, Uterus, Suspension; Revision

**Cotton Procedure**
Bohler Procedure ....28405

**Counseling**
*See* Preventive Medicine

**Counseling and/or Risk Factor Reduction Intervention - Preventive Medicine, Individual Counseling**
*See* Preventive Medicine, Counseling and/or Risk Factor Reduction Intervention, Individual Counseling

**Count, Blood Cell**
*See* Blood Cell Count

**Count, Blood Platelet**
*See* Blood, Platelet, Count

**Count, Cell**
*See* Cell Count

**Count, Complete Blood**
*See* Complete Blood Count (CBC)

**Count, Erythrocyte**
*See* Red Blood Cell (RBC), Count

**Count, Leukocyte**
*See* White Blood Cell, Count

**Count, Reticulocyte**
*See* Reticulocyte, Count

**Counterimmuno-electrophoresis** ....86185

**Counters, Cell**
*See* Cell Count

**Countershock, Electric**
*See* Cardioversion

**Coventry Tibial Wedge Osteotomy**
*See* Osteotomy, Tibia

**Cowper's Gland**
Excision ....53250

**Coxa**
*See* Hip

**Coxiella Burnetii**
Antibody ....86638

**Coxsackie**
Antibody ....86658

**CPAP**
*See* Continuous Positive Airway Pressure

**CPK**
Blood ....82550-82552

**CPR (Cardiopulmonary Resuscitation)** ....92950

**Cranial Bone**
Halo
Thin Skull Osteology ....20664
Reconstruction
Extracranial ....21181-21184
Tumor
Excision ....61563-61564

**Cranial Halo** ....20661

**Cranial Nerve**
*See* Specific Nerve
Avulsion ....64732-64760, 64771
Decompression ....61458, 64716
Implantation
Electrode ....64553, 64573
Incision ....64732-64746, 64752, 64760, 65771
Injection
Anesthetic ....64400, 64402, 64405, 64408, 64412
Neurolytic ....64600, 64605, 64610
Insertion
Electrode ....64553, 64573
Neuroplasty ....64716
Release ....64716
Repair
Suture, with or without Graft ....64864-64865
Section ....61460
Transection ....64732-64746, 64752, 64755, 64760, 64771
Transposition ....64716

**Cranial Nerve II**
*See* Optic Nerve

**Cranial Nerve V**
*See* Trigeminal Nerve

**Cranial Nerve VII**
*See* Facial Nerve

**Cranial Nerve X**
*See* Vagus Nerve

**Cranial Nerve XI**
*See* Accessory Nerve

**Cranial Nerve XII**
*See* Hypoglossal Nerve

**Cranial Tongs**
Application/Removal ....20660
Removal ....20665

**Craniectomy** ....61501
*See* Craniotomy
Decompression ....61343
Exploratory ....61304-61305
Extensive, for Multiple Suture Craniosynostosis ....61558, 61559
for Electrode ....61860-61875
Release Stenosis ....61550-61552
Surgical ....61312-61315, 61320-61321, 61440, 61450, 61458-61480, 61500-61501, 61510-61516, 61518-61522

**Craniofacial Procedures**
Unlisted Services and Procedures ....21299

**Craniofacial Separation**
Closed Treatment ....21431
Open Treatment ....21432-21436
Wire Fixation ....21431

**Craniomegalic Skull**
Reduction ....62115-62117

**Craniopharyngioma**
Excision ....61545

**Cranioplasty** ....62120
Encephalocele Repair ....62120
for Defect ....62140-62141, 62145
with Autograft ....62146-62147
with Bone Graft ....62146-62147

Other .87102
Skin .87101
Lymphocyte
Chromosome Analysis .88230
Mycobacteria .87116-87118
Mycoplasma .87109
Oocyte
Co-Culture of Embryo .89250-89251
Pathogen
by Kit .87082-87085
Skin
Chromosome Analysis .88233
Tissue
Toxin/Antitoxin .87230
Virus .87252-87253
Tubercle Bacilli .87116-87117
Typing .87140-87158
Unlisted Services and
Procedures .87163, 87999

**Curettage**
*See* Dilation and Curettage
Cervix
Endocervical .57454, 57505
Cornea .65435-65436
Chelating Agent .65436
Hydatidiform Mole .59870
Postpartum .59160

**Curettage, Uterus**
*See* Uterus, Curettage

**Curettage and Dilatation**
*See* Dilation and Curettage

**Curettement**
Skin Lesion .11055-11057

**Curietherapy**
*See* Brachytherapy

**Custodial Care**
*See* Domiciliary Services; Nursing Facility Services

**Cutaneolipectomy**
*See* Lipectomy

**Cutaneous-Vesicostomy**
*See* Vesicostomy, Cutaneous

**Cutaneous Electrostimulation, Analgesic**
*See* Application, Neurostimulation

**Cutaneous Tag**
*See* Skin, Tags

**Cutaneous Tissue**
*See* Integumentary System

**CVS**
*See* Biopsy, Chorionic Villus

**Cyanacobalamin**
*See* Cyanocobalamin

**Cyanide**
Blood .82600
Tissue .82600

**Cyanocobalamin** .82607-82608

**Cyclic AMP** .82030

**Cyclic GMP** .83008

**Cyclic Somatostatin**
*See* Somatostatin

**Cyclocryotherapy**
*See* Cryotherapy, Destruction, Ciliary Body

**Cyclodialysis**
Destruction
Ciliary Body .66740

**Cyclophotocoagulation**
Destruction
Ciliary Body .66710

**Cyclosporine**
Assay .80158

**Cyst**
Abdomen
Destruction/Excision .49200-49201
Ankle
Capsule .27630
Tendon Sheath .27630
Aspiration
CAT Scan Guide .76365
Bartholin's Gland Excision .56740
*See* Bartholin's Gland, Cyst
Repair .56440
Bile Duct .47715, 47716
Bladder
Excision .51500
Bone
Drainage .20615
Injection .20615
Brain
Drainage .61150-61151, 61156
Excision .61516, 61524
Branchial Cleft
Excision .42810, 42815
Breast
Incision and Drainage .19020
Puncture Aspiration .19000-19001
Calcaneus .28100-28103
Carpal .25130, 25135-25136
Choledochal .47715-47716
Ciliary Body
Destruction .66770
Clavicle
Excision .23140-23146
Conjunctiva .68020
Dermoid
Nose
Excision .30124-30125
Drainage
Contrast Injection .49424
with X-Ray .76080
Excision
Clavicle .23140
with Allograft .23146
with Autograft .23145
Femur .27355-27358
Ganglion
*See* Ganglion
Hydatid
*See* Echinococcosis
Humerus
with Allograft .23156
with Autograft .23155
Lymphatic
*See* Lymphocele
Mediastinum .32662
Olecranon Process
with Allograft .24126
with Autograft .24125
Pericardial .32661
Pilonidal .11770-11772
Radius
with Allograft .24126
with Autograft .24125
Scapula .23140
with Allograft .23146
with Autograft .23145
Ulna
with Allograft .24126
with Autograft .24125
Facial Bones
Excision .21030
Femur .27065-27067
Fibula .27635-27638
Gums
Incision and Drainage .41800
Hip .27065-27067
Humerus
Excision .23150-23156, 24110
with Allograft .24116
with Autograft .24115
Ileum .27065-27067
Incision and Drainage .10060-10061
Pilonidal .10080-10081
Iris
Destruction .66770
Kidney
Ablation .50541
Aspiration .50390
Excision .50280-50290
Injection .50390
X-Ray .74470
Knee
Baker's .27345
Excision .27347
Leg, Lower
Capsule .27630
Tendon Sheath .27630
Liver .47010
Drainage .47010
Open .47010
Repair .47300
Lung
Incision and Drainage .32200
Removal .32140
Lymph Node
Axillary/Cervical
Excision .38550-38555

# D

- Chemical Cauterization
  - Granulation Tissue . . . . . . . . . . . .17250
- Ciliary Body
  - Cryotherapy . . . . . . . . . . . . . . . . . .66720
  - Cyclodialysis . . . . . . . . . . . . . . . . .66740
  - Cyclophotocoagulation . . . . . . . . .66710
  - Diathermy . . . . . . . . . . . . . . . . . . .66700
- Cyst
  - Abdomen . . . . . . . . . . . . . .49200-49201
  - Ciliary Body . . . . . . . . . . . . . . . . .66770
  - Iris . . . . . . . . . . . . . . . . . . . . . . . .66770
  - Retroperitoneal . . . . . . . . .49200-49201
- Endometriomas
  - Abdomen . . . . . . . . . . . . . .49200-49201
  - Retroperitoneal . . . . . . . . .49200-49201
- Fissure
  - Anal . . . . . . . . . . . . . . . . . .46940, 46942
- Hemorrhoids . . . . . . . . . . . . . . .46934-46936
- Kidney
  - Endoscopic . . . . . . . . . . . .50557, 50576
- Lesion
  - Anal . . . . . . . . . . . .46900-46917, 46924
  - Bladder . . . . . . . . . . . . . . . . . . . . .51030
  - Ciliary Body . . . . . . . . . . . . . . . . .66770
  - Colon . . . . . . . . . . . . . . . . . . . . . . .45303
  - Conjunctiva . . . . . . . . . . . . . . . . .68135
  - Cornea . . . . . . . . . . . . . . . . . . . . .65450
  - Choroid . . . . . . . . . . . . . . . . . . . .67220
  - Eyelid . . . . . . . . . . . . . . . . . . . . . .67850
  - Facial . . . . . .17000-17011, 17280-17286
  - Gastrointestinal, Upper . . . . . . . . .43258
  - Gums . . . . . . . . . . . . . . . . . . . . . .41850
  - Intestines
    - Large . . . . . . . . . . . . . . . . . . . . .44393
    - Small . . . . . . . . . . . . . . . . . . . .44369
  - Iris . . . . . . . . . . . . . . . . . . . . . . . .66770
  - Mouth . . . . . . . . . . . . . . . . . . . . .40820
  - Nose
    - Intranasal . . . . . . . . . . . .30117-30118
  - Palate . . . . . . . . . . . . . . . . . . . . .42160
  - Penis
    - Cryosurgery . . . . . . . . . . . . . . . .54056
    - Electrodesiccation . . . . . . . . . . .54055
    - Extensive . . . . . . . . . . . . . . . . . .54065
    - Laser Surgery . . . . . . . . . . . . . . .54057
    - Simple . . . . . . . . . . . . . . .54050-54060
    - Surgical Excision . . . . . . . . . . . .54060
  - Pharynx . . . . . . . . . . . . . . . . . . . .42808
  - Prostate . . . . . . . . . . . . . . . . . . . .45320
    - Thermotherapy . . . . . . . .53850-53852
      - Microwave . . . . . . . . . . . . . . .53850
      - Radio Frequency . . . . . . . . . .53852
  - Rectum . . . . . . . . . . . . . . . . . . . .45320
  - Retina
    - Cryotherapy, Diathermy .67208, 67227
    - Photocoagulation . . . . . .67210, 67228
    - Radiation by Implantation of Source . . . . . . . . . . . . . . . . .67218
  - Skin
    - Benign . . . . . . . . . . . . . . .17000-17250
    - Malignant . . . . . . . . . . . .17260-17286
  - Spinal Cord . . . . . . . . . . . . .62280-62282
  - Ureter . . . . . . . . . . . . . . . . . . . . . .52338
  - Urethra . . . . . . . . . . . . . . . . . . . . .53265
  - Uvula . . . . . . . . . . . . . . . . . . . . . . .42160
  - Vagina
    - Extensive . . . . . . . . . . . . . . . . . .57065
    - Simple . . . . . . . . . . . . . . . . . . . .57061
  - Vascular, Cutaneous . . . . . .17106-17108
  - Vulva
    - Extensive . . . . . . . . . . . . . . . . . .56515
    - Simple . . . . . . . . . . . . . . . . . . . .56501
- Molluscum Contagiosum . . . . . . . . . .17110
- Muscle Endplate
  - Cervical Spine . . . . . . . . . . . . . . .64613
  - Extraocular . . . . . . . . . . . . . . . . .67345
  - Facial . . . . . . . . . . . . . . . . . . . . . .64612
- Nerve . . . . . . . . . . . . . . . . . . . .64600-64680
  - Laryngeal, Recurrent . . . . . . . . . . .31595
- Polyp
  - Aural . . . . . . . . . . . . . . . . . . . . . . .69540
  - Nose . . . . . . . . . . . . . . . . . .30110-30115
  - Urethra . . . . . . . . . . . . . . . . . . . . .53260
- Prostate Tissue
  - Transurethral
    - Thermotherapy . . . . . . . .53850-53852
- Sinus
  - Frontal . . . . . . . . . . . . . . . .31080-31085
- Skene's Gland . . . . . . . . . . . . . . . . . . .53270
- Skin Lesion
  - Benign . . . . . . . . . . . . . . . .17000-17004
    - Fifteen or More Lesions . . . . . .17004
    - Two - Fourteen Lesions . . . . . . .17003
  - Malignant . . . . . . . . . . . . . .17260-17286
  - Premalignant . . . . . . . . . . .17000-17004
    - Fifteen or More Lesions . . . . . . .17004
    - Two - Fourteen Lesions . . . . . . .17003
- Tonsil
  - Lingual . . . . . . . . . . . . . . . . . . . . . .42870
- Tumor
  - Abdomen . . . . . . . . . . . . . .49200-49201
  - Bile Duct . . . . . . . . . . . . . . . . . . . .43272
  - Chemosurgery . . . . . . . . . .17304-17310
  - Colon . . . . . . . . . . . . . . . . . . . . . . .45383
  - Intestines
    - Large . . . . . . . . . . . . . . . . . . . . .44393
    - Small . . . . . . . . . . . . . . . . . . . .44369
  - Pancreatic Duct . . . . . . . . . . . . . . .43272
  - Rectum . . . . . . . . . .45190, 46937-46938
  - Retroperitoneal . . . . . . . . .49200-49201
  - Urethra . . . . . . . . . . . . . . . . . . . . .53220
- Tumor or Polyp
  - Rectum . . . . . . . . . . . . . . . . . . . . .45320
- Turbinate Mucosa . . . . . . . . . .30801-30802
- Ureter
  - Endoscopic . . . . . . . . . . . .50957-50959, 50976-50978
- Urethra . . . . . . . . . . . . . . . . . . .52214-52224
  - Prolapse . . . . . . . . . . . . . . . . . . . .53275
- Warts
  - Flat . . . . . . . . . . . . . . . . . . . .17110-17111

**Determination, Blood Pressure**
*See* Blood Pressure

**Developmental Testing** . .96110-96111

**Device**
- Venous Access
  - Insertion . . . . . . . . . . . . . . . . . . . .36533
  - Removal . . . . . . . . . . . . . . . . . . . . .36535
  - Revision . . . . . . . . . . . . . . . . . . . .36534

**Device, Intrauterine**
*See* Intrauterine Device (IUD)

**Device, Orthotic**
*See* Orthotics

**Device Handling** . . . . . . . . . . . . . .99002

**DEXA**
*See* Dual Energy X-Ray Absorptiometry (DEXA)

**Dexamethasone**
Suppression Test . . . . . . . . . . . . . . . . .80420

**de Quervain's Disease Treatment** . . . . . . . . . . . . . . . . . . . .25000

**DHA Sulfate**
*See* Dehydroepiandrosterone Sulfate

**DHEA**
*See* Dehydroepiandrosterone

**DHEA Sulfate**
*See* Dehydroepiandrosterone Sulfate

**DHT**
*See* Dihydrotestosterone

**Diagnosis, Psychiatric**
*See* Psychiatric Diagnosis

**Diagnostic Amniocentesis**
*See* Amniocentesis

**Diagnostic Aspiration of Anterior Chamber of Eye**
*See* Eye, Paracentesis, Anterior Chamber, with Diagnostic Aspiration of Aqueous

**Diagnostic Radiologic Examination**
*See* Radiology, Diagnostic

**Diagnostic Skin and Sensitization Tests**
*See* Allergy Tests

**Diagnostic Ultrasound**
*See* Echography

**Diagnostic Ultrasound of Heart**
*See* Echocardiography

**Dialyses, Peritoneal**
*See* Dialysis, Peritoneal

**Dialysis**
- Arteriovenous Fistula
  - Revision
    - without Thrombectomy . . . . . . .36832
- Arteriovenous Shunt . . . . . . . . . . . . . .36145

**Diphosphate, Adenosine**
- *See* Adenosine Diphosphate

**Diphtheria**
- *See* Vaccines
- Antibody ....86648

**Dipropylacetic Acid**
- Assay ....80164

**Direct Pedicle Flap**
- Formation ....15570-15576

**Disability Evaluation Services**
- Basic Life and/or Disability Evaluation ....99450
- Work-Related or Medical Disability Evaluation ....99455-99456

**Disarticulation**
- Ankle ....27889
- Hip ....27295
- Knee ....27598
- Wrist ....25920, 25924
  - Revision ....25922

**Disarticulation of Shoulder**
- *See* Shoulder, Disarticulation

**Disc, Intervertebral**
- *See* Intervertebral Disk

**Discectomies**
- *See* Diskectomy

**Discectomies, Percutaneous**
- *See* Diskectomy, Percutaneous

**Discharge, Body Substance**
- *See* Drainage

**Discharge Services**
- *See* Hospital Services
- Hospital ....99238-99239
- Nursing Facility ....99315-99316
- Observation Care ....99234-99236

**Discission**
- Cataract
  - Laser Surgery ....66821
  - Stab Incision ....66820
- Vitreous Strands ....67030

**Discography**
- *See* Diskography

**Discolysis**
- *See* Chemonucleolysis

**Disease**
- Durand-Nicolas-Favre
  - *See* Lymphogranuloma Venereum
- Erb-Goldflam
  - *See* Myasthenia Gravis
- Heine-Medin
  - *See* Polio
- Hydatid
  - *See* Echinococcosis
- Lyme
  - *See* Lyme Disease
- Ormond
  - *See* Retroperitoneal Fibrosis
- Peyronie
  - *See* Peyronie Disease
- Posada-Wernicke
  - *See* Coccidioidomycosis

**Disease/Organ Panel**
- *See* Organ/Disease Panel

**Diskectomy** ....63075-63078
- Additional Segment ....22226
- Arthrodesis
  - Additional Interspace ....22585
  - Cervical ....22554
  - Lumbar ....22558, 22630
  - Thoracic ....22556
- Cervical ....22220
- Lumbar ....22224, 22630
- Percutaneous ....62287
- Thoracic ....22222

**Diskography**
- Cervical Disk ....72285
- Injection ....62290-62291
- Lumbar Disk ....72295
- Thoracic ....72285

**Disk Chemolyses, Intervertebral**
- *See* Chemonucleolysis

**Dislocated Elbow**
- *See* Dislocation, Elbow

**Dislocated Hip**
- *See* Dislocation, Hip Joint

**Dislocated Jaw**
- *See* Dislocation, Temporomandibular Joint

**Dislocated Joint**
- *See* Dislocation

**Dislocated Shoulder**
- *See* Dislocation, Shoulder

**Dislocation**
- Acromioclavicular Joint
  - Open Treatment ....23550-23552
- Ankle
  - Closed Treatment ....27840-27842
  - Open Treatment ....27846-27848
- Carpal
  - Closed Treatment ....25690
  - Open Treatment ....25695
- Carpometacarpal Joint ....26670
  - Closed Treatment
    - with Manipulation ....26675-26676
  - Open Treatment ....26685-26686
  - Percutaneous Fixation ....26676
- Clavicle
  - Closed Treatment ....23540-23545
  - Open Treatment ....23550-23552
  - without Manipulation ....23540
  - with Manipulation ....23545
- Closed Treatment
  - Carpometacarpal Joint ....26670, 26675
  - Metacarpophalangeal ....26700, 26705-26706
  - Thumb ....26641
- Elbow
  - Closed Treatment ....24600-24605, 24640
  - Open Treatment ....24615
- Hip Joint
  - Closed Treatment ....27250-27252, 27265-27266
  - Congenital ....27256-27259
  - Open Treatment ....27253-27254, 27258-27259
  - without Trauma ....27265-27266
- Interphalangeal Joint
  - Closed Treatment ....26770, 26775
  - Open Treatment ....26785
  - Percutaneous Fixation ....26776
  - Toe
    - Closed Treatment ....28660-28665
    - Open Treatment ....28675
    - Percutaneous Fixation ....28666, 26770-26776
  - with Manipulation ....26770
- Knee ....27560-27562
  - Closed Treatment ....27550-27552, 27550-27752
  - Open Treatment ....27556-27558, 27566
  - Recurrent ....27420-27424
- Lunate
  - Closed Treatment ....25690
  - Open Treatment ....25695
  - with Manipulation ....25690, 26670, 26675-26676, 26700, 26705-26706
- Metacarpophalangeal Joint
  - Closed Treatment ....26700, 26705-26706
  - Open Treatment ....26715
- Metatarsophalangeal Joint
  - Closed Treatment ....28630-28635
  - Open Treatment ....28645
  - Percutaneous Fixation ....28636
- Open Treatment ....26685-26686
- Patella
  - Closed Treatment ....27560-27562
  - Open Treatment ....27566
  - Recurrent ....27420-27424
- Pelvic Ring
  - Closed Treatment ....27193-27194
  - Open Treatment ....27217-27218
  - Percutaneous Fixation ....27216
  - without Manipulation ....27193-27194

Percutaneous Fixation
Metacarpophalangeal ..........26705
Peroneal Tendons ...........27675-27676
Radio-Ulnar Joint .....25520, 25525-25526
Radius
Closed Treatment .............24640
with Fracture
Closed Treatment ............24620
Open Treatment .............24635
Shoulder
Closed Treatment
with Manipulation .....23650-23655
Open Treatment with Surgical or Anatomical Neck Fracture .......23660
Closed Treatment with Manipulation ...............23675
Open Treatment .............23680
with Greater Tuberosity Fracture
Closed Treatment ............23665
Open Treatment .............23670
Skin
Debridement ...........11010-11012
Sternoclavicular Joint
Closed Treatment
without Manipulation ........23520
with Manipulation ............23525
Open Treatment .........23530-23532
Talotarsal Joint
Closed Treatment ........28570-28575
Open Treatment ...............28546
Percutaneous Fixation ..........28576
Tarsal
Closed Treatment ........28540-28545
Open Treatment ...............28555
Percutaneous Fixation ..........28546
Tarsometatarsal Joint
Closed Treatment ........28600-28605
Open Treatment ...............28615
Percutaneous Fixation ..........28606
Temporomandibular Joint
Closed Treatment ........21480-21485
Open Treatment ...............21490
Thumb
Closed Treatment .......26641, 26645
Open Treatment ...............26665
Percutaneous Fixation ..........26650
with Fracture ................26645
Open Treatment .............26665
Percutaneous Fixation ..26650, 26665
with Manipulation ......26641, 26645, 26650
Tibiofibular Joint
Closed Treatment ........27830-27831
Open Treatment ...............27832
Vertebra
Additional Segment
Open Treatment .............22328
Cervical
Open Treatment .............22326
Closed Treatment .............22305
without Manipulation ........22310
with Manipulation, Casting and/or Bracing ....................22315
Lumbar
Open Treatment .............22325
Thoracic
Open Treatment .............22327
Wrist
Closed Treatment .......25660, 25675, 25680
Intercarpal ...................25660
Open Treatment .............25670
Open Treatment .........25670, 25685
Radiocarpal ..................25660
Open Treatment .............25670
Radioulnar
Closed Treatment ............25675
Open Treatment .............25676
with Fracture
Closed Treatment ............25680
Open Treatment .............25685
with Manipulation ......25660, 25675, 25680

**Dislocation, Radiocarpal Joint**
*See* Radiocarpal Joint, Dislocation

**Disorder**
Blood Coagulation
*See* Coagulopathy
Penis
*See* Penis
Retinal
*See* Retina

**Displacement Therapy**
Nose ..........................30210

**Dissection**
Hygroma, Cystic
Axillary/Cervical .........38550-38555
Lymph Nodes ...................38542

**Dissection, Neck, Radical**
*See* Radical Neck Dissection

**Distention**
*See* Dilation

**Diverticula, Meckel's**
*See* Diverticulum, Meckel's

**Diverticulectomy** .............44800
Esophagus ................43130, 43135

**Diverticulectomy, Meckel's**
*See* Meckel's Diverticulum, Excision

**Diverticulum**
Bladder
*See* Bladder, Diverticulum
Meckel's
Excision ......................44800
Repair
Urethra ................53400-53405

**Division**
Muscle
Foot ..........................28250
Plantar Fascia
Foot ..........................28250

**Division, Isthmus, Horseshoe Kidney**
*See* Symphysiotomy, Horseshoe Kidney

**Division, Scalenus Anticus Muscle**
*See* Muscle Division, Scalenus Anticus

**Dl-Amphetamine**
*See* Amphetamine

**DMO**
*See* Dimethadione

**DNA**
Antibody ..................86225-86226

**DNAse**
Antibody ........................86215

**DNA Endonuclease**
*See* DNAse

**DNA Probe**
*See* Cytogenetics Studies; Nucleic Acid Probe

**Domiciliary Services**
*See* Nursing Facility Services
Discharge Services .........99315-99316
Established Patient .........99331-99333
New Patient ...............99321-99323

**Donor Procedures**
Heart/Lung Excision ..............33930
Heart Excision ...................33940

**Dopamine**
*See* Catecholamines
Blood ....................82383-82384
Urine ....................82382, 82384

**Doppler Echocardiography** ...76827-76828, 93307-93308, 93320-93321, 93325, 93350
Extracranial .....................93875
Transthoracic ..............93303-93317

**Doppler Scan**
Arterial Studies, Extremities ..93922-93924
Extremities .....................93965
Intracranial Arteries .........93886-93888

**Dorsal Vertebra**
*See* Vertebra, Thoracic

**Dose Plan**
*See* Dosimetry

**Dosimetry**
Radiation Therapy ..........77300, 77331
Brachytherapy ..........77326-77328
Teletherapy ............77305-77321

**Double-Stranded DNA**
*See* Deoxyribonucleic Acid

**Doxepin**
Assay ........ 80166

**DPH**
*See* Phenytoin

**Drainage**
*See* Excision; Incision; Incision and Drainage
Abdomen
  Abdomen Fluid ........ 49080-49081
Abscess
  Appendix ........ 44900-44901
    Percutaneous ........ 44901
  Brain ........ 61150-61151
  Eyelid ........ 67700
  Liver ........ 47010-47011
  Ovary
    Percutaneous ........ 58823
  Pelvic
    Percutaneous ........ 58823
  Pericolic
    Percutaneous ........ 58823
  Perirenal or Renal ........ 50020-50021
    Percutaneous ........ 50021
  Prostate ........ 52700
  Retroperitoneal ........ 49060-49061
    Percutaneous ........ 49061
  Subdiaphragmatic or Subphrenic ........ 49040-49041
    Percutaneous ........ 49040-49041
  with X-Ray ........ 75989
Bile Duct
  Transhepatic ........ 75980
Brain Fluid ........ 61070
Bursa ........ 20600, 20600-20610
Cerebrospinal Fluid ........ 61000-61001, 61020, 61050, 61070, 62272
Cervical Fluid ........ 61050
Cisternal Fluid ........ 61050
Cyst
  Bone ........ 20615
  Brain ........ 61150-61151
  Breast ........ 19000-19001
  Ganglion ........ 20600
  Liver ........ 47010-47011
    Percutaneous ........ 47011
  Salivary Gland ........ 42409
  Sublingual Gland ........ 42409
  with Fistula ........ 42325-42326
Extraperitoneal Lymphocele
  Laparoscopic ........ 49323
  Open ........ 49062
Eye
  Anterior Chamber Paracentesis
    with Diagnostic Aspiration of Aqueous ........ 65800
    with Therapeutic Release of Aqueous ........ 65805
  Removal Blood ........ 65815
  Removal of Vitreous and/or Discission Anterior Hyaloid Membrane ........ 65810
Ganglion Cyst ........ 20600-20605
Hematoma
  Brain ........ 61154, 61156
Hematoma, Subungual ........ 11740
Joint ........ 20600, 20600-20610
Liver
  Abscess or Cyst ........ 47010-47011
    Percutaneous ........ 47011
Lymphocele
  Endoscopic ........ 49323
Onychia ........ 10060-10061
Orbit ........ 67405, 67440
Pancreas
  *See* Anastomosis, Pancreas to Intestines
  Pseudocyst ........ 48510-48511
    Percutaneous ........ 48511
Paronychia ........ 10060-10061
Pericardial Sac ........ 32659
Pericardium
  *See* Aspiration, Pericardium
Pseudocyst
  Pancreas ........ 48510
    Open ........ 48510
    Percutaneous ........ 48511
Puncture
  Chest ........ 32000-32002
Skin ........ 10040-10180
Spinal Cord
  Cerebrospinal Fluid ........ 62272
Subdural Fluid ........ 61000-61001
Urethra
  Extravasation ........ 53080-53085
Ventricular Fluid ........ 61020

**Drainage Implant, Glaucoma**
*See* Aqueous Shunt

**Dressings**
Burns ........ 16010-16030
Change
  Anesthesia ........ 15852

**DREZ Procedure**
*See* Incision, Spinal Cord; Incision and Drainage

**Drill Hole**
Skull
  Catheter ........ 61107
  Drain Hematoma ........ 61108
  Exploration ........ 61105
  Implant Electrode ........ 61850, 61862

**Drinking Test for Glaucoma**
*See* Glaucoma, Provocative Test

**Drug**
*See* Drug Assay; Specific Drug
Analysis
  Tissue Preparation ........ 80103
Confirmation ........ 80102
Infusion ........ 62360-62362

**Drugs, Anticoagulant**
*See* Clotting Inhibitors

**Drug Assay**
Amikacin ........ 80150
Amitriptyline ........ 80152
Benzodiazepine ........ 80154
Carbamazepine ........ 80156
Cyclosporine ........ 80158
Desipramine ........ 80160
Digoxin ........ 80162
Dipropylacetic Acid ........ 80164
Doxepin ........ 80166
Ethosuximide ........ 80168
Gentamicin ........ 80170
Gold ........ 80172
Imipramine ........ 80174
Lidocaine ........ 80176
Lithium ........ 80178
Nortriptyline ........ 80182
Phenobarbital ........ 80184
Phenytoin ........ 80185-80186
Primidone ........ 80188
Procainamide ........ 80190-80192
Quantitative
  Other ........ 80299
Quinidine ........ 80194
Salicylate ........ 80196
Tacrolimus ........ 80197
Theophylline ........ 80198
Tobramycin ........ 80200
Topiramate ........ 80201
Vancomycin ........ 80202

**Drug Instillation**
*See* Instillation, Drugs

**Drug Management**
Psychiatric ........ 90862

**Drug Screen** ........ 80100-80101, 82486

**DST**
*See* Dexamethasone, Suppression Test

**DTaP Immunization** ........ 90721

**DTP Immunization** ........ 90701, 90720

**DT Shots** ........ 90702

**Dual Energy X-Ray Absorptiometry (DEXA)** ........ 76075
Appendicular ........ 76076
Axial Skeleton ........ 76075

**Dual Photon Absorptiometry**
*See* Absorptiometry, Dual Photon

**Duct, Bile**
*See* Bile Duct

**Duct, Hepatic**
*See* Hepatic Duct

**Duct, Nasolacrimal**
*See* Nasolacrimal Duct

**Duct, Omphalomesenteric**
*See* Omphalomesenteric Duct

**Duct, Pancreatic**
*See* Pancreatic Duct

**Duct, Salivary**
*See* Salivary Duct

**Duct, Stensen's**
*See* Parotid Duct

**Duct, Thoracic**
*See* Thoracic Duct

**Ductogram, Mammary**
*See* Galactogram

**Ductus Arteriosus**
Repair ....................33820-33824

**Ductus Deferens**
*See* Vas Deferens

**Duhamel Procedure**
*See* Proctectomy, Total

**Dunn Operation**
*See* Arthrodesis, Foot Joint

**Duodenotomy** ................44010

**Duodenum**
Biopsy .........................44010
Exclusion ......................48547
Exploration ....................44010
Incision .......................44010
Removal
  Foreign Body ................44010
X-Ray ..........................74260

**Duplex Scan**
*See* Vascular Studies
Arterial Studies
  Aorta ................93978-93979
  Extracranial ............93880-93882
  Lower Extremity .........93925-93926
  Penile .................93980-93981
  Upper Extremity .........93930-93931
  Visceral ...............93975-93979
Hemodialysis Access ............93990
Venous Studies
  Extremity .............93970-93971
  Penile .................93980-93981

**Dupuy-Dutemp Operation**
*See* Reconstruction, Eyelid; Revision

**Dupuytren's Contracture** ............26040, 26045

**Durand-Nicolas-Favre Disease**
*See* Lymphogranuloma Venereum

**Dust, Angel**
*See* Phencyclidine

**Duvries Operation**
*See* Tenoplasty

**Dwyer Procedure**
*See* Osteotomy, Calcaneus

**Dynamometry**
  with Ophthalmoscopy ..........92260

**D & C Yellow No. 7**
*See* Fluorescein

**D 2, Vitamin**
*See* Calciferol

**D and C**
*See* Dilation and Curettage

**D and E**
*See* Dilation and Evacuation

**D Galactose**
*See* Galactose

**D Glucose**
*See* Glucose

**D Vitamin**
*See* Vitamin, D

# E

**E1**
*See* Estrone

**E2**
*See* Estradiol

**E3**
*See* Estriol

**Ear**
Collection of Blood ...............36415
Drum ........69420-69421, 69433, 69436, 69450, 69610, 69620
  *See* Tympanic Membrane
External
  Abscess Incision and Drainage
    Complicated ................69005
    Simple ....................69000
  Biopsy .......................69100
  Excision
    Partial ....................69110
    Total ......................69120
  Hematoma
    Incision and Drainage ..69000, 69005
  Reconstruction ...............69300
  Unlisted Services and Procedures ..................69399
Inner
  CAT Scan ........70480, 70481, 70482
  Excision
    Labyrinth ............69905, 69910
  Exploration
    Endolymphatic Sac .....69805-69806
  Incision .....................69820
    Labyrinth .............69801-69802
    Semicircular Canal ..........69840
  Insertion
    Cochlear Device .............69930
  Semicircular Canal ............69820
  Unlisted Services and Procedures ..................69949
Middle
  Catheterization ...............69405
  CAT Scan ........70480, 70481, 70482
  Exploration ..................69440
  Inflation
    without Catheterization .......69401
    with Catheterization ..........69400
  Insertion
    Baffle .....................69410
    Catheter ...................69405
  Lesion
    Excision ...................69540
  Reconstruction
    Tympanoplasty without Mastoidectomy ........69631-69633
    Tympanoplasty with Antrotomy or Mastoidotomy .........69635-69637
    Tympanoplasty with Mastoidectomy ........69641-69646
  Removal
    Ventilating Tube .............69424
  Repair
    Oval Window ...............69666
    Round Window ..............69667
  Revision
    Stapes ....................69662
  Tumor
    Excision .......69550, 69552, 69554
  Unlisted Services and Procedures ..................69799
Outer
  CAT Scan ..............70480-70482

**Ear, Nose, and Throat**
*See* Hearing Aid Services; Otorhinolaryngology, Diagnostic
Audiologic Function Tests
  Acoustic Reflex ...............92568
  Acoustic Reflex Decay .........92569
  Audiometry
    Bekesy ...............92560-92561
    Comprehensive ..............92557
    Conditioning Play ...........92582
    Evoked Response ............92585
    Groups ....................92559
    Pure Tone ...........92552, 92553
    Select Picture ...............92583
    Speech ..............92555-92556
  Brainstem Evoked Response .....92585
  Central Auditory Function .......92589
  Ear Protector Evaluation ........92596

**Embolectomy**
Aortoiliac Artery ............34151-34201
Axillary Artery ..................34101
Brachial Artery ..................34101
Carotid Artery ...................34001
Celiac Artery ....................34151
Femoral ..........................34201
Iliac .......................34151-34201
Innominate Artery ..........34001-34101
Mesentery Artery ................34151
Peroneal Artery ..................34203
Popliteal Artery ..................34203
Pulmonary Artery ...........33910-33916
Radial Artery ....................34111
Renal Artery .....................34151
Subclavian Artery ...........34001-34101
Tibial Artery .....................34203
Ulnar Artery ......................34111

**Embryo**
Cryopreservation .................89258
Cryopreserved
Preparation
Transfer ...................89256
Culture
with Culture
Fertilized Oocyte .............89251
Hatching
Assisted
Microtechnique .............89253
Preparation
for Transfer ..................89255

**Embryonated Eggs**
Inoculation .......................87250

**Embryo /Fetus Monitoring**
*See* Monitoring, Fetal

**Embryo Implantation**
*See* Implantation

**Embryo Transfer**
In Vitro Fertilization .........58974, 58976
Intrafallopian Transfer ..........58976
Intrauterine Transfer ...........58974

**Emergency Department Services** ..........99281-99288, 99288
*See* Critical Care; Emergency Department Services
Anesthesia .......................99140
Physician Direction of Advanced Life Support ........................99288

**Emesis Induction** ............99175

**EMG**
*See* Electromyography, Needle

**Emission-Computed Tomography, Single-Photon**
*See* SPECT

**Emission Computerized Tomography** ..................78607

**EMI Scan**
*See* CAT Scan

**Emmet Operation**
*See* Vagina, Repair, Obstetric

**Empyema**
Closure
Chest Wall ...................32810
Thoracostomy ........32020, 32035-32036

**Empyema, Lung**
*See* Abscess, Thorax

**Empyemectomy** ...............32540

**Encephalitis**
Antibody ..................86651-86654

**Encephalitis Virus Vaccine**

**Encephalocele**
Repair ..........................62120
Craniotomy ..................62121

**Encephalon**
*See* Brain

**End-Expiratory Pressure, Positive**
*See* Pressure Breathing, Positive

**Endarterectomy**
Coronary Artery .................33572
Pulmonary .......................33916

**Endemic Flea-Borne Typhus**
*See* Murine Typhus

**Endocavitary Fulguration**
*See* Electrocautery

**Endocrine, Pancreas**
*See* Islet Cell

**Endocrine System**
Unlisted Services and Procedures ...............60699, 78099

**Endolymphatic Sac**
Exploration
without Shunt ...............69805
with Shunt ...................69806

**Endometrial Ablation**
Exploration
via Hysteroscopy ..............58563

**Endometrioma**
Abdomen
Destruction/Excision .....49200-49201
Retroperitoneal
Destruction/Excision .....49200-49201

**Endometriosis, Adhesive**
*See* Adhesions, Intrauterine

**Endometrium**
Biopsy ...................58100, 58558

**Endonuclease, DNA**
*See* DNAse

**Endorectal Pull-through**

**Endoscopic Retrograde Cannulation of Pancreatic Duct (ERCP)**
*See* Cholangiopancreatography

**Endoscopies, Pleural**
*See* Thoracoscopy

**Endoscopy**
*See* Arthroscopy; Thoracoscopy
Adrenal Gland
Biopsy ......................60650
Excision .....................60650
Anus
Biopsy ......................46606
Dilation .....................46604
Exploration ..................46600
Hemorrhage .................46614
Removal
Foreign Body ...............46608
Polyp ...............46610, 46612
Tumor ..............46610, 46612
Bile Duct
Biopsy ......................47553
Destruction
Calculi (Stone) ...........43265
Tumor ....................43272
Dilation ..........43271, 47555-47556
Exploration ..................47552
Intraoperative ................47550
Percutaneous ...........47552-47555
Removal
Calculi (Stone) ........43264, 47554
Foreign Body ...............43269
Stent .......................43269
Specimen Collection ..........43260
Sphincterotomy ...............43262
Sphincter Pressure ...........43263
Tube Placement .........43267, 43268
Bladder .........................52000
Biopsy ......................52204
Catheterization .........52005, 52010
Resection ....................52340
Urethral Stent ................52282
Bladder Neck
Injection of Implant Material ....51715
Bronchi
Aspiration ..............31645-31646
Biopsy ................31625-31629
Destruction
Lesion .....................31641
Tumor .....................31641
Dilation ...............31630-31631
Exploration ..................31622
Injection ....................31656
Lesion
Destruction ................31641
Needle Biopsy ...............31629
Placement
Stent ......................31631
Stenosis .....................31641

Uterus
  Anesthesia ..................00952
  Hysteroscopy
    Diagnostic .................58555
    with Division/Resection Intrauterine Septum ....................58560
    with Lysis of Intrauterine Adhesions ..................58559
  Removal
    Endometrial ................58563
    Impacted Foreign Body ........58562
    Leiomyomata ...............58561
  Surgical with Biopsy ...........58558
Vagina
  Anesthesia ..................00950
  Biopsy ......................57454
  Exploration ..................57452

**Endosteal Implant**
Reconstruction
  Mandible ..............21248-21249
  Maxilla ................21248-21249

**Endothelioma, Dural**
*See* Meningioma

**Endotoxin**
Bacteria ..................87174-87176

**Endotracheal Intubation**
*See* Insertion, Endotracheal Tube

**Endotracheal Tube**
Intubation ......................31500

**End Stage Renal Disease Services** ................90918-90925

**Enema**
Intussusception ..................74283
Therapeutic
  for Intussusception ............74283

**Energies, Electromagnetic**
*See* Irradiation

**ENT**
*See* Ear, Nose, and Throat; Otorhinolaryngology, Diagnostic

**Enterectomy** ............44120-44121
with Enterostomy ................44125

**Enterocele**
Repair .........................57556
  Hysterectomy
    with Colpectomy ............58280

**Enterocystoplasty** ............51960
Camey .........................50825

**Enteroenterostomy**
*See* Anastomosis, Intestines

**Enterolysis** ...................44005
Laparoscopic ....................44200

**Enteropancreatostomy**
*See* Anastomosis, Pancreas to Intestines

**Enterorrhaphy** .....44602-44603, 44615

**Enterostomy** ..................44300
Closure ..................44625-44626
with Enterectomy
  Intestine, Small ...............44125

**Enterotomy** ..................44615

**Enterovirus**
Antibody .......................86658

**Entropion**
Repair ....................67921-67924
  Blepharoplasty
    Excision Tarsal Wedge ........67923
  Suture .....................67921
  Thermocauterization ...........67922

**ENT (Ear Nose Throat)**
*See* Otorhinolaryngology

**Enucleation**
Eye
  without Implant ...............65101
  with Implant .................65103
    Muscles Attached ...........65105
Pleural .........................32540

**Enucleation, Cyst, Ovarian**
*See* Cystectomy, Ovarian

**Environmental Intervention**
for Psychiatric Patients ............90882

**Enzyme, Angiotensin-Forming**
*See* Renin

**Enzyme, Angiotensin Converting**
*See* Angiotensin Converting Enzyme (ACE)

**Enzyme Activity** ...............82657
Radioactive Substrate .............82658

**EOG**
*See* Electro-oculography

**Eosinocyte**
*See* Eosinophils

**Eosinophils**
Nasal Smear ....................89190

**Epiandrosterone** ..............82666

**Epicondylitides, Lateral Humeral**
*See* Tennis Elbow

**Epicondylitis, Radiohumeral**
*See* Tennis Elbow

**Epidemic Parotitis**
*See* Mumps

**Epididymectomy**
Bilateral ........................54861
Unilateral .......................54860

**Epididymis**
Abscess
  Incision and Drainage ..........54700
Anastomosis
  to Vas Deferens
    Bilateral ...................54901
    Unilateral ..................54900
Biopsy ....................54800-54820
Epididymography .................74440
Excision
  Bilateral ......................54861
  Unilateral .....................54860
Exploration
  Biopsy ......................54820
Hematoma
  Incision and Drainage ..........54700
Lesion
  Excision
    Local ......................54830
    Spermatocele ...............54840
Needle Biopsy ...................54800
Spermatocele
  Excision .....................54840
Unlisted Services and Procedures ...55899
X-Ray with Contrast ..............74440

**Epididymograms** ..............55300

**Epididymography** .............74440

**Epididymoplasty**
*See* Repair, Epididymis

**Epididymovasostomy**
Bilateral ........................54901
Unilateral .......................54900

**Epidural**
Electrode
  Insertion ....................61531
  Removal .....................61535
Injection .................62281-62282, 62310-62319, 64479-64484
  Lysis ........................62263

**Epidural Anesthesia**
*See* Anesthesia, Epidural

**Epidurography** ...............72275

**Epigastric**
Hernia Repair ...................49572

**Epiglottidectomy** .............31420

**Epiglottis**
Excision ........................31420

**Epikeratoplasty** ..............65767

**Epilation**
*See* Removal, Hair

**Epinephrine**
*See* Catecholamines
Blood ....................82383-82384
Urine ..........................82384

**Epiphysis**
*See* Bone; Specific Bone

**Epiphyseal Arrest**
Femur ............20150, 27185, 27475, 27479, 27485, 27742
Fibula ............20150, 27477-27485, 27730, 27732, 27734, 27740-27742
Radius ............20150, 25450, 25455
Tibia ............20150, 27477-27485, 27730, 27734, 27740-27742
Ulna ............20150, 25450, 25455

**Epiphyseal Separation**
Radius
  Closed Treatment ............25600
  Open Treatment ............25620

**Epiphysiodesis**
*See* Epiphyseal Arrest

**Epiploectomy** ............49255

**Episiotomy** ............59300

**Epispadias**
Penis
  Reconstruction ............54385
Repair ............54380-54390
  with Exstrophy of Bladder ............54390
  with Incontinence ............54380-54390

**Epistaxis** ............30901-30906
with Nasal/Sinus Endoscopy ............31238

**EPO**
*See* Erythropoietin

**Epstein-Barr Virus**
Antibody ............86663-86665

**Equina, Cauda**
*See* Cauda Equina

**ERCP**
*See* Bile Duct; Cholangiopancreatography; Pancreatic Duct

**ERG**
*See* Electroretinography

**Ergocalciferol**
*See* Calciferol

**Ergocalciferols**
*See* Calciferol

**Ergonovine Provocation Test** ............93024

**Erythrocyte**
*See* Red Blood Cell (RBC)

**Erythrocyte ab**
*See* Antibody, Red Blood Cell

**Erythrocyte Count**
*See* Red Blood Cell (RBC), Count

**Erythropoietin** ............82668

**Escharotomy**
Burns ............16035

**Escherichia coli 0157**
Antigen Detection
  Enzyme Immunoassay ............87335

**ESD**
*See* Endoscopy, Gastrointestinal, Upper

**Esophageal Acid Infusion Test**
*See* Acid Perfusion Test

**Esophageal Polyp**
*See* Polyp, Esophagus

**Esophageal Tumor**
*See* Tumor, Esophagus

**Esophageal Varices**
Ligation ............43205, 43400
Transection/Repair ............43401

**Esophagectomy**
Partial ............43116-43118, 43121-43124
Total ............43107-43108, 43112-43113, 43124

**Esophagoenterostomy**
with Total Gastrectomy ............43620

**Esophagogastroduodenoscopies**
*See* Endoscopy, Gastrointestinal, Upper

**Esophagogastromyotomy**
*See* Esophagomyotomy

**Esophagogastrostomy** ............43320

**Esophagojejunostomy** ............43340-43341

**Esophagomyotomy** ............32665, 43330-43331

**Esophagorrhaphy**
*See* Esophagus, Suture

**Esophagoscopies**
*See* Endoscopy, Esophagus

**Esophagostomy** ............43350-43352
Closure ............43420, 43425

**Esophagotomy** ............43020, 43045

**Esophagotracheal Fistula**
*See* Fistula, Tracheoesophageal

**Esophagus**
Acid Perfusion Test ............91030
Acid Reflux Tests ............91032-91033
Biopsy
  Endoscopy ............43202
Cineradiography ............74230
Dilation ............43450, 43453, 43456, 43458
  Endoscopic ............43220, 43226, 43248-43249
  Surgical ............43510
Endoscopy
  Biopsy ............43202
  Dilation ............43220, 43226
  Exploration ............43200
  Hemorrhage ............43227
  Injection ............43204
  Insertion Stent ............43219
  Removal
    Foreign Body ............43215
    Polyp ............43216-43217, 43228
    Tumor ............43216, 43228
  Vein Ligation ............43205
Excision
  Diverticula ............43130, 43135
  Partial ............43116-43118, 43121-43124
  Total ............43107-43108, 43112-43113, 43124
Exploration
  Endoscopy ............43200
Hemorrhage
  Endoscopic Control ............43227
Incision ............43020, 43045
  Muscle ............43030
Injection
  Sclerosing Agent ............43204
Insertion
  Stent ............43219
  Tamponade ............43460
  Tube ............43510
Intubation with Specimen Collection ............91000
Lesion
  Excision ............43100-43101
Ligation ............43405
Motility Study ............78258, 91010-91012
Nuclear Medicine
  Imaging (Motility) ............78258
  Reflux Study ............78262
Reconstruction ............43300, 43310
  Creation
    Stoma ............43350-43352
  Esophagostomy ............43350
  Fistula ............43305, 43312
  Gastrointestinal ............43360-43361
Removal
  Foreign Bodies ............43020, 43045, 43215, 74235
  Lesion ............43216
  Polyp ............43216-43217, 43228
Repair ............43300, 43310
  Esophagogastric Fundoplasty ............43324-43325
    Laparoscopic ............43280
  Esophagogastrostomy ............43320
  Esophagojejunostomy ............43340-43341
  Fistula ............43305, 43312, 43420, 43425
  Muscle ............43330-43331
  Pre-existing Perforation ............43405
  Varices ............43401
  Wound ............43410, 43415
Suture ............43405
  Wound ............43410, 43415
Unlisted Services and Procedures ............43289, 43499
Vein
  Ligation ............43205, 43400
Video ............74230
X-Ray ............74220

**Esophagus, Varix**
*See* Esophageal Varices

**Esophagus Neoplasm**
*See* Tumor, Esophagus

**Established Patient**
Confirmatory Consultations . . . 99271-99275
Domiciliary or Rest Home Visit . . . 99331-99333
Emergency Department Services . . . 99281-99285
Home Services . . . 99347-99350
Hospital Inpatient Services . . . 99221-99239
Hospital Observation Services . . . 99217-99220
Initial Inpatient Consultations . . . 99251-99255
Office and/or Other Outpatient Consultations . . . 99241-99245
Office Visit . . . 99211-99215
Outpatient Visit . . . 99211-99215

**Establishment**
Colostomy
Abdominal . . . 50810
Perineal . . . 50810

**Estes Operation**
*See* Ovary, Transposition

**Estlander Procedure** . . . 40525

**Estradiol** . . . 82670
Response . . . 80414

**Estriol**
Blood or Urine . . . 82677

**Estrogen**
Blood or Urine . . . 82671-82672
Receptor . . . 84233

**Estrone**
Blood or Urine . . . 82679

**Ethanediols**
*See* Ethylene Glycol

**Ethanol**
Blood . . . 82055
Breath . . . 82075
Urine . . . 82055

**Ethchlorovynol**
*See* Ethchlorvynol

**Ethchlorvinol**
*See* Ethchlorvynol

**Ethchlorvynol**
Blood . . . 82690
Urine . . . 82690

**Ethmoid**
Fracture
with Fixation . . . 21340

**Ethmoid, Sinus**
*See* Sinus, Ethmoid

**Ethmoidectomy** . . . 31200-31205
Endoscopic . . . 31254-31255
Skull Base Surgery . . . 61580-61581
with Nasal/Sinus Endoscopy . . 31254-31255

**Ethosuccimid**
*See* Ethosuximide

**Ethosuximide** . . . 80168
Assay . . . 80168

**Ethylene Dichlorides**
*See* Dichloroethane

**Ethylene Glycol** . . . 82693

**Ethylmethylsuccimide**
*See* Ethosuximide

**Ethyl Alcohol**
*See* Ethanol

**Etiocholanalone Measurement**
*See* Etiocholanolone

**Etiocholanolone** . . . 82696

**ETOH**
*See* Alcohol, Ethyl

**Euglobulin Lysis** . . . 85360

**European Blastomycosis**
*See* Cryptococcus

**Eustachian Tube**
Catheterization . . . 69405
Inflation
Myringotomy . . . 69420
Anesthesia . . . 69421
without Catheterization . . . 69401
with Catheterization . . . 69400
Insertion
Catheter . . . 69405

**Eutelegenesis**
*See* Artificial Insemination

**Evacuation**
Cervical Pregnancy . . . 59140
Hematoma
Brain . . . 61312-61315
Subungual . . . 11740
Hydatidiform Mole . . . 59870

**Evaluation and Management**
Basic Life and/or Disability Evaluation Services . . . 99450
Care Plan Oversight Services . . 99374-99380
Home Health Agency Care . . . 99374
Hospice . . . 99377-99378
Nursing Facility . . . 99379-99380
Case Management Services . . . 99361-99373
Consultation . . . 99241-99245, 99251-99255, 99261-99263, 99271-99275
Critical Care . . . 99291-99292
Domiciliary or Rest Home . . . 99321-99333
Emergency Department . . . 99281-99285, 99288
Home Services . . . 99341-99350
Hospital . . . 99221-99223, 99231-99233
Discharge . . . 99238-99239
Hospital Services
Observation Care . . . 99217-99220
Insurance Exam . . . 99455-99456
Medical
with Individual Psychotherapy
Hospital or Residential Care . . . 90817, 90819, 90822, 90824, 90827, 90829
Office or Outpatient . . . 90805, 90807, 90809
with Individual Psychotherapy, Interactive
Office or Outpatient . . . 90811, 90813, 90815
Neonatal Intensive Care . . . 99295-99297
Newborn Care . . . 99431-99440
Nursing Facility . . . 99301-99313
*See* Nursing Facility Services
Occupation Therapy Evaluation . . . 97003
Re-evaluation . . . 97004
Office and Other Outpatient . . . 99201-99205, 99211-99215
Physical Therapy Evaluation . . . 97001
Re-evaluation . . . 97002
Physician Standby Services . . . 99360
Preventive Services . . . 99381-99387, 99381-99397, 99401-99429, 99411-99412
Prolonged Services . . . 99356-99357
Psychiatric
Records or Reports . . . 90885
Psychiatric Residential Treatment Facility Care . . . 99301-99313
Unlisted Services and Procedures . . . 99499
Work-Related and/or Medical Disability Evaluation . . . 99450

**Evaluation Studies, Drug, Pre-Clinical**
*See* Drug Screen

**Evisceration**
Ocular Contents
without Implant . . . 65091
with Implant . . . 65093

**Evisceration, Pelvic**
*See* Exenteration, Pelvis

**Evocative/Suppression Test** . . . 80400-80440
Stimulation Panel . . . 80410

**Evoked Potential**
*See* Audiologic Function Tests
Auditory Brainstem . . . 92585
Somatosensory Testing . . . 95925-95927
Visual, CNS . . . 95930

**Evoked Potential, Auditory**
*See* Auditory Evoked Potentials

**Ewart Procedure**
*See* Palate, Reconstruction, Lengthening

**Excavatum, Pectus**
*See* Pectus Excavatum

**Exchange**
Arterial Catheter . . . 37209, 75900
Drainage Catheter
Under Radiologic Guidance . . . 49423

Radius ....24120, 25120, 25125-25126
with Allograft ....24126
with Autograft ....24125
Salivary Gland ....42408
Scapula ....23140
with Allograft ....23146
with Autograft ....23145
Seminal Vesicle ....55680
Sublingual Gland ....42408
Talus ....28100-28103
Tarsal ....28104-28107
Thyroglossal Duct ....60280-60281
Thyroid Gland ....60200
Tibia ....27635-27638
Toe ....28092
Ulna ....24120, 25120, 25125-25126
with Allograft ....24126
with Autograft ....24125
Urachal
Bladder ....51500
Vaginal ....57135
Destruction of the Vestibule of the Mouth
*See* Mouth, Vestibule of, Excision, Destruction
Diverticulum, Meckel's
*See* Meckel's Diverticulum, Excision
Ear, External
Partial ....69110
Total ....69120
Elbow Joint ....24155
Electrode ....57522
Embolectomy/Thrombectomy
Aortoiliac Artery ....34151-34201
Axillary Artery ....34101
Brachial Artery ....34101
Carotid Artery ....34001
Celiac Artery ....34151
Femoral Artery ....34201
Iliac Artery ....34151-34201
Innominate Artery ....34001-34101
Mesentery Artery ....34151
Peroneal Artery ....34203
Popliteal Artery ....34203
Radial Artery ....34111
Renal Artery ....34151
Subclavian Artery ....34001-34101
Tibial Artery ....34203
Ulnar Artery ....34111
Embolism
Pulmonary Artery ....33910-33916
Empyema
Lung ....32540
Pleural ....32540
Epididymis
Bilateral ....54861
Unilateral ....54860
Epiglottis ....31420
Esophagus
Diverticula ....43130, 43135
Partial ....43116-43118, 43121-43124
Total ....43107-43108, 43112-43113, 43124
Eye
*See* Enucleation, Eye
Fallopian Tube
Salpingectomy ....58700
Salpingo-Oophorectomy ....58720
Fascia
*See* Fasciectomy
Femur ....27360
Partial ....27070-27071
Fibula ....27360, 27455-27457, 27641
Fistula
Anal ....46270, 46275, 46280, 46285
Foot
Fasciectomy ....28060
Radical ....28060-28062
Gallbladder ....47600-47605, 47610-47620
Cholecystectomy ....47562-47564
with Cholangiography ....47563
with Exploration Common Duct ....47564
Ganglion Cyst
Knee ....27347
Wrist ....25111-25112
Gingiva ....41820
Gums ....41820
Alveolus ....41830
Operculum ....41821
Heart
Donor ....33940
Heart/Lung
Donor ....33930
Hemangioma ....11400-11446
Hemorrhoids ....46221, 46250
Clot ....46320
Complex ....46260-46262
Simple ....46255
with Fissurectomy ....46257-46258
Hip
Partial ....27070-27071
Humeral Head
Resection ....23195
Sequestrectomy ....23174
Humerus ....23184, 23220-23222, 24134, 24140, 24150-24151
Hydrocele
Spermatic Cord ....55500
Tunica Vaginalis ....55040-55041
Bilateral ....55041
Unilateral ....55040
Hygroma, Cystic
Axillary/Cervical ....38550-38555
Hymenotomy ....56700
*See* Hymen, Excision
Ileum
Partial ....27070-27071
Inner Ear
*See* Ear, Inner, Excision
Interphalangeal Joint
Toe ....28160
Intervertebral Disk
Decompression ....63075-63078
Hemilaminectomy ....63040
Herniated ....63020-63042, 63055-63066, 63066
Intestine
Laparoscopic
with Anastomosis ....44202
Intestines, Small ....44120-44121, 44125
Iris
Iridectomy
Optical ....66635
Peripheral ....66625
Sector ....66630
with Corneoscleral or Corneal Section ....66600
with Cyclectomy ....66605
Kidney
Donor ....50300-50320, 50547
Partial ....50240
Recipient ....50340
Transplantation ....50370
with Ureters ....50220-50236
Kneecap ....27350
Labyrinth
Transcanal ....69905
with Mastoidectomy ....69910
Lacrimal Gland
Partial ....68505
Total ....68500
Lacrimal Sac ....68520
Larynx
Partial ....31367-31382
Total ....31360-31365
with Pharynx ....31390-31395
Lesion
Anal ....45108, 46922
Ankle ....27630
Arthroscopic ....29891
Auditory Canal, External
Exostosis ....69140
Radical without Neck Dissection ....69150
Radical with Neck Dissection ....69155
Soft Tissue ....69145
Bladder ....52224
Brain ....61534, 61536
Brainstem ....61575-61576
Carotid Body ....60600-60605
Colon ....44110-44111
Conjunctiva ....68110-68130
Over 1cm ....68115
with Adjacent Sclera ....68130
Cornea ....65400
without Graft ....65420
Ear, Middle ....69540
Epididymis
Local ....54830
Spermatocele ....54840
Esophagus ....43100-43101
Eye ....65900

## Exclusion



## Exenteration

**Extracorporeal Circulation** .............33960-33961
for Regional Chemotherapy
Extremity ...................36823

**Extracorporeal Dialyses**
*See* Hemodialysis

**Extracorporeal Membrane Oxygenation**
Cannulization ...................36822

**Extracorporeal Photochemotherapies**
*See* Photopheresis

**Extraction**
Lens
Extracapsular ................66940
Intracapsular ................66920
for Dislocated Lens .........66930

**Extraction, Cataract**
*See* Cataract, Excision

**Extradural Anesthesia**
*See* Anesthesia, Epidural

**Extradural Injection**
*See* Epidural, Injection

**Extraocular Muscle**
*See* Eye Muscles

**Extrauterine Pregnancy**
*See* Ectopic Pregnancy

**Extravasation Blood**
*See* Hemorrhage

**Extremity**
Lower
Harvest of Vein for Bypass
Graft ......................35500
Revision ..............35879, 35881
Upper
Harvest of Vein for Bypass
Graft ......................35500
Repair
Blood Vessel ...............35206
Wound Exploration
Penetrating Wound ...........20103

**Eye**
*See* Ciliary Body; Cornea; Iris; Lens; Retina; Sclera; Vitreous
Biometry .................76516-76519
Drainage
Anterior Chamber
Discission of Anterior Hyaloid
Membrane ................65810
with Diagnostic Aspiration
of Aqueous ................65800
with Removal of Blood ........65815
with Removal of Vitreous and/or
with Therapeutic Release
of Aqueous ................65805
Goniotomy .....................65820
Incision
Adhesions
Anterior Synechiae .....65860, 65870
Corneovitreal Adhesions ......65880
Goniosynechiae ............65865
Posterior Synechiae ..........65875
Anterior Chamber ............65820
Trabeculae ..................65850
Injection
Air .........................66020
Medication ..................66030
Insertion
Implantation
Drug Delivery System .........67027
Foreign Material for
Reinforcement .............65155
Muscles Attached ...........65140
Muscles, Not Attached .......65135
Reinsertion ................65150
Scleral Shell ...............65130
Lesion
Excision ....................65900
Nerve
Destruction .................67345
Paracentesis
Anterior Chamber
Removal of Blood ...........65815
Removal or Vitreous and/or
Discission Anterior Hyaloid
Membrane ................65810
with Diagnostic Aspiration
of Aqueous ................65800
with Therapeutic Release of
Aqueous ..................65805
Radial Keratotomy ...............65771
Removal
Blood Clot ..................65930
Bone .......................65112
Foreign Body
Conjunctival Embedded .......65210
Conjunctival Superficial .......65205
Corneal without Slit Lamp .....65220
Corneal with Slit Lamp .......65222
Intraocular .....65235, 65260, 65265
Implant ....................65175
Anterior Segment ...........65920
Muscles, Not Attached .......65103
Posterior Segment .....67120-67121
Repair
Conjunctiva
by Mobilization and Rearrangement
without Hospitalization .......65272
by Mobilization and Rearrangement
with Hospitalization .........65273
Direct Closure ...............65270
Cornea
Nonperforating .............65275
Perforating ...........65280-65285
Muscles ....................65290
Sclera
Anterior Segment ...........66250
without Graft ..............66220
with Graft .................66225
with Tissue Glue ............65286
Trabeculae ..................65855
Wound
by Mobilization and
Rearrangement ........65272-65273
Direct Closure ..............65270
Shunt, Aqueous
to Extraocular Reservoir ........66180
Ultrasound ................76511-76513
Biometry ...............76516-76519
Foreign Body ................76529
Unlisted Services and Procedures
Anterior Segment ............66999
Posterior Segment ............67299
with Muscle or Myocutaneous Flap ..65114
Muscles Attached ............65105
Ocular Contents
without Implant .............65091
with Implant ................65093
Orbital Contents ..............65110
without Implant .............65101
X-Ray .........................70030

**Eyebrow**
Repair
Ptosis .......................67900

**Eyeglasses**
*See* Spectacle Services

**Eyelashes**
Repair Trichiasis
Epilation
by Forceps Only .............67820
by Other than Forceps ........67825
Incision of Lid Margin ..........67830
with Free Mucous Membrane
Graft ......................67835

**Eyelid**
Abscess
Incision and Drainage ..........67700
Biopsy .........................67810
Blepharoplasty ............15820-15823
Chalazion
Excision .....................67805
Multiple .............67801, 67805
Single ....................67800
with Anesthesia .............67808
Closure by Suture ................67875
Incision
Canthus .....................67715
Sutures .....................67710
Injection
Subconjunctival ...............68200
Lesion
Destruction ..................67850
Excision
Multiple .............67801, 67805
Single ....................67800

# F

**Factor, Blood Coagulation**
*See* Clotting Factor

**Factor, Fitzgerald**
*See* Fitzgerald Factor

**Factor, Fletcher**
*See* Fletcher Factor

**Factor, Hyperglycemic-Glycogenolytic**
*See* Glucagon

**Factor, Intrinsic**
*See* Intrinsic Factor

**Factor, Sulfation**
*See* Somatomedin

**Factor I**
*See* Fibrinogen

**Factor II**
*See* Prothrombin

**Factor III**
*See* Thromboplastin

**Factor Inhibitor Test** .......... 85335

**Factor IV**
*See* Calcium

**Factor IX**
*See* Christmas Factor

**Factor Rheumatoid**
*See* Rheumatoid Factor

**Factor VII**
*See* Proconvertin

**Factor VIII**
*See* Clotting Factor

**Factor X**
*See* Stuart-Prower Factor

**Factor X, Activated**
*See* Thrombokinase

**Factor Xa Inhibitor**
*See* Antithrombin III

**Factor XI**
*See* Plasma Thromboplastin, Antecedent

**Factor XII**
*See* Hageman Factor

**Factor XIII**
*See* Fibrin Stabilizing Factor

**Fallopian Tube**
Anastomosis .................... 58750
Catheterization ............ 58345, 74742
Destruction
  Endoscopy .................. 58670
Ectopic Pregnancy ................ 59121
  with Salpingectomy and/or Oophorectomy ............... 59120
Excision .................. 58700-58720
Ligation .................. 58600-58611
Lysis
  Adhesions ................... 58740
Occlusion ....................... 58615
  Endoscopy ................... 58671
Repair ......................... 58752
  Anastomosis ................ 58750
  Create Stoma ................ 58770
Unlisted Services and Procedures ... 58999
X-Ray ......................... 74742

**Fallopian Tube Pregnancy**
*See* Ectopic Pregnancy, Tubal

**Fallot, Tetralogy of**
*See* Tetralogy of Fallot

**Family Psychotherapy**
*See* Psychotherapy, Family

**Fanconi Anemia**
Chromosome Analysis ............ 88248

**Farnsworth-Munsell Color Test**
*See* Color Vision Examination

**Farr Test**
*See* Gammaglobulin, Blood

**Fasanella-Servat Procedure** .................... 67908

**Fascial Defect**
Repair ......................... 50728

**Fascial Graft**
Free
  Microvascular Anastomosis ..... 15758
Open Treatment
  Sternoclavicular Dislocation ..... 23532

**Fascia Graft** .................. 15840

**Fascia Lata Graft**
Harvesting ................ 20920-20922

**Fasciectomy**
Foot .......................... 28060
  Radical ................ 28060-28062
Palm ............... 26121, 26123, 26125

**Fasciocutaneous Flaps** .................... 15732-15738

**Fasciotomy**
Arm, Lower ......... 24495, 25020, 25023
Elbow .................... 24350-24356
Foot .......................... 28008
Hand Decompression ............ 26037
Hip ........................... 27025
Knee ............... 27305, 27496-27499
Leg, Lower .... 27600-27602, 27892-27894
Leg, Upper .......... 27305, 27496-27499, 27892-27894
Palm ..................... 26040, 26045
Plantar
  Endoscopic ................. 29893
Thigh ......................... 27025
Toe ........................... 28008
Wrist .................... 25020, 25023

**FAST**
*See* Allergen Immunotherapy

**Fat**
Feces .................... 82705-82715
Removal
  Lipectomy .............. 15876-15879

**Fatty Acid**
Blood ......................... 82725
Very Long Chain ................. 82726

**Fat Stain**
Feces ......................... 89125
Sputum ........................ 89125
Urine ......................... 89125

**Favre-Durand Disease**
*See* Lymphogranuloma Venereum

**FC Receptor** .................. 86243

**FDP**
*See* Fibrin Degradation Products

**Feedback, Psychophysiologic**
*See* Biofeedback

**Female Castration**
*See* Oophorectomy

**Female Gonad**
*See* Ovary

**Femoral Arteries**
*See* Artery, Femoral

**Femoral Stem Prosthesis**
*See* Arthroplasty, Hip

**Femoral Vein**
*See* Vein, Femoral

**Femur**
*See* Hip; Knee; Leg, Upper
Abscess
  Incision .................... 27303
Bursa
  Excision .................... 27062
Craterization ............. 27070, 27360
Cyst
  Excision .... 27065-27067, 27355-27358
Diaphysectomy ................. 27360
Drainage ...................... 27303
Excision ................. 27070, 27360
  Epiphyseal Bar ............... 20150
Fracture
  Closed Treatment ........ 27501-27503
  Distal ........... 27508, 27510, 27514
  Distal, Medial or Lateral Condyle .................... 27509
  Epiphysis ........ 27516-27517, 27519
  Intertrochanteric
    Closed Treatment ........... 27238
    Open Treatment ............ 27244
    with Implant ............... 27245
    with Manipulation .......... 27240
  Neck
    Closed Treatment ..... 27230, 27232
    Open Treatment ............ 27236
    Percutaneous Fixation ........ 27235

**Fixation**
Interdental
without Fracture .............. 21497

**Fixation, External**
*See* External Fixation

**Fixation, Kidney**
*See* Nephropexy

**Fixation, Rectum**
*See* Proctopexy

**Fixation, Tongue**
*See* Tongue, Fixation

**Fixation (Device)**
*See* Application; Bone, Fixation; Spinal Instrumentation
Application
External ............... 20690-20692
Pelvic
Insertion .................... 22848
Removal
Internal ................ 20670-20680
External ..................... 20694
Sacrospinous Ligament
Vaginal Prolapse .............. 57202
Shoulder ....................... 23700
Skeletal
Humeral Epycondyle
Percutaneous ............... 24566
Spinal
Insertion ............... 22841-22847
Prosthetic .................. 22851
Reinsertion .................. 22849

**Fixation Test, Complement**
*See* Complement, Fixation Test

**Flank**
*See* Back/Flank

**Flap**
*See* Skin Graft and Flap
Free
Breast Reconstruction .......... 19364
Grafts .................... 15574-15650
Latissimus Dorsi
Breast Reconstruction .......... 19361
Omentum
Free
with Microvascular Anastomosis ................ 49906
Transverse Rectus Abdominis Myocutaneous
Breast Reconstruction .... 19367-19369

**Flatfoot Correction** ........... 28735

**Flea Typhus**
*See* Murine Typhus

**Fletcher Factor** ............... 85292

**Flow-Volume Loop**
*See* Pulmonology, Diagnostic
Pulmonary ...................... 94375

**Flow Cytometry** ......... 88180-88182

**Fluid, Amniotic**
*See* Amniotic Fluid

**Fluid, Body**
*See* Body Fluid

**Fluid, Cerebrospinal**
*See* Cerebrospinal Fluid

**Fluid Collection**
Incision and Drainage
Skin ........................ 10140

**Fluorescein**
Angiography, Ocular .............. 92287
Intravenous Injection
Blood Flow Check, Graft ........ 15860

**Fluorescein Angiography**
*See* Angiography, Fluorescein

**Fluoride**
Blood .......................... 82735
Urine .......................... 82735

**Fluoroscopy**
Bile Duct
Guido Catheter ........ 74328, 74330
Guide Stone Removal .......... 74327
Chest .......................... 31628
Complete (Four Views) ......... 71034
Partial (Two Views) ........... 71023
Drain Abscess ................... 75989
GI Tract
Guide Intubation .............. 74340
Hourly .................... 76000-76001
Introduction
GI Tube ...................... 74340
Larynx ......................... 70370
Needle Biopsy ................... 76003
Pancreatic Duct
Guide Catheter ......... 74329, 74330
Pharynx ........................ 70370
Renal
Guide Catheter ............... 74475
Spine/Paraspinous
Guide Catheter/Needle ......... 76005
Ureter
Guide Catheter ............... 74480

**Flurazepam**
Blood or Urine ................... 82742

**Flush Aortogram** ........ 75722-75724

**Flu Vaccines**

**FNA**
*See* Fine Needle Aspiration

**Foam Stability Test** ........... 83662

**Fold, Vocal**
*See* Vocal Cords

**Foley Operation Pyeloplasty**
*See* Pyeloplasty

**Foley Y-Pyeloplasty** ..... 50400-50405

**Folic Acid** .................... 82747
Blood .......................... 82746

**Follicle Stimulating Hormone (FSH)** ............ 80418, 80426, 83001

**Folliculin**
*See* Estrone

**Follitropin**
*See* Follicle Stimulating Hormone (FSH)

**Follow-up Inpatient Consultations**
*See* Consultation, Follow-up Inpatient

**Follow-up Services**
*See* Hospital Services; Office and/or Other Outpatient Services
Inpatient Consultations ...... 99261-99263
Post-Op ........................ 99024

**Fontan Procedure**
*See* Repair, Heart, Anomaly; Revision

**Food Allergy Test** ............. 95075
*See* Allergy Tests

**Foot**
*See* Metatarsal; Tarsal
Amputation ............... 28800-28805
Bursa
Incision and Drainage .......... 28001
Capsulotomy ........ 28260-28262, 28264
Cast ........................... 29450
Fasciectomy ..................... 28060
Radical ................ 28060-28062
Fasciotomy ...................... 28008
Endoscopic .................. 29893
Incision ............ 28002-28003, 28005
Joint
*See* Talotarsal Joint; Tarsometatarsal Joint
(MRI) ....................... 73721
Magnetic Resonance Imaging
Lesion
Excision ............... 28080, 28090
Magnetic Resonance Imaging (MRI) .................. 73720
Nerve
Excision ..................... 28030
Incision ..................... 28035
Neuroma
Excision ..................... 28080
Reconstruction
Cleft Foot ................... 28360
Removal
Foreign Body ........... 28190-28193
Repair
Muscle ...................... 28250
Tendon .... 28200-28210, 28220-28226, 28230, 28234, 28238
Replantation .................... 20838
Sesamoid
Excision ..................... 28315
Splint .......................... 29590
Strapping ....................... 29590

**Fundoplication**
*See* Fundoplasty, Esophagogastric

**Fungus**
Antibody ....................... 86671
Culture
  Blood ....................... 87103
  Identification ................ 87106
  Other ....................... 87102
  Skin ........................ 87101
Tissue Exam .................... 87220

**Funnel Chest**
*See* Pectus Excavatum

**Furuncle**
Incision and Drainage ....... 10060-10061

**Furuncle, Vulva**
*See* Abscess, Vulva

**Fusion**
*See* Arthrodesis
Pleural Cavity .................. 32005
Thumb
  in Opposition ................ 26820

**Fusion, Epiphyseal-Diaphyseal**
*See* Epiphyseal Arrest

**Fusion, Joint**
*See* Arthrodesis

**Fusion, Joint, Ankle**
*See* Ankle, Arthrodesis

**Fusion, Joint, Interphalangeal, Finger**
*See* Arthrodesis, Finger Joint, Interphalangeal

# G

**Gago Procedure**
*See* Repair, Tricuspid Valve; Revision

**Gait Training** .................. 97116
*See* Physical Medicine/Therapy/ Occupational Therapy

**Galactogram** ........... 76086-76088
Injection ........................ 19030

**Galactokinase**
Blood .......................... 82759

**Galactose**
Blood .......................... 82760
Urine .......................... 82760

**Galactose-1-Phosphate**
Uridyl Transferase .......... 82775-82776

**Gallbladder**
*See* Bile Duct
Anastomosis
  with Intestines ......... 47720-47721, 47740, 47741
Excision ....... 47600-47620, 47562-47564
Exploration ..................... 47480
Incision ........................ 47490
Incision and Drainage ............ 47480
Nuclear Medicine
  Imaging ..................... 78223
Removal
  Calculi (Stone) ............... 47480
Repair
  with Gastroenterostomy ........ 47741
  with Intestines .... 47720-47721, 47740
Unlisted Services and Procedures ... 47999
X-Ray with Contrast ......... 74290-74291

**Gall Bladder**
*See* Gallbladder

**Galvanocautery**
*See* Electrocautery

**Galvanoionization**
*See* Iontophoresis

**Gamete Intrafallopian Transfer**
*See* GIFT

**Gamete Transfer**
In Vitro Fertilization ............... 58976

**Gammacorten**
*See* Dexamethasone

**Gammaglobulin**
Blood .................... 82784-82785

**Gamma Camera Imaging**
*See* Nuclear Medicine

**Gamma Glutamyl Transferase** .................. 82977

**Gamma Seminoprotein**
*See* Antigen, Prostate Specific

**Gamulin Rh**
*See* Immune Globulins, Rho (D)

**Ganglia, Trigeminal**
*See* Gasserian Ganglion

**Ganglion**
*See* Gasserian Ganglion
Cyst
  Drainage .............. 20600-20605
  Injection ............... 20550-20605
  Wrist
    Excision .............. 25111-25112
Injection
  Anesthetic ............. 64505, 64510

**Ganglion, Gasser's**
*See* Gasserian Ganglion

**Ganglion Cervicothoracicum**
*See* Stellate Ganglion

**Ganglion Pterygopalatinum**
*See* Sphenopalatine Ganglion

**Gardnerella Vaginalis Detection** ............... 87510-87512

**Gardner Operation**
*See* Meningocele Repair

**Gasserian Ganglion**
Sensory Root
  Decompression ............... 61450
  Section ..................... 61450
Stereotactic ..................... 61790

**Gasser Ganglion**
*See* Gasserian Ganglion

**Gastrectomy**
Partial ........ 43631-43635, 43638-43639
  with Gastrojejunostomy ........ 43632
Total ................... 43621-43622
  with Esophagoenterostomy ..... 43620
with Gastroduodenostomy ......... 43631

**Gastric Acid** ............ 82926-82928

**Gastric Analysis Test** ......... 91052

**Gastric Intubation** ......... 89130-89141, 91105

**Gastric Lavage, Therapeutic** .. 91105

**Gastric Tests**
Manometry ..................... 91020

**Gastric Ulcer Disease**
*See* Stomach, Ulcer

**Gastrin** .................. 82938-82941

**Gastrocnemius Recession**
Leg, Lower ...................... 27687

**Gastroduodenostomy** ......... 43810, 43850, 43855

**Gastroenterology, Diagnostic**
Breath Hydrogen Test ............. 91065
Esophagus Tests
  Acid Perfusion ................ 91030
  Acid Reflux ............. 91032-91033
  Intubation with Specimen Collection .................... 91000
  Motility Study .......... 91010-91012
Gastric Tests
  Manometry .................. 91020
Intestine
  Bleeding Tube ................ 91100
Manometry ...................... 91020
Rectum/Anus
  Manometry .................. 91122
Stomach
  Intubation with Specimen Prep ........................ 91055
  Saline Load Test ............. 91060
  Stimulation of Secretion ........ 91052
Unlisted Services and Procedures .. 91299

**Gastroenterostomy**
for Obesity ..................... 43846

**Gastrointestinal, Upper**
Biopsy
  Endoscopy .................. 43239

**Glaucoma**
Fistulization of Sclera .............66150
Provocative Test .................92140

**Glaucoma Drainage Implant**
*See* Aqueous Shunt

**Gla Protein (Bone)**
*See* Osteocalcin

**Glenn Procedure** ........33766-33767

**Glenohumeral Joint**
Arthrotomy .....................23040
  with Biopsy ..................23100
  with Synovectomy ............23105
Exploration .....................23107
Removal
  Foreign or Loose Body ..........23107

**Glenoid Fossa**
Reconstruction ..................21255

**GLN**
*See* Glutamine

**Globulin**
Antihuman ................86880-86886
Immune .................90281-90399
Sex Hormone Binding .............84270

**Globulin, Corticosteroid-Binding**
*See* Transcortin

**Globulin, Rh Immune**
*See* Immune Globulins, Rho (D)

**Globulin, Thyroxine-Binding**
*See* Thyroxine Binding Globulin

**Glomerular Procoagulant Activity**
*See* Thromboplastin

**Glomus Caroticum**
*See* Carotid Body

**Glossectomies**
*See* Excision, Tongue

**Glossopexy**
*See* Tongue, Fixation

**Glossorrhaphy**
*See* Suture, Tongue

**Glucagon** .....................82943
Tolerance Panel ............80422, 80424
Tolerance Test ...................82946

**Glucose** .....80422-80424, 80430-80435
Blood Test .........82947-82950, 82962
Joint Fluid ......................82947
Spinal Fluid .....................82947
Tolerance Test .............82951-82952
  with Tolbutamide ...............82953

**Glucose-6-Phosphate**
Dehydrogenase ............82955-82960

**Glucose Phosphate Isomerase**
*See* Phosphohexose Isomerase

**Glucose Phosphate Isomerase Measurement**
*See* Phosphohexose Isomerase

**Glucosidase** ..................82963

**Glucuronide Androstanediol** ...............82154

**Glue**
Cornea Wound ..................65286
Sclera Wound ..................65286

**Glukagon**
*See* Glucagon

**Glutamate Dehydrogenase**
Blood ..........................82965

**Glutamate Pyruvate Transaminase**
*See* Transaminase, Glutamic Pyruvic

**Glutamic Alanine Transaminase**
*See* Transaminase, Glutamic Pyruvic

**Glutamic Aspartic Transaminase**
*See* Transaminase, Glutamic Oxaloacetic

**Glutamic Dehydrogenase**
*See* Glutamate Dehydrogenase

**Glutamine** ....................82975

**Glutamyltransferase, Gamma** .......................82977

**Glutathione** ...................82978

**Glutathione Reductase** .......82979

**Glutethimide** .................82980

**Glycanhydrolase, N-Acetylmuramide**
*See* Lysozyme

**Glycated Protein** ..............82985

**Glycerol, Phosphatidyl**
*See* Phosphatidylglycerol

**Glycerol Phosphoglycerides**
*See* Phosphatidylglycerol

**Glycerophosphatase**
*See* Alkaline Phosphatase

**Glycinate, Theophylline Sodium**
*See* Theophylline

**Glycocholic Acid**
*See* Cholylglycine

**Glycohemoglobin** .............83036

**Glycol, Ethylene**
*See* Ethylene Glycol

**Glycols, Ethylene**
*See* Ethylene Glycol

**Glycosaminoglycan**
*See* Mucopolysaccharides

**GMP**
*See* Guanosine Monophosphate

**GMP, Cyclic**
*See* Cyclic GMP

**Goeckerman Treatment** ..............96910-96913

**Gol-Vernet Operation**
*See* Pyelotomy, Exploration

**Gold**
Assay ..........................80172

**Goldwaite Procedure** .........27422

**Golfer's Elbow**
*See* Tennis Elbow

**Gonadectomy, Female**
*See* Oophorectomy

**Gonadectomy, Male**
*See* Excision, Testis

**Gonadotropin**
Chorionic ................84702-84703
FSH ...........................83001
ICSH ..........................83002
LH ............................83002

**Gonadotropin Panel** ..........80426

**Gonioscopy** ...................92020

**Goniotomy** ....................65820

**Gonoooccus**
*See* Neisseria Gonorrhoeae

**Goodenough Harris Drawing Test** ................96100

**GOTT**
*See* Transaminase, Glutamic Oxaloacetic

**GPUT**
*See* Galactose-1-Phosphate, Uridyl Transferase

**Graft**
*See* Bone Graft; Bypass Graft
Anal ..........................46753
Aorta .........33840-33851, 33860-33877
Artery
  Coronary ...............33503-33505
Bone
  *See* Bone Marrow, Transplantation
  Harvesting .............20900-20902
  Microvascular Anastomosis ...........20955-20962
  Osteocutaneous Flap with Microvascular Anastomosis ...........20969-20973
Bone and Skin .............20969-20973
Cartilage
  Ear to Face ..................21235
  Harvesting .............20910-20912
    *See* Cartilage Graft
  Rib to Face ..................21230
Cornea
  with Lesion Excision ..........65426
Cornea Transplant
  in Aphakia ...................65750
  in Pseudophakia .............65755

Lamellar .................... 65710
Penetrating .................. 65730
Dura
Spinal Cord .................. 63710
Facial Nerve Paralysis ....... 15840-15845
Fascia
Cheek ........................ 15840
Fascia Lata
Harvesting ............ 20920-20922
Gum Mucosa .................... 41870
Heart
*See* Heart, Transplantation
Heart Lung
*See* Transplantation, Heart-Lung
Kidney
*See* Kidney, Transplantation
Liver
*See* Liver, Transplantation
Lung
*See* Lung, Transplantation
Muscle
Cheek ................. 15841-15845
Nail Bed
Reconstruction ............... 11762
Nerve .................... 64885-64907
Oral Mucosa .................. 40818
Organ
*See* Transplantation
Pancreas
*See* Pancreas, Transplantation
Skin
Biological
*See* Allograft, Skin
Blood Flow Check, Graft ........ 15860
*See* Skin Graft and Flap
Tendon
Finger ....................... 26392
Hand ......................... 26392
Harvesting ................... 20924
Tissue
Harvesting ................... 20926
Vein
Cross-Over ................... 34520

**Grain Alcohol**
*See* Alcohol, Ethyl

**Granulation Tissue**
Cauterization, Chemical .......... 17250

**Gravi, Myasthenia**
*See* Myasthenia Gravis

**Gravities, Specific**
*See* Specific Gravity

**Greater Tuberosity Fracture**
with Shoulder Dislocation
Closed Treatment ............ 23665
Open Treatment .............. 23670

**Greater Vestibular Gland**
*See* Bartholin's Gland

**Great Toe**
Free Osteocutaneous Flap with
Microvascular Anastomosis ........ 20973

**Great Vessels**
Shunt
Aorta to Pulmonary Artery
Ascending ................... 33755
Descending .................. 33762
Central ..................... 33764
Subclavian to Pulmonary
Artery ...................... 33750
Vena Cava to Pulmonary
Artery ............... 33766-33767
Unlisted Services and Procedures ... 33999

**Great Vessels Transposition**
*See* Transposition, Great Arteries

**Green Operation**
*See* Scapulopexy

**Gridley Stain** ................. 88312

**Grippe, Balkan**
*See* Q Fever

**Gritti Operation**
*See* Amputation, Leg, Upper; Radical Resection; Replantation

**Groin Area**
Repair
Hernia ................ 49550-49557

**Grouping, Blood**
*See* Blood Typing

**Group Health Education** ...... 99078

**Growth Factors, Insulin-Like**
*See* Somatomedin

**Growth Hormone** ............ 83003
Human ....... 80418, 80428-80430, 86277

**Growth Hormone Release Inhibiting Factor**
*See* Somatostatin

**GTT**
*See* Hydatidiform Mole

**Guaiac Test**
*See* Blood, Feces

**Guanosine Monophosphate** ... 83008

**Guanosine Monophosphate, Cyclic**
*See* Cyclic GMP

**Guanylic Acids**
*See* Guanosine Monophosphate

**Guard Stain** .................. 88313

**Gullet**
*See* Esophagus

**Gums**
Abscess
Incision and Drainage .......... 41800
Alveolus
Excision .................... 41830
Cyst
Incision and Drainage .......... 41800
Excision
Gingiva ..................... 41820
Operculum ................... 41821
Graft
Mucosa ...................... 41870
Hematoma
Incision and Drainage .......... 41800
Lesion
Destruction .................. 41850
Excision ............. 41822-41828
Mucosa
Excision ..................... 41828
Reconstruction
Alveolus ..................... 41874
Gingiva ...................... 41872
Removal
Foreign Body ................. 41805
Tumor
Excision ............. 41825-41827
Unlisted Services and Procedures .. 41899

**Gunning-Lieben Test**
*See* Acetone, Blood or Urine

**Guthrie Test** ................. 84030

**H-Reflex Study** ......... 95934, 95936

**HAAb**
*See* Antibody, Hepatitis

**HAA (Hepatitis Associated Antigen)**
*See* Hepatitis Antigen, B Surface

**Haemoglobin F**
*See* Fetal Hemoglobin

**Haemorrhage**
*See* Hemorrhage

**Haemorrhage Rectum**
*See* Hemorrhage, Rectum

**Hageman Factor** .............. 85280

**Hair**
Electrolysis ................... 17380
Microscopic Evaluation ........... 96902
Transplant
Punch Graft ........... 15775-15776
Strip Graft ............ 15220-15221

**Hair Removal**
*See* Removal, Hair

**HAI Test**
*See* Hemagglutination Inhibition Test

**Hallux**
*See* Great Toe

**Halo**
Body Cast .....29000
Cranial .....20661
for Thin Skull Osteology .....20664
Femur .....20663
Maxillofacial .....21100
Pelvic .....20662
Removal .....20665

**Halsted Mastectomy**
*See* Mastectomy, Radical

**Halsted Repair**
*See* Hernia, Repair, Inguinal

**Hammertoe Repair** .....28285-28286

**Hamster Penetration Test** .....89329

**Ham Test**
*See* Hemolysins

**Hand**
*See* Carpometacarpal Joint; Intercarpal Joint
Amputation
at Metacarpal .....25927
at Wrist .....25920
Revision .....25922
Revision .....25924, 25929, 25931
Arthrodesis
Carpometacarpal Joint .....26843-26844
Intercarpal Joint .....25820, 25825
Bone
Incision and Drainage .....26034
Cast .....29085
Decompression .....26035, 26037
Fracture
Metacarpal .....26600
Insertion
Tendon Graft .....26392
Magnetic Resonance Imaging (MRI) .....73220, 73221
Reconstruction
Tendon Pulley .....26500, 26502, 26504
Removal
Implantation .....26320
Tube/Rod .....26392, 26416
Repair
Blood Vessel .....35207
Cleft Hand .....26580
Muscle .....26591, 26593
Scar Contracture .....26597
Tendon
Extensor .....26410-26412, 26415-26416, 26426-26428, 26433-26434, 26437
Flexor .....26350, 26352, 26356-26358, 26440
Profundus .....26370, 26372-26373
Replantation .....20808
Strapping .....29280
Tendon
Excision .....26390
Extensor .....26415
Tenotomy .....26450, 26460
Tumor
Excision .....26115-26117
Unlisted Services and Procedures .....26989
X-Ray .....73120-73130

**Hand(s) Dupuytrens Contracture(s)**
*See* Dupuytren's Contracture

**Handling**
Device .....99002
Radioelement .....77790
Specimen .....99000-99001

**Hand Abscess**
*See* Abscess, Hand

**Hand Phalange**
*See* Finger, Bone

**Hanganutziu Deicher Antibodies**
*See* Antibody, Heterophile

**Haptoglobin** .....83010-83012

**Hard Palate**
*See* Palate

**Harelip Operation**
*See* Cleft Lip, Repair

**Harrington Rod**
Insertion .....22840
Removal .....22850

**Hartmann Procedure** .....44143

**Harvesting**
Bone Graft .....20900-20902
Bone Marrow .....38230
Cartilage Graft .....20910-20912
Eggs
In Vitro Fertilization .....58970
Fascia Lata Graft .....20920-20922
Kidney .....50300-50320, 50547
Liver .....47133, 47134
Stem Cell .....38231
Tendon Graft .....20924
Tissue Grafts .....20926
Upper Extremity Vein
for Bypass Graft .....35500

**Hauser Procedure** .....27420

**Hayem's Elementary Corpuscle**
*See* Blood, Platelet

**Haygroves Procedure**
*See* Reconstruction, Acetabulum; Revision

**HBcAb**
*See* Antibody, Hepatitis

**HBeAb**
*See* Antibody, Hepatitis

**HBeAg**
*See* Hepatitis Antigen, Be

**HBsAb**
*See* Antibody, Hepatitis

**HBsAg**
*See* Hepatitis Antigen, B Surface

**HBsAg (Hepatitis B Surface Antigen)**
*See* Hepatitis Antigen, B Surface

**HCG**
*See* Chorionic Gonadotropin

**HCO3**
*See* Bicarbonate

**HCV Antibodies**
*See* Antibody, Hepatitis C

**HDL**
*See* Lipoprotein

**Head**
CAT Scan .....70450, 70460, 70470
Excision .....21015-21070
Fracture and/or Dislocation .....21300-21497
Incision .....21010
Introduction or Removal .....21076-21116
Lipectomy, Suction Assisted .....15876
Nerve
Graft .....64885-64886
Other Procedures .....21299, 21499
Repair/Revision and/or Reconstruction .....21120-21296
Ultrasound Exam .....76506, 76536
Unlisted Services and Procedures .....21499
X-Ray .....70350

**Headbrace**
Application .....21100
Application/Removal .....20661

**Head Rings, Stereotactic**
*See* Stereotactic Frame

**Heaf Test**
*See* TB Test

**Health Risk Assessment Instrument**
*See* Preventive Medicine

**Hearing Aid**
Bone Conduction
Implantation .....69710
Removal .....69711
Repair .....69711
Replacement .....69710

**Hearing Aid Check** .....92592-92593

**Hearing Aid Services**
Electroacoustic Test .....92594-92595
Examination .....92590-92591

**Hearing Evaluation** .....92510

**Hearing Tests**
*See* Audiologic Function Tests; Hearing Evaluation

**Hearing Therapy** .....92507-92508, 92510

Replacement
Electrode ........33210-33211, 33217
Mitral Valve ..................33430
Tricuspid Valve ...............33465
Repositioning
Electrode ..............33216-33217
Tricuspid Valve ...............33468
Resuscitation ....................92950
Septal Defect
*See* Septal Defect
Stimulation and Pacing ............93623
Transplantation ............33935, 33945
Tricuspid Valve
*See* Tricuspid Valve
Tumor
Excision ...............33120-33130
Unlisted Services and Procedures ...33999
Ventriculography
*See* Ventriculography
Ventriculomyectomy ..............33416
Wound
Repair .................33300-33305

**Heart Vessels**
Angioplasty
Percutaneous ...........92982-92984
*See* Angioplasty; Percutaneous Transluminal Angioplasty
Insertion
Graft ..................33330-33335
Thrombolysis ..............92975, 92977
Valvuloplasty
*See* Valvuloplasty
Percutaneous ...........92986-92990

**Heat Unstable Haemoglobin**
*See* Hemoglobin, Thermolabile

**Heavy Lipoproteins**
*See* Lipoprotein

**Heavy Metal** ............83015-83018

**Heel**
*See* Calcaneus
Collection of Blood ...............36415
X-Ray ..........................73650

**Heel Bone**
*See* Calcaneus

**Heel Fracture**
*See* Calcaneus, Fracture

**Heel Spur**
Excision ........................28119

**Heine-Medin Disease**
*See* Polio

**Heine Operation**
*See* Cyclodialysis

**Heinz Bodies** ............85441-85445

**Helicobacter Pylori**
Antibody .......................86677
Breath Test ...78267, 78268, 83013, 83014
Stool ..........................87338

**Heller Operation**
*See* Esophagomyotomy

**Heller Procedure** .............32665, 43330-43331

**Helminth**
Antibody .......................86682

**Hemagglutination Inhibition Test** ..........................86280

**Hemangioma**
*See* Lesion, Skin; Tumor

**Hemapheresis**
*See* Apheresis

**Hematochezia**
*See* Blood, Feces

**Hematologic Test**
*See* Blood Tests

**Hematology**
Unlisted Services and Procedures ...85999

**Hematoma**
Ankle ..........................27603
Arm, Lower .....................25028
Arm, Upper
Incision and Drainage ..........23930
Brain
Drainage .............61154, 61156
Evacuation ............61312-61315
Incision and Drainage ....61312-61315
Drain ..........................61108
Ear, External
Complicated ...................69005
Simple ........................69000
Elbow
Incision and Drainage ..........23930
Epididymis
Incision and Drainage ..........54700
Gums
Incision and Drainage ..........41800
Hip ............................26990
Incision and Drainage
Neck .................21501-21502
Skin ..........................10140
Thorax ...............21501-21502
Knee ...........................27301
Leg, Lower .....................27603
Leg, Upper .....................27301
Mouth ........41005-41009, 41015-41018
Incision and Drainage ....40800-40801
Nasal Septum
Incision and Drainage ..........30020
Nose
Incision and Drainage ....30000-30020
Pelvis ..........................26990
Scrotum
Incision and Drainage ..........54700
Shoulder
Drainage ......................23030
Skin
Puncture Aspiration ............10160
Subdural ........................61108
Subungual
Evacuation ....................11740
Testis
Incision and Drainage ..........54700
Tongue .......41000, 41005-41006, 41015
Wrist ..........................25028

**Hematopoietic Stem Cell Transplantation**
*See* Stem Cell, Transplantation

**Hematopoietin**
*See* Erythropoietin

**Hematuria**
*See* Blood, Urine

**Hemic System**
Unlisted Procedure ...............38999

**Hemiepiphyseal Arrest**
Elbow ..........................24470

**Hemifacial Microsomia**
Reconstruction
Mandibular Condyle ............21247

**Hemilaminectomy** .......63020-63042

**Hemilaryngectomy** ......31370-31382

**Hemipelvectomies**
*See* Amputation, Interpelviabdominal

**Hemiphalangectomy**
Toe ............................28160

**Hemispherectomy**
Partial .........................61543
Total ..........................61542

**Hemocytoblast**
*See* Stem Cell

**Hemodialyses**
*See* Hemodialysis

**Hemodialysis** ...........90935, 90937
Duplex Scan of Access ............93990

**Hemofiltration** ..........90945-90947

**Hemoglobin** ...................83036
Analysis
O2 Affinity ...................82820
Carboxyhemoglobin .........82375-82376
Chromatography .................83021
Concentration ..................85046
Electrophoresis .................83020
Fetal .........83030-83033, 85460, 85461
Fractionation and Quantitation ......83020
Methemoglobin ............83045-83050
Non-Automated ..................83026
Plasma .........................83051
Sulfhemoglobin ............83055-83060
Thermolabile ..............83065-83068
Urine ..........................83069

Laparoscopic . . . . . . . . . .49650-49651
Recurrent . . . . . . . . . . . . . . . . . .49520
Sliding . . . . . . . . . . . . . . . . . . . .49525
Lumbar . . . . . . . . . . . . . . . . . . . . .49540
Lung . . . . . . . . . . . . . . . . . . . . . . .32800
Orchiopexy . . . . . . . . . . . . . . . . . .54640
Recurrent Incisional
Incarcerated . . . . . . . . . . . . . . . .49566
Umbilicus . . . . . . . . . . . . . .49580, 49585
Incarcerated . . . . . . . . . .49582, 49587
with Spermatic Cord . . . . . . . . . . .55540
Spigelian . . . . . . . . . . . . . . . . . . . . . .49590

**Hernia, Cerebral**
*See* Encephalocele

**Hernia, Rectovaginal**
*See* Rectocele

**Hernia Umbilical**
*See* Omphalocele

**Heroin, Alkaloid Screening** . . .82101

**Heroin Screen** . . . . . . . . . . . . . . . .82486

**Herpesvirus 4 (Gamma), Human**
*See* Epstein-Barr Virus

**Herpes Simplex**
Antigen Detection
Direct Fluorescence . . . . . . . . . . . .87274
Nucleic Acid . . . . . . . . . . . .87528-87530

**Herpes Smear** . . . . . . . . . . . . . . . .87207
Herpes Virus-6 Detection . . . . .87531-87533

**Herpes Virus-6 Detection** . . . . . . . . . . . . . . .87531-87533

**Herpetic Vesicle**
Destruction . . . . . . . . . . . . . . . .54050-54065

**Heteroantibodies**
*See* Antibody, Heterophile

**Heterograft**
Skin . . . . . . . . . . . . . . . . . . . . . . . . . .15400

**Heterologous Transplant**
*See* Xenograft

**Heterologous Transplantation**
*See* Heterograft

**Heterophile Antibody** . . .86308-86310

**Heterotropia**
*See* Strabismus

**Hexadecadrol**
*See* Dexamethasone

**Hexosephosphate Isomerase**
*See* Phosphohexose Isomerase

**Hex B**
*See* b-Hexosaminidase

**Heyman Procedure** . . . . .27179, 28264

**HGB**
*See* Hemoglobin, Concentration

**HGH**
*See* Growth Hormone, Human

**Hg Factor**
*See* Glucagon

**HHV-4**
*See* Epstein-Barr Virus

**HIAA**
*See* Hydroxyindolacetic Acid, Urine

**Hibb Operation**
*See* Spinal Cord; Spine, Fusion; Vertebra; Vertebral Body; Vertebral Process

**Hib Vaccine**
4 Dose Schedule
HbOC . . . . . . . . . . . . . . . . . . . . . . .90645
PRP-T . . . . . . . . . . . . . . . . . . . . . .90648
PRP-D
Booster . . . . . . . . . . . . . . . . . . . . .90646
PRP-OMP
3 Dose Schedule . . . . . . . . . . . . . .90647

**Hickmann Catheterization**
*See* Cannulization; Catheterization, Venous, Central Line; Venipuncture

**Hidradenitis**
*See* Sweat Gland
Excision . . . . . . . . . . . . 11450-11471
Suppurative
Incision and Drainage . . . .10060-10061

**Highly Selective Vagotomy**
*See* Vagotomy, Highly Selective

**Highmore Antrum**
*See* Sinus, Maxillary

**High Density Lipoprotein**
*See* Lipoprotein

**High Molecular Weight Kininogen**
*See* Fitzgerald Factor

**Hill Procedure** . . . . . . . . . . . . . . . .43324
Laparoscopic . . . . . . . . . . . . . . . . . . .43280

**Hinton Positive**
*See* RPR

**Hip**
*See* Femur; Pelvis
Abscess
Incision and Drainage . . . . . . . . . .26990
Arthroscopy . . . . . . . . . . . . . .29860-29863
Arthrocentesis . . . . . . . . . . . . . . . . . . .20610
Arthrodesis . . . . . . . . . . . . . . . .27284-27286
Arthrography . . . . . . . . . . . . . . . . . . .73525
Arthroplasty . . . . . . . . . . . . . .27130, 27132
Arthrotomy . . . . . . . . . . . . . .27030, 27033
Biopsy . . . . . . . . . . . . . . . . . . . .27040-27041
Bone
Drainage . . . . . . . . . . . . . . . . . . . .26992
Bursa
Incision and Drainage . . . . . . . . . .26991
Capsulectomy
with Release, Flexor Muscles . . . .27036
Cast . . . . . . . . . . . . . . . . . . . .29305, 29325
Craterization . . . . . . . . . . . . . . . . . . . .27070
Cyst
Excision . . . . . . . . . . . . . . .27065-27067
Denervation . . . . . . . . . . . . . . . . . . . .27035
Echography
Infant . . . . . . . . . . . . . . . . .76885-76886
Endoprosthesis
*See* Prosthesis, Hip
Excision . . . . . . . . . . . . . . . . . . . . . . . .27070
Exploration . . . . . . . . . . . . . . . . . . . . .27033
Fasciotomy . . . . . . . . . . . . . . . . . . . . .27025
Fusion . . . . . . . . . . . . . . . . . . . .27284-27286
Hematoma
Incision and Drainage . . . . . . . . . .26990
Injection
Radiologic . . . . . . . . . . . . .27093-27096
Reconstruction
Total Replacement . . . . . . . . . . . .27130
Removal
Cast . . . . . . . . . . . . . . . . . . . . . . . .29710
Foreign Body . . . . .27033, 27086-27087
Arthroscopic . . . . . . . . . . . . . . . .29861
Loose Body
Arthroscopic . . . . . . . . . . . . . . . .29861
Prosthesis . . . . . . . . . . . . . .27090-27091
Repair
Muscle Transfer . . . . . . . .27100, 27105, 27110-27111
Osteotomy . . . . . . . . . . . . .27146-27147, 27151, 27156
Tendon . . . . . . . . . . . . . . . . . . . . . .27097
Saucerization . . . . . . . . . . . . . . . . . . . .27070
Stem Prostheses
*See* Arthroplasty, Hip
Strapping . . . . . . . . . . . . . . . . . . . . . . .29520
Tenotomy
Abductor Tendon . . . . . . . . . . . . . .27006
Adductor Tendon . .27000-27001, 27003
Iliopsoas . . . . . . . . . . . . . . . . . . . .27005
Total Replacement . . . . . . . . .27130, 27132
Tumor
Excision . . . .27047-27049, 27065-27067
Radical . . . . . . . . . . . . . .27075-27076
X-Ray . . . . . . . . . . . . . .73500-73520, 73540
Intraoperative . . . . . . . . . . . . . . . .73530
with Contrast . . . . . . . . . . . . . . . . .73525

**Hip Joint**
Arthroplasty . . . . . . . . . . . . . . . . . . . .27132
Revision . . . . . . . . .27134, 27137-27138
Arthrotomy . . . . . . . . . . . . . . . . . . . . .27052
Biopsy . . . . . . . . . . . . . . . . . . . . . . . . .27052
Capsulotomy
with Release, Flexor Muscles . . . .27036
Dislocation . . . . . . . . . . . . . . . .27250-27252
Congenital . . . . . . . . . . . . .27256-27259
Open Treatment . . . . . . . . .27253-27254
without Trauma . . . . . . . . .27265-27266
Manipulation . . . . . . . . . . . . . . . . . . .27275
Reconstruction
Revision . . . . . . . . .27134, 27137-27138

Synovium
Excision .....................27054
Arthroscopic ................29863
Total Replacement ...............27132

**Hip Stem Prostheses**
*See* Arthroplasty, Hip

**Histamine** ....................83088

**Histamine Release Test** .......86343

**Histochemistry** ..........88318-88319

**Histocompatibility Testing**
*See* Tissue Typing

**Histoplasma**
Antibody .......................86698
Antigen ........................87385

**Histoplasma capsulatum**
Antigen Detection
Enzyme Immunoassay ..........87385

**Histoplasmin Test**
*See* Histoplasmosis, Skin Test

**Histoplasmoses**
*See* Histoplasmosis

**Histoplasmosis**
Skin Test .......................86510

**History and Physical**
*See* Evaluation and Management, Office and/or Other Outpatient Services
Pelvic Exam .....................57410

**HIV**
Antibody ..................86701-86703
Confirmation Test .............86689

**HIV-1**
Antigen Detection
Enzyme Immunoassay ..........87390

**HIV-2**
Antigen Detection
Enzyme Immunoassay ..........87391

**HK3 Kallikrein**
*See* Antigen, Prostate Specific

**HLA Typing** .............86812-86817

**HMRK**
*See* Fitzgerald Factor

**HMW Kininogen**
*See* Fitzgerald Factor

**Hoffman Apparatus** ...........20690

**Hofmeister Operation**
*See* Gastrectomy, Total

**Holographic Imaging** .........76375

**Holten Test**
*See* Creatinine, Urine, Clearance

**Home Services**
Established Patient .........99347-99350
New Patient ...............99341-99345

**Home Visit**
*See* House Calls

**Homocystine**
Urine ..........................82615

**Homograft**
Skin ...........................15350

**Homologous Grafts**
*See* Graft

**Homologous Transplantation**
*See* Homograft

**Homovanillic Acid**
Urine ..........................83150

**Hormone, Adrenocorticotrophic**
*See* Adrenocorticotropic Hormone (ACTH)

**Hormone, Corticotropin-Releasing**
*See* Corticotropic Releasing Hormone (CRH)

**Hormone, Growth**
*See* Growth Hormone

**Hormone, Human Growth**
*See* Growth Hormone, Human

**Hormone, Interstitial Cell-Stimulating**
*See* Luteinizing Hormone (LH)

**Hormone, Parathyroid**
*See* Parathormone

**Hormone, Pituitary Lactogenic**
*See* Prolactin

**Hormone, Placental Lactogen**
*See* Lactogen, Human Placental

**Hormone, Somatotropin Release-Inhibiting**
*See* Somatostatin

**Hormone, Thyroid-Stimulating**
*See* Thyroid Stimulating Hormone (TSH)

**Hormone-Binding Globulin, Sex**
*See* Globulin, Sex Hormone Binding

**Hormones, Adrenal Cortex**
*See* Corticosteroids

**Hormones, Antidiuretic**
*See* Antidiuretic Hormone

**Hormone Assay**
ACTH ..........................82024
Aldosterone
Blood or Urine ................82088
Androstenedione
Blood or Urine ................82157
Androsterone
Blood or Urine ................82160
Angiotensin II ..................82163
Corticosterone ..................82528
Cortisol
Total ..........................82533
Dehydroepiandrosterone ...........82626
Dihydroelestosterone .............82651
Dihydrotestosterone .............82651
Epiandrosterone ................82666
Estradiol .......................82670
Estriol .........................82677
Estrogen .................82671-82672
Estrone ........................82679
Follicle Stimulating Hormone .......83001
Growth Hormone .................83003
Hydroxyprogesterone ........83498-83499
Luteinizing Hormone ..............83002
Somatotropin ....................83003
Testosterone ....................84403
Vasopressin .....................84588

**Hormone Pellet Implantation** ..................11980

**Hospital Discharge Services**
*See* Discharge Services, Hospital

**Hospital Services**
Inpatient Services ..........99238-99239
Discharge Services ......99238-99239
Initial Care
New or Established Patient ...............99221-99233
Initial Hospital Care ......99221-99223
Newborn ..............99431-99433
Prolonged Services ......99356-99357
Subsequent Hospital Care ..................99231-99233
Observation
Discharge Services ......99234-99236
Initial Care .............99218-99220
New or Established Patient ...............99218-99220
Same Day Admission
Discharge Services ......99234-99236
Subsequent Newborn Care .........99433

**Hot Pack Treatment** ...........97010
*See* Physical Medicine and Rehabilitation

**House Calls** .............99341-99350

**Howard Test**
*See* Cystourethroscopy, Catheterization, Ureter

**HPL**
*See* Lactogen, Human Placental

**HTLV-IV**
*See* HIV-2

**HTLV I**
Antibody
Confirmatory Test ............86689
Detection ....................86687

**HTLV II**
Antibody .......................86688

**HTLV III**
*See* HIV

**HTLV III Antibodies**
*See* Antibody, HIV

**Hubbard Tank Therapy** . . . . . . . .97036
*See* Physical Medicine/Therapy/ Occupational Therapy

**Hue Test** . . . . . . . . . . . . . . . . . . . . . .92283

**Huggin Operation**
*See* Orchiectomy, Simple

**Huhner Test** . . . . . . . . . . . . .89300-89320

**Human Chorionic Gonadotropin**
*See* Chorionic Gonadotropin

**Human Chorionic Somatomammotropin**
*See* Lactogen, Human Placental

**Human Cytomegalovirus Group**
*See* Cytomegalovirus

**Human Growth Hormone (HGH)** . . . . . . . . . . . . .80418, 80428-80430

**Human Herpes Virus 4**
*See* Epstein-Barr Virus

**Human Immunodeficiency Virus**
*See* HIV

**Human Immunodeficiency Virus 1**
*See* HIV-1

**Human Immunodeficiency Virus 2**
*See* HIV-2

**Human Papillomavirus Detection** . . . . . . . . . . . . . . .87620-87622

**Human Placental Lactogen**
*See* Lactogen, Human Placental

**Human T Cell Leukemia Virus I**
*See* HTLV I

**Human T Cell Leukemia Virus II**
*See* HTLV II

**Human T Cell Leukemia Virus II Antibodies**
*See* Antibody, HTLV-II

**Human T Cell Leukemia Virus I Antibodies**
*See* Antibody, HTLV-I

**Humeral Epicondylitides, Lateral**
*See* Tennis Elbow

**Humeral Fracture**
*See* Fracture, Humerus

**Humerus**
*See* Arm, Upper; Shoulder
Abscess
Incision and Drainage . . . . . . . . . .23935
Craterization . . . . . . . . . . . . .23184, 24140
Cyst
Excision . . . . . . . . . . . . . . .23150, 24110
with Allograft . . . . . . . . .23156, 24116
with Autograft . . . . . . . .23155, 24115
Diaphysectomy . . . . . . . . . . . .23184, 24140
Excision . . . . .23174, 23184, 23195, 24134, 24140, 24150-24151
Fracture
Closed Treatment . . . . . . . .24500-24505
without Manipulation . . . . . . . .23600
with Manipulation . . . . . . . . . . .23605
Condyle
Closed Treatment . . . . . .24576-24577
Open Treatment . . . . . . . . . . . . .24579
Percutaneous Fixation . . . . . . . .24582
Epicondyle
Closed Treatment . . . . . .24560-24565
Open Treatment . . . . . . . . . . . . .24575
Skeletal Fixation
Percutaneous . . . . . . . . . . . . .24566
Greater Tuberosity Fracture
Closed Treatment without Manipulation . . . . . . . . . . . . . . .23620
Closed Treatment with Manipulation . . . . . . . . . . . . . . .23625
Open Treatment . . . . . . . . . . . . .23630
Open Treatment . . . . . . . . .23615-23616
Shaft . . . . . . . . . . . . . . . . . .24500-24505
Open Treatment . . . . . . .24515-24516
Supracondylar
Closed Treatment . . . . . .24530-24535
Open Treatment . . . . . . .24545-24546
Percutaneous Fixation . . . . . . . .24538
Transcondylar
Closed Treatment . . . . . .24530-24535
Open Treatment . . . . . . .24545-24546
Percutaneous Fixation . . . . . . . .24538
with Dislocation . . . . . . . .23665, 23670
Osteomyelitis . . . . . . . . . . . . . . . . . .24134
Pinning, Wiring . . . . . . . . . . . .23491, 24498
Prophylactic Treatment . . . . . .23491, 24498
Radical Resection . . . . . . . . . .23220-23222
Repair . . . . . . . . . . . . . . . . . . . . . . . .24430
Nonunion, Malunion . . . . .24430-24435
Osteoplasty . . . . . . . . . . . . . . . . . .24420
Osteotomy . . . . . . . . . . . . .24400-24410
with Graft . . . . . . . . . . . . . . . . . .24435
Resection Head . . . . . . . . . . . . . . . . .23195
Saucerization . . . . . . . . . . . . . .23184, 24140
Sequestrectomy . . . . . . . . . . .23174, 24134
Tumor
Excision . . .23150, 23220-23222, 24110
with Allograft . . . . . . . . .23156, 24116
with Autograft . . . . . . . .23155, 24115
X-Ray . . . . . . . . . . . . . . . . . . . . . . . .73060

**Hummelshein Operation**
*See* Strabismus, Repair

**Humor Shunt, Aqueous**
*See* Aqueous Shunt

**HVA**
*See* Homovanillic Acid

**Hybridization Probes, DNA**
*See* Nucleic Acid Probe

**Hydatidiform Mole**
Evacuation and Curettage . . . . . . . . . .59870
Excision . . . . . . . . . . . . . . . . . . . . . . .59100

**Hydatid Disease**
*See* Echinococcosis

**Hydatid Mole**
*See* Hydatidiform Mole

**Hydrocarbons, Chlorinated**
*See* Chlorinated Hydrocarbons

**Hydrocele**
Aspiration . . . . . . . . . . . . . . . . . . . . . .55000
Excision
Bilateral
Tunica Vaginalis . . . . . . . . . . . . .55041
Unilateral
Spermatic Cord . . . . . . . . . . . . .55500
Tunica Vaginalis . . . . . . . . . . . . .55040
Repair . . . . . . . . . . . . . . . . . . . . . . . . .55060

**Hydrocele, Tunica Vaginalis**
*See* Tunica Vaginalis, Hydrocele

**Hydrochloric Acid, Gastric**
*See* Acid, Gastric

**Hydrochloride, Vancomycin**
*See* Vancomycin

**Hydrocodon**
*See* Dihydrocodeinone

**Hydrogen Ion Concentration**
*See* pH

**Hydrolase, Acetylcholine**
*See* Acetylcholinesterase

**Hydrolase, Triacylglycerol**
*See* Lipase

**Hydrolases, Phosphoric Monoester**
*See* Phosphatase

**Hydrotherapy (Hubbard Tank)** . . . . . . . . . . . . . . . . . . . . . . . .97036
*See* Physical Medicine/Therapy/ Occupational Therapy

**Hydrotubation** . . . . . . . . . . . . . . . .58350

**Hydroxyacetanilide**
*See* Acetaminophen

**Hydroxycorticosteroid** . . . . . . . .83491

**Hydroxyindolacetic Acid** . . . . .83497
Urine . . . . . . . . . . . . . . . . . . . . . . . . .83497

**Hydroxypregnenolone** . .80406, 84143

**Hydroxyprogesterone** . . .80402-80406, 83498-83499

**Hydroxyproline** . . . . . . . . .83500-83505

**Hydroxytyramine**
*See* Dopamine

**Hygroma**
Cystic
Axillary/Cervical
Excision . . . . . . . . . . . . . .38550-38555

**Hymen**
Excision . . . . . . . . . . . . . . . . . . . . . . .56700
Incision . . . . . . . . . . . . . . . . . . . . . . .56720

# I

**Ilium**
Craterization .....27070
Cyst
  Excision .....27065-27067
Excision .....27070
Fracture
  Open Treatment .....27215, 27218
Saucerization .....27070
Tumor
  Excision .....27065-27067

**Ilizarov Procedure**
Monticelli Type .....20692
  *See* Application, Bone Fixation Device

**Imaging**
*See* Vascular Studies

**Imaging, Gamma Camera**
*See* Nuclear Medicine

**Imaging, Magnetic Resonance**
*See* Magnetic Resonance Imaging (MRI)

**Imaging, Ultrasonic**
*See* Echography

**Imbrioation**
Diaphragm .....39545

**Imidobenzyle**
*See* Imipramine

**Imipramine**
Assay .....80174

**Immune Complex Assay** .....86332

**Immune Globulins**
Antitoxin
  Botulinum .....90287
  Diphtheria .....90296
Botulism .....90288
Cytomegalovirus .....90291
Hepatitis B .....90371
Human .....90281, 90283
Rabies .....90375, 90376
Respiratory Syncytial Virus .....90378-90379
Rho (D) .....90384-90386
Tetanus .....90389
Unlisted Immune Globulin .....90399
Vaccinia .....90393
Varicella-Zoster .....90396

**Immune Globulin Administration** .....90780-90784

**Immune Globulin E**
*See* IgE

**Immunization, Mumps**
*See* Mumps, Immunization

**Immunization Administration**
One Vaccine/Toxoid .....90471
Each Additional Vaccine/Toxoid .....90472

**Immunoassay**
Analyte .....83519, 83520
Infectious Agent .....86317-86318, 87449-87450
Nonantibody .....83516-83518, 83519
Tumor Antigen .....86316

**Immunoblotting, Western**
*See* Western Blot

**Immunochemical, Lysozyme (Muramidase)**
*See* Lysozyme

**Immunocytochemistry** .....88342

**Immunodeficiency Virus, Human**
*See* HIV

**Immunodeficiency Virus Type 1, Human**
*See* HIV-1

**Immunodeficiency Virus Type 2, Human**
*See* HIV-2

**Immunodiffusion** .....86329-86331

**Immunoelectrophoresis** .....86320-86327, 86334

**Immunofixation Electrophoresis** .....86334

**Immunofluorescent Study** .....88346-88347

**Immunogen**
*See* Antigen

**Immunoglobulin** .....82787
Platelet Associated .....86023
Thyroid Stimulating .....84445

**Immunoglobulin E**
*See* IgE

**Immunoglobulin Receptor Assay** .....86243

**Immunologic Skin Test**
*See* Skin, Tests

**Immunology**
Unlisted Services and Procedures .....86849

**Immunotherapies, Allergen**
*See* Allergen Immunotherapy

**Impedance Testing** .....92567
*See* Audiologic Function Tests

**Imperfectly Descended Testis**
*See* Testis, Undescended

**Implant, Breast**
*See* Breast, Implants

**Implant, Glaucoma Drainage**
*See* Aqueous Shunt

**Implant, Orbital**
*See* Orbital Implant

**Implant, Penile**
*See* Penile Prosthesis

**Implant, Penile Prosthesis, Inflatable**
*See* Penile Prosthesis, Insertion, Inflatable

**Implant, Subperiosteal**
*See* Subperiosteal Implant

**Implant, Ureters into, Bladder**
*See* Anastomosis, Ureter, to Bladder

**Implantation**
Cardiac Event Recorder .....33282
Contraceptive Capsules .....11975, 11977
Electrode
  Brain .....61850-61875
  Nerve .....64553-64580
  Spinal Cord .....63650-63655
Eye
  Anterior Segment .....65920
  Aqueous Shunt to Extraocular Placement or Replacement of Pegs .....65125
  Posterior Segment
    Extraocular .....67120
    Intraocular .....67121
  Reservoir .....66180
  Vitreous
    Drug Delivery System .....67027
Hearing Aid Hormone Pellet(s)
  Bone Conduction .....69710
Hip Prosthesis
  *See* Arthroplasty, Hip
Hormone Pellet .....11980
Intraocular Lens
  *See* Insertion, Intraocular Lens
Joint
  *See* Arthroplasty
Mesh
  Hernia Repair .....49568
Nerve
  into Bone .....64787
  into Muscle .....64787
Neurostimulators
  Pulse Generator .....61885
  Receiver .....61886
Pulse Generator
  Brain .....61885-61886
  Spinal Cord Electrode Array .....63685
Receiver
  Brain .....61885-61886
  Spinal Cord .....63685
Removal .....20670-20680
  Elbow .....24164
  Radius .....24164
Reservoir Vascular Access Device
  Declotting .....36550
Tubouterine .....58752
Ventricular Assist Device .....33975-33976

**Implant Removal**
*See* Specific Anatomical Site

**Impression, Maxillofacial**
Auricular Prosthesis .....21086
Definitive Obturator Prosthesis .....21080
Facial Prosthesis .....21088
Interim Obturator .....21079
Mandibular Resection Prosthesis .....21081

Nasal Prosthesis . . . . . . . . . . . . . . . . .21087
Oral Surgical Splint . . . . . . . . . . . . . . .21085
Orbital Prosthesis . . . . . . . . . . . . . . . .21077
Palatal Augmentation Prosthesis . . . .21082
Palatal Lift Prosthesis . . . . . . . . . . . . .21083
Speech Aid Prosthesis . . . . . . . . . . . .21084
Surgical Obturator . . . . . . . . . . . . . . . .21076

**IM Injection**
*See* Injection, Intramuscular

**Incision**
*See* Incision and Drainage
Abdomen . . . . . . . . . . . . . . . . . . . . . . .49000
  Exploration . . . . . . . . . . . . . . . . . .58960
Abscess
  Soft Tissue . . . . . . . . . . . . .20000-20005
Accessory Nerve . . . . . . . . . . . . . . . .63191
Anal
  Fistula . . . . . . . . . . . . . . . .46270, 46280
  Septum . . . . . . . . . . . . . . . . . . . . .46070
  Sphincter . . . . . . . . . . . . . . . . . . . .46080
Ankle . . . . . . . . . . . . . . . . . . . . . . . . .27607
  Tendon . . . . . . . . . . . . . . . .27605-27606
Anus
  *See* Anus, Incision
Aortic Valve
  for Stenosis . . . . . . . . . . . . . . . . . .33415
Artery
  Nose . . . . . . . . . . . . . . . . . .30915-30920
Atrial Septum . . . . . . . . . . . . .33735-33737
Bile Duct
  Sphincter . . . . . . . . . . . . . .43262, 47460
Bladder
  Catheterization . . . . . . . . . . . . . . .51045
  with Destruction . . . . . . . .51020-51030
  with Radiotracer . . . . . . . . . . . . . .51020
Bladder Diverticulum . . . . . . . . . . . . . .52305
Breast
  Capsules . . . . . . . . . . . . . . . . . . . .19370
Burn Scalp . . . . . . . . . . . . . . . . . . . . . .16035
Cataract
  Secondary
    Laser Surgery . . . . . . . . . . . . . . .66821
    Stab Incision Technique . . . . . . .66820
Chest
  Biopsy . . . . . . . . . . . . . . . . .32095-32100
Colon
  Exploration . . . . . . . . . . . . . . . . . .44025
  Stoma
    Creation . . . . . . . . . . . . .44320, 44322
    Revision . . . . . . . .44340, 44345-44346
Cornea
  for Astigmatism . . . . . . . . . . . . . . .65772
Corpus Callosum . . . . . . . . . . . . . . . . .61541
Cricothyroid Membrane . . . . . . . . . . .31605
Dentate Ligament . . . . . . . . . .63180, 63182
Duodenum . . . . . . . . . . . . . . . . . . . . .44010
Ear, Inner
  Labyrinth
    with Mastoidectomy . . . . . . . . .69802
    with or without Cryosurgery . . .69801
Elbow . . . . . . . . . . . . . . . . . . . . . . . . .24000
Esophagus . . . . . . . . . . . . . . . .43020, 43045
  Muscle . . . . . . . . . . . . . . . . . . . . . .43030
Exploration
  Kidney . . . . . . . . . . . . . . . . . . . . . .50010
Eye
  Adhesions . . . . . . . . . . . . . . . . . . .65880
    Anterior Segment . . . . . .65860, 65865
    Anterior Synechiae . . . . . . . . . . .65870
    Corneovitreal . . . . . . . . . . . . . . .65880
    Posterior . . . . . . . . . . . . . . . . . . .65875
  Anterior Chamber . . . . . . . . . . . . .65820
  Trabeculae . . . . . . . . . . . . . . . . . .65850
Eyelid
  Canthus . . . . . . . . . . . . . . . . . . . . .67715
  Sutures . . . . . . . . . . . . . . . . . . . . .67710
Fibula . . . . . . . . . . . . . . . . . . . . . . . . .27607
Finger
  Decompression . . . . . . . . . . . . . . .26035
  Tendon . . . . . . . . . .26060, 26455, 26460
  Tendon Sheath . . . . . . . . . . . . . . .26055
Foot . . . . . . . . . . . . . . . . . . . . . . . . . .28005
  Capsule . . . . . . . . .28260-28262, 28264
  Fasciotomy . . . . . . . . . . . . . . . . . .28008
  for Infection . . . . . . . . . . . .28002-28003
  Tendon . . . . . . . . . . . . . . . .28230, 28234
Frontal Lobe . . . . . . . . . . . . . . . . . . . .61490
Gallbladder . . . . . . . . . . . . . . . . . . . .47490
Hand Decompression . . . . . . .26035, 26037
  Tendon . . . . . . . . . . . . . . . .26450, 26460
Heart
  Exploration . . . . . . . . . . . .33310, 33315
Hemorrhoids
  External . . . . . . . . . . . . . . . . . . . .46083
Hepatic Ducts
  *See* Hepaticostomy
Hip
  Denervation . . . . . . . . . . . . . . . . .27035
  Exploration . . . . . . . . . . . . . . . . . .27033
  Fasciotomy . . . . . . . . . . . . . . . . . .27025
  Joint Capsule
    for Flexor Release . . . . . . . . . . .27036
  Tendon
    Abductor . . . . . . . . . . . . . . . . . .27006
    Adductor . . . . . . .27000-27001, 27003
    Iliopsoas . . . . . . . . . . . . . . . . . .27005
Hymen
  *See* Hymen, Incision
Hymenotomy . . . . . . . . . . . . . . . . . . . .56720
Intercarpal Joint
  Dislocation . . . . . . . . . . . . . . . . . .25670
Interphalangeal Joint
  Capsule . . . . . . . . . . . . . . . . . . . . .26525
Intestines (Except Rectum)
  *See* Enterotomy
Intestines, Small . . . . . . . . . . . . . . . .44010
  Biopsy . . . . . . . . . . . . . . . . . . . . . .44020
  Creation
    Pouch . . . . . . . . . . . . . . . . . . . . .44316
    Stoma . . . . . . . . .44300, 44310, 44314
  Decompression . . . . . . . . . . . . . . .44021
  Exploration . . . . . . . . . . . . . . . . . .44020
  Incision . . . . . . . . . . . . . . . . . . . . .44020
  Removal
    Foreign Body . . . . . . . . . . . . . . .44020
  Revision
    Stoma . . . . . . . . . . . . . . . . . . . . .44312
Iris . . . . . . . . . . . . . . . . . . . . .66500, 66505
Kidney . . . . . . . . . . . . . . . . . . .50010, 50045
Knee
  Capsule . . . . . . . . . . . . . . . . . . . . .27435
  Exploration . . . . . . . . . . . . . . . . . .27310
  Fasciotomy . . . . . . . . . . . . . . . . . .27305
  Removal of Foreign Body . . . . . . .27310
Lacrimal Punctum . . . . . . . . . . . . . . . .68440
Lacrimal Sac
  *See* Dacryocystotomy
Larynx . . . . . . . . . . . . . . . . . . .31300-31320
Leg, Lower
  Fasciotomy . . . . . . . . . . . . .27600-27602
Leg, Upper
  Fasciotomy . . . . . . . . . . . . . . . . . .27305
  Tenotomy . . . . . . . . . . . . . .27306-27307,
    27390-27392
Lip
  Frenum . . . . . . . . . . . . . . . . . . . . . .40806
Liver
  *See* Hepatotomy
Lung
  Biopsy . . . . . . . . . . . . . . . . .32095-32100
  Decortication
    Partial . . . . . . . . . . . . . . . . . . . .32225
    Total . . . . . . . . . . . . . . . . . . . . . .32220
Lymphatic Channels . . . . . . . . . . . . . .38308
Mastoid
  *See* Mastoidotomy
Medullary Tract . . . . . . . . . . . . . . . . . .61470
Mesencephalic Tract . . . . . . . . . . . . . .61480
Metacarpophalangeal Joint
  Capsule . . . . . . . . . . . . . . . . . . . . .26520
Mitral Valve . . . . . . . . . . . . . . .33420-33422
Muscle
  *See* Myotomy
Nerve . . . . . . . . . . . . . . . . . . . .64400-64772
  Foot . . . . . . . . . . . . . . . . . . . . . . . .28035
  Root . . . . . . . . . . . . . . . . . . .63185, 63190
  Vagus . . . . . . . . . . . . . . . . . .43640-43641
Nose
  *See* Rhinotomy
Orbit
  *See* Orbitotomy
Palm
  Fasciotomy . . . . . . . . . . . . .26040, 26045
Pancreas
  Sphincter . . . . . . . . . . . . . . . . . . . .43262
Penis
  Prepuce . . . . . . . . . . . . . . . .54000-54001
    Newborn . . . . . . . . . . . . . . . . . . .54000
Pericardium
  with Clot Removal . . . . . . . . . . . . .33020
  with Foreign Body Removal . . . . .33020
  with Tube . . . . . . . . . . . . . . . . . . . .33015

## Incisional Hernia Repair



## Incision and Drainage

Excision
Iridectomy
Optical ....66635
Peripheral ....66625
Sector ....66630
with Corneoscleral or Corneal Section ....66600
with Cyclectomy ....66605
Incision
Iridotomy
Stab ....66500
with Transfixion as for Iris Bombe ....66505
Lesion
Destruction ....66770
Repair
with Ciliary Body ....66680
Suture ....66682
Revision
Laser Surgery ....66761
Photocoagulation ....66762
Suture
with Ciliary Body ....66682

**Iron** ....83540
Absorption ....78162
Chelatable
Total Body Iron ....78172
Turnover Rate ....78160
Utilization ....78170

**Iron Binding Capacity** ....83550

**Iron Hematoxylin Stain** ....88312

**Iron Stain** ....85535, 88313

**Irradiation**
Blood Products ....86945

**Irrigation**
Bladder ....51700
Catheter
Brain ....62194, 62225
Corpora Cavernosa
Priapism ....54220
Penis
Priapism ....54220
Peritoneal
*See* Peritoneal Lavage
Shunt
Spinal Cord ....63744
Sinus
Maxillary ....31000
Sphenoid ....31002
Vagina ....57150

**Irving Sterilization**
*See* Ligation, Fallopian Tube, Oviduct

**Ischial**
Bursa
Excision ....27060
Tumor
Excision ....27078, 27079

**Ischiectomy** ....15941

**Islands of Langerhans**
*See* Islet Cell

**Island Pedicle Flaps** ....15740

**Islet Cell**
Antibody ....86341

**Isocitrate Dehydrogenase**
*See* Isocitric Dehydrogenase

**Isocitric Dehydrogenase**
Blood ....83570

**Isolation**
Sperm ....89260-89261

**Isomerase, Glucose 6 Phosphate**
*See* Phosphohexose Isomerase

**Isopropanol**
*See* Isopropyl Alcohol

**Isopropyl Alcohol** ....84600

**Isthmusectomy**
Thyroid Gland ....60210-60225

**IUD**
*See* Intrauterine Device (IUD)

**IV**
*See* Injection, Chemotherapy; Intravenous Therapy

**IV, Coagulation Factor**
*See* Calcium

**IVC Filter**
Placement ....75940

**IVF**
*See* Artificial Insemination; In Vitro Fertilization

**Ivy Bleeding Time** ....85002

**IV Infusion Therapy**
*See* Allergen Immunotherapy; Chemotherapy; Infusion; Injection, Chemotherapy

**IV Injection**
*See* Injection, Intravenous

**IX Complex, Factor**
*See* Christmas Factor

**I Antibodies, HTLV**
*See* Antibody, HTLV-I

# J

**Jaboulay Operation**
*See* Gastroduodenostomy

**Jaboulay Operation Gastroduodenostomy**
*See* Gastroduodenostomy

**Jannetta Procedure**
*See* Decompression, Cranial Nerve; Section

**Japanese, River Fever**
*See* Scrub Typhus

**Jatene Type** ....33770-33781

**Jaws**
Muscle Reduction ....21295-21296
X-Ray
for Orthodontics ....70355

**Jaw Joint**
*See* Facial Bones; Mandible; Maxilla

**Jejunostomy**
Catheterization ....44015
Insertion
Catheter ....44015
Laparoscopic ....44201
Non-Tube ....44310
with Pancreatic Drain ....48001

**Jejunum**
Creation
Stoma
Laparoscopic ....44201
Transfer
with Microvascular Anastomosis
Free ....43496

**Johannsen Procedure** ....53400

**Johanson Operation**
*See* Reconstruction, Urethra

**Joint**
*See* Specific Joint
Acromioclavicular
*See* Acromioclavicular Joint
Arthrocentesis ....20600-20610
Aspiration ....20600-20610
Dislocation
*See* Dislocation
Drainage ....20600-20610
Finger
*See* Intercarpal Joint
Fixation (Surgical)
*See* Arthrodesis
Foot
*See* Foot, Joint
Hip
*See* Hip Joint
Injection ....20600-20610
Intertarsal
*See* Intertarsal Joint
Knee
*See* Knee Joint
Ligament
*See* Ligament
Metacarpophalangeal
*See* Metacarpophalangeal Joint
Metatarsophalangeal
*See* Metatarsophalangeal Joint

# K

**Kinetic Therapy** ....97530
*See* Physical Medicine/Therapy/Occupational Therapy

**Kininase A**
*See* Angiotensin Converting Enzyme (ACE)

**Kininogen** ....85293

**Kininogen, High Molecular Weight**
*See* Fitzgerald Factor

**Kleihauer-Betke Test** ....85460

**Kloramfenikol**
*See* Chloramphenicol

**Knee**
*See* Femur; Fibula; Patella; Tibia
Abscess ....27301
Arthrocentesis ....20610
Arthrodesis ....27580
Arthroplasty ....27440-27443, 27445
  Revision ....27486-27487
Arthroscopy
  Diagnostic ....29870
  Surgical ....29871-29889
Arthrotomy ....27310, 27330-27331, 27332, 27333, 27334-27335, 27403
Biopsy ....27323-27324, 27330-27331
  Synovium ....27330
Bone
  Drainage ....27303
Bursa ....27301
  Excision ....27340
Cyst
  Excision ....27345, 27347
Disarticulation ....27598
Dislocation ....27550-27552, 27560-27562
  Open Treatment ....27556-27558, 27566
Drainage ....27310
Excision
  Cartilage ....27332-27333
  Ganglion ....27347
  Lesion ....27347
  Synovial Lung ....27334-27335
Exploration ....27310, 27331
Fasciotomy ....27305, 27496-27499
Fracture ....27520, 27524
  Arthroscopic Treatment ....29850-29851
Fusion ....27580
Hematoma ....27301
Incision
  Capsule ....27435
Injection
  X-Ray ....27370
Magnetic Resonance Imaging (MRI) ....73721
Manipulation ....27570
Meniscectomy ....27332-27333
Reconstruction ....27437-27438
  Ligament ....27427-27429
  with Prosthesis ....27445
Removal
  Foreign Body ....27310, 27331, 27372
  Loose Body ....27331
  Prosthesis ....27488
Repair
  Ligament ....27405-27409
    Collateral ....27405
    Collateral and Cruciate ....27409
    Cruciate ....27407-27409
  Meniscus ....27403
  Tendon ....27380-27381
Replacement ....27447
Retinacular
  Release ....27425
Strapping ....29530
Suture
  Tendon ....27380-27381
Tumor
  Excision ....27327-27329, 27365
Unlisted Services and Procedures ....27599
X-Ray ....73560-73564
  Arthrography ....73580
  Bilateral ....73565
X-Ray with Contrast
  Arthrography ....73580

**Kneecap**
Excision ....27350
Repair
  Instability ....27420-27424

**Knee Joint**
Arthroplasty ....27446

**Knee Prosthesis**
*See* Prosthesis, Knee

**Knock-Knee Repair** ....27455-27457

**Kocher Operation** ....23650-23655, 23660, 23665, 23670, 23675, 23680
*See* Clavicle; Scapula; Shoulder, Dislocation, Closed Treatment

**Kocher Pylorectomy**
*See* Gastrectomy, Partial

**Kock Pouch** ....44316
Formation ....50825

**Kock Procedure** ....44316

**KOH**
*See* Tissue, Examination for Fungi

**Kraske Procedure** ....45116

**Krause Operation**
*See* Gasserian Ganglion, Sensory Root, Decompression

**Kroenlein Procedure** ....67420

**Krukenberg Procedure** ....25915

**Kuhlmann Test** ....96100

**Kuhnt-Szymanowski Procedure** ....67917

**Kyphectomy**
More than Two Segments ....22819
Up to Two Segments ....22818


# L


**L-Alanine**
*See* Aminolevulinic Acid (ALA)

**L-Leucylnaphthylamidase**
*See* Leucine Aminopeptidase

**L/S Ratio**
Amniotic Fluid ....83661

**Labial Adhesions**
Lysis ....56441

**Labyrinth**
*See* Ear, Inner

**Labyrinthectomy** ....69905
with Mastoidectomy ....69910
with Skull Base Surgery ....61596

**Labyrinthotomy**
with/without Cryosurgery ....69801
with Mastoidectomy ....69802

**Laceration Repair**
*See* Specific Site

**Lacrimal Duct**
Canaliculi
  Repair ....68700
Exploration ....68810
  Canaliculi ....68840
  Stent ....68815
  with Anesthesia ....68811
Insertion
  Stent ....68815
Removal
  Dacryolith ....68530
  Foreign Body ....68530
X-Ray with Contrast ....70170

**Lacrimal Gland**
Biopsy ....68510
Close Fistula ....68770
Excision
  Partial ....68505
  Total ....68500
Fistulization ....68720
Incision and Drainage ....68400
Injection
  X-Ray ....68850
Nuclear Medicine
  Tear Flow ....78660
Removal
  Dacryolith ....68530
  Foreign Body ....68530
Repair
  Fistula ....68770
Tumor
  Excision
    without Closure ....68540
    with Osteotomy ....68550

Exploration ....31505, 31520-31526, 31575
Fiberoptic ................31575-31579
with Stroboscopy ............31579
Indirect ..................31505-31513
Newborn ......................31520
Operative ................31530-31561

**Laryngotomy** ..................31300
Diagnostic ......................31320
Total ....................31360-31368

**Larynx**
Aspiration
Endoscopy ..................31515
Biopsy
Endoscopy .31510, 31535-31536, 31576
Dilation
Endoscopic ............31528-31529
Endoscopy
Direct ................31515-31571
Exploration .................31505, 31520-31526, 31575
Fiberoptic ..............31575-31579
with Stroboscopy ...........31579
Indirect ...............31505-31513
Operative ..............31530-31561
Excision
Lesion ................31512, 31578
Partial ................31367-31382
Total ..................31360-31365
with Pharynx ...........31390-31395
Exploration
Endoscopic .................31505, 31520-31526, 31575
Fracture
Closed Treatment
without Manipulation ........31585
with Manipulation ...........31586
Open Treatment ..............31584
Insertion
Obturator ...................31527
Nerve
Destruction .................31595
Reconstruction
Burns .......................31588
Cricoid Split ...............31587
Other .......................31588
Stenosis ....................31582
Web .........................31580
Removal
Foreign Body
Endoscopic ...............31511, 31530-31531, 31577
Lesion
Endoscopic ..........31512, 31578
Repair
Reinnervation Neuromuscular
Pedicle .....................31590
Stroboscopy ....................31579
Tumor
Excision ....................31300
Endoscopic ..........31540-31541
Unlisted Services and Procedures ...31599

Vocal Cord(s)
Injection .........31513, 31570-31571
X-Ray ..........................70370
with Contrast ................70373

**Laser Surgery**
Anal ...........................46917
Lesion
Mouth ......................40820
Nose ..................30117-30118
Penis ......................54057

**Laser Treatment** ........17000-17250, 17260-17286
*See* Destruction

**Lateral Epicondylitis**
*See* Tennis Elbow

**Latex Fixation** ...........86403-86406

**LATS**
*See* Thyrotropin Releasing Hormone (TRH)

**Latzko Operation**
*See* Repair, Vagina, Fistula; Revision

**LAV**
*See* HIV

**LAV-2**
*See* HIV-2

**Lavage, Bronchioalveolar**
*See* Lung, Lavage

**Lavage, Peritoneal**
*See* Peritoneal Lavage

**Lav Antibodies**
*See* Antibody, HIV

**LCM**
*See* Lymphocytic Choriomeningitis

**LD**
*See* Lactic Dehydrogenase

**LDH** ....................83615-83625

**LDL**
*See* Lipoprotein, LDL

**Lead** .........................83655

**Leadbetter Procedure** .........53443

**Lecithin-Sphingomyelin Ratio** ...................83661-83662

**Lecithinase C**
*See* Tissue Typing

**LEEP Procedure** ..............57460

**Lee and White Test** ...........85345

**LeFort Procedure**
Vagina .........................57120

**LeFort III Procedure**
Craniofacial Separation ......21431-21436
Midface Reconstruction ......21154-21159

**LeFort II Procedure**
Midface Reconstruction ......21150-21151
Nasomaxillary Complex
Fracture .................21345-21348

**LeFort I Procedure**
Midface Reconstruction .....21141-21147, 21155, 21160
Palatal or Maxillary
Fracture .................21421-21423

**Left Atrioventricular Valve**
*See* Mitral Valve

**Left Heart Cardiac Catheterization**
*See* Cardiac Catheterization, Left Heart

**Leg**
Cast
Rigid Total Contact ...........29445
Lower
*See* Ankle; Fibula; Knee; Tibia
(MRI) ......................73720
Abscess
Incision and Drainage ........27603
Amputation ......27598, 27880-27882
Revision ..............27884-27886
Artery
Ligation ...................37618
Biopsy .................27613-27614
Bursa
Incision and Drainage ........27604
Bypass Graft ...............35903
Cast ......29405, 29425, 29435, 29450
CAT Scan ..............73700-73702
Decompression .........27600-27602
Exploration
Blood Vessel ...............35860
Fasciotomy ............27600-27602, 27892-27894
Hematoma
Incision and Drainage ........27603
Lesion
Excision ...................27630
Magnetic Resonance Imaging
Repair
Blood Vessel ...............35226
Blood Vessel with Other Graft ..35286
Blood Vessel with Vein Graft ...35256
Fascia .....................27656
Tendon ..............27658-27665, 27675-27676, 27680-27681, 27685-27687, 27690-27692
Splint .......................29515
Strapping ...................29580
Suture
Tendon ...............27658-27665
Tumor
Excision ........27615, 27618-27619
Ultrasound ..................76880
Unlisted Services and
Procedures ..................27899
Unna Boot ...................29580
X-Ray .......................73592
Upper
*See* Femur
Abscess .....................27301
MRI .........................73720

Iris
Destruction ....66770
Leg, Lower
Tendon Sheath ....27630
Lymph Node
Incision and Drainage ....38300-38305
Mesentery
Excision ....44820
Mouth
Destruction ....40820
Excision ....40810, 40812, 40814, 40816, 41116
Vestibule
Destruction ....40820
Repair ....40830
Nerve
Excision ....64774-64792
Nose
Intranasal
External Approach ....30118
Internal Approach ....30117
Orbit
Excision ....61333, 67412
Palate
Destruction ....42160
Excision ....42104, 42106-42107, 42120
Pancreas
Excision ....48120
Pelvis
Destruction ....58662
Penis
Destruction
Cryosurgery ....54056
Electrodesiccation ....54055
Extensive ....54065
Laser Surgery ....54057
Simple ....54050-54060
Surgical Excision ....54060
Excision ....54060
Penile Plague ....54110-54112
Pharynx
Destruction ....42808
Excision ....42808
Rectum
Excision ....45108
Removal
Larynx ....31512, 31578
Resection ....52338
Retina
Destruction
Extensive ....67227-67228
Localized ....67208, 67210
Radiation by Implantation of Source ....67218
Sclera
Excision ....66130
Skin
Abrasion ....15786-15787
Biopsy ....11100-11101
Destruction
Benign ....17000-17250
Malignant ....17260-17286
Excision
Benign ....11400-11471
Malignant ....11600-11646
Injection ....11900-11901
Paring or Curettement ....11055-11057
Shaving ....11300-11313
Skin Tags
Removal ....11200-11201
Skull
Excision ....61500, 61600-61608, 61615-61616
Spermatic Cord
Excision ....55520
Spinal Cord
Destruction ....62280-62282
Excision ....63265-63268, 63270-63273
Stomach
Excision ....43611
Testis
Excision ....54510
Toe
Excision ....28092
Tongue
Excision ....41110, 41112-41114
Uvula
Destruction ....42145
Excision ....42104, 42106-42107
Vagina
Destruction ....57061-57065
Vulva
Destruction
Extensive ....56515
Simple ....56501
Wrist Tendon
Excision ....25110

**Lesion of Sciatic Nerve**
*See* Sciatic Nerve, Lesion

**Leucine Aminopeptidase** ....83670

**Leukemia Lymphoma Virus I, Adult T Cell**
*See* HTLV I

**Leukemia Lymphoma Virus II Antibodies, Human T Cell**
*See* Antibody, HTLV-II

**Leukemia Lymphoma Virus I Antibodies, Human T Cell**
*See* Antibody, HTLV-I

**Leukemia Virus II, Hairy Cell Associated, Human T Cell**
*See* HTLV II

**Leukoagglutinins** ....86021

**Leukocyte**
*See* White Blood Cell
Alkaline Phosphatase ....85540
Antibody ....86021
Histamine Release Test ....86343
Phagocytosis ....86344
Transfusion ....86950

**Leukocyte Count**
*See* White Blood Cell, Count

**Leu 2 Antigens**
*See* CD8

**Levarterenol**
*See* Noradrenalin

**Levator Muscle Rep**
*See* Blepharoptosis, Repair

**LeVeen Shunt**
Insertion ....49425
Patency Test ....78291
Revision ....49426

**Levulose**
*See* Fructose

**LGV**
*See* Lymphogranuloma Venereum

**LH**
*See* Luteinizing Hormone (LH)

**LHR**
*See* Leukocyte Histamine Release Test

**Lidocaine**
Assay ....80176

**Lid Suture**
*See* Blepharoptosis, Repair

**Lift, Face**
*See* Face Lift

**Ligament**
*See* Specific Site
Collateral
Repair
Knee
with Cruciate Ligament ....27409
Dentate
Incision ....63180-63182
Section ....63180-63182
Injection ....20550
Release
Coracoacromial ....23415
Transverse Carpal ....29848
Repair
Knee Joint ....27405-27409

**Ligation**
Artery
Abdomen ....37617
Carotid ....37600-37606
Chest ....37616
Coronary ....33502
Coronary Artery ....33502
Ethmoidal ....30915
Extremity ....37618
Fistula ....37607
Maxillary ....30920
Neck ....37615
Temporal ....37609
Esophageal Varices ....43204, 43400
Fallopian Tube
Oviduct ....58670, 58600-58611

**Local Excision of Lesion or Tissue of Femur**
*See* Excision, Lesion, Femur

**Log Hydrogen Ion Concentration**
*See* pH

**Lombard Test**
*See* Audiologic Function Test

**Longmire Operation**
*See* Anastomosis, Hepatic Duct to Intestines

**Long Acting Thyroid Stimulator**
*See* Thyrotropin Releasing Hormone (TRH)

**Long Term Care Facility Visits**
*See* Nursing Facility Services

**Loopogram**
*See* Urography, Antegrade

**Loose Body**
Removal
- Ankle .....27620
- Carpometacarpal Joint .....26070
- Elbow .....24101
- Interphalangeal Joint .....28020
  - Toe .....28024
- Knee Joint .....27331
- Metatarsophalangeal Joint .....28022
- Tarsometatarsal Joint .....28020
- Toe .....28022
- Wrist .....25101

**Lord Procedure**
*See* Anal Sphincter, Dilation

**Louis Bar Syndrome**
*See* Ataxia Telangiectasia

**Lower Extremities**
*See* Extremity, Lower

**Lower GI Series**
*See* Barium Enema

**Low Density Lipoprotein**
*See* Lipoprotein, LDL

**Low Vision Aids**
*See* Spectacle Services
Fitting .....92354-92355
Supply .....92392

**LRH**
*See* Luteinizing Releasing Factor

**LSD**
*See* Lysergic Acid Diethylamide

**LTH**
*See* Prolactin

**Lumbar**
*See* Spine
Aspiration, Disk
- Percutaneous .....62287

**Lumbar Plexus**
Decompression .....64714
Neuroplasty .....64714
Release .....64714
Repair/Suture .....64862

**Lumbar Puncture**
*See* Spinal Tap

**Lumbar Spine Fracture**
*See* Fracture, Vertebra, Lumbar

**Lumbar Sympathectomy**
*See* Sympathectomy, Lumbar

**Lumbar Vertebra**
*See* Vertebra, Lumbar

**Lumen Dilation** .....74360

**Lumpectomies**
*See* Breast, Excision, Lesion

**Lunate**
Arthroplasty
- with Implant .....25444

Dislocation
- Closed Treatment .....25690
- Open Treatment .....25695

**Lung**
Abscess
- Incision and Drainage
  - Open .....32200
  - Percutaneous .....32200-32201

Aspiration .....32420
Biopsy .....32095-32100
Bullae
- Excision .....32141
  - Endoscopic .....32655

Cyst
- Incision and Drainage
  - Open .....32200
- Removal .....32140

Decortication
- Endoscopic .....32651-32652
- Partial .....32225
- Total .....32220
- with Parietal Pleurectomy .....32320

Empyema
- Excision .....32540

Excision
- Bronchus Resection .....32486
- Chest Resection .....32520-32525
- Completion .....32488
- Donor .....33930
- Emphysematous .....32491
- Lobe .....32480-32482
- Segment .....32484
- Total .....32440-32445
- Wedge Resection .....32500
  - Endoscopic .....32657

Foreign Body
- Removal .....32151

Hemorrhage .....32110
Lavage
- Bronchial .....31624
- Total .....32997

Lysis
- Adhesions .....32124

Needle Biopsy .....32405
Nuclear Medicine
- Imaging, Perfusion .....78580-78585
- Imaging, Ventilation .....78586-78594
- Unlisted Services and Procedures .....78599

Pneumocentesis .....32420
Pneumolysis .....32940
Pneumothorax .....32960
Puncture .....32420
Removal
- Bronchoplasty .....32501
- Completion Pneumonectomy .....32488
- Extrapleural .....32445
- Single Lobe .....32480
- Single Segment .....32484
- Sleeve Lobectomy .....32486
- Sleeve Pneumonectomy .....32442
- Total Pneumonectomy .....32440-32445
- Two Lobes .....32482
- Volume Reduction .....32491
- Wedge Resection .....32500

Repair
- Hernia .....32800

Segmentectomy .....32484
Tear
- Repair .....32110

Thoracotomy
- Biopsy .....32095-32100
- Cardiac Massage .....32160
- for Post-Op Complications .....32120
- Removal
  - Bullae .....32141
  - Cyst .....32140
  - Intrapleural Foreign Body .....32150
  - Intrapulmonary Foreign Body .....32151
- Repair .....32110
- with Excision-Plication of Bullae .....32141
- with Open Intrapleural Pneumonolysis .....32124

Transplantation .....32851-32854, 33935
Unlisted Services and Procedures .....32999

**Lung Function Tests**
*See* Pulmonology, Diagnostic

**Lung Volume Reduction**
Emphysematous .....32491

**Lupus Anticoagulant Assay** .....85705

**Lupus Band Test**
*See* Immunofluorescent Study

**Luteinizing Hormone (LH)** .....80418, 80426, 83002

**Luteinizing Releasing Factor** .....83727

**Lutenizing Hormone**
*See* Luteinizing Hormone (LH)

**Luteotropic Hormone**
*See* Prolactin

**Luteotropin**
*See* Prolactin

**Luteotropin, Placental**
*See* Lactogen, Human Placental

**Lyme Disease** .......... 86617, 86618

**Lyme Disease ab**
*See* Antibody, Lyme Disease

**Lyme Disease Vaccine**
*See* Vaccination

**Lymphadenectomy**
Abdominal .......... 38747
Bilateral Inguinofemoral .......... 54130, 56632, 56637
Bilateral Pelvic .......... 51575, 51585, 51595, 54135, 55845, 55865
  Total .......... 38571-38572, 57531, 58210
Diaphragmatic Assessment .......... 58960
Gastric .......... 38747
Inguinofemoral .......... 38760-38765
Inguinofemoral, Iliac and Pelvic .......... 56640
Injection
  Sentinel Node .......... 38792
Limited, for Staging
  Para-Aortic .......... 38562
  Pelvic .......... 38562
  Retroperitoneal .......... 38564
Limited Para-Aortic, Resection of Ovarian Malignancy .......... 58951
Limited Pelvic .......... 55842, 55862
Mediastinal .......... 21632
Peripancreatic .......... 38747
Portal .......... 38747
Radical
  Axillary .......... 38740-38745
  Cervical .......... 38720-38724
  Pelvic .......... 54135, 55845
  Suprahyoid .......... 38700
Regional .......... 50230
Retroperitoneal Transabdominal .......... 38780
Thoracic .......... 38746
Unilateral Inguinofemoral .......... 56631, 56634

**Lymphadenitis**
Incision and Drainage .......... 38300-38305

**Lymphadenopathy Associated Antibodies**
*See* Antibody, HIV

**Lymphadenopathy Associated Virus**
*See* HIV

**Lymphangiogram, Abdominal**
*See* Lymphangiography, Abdomen

**Lymphangiography**
Abdomen .......... 75805-75807
Arm .......... 75801-75803
Injection .......... 38790
Leg .......... 75801-75803
Pelvis .......... 75805-75807

**Lymphangioma, Cystic**
*See* Hygroma

**Lymphangiotomy** .......... 38308

**Lymphatics**
*See* Specific Procedure

**Lymphatic Channels**
Incision .......... 38308

**Lymphatic Cyst**
*See* Lymphocele

**Lymphatic System**
Unlisted Procedure .......... 38999

**Lymphoblast Transformation**
*See* Blastogenesis

**Lymphocele**
Drainage
  Laparoscopic .......... 49323
Extraperitoneal
  Open Drainage .......... 49062

**Lymphocoele**
*See* Lymphocele

**Lymphocyte**
Culture .......... 86821-86822
Toxicity Assay .......... 86805-86806
Transformation .......... 86353

**Lymphocyte, Thymus-Dependent**
*See* T-Cells

**Lymphocytes, CD4**
*See* CD4

**Lymphocytes, CD8**
*See* CD8

**Lymphocytic Choriomeningitis**
Antibody .......... 86727

**Lymphocytotoxicity** .......... 86805-86806

**Lymphogranuloma Venereum**
Antibody .......... 86729

**Lymphoma Virus, Burkitt**
*See* Epstein-Barr Virus

**Lymph Duct**
Injection .......... 38790

**Lymph Nodes**
Abscess
  Incision and Drainage .......... 38300-38305
Biopsy .......... 38500, 38510-38530, 38570
  Needle .......... 38505
Dissection .......... 38542
Excision .......... 38500, 38510-38530
  Abdominal .......... 38747
  Inguinofemoral .......... 38760-38765
  Laparoscopic .......... 38571-38572
  Limited, for Staging
    Para-Aortic .......... 38562
    Pelvic .......... 38562
    Retroperitoneal .......... 38564
  Pelvic .......... 38770
  Radical
    Axillary .......... 38740-38745
    Cervical .......... 38720-38724
    Suprahyoid .......... 38720-38724
  Retroperitoneal
    Transabdominal .......... 38780
    Thoracic .......... 38746
Exploration .......... 38542
Hygroma, Cystic
  Axillary/Cervical
    Excision .......... 38550-38555
Nuclear Medicine
  Imaging .......... 78195
Removal
  Abdominal .......... 38747
  Inguinofemoral .......... 38760-38765
  Pelvic .......... 38770
  Retroperitoneal
  Transabdominal .......... 38780
  Thoracic .......... 38746

**Lymph Vessels**
Abdomen
  Lymphangiography .......... 75805-75807
Arm
  Lymphangiography .......... 75801-75803
Leg
  Lymphangiography .......... 75801-75803
Nuclear Medicine
  Imaging .......... 78195
Pelvis
  Lymphangiography .......... 75805-75807

**Lynch Procedure** .......... 31075

**Lysergic Acid Diethylamide** .......... 80100-80103, 80299

**Lysergide**
*See* Lysergic Acid Diethylamide

**Lysis**
Adhesions
  Epidural .......... 62263
  Fallopian Tube .......... 58740
  Foreskin .......... 54450
  Intestinal .......... 44005
  Labial .......... 56441
  Lung .......... 32124
  Nose .......... 30560
  Ovary .......... 58740
  Oviduct .......... 58740
  Ureter .......... 50715-50725
  Uterus .......... 58559
Euglobulin .......... 85360
Labial
  Adhesions .......... 56441
Nose
  Intranasal Synechia .......... 30560

**Lysozyme** .......... 85549

**L Ascorbic Acid**
*See* Ascorbic Acid

**L Aspartate 2 Oxoglutarate Aminotransferase**
*See* Transaminase, Glutamic Oxaloacetic

**L Glutamine**
*See* Glutamine

**MacEwen Operation**
*See* Hernia, Repair, Inguinal

**Machado Test**
*See* Complement, Fixation Test

**MacLean-De Wesselow Test**
*See* Blood Urea Nitrogen; Urea Nitrogen, Clearance

**Macrodactylia**
Repair ........................26590

**Madlener Operation**
*See* Tubal Ligation

**Magnesium** ..................83735

**Magnetic Resonance Angiography (MRA)**
Abdomen ......................74185
Arm ..........................73225
Chest ........................71555
Head .........................70541
Leg ..........................73725
Neck .........................70541
Pelvis .......................72198
Spine ........................72159

**Magnetic Resonance Imaging (MRI)**
Abdomen ......................74181
Ankle ........................73721
Arm ..........................73220
Bone Marrow Study ............76400
Brain ...............70551-70553
Breast ..............76093-76094
Chest ........................71550
Elbow ........................73221
Face .........................70540
Finger Joint .................73221
Foot Joints ..................73721
Hand .........................73220
Heart ........................75552
Complete Study ...............75554
Flow Mapping .................75556
Limited Study ................75555
Morphology ...................75553
Knee .........................73721
Leg ..........................73720
Neck .........................70540
Orbit ........................70540
Pelvis .......................72196
Radiology
Diagnostic
Procedures ...................76499
Unlisted Services and
Spectroscopy .................76390
Spine
Cervical ....72141-72142, 72156-72158
Lumbar ....72148-72149, 72156-72158
Thoracic ...72146-72147, 72156-72158
Temporomandibular Joint (TMJ) .....70336
Toe ..........................73721
Wrist ........................73221

**Magnetic Resonance Spectroscopy** ................76390

**Magnet Operation**
*See* Ciliary Body; Cornea; Eye, Removal, Foreign Body; Iris; Lens; Retina; Sclera; Vitreous

**Magnuson Procedure** .........23450

**Magpi Operation** .............54322

**Magpi Procedure**
*See* Hypospadias, Repair

**Major Vestibular Gland**
*See* Bartholin's Gland

**Malaria Antibody** ............86750

**Malaria Smear** ...............87207

**Malar Area**
Augmentation .................21270
Bone Graft ...................21210
Fracture
Open Treatment .........21360-21366
with Bone Graft ..............21366
with Manipulation ............21355
Reconstruction ...............21270

**Malar Bone**
*See* Cheekbone

**Malate Dehydrogenase** .......83775

**Maldescent, Testis**
*See* Testis, Undescended

**Male Circumcision**
*See* Circumcision

**Malformation, Arteriovenous**
*See* Arteriovenous Malformation

**Malic Dehydrogenase**
*See* Malate Dehydrogenase

**Malleolus**
*See* Ankle; Fibula; Leg, Lower; Tibia; Tibiofibular Joint
Metatarsophalangeal Joint ........27889

**Mallet Finger Repair** ..........26432

**Maltose**
Tolerance Test ............82951-82952

**Malunion Repair**
Femur
without Graft ................27470
with Graft ...................27472
Metatarsal ...................28322
Tarsal Joint .................28320

**Mammalian Oviduct**
*See* Fallopian Tube

**Mammaplasties**
*See* Breast, Reconstruction

**Mammary Abscess**
*See* Abscess, Breast

**Mammary Arteries**
*See* Artery, Mammary

**Mammary Duct**
X-Ray with Contrast .........76086-76088

**Mammary Ductogram**
Injection ....................19030

**Mammary Stimulating Hormone**
*See* Prolactin

**Mammilliplasty**
*See* Nipples, Reconstruction

**Mammography** ..........76090-76092
Screening ....................76092

**Mammoplasty**
Augmentation .............19324-19325
Reduction ....................19318

**Mammotomy**
*See* Mastotomy

**Mammotropic Hormone, Pituitary**
*See* Prolactin

**Mammotropic Hormone, Placental**
*See* Lactogen, Human Placental

**Mammotropin**
*See* Prolactin

**Mandible**
*See* Facial Bones; Maxilla; Temporomandibular Joint (TMJ)
Abscess
Excision .....................21025
Bone Graft ...................21215
Fracture
Closed Treatment
without Manipulation .........21450
with Interdental Fixation ......21453
with Manipulation ............21451
Open Treatment .........21454-21470
External Fixation .............21454
without Interdental Fixation ....21461
with Interdental Fixation ......21462
Percutaneous Treatment ........21452
Osteotomy ....................21198
Reconstruction
with Implant ...........21244-21246, 21248-21249
Removal
Foreign Body .................41806

**Mastoidectomy**
with Apicectomy . . . . 69605
with Skull Base Surgery . . . . 61590, 61597
Decompression . . . . 61595
Facial Nerve . . . . 61595
with Tympanoplasty . . . 69604, 69641-69646
Cochlear Device Implantation . . . . 69930
Complete . . . . 69502
Revision . . . . 69601
Ossicular Chain
Reconstruction . . . . 69605
Radical . . . . 69511
Modified . . . . 69505
Revision . . . . 69602-69603
Simple . . . . 69501
with Labyrinthectomy . . . . 69910
with Labyrinthotomy . . . . 69802
with Petrous Apicectomy . . . . 69530

**Mastoidotomy** . . . . 69635-69637
with Tympanoplasty . . . . 69635
Ossicular Chain Reconstruction . . 69636
and Synthetic Prosthesis . . . . 69636

**Mastoids**
Polytomography . . . . 76101-76102
X-Ray . . . . 70120-70130

**Mastoid Cavity**
Debridement . . . . 69220, 69222

**Mastopexy** . . . . 19316

**Mastotomy** . . . . 19020

**Maternity Care**
*See* Abortion; Cesarean Delivery; Ectopic Pregnancy; Obstetrical Care

**Maternity Care and Delivery** . . . . 59612, 59614, 59618, 59620, 59622, 59898

**Maxilla**
*See* Facial Bones; Mandible
Bone Graft . . . . 21210
CAT Scan . . . . 70486, 70487, 70488
Excision . . . . 21032
Fracture
Closed Treatment . . . . 21345, 21421
Open Treatment . . . . 21346-21348, 21422-21423
with Fixation . . . . 21345-21347
Osteotomy . . . . 21206
Reconstruction
with Implant . . . . 21245-21246, 21248-21249

**Maxillary Arteries**
*See* Artery, Maxillary

**Maxillary Sinus**
*See* Sinus, Maxillary

**Maxillary Torus Palatinus**
Tumor Excision . . . . 21032

**Maxillectomy** . . . . 31225-31230

**Maxillofacial Fixation**
Application
Halo Type Appliance . . . . 21100

**Maxillofacial Impressions**
Auricular Prosthesis . . . . 21086
Definitive Obturator Prosthesis . . . . 21080
Facial Prosthesis . . . . 21088
Interim Obturator Prosthesis . . . . 21079
Mandibular Resection Prosthesis . . . . 21081
Nasal Prosthesis . . . . 21087
Oral Surgical Splint . . . . 21085
Orbital Prosthesis . . . . 21077
Palatal Augmentation Prosthesis . . . . 21082
Palatal Lift Prosthesis . . . . 21083
Speech Aid Prosthesis . . . . 21084
Surgical Obturator Prosthesis . . . . 21076

**Maxillofacial Procedures**
Unlisted Services and Procedures . . . 21299

**Maxillofacial Prosthetics** . . . . 21076-21089
Unlisted Services and Procedures . . . 21089

**Maydl Operation** . . . . 45563, 50810
*See* Colostomy

**Mayo Hernia Repair**
*See* Hernia, Repair, Umbilicus

**Mayo Operation**
*See* Varicose Vein, Removal

**Mayo Procedure** . . . . 28292

**MBC**
*See* Minimum Bactericidal Concentration

**McBride Procedure** . . . . 28292

**McBurney Operation**
*See* Hernia, Repair, Inguinal

**McCannel Procedure** . . . . 66682

**McDonald Operation**
*See* Repair, Cervix, Cerclage, Abdominal; Revision

**McIndoe Procedure**
*See* Vagina, Construction

**McKissock Surgery**
*See* Breast, Reduction

**McVay Operation**
*See* Hernia, Repair, Inguinal

**Measles, German**
*See* Rubella

**Measles Uncomplicated**
*See* Rubeola

**Measles Vaccine**
*See* Vaccines

**Meatoplasty** . . . . 69310

**Meatotomy** . . . . 53020-53025
Contact Laser Vaporization with/without Transurethral Resection of
Prostate . . . . 52648
with Cystourethroscopy . . . . 52281
Infant . . . . 53025
Non-Contact Laser Coagulation
Prostate . . . . 52647
Transurethral Electrosurgical Resection
Prostate . . . . 52601
Ureter . . . . 52290
Ureteral
Cystourethroscopy . . . . 52290-52305

**Meat Fibers**
Feces . . . . 89160

**Meckel's Diverticulum**
Excision . . . . 44800
Unlisted Services and Procedures . . . 44899

**Median Nerve**
Decompression . . . . 64721
Neuroplasty . . . . 64721
Release . . . . 64721
Repair/Suture
Motor . . . . 64835
Transposition . . . . 64721

**Median Nerve Compression**
*See* Carpal Tunnel Syndrome

**Mediastinal Cyst**
*See* Cyst, Mediastinal

**Mediastinoscopy** . . . . 39400

**Mediastinotomy**
Cervical Approach . . . . 39000
Transthoracic Approach . . . . 39010

**Mediastinum**
*See* Chest; Thorax
Cyst
Excision . . . . 32662, 39200
Endoscopy
Biopsy . . . . 39400
Exploration . . . . 39400
Exploration . . . . 39000-39010
Incision and Drainage . . . . 39000-39010
Needle Biopsy . . . . 32405
Removal
Foreign Body . . . . 39000-39010
Tumor
Excision . . . . 32662, 39220
Unlisted Procedures . . . . 39499

**Medical Disability Evaluation Services** . . . . 99455-99456

**Medical Testimony** . . . . 99075

**Medicine, Preventive**
*See* Preventive Medicine

**Medicine, Pulmonary**
*See* Pulmonology

**Medulla**
Tractotomy .......61470

**Medullary Tract**
Incision .......61470
Section .......61470

**Meibomian Cyst**
*See* Chalazion

**Membrane, Mucous**
*See* Mucosa

**Membrane, Tympanic**
*See* Ear, Drum

**Membrane Oxygenation, Extracorporeal**
*See* Extracorporeal Membrane Oxygenation

**Meninges**
Tumor
  Excision .......61512, 61519

**Meningioma**
Excision .......61512, 61519
Tumor
  Excision .......61512, 61519

**Meningitis, Lymphocytic Benign**
*See* Lymphocytic Choriomeningitis

**Meningocele Repair** .......63700, 63702

**Meningococcal**
*See* Vaccines

**Meningococcal Vaccine**
*See* Vaccines

**Meningococcus**
*See* Neisseria Meningitidis

**Meningomyelocele**
*See* Myelomeningocele

**Meniscectomy**
Knee Joint .......27332-27333
Temporomandibular Joint .......21060

**Meniscus**
Knee
  Excision .......27332-27333
  Repair .......27403

**Mental Nerve**
Avulsion .......64736
Incision .......64736
Transection .......64736

**Meprobamate** .......83805

**Mercury** .......83015, 83825

**Merskey Test**
*See* Fibrin Degradation Products

**Mesencephalic Tract**
Incision .......61480
Section .......61480

**Mesencephalon**
Tractotomy .......61480

**Mesenteric Arteries**
*See* Artery, Mesenteric

**Mesentery**
Lesion
  Excision .......44820
Repair .......44850
Suture .......44850
Unlisted Services and Procedures .......44899

**Metabisulfite Test**
*See* Red Blood Cell (RBC), Sickling

**Metabolite** .......82520

**Metacarpal**
Amputation .......26910
Craterization .......26230
Cyst
  Excision .......26200, 26205
Diaphysectomy .......26230
Excision .......26230
  Radical
    for Tumor .......26250, 26255
Fracture
  Closed Treatment .......26605
    with Fixation .......26607
  Open Treatment .......26615
  Percutaneous Fixation .......26608
  without Manipulation .......26600
  with Manipulation .......26605, 26607
Ostectomy
  Radical
    for Tumor .......26250, 26255
Repair
  Lengthening .......26568
  Nonunion .......26546
  Osteotomy .......26565
Saucerization .......26230
Tumor
  Excision .......26200, 26205

**Metacarpophalangeal Joint**
Arthrodesis .......26850, 26852
Arthroplasty .......26530-26531
Arthrotomy .......26075
Biopsy
  Synovium .......26105
Capsule
  Excision .......26520
  Incision .......26520
Capsulodesis .......26516-26518
Dislocation
  Closed Treatment .......26700
  Open Treatment .......26715
  Percutaneous Fixation .......26705-26706
Exploration .......26075
Fracture
  Closed Treatment .......26740
  Open Treatment .......26746
  with Manipulation .......26742
Fusion .......26516-26518, 26850, 26852
Removal of Foreign Body .......26075
Repair
  Collateral Ligament .......26540-26542
Synovectomy .......26135

**Metadrenaline**
*See* Metanephrines

**Metals, Heavy**
*See* Heavy Metal

**Metamfetamine**
*See* Methamphetamine

**Metanephrines** .......83835

**Metatarsal**
*See* Foot
Amputation .......28810
Condyle
  Excision .......28288
Craterization .......28122
Cyst
  Excision .......28104-28107
Diaphysectomy .......28122
Excision .......28110-28114, 28122, 28140
Fracture
  Closed Treatment
    without Manipulation .......28470
    with Manipulation .......28475-28476
  Open Treatment .......28485
  Percutaneous Fixation .......28476
Free Osteocutaneous Flap with Microvascular Anastomosis .......20972
Repair .......28322
  Lengthening .......28306-28307
  Osteotomy .......28306-28308, 28309
Saucerization .......28122
Tumor
  Excision .......28104-28107, 28173

**Metatarsectomy** .......28140

**Metatarsophalangeal Joint**
Arthrotomy .......28022, 28052
Cheilectomy .......28289
Dislocation .......28630-28635, 28645
  Percutaneous Fixation .......28636
Exploration .......28022
Great Toe
  Arthrodesis .......28750
  Fusion .......28750
Removal
  of Foreign Body .......28022
  of Loose Body .......28022
Repair
  Hallux Rigidus .......28289
Synovial
  Biopsy .......28052
  Excision .......28072
Toe .......28270

**Methadone** .......83840

**Methaemoglobin**
*See* Methemoglobin

**Methamphetamine**
Blood or Urine .......82145

**Methanol** .......84600

**Methbipyranone**
*See* Metyrapone

**Methemalbumin** .............83857

**Methemoglobin** .........83045-83050

**Methenamine Silver Stain** ....88312

**Methopyrapone**
*See* Metyrapone

**Methoxyhydroxymandelic Acid**
*See* Vanillylmandelic Acid

**Methsuximide** ................83858

**Methylamphetamine**
*See* Methamphetamine

**Methylene Bichloride**
*See* Dichloromethane

**Methylfluorprednisolone**
*See* Dexamethasone

**Methylmorphine**
*See* Codeine

**Methyl Alcohol**
*See* Methanol

**Metroplasty**
*See* Hysteroplasty

**Metyrapone** ..................80436

**MIC**
*See* Minimum Inhibitory Concentration

**Micro-Ophthalmia**
Orbit Reconstruction ..............21256

**Microalbumin**
Urine .....................82043-82044

**Microbial Identification**

**Microbiology** ..........87001-87999

**Microfluorometries, Flow**
*See* Flow Cytometry

**Microglobulin, Beta 2**
Blood .........................82232
Urine .........................82232

**Micrographic Surgery**
Moh's Technique ...........17304-17310

**Micrographic Surgery, Moh**
*See* Moh's Micrographic Surgery

**Micropigmentation**
Correction.................11920-11922

**Microscope, Surgical**
*See* Operating Microscope

**Microscopic Evaluation**
Hair ...........................96902

**Microscopies, Electron**
*See* Electron Microscopy

**Microscopy**
Ear Exam ......................92504

**Microsomal Antibody** .........86376

**Microsomia, Hemifacial**
*See* Hemifacial Microsomia

**Microsurgery**
Operating Microscope .............69990

**Microvascular Anastomosis**
Bone Graft
  Fibula .......................20955
  Other ........................20962
Fascial Flap, Free ................15758
Muscle Flap, Free ................15756
Osteocutaneous Flap with ....20969-20973
Skin Flap, Free ...................15757

**Microvite A**
*See* Vitamin, A

**Microwave Therapy** ..........97020
*See* Physical Medicine/Therapy/ Occupational Therapy

**Midbrain**
*See* Brain; Brainstem; Mesencephalon; Skull Base Surgery

**Midcarpal Medioccipital Joint**
Arthrotomy .....................25040

**Middle Ear**
*See* Ear, Middle

**Midface**
Reconstruction
  Forehead Advancement ...21159-21160
  without Bone Graft ......21141-21143
  with Bone Graft ...21145-21160, 21188

**Migration Inhibitory Factor (MIF)** .................86378

**Mile Operation**
*See* Colectomy, Total, with Proctectomy

**Milia, Multiple**
Removal .......................10040

**Miller-Abbott Intubation** .............44500, 74340

**Miller Procedure** ............28737

**Minerva Cast** .................29035
Removal .......................29710

**Minimum Bactericidal Concentration** ................87187

**Minimum Inhibitory Concentration** ................87186

**Minnesota Multiphasic Personality Inventory**
*See* MMPI

**Miscarriage**
Incomplete Abortion .............59812
Missed Abortion
  First Trimester ...............59820
  Second Trimester .............59821
Septic Abortion .................59830

**Missed Abortion**
*See* Abortion

**Mitchell Procedure** ...........28296

**Mitogen Blastogenesis** .......86353

**Mitral Valve**
Incision ...................33420-33422
Repair ........33420-33422, 33425-33427
  Incision ................33420-33422
Replacement ....................33430

**Mitrofanoff Operation** .........50845
*See* Appendico-Vesicostomy

**Miyagawanella**
*See* Chlamydia

**MMPI** ........................96100

**MMR Shots** ...................90707
*See* Vaccines

**Mobilization**
Splenic Flexure ..................44139
Stapes .........................69650

**Modified Radical Mastectomy**
*See* Mastectomy, Modified Radical

**Moh's Micrographic Surgery** .................17304-17310

**Molar Pregnancy**
*See* Hydatidiform Mole

**Mole, Carneous**
*See* Abortion

**Mole, Hydatid**
*See* Hydatidiform Mole

**Molecular Cytogenetics** ............88271-88275
Interpretation and Report ..........88291

**Molecular Diagnostics** .............83890-83898
Amplification ..............83898, 83901
Dot/Slot Production ..............83893
Enzymatic Digestion ..............83892
Extraction ................83890-83891
Interpretation ...................83912
Molecular Isolation (Extraction) .....83890
Mutation Identification ......83904-83906
Mutation Scanning ...............83903
Nucleic Acid Probe ...............83896
Nucleic Acid Transfer .............83897
Polymerase Reaction Chain ........83898
Reverse Transcription .............83902
Separation ......................83894

**Molecular Oxygen Saturation**
*See* Oxygen Saturation

**Molluscum Contagiosum**
Destruction ....17110-17111, 54050-54065

**Molteno Procedure** ...........66180

**Monilia**
*See* Candida

**Monitoring**
Blood Pressure, 24 Hour .....93784-93790
Electrocardiogram ..........93224-93237
  *See* Electrocardiography

Electroencephalogram . . . . . .95812-95813, 95950-95953, 95956
with Drug Activation . . . . . . . . . . .95954
with Physical Activation . . . . . . . .95954
with WADA Activation . . . . . . . . .95958
Fetal
During Labor . . . . . . . . . . . .59050-59051
Interpretation Only . . . . . . . . . . .59051
Interstitial Fluid Pressure . . . . . . . . . .20950
Seizure . . . . . . . . . . . . . . . . . . . .61531, 61760

**Monitoring, Sleep**
*See* Polysomnography

**Monoethylene Glycol**
*See* Ethylene Glycol

**Mononucleosis Virus, Infectious**
*See* Epstein-Barr Virus

**Monophosphate, Adenosine**
*See* Adenosine Monophosphate (AMP)

**Monophosphate, Adenosine Cyclic**
*See* Cyclic AMP

**Monophosphate, Guanosine**
*See* Guanosine Monophosphate

**Monophosphate, Guanosine Cyclic**
*See* Cyclic GMP

**Monospot Test**
*See* Rapid Test for Infection

**Monoxide, Carbon**
*See* Carbon Monoxide

**Monteggia Fracture** . . . . .24620, 24635

**Monticelli Procedure**
*See* Application, Bone Fixation Device

**Morbilli**
*See* Rubeola

**Morphine Methyl Ether**
*See* Codeine

**Morphometric Analysis**
Nerve . . . . . . . . . . . . . . . . . . . . . . . . .88356
Skeletal Muscle . . . . . . . . . . . . . . . . .88355
Tumor . . . . . . . . . . . . . . . . . . . . . . . . .88358

**Morton's Neuroma**
Excision . . . . . . . . . . . . . . . . . . . . . . .28080

**Moschcowitz Operation**
*See* Repair, Hernia, Femoral; Revision

**Mosenthal Test**
*See* Urinalysis, Routine

**Mother Cell**
*See* Stem Cell

**Motility Study**
Esophagus . . . . . . . . . . . . . . . .91010-91012

**Mouth**
Abscess
Incision and Drainage . . . .40800-40801, 41005-41009, 41015-41018
Biopsy . . . . . . . . . . . . . . . . . . .40808, 41108
Cyst
Incision and Drainage . . . .40800-40801, 41005-41009, 41015-41018
Excision
Frenum . . . . . . . . . . . . . . . . . . . . . .40819
Hematoma
Incision and Drainage . . . .40800-40801, 41005-41009, 41015-41018
Lesion
Destruction . . . . . . . . . . . . . . . . . .40820
Excision . . . . . . . .40810, 40812, 40814, 40816, 41116
Vestibule of
Destruction . . . . . . . . . . . . . . . . .40820
Repair . . . . . . . . . . . . . . . . . . . . .40830
Mucosa
Excision . . . . . . . . . . . . . . . . . . . . .40818
Reconstruction . . . . . . .40840, 40842-40845
Removal
Foreign Body . . . . . . . . . . .40804-40805
Repair
Laceration . . . . . . . . . . . . .40830-40831
Unlisted Services and Procedures . . . . . . . . . . . . . . . .40899, 41599
Vestibule of
Excision
Destruction . . . .40808, 40810, 40812, 40814, 40816, 40818-40820
Incision . . . .40800-40801, 40804-40806
Other Procedures . . . . . . . . . . . . .40899
Removal
Foreign Body . . . . . . . . . . . . . . .40804
Repair . . . . . . . . . .40830-40831, 40840, 40842-40845

**Move**
*See* Transfer
Finger . . . . . . . . . . . . . . . . . . . . . . . . .26555
Toe Joint . . . . . . . . . . . . . . . . . . . . . .26556
Toe to Hand . . . . . . . . . . . . . . .26551-26554

**Moynihan Test**
*See* Gastrointestinal Tract, X-Ray, with Contrast

**MPD Syndrome**
*See* Temporomandibular Joint (TMJ)

**MPR**
*See* Multifetal Pregnancy Reduction

**MRA**
*See* Magnetic Resonance Angiography

**MRI**
*See* Magnetic Resonance Imaging (MRI)

**MR Spectroscopy**
*See* Magnetic Resonance Spectroscopy

**MSLT**
*See* Multiple Sleep Latency Testing (MSLT)

**Mucin**
Synovial Fluid . . . . . . . . . . . . . . . . . .83872

**Mucocele**
Sinusotomy
Frontal . . . . . . . . . . . . . . . . . . . . . .31075

**Mucopolysaccharides** . .83864-83866

**Mucormycoses**
*See* Mucormycosis

**Mucormycosis**
Antibody . . . . . . . . . . . . . . . . . . . . . .86732

**Mucosa**
Ectopic Gastric Imaging . . . . . . . .78290
Excision of Lesion
Alveolar, Hyperplastic . . . . . . . .41828
Vestibule of Mouth . . . . .40810-40818
via Esophagoscopy . . . . . . . . . . .43228
via Small Intestinal Endoscopy . . . . . . . . . . . . . . . .44369
via Upper GI Endoscopy . . . . . . .43258
Periodontal Grafting . . . . . . . . . . .41870
Urethra, Mucosal Advancement . . . . . . . . . . . . . . . .53450
Vaginal Biopsy . . . . . . . . . .57100, 57105

**Mucosa, Buccal**
*See* Mouth, Mucosa

**Mucous Cyst**
Hand or Finger . . . . . . . . . . . . . . . .26160

**Mucous Membrane**
Buccal
Conjunctivoplasty . . . . . .68325, 68328
Repair Symblepharon . . . . . . . . .68335
Cutaneous
Biopsy . . . . . . . . . . . . . . .11100, 11101
Excision, Benign Lesion . . . . . . . . . . . . . . .11440-11446
Layer Closure, Wounds . .12051-12057
Simple Repair, Wounds . . . . . . . . . . . . .12011-12018
Excision
Sphenoid Sinus . . . . . . . . . . . . .31288
Lid Margin
Correction of Trichiasis . . . . . . .67835
Nasal Test . . . . . . . . . . . . . . . . .95065
Ophthalmic Test . . . . . . . . . . . . .95060
Rectum
Proctoplasty for Prolapse . . . . . .45505

**Mucus Cyst**
*See* Mucous Cyst

**MUGA (Multiple Gated Acquisition)** . . . . . .78472-78478, 78483

**Muller Procedure**
*See* Sleep Study

**Multifetal Pregnancy Reduction** . . . . . . . . . . . . . . . . . . . .59866

**Multiple Sleep Latency Testing (MSLT)** . . . . . . . . . . . . . . . . . . . . . .95805

**Multiple Valve Procedures**
*See* Valvuloplasty

**Mumford Operation**
*See* Claviculectomy, Partial

**Mumps**
Antibody .....86735
Immunization .....90704, 90707, 90709, 90710
Vaccine .....90704
MMR .....90707
MMRV .....90710
Rubella and Mumps .....90709

**Muramidase** .....85549

**Murine Typhus** .....86000

**Muscle**
*See* Specific Muscle
Abdomen
*See* Abdominal Wall
Biopsy .....20200-20206
Heart
*See* Myocardium
Neck
*See* Neck Muscle
Removal
Foreign Body .....20520-20525
Repair
Forearm .....25260-25274
Wrist .....25260-25274
Revision
Arm, Upper .....24330, 24331
Transfer
Arm, Upper .....24301, 24320
Elbow .....24301
Hip .....27100-27111
Shoulder ...23395-23397, 24301, 24320

**Muscle, Oculomotor**
*See* Eye Muscles

**Muscles**
Repair
Extraocular .....65290

**Muscle Compartment Syndrome**
Detection .....20950

**Muscle Denervation**
*See* Denervation

**Muscle Division**
Scalenus Anticus .....21700-21705
Sternocleidomastoid .....21720-21725

**Muscle Flaps** .....15732-15738
Free .....15756

**Muscle Grafts** .....15841-15845

**Muscle Testing**
Dynamometry, Eye .....92260
Extraocular Multiple Muscles .....92265
Manual .....95831-95834

**Musculo-Skeletal System**
*See* Musculoskeletal System

**Musculoplasty**
*See* Muscle, Repair

**Musculoskeletal System**
Unlisted Services and Procedures ...20999, 24999, 25999, 26989, 27299, 27599, 27899
Unlisted Services and Procedures, Head .....21499

**Musculotendinous (Rotator) Cuff**
Repair .....23410-23412

**Mustard Procedure**
*See* Repair, Great Arteries; Revision

**Myasthenia Gravis**
Tensilon Test .....95857-95858

**Myasthenic, Gravis**
*See* Myasthenia Gravis

**Mycobacteria**
Culture .....87116-87117
Identification .....87118
Detection .....87550-87552, 87555-87557, 87560-87562

**Mycoplasma**
Antibody .....86738
Culture .....87109
Detection .....87580-87582

**Mycota**
*See* Fungus

**Myectomy, Anorectal**
*See* Myomectomy, Anorectal

**Myelencephalon**
*See* Medulla

**Myelin Basic Protein**
Cerebrospinal Fluid .....83873

**Myelography**
Brain .....70010
Spine
Cervical .....72240
Lumbosacral .....72265
Thoracic .....72255
Total .....72270

**Myelomeningocele**
Repair .....63704, 63706

**Myelotomy** .....63170

**Myocardial**
Perfusion Imaging .....78460-78465, 78478, 78480
*See* Nuclear Medicine
Positron Emission Tomography (PET) .....78459

**Myocardial Imaging** ....78466-78469
Positron Emission Tomography
Perfusion Study .....78491-78492
Repair
Postinfarction .....33542

**Myocutaneous Flaps** ....15732-15738

**Myofascial Pain Dysfunction Syndrome**
*See* Temporomandibular Joint (TMJ)

**Myofibroma**
*See* Leiomyomata

**Myoglobin** .....83874

**Myomectomy**
Anorectal .....45108
Uterus .....58140-58145

**Myoplasty**
*See* Muscle, Repair

**Myotomy**
Esophagus .....43030

**Myringoplasty** .....69620

**Myringostomy**
*See* Myringotomy

**Myringotomy** .....69420-69421

**Myxoid Cyst**
*See* Ganglion


# N


**N. Meningitidis**
*See* Neisseria Meningitidis

**Naffziger Operation**
*See* Decompression, Orbit; Section

**Nagel Test**
*See* Color Vision Examination

**Nails**
Avulsion .....11730-11732
Biopsy .....11755
Debridement .....11720-11721
Evacuation
Hematoma, Subungual .....11740
Excision .....11750-11752
Cyst
Pilonidal .....11770-11772
Removal ......11730-11732, 11750-11752
Trimming .....11719

**Nail Bed**
Reconstruction .....11762
Repair .....11760

**Nail Fold**
Excision
Wedge .....11765

**Nail Plate Separation**
*See* Onychia

**Narcosynthesis**
Diagnostic and Therapeutic .....90865

Esophageal
  *See* Tumor, Esophagus
Spinal Cord
  *See* Spinal Cord, Neoplasm
Unspecified Nature of Brain
  *See* Brain, Tumor
Cancer Photoradiation Therapy
  *See* Photochemotherapy

**Neoplastic Growth**
*See* Tumor

**Nephelometry** .....83883

**Nephrectomy**
Donor .....50300-50320, 50547
Laparoscopic .....50546-50547
Partial .....50240
Recipient .....50340
with Ureters .....50220-50236

**Nephrolith**
*See* Calculus, Removal, Kidney

**Nephrolithotomy** .....50060-50075

**Nephropexy** .....50400-50405

**Nephroplasty**
*See* Kidney, Repair

**Nephropyeloplasty**
*See* Pyeloplasty

**Nephrorrhaphy** .....50500

**Nephroscopy**
*See* Endoscopy, Kidney

**Nephrostogram** .....50394

**Nephrostolithotomy**
Percutaneous .....50080-50081

**Nephrostomy** .....50040
Change Tube .....50398
Endoscopic .....50570
Percutaneous .....52334
with Drainage .....50040
X-Ray with Contrast
  Guide Dilation .....74485

**Nephrostomy Tract**
Establishment .....50395

**Nephrotomogram**
*See* Nephrotomography

**Nephrotomography** .....74415

**Nephrotomy** .....50040-50045
with Exploration .....50045

**Nephroureterectomy (Laparoscopically Assisted)** .....50548

**Nerve**
Cranial
  *See* Cranial Nerve
Intercostal
  *See* Intercostal Nerve
Lingual
  *See* Lingual Nerve
Median
  *See* Median Nerve
Obturator
  *See* Obturator Nerve
Peripheral
  *See* Peripheral Nerve
Phrenic
  *See* Phrenic Nerve
Sciatic
  *See* Sciatic Nerve
Spinal
  *See* Spinal Nerve
Tibial
  *See* Tibial Nerve
Ulnar
  *See* Ulnar Nerve
Vestibular
  *See* Vestibular Nerve

**Nerves**
Anastomosis
  Facial to Hypoglossal .....64868
  Facial to Phrenic .....64870
  Facial to Spinal Accessory .....64866
Avulsion .....64732-64772
Biopsy .....64795
Decompression .....64702-64727
Destruction .....64600-64680
  Laryngeal, Recurrent .....31595
Foot
  Excision .....28030
  Incision .....28035
Graft .....64885-64907
Implantation
  Electrode .....64553-64580
  to Bone .....64787
  to Muscle .....64787
Incision .....43640-43641, 64732-64772
Injection
  Anesthetic .....64400-64530
  Neurolytic Agent .....64600-64680
Insertion
  Electrode .....64553-64580
Lesion
  Excision .....64774-64792
Neurofibroma
  Excision .....64788-64792
Neurolemmoma
  Excision .....64788-64792
Neurolytic
  Internal .....64727
Neuroma
  Excision .....64774-64786
Neuroplasty .....64702-64721
Removal
  Electrode .....64585
Repair
  Graft .....64885-64907
  Microdissection .....69990
  Suture .....64831-64876
Spinal Accessory
  Incision .....63191
  Section .....63191
Suture .....64831-64876
Sympathectomy
  Excision .....64802-64818
Transection .....43640-43641, 64732-64772
Transposition .....64718-64719, 64721
Unlisted Services and Procedures .....64999

**Nerve Conduction**
Motor Nerve .....95900-95903
Sensory Nerve or Mixed .....95904

**Nerve II, Cranial**
*See* Optic Nerve

**Nerve Root**
*See* Cauda Equina; Spinal Cord
Decompression .....63020-63091
Incision .....63185, 63190
Section .....63185, 63190

**Nerve Stimulation, Transcutaneous**
*See* Application, Neurostimulation

**Nerve Teasing** .....88362

**Nerve V, Cranial**
*See* Trigeminal Nerve

**Nerve VII, Cranial**
*See* Facial Nerve

**Nerve X, Cranial**
*See* Vagus Nerve

**Nerve XI, Cranial**
*See* Accessory Nerve

**Nerve XII, Cranial**
*See* Hypoglossal Nerve

**Nervous System**
Nuclear Medicine
  Unlisted Services and
  Procedures .....78699

**Nesidioblast**
*See* Islet Cell

**Neural Conduction**
*See* Nerve Conduction

**Neural Ganglion**
*See* Ganglion

**Neurectomy**
Foot .....28030
Gastrocnemius .....27320
Hamstring Muscle .....27315
Leg, Upper .....27315, 27320
Popliteal .....27320
Tympanic .....69676

**Neurofibroma**
Cutaneous Nerve
  Excision .....64788
Extensive
  Excision .....64792
Peripheral Nerve
  Excision .....64790

**Nissen Operation**
*See* Fundoplasty, Esophagogastric

**Nissen Procedure** ............43324
Laparoscopic ....................43280

**Nitrate Reduction Test**
*See* Urinalysis

**Nitroblue Tetrazolium Dye Test** ....................86384

**Nitrogen, Blood Urea**
*See* Blood Urea Nitrogen

**NMR Imaging**
*See* Magnetic Resonance Imaging (MRI)

**NMR Spectroscopies**
*See* Magnetic Resonance Spectroscopy

**Noble Procedure**
*See* Repair; Suture

**Nocardia**
Antibody ......................86744

**Nocturnal Penile Rigidity Test** ..................54250

**Nocturnal Penile Tumescence Test** .............54250

**Node, Lymph**
*See* Lymph Nodes

**Nodes**
*See* Lymph Nodes

**Node Dissection, Lymph**
*See* Dissection, Lymph Nodes

**Non-Invasive Vascular Imaging**
*See* Vascular Studies

**Non-Office Medical Services** .....................99056

**Non-Stress Test, Fetal** ........59025

**Nonunion Repair**
Femur
without Graft .................27470
with Graft ...................27472
Metatarsal ......................28322
Tarsal Joint .....................28320

**Noradrenalin**
Blood ...................82383-82384
Urine ..........................82384

**Norchlorimipramine**
*See* Imipramine

**Norepinephrine**
*See* Catecholamines
Blood ...................82383-82384
Urine ..........................82384

**Norwood Procedure** .......33611-33612, 33619
*See* Repair, Heart, Ventricle; Revision

**Nose**
Abscess
Incision and Drainage ....30000-30020
Artery
Incision ................30915-30920
Biopsy
Intranasal ..................30100
Dermoid Cyst
Excision
Complex ..................30125
Simple ....................30124
Displacement Therapy ............30210
Endoscopy
Diagnostic .............31231-31235
Surgical ...............31237-31294
Excision
Rhinectomy ............30150-30160
Fracture
Closed Treatment .............21345
Open Treatment ........21325-21336, 21338-21339, 21346-21347
Percutaneous Treatment ........21340
with Fixation ...........21330, 21340, 21345-21347
Hematoma
Incision and Drainage ....30000-30020
Hemorrhage
Cauterization ...........30901-30906
Insertion
Septal Prosthesis .............30220
Intranasal
Lesion
External Approach ...........30118
Internal Approach ...........30117
Lysis of Adhesions ...............30560
Polyp
Excision
Extensive ..................30115
Simple ....................30110
Reconstruction
Cleft Lip/Cleft Palate .....30460-30462
Dermatoplasty ................30620
Primary ................30400-30420
Secondary ............30430-30450
Septum .....................30520
Removal
Foreign Body .................30300
Anesthesia .................30310
Lateral Rhinotomy ...........30320
Repair
Adhesions ..................30560
Cleft Lip ...40700-40702, 40720, 40761
Fistula ...........30580-30600, 42260
Rhinophyma ..................30120
Septum .........30540-30545, 30630
Synechia ....................30560
Skin
Excision ....................30120
Surgical Planing ..............30120
Submucous Resection Turbinate
Excision ....................30140
Turbinate
Excision ...............30130-30140
Fracture .....................30930
Injection ....................30200
Turbinate Mucosa
Cauterization ...........30801-30802
Unlisted Services and Procedures ...30999

**Nose Bleed** .............30901-30906
*See* Hemorrhage, Nasal

**Nortriptyline**
Assay ..........................80182

**No Man's Land**
Tendon Repair .............26356-26358

**NTD** ..........................86384
*See* Nitroblue Tetrazolium Dye Test

**Nuclear Antigen**
Antibody ......................86235

**Nuclear Imaging**
*See* Nuclear Medicine

**Nuclear Magnetic Resonance Imaging**
*See* Magnetic Resonance Imaging (MRI)

**Nuclear Magnetic Resonance Spectroscopy**
*See* Magnetic Resonance Spectroscopy

**Nuclear Medicine**
Abscess Localization ........78805-78806, 78807
Adrenal Gland Imaging ............78075
Automated Data ...........78890-78891
Bile Duct
Imaging ....................78223
Bladder
Residual Study ...............78730
Blood
Flow Imaging .................78445
Iron
Absorption ................78162
Chelatable .................78172
Plasma ....................78160
Red Cells ..................78140
Utilization .................78170
Platelet Survival .........78190-78191
Red Cells ..............78120-78121
Red Cell Survival ........78130-78135
Unlisted Services and Procedures ..................78199
Whole Blood Volume .........78122
Bone
Density Study .........78350-78351
Imaging .......78300-78315, 78320
SPECT .....................78320
Ultrasound .................76977
Unlisted Services and Procedures .................78399
Bone Marrow
Imaging ..............78102-78104

## Nucleases, DNA



## Nucleic Acid Probe ...........83896

HIV-1 . . . . . 87536
HIV-2 . . . . . 87539
Legionella Pneumophila . . . . . 87542
Mycobacteria avium-intracellulare . . . . . 87562
Mycobacteria species . . . . . 87552
Mycobacteria tuberculosis . . . . . 87557
Mycoplasma pneumoniae . . . . . 87582
Neisseria gonorrhoeae . . . . . 87592
Not Otherwise Specified . . . . . 87799
Papillomavirus, Human . . . . . 87622
Streptococcus, Group A . . . . . 87652

**Nucleolysis, Intervertebral Disk**
*See* Chemonucleolysis

**Nucleotidase** . . . . . 83915

**Nursemaid Elbow** . . . . . 24640

**Nursing Facility Discharge Services**
*See* Discharge Services, Nursing Facility

**Nursing Facility Services**
Care Plan Oversight Services . . . . . 99379-99380
Comprehensive Assessments
New or Established Patient . . . . . 99301-99303
Discharge Services . . . . . 99315-99316
Subsequent Care
New or Established Patient . . . . . 99311-99313
*See* Domiciliary Services

**Nystagmus Tests**
*See* Vestibular Function Tests
Optokinetic . . . . . 92534, 92544
Positional . . . . . 92532, 92542
Spontaneous . . . . . 92531, 92541


# O


**O2 Saturation**
*See* Oxygen Saturation

**Ober-Yount Procedure** . . . . . 27025
*See* Fasciotomy, Hip

**Obliteration**
Mastoid . . . . . 69670

**Obliteration, Total Excision of Vagina**
*See* Excision, Vagina, Complete

**Obliteration, Vaginal Vault**
*See* Vagina, Closure

**Oblongata, Medulla**
*See* Medulla

**Observation** . . . . . 99234-99236
*See* Evaluation and Management; Hospital Services

**Obstetrical Care**
Abortion
Induced
by Amniocentesis
Injection . . . . . 59850-59852
*See* Abortion; Cesarean Delivery; Ectopic Pregnancy
by Dilation and Curettage . . . . . 59840
by Dilation and Evaluation . . . . . 59841
Missed
First Trimester . . . . . 59820
Second Trimester . . . . . 59821
Spontaneous . . . . . 59812
Therapeutic . . . . . 59840, 59841, 59850-59852
Antepartum Care . . . . . 59425-59426
Cesarean Delivery . . . . . 59618, 59620, 59622
Only . . . . . 59514
Postpartum Care . . . . . 59515
Routine . . . . . 59510
with Hysterectomy . . . . . 59525
Curettage
Hydatidiform Mole . . . . . 59870
Evacuation
Hydatidiform Mole . . . . . 59870
External Cephalic Version . . . . . 59412
Miscarriage
Surgical Completion . . . . . 59812, 59820-59821
Placenta Delivery . . . . . 59414
Postpartum Care . . . . . 59430, 59514
Septic Abortion . . . . . 59830
Total (Global) . . . . . 59400, 59610, 59618
Unlisted Services and Procedures . . . . . 59898, 59899
Vaginal
after Cesarean . . . . . 59610, 59612, 59614
Vaginal Delivery . . . . . 59409-59410
Delivery after Cesarean . . . . . 59610, 59612, 59614

**Obstruction**
*See* Occlusion

**Obstruction Colon**
*See* Colon, Obstruction

**Obturator Nerve**
Avulsion . . . . . 64763-64766
Incision . . . . . 64763-64766
Transection . . . . . 64763-64766

**Obturator Prosthesis** . . . . . 21076
Definitive . . . . . 21080
Insertion
Larynx . . . . . 31527
Interim . . . . . 21079

**Occipital Nerve, Greater**
Avulsion . . . . . 64744
Incision . . . . . 64744
Injection
Anesthetic . . . . . 64405
Transection . . . . . 64744

**Occlusion**
Fallopian Tube
Oviduct . . . . . 58615
Penis
Vein . . . . . 37790

**Occlusive Disease of Artery**
*See* Repair, Artery; Revision

**Occult Blood** . . . . . 82270

**Occupational Therapy**
Evaluation . . . . . 97003-97004

**Ocular Implant** . . . . . 65175
*See* Orbital Implant
Insertion
in Scleral Shell . . . . . 65130
Muscles Attached . . . . . 65140
Muscles, Not Attached . . . . . 65135
Modification . . . . . 65125
Reinsertion . . . . . 65150
with Foreign Material . . . . . 65155
Removal . . . . . 65175

**Ocular Muscle**
*See* Eye Muscles

**Ocular Orbit**
*See* Orbit

**Ocular Prostheses**
*See* Prosthesis, Ocular

**Oculomotor Muscle**
*See* Eye Muscles

**Oddi Sphincter**
*See* Sphincter of Oddi

**Odontoid Dislocation**
Open Treatment/Reduction . . . . . 22318
with Grafting . . . . . 22319

**Odontoid Fracture**
Open Treatment/Reduction . . . . . 22318
with Grafting . . . . . 22319

**Odontoid Process**
Excision . . . . . 22548

**Oesophageal Neoplasm**
*See* Tumor, Esophagus

**Oesophageal Varices**
*See* Esophageal Varices

**Oesophagus**
*See* Esophagus

**Oestradiol**
*See* Estradiol

**Office and/or Other Outpatient Services**
*See* History and Physical
Consultation
  Confirmatory
  Consultations ..........99271-99275
Established Patient ........99211-99215
New Patient ..............99201-99205
Normal Newborn ................99432
Office Visit
  Established Patient ......99211-99215
  New Patient ...........99201-99205
Outpatient Visit
  Established Patient ......99211-99215
  New Patient ...........99201-99205
  Prolonged Services ......99354-99355
with Surgical Procedure ..........99025

**Office Medical Services**
After Hours ...............99050-99054
Emergency Care ................99058

**Office or Other Outpatient Consultations**
*See* Consultation, Office and/or Other Outpatient

**Olecranon**
*See* Elbow; Humerus; Radius; Ulna
Bursa
  Arthrocentesis ................20605
Cyst
  Excision ..............24125-24126
Tumor
  Cyst .......................24120
  Excision ..............24125-24126

**Olecranon Process**
Craterization ....................24147
Diaphysectomy ..................24147
Excision .........................24147
  Abscess .....................24138
Fracture
  *See* Elbow; Humerus; Radius
  Closed Treatment ........24670-24675
  Open Treatment ...............24685
Osteomyelitis ............24138, 24147
Saucerization ....................24147
Sequestrectomy .................24138

**Oligoclonal Immunoglobulin** .............83916

**Omentectomy** .....49255, 58950-58952
Laparotomy .....................58960
Oophorectomy ..................58943
Resection Ovarian
Malignancy ..............58950-58952

**Omentum**
Excision ...........49255, 58950-58952
Flap ...........................49905
  Free
    with Microvascular
    Anastomosis ...............49906

Unlisted Services and Procedures ...49999

**Omphalectomy** ..............49250

**Omphalocele**
Repair ............49600, 49605-49606, 49610-49611

**Omphalomesenteric Duct**
Excision .........................44800

**Omphalomesenteric Duct, Persistent**
*See* Diverticulum, Meckel's

**One Stage Prothrombin Time** ...................85610-85611
*See* Prothrombin Time

**Onychectomy**
*See* Excision, Nails

**Onychia**
Drainage .................10060-10061

**Oocyte**
Assisted Fertilization
  Microtechnique ...............89252
Culture
  for In Vitro Fertilization .........89250
Identification
  Follicular Fluid ...............89254
Retrieval
  for In Vitro Fertilization .........58970

**Oophorectomy** ....58262-58263, 58661, 58940-58943
Ectopic Pregnancy
  Laparoscopic Treatment ........59120
  Surgical Treatment ............59120

**Oophorectomy, Partial**
*See* Excision, Ovary, Partial

**Oophorocystectomy**
*See* Cystectomy, Ovarian

**Open Biopsy, Adrenal Gland**
*See* Adrenal Gland, Biopsy

**Operating Microscope** ........69990

**Operation**
Blalock-Hanlon
  *See* Septostomy, Atrial
Blalock-Taussig Subclavian-Pulmonary Anastomosis
  *See* Pulmonary Artery, Shunt, Subclavian
Borthen
  *See* Iridotasis
Dana
  *See* Rhizotomy
Dunn
  *See* Arthrodesis, Foot Joint
Duvries
  *See* Tenoplasty
Estes
  *See* Ovary, Transposition
Foley Pyeloplasty
  *See* Pyeloplasty
Fontan
  *See* Repair, Heart, Anomaly
Fox
  *See* Fox Operation
Gardner
  *See* Meningocele Repair
Green
  *See* Scapulopexy
Harelip
  *See* Cleft Lip, Repair
Heine
  *See* Cyclodialysis
Heller
  *See* Esophagomyotomy
Iris, Inclusion
  *See* Iridencleisis
Jaboulay Gastroduodenostomy
  *See* Gastroduodenostomy
Johanson
  *See* Reconstruction, Urethra
Keller
  *See* Keller Procedure
Krause
  *See* Gasserian Ganglion, Sensory Root, Decompression
Kuhnt-Szymanowski
  *See* Ectropion, Repair, Blepharoplasty
Mumford
  *See* Claviculectomy, Partial
Nissen
  *See* Fundoplasty, Esophagogastric
Peet
  *See* Nerves, Sympathectomy, Excision
Ramstedt
  *See* Pyloromyotomy
Richardson Hysterectomy
  *See* Hysterectomy, Abdominal, Total
Schanz
  *See* Femur, Osteotomy
Schlatter Total Gastrectomy
  *See* Excision, Stomach, Total
Smithwick
  *See* Excision, Nerve, Sympathetic
Winiwarter Cholecystoenterostomy
  *See* Anastomosis, Gallbladder to Intestines

**Operation Microscopes**
*See* Operating Microscope

**Operculectomy** ...............41821

**Operculum**
*See* Gums

**Ophthalmic Mucous Membrane Test** ............................95060
*See* Allergy Tests

**Ophthalmology**
Unlisted Services and Procedures ...92499
  *See* Ophthalmology, Diagnostic

with Graft
Reconstruction
Periorbital Region . . . . . .21267-21268

**Os Calcis Fracture**
*See* Calcaneus, Fracture

**Otolaryngology**
Diagnostic
Exam Under Anesthesia . . . . . . . .92502

**Otomy**
*See* Incision

**Otoplasty** . . . . . . . . . . . . . . . . . . . .69300

**Otorhinolaryngology**
Unlisted Services and Procedures . . .92599

**Ouchterlony Immunodiffusion** . . . . . . . . . . . . . .86331

**Outer Ear**
*See* Ear, Outer

**Outpatient Visit**
*See* History and Physical; Office and/or Other Outpatient Services

**Output, Cardiac**
*See* Cardiac Output

**Ova**
Smear . . . . . . . . . . . . . . . . . . . . . . . .87177

**Oval Window**
Repair Fistula . . . . . . . . . . . . . . . . . . .69666

**Oval Window Fistula**
*See* Fistula, Oval Window

**Ovarian Cyst**
*See* Cyst, Ovarian

**Ovarian Vein Syndrome**
Ureterolysis . . . . . . . . . . . . . . . . . . . .50722

**Ovariectomies**
*See* Oophorectomy

**Ovariolysis** . . . . . . . . . . . . . . . . . . .58740

**Ovary**
Abscess
Incision and Drainage . . . .58820-58822
Abdominal Approach . . . . . . . . .58822
Biopsy . . . . . . . . . . . . . . . . . .49321, 58900
Cyst
Incision and Drainage . . . .58800-58805
Excision . . . . . . . . . . . . . . . . .58662, 58720
Cyst . . . . . . . . . . . . . . . . . . . . . . . .58925
Partial
Oophorectomy . . . . . . . .58661, 58940
Ovarian Malignancy . . . . . . . . . .58943
Wedge Resection . . . . . . . . . . .58920
Total . . . . . . . . . . . . . . . . . .58940-58943
Laparoscopy . . . . . . . .58660-58662, 58679
Lysis
Adhesions . . . . . . . . . . . . .58660, 58740
Radical Resection . . . . . . . . . .58950-58952
Transposition . . . . . . . . . . . . . . . . . . .58825
Tumor
Resection . . . . . . . . . . . . . .58950-58952
Unlisted Services and Procedures . . . . . . . . . . . . . . . .58679, 58999
Wedge Resection . . . . . . . . . . . . . . . .58920

**Oviduct**
Anastomosis . . . . . . . . . . . . . . . . . . .58750
Chromotubation . . . . . . . . . . . . . . . . . .58350
Ectopic Pregnancy . . . . . . . . . .59120-59121
Excision . . . . . . . . . . . . . . . . . .58700-58720
Fulguration
Laparoscopic . . . . . . . . . . . . . . . . .58670
Hysterosalpingography . . . . . . . . . . . .74740
Laparoscopy . . . . . . . . . . . . . . . . . . . .58679
Ligation . . . . . . . . . . . . . . . . . .58600-58611
Lysis
Adhesions . . . . . . . . . . . . . . . . . . .58740
Occlusion . . . . . . . . . . . . . . . . . . . . . .58615
Laparoscopic . . . . . . . . . . . . . . . . .58671
Repair . . . . . . . . . . . . . . . . . . . . . . . . .58752
Anastomosis . . . . . . . . . . . . . . . . .58750
Create Stoma . . . . . . . . . . . . . . . .58770
Unlisted Services and Procedures . . . . . . . . . . . . . . . .58679, 58999
X-Ray with Contrast . . . . . . . . . . . . . .74740

**Ovocyte**
*See* Oocyte

**Ovulation Tests** . . . . . . . . . . . . . . .84830

**Ovum Implantation**
*See* Implantation

**Ovum Transfer Surgery**
*See* GIFT

**Oxalate** . . . . . . . . . . . . . . . . . . . . . . .83945

**Oxidase, Ceruloplasmin**
*See* Ceruloplasmin

**Oxidoreductase, Alcohol-Nad+**
*See* Antidiuretic Hormone

**Oximetry (Noninvasive)**
*See* Pulmonology, Diagnostic
Blood O2 Saturation
Ear or Pulse . . . . . . . . . . . .94760-94762

**Oxoisomerase**
*See* Phosphohexose Isomerase

**Oxosteroids**
*See* Ketosteroids

**Oxycodinone** . . . . . .80100-80103, 83925

**Oxygenation, Extracorporeal Membrane**
*See* Extracorporeal Membrane Oxygenation

**Oxygen Saturation** . . . . . .82805-82810

**Oxyproline**
*See* Hydroxyproline

**Oxytocin Stress Test, Fetal** . . . .59020

# P


**P-Acetamidophenol**
*See* Acetaminophen

**Pacemaker, Heart**
*See* Defibrillator, Heart
Conversion . . . . . . . . . . . . . . . . . . . . . .33214
Electronic Analysis . . . . . . . . . .93641-93642
Antitachycardia System . . . . . . . .93724
Dual Chamber . . . . . . . . . .93731-93732
Single Chamber . . . . . . . . .93734-93735
Insertion . . . . . .33200-33201, 33206-33208
Electrode . . .33210-33211, 33216-33217
Pulse Generator Only . . . . .33212-33213
Removal . . . . . . . . . . . . . . . . .33233-33237
via Thoracotomy . . . . . . . . .33236-33237
Repair
Electrode . . . . . . . . . . . . . .33218, 33220
Replacement
Catheter . . . . . . . . . . . . . . . . . . . . .33210
Electrode . . . . . . . .33210-33211, 33217
Insertion . . .33200-33201, 33206-33208
Pulse Generator . . . . . . . . .33212-33213
Revise Pocket
Chest . . . . . . . . . . . . . . . . . . . . . . .33222
Telephonic Analysis . . . . . . . .93733, 93736
Upgrade . . . . . . . . . . . . . . . . . . . . . . . .33214

**Packing**
Nasal Hemorrhage . . . . . . . . . .30901-30906

**Pain Management**
*See* Injection, Chemotherapy
Epidural/Intrathecal . . . . . . . .62350-62351, 62360-62362
Intravenous Therapy . . . . . . . .90783-90784

**Palatal Augmentation Prosthesis** . . . . . . . . . . . . . . . . . . . .21082

**Palatal Lift Prosthesis** . . . . . . . .21083

**Palate**
Abscess
Incision and Drainage . . . . . . . . . .42000
Biopsy . . . . . . . . . . . . . . . . . . . . . . . . .42100
Excision . . . . . . . . . . . . . . . . . .42120, 42145
Fracture
Closed Treatment . . . . . . . . . . . . .21421
Open Treatment . . . . . . . . .21422-21423
Lesion
Destruction . . . . . . . . . . . . . . . . . .42160
Excision . . .42104, 42106-42107, 42120
Prosthesis . . . . . . . . . . . . . . . .42280-42281
Reconstruction
Lengthening . . . . . . . . . . . .42226, 42227
Repair
Cleft Palate . . . . . . . . . . . .42200-42225
Laceration . . . . . . . . . . . . .42180, 42182
Vomer Flap . . . . . . . . . . . . . . . . . .42235
Unlisted Services and Procedures . . .42299

**Parathyroid Autotransplantation** .......... 60512

**Parathyroid Gland**
Autotransplant .......... 60512
Excision .......... 60500-60502
Exploration .......... 60500-60505
Nuclear Medicine
  Imaging .......... 78070

**Parathyroid Hormone** .......... 83970

**Parathyroid Hormone Measurement**
*See* Parathormone

**Parathyroid Transplantation**
*See* Transplantation, Parathyroid

**Paraurethral Gland**
Abscess
  Incision and Drainage .......... 53060

**Paravertebral Nerve**
Destruction .......... 64622-64627
Injection
  Anesthetic .. 64475-64484, 64470-64472
  Neurolytic .......... 64622-64627

**Parietal Cell Vagotomies**
*See* Vagotomy, Highly Selective

**Parietal Craniotomy** .......... 61556

**Paring**
Skin Lesion
  Benign Hyperkeratotic
    More than Four Lesions .......... 11057
    Single Lesion .......... 11055
    Two to Four Lesions .......... 11056

**Paronychia**
Incision and Drainage .......... 10060-10061

**Parotid Duct**
Diversion .......... 42507-42510
Reconstruction .......... 42507-42510

**Parotid Gland**
Abscess
  Incision and Drainage .... 42300, 42305
Calculi (Stone)
  Excision .......... 42330, 42340
Excision
  Partial .......... 42410, 42415
  Total .......... 42420, 42425-42426
Tumor
  Excision ........ 42410, 42415, 42420, 42425-42426

**Parotitides, Epidemic**
*See* Mumps

**Pars Abdominalis Aortae**
*See* Aorta, Abdominal

**Partial Colectomy**
*See* Colectomy, Partial

**Partial Cystectomy**
*See* Cystectomy, Partial

**Partial Esophagectomy**
*See* Esophagectomy, Partial

**Partial Gastrectomy**
*See* Excision, Stomach, Partial

**Partial Glossectomy**
*See* Excision, Tongue, Partial

**Partial Hepatectomy**
*See* Excision, Liver, Partial

**Partial Mastectomies**
*See* Breast, Excision, Lesion

**Partial Nephrectomy**
*See* Excision, Kidney, Partial

**Partial Pancreatectomy**
*See* Pancreatectomy, Partial

**Partial Splenectomy**
*See* Splenectomy, Partial

**Partial Thromboplastin Time**
*See* Thromboplastin, Partial, Time

**Partial Ureterectomy**
*See* Ureterectomy, Partial

**Particle Agglutination** .......... 86403-86406

**Parvovirus**
Antibody .......... 86747

**Patch**
Allergy Tests .......... 95044
  *See* Allergy Tests

**Patella**
*See* Knee
Dislocation .......... 27560-27562, 27566
Excision .......... 27350
  with Reconstruction .......... 27424
Fracture .......... 27520, 27524
Reconstruction .......... 27437-27438
Repair
  Chondromalacia .......... 27418
  Instability .......... 27420-27424

**Patella, Chondromalacia**
*See* Chondromalacia Patella

**Patellar Tendon Bearing (PTB) Cast** .......... 29435

**Patellectomy**
with Reconstruction .......... 27424

**Paternity Testing** .......... 86910-86911

**Patey's Operation**
*See* Mastectomy, Radical

**Pathologic Dilatation**
*See* Dilation

**Pathology**
Clinical
  Consultation .......... 80500-80502
Surgical .......... 88355
  Consultation .......... 88321-88325
    Intraoperative .......... 88329-88332
  Decalcification Procedure .......... 88311
  Electron Microscopy .......... 88348-88349
  Gross and Micro Exam
    Level II .......... 88302
    Level III .......... 88304
    Level IV .......... 88305
    Level V .......... 88307
    Level VI .......... 88309
  Gross Exam
    Level I .......... 88300
  Histochemistry .......... 88318-88319
  Immunocytochemistry .......... 88342
  Immunofluorescent Study .......... 88346-88347
  Morphometry
    Nerve .......... 88356
    Skeletal Muscle .......... 88355
    Tumor .......... 88358
  Nerve Teasing .......... 88362
  Special Stain .......... 88312-88314
  Staining .......... 88312-88314
  Tissue Hybridization .......... 88365
  Unlisted Services and Procedures .......... 88399, 89399

**Patterson's Test**
*See* Blood Urea Nitrogen

**Paul-Bunnell Test**
*See* Antibody; Antibody Identification; Microsomal Antibody

**PBG**
*See* Porphobilinogen

**PCP**
*See* Phencyclidine

**PCR**
*See* Polymerase Chain Reaction

**Peans' Operation**
*See* Amputation, Leg, Upper, at Hip; Radical Resection; Replantation

**Pectoral Cavity**
*See* Chest Cavity

**Pectus Carinatum**
Reconstructive Repair .......... 21740

**Pectus Excavatum**
Reconstructive Repair .......... 21740

**Pedicle Fixation**
Insertion .......... 22842-22844

**Pedicle Flap**
Formation .......... 15570-15576
Island .......... 15740
Neurovascular .......... 15750
Transfer .......... 15650

**PEEP**
*See* Pressure Breathing, Positive

**Peet Operation**
*See* Nerves, Sympathectomy, Excision

**Pelvi-Ureteroplasty**
*See* Pyeloplasty

**Pelvic Adhesions**
*See* Adhesions, Pelvic

**Pelvic Exam** .................57410

**Pelvic Exenteration** ...........51597

**Pelvic Fixation**
Insertion .......................22848

**Pelvic Lymphadenectomy** .....58240

**Pelvimetry** ....................74710

**Pelviolithotomy** ...............50130

**Pelvis**
*See* Hip
Abscess
  Incision and Drainage ....26990, 45000
Biopsy ...................27040-27041
Bone
  Drainage ...................26992
Brace Application ...............20662
Bursa
  Incision and Drainage ..........26991
CAT Scan ..................72192-72194
Cyst
  Aspiration ..................50390
  Injection .....................50390
Destruction
  Lesion ......................58662
Endoscopy
  Destruction of Lesion .........58662
  Lysis of Adhesions ............58660
  Oviduct Surgery .........58670-58671
Exclusion
  Small Bowel .................44700
Exenteration .............45126, 58240
Halo ...........................20662
Hematoma
  Incision and Drainage ..........26990
Lysis
  Adhesions ...................58660
Magnetic Resonance Angiography ...72198
Magnetic Resonance Imaging ......72196
Removal
  Foreign Body ...........27086-27087
Repair
  Osteotomy ..................27158
  Tendon ......................27098
Ring
  Dislocation ...........27193-27194, 27216-27218
  Fracture ..............27216-27218
    Closed Treatment ......27193-27194
Tumor
  Excision ..............27047-27049
Ultrasound ...............76856-76857
Unlisted Services and Procedures
for Hips and Hip Joint ............27299
X-Ray .............72170-72190, 73540
  Manometry ..................74710

**Pemberton Osteotomy of Pelvis**
*See* Osteotomy, Pelvis

**Penectomy**
*See* Amputation, Penis

**Penetrating Keratoplasties**
*See* Keratoplasty, Penetrating

**Penile Induration**
*See* Peyronie Disease

**Penile Prosthesis**
Insertion
  Inflatable ..............54401, 54405
  Noninflatable ................54400
Removal
  Inflatable ..............54402, 54407
  Semi-Rigid ...................54402
Repair
  Inflatable ....................54407

**Penile Rigidity Test** ...........54250

**Penile Tumescence Test** ......54250

**Penis**
Amputation
  Partial ......................54120
  Radical ................54130-54135
  Total ........................54125
Biopsy ...................54100-54105
Circumcision
  Surgical Excision
    Newborn ...................54160
  with Clamp or Other Device .....54152
    Newborn ...................54150
Excision
  Partial ......................54120
  Prepuce ...............54150-54161
  Total ...........54125, 54130-54135
Incision
  Prepuce ...............54000-54001
Incision and Drainage ............54015
Injection
  for Erection .................54235
  Peyronie Disease ..............54200
    Surgical Exposure Plague ......54205
  Vasoactive Drugs .............54231
  X-Ray .......................54230
Insertion
  Prosthesis
    Inflatable ............54401, 54405
    Noninflatable ..............54400
Irrigation
  Priapism ....................54220
Lesion
  Destruction
    Cryosurgery ...............54056
    Electrodesiccation ..........54055
    Extensive ..................54065
    Laser Surgery ..............54057
    Simple ...............54050-54060
    Surgical Excision ...........54060
  Excision .....................54060
    Penile Plague .........54110-54112
Nocturnal Penile Tumescence Test ...54250
Occlusion
  Vein ........................37790
Plaque
  Excision ..............54110-54112
Plethysmography ................54240
Prepuce
  Stretch ......................54450
Reconstruction
  Angulation ...................54360
  Chordee .........54300-54304, 54328
  Complications ..........54340-54348
  Epispadias ............54380-54390
  Hypospadias ...........54328-54352
  Injury .......................54440
Removal
  Foreign Body .................54115
  Prosthesis
    Inflatable ............54402, 54407
    Semi-Rigid .................54402
Repair
  Fistulization .................54435
  Priapism with Shunt ......54420-54430
  Prosthesis ............54407, 54409
Revascularization ................37788
Rigidity Test ....................54250
Test Erection ...................54250
Unlisted Services and Procedures ...55899
Venous Studies ...........93980-93981

**Penis Prostheses**
*See* Penile Prosthesis

**Pentagastrin Test**
*See* Gastric Analysis Test

**Pentamidine**
*See* Inhalation Treatment

**Peptidase P**
*See* Angiotensin Converting Enzyme (ACE)

**Peptidase S**
*See* Leucine Aminopeptidase

**Peptide, Connecting**
*See* C-Peptide

**Peptide, Vasoactive Intestinal**
*See* Vasoactive Intestinal Peptide

**Peptidyl Dipeptidase A**
*See* Angiotensin Converting Enzyme (ACE)

**Percutaneous Abdominal Paracentesis**
*See* Abdomen, Drainage

**Percutaneous Atherectomies**
*See* Artery, Atherectomy

**Percutaneous Biopsy, Gallbladder/Bile Ducts**
*See* Bile Duct, Biopsy

**Percutaneous Discectomies**
*See* Diskectomy, Percutaneous

**Percutaneous Electric Nerve Stimulation**
*See* Application, Neurostimulation

**Percutaneous Lumbar Diskectomy** .................. 62287
*See* Aspiration, Nucleus of Disk, Lumbar; Puncture Aspiration

**Percutaneous Lysis** ........... 62263

**Percutaneous Nephrostomies**
*See* Nephrostomy, Percutaneous

**Percutaneous Transluminal Angioplasty**
Artery
- Aortic ....................... 35472
- Brachiocephalic ............... 35475
- Coronary ............... 92982-92984
- Femoral-Popliteal ............. 35474
- Iliac ........................ 35473
- Pulmonary ............. 92997-92998
- Renal ....................... 35471
- Tibioperoneal ................. 35470
- Visceral ..................... 35471

Venous ......................... 35476

**Percutaneous Transluminal Coronary Angioplasty**
*See* Percutaneous Transluminal Angioplasty

**Pereyra Procedure** ........... 51845, 57289, 58267

**Performance Test** ............. 96100
*See* Physical Medicine/Therapy/ Occupational Therapy
Physical Therapy ................. 97750

**Perfusion**
Myocardial .... 78460-78465, 78478, 78480
- Imaging ............... 78466-78469

Positron Emission Tomography (PET)
- Myocardial Imaging ...... 78491-78492

**Perfusion, Intracranial Arterial**
Thrombolysis .................... 61624

**Perfusion Pump**
*See* Infusion Pump

**Pericardectomies**
*See* Excision, Pericardium

**Pericardial Cyst**
*See* Cyst, Pericardial

**Pericardial Sac**
Drainage ...................... 32659

**Pericardial Window**
for Drainage ..................... 33025

**Pericardial Window Technic**
*See* Pericardiostomy

**Pericardiectomy**
Complete ................. 33030-33031
Subtotal .................. 33030-33031
Total
- Endoscopic .................. 32660

**Pericardiocentesis** ...... 33010-33011
Ultrasound Guidance .............. 76930

**Pericardiostomy**
Tube ........................... 33015

**Pericardiotomy**
Removal
- Clot ........................ 33020
- Foreign Body ................ 33020

**Pericardium**
Cyst
- Excision ............... 32661, 33050

Excision ............ 32659, 33030-33031
Incision
- Removal
  - Clot ....................... 33020
  - Foreign Body ................ 33020
- with Tube .................... 33015

Incision and Drainage ............. 33025
Puncture Aspiration ......... 33010-33011
Removal
- Clot
  - Endoscopic ................. 32658
- Foreign Body
  - Endoscopic ................. 32658

Tumor
- Excision ............... 32661, 33050

**Peridural Anesthesia**
*See* Anesthesia, Epidural

**Peridural Injection**
*See* Epidural, Injection

**Perineal Prostatectomy**
*See* Prostatectomy, Perineal

**Perineoplasty** ................. 56810

**Perineorrhaphy**
Repair
- Rectocele .................... 57250

**Perineum**
Abscess
- Incision and Drainage .......... 56405

Colposcopy ..................... 99170
Removal
- Prosthesis ................... 53442

Repair ......................... 56810
X-Ray with Contrast ............. 74775

**Perionychia**
*See* Paronychia

**Periorbital Region**
Reconstruction
- Osteotomy with Graft .... 21267-21268

Repair-Osteotomy .......... 21260-21263

**Peripheral Nerve**
Repair/Suture
- Major ................. 64856, 64859

**Periprosthetic Capsulectomy**
Breast .......................... 19371

**Peristaltic Pumps**
*See* Infusion Pump

**Peritoneal Dialysis** ...... 90945-90947

**Peritoneal Free Air**
*See* Pneumoperitoneum

**Peritoneal Lavage** ............ 49080

**Peritoneocentesis** ...... 49080-49081

**Peritoneoscopy**
*See* Endoscopy, Peritoneum

**Peritoneum**
Abscess
- Incision and Drainage .......... 49020
  - Percutaneous ............... 49021

Chemotherapy Administration ...... 96445
- *See* Chemotherapy

Endoscopy
- Biopsy ...................... 47561
- Drainage
  - Lymphocele ................ 49323
- X-Ray ....................... 47560

Exchange
- Drainage Catheter ............. 49423

Injection
- Contrast
  - via Catheter ................ 49424

Ligation
- Shunt ....................... 49428

Removal
- Cannula/Catheter ............. 49422
- Foreign Body ................. 49085
- Shunt ....................... 49429

Unlisted Services and Procedures ... 49999
Venous Shunt
- Injection ..................... 49427

X-Ray .......................... 74190

**Persistent, Omphalomesenteric Duct**
*See* Diverticulum, Meckel's

**Persistent Truncus Arteriosus**
*See* Truncus Arteriosus

**Personal Care**
*See* Self Care

**Pessary**
Insertion ....................... 57160

**Pesticides**
Chlorinated Hydrocarbons .......... 82441

**PET**
*See* Positron Emission Tomography

**Phosphocreatine Phosphotransferase, ADP**
*See* CPK

**Phosphogluconate-6**
Dehydrogenase . . . . . . . . . . . . . . . . . . 84085

**Phosphoglycerides, Glycerol**
*See* Phosphatidylglycerol

**Phosphohexose Isomerase** . . . 84087

**Phosphohydrolases**
*See* Phosphatase

**Phosphokinase, Creatine**
*See* CPK

**Phospholipase C**
*See* Tissue Typing

**Phospholipid Antibody** . . . . . . . . 86147

**Phosphomonoesterase**
*See* Phosphatase

**Phosphoric Monoester Hydrolases**
*See* Phosphatase

**Phosphorus** . . . . . . . . . . . . . . . . . . 84100
Urine . . . . . . . . . . . . . . . . . . . . . . . . . . 84105

**Phosphotransferase, ADP Phosphocreatine**
*See* CPK

**Photochemotherapies, Extracorporeal**
*See* Photopheresis

**Photochemotherapy** . . . . . 96910-96913
*See* Dermatology
Endoscopic Light . . . . . . . . . . . 96570-96571

**Photocoagulation**
Endolaser Panretinal
  Vitrectomy . . . . . . . . . . . . . . . . . . 67040
Focal Endolaser
  Vitrectomy . . . . . . . . . . . . . . . . . . 67040
Iridoplasty . . . . . . . . . . . . . . . . . . . . . 66762
Lesion
  Cornea . . . . . . . . . . . . . . . . . . . . . . 65450
  Retina . . . . . . . . . . . 67210, 67227-67228
Retinal Detachment
  Prophylaxis . . . . . . . . . . . . . . . . . 67145
  Repair . . . . . . . . . . . . . . . . . . . . . . 67105

**Photodensity**
Radiographic
  Absorptiometry . . . . . . . . . . . . . . . 76078

**Photodynamic Therapies**
*See* Photochemotherapy

**Photography, Ocular**
*See* Ophthalmosocpy, Diagnostic

**Photopheresis**
Extracorporeal . . . . . . . . . . . . . . . . . . 36522

**Photophoresis**
*See* Actinotherapy; Photochemotherapy

**Photoradiation Therapies**
*See* Actinotherapy

**Photosensitivity Testing** . . . . . . 95056
*See* Allergy Tests

**Phototherapies**
*See* Actinotherapy

**Phototherapy, Ultraviolet**
*See* Actinotherapy

**Photo Patch**
Allergy Test . . . . . . . . . . . . . . . . . . . . 95052
  *See* Allergy Tests

**Phrenic Nerve**
Anastomosis
  to Facial Nerve . . . . . . . . . . . . . . . 64870
Avulsion . . . . . . . . . . . . . . . . . . . . . . . . 64746
Incision . . . . . . . . . . . . . . . . . . . . . . . . 64746
Injection
  Anesthetic . . . . . . . . . . . . . . . . . . . 64410
Transection . . . . . . . . . . . . . . . . . . . . . 64746

**Physical Medicine/Therapy/ Occupational Therapy**
*See* Neurology, Diagnostic
Activities of Daily Living . . . . . . . . . . . 97535
Aquatic Therapy
  with Exercises . . . . . . . . . . . . . . . . 97113
Check-Out
  Orthotic/Prosthetic . . . . . . . . . . . . 97703
Cognitive Skills Development . . . . . . . 97770
Community/Work Reintegration . . . . . 97537
Evaluation . . . . . . . . . . . . . . . . 97001-97002
Kinetic Therapy . . . . . . . . . . . . . . . . . 97530
Manual Therapy . . . . . . . . . . . . . . . . . 97140
Modalities
  Contrast Baths . . . . . . . . . . . . . . . . 97034
  Diathermy Treatment . . . . . . . . . . 97024
  Electric Simulation
    Unattended . . . . . . . . . . . . . . . . . 97014
  Electric Stimulation
    Attended, Manual . . . . . . . . . . . 97032
  Hot or Cold Pack . . . . . . . . . . . . . . 97010
  Hydrotherapy (Hubbard Tank) . . . . 97036
  Infrared Light Treatment . . . . . . . . 97026
  Iontophoresis . . . . . . . . . . . . . . . . . 97033
  Microwave Therapy . . . . . . . . . . . 97020
  Paraffin Bath . . . . . . . . . . . . . . . . . 97018
  Traction . . . . . . . . . . . . . . . . . . . . . 97012
  Ultrasound . . . . . . . . . . . . . . . . . . . 97035
  Ultraviolet Light . . . . . . . . . . . . . . . 97028
  Unlisted Services and
  Procedures . . . . . . . . . . . . . . . . . . . 97039
  Vasopneumatic Device . . . . . . . . . 97016
  Whirlpool Therapy . . . . . . . . . . . . . 97022
Orthotics Training . . . . . . . . . . . . . . . . 97504
Osteopathic Manipulation . . . . 98925-98929
Procedures
  Aquatic Therapy . . . . . . . . . . . . . . 97113
  Gait Training . . . . . . . . . . . . . . . . . 97116
  Group Therapeutic . . . . . . . . . . . . . 97150
  Massage Therapy . . . . . . . . . . . . . 97124
  Neuromuscular Reeducation . . . . . 97112
  Physical Performance Test . . . . . . 97750
  Therapeutic Exercises . . . . . . . . . . 97110
  Traction Therapy . . . . . . . . . . . . . . 97140
  Work Hardening . . . . . . . . . 97545-97546
Prosthetic Training . . . . . . . . . . . . . . . 97520
Therapeutic Activities . . . . . . . . . . . . . 97530
Unlisted Services and
Procedures . . . . . . . . . . . . . . . . 97139, 97799
Wheelchair Management/
Propulsion . . . . . . . . . . . . . . . . . . . . . . 97542
Work Reintegration . . . . . . . . . . . . . . . 97537

**Physical Therapy**
*See* Physical Medicine/Therapy/ Occupational Therapy

**Physician Services**
Care Plan Oversight Services . . 99374-99380
  Home Health Agency Care . . . . . . 99374
  Hospice . . . . . . . . . . . . . . . 99377-99378
  Nursing Facility . . . . . . . . . 99379-99380
Direction, Advanced Life Support . . . . 99288
Prolonged
  without Direct Patient
  Contact . . . . . . . . . . . . . . . . 99358-99359
  with Direct Patient
  Contact . . . . . . . . . . . . . . . . 99354-99357
    Outpatient/Office . . . . . . 99354-99355
  with Direct Patient Services
    Inpatient . . . . . . . . . . . . . 99356-99357
Standby . . . . . . . . . . . . . . . . . . . . . . . . 99360
Supervision, Care Plan Oversight
Services . . . . . . . . . . . . . . . . . . 99374-99380

**Pierce Ears** . . . . . . . . . . . . . . . . . . . 69090

**Piercing of Ear Lobe**
*See* Ear Lobes, Pierce

**Piles**
*See* Hemorrhoids

**Pilonidal Cyst**
Excision . . . . . . . . . . . . . . . . . . 11770-11772
Incision and Drainage . . . . . . . 10080-10081

**Pin**
*See* Wire
Insertion/Removal
  Skeletal Traction . . . . . . . . . . . . . . 20650
Prophylactic Treatment
  Femur . . . . . . . . . . . . . . . . . . . . . . . 27187
  Humerus . . . . . . . . . . . . . . . . . . . . . 24498
  Shoulder . . . . . . . . . . . . . . . 23490-23491

**Pinch Graft** . . . . . . . . . . . . . . . . . . . 15050

**Pinna**
*See* Ear, External

**Pirogoff Procedure** . . . . . . . . . . . 27888

**Pituitary Epidermoid Tumor**
*See* Craniopharyngioma

**Pneumonectomy** ........32440-32500
Completion ......................32488
Donor ....................32850, 33930
Sleeve ..........................32442
Total ....................32440-32445

**Pneumonology**
*See* Pulmonology

**Pneumonolysis** ...............32940
Intrapleural .....................32652
Open Intrapleural ................32124

**Pneumonostomy** ........32200-32201

**Pneumonotomy**
*See* Incision, Lung

**Pneumoperitoneum** ...........49400

**Pneumoplethysmography**
Ocular ..........................93875

**Pneumothorax**
Chemical Pleurodesis .............32005
Pleural Scarification for Repeat .....32215
Therapeutic
  Injection Intrapleural Air ........32960
Thoracentesis with Tube Insertion ...32002

**Pollo**
Antibody .......................86658
Vaccine ..................90712-90713

**Pollicization**
Digit ...........................26550

**Polya Gastrectomy**
*See* Gastrectomy, Partial

**Polydactylism**
*See* Supernumerary Digit

**Polydactyly, Toes** .............28344

**Polymerase Chain Reaction** ..83898,

**Polyp**
Antrochoanal
  Removal .....................31032
Esophagus
  Ablation .....................43228
Nose
  Excision
    Endoscopic ...........31237-31240
    Extensive ..................30115
    Simple ....................30110
Sphenoid Sinus
  Removal .....................31051
Urethra
  Excision .....................53260

**Polypectomy**
Nose
  Endoscopic ..................31237
Uterus ..........................58558

**Polypeptide, Vasoactive Intestinal**
*See* Vasoactive Intestinal Peptide

**Polysomnography** .......95808-95811

**Polyuria Test**
*See* Water Load Test

**Pomeroy's Operation**
*See* Tubal Ligation

**Pooling**
Blood Products ..................86965

**Popliteal Arteries**
*See* Artery, Popliteal

**Popliteal Synovial Cyst**
*See* Baker's Cyst

**Poradenitistras**
*See* Lymphogranuloma Venereum

**Porphobilinogen**
Urine ....................84106-84110

**Porphyrins**
Feces ....................84126-84127
Urine ....................84119-84120

**Porphyrin Precursors** .........82135

**PORP (Partial Ossicular Replacement Prosthesis)** .............69633, 69637

**Portal Vein**
*See* Vein, Hepatic Portal

**Porter-Silber Test**
*See* Corticosteroid, Blood

**Portoenterostomies, Hepatic**
*See* Hepaticoenterostomy

**Portoenterostomy** .............47701

**Port Film** .....................77417

**Posadas-Wernicke Disease**
*See* Coccidioidomycosis

**Positional Nystagmus Test**
*See* Nystagmus Tests, Positional

**Positive-Pressure Breathing, Inspiratory**
*See* Intermittent Positive Pressure Breathing (IPPB)

**Positive End Expiratory Pressure**
*See* Pressure Breathing, Positive

**Positron Emission Tomography (PET)**
Brain ....................78608-78609
Heart ..........................78459
Myocardial Imaging
  Perfusion Study .........78491-78492
Tumor ..........................78810

**Post-Op Visit** .................99024

**Postauricular Fistula**
*See* Fistula, Postauricular

**Postcaval Ureter**
*See* Retrocaval Ureter

**Postmortem**
*See* Autopsy

**Postoperative Wound Infection**
Incision and Drainage .............10180

**Postop Vas Reconstruction**
*See* Vasovasorrhaphy

**Postpartum Care**
Cesarean Delivery ................59515
  after Attempted Vaginal Delivery .....................59622
  Previous ...59610, 59614, 59618, 59622
Vaginal Delivery .................59430
  after Previous Cesarean Delivery .....................59614

**Potassium** ....................84132
Urine ..........................84133

**Potential, Auditory Evoked**
*See* Auditory Evoked Potentials

**Potential, Evoked**
*See* Evoked Potential

**Potts-Smith Procedure** ........33762

**Pouch, Kock**
*See* Kock Pouch

**PPP**
*See* Fibrin Degradation Products

**PRA**
*See* Cytotoxic Screen

**Prealbumin** ...................84134

**Prebeta Lipoproteins**
*See* Lipoprotein, Blood

**Pregl's Test**
*See* Cystourethroscopy, Catheterization, Urethral

**Pregnancy**
Abortion
  Induced ...............59855-59857
    by Amniocentesis Injection ............59850-59852
    by Dilation and Curettage .....59840
    by Dilation and Evaluation .....59841
  Septic ........................59830
  Therapeutic
    by Dilation and Curettage .....59851
    by Hysterectomy ............59852
    by Saline ...................59850
Cesarean Delivery ....59618, 59620, 59622
  Only ..........................59514
  Postpartum Care ........59514-59515
  Routine Care ..................59510
  Vaginal Birth After ...........59610, 59612, 59614
  with Hysterectomy ............59525

Ectopic
Abdominal .....59130
Cervix .....59140
Interstitial
Partial Resection Uterus .....59136
Total Hysterectomy .....59135
Laparoscopy
without Salpingectomy and/or Oophorectomy .....59150
with Salpingectomy and/or Oophorectomy .....59151
Tubal .....59121
with Salpingectomy and/or Oophorectomy .....59120
Miscarriage
Surgical Completion
Any Trimester .....59812
First Trimester .....59820
Second Trimester .....59821
Molar
*See* Hydatidiform Mole
Multifetal Reduction .....59866
Placenta Delivery .....59414
Vaginal Delivery .....59409-59410
Antepartum Care .....59425-59426
after Cesarean Delivery .....59610, 59612, 59614
Postpartum Care .....59430
Total Obstetrical Care .....59400, 59610, 59618

**Pregnancy Test** .....84702-84703
Urinalysis .....81025

**Pregnanediol** .....84135

**Pregnanetriol** .....84138

**Pregnenolone** .....84140

**Prekallikrein**
*See* Fletcher Factor

**Prekallikrein Factor** .....85292

**Premature, Closure, Cranial Suture**
*See* Craniosynostosis

**Prenatal Testing**
Amniocentesis .....59000
Chorionic Villus Sampling .....59015
Cordocentesis .....59012
Fetal Blood Sample .....59030
Fetal Monitoring .....59050
Interpretation Only .....59051
Non-Stress Test, Fetal .....59025
Oxytocin Stress Test .....59020
Stress Test
Oxytocin .....59020
Ultrasound .....76805-76816
Fetal Biophysical Profile .....76818
Fetal Heart .....76825

**Prentiss Operation**
*See* Orchiopexy, Inguinal Approach

**Preparation**
for Transfer
Embryo .....89255
Cryopreserved .....89256

**Presacral Sympathectomy**
*See* Sympathectomy, Presacral

**Prescription**
Contact Lens .....92310-92317
*See* Contact Lens Services
Ocular Prosthesis .....92330, 92335
*See* Prosthesis, Ocular

**Pressure, Blood**
*See* Blood Pressure

**Pressure, Venous**
*See* Blood Pressure, Venous

**Pressure Breathing**
*See* Pulmonology, Therapeutic
Negative
Continuous (CNP) .....94662
Positive
Continuous (CPAP) .....94660
Intermittent (IPPB) .....94650-94652

**Pressure Measurement of Sphincter of Oddi**
*See* Sphincter of Oddi, Pressure Measurement

**Pressure Ulcers**
Excision .....15920-15999

**Pressure Ulcer (Decubitus)**
*See* Debridement; Skin Graft and Flap
Excision
Unlisted Services and Procedures .....15999

**Pretreatment**
Red Blood Cell
Antibody Identification .....86970-86972
Serum
Antibody Identification .....86975-86978

**Prevention & Control**
*See* Prophylaxis

**Preventive Medicine** .....99381-99397
*See* Immunization; Newborn Care, Normal; Office and/or Other Outpatient Services; Prophylactic Treatment
Administration/Interpretation of Health Risk Assessment .....99420
Counseling and/or Risk Factor Reduction Intervention .....99401-99429
Group Counseling .....99411-99412
Individual Counseling .....99401-99404
Established Patient .....99381-99397
Newborn Care .....99432
New Patient .....99381-99387
Respiratory Pattern Recording .....94772
Unlisted Services and Procedures .....99429

**Priapism**
Repair
Fistulization .....54435
with Shunt .....54420-54430

**Primidone**
Assay .....80188

**PRL**
*See* Prolactin

**Pro-Insulin C Peptide**
*See* C-Peptide

**Proalbumin**
*See* Prealbumin

**Probes, DNA**
*See* Nucleic Acid Probe

**Probes, Nucleic Acid**
*See* Nucleic Acid Probe

**Procainamide**
Assay .....80190-80192

**Procedure, Fontan**
*See* Repair, Heart, Anomaly

**Procedure, Maxillofacial**
*See* Maxillofacial Procedures

**Process, Odontoid**
*See* Odontoid Process

**Procidentia**
Rectum
Excision .....45130, 45135
Repair .....45900

**Procoagulant Activity, Glomerular**
*See* Thromboplastin

**Proconvertin** .....85230

**Proctectasis**
*See* Dilation, Rectum

**Proctectomy**
Partial .....45111, 45113, 45114, 45116, 45123
Total .....45110, 45112, 45120
with Colon .....45121

**Proctocele**
*See* Rectocele

**Proctopexy** .....45540-45541
with Sigmoid Excision .....45550

**Proctoplasty** .....45500, 45505

**Proctorrhaphy**
*See* Rectum, Suture

**Proctoscopies**
*See* Anoscopy

**Proctosigmoidoscopy**
Ablation
Polyp or Lesion .....45320
Biopsy .....45305
Destruction
Tumor .....45320

Dilation .......... 45303
Exploration .......... 45300
Hemorrhage Control .......... 45317
Removal
Foreign Body .......... 45307
Polyp .......... 45308-45309, 45315
Tumor .......... 45315
Volvulus Repair .......... 45321

**Products, Gene**
*See* Protein

**Proetz Therapy**
Nose .......... 30210

**Profibrinolysin**
*See* Plasminogen

**Progenitor Cell**
*See* Stem Cell

**Progesterone** .......... 84144

**Progesterone Receptors** .......... 84234

**Progestin Receptors**
*See* Progesterone Receptors

**Proinsulin** .......... 84206

**Projective Test** .......... 96100

**Prokallikrein**
*See* Fletcher Factor

**Prokallikrein, Plasma**
*See* Fletcher Factor

**Prokinogenase**
*See* Fletcher Factor

**Prolactin** .......... 80418, 80440, 84146

**Prolapse**
*See* Procidentia

**Prolapse, Rectal**
*See* Procidentia, Rectum

**Prolastin**
*See* Alpha-1 Antitrypsin

**Prolonged Services** .......... 99354-99357, 99360
without Direct Patient Contact .......... 99358-99359

**Prophylactic Treatment**
*See* Preventive Medicine
Femur .......... 27495
Pinning .......... 27187
Humerus
Pinning, Wiring .......... 24498
Radius .......... 25490, 25492
Nailing .......... 25490, 25492
Pinning .......... 25490, 25492
Plating .......... 25490, 25492
Wiring .......... 25490, 25492
Shoulder
Clavicle .......... 23490
Humerus .......... 23491
Tibia .......... 27745
Ulna .......... 25491-25492
Nailing .......... 25491-25492
Pinning .......... 25491-25492
Plating .......... 25491-25492
Wiring .......... 25491-25492

**Prophylaxis**
Retina
Detachment
Cryotherapy, Diathermy .......... 67141
Photocoagulation .......... 67145

**Prostaglandin** .......... 84150
Insertion .......... 59200

**Prostanoids**
*See* Prostaglandin

**Prostate**
Abscess
Drainage .......... 52700
Incision and Drainage .......... 55720-55725
Biopsy .......... 55700-55705
Brachytherapy
Needle Insertion .......... 55859
Coagulation
Laser .......... 52647
Destruction
Thermotherapy .......... 53850, 53852
Microwave .......... 53850
Radio Frequency .......... 53852
Excision
Partial .......... 55801, 55821-55831
Perineal .......... 55801-55815
Radical .......... 55810-55815, 55840-55845
Retropubic .......... 55831, 55840-55845
Suprapubic .......... 55821
Transurethral .......... 52601, 52612-52614
Exploration
Exposure .......... 55860
with Nodes .......... 55862, 55865
Incision
Exposure .......... 55860-55865
Transurethral .......... 52450
Insertion
Radioactive Substance .......... 55860
Needle Biopsy .......... 55700
Thermotherapy
Transurethral .......... 53850-53852
Ultrasound .......... 76872-76873
Unlisted Services and Procedures .......... 55899
Urinary System .......... 53899
Urethra
Transurethral Balloon Dilation .......... 52510
Vaporization
Laser .......... 52648

**Prostatectomy** .......... 52601
Perineal
Partial .......... 55801
Radical .......... 55810-55815
Retropubic
Partial .......... 55831
Radical .......... 55840-55845
Suprapubic
Partial .......... 55821
Transurethral .......... 52612-52614

**Prostate Specific Antigen** .......... 84153-84154, 86316

**Prostatic Abscess**
*See* Abscess, Prostate

**Prostatotomy** .......... 55720-55725

**Prosthesis**
Augmentation
Mandibular Body .......... 21125
Auricular .......... 21086
Breast
Insertion .......... 19340-19342
Removal .......... 19328-19330
Supply .......... 19396
Check-Out .......... 97703
*See* Physical Medicine/Therapy/Occupational Therapy
Cornea .......... 65770
Facial .......... 21088
Hernia
Mesh .......... 49568
Hip
Removal .......... 27090-27091
Intestines .......... 44700
Knee
Insertion .......... 27438, 27445
Lens
Insertion .......... 66983-66985
Manual or Mechanical Technique .......... 66984
Not Associated with Concurrent Cataract Removal .......... 66985
Mandibular Resection .......... 21081
Nasal .......... 21087
Nasal Septum
Insertion .......... 30220
Obturator .......... 21076
Definitive .......... 21080
Interim .......... 21079
Ocular .......... 21077, 65770, 66983-66985, 92330, 92335, 92358, 92393
Fitting and Prescription .......... 92330
Loan .......... 92358
Prescription .......... 92335
Supply .......... 92393
Orbital .......... 21077
Partial or Total .......... 69633, 69637
Ossicle Reconstruction
Chain .......... 69633
Palatal Augmentation .......... 21082
Palatal Lift .......... 21083
Palate .......... 42280-42281

Penile
Insertion ........ 54400-54401, 54405
Removal ........ 54402, 54407
Repair ........ 54407, 54409
Replacement ........ 54402, 54407
Perineum
Removal ........ 53442
Skull Plate
Removal ........ 62142
Replacement ........ 62143
Spectacle
Fitting ........ 92352-92353
Repair ........ 92371
Speech Aid ........ 21084
Spinal
Insertion ........ 22851
Synthetic ........ 69633, 69637
Temporomandibular Joint
Arthroplasty ........ 21243
Testicular
Insertion ........ 54660
Training ........ 97520
Urethral Sphincter
Removal ........ 53447
Wrist
Removal ........ 25250-25251

**Protease F**
*See* Plasmin

**Proctectomy**
Total ........ 45119-45120

**Protein**
C-Reactive ........ 86140
Glycated ........ 82985
Myelin Basic ........ 83873
Osteocalcin ........ 83937
Prealbumin ........ 84134
Serum ........ 84160-84165
Total ........ 84155
Western Blot ........ 84181-84182, 88372

**Protein Analysis, Tissue**
Western Blot ........ 88371

**Protein Blotting**
*See* Western Blot

**Protein C Activator** ........ 85337

**Protein C Antigen** ........ 85302

**Protein C Assay** ........ 85303

**Protein S**
Assay ........ 85306
Total ........ 85305

**Prothrombase**
*See* Thrombokinase

**Prothrombin** ........ 85210

**Prothrombinase**
*See* Thromboplastin

**Prothrombin Time** ........ 85610-85611

**Prothrombokinase** ........ 85230

**Protime**
*See* Prothrombin Time

**Proton Beam Delivery**
Single Area ........ 77520
Two Areas ........ 77523

**Protoporphyrin** ........ 84202-84203

**Protozoa**
Antibody ........ 86753

**Provitamin A**
*See* Vitamin, A

**Provocation Test**
for Allergies ........ 95078
*See* Allergy Tests
for Glaucoma ........ 92140

**Provocation Tonography** ........ 92130

**Prower Factor**
*See* Stuart-Prower Factor

**PSA**
*See* Prostate Specific Antigen

**Pseudocyst, Pancreas**
*See* Pancreas, Pseudocyst

**PSG**
*See* Polysomnography

**Psoriasis Treatment** ........ 96910-96913
*See* Dermatology; Photochemotherapy

**Psychiatric Diagnosis**
Evaluation of Records or Reports ........ 90885
Interventional Evaluation
Interactive ........ 90802
Interview and Evaluation ........ 90802
Psychological Testing ........ 96100
Unlisted Services and Procedures ........ 90899

**Psychiatric Treatment**
*See* Psychotherapy
Biofeedback Training ........ 90875-90876
Consultation with Family ........ 90887
Drug Management ........ 90862
Electroconvulsive Therapy ........ 90870-90871
Environmental Intervention ........ 90882
Family ........ 90846-90849
Group ........ 90853, 90857
Hypnotherapy ........ 90880
Individual
Insight-Oriented
Hospital or Residential
Care ........ 90816-90822
Office or Outpatient ........ 90804-90809
Interactive
Hospital or Residential
Care ........ 90823-90829
Office or Outpatient ........ 90810-90815
Narcosynthesis Analysis ........ 90865
Psychoanalysis ........ 90845
Report Preparation ........ 90889
Residential
Facility Care ........ 90816-90829
Unlisted Services and Procedures ........ 90899

**Psychoanalysis** ........ 90845

**Psychophysiologic Feedback**
*See* Biofeedback

**Psychotherapy**
Family ........ 90846-90849
Group ........ 90853, 90857
Insight-Oriented
Hospital or Residential
Care ........ 90816-90822
Office or Outpatient ........ 90804-90809
Interactive
Hospital or Residential
Care ........ 90823-90829
Office or Outpatient ........ 90810-90815

**PTA** ........ 85270

**PTA (Factor XI)**
*See* Clotting Factor

**PTC**
*See* Christmas Factor

**PTCA**
*See* Percutaneous Transluminal Angioplasty

**PTC Factor** ........ 85250

**Pteroylglutamic Acid**
*See* Folic Acid

**Pterygium**
Excision ........ 65420
with Graft ........ 65426

**Pterygomaxillary Fossa**
Incision ........ 31040

**Pterygopalatine Ganglion**
*See* Sphenopalatine Ganglion

**PTH**
*See* Parathormone

**Ptosis**
*See* Blepharoptosis; Procidentia

**PTT**
*See* Thromboplastin, Partial, Time

**Ptyalectasis**
*See* Dilation, Salivary Duct

**Pubic Symphysis** ........ 27282

**Pubis**
Craterization ........ 27070
Cyst
Excision ........ 27065-27067
Excision ........ 27070
Saucerization ........ 27070
Tumor
Excision ........ 27065-27067

**Pudendal Nerve**
Avulsion ........ 64761
Destruction ........ 64630
Incision ........ 64761
Injection
Anesthetic ........ 64430
Neurolytic ........ 64630
Transection ........ 64761

# Q



# R

**Radioactive Substance**
Insertion
Kidney ....................50578
Prostate ....................55860
Ureteral Endoscopic ..........50978
Urethral Endoscopic ..........50959

**Radiocarpal Joint**
Arthrotomy ....................25040
Dislocation
Closed Treatment ............25660

**Radiocinematographies**
*See* Cineradiography

**Radioelement**
Application ...............77761-77778
Surface ....................77789
with Ultrasound ..............76965
Handling ......................77790
Infusion .......................77750

**Radioelement Substance**
Catheterization ..................55859
Catheter Placement
Bronchus ...................31643

**Radiography**
*See* Radiology, Diagnostic; X-Ray

**Radioimmunosorbent Test**
*See* Gammaglobulin, Blood

**Radioisotope Brachytherapy**
*See* Brachytherapy

**Radioisotope Scan**
*See* Nuclear Medicine

**Radiological Marker**
Preoperative Placement
Excision of Breast
Lesion .................19125-19126

**Radiology**
Diagnostic
Unlisted Services and
Procedures ..................76499
Examination .....................70030
Stress Views ................76006
Therapeutic
*See* Specific Procedure
Field Set-up ...........77280-77290
Planning ........77261-77263, 77299
Port Film ....................77417

**Radionuclide CAT Scan**
*See* Emission Computerized Tomography

**Radionuclide Imaging**
*See* Nuclear Medicine

**Radionuclide Therapy**
Intra-articular ..................79440
Intravascular ....................79420
Leukemia ......................79100
Other .........................79400
Polycythemia Vera ................79100
Thyroid Gland .......79000-79001, 79020, 79030, 79035
Unlisted Services and Procedures ...79999

**Radionuclide Tomography, Single-Photon Emission-Computed**
*See* SPECT

**Radiopharmaceutical Therapy**
Heart .........................79440
Intravascular ...................79420
Leukemia ......................79100
Other .........................79400
Polycythemia Vera ...............79100
Thyroid Gland .......79020, 79030, 79035
Unlisted Services and Procedures ...79999

**Radiotherapeutic**
*See* Radiation Therapy

**Radiotherapies**
*See* Irradiation

**Radiotherapy, Surface**
*See* Application, Radioelement, Surface

**Radioulnar Joint**
Arthrodesis
with Resection of Ulna .........25830
Dislocation
Closed Treatment .............25675
Open Treatment ...............25676

**Radius**
*See* Arm, Lower; Elbow; Ulna
Arthroplasty ....................24365
with Implant ...........24366, 25441
Craterization ..............24145, 25151
Cyst
Excision .........24125-24126, 25120, 25125-25126
Diaphysectomy ...........24145, 25151
Dislocation
Partial ......................24640
Subluxate ..................24640
with Fracture
Closed Treatment ...........24620
Open Treatment .............24635
Excision ...........24130, 24136, 24145, 24152-24153
Epiphyseal Bar ................20150
Partial .....................25145
Styloid Process ..............25230
Fracture .......................25605
Closed Treatment .......25500, 25505, 25520, 25600, 25605
without Manipulation ........25600
with Manipulation ..........25605
Distal ..........25600, 25605, 25611
Open Treatment .............25620
Head/Neck
Closed Treatment ......24650-24655
Open Treatment .......24665-24666
Open Treatment .............25515, 25525-25526, 25574
Percutaneous Fixation ..........25611
Shaft ...........25500, 25505, 25515, 25520, 25525-25526
Open Treatment .............25574
with Ulna ..............25560, 25565
Open Treatment .............25575
Implant
Removal .....................24164
Incision and Drainage .............25035
Osteomyelitis .............24136, 24145
Osteoplasty ...............25390-25393
Prophylactic Treatment ......25490, 25492
Repair
Epiphyseal Arrest .......25450, 25455
Epiphyseal Separation
Closed .....................25600
Closed with Manipulation .....25605
Open Treatment .............25620
Percutaneous Fixation ........25611
Malunion or Nonunion ...25400, 25415
Osteotomy ............25350, 25355, 25370, 25375
and Ulna ...................25365
with Graft .............25405, 25420, 25425-25426
Saucerization .............24145, 25151
Sequestrectomy ...........24136, 25145
Tumor
Cyst ........................24120
Excision .........24125-24126, 25120, 25125-25126, 25170

**Ramstedt Operation**
*See* Pyloromyotomy

**Ramus Anterior, Nervus Thoracicus**
*See* Intercostal Nerve

**Range of Motion Test**
Extremities or Trunk ..............95851
Eye ......................92018-92019
Hand ..........................95852

**Rapid Heart Rate**
*See* Tachycardia

**Rapid Plasma Reagin Test** .....................86592-86593

**Rapid Test for Infection** ...............86403-86406

**Rapoport Test** ................52005

**Raskind Procedure** ......33735-33737

**Rathke Pouch Tumor**
*See* Craniopharyngioma

**Rat Typhus**
*See* Murine Typhus

**Rays, Roentgen**
*See* X-Ray

**Raz Procedure** ...............51845
*See* Repair, Bladder, Neck

**RBC**
*See* Red Blood Cell (RBC)

## RBC ab


*See* Antibody, Red Blood Cell


## Reaction


Lip
without Reconstruction .........40530


## Reaction, Polymerase Chain


*See* Polymerase Chain Reaction


## Realignment


Femur
with Osteotomy ...............27454
Knee
Extensor .....................27422


## Receptor


*See* CD4; Estrogen, Receptor; FC Receptor; Progesterone Receptors


## Receptor Assay


Hormone ..................84233-84235
Non Hormone ..................84238


## Recession


Gastrocnemius
Leg, Lower ...................27687


## Reconstruction


*See* Revision
Acetabulum ...............27120, 27122
Anal
Congenital Absence .....46730, 46735, 46740
Fistula .....................46742
Graft .......................46753
Sphincter . . .46750-46751, 46760-46762
with Implant ................46762
Ankle ....................27700-27703
Apical-Aortic Conduit ............33404
Atrial ..........................33253
Auditory Canal, External .....69310, 69320
Bile Duct
Anastomosis ................47800
Bladder
and Urethra ............51800-51820
from Colon ...................50810
from Intestines .........50820, 51960
Breast ...................19357-19369
Augmentation ...........19324-19325
Mammoplasty ..........19318-19325
Nipple .................19350-19355
Revision .....................19380
Transverse Rectus Abdominis
Myocutaneous Flap ......19367-19369
with Free Flap ...............19364
with Latissimus Dorsi Flap ......19361
with Other Techniques ..........19366
with Tissue Expander ..........19357
Bronchi .........................32501
Graft Repair ..................31770
Stenosis .....................31775
Canthus .........................67950
Cheekbone .......................21270
Chest Wall
Omental Flap ................49905
Trauma ......................32820
Cleft Palate ...............42200-42225
Conduit
Apical-Aortic .................33404
Conjunctiva ..............68320-68335
with Flap
Bridge or Partial .............68360
Total .......................68362
Cranial Bone
Extracranial ............21181-21184
Ear, Middle
Tympanoplasty without
Mastoidectomy ...............69631
with Ossicular Chain
Reconstruction ........69632-69633
Tympanoplasty with Antrotomy or
Mastoidotomy
with Ossicular Chain
Reconstruction ........69636-69637
Tympanoplasty with
Mastoidectomy ...............69641
Radical or Complete ....69644-69645
with Intact or Reconstructed
Wall ................69643-69644
with Ossicular Chain
Reconstruction ..............69642
Elbow .........................24360
Total Replacement ............24363
with Implant ............24361-24362
Esophagus ...............43300, 43310
Creation
Stoma .........43350, 43351, 43352
Esophagostomy ..............43350
Fistula ...............43305, 43312
Gastrointestinal .........43360-43361
Eyelid
Canthus .....................67950
Second Stage ................67975
Total ..................67973-67975
Total Eyelid
Lower, One Stage ...........67973
Upper, One State ...........67974
Transfer Tarsoconjunctival Flap from
Opposing Eyelid ..............67971
Facial Bones
Secondary ..................21275
Fallopian Tube
*See* Repair
Femur
Lengthening ...........27466, 27468
Shortening ............27465, 27468
Fibula
Lengthening .................27715
Finger
Supernumerary ..............26587
Foot
Cleft .......................28360
Forehead ......21172-21180, 21182-21184
Glenoid Fossa ...................21255
Gums
Alveolus ....................41874
Gingiva .....................41872
Hand
Tendon Pulley ...............26500, 26502, 26504
Toe to Finger Transfer ....26551-26556
Heart
Atrial .......................33253
Atrial Septum ...........33735-33737
Pulmonary Artery Shunt ........33924
Vena Cava ..................34502
Hip
Replacement ...........27130, 27132
Secondary .......27134, 27137-27138
Hip Joint
with Prosthesis ...............27125
Interphalangeal Joint ........26535-26536
Collateral Ligament ............26545
Intestines, Small
Anastomosis .................44130
Knee .....................27437-27438
Femur ..........27442-27443, 27446
Ligament ..............27427-27429
Replacement ................27447
Revision ..............27486-27487
Tibia ............27440-27443, 27446
with Prosthesis .........27438, 27445
Kneecap
Instability .............27420-27424
Larynx
Burns .......................31588
Cricoid Split .................31587
Other .......................31588
Stenosis .....................31582
Web ........................31580
Lip ...............40525, 40527, 40761
Lunate ..........................25444
Malar Augmentation
Prosthetic Material ............21270
with Bone Graft ..............21210
Mandible
with Implant ..........21244-21246, 21248-21249
Mandibular Condyle ..............21247
Mandibular Rami
without Bone Graft ............21193
without Internal Rigid Fixation . . .21195
with Bone Graft ..............21194
with Internal Rigid Fixation ......21196
Maxilla
with Implant ..........21245-21246, 21248-21249
Metacarpophalangeal
Joint ....................26530-26531
Midface
Forehead Advancement . . .21159-21160
without Bone Graft ......21141-21143
with Bone Graft . . .21145-21160, 21188
Mouth ..............40840, 40842-40845
Nail Bed .........................11762

Stricture
  Excision ....................45150
Suture
  Fistula ................45800-45825
  Prolapse ..............45540-45541
Tumor
  Destruction ...........45190, 45320, 46937-46938
  Excision ..............45160, 45170
Unlisted Services and Procedures ...45999

**Reductase, Glutathione**
*See* Glutathione Reductase

**Reductase, Lactic Cytochrome**
*See* Lactic Dehydrogenase

**Reduction**
Forehead ................21137-21139
Lung Volume ....................32491
Mammoplasty ...................19318
Masseter Muscle/Bone ......21295-21296
Osteoplasty
  Facial Bones ................21209
Pregnancy
  Multifetal ...................59866
Skull
  Craniomegalic ..........62115-62117

**Red Blood Cell (RBC)**
Antibody .................86850-86870
  Pretreatment ..........86970-86972
Count ..........................85041
Fragility
  Mechanical ..................85547
  Osmotic ..............85555-85557
Hematocrit ......................85014
Iron Utilization ..................78170
Morphology ......................85007
Platelet Estimation ...............85007
Sedimentation Rate
  Automated ...................85652
  Manual .......................85651
Sequestration ....................78140
Sickling .........................85660
Survival Test ..............78130-78135
Volume Determination .......78120-78121

**Red Blood Cell ab**
*See* Antibody, Red Blood Cell

**Reflex Test**
Blink Reflex .....................95933
H-Reflex ................95934, 95936

**Reflux Study** .................78262

**Refraction** ....................92015

**Rehabilitation**
Aural ..........................92510
Cardiac ..................93797-93798

**Rehabilitative**
*See* Rehabilitation

**Rehfuss Test**
*See* Gastroenterology, Diagnostic, Stomach

**Reichstein's Substance S**
*See* Deoxycortisol

**Reimplantation**
Arteries
  Carotid ..........35691, 35694-35695
  Subclavian .............35693-35695
  Vertebral ..............35691, 35693
Kidney ..........................50380
Ovary ...........................58825
Pulmonary Artery .................33788
Ureters ..........................51565
Ureter, to Bladder ...........50780-50785

**Reinnervation**
Larynx
  Neuromuscular Pedicle .........31590

**Reinsch Test** .................83015

**Reinsertion**
Implantable Contraceptive
Capsules .......................11977
Spinal Fixation Device .............22849

**Relative Density**
*See* Specific Gravity

**Release**
Carpal Tunnel ...................64721
Elbow Contracture
  with Radical Release of
  Capsule ......................24149
Flexor Muscles
  Hip ..........................27036
Muscle
  Knee .........................27422
Nerve ...................64702-64726
  Neurolytic ...................64727
Retina
  Encircling Material ...........67115
Spinal Cord .....................63200
Stapes ..........................69650
Tarsal Tunnel ....................28035
Tendon ..........................25295

**Release-Inhibiting Hormone, Somatotropin**
*See* Somatostatin

**Removal**
Balloon
  Intra-Aortic ..................33974
Balloon Assist Device
  Intra-Aortic ...........33968, 33971
Blood Clot
  Eye ..........................65930
Blood Component
  Apheresis .............36520-36521
Breast
  Capsules ....................19371
  Implants ...............19328-19330
  Modified Radical .............19240
  Partial ................19140-19162
  Radical ...............19200-19220
  Simple, Complete .............19180
  Subcutaneous ................19182
Calcareous Deposits
  Subdeltoid ...................23000
Calculi (Stone)
  Bile Duct ........43264, 47420, 47425
    Percutaneous .........47554, 47630
  Bladder .........51050, 52310-52315, 52317-52318
  Gallbladder ..................47480
  Hepatic Duct .................47400
  Kidney ..........50060-50081, 50130, 50561, 50580
  Pancreas .....................48020
  Pancreatic Duct ...............43264
  Salivary Gland ..........42330-42340
  Ureter ....50610-50630, 50961, 50980, 51060-51065, 52320-52330, 52336-52337
  Urethra ...............52310-52315
Cardiac Event Recorder ............33284
Cast .........29700, 29705, 29710, 29715
Cataract
  with Replacement
    Not Associated with
    Concurrent .................66983
    Extracapsular ...............66984
    Intracapsular ...............66983
Catheter
  Fractured ....................75961
  Peritoneum ..................49422
  Spinal Cord ..................62355
Cerclage
  Cervix .......................59871
Cerumen
  Auditory Canal, External ........69210
Clot
  Pericardium ..................33020
    Endoscopic .................32658
Comedones ......................10040
Contraceptive Capsules ......11976-11977
Cranial Tongs ....................20665
Cyst ............................10040
Dacryolith
  Lacrimal Duct ................68530
  Lacrimal Gland ...............68530
Defibrillator
  Heart ........................33244
    Pulse Generator Only .........33241
    via Thoracotomy .............33243
Ear Wax
  Auditory Canal, External ........69210
Electrode
  Brain .................61535, 61880
  Heart ........................33238
  Nerve ........................64585
  Spinal Cord ..................63660
Embolus
  *See* Embolectomy
External Fixation System ...........20694

Eye
Bone ....67414, 67445
Ocular Contents
without Implant ....65091
with Implant ....65093
Orbital Contents Only ....65110
without Implant ....65101
with Bone ....65112
with Implant
Muscles Attached ....65105
Muscles, Not Attached ....65103
with Muscle or Myocutaneous Flap ....65114
Fallopian Tube
Laparoscopy ....58661
Fat
Lipectomy ....15876-15879
Fecal Impaction
Rectum ....45915
Fibrin Deposit ....32150
Fixation Device ....20670-20680
Foreign Bodies ....65205-65265
Anal ....46608
Ankle Joint ....27610, 27620
Arm
Lower ....25248
Upper ....24200-24201
Auditory Canal, External ....69200
with Anesthesia ....69205
Bile Duct ....43269
Bladder ....52310-52315
Brain ....61570
Bronchi ....31635
Colon ....44025, 44390, 45379
Colon-Sigmoid ....45332
Conjunctival Embedded ....65210
Cornea
without Slit Lamp ....65220
with Slit Lamp ....65222
Duodenum ....44010
Elbow ....24000, 24101, 24200-24201
Esophagus ....43020, 43045, 43215, 74235
External Eye ....65205
Eyelid ....67938
Finger ....26075, 26080
Foot ....28190-28193
Gastrointestinal, Upper ....43247
Gum ....41805
Hand ....26070
Hip ....27033, 27086-27087
Hysteroscopy ....58562
Interphalangeal Joint
Toe ....28024
Intertarsal Joint ....28020
Intestines, Small ....44020, 44363
Intraocular ....65235
Kidney ....50561, 50580
Knee Joint ....27310, 27331, 27372
Lacrimal Duct ....68530
Lacrimal Gland ....68530
Larynx ....31511, 31530-31531, 31577
Leg, Upper ....27372
Lung ....32151
Mandible ....41806
Mediastinum ....39000-39010
Metatarsophalangeal Joint ....28022
Mouth ....40804-40805
Muscle ....20520-20525
Nose ....30300
Anesthesia ....30310
Lateral Rhinotomy ....30320
Orbit ....61334, 67413, 67430
without Bone Flap ....67413
with Bone Flap ....67430
Pancreatic Duct ....43269
Patella
*See* Patellectomy
Pelvis ....27086-27087
Penile Tissue ....54115
Penis ....54115
Pericardium ....33020
Endoscopic ....32658
Peritoneum ....49085
Pharynx ....42809
Pleura ....32150-32151
Endoscopic ....32653
Posterior Segment
Magnetic Extraction ....65260
Nonmagnetic Extraction ....65265
Rectum ....45307, 45915
Scrotum ....55120
Shoulder ....23040-23044
Complicated ....23332
Deep ....23331
Subcutaneous ....23330
Skin
with Debridement ....11010-11012
Stomach ....43500
Subcutaneous Tissue ....10120-10121
with Debridement ....11010-11012
Tarsometatarsal Joint ....28020
Tendon Sheath ....20520-20525
Toe ....28022
Ureter ....50961, 50980
Urethra ....52310-52315
Uterus ....58562
Vagina ....57415
Wrist ....25040, 25101, 25248
Foreign Body
Elbow ....24101
Hair
Electrolysis ....17380
Halo ....20665
Hearing Aid
Bone Conduction ....69711
Hematoma
Brain ....61312-61315
Implantation ....20670-20680
Ankle ....27704
Contraceptive Capsules ....11976-11977
Elbow ....24160
Eye ....67120-67121
Finger ....26320
Hand ....26320
Radius ....24164
Wrist ....25449
Infusion Pump
Intraarterial ....36262
Intravenous ....36532
Spinal Cord ....62365
Intra-Aortic Balloon ....33974
Assist Device ....33968, 33971
Intrauterine Device (IUD) ....58301
Keel
Laryngoplasty ....31580
Lacrimal Gland
Partial ....68505
Total ....68500
Lacrimal Sac
Excision/(Optional) ....68520
Laryngocele ....31300
Leiomyomata ....58551, 58561
Lens ....66920-66940
Lens Material ....66840-66852
Lesion
Conjunctiva ....68040
Larynx ....31512, 31578
Loose Body
Ankle ....27620
Carpometacarpal Joint ....26070
Elbow ....24101
Interphalangeal Joint
Toe ....28024
Intertarsal Joint ....28020
Knee Joint ....27331
Metatarsophalangeal Joint ....28022
Tarsometatarsal Joint ....28020
Toe ....28022
Wrist ....25101
Lung
Bronchoplasty ....32501
Completion Pneumonectomy ....32488
Cyst ....32140
Extrapleural ....32445
Single Lobe ....32480
Single Segment ....32484
Sleeve Lobectomy ....32486
Sleeve Pneumonectomy ....32442
Total Pneumonectomy ....32440-32445
Two Lobes ....32482
Volume Reduction ....32491
Wedge Resection ....32500
Lymph Nodes
Abdominal ....38747
Inguinofemoral ....38760-38765
Pelvic ....38770
Retroperitoneal
Transabdominal ....38780
Thoracic ....38746
Mammary Implant ....19328-19330
Mastoid
Air Cells ....69670

Thorax ....................35182
Acquired or Traumatic ........35189
Upper Extremity ...............35184
Acquired or Traumatic ........35190
Arteriovenous Malformation
Intracranial .............61680-61692
Intracranial Artery .......61705, 61708
Spinal Artery ................62294
Spinal Cord .............63250-63252
Artery
Angioplasty ............75962-75968
Aorta ................35452, 35472
Axillary ....................35458
Brachiocephalic .........35458, 35475
Bypass Graft ...........35501-35571, 35601-35700
Bypass In-Situ ..........35582-35583, 35585, 35587
Bypass Venous Graft .....33510-33516
Femoral ...............35456, 35474
Iliac .................35454, 35473
Occlusive Disease ......35001, 35005, 35011-35013, 35021, 35045, 35081, 35091, 35102, 35111, 35121, 35131, 35141, 35151, 35161
Popliteal ..............35456, 35474
Pulmonary ...................33690
Renal .......................35450
Renal or Visceral ..............35471
Subclavian ...................35458
Thromboendarterectomy .......35301, 35311, 35321, 35341, 35351-35390
Tibioperoneal ...........35459, 35470
Viscera ...............35450, 35471
Arytenoid Cartilage ...............31400
Atrial Fibrillation ...............33253
Bile Duct .......................47701
Cyst ........................47716
with Intestines ...47760, 47780, 47785
Wound ......................47900
Bladder
Exstrophy ....................51940
Fistula ....44660-44661, 45800, 45805, 51880-51925
Neck ........................51845
Resection .............52340, 52500
Wound ................51860-51865
Blepharoptosis
Frontalis Muscle Technique
with Fascial Sling ............67902
Blood Vessel
Abdomen ....................35221
with Other Graft .............35281
with Vein Graft ..............35251
Chest ................35211-35216
with Other Graft .......35271-35276
with Vein Graft ........35241-35246
Finger .......................35207
Graft Defect ..................35870
Hand ........................35207
Kidney ......................50100
Lower Extremity ..............35226
with Other Graft .............35286
with Vein Graft ..............35256
Neck ........................35201
with Other Graft .............35261
with Vein Graft ..............35231
Upper Extremity ...............35206
with Other Graft .............35266
with Vein Graft ..............35236
Body Cast .......................29720
Brain
Wound ......................61571
Breast
Suspension ..................19316
Bronchi
Fistula ......................32815
Brow Pyrosis ....................67900
Bunion .............28290, 28292-28294, 28296-28299
Bypass Graft ...............35901-35907
Fistula ......................35870
Calcaneus
Osteotomy ...................28300
Cannula .................36860-36861
Cervix
Cerclage ....................57700
Abdominal ...........59320, 59325
Suture ......................57720
Chest Wall ......................32905
Closure .....................32810
Fistula ......................32906
Chin
Augmentation ..........21120, 21123
Osteotomy .............21121-21123
Clavicle
Osteotomy .............23480-23485
Cleft Hand ......................26580
Cleft Lip ......40525, 40527, 40700-40702, 40720, 40761
Nasal Deformity ........40700-40701, 40720, 40761
Cleft Palate
*See* Cleft Palate Repair
Colon
Fistula ...........44650, 44660-44661
Hernia ......................44050
Malrotation ..................44055
Obstruction ..................44050
Cornea
*See* Cornea, Repair
Coronary Chamber Fistula ....33500-33501
Cyst
Bartholin's Gland .............56440
Liver .......................47300
Repair ......................47716
Defibrillator
Heart .......................33242
Diaphragm
for Eventration ................39545
Hernia ................39502-39541
Laceration ...................39501
Ductus Arteriosus ..........33820-33824
Ear, Middle
Oval Window Fistula ...........69666
Round Window Fistula .........69667
Elbow
Fasciotomy .............24350-24356
Hemiepiphyseal Arrest .........24470
Muscle ......................24341
Muscle Transfer ..............24301
Tendon ................24340-24342
Each ......................24341
Tendon Lengthening ...........24305
Tendon Transfer ...............24301
Tennis Elbow ...........24350-24356
Encephalocele ...................62121
Enterocele
Hysterectomy ................58270
Epididymis ................54900-54901
Epispadias ................54380-54390
Esophagus ................43300, 43310
Esophagogastrostomy ..........43320
Esophagojejunostomy ....43340-43341
Fistula ....43305, 43312, 43420, 43425
Fundoplasty ...........43324-43325
Muscle ...............43330-43331
Pre-existing Perforation ........43405
Varices ......................43401
Wound ................43410, 43415
Eye
Ciliary Body .................66680
Suture ....................66682
Conjunctiva ...........65270-65273
Wound ........65270, 65272, 65273
Cornea ......................65275
Astigmatism ..........65772, 65775
with Glue .................65286
Wound .........65275, 65280-65285
Fistula
Lacrimal Gland ..............68770
Iris
Suture ....................66682
with Ciliary Body ............66680
Lacrimal Duct
Canaliculi ..................68700
Lacrimal Punctum .............68705
Retina
Detachment ..........67101, 67105, 67107-67108, 67110, 67112
Sclera
Reinforcement ........67250, 67255
Staphyloma ..........66220, 66225
with Glue .................65286
with Graft .................66225
Wound ..............65286, 66250
Strabismus
Chemodenervation ...........67345
Symblepharon
Division ...................68340
without Graft ...............68330
with Graft .................68335
Trabeculae ...................65855

Vagina
Anterior
*See* Colporrhaphy, Anterior
Cystocele ..............57240, 57260
Enterocele ..................57265
Fistula ...........46715-46716, 51900
Rectovaginal ..........57300-57307
Transvesical and Vaginal Approach ..................57330
Urethrovaginal ........57310-57311
Vesicovaginal .........57320-57330
Hysterectomy ................58267
Incontinence ...........57284, 57288
Pereyra Procedure .............57289
Postpartum ...................59300
Prolapse ...............57282, 57284
Rectocele ..............57250, 57260
Suspension ............57280, 57284
Wound ................57200, 57210
Vaginal Wall Prolapse
*See* Colporrhaphy
Vas Deferens
Suture .......................55400
Vein
Angioplasty ....35460, 35476, 75978
Femoral .....................34501
Graft .......................34520
Pulmonary ...................33730
Transposition ................34510
Vulva
Postpartum ..................59300
Wound
Complex ...............13100-13160
Intermediate ............12031-12057
Simple ................12001-12021
Wound Dehiscence
Complex .....................13160
Simple ................12020-12021
Wrist ........25260, 25263, 25270, 25447
Bone ........................25440
Cartilage ....................25107
Removal
Implant ....................25449
Secondary .......25265, 25272, 25274
Tendon .........25280, 25290, 25295, 25300-25301, 25310-25312, 25315-25316
Total Replacement ............25446

**Repeat Surgeries**
*See* Reoperation

**Replacement**
Arthroplasties, Hip
*See* Arthroplasty, Hip
Aortic Valve ..............33405-33413
Cerebrospinal Fluid Shunt .........62194, 62225, 62230
Contact Lens
*See* Contact Lens Services
Elbow
Total ........................24363
Electrode
Heart ......33210-33211, 33216-33217
Eye
Drug Delivery System ..........67121
Gastrostomy Tube ................43760
Hearing Aid
Bone Conduction ..............69710
Hip .......................27130, 27132
Revision .........27134, 27137-27138
Knee
Total ........................27447
Mitral Valve .....................33430
Nephrostomy Tube
*See* Nephrostomy, Change Tube
Nerve ..........................64726
Ossicles
with Prosthesis .........69633, 69637
Ossicular Replacement
*See* TORP (Total Ossicular Replacement Prosthesis)
Pacemaker ................33206-33208
Catheter .....................33210
Electrode ...33210-33211, 33216-33217
Pacing Cardioverter-Defibrillator
Pulse Generator Only ..........33241
Leads ..................33243-33244
Penile
Prosthesis .............54402, 54407
Prosthesis
Skull ........................62143
Pulmonary Valve ................33475
Skull Plate .....................62143
Spinal Cord
Reservoir ....................62360
Tissue Expanders
Skin ........................11970
Total Replacement
*See* Hip, Total Replacement
Tricuspid Valve .................33465
Ureter
with Intestines ...............50840

**Replantation**
Arm, Upper .....................20802
Digit ....................20816-20822
Foot ...........................20838
Forearm ........................20805
Hand ...........................20808
Thumb ...................20824-20827

**Report Preparation**
Extended, Medical ...............99080
Psychiatric .....................90889

**Reposition**
Toe to Hand ..............26551-26556

**Repositioning**
Central Venous Catheter ...........36493
Electrode
Heart .................33216-33217
Gastrostomy Tube ................43761
Heart
Defibrillator
Leads ...............33216, 33249
Intraocular Lens .................66825
Tricuspid Valve ..................33468

**Reptilase Test** ................85635

**Reptilase Time**
*See* Thrombin Time

**Resection**
Aortic Valve
Stenosis .....................33415
Bladder ........................52340
Bladder Diverticulum ..............52305
Bladder Neck
Transurethral .................52500
Brain Lobe
*See* Lobectomy, Brain
Diaphragm ................39560-39561
Endaural
*See* Ear, Inner, Excision
Humeral Head ...................23195
Intestines, Small
Laparoscopic .................44202
Lung ....................32520-32525
Mouth
with Tongue Excision ..........41153
Myocardium
Aneurysm ...................33542
Septal Defect ................33545
Nasal Septum Submucous
*See* Nasal Septum, Submucous Resection
Nose
Septum .....................30520
Ovary, Wedge
*See* Overy, Wedge Resection
Palate .........................42120
Phalangeal Head
Toe ........................28153
Prostate Transurethral
*See* Prostatectomy, Transurethral
Radical
Arm, Upper ..................24077
Elbow .......................24077
with Contracture Release .....24149
Foot ........................28046
Humerus ...............24150-24151
Radius ................24152-24153
Tumor
Ankle ......................27615
Calcaneus or Talus ..........27647
Clavicle ....................23200
Femur ......................27365
Fibula ......................27646
Humerus ....................23220
Humerus with Autograft ......23221
Humerus with Prosthetic Replacement ...............23222
Knee ...............27329, 27365
Leg, Lower .................27615

**Rhinectomy**
Partial ... 30150
Total ... 30160

**Rhinomanometry** ... 92512

**Rhinopharynx**
*See* Nasopharynx

**Rhinophyma**
Repair ... 30120

**Rhinoplasty**
Cleft Lip/Cleft Palate ... 30460-30462
Primary ... 30400-30420
Secondary ... 30430-30450

**Rhinoscopy**
*See* Endoscopy, Nose

**Rhinotomy**
Lateral ... 30118, 30320

**Rhizotomy** ... 63185, 63190

**Rho Variant Du** ... 86905

**Rhytidectomy** ... 15824-15829

**Rhytidoplasties**
*See* Face Lift

**Rh Immune Globulin**
*See* Immune Globulins, Rho (D)

**Rib**
Excision ... 21600-21616, 32900
Fracture
  Closed Treatment ... 21800
  External Fixation ... 21810
  Open Treatment ... 21805
Graft
  to Face ... 21230
Resection ... 32900
X-Ray ... 71100-71111

**Riboflavin** ... 84252

**Richardson Operation Hysterectomy**
*See* Hysterectomy, Abdominal, Total

**Richardson Procedure** ... 53460

**Ridell Operation**
*See* Sinusotomy, Frontal

**Ridge, Alveolar**
*See* Alveolar Ridge

**Right Atrioventricular Valve**
*See* Tricuspid Valve

**Right Heart Cardiac Catheterization**
*See* Cardiac Catheterization, Right Heart

**Ripstein Operation**
*See* Proctopexy

**Risk Factor Reduction Intervention**
*See* Preventive Medicine

**Risser Jacket** ... 29010-29015
Removal ... 29710

**Rocky Mountain Spotted Fever** ... 86000

**Roentgenographic**
*See* X-Ray

**Roentgenography**
*See* Radiology, Diagnostic

**Roentgen Rays**
*See* X-Ray

**Ropes Test** ... 83872

**Rorschach Test** ... 96100

**Ross Procedure** ... 33413

**Rotation Flap**
*See* Skin, Adjacent Tissue Transfer

**Rotator Cuff**
Repair ... 23410-23412, 23415-23420

**Rotavirus**
Antibody ... 86759
Antigen Detection
  Enzyme Immunoassay ... 87425

**Rotavirus Vaccine**

**Round Window**
Repair Fistula ... 69667

**Round Window Fistula**
*See* Fistula, Round Window

**Roux-En-Y Procedure** ... 43621, 43633-43634, 43846, 47740-47741, 47780, 47785, 48540

**RPR** ... 86592-86593

**RSV**
*See* Immune Globulins; Respiratory Syncytial Virus

**RT3**
*See* Triiodothyronine, Reverse

**Rubbing Alcohol**
*See* Isopropyl Alcohol

**Rubella**
Antibody ... 86762
Vaccine ... 90706, 90709

**Rubella/Mumps**
*See* Vaccines

**Rubella HI Test**
*See* Hemagglutination Inhibition Test

**Rubeola**
Antibody ... 86765

**Rubeolla**
*See* Rubeola

**Russell Viper Venom Time** ... 85612-85613


# S


**Sac, Endolymphatic**
*See* Endolymphatic Sac

**Saccomanno Technique** ... 88108

**Sacroiliac Joint**
Arthrodesis ... 27280
Arthrotomy ... 27050
Biopsy ... 27050
Dislocation
  Open Treatment ... 27218
Fusion ... 27280
Injection for Arthrography ... 27096
X-Ray ... 72200-72202, 73542

**Sacrum**
Tumor
  Excision ... 49215
X-Ray ... 72220

**Sahli Test**
*See* Gastroenterology, Diagnostic, Stomach

**Salabrasion** ... 15810-15811

**Salicylate**
Assay ... 80196

**Saline-Solution Abortion**
*See* Abortion, Induced, by Saline

**Saline Load Test** ... 91060

**Salivary Duct**
Catheterization ... 42660
Dilation ... 42650, 42660
Ligation ... 42665
Repair ... 42500, 42505
  Fistula ... 42600

**Salivary Glands**
Abscess
  Incision and Drainage ... 42310, 42320
Biopsy ... 42405
Calculi (Stone)
  Excision ... 42330, 42335, 42340
Cyst
  Creation
    Fistula ... 42325-42326
  Drainage ... 42409
  Excision ... 42408
Injection
  X-Ray ... 42550
Needle Biopsy ... 42400
Nuclear Medicine
  Function Study ... 78232
  Imaging ... 78230-78231
Parotid
  Abscess ... 42300, 42305

Unlisted Services and Procedures . . . 42699
X-Ray . . . . . . . . . . 70380-70390
with Contrast . . . . . . . . 70390

**Salivary Gland Virus**
*See* Cytomegalovirus

**Salmonella**
Antibody . . . . . . . . . . 86768

**Salpingectomy** . . . . . . 58262-58263, 58661, 58700
Ectopic Pregnancy
Laparoscopic Treatment . . . . . . 59151
Surgical Treatment . . . . . . 59120
Oophorectomy . . . . . . . . 58943

**Salpingo-Oophorectomy** . . . . . . 58720
Resection Ovarian
Malignancy . . . . . . . . 58950-58952

**Salpingohysterostomy**
*See* Implantation, Tubouterine

**Salpingolysis** . . . . . . . . 58740

**Salpingoneostomy** . . . . . . 58673, 58770

**Salpingoplasty**
*See* Fallopian Tube, Repair

**Salpingostomy** . . . . . . . 58673, 58770
Laparoscopic . . . . . . . . . 58673

**Salter Osteotomy of the Pelvis**
*See* Osteotomy, Pelvis

**Sampling**
*See* Biopsy; Brush Biopsy; Needle Biopsy

**Sang-Park Procedure** . . . 33735-33737

**Sao Paulo Typhus**
*See* Rocky Mountain Spotted Fever

**Saucerization**
Calcaneus . . . . . . . . . . 28120
Clavicle . . . . . . . . . . 23180
Femur . . . . . . . . . . 27070, 27360
Fibula . . . . . . . . . . 27360, 27641
Hip . . . . . . . . . . 27070
Humerus . . . . . . . . . . 23184, 24140
Ileum . . . . . . . . . . 27070
Metacarpal . . . . . . . . . . 26230
Metatarsal . . . . . . . . . . 28122
Olecranon Process . . . . . . . . 24147
Phalanges
Finger . . . . . . . . . . 26235-26236
Toe . . . . . . . . . . 28124
Pubis . . . . . . . . . . 27070
Radius . . . . . . . . . . 24145, 25151
Scapula . . . . . . . . . . 23182
Talus . . . . . . . . . . 28120
Tarsal . . . . . . . . . . 28122
Tibia . . . . . . . . . . 27360, 27640
Ulna . . . . . . . . . . 24147, 25150

**Saundby Test**
*See* Blood, Feces

**Scalenotomy**
*See* Muscle Division, Scalenus Anticus

**Scalenus Anticus**
Division . . . . . . . . . . 21700-21705

**Scaling**
*See* Exfoliation

**Scalp**
Tumor Resection
Radical . . . . . . . . . . 21015

**Scalp Blood Sampling** . . . . . . . 59030

**Scan**
*See* Specific Site, Nuclear Medicine
C.A.T.
*See* C.A.T. Scan
Abdomen
*See* Abdomen, C.A.T. Scan
MRI
*See* Magnetic Resonance Imaging
PET
*See* Positron Emission Tomography
Radionuclide
*See* Emission Computerized Tomography

**Scanning, Radioisotope**
*See* Nuclear Medicine

**Scanogram** . . . . . . . . . . 76040

**Scaphoid**
Arthroplasty
with Implant . . . . . . . . . . 25443
Fracture
Closed Treatment . . . . . . . . 25622
Open Treatment . . . . . . . . 25628
with Manipulation . . . . . . . . 25624
Repair . . . . . . . . . . 25440

**Scapula**
Craterization . . . . . . . . . . 23182
Cyst
Excision . . . . . . . . . . 23140
with Allograft . . . . . . . . 23146
with Autograft . . . . . . . . 23145
Diaphysectomy . . . . . . . . . . 23182
Excision . . . . . . . . . . 23172, 23190
Partial . . . . . . . . . . 23182
Fracture
Closed Treatment
without Manipulation . . . . . . . 23570
with Manipulation . . . . . . . 23575
Open Treatment . . . . . . . . 23585
Ostectomy . . . . . . . . . . 23190
Repair
Fixation . . . . . . . . . . 23400
Scapulopexy . . . . . . . . . . 23400
Saucerization . . . . . . . . . . 23182
Sequestrectomy . . . . . . . . . . 23172
Tumor
Excision . . . . . . . . . . 23140, 23210
with Allograft . . . . . . . . 23146
with Autograft . . . . . . . . 23145
Radical Resection . . . . . . . . 23210
X-Ray . . . . . . . . . . 73010

**Scapulopexy** . . . . . . . . . . 23400

**Scarification**
Pleural . . . . . . . . . . 32215

**Scarification of Pleura**
*See* Pleurodesis

**Schanz Operation**
*See* Femur, Osteotomy

**Schauta Operation**
*See* Hysterectomy, Vaginal, Radical

**Schede Procedure** . . . . . . 32905-32906

**Scheie Procedure**
*See* Iridectomy

**Schilling Test** . . . . . . . . . . 78270
*See* Vitamin B-12 Absorption Study

**Schlatter Operation Total Gastrectomy**
*See* Excision, Stomach, Total

**Schlicter Test** . . . . . . . . . . 87197
*See* Bactericidal Titer, Serum

**Schocket Procedure** . . . . . . . . 66180
*See* Aqueous Shunt

**Schonbein Test**
*See* Blood, Feces

**Schuchard Procedure**
Osteotomy
Maxilla . . . . . . . . . . 21206

**Schwannoma, Acoustic**
*See* Brain, Tumor, Excision

**Sciatic Nerve**
Decompression . . . . . . . . . . 64712
Injection
Anesthetic . . . . . . . . . . 64445
Lesion
Excision . . . . . . . . . . 64786
Neuroma
Excision . . . . . . . . . . 64786
Neuroplasty . . . . . . . . . . 64712
Release . . . . . . . . . . 64712
Repair/Suture . . . . . . . . . . 64858

**Scintigraphy**
*See* Nuclear Medicine
Computed Tomographic
*See* Emission Computerized Tomography

**Scissoring**
Skin Tags . . . . . . . . . . 11200-11201

**Sclera**
Excision
Sclerectomy with Punch or Scissors .......66160
Fistulization
Iridencleisis or Iridotasis .......66165
Sclerectomy with Punch or Scissors with Iridectomy .......66160
Thermocauterization with Iridectomy .......66155
Trabeculectomy ab Externo in Absence of Previous Surgery .......66170
Trephination with Iridectomy .......66150
Incision
Fistulization
Iridencleisis or Iridotasis .......66165
Sclerectomy with Punch or Scissors with Iridectomy .......66160
Thermocauterization with Iridectomy .......66155
Trabeculectomy ab Externo in Absence of Previous Surgery .......66170
Trephination with Iridectomy .......66150
Lesion
Excision .......66130
Repair
Reinforcement
without Graft .......67250
with Graft .......67255
Staphyloma
without Graft .......66220
with Graft .......66225
with Glue .......65286
Wound
Operative .......66250
Tissue Glue .......65286

**Scleral Buckling Operation**
*See* Retina, Repair, Detachment

**Scleral Ectasia**
*See* Staphyloma, Sclera

**Sclerectomy** .......66160

**Sclerotherapy**
Venous .......36468-36471

**Sclerotomy**
*See* Incision, Sclera

**Screening, Drug**
*See* Drug Screen

**Scribner Cannulization** .......36810

**Scrotal Varices**
*See* Varicocele

**Scrotoplasty** .......55175-55180

**Scrotum**
Abscess
Incision and Drainage .......54700, 55100
Excision .......55150
Exploration .......55110
Hematoma
Incision and Drainage .......54700
Removal
Foreign Body .......55120
Repair .......55175-55180
Ultrasound .......76870
Unlisted Services and Procedures .......55899

**Scrub Typhus** .......86000

**Second Look Surgery**
*See* Reoperation

**Second Opinion**
*See* Confirmatory Consultations

**Section**
*See* Decompression
Cesarean
*See* Cesarean Delivery
Cranial Nerve .......61460
Spinal Access .......63191
Dentate Ligament .......63180, 63182
Gasserian Ganglion
Sensory Root .......61450
Medullary Tract .......61470
Mesencephalic Tract .......61480
Nerve Root .......63185, 63190
Spinal Accessory Nerve .......63191
Spinal Cord Tract .......63194-63199
Tentorium Cerebelli .......61440
Vestibular Nerve
Transcranial Approach .......69950
Translabyrinthine Approach .......69915

**Sedation**
with or without Analgesia .......99141-99142

**Seddon-Brookes Procedure** .......24320

**Sedimentation Rate**
Blood Cell
Automated .......85652
Manual .......85651

**Segmentectomy**
Lung .......32484

**Seidlitz Powder Test**
*See* X-Ray, with Contrast

**Selenium** .......84255

**Self Care**
*See* Physical Medicine/Therapy/ Occupational Therapy
Training .......97535

**Sella Turcica**
CAT Scan .......70480, 70481, 70482
X-Ray .......70240

**Semenogelase**
*See* Antigen, Prostate Specific

**Semen Analysis** .......89300-89320
Sperm Analysis
Antibodies .......89325
with Sperm Isolation .......89260-89261

**Semicircular Canal**
Incision
Fenestration .......69820
Revised .......69840

**Semilunar**
Bone
*See* Lunate
Ganglion
*See* Gasserian Ganglion

**Seminal Vesicle**
Cyst
Excision .......55680
Excision .......55650
Incision .......55600-55605
Mullerian Duct
Excision .......55680
Unlisted Services and Procedures .......55899

**Seminal Vesicles**
Vesiculography .......74440
X-Ray with Contrast .......74440

**Seminin**
*See* Antigen, Prostate Specific

**Semiquantitative** .......81005

**Sengstaaken Tamponade**
Esophagus .......43460

**Senning Procedure** .......33774-33777
*See* Repair, Great Arteries; Revision

**Senning Type** .......33774-33777

**Sensitivity Study**
Antibiotic
Agar .......87181
Disc .......87184
Fungus .......87192
Macrotube .......87188
MBC .......87187
MIC .......87186
Microtiter .......87186
Tubercle Bacillus (TB) .......87190

**Sensorimotor Exam** .......92060

**Sensory Nerve**
Common
Repair/Suture .......64834

**Sentinel Node**
Injection Procedure .......38792

**Separation**
Craniofacial
Closed Treatment .......21431
Open Treatment .......21432-21436

**Septal Defect**
Repair .......33813-33814

**Septectomy**
Atrial ....................33735-33737
Balloon (Rashkind Type) ........92992
Blade Method (Park) ...........92993
Closed
*See* Septostomy, Atrial
Submucous Nasal
*See* Nasal Septum, Submucous Resection

**Septic Abortion**
*See* Abortion, Septic

**Septoplasty** ..................30520

**Septostomy**
Atrial ....................33735-33737
Balloon (Rashkind Type) ........92992
Blade Method (Park) ...........92993

**Septum, Nasal**
*See* Nasal Septum

**Sequestrectomy**
Carpal .........................25145
Clavicle .........................23170
Humeral Head ..................23174
Humerus ........................24134
Olecranon Process ...............24138
Radius ..................24136, 25145
Scapula ........................23172
Skull ...........................61501
Ulna ....................24138, 25145

**Serialography**
Aorta ..........................75625

**Serodiagnosis, Syphilis**
*See* Serologic Test for Syphilis

**Serologic Test for Syphilis** ................86592-86593

**Seroma**
Incision and Drainage
Skin .........................10140

**Serotonin** ....................84260

**Serum**
Albumin
*See* Albumin, Serum
Antibody Identification
Pretreatment ...........86975-86978
CPK
*See* Creatine Kinase, Total
Serum Immune Globulin .....90281, 90283

**Sesamoidectomy**
Toe ............................28315

**Sesamoid Bone**
Excision .......................28315
Finger
Excision .....................26185
Foot
Fracture ...............28530-28531
Thumb
Excision .....................26185

**Severing of Blepharorrhaphy**
*See* Tarsorrhaphy, Severing

**Sever Procedure**
*See* Contracture, Palm, Release

**Sex-Linked Ichthyoses**
*See* Syphilis Test

**Sex Change Operation**
Female to Male ..................55980
Male to Female .................55970

**Sex Chromatin**
*See* Barr Bodies

**Sex Chromatin Identification** ...........88130, 88140

**Sex Hormone Binding Globulin** ......................84270

**SGOT** .........................84450

**SGPT** .........................84460

**Shaving**
Skin Lesion ................11300-11313

**SHBG**
*See* Sex Hormone Binding Globulin

**Shelf Procedure**
*See* Osteotomy, Hip

**Shigella**
Antibody .......................86771

**Shirodkar Operation**
*See* Repair, Cervix, Cerclage, Abdominal

**Shock Wave, Ultrasonic**
*See* Ultrasound

**Shock Wave Lithotripsy** .......50590

**Shop Typhus of Malaya**
*See* Murine Typhus

**Shoulder**
*See* Clavicle; Scapula
Abscess
Drainage ....................23030
Amputation ...............23900-23921
Arthrocentesis ..................20610
Arthrodesis .....................23800
with Autogenous Graft .........23802
Arthrography
Injection
Radiologic .................23350
Arthroscopy
Diagnostic ...................29815
Surgical ...............29819-29826
Arthrotomy
with Removal Loose or Foreign Body ................23107
Biopsy
Deep .......................23066
Soft Tissue ..................23065
Blade
*See* Scapula
Bone
Excision
Acromion .................23130
Clavicle .............23120-23125
Incision ....................23035
Tumor
Excision .............23140-23146
Bursa
Drainage ....................23031
Capsular Contracture Release ......23020
Cast
Figure Eight .................29049
Removal ....................29710
Spica .......................29055
Velpeau .....................29058
Disarticulation .............23920-23921
Dislocation
Closed Treatment
with Manipulation .....23650-23655
Exploration .....................23107
Hematoma
Drainage ....................23030
Manipulation
Application of Fixation Apparatus ..................23700
Prophylactic Treatment ......23490-23491
Radical Resection ................23077
Removal
Calcareous Deposits ...........23000
Cast .......................29710
Foreign Body
Complicated ................23332
Deep ......................23331
Subcutaneous ...............23330
Foreign or Loose Body ..........23107
Repair
Capsule ...............23450-23466
Ligament Release ............23415
Muscle Transfer .........23395-23397
Rotator Cuff ...........23410-23412, 23415-23420
Tendon ...............23410-23412, 23430-23440
Tenomyotomy ...........23405-23406
Strapping .......................29240
Surgery
Unlisted Services and Procedures ...................23929
Tumor
Excision ...............23075-23077
Unlisted Services and Procedures ...23929
X-Ray ...................73020-73030
X-Ray with Contrast .............73040

**Shoulder Joint**
*See* Clavicle; Scapula
Arthroplasty
with Implant ...........23470-23472
Arthrotomy
with Biopsy ............23100-23101
with Synovectomy .......23105-23106

Dislocation
Open Treatment .23660
with Greater Tuberosity Fracture
Closed Treatment .23665
Open Treatment .23670
with Surgical or Anatomical Neck Fracture
Closed Treatment with Manipulation .23675
Open Treatment .23680
Excision
Torn Cartilage .23101
Exploration .23040-23044
Incision and Drainage .23040-23044
Removal
Foreign Body .23040-23044
X-Ray .73050

**Shunt(s)**
Aqueous
to Extraocular Reservoir .66180
Revision .66185
Arteriovenous
*See* Arteriovenous Shunt
Brain
Creation .62180-62223
Removal .62256, 62258
Replacement .62194, 62225, 62230, 62258
Cerebrospinal Fluid
*See* Cerebrospinal Fluid Shunt
Creation
Arteriovenous
Direct .36821
ECMO .36822
Thomas Shunt .36835
with Graft .36825-36830
Cerebrospinal Fluid .62200
Thomas Shunt .36835
Great Vessel
Aorta
Pulmonary .33924
Aorta to Pulmonary Artery
Ascending .33755
Descending .33762
Central .33764
Subclavian Pulmonary Artery .33750
Vena Cava to Pulmonary Artery .33766-33767
Intra-atrial .33735-33737
LeVeen
*See* LeVeen Shunt
Nonvascular
X-Ray .75809
Peritoneal
Venous
Injection .49427
Ligation .49428
Removal .49429
X-Ray .75809
Pulmonary Artery
*See* Pulmonary Artery, Shunt
Revision
Arteriovenous .36832
Spinal Cord
Creation .63740-63741
Irrigation .63744
Removal .63746
Replacement .63744
Superior Mesenteric-Caval
*See* Anastomosis, Caval to Mesenteric
Ureter to Colon .50815
Ventriculocisternal with Valve
*See* Ventriculocisternostomy

**Shuntogram** .75809

**Sialic Acid** .84275

**Sialodochoplasty** .42500, 42505

**Sialogram**
*See* Sialography

**Sialography** .70390

**Sickling**
Electrophoresis .83020

**Siderocytes** .85535

**Siderophilin**
*See* Transferrin

**Sigmoid**
*See* Colon-Sigmoid

**Sigmoidoscopy**
Ablation
Polyp .45339
Tumor .45339
Biopsy .45331
Collection
Specimen .45331
Exploration .45330
Hemorrhage Control .45334
Removal
Foreign Body .45332
Polyp .45333, 45338
Tumor .45333, 45338
Repair
Volvulus .45337

**Sigmoid Bladder**
Cystectomy .51590

**Signal-Averaged Electrocardiography**
*See* Electrocardiogram

**Silica** .84285

**Silicone**
Contouring Injections .11950-11954

**Silicon Dioxide**
*See* Silica

**Silver Operation**
*See* Keller Procedure

**Silver Procedure** .28290

**Simple Mastectomies**
*See* Mastectomy

**Single Photon Absorptiometry**
*See* Absorptiometry, Single Photon

**Single Photon Emission Computed Tomography**
*See* SPECT

**Sinu, Sphenoid**
*See* Sinuses, Sphenoid

**Sinus**
Ethmoidectomy
Excision .31254
Pilonidal
*See* Cyst, Pilonidal

**Sinusectomy, Ethmoid**
*See* Ethmoidectomy

**Sinuses**
Ethmoid
Excision .31200-31205
with Nasal/Sinus Endoscopy .31254-31255
Repair of Cerebrospinal Leak .31290
Frontal
Destruction .31080-31085
Exploration .31070-31075
with Nasal/Sinus Endoscopy .31276
Fracture
Open Treatment .21343-21344
Incision .31070-31087
Injection .20500
Diagnostic .20501
Maxillary
Antrostomy .31256-31267
Excision .31225-31230
Exploration .31020-31032
with Nasal/Sinus Endoscopy .31233
Incision .31020-31032, 31256-31267
Irrigation .31000
Skull Base .61581
Surgery .61581
Multiple
Incision .31090
Paranasal
Incision .31090
Sphenoid
Biopsy .31050-31051
Exploration .31050-31051
with Nasal/Sinus Endoscopy .31235
Incision .31050-31051
with Nasal/Sinus Endoscopy .31287-31288
Irrigation .31002
Repair of Cerebrospinal Leak .31291
Sinusotomy .31050-31051
Skull Base Surgery .61580-61581
Unlisted Services and Procedures .31299
X-Ray .70210-70220

**STH (Somatotropic Hormone)**
*See* Growth Hormone

**Stimulating Antibody, Thyroid**
*See* Immunoglobulin, Thyroid Stimulating

**Stimulation**
Electric
  *See* Electrical Stimulation
Lymphocyte
  *See* Blastogenesis
Spinal Cord
  Stereotaxis .................. 63610
Transcutaneous Electric
  *See* Application, Neurostimulation

**Stimulator, Long-Acting Thyroid**
*See* Thyrotropin Releasing Hormone (TRH)

**Stimulators, Cardiac**
*See* Heart, Pacemaker

**Stimulus Evoked Response** ... 51792

**Stoffel Operation**
*See* Rhizotomy

**Stoma**
Creation
  Bladder ..................... 51980
  Kidney ................ 50551-50561
  Stomach
    Neonatal ................... 43831
    Temporary ............ 43830-43831
  Ureter ...................... 50860
Ureter
  Endoscopy via .......... 50951-50961

**Stomach**
Anastomosis
  with Duodenum ... 43810, 43850, 43855
  with Jejunum .......... 43820, 43825, 43860, 43865
Biopsy ................... 43600, 43605
Creation
  Stoma
    Temporary ............ 43830-43831
  Temporary Stoma
    Laparoscopic ............... 43653
Excision
  Partial ..... 43631-43635, 43638-43639
  Total .................. 43620-43622
Exploration ..................... 43500
Gastric Bypass .................. 43846
  Revision ...................... 43848
Incision .................. 43830-43832
  Exploration .................. 43500
  Pyloric Sphincter .............. 43520
  Removal
    Foreign Body ................ 43500
Intubation with Specimen Prep ...... 91055
Nuclear Medicine
  Blood Loss Study .............. 78278
  Emptying Study ............... 78264
  Imaging ..................... 78261
  Protein Loss Study ............ 78282
  Reflux Study ................. 78262
  Vitamin B-12
    Absorption ............. 78270-78272
Reconstruction
  for Obesity ............. 43842-43843, 43846-43847
  Roux-En-Y .................. 43846
Removal
  Foreign Body ................. 43500
Repair ......................... 48547
  Fistula ...................... 43880
  Fundoplasty ............ 43324-43325
    Laparoscopic ............... 43280
  Laceration ............. 43501-43502
  Stoma ...................... 43870
  Ulcer ....................... 43501
Saline Load Test ................. 91060
Specimen Collection ........ 89130-89141
Stimulation of Secretion ........... 91052
Suture
  Fistula ...................... 43880
  for Obesity ............. 43842-43843
  Stoma ...................... 43870
  Ulcer ....................... 43840
  Wound ...................... 43840
Tumor
  Excision ............... 43610-43611
Ulcer
  Excision .................... 43610
Unlisted Services and
Procedures ............... 43659, 43999

**Stomatoplasty**
*See* Mouth, Repair

**Stone, Kidney**
*See* Calculus, Removal, Kidney

**Stookey-Scarff Procedure**
*See* Ventriculocisternostomy

**Stool Blood**
*See* Blood, Feces

**Strabismus**
Chemodenervation ............... 67345
Repair
  Adjustable Sutures ............ 67335
  Extraocular Muscles ........... 67340
  One Horizontal Muscle ......... 67311
  One Vertical Muscle ........... 67314
  Posterior Fixation Suture
  Technique ............. 67334-67335
  Previous Surgery, Not Involving
  Extraocular Muscles ........... 67331
  Release Extensive Scar Tissue ... 67343
  Superior Oblique Muscle ....... 67318
  Transposition ................. 67320
  Two Horizontal Muscles ........ 67312
  Two or More Vertical Muscles ... 67316

**Strapping**
*See* Cast; Splint
Ankle ......................... 29540
Back .......................... 29220
Chest ......................... 29200
Elbow ......................... 29260
Finger ........................ 29280
Foot .......................... 29590
Hand .......................... 29280
Hip ........................... 29520
Knee .......................... 29530
Shoulder ...................... 29240
Thorax ........................ 29200
Toes .......................... 29550
Unlisted Services and Procedures ... 29799
Unna Boot ..................... 29580
Wrist ......................... 29260

**Strassman Procedure** ......... 58540

**Streptococcus, Group A**
Antigen Detection
  Enzyme Immunoassay .......... 87430
  Nucleic Acid ........... 87650-87652
Direct Optical Observation ......... 87880

**Streptococcus pneumoniae Vaccine**
*See* Vaccines

**Streptokinase, Antibody** ...... 86590

**Stress Tests**
Cardiovascular ....... 93015-93018, 93024
Multiple Gated Acquisition
(MUGA) ................. 78472-78473
Myocardial Perfusion
Imaging ................. 78460-78465
Pulmonary ............... 94620, 94621
  *See* Pulmonology, Diagnostic

**Stricture**
Repair
  Urethra ............... 53400-53405
Urethra
  *See* Urethral Stenosis

**Stricturoplasty**
Intestines ...................... 44615

**Stroboscopy**
Larynx ......................... 31579

**Strayer Procedure**
Leg, Lower ..................... 27687

**STS** ..................... 86592-86593
*See* Syphilis Test

**Stuart-Prower Factor** ......... 85260

**Study, Color Vision**
*See* Color Vision Examination

**Sturmdorf Procedure** ......... 57520

**Styloidectomy**
Radial ......................... 25230

**Styloid Process**
Radial
Excision .....................25230

**Stypven Time**
*See* Russell Viper Venom Time

**Subacromial Bursa**
Arthrocentesis ...................20610

**Subclavian Arteries**
*See* Artery, Subclavian

**Subcutaneous Injection**
*See* Injection, Subcutaneous

**Subcutaneous Mastectomies**
*See* Mastectomy, Subcutaneous

**Subcutaneous Tissue**
Excision ..................15831-15839

**Subdiaphragmatic Abscess**
*See* Abscess, Subdiaphragmatic

**Subdural Electrode**
Insertion .................61531, 61533
Removal ........................61535

**Subdural Hematonia**
*See* Hematoma, Subdural

**Subdural Puncture** ......61105-61108

**Subdural Tap** ...........61000-61001

**Sublingual Gland**
Abscess
Incision and Drainage ....42310, 42320
Calculi (Stone)
Excision .....................42330
Cyst
Drainage ....................42409
Excision .....................42408
Excision ........................42450

**Subluxation**
Elbow ..........................24640

**Submandibular Gland**
Calculi (Stone)
Excision ...............42330, 42335
Excision ........................42440

**Submaxillary Gland**
Abscess
Incision and Drainage ....42310, 42320

**Submucous Resection of Nasal Septum**
*See* Nasal Septum, Submucous Resection

**Subperiosteal Implant**
Reconstruction
Mandible ..............21245-21246
Maxilla ................21245-21246

**Subphrenic Abscess**
*See* Abscess, Subdiaphragmatic

**Substance S, Reichstein's**
*See* Deoxycortisol

**Subtrochanteric Fracture**
*See* Femur, Fracture, Subtrochanteric

**Sucrose Hemolysis Test**
*See* Red Blood Cell (RBC), Fragility, Osmotic

**Suction Lipectomies**
*See* Liposuction

**Sudiferous Gland**
*See* Sweat Glands

**Sugars** ..................84375-84379

**Sugar Water Test**
*See* Red Blood Cell (RBC), Fragility, Osmotic

**Sugiura Procedure**
*See* Esophagus, Repair, Varices

**Sulfate**
Chondroitin
*See* Chondroitin Sulfate
DHA
*See* Dehydroepiandrosterone Sulfate
Urine ..........................84392

**Sulfation Factor**
*See* Somatomedin

**Sulphates**
*See* Sulfate

**Sumatran Mite Fever**
*See* Scrub Typhus

**Superficial Musculoaponeurotic System (SMAS) Flap**
Rhytidectomy ....................15829

**Supernumerary Digit**
Reconstruction ..................26587
Repair ..........................26587

**Supply**
Chemotherapeutic Agent ..........96545
*See* Chemotherapy
Contact Lenses ...........92391, 92396
Educational Materials ............99071
Low Vision Aids .................92392
*See* Spectacle Services
Materials .......................99070
Ocular Prosthesis ...............92393
Prosthesis
Breast .....................19396
Radionuclide ....................78990
Radionuclide Therapy ............79900
Radiopharmaceutical .............78990
Radiopharmaceutical Therapy ......79900
Spectacles ......................92390
Spectacle Prosthesis .............92395

**Suppositories, Vaginal**
*See* Pessary

**Suppression** ...........80400-80408

**Suppression/Testing**
*See* Evocative/Suppression Test

**Suppressor T Lymphocyte Marker**
*See* CD8

**Suppurative Hidradenitides**
*See* Hidradenitis, Suppurative

**Suprahyoid**
Lymphadenectomy ...............38700

**Supraorbital Nerve**
Avulsion ........................64732
Incision ........................64732
Transection .....................64732

**Supraorbital Rim and Forehead**
Reconstruction .............21179-21180

**Suprapubic Prostatectomies**
*See* Prostatectomy, Suprapubic

**Suprarenal**
Gland
*See* Adrenal Gland
Vein
*See* Vein, Adrenal

**Suprascapular Nerve**
Injection
Anesthetic ...................64418

**Suprasellar Cyst**
*See* Craniopharyngioma

**Surface CD4 Receptor**
*See* CD4

**Surface Radiotherapy**
*See* Application, Radioelement, Surface

**Surgeries**
Breast-Conserving
*See* Breast, Excision, Lesion
Repeat
*See* Reoperation
Conventional
*See* Celiotomy
Laser
*See* Laser Surgery
Moh's
*See* Moh's Micrographic Surgery

**Surgical**
Avulsion
*See* Avulsion
Cataract Removal
*See* Cataract, Excision
Collapse Therapy; Thoracoplasty
*See* Thoracoplasty
Diathermy
*See* Electrocautery
Galvanism
*See* Electrolysis
Incision
*See* Incision
Microscopes
*See* Operating Microscope

Pathology
  *See* Pathology, Surgical
Planing
  Nose
    Skin . . . . . . . . . . . . . . . . . . . . . .30120
Pneumoperitoneum
  *See* Pneumoperitoneum
Removal, Eye
  *See* Enucleation, Eye
Revision
  *See* Reoperation
Services
  Post-Op Visit . . . . . . . . . . . . . . . . .99024

**Surveillance**
*See* Monitoring

**Suspension**
Aorta . . . . . . . . . . . . . . . . . . . . . . . . . .33800
Kidney
  *See* Nephropexy
Vagina
  *See* Colpopexy

**Suture**
*See* Repair
Abdomen . . . . . . . . . . . . . . . . . . . . . . . .49900
Aorta . . . . . . . . . . . . . . . . . . . .33320-33322
Bile Duct
  Wound . . . . . . . . . . . . . . . . . . . . . .47900
Bladder
  Fistulization . . . . . .44660-44661, 45800, 45805, 51880-51925
    Vesicouterine . . . . . . . . .51920-51925
    Vesicovaginal . . . . . . . . . . . . . . .51900
  Wound . . . . . . . . . . . . . . . .51860-51865
Cervix . . . . . . . . . . . . . . . . . . . . . . . . . .57720
Colon
  Diverticula . . . . . . . . . . . . .44604-44605
  Fistula . . . . . . . . . . .44650, 44660-44661
  Plication . . . . . . . . . . . . . . . . . . . . .44680
  Stoma . . . . . . . . . . . . . . . .44620, 44625
  Ulcer . . . . . . . . . . . . . . . . . . .44604-44605
  Wound . . . . . . . . . . . . . . . .44604-44605
Esophagus
  Wound . . . . . . . . . . . . . . . .43410, 43415
Eyelid . . . . . . . . . . . . . . . . . . . . . . . . . .67880
  Closure of . . . . . . . . . . . . . . . . . . .67875
  with Transposition of Tarsal Plate . . . . . . . . . . . . . . . . . . . . . .67882
  Wound
    Full Thickness . . . . . . . . . . . . . . .67935
    Partial Thickness . . . . . . . . . . . .67930
Facial Nerve
  Intratemporal
    Lateral to Geniculate Ganglion . . . . . . . . . . . . . . . . . . .69740
    Medial to Geniculate Ganglion . . . . . . . . . . . . . . . . . . .69745
Foot
  Tendon . . . . . . . . . . . . . . . .28200-28210
Gastroesophageal . . . . . . . . . . . . . . . .43405
Great Vessel . . . . . . . . . . . . . . .33320-33322
Hepatic Duct
  *See* Hepatic Duct, Repair
Hemorrhoids . . . . . . . . . . . . . . .46945-46946
Intestine
  Large
    Diverticula . . . . . . . . . . . . . . . . .44605
    Ulcer . . . . . . . . . . . . . . . . . . . . . .44605
    Wound . . . . . . . . . . . . . . . . . . . .44605
Intestines
  Large
    Diverticula . . . . . . . . . . . . . . . . .44604
    Ulcer . . . . . . . . . . . . . . . . . . . . . .44604
    Wound . . . . . . . . . . . . . . . . . . . .44604
  Small
    Diverticula . . . . . . . . . . . .44602-44603
    Fistula . . .44640, 44650, 44660-44661
    Plication . . . . . . . . . . . . . . . . . . .44680
    Ulcer . . . . . . . . . . . . . . . .44602-44603
    Wound . . . . . . . . . . . . . . .44602-44603
  Stoma . . . . . . . . . . . . . . . .44620, 44625
Iris
  with Ciliary Body . . . . . . . . . . . . . .66682
Kidney
  Fistula . . . . . . . . . . . . . . . . .50520-50526
  Horseshoe . . . . . . . . . . . . . . . . . . .50540
  Wound . . . . . . . . . . . . . . . . . . . . . .50500
Leg, Lower
  Tendon . . . . . . . . . . . . . . . .27658-27665
Leg, Upper
  Muscle . . . . . . . . . . . . . . . .27385-27386
Liver
  Wound . . . . . . . . . .47350, 47360, 47361
Mesentery . . . . . . . . . . . . . . . . . . . . . .44850
Nerve . . . . . . . . . . . . . . . . . . . .64831-64876
Pancreas . . . . . . . . . . . . . . . . . . . . . . .48545
Pharynx
  Wound . . . . . . . . . . . . . . . . . . . . . .42900
Rectum
  Fistula . . . . . . . . . . . . . . . . .45800-45825
  Prolapse . . . . . . . . . . . . . . .45540-45541
Removal
  Anesthesia . . . . . . . . . . . . .15850-15851
Spleen
  *See* Splenorrhapy
Stomach
  Fistula . . . . . . . . . . . . . . . . . . . . . .43880
  Laceration . . . . . . . . . . . . .43501, 43502
  Stoma . . . . . . . . . . . . . . . . . . . . . .43870
  Ulcer . . . . . . . . . . . . . . . . .43501, 43840
  Wound . . . . . . . . . . . . . . . . . . . . . .43840
Tendon
  Foot . . . . . . . . . . . . . . . . . .28200-28210
  Knee . . . . . . . . . . . . . . . . . .27380-27381
Testis
  Injury . . . . . . . . . . . . . . . . . . . . . . .54670
  Suspension . . . . . . . . . . . .54620-54640
Thoracic Duct
  Abdominal Approach . . . . . . . . . . .38382
  Cervical Approach . . . . . . . . . . . .38380
  Thoracic Approach . . . . . . . . . . . .38381
Throat
  Wound . . . . . . . . . . . . . . . . . . . . . .42900
Tongue
  to Lip . . . . . . . . . . . . . . . . . . . . . . .41510
Trachea
  Fistula
    without Plastic Repair . . . . . . . .31820
    with Plastic Repair . . . . . . . . . . .31825
  Stoma
    without Plastic Repair . . . . . . . .31820
    with Plastic Repair . . . . . . . . . . .31825
  Wound
    Cervical . . . . . . . . . . . . . . . . . . . .31800
    Intrathoracic . . . . . . . . . . . . . . . .31805
Ulcer . . . . . . . . . . . . . . . . . . . . .44604-44605
Ureter . . . . . . . . . . . . . . . . . . . . . . . . .50900
  Deligation . . . . . . . . . . . . . . . . . . .50940
  Fistula . . . . . . . . . . . . . . . . .50920-50930
Urethra
  Fistula . . . . . . . . . .45820, 45825, 53520
  Stoma . . . . . . . . . . . . . . . . . . . . . .53520
  to Bladder . . . . . . . . . . . . . .51840-51841
  Wound . . . . . . . . . . . . . . . .53502-53515
Uterus
  Fistula . . . . . . . . . . . . . . . . .51920-51925
  Rupture . . . . . . . . . . . . . . .58520, 59350
  Suspension . . . . . . . . . . . . .58400-58410
Vagina
  Cystocele . . . . . . . . . . . . . .57240, 57260
  Enterocele . . . . . . . . . . . . . . . . . . .57265
  Fistula
    Rectovaginal . . . . . . . . . .57300-57307
    Transvesical and Vaginal Approach . . . . . . . . . . . . . . . . . .57330
    Urethrovaginal . . . . . . . .57310-57311
    Vesicovaginal . . .51900, 57320-57330
  Rectocele . . . . . . . . . . . . . .57250, 57260
  Suspension . . . . . . . . . . . . . . . . . .57280
  Wound . . . . . . . . . . . . . . . .57200, 57210
Vas Deferens . . . . . . . . . . . . . . . . . . . .55400
Vein
  Femoral . . . . . . . . . . . . . . . . . . . . .37650
  Iliac . . . . . . . . . . . . . . . . . . . . . . . .37660
  Vena Cava . . . . . . . . . . . . . . . . . . .37620
Wound . . . . . . . . . . . . . . . . . . .44604-44605

**Swallowing Evaluation** . . . . . .92525, 92525-92526
Cine . . . . . . . . . . . . . . . . . . . . . . . . . . .74230
Treatment . . . . . . . . . . . . . . . . . . . . . .92526
Video . . . . . . . . . . . . . . . . . . . . . . . . . .74230

**Swanson Procedure** . . . . . . . . . .28309

**Sweat Collection**
Iontophoresis . . . . . . . . . . . . . . . . . . .89360

**Sweat Glands**
Excision
  Axillary . . . . . . . . . . . . . . . .11450-11451
  Inguinal . . . . . . . . . . . . . . . .11462-11463
  Perianal . . . . . . . . . . . . . . .11470-11471
  Perineal . . . . . . . . . . . . . . .11470-11471
  Umbilical . . . . . . . . . . . . . .11470-11471

# T

Arthroscopy
Surgical ...............29891, 29892
Craterization ....................28120
Cyst
Excision ...............28100-28103
Diaphysectomy ..................28120
Excision ..................28120, 28130
Fracture
Open Treatment ...............28445
Percutaneous Fixation ..........28436
without Manipulation ..........28430
with Manipulation .......28435-28436
Repair
Osteochondritis Dissecans ......29892
Osteotomy ..................28302
Saucerization ....................28120
Tumor
Excision .........27647, 28100-28103

**Tap**
Cisternal
*See* Cisternal Puncture
Lumbar Diagnostic
*See* Spinal Tap

**Tarsal**
Fracture
Percutaneous Fixation ..........28456

**Tarsal Bone**
*See* Ankle Bone

**Tarsal Joint**
*See* Foot
Arthrodesis ..........28730-28735, 28740
with Advancement ............28737
with Lengthening .............28737
Craterization ....................28122
Cyst
Excision ...............28104-28107
Diaphysectomy ..................28122
Dislocation ..........28540-28545, 28555
Percutaneous Fixation ....28545-28546
Excision ..................28116, 28122
Fracture
Open Treatment ...............28465
without Manipulation ..........28450
with Manipulation .......28455-28456
Fusion ..............28730-28735, 28740
with Advancement ............28737
with Lengthening .............28737
Repair ........................28320
Osteotomy .............28304-28305
Saucerization ....................28122
Tumor
Excision .........28104-28107, 28171

**Tarsal Strip Procedure** ........67917

**Tarsal Tunnel Release** ........28035

**Tarsometatarsal Joint**
Arthrodesis ..........28730-28735, 28740
Arthrotomy ...............28020, 28050
Dislocation ..........28600-28605, 28615
Percutaneous Fixation ..........28606
Exploration .....................28020
Fusion ..............28730-28735, 28740
Removal
Foreign Body .................28020
Loose Body ..................28020
Synovial
Biopsy ......................28050
Excision .....................28070

**Tarsorrhaphy** .................67875
Median ........................67880
Severing .......................67710
with Transposition of
Tarsal Plate ..................67882

**Tattoo**
Cornea .........................65600
Skin .....................11920-11922

**TBG**
*See* Thyroxine Binding Globulin

**TBS**
*See* Bethesda System

**TB Test**
Skin Test ...............86580-86585

**TCT**
*See* Thrombin Time

**Td Shots**
*See* Tetanus Immunization; Vaccines

**Team Conference**
Case Management
Services ..................99361-99373

**Tear Duct**
*See* Lacrimal Duct

**Tear Gland**
*See* Lacrimal Gland

**Technique**
Pericardial Window
*See* Pericardiostomy
Projective
*See* Projective Test

**Teeth**
X-Ray ....................70300-70320

**Telangiectasia**
Chromosome Analysis .............88248
Injection .......................36468

**Telangiectasia, Cerebello-Oculocutaneous**
*See* Ataxia Telangiectasia

**Telephone**
Case Management
Services ..................99361-99373
Pacemaker Analysis ........93733, 93736
Transmission of ECG ..............93012

**Teletherapy**
Dose Plan .................77305-77321

**Temperature Gradient Studies** .......................93740

**Temporal, Petrous**
Excision
Apex .......................69530

**Temporal Arteries**
*See* Artery, Temporal

**Temporal Bone**
Electromagnetic Bone Conduction Hearing Device
Implantation/Replacement ......69710
Removal/Repair ...............69711
Excision ........................69535
Resection .......................69535
Tumor
Removal .....................69970
Unlisted Services and Procedures ...69979

**Temporomandibular Joint (TMJ)**
Arthrocentesis ...................20605
Arthrography ..............70328-70332
Injection .....................21116
Arthroplasty ...............21240-21243
Arthroscopy
Diagnostic ...................29800
Surgical .....................29804
Arthrotomy .....................21010
Cartilage
Excision .....................21060
Condylectomy ...................21050
Coronoidectomy .................21070
Dislocation
Closed Treatment ........21480-21485
Open Treatment ...............21490
Injection
Radiologic ...................21116
Magnetic Resonance Imaging (MRI) ..........................70336
Meniscectomy ...................21060
Prostheses
*See* Prosthesis, Temporomandibular Joint
Reconstruction
*See* Reconstruction, Temporomandibular Joint
X-Ray with Contrast .........70328-70332

**Tenago Procedure** ............53443

**Tendinosuture**
*See* Suture, Tendon

**Tendon**
Achilles
*See* Achilles Tendon
Arm, Upper
Revision .....................24320

Rorschach
  *See* Rorschach Test
Schilling
  *See* Schilling Test
Skin
  *See* Skin, Tests
Stanford-Binet
  *See* Psychiatric Diagnosis
Tuberculin
  *See* Skin, Tests, Tuberculosis

**Tester, Color Vision**
*See* Color Vision Examination

**Testes**
Nuclear Medicine
  Imaging ............... 78760-78761
Undescended
  *See* Testis, Undescended

**Testicular Vein**
*See* Spermatic Veins

**Testimony, Medical** ........... 99075

**Testing, Histocompatibility**
*See* Tissue Typing

**Testing, Neurophysiologic**
Intraoperative ........ 95920

**Testing, Neuropsychological** .......... 96117

**Testing, Range of Motion**
*See* Range of Motion Test

**Testis**
Abscess
  Incision and Drainage .......... 54700
Biopsy ................... 54500-54505
Excision
  Laparoscopic ................. 54690
  Radical ............... 54530-54535
  Simple ...................... 54520
Hematoma
  Incision and Drainage .......... 54700
Insertion
  Prosthesis .................. 54660
Lesion
  Excision .................... 54510
Needle Biopsy .................. 54500
Repair
  Injury ...................... 54670
  Suspension ........... 54620, 54640
  Torsion ..................... 54600
Suture
  Injury ...................... 54670
  Suspension ........... 54620, 54640
Transplantation
  to Thigh .................... 54680
Tumor
  Excision .............. 54530-54535
Undescended
  Exploration ............ 54550-54560
Unlisted Services and Procedures ............... 54699, 55899

**Testosterone** .................. 84402
Response ........................ 80414
  Stimulation ............ 80414-80415
Total ........................... 84403

**Testosterone Estradiol Binding Globulin**
*See* Globulin, Sex Hormone Binding

**Test Tube Fertilization**
*See* In Vitro Fertilization

**Tetanus** ....................... 86280
Antibody ....................... 86774
Immunoglobulin .................. 90389
Vaccine ........................ 90703

**Tetrachloride, Carbon**
*See* Carbon Tetrachloride

**Tetralogy of Fallot** ............. 33692-33697, 33924

**Thal-Nissen Procedure** ....... 43325

**Thawing and Expansion**
of Frozen Cell .................... 88241

**THBR**
*See* Thyroid Hormone Binding Ratio

**Theleplasty**
*See* Nipples, Reconstruction

**Theophylline**
Assay .......................... 80198

**Therapeutic**
Abortion
  *See* Abortion, Therapeutic
Apheresis
  *See* Apheresis, Therapeutic
Drug Assay
  *See* Drug Assay
Mobilization
  *See* Mobilization
Photopheresis
  *See* Photopheresis
Radiology
  *See* Radiology, Therapeutic

**Therapies**
Cold
  *See* Cryotherapy
Exercise
  *See* Exercise Therapy
Family
  *See* Psychotherapy, Family
Language
  *See* Language Therapy
Milieu
  *See* Environmental Intervention
Occupational
  *See* Occupational Therapy
Photodynamic
  *See* Photochemotherapy
Photoradiation
  *See* Actinotherapy
Physical
  *See* Physical Medicine/Therapy/Occupational Therapy
Speech
  *See* Speech Therapy
Tocolytic
  *See* Tocolysis
Ultraviolet
  *See* Actinotherapy

**Therapy**
Desensitization
  *See* Allergen Immunotherapy
Hemodialysis
  *See* Hemodialysis
Hot Pack
  *See* Hot Pack Treatment
Radiation
  *See* Irradiation
Speech
  *See* Speech Therapy

**Thermocauterization**
Ectropion
  Repair ...................... 67922
Lesion
  Cornea ...................... 65450

**Thermocoagulation**
*See* Electrocautery

**Thermogram**
Cephalic ........................ 93760
Peripheral ...................... 93762

**Thermographies**
*See* Thermogram

**Thermography, Cerebral**
*See* Thermogram, Cephalic

**Thermotherapy**
Prostate ................. 53850-53852
  Microwave ................. 53850
  Radiofrequency ............... 53852

**Thiamine** ...................... 84425

**Thiersch Operation** ........... 15050
*See* Pinch Graft

**Thiersch Procedure** ........... 46753

**Thigh**
Fasciotomy ..................... 27025
  *See* Femur; Leg, Upper

**Thin Layer Chromatographies**
*See* Chromatography, Thin-Layer

**Thiocyanate** .................. 84430

**Third Disease**
*See* Rubella

**Third Opinion**
*See* Confirmatory Consultations

**Thompson Procedure** ......... 27430

**Thompson Test**
*See* Smear and Stain, Routine

Peroneal Artery .................. 35381
Popliteal Artery .................. 35381
Renal Artery .................... 35341
Subclavian Artery .......... 35301, 35311
Tibial Artery ..................... 35381
Vertebral Artery .................. 35301

**Thrombokinase** ............... 85260

**Thrombolysin**
*See* Plasmin

**Thrombolysis**
Catheter Exchange
  Arterial ............... 37209, 75900
Cerebral
  Intravenous Infusion ........... 37195
Coronary Vessels ........... 92975, 92977
Cranial Vessels .................. 37195

**Thrombolysis Biopsy Intracranial**
Arterial Perfusion ................ 61624

**Thrombolysis Intracranial** .... 65205
*See* Ciliary Body; Cornea; Eye, Removal, Foreign Body; Iris; Lens; Retina; Sclera; Vitreous

**Thrombomodulin** ......... 85337

**Thromboplastin**
Inhibition ....................... 85705
Inhibition Test ................... 85347
Partial Time ............... 85730-85732

**Thromboplastinogen**
*See* Clotting Factor

**Thromboplastinogen B**
*See* Christmas Factor

**Thromboplastin Antecedent, Plasma**
*See* Plasma Thromboplastin, Antecedent

**Thumb**
*See* Phalanx
Amputation ......... 26910, 26951-26952
Arthrodesis
  Carpometacarpal Joint ... 26841-26842
Dislocation
  with Fracture ........... 26645, 26650
    Open Treatment ............. 26665
  with Manipulation ............. 26641
Fracture
  with Dislocation ........ 26645, 26650
    Open Treatment ............. 26665
Fusion
  in Opposition .................. 26820
Reconstruction
  from Finger .................. 26550
  Opponensplasty ........ 26490, 26492, 26494, 26496
Repair
  Muscle ...................... 26508
  Muscle Transfer .............. 26494
  Tendon Transfer ............... 26510

Replantation ............... 20824-20827
Sesamoidectomy ................. 26185
Unlisted Services and Procedures ... 26989

**Thymectomy** ............ 60520-60521
Sternal Split/Transthoracic Approach ................ 60521-60522
Transcervical Approach ............ 60520

**Thymotaxin**
*See* Beta-2-Microglobulin

**Thymus Gland** ................ 60520
Excision .................. 60520-60521

**Thyramine**
*See* Amphetamine

**Thyrocalcitonin**
*See* Calcitonin

**Thyroglobulin** ................. 84432
Antibody ....................... 86800

**Thyroglossal Duct**
Cyst
  Excision ............... 60280-60281

**Thyroidectomy**
Partial ....... 60210, 60212, 60220, 60225
Secondary ..................... 60260
Total ..................... 60240, 60271
  Cervical Approach ............. 60271
  for Malignancy
    Limited Neck Dissection ...... 60252
    Radical Neck Dissection ...... 60254
  Removal All Thyroid Tissue ...... 60260
  Sternal Split/Transthoracic Approach ................... 60270

**Thyroid Gland**
Cyst
  Aspiration ................... 60001
  Excision ..................... 60200
  Incision and Drainage .......... 60000
  Injection ..................... 60001
Excision
  for Malignancy
    Limited Neck Dissection ...... 60252
    Radical Neck Dissection ...... 60254
  Partial .... 60210, 60212, 60220, 60225
  Secondary ................... 60260
  Total .................. 60240, 60271
    Cervical Approach ........... 60271
    Removal All Thyroid Tissue .... 60260
    Sternal Split/Transthoracic Approach ................. 60270
    Transcervical Approach ....... 60520
Metastatic Cancer
  Nuclear Imaging ......... 78015-78018
Needle Biopsy ................... 60100
Nuclear Medicine
  Imaging ..................... 78010
  Imaging for Metastases ... 78015-78018
  Imaging with Flow ............ 78011
  Imaging with Uptake ..... 78006, 78007
  Metastases Uptake ............ 78020
  Uptake ................ 78000-78003
Radionuclide Therapy
  Ablation ..................... 79030
  Hyperthyroidism ......... 79000-79001
  Metastases .................. 79035
  Suppression .................. 79020
Radiopharmaceutical Therapy
  Ablation ..................... 79030
  Metastases .................. 79035
  Suppression .................. 79020
Tumor
  Excision ..................... 60200

**Thyroid Hormone Binding Ratio** ........................ 84479

**Thyroid Hormone Uptake** ..... 84479

**Thyroid Stimulating Hormone (TSH)** ....... 80418, 80438-80440, 84443

**Thyroid Stimulating Hormone Receptor ab**
*See* Thyrotropin Releasing Hormone (TRH)

**Thyroid Stimulating Immunoglobulins** ............. 84445

**Thyroid Stimulator, Long Acting**
*See* Thyrotropin Releasing Hormone (TRH)

**Thyroid Suppression Test**
*See* Nuclear Medicine, Thyroid, Uptake

**Thyrolingual Cyst**
*See* Cyst, Thyroglossal Duct

**Thyrotomy** .................... 31300

**Thyrotropin Receptor ab**
*See* Thyrotropin Releasing Hormone (TRH)

**Thyrotropin Releasing Hormone (TRH)** .................. 80438-80439

**Thyroxine**
Free .......................... 84439
Neonatal ...................... 84437
Total .......................... 84436
True .......................... 84436

**Thyroxine Binding Globulin** .. 84442

**Tibia**
*See* Ankle
Arthroscopy Surgical ........ 29891, 29892
Craterization ............. 27360, 27640
Cyst
  Excision .............. 27635-27638
Diaphysectomy ........... 27360, 27640
Excision ................. 27360, 27640
  Epiphyseal Bar ............... 20150
Fracture
  Arthroscopic Treatment ... 29855-29856
    Plafond .................. 29892
  Closed Treatment ........ 27824-27825
  Distal ................ 27824-27828

Intercondylar . . . . . . . . . . .27538, 27540
Malleolus . . . . . . .27760-27762, 27762, 27766, 27808-27810, 27814
Open Treatment . . . . . . . .27535-27536, 27758-27759, 27826-27828
Plateau . . . . . . . . . . . . . . . .29855-29856
Closed Treatment . . . . .27530, 27532, 27535-27536
Shaft . . . . . .27752, 27756, 27758-27759
without Manipulation . . . . . . . . . .27824
with Manipulation . . . . . . . . . . . . .27825
Incision . . . . . . . . . . . . . . . . . . . . . . . . .27607
Osteoplasty
Lengthening . . . . . . . . . . . . . . . . . .27715
Prophylactic Treatment . . . . . . . . . . .27745
Reconstruction . . . . . . . . . . . . . . . . . . .27418
at Knee . . . . . . . . . .27440-27443, 27446
Repair . . . . . . . . . . . . . . . . . . . . .27720-27725
Epiphysis . . . . . . . . . . . . . .27477-27485, 27730-27740, 27742
Osteochondritis Dissecans Arthroscopy . . . . . . . . . . . . . . . . . . .29892
Osteotomy . . . . . . .27455-27457, 27705, 27709, 27712
Pseudoarthrosis . . . . . . . . . . . . . . .27727
Saucerization . . . . . . . . . . . . .27360, 27640
Tumor
Excision . . . . . . . . .27635-27638, 27645
X-Ray . . . . . . . . . . . . . . . . . . . . . . . . .73590

**Tibial**
Arteries
*See* Artery, Tibial
Nerve
Repair/Suture
Posterior . . . . . . . . . . . . . . . . . . .64840

**Tibiofibular Joint**
Arthrodesis . . . . . . . . . . . . . . . . . . . . .27871
Dislocation . . . . . . . . . .27830-27831, 27832
Disruption
Open Treatment . . . . . . . . . . . . . . .27829
Fusion . . . . . . . . . . . . . . . . . . . . . . . .27871

**TIG**
*See* Immune Globulins, Tetanus

**Time**
Bleeding
*See* Bleeding Time
Prothrombin
*See* Prothrombin Time
Reptilase
*See* Thrombin Time

**Tissue**
Culture
Chromosome Analysis . . . .88230-88239
Non-neoplastic Disorder . . . . . . . . . . . . . .88230, 88237
Skin Grafts . . . . . . . . . . . .15100-15121
Solid Tumor . . . . . . . . . . . . . . . . . .88239
Toxin/Antitoxin . . . . . . . . . . . . . . .87230
Virus . . . . . . . . . . . . . . . . . .87252-87253
Enzyme Activity . . . . . . . . . . . . . . . . . .82657
Examination for Fungi . . . . . . . . . . . . .87220
Expander
Breast Reconstruction with . . . . . .19357
Insertion
Skin . . . . . . . . . . . . . . . . . . . . . . . .11960
Removal
Skin . . . . . . . . . . . . . . . . . . . . . . .11971
Replacement
Skin . . . . . . . . . . . . . . . . . . . . . . .11970
Grafts
Harvesting . . . . . . . . . . . . . . . . . . .20926
Granulation
*See* Granulation Tissue
Hybridization In Situ . . . . . . . . . . . . . .88365
Mucosal
*See* Mucosa
Preparation
Drug Analysis . . . . . . . . . . . . . . . . .80103
Soft
Abscess . . . . . . . . . . . . . . .20000-20005
Transfer
Adjacent
Eyelids . . . . . . . . . . . . . . . . . . . .67961
Skin . . . . . . . . . . . . . . . . .14000-14350
Facial Muscles . . . . . . . . . . . . . . .15845
Finger Flap . . . . . . . . . . . . . . . . . . .14350
Toe Flap . . . . . . . . . . . . . . . . . . . . .14350
Typing
HLA Antibodies . . . . . . . . .86812-86817
Lymphocyte Culture . . . . . .86821-86822

**Tissue Factor**
*See* Thromboplastin

**TLC**
*See* Chromatography, Thin-Layer
Screen . . . . . . . . . . . . . . . . . . . . . . . . .84375

**TMJ**
*See* Temporomandibular Joint (TMJ)
Prostheses
*See* Prosthesis, Temporomandibular Joint

**Tobramycin**
Assay . . . . . . . . . . . . . . . . . . . . . . . . . .80200

**Tocolysis** . . . . . . . . . . . . . . . . . . . . .59412
External Cephalic Version . . . . . . . . . .59412

**Tocopherol** . . . . . . . . . . . . . . . . . .84446

**Toe**
*See* Interphalangeal Joint, Toe; Metatarsophalangeal Joint; Phalanx
Amputation . . . . . . . . .28810, 28820-28825
Capsulotomy . . . . . . . . . . . . . .28270, 28272
Fasciotomy . . . . . . . . . . . . . . . . . . . .28008
Fracture
*See* Fracture, Phalanges, Toe
Lesion
Excision . . . . . . . . . . . . . . . . . . . . .28092
Reconstruction
Angle Deformity . . . . . . . . . . . . . .28313
Extra Toes . . . . . . . . . . . . . . . . . . .28344
Hammertoe . . . . . . . . . . . .28285-28286
Macrodactyly . . . . . . . . . . .28340-28341
Syndactyly . . . . . . . . . . . . . . . . . . .28345
Webbed Toe . . . . . . . . . . . . . . . . .28345
Repair
Bunion . . . . . . . . . .28290, 28292-28294, 28296-28299
Muscle . . . . . . . . . . . . . . . . . . . . . .28240
Tendon . . . . . . . . . .28232, 28234, 28240
Webbed . . . . . . . . . . . . . . . . . . . . .28280
Webbed Toe . . . . . . . . . . . . . . . . .28345
Tenotomy . . . . .28010-28011, 28232, 28234
Unlisted Services and Procedures . . .28899

**Toes**
Arthrocentesis . . . . . . . . . . . . . . . . . . .20600
Dislocation
*See* Specific Joint
Magnetic Resonance Imaging (MRI) . . . . . . . . . . . . . . . . . . . . . . . . . .73721
Reconstruction
Extra Digit . . . . . . . . . . . . . . . . . . .26587
Repair
Bifid Toe . . . . . . . . . . . . . . . . . . . .26585
Extra Digit . . . . . . . . . . . . . . . . . . .26587
Macrodactylia . . . . . . . . . . . . . . . .26590
Reposition to Hand . . . . . . . . .26551-26556
Strapping . . . . . . . . . . . . . . . . . . . . . . .29550
X-Ray . . . . . . . . . . . . . . . . . . . . . . . . . .73660

**Toe Flap**
Tissue Transfer . . . . . . . . . . . . . . . . . .14350

**Tolbutamide Tolerance Test** . . .82953

**Tolerance Test**
Glucagon . . . . . . . . . . . . . . . . . . . . . . .82946
Glucose . . . . . . . . . . . . . . . . . .82951-82952
with Tolbutamide . . . . . . . . . . . . .82953
Heparin-Protamine . . . . . . . . . . . . . . .85530
Insulin . . . . . . . . . . . . . . . . . . . .80434-80435
Maltose . . . . . . . . . . . . . . . . . .82951-82952
Tolbutamide . . . . . . . . . . . . . . . . . . . .82953

**Tomodensitometries**
*See* CAT Scan

**Tomographic Scintigraphy, Computed**
*See* Emission Computerized Tomography

**Tomographic SPECT**
Myocardial Imaging . . . . . . . . . . . . . .78469

**Tomographies, Computed X-Ray**
*See* CAT Scan

**Tomography, Computerized Axial**
Abdomen
*See* Abdomen, CAT Scan
Head
*See* Head, CAT Scan

**Tomography, Emission Computed**
*See* Positron Emission Tomography
Single Photon
*See* SPECT

**Tompkins Metroplasty** ........58540
*See* Uterus, Reconstruction

**Tongue**
Abscess
  Incision and Drainage .........41000, 41005-41006, 41015
Biopsy ..................41100, 41105
Cyst
  Incision and Drainage .........41000, 41005-41006, 41015, 60000
Excision
  Complete .......41140, 41145, 41150, 41153, 41155
  Frenum .....................41115
  Partial ..........41120, 41130, 41135
  with Mouth Resection ....41150, 41153
  with Radical Neck ......41135, 41145, 41153, 41155
Fixation ........................41500
Hematoma
  Incision and Drainage .........41000, 41005-41006, 41015
Incision
  Frenum ......................41010
Lesion
  Excision .........41110, 41112-41114
Reconstruction
  Frenum ......................41520
Repair
  *See* Repair, Tongue
  Laceration .............41250-41252
  Suture ......................41510
Suture .........................41510
Unlisted Services and Procedures ...41599

**Tonography** ..................92120
with Provocation .................92130

**Tonometry, Serial** .............92100

**Tonsil, Pharyngeal**
*See* Adenoids

**Tonsillectomy** ..........42820-42821, 42825-42826

**Tonsils**
Abscess
  Incision and Drainage ..........42700
Excision ..................42825-42826
  Lingual ......................42870
  Radical ..........42842, 42844-42845
  Tag .........................42860
  with Adenoids ..........42820-42821
Lingual
  Destruction ..................42870
Unlisted Services and Procedures ...42999

**Topiramate**
Assay ..........................80201

**TORCH Antibody Panel** .......80090

**Torek Procedure**
*See* Orchiopexy

**Torkildsen Procedure** .........62180

**TORP (Total Ossicular Replacement Prosthesis)** .............69633, 69637

**Torsion Swing Test** ...........92546

**Torula**
*See* Cryptococcus

**Torus Mandibularis**
Tumor Excision ..................21031

**Total**
Abdominal Hysterectomy
  *See* Hysterectomy, Abdominal, Total
Bilirubin Level
  *See* Bilirubin, Total
Catecholamines
  *See* Catecholamines, Urine
Cystectomy
  *See* Bladder, Excision, Total
Dacryoadenectomy
  *See* Dacryoadenectomy, Total
Elbow Replacement
  *See* Replacement, Elbow, Total
Esophagectomy
  *See* Esophagectomy, Total
Gastrectomy
  *See* Excision, Stomach, Total
Hemolytic Complement
  *See* Complement, Hemolytic, Total
Hip Arthroplasty
  *See* Hip, Total Replacement
Knee Arthroplasty
  *See* Prosthesis, Knee
Mastectomies
  *See* Mastectomy
Ostectomy of Patella
  *See* Patellectomy
Splenectomy
  *See* Splenectomy, Total

**Touroff Operation** .............37615
*See* Ligation, Artery, Neck

**Toxicology Screen** ......80100-80103

**Toxin, Botulinum**
*See* Chemodenervation

**Toxin Assay** ..................87230

**Toxoplasma**
Antibody .................86777-86778

**Trabeculectomies**
*See* Trabeculoplasty

**Trabeculectomy ab Externo**
in Absence of Previous Surgery .....66170
with Scarring Previous Surgery ......66172

**Trabeculoplasty**
by Laser Surgery ................65855

**Trabeculotomy ab Externo**
Eye ............................65850

**Trachea**
Aspiration .....................31720
  Catheter ..............31720-31725
Catheterization .................31700
Dilation ..................31630-31631
Endoscopy
  via Tracheostomy .............31615
Excision
  Stenosis ..............31780-31781
Fistula
  without Plastic Repair ..........31820
  with Plastic Repair ............31825
Fracture
  Endoscopy ...................31630
Incision
  Emergency .............31603-31605
  Planned ..............31600-31601
  with Flaps ...................31610
Instillation
  Contrast Material .............31708
Introduction
  Needle Wire .................31730
Puncture
  Aspiration and/or Injection ......31612
Reconstruction
  Carina ......................31766
  Cervical .....................31750
  Fistula ......................31755
  Intrathoracic .................31760
Repair
  Cervical .....................31750
  Fistula ......................31755
  Intrathoracic .................31760
  Stoma ................31613-31614
Revision
  Stoma
    Scars ......................31830
Scar
  Revision .....................31830
Stenosis
  Excision ..............31780-31781
  Repair ...............31780, 31781
Stoma
  Repair
    without Plastic Repair ........31820
    with Plastic Repair ...........31825
  Revision
    Scars ......................31830
Tumor
  Excision
    Cervical ....................31785
    Thoracic ...................31786
Unlisted Services and Procedures
  Bronchi .....................31899
Wound
  Suture
    Cervical ....................31800
    Intrathoracic ................31805

Hair
  Punch Graft . . . . 15775-15776
  Strip . . . . 15220-15221
Heart . . . . 33945
Heart-Lung . . . . 33935
Heterologous
  *See* Heterograft
Liver . . . . 47135
  Heterotopic . . . . 47136
Lung
  Anesthesia . . . . 00580
  Donor Pneumonectomy . . . . 32850
  Double
    with Cardiopulmonary
    Bypass . . . . 32854
  Double, without Cardiopulmonary
  Bypass . . . . 32853
  Single, without Cardiopulmonary
  Bypass . . . . 32851
  Single, with Cardiopulmonary
  Bypass . . . . 32852
Muscle
  *See* Muscle Flaps
Pancreas . . . . 48160, 40550, 48554, 48556
Parathyroid . . . . 60512
Renal
  Allotransplantation . . . . 50360
    with Recipient Nephrectomy . . . 50365
  Autotransplantation . . . . 50380
  Donor Nephrectomy . . . . 50300-50320, 50547
  Recipient Nephrectomy . . . . 50340
  Removal Transplanted Renal
  Allograft . . . . 50370
Skin
  *See* Dermatology
Stem Cells . . . . 38240-38241
  Harvesting . . . . 38231
Testis
  to Thigh . . . . 54680
Tissue, Harvesting
  *See* Graft, Tissue, Harvesting

**Transpleural Thoracoscopy**
*See* Thoracoscopy

**Transposition**
Arteries
  Carotid . . . . 35691, 35694-35695
  Subclavian . . . . 35693-35695
  Vertebral . . . . 35691, 35693
Cranial Nerve . . . . 64716
Eye Muscles . . . . 67320
Great Arteries
  Repair . . . . 33770-33781
Nerve . . . . 64718-64721
Ovary . . . . 58825
Peripheral Nerve
  Major . . . . 64856
Vein Valve . . . . 34510

**Transthoracic Echocardiography**
*See* Echocardiography

**Transthyretin**
*See* Prealbumin

**Transureteroureterostomy** . . . . 50770

**Transurethral Balloon Dilation**
Prostatic Urethra . . . . 52510

**Transurethral Fulguration**
Postoperative Bleeding . . . . 52606

**Transurethral Procedure**
*See* Specific Procedure
Prostate
  Incision . . . . 52450
  Resection . . . . 52612-52614
  Thermotherapy . . . . 53850-53852
    Microwave . . . . 53850
    Radiofrequency . . . . 53852

**Trapezium**
Arthroplasty
  with Implant . . . . 25445

**Travel, Unusual** . . . . 99082

**Treacher-Collins Syndrome**
Midface Reconstruction . . . . 21150-21151

**Treatment, Tocolytic**
*See* Tocolysis

**Trendelenburg Operation**
*See* Varicose Vein, Removal, Secondary Varicosity

**Trephine Procedure**
Sinusotomy
  Frontal . . . . 31070

**Treponema Pallidum**
Antibody
  Confirmation Test . . . . 86781
Antigen Detection
  Direct Fluorescence . . . . 87285

**TRH**
*See* Thyrotropin Releasing Hormone (TRH)

**Triacylglycerol**
*See* Triglycerides

**Triacylglycerol Hydrolase**
*See* Lipase

**Tributyrinase**
*See* Lipase

**Trichiasis**
Repair . . . . 67825
  Epilation, by Forceps . . . . 67820
  Epilation, by Other than
  Forceps . . . . 67825
  Incision of Lid Margin . . . . 67830
    with Free Mucous Membrane
    Graft . . . . 67835

**Trichina**
*See* Trichinella

**Trichinella**
Antibody . . . . 86784
Trichogram . . . . 96902

**Trichrome Stain** . . . . 88313

**Tricuspid Valve**
Excision . . . . 33460
Repair . . . . 33463-33465
Replacement . . . . 33465
Repositioning . . . . 33468

**Tridymite**
*See* Silica

**Trigeminal Ganglia**
*See* Gasserian Ganglion

**Trigeminal Nerve**
Destruction . . . . 64600, 64605, 64610
Injection
  Anesthetic . . . . 64400
  Neurolytic . . . . 64600-64610

**Trigeminal Tract**
Stereotactic
  Create Lesion . . . . 61791

**Trigger Finger Repair** . . . . 26055

**Trigger Point Injection** . . . . 20550

**Triglyceridase**
*See* Lipase

**Triglycerides** . . . . 84478

**Triglyceride Lipase**
*See* Lipase

**Trigonocephaly** . . . . 21175

**Triiodothyronine**
Free . . . . 84481
Reverse . . . . 84482
Total . . . . 84480
True . . . . 84480

**Triolean Hydrolase**
*See* Lipase

**Trioxopurine**
*See* Uric Acid

**Tripcellim**
*See* Trypsin

**Trisegmentectomy** . . . . 47122

**Trocar Biopsy**
Bone Marrow . . . . 85102

**Trochanteric Femur Fracture**
*See* Femur, Fracture, Trochanteric

**Trophoblastic Tumor GTT**
*See* Hydatidiform Mole

**Troponin** . . . . 84484
Qualitative . . . . 84512
Quantitative . . . . 84484

**Truncal Vagotomies**
*See* Vagotomy, Truncal

**Truncus Arteriosus**
Repair . . . . 33786

**Truncus Brachiocephalicus**
*See* Artery, Brachiocephalic

Localization
  Nuclear Medicine .78800-78802, 78803
Mandible .21040-21045
Maxillary Torus Palatinus .21032
Mediastinal
  Excision .39220
Mediastinum .32662
Meningioma .61512
  Excision .61519
Metacarpal .26200-26205, 26250-26255
Metatarsal .28104-28107
  Excision .28173
Neck
  Excision .21555-21556
  Radical Resection .21557
Olecranon
  Excision .24120
Olecranon Process
  with Allograft
    Excision .24126
  with Autograft
    Excision .24125
Ovary
  Resection .58060-58952
Pancreatic Duct
  Destruction .43272
Parotid Gland
  Excision .42410, 42415, 42420, 42425-42426
Pelvis .27047-27049
Pericardial
  Endoscopic .32661
  Excision .33050
Phalanges
  Finger .26210-26215, 26260-26262
  Toe .28108
    Excision .28175
Pituitary Gland
  Excision .61546, 61548
Positron Emission Tomography (PET) .78810
Pubis .27065-27067
Radiation Therapy .77295
Radius .25120, 25125-25126, 25170
  Excision .24120
  with Allograft
    Excision .24126
  with Autograft
    Excision .24125
Rathke's Pouch
  *See* Craniopharyngioma
Rectum
  Destruction .45190, 45320, 46937-46938
  Excision .45160, 45170
Resection
  Face .21015
  Scalp .21015
  with Cystourethroscopy .52339
Retroperitoneal
  Destruction/Excision .49200-49201
Sacrum .49215
Scapula
  Excision .23140, 23210
    with Allograft .23146
    with Autograft .23145
Shoulder
  Excision .23075-23077
Skull
  Excision .61500
Soft Tissue
  Forearm
    Radical Resection .25077
  Wrist
    Radical Resection .25077
Spinal Cord
  Excision .63275-63290
Stomach
  Excision .43610, 43611
Talus .28100-28103
  Excision .27647
Tarsal .28104-28107
  Excision .28171
Temporal Bone
  Removal .69970
Testis
  Excision .54530-54535
Thorax
  Excision .21555-21556
  Radical Resection .21557
Thyroid
  Excision .60200
Tibia .27365-27638, 27635-27638
  Excision .27645
Torus Mandibularis .21031
Trachea
  Excision
    Cervical .31785
    Thoracic .31786
Ulna .25120, 25125-25126, 25170
  Excision .24120
  with Allograft
    Excision .24126
  with Autograft
    Excision .24125
Urethra .52234-52240, 53220
Uterus
  Excision .58140-58145
Vagina
  Excision .57135
Vertebra
  Additional Segment
    Excision .22116
  Cervical
    Excision .22100
  Lumbar .22102
  Thoracic
    Excision .22101
Wrist .25075-25077, 25135, 25136
  Radical Resection .25077

**Tunica Vaginalis**
Hydrocele
  Aspiration .55000
  Excision .55040-55041
  Repair .55060

**Turbinate**
Excision .30130-30140
Fracture
  Therapeutic .30930
Injection .30200
Submucous Resection
  Nose Excision .30140

**Turbinate Mucosa**
Cauterization .30801-30802

**Turcica, Sella**
*See* Sella Turcica

**Turnbuckle Jacket** .29020-29025
Removal .29715

**TURP**
*See* Prostatectomy, Transurethral

**Tylectomy**
*See* Breast, Excision, Lesion

**Tylonol**
Urine .82003

**Tympanic Membrane**
Create Stoma .69433, 69436
Incision .69420-69421
Reconstruction .69620
Repair .69450, 69610

**Tympanic Nerve**
Excision .69676

**Tympanolysis** .69450

**Tympanometry** .92567
*See* Audiologic Function Tests

**Tympanoplasty**
*See* Myringoplasty
Radical or Complete .69645
  with Ossicular Chain Reconstruction .69646
without Mastoidectomy .69631
  with Ossicular Chain Reconstruction .69632
    and Synthetic Prosthesis .69633
with Antrotomy or Mastoidotomy .69635
  with Ossicular Chain Reconstruction .69636
    and Synthetic Prosthesis .69637
with Mastoidectomy .69641
  with Intact or Reconstructed Wall .69643
    and Ossicular Chain Reconstruction .69644
  with Ossicular Chain Reconstruction .69642

**Tympanostomy** .69433-69436

**Tympanotomy**
*See* Myringotomy

**Typhoid Vaccine**

**Typhus**
Endemic
*See* Murine Typhus
Mite-Borne
*See* Scrub Typhus
Sao Paulo
*See* Rocky Mountain Spotted Fever
Tropical
*See* Scrub Typhus

**Typing, Blood**
*See* Blood Typing

**Typing, HLA**
*See* HLA Typing

**Typing, Tissue**
*See* Tissue Typing

**Tyrosine** .......................84510

**Tzank Smear** ...................87207

**T Cell Leukemia Virus I, Human**
*See* HTLV I

**T Cell Leukemia Virus I Antibodies, Adult**
*See* Antibody, HTLV-I

**T Cell Leukemia Virus II, Human**
*See* HTLV II

**T Cell Leukemia Virus II Antibodies, Human**
*See* Antibody, HTLV-II

**T Lymphotropic Virus Type III Antibodies, Human**
*See* Antibody, HIV

# U

**Uchida Procedure**
*See* Tubal Ligation

**UDP Galactose Pyrophosphorylase**
*See* Galactose-1-Phosphate, Uridyl Transferase

**UFR**
*See* Uroflowmetry

**Ulcer**
Anal
*See* Anus, Fissure
Decubitus
*See* Debridement; Pressure Ulcer (Decubitus); Skin Graft and Flap
Pinch Graft .......................15050
Pressure ..................15920-15999
Stomach
Excision .....................43610

**Ulcerative, Cystitis**
*See* Cystitis, Interstitial

**Ulna**
*See* Arm, Lower; Elbow; Humerus; Radius
Arthrodesis
Radioulnar Joint
with Resection ..............25830
Arthroplasty
with Implant .................25442
Centralization or Wrist ...........25335
Craterization .........24147, 25150-25151
Cyst
Excision .........24125-24126, 25120, 25125-25126
Diaphysectomy .......24147, 25150-25151
Excision .........................24147
Abscess .....................24138
Complete ....................25240
Epiphyseal Bar ...............20150
Partial .....25145, 25150-25151, 25240
Fracture
Closed Treatment .......25530, 25535
Olecranon ..............24670-24675
Open Treatment ............24685
Open Treatment ...............25545
Shaft ...........25530, 25535, 25545
Open Treatment ............25574
Styloid
Closed Treatment ...........25650
without Manipulation .........25530
with Dislocation
Closed Treatment ...........24620
Open Treatment ............24635
with Manipulation .............25535
with Radius ............25560, 25565
Open Treatment ............25575
Incision and Drainage .............25035
Osteoplasty ..............25390-25393
Prophylactic Treatment ......25491-25492
Reconstruction
Radioulnar ..................25337
Repair
Epiphyseal Arrest .......25450, 25455
Malunion or Nonunion ...25400, 25415
Osteotomy .......25360, 25370, 25375
and Radius .................25365
with Graft ............25405, 25420, 25425-25426
Saucerization ........24147, 25150-25151
Sequestrectomy ...........24138, 25145
Tumor
Cyst ........................24120
Excision .........24125-24126, 25120, 25125-25126, 25170

**Ulnar Arteries**
*See* Artery, Ulnar

**Ulnar Nerve**
Decompression ..................64718
Neuroplasty ...............64718-64719
Reconstruction .............64718-64719
Release ..................64718-64719
Repair/Suture
Motor ........................64836
Transposition ..............64718-64719

**Ultrasonic**
*See* Ultrasound

**Ultrasonic Cardiography**
*See* Echocardiography

**Ultrasonic Procedure** .........52325

**Ultrasonography**
*See* Echography

**Ultrasound**
*See* Echocardiography; Echography
Abdomen .................76700-76705
Arm ............................76880
Bone Density Study ...............76977
Breast ..........................76645
Chest ..........................76604
Drainage
Abscess .....................75989
Echoencephalography
*See* Echoencephalography
Eye .....................76511-76513
Arteries .....................93875
Biometry ...............76516-76519
Foreign Body ................76529
Fetus ...........................76818
Follow-up .......................76970
for Physical Therapy ..............97035
Gastrointestinal ..................76975
Gastrointestinal, Upper
Endoscopic ..................43259
Guidance
Amniocentesis ................76946
Arteriovenous Fistulae .........76936
Aspiration ..................76938
Chorionic Villus Sampling .......76945
Fetal Cordocentesis ............76941
Fetal Transfusion .............76941
Heart Biopsy ................76932
Needle Biopsy ................76942
Ova Retrieval ................76948
Pericardiocentesis .............76930
Pseudoaneurysm ..............76936
Radiation Prescription ....76950-76960
Radioelement ................76965
Thoracentesis ................76934
Head ...................76506, 76536
Heart
Fetal ........................76825
Hips
Infant .................76885, 76886
Hysterosonography ...............76831
Intraoperative ...................76986

Intravascular
Intraoperative ..........37250-37251
Kidney
Transplant ..................76778
Leg ............................76880
Neck ..........................76536
Non-Coronary
Intravascular ..........75945-75946
Pelvis ....................76856-76857
Pregnant Uterus ..........76805-76816
Prostate .................76872-76873
Rectal ....................76872-76873
Retroperitoneal ..........76770-76775
Scrotum .......................76870
Spine ..........................76800
Stimulation to Aid Bone Healing ....20979
Unlisted Services and Procedures ...76999
Vagina .........................76830

**Ultraviolet Light Therapy**
Dermatology
Ultraviolet A ................96912
Ultraviolet B ................96910
for Dermatology ................96900
for Physical Medicine ............97028

**Umbilectomy** ................49250

**Umbilical**
Hernia
*See* Omphalocele
Vein Catheterization
*See* Catheterization, Umbilical Vein

**Umbilicus**
Excision .......................49250
Repair
Hernia ................49580-49587
Omphalocele .....49600, 49605-49606, 49610-49611

**Undescended Testicle**
*See* Testis, Undescended

**Unfertilized Egg**
*See* Ova

**Unguis**
*See* Nails

**Unilateral Simple Mastectomy**
*See* Mastectomy

**Unlisted Services and Procedures** ..................99499
Abdomen ..........22999, 49329, 49999
Allergy/Immunology .............95199
Anal ............................46999
Anesthesia .....................01999
Arm ............................25999
Arthroscopy ....................29909
Autopsy ........................88099
Bile Duct .......................47999
Brachytherapy ..................77799
Breast ..........................19499
Bronchi ........................31899
Cardiac ........................33999
Cardiovascular Studies ...........93799
Casting .........................29799
Cervix ..........................58999
Chemistry Procedure .............84999
Chemotherapy ..................96549
Chest ..........................32999
Coagulation .....................85999
Colon ..........................44799
Conjunctiva Surgery .............68399
Craniofacial .....................21299
Cytogenetic Study ...............88299
Cytopathology ..................88199
Dermatology ....................96999
Dialysis ........................90999
Diaphragm .....................39599
Ear
External ....................69399
Inner .......................69949
Middle .....................69799
Endocrine System ...............60699
Epididymis .....................55899
Esophagus ................43289, 43499
Evaluation and Management Services ........................99499
Eyelid .........................67999
Eye Muscle .....................67399
Eye Surgery
Anterior Segment ............66999
Posterior Segment ............67299
Forearm ........................25999
Gallbladder .....................47999
Gastroenterology Test ............91299
Gum ...........................41899
Hand ..........................26989
Hemic System ..................38999
Hepatic Duct ...................47999
Hip Joint .......................27299
Hysteroscopy ...................58579
Immunization ...................90749
Immunology ....................86849
Injection .......................90799
Injection of Medication ...........90799
Intestine ................44209, 44799
Kidney ........................49659
Lacrimal System ................68899
Laparoscopy ........38129, 38589, 43289, 43659, 44209, 44979, 47579, 49329, 49659, 50549, 54699, 55559, 58578, 58679, 59898, 60659
Larynx .........................31599
Lip ............................40799
Liver ..........................47399
Lungs .........................32999
Lymphatic System ...............38999
Maxillofacial ...................21299
Maxillofacial Prosthetics ..........21089
Meckel's Diverticulum ...........44899
Mediastinum ...................39499
Mesentery Surgery ..............44899
Microbiology ...................87999
Mouth ...................40899, 41599
Musculoskeletal ..........25999, 26989
Musculoskeletal Surgery
Abdominal Wall .............22999
Neck .......................21899
Spine ......................22899
Thorax .....................21899
Musculoskeletal System ...........20999
Ankle ......................27899
Arm, Upper .................24999
Elbow ......................24999
Head .......................21499
Knee .......................27599
Leg, Lower ..................27899
Leg, Upper ..................27599
Necropsy .......................88099
Nervous System Surgery ..........64999
Neurology/Neuromuscular Testing ...95999
Nose ...........................30999
Nuclear Medicine ...............78999
Blood ......................78199
Bone .......................78399
Endocrine System ............78099
Genitourinary System .........78799
Heart ......................78499
Hematopoietic System ........78199
Lymphatic System ............78199
Musculoskeletal System .......78399
Nervous System .............78699
Therapeutic .................79999
Obstetrical Care ..........59898, 59899
Omentum ................49329, 49999
Ophthalmology .................92499
Orbit ..........................67599
Otorhinolaryngology .............92599
Ovary ...................58679, 58999
Oviduct .................58679, 58999
Palate .........................42299
Pancreas Surgery ...............48999
Pathology ......................89399
Pelvis .........................27299
Penis ..........................55899
Peritoneum ..............49329, 49999
Pharynx ........................42999
Physical Therapy .....97039, 97139, 97799
Pleura .........................32999
Pressure Ulcer ..................15999
Preventive Medicine .............99429
Prostate .......................55899
Psychiatric ....................90899
Pulmonology ...................94799
Radiation Physics ...............77399
Radiation Therapy ...............77499
Planning ....................77299
Radiology, Diagnostic ............76499
Radionuclide Therapy ............79999
Radiopharmaceutical Therapy ......79999
Rectum ........................45999
Salivary Gland ..................42699
Scrotum .......................55899
Seminal Vesicle .................55899
Shoulder Surgery ................23929
Sinuses ........................31299

**Uric Acid**
Blood .....84550
Other Source .....84560
Urine .....84560

**Uridyltransferase, Galactose-1-Phosphate**
*See* Galactose-1-Phosphate, Uridyl Transferase

**Uridylyltransferase, Galactosephosphate**
*See* Galactose-1-Phosphate, Uridyl Transferase

**Urinalysis** .....81000-81099
Automated .....81001, 81003
Glass Test .....81020
Microalbumin .....82043-82044
Microscopic .....81015
Pregnancy Test .....81025
Qualitative .....81005
Routine .....81002
Screen .....81007
Semiquantitative .....81005
Unlisted Services and Procedures .....81099
Volume Measurement .....81050
without Microscopy .....81002

**Urinary Bladder**
*See* Bladder

**Urinary Catheter Irrigation**
*See* Irrigation, Catheter

**Urinary Concentration Test**
*See* Water Load Test

**Urinary Sphincter, Artificial**
*See* Prosthesis, Urethral Sphincter

**Urinary Tract**
X-Ray with Contrast .....74400-74425

**Urine**
Albumin
*See* Albumin, Urine
Blood
*See* Blood, Urine
Colony Count .....87086
Pregnancy Test .....81025
Tests .....81001

**Urobilinogen**
Feces .....84577
Urine .....84578-84583

**Urodynamic Tests**
Cystometrogram .....51725-51726
Electromyography Studies
Needle .....51785
Stimulus Evoked Response .....51792
Urethra Pressure Profile .....51772
Uroflowmetry .....51736-51741
Voiding Pressure Studies
Bladder .....51795
Intra-Abdominal .....51797

**Uroflowmetry** .....51736-51741

**Urography**
Antegrade .....74425
Infusion .....74410-74415
Intravenous .....74400-74410, 74415
Retrograde .....74420

**Uroporphyrin** .....84120

**Urothromboplastin**
*See* Thromboplastin

**Uterine**
Adhesion
*See* Adhesions, Intrauterine
Cervix
*See* Cervix
Endoscopies
*See* Endoscopy, Uterus
Haemorrhage
*See* Hemorrhage, Uterus

**Uterus**
Biopsy
Endometrium .....58100
Endoscopic .....58558
Catheterization
X-Ray .....58340
Chromotubation .....58350
Curettage
Postpartum .....59160
Dilation and Curettage .....58120
Postpartum .....59160
Ectopic Pregnancy
Interstitial
Partial Resection Uterus .....59136
Total Hysterectomy .....59135
Endoscopy
Endometrial Ablation .....58563
Exploration .....58555
Surgery .....58558-58563
Treatment .....58558-58563
Excision
Laparoscopic .....58550
Partial .....58180
Radical .....58210, 58285
Removal of Tubes and/or Ovaries .....58262-58263
Total .....58150-58152, 58200
Vaginal .....58260-58270, 58550
with Colpectomy .....58275-58280
with Colpo-Urethrocystopexy .....58267
with Repair of Enterocele .....58270
Hemorrhage
Postpartum .....59160
Hydatidiform Mole
Excision .....59100
Hydrotubation .....58350
Hysterosalpingography .....74740
Hysterosonography .....76831
Incision
Remove Lesion .....59100
Insertion
Intrauterine Device (IUD) .....58300
Laparoscopy .....58578
Lesion
Excision .....58551, 59100
Reconstruction .....58540
Removal
Intrauterine Device (IUD) .....58301
Repair
Fistula .....51920-51925
Rupture .....58520, 59350
Suspension .....58400
with Presacral Sympathectomy .....58410
Suture
Rupture .....59350
Tumor
Excision
Abdominal Approach .....58140
Vaginal Approach .....58145
Unlisted Services and Procedures .....58578, 58999
X-Ray with Contrast .....74740

**UTP Hexose 1 Phosphate Uridylyltransferase**
*See* Galactose-1-Phosphate, Uridyl Transferase

**Uvula**
Abscess
Incision and Drainage .....42000
Biopsy .....42100
Excision .....42140, 42145
Lesion
Destruction .....42145
Excision .....42104, 42106-42107
Unlisted Services and Procedures .....42299

**Uvulectomy** .....42140

**UV Light Therapy**
*See* Actinotherapy


# V


**V, Cranial Nerve**
*See* Trigeminal Nerve

**V-Y Operation, Bladder, Neck**
*See* Bladder, Repair, Neck

**V-Y Plasty**
*See* Skin, Adjacent Tissue Transfer

**Vaccination**
*See* Allergen Immunotherapy; Immunization; Vaccines

**Vaginoscopy**
Biopsy .....57454
Exploration .....57452

**Vaginotomy**
*See* Colpotomy

**Vagotomy**
Abdominal .....64760
Highly Selective .....43641
Parietal Cell .....43641, 64755
Selective .....43640
Transthoracic .....64752
Truncal .....43640
with Gastroduodenostomy Revision, Reconstruction .....43855
with Gastrojejunostomy Revision, Reconstruction .....43865
with Partial Distal Gastrectomy .....43635

**Vagus Nerve**
Avulsion
Abdominal .....64760
Selective .....64755
Thoracic .....64752
Incision .....43640-43641
Abdominal .....64760
Selective .....64755
Thoracic .....64752
Injection
Anesthetic .....64408
Transection .....43640-43641
Abdominal .....64760
Selective .....43652, 64755
Thoracic .....64752
Truncal .....43651

**Valentine's Test**
*See* Urinalysis, Glass Test

**Valproic Acid**
*See* Dipropylacetic Acid

**Valproic Acid Measurement**
*See* Dipropylacetic Acid

**Valsalva Sinus**
*See* Sinus of Valsalva

**Valva Atrioventricularis Sinistra (Valva Mitralis)**
*See* Mitral Valve

**Valve**
Aortic
*See* Heart, Aortic Valve
Bicuspid
*See* Mitral Valve
Mitral
*See* Mitral Valve
Pulmonary
*See* Pulmonary Valve
Tricuspid
*See* Tricuspid Valve

**Valvectomy**
Tricuspid Valve .....33460

**Valve Stenoses, Aortic**
*See* Aortic Stenosis

**Valvotomy**
Mitral Valve .....33420-33422
Pulmonary Valve .....33470-33474
Reoperation .....33530

**Valvuloplasty**
Aortic Valve .....33400-33403
Femoral Vein .....34501
Mitral Valve .....33425-33427
Percutaneous Balloon
Aortic Valve .....92986
Mitral Valve .....92987
Pulmonary Valve .....92990
Prosthetic Valve .....33496
Reoperation .....33530
Tricuspid Valve .....33463-33465

**Vancomycin**
Assay .....80202

**Vanillylmandelic Acid**
Urine .....84585

**Vanilmandelic Acid**
*See* Vanillylmandelic Acid

**Van Deen Test**
*See* Blood, Feces

**Van Den Bergh Test**
*See* Bilirubin, Blood

**Varicella (Chicken Pox)**
*See* Vaccines

**Varicella-Zoster**
Antibody .....86787
Antigen Detection
Direct Fluorescence .....87290

**Varices Esophageal**
*See* Esophageal Varices

**Varicocele**
Spermatic Cord
Excision .....55530-55540

**Varicose Vein**
Removal .....37720, 37730, 37780, 37785
Secondary Varicosity .....37785
with Tissue Excision .....37735, 37760

**Vascular Injection**
Unlisted Services and Procedures .....36299

**Vascular Lesion**
Cranial
Excision .....61600-61608, 61615-61616
Cutaneous
Destruction .....17106-17108

**Vascular Malformation**
Cerebral
Repair .....61710
Finger
Excision .....26115
Hand
Excision .....26115

**Vascular Procedure**
Intravascular Ultrasound
Coronary Vessels .....92978-92979
Stent
Intracoronary .....92980-92981

**Vascular Procedures**
Angioscopy
Non-Coronary Vessels .....35400
Intravascular Ultrasound
Non-Coronary Vessels .....75945-75946
Thrombolysis
Coronary Vessels .....92975, 92977
Cranial Vessels .....37195

**Vascular Studies**
*See* Doppler Scan, Duplex, Plethysmography
Angioscopy
Non-Coronary Vessels .....35400
Aorta .....93978-93979
Arterial Studies (Non-Invasive)
Extracranial .....93875-93882
Extremities .....93922-93924
Intracranial .....93886-93888
Lower Extremity .....93925-93926
Artery Studies
Upper Extremity .....93930-93931
Blood Pressure Monitoring, 24 Hour .....93784-93790
Cardiac Catheterization
Imaging .....93555-93556
Hemodialysis Access .....93990
Kidney
Multiple Study
with Pharmacological Intervention .....78709
Single Study
with Pharmacological Intervention .....78708
Penile Vessels .....93980-93981
Plethysmography
Total Body .....93720-93722
Temperature Gradient .....93740
Thermogram
Cephalic .....93760
Peripheral .....93762
Unlisted Services and Procedures .....93799
Venous Studies
Extremity .....93965-93971
Venous Pressure .....93770
Visceral Studies .....93975-93979

**Vascular Surgery**
Arm, Upper
Anesthesia .....01770-01784
Elbow
Anesthesia .....01770-01784
Unlisted Services and Procedures .....37799

**Vasectomy** .....55250
Contact Laser Vaporization with/without Transurethral Resection
of Prostate .....52648

Non-Contact Laser Coagulation of Prostate . . . . . 52647
Transurethral Electrosurgical Resection of Prostate . . . . . 52601, 52648
Reversal
  *See* Vasovasorrhaphy

**Vasoactive Drugs**
Injection
  Penis . . . . . 54231

**Vasoactive Intestinal Peptide** . 84586

**Vasogram**
*See* Vasography

**Vasography** . . . . . 74440

**Vasointestinal Peptide**
*See* Vasoactive Intestinal Peptide

**Vasopneumatic Device Therapy** . . . . . 97016
*See* Physical Medicine/Therapy/ Occupational Therapy

**Vasopressin** . . . . . 84588

**Vasotomy** . . . . . 55200, 55300

**Vasovasorrhaphy** . . . . . 55400

**Vasovasostomy** . . . . . 55400

**Vas Deferens**
Anastomosis
  to Epididymis . . . . . 54900-54901
Excision . . . . . 55250
Incision . . . . . 55200
  for X-Ray . . . . . 55300
Ligation . . . . . 55450
Repair
  Suture . . . . . 55400
Unlisted Services and Procedures . . 55899
Vasography . . . . . 74440
X-Ray with Contrast . . . . . 74440

**VATS**
*See* Thoracoscopy

**VDRL** . . . . . 86592-86593

**Vein**
Adrenal
  Venography . . . . . 75840-75842
Anastomosis
  Caval to Mesenteric . . . . . 37160
  Portocaval . . . . . 37140
  Reniportal . . . . . 37145
  Saphenopopliteal . . . . . 34530
  Splenorenal . . . . . 37180-37181
  to Vein . . . . . 37140, 37145, 37160
Angioplasty . . . . . 75978
  Transluminal . . . . . 35460
Arm
  Harvest of Vein for Bypass Graft . . . . . 35500
  Venography . . . . . 75820-75822
Axillary
  Thrombectomy . . . . . 34490
Biopsy
  Transcatheter . . . . . 75970
Cannulization
  to Artery . . . . . 36810-36815
  to Vein . . . . . 36800
Catheterization
  Cutdown . . . . . 36490-36491
  Organ Blood . . . . . 36500
  Percutaneous . . . . . 36488-36489
  Umbilical . . . . . 36510
External Cannula
  Declotting . . . . . 36860-36861
Femoral
  Repair . . . . . 34501
Femoropopliteal
  Thrombectomy . . . . . 34421-34451
Hepatic Portal
  Splenoportography . . . . . 75810
  Venography . . . . . 75885-75887
Iliac
  Thrombectomy . . . . . 34401-34451
Injection
  Sclerosing Agent . . . . . 36468-36471
Insertion
  IVC Filter . . . . . 75940
Interrupt
  Femoral . . . . . 37650
  Iliac . . . . . 37660
  Vena Cava . . . . . 37620
Jugular
  Venography . . . . . 75860
Leg
  Venography . . . . . 75820-75822
Ligation
  Esophagus . . . . . 43205
  Jugular . . . . . 37565
  Perforation . . . . . 37760
  Saphenous . . . . . 37700, 37720, 37730, 37735, 37780
  Secondary . . . . . 37785
Liver
  Venography . . . . . 75889-75891
Neck
  Venography . . . . . 75860
Nuclear Medicine
  Thrombosis Imaging . . . . . 78455-78458
Orbit
  Venography . . . . . 75880
Placement
  IVC Filter . . . . . 75940
Portal
  Catheterization . . . . . 36481
Pulmonary
  Repair . . . . . 33730
Removal
  Saphenous . . . . . 37720, 37730, 37735, 37780
  Secondary . . . . . 37785
Renal
  Venography . . . . . 75831-75833
Repair
  Aneurysm . . . . . 36834
  Angioplasty . . . . . 75978
  Graft . . . . . 34520
Sampling
  Venography . . . . . 75893
Sinus
  Venography . . . . . 75870
Skull
  Venography . . . . . 75870-75872
Spermatic
  Excision . . . . . 55530-55540
  Ligation . . . . . 55550
Splenic
  Splenoportography . . . . . 75810
Stripping
  Saphenous . . . . . 37720, 37730, 37735
Subclavian
  Thrombectomy . . . . . 34471-34490
Thrombectomy
  Other than Hemodialysis Graft or Fistula . . . . . 35875-35876
Unlisted Services and Procedures . . 37799
Valve Transposition . . . . . 34510
Varicose
  *See* Varicose Vein
Vena Cava
  Thrombectomy . . . . . 34401-34451
  Venography . . . . . 75825-75827

**Velpeau Cast** . . . . . 29058

**Vena Cava**
Catheterization . . . . . 36010
Reconstruction . . . . . 34502
Resection with Reconstruction . . . . . 37799

**Vena Caval**
Thrombectomy . . . . . 50230

**Venereal Disease Research Laboratory**
*See* VDRL

**Venesection**
*See* Phlebotomy

**Venipuncture**
*See* Cannulation; Catheterization
Child/Adult
  Cutdown . . . . . 36425
  Percutaneous . . . . . 36410
Infant
  Cutdown . . . . . 36420
  Percutaneous . . . . . 36400-36406
Routine . . . . . 36415

**Venography**
Adrenal . . . . . 75840-75842
Arm . . . . . 75820-75822
Epidural . . . . . 75872
Hepatic Portal . . . . . 75885-75887
Injection . . . . . 36005
Jugular . . . . . 75860
Leg . . . . . 75820-75822

Partial
with Bilateral Inguinofemoral
Lymphadenectomy . . . . . . . . . . .56632
with Unilateral Inguinofemoral
Lymphadenectomy . . . . . . . . . . .56631
Simple
Complete . . . . . . . . . . . . . . . . . . . .56625
Partial . . . . . . . . . . . . . . . . . . . . . .56620

**VZIG**
*See* Immune Globulins, Varicella-Zoster

**V Flap Procedure**
One Stage Distal Hypospadias Repair 54322


# W


**W-Plasty**
*See* Skin, Adjacent Tissue Transfer

**WADA Activation Test** . . . . . . . .95958
*See* Electroencephalography

**WAIS-R** . . . . . . . . . . . . . . . . . . . . . . .96100

**Waldius Procedure** . . . . . . . . . . .27445

**Wall, Abdominal**
*See* Abdominal Wall

**Walsh Modified Radical Prostatectomy**
*See* Prostatectomy

**Warts**
Flat
Destruction . . . . . . . . . . . . .17110-17111

**Washing**
Sperm . . . . . . . . . . . . . . . . . . . . . . . . .58323

**Wasserman Test**
*See* Syphilis Test

**Wassmund Procedure**
Osteotomy
Maxilla . . . . . . . . . . . . . . . . . . . . .21206

**Waterston Procedure** . . . . . . . . .33755

**Water Load Test** . . . . . . . . . . . . . .89365

**Water Wart**
*See* Molluscum Contagiosum

**Watson-Jones Procedure** . . . . . . . . . . . . .27695-27698

**Wave, Ultrasonic Shock**
*See* Ultrasound

**WBC**
*See* White Blood Cell

**Webbed**
Toe
Repair . . . . . . . . . . . . . . . . . . . . . . .28280

**Wedge Excision**
Osteotomy . . . . . . . . . . . . . . . . . . . . . .21122

**Wedge Resection**
Ovary . . . . . . . . . . . . . . . . . . . . . . . . . .58920

**Well-Baby Care** . . . . . . . .99391, 99432

**Wernicke-Posadas Disease**
*See* Coccidioidomycosis

**Westergren Test**
*See* Sedimentation Rate, Blood Cell

**Western Blot**
HIV . . . . . . . . . . . . . . . . . . . . . . . . . . . .86689
Protein . . . . . . . . . . . . . . . . . . .84181-84182
Tissue Analysis . . . . . . . . . . . .88371-88372

**Wheelchair Management/ Propulsion**
*See* Physical Medicine/Therapy/ Occupational Therapy
Training . . . . . . . . . . . . . . . . . . . . . . . .97542

**Wheeler Knife Procedure**
*See* Discission, Cataract

**Wheeler Procedure**
*See* Blepharoplasty, Entropion
Blepharoplasty . . . . . . . . . . . . . . . . . .67924
Discission Secondary Membranous Cataract . . . . . . . . . . . . . . . . . . . . . . . .66820

**Whipple Procedure** . . . . . . . . . . .48150

**Whirlpool Therapy** . . . . . . . . . . . .97022
*See* Physical Medicine/Therapy/ Occupational Therapy

**White Blood Cell**
Alkaline Phosphatase . . . . . . . . . . . . .85540
Antibody . . . . . . . . . . . . . . . . . . . . . .86021
Count . . . . . . . . . . . . . . . . . . . . . . . . . .85048
Differential . . . . . . . . . . . . . . .85007, 85009
Histamine Release Test . . . . . . . . . . .86343
Phagocytosis . . . . . . . . . . . . . . . . . . . .86344
Transfusion
*See* Leukocyte, Transfusion

**Whitemead Operation**
*See* Hemorrhoidectomy, Complex

**Whitman Astragalectomy**
*See* Talus, Excision

**Whitman Procedure** . . . . . . . . . .27120

**Wick Catheter Technique** . . . . .20950

**Widal Serum Test**
*See* Agglutinin, Febrile

**Window**
Oval
*See* Oval Window
Round
*See* Round Window

**Window Technic, Pericardial**
*See* Pericardiostomy

**Windpipe**
*See* Trachea

**Winiwarter Operation**
*See* Anastomosis, Gallbladder to Intestines

**Winter Procedure** . . . . . . . . . . . .54435

**Wintrobe Test**
*See* Sedimentation Rate, Blood Cell

**Wire**
*See* Pin
Insertion/Removal
Skeletal Traction . . . . . . . . . . . . . .20650
Interdental
without Fracture . . . . . . . . . . . . . .21497

**Wiring**
Prophylactic Treatment
Humerus . . . . . . . . . . . . . . . . . . . .24498

**Wirsung Duct**
*See* Pancreatic Duct

**Witzel Operation** . . . . . . .43500, 43520, 43830-43832
*See* Incision, Stomach, Creation, Stoma; Incision and Drainage

**Womb**
*See* Uterus

**Wood Alcohol**
*See* Methanol

**Work Hardening** . . . . . . . .97545-97546
*See* Physical Medicine/Therapy/ Occupational Therapy

**Work Related Evaluation Services** . . . . . . . . . . . . . . . .99455-99456

**Worm**
*See* Helminth

**Wound**
Dehiscence
Repair . . . . . . . . . . .12020-12021, 13160
Exploration
Penetrating
Abdomen/Flank/Back . . . . . . . . .20102
Chest . . . . . . . . . . . . . . . . . . . . .20101
Extremity . . . . . . . . . . . . . . . . . .20103
Neck . . . . . . . . . . . . . . . . . . . . . .20100
Penetrating Trauma . . . . . .20100-20103
Infection
Incision and Drainage
Postoperative . . . . . . . . . . . . . . .10180
Repair
Complex . . . . . . . . . . . . . . .13100-13160
Intermediate . . . . . . . . . . . .12031-12057
Simple . . . . . . . . . . . . . . . .12001-12021
Urethra . . . . . . . . . . . . . . . .53502-53515
Suture
Bladder . . . . . . . . . . . . . . . .51860-51865
Kidney . . . . . . . . . . . . . . . . . . . . . .50500
Trachea
Cervical . . . . . . . . . . . . . . . . . . . .31800
Intrathoracic . . . . . . . . . . . . . . . .31805
Urethra . . . . . . . . . . . . . . . .53502-53515

# X

**XIII, Coagulation Factor**
*See* Fibrin Stabilizing Factor

**Xylose Absorption Test**
Blood ..........................84620
Urine ..........................84620

**Yellow Fever Vaccine**

**Yersinia**
Antibody .......................86793

## Z

**Ziegler Procedure**
Discission Secondary Membranous
Cataract ........................66820

**Zinc** ..........................84630

**Zinc Manganese Leucine Aminopeptidase**
*See* Leucine Aminopeptidase

**Zygoma**
*See* Cheekbone

**Zygomatic Arch**
Fracture
  Open Treatment .........21356-21366
  with Manipulation .............21355

# A CPT™ coding resource for every need.

*The CPT™ coding authority, the American Medical Association, offers every coding professional a family of tools designed to make your coding process faster, easier and more accurate.*

**CPT™ 2000 Professional Edition**

The industry's definitive CPT™ coding resource. Features include color coding, pre-installed tabs, more than 120 (including 25 new) procedural and anatomical illustrations, references to the *CPT™ Assistant Newsletter*, enhanced index... and more than 300 coding changes. Spiral-bound or 3-ring format.

**Spiral Bound**
*Order #: EP054100AWW*
AMA member price: $ 56.95
Nonmember price: $ 66.95

**3-Ring Binder**
*Order #: LP054100AWW*
AMA member price: $ 61.95
Nonmember price: $ 74.95

**CPT™ Spanish 2000**

The official Spanish language version of CPT, for everyday coding or for handy reference. Translated from the *CPT Standard* edition by linguists from various Spanish-speaking countries.

*Order #: OP052200AWW*
AMA member price: $ 41.95 Nonmember price: $ 51.95

NEW! **CPT™ Companion 2000 (Available January 2000)**

Invaluable updated reference and training manual is indexed by both code and procedure description, and answers virtually every frequently asked CPT question from both coders and physicians. Organization corresponds to CPT code book for faster and simpler use.
*Order #: OP083100AWW*
AMA member price: $ 39.95 Nonmember price: $ 49.95

NEW! **Principles of CPT™ Coding (Available January 2000)**

The comprehensive CPT™ coding instruction manual from the CPT originators, the American Medical Association. Simple and easy-to-understand, *Principles of CPT™ Coding* is designed to guide you through the process of procedural coding.

*Order #: OP501099AWW*
AMA member price: $ 39.95 Nonmember price: $ 49.95

**CPT™ Assistant Newsletter**

Get accurate information and guidance on current CPT coding issues with a subscription to the monthly *CPT™ Assistant*, the only newsletter from the source of CPT, the American Medical Association.

*Order #: CA500996AWW*
AMA member price: $ 99/one year, $ 179/two years
Nonmember price: $ 139/one year, $ 249/two years

**CPT™ Assistant Archives on CD-ROM *(New)***

Immediate access to every issue of the *CPT™ Assistant* from its beginning in 1990 through 1998. Single CD-ROM offers an advanced search engine to find coding examples, charts and illustrations, questions and answers, and case histories... putting all the insights of nine years of the AMA's authoritative newsletter at your fingertips. Special Bonus: includes at least two FREE inquiries to *CPT™ Information Services*.

*Order #: OP510099AWW*
Single User
AMA member price: $ 175
Nonmember price: $ 220

*Order #: OP510199AWW*
2-5 Users
AMA member price: $ 655
Nonmember price: $ 825

*Order #: OP510299AWW*
6-10 Users
AMA member price $ 1,315
Nonmember price $ 1,650

Call 800 621-8335 for pricing on 11+ users.

**CPT™ IS**

Through *CPT™ Information Services*, coding professionals who helped develop CPT™ provide complete, accurate answers to all your coding questions... by phone, fax, or mail. Choose the subscription that best meets your needs.

*Order #: CRS00075AWW*
Subscription A: 75 inquiries per year $1,500

*Order #: CRS00024AWW*
Subscription B: 24 inquiries per year $ 600

*Order #: CRS00005AWW*
Subscription C: 5 inquiries per year $ 150

**Order now toll free: Call 800-621-8335**
**Mention priority code AWW**

**To order on the Web: www.ama-assn.org/catalog**
**Visit CPT™ on the Web at www.ama-assn.org/cpt**

American Medical Association
Physicians dedicated to the health of America

Visa, MasterCard, American Express, and Optima accepted. Shipping/handling and state sales taxes apply. Satisfaction Guaranteed! If not satisfied, return within 30 days for complete refund. CPT™ is a trademark of the American Medical Association.

# CPT™ references that simplify, amplify, and clarify the coding process.

*Three affordable CPT™ reference products that provide the most accurate and up-to-date coding information, plus invaluable guidance, insights, and answers.*

**CPT™ Assistant Newsletter**
*Order #: CA500996AWW*

| | |
|---|---|
| AMA member price: | $ 99/one year |
| | $ 179/two years |
| Nonmember price: | $ 139/one year |
| | $ 249/two years |

**CPT™ Assistant Archives on CD-ROM**
*Order #: OP510099AWW*
**Single User**

| | |
|---|---|
| AMA member price: | $ 175 |
| Nonmember price: | $ 220 |

*Order #: OP510199AWW*
**2-5 Users**

| | |
|---|---|
| AMA member price: | $ 655 |
| Nonmember price: | $ 825 |

*Order #: OP510299AWW*
**6-10 Users**

| | |
|---|---|
| AMA member price: | $ 1,315 |
| Nonmember price: | $ 1,650 |

**Special Bonus:** Get two free inquiries from CPT-IS with the single user CD-ROM, ten free inquiries with the 2-5 user version, and twenty free inquiries with the 6-10 user version.

Call 800 621-8335 for pricing on 11+ users.

**CPT™ IS**
*Order #: CRS00075AWW*
Subscription A:
75 inquiries per year $1,500

*Order #: CRS00024AWW*
Subscription B:
24 inquiries per year $ 600

*Order #: CRS00005AWW*
Subscription C:
5 inquiries per year $ 150

## CPT™ Assistant Newsletter

A subscription to the AMA's monthly *CPT™ Assistant* brings you the most current coding information, plus expert tips and advice, answers to frequently asked questions, insights and analyses, and case histories to illustrate coding practices. Easy-to-understand and simple-to-use format enables you to keep your claims system running smoothly and efficiently. For the most current guidance on coding issues of all types, subscribe to *CPT™ Assistant*, the only newsletter from the source of CPT, the American Medical Association.

## CPT™ Assistant Archives on CD-ROM

Immediate access to every issue of the *CPT™ Assistant* from its beginning in 1990 through 1998. The single CD-ROM archive offers an advanced search engine to help you quickly find coding examples, charts and illustrations, questions and answers, and case histories. You can search by codes, key terms, or subjects. *CPT™ Assistant Archives* puts the insights and guidance of nine years of the AMA's authoritative newsletter at your fingertips.

## CPT™ IS

Through *CPT™ Information Services*, AMA coding professionals who helped develop CPT™ provide the most up-to-date information, as well as complete, accurate answers to all your coding questions, on a query basis. You can elect to receive your answers by phone, fax, or mail. Available in three subscription levels to meet your needs accurately and affordably.

**Order now toll free: Call 800-621-8335**
**Mention priority code AWW**

**To order on the Web: www.ama-assn.org/catalog**
**Visit CPT™ on the Web at www.ama-assn.org/cpt**

American Medical Association
Physicians dedicated to the health of America

Visa, MasterCard, American Express, and Optima accepted. Shipping/handling and state sales taxes apply. Satisfaction Guaranteed! If not satisfied, return within 30 days for complete refund.
*CPT™* is a trademark of the American Medical Association.